Thomas Aquinas

BASIC WRITINGS OF SAINT THOMAS AQUINAS I

〔意〕托马斯·阿奎那 著

圣托马斯基本著作

（第一卷）

方补课 导读 注释

上海译文出版社

图书在版编目（CIP）数据

圣托马斯基本著作. 第一、二卷=Basic Writings of Saint Thomas Aquinas（I, II）：导读注释本：英文 /（意）托马斯 · 阿奎那（Thomas Aquinas）著；方补课注释. — 上海：上海译文出版社，2019.8
（世界学术经典系列）
ISBN 978-7-5327-8242-0

Ⅰ. ①圣… Ⅱ. ①托… ②方… Ⅲ. ①神学—英文
Ⅳ. ①B972

中国版本图书馆CIP数据核字（2019）第125161号

Thomas Aquinas
Basic Writings of Saint Thomas Aquinas (I, II)

圣托马斯基本著作（第一卷、第二卷）（导读注释版）
［意］托马斯 · 阿奎那　著　方补课　导读　注释
责任编辑 / 谭春惠　装帧设计 / 张志全工作室

上海译文出版社有限公司出版、发行
网址：www.yiwen.com.cn
200001 上海福建中路 193 号
江阴金马印刷有限公司印刷

开本 890 × 1240　1/32　印张 55　插页 11　字数 1,563,000
2019 年 8 月第 1 版　2019 年 8 月第 1 次印刷
印数：0,001—3,000 册

ISBN 978-7-5327-8242-0/B · 473
定价：288.00 元（第一、二卷）

WAC

World Academic Classics

世界学术经典·英文版

总策划／总主编

庄智象　林骧华

上海时代教育出版研究中心 研发

Shanghai Epoch Education Publishing Research Center

编辑委员会

世界学术经典（英文版）

总　序

书之成为经典，乃人类在不同时代的思想、智慧与学术的结晶，优秀文化之积淀，具有不随时代变易的永恒价值。有道是读书须读经典，这是智者的共识。

对于中外经典著作中的思想表述，仅读外文书的中译本或文言著作的白话释文是不够的，尤其是当误译、误释发生的时候，读者容易被误导，或望文生义，或以讹传讹，使原有的文化差异变成更深的文化隔阂。因此，在“世界学术经典（英文版）”的选目中，大部分作品为英文原著；原作是其他语种的经典，则选用相对可靠的英文译本；至于中国古代经典，则采用汉英对照的方式呈现，旨在向西方阐释中国的思想和文化。其中，精选的中国经典是整个系列的重要组成部分。有了这一部分的经典，才真正体现出“世界性”。

以原典和英文方式出版，是为了使读者通过研读，准确理解以英文表达的思想、理论和方法，力求避免舛误，进而通过批判和接受，化为智慧力量。这有利于思想的传播，裨益于新思想的产生，同时亦可提高英语修养。

经典名著的重要性是不言而喻的，但是以下几点意义值得一再重申。

（一）学术经典提供思想源泉

两千六百年来的世界学术经典凝聚了人类思想的精华，世世代代的优秀思想家以他们独特的见识和智慧，留给后人取之不竭、用之不尽的思想源泉。从老子、孔子、柏拉图、亚里士多德以降，天才辈出，思想闪光，精彩纷呈。思想界的大师、名家们在人类思想史传统链条上的每一个环节，都启发后人开拓新的思想领域，探究生命的本质，直抵人性的深层。随着人类思想的不断成熟和完善，各个学科领域的理论从本体论、认识论、方法论、实践论、价值论等维度不断深化。后人继承前人的思想，借经典的滋养保持思想活力，丰富和发展前人的观点，使之形成一波又一波的思想洪流，从而改变人的思想和世界观，改变人类社会的进程。历史已经证明：人类社会的进步，思想的力量大于一切。

（二）学术经典传承精神力量

经典名著中蕴含的人类精神，传承的人类守望的共同价值原则和社会理想，在每一个具体领域里都有诸多丰富的表述，它们从整体上构成了推动人类进步的精神力量。研习和传承人类两千六百多年来的优秀思想，并将它化作求新求变的灵感，是人类文明的要义所在。仅有技术进步，还不足以表明人类的文明程度。若无优秀的思想底蕴，人类存在的意义将大打折扣。

中国思想传统中的基本理念和西方思想传统中的基本理念分别形成了东西方两大具有普遍价值的道德观念和价值系统。值得注意的是：（1）这两大道德系统应该是一个互补、互鉴的整体，两者都不可偏废，因为人类的思想是个多元整体。任何一个民族，缺少其中之一，在精神上都可能是不完整的；(2) 这些基本理念都不是抽象概念，它们都具有很强的实践意义，并且必须由实践来考察，否则就很难体现其价值。

精神传承必然是一种自觉的过程，它靠习得，不靠遗传，因此我们需要研读经典。

（三）学术经典构成文化积淀

“文化”包含三大部分：(1) 思想与精神现象；(2) 制度与习俗；(3) 有形的事物。学术经典是对思想与精神现象的归纳和提炼，对制度与习俗的探究和设计，对有形事物的形而上思考和描述。

每一个学科领域的经典著作中都会提出一些根本性的问题，这些问题直面人的困惑，思考人类社会的疑难，在新思想和新知识中展现人类的智慧。当这些思想成果积淀下来，就构成人类文化的主要组成部分。文化不只是制度或器物的外在形式，更重要的是凝结在其背后的精神与思想。

每一个学科的学术本身都要面对一些形而上的（超越性的、纯理论性的）文化问题。在很多人看来，理性的思考和理论的表述都是很枯燥的，但是热爱真理并且对思想情有独钟的人会从学术经典的理论中发现无限生动的天地，从而产生获得真理的快乐，这才是我们追求的真正文化。

大量阅读经典名著是一种学习、积累文化的根本方法，深度阅读和深刻记忆能使文化积淀在人的身上，并且代代相传。假如这一过程中断了，人世间只剩下花天酒地、歌舞升平，文化也就湮灭了。

（四）学术经典推动社会进步

毫无疑问，凡属学术经典，都必须含有新的学术成果——新思想、新理论、新方法，或者新探索。这样的原创性学术成果越多，人类的思想就越深邃，视野越开阔，理论更全面、完美，方法更先进、有效，社会的进步才能获得新的动力和保障。

人文主义推翻神学，理性主义旨在纠正人的偏激，启蒙精神主张打破思想束缚，多元主义反抗绝对理念。各种新思想层出不穷，带来了学术的进步，启发并推动了更大的社会变革。这些原创思想在历史长河中经过漫长的时间考验，成为经典，在任何一种文明中都是社会进步和发展的动力。

当我们研读完一部学术经典，分析和归纳其原创的思想观点时，可以很清晰地理解和感悟它在同时代的环境里对于社会的变革和进步有着何种意义，以及它对当下有哪些启迪。

相比技术的发展，思想并不浮显在社会的表层，它呈现在书本的字里行间，渗透于人的心智，在人的灵魂中闪光。每当社会需要时，它能让我们看到无形的巨大力量。

温故而知新。今日世界纷乱依旧，但时代已不再朦胧。人类思想史上的各种主张，在实践中都已呈现清晰的面貌。当我们重新梳理各种思想和理论时，自然不会再返回到“全盘接受”或者“全盘否定”的幼稚阶段。二十一世纪人类正确的世界观、人生观、价值观需要优秀思想传统的支撑，并通过批判继承，不断推陈出新，滋衍出磅礴之推力。

我们所选的这些学术经典，成书于不同的时代，代表了不同的思想与理论主张。有些著作带有时代烙印，有其局限性或片面性；有些观点不一定正确，但从另一个方面显示出人类思想的丰富性和复杂性。各门学科建立、各种主张提出之后，都曾经在历代思想的实验场上经受碰撞和检验，被接受或者被批判。我们的学者需要研读这些书，而青年学生们的思想成长更需要读这些书。当然，批评与分析是最有效和最有益的阅读方法。

有鉴于此，我们希望“世界学术经典（英文版）”能够真正做到“开卷有益”，使我们自己在潜移默化中都成长为有思想、有理想、有品位的人。

上海时代教育出版研究中心

2018 年 10 月

目录

导读
— 001 —

THE SUMMA THEOLOGICA
— 001 —

Question I
THE NATURE AND DOMAIN OF SACRED DOCTRINE
(*In Ten Articles*)
— 003 —

Question II
THE EXISTENCE OF GOD
(*In Three Articles*)
— 024 —

Question III
ON THE SIMPLICITY OF GOD
(*In Eight Articles*)
— 034 —

Question IV
THE PERFECTION OF GOD
(*In Three Articles*)
— 053 —

Question V
ON GOODNESS IN GENERAL
(*In Six Articles*)
— 061 —

Question VI
THE GOODNESS OF GOD
(*In Four Articles*)
— 076 —

Question VII
THE INFINITY OF GOD
(*In Four Articles*)
— 084 —

Question VIII
THE EXISTENCE OF GOD IN THINGS
(*In Four Articles*)
— 095 —

Question IX
THE IMMUTABILITY OF GOD
(*In Two Articles*)
— 106 —

Question X
THE ETERNITY OF GOD
(*In Six Articles*)
— 113 —

Question XI
THE UNITY OF GOD
(*In Four Articles*)
— 130 —

Question XII
HOW GOD IS KNOWN BY US
(*In Thirteen Articles*)
— 140 —

Question XIII
THE NAMES OF GOD
(*In Twelve Articles*)
— 172 —

Question XIV
ON GOD'S KNOWLEDGE
(*In Sixteen Articles*)
— 208 —

Question XV
ON IDEAS
(*In Three Articles*)
— 250 —

Question XVI
ON TRUTH
(*In Eight Articles*)
— 259 —

Question XVII
CONCERNING FALSITY
(*In Four Articles*)
— 277 —

Question XVIII
THE LIFE OF GOD
(*In Four Articles*)
— 288 —

Question XIX
THE WILL OF GOD
(*In Twelve Articles*)
— 300 —

Question XX
GOD'S LOVE
(*In Four Articles*)
— 330 —

Question XXI
THE JUSTICE AND MERCY OF GOD
(*In Four Articles*)
— 342 —

Question XXII
THE PROVIDENCE OF GOD
(*In Four Articles*)
— 352 —

Question XXIII
PREDESTINATION
(*In Eight Articles*)
— 365 —

Question XXIV
THE BOOK OF LIFE
(*In Three Articles*)
— 389 —

Question XXV
THE POWER OF GOD
(*In Six Articles*)
— 396 —

Question XXVI
THE DIVINE BEATITUDE
(*In Four Articles*)
— 414 —

TREATISE ON THE TRINITY
— 421 —

Question XXVII
THE PROCESSION OF THE DIVINE PERSONS
(*In Five Articles*)
— 423 —

Question XXVIII
THE DIVINE RELATIONS
(*In Four Articles*)
— 436 —

Question XXIX
THE DIVINE PERSONS
(*In Four Articles*)
— 448 —

Question XXX
THE PLURALITY OF PERSONS IN GOD
(*In Four Articles*)
— 463 —

Question XXXI
WHAT BELONGS TO THE UNITY OR PLURALITY IN GOD
(*In Four Articles*)
— 475 —

Question XXXII
THE KNOWLEDGE OF THE DIVINE PERSONS
(*In Four Articles*)
— 487 —

Question XXXIII
THE PERSON OF THE FATHER
(*In Four Articles*)
— 502 —

Question XXXIV
THE PERSON OF THE SON
(*In Three Articles*)
— 514 —

Question XXXV
THE IMAGE
(*In Two Articles*)
— 525 —

Question XXXVI
THE PERSON OF THE HOLY GHOST
(*In Four Articles*)
— 530 —

Question XXXVII
THE NAME OF THE HOLY GHOST: LOVE
(*In Two Articles*)
— 547 —

Question XXXVIII
THE NAME OF THE HOLY GHOST AS *GIFT*
(*In Two Articles*)
— 556 —

Question XXXIX
THE PERSONS IN REFERENCE TO THE ESSENCE
(*In Eight Articles*)
— 561 —

Question XL
THE PERSONS AS COMPARED TO THE RELATIONS OR PROPERTIES
(*In Four Articles*)
— 590 —

Question XLI
THE PERSONS IN REFERENCE TO THE NOTIONAL ACTS
(*In Six Articles*)
— 602 —

Question XLII
EQUALITY AND LIKENESS AMONG THE DIVINE PERSONS
(*In Six Articles*)
— 620 —

Question XLIII
THE MISSION OF THE DIVINE PERSONS
(*In Eight Articles*)
— 637 —

TREATISE ON CREATION
— 657 —

Question XLIV
THE PROCESSION OF CREATURES FROM GOD, AND THE FIRST CAUSE OF ALL THINGS
(*In Four Articles*)
— 659 —

Question XLV
THE MODE OF EMANATION OF THINGS FROM THE FIRST PRINCIPLE
(*In Eight Articles*)
— 670 —

Question XLVI
ON THE BEGINNING OF THE DURATION OF CREATURES
(*In Three Articles*)
— 692 —

Question XLVII
ON THE DISTINCTION OF THINGS IN GENERAL
(*In Three Articles*)
— 708 —

Question XLVIII
THE DISTINCTION OF THINGS IN PARTICULAR
(*In Six Articles*)
— 717 —

Question XLIX
THE CAUSE OF EVIL
(*In Three Articles*)
— 732 —

TREATISE ON THE ANGELS
— 743 —

Question L
THE SUBSTANCE OF THE ANGELS ABSOLUTELY CONSIDERED
(*In Five Articles*)
— 745 —

Question LI
THE ANGELS IN COMPARISON WITH BODIES
(*In Three Articles*)
— 762 —

Question LII
THE ANGELS IN RELATION TO PLACE
(*In Three Articles*)
— 772 —

Question LIII
ON THE LOCAL MOVEMENT OF THE ANGELS
(*In Three Articles*)
— 778 —

Question LIV
THE KNOWLEDGE OF THE ANGELS
(*In Five Articles*)
— 789 —

Question LV
THE MEDIUM OF THE ANGELIC KNOWLEDGE
(*In Three Articles*)
— 801 —

Question LVI
THE ANGELS' KNOWLEDGE OF IMMATERIAL THINGS
(*In Three Articles*)
— 810 —

Question LVII
THE ANGELS' KNOWLEDGE OF MATERIAL THINGS
(*In Five Articles*)
— 819 —

Question LVIII
THE MODE OF THE ANGELIC KNOWLEDGE
(*In Seven Articles*)
— 834 —

Question LIX
THE WILL OF THE ANGELS
(*In Four Articles*)
— 851 —

Question LX
THE LOVE OR DILECTION OF THE ANGELS
(*In Five Articles*)
— 862 —

Question LXI
THE PRODUCTION OF THE ANGELS IN THE ORDER OF NATURAL BEING
(*In Four Articles*)
— 875 —

Question LXII
THE PERFECTION OF THE ANGELS IN THE ORDER OF GRACE AND OF GLORY
(*In Nine Articles*)
— 883 —

Question LXIII
THE MALICE OF THE ANGELS WITH REGARD TO SIN
(*In Nine Articles*)
— 904 —

Question LXIV
THE PUNISHMENT OF THE DEMONS
(*In Four Articles*)
— 927 —

TREATISE ON THE WORK OF THE SIX DAYS
— 941 —

Question LXV
THE WORK OF CREATION OF CORPOREAL CREATURES
(*In Four Articles*)
— 943 —

Question LXVI
THE ORDER OF CREATION TOWARDS DISTINCTION
(*In Four Articles*)
— 955 —

Question LXVII
THE WORK OF DISTINCTION IN ITSELF
(*In Four Articles*)
— 972 —

Question LXVIII
THE WORK OF THE SECOND DAY
(*In Four Articles*)
— 984 —

Question LXIX
THE WORK OF THE THIRD DAY
(*In Two Articles*)
— 999 —

Question LXX
THE WORK OF ADORNMENT, AS REGARDS THE FOURTH DAY
(*In Three Articles*)
— 1008 —

Question LXXI
THE WORK OF THE FIFTH DAY
(*In One Article*)
— 1021 —

Question LXXII
THE WORK OF THE SIXTH DAY
(*In One Article*)
— 1025 —

Question LXXIII
THE THINGS THAT BELONG TO THE SEVENTH DAY
(*In Three Articles*)
— 1029 —

Question LXXIV
ON ALL THE SEVEN DAYS IN COMMON
(*In Three Articles*)
— 1037 —

TREATISE ON MAN
— 1051 —

Question LXXV
ON MAN WHO IS COMPOSED OF A SPIRITUAL AND A CORPOREAL SUBSTANCE: AND FIRST, CONCERNING WHAT BELONGS TO THE ESSENCE OF THE SOUL.
(*In Seven Articles*)
— 1053 —

Question LXXVI
THE UNION OF BODY AND SOUL
(*In Eight Articles*)
— 1074 —

Question LXXVII
WHAT BELONGS TO THE POWERS OF THE SOUL IN GENERAL
(*In Eight Articles*)
— 1111 —

Question LXXVIII
THE POWERS OF THE SOUL IN PARTICULAR
(*In Four Articles*)
— 1132 —

Question LXXIX
THE INTELLECTUAL POWERS
(*In Thirteen Articles*)
— 1150 —

Question LXXX
THE APPETITIVE POWERS IN GENERAL
(*In Two Articles*)
— 1186 —

Question LXXXI
THE POWER OF SENSUALITY
(*In Three Articles*)
— 1191 —

Question LXXXII
THE WILL
(*In Five Articles*)
— 1199 —

Question LXXXIII
FREE CHOICE
(*In Four Articles*)
— 1213 —

Question LXXXIV
HOW THE SOUL WHILE UNITED TO THE BODY UNDERSTANDS CORPOREAL THINGS BENEATH IT
(*In Eight Articles*)
— 1223 —

Question LXXXV
THE MODE AND ORDER OF UNDERSTANDING
(*In Eight Articles*)
— 1253 —

Question LXXXVI
WHAT OUR INTELLECT KNOWS IN MATERIAL THINGS
(*In Four Articles*)
— 1280 —

Question LXXXVII
HOW THE INTELLECTUAL SOUL KNOWS ITSELF AND ALL THAT IS WITHIN ITSELF
(*In Four Articles*)
— 1290 —

Question LXXXVIII
HOW THE HUMAN SOUL KNOWS WHAT IS ABOVE ITSELF
(*In Three Articles*)
— 1301 —

Question LXXXIX
THE KNOWLEDGE OF THE SEPARATED SOUL
(*In Eight Articles*)
— 1313 —

Question XC
THE FIRST PRODUCTION OF MAN'S SOUL
(*In Four Articles*)
— 1333 —

Question XCI
THE PRODUCTION OF THE BODY OF THE FIRST MAN
(*In Four Articles*)
— 1343 —

Question XCII
THE PRODUCTION OF WOMAN
(*In Four Articles*)
— 1356 —

Question XCIII
THE END OR TERM OF THE PRODUCTION OF MAN
(*In Nine Articles*)
— 1365 —

Question XCIV
THE STATE AND CONDITION OF THE FIRST MAN AS REGARDS HIS INTELLECT
(*In Four Articles*)
— 1390 —

Question XCV
OF THINGS PERTAINING TO THE FIRST MAN'S WILL, NAMELY, GRACE AND JUSTICE
(*In Four Articles*)
— 1403 —

Question XCVI
THE MASTERSHIP BELONGING TO MAN IN THE STATE OF INNOCENCE
(*In Four Articles*)
— 1414 —

Question XCVII
THE PRESERVATION OF THE INDIVIDUAL IN THE FIRST STATE
(*In Four Articles*)
— 1424 —

Question XCVIII
THE PRESERVATION OF THE SPECIES
(*In Two Articles*)
— 1433 —

Question XCIX
THE CONDITION OF THE OFFSPRING AS TO THE BODY
(*In Two Articles*)
— 1440 —

Question C
THE CONDITION OF THE OFFSPRING AS REGARDS JUSTICE
(*In Two Articles*)
— 1445 —

Question CI
THE CONDITION OF THE OFFSPRING AS REGARDS KNOWLEDGE
(*In Two Articles*)
— 1450 —

Question CII
ON MAN'S ABODE, WHICH IS PARADISE
(*In Four Articles*)
— 1454 —

TREATISE ON THE DIVINE GOVERNMENT
— 1465 —

Question CIII
THE GOVERNMENT OF THINGS IN GENERAL
(*In Eight Articles*)
— 1467 —

Question CIV
THE SPECIAL EFFECTS OF THE DIVINE GOVERNMENT
(*In Four Articles*)
— 1484 —

Question CV
THE MOVEMENT OF GOD IN CREATURES
(*In Eight Articles*)
— 1495 —

Question CVI
HOW ONE CREATURE MOVES ANOTHER
(*In Four Articles*)
— 1513 —

Question CVII
THE SPEECH OF THE ANGELS
(*In Five Articles*)
— 1524 —

Question CVIII
THE ANGELIC DEGREES OF HIERARCHIES AND ORDERS
(*In Eight Articles*)
— 1533 —

Question CIX
THE ORDERING OF THE BAD ANGELS
(*In Four Articles*)
— 1559 —

Question CX
HOW ANGELS ACT ON BODIES
(*In Four Articles*)
— 1566 —

Question CXI
THE ACTION OF THE ANGELS ON MAN
(*In Four Articles*)
— 1577 —

Question CXII
THE MISSION OF THE ANGELS
(*In Four Articles*)
— 1587 —

Question CXIII
THE GUARDIANSHIP OF THE GOOD ANGELS
(*In Eight Articles*)
— 1598 —

Question CXIV
THE ASSAULTS OF THE DEMONS
(*In Five Articles*)
— 1614 —

Question CXV
THE ACTION OF THE CORPOREAL CREATURE
(*In Six Articles*)
— 1625 —

Question CXVI
ON FATE
(*In Four Articles*)
— 1644 —

Question CXVII
OF THINGS PERTAINING TO THE ACTION OF MAN
(*In Four Articles*)
— 1653 —

Question CXVIII
THE PRODUCTION OF MAN FROM MAN AS TO THE SOUL
(*In Three Articles*)
— 1665 —

Question CXIX
THE PROPAGATION OF MAN AS TO THE BODY
(*In Two Articles*)
— 1677 —

术语汇编与简释
— 1689 —

导 读

方补课

一

《圣托马斯基本著作》的作者托马斯·阿奎那（Thomas Aquinas，1225—1274）生于意大利那不勒斯附近的洛卡塞卡城堡，该城堡距离罗马与拿坡里之间的阿奎诺（Aquino）小城不远。他的祖先是伦巴德（Lombard）望族，他父亲是阿奎诺的首席长官，全家都信奉天主教。托马斯5岁就被送入卡西诺山天主教本笃会隐修院接受初级教育。

1241年，托马斯进入那不勒斯大学，在读大学期间，他出人意料地决意要加入刚成立不久的天主教修会——道明会（Dominican Order）。他的这个决定让他的家人很不悦并横加干涉，就在他准备前往罗马的路上让他的几个兄弟拦截他并押送回家，还监禁了他一两年，甚至安排娼妓去诱惑他，以迫使他放弃弃俗修道，加入道明会的志向，但他始终意志坚定，毫不妥协。最后，教宗伊诺森四世出面干预此事，他的家人才只好作罢。

1242年，托马斯正式接受了入会礼，成为道明会会士。修会长上看到他的天赋异禀，于1244年送他去科隆的道明会神学院，师从阿尔伯特神父学习神哲学。阿尔伯特神父博学多才，不但获得“万能博士”的称号，还常被人们尊称为“伟大的阿尔伯特”，由此得名“大阿尔伯特”（Albert the Great）。在当时西欧流行的亚里士多德的自然哲学新思潮的影响下，大阿尔伯特除了神哲学，也投身于实验科学的研究，而且成果显著，因此被天主教会称为“自然科学的捍卫者”。他先执教于科隆的道明会神学院、弗莱堡大学等学府，后来又获得巴黎大学神学教授的教职。大阿尔伯特独具慧眼，他有意让托马斯参加诸如汇编和注释亚里士多德的著作、撰写大学教材等工作，对他精心加以培养。

1245 年，托马斯随从大阿尔伯特转学到巴黎大学，三年后获得神学学士学位，于 1248 年回到科隆担任神学讲师。托马斯升为神父不久，即 1252 年，在导师大阿尔伯特的大力推荐下，登上了巴黎大学的讲坛。由于托马斯教学成绩优异，1257 年，他被授予神学博士学位，并被破格晋升为巴黎大学教授。托马斯在讲学、查阅、印证、辩论的基础上，先后撰写了大量的专著、论文和评注。在所有论著中，《反异教大全》和《神学大全》是托马斯的代表作，特别是后者，系统而完整地反映了托马斯的思想与理论体系。

托马斯卒于 1274 年，享年 49 岁。1323 年被教宗若望二十二世册封为“圣人”。因为其卓越的学术才能和举世瞩目的学术成就，1563 年，他被誉为“天使博士”，成为经院哲学最大的权威。1567 年被教宗庇护五世加封为“圣师”，从而与安布罗斯（Ambrose of Milan，339—397）、哲罗姆（Jerome，347—419）、奥古斯丁（Augustine of Hippo，354—430）和格列高利（Gregory the Great，540—604）齐名。在基督宗教（包括天主教、基督新教和东正教）神哲学界，托马斯至今享有无人可及的至高地位。

天主教会甚至规定，凡有志献身于教会工作的神职人员，特别要“以圣托马斯为师表”（《天主教法典》252条3项），用推理的方法深入探讨神哲学；而且规定，“至少该满六年，即专攻哲学的时间应满2年，神学应满4年”（《天主教法典》250条）。

托马斯在人类思想史上享有独特的地位，他在神学思想发展史上的重要性只有圣奥古斯丁能够与他相提并论。他的学术地位与社会影响力能与柏拉图、亚里士多德、康德、黑格尔等人相媲美，甚至有所胜过。托马斯对西方思想史最大的贡献在于他把亚里士多德主义与基督宗教学说融合为一，并在此基础上建立起自己庞大的基督宗教亚里士多德主义体系，从而取代了数百年来在思想界占据统治地位的奥古斯丁的基督宗教柏拉图主义，为基督宗教带来了强大的思想活力，也极大地推动了人类社会的文明进步。在构筑基督宗教亚里士多德主义体系的时候，他除了对前人思想成果的汲取和综合，也提出了许多个人的独到见解。例如，针对在近现代哲学中争论颇多的自明真理问题，托马斯的见解至今仍不失为非常有说服力的观点。托马斯认为，自明真理的确是只要知道其主词就能知道其谓词的命题，但却不能就此而说它是完全独立于经验的。因为即使这种命题只是概念的展开，但概念本身却是依赖经验而存在的。而且与今天大多数人所持的观点不同，他认为自明真理不仅仅适用于数学和逻辑领域，而且遍布各学科领域。因为任何学科中都有定义性命题，而任何定义性命题都是自明真理，所以任何学科都有自明真理。只是在托马斯看来“自明”有“本身自明”和“对人自明”之别。自明真理本身都是自明的，但是对于不熟悉它的人来说就不是自明的。比如，对于不懂三角几何的人来说，三角形的三个内角之和等于180°就不是自明的，尽管它本身是自明的。

《圣托马斯基本著作》收录的《神学大全》是托马斯的无可替代的历史标签，是奠定托马斯历史地位的一部思想杰作。这部巨著不仅是一部“神学”大全，而且也是一部“哲学”大全，因为它所论述的问题几乎涉及哲学和神学的所有重要内容。它博大精深，对于每一个问题都探讨和分析得透彻精微，鞭辟入里。这部著作不但是基督教会取之不尽，用之不竭的一份信仰财富，而且是人类文化遗产中的一块精神珍宝。

二

《神学大全》这一书名译自本书的拉丁文原文书名 *Summa Theologiae*。全书共分三集，共计 160 余万字。托马斯从 1266 年开始进行本书的写作，至 1273 年结束，历时八年。其中第一集的主题是“天主及其创造的秩序”（天主论），是他在罗马任教廷做顾问期间（1266—1268 年）所写，共有 119 题；第二集的主题是“伦理学”，是他在巴黎大学任教期间（1268—1272 年）写的，共有 392 题；第三集的主题为“信理神学”，是他在意大利那不勒斯大学任教期间（1272—1273 年）写的，但他只写了 90 题就停笔了，至于他为何不继续写下去，至今众说纷纭。但总的来说，该书已经充分体现了托马斯的全部思想和理论体系，所欠缺的部分无关大局。第三集 90 题之后的 101 题是后人按照他早年的著作补充的，所以补充的这部分内容叫“补篇”。《神学大全》共讨论了 613 题。

《神学大全》的原著是按照当时大学教材的体例，以论辩问题的形式进行编写的。在每一个“题”之下，都设有若干个子论题，被称为“条”。对于每个“条”的论述，都遵循同一个格式：先以若干论据该“条”的论点提出质疑（Objection），再对质疑进行反驳（On the contrary），然后给出正面解释，即正解（I answer that），最后对质疑所持有的论据逐一进行解释，即释疑（Reply Objection）。

《神学大全》全书不分卷，也不分章节，只有“题”。但为了方便读者阅读和理解，《圣托马斯基本著作》根据内容把每一集分为若干“卷”。我们在此只简单地介绍第一集的主要内容。第一集主要论证的是人和天主的关系。托马斯认为，人虽然是最高级的受造物，是世界的主人，享有充分的自由，但他同其他所有受造物一样，也必然以其造物主为最高原则和最终目的。人生的意义在于崇拜天主，归向天主，其最终目的是与天主结合为一。

第一集共分为七卷：1. 论天主的本性（1—26 题）；2. 论天主三位一体（27—43 题）；3. 论创造（44—49 题）；4. 论天使（50—64 题）；5. 论六天的工作（65—74 题）；6. 论人（75—102 题）；7. 论天主的管理（103—119 题）。

在第一卷中，托马斯从三个子问题出发讨论了“天主的本性”：(1) 天主的存在（1—2 题）；(2) 天主的存在方式（3—13 题）；(3) 天主的运作（14—26 题）。在对“天主是否存在”的问题上，托马斯运用了著名的“五路论证”：第一路乃从变动中推论出第一不动的原动者；第二路乃从动力因的本性推论出一个首要的动力因的存在；第三路乃从事物的偶然性推论出一个必然者的存在；第四路乃从万物的等级层次推论出最美善的实有的存在；第五路乃通过对万物秩序的观察推论出宇宙万物必有一个终极的目的因。在讨论“天主的存在方式”这个子问题时，托马斯采取的是一种排除法。他先后论证了天主不是合成的、不是不完满的、不是有限的、不是变动的和多元的，从而就间接地证明了天主的单纯性、完满性、无限性、永恒性和唯一性。在卷一的最后，托马斯从天主的知识、意志、能力和幸福四个层面论述了天主的运作。

在第二卷中，托马斯从三个子问题讨论了三位一体的“天主的位格”：(1) 天主位格的起源（27 题）；(2) 天主内在的关系（28 题）；(3) 天主的位格（29—43 题）。在讨论天主位格的起源问题时，托马斯把“存在”本身定义为“运行”或者“活动”。按照他的观点，在天主内存在两种运行：“道的运行”和“爱的运行”。前者关涉天主的理智，关涉到创造，即“从非存在到存在的转变”，从而可称之为“生育”，此乃圣三的第二位，即降生成人的圣子的活动；而后者则关涉天主的意志，关涉生命的运动或冲力，托马斯称之为“发出”，此乃圣三的第三位，即圣神的活动。在论述天主内在的关系问题时，托马斯强调三位一体的天主内存在着父子、子父、发出和运行四种关系。在讨论天主位格的问题时，托马斯强调了位格的个体性，他将位格界定为“一个具有理性本能的个别实体”。而且他强调指出：天主位格的“多”（三个）并不影响天主为“一”（独一无二）。

在第三卷中，托马斯依次讨论了以下四个子问题：(1) 受造物的第一因（44 题）；(2) 受造物的受造（45 题）；(3) 受造物的开端（46 题）；(4) 受造物的区别（47—50 题）。在阐述受造物的第一因时，托马斯强调，天主不但是万物的动力因和第一原型因，而且还是万物的目的因。在阐述受造物的受造时，他强调天主以“溢出”（或“无中生有”）的方式创造了万物。在阐述受造物的开端时，他批判了有关世界永恒论的观点，而把它归结为“信德”，因为不能以论证加以证明。关于受造物的区别，托马斯从两个层面进行讨论：一是受造物区别的根源；二是受造物区别的类型。在他看来，既然受造物来自天主的创造，那么其区别便来自天主。关于受造物的类型，他总结了两种基本类型：一是“善恶”之别（48—49题）；二是“有形无形”之别（50—112题）。鉴于对“善”的问题的讨论主要集中在《神学大全》的第二集，因此他在这里只是扼要地考察了恶的本性及其原因。关于恶，托马斯强调说，恶不可能表示存在，它只是善在一定程度上的缺乏；而且天主一定不是恶的创造者，但祂是恶的惩罚者。“有形无形”之别也是个大问题，所以，托马斯用了整整三卷（4—6卷）的篇幅对此加以讨论，为了厘清这一区别，他分别讨论了天使、物体和人。

在卷四中，托马斯专题讨论了作为精神受造物的天使。为此，他用以下四个子问题进行讨论：(1) 天使的实体（50—53题）；(2) 天使的理智（54—58题）；(3) 天使的意志（59—60题）；(4) 天使的创造（61—64题）。在讨论天使实体时，托马斯强调了天使与物质和人的本质区别，天使的本质是完全无形的精神体，而物质和人是由质料和形式组合而成的。在讨论天使的理智和意志时，托马斯强调，天使比人具有更高程度的理智和自由意志。在讨论天使的创造的时候，托马斯指出，天使与物质和人一样，都来自天主的创造，而且是同时被造的。另外，天使都是在恩宠中受造的，但因为有的天使对抗天主而遭永远的判罚，变成了魔鬼。

在卷五中，关于天主创造天地的“六天工作”，托马斯着重强调了两个问题：一是有形事物是因天主的善而受造的，二是物体的最初形式来自天主的创造。他认为天主创造天地的过程是一种不断赋予无形式的质料以有形形式的过程，祂“六天的工作”所展现的正是这样一个过程。

在第六卷中，托马斯讨论了人的问题。他着重讨论了人的本性问题（75—89题）和人的受造问题（90—102题）。他在考察人的本性时，重点考察了人的灵魂。关于人的灵魂，他讨论了三个问题：(1) 灵魂的本质；(2) 灵魂的能力；(3) 灵魂的运作。关于灵魂的本质，托马斯认为，人的灵魂虽然不是形体，但与天使并不属于同一个种相，它是作为人的身体的形式与人的身体结合在一起的。关于灵魂的能力，他将其划分为三种：(1) 作为理智前奏的能力，如感官能力；(2) 理智能力（不仅有别于天主的理智，也有别于天使的理智）；(3) 欲望能力（感觉欲望和理智欲望）。至于灵魂的运作，是一个范围极其广泛的话题，不仅关涉到人的理智活动和认识论，而且也关涉到人的意志活动和整个道德哲学。后者是《神学大全》第二集所讨论的基本话题。而托马斯在这里只讨论其理智活动和认识论的问题。他分为“灵魂与身体结合在一起的时候”和“灵魂离开身体的时候”两种情况下人的理性活动的问题，即今生和来世的两种情况。在讨论今生的理性活动的时候，托马斯强调了理性知识对于感性知识的依赖性，也强调了理智基于心像的抽象活动。在讨论来世的理性活动的时候，他虽然认为脱离了身体的灵魂无需再回到心像也能够理解事物，但他还是认为，无论在今生获得的知识习性还是今生获得的认识活动，都依然存在于脱离了身体的灵魂内。关于人的受造，托马斯讨论了四个问题：(1) 人的产生；(2) 产生人的目的；(3) 首生人的状态；(4) 人的居所。在讨论这些问题时，托马斯提出，人的灵魂和人的身体是同时受造的；人是天主的肖像；儿童在刚出生的时候不能完满地运用理性；人被安排在伊甸园是为了治理和看守它。

在卷七中，托马斯讨论的是天主对受造物的管理。对这个问题他从受造物的存在（104 题）和受造物的改变（105—119 题）两个层面进行了讨论。在讨论受造物的存在时，托马斯主要强调两点：一是所有的受造物都因天主而得以存在和维持；二是天主藉一些中间原因维系受造物的存在。在讨论受造物的改变时，托马斯区分了天主对受造物的改变和一个受造物对另一个受造物的改变。在谈到天主对受造物的改变时，他强调了天主的万能。而在考察一个受造物对另一个受造物的改变时，他区分了三种情况：(1) 来自天使的改变；(2) 来自物体的改变；(3) 来自人的改变。托马斯认为，在天使和天使之间、在天使和有形的受造物之间、在天使和人之间、在物体和物体之间、在个人和个人之间都存在着一种普遍的联系和作用。

旁征博引是托马斯论证的特色，以下是他在《神学大全》中经常引用的作品、作品简称和著作者，我虽勉力查找但仍有遗缺。希望以下信息，能为进一步了解托马斯有所助益：

主要文献出处简表

文献作者及书名原名	文献名缩写	文献作者及书名翻译
Aristotle		亚里士多德
D Anima	***De An.***	亚里士多德的《论灵魂》
De Animalibus	***De Anim.***	亚里士多德的《论动物》

（续表）

文献作者及书名原名	文献名缩写	文献作者及书名翻译
De Partibus Animalium	***De Part. Anim.***	亚里士多德的《论动物之部分》
De Causa Motus Animalium	***De Causa Mot. Anim.***	亚里士多德的《动物行动原因论》
De Caeli et Mundi	***De Caeli***	亚里士多德的《天地论》
De Caelo	***De Caelo***	亚里士多德的《天界论》
De Plantis	***De Plant.***	亚里士多德的《论植物》
De Sophisticis Elenchis	***Soph. Elench.***	亚里士多德的《论诡辩的谬论》
Ethic	***Eth.***	亚里士多德的《伦理学》
Meteorologica	***Meteor.***	亚里士多德的《气象论》
Metaphysics	***Metaph.***	亚里士多德的《形上学》
Periherm	***Perih.***	亚里士多德的《解释论》
Analytica Posteriora	***Post. Anal.***	亚里士多德的《分析后论》
Physica	***Phys.***	亚里士多德的《物理学》
Topica	***Top.***	亚里士多德的《辨证论》
De Somno et Vigilia	***De Somno***	亚里士多德的《论睡眠与醒悟》
De Generatione et Corruptione	***De. Gener.***	亚里士多德的《生灭论》
Ars Rhetorica	***Rhetor.***	亚里士多德的《修辞学》
Ethica Eudemia	***Eth. Eudem.***	亚里士多德的《幸福伦理学》
Politica	***Polit.***	亚里士多德的《政治学》
De Generationibus Animalium	***De Gener. Anim.***	亚里士多德的《论动物之生殖》
Averroes Mohammed Ibn Rushd		亚威洛哀
Metaphysics	***In Metaph.***	亚威洛哀的《形上学注疏》

（续表）

文献作者及书名原名	文献名缩写	文献作者及书名翻译
De Anima	***De An.***	亚威洛哀的《灵魂论注疏》
Physic	***Phys.***	亚威洛哀的《物理学注释》
De Generationibus	***In De Gener.***	亚威洛哀的《生殖论注疏》
Anselm		安瑟谟
Monologium	***Monolog.***	安瑟谟的《独语录》
De Conceptu Virginali	***De Concep. Virg.***	安瑟谟的《论童贞女受孕与原罪》
De Casu Diaboli	***De Casu Diab.***	安瑟谟的《论魔鬼之堕落》
Cur Deus Homo	***Cur Deus Homo***	安瑟谟的《天主为何成人》
Gulielmus Altissiodus		吉勒莫安迪萧
Summa Aurea	***Summa Aurea***	吉勒莫安迪萧的《金言全集》
Altissiodorensis		亚提书
Summa Aurea	***Summa Aurea***	亚提书的《金言全集》
William of Auxerre		欧塞尔
Summa Aurea	***Summa Aurea***	欧塞尔的《金言全集》
Petrus Lombard		彼得隆巴
Sententiis	***Sent.***	彼得隆巴的《语录》
Anicius Manlius Boethius		波其武
De Hebdomadibus	***De Hedom.***	波其武的《论七天创造工程》
De Consolatione	***De Consol.***	波其武的《哲学的慰藉》
De Dualibus Nataralibus	***De Duab. Nat.***	波其武的《论二天性》
Topica Ciceronis	***In Top. Cicer.***	波其武的《论题之分类》
De Differenctia Topica	***De Differ. Top.***	波其武的《论辩的区分》
De Trinitate	***De Trin.***	波其武的《论天主圣三》

（续表）

文献作者及书名原名	文献名缩写	文献作者及书名翻译
Cyprianus		西彼莲
Epistola/Epistle	***Epist.***	西彼莲的《书信》
Tully Cicero		西塞罗
De Officiis	***De Officiis***	西塞罗的《论职务》
De Inventio	***De Invent.***	西塞罗的《修辞学》
De Divinatio	***De Divinat.***	西塞罗的《论占卜》
De Natura Deorum	***De Nat. Deor.***	西塞罗的《论神之性质》
Bernard of Clairvaus		伯尔纳铎
De Consideratione	***De Consider.***	伯尔纳铎的《论审察》
Homilia Super Canticos	***Hom. Cant.***	伯尔纳铎的《雅歌释义》
De Gratia et Libero Arbitrio	***De Gratia et Lib. Arb.***	伯尔纳铎的《论恩宠与抉择》
Hilary of Poitiers		希拉利
De Trinitate	***De Trin.***	希拉利的《论天主圣三》
De Synodis	***De Synod.***	希拉利的《论主教会议》
Commentarius in Matthaeum	***In Matth.***	希拉利的《玛窦福音释义》
Dionysius Exiguus		狄奥尼修
Caelestis Hierarchiae	***De Cael. Hier.***	狄奥尼修的《上天阶级论》
De Causis	***De Causis***	狄奥尼修的《论原因》
De Mystica Theologia	***Myst. Theol.***	狄奥尼修的《神秘神学》
De Divinis Nominibus	***De Div. Nom.***	狄奥尼修的《神名论》
Ecclesiastica Hierarchia	***De Eccles. Hier.***	狄奥尼修的《教会阶级论》
Epistola ad Polycarpum	***Epist. ad Poly.***	狄奥尼修的《致波利卡普书》

（续表）

文献作者及书名原名	文献名缩写	文献作者及书名翻译
Epistola	***Epist.***	狄奥尼修的《书信集》
Ad Ioannem Evangelistam	***Ad Ioann. Evanglist.***	狄奥尼修的《致圣史若望》
Ioannes Chrysostom		金口若望
Homiilia (Super Ioannem)	***Hom. In Ioan.***	金口若望的《若望福音论赞》
In Matthaeum	***In Matt.***	金口若望的《玛窦福音论赞》
Homilia in Geneim	***In Genesim***	金口若望的《创世纪论赞》
Homilia in Epistola Ad Romanos	***Hom. Ad Roman.***	金口若望的《罗马书论赞》
Homila in Epistola Ad Hebraeus	***Hom. Ad Hebrae.***	金口若望的《希伯来书论赞》
Ambrose		盎博罗修
De Fide Catholica	***De Fide***	盎博罗修的《论天主教信德》
De Officiis	***De Officiis***	盎博罗修的《论神职职务》
De Spiritu Sancto	***De Spir. Sacto***	盎博罗修的《论天主圣神》
Hexaemerom	***Hexaem.***	盎博罗修的《六天创世注疏》
De Trinit	***De Trin.***	盎博罗修的《论天主圣三》
De Fide	***De Fide***	盎博罗修的《论信德》
Gregory of Nazianzus		纳西盎的额我略
Prologus in Oratione	***Orat.***	纳西盎的额我略的《演讲集》
Epistola	***Epist.***	纳西盎的额我略的《书信集》
Gregory I		教宗额我略一世
Dialogorum Libri	***Dial.***	教宗额我略一世的《对话录》
Moralium Libri	***Moral.***	教宗额我略一世的《伦理纵谈》

（续表）

文献作者及书名原名	文献名缩写	文献作者及书名翻译
Homilia in Ezechiel	***In Ezech.***	教宗额我略一世的《厄则克耳论赞》
Evangeliorum Libri	***In Evang.***	教宗额我略一世的《福音论赞》
Rabbi Moses		梅瑟教师
Doctor Perplexorum	***Doct. Perpl.***	梅瑟教师的《疑问指南》
Origen		奥利振
Peri Archon	***Peri Archon***	奥利振的《原则论》
Super Epistolam ad Romanos	***In Rom.***	奥利振的《罗马书释义》
On Jesus' Nativity	***In Lib. Iesu Nave***	奥利振的《论耶稣圣诞》
Augustine		奥古斯丁
Contra Faustum Manichaeum	***Contra Faust.***	奥古斯丁的《驳摩尼教徒福斯德》
Confessiones	***Confess.***	奥古斯丁的《忏悔录》
Contra Maximinum Arianorcem	***Contra Maximin.***	奥古斯丁的《驳马西米诺》
De Civitate Dei	***De Civit. Dei***	奥古斯丁的《天主之城》
De Natura Boni	***De Nat. Boni***	奥古斯丁的《论善之性质》
De Doctrina Christiana	***De Doct. Christ.***	奥古斯丁的《论基督圣道》
De Trinitate	***De Trin.***	奥古斯丁的《论天主圣三》
De Vera Religione	***De Vera Relig.***	奥古斯丁的《论真宗教》
De Utilitate Credendi	***De Util. Cred.***	奥古斯丁的《论信仰的益处》
De Correptione et Gratia	***De Corrept. et Grat.***	奥古斯丁的《论劝诫与恩宠》
Enchiridion	***Enchir.***	奥古斯丁的《基本教理手册》
Epistola	***Epist.***	奥古斯丁的《书信集》

（续表）

文献作者及书名原名	文献名缩写	文献作者及书名翻译
Octoginta Trium Quaestionibus	***Lib. 83 Quaest.***	奥古斯丁的《杂题八十三》
Retractationum	***Retract.***	奥古斯丁的《订正录》
Super Genesis ad Litteram	***De Genesi ad Litt.***	奥古斯丁的《创世纪字义新探》
Soliloquium	***Solil.***	奥古斯丁的《独语》
Enarrationes in Psalmos	***Enarr. In Psalm.***	奥古斯丁的《圣咏讲述》
In Epistolam Joannis ad Parthos	***Epist.***	奥古斯丁的《公函若望一书释义》
Sermo de Fide	***Serm.***	奥古斯丁的《论信德》
De Cura Pro Mortuis Gerenda	***De Cura pro Mort.***	奥古斯丁的《论追念亡者》
Contra Adversarium Legis et Prophetarum	***Contra Adv. Legis et Proph.***	奥古斯丁的《法律和先知恶评批驳》
De Divinatione Daemonum	***De Divinat. Daemon.***	奥古斯丁的《论魔鬼之预言》
Adversus Quinque Haereses	***De Haere.***	奥古斯丁的《驳五种异端》
Contra Julianum	***Contra Julian.***	奥古斯丁的《驳朱利安》
Merits and Rmission of Sin, and Infant Baptism	***De Pecc. Remiss. Et Bapt. Parv.***	奥古斯丁的《功绩和罪的赦免以及婴儿洗礼》
Hugh of St. Victor		圣维克多之雨果
Sententiarum	***Sent.***	圣维克多的雨果的《语录大全》
De Sacramentum	***De Sacram.***	圣维克多的雨果的《论圣事》
Avicenna		亚维采那
Sufficientiae	***Sufficientia***	亚维采那的《哲学集成》

（续表）

文献作者及书名原名	文献名缩写	文献作者及书名翻译
Metaphysics	***Metaph.***	亚维采那的《形上学》
De Naturalibus	***De Natur.***	亚维采那的《论自然物》
Jerome		热罗尼莫
Epistole	***Epist.***	热罗尼莫的《书信》
John of Damascene		大马士革的若望
De Fide Orthodoxa	***De Fide Orth.***	大马士革的若望的《论正统信仰》
De Suffragiis Mortuorum	***Suffrag.***	大马斯革的《论救助死人》
Alexander of Hales		哈勒士的亚历山大
Summa Theologica	***Summa Theol.***	哈勒士的亚历山大的《神学大全》
Pelagius		贝拉
Symboli Explanetiones Ad Damasum	***Symb.***	贝拉的《信德发徵》
St. Thomas Aquinas		圣托马斯 · 阿奎那
Contra Errors Graecorum	***Contra Err.***	圣托马斯的《反对希腊人的错误》
Questiones Disputatae De Potential	***De Pot.***	圣托马斯的《论能力》
Summa Theologica, Suppl.	***S. T., Suppl.***	《神学大全》补录
Beda/Bede the Venerable		伯达
Commentarium in Lucam	***In Luc.***	伯达的《路加福音注释》
Glossa	***Glossa***	伯达的《圣经注释》
Gregory of Nyssa		尼沙的额我略
De Hominis Opificio	***De Hom. Opif.***	尼沙的额我略的《论人的工作》
Fulgentius of Ruspe		富振秋
De Fide ad Petrum	***De Fide ad Petrum***	富振秋的《与伯铎论信仰》

（续表）

文献作者及书名原名	文献名缩写	文献作者及书名翻译
Isidor of Sevilla		依希道
Etymologiae	***Etym.***	依希道的《语源学》
De Ecclesiasticis Officiis	***Eccles. Officiis***	依希道的《论教会的职责》
De Ordine Creatur	***De Ord. Creatur***	依希道的《论受造物的秩序》
Plato		柏拉图
Meno	***Meno***	柏拉图的《美诺篇》
Timaeus	***Timaeus***	柏拉图的《蒂迈欧篇》
Phaedo	***Phaedo***	柏拉图的《费多篇》
Avicebron		亚维采布隆
Fons Vitae	***Fons Vitae***	亚维采布隆的《生命之泉源》
Issac Israeli		依撒格
De Definitionibus	***De Defin.***	依撒格的《论定义》
Basil		巴西略
Homilia in Hexaem	***In Hexaem.***	巴西略的《六天创世论赞》
Gennadius de Marseille		马赛的吉南德
De Ecclesiasticis Dogmatibus	***De Eccles. Dogm.***	吉南德的《论圣教信端》
Ptolomaeus		托勒密
Syntaxis Matkematica	***Syntaxis Matkematica***	托勒密的《天文学大成》
Alpharabius		亚丰拉比
Ethicae	***Eth.***	亚丰拉比的《伦理学》
Bonaventure		波那文都
Commentaria in IV Libros Sententiarum Petri Lombardi	***In Sent.***	波那文都的《隆巴思想注疏》

（续表）

文献作者及书名原名	文献名缩写	文献作者及书名翻译
St. Albert the Great		阿尔伯特
Commentary on Aristotle's Physics	***Sent.***	阿尔伯特的《亚里士多德的物理学注疏》
Opera Omnia	***Opera Omnia***	阿尔伯特的《阿尔伯特全集》
De Animalibus	***De Anim.***	阿尔伯特的《论动物》
Nemesius of Emesa		尼莫修斯
De Natura Hominis	***De Nat. Hom.***	尼莫修斯的《论人的本性》
Robert Grosseteste		格罗斯泰斯特
DeLibero Arbitrio	***De Lib. Arb.***	格罗斯泰斯特的《论自由抉择》
Maimonides		迈蒙尼德
Guide for Perplexed	***Guide***	迈蒙尼德的《解惑指南》

文献中相关符号的指示意义说明如下：

1.《神学大全》第一集用 I 表示，第二集是 II，第三集是 III，补编用 suppl. 表示。集下的“问题”用大写英文字母 Q 或小写字母 q 表示；问题之下的条用 Art. 或 a 表示；每条下面的质疑是“arg.”，反证是“sed contra”，正解是“c”，释疑是“ad”。如“I, Q25, a. 3, ad. 4”就表示“《神学大全》第一集第 25 题第三条的释疑 4”。

2. 书中引用文献时出现的符号有罗马数字代表文献的不同部分；p. 加数字代表页数；PG 加数字代表段落（如 PG4 代表第四段）；PL 加数字则代表行数（如 PL5 代表第五行）。

3. 符号“*op. cit.*”是拉丁文 opere citato 的缩写，意思是“在已引用的著作中”，其后面所加的字母或者数字，通常指的是在前文中刚刚引用过的文献的出处。

以上就是《圣托马斯基本著作》两卷本所收《神学大全》第一卷的全部内容结构及托马斯的主要学术观点，并附带说明了所引文献出处及相关符号指示意义。简述于此，供读者参考。

THE SUMMA THEOLOGICA[1]

PART ONE

1. The Summa Theologica：神学总论；神学大全

Question I
THE NATURE AND DOMAIN OF SACRED DOCTRINE
(*In Ten Articles*)

TO place our purpose within definite limits, we must first investigate the nature and domain of sacred doctrine. Concerning this there are ten points of inquiry:—

(1) Whether sacred doctrine is necessary? (2) Whether it is a science? (3) Whether it is one or many? (4) Whether it is speculative or practical? (5) How it is compared with other sciences? (6) Whether it is a wisdom? (7) Whether God is its subject-matter[2]? (8) Whether it is argumentative[3]? (9) Whether it rightly employs metaphors[4] and similes? (10) Whether the Sacred Scripture[5] of this doctrine may be expounded in different senses?

First Article
WHETHER, BESIDES THE PHILOSOPHICAL SCIENCES, ANY FURTHER DOCTRINE IS REQUIRED?

We proceed thus to the First Article: —

Objection 1. It seems that, besides the philosophical sciences, we have

---

1. speculative：思考的；思辨的
2. subject-matter：主题；研究对象
3. argumentative：论证性的
4. metaphors：隐喻
5. the Sacred Scripture：《圣经》

no need of any further knowledge. For man should not seek to know what is above reason: *Seek not the things that are too high for thee* (*Ecclus.* iii. 22). But whatever is not above reason is sufficiently considered in the philosophical sciences. Therefore any other knowledge besides the philosophical sciences is superfluous.

Obj. 2. Further, knowledge can be concerned only with being, for nothing can be known, save the true, which is convertible with being. But everything that is, is considered in the philosophical sciences — even God Himself; so that there is a part of philosophy called theology[1], or the divine science, as is clear from Aristotle.[2] Therefore, besides the philosophical sciences, there is no need of any further knowledge.

On the contrary, It is written (*2 Tim.* iii. 16): *All Scripture inspired of God is profitable to teach, to reprove, to correct, to instruct in justice.* Now Scripture, inspired of God, is not a part of the philosophical sciences discovered by human reason. Therefore it is useful that besides the philosophical sciences there should be another science — *i.e.*, inspired of God.

I answer that, It was necessary for man's salvation[3] that there should be a knowledge revealed by God, besides the philosophical sciences investigated by human reason. First, because man is directed to God as to an end that surpasses the grasp of his reason: *The eye hath not seen, O God, besides Thee, what things Thou hast prepared for them that wait for Thee* (*Isa.* lxiv. 4). But the end must first be known by men who are to direct their thoughts and actions to the end. Hence it was necessary for the salvation of man that certain truths which exceed human reason should be made known to him by divine revelation[4]. Even as regards those truths about God which human reason can investigate, it was

---

1. theology：神学
2. 参见 *Metaph.*, V, 1 (1026a 19).
3. salvation：救恩
4. revelation：启示

necessary that man be taught by a divine revelation. For the truth about God, such as reason can know it, would only be known by a few, and that after a long time, and with the admixture of many errors; whereas man's whole salvation, which is in God, depends upon the knowledge of this truth. Therefore, in order that the salvation of men might be brought about more fitly and more surely, it was necessary that they be taught divine truths by divine revelation. It was therefore necessary that, besides the philosophical sciences investigated by reason, there should be a sacred science by way of revelation.

Reply Obj. 1. Although those things which are beyond man's knowledge may not be sought for by man through his reason, nevertheless, what is revealed by God must be accepted through faith. Hence the sacred text continues, *For many things are shown to thee above the understanding of man* (*Ecclus.* iii. 25). And in such things sacred science consists.

Reply Obj. 2. Sciences are diversified according to the diverse nature of their knowable objects. For the astronomer and the physicist both prove the same conclusion — that the earth, for instance, is round: the astronomer by means of mathematics (*i.e.*, abstracting from matter), but the physicist by means of matter itself. Hence there is no reason why those things which are treated by the philosophical sciences, so far as they can be known by the light of natural reason, may not also be treated by another science so far as they are known by the light of the divine revelation. Hence the theology included in sacred doctrine differs in genus from that theology which is part of philosophy.

Second Article
WHETHER SACRED DOCTRINE IS A SCIENCE?

We proceed thus to the Second Article: —

---

1. doctrine：教义；教理

Objection 1. It seems that sacred doctrine is not a science. For every science proceeds from self-evident principles. But sacred doctrine proceeds from articles of faith[1] which are not self-evident, since their truth is not admitted by all: *For all men have not faith* (*2 Thess.* iii. 2). Therefore sacred doctrine is not a science.

Obj. 2. Further, science is not of individuals. But sacred doctrine treats of individual facts, such as the deeds of Abraham, Isaac and Jacob, and the like. Therefore sacred doctrine is not a science.

On the contrary, Augustine says that *to this science alone belongs that whereby saving faith is begotten, nourished, protected and strengthened.*[2] But this can be said of no science except sacred doctrine. Therefore sacred doctrine is a science.

I answer that, Sacred doctrine is a science. We must bear in mind that there are two kinds of sciences. There are some which proceed from principles known by the natural light of the intellect, such as arithmetic and geometry and the like. There are also some which proceed from principles known by the light of a higher science: thus the science of optics proceeds from principles established by geometry, and music from principles established by arithmetic. So it is that sacred doctrine is a science because it proceeds from principles made known by the light of a higher science, namely, the science of God and the blessed. Hence, just as music accepts on authority the principles taught by the arithmetician, so sacred science accepts the principles revealed by God.

Reply Obj. 1. The principles of any science are either in themselves selfevident, or reducible to the knowledge of a higher science; and such, as we have said, are the principles of sacred doctrine.

Reply Obj. 2. Individual facts are not treated in sacred doctrine because it is concerned with them principally; they are rather

---

1. faith：信仰
2. 参见 *De Trin.*, XIV, 1 (PL 42, 1037).

introduced as examples to be followed in our lives (as in the moral sciences), as well as to establish the authority of those men through whom the divine revelation, on which this sacred scripture or doctrine is based, has come down to us.

Third Article
WHETHER SACRED DOCTRINE IS ONE SCIENCE?

We proceed thus to the Third Article: —

Objection 1. It seems that sacred doctrine is not one science, for according to the Philosopher *that science is one which treats only of one class of subjects.*[1] But the creator and the creature, both of whom are treated in sacred doctrine, cannot be grouped together under one class of subjects. Therefore sacred doctrine is not one science.

Obj. 2. Further, in sacred doctrine we treat of angels, corporeal creatures and human morality. But these belong to separate philosophical sciences. Therefore sacred doctrine cannot be one science.

On the contrary, Holy Scripture speaks of it as one science: *Wisdom gave him the knowledge* [*scientiam*] *of holy things* (*Wis.* x. 10).

I answer that, Sacred doctrine is one science. The unity of a power or habit is to be gauged by its object, not indeed, in its material aspect, but as regards the formality under which it is an object. For example, man, ass, stone, agree in the one formality of being colored; and color is the formal object of sight. Therefore, because Sacred Scripture (as we have said) considers some things under the formality of being divinely revealed, all things which have been divinely revealed have in common the formality of the object of this science. Hence, they are included under sacred doctrine as under one science.

---

1. 参见 *Post. Anal.*, I, 28 (87a 38).

Reply Obj. 1. Sacred doctrine does not treat of God and creatures equally, but of God primarily, and of creatures only so far as they are referable to God as their beginning or end. Hence the unity of this science is not impaired.

Reply Obj. 2. Nothing prevents inferior powers or habits from being diversified by objects which yet agree with one another in coming together under a higher power or habit; because the higher power or habit regards its own object under a more universal formality. Thus, the object of the *common sense*[1] is the sensible, including, therefore, whatever is visible or audible. Hence the *common sense*, although one power, extends to all the objects of the five senses. Similarly, objects which are the subject-matter of different philosophical sciences can yet be treated by this one single sacred science under one aspect, namely, in so far as they can be included in revelation. So that in this way sacred doctrine bears, as it were, the stamp of the divine science, which is one and simple, yet extends to everything.

Fourth Article
WHETHER SACRED DOCTRINE IS A PRACTICAL SCIENCE?

We proceed thus to the Fourth Article: —

Objection 1. It seems that sacred doctrine is a practical science, for a practical science is that which ends in action, according to the Philosopher.[2] But sacred doctrine is ordained to action: *Be ye doers of the word, and not hearers only* (*Jas.* i. 22). Therefore sacred doctrine is a practical science.

Obj. 2. Further, sacred doctrine is divided into the Old and the New Law. But law belongs to moral science, which is a practical science. Therefore sacred doctrine is a practical science.

---

1. common sense：共同意识
2. 参见 *Metaph.*, Ia, 1 (993b 21).

On the contrary, Every practical science is concerned with the things man can do; as moral science is concerned with human acts, and architecture with buildings. But sacred doctrine is chiefly concerned with God, Who is rather the Maker of man. Therefore it is not a practical but a speculative science.

I answer that, Sacred doctrine, being one, extends to things which belong to the different philosophical sciences, because it considers in each the same formal aspect, namely, so far as they can be known through the divine light. Hence, although among the philosophical sciences some are speculative and others practical, nevertheless sacred doctrine includes both; as God, by one and the same science, knows both Himself and His works.

Still, it is more speculative than practical, because it is more concerned with divine things than with human acts; though even of these acts it treats inasmuch as man is ordained by them to the perfect knowledge of God, in which consists eternal beatitude[1].

This is a sufficient answer to the Objections.

Fifth Article
WHETHER SACRED DOCTRINE IS NOBLER THAN OTHER SCIENCES?

We proceed thus to the Fifth Article: —

Objection 1. It seems that sacred doctrine is not nobler than other sciences, for the nobility of a science depends on its certitude. But other sciences, the principles of which cannot be doubted, seem to be more certain than sacred doctrine; for its principles — namely, articles of faith — can be doubted. Therefore other sciences seem to be nobler.

Obj. 2. Further, it is the part of a lower science to draw upon a

---

1. beatitude：真福；全福；至福：指圆满的幸福。

higher; as music draws upon arithmetic. But sacred doctrine does draw upon the philosophical sciences; for Jerome observes, in his Epistle to Magnus, that *the ancient doctors so enriched their books with the doctrines and thoughts of the philosophers, that thou knowest not what more to admire in them, their profane erudition or their scriptural learning.*[1] Therefore sacred doctrine is inferior to other sciences.

On the contrary, Other sciences are called the handmaidens of this one: *Wisdom sent her maids to invite to the tower* (*Prov.* ix. 3).

I answer that, Since this science is partly speculative and partly practical, it transcends all other sciences, speculative and practical. Now one speculative science is said to be nobler than another either by reason of its greater certitude, or by reason of the higher dignity of its subject-matter. In both these respects this science surpasses other speculative sciences: in point of greater certitude, because other sciences derive their certitude from the natural light of human reason, which can err, whereas this derives its certitude from the light of the divine knowledge, which cannot err; in point of the higher dignity of its subject-matter, because this science treats chiefly of those things which by their sublimity transcend human reason, while other sciences consider only those things which are within reason's grasp. Of the practical sciences, that one is nobler which is ordained to a more final end, as political science is nobler than military science; for the good of the army is directed to the good of the state. But the purpose of this science, in so far as it is practical, is eternal beatitude, to which as to an ultimate end the ends of all the practical sciences are directed. Hence it is clear that from every standpoint it is nobler than other sciences.

Reply Obj. 1. It may well happen that what is in itself the more certain may seem to us the less certain because of the weakness of our

---

1. 参见 *Epist.* LXX (PL 22, 668).

intellect, *which is dazzled by the clearest objects of nature; as the owl is dazzled by the light of the sun.*[1] Hence the fact that some happen to doubt about the articles of faith is not due to the uncertain nature of the truths, but to the weakness of the human intellect; yet the slenderest knowledge that may be obtained of the highest things is more desirable than the most certain knowledge obtained of the lowest things, as is said in *De Animalibus* xi.[2]

Reply Obj. 2. This science can draw upon the philosophical sciences, not as though it stood in need of them, but only in order to make its teaching clearer. For it accepts its principles, not from the other sciences, but immediately from God, by revelation. Therefore it does not draw upon the other sciences as upon its superiors, but uses them as its inferiors and handmaidens: even so the master sciences make use of subordinate sciences, as political science of military science. That it thus uses them is not due to its own defect or insufficiency, but to the defect of our intellect, which is more easily led by what is known through natural reason (from which proceed the other sciences), to that which is above reason, such as are the teachings of this science.

Sixth Article
WHETHER THIS DOCTRINE IS A WISDOM?

We proceed thus to the Sixth Article: —

Objection 1. It seems that this doctrine is not a wisdom. For no doctrine which borrows its principles is worthy of the name of wisdom, seeing that the wise man directs, and is not directed.[3] But this doctrine borrows its principles. Therefore it is not a wisdom.

---

1. 参见 Aristotle, *Metaph.*, Ia, 1 (993b 9).
2. 参见 Aristotle, *De Part. Anim.*, I, 5 (644b 31).
3. 参见 Aristotle, *Metaph.*, I, 2 (982a 18).

Obj. 2. Further, it is a part of wisdom to prove the principles of other sciences. Hence it is called the chief of sciences, as is clear in *Ethics* vi.[1] But this doctrine does not prove the principles of other sciences. Therefore it is not a wisdom.

Obj. 3. Further, this doctrine is acquired by study, whereas wisdom is acquired by God's inspiration, and is accordingly numbered among the gifts of the Holy Spirit[2] (*Isa.* xi. 2). Therefore this doctrine is not a wisdom.

On the contrary, It is written (*Deut.* iv. 6): *This is your wisdom and understanding in the sight of nations.*

I answer that, This doctrine is wisdom above all human wisdoms not merely in any one order, but absolutely. For since it is the part of a wise man to order and to judge, and since lesser matters can be judged in the light of some higher cause, he is said to be wise in any genus who considers the highest cause in that genus. Thus in the realm of building, he who plans the form of the house is called wise and architect, in relation to the subordinate laborers who trim the wood and make ready the stones: thus it is said, *As a wise architect I have laid the foundation* (*1 Cor.* iii. 10). Again, in the order of all human life, the prudent man is called wise, inasmuch as he directs his acts to a fitting end: thus it is said, *Wisdom is prudence to a man* (*Prov.* x. 23). Therefore, he who considers absolutely the highest cause of the whole universe, namely God, is most of all called wise. Hence wisdom is said to be the knowledge of divine things, as Augustine says.[3] But sacred doctrine essentially treats of God viewed as the highest cause, for it treats of Him not only so far as He can be known through creatures just as philosophers knew Him — *That which is known of God is manifest in them* (*Rom.* i. 19) — but also so far as He is known

1. 参见 Aristotle, *Eth.*, VI, 7 (1141a 20).
2. the Holy Spirit：圣神；圣灵，指三位一体的天主的第三位
3. 参见 *De Trin.*, XII, 14 (PL 42, 1009).— Cf. Cicero, *De Officiis*, II, 2 (p. 80).

to Himself alone and revealed to others. Hence sacred doctrine is especially called a wisdom.

Reply Obj. 1. Sacred doctrine derives its principles, not from any human knowledge, but from the divine knowledge, by which, as by the highest wisdom[1], all our knowledge is ordered.

Reply Obj. 2. The principles of the other sciences either are evident and cannot be proved, or they are proved by natural reason in some other science. But the knowledge proper to this science comes through revelation, and not through natural reason. Therefore it is not its business to prove the principles of the other sciences, but only to judge them. For whatsoever is found in the other sciences contrary to the truth of this science must be condemned as false. Hence, it is said: *Destroying counsels and every height that exalteth itself against the knowledge of God* (*2 Cor.* x. 4, 5).

Reply Obj. 3. Since judgment pertains to wisdom, in accord with a twofold manner of judging there is a twofold wisdom. A man may judge in one way by inclination, as whoever has the habit of a virtue judges rightly of what is virtuous by his very inclination towards it. Hence it is the virtuous man, as we read, [2] who is the measure and rule of human acts. In another way, a man may judge by knowledge, just as a man learned in moral science might be able to judge rightly about virtuous acts, though he had not virtue. The first manner of judging divine things belongs to that wisdom which is numbered as a gift of the Holy Ghost: *The spiritual man judgeth all things* (*1 Cor.* ii. 15). And Dionysius says: *Hierotheus is taught not only as one learning, but also as experiencing divine things.*[3] The second manner of judging belongs to this doctrine, inasmuch as it is acquired by study, though its principles are obtained by revelation.

---

1. the highest wisdom：最高的智慧：指天主。
2. 参见 Aris- totle, *Eth.*, X, 5 (1176a 17).
3. 参见 *De Div. Nom.*, II, 9 (PG 3, 648).

Seventh Article

WHETHER GOD IS THE SUBJECT-MATTER OF THIS SCIENCE?

We proceed thus to the Seventh Article: —

Objection 1 . It seems that God is not the subject-matter of this science. For, according to the Philosopher,[1] in every science the essence of its subject is presupposed. But this science cannot presuppose the essence of God, for Damascene says: *It is impossible to express the essence of God.*[2] Therefore God is not the subject-matter of this science.

Obj. 2. Further, whatever conclusions are reached in any science must be comprehended under the subject-matter of that science. But in Holy Scripture we reach conclusions not only concerning God, but concerning many other things, such as creatures and human morality. Therefore God is not the subject-matter of this science.

On the contrary, The subject-matter of a science is that of which it principally treats. But in this science the treatment is mainly about God; for it is called theology, as treating of God. Therefore God is the subject-matter of this science.

I answer that, God is the subject-matter of this science. The relation between a science and its subject-matter is the same as that between a habit or a power and its object. Now properly speaking the object of a power or habit is that under whose formality all things are referred to that power or habit, as man and stone are referred to sight in that they are colored. Hence colored things are the proper object of sight. But in sacred doctrine all things are treated under the aspect of God, either because they are God Himself, or because they refer to God as to their beginning and end. Hence it follows that God is in very truth the subject-matter of this science. This is made clear also from the

1. 参见 *Post. Anal.*, I, 1 (71a 13).
2. 参见 *De Fide Orth.*, I, 4 (PG 94, 797).

principles of this science, namely, the articles of faith, for faith is about God. The subject-matter of the principles and of the whole science must be the same, since the whole science is contained virtually in its principles.

Some, however, looking to what is treated in this science, and not to the aspect under which it is treated, have asserted the subject-matter of this science to be something other than God — that is, either things and signs,[1] or the works of salvation,[2] or the whole Christ[3], that is, the head and members.[4] Of all these things, in truth, we treat in this science, but so far as they are ordered to God.

Reply Obj. 1. Although we cannot know in what consists the essence of God, nevertheless in this doctrine we make use of His effects, either of nature or of grace[5], in the place of a definition, in regard to whatever is treated in this doctrine concerning God; even as in some philosophical sciences we demonstrate something about a cause from its effect, by taking the effect in the place of a definition of the cause.

Reply Obj. 2. Whatever other conclusions are reached in this sacred science are comprehended under God, not as parts or species or accidents, but as in some way ordained to Him.

Eighth Article
WHETHER SACRED DOCTRINE IS ARGUMENTATIVE?

We proceed thus to the Eighth Article: —

Objection 1. It seems this doctrine is not argumentative. For Ambrose

---

1. 参见 Peter Lombard, *Sent.*, I, i, 1 (I, 14); cf. St. Augustine, *De Doc. Christ.*, I, 2 (PL 34, 19).
2. 参见 Hugh of St. Victor, *De Sacram.*, Prol2 (PL 176, 183).
3. Christ：基督
4. 参见 Robert Grosseteste, *Hexaëm.* (p. 176); Robert Kilwardby, *De Nat. Theol.* (p. 17).
5. grace：恩宠；恩典

says: *Put arguments aside where faith is sought.*[1] But in this doctrine faith especially is sought: *But these things are written that you may believe* (*Jo.* xx. 31). Therefore sacred doctrine is not argumentative.

Obj. 2. Further, if it is argumentative, the argument is either from authority or from reason. If it is from authority, it seems unbefitting its dignity, for the proof from authority is the weakest form of proof according to Boethius.[2] But if from reason, this is unbefitting its end, because, according to Gregory, *faith has no merit in those things of which human reason brings its own experience.*[3] Therefore sacred doctrine is not argumentative.

On the contrary, The Scripture says that a bishop should *embrace that faithful word which is according to doctrine, that he may be able to exhort in sound doctrine and to convince the gainsayers* (*Tit.* i. 9).

I answer that, As the other sciences do not argue in proof of their principles, but argue from their principles to demonstrate other truths in these sciences, so this doctrine does not argue in proof of its principles, which are the articles of faith[4], but from them it goes on to prove something else; as the Apostle argues from the resurrection of Christ in proof of the general resurrection (*1 Cor.* xv, 12). However, it is to be borne in mind, in regard to the philosophical sciences, that the inferior sciences neither prove their principles nor dispute with those who deny them, but leave this to a higher science; whereas the highest of them, viz., metaphysics[5], can dispute with one who denies its principles, if only the opponent will make some concession; but if he concedes nothing, it can have no dispute with him, though it can answer his arguments. Hence Sacred Scripture, since it has no science above itself, disputes

---

1. 参见 *De Fide*, I, 13 (PL 16, 570).
2. 参见 *In Top. Cicer.*, I (PL 64, 1166); *De Differ. Top.*, III (PL 64, 1199).
3. 参见 *In Evang.*, II, hom. 26 (PL 76, 1197).
4. the articles of faith：信条
5. metaphysics：形而上学；玄学

argumentatively with one who denies its principles only if the opponent admits some at least of the truths obtained through divine revelation. Thus, we can argue with heretics[1] from texts in Holy Scripture[2], and against those who deny one article of faith we can argue from another. If our opponent believes nothing of divine revelation, there is no longer any means of proving the articles of faith by argument, but only of answering his objections — if he has any — against faith. Since faith rests upon infallible truth[3], and since the contrary of a truth can never be demonstrated, it is clear that the proofs brought against faith are not demonstrations, but arguments that can be answered.

Reply Obj. 1. Although arguments from human reason cannot avail to prove what belongs to faith, nevertheless, this doctrine argues from articles of faith to other truths.

Reply Obj. 2. It is especially proper to this doctrine to argue from authority, inasmuch as its principles are obtained by revelation; and hence we must believe the authority of those to whom the revelation has been made. Nor does this take away from the dignity of this doctrine, for although the argument from authority based on human reason is the weakest, yet the argument from authority based on divine revelation is the strongest. But sacred doctrine also makes use of human reason, not, indeed, to prove faith (for thereby the merit of faith would come to an end), but to make clear other things that are set forth in this doctrine. Since therefore grace does not destroy nature, but perfects it, natural reason should minister to faith as the natural inclination of the will ministers to charity. Hence the Apostle says: *Bringing into captivity every understanding unto the obedience of Christ* (*2 Cor.* x. 5). Hence it is that sacred doctrine makes use also of the authority of philosophers in those questions in which they were able to

---

1. heretics：异教徒
2. Holy Scripture：《圣经》
3. infallible truth：绝对可靠的真理；确凿的真理

know the truth by natural reason, as Paul quotes a saying of Aratus: *As some also of your own poets said: For we are also His offspring* (*Acts* xvii. 28). Nevertheless, sacred doctrine makes use of these authorities as extrinsic and probable arguments, but properly uses the authority of the canonical Scriptures as a necessary demonstration, and the authority of the doctors of the Church as one that may properly be used, yet merely as probable. For our faith rests upon the revelation made to the apostles[1] and prophets[2], who wrote the canonical books[3], and not on the revelations (if any such there are) made to other doctors. Hence Augustine says: *Only those books of Scripture which are called canonical have I learned to hold in such honor as to believe their authors have not erred in any way in writing them. But other authors I so read as not to deem anything in their works to be true, merely because of their having so thought and written, whatever may have been their holiness and learning.*

Ninth Article
WHETHER HOLY SCRIPTURE SHOULD USE METAPHORS ?

We proceed thus to the Ninth Article: —

Objection 1. It seems that Holy Scripture should not use metaphors. For that which is proper to the lowest science seems not to befit this science which holds the highest place of all. But to proceed by the aid of various similitudes and figures is proper to poetic, the least of all the sciences. Therefore it is not fitting that this science should make use of such similitudes.

Obj, 2. Further, this doctrine seems to be intended to make truth clear. Hence a reward is held out to those who manifest it: *They*

---

1. apostle：宗徒；使徒，通常指耶稣的十二门徒，但这里指十二门徒之外由耶稣亲选的保禄宗徒。
2. prophet：先知
3. the canonical books：指被定为正典的圣经内各书卷。

that explain me shall have life everlasting[1] (*Ecclus*. xxiv. 31). But by such similitudes truth is obscured. Therefore to put forward divine truths under the likeness of corporeal things does not befit this doctrine.

Obj. 3. Further, the higher creatures are, the nearer they approach to the divine likeness. If therefore any creature be taken to represent God, this representation ought chiefly to be taken from the higher creatures, and not from the lower; yet this is often found in the Scriptures.

On the contrary, It is written (*Osee* xii. 10): *I have multiplied visions, and I have used similitudes by the ministry of the prophets*. But to put forward anything by means of similitudes is to use metaphors. Therefore sacred doctrine may use metaphors.

I answer that, It is befitting Holy Scripture to put forward divine and spiritual truths[2] by means of comparisons with material things. For God provides for everything according to the capacity of its nature. Now it is natural to man to attain to intellectual truths through sensible things, because all our knowledge originates from sense. Hence in Holy Scripture spiritual truths are fittingly taught under the likeness of material things. This is what Dionysius says: *We cannot be enlightened by the divine rays except they be hidden within the covering of many sacred veils*.[3] It is also befitting Holy Scripture which is proposed to all without distinction of persons — *To the wise and to the unwise I am a debtor* (*Rom*. i. 14) — that spiritual truths be expounded by means of figures taken from corporeal things, in order that thereby even the simple who are unable by themselves to grasp intellectual things may be able to understand it.

Reply Obj. 1. Poetry makes use of metaphors to produce a representation for it is natural to man to be pleased with representations. But sacred doctrine makes use of metaphors as both necessary and useful.

Reply Obj. 2. The ray of divine revelation is not extinguished by the

---

1. life everlasting：永恒的生命
2. spiritual truth：属灵的真理
3. 参见 *De Cael. Hier*., I, 2 (PG 3, 121).

sensible imagery wherewith it is veiled, as Dionysius says;[1] and its truth so far remains that it does not allow the minds of those to whom the revelation has been made, to rest in the likenesses, but raises them to the knowledge of intelligible truths; and through those to whom the revelation has been made others also may receive instruction in these matters. Hence those things that are taught metaphorically in one part of Scripture, in other parts are taught more openly. The very hiding of truth in figures is useful for the exercise of thoughtful minds, and as a defense against the ridicule of the unbelievers according to the words, *Give not that which is holy to dogs* (*Matt.* vii.6)

Reply Obj. 3. As Dionysius says,[2] it is more fitting that divine truths should be expounded under the figure of less noble than of nobler bodies; and this for three reasons. First, because thereby men's minds are the better freed from error. For then it is clear that these things are not literal descriptions of divine truths, which might have been open to doubt had they been expressed under the figure of nobler bodies, especially in the case of those who could think of nothing nobler than bodies. Second, because this is more befitting the knowledge of God that we have in this life. For what He is not is clearer to us than what He is. Therefore similitudes drawn from things farthest away from God form within us a truer estimate that God is above whatsoever we may say or think of Him. Third, because thereby divine truths are the better hidden, from the unworthy.

Tenth Article
WHETHER IN HOLY SCRIPTURE A WORD MAY HAVE SEVERAL SENSES ?

We proceed thus to the Tenth Article: —

1. 参见 *De Cael. Hier.*, I, 2 (PG 3, 121).
2. 参见 *Op. cit.*, II, 2 (PG 3, 136) .

Objection 1. It seems that in Holy Scripture a word cannot have several senses, historical or literal, allegorical, tropological or moral, and anagogical. For many different senses in one text produce confusion and deception and destroy all force of argument. Hence no argument, but only fallacies, can be deduced from a multiplicity of propositions. But Holy Scripture ought to be able to state the truth without any fallacy. Therefore in it there cannot be several senses to a word.

Obj. 2. Further, Augustine says that *the Old Testament has a fourfold division: according to history, etiology, analogy, and allegory.*[1] Now these four seem altogether different from the four divisions mentioned in the first objection. Therefore it does not seem fitting to explain the same word of Holy Scripture according to the four different senses mentioned above.

Obj. 3. Further, besides these senses, there is the parabolical, which is not one of these four.

On the contrary, Gregory says: *Holy Scripture by the manner of its speech transcends every science, because in one and the same sentence, while it describes a fact, it reveals a mystery.*[2]

I answer that, The author of Holy Scripture is God[3], in Whose power it is to signify His meaning, not by words only (as man also can do), but also by things themselves. So, whereas in every other science things are signified by words, this science has the property that the things signified by the words have themselves also a signification. Therefore that first signification whereby words signify things belongs to the first sense, the historical or literal. That signification whereby things signified by words have themselves also a signification is called the

1. 参见 *De Util. Cred.*, III (PL 42, 68).
2. 参见 *Moral*, XX, 1 (PL 76, 135).
3. The author of Holy Scripture is God：天主是《圣经》的作者。指《圣经》是在天主圣神的启示下写成的。

spiritual sense, which is based on the literal, and presupposes it. Now this spiritual sense has a threefold division. For as the Apostle says (*Heb.* x. 1) the Old Law[1] is a figure of the New Law[2], and Dionysius says *the New Law itself is a figure of future glory.*[3] Again, in the New Law, whatever our Head has done is a type of what we ought to do. Therefore, so far as the things of the Old Law signify the things of the New Law, there is the allegorical sense; so far as the things done in Christ, or so far as the things which signify Christ, are signs of what we ought to do, there is the moral sense. But so far as they signify what relates to eternal glory, there is the anagogical sense. Since the literal sense is that which the author intends, and since the author of Holy Scripture is God, Who by one act comprehends all things by His intellect, it is not unfitting, as Augustine says,[4] if, even according to the literal sense, one word in Holy Scripture should have several senses.

Reply Obj. 1. The multiplicity of these senses does not produce equivocation or any other kind of multiplicity, seeing that these senses are not multiplied because one word signifies several things, but because the things signified by the words can be themselves signs of other things. Thus in Holy Scripture no confusion results, for all the senses are founded on one — the literal — from which alone can any argument be drawn, and not from those intended allegorically, as Augustine says.[5] Nevertheless, nothing of Holy Scripture perishes because of this, since nothing necessary to faith is contained under the spiritual sense which is not elsewhere put forward clearly by the Scripture in its literal sense.

Reply Obj. 2. These three — history, etiology, analogy — are grouped

---

1. the Old Law：《圣经 · 旧约》
2. the New Law：《圣经 · 新约》
3. 参见 *De Eccles. Hier.*, V, 2 (PG 3, 501).
4. 参见 *Confess.*, XII, 31 (PL 32, 844).
5. 参见 *Epist.* XCIII, 8 (PL 33, 334).

under the literal sense. For it is called history, as Augustine expounds,[1] whenever anything is simply related; it is called etiology when its cause is assigned, as when Our Lord gave the reason why Moses allowed the putting away of wives — namely, because of the hardness of men's hearts (*Matt.*, xix, 8); it is called analogy whenever the truth of one text of Scripture is shown not to contradict the truth of another. Of these four, allegory alone stands for the three spiritual senses. Thus Hugh of St. Victor includes the anagogical under the allegorical sense, laying down three senses only — the historical, the allegorical and the tropological.[2]

Reply Obj. 3. The parabolical sense is contained in the literal, for by words things are signified properly and figuratively. Nor is the figure itself, but that which is figured, the literal sense. When Scripture speaks of God's arm, the literal sense is not that God has such a member, but only what is signified by this member, namely, operative power. Hence it is plain that nothing false can ever underlie the literal sense of Holy Scripture.

---

1. 参见 *De Util. Cred.*, 3 (PL 42, 68).
2. 参见 Cf. *De Sacram.*, I, 4 (PL 176, 184).— Cf. also *De Scriptur. et Scriptor. Sacris*, 3 (PL 175, 11).

Question II
THE EXISTENCE OF GOD
(*In Three Articles*)

BECAUSE the chief aim of sacred doctrine is to teach the knowledge of God not only as He is in Himself, but also as He is the beginning of things and their last end, and especially of rational creatures, as is clear from what has been already said,[1] therefore, in our endeavor to expound this science, we shall treat: (1) of God; (2) of the rational creature's movement towards God;[2] (3) of Christ Who as man is our way to God.[3]

In treating of God there will be a threefold division:—

For we shall consider (1) whatever concerns the divine essence. (2) Whatever concerns the distinctions of Persons.[4] (3) Whatever concerns the procession of creatures from Him.[5]

Concerning the divine essence, we must consider:—

(1) Whether God exists? (2) The manner of His existence, or, rather, what is *not* the manner of His existence.[6](3) Whatever concerns His operations — namely, His knowledge, [7] will,[8] power.[9]

Concerning the first, there are three points of inquiry:—

---

1. 参见 Q. 1, a. 7.
2. 参见 *S. T.*, II.
3. 参见 *S. T.*, III.
4. 参见 Q. 27.
5. 参见 Q. 44.
6. 参见 Q. 3.
7. 参见 Q. 14.
8. 参见 Q. 19.
9. 参见 Q. 25.

(1) Whether the proposition *God exists* is self-evident? (2) Whether it is demonstrable? (3) Whether God exists?

First Article
WHETHER THE EXISTENCE OF GOD IS SELF-EVIDENT?

We proceed thus to the First Article: —

Objection 1. It seems that the existence of God is self-evident. For those things are said to be self-evident to us the knowledge of which exists naturally in us, as we can see in regard to first principles. But as Damascene says, *the knowledge of God is naturally implanted in all.*[1] Therefore the existence of God is self-evident.

Obj. 2. Further, those things are said to be self-evident[2] which are known as soon as the terms are known, which the Philosopher says is true of the first principles of demonstration.[3] Thus, when the nature of a whole and of a part is known, it is at once recognized that every whole is greater than its part. But as soon as the signification of the name God is understood, it is at once seen that God exists. For by this name is signified that thing than which nothing greater can be conceived. But that which exists actually and mentally is greater than that which exists only mentally. Therefore, since as soon as the name *God* is understood it exists mentally, it also follows that it exists actually. Therefore the proposition *God exists* is self-evident.

Obj. 3. Further, the existence of truth is self-evident. For whoever denies the existence of truth grants that truth does not exist: and, if truth does not exist, then the proposition *Truth does not exist* is true: and if there is anything true, there must be truth. But God is truth itself: *I am the way, the truth, and the life* (*Jo.* xiv. 6). Therefore *God exists* is self-evident.

---

1. 参见 *De Fide Orth.*, I, 1; 3 (PG 94, 789; 793).
2. self-evident：不证自明的，不言而喻的
3. 参见 *Post. Anal.*, I, 3 (72b 18).

On the contrary, No one can mentally admit the opposite of what is self-evident, as the Philosopher states concerning the first principles of demonstration.[1] But the opposite of the proposition *God is* can be mentally admitted: *The fool said in his heart, There is no God* (*Ps.* lii. 1). Therefore, that God exists is not self-evident.

I answer that, A thing can be self-evident in either of two ways: on the one hand, self-evident in itself, though not to us; on the other, self-evident in itself, and to us. A proposition is self-evident because the predicate is included in the essence of the subject: *e.g.*, *Man is an animal*, for animal is contained in the essence of man. If, therefore, the essence of the predicate and subject be known to all, the proposition will be self-evident to all; as is clear with regard to the first principles of demonstration, the terms of which are certain common notions that no one is ignorant of, such as being and non-being, whole and part, and the like. If, however, there are some to whom the essence of the predicate and subject is unknown, the proposition will be self-evident in itself, but not to those who do not know the meaning of the predicate and subject of the proposition. Therefore, it happens, as Boethius says, that there are some notions of the mind which are common and self- evident only to the learned, as that incorporeal substances[2] are not in space.[3] Therefore I say that this proposition, *God exists*, of itself is self-evident, for the predicate is the same as the subject, because God is His own existence as will be hereafter shown.[4] Now because we do not know the essence of God, the proposition is not self-evident to us, but needs to be demonstrated by things that are more known to us, though less known in their nature — namely, by His effects.

Reply Obj. 1. To know that God exists in a general and confused way

---

1. 参见 *Metaph.*, III, 3 (1005b 11); *Post. Anal.*, I, 10 (76b 23).
2. incorporeal substances：非有形物
3. 参见 *De Hebdom.* (PL 64, 1311).
4. 参见 Q. 3, a. 4.

is implanted in us by nature, inasmuch as God is man's beatitude. For man naturally desires happiness, and what is naturally desired by man is naturally known by him. This, however, is not to know absolutely that God exists; just as to know that someone is approaching is not the same as to know that Peter is approaching, even though it is Peter who is approaching; for there are many who imagine that man's perfect good, which is happiness, consists in riches, and others in pleasures, and others in something else.

Reply Obj. 2. Perhaps not everyone who hears this name *God* understands it to signify something than which nothing greater can be thought, seeing that some have believed God to be a body.[1] Yet, granted that everyone understands that by this name *God* is signified something than which nothing greater can be thought, nevertheless, it does not therefore follow that he understands that what the name signifies exists actually, but only that it exists mentally. Nor can it be argued that it actually exists, unless it be admitted that there actually exists something than which nothing greater can be thought; and this precisely is not admitted by those who hold that God does not exist.

Reply Obj. 3. The existence of truth in general is self-evident, but the existence of a Primal Truth[2] is not self-evident to us.

Second Article
WHETHER IT CAN BE DEMONSTRATED THAT GOD EXISTS?

We proceed thus to the Second Article: —

Objection 1. It seems that the existence of God cannot be

---

1. 参见 Cf. *C. G.*, I, 20.— Cf. also Aristotle, *Phys.*, I, 4 (187a 12); St. Augustine, *De Civit. Dei*, VIII, 2; 5 (PL 41, 226; 239); *De Haeres.*, 46, 50, 86 (PL 42, 35; 39; 46); *De Genesi ad Litt.*, X, 25 (PL 34, 427); Maimonides, *Guide*, I, 53 (p. 72).
2. Primal Truth：这里指元真理，真理根源，即天主。

demonstrated. For it is an article of faith that God exists. But what is of faith cannot be demonstrated, because a demonstration produces scientific knowledge, whereas faith is of the unseen, as is clear from the Apostle (*Heb.* xi. 1). Therefore it cannot be demonstrated that God exists.

Obj. 2. Further, essence is the middle term of demonstration. But we cannot know in what God's essence consists, but solely in what it does not consist, as Damascene says.[1] Therefore we cannot demonstrate that God exists.

Obj. 3. Further, if the existence of God were demonstrated, this could only be from His effects. But His effects are not proportioned to Him, since He is infinite and His effects are finite, and between the finite and infinite there is no proportion. Therefore, since a cause cannot be demonstrated by an effect not proportioned to it, it seems that the existence of God cannot be demonstrated.

On the contrary, The Apostle says: *The invisible things of Him are clearly seen, being understood by the things that are made* (*Rom.* i. 20). But this would not be unless the existence of God could be demonstrated through the things that are made; for the first thing we must know of anything is, whether it exists.

I answer that, Demonstration can be made in two ways: One is through the cause, and is called *propter quid*, and this is to argue from what is prior absolutely. The other is through the effect, and is called a demonstration *quia*; this is to argue from what is prior relatively only to us. When an effect is better known to us than its cause, from the effect we proceed to the knowledge of the cause. And from every effect the existence of its proper cause can be demonstrated, so long as its effects are better known to us; because, since every effect depends upon its cause, if the effect exists, the cause must preexist. Hence the existence

---

1. 参见 *De Fide Orth.*, I, 4 (PG 94, 800).

of God, in so far as it is not self-evident to us, can be demonstrated from those of His effects which are known to us.

Reply Obj. 1. The existence of God and other like truths about God, which can be known by natural reason, are not articles of faith, but are preambles to the articles; for faith presupposes natural knowledge, even as grace presupposes nature and perfection the perfectible. Nevertheless, there is nothing to prevent a man, who cannot grasp a proof, from accepting, as a matter of faith, something which in itself is capable of being scientifically known and demonstrated.

Reply Obj. 2. When the existence of a cause is demonstrated from an effect, this effect takes the place of the definition of the cause in proving the cause's existence. This is especially the case in regard to God, because, in order to prove the existence of anything, it is necessary to accept as a middle term the meaning of the name, and not its essence, for the question of its essence follows on the question of its existence. Now the names given to God are derived from His effects, as will be later shown.[1] Consequently, in demonstrating the existence of God from His effects, we may take for the middle term the meaning of the name *God.*

Reply Obj. 3. From effects not proportioned to the cause no perfect knowledge of that cause can be obtained. Yet from every effect the existence of the cause can be clearly demonstrated, and so we can demonstrate the existence of God from His effects; though from them we cannot know God perfectly as He is in His essence.

Third Article
WHETHER GOD EXISTS?

We proceed thus to the Third Article: —

---

1. 参见 Q. 13, a. 1.

Objection 1. It seems that God does not exist; because if one of two contraries be infinite, the other would be altogether destroyed. But the name *God* means that He is infinite goodness. If, therefore, God existed, there would be no evil discoverable; but there is evil in the world. Therefore God does not exist.

Obj. 2. Further, it is superfluous to suppose that what can be accounted for by a few principles has been produced by many. But it seems that everything we see in the world can be accounted for by other principles, supposing God did not exist. For all natural things can be reduced to one principle, which is nature; and all voluntary things can be reduced to one principle, which is human reason, or will. Therefore there is no need to suppose God's existence.

On the contrary, It is said in the person of God: *I am Who am*[1] (*Exod.* iii. 14).

I answer that, The existence of God can be proved in five ways.

The first and more manifest way is the argument from motion. It is certain, and evident to our senses, that in the world some things are in motion. Now whatever is moved is moved by another, for nothing can be moved except it is in potentiality to that towards which it is moved; whereas a thing moves inasmuch as it is in act. For motion is nothing else than the reduction of something from potentiality to actuality. But nothing can be reduced from potentiality to actuality, except by something in a state of actuality. Thus that which is actually hot, as fire, makes wood, which is potentially hot, to be actually hot, and thereby moves and changes it. Now it is not possible that the same thing should be at once in actuality and potentiality in the same respect, but only in different respects. For what is actually hot cannot simultaneously be potentially hot; but it is simultaneously potentially cold. It is therefore impossible that in the same respect and

1. I am Who am.：我是自有者。《圣经·创世纪》中记载，梅瑟问怎么称呼天主，天主说了这句话。

in the same way a thing should be both mover and moved, *i.e.*, that it should move itself. Therefore, whatever is moved must be moved by another. If that by which it is moved be itself moved, then this also must needs be moved by another, and that by another again. But this cannot go on to infinity, because then there would be no first mover, and, consequently, no other mover, seeing that subsequent movers move only inasmuch as they are moved by the first mover; as the staff moves only because it is moved by the hand. Therefore it is necessary to arrive at a first mover, moved by no other; and this everyone understands to be God.

The second way is from the nature of efficient cause. In the world of sensible things we find there is an order of efficient causes. There is no case known (neither is it, indeed, possible) in which a thing is found to be the efficient cause of itself; for so it would be prior to itself, which is impossible. Now in efficient causes it is not possible to go on to infinity, because in all efficient causes following in order, the first is the cause of the intermediate cause, and the intermediate is the cause of the ultimate cause, whether the intermediate cause be several, or one only. Now to take away the cause is to take away the effect. Therefore, if there be no first cause among efficient causes, there will be no ultimate, nor any intermediate, cause. But if in efficient causes it is possible to go on to infinity, there will be no first efficient cause, neither will there be an ultimate effect, nor any intermediate efficient causes; all of which is plainly false. Therefore it is necessary to admit a first efficient cause, to which everyone gives the name of God.

The third way is taken from possibility and necessity, and runs thus. We find in nature things that are possible to be and not to be, since they are found to be generated, and to be corrupted, and consequently, it is possible for them to be and not to be. But it is impossible for these always to exist, for that which can not-be at some time is not. Therefore, if everything can not-be, then at one time there was nothing in existence. Now if this were true, even now there would be nothing in existence, because that which does not exist begins to exist only through something already existing. Therefore, if at one time nothing was in existence, it would have been impossible for anything to have begun to exist; and thus even now nothing would be in existence — which is absurd. Therefore, not all beings are merely possible, but there must exist something the existence of which is necessary. But every necessary thing either has its necessity caused by another, or not. Now it is impossible to go on to infinity in necessary things which have their necessity caused by another, as has been already proved in regard to efficient causes. Therefore we cannot but admit the existence of some being having of itself its own necessity, and not receiving it from another, but rather causing in others their necessity. This all men speak of as God.

The fourth way is taken from the gradation to be found in things. Among beings there are some more and some less good, true, noble, and the like. But *more* and *less* are predicated of different things according as they resemble in their different ways something which is the maximum, as a thing is said to be hotter according as it more nearly resembles that which is hottest; so that there is something which is truest, something best, something noblest, and, consequently, something which is most being, for those things that are greatest in truth are greatest in being, as it is written in *Metaph.* ii.[1] Now the maximum in any genus is the cause of all in that genus, as fire, which is the maximum of heat, is the cause of all hot things, as is said in the same book.[2] Therefore there must also be something which is to all beings the cause of their being, goodness, and every other perfection; and this we call God.

The fifth way is taken from the governance of the world. We see that things which lack knowledge, such as natural bodies, act for an

---

1. 参见 *Metaph.* Ia, 1 (993b 30).
2. 同上 (993b 25).

end, and this is evident from their acting always, or nearly always, in the same way, so as to obtain the best result. Hence it is plain that they achieve their end, not fortuitously, but designedly. Now whatever lacks knowledge cannot move towards an end, unless it be directed by some being endowed with knowledge and intelligence; as the arrow is directed by the archer. Therefore some intelligent being exists by whom all natural things are directed to their end; and this being we call God.

Reply Obj. 1. As Augustine says: *Since God is the highest good, He would not allow any evil to exist in His works, unless His omnipotence*[1] *and goodness were such as to bring good even out of evil.*[2] This is part of the infinite goodness of God, that He should allow evil to exist, and out of it produce good.

Reply Obj. 2. Since nature works for a determinate end under the direction of a higher agent, whatever is done by nature must be traced back to God as to its first cause. So likewise whatever is done voluntarily must be traced back to some higher cause other than human reason and will, since these can change and fail; for all things that are changeable and capable of defect must be traced back to an immovable and self-necessary[3] first principle, as has been shown.

---

1. omnipotence：全能
2. 参见 *Enchir.*, XI (PL 40, 236).
3. self-necessary：本身必然存在的

Question III
ON THE SIMPLICITY OF GOD
(*In Eight Articles*)

WHEN the existence of a thing has been ascertained, there remains the further question of the manner of its existence, in order that we may know its essence. Now because we cannot know what God is, but rather what He is not, we have no means for considering how God is, but rather how He is not.

Therefore, we must consider (1) how He is not; (2) how He is known by us;[1] (3) how He is named.[2]

Now it can be shown how God is not, by removing from Him whatever does not befit Him — viz., composition, motion, and the like. Therefore (1) we must discuss His simplicity[3], whereby we remove composition from Him. And because whatever is simple in material things is imperfect and a part of something else, we shall discuss (2) His perfection;[4] (3) His infinity;[5] (4) His immutability[6];[7] (5) His unity.[8]

Concerning His simplicity, there are eight points of inquiry: (1) Whether God is a body? (2) Whether He is composed of matter and form? (3) Whether in Him there is composition of quiddity or essence

---

1. 参见 Q. 12.
2. 参见 Q. 13.
3. simplicity：单纯性
4. 参见 Q. 4.
5. 参见 Q. 7.
6. immutability：不变性，永恒性
7. 参见 Q. 9.
8. 参见 Q. 11.

(or nature) and subject? (4) Whether there is in Him a composition of essence and being? (5) Whether He is composed of genus and difference? (6) Whether He is composed of subject and accident? (7) Whether He is in any way composite, or wholly simple? (8) Whether He enters into composition with other things?

First Article

WHETHER GOD IS A BODY?

We proceed thus to the First Article: —

Objection 1. It seems that God is a body. For a body is that which has three dimensions. But Holy Scripture attributes three dimensions to God, for it is written: *He is higher than Heaven, and what wilt thou do? He is deeper than Hell, and how wilt thou know? The measure of Him is longer than the earth and broader than the sea* (*Job* xi. 8, 9). Therefore God is a body.

Obj. 2. Further, everything that has figure is a body, since figure is a quality of quantity. But God seems to have figure, for it is written: *Let us make man to our image and likeness* (*Gen.* i. 26). Now a figure is called an image, according to the text: *Who being the brightness of His glory and the figure i.e.*, the image of His substance (Heb. i. 3). Therefore God is a body.

Obj, 3. Further, whatever has corporeal parts is a body. Now Scripture attributes corporeal parts to God. *Hast thou an arm like God?* (*Job* xl. 4); and *The eyes of the Lord are upon the just* (*Ps.* xxxiii. 16); and *The right hand of the Lord hath wrought strength* (*Ps.* cxvii. 16). Therefore God is a body.

Obj. 4. Further, posture belongs only to bodies. But something which supposes posture is said of God in the Scriptures: *I saw the Lord sitting* (*Isa.* vi. 1), and *He standeth up to judge* (*Isa.* iii. 13). Therefore God is a body.

Obj. 5. Further, only bodies or things corporeal can be a local terminus *wherefrom or whereto*. But in the Scriptures God is spoken of as a local terminus *whereto*, according to the words, *Come ye to Him and be enlightened* (*Ps.* xxxiii. 6), and as a term *wherefrom: All they that depart from Thee shall be written in the earth* (*Jer.* xvii. 13). Therefore God is a body.

On the contrary, It is written in the Gospel of St. John (iv. 24): *God is a spirit.*

I answer that, It is absolutely true that God is not a body, and this can be shown in three ways. First, because no body moves unless it be moved, as is evident from induction. Now it has been already proved that God is the First Mover[1], Himself unmoved.[2] Therefore it is clear that God is not a body. Second, because the first being must of necessity be in act, and in no way in potentiality. For although in any single thing that passes from potentiality to actuality, the potentiality is prior in time to the actuality, nevertheless, absolutely speaking, actuality is prior to potentiality; for whatever is in potentiality is reduced to actuality only by some being in actuality. Now it has been already proved that God is the First Being[3].[4] It is therefore impossible that in God there should be any potentiality. But every body is in potentiality, because the continuous, as such, is divisible to infinity. It is therefore impossible that God should be a body. Third, because God is the most noble of beings, as is clear from what has been said.[5] Now it is impossible for a body to be the most noble of beings. For a body is either animate or inanimate; and an animate body is manifestly nobler than any inanimate body. But an animate body is not animate precisely as body, or otherwise all bodies would be animate. Therefore

1. the First Mover：第一推动者
2. 参见 Q. 2, a. 3.
3. the First Being：第一存在者
4. 参见 Q. 2, a. 3.
5. 同上

its animation depends upon some other thing, as our body depends for its animation on the soul. Hence that by which a body is animated is nobler than the body. Therefore it is impossible that God should be a body.

Reply Obj. 1. As we have said above, Holy Scripture puts before us spiritual and divine things under the likenesses of corporeal things.[1] Hence, when it attributes three dimensions to God, under the comparison of corporeal quantity it designates His virtual quantity: thus, by depth, it signifies His power of knowing hidden things; by height, the transcendence of His excelling power; by length, the duration of His existence; by breadth, His act of love for all. Or, as says Dionysius,[2] by the depth of God is meant the incomprehensibility[3] of His essence, by length, the procession of His allpervading power, by breadth, His overspreading all things, inasmuch as all things lie under His protection.

Reply Obj. 2. Man is said to be in the image of God[4], not as regards his body, but as regards that whereby he excels other animals. Hence, when it is said, *Let us make man to our image and likeness*, it is added, *And let him have dominion over the fishes of the sea* (*Gen.* i. 26). Now man excels all animals by his reason and intellect; hence it is according to his intellect and reason, which are incorporeal, that man is said to be in the image of God.

Reply Obj. 3. Corporeal parts are attributed to God in Scripture because of His actions, and this is owing to a certain likeness. For instance, the act of the eye is to see, and hence the eye attributed to God signifies His power of seeing intellectually, not sensibly; and so on with the other parts.

---

1. 参见 Q. 1, a. 9.
2. 参见 *De Div. Nom.*, IX, 5 (PG 3, 913).
3. incomprehensibility：高深莫测
4. the image of God：天主的肖像

Reply Obj. 4. Whatever pertains to posture, likewise, is attributed to God only by a sort of likeness. He is spoken of as sitting, because of His unchangeableness and dominion; and as standing, because of His power of overcoming whatever withstands Him.

Reply Obj. 5. We draw near to God by no corporeal steps, since He is everywhere, but by the affections of the soul, and by the actions of that same soul do we withdraw from Him. Hence, to draw near or to withdraw signifies merely spiritual affection under the likeness of local motion.

Second Article
WHETHER GOD IS COMPOSED OF MATTER AND FORM?

We proceed thus to the Second Article: —

Objection 1. It seems that God is composed of matter and form[1]. For what ever has a soul is composed of matter and form; since the soul is the form of the body. But Scripture attributes a soul to God; for it is mentioned in *He brews* (x. 38), where God says: *But My just man liveth by faith; but if he withdraw himself, he shall not please My soul.* Therefore God is composed of matter and form.

Obj. 2. Further, anger, joy, and the like are passions of the composite, as is said in *De Anima*, i.[2] But these are attributed to God in Scripture: *The Lord was exceeding angry with His people* (*Ps.* cv. 40). Therefore God it composed of matter and form.

Obj. 3. Further, matter is the principle of individuation. But God seems to be individual, for He cannot be predicated of many. Therefore He is composed of matter and form.

On the contrary, Whatever is composed of matter and form is a body, for dimensive quantity is the first property of matter. But God is not

1. matter and form：质素和形素
2. 参见 Aristotle, *De An.*, I, 1 (403a 3).

a body, as has been proved. Therefore, He is not composed of matter and form.

I answer that, It is impossible that matter be in God. First, because matter is that which exists in potentiality. But we have shown that God is pure act, without any potentiality. Hence it is impossible that God be composed of matter and form. Second, because everything composed of matter and form owes its perfection and goodness to its form, and therefore its goodness is participated, inasmuch as matter participates the form. Now the first good and the best — viz., God — is not a participated good, because the essential good is prior to the participated good. Hence it is impossible that God should be composed of matter and form. Third, because every agent acts by its form, and so the manner in which it has its form is the manner in which it is an agent. Therefore whatever is primarily and essentially an agent must be primarily and essentially form. Now God is the first agent, since He is the first efficient cause, as has been shown.[1] He is therefore of His essence a form, and not composed of matter and form.

Reply Obj. 1. A soul is attributed to God because of a similitude in acts; for, that we will anything, is due to our soul. Hence what is pleasing to His will is said to be pleasing to His soul.

Reply Obj. 2. Anger and the like are attributed to God because of a similitude in effects. Thus, because to punish is properly the act of an angry man, God's punishment is metaphorically spoken of as His anger.

Reply Obj. 3. Forms which can be received in matter are individuated by matter, which cannot be in another as in a subject since it is the first underlying subject; although form of itself, unless something else prevents it, can be received by many. But that form which cannot

1. 参见 Q. 2, a. 3.

be received in matter, but is self-subsisting, is individuated precisely because it cannot be received in a subject; and such a form is God. Hence it does not follow that matter exists in God.

Third Article
WHETHER GOD IS THE SAME AS HIS ESSENCE OR NATURE?

We proceed thus to the Third Article: —

Objection 1. It seems that God is not the same as His essence or nature. For nothing is in itself. But the essence or nature of God — *i.e.*, the Godhead — is said to be in God. Therefore it seems that God is not the same as His essence or nature.

Obj. 2. Further, the effect is assimilated to its cause; for every agent produces its like. But in created things the *suppositum* is not identical with its nature; for a man is not the same as his humanity. Therefore God is not the same as His Godhead.

On the contrary, It is said of God that He is life itself, and not only that He is a living thing: *I am the way, the truth, and the life* (*Jo.* xiv. 6). Now the relation between Godhead and God is the same as the relation between life and a living thing. Therefore God is His very Godhead.

I answer that, God is the same as His essence or nature. To understand this, it must be noted that in things composed of matter and form, the nature or essence must differ from the *suppositum*, for the essence or nature includes only what falls within the definition of the species; as humanity includes all that falls within the definition of man, for it is by this that man is man, and it is this that humanity signifies, that, namely, whereby man is man. Now individual matter, with all the individuating accidents, does not fall within the definition of the species. For this particular flesh, these bones, this blackness or whiteness, etc., do not fall within the definition of a man. Therefore this flesh, these bones, and the accidental qualities designating this particular matter, are not included in humanity; and yet they are included in the reality which is a man. Hence, the reality which is a man has something in it that humanity does not have. Consequently, humanity and a man are not wholly identical; but humanity is taken to mean the formal part of a man, because the principles whereby a thing is defined function as the formal constituent in relation to individuating matter. The situation is different in things not composed of matter and form, in which individuation is not due to individual matter — that is to say, to *this* matter — but the forms themselves are individuated of themselves. Here it is necessary that the forms themselves should be subsisting *supposita*. Therefore *suppositum* and nature in them are identified. Since, then, God is not composed of matter and form, He must be His own Godhead, His own Life, and whatever else is so predicated of Him.

Reply Obj. 1. We can speak of simple things only as though they were like the composite things from which we derive our knowledge. Therefore, in speaking of God, we use concrete nouns to signify His subsistence, because with us only those things subsist which are composite, and we use abstract nouns to signify His simplicity. In speaking therefore of Godhead, or life, or the like as being in God, we indicate the composite way in which our intellect understands, but not that there is any composition in God.

Reply Obj. 2. The effects of God do not imitate Him perfectly, but only as far as they are able. It pertains to defect in imitation that what is simple and one can be represented only by a multiplicity. This is the source of composition in God's effects, and therefore in them *suppositum* is not the same as nature.

Fourth Article
WHETHER ESSENCE AND BEING ARE THE SAME IN GOD?

We proceed thus to the Fourth Article: —

Objection 1. It seems that essence and being [*esse*] are not the same in God. For if it be so, then the divine being has nothing added to it. Now being to which no addition is made is the being-in-general which is predicated of all things. Therefore it follows that God is being-in-general which can be predicated of everything. But this is false: *For men gave the incommunicable name to stones and wood* (*Wisd.* xiv. 21). Therefore God's being is not His essence.

Obj. 2. Further, we can know *whether* God exists, as was said above,[1] but we cannot know *what* He is. Therefore God's being is not the same as His essence — that is, as His quiddity or nature.

On the contrary, Hilary says: *In God being is not an accidental quality*[2], *but subsisting truth*[3].[4] Therefore what subsists in God is His being.

I answer that, God is not only His own essence, as has been shown, but also His own being. This may be shown in several ways. First, whatever a thing has besides its essence must be caused either by the constituent principles of that essence (like a proper accident that necessarily accompanies the species — as the faculty of laughing is proper to a man — and is caused by the constituent principles of the species), or by some exterior agent,— as heat is caused in water by fire. Therefore, if the being of a thing differs from its essence, this being must be caused either by some exterior agent or by the essential principles of the thing itself. Now it is impossible for a thing's being to be caused only by its essential constituent principles, for nothing can be the sufficient cause of its own being, if its being is caused. Therefore that thing, whose being differs from its essence, must have its being caused by another. But this cannot be said of God, because we call God the first efficient cause. Therefore it is impossible that in God His

1. 参见 Q. 2, a. 2.
2. accidental quality：依附体，指不能自主行动或存在的东西，如颜色
3. subsisting truth：自立的真理；现存的真理
4. 参见 De Trin.,VII (PL 10, 208).

being should differ from His essence.

Second, being is the actuality of every form or nature; for goodness and humanity are spoken of as actual, only because they are spoken of as being. Therefore, being must be compared to essence, if the latter is distinct from it, as actuality to potentiality. Therefore, since in God there is no potentiality, as shown above, it follows that in Him essence does not differ from being. Therefore His essence is His being. Third, just as that which has fire, but is not itself fire, is on fire by participation, so that which has being, but is not being, is a being by participation. But God is His own essence, as was shown above. If, therefore, He is not His own being, He will be not essential, but participated, being. He will not therefore be the first being — which is absurd. Therefore, God is His own being, and not merely His own essence.

Reply Obj. 1. A thing-that-has-nothing-added-to-it[1] can be understood in two ways. Either its essence precludes any addition (thus, for example, it is of the essence of an irrational animal to be without reason), or we may understand a thing to have nothing added to it, inasmuch as its essence does not require that anything should be added to it (thus the genus animal is without reason, because it is not of the essence of animal in general to have reason; but neither is it of the essence of animal to lack reason). And so the divine being has nothing added to it in the first sense; whereas being-in-general has nothing added to it in the second sense.

Reply Obj. 2. *To be* can mean either of two things. It may mean the act of being, or it may mean the composition of a proposition effected by the mind in joining a predicate to a subject. Taking *to be* in the first sense, we cannot understand God's being (or His essence); but only in the second sense. We know that this proposition which we form about

---

1. thing-that-has-nothing-added-to-it：不为自己添加什么的事物

God when we say *God is*, is true; and this we know from His effects, as was said above.[1]

Fifth Article
WHETHER GOD IS CONTAINED IN A GENUS?

We proceed thus to the Fifth Article: —

Objection 1. It seems that God is contained in a genus. For a substance is a being that subsists of itself. But to be such a being is especially true of God. Therefore God is in the genus of substance.

Obj. 2. Further, each thing is measured by something of its own genus; as length is measured by length and numbers by number. But God is the measure of all substances, as the Commentator shows.[2] Therefore God is in the genus of substance.

On the contrary, Genus is prior in meaning to what it contains. But nothing is prior to God either really or in meaning. Therefore God is not in any genus.

I answer that, A thing can be in a genus in two ways: either absolutely and properly, as a species contained under a genus; or as being reducible to it, as principles and privations. For example, *point* and *unity* are reduced to the genus of quantity as its principles, while blindness and all other privations are reduced to the genus of habit. But in neither of these ways is God in a genus. That He cannot be a species of any genus may be shown in three ways. First, because a species is constituted of genus and difference. Now that from which the difference constituting the species is derived is always related to that from which the genus is derived as actuality is related to potentiality. For *animal* is derived from sensitive nature by concretion, for that is animal which has a sensitive nature. *Rational*, on the other hand, is

---

1. 参见 Q. 2, a. 2.
2. 参见 *In Metaph.*, X, comm. 7 (VIII, 120 v).

derived from intellectual nature, because that is rational which has an intellectual nature. Now the intellectual is compared to the sensitive as actuality is to potentiality. The same argument holds good in other things. Hence, since in God potentiality is not added to actuality, it is impossible that He should be in any genus as a species. Second, since the being of God is His essence, if God were in any genus, He would have to be in the genus *being*, because, since genus is predicated essentially, it refers to the essence of a thing. But the Philosopher has shown that being cannot be a genus, for every genus has differences outside the generic essence.[1] Now no difference can exist distinct from being, for non-being cannot be a difference. It follows then that God is not in a genus. Third, because all members of one genus share in the quiddity or essence of the genus which is predicated of them essentially, but they differ in their being. For the being of man and of horse is not the same; nor is the being of this man and that man. Thus, in every member of a genus, being and quiddity — *i.e.*, essence —must differ. But in God they do not differ, as was shown in the preceding article. Therefore it is plain that God is not in a genus as if He were a species. From this it is also plain that He has no genus or difference, nor can there be any definition of Him; nor, save through His effects, a demonstration of Him; for a definition is from genus and difference, and the means of a demonstration is a definition.

That God is not in a genus, as reducible to it as its principle, is clear from this, that a principle reducible to any genus does not extend beyond that genus: *e.g.*, a point is the principle of continuous quantity alone, and unity, of discontinuous quantity. But God is the principle of all being, as will later be shown.[2] Therefore He is not contained in any genus as its principle.

Reply Obj. 1. The name *substance* signifies not only what is being of

---

1. 参见 *Metaph.*, II, 3 (998b 22).
2. 参见 Q. 44, a. 1.

itself — for being cannot of itself be a genus, as has been shown; but it also signifies an essence to which it belongs to be in this way — namely, of itself, which being, however, is not its essence. Thus it is clear that God is not in the genus of substance.

Reply Obj. 2. This objection turns upon proportionate measure, which must be homogeneous[1] with what is measured. Now, God is not a measure proportionate to anything. Still, He is called the measure of all things, in the sense that everything has being only according as it resembles Him.

Sixth Article
WHETHER IN GOD THERE ARE ANY ACCIDENTS?

We proceed thus to the Sixth Article: —

Objection 1. It seems that there are accidents in God. For substance cannot be an accident, as Aristotle says.[2] Therefore that which is an accident in one, cannot, in another, be a substance. Thus it is proved that heat cannot be the substantial form of fire, because it is an accident in other things. But wisdom, power, and the like, which are accidents in us, are attributes of God. Therefore in God there are accidents.

Obj, 2. Further, in every genus there is a first principle. But there are many *genera* of accidents. If, therefore, the primal members of these genera are not in God, there will be many primal beings other than God — which is absurd.

On the contrary, Every accident is in a subject. But God cannot be a subject, for *no simple form can be a subject*, as Boethius says.[3] Therefore in God there cannot be any accident.

---

1. homogeneous：同质的；同类的
2. 参见 *Phys*. I, 3 (186b 4).
3. 参见 *De Trin*., II (PL 64, 1250).

I answer that, From all we have said, it is clear there can be no accident in God. First, because a subject is compared to its accidents as potentiality to actuality; for a subject is in some sense made actual by its accidents. But there can be no potentiality in God, as was shown. Second, because God is His own being, and as Boethius says, although that which is may have something superadded to it, this cannot happen to being itself.[1] Thus, a heated substance can have something extraneous to heat added to it, as whiteness, but heat itself can have nothing else than heat. Third, because what is essential is prior to what is accidental. Whence, as God is absolute primal being, there can be in Him nothing accidental. Neither can He have any essential accidents (as the capability of laughing is an essential accident of man), because such accidents are caused by the constituent principles of the subject. Now there can be nothing caused in God, since He is the first cause. Hence it follows that there is no accident in God.

Reply Obj. 1. Power and wisdom are not predicated of God and of us univocally, as will later be clear.[2] Hence it does not follow that there are accidents in God as there are in us.

Reply Obj. 2. Since substance is prior to its accidents, the principles of accidents are reducible to the principles of the substance as to that which is prior. Now God is not first as contained in the genus of substance; He is first in respect to all being, outside every genus.

Seventh Article
WHETHER GOD IS ALTOGETHER SIMPLE?

We proceed thus to the Seventh Article: —

Objection 1. It seems that God is not altogether simple. For whatever is from God imitates Him. Thus from the first being are all beings,

---

1. 参见 *De Hebdom.* (PL 64, 1311).
2. 参见 Q. 13, a. 5.

and from the first good are all goods. But in the things which God has made, nothing is altogether simple. Therefore neither is God altogether simple.

Obj. 2. Further, whatever is better must be attributed to God. But with us that which is composite is better than that which is simple: thus, chemical compounds are better than elements, and elements than the parts that compose them. Therefore it cannot be said that God is altogether simple.

On the contrary, Augustine says, *God is truly and absolutely simple.*[1]

I answer that, The absolute simplicity of God may be shown in many ways. First, from the previous articles of this question. For there is neither composition of quantitative parts in God, since He is not a body; nor composition of form and matter; nor does His nature differ from His *suppositum*; nor His essence from His being; neither is there in Him composition of genus and difference, nor of subject and accident. Therefore, it is clear that God is in no way composite, but is altogether simple. Secondly, because every composite is posterior to its component parts, and is dependent on them; but God is the first being, as has been shown above.[2] Thirdly, because every composite has a cause, for things in themselves diverse cannot unite unless something causes them to unite. But God is uncaused, as has been shown above,[3] since He is the first efficient cause. Fourthly, because in every composite there must be potentiality and actuality (this does not apply to God) for either one of the parts actualizes another, or at least all the parts are as it were in potency with respect to the whole. Fifthly, because nothing composite can be predicated of any one of its parts. And this is evident in a whole made up of dissimilar parts; for no part of a man is a man, nor any of the parts of the foot, a foot.

---

1. 参见 *De Trin.*, VI, 6 (PL 42, 928).
2. 参见 Q. 2, a. 3.
3. 同上

But in wholes made up of similar parts, although something which is predicated of the whole may be predicated of a part (as a part of the air is air, and a part of water, water), nevertheless certain things are predicable of the whole which cannot be predicated of any of the parts; for instance, if the whole volume of water is two cubits, no part of it can be two cubits. Thus in every composite there is something which is not it itself. But, even if this could be said of whatever has a form, viz., that it has something which is not it itself, as in a white object there is something which does not belong to the essence of white, nevertheless, in the form itself there is nothing besides itself. And so, since God is absolute form, or rather absolute being, He can be in no way composite. Hilary touches upon this argument when he says: *God, Who is strength, is not made up of things that are weak*; *nor is He*, *Who is light, composed of things that are dark.*[1]

Reply Obj, 1. Whatever is from God imitates Him, as caused things imitate the first cause. But it is of the essence of a thing caused to be in some way composite; because at least its being differs from its essence, as will be shown hereafter.[2]

Reply Obj. 2. With us composite things are better than simple things, because the perfection of created goodness is not found in one simple thing, but in many things. But the perfection of divine goodness is found in one simple thing, as will be shown hereafter.[3]

Eighth Article
WHETHER GOD ENTERS INTO THE COMPOSITION OF OTHER THINGS ?

We proceed thus to the Eighth Article: —

---

1. 参见 *De Trin.*, VII (PL10, 223).
2. 参见 Q. 50, a. 2.
3. 参见 Q. 4, a. 1; Q. 6, a. 3.

Objection 1. It seems that God enters into the composition of other things, for Dionysius says: *The being of all things is that which is above being — the Godhead.*[1] But the being of all things enters into the composition of everything. Therefore God enters into the composition of other things.

Obj. 2. Further, God is a form; for Augustine says that, *the word of God, which is God, is an uncreated form.*[2] But a form is part of a composite. Therefore God is part of some composite.

Obj. 3. Further, whatever things exist, in no way differing from each other, are the same. But God and primary matter exist, and in no way differ from each other. Therefore they are absolutely the same. But primary matter enters into the composition of things. Therefore so does God. Proof of the minor: whatever things differ, they differ by some differences, and therefore must be composite. But God and primary matter are altogether simple. Therefore they nowise differ from each other.

On the contrary, Dionysius says: *There can be no touching Him*, i.e., God, *nor any other union with Him by mingling part with part.*[3]

Further, the first cause rules all things without commingling with them, as it is said in the *Book of Causes.*[4]

I answer that, On this point there have been three errors. Some have affirmed that God is the world-soul, as is clear from Augustine.[5] This is also the opinion of those who assert that God is the soul of the first heavens. Again, others[6] have said that God is the formal principle of all things; and this is said to have been the theory of the Almaricians.[7]

---

1. 参见 *De Cael. Hier.*, IV, 1 (PG 3, 177).
2. 参见 *Serm.* CXVII, 2 (PL 38, 662).
3. 参见 *De Div. Nom.*, II, 5 (PG 3, 643).
4. 参见 *De Causis*, XX (p. 177).
5. 参见 *De Civit Dei*, VII, 6 (PL 41, 199).
6. 参见 Cf. C. G., I, 27.
7. 参见 Cf. G. C. Capelle, *Amaury de Bène* (Paris: J. Vrin, 1932), pp. 42–50.

The third error is that of David of Dinant,[1] who most stupidly taught that God was primary matter. Now all these contain manifest untruth, since it is not possible for God to enter into the composition of anything, either as a formal or a material principle. First, because we pointed out above that God is the first efficient cause.[2] Now the efficient cause is not identical numerically with the form of the thing caused, but only specifically: for man begets man. But primary matter can be neither numerically nor specifically identical with an efficient cause; for primary matter exists potentially, while the efficient cause exists actually. Secondly, because, since God is the first efficient cause, to act belongs to Him primarily and essentially. But that which enters into composition with anything does not act primarily and essentially, but rather the composite so acts; for the hand does not act, but the man by his hand, and fire warms by its heat. Hence God cannot be part of a composite. Thirdly, because no part of a composite can be absolutely first among beings — not even matter, nor form, though they are the first parts of composites. For matter is merely potential, and potentiality is posterior absolutely to actuality, as is clear from the foregoing, while a form which is part of a composite is a participated form; and as that which participates is posterior to that which is essential, so likewise is that which is participated, as fire in ignited things is posterior to fire that is essentially such. Now it has been proved that God is absolutely the first being.

Reply Obj. 1. The Godhead is called the being of all things as their efficient and exemplar cause, but not as being their essence.

Reply Obj. 2. The Word is an exemplar form[3], but not a form that is part of a composite.

Reply Obj. 3. Simple things do not differ by added differences,—

---

1. 参见 Cf. G. Théry, *David de Dinant* (Paris: J. Vrin, 1925), pp. 34–45.
2. 参见 Q. 2, a. 3.
3. exemplar form：模型形式

for this belongs to composites. Thus man and horse differ by their differences, rational and irrational; which differences, however, do not differ from each other by other differences. Hence, to be quite accurate, it is better to say that they are, not different, but diverse. Hence, according to the Philosopher, *things are said to be diverse absolutely, but things which are different differ by something.*[1] Therefore, strictly speaking, primary matter and God do not differ, but are by their very being diverse. Hence it does not follow that they are the same.

---

1. 参见 *Metaph.*, IX, 3 (1054b 24).

Question IV
THE PERFECTION OF GOD
(*In Three Articles*)

HAVING considered the divine simplicity, we treat next of God's perfection. Now because it is in so far as it is perfect that everything is called good, we shall speak first of the divine perfection[1]; secondly of the divine goodness[2].[3]

Concerning the first there are three points of inquiry:—

(1) Whether God is perfect? (2) Whether God is perfect universally, as having in Himself the perfections of all things? (3) Whether creatures can be said to be like God?

First Article
WHETHER GOD IS PERFECT?

We proceed thus to the First Article: —

Objection 1. It seems that to be perfect does not belong to God. For we say that a thing is perfect if it is completely made. But it does not befit God to be made. Therefore, neither does it befit Him to be perfect.

Obj. 2. Further, God is the first beginning of things. But the beginnings of things seem to be imperfect, for a seed is the beginning of animals and plants. Therefore God is imperfect.

---

1. the divine perfection：神圣的完美
2. the divine goodness：神圣的善
3. 参见 Q. 5.

Obj. 3. Further, as has been shown above, God's essence is being itself.[1] But being itself seems most imperfect, since it is most universal and receptive of all modification. Therefore God is imperfect.

On the contrary, It is written: *Be you perfect as also your heavenly Father is perfect* (*Matt*. v. 48).

I answer that, As the Philosopher relates,[2] some ancient philosophers, namely, the Pythagoreans and Speusippus[3], did not predicate *best* and *most perfect* of the first principle. The reason was that the ancient philosophers considered only a material principle; and a material principle is most imperfect. For since matter as such is merely potential, the first material principle must be absolutely potential, and thus most imperfect. Now God is the first principle, not material, but in the order of efficient cause, which must be most perfect. For just as matter, as such, is merely potential, so an agent, as such, is in a state of actuality. Hence, the first active principle must needs be most actual, and therefore most perfect; for a thing is said to be perfect in proportion to its actuality, because we call that perfect which lacks nothing of the mode of its perfection.

Reply Obj. 1. As Gregory says: *Though our lips can only stammer*, *we yet chant the high things of God*.[4] For that which has not been made is improperly called perfect. Nevertheless, because things which come to be are then called perfect when from potentiality they are brought into actuality, this term *perfect* signifies by extension whatever is not wanting in actual being, whether this be by way of having been produced or not.

Reply Obj. 2. The material principle which with us is found to be imperfect, cannot be absolutely first, but is preceded by something

---

1. 参见 Q. 3, a. 4.
2. 参见 *Metaph*., XI, 7 (1072b 30).
3. the Pythagoreans and Speusippus：毕达哥拉斯和斯波西比斯
4. 参见 *Moral*., V, 36 (PL 75, 715).

perfect. For the seed, though it be the principle of the animal generated through it, has previous to it the animal or plant from which it came. Because, previous to that which is potential, must be that which is actual, since a potential being can be reduced to act only by some being already actual.

Reply Obj. 3. Being itself is the most perfect of all things, for it is compared to all things as that which is act; for nothing has actuality except so far as it is. Hence being is the actuality of all things, even of forms themselves. Therefore it is not compared to other things as the receiver is to the received, but rather as the received to the receiver. When therefore I speak of the being of man, or of a horse or of anything else, being is considered as a formal principle, and as something received, and not as that to which being belongs.

Second Article
WHETHER THE PERFECTIONS OF ALL THINGS ARE IN GOD?

We proceed thus to the Second Article: —

Objection 1. It seems that the perfections of all things are not in God For God is simple, as has been shown above,[1] whereas the perfections of things are many and diverse. Therefore the perfections of all things are not in God.

Obj. 2. Further, opposites cannot coexist. Now the perfections of things are opposed to each other, for each species is perfected by its own specific difference. But the differences by which a *genus* is divided, and *species* constituted, are opposed to each other. Therefore because opposites cannot coexist in the same subject, it seems that the perfections of all things are not in God.

---

1. 参见 Q. 3, a. 7.

Obj. 3. Further, a living thing is more perfect than what merely exists, and an intelligent thing than what merely lives. Therefore, to live is more perfect than to be, and to know than to live. But the essence of God is being itself. Therefore He has not the perfections of life, and knowledge, and other similar perfections.

On the contrary, Dionysius says that *God in His one existence prepossesses all things.*[1]

I answer that, All the perfections of all things are in God. Hence He is spoken of as universally perfect, because He lacks not (says the Commentator) any excellence which may be found in any genus. This may be seen from two considerations.

First, because whatever perfection exists in an effect must be found in the producing cause: either in the same formality, if it is a univocal agent[2] — as when man reproduces man; or in a more eminent degree, if it is an equivocal agent[3]— thus in the sun is the likeness of whatever is generated by the sun's power. Now it is plain that the effect pre-exists virtually in the efficient cause; and although to pre-exist in the potentiality of a material cause is to pre-exist in a more imperfect way, since matter as such is imperfect, and an agent as such is perfect, still to pre-exist virtually in the efficient cause is to pre-exist not in a more imperfect, but in a more perfect, way. Since therefore God is the first producing cause of things, the perfections of all things must pre-exist in God in a more eminent way. Dionysius touches upon this argument by saying of God: *It is not that He is this and not that, but that He is all, as the cause of all.*[4]

Secondly, from what has been already proved, God is being itself, of itself subsistent. Consequently, He must contain within Himself

1. 参见 *De Div. Nom.*, V, 9 (PG 3, 825).
2. univocal agent：意义明确的主体
3. equivocal agent：模棱两可的主体
4. 参见 *De Div. Nom.*, V, 8 (PG 3 , 824).

the whole perfection of being. For it is clear that if some hot thing has not the whole perfection of heat, this is because heat is not participated in its full perfection; but if this heat were self-subsisting, nothing of the virtue of heat would be wanting to it. Since therefore God is subsisting being itself, nothing of the perfection of being can be wanting to Him. Now all the perfections of all things pertain to the perfection of being; for things are perfect precisely so far as they have being after some fashion. It follows therefore that the perfection of no thing is wanting to God. This line of argument, too, is touched upon by Dionysius when he says that *God exists not in any single mode, but embraces all being within Himself, absolutely, without limitation, uniformly*;[1] and afterwards he adds that *He is very being to subsisting things.*[2]

Reply Obj. 1. Even as the sun, as Dionysius remarks, *while remaining one and shining uniformly, contains within itself first and uniformly the substances of sensible things, and many and diverse qualities; a fortiori should all things in a kind of natural unity pre-exist in the cause of all things*;[3] and thus things diverse and in themselves opposed to each other pre-exist in God as one, without injury to His simplicity.

This suffices for the *Reply to the Second Objection.*

Reply Obj. 3. The same Dionysius says that, although being itself is more perfect than life, and life than wisdom, if they are considered as distinguished in idea, nevertheless, a living thing is more perfect than what merely is, because a living thing is also a being, and an intelligent thing is both a being and alive.[4] Although therefore being does not include life and wisdom, because that which participates being need not participate in every mode of being, nevertheless God's being

---

1. 参见 *De Div. Nom.*, V, 4 (PG 3, 817).
2. 同上
3. 参见 *Op. cit.*, V, 8 (PG 3, 824).
4. 参见 *Op. cit.*, V, 3 (PG 3, 817).

includes in itself life and wisdom, because nothing of the perfection of being can be wanting to Him Who is subsisting being itself.

Third Article
WHETHER ANY CREATURE CAN BE LIKE GOD?

We proceed thus to the Third Article: —

Objection 1. It seems that no creature can be like God. For it is written (*Ps*. lxxxv. 8): *There is none among the gods like unto Thee, O Lord.* But of all creatures the most excellent are those which are called by participation gods. Therefore still less can other creatures be said to be like to God.

Obj. 2. Further, a likeness is a certain comparison. But there can be no comparison between things in diverse genera. Therefore neither can there be any likeness. Thus we do not say that sweetness is like whiteness. But no creature is in the same genus as God, since God is in no genus, as has been shown above.[1] Therefore no creature is like God.

Obj. 3. Further, we speak of those things as like which agree in form. But nothing can agree with God in form; for only in God is the essence being itself. Therefore no creature can be like to God.

Obj. 4. Further, among like things there is mutual likeness; for like is like to like. If therefore any creature is like God, God will be like some creature, which is against what is said by Isaias: *To whom have you likened God?* (xl. 18).

On the contrary, It is written: *Let us make man to our image and likeness* (*Gen*. i. 26), and: *When He shall appear, we shall be like to Him* (*1 John* iii. 2).

I answer that, Since likeness is based upon agreement or communication in form, it varies according to the many modes

1. 参见 Q. 3, a. 5.

of communication in form. Some things are said to be like, which communicate in the same form according to the same formality, and according to the same measure; and these are said to be not merely like, but equal in their likeness, as two things equally white are said to be alike in whiteness; and this is the most perfect likeness. In another way, we speak of things as alike which communicate in form according to the same formality, though not according to the same measure, but according to more or less, as something less white is said to be like another thing more white; and this is imperfect likeness. In a third way some things are said to be alike which communicate in the same form, but not according to the same formality; as we see in non-univocal agents[1]. For since every agent reproduces itself so far as it is an agent, and everything acts in accord with its form, the effect must in some way resemble the form of the agent. If therefore the agent is contained in the same species as its effect, there will be a likeness in form between that which makes and that which is made, according to the same formality of the species; as man reproduces man. If however the agent and its effect are not contained in the same species, there will be a likeness, but not according to the formality of the same species as things generated by the sun's power may reach some likeness of the sun, not indeed so as to receive the form of the sun in its specific likeness, but only in its generic likeness. Therefore, if there is an agent not contained in any genus, its effects will still more distantly reproduce the form of the agent, not, that is, so as to participate in the likeness of the agent's form according to the same specific or generic formality, but only according to some sort of analogy; as being itself is common to all. In this way all created things, so far as they are beings, are like God as the first and universal principle of all being.

Reply Obj. 1. As Dionysius says, when Holy Scripture declares that

---

1. Non-univocal agents：不同质的主动者

nothing is like God, it does not mean to deny all likeness to Him. For, *the same things can be like and unlike to God: like, according as they imitate Him, as far as He, Who is not imitable perfectly, can be imitated; unlike, according as they fall short of their cause,*[1] not merely in intensity and remission, as that which is less white falls short of that which is more white, but because they are not in agreement, specifically or generically.

Reply Obj. 2. God is not related to creatures as though belonging to a different genus, but as transcending every genus, and as the principle of all genera.

Reply Obj. 3. Likeness of creatures to God is not affirmed because of agreement in form according to the same formality of genus or species, but solely according to analogy, viz., inasmuch as God is essential being, whereas other things are beings by participation.

Reply Obj. 4. Although it may be admitted that creatures are in some way like God, it can in no way be admitted that God is like creatures; because, as Dionysius says: *A mutual likeness may be found, between things of the same order, but not between a cause and that which is caused.*[2] For we say that a statue is like a man, but not conversely; so also a creature can be spoken of as in some way like God, but not that God is like a creature.

1. 参见 *De Div. Nom.*, X, 7 (PG 3, 916).
2. 参见 *Op. cit.*, IX, 6 (PG 3, 913).

Question V
ON GOODNESS IN GENERAL
(*In Six Articles*)

WE next consider goodness:—

First, goodness in general. Secondly, the goodness of God[1].[2]

Under the first head there are six points of inquiry:—

(1) Whether goodness and being are the same really? (2) Granted that they differ only in idea, which is prior in thought? (3) Granted that being is prior, whether every being is good? (4) To what cause should goodness be reduced? (5) Whether goodness consists in limit, species and order? (6) Whether goodness is divided into the befitting, the useful, and the pleasant?

First Article
WHETHER GOODNESS DIFFERS REALLY FROM BEING?

We proceed thus to the First Article: —

Objection 1. It seems that goodness differs really from being. For Boethius says: *I perceive that in nature the fact that things are good is one thing, that they are is another.*[3] Therefore goodness and being differ really.

Obj. 2. Further, nothing can be its own form. *But that is called good which has the form of being*, according to the commentary on the *Book of*

---

1. the goodness of God：天主的善
2. 参见 Q. 6.
3. 参见 *De Hebdom.* (PL 64, 1312).

Causes.[1] Therefore goodness differs really from being.

Obj. 3. Further, goodness is receptive of more and less. But being cannot receive more and less. Therefore goodness differs really from being.

On the contrary, Augustine says that, *inasmuch as we are, we are good.*[2]

I answer that, Goodness and being are really the same, and differ only in idea; which is clear from the following argument. The essence of goodness consists in this, that it is in some way desirable. Hence the Philosopher says: *Goodness is what all desire.*[3] Now it is clear that a thing is desirable only in so far as it is perfect, for all desire their own perfection. But everything is perfect so far as it is actual. Therefore it is clear that a thing is perfect so far as it is being; for being is the actuality of every thing, as is clear from the foregoing.[4] Hence it is clear that goodness and being are the same really. But goodness expresses the aspect of desirableness, which being does not express.

Reply Obj. 1. Although goodness and being are the same really, nevertheless, since they differ in thought, they are not predicated of a thing absolutely in the same way. For since being properly signifies that something actually is, and actuality properly correlates to potentiality, a thing is, in consequence, said absolutely to have being accordingly as it is primarily distinguished from that which is only in potentiality; and this is precisely each thing's substantial being. Hence it is by its substantial being that everything is said to have being absolutely; but by any further actuality it is said to have being relatively. Thus to be white signifies being relatively, for to be white does not take a thing out of absolutely potential being, since it is added to a thing that actually has being. But goodness expresses perfection, which is

---

1. 参见 *De Causis*, XX (p. 177).
2. 参见 *De Doct. Christ.*, I, 32 (PL 34, 32).
3. 参见 *Eth.*, I, 1 (1094a 3).
4. 参见 Q. 3, a. 4; q. 4, a. 1, ad 3.

something desirable, and hence it expresses something final. Hence, that which has ultimate perfection is said to be absolutely good, but that which has not the ultimate perfection it ought to have (although, in so far as it is at all actual , it has some perfection) is not said to be perfect absolutely nor good absolutely, but only relatively. In this way, therefore, viewed in its first (*i.e.*, substantial) being, a thing is said to be absolutely, and to be good relatively (*i.e.*, in so far as it has being); but viewed in its complete actuality a thing is said to be relatively, and so be good absolutely. Hence the saying of Boethius, *that in nature the fact that things are good is one thing, that they are is another,*[1] is to be referred to being good absolutely, and being absolutely. Because, regarded in its first actuality, a thing is a being absolutely; and regarded in its complete actuality, it is good absolutely, though even in its first actuality, it is in some way good, and even in its complete actuality, it is in some way being.

Reply Obj. 2. Goodness is a form so far as it is understood absolutely according to complete actuality.

Reply Obj. 3. Again, goodness is spoken of as more or less according to a superadded actuality, for example, according to knowledge or virtue.

Second Article

WHETHER GOODNESS IS PRIOR IN IDEA TO BEING?

We proceed thus to the Second Article: —

Objection 1. It seems that goodness is prior in idea to being. For names are arranged according to the arrangement of the things signified by the names. But Dionysius assigned the first place, among other names of God, to His goodness rather than to His being.[2]

1. 参见 *De Hebdom.* (PL 64, 1312).
2. 参见 *De Div. Nom.*, III, 1 (PG 3, 680).

Therefore in idea goodness is prior to being.

Obj. 2. Further, that which is the more extensive is prior in idea. But goodness is more extensive than being, because, as Dionysius notes,[1] *goodness extends to things both existing and non-existing; whereas being extends to existing things alone.* Therefore goodness is in idea prior to being.

Obj. 3. Further, what is more universal is prior in idea. But goodness seems to be more universal than being, since goodness has the aspect of the desirable. Now to some non-existence is desirable, for it is said of Judas: *It were better for him, if that man had not been born* (*Matt.* xxvi. 24). Therefore in idea goodness is prior to being.

Obj. 4. Further, not only is being desirable, but life, knowledge, and many other things besides. Thus it seems that being is a particular appetible, and goodness a universal appetible. Therefore, absolutely, goodness is prior in idea to being.

On the contrary, It is said in the *Book of Causes that the first of created things is being.*[2]

I answer that, In idea being is prior to goodness. For the meaning signified by the name of a thing is that which the intellect conceives of the thing and intends by the word that stands for it. Therefore, that is prior in idea which is first conceived by the intellect. Now the first thing conceived by the intellect is being, because everything is knowable only inasmuch as it is actually.[3] Hence, being is the proper object of the intellect, and is thus the first intelligible, as sound is the first audible. Therefore in idea being is prior to goodness.

Reply Obj. 1. Dionysius defines the divine names according as they imply some causal relation in God; for we name God, as he says,[4] from creatures, as a cause from its effects. But goodness, since it has the

---

1. 参见 *Op. cit.*, V, 1(PG 3 , 816).
2. 参见 *De Causis*, IV (p. 164).
3. 参见 Aristotle, *Metaph.*, VIII, 9 (1051a 31).
4. 参见 *De Div. Nom.*, I, 7 (PG 3, 596).

aspect of the desirable, implies the idea of a final cause, the causality of which is first among causes, since an agent does not act except for some end; and by an agent matter is moved to its form. Hence the end is called the cause of causes. Thus goodness, as a cause, is prior to being, as is the end to the form. Therefore among the names signifying the divine causality, goodness precedes being. Again, according to the Platonists, who, through not distinguishing primary matter from privation,[1] said that matter was non-being,[2] goodness is more extensively participated than being; for primary matter participates in goodness as seeking it, for all seek their like, but it does not participate in being, since it is presumed to be non-being. Therefore Dionysius says that *goodness extends to the non-existent.*[3]

Reply Obj. 2. The same solution applies to this objection. Or it may be said that goodness extends to existing and non-existing things, not so far as it can be predicated of them, but so far as it can cause them — if, indeed, by the non-existent we understand not unqualifiedly those things which do not exist, but those which are potential, and not actual. For goodness has the aspect of the end in which not only actual things find their completion, but also towards which tend even those things which are not actual, but merely potential. But being implies the relation of a formal cause only, either inherent or exemplar; and its causality does not extend save to those things which are actual.

Reply Obj. 3. Non-being is desirable, not of itself, but only relatively — *i.e.*, inasmuch as the removal of an evil, which is removed by non-being, is desirable. Now the removal of an evil cannot be desirable, except so far as this evil deprives a thing of some being. Therefore it is being which is desirable of itself, while non-being is desirable only

---

1. 参见 Cf. Aristotle, *Phys.*, I, 9 (192a 2).
2. 参见 Cf. Aristotle, *ibid.* (192a 3).
3. 参见 *De Div. Nom.*, V, 1 (PG 3, 816).

relatively, viz., inasmuch as one seeks some being of which one cannot bear to be deprived; and thus it happens that even non-being can be spoken of as relatively good.

Reply Obj. 4. Life, wisdom, and the like, are desirable only so far as they are actual. Hence in each one of them some sort of being is desired. And thus nothing is desirable except being, and consequently nothing is good except being.

Third Article
WHETHER EVERY BEING IS GOOD?

We proceed thus to the Third Article: —

Objection 1. It seems that not every being is good. For goodness is something superadded to being, as is clear from what has been said. But whatever is added to being limits it; as substance, quantity, quality, etc. Therefore goodness limits being. Therefore not every being is good.

Obj. 2. Further, no evil is good: *Woe to you that call evil good, and good evil* (*Isa.* v. 20). But some things are called evil. Therefore not every being is good.

Obj. 3. Further, goodness implies desirability[1]. Now primary matter does not imply desirability, but rather that which desires. Therefore primary matter does not contain the formality of goodness. Therefore not every being is good.

Obj. 4. Further, the Philosopher observes that in *mathematics goodness does not exists.*[2] But mathematicals are entities, or otherwise there would be no science of mathematics. Therefore not every being is good.

On the contrary, Every being that is not God, is God's creature[3]. Now

1. desirability：愿望；希求
2. 参见 *Metaph.*, II, 2 (996b 1).
3. God's creature：天主的受造物

every creature of God is good (*1 Tim.* iv. 4): and God is the greatest good. Therefore every being is good.

I answer that, Every being, as being, is good. For all being, as being, has actuality and is in some way perfect, since every act is some sort of perfection, and perfection implies desirability and goodness, as is clear from what has been said. Hence it follows that every being as such is good.

Reply Obj. 1. Substance, quantity, quality, and everything included in them, limit being by applying it to some essence or nature. Now in this sense, goodness does not add anything to being beyond the aspect of desirability and perfection, which is also proper to being, whatever its nature. Hence goodness does not limit being.

Reply Obj. 2. No being is said to be evil, considered as being, but only so far as it lacks being. Thus a man is said to be evil, because he lacks the being of virtue; and an eye is said to be evil, because it lacks the power to see well.

Reply Obj. 3. As primary matter has only potential being, so is it only potentially good. Although, according to the Platonists,[1] primary matter may be said to be a non-being because of the privation added to it, nevertheless, it does participate to a certain extent in goodness, viz., by its ordination to, or aptitude for, goodness. Consequently, not to be desirable, but to desire, befits it.

Reply Obj. 4. Mathematicals do not subsist as separate beings, for if they subsisted there would be in them some good, viz., their very being; but they have a separate existence only in the reason, inasmuch as they are abstracted from motion and matter; and it is thus that they are abstracted from an end whose nature it is to act as a moving cause. Nor is it repugnant[2] that in some logical entity we do not find the good, or the character of goodness; for the idea of being is prior to the

---

1. 参见 Cf. Aristotle, *Phys.*, I, 9 (192a 2).
2. repugnant：令人厌恶的；矛盾的

idea of goodness, as was said in the preceding article.

Fourth Article
WHETHER GOODNESS HAS THE ASPECT OF A FINAL CAUSE?

We proceed thus to the Fourth Article: —

Objection 1. It seems that goodness has not the aspect of a final cause, but rather of the other causes. For, as Dionysius says, *Goodness is praised, as beauty*.[1] But beauty has the aspect of a formal cause. Therefore goodness has the aspect of a formal cause.

Obj. 2. Further, goodness is self-diffusive; for Dionysius says that goodness is that whereby all things subsist, and are.[2] But to be self-giving implies the aspect of an efficient cause. Therefore goodness has the aspect of an efficient cause.

Obj. 3. Further, Augustine says that *we exist, because God is good*.[3] But we are from God as from an efficient cause. Therefore goodness implies the aspect of an efficient cause.

On the contrary, The Philosopher says that *that is to be considered as the end and the good of other things, for the sake of which something is*.[4] Therefore goodness has the aspect of a final cause.

I answer that, Since goodness is that which all things desire, and since this has the aspect of an end, it is clear that goodness implies the aspect of an end. Nevertheless, the idea of goodness presupposes the idea of an efficient cause[5], and also of a formal cause[6]. For we se

---

1. 参见 *Dc Div. Nom.*, IV, 7 (PG 3, 701).
2. 参见 *Op. cit.*, IV, 4; 20 (PG 3, 700; 720); cf. also, *op. cit.*, IV, 1 and 4 (PG 3, 693; 697).
3. 参见 *De Doc. Christ.*, I, 32 (PL 34, 32).
4. 参见 *Phys.*, II, 3 (195a 23).
5. efficient cause：直接原因；动力因
6. formal cause：形式因

that what is first in causing is last in the thing caused. Fire, *e.g.*, heats first of all before it reproduces the form of fire, though the heat in the fire follows from its substantial form. Now in causing, first comes goodness and the end, moving the agent to act; secondly, the action of the agent moving to the form; thirdly, comes the form. Hence in that which is caused the converse ought to take place, so that there should be, first, the form whereby it is a being; secondly, we consider in it its effective power, whereby it is perfect in being, *for a thing is perfect when it can reproduce its like*, as the Philosopher says;[1] thirdly, there follows the formality of goodness which is the basic principle of perfection in a being.

Reply Obj. 1. Beauty and goodness in a thing are identical fundamentally, for they are based upon the same thing, namely, the form; and this is why goodness is praised as beauty. But they differ logically, for goodness properly relates to appetite (goodness being what all things desire), and therefore it has the aspect of an end (the appetite being a kind of movement towards a thing). On the other hand, beauty relates to a cognitive power, for those things are said to be beautiful which please when seen. Hence beauty consists in due proportion, for the senses delight in things duly proportioned, as in what is like them — because the sense too is a sort of reason, as is every cognitive power. Now, since knowledge is by assimilation, and likeness relates to form, beauty properly belongs to the nature of a formal cause.

Reply Obj. 2. Goodness is described as self-diffusive in the sense that an end is said to move.

Reply Obj. 3. He who has a will is said to be good, so far as he has a good will; because it is by our will that we employ whatever powers we may have. Hence a man is said to be good, not because he has a good

---

1. 参见 *Meteor.*, IV, 3 (380a 12).

intellect, but because he has a good will. Now the will relates to the end as to its proper object. Thus the saying, *we exist because God is good*[1] has reference to the final cause.

Fifth Article
WHETHER THE ESSENCE OF GOODNESS CONSISTS IN LIMIT SPECIES AND ORDER?

We proceed thus to the Fifth Article: —

Objection 1. It seems that the essence of goodness does not consist in limit, species and order. For goodness and being differ logically. But limit, species and order seem to belong to the nature of being, for it is written: *Thou hast ordered all things in measure, and number and weight* (*Wis.* xi. 21). And to these three can be reduced species, limit and order, as Augustine says: *Measure fixes the limit of everything, number gives it its species, and weight gives it rest and stability.*[2] Therefore the essence of goodness does not consist in limit, species and order.

Obj. 2. Further, limit, form, and order are themselves good. Therefore if the essence of goodness consists in limit, species and order, then every limit must have its own limit, species and order. The same would be the case with species and order in endless succession.

Obj. 3. Further, evil is the privation of limit, species and order. But evil is not the total absence of goodness. Therefore the essence of goodness does not consist in limit, species and order.

Obj. 4. Further, that wherein consists the essence of goodness cannot be spoken of as evil. Yet we can speak of an evil limit, species and order. Therefore the essence of goodness does not consist in limit, species and order.

Obj. 5. Further, limit, species and order are caused by weight,

---

1. 参见 St. Augustine, *De Doc. Christ.*, I, 32 (PL 34, 32).
2. 参见 *De Genesi ad Litt.*, IV, 3 (PL 34, 299).

number and measure, as appears from the quotation from Augustine.[1] But not every good thing has weight, number and measure; for Ambrose says: *It is of the nature of light not to have been created in number, weight and measure.*[2] Therefore the essence of goodness does not consist in limit, species and order.

On the contrary, Augustine says: *These three — limit, species, order — as common good things, are in everything God has made; thus, where these three abound the things are very good; where they are less, the things are less good; where they do not exist at all, there can be nothing good.*[3] But this would not be unless the essence of goodness consisted in them. Therefore the essence of goodness consists in limit, species and order.

I answer that, Everything is said to be good so far as it is perfect; for in that way is it desirable(as has been shown above). Now a thing is said to be perfect if it lacks nothing according to the mode of its perfection. But since everything is what it is by its form (and since the form presupposes certain things, and from the form certain things necessarily follow), in order for a thing to be perfect and good it must have a form, together with all that precedes and follows upon that form. Now the form presupposes determination or commensuration[4] of its principles, whether material or efficient, and this is signified by the limit: hence it is said that *measure fixes the limit.*[5] But the form itself is signified by the species, for everything is placed in its species by its form. Hence number is said to give the species, for *definitions signifying species are like numbers*, according to the Philosopher;[6] for as a unit added to, or taken from, a number, changes its species, so a difference added to, or taken from, a definition, changes its species. Further,

1. 参见 *De Genesi ad Litt.*, IV, 3 (PL 34, 299).
2. 参见 *Hexaëm.*, I, 9 (PL 14, 154).
3. 参见 *De Nat. Boni*, 3 (PL 42, 553).
4. commensuration：同量；同大
5. 参见 St. Augustine, *De Genesi ad Litt.*, IV, 3 (PL 34, 299).
6. 参见 *Metaph.*, VIII, 3 (1043b 34).

upon the form follows an inclination to the end, or to an action, or something of the sort; for everything, in so far as it is in act, acts and tends towards that which befits it according to its form; and this belongs to weight and order. Hence the essence of goodness, so far as it consists in perfection, consists also in limit, species and order.

Reply Obj. 1. These three follow upon being, only so far as it is perfect; and according to this perfection it is good.

Reply Obj. 2. Limit, species and order are said to be good, and to be beings, not as though they themselves were subsistents, but because through them other things are both beings and good. Hence they have no need of other things whereby to be good, for they are spoken of as good, not as though formally so constituted by something else, but as formally constituting others good: thus whiteness is not said to be a being because it exists in anything else, but because, by it, something else has accidental being[1], viz., a thing that is white.

Reply Obj. 3. All being is through some form. Hence, according to the particular being of a thing is its limit, species, order. Thus, a man has a limit, species and order, as a man; and another limit, species, and order, as he is white, virtuous, knowing, and so on, according to everything predicated of him. But evil deprives a thing of some sort of being, as blindness deprives us of that being which is sight; and so it does not destroy every limit, species and order, but only such as follow upon the being of sight.

Reply Obj. 4. As Augustine says, *Every limit, as limit, is good* (and the same can be said of species and order). *But an evil limit, species and order are so called as being less than they ought to be, or as not belonging to that to which they ought to belong; or they are called evil, because they are out of place and incongruous*[2].[3]

---

1. accidental being：偶然的存在
2. incongruous：不协调的；不一致的
3. 参见 *De Nat. Boni*, 22 (PL 42, 558).

Reply Obj. 5. The nature of light is spoken of as being without number, weight and measure, not absolutely, but in comparison with corporeal things, because the power of light extends to all corporeal things inasmuch as it is an active quality of the first body that causes change, *i.e.*, the heavens.

Sixth Article

WHETHER GOODNESS IS RIGHTLY DIVIDED INTO THE BEFITTING, THE USEFUL AND THE PLEASANT?

We proceed thus to the Sixth Article: —

Objection 1. It seems that goodness is not rightly divided into the befitting, the useful and the pleasant. For goodness is divided by the ten predicaments[1], as the Philosopher says.[2] But the befitting, the useful and the pleasant can be found under one predicament. Therefore goodness is not rightly divided by them.

Obj. 2. Further, every division is made by opposites. But these three do not seem to be opposites, for the befitting is pleasing, and nothing unbefitting is useful; whereas this ought to be the case if the division were made by opposites, for then the befitting and the useful would be opposed, as also Tully observes.[3] Therefore the division is improper.

Obj. 3. Further, where one thing is because of another, there is only one thing. But the useful is not good, except so far as it is pleasing and befitting. Therefore the useful ought not to be divided from the pleasant and the befitting.

On the contrary, Ambrose makes use of this division of goodness in his *De Officiis*.[4]

---

1. predicaments：困难的处境；窘境
2. 参见 *Eth.*, I, 6 (1096a 19).
3. 参见 *De Off.*, II, 3 (PP. 81–82).
4. 参见 *De Off.*, I, 9 (PL 16, 35).

I answer that, This division properly concerns human goodness. But if we consider the nature of goodness from a higher and more universal point of view, we shall find that this division properly concerns goodness as such. For a thing is good so far as it is desirable, and is a term of the movement of appetite. The term of this movement can be seen from a consideration of the movement of a natural body. The movement of a natural body terminates absolutely in the end, and relatively in the means through which it comes to the end, where the movement ceases; so that a term of movement is so called in so far as it terminates any part of that movement. Now the ultimate term of movement can be taken in two ways: either as the thing itself towards which it tends, *e.g.*, a place or form; or as a state of rest in that thing. Thus, in the movement of appetite, the thing desired that terminates the movement of appetite relatively, as a means of tending towards something else, is called the *useful*; that sought after as the last thing absolutely terminating the movement of the appetite, as a thing towards which for its own sake the appetite tends, is called the *befitting*, for the *befitting* is that which is desired for its own sake; but that which terminates the movement of appetite in the form of rest in the thing desired, is called the *pleasant*.

Reply Obj. 1. Goodness, so far as it is really identical with being, is divided by the ten predicaments. But this division belongs to it according to its proper formality.

Reply Obj. 2. This division is not by opposite things, but by opposite aspects. Now those things are properly called pleasing which have no other formality under which they are desirable except the pleasant, although at times they are harmful and unbefitting. Whereas the useful applies to such as are undesirable in themselves, but are desired only as helpful to something further: *e.g.*, the taking of bitter medicine; while the befitting are said to be such as are desirable in themselves.

Reply Obj. 3. Goodness is not divided into these three as something univocal which is predicated equally of them all, but as something analogical which is predicated of them according to priority and posteriority[1]. For it is predicated by priority of the befitting, then of the pleasant, and lastly of the useful.

1. priority and posteriority：优先性和后天性

Question VI
THE GOODNESS OF GOD
(*In Four Articles*)

WE next consider the goodness of God, under which head there are four points of inquiry: (1) Whether to be good belongs to God? (2) Whether God is the highest good? (3) Whether He alone is essentially good? (4) Whether all things are good by the divine goodness?

First Article
WHETHER TO BE GOOD BELONGS TO GOD?

We proceed thus to the First Article: —

Objection 1. It seems that to be good does not belong to God. For goodness consists in limit, species and order. But these do not seem to belong to God, since God is immense, and is not ordered to anything. Therefore to be good does not belong to God.

Obj. 2. Further, the good is what all things desire. But all things do not desire God, because all things do not know Him; and nothing is desired unless it is known. Therefore to be good does not belong to God.

On the contrary, It is written (*Lam.* iii. 25): *The Lord is good to them that hope in Him, to the soul that seeketh Him.*

I answer that, To be good belongs pre-eminently[1] to God. For a thing is good according to its desirableness. Now everything seeks after its

---

1. pre-eminently：卓越地；杰出地

own perfection, and the perfection and form of an effect consist in a certain likeness to the agent, since every agent makes its like; and hence the agent itself is desirable and has the nature of good. For the very thing which is desirable in it is the participation of its likeness. Therefore, since God is the first producing cause of all things, it is manifest that the aspect of good and of desirableness belong to Him; and hence Dionysius attributes good to God as to the first efficient cause, saying that *God is called good as by Whom all things subsist.*[1]

Reply Obj. 1. To have limit, species and order belongs to the essence of caused good; but good is in God as in its cause, and hence it belongs to Him to impose limit, species and order on others; wherefore these three things are in God as in their cause.

Reply Obj. 2. All things, by desiring their own perfection, desire God Himself, inasmuch as the perfections of all things are so many similitudes of the divine being, as appears from what is said above.[2] And so of those beings which desire God, some know Him as He is in Himself, and this is proper to a rational creature; others know some participation of His goodness, and this belongs also to sensible knowledge; and others have a natural desire without knowledge, as being directed to their ends by a higher knower.

Second Article
WHETHER GOD IS THE HIGHEST GOOD?

We proceed thus to the Second Article: —

Objection 1. It seems that God is not the *highest* good[3]. For the *highest* good adds something to good, or otherwise it would belong to every good. But everything which is an addition to anything else is

---

1. 参见 *De Div. Nom.*, 4 (PG 3, 700).
2. 参见 Q. 4, a. 3.
3. the highest good：至善者

a composite thing: therefore the highest good is composite. But God is supremely simple, as was shown above.[1] Therefore God is not the highest good.

Obj. 2. Further, *Good is what all desire*, as the Philosopher says.[2] Now what all desire is nothing but God, Who is the end of all things: therefore there is no other good but God. This appears also from what is said (*Luke* xviii. 19): *None is good but God alone*. But we use the word highest in comparison with others, as, *e.g.*, the highest hot thing is used in comparison with all other hot things. Therefore God cannot be called the highest good.

Obj. 3. Further, highest implies comparison. But things not in the same genus are not comparable; as sweetness is not properly called greater or less than a line. Therefore, since God is not in the same genus as other good things, as appears above,[3] it seems that God cannot be called the highest good in relation to them.

On the contrary, Augustine says that the Trinity[4] of the divine persons *is the highest good, discerned by purified minds.*[5]

I answer that, God is the highest good absolutely, and not only in any genus or order of things. For good is attributed to God, as was said, inasmuch as all desired perfections flow from Him as from the first cause. They do not, however, flow from Him as from a univocal agent, as was shown above,[6] but as from an agent that does not agree with its effects either in species or genus. Now the likeness of an effect in the univocal cause is found uniformly; but in the equivocal cause it is found more excellently, as heat is in the sun more excellently than it is in fire. Therefore as good is in God as in the first, but not the

1. 参见 Q. 3, a. 7.
2. 参见 *Eth.*, I, 1 (1094a 3).
3. 参见 Q. 3, a. 5; q. 4. a. 3.
4. Trinity：三位一体
5. 参见 *De Trin.*, I, 2 (PL 42, 822).
6. 参见 Q. 4, a. 2 and 3.

univocal, cause of all things, it must be in Him in a most excellent way; and therefore He is called the highest good.

Reply Obj. 1. The highest good does not add to good any absolute thing, but only a relation. Now a relation, by which something is said of God relatively to creatures, is not really in God, but in the creature, for it is in God in our idea only. In the same way, what is knowable is so called with relation to knowledge, not that it depends on knowledge, but because knowledge depends on it. Thus it is not necessary that there should be composition in the highest good, but only that other things be deficient in comparison with it.

Reply Obj. 2. When we say that *good is what all desire*, it is not to be understood that every kind of good thing is desired by all, but that whatever is desired has the nature of good. And when it is said, *None is good but God alone*[1], this is to be understood of the essentially good, as will be explained.[2]

Reply Obj. 3. Things not of the same genus are in no way comparable to each other if they are in diverse genera. Now we say that God is not in the same genus with other good things. This does not mean that He is in any other genus, but that He is outside genus, and is the principle of every genus. Thus He is compared to others by excess, and it is this kind of comparison that the highest good implies.

Third Article
WHETHER TO BE ESSENTIALLY GOOD BELONGS TO GOD ALONE?

We proceed thus to the Third Article: —

Objection 1. It seems that to be essentially good does not belong to God alone. For as *one* is convertible with *being*, so is *good*, as we

---

1. None is good but God alone：除了天主没有其他善。
2. 参见 A. 3.

said above.[1] But every being is one essentially, as appears from the Philosopher.[2] Therefore every being is good essentially.

Obj. 2. Further, if good is what all things desire, since being itself is desired by all, then the being of each thing is its good. But everything is a being essentially: therefore every being is good essentially.

Obj. 3. Further, everything is good by its own goodness. Therefore if there is anything which is not good essentially, it is necessary to say that its goodness is not its own essence. Therefore its goodness, since it is a being, must be good; and if it is good by some other goodness, the same question applies to that goodness also. Therefore we must either proceed to infinity, or come to some goodness which is not good by any other goodness. Therefore the first supposition holds good. Therefore everything is good essentially.

On the contrary, Boethius says that *all things but God are good by participation*[3] .[4] Therefore they are not good essentially.

I answer that, God alone is good essentially. For everything is called good according to its perfection. Now perfection in a thing is threefold: first, according to the constitution of its own being; secondly, in respect of any accidents being added as necessary for its perfect operation; thirdly, perfection consists in the attaining to something else as the end. Thus, for instance, the first perfection of fire consists in its being, which it has through its own substantial form; its secondary perfection consists in heat, lightness and dryness, and the like; its third perfection is to rest in its own place. This triple perfection belongs to no creature by its own essence; it belongs to God only, Whose essence alone is His being, in Whom there are no accidents, since whatever belongs to others accidentally belongs to Him essentially: *e.g.*, to be

---

1. 参见 Q. 5, a. 1.
2. 参见 *Metaph.*, III, 2 (1003b 32).
3. All things but God are good by participation：除了天主没有全善。
4. 参见 *De Hebdom.* (PL 64, 1313).

powerful, wise, and the like, as appears from what is stated above.[1] Furthermore, He is not directed to anything else as to an end, but is Himself the last end of all things. Hence it is manifest that God alone has every kind of perfection by His own essence, and therefore He alone is good essentially.

Reply Obj. 1. *One* does not include the idea of perfection, but only of indivision, which belongs to everything according to its own essence. Now the essences of simple things are undivided both actually and potentially, but the essences of composite things are undivided only actually; and therefore everything must be one essentially, but not good essentially, as was shown above.

Reply Obj. 2. Although everything is good in that it has being, yet the essence of a creature is not being itself, and therefore it does not follow that a creature is good essentially.

Reply Obj. 3. The goodness of a creature is not its very essence, but something superadded; it is either its being, or some added perfection, or the order to its end. Still, the goodness itself thus added is called good, just as it is called being. But it is called being because by it something has being, not because it itself has being through something else. Hence it is called good because by it something is good, and not because it itself has some other goodness whereby it is good.

Fourth Article
WHETHER ALL THINGS ARE GOOD BY THE DIVINE GOODNESS?

We proceed thus to the Fourth Article: —

Objection 1. It seems that all things are good by the divine goodness. For Augustine says: *This and that are good. Take away this and that, and*

1. 参见 Q. 3, a. 6.

see good itself if thou canst; and so thou shalt see God, good not by any other good, but the good of every good.[1] But everything is good by its own good: therefore everything is good by that very good which is God.

Obj. 2. Further, as Boethius says,[2] all things are called good according as they are directed to God, and this is by reason of the divine goodness: therefore all things are good by the divine goodness.

On the contrary, All things are good inasmuch as they have being. But they are not called beings through the divine being, but through their own being: therefore all things are not good by the divine goodness, but by their own goodness.

I answer that, As regards relative things, we may admit extrinsic denomination. Thus, a thing is denominated *placed* from *place*, and *measured* from *measure*. But as regards what is said absolutely, opinions differ. Plato held the separate existence of the essences of all things, and that individuals were denominated by them as participating in the separate essences; for instance, that Socrates is called man according to the separate Form of man.[3] Now just as he laid down separate Forms of man and horse which he called absolute man and absolute horse,[4] so likewise he laid down separate Forms of *being* and of *one*, and these he called absolute being and absolute oneness,[5] and by participation in these everything was called *being* or *one*. What was thus absolute being and absolute one, he said was the highest good.[6] And because good is convertible with being, as is also one, he called the absolute good God,[7] from whom all things are called good by way of

1. 参见 *De Trin.*, VIII, 3 (PL 42, 949).
2. 参见 *De Hebdom.* (PL 64, 1312).
3. 参见 Cf. Aristotle, *Metaph.*, I, 6 (987b 7) ; St. Augustine, *Lib.* 83 *Quaest.*, q. 46 (PL 40, 30).
4. 参见 Aristotle, *Metaph.*, II, 2 (997b 8).
5. 参见 *Op. cit.*, II, 4 (999b 26).
6. 参见 Cf. Aristotle, *Eth.*, I, 6 (1096a 23); Macrobius, *In Somn. Scipion.*, I, 2 (p. 482).
7. 参见 St. Augustine, *De Civit. Dei*, VIII, 8 (PL 41, 233); Plato, *Republic*, VI (p. 508c) .

participation.[1]

Although this opinion appears to be unreasonable in affirming that there are separate forms of natural things subsisting of themselves — as Aristotle argues in many ways[2] — still, it is absolutely true that there is something first which is essentially being and essentially good, which we call God, as appears from what is shown above.[3] Aristotle agrees with this.[4] Hence from the first being, essentially being and good, everything can be called good and a being inasmuch as it participates in the first being by way of a certain assimilation, although distantly and defectively, as appears from the above.[5]

Everything is therefore called good from the divine goodness, as from the first exemplary, effective and final principle of all goodness. Nevertheless, everything is called good by reason of the likeness of the divine goodness belonging to it, which is formally its own goodness, whereby it is denominated good. And so of all things there is one goodness, and yet many goodnesses.

This is a sufficient Reply to the Objections.

1. 参见 Cf. St. Augustine, *De Trin.*, VIII, 3 (PL 42, 949) ; St. Albert, *In Eth.*, I, tr. 5, ch. 13 (VII, 76).
2. 参见 *Metaph.*, I, 9 (990a 33); VI, 7–8 (1031a 15); *Eth.*, I, 6 (1096a 11).
3. 参见 Q. 2, a. 3.
4. 参见 *Metaph.*, Ia, 1 (993b 24); cf. above, q. 2, a. 3.
5. 参见 Q. 4, a. 3.

Question VII
THE INFINITY OF GOD
(*In Four Articles*)

AFTER considering the divine perfection, we must consider God's infinity[1], and His existence in things;[2] for God is said to be everywhere, and in all things, inasmuch as He is boundless and infinite.

Concerning the first, there are four points of inquiry: (1) Whether God is infinite? (2) Whether anything besides Him is infinite in essence? (3) Whether anything can be infinite in magnitude? (4) Whether an infinite multitude can exist?

First Article
WHETHER GOD IS INFINITE?

We proceed thus to the First Article: —

Objection 1. It seems that God is not infinite. For everything infinite is imperfect, as the Philosopher says, because it has parts and matter, as is said in *Physics* iii.[3] But God is most perfect: therefore He is not infinite.

Obj. 2. Further, according to the Philosopher,[4] finite and infinite belong to quantity. But there is no quantity in God, for He is not a

---

1. God's infinity：天主的无限性
2. 参见 Q. 8.
3. 参见 Aristotle, *Phys.*, III, 6 (207a 27).
4. 参见 *Op. cit.*, I, 2 (185b 2).

body, as was shown above.[1] Therefore it does not belong to Him to be infinite.

Obj. 3. Further, what is here in such a way as not to be elsewhere is finite according to place. Therefore, that which is this thing in such a way as not to be another thing is finite according to substance. But God is this, and not another; for He is not a stone or wood. Therefore God is not infinite in substance.

On the contrary, Damascene says that *God is infinite and eternal and boundless.*[2]

I answer that, All the ancient philosophers attribute infinitude to the first principle, as it is said,[3] and this *with reason*;[4] for they considered that things flow forth infinitely from the first principle. But because some erred concerning the nature of the first principle, as a consequence they erred also concerning its infinity. For they asserted that matter was the first principle;[5] and consequently they attributed to the first principle a material infinity, asserting that some infinite body was the first principle of things.

We must consider therefore that a thing is called infinite because it is not finite. Now matter is in a way made finite by form, and the form by matter. Matter is made finite by form inasmuch as matter, before it receives its form, is in potentiality to many forms; but on receiving a form, it is terminated by that one. Again, form is made finite by matter inasmuch as form, considered in itself, is common to many; but when received in matter, the form is determined to this one particular thing. Now matter is perfected by the form by which it is made finite, and therefore infinity as attributed to matter has the nature of

1. 参见 Q. 3, a. 1.
2. 参见 *De Fide Orth.*, I, 4 (PG 94, 800).
3. 参见 Aristotle, *Phys.*, III, 4 (203a 1).
4. 同上 (203b 4).
5. 参见 Aristotle, *Metaph.*, I, 3 (983b 6).

something imperfect, for it is as it were formless matter. On the other hand, form is not made perfect by matter, but rather is contracted by matter; and hence the infinite, regarded on the part of the form not determined by matter, has the nature of something perfect. Now being is the most formal of all things, as appears from the above.[1] Since therefore the divine being is not a being received in anything, but God is His own subsistent being[2] (as was shown above[3]), it is clear that God Himself is infinite and perfect.

From this appears the Reply to the First Objection.

Reply Obj. 2. The term of quantity is, as it were, its form, and this can be seen in the fact that a figure which consists in the termination of quantity is a kind of quantitative form. Hence the infinite of quantity is in the order of matter, and such a kind of infinite cannot be attributed to God, as was said above.

Reply Obj. 3. The fact that the being of God is self-subsisting, not received in any other, and is thus called infinite, shows God to be distinguished from all other beings, and all others to be apart from Him; much as, were there such a thing as a self-subsisting whiteness, the very fact that it did not exist in anything else would make it distinct from every other whiteness existing in a subject.

Second Article
WHETHER ANYTHING BUT GOD CAN BE ESSENTIALLY INFINITE?

We proceed thus to the Second Article: —

Objection 1. It seems that something else besides God can be essentially infinite. For the power of anything is proportioned to its

---

1. 参见 Q. 4, a. 1.
2. subsistent being：独立存有
3. 参见 Q. 3, a. 4.

essence. Now if the essence of God is infinite, His power must also be infinite. Therefore He can produce an infinite effect, since the extent of a power is known by its effect.

Obj. 2. Further, whatever has infinite power has an infinite essence. Now the created intellect has an infinite power, for it apprehends the universal, which can extend itself to an infinitude of singulars. Therefore every created intellectual substance is infinite.

Obj. 3. Further, primary matter is something other than God, as was shown above.[1] But primary matter is infinite. Therefore something besides God can be infinite.

On the contrary, The infinite cannot be from some principle, as is said in *Physics* iii.[2] But everything outside God is from God as from its first principle. Therefore nothing besides God can be infinite.

I answer that, Things other than God can be relatively infinite[3], but not absolutely infinite[4]. For with regard to the infinite as applied to matter, it is manifest that everything actually existing possesses a form; and thus its matter is determined by form. But because matter, considered as existing under some substantial form, remains in potentiality to many accidental forms, what is absolutely finite can be relatively infinite. For example, wood is finite according to its own form, but still it is relatively infinite inasmuch as it is in potentiality to an infinite number of shapes. But if we speak of the infinite in reference to form, it is manifest that those things, the forms of which are in matter, are absolutely finite, and in no way infinite. If, however, any created forms are not received into matter, but are self-subsisting, as some think to be the case with the angels,[5] these will be relatively

1. 参见 Q. 3, a. 8.
2. 参见 Aristotle, *Phys.* III, 4 (203b 7).
3. relatively infinite：相对无限
4. absolutely infinite：绝对无限
5. 参见 Cf. below, q. 50, a. 2.

infinite, inasmuch as such forms are not terminated, nor contracted, by any matter. But because a created form thus subsisting has being, and yet is not its own being, it follows that its being is received and contracted to a determinate nature. Hence it cannot be absolutely infinite.

Reply Obj. 1. It is against the nature of a produced thing for its essence to be its being, because subsisting being is not a created being; and hence it is against the nature of a produced thing to be absolutely infinite. Therefore, as God, although He has infinite power, cannot make a thing to be not made (for this would imply that two contradictories are true at the same time), so likewise He cannot make anything to be absolutely infinite.

Reply Obj. 2. The reason why the power of the intellect in a way extends itself to an infinity of things is that the intellect is a form not in matter; but it is either wholly separated from matter, as are angelic substances, or at least there is the separation of an intellectual power, which is not the act of any organ, in the intellectual soul joined to a body.

Reply Obj. 3. Primary matter does not exist by itself in nature, since it is not actual being, but only potential. Hence it is something concreated rather than created. Nevertheless, primary matter even as a potentiality is not absolutely infinite, but relatively, because its potentiality extends only to natural forms.

Third Article
WHETHER AN ACTUALLY INFINITE MAGNITUDE[1] CAN EXIST?

We proceed thus to the Third Article: —

---

1. infinite magnitude：无限大

Objection 1. It seems that there can be something actually infinite in magnitude. For in mathematics there is no error, since *there is no lie in things abstract*, as the Philosopher says.[1] But mathematics uses the infinite in magnitude; and thus, the geometrician in his demonstrations says, *Let this line be infinite*. Therefore it is not impossible for a thing to be infinite in magnitude.

Obj. 2. Further, what is not against the nature of anything can agree with it. Now to be infinite is not against the nature of magnitude, but rather both the finite and the infinite seem to be attributes of quantity. Therefore it is not impossible for some magnitude to be infinite.

Obj. 3. Further, magnitude is infinitely divisible, for the continuous is defined as *that which is infinitely divisible*, as is clear from *Physics* iii.[2] But contraries are concerned about one and the same thing. Since, therefore, addition is opposed to division, and increase is opposed to diminution, it appears that magnitude can be increased to infinity. Therefore it is possible for magnitude to be infinite.

Obj. 4. Further, movement and time have quantity and continuity derived from the magnitude over which movement passes, as it is said in *Physics* iv.[3] But it is not against the nature of time and movement to be infinite, since every determinate indivisible in time and circular movement is both a beginning and an end. Therefore neither is it against the nature of magnitude to be infinite.

On the contrary, Every body has a surface. But every body which has a surface is finite, because surface is the term of a finite body. Therefore all bodies are finite. The same applies also to surface and to a line. Therefore nothing is infinite in magnitude.

I answer that, It is one thing to be infinite in essence, and another to be infinite in magnitude. For granted that there exists a body which

---

1. 参见 Aristotle, *Phys*. II, 2 (193b 35).
2. 参见 *Op. cit*. III, 1 (200b 20).
3. 参见 *Op. cit*., IV, 11 (219a 12).

is infinite in magnitude, as fire or air, yet this would not be infinite in essence, because its essence would be terminated in a species by its form, and confined to some individual by matter. And so, assuming from what has preceded that no creature is infinite in essence, it still remains to inquire whether any creature can be infinite in magnitude.

We must therefore observe that a body, which is a complete magnitude, can be considered in two ways: *mathematically*, in which case we consider its quantity only; and *naturally*, in which case we consider its matter and form.

Now it is manifest that a natural body cannot be actually infinite. For every natural body has some determined substantial form. Therefore, since accidents follow upon the substantial form, it is necessary that determinate accidents should follow upon a determinate form; and among these accidents is quantity. So every natural body has a greater or smaller determinate quantity. Hence it is impossible for a natural body to be infinite. The same appears from movement, because every natural body has some natural movement, whereas an infinite body could not have any natural movement. It cannot have one in a straight line, because nothing moves naturally by such a movement unless it is out of its place; and this could not happen to an infinite body, for it would occupy every place, and thus every place would be indifferently its own place. Neither could it move circularly, since circular motion requires that one part of the body be necessarily transferred to a place which had been occupied by another part, and this could not happen as regards an infinite circular body: for if two lines be drawn from the center, the farther they extend from the center, the farther they are from each other; and therefore, if a body were infinite, the lines would be infinitely distant from each other, and thus one could never occupy the place belonging to the other.

The same applies to a mathematical body. For if we imagine a mathematical body actually existing, we must imagine it under some form, because nothing is actual except by its form. Hence, since the form of quantity as such is figure, such a body must have some figure. It would therefore be finite, for figure is confined by a term or boundary.

Reply Obj. 1. A geometrician does not need to assume that a given line is actually infinite: he needs to take some actually finite line, from which he can subtract whatever he finds necessary; which line he calls infinite.

Reply Obj. 2. Although the infinite is not against the nature of magnitude in general, it is against the nature of any species of it. Thus, for instance, it is against the nature of a bicubical or tricubical magnitude, whether circular or triangular, and so on. Now what is not possible in any species cannot exist in the genus, and hence there cannot be any infinite magnitude, since no species of magnitude is infinite.

Reply Obj. 3. The infinite in quantity, as was shown above, belongs to matter. Now by division of the whole we approach to matter, since parts are as matter; but by addition we approach to the whole which is as a form. Therefore, the infinite is not found in the addition of magnitude, but only in division.

Reply Obj. 4. Movement and time are not actual as wholes, but successively, and hence they have potentiality mixed with actuality. But magnitude is an actual whole, and therefore the infinite in quantity refers to matter, and does not agree with the totality of magnitude; yet it agrees with the totality of time or movement: for to be in potentiality befits matter.

Fourth Article
WHETHER AN INFINITE MULTITUDE CAN EXIST?

We proceed thus to the Fourth Article: —

Objection 1. It seems that an actually infinite multitude[1] is possible.

---

1. infinite multitude：无限多

For it is not impossible for a potentiality to be made actual. But number can be multiplied to infinity. Therefore it is possible for an infinite multitude actually to exist.

Obj. 2. Further, it is possible for any individual of any species to be actual. But the species of figures are infinite. Therefore an infinite number of actual figures is possible.

Obj. 3. Further, things not opposed to each other do not obstruct each other. But supposing a multitude of things to exist, there can still be many others not opposed to them. Therefore it is not impossible for others also to coexist with them, and so on to infinitude. Therefore an actual infinite number of things is possible.

On the contrary, It is written, *Thou hast ordered all things in measure, and number and weight* (*Wis*. xi. 21).

I answer that, A twofold opinion has obtained on this subject. Some, as Avicenna and Algazel,[1] said that *it was impossible for an absolutely infinite multitude to exist actually, but that an accidentally infinite multitude was not impossible. A multitude is said to be infinite absolutely, when an infinite multitude is necessary that something may exist.* Now this is impossible, because it would mean that something is dependent on an infinity for its existence; and hence its generation would never be accomplished, because it is impossible to traverse what is infinite.

A multitude is said to be accidentally infinite when its existence as such is not necessary, but accidental. This can be shown, for example, in the work of an artisan requiring a certain absolute multitude, namely, art in the soul, the movement of the hand and a hammer; and supposing that such things were infinitely multiplied, the work would never be finished, since it would depend on an infinite number of causes. But the multitude of hammers, which results when one hammer is broken and is replaced by another, is an accidental

1. 参见 Cf. Averroes. *Destruct. Destruct.*, I (IX, 12vab).

multitude; for it happens by accident that many hammers are used, and it matters little whether one or two, or many are used, or an infinite number, if the work is carried on for an infinite time. In this way they said that there can be actually an accidentally infinite multitude.

This, however, is impossible, since every kind of multitude must belong to a species of multitude. Now the species of multitude are to be reckoned by the species of numbers. But no species of number is infinite, for every number is multitude measured by one. Hence it is impossible that there be an actually infinite multitude, either absolutely or accidentally. Furthermore, multitude in the world is created, and everything created is comprehended under some definite intention of the Creator; for no agent acts aimlessly. Hence everything created must be comprehended under a certain number. Therefore it is impossible for an actually infinite multitude to exist, even accidentally.

But a potentially infinite multitude is possible, because the increase of multitude follows upon the division of a magnitude, since the more a thing is divided, the greater number of things result. Hence, just as the infinite is to be found potentially in the division of the continuous, because we thus approach matter, as was shown above, in the same way the infinite can also be found potentially in the addition of multitude.

Reply Obj. 1. Whatever exists potentially is made actual according to its mode of being. For instance, a day is reduced to act successively, and not all at once. Likewise the infinite in multitude is reduced to act successively, and not all at once, because every multitude can be succeeded by another multitude to infinity.

Reply Obj. 2. Species of figures are infinite by the infinitude of number. Now there are various species of figures, such as trilateral, quadrilateral and so on; and as an infinitely numerable multitude is not all at once reduced to act, so neither is the multitude of figures.

Reply Obj. 3. Although the supposition of some things does not preclude the supposition of others, still the supposition of an infinite number is opposed to any single species of multitude. Hence it is not possible for any actually infinite multitude to exist.

Question VIII
THE EXISTENCE OF GOD IN THINGS
(*In Four Articles*)

SINCE it evidently belongs to the infinite to be present everywhere and in all things, we must now consider whether this belongs to God; and concerning this there arise four points of inquiry: (1) Whether God is in all things? (2) Whether God is everywhere? (3) Whether God is everywhere by essence, power and presence? (4) Whether to be everywhere belongs to God alone?

First Article
WHETHER GOD IS IN ALL THINGS?

We proceed thus to the First Article: —

Objection 1. It seems that God is not in all things. For what is above all things is not in all things. But God is above all, according to the Psalm (cxii. 4): *The Lord is high above all nations*, etc. Therefore God is not in all things.

Obj. 2. Further, what is in anything is thereby contained. Now God is not contained by things, but He rather contains them. Therefore God is not in things, but things are rather in Him. Hence Augustine says that *things are in Him, rather than that He is in any place.*[1]

Obj. 3. Further, the more powerful an agent is, the more extended is its action. But God is the most powerful of all agents. Therefore, His

1. 参见 *Lib. 83 Quaest.*, q. 20 (PL 40, 15).

action can extend even to things which are far removed from Him, and it is not necessary that He should be in all things.

Obj. 4. Further, the demons[1] are beings. But God is not in the demons, for there is no *fellowship between light and darkness* (*2 Cor.* vi. 14). Therefore God is not in all things.

On the contrary, A thing is wherever it operates. But God operates in all things, according to *Isa.* xxvi. 12, *Lord . . . Thou hast wrought all our works in us*. Therefore God is in all things.

I answer that, God is in all things, not, indeed, as part of their essence, nor as an accident, but as an agent is present to that upon which it acts. For an agent must be joined to that on which it acts immediately, and reach it by its power; hence it is proved in *Physics* vii. that the thing moved and the mover must exist together.[2] Now, since God is being itself by His own essence, created being must be His proper effect; as to ignite is the proper effect of fire. But God causes this effect in things not only when they first begin to be, but as long as they are preserved in being; as light is caused in the air by the sun as long as the air remains illuminated. Therefore, as long as a thing has being, so long must God be present to it, according to its mode of being. But being is innermost in each thing and most fundamentally present within all things, since it is formal in respect of everything found in a thing, as was shown above.[3] Hence it must be that God is in all things, and innermostly.

Reply Obj. 1. God is above all things by the excellence of His nature; nevertheless, He is in all things as causing the being of all things, as was shown above.

Reply Obj. 2. Although corporeal things are said to be *in* something as in that which contains them, nevertheless spiritual beings contain

---

1. demons：恶魔，邪灵
2. 参见 Aristotle, *Phys*., VII, 2 (243a 4).
3. 参见 Q. 4, a. 1, ad 3; q. 7, a. 1.

those things in which they are; as the soul contains the body. So, too, God is in things as containing them. Nevertheless, by a certain similitude[1] to corporeal things it is said that all things are in God inasmuch as they are contained by Him.

Reply Obj. 3. No action of an agent, however powerful it may be, acts at a distance, except through a medium. But it belongs to the supreme power of God that He acts immediately in all things. Hence nothing is distant from Him, as if it could be without God in itself. But things are said to be distant from God by unlikeness to Him in nature or grace; just as He is above all by the excellence of His own nature.

Reply Obj. 4. In the demons there is their nature which is from God, and also the deformity[2] of sin which is not from Him. Therefore, it is not to be absolutely conceded that God is in the demons, except with the addition, *inasmuch as they are beings.* But in things not deformed in their nature, we must say absolutely that God is present.

Second Article
WHETHER GOD IS EVERYWHERE?

We proceed thus to the Second Article: —

Objection 1. It seems that God is not everywhere. For to be everywhere means to be in every place. But to be in every place does not belong to God, to Whom it does not belong to be in place at all; for *incorporeal beings*, as Boethius says,[3] *are not in place.* Therefore God is not everywhere.

Obj. 2. Further, the relation of time to succession is the same as the relation of place to permanence. But one indivisible part of action or movement cannot exist in different times. Therefore neither can one

1. similitude：相似性
2. deformity：畸形状态；（道德方面的）缺陷
3. 参见 *De Hebdom.* (PL 64, 1311).

indivisible part in the genus of permanent things be in every place. Now the divine being is not successive, but permanent. Therefore God is not in many places; and thus He is not everywhere.

Obj. 3. Further, what is wholly in any one place is not in part elsewhere But if God is in any one place He is all there; for He has no parts. No part of Him then is elsewhere; and therefore God is not everywhere.

On the contrary, It is written, *I fill heaven and earth* (*Jer.* xxiii. 24).

I answer that, Since place is a reality, to be in place can be understood in a twofold sense: either after the manner of other realities — *i.e.*, as one thing is said to be in another in any way whatever, and thus the accidents of a place are in place; or in a manner proper to place, and thus things placed are in place. Now in both these senses in some way God is in every place; and this is to be everywhere. First, He is in all things as giving them being, power and operation; so He is in every place as giving it being and locative power. Again, things placed are in place inasmuch as they fill place: so, too, God fills every place; not, indeed, like a body, for a body is said to fill place inasmuch as it excludes the co-occupancy of another body, whereas by the fact that God is in a place, others are not thereby excluded from it. Indeed, He fills every place by the very fact that He gives being to the things that fill all places.

Reply Obj. 1. Incorporeal things are in place not by contact of dimensive quantity, as bodies are, but by contact of power.

Reply Obj. 2. The indivisible is twofold. One is the term of the continuous: *e.g.*, a point in permanent things, and a moment in the successive. This kind of indivisible in permanent things, since it has a determinate site, cannot be in many parts of place, or in many places; likewise the indivisible of action or movement, since it has a determinate order in movement or action, cannot be in many parts of time. Another kind of indivisible is outside of the whole genus of the continuous; and in this way incorporeal substances, like God, angel, and soul, are called indivisible. Such a kind of indivisible does not belong to the continuous as a part of it, but as touching it by its power.

Hence, according as its power can extend itself to one or to many, to a small thing, or to a great one, in this way it is in one or in many places, and in a small or large place.

Reply Obj. 3. A whole is so called with reference to its parts. Now a *part* is twofold: viz., a part of the essence, as the form and the matter are called parts of the composite, while genus and difference are called parts of species. There is also a part of quantity, into which any quantity is divided. What therefore is wholly in any place by totality of quantity cannot be outside of that place, because the quantity of anything placed is commensurate[1] with the quantity of the place; and hence there is no totality of quantity without totality of place. But the totality of essence is not commensurate with the totality of place. Hence it is not necessary for that which is wholly in a thing by totality of essence, not to be at all outside it. This appears also in accidental forms, which have quantity accidentally. For example, whiteness is whole in each part of the surface if we speak of its totality of essence, because it is found to exist in every part of the surface according to the perfection of its nature. But if its totality be considered according to quantity, which it has accidentally, then it is not wholly in every part of the surface. On the other hand, incorporeal substances have no totality either essentially or accidentally, except according to the perfect idea of their essence. Hence, as the soul is wholly in every part of the body, so God is wholly in all things and in each one.

Third Article
WHETHER GOD IS EVERYWHERE BY ESSENCE, PRESENCE AND POWER ?

We proceed thus to the Third Article:–

---

1. commensurate：相称的；相当的

Objection 1. It seems that the mode of God's existence in things is badly explained by saying that God is present in all things by essence, presence and power.[1] For what is by essence in anything, is in it essentially. But God is not essentially in things, for He does not belong to the essence of anything. Therefore it ought not to be said that God is in things by essence, presence and power.

Obj. 2. Further, to be present to anything means not to be absent from it. Now this is the meaning of God being in things by his essence, that He is not absent from anything. Therefore the presence of God in all things by essence and presence means the same thing. Therefore it is superfluous to say that God is present in things by His essence, presence and power.

Obj. 3. Further, as God by His power is the principle of all things, so He is the same likewise by His knowledge and will. But it is not said that He is in things by knowledge and will. Therefore neither is He present by His power.

Obj. 4. Further, as grace is a perfection added to the substance of a thing, so many other perfections are likewise added. Therefore if God is said to be in certain beings in a special way by grace, it seems that according to every perfection there ought to be a special mode of God's existence in things.

On the contrary, Gregory, commenting on the *Canticle of Canticles*, says that *God is in all things in a general manner by His presence, power and substance; but He is said to be present more familiarly in some by grace.*[2]

I answer that, God is said to be in a thing in two ways: in one way, after the manner of an efficient cause, and thus He is in all things created by Him; in another way, He is in things as the object of operation is in the operator, and this is proper to the operations of the soul, according as the thing known is in the one who knows,

---

1. 参见 Cf. Peter Lombard, *Sent.*, I, xxxvii, 1 (I, 229).
2. 参见 Cf. Peter Lombard, *ibid.* (I, 230), with the note of the editors.

and the thing desired in the one desiring. In this second way God is especially in the rational creature[1], which knows and loves Him actually or habitually. And because the rational creature possesses this prerogative by grace, as will be shown later,[2] He is said to be thus in the saints by grace.

But how He is in other things created by Him may be considered from human affairs. A king, for example, is said to be in the whole kingdom by his power, although he is not everywhere present. Again, a thing is said to be by its presence in other things which are subject to its inspection[3]; as things in a house are said to be present to anyone, who nevertheless may not be in substance in every part of the house. Lastly, a thing is said to be substantially or essentially in that place in which its substance is. Now there were some (the Manichees[4]) who said that spiritual and incorporeal things were subject to the divine power, but that visible and corporeal things were subject to the power of a contrary principle. Therefore against these it is necessary to say that God is in all things by His power.

But others,[5] though they believed that all things were subject to the divine power, still did not think that the divine providence extended to these inferior bodies, and in the person of these it is said, *He walketh about the poles of the heavens, and He doth not consider our things* (*Job* xxii. 14). Against these it has been necessary to say that God is in all things by His presence.

Further, others[6] said that, although all things are subject to God's providence[7], still all things are not immediately created by God, but that He immediately created the first creatures, and these created the others.

---

1. rational creature：有理性的受造物
2. 参见 *S.T.*, I-II, q. 109, a. 1 and 3.
3. inspection：检查
4. 参见 Cf. St. Augustine, *De Haeres.*, 46 (PL 42, 35).
5. 参见 Cf. below, q. 22, a. 2.
6. 参见 Cf. below, q. 45, a. 5.
7. God's providence：天主的眷顾

Against these it is necessary to say that He is in all things by His essence.

Therefore, God is in all things by His power, inasmuch as all things are subject to His power; He is by His presence in all things, inasmuch as all things are bare and open to His eyes; He is in all things by His essence, inasmuch as He is present to all as the cause of their being.

Reply Obj. 1. God is said to be in all things by essence, not indeed by the essence of the things themselves, as if He were of their essence, but by His own essence, because His substance is present to all things as the cause of their being.

Reply Obj. 2. A thing can be said to be present to another when it lies within its sight, though the thing may be distant in substance, as has been shown; and therefore two modes of presence are necessary, viz., by essence and by presence.

Reply Obj. 3. Knowledge and will require that the thing known should be in the one who knows, and the thing willed in the one who wills. Hence by knowledge and will things are more truly in God than God in things. But power is the principle of acting on another. Hence by power the agent is related and applied to an external thing; and thus by power an agent may be said to be in another.

Reply Obj. 4. No other perfection, except grace, added to substance, renders God present in anything as the object known and loved; therefore only grace constitutes a special mode of God's existence in things. There is, however, another special mode of God's existence in man by union, which will be treated in its own place.[1]

Fourth Article
WHETHER TO BE EVERYWHERE BELONGS TO GOD ALONE?

We proceed thus to the Fourth Article:–

---

1. 参见 *S.T.*, III, q. 2.

Objection 1. It seems that to be everywhere does not belong to God alone. For the universal, according to the Philosopher,[1] is everywhere and always; and primary matter also, since it is in all bodies, is everywhere. But neither of these is God, as appears from what is said above.[2] Therefore to be everywhere does not belong to God alone.

Obj. 2. Further, number is in things numbered. But the whole universe is constituted in number, as appears from *Wisdom* (xi. 21). Therefore, there is some number which is in the whole universe, and is thus everywhere.

Obj. 3. Further, the universe is a kind of whole perfect body.[3] But the whole universe is everywhere, because there is no place outside of it. Therefore to be everywhere does not belong to God alone.

Obj. 4. Further, if any body were infinite, no place would exist outside of it, and so it would be everywhere. Therefore to be everywhere does not appear to belong to God alone.

Obj. 5. Further, the soul, as Augustine says, is *whole in the whole body, and whole in every one of its parts.*[4] Therefore if there were in the world only one animal, its soul would be everywhere; and thus to be everywhere does not belong to God alone.

Obj. 6. Further, as Augustine says, *The soul feels where it sees, and lives where it feels, and is where it lives.*[5] But the soul sees as it were everywhere: for in a succession of glances it comprehends the entire space of the heavens in its sight. Therefore the soul is everywhere.

On the contrary, Ambrose says: *Who dares to call the Holy Ghost a creature, Who is in all things, and everywhere, and always, which assuredly*

---

1. 参见 *Post. Anal.*, I, 31 (87b 33).
2. 参见 Q. 3, a. 5 and 8.
3. 参见 Aristotle, *De Caelo*, I, 1 (268b 8).
4. 参见 *De Trin.*, VI, 6 (PL 42, 929).
5. 参见 *Epist.* CXXXVII, 2(PL 33, 518).

belongs to the divinity[1] *alone*?[2]

I answer that, To be everywhere primarily and essentially is proper to God. Now to be everywhere primarily is said of that which in its whole self is everywhere; for if a thing were everywhere according to diverse parts in diverse places, it would not be primarily everywhere, for what belongs to anything according to a part does not belong to it primarily. Thus, if a man has white teeth, whiteness belongs primarily not to the man but to his teeth. But a thing is everywhere essentially when it does not belong to it to be everywhere accidentally, that is, merely on some supposition; as a grain of millet would be everywhere, supposing that no other body existed. It belongs therefore to a thing to be everywhere essentially when, on any supposition, it must be everywhere; and this properly belongs to God alone. For whatever number of places be supposed, even if an infinite number be supposed besides what already exist, it would be necessary that God should be in all of them; for nothing can exist except by Him. Therefore to be everywhere primarily and essentially belongs to God, and is proper to Him;[3] because whatever number of places be supposed to exist, God must be in all of them, not by a part of Him, but by His very self.

Reply Obj. 1. The universal and primary matter are indeed everywhere, but not according to the same being.

Reply Obj. 2. Number, since it is an accident, is not found in place essentially, but accidentally; neither is the whole but only part of it in each of the things numbered. Hence it does not follow that it is primarily and essentially everywhere.

Reply Obj. 3. The whole body of the universe is everywhere, but not primarily, since it is not wholly in each place, but according to its parts; nor again is it everywhere essentially, because, supposing that

1. *divinity*：神，神学，神性
2. 参见 *De Spir. Sancto*, I, 7 (PL 16, 753).
3. 参见 Q. 10.

other places existed, it would not be in them.

Reply Obj. 4. If an infinite body existed, it would be everywhere, but according to its parts.

Reply Obj. 5. Were there one animal only, its soul would be everywhere primarily indeed, but accidentally.

Reply Obj. 6. When it is said that the soul sees anywhere, this can be taken in two senses. In one sense, the adverb *anywhere* modifies the act of seeing on the part of the object, and in this sense it is true that while it sees the heavens, it sees in the heavens, and in the same way it feels in the heavens; but it does not follow that it lives or exists in the heavens, because to live and to exist do not import an act passing to an exterior object[1]. In another sense, it can be understood according as the adverb modifies the act of the seer, as proceeding from the seer; and thus it is true that where the soul feels and sees, there it is, and there it lives, according to this mode of speaking; and thus it does not follow that it is everywhere.

1. exterior object：外在目标

Question IX
THE IMMUTABILITY OF GOD
(*In Two Articles*)

WE next consider the divine immutability and the divine eternity which follows from it.

On the immutability of God there are two points of inquiry: (1) Whether God is altogether immutable? (2) Whether to be immutable belongs to God alone?

First Article
WHETHER GOD IS ALTOGETHER IMMUTABLE?

We proceed thus to the First Article: —

Objection 1. It seems that God is not altogether immutable. For whatever moves itself is in some way mutable. But, as Augustine says, *The Creator Spirit moves Himself neither by time, nor by place.*[1] Therefore God is in some way mutable.

Obj. 2. Further, it is said of Wisdom that *it is more mobile than all active things* (*Wis.* vii. 24). But God is wisdom itself; therefore God is movable.

Obj. 3. Further, to approach and to recede signify movement. But these are said of God in Scripture: *Draw nigh to God, and He will draw nigh to you* (*Jas.* iv. 8). Therefore God is mutable.

On the contrary, It is written, *I am the Lord, and I change not* (*Mal.* iii. 6).

I answer that, From what precedes, here is the proof that God is

---

1. 参见 *De Genesi ad Litt.*, VIII, 20 (PL 34, 388).

altogether immutable. First, because it was shown above that there is some first being, whom we call God,[1] and that this first being must be pure act, without the admixture of any potentiality, for the reason that, absolutely, potentiality is posterior to act.[2] Now everything which is in any way changed, is in some way in potentiality. Hence it is evident that it is impossible for God to change in any way. Secondly, because everything which is moved remains in part as it was, and in part passes away, as what is moved from whiteness to blackness remains the same as to substance; and thus in everything which is moved there is some kind of composition to be found. But it has been shown above that in God there is no composition, for He is altogether simple.[3] Hence it is manifest that God cannot be moved. Thirdly, because everything which is moved acquires something by its movement, and attains to what it had not attained previously. But since God is infinite, comprehending in Himself all the plenitude of the perfection[4] of all being, He cannot acquire anything new, nor extend Himself to anything whereto He was not extended previously. Hence movement in no way belongs to Him. So it is that some of the ancients, constrained, as it were, by the truth, held that the first principle was immovable.[5]

Reply Obj. 1. Augustine there[6] speaks in a similar way to Plato, who said that the first mover moves Himself,[7] thus calling every operation a movement, according to which even the acts of understanding, and willing, and loving, are called movements. Therefore, because God understands and loves Himself, in that respect they said that

---

1. 参见 Q. 2, a. 3.
2. 参见 Q. 3, a. 3.
3. 参见 Q. 3, a. 7.
4. plenitude of the perfection：丰富的圆满性
5. 参见 Parmenides and Melissus, according to Aristotle, *Phys.*, I, 2 (184b 16).
6. 参见 *De Genesi ad Litt.*, VIII, 20 (PL 34, 388).
7. 参见 Aristotle, *Metaph.*, XI, 6 (1071b 37); cf. Plato, *Timaeus* (pp. 30a, 34b); *Phaedrus* (p. 245c).— Cf. also Averroes, *In Phys.*, VIII, comm. 40 (IV, 173r).

God moves Himself; not, however, as movement and change belong to a thing existing in potentiality, as we now speak of change and movement.

Reply Obj. 2. Wisdom is called mobile by way of similitude, according as it diffuses its likeness[1] even to the outermost of things[2], for nothing can exist which does not proceed from the divine wisdom[3], by way of some kind of imitation, as from the first effective and formal principle; as also works of art proceed from the wisdom of the artist. And so in the same way, inasmuch as the similitude of the divine wisdom proceeds in degrees from the highest things, which participate more fully of its likeness, to the lowest things which participate of it in a lesser degree, there is said be a kind of procession and movement of the divine wisdom to things; as if we should say that the sun proceeds to the earth, inasmuch as a ray of its light reaches the earth. In this way Dionysius expounds the matter, saying that every procession of the divine manifestation comes to us from the movement of the Father of lights.[4]

Reply Obj. 3. These things are said of God in Scripture metaphorically. For as the sun is said to enter a house, or to go out, according as its rays reach the house, so God is said to approach to us, or to recede from us, when we receive the influx of His goodness or fall away from Him.

Second Article
WHETHER TO BE IMMUTABLE BELONGS TO GOD ALONE?

We proceed thus to the Second Article:—

Objection 1. It seems that to be immutable does not belong to God alone.

---

1. diffuses its likeness：传播其相似性
2. outermost of things：事物的最外围
3. divine wisdom：神圣的智慧；天主的智慧
4. 参见 *De Cael. Hier.*, I, 1 (PG 3, 120).

For the Philosopher says that *matter is in everything which is moved.*[1] But, according to some,[2] certain created substances, as angels and souls, have not matter. Therefore to be immutable does not belong to God alone.

Obj. 2. Further, everything in motion moves for some end. What therefore has already attained its ultimate end is not in motion. But some creatures have already attained to their ultimate end; as all the blessed in heaven. Therefore some creatures are immovable.

Obj. 3. Further, everything mutable is variable. But forms are invariable[3], for it is said that *form consists of a simple and invariable essence.*[4] Therefore it does not belong to God alone to be immutable.

On the contrary, Augustine says, *God alone is immutable; but whatever things He has made, being from nothing, are mutable.*[5]

I answer that, God alone is altogether immutable, whereas every creature is in some way mutable. We must observe therefore that a mutable thing can be so called in two ways: by a power in itself, and by a power possessed by another. For all creatures, before they existed, were possible, not by any created power, since no creature is eternal, but by the divine power alone, inasmuch as God could bring them into being. Thus, just as to bring a thing into being depends on the will of God[6], so likewise it depends on His will that things should be preserved in being, for He does not preserve them in being otherwise than by ever giving them being; and so if He took away His action from them, all things would be reduced to nothing, as appears from Augustine.[7] Therefore, as it was in the Creator's power to produce

---

1. 参见 *Metaph.*, I a, 2 (994b 26).
2. 参见 St. Thomas himself (cf. below, q. 50, a. 2) ; William of Auvergne, *De Univ.*, IIa-IIae, 8 (I, pt. II, 851); John of Rochelle, *Summa de An.*, XI, XXIII; St. Albert, *In II Sent.*, d. iii, a. 7 (XXVIII, 68).
3. invariable：恒定的，始终如一的
4. 参见 Gilbert de la Porrée (?), *De sex Princ.*, I (PL 188, 1257).
5. 参见 *De Nat. Boni*, I(PL 42, 551).
6. the will of God：天主的旨意
7. 参见 *De Genesi ad Litt.*, IV, 12 (PL 34, 305).

them before they existed in themselves, so likewise it is in the Creator's power, when they exist in themselves, to bring them to nothing. In this way, therefore, by the power of another — namely, of God — they are mutable, inasmuch as they were producible from nothing by Him, and are by Him reducible from being to non-being.

If, however, a thing is called mutable by a power existing in it, in this way also every creature is in some manner mutable. For every creature has a twofold power, active and passive; and I call that power passive which enables anything to attain its perfection, either in being, or in reaching its end. Now if the mutability[1] of a thing be considered according to its power for being, in that way all creatures are not mutable, but those only in which what is possible in them is consistent with non-being[2]. Hence, in the inferior bodies there is mutability both as regards substauntial being[3], inasmuch as their matter can exist with the privation of their substantial form[4], and also as regards their accidental being, supposing that the subject can be with the privation of an accident; as, for example, this subject *man* can exist with *not-whiteness*, and can therefore be changed from white to not-white. But supposing the accident to be such as to follow on the essential principles of the subject, then the privation[5] of such an accident cannot coexist with the subject. Hence the subject cannot be changed as regards that kind of accident; as, for example, snow cannot be made black. Now in the celestial bodies[6] matter is not consistent with the privation of form, because the form perfects the whole potentiality of the matter; and so these bodies are not mutable as to substantial being, but only as to being in place, because the subject is consistent

1. mutability：易变性；性情不定
2. non-being：不存在的事物；无
3. substauntial being：实体存有
4. substantial form：实体形式
5. privation：缺乏；缺陷
6. celestial bodies：天体

with privation of this or that place. On the other hand, incorporeal substances, being subsistent forms which, although with respect to their own being they are as potentiality to act, are not consistent with the privation of this act, since being is consequent upon form, and nothing is corrupted except it lose its form. Hence, in the form itself there is no potency to non-being; and so such substances are immutable and invariable as regards their being. Therefore Dionysius says that *created intellectual substances are pure from generation and from every variation, and they are likewise incorporeal and immaterial.*[1] Still, there remains in them a twofold mutability: one, inasmuch as they are in potency to their end, and in that way there is in them a mutability, through choice, from good to evil, as Damascene says;[2] the other, as regards place, inasmuch as by their finite power they can attain to certain new and hitherto unattained places — which cannot be said of God, Who by His infinity fills all places, as was shown above.[3]

Thus in every creature there is a potentiality to change: either as regards substantial being as in the case of corruptible things; or as regards being in place only, as in the case of the celestial bodies; or as regards the order to their end, and the application of their powers to divers objects, as is the case with the angels; and universally all creatures generally are mutable by the power of the Creator, in Whose power is their being and non-being. Hence, since God is mutable in none of these ways, it belongs to Him alone to be altogether immutable.

Reply Obj. 1. This objection proceeds from mutability as regards substantial or accidental being; for it was such movement that philosophers considered.

Reply Obj. 2. The good angels, besides their natural endowment of

---

1. 参见 *De Div. Nom.*, IV, 1 (PG 3, 693).
2. 参见 *De Fide Orth.*, II, 3 (PG 94, 868).
3. 参见 Q. 8, a. 2.

immutability of being, have also immutability of election by divine power. Nevertheless there remains in them mutability as regards place.

Reply Obj. 3. Forms are called invariable inasmuch as they cannot be subjects of variation; but they are subject to variation because according to them their subject is variable. Hence it is clear that they vary in so far as they are; for they are not called beings as though they were the subject of being, but because through them something has being.

Thus we have the answers to the objections.

Question X
THE ETERNITY OF GOD
(*In Six Articles*)

WE must now consider the eternity of God[1], concerning which arise six points of inquiry: (1) What is eternity? (2) Whether God is eternal? (3) Whether to be eternal belongs to God alone? (4) Whether eternity differs from time? (5) The difference of æviternity[2] and of time. (6) Whether there is only one æviternity, as there is one time, and one eternity?

First Article
WHETHER THIS IS A GOOD DEFINITION OF ETERNITY, *THE SIMULTANEOUSLY-WHOLE AND PERFECT POSSESSION OF INTERMINABLE LIFE?*

We proceed thus to the First Article: —

Objection 1. It seems that the definition of eternity given by Boethius is not a good one: *Eternity is the simultaneously-whole*[3] *and perfect possession of interminable life*[4].[5] For the word *interminable* is a negative one. But negation belongs only to what is defective, and this does not befit eternity. Therefore in the definition of eternity the word *interminable*

---

1. the eternity of God：天主的永恒性
2. æviternity：永久性
3. simultaneously-whole：完整而同时地
4. interminable life：无限的生命
5. 参见 *De Consol.*, V, prose 6 (PL 63, 858). Cf. *op. cit.*, III, prose 2 (c. 724).

ought not to be found.

Obj. 2. Further, eternity signifies a certain kind of duration. But duration regards being rather than life. Therefore the word *life* ought not to come into the definition of eternity, but rather the word *being*.

Obj. 3. Further, a whole is what has parts. But this is alien to eternity, which is simple. Therefore it is improperly said to be *whole*.

Obj. 4. Many days cannot exist together, nor can many times. But in eternity days and times are referred to in the plural, for it is said, *His going forth is from the beginning, from the days of eternity* (*Mic.* v. 2); and it is also said, *According to the revelation of the mystery which was kept secret from eternity* (*Rom.* xvi. 25). Therefore eternity is not omnisimultaneous[1].

Obj. 5. Further, the whole and the perfect are the same thing. Supposing, therefore, that it is *whole*, it is superfluously described as *perfect*.

Obj. 6. Further, duration does not imply *possession*. But eternity is a kind of duration. Therefore eternity is not possession.

I answer that, Just as we attain to the knowledge of simple things by way of composite things, so we must reach to the knowledge of eternity by means of time, which is nothing but *the number of movement according to before and after.*[2] For since succession occurs in every movement, and one part comes after another, the fact that we reckon before and after in movement makes us apprehend time, which is nothing else but the number of before and after in movement. Now in a thing lacking movement, and which is always the same, there is no before and after. Just as therefore the nature of time consists in the numbering of before and after in movement, so likewise in the apprehension of the uniformity of what is absolutely outside of movement consists the nature of eternity.

---

1. omnisimultaneous：完整而同时的
2. 参见 Aristotle, *Phys.*, IV, 11 (220a 25).

Further, *those things are said to be measured by time which have a beginning and an end in time*, as it is said in *Physics* iv,[1] because in everything which is moved there is a beginning, and there is an end. But as whatever is wholly immutable can have no succession, so it has no beginning, and no end.

Thus eternity is known from two facts: first, because what is eternal is interminable — that is, has no beginning or end (that is, no term either way); secondly, because eternity itself has no succession, being simultaneously whole.

Reply Obj. 1. Simple things are usually defined by way of negation e.g., *a point is that which has no parts*. Yet this is not to be taken as if the negation belonged to their essence, but because our intellect, which first apprehends composite things, cannot attain to the knowledge of simple things except by removing the composition.

Reply Obj. 2. What is truly eternal is not only being, but also living; and life extends to operation, which is not true of being. Now the protraction of duration[2] seems to belong to operation rather than to being; hence time is the numbering of movement.

Reply Obj. 3. Eternity is called whole, not because it has parts, but because it is wanting in nothing.

Reply Obj. 4. As God, although incorporeal, is named in Scripture metaphorically by corporeal names, so eternity, though simultaneously whole, is called by names implying time and succession.

Reply Obj. 5. Two things are to be considered in time: time itself, which is successive; and the *now* of time, which is imperfect. Hence the expression *simultaneously-whole* is used to remove the idea of time, and the word *perfect* is used to exclude the *now* of time.

Reply Obj. 6. Whatever is possessed is held firmly and imperturbably. Therefore, to designate the immutability and permanence of eternity,

---

1. 参见 *Op. cit.*, IV, 13 (221b 28).
2. the protraction of duration：持续的延展

we use the word *possession*.

Second Article
WHETHER GOD IS ETERNAL?

We proceed thus to the Second Article: —

Objection 1. It seems that God is not eternal. For nothing made can be predicated of God. But eternity is a thing made, for Boethius says that *The now that flows away makes time, the now that stands still makes eternity*;[1] and Augustine says that *God is the author of eternity.*[2] Therefore God is not eternal.

Obj. 2. Further, what is before eternity, and after eternity, is not measured by eternity. But, as it is stated in the *Book of Causes*,[3] *God is before eternity*; and He is after eternity; for it is written that *the Lord shall reign for eternity, and beyond* (*Exod.* xv. 18). Therefore to be eternal does not belong to God.

Obj. 3. Further, eternity is a kind of measure. But to be measured belongs not to God. Therefore it does not belong to Him to be eternal.

Obj. 4. Further, in eternity there is no present, past, nor future, since it is simultaneously whole, as was said. But words denoting present, past and future time are applied to God in Scripture. Therefore God is not eternal.

On the contrary, Athanasius says: *The Father is eternal, the Son is eternal, the Holy Ghost is eternal.*[4]

I answer that, The notion of eternity follows immutability, as the notion of time follows movement, as appears from the preceding article. Hence, as God is supremely immutable, it supremely belongs to

---

1. 参见 *De Trin.*, IV (PL 64, 1253).
2. 参见 *Lib. 83 Quaest.*, q. 23 (PL 40, 16).
3. 参见 *De Causis*, II (p. 162).
4. 参见 Pseudo - Athanasius, *Symb. "Quicumque"* (Denzinger, no. 39).

Him to be eternal. Nor is He eternal only, but He is His own eternity; whereas no other being is its own duration, since it is not its own being. Now God is His own uniform being; and hence, as He is His own essence, so He is His own eternity.

Reply Obj. 1. The *now* that stands still is said to make eternity according to our apprehension. For just as the apprehension of time is caused in us by the fact that we apprehend the flow of the *now*, so the apprehension of eternity is caused in us by our apprehending the *now* standing still. When Augustine says that *God is the author of eternity*[1],[2] this is to be understood of participated eternity. For God communicates His eternity to some in the same way as He communicates His immutability.

Reply Obj. 2. From this appears the answer to the second objection. For God is said to be before eternity according as it is shared by immaterial substances. Hence, also, in the same book it is said that *intelligence ranks with eternity.*[3] In the words of *Exodus* (xv. 18), *The Lord shall reign for eternity, and beyond*, eternity stands for *age*, as another translation has it. Thus, it is said that the Lord will reign beyond eternity, inasmuch as He endures beyond every age, that is, beyond every kind of given duration. For age is nothing more than the period of each thing, as is said in the first book of the treatise *On the Heavens.*[4] Or to reign beyond eternity can be taken to mean that if any other thing were conceived to exist forever, *e.g.*, the movement of the heavens according to some philosophers,[5] then God still reigns *beyond*, inasmuch as His reign is simultaneously whole.

Reply Obj. 3. Eternity is nothing else but God Himself. Hence God is

---

1. God is the author of eternity.：天主是永恒的创造者。
2. 参见 *Lib.83 Quaest.*, q. 23 (PL 40, . 16).
3. 参见 *De Causis, II* (p. 163).
4. 参见 Aristotle, *De Caelo*, I, 9 (279a 23).
5. 参见 Cf. below, q. 46, a. 1, ad 3 and 5.

not called eternal, as if He were in any way measured; but the notion of measurement is there understood only according to the manner of our apprehension.

Reply Obj. 4. Words denoting different times are applied to God because His eternity includes all times, and not as if He Himself were altered through present, past and future.

Third Article
WHETHER TO BE ETERNAL BELONGS TO GOD ALONE?

We proceed thus to the Third Article: —

Objection 1. It seems that it does not belong to God alone to be eternal. For it is written that *those who instruct many to justice* shall be *as stars unto perpetual eternities* (*Dan.* xii. 3). Now if God alone were eternal, there could not be many eternities. Therefore God alone is not the only eternal.

Obj. 2. Further, it is written, *Depart, ye cursed, into eternal fire* (*Matt.* xxv. 41). Therefore God is not the only eternal.

Obj. 3. Further, every necessary thing is eternal. But there are many necessary things; as, for instance, all principles of demonstration, and all demonstrative propositions. Therefore God is not the only eternal.

On the contrary, Augustine says that *God is the only one who has no beginning.*[1] Now whatever has a beginning is not eternal. Therefore God alone is eternal.

I answer that, Eternity truly and properly so called is in God alone, because eternity follows on immutability, as appears from the above. But God alone is altogether immutable, as was shown above.[2] According, however, as some beings receive immutability from Him, they share in His eternity. Thus some receive immutability from God in the way of never ceasing to exist; in which sense it is said of the earth, that *it standeth*

1. 参见 Cf. St. Jerome, *Epist.* XV (PL 22, 357).
2. 参见 Q. 9, a. 2.

for ever (*Eccles.* i. 4). In this sense, eternity can be attributed to the angels, according to the *Psalms* (lxxv. 5): *Thou enlightenest wonderfully from the everlasting hills.* Again, some things are called eternal in Scripture because of the length of their duration, although they are in nature corruptible; and thus the hills are called *eternal*, and we read *of the fruits of the eternal hills* (*Deut.* xxxiii. 15). Some, again, share more fully than others in the nature of eternity, inasmuch as they possess unchangeableness either in being or further still in operation; like the angels, and the blessed, who enjoy the Word, because *as regards that vision of the Word, no changing thoughts exist in the saints*, as Augustine says.[1] Hence those who see God are said to have eternal life, according to the text, *This is eternal life, that they may know Thee the only true God, etc.* (*Jo.* xvii. 3).

Reply Obj. 1. There are said to be many eternities according as many share in eternity, by the contemplation of God.

Reply Obj. 2. The fire of hell is called eternal only because it never ends. Still, there is change in the pains of the lost, according to the words, To *extreme heat they will pass from snowy waters* (*Job* xxiv. 19). Hence in hell true eternity does not exist, but rather time, according to the text of the Psalm, *Their time will be for ever* (*Ps.* lxxx. 16).

Reply Obj. 3. *Necessary* means a certain mode of truth; and truth, according to the Philosopher,[2] is *in the intellect.* Therefore, in this sense the true and the necessary are eternal, because they are in an eternal intellect, which is the divine intellect alone. Hence it does not follow that anything beside God is eternal.

Fourth Article
WHETHER ETERNITY DIFFERS FROM TIME?

We proceed thus to the Fourth Article: —

1. 参见 *De Trin.*, XV, 16 (PL 42, 1079).
2. 参见 *Metaph.*, V, 4 (1027b 27).

Objection 1. It seems that eternity does not differ from time. For two measures of duration cannot exist together, unless one is part of the other. For instance, two days or two hours cannot be together; nevertheless, we may say that a day and an hour are together, because an hour is part of a day. But eternity and time occur together, and each of them imports a certain measure of duration. Since therefore eternity is not a part of time, since eternity exceeds time, and includes it, it seems that time is a part of eternity, and is not a different thing from eternity.

Obj. 2. Further, according to the Philosopher,[1] the *now* of time remains the same in the whole of time. But the nature of eternity seems to be that it maintains itself indivisible in the whole course of time. Therefore eternity is the *now* of time. But the *now* of time is not in substance other than time. Therefore eternity is not in substance other than time.

Obj. 3. Further, as the measure of the first movement is the measure of every movement, as said in *Physics* iv.,[2] so it appears that the measure of the first being is that of every being. But eternity is the measure of the first being, which is the divine being. Therefore eternity is the measure of every being. But the being of things corruptible is measured by time. Time, therefore, is either eternity or a part of eternity.

On the contrary, Eternity is simultaneously whole. But time has a before and an after. Therefore time and eternity are not the same thing.

I answer that, It is manifest that time and eternity are not the same. Some have founded this diversity on the fact that eternity has neither beginning nor an end, whereas time has a beginning and an

---

1. 参见 *Phys.*, IV, 11 (219b 11); 13 (222a 15).
2. 参见 *Op. cit.*, IV, 14 (223b 18).

end.[1] This, however, makes a merely accidental, and not an essential, difference; because, granted that time always was and always will be (according to the view of those who think the movement of the heavens goes on for ever,[2]), there would yet remain a difference between eternity and time, as Boethius says,[3] arising from the fact that eternity is simultaneously whole, which cannot be applied to time; for eternity is the measure of a permanent being, while time is the measure of movement. Supposing, however, that the aforesaid difference be considered from the side of the things measured, and not from the side of the measures, then there is some reason for it, inasmuch as that alone is measured by time which has a beginning and an end in time, as is said in *Physics* iv.[4] Hence, if the movement of the heavens lasted always, time would not be its measure as regards the whole of its duration, since the infinite is not measurable; but it would be the measure of any part of its revolution which has a beginning and an end in time.

Another reason for this position can be taken from these measures in themselves, if we consider the end and the beginning in potency; because, granted even that time always goes on, yet it is possible to mark in time both the beginning and the end, by considering its parts:— thus we speak of the beginning and the end of a day, or of a year; which cannot be applied to eternity.

Still these differences follow upon the essential and primary difference, viz., that eternity is simultaneously whole, but that time is not so.

Reply Obj. 1. Such a reason would be a valid one if time and eternity were the same kind of measure; but this is seen not to be the case when

---

1. 参见 Alex. of Hales, *Summa Theol.*, I, no. 65 (I, 100).
2. 参见 The texts are cited by St. Thomas; cf. below, q. 46, a. 1, ad 3 and 5.
3. 参见 *De Consol.*, V, prose 6 (PL 63, 858).
4. 参见 Aristotle, *Phys.* IV, 12 (221b 28).

we consider those things of which the respective measures are time and eternity.

Reply Obj. 2. The *now* of time is the same as regards its subject in the whole course of time, but it differs in aspect. For just as time corresponds to movement, so its *now* corresponds to what is movable; and the thing movable has one and the same subject in all time, but differs in aspect as being here and there; and such alternation is movement. Likewise the flow of the *now*, as altering in aspect, is time. But eternity remains the same according to both subject and aspect; and hence eternity is not the same as the *now* of time.

Reply Obj. 3. As eternity is the proper measure of being, so time is the proper measure of movement; and hence, according as any being recedes from permanence of being, and is subject to change, it recedes from eternity, and is subject to time. Therefore, the being of corruptible things, because it is changeable, is not measured by eternity, but by time. For time measures not only things actually changing, but also things changeable; hence it not only measures movement, but it also measures repose[1], which belongs to whatever is naturally movable, but is not actually in motion.

Fifth Article
THE DIFFERENCE OF ÆVITERNITY AND TIME.

We proceed thus to the Fifth Article: —

Obj. 1. It seems that æviternity is the same as time. For Augustine says that *God moves the spiritual creature through time.*[2] But æviternity is said to be the measure of spiritual substances. Therefore time is the same as æviternity.

Obj. 2. Further, it is essential to time to have before and after; but it is essential to eternity to be simultaneously whole, as was shown above.

---

1. repose：休息；睡眠。这里指一切静止不动者。
2. 参见 *De Genesi ad Litt.*, VIII, 20; 22 (PL 34, 388; 389).

Now æviternity is not eternity, for it is written (*Ecclus.* i. 1) that eternal *Wisdom is before age*. Therefore it is not simultaneously whole but has before and after; and thus it is the same as time.

Obj. 3. Further, if there is no before and after in æviternity, it follows that in æviternal things there is no difference between being, having been, or going to be. Since then it is impossible for æviternal things not to have been, it follows that it is impossible for them not to be in the future; which is false, since God can reduce them to nothing.

Obj. 4. Further, since the duration of æviternal things is infinite as to subsequent duration, if æviternity is simultaneously whole, it follows that some creature is actually infinite; which is impossible. Therefore æviternity does not differ from time.

On the contrary, Boethius says, *Who commandest time to go forth from æviternity.*[1]

I answer that, Æviternity differs from time, and from eternity, as the mean between them both. This difference is explained by some[2] to consist in the fact that eternity has neither beginning nor end, æviternity, a beginning but no end, and time both beginning and end. This difference, however, is an accidental one, as was shown above, because even if æviternal things had always been, and would always be, as some[3] think, or even if they might sometime fail to be, which is possible to God to allow, even granted this, æviternity would still be distinguished from eternity, and from time.

Others[4] assign the difference among these three as consisting in the fact that eternity has no before and after; but that time has both, together with innovation and veteration[5]; and that æviternity

1. 参见 *De Consol.*, III, verse 9 (PL 63, 758).
2. 参见 Alex. of Hales, *Summa Theol.*, I, no. 65 (I, 100).
3. 参见 Cf. below, q. 46, a. 1, ad 3 and 5.
4. 参见 St. Bonaventure, *In II Sent.*, d. ii, pt. 1, a. 1, q. 3 (II, 62).
5. veteration：变旧，这里指消失或毁灭

has before and after without innovation and veteration. This theory, however, involves a contradiction, which manifestly appears if innovation and veteration be referred to the measure itself. For since the before and after of duration cannot exist together, if æviternity has a before and after, it must follow that with the receding of the first part of æviternity, the after part of æviternity must newly appear; and thus innovation would occur in æviternity itself, as it does in time. And if they be referred to the things measured, even then an incongruity would follow. For a thing which exists in time grows old with time, because it has a changeable existence, and from the changeableness of what is measured there follows the before and after in the measure, as is clear from *Physics* iv.[1] Therefore, the fact that an æviternal thing is neither inveterable nor subject to innovation comes from its changelessness; and consequently its measure does not contain a before and after.

We must say, then, that since eternity is the measure of a permanent being, in so far as anything recedes from permanence of being, it recedes from eternity. Now some things recede from permanence of being, so that their being is subject to change, or consists in change; and these things are measured by time, *e.g.*, all movements, and also the being of all things corruptible. But others recede less from permanence of being, since their being neither consists in change, nor is the subject of change; although they have change annexed to them either actually or potentially. This appears in the heavenly bodies, the substantial being of which is unchangeable; and yet with unchangeable being they have changeableness of place. The same applies to the angels, who have, as regards their nature, an unchangeable being with changeableness as regards choice; moreover with changeableness of acts of understanding, of affections, and of places, in their own degree.

---

1. 参见 Aristotle, *Phys.*, IV, 12 (221a 31; 220b 9).

Therefore, these are measured by æviternity, which is a mean between eternity and time. But the being that is measured by eternity is not changeable, nor is it joined to changeability[1]. In this way, time has a before and after; æviternity in itself has no before and after, which can, however, be joined to it; while eternity has neither before nor after, nor is it compatible with such at all.

Reply Obj. 1. Spiritual creatures, as regards successive affections and acts of understanding, are measured by time. Hence also Augustine says that to be moved through time is to be moved by the affections.[2] But as regards the being of their nature, they are measured by æviternity; whereas as regards the vision of glory, they share in eternity.

Reply Obj. 2. Æviternity is simultaneously whole; yet it is not eternity, because before and after are compatible with it.

Reply Obj. 3. In the very being of an angel, considered absolutely, there is no difference of past and future, but only as regards accidental changes. Now to say that an angel was, or is, or will be, is to be taken in a different sense according to the acceptation of our intellect, which apprehends the angelic being by comparison with different parts of time. But when we say that an angel is, or was, we suppose something, which being supposed, its opposite is not subject to the divine power. Whereas when we say he will be, we do not as yet suppose anything. Hence, since the being and non-being of an angel considered absolutely is subject to the divine power, God can make the being of an angel not to be future; but He cannot cause him not to be while he is, or not to have been, after he has been.

Reply Obj. 4. The duration of æviternity is infinite, inasmuch as it is not limited by time. Hence, there is no incongruity[3] in saying that

---

1. changeability：可变性；易变性
2. 参见 *De Genesi ad Litt.*, VIII, 20 (PL 34, 388).
3. incongruity：不合适；不一致

a creature is infinite in the sense that it is not limited by any other creature.

Sixth Article
WHETHER THERE IS ONLY ONE ÆVITERNITY?

We proceed thus to the Sixth Article: —

Objection 1. It seems that there is not only one æviternity; for it is written in the apocryphal books[1] of Esdras: *Majesty and power of ages are with Thee, O Lord.*

Obj. 2. Further, diverse genera have diverse measures. But some æviternal things belong to the corporeal genus, as the heavenly bodies; and others are spiritual substances, as the angels. Therefore there is not only one æviternity.

Obj. 3. Further, since æviternity is a term of duration, where there is one æviternity, there is also one duration. But not all æviternal things have one duration, for some begin to exist after others; as appears especially in the case of human souls. Therefore there is not only one æviternity.

Obj. 4. Further, things not dependent on each other do not seem to have one measure of duration; for there appears to be one time for all temporal things for the reason that the first movement, measured first by time, is in some way the cause of all movement. But æviternal things do not depend on each other, for one angel is not the cause of another angel. Therefore there is not only one æviternity.

On the contrary, Æviternity is a more simple thing than time, and is nearer to eternity. But time is one only. Therefore much more is æviternity one only.

I answer that, A twofold opinion exists on this subject. Some[2] say

---

1. apocryphal books：伪经
2. 参见 Alex. of Hales, *Summa Theol.*, I, no. 66 (I, 102).

there is only one æviternity; others,[1] that there are many. Which of these is true, may be considered from the reason why time is one; for we can rise to the knowledge of spiritual things from corporeal things.

Now some[2] say that there is only one time for all temporal things because one number exists for all things numbered; and *time is a number*, according to the Philosopher.[3] This, however, is not a sufficient reason, because *time is not a number* as abstracted from the thing numbered, but *as existing in the thing numbered*; otherwise it would not be continuous. For ten ells of cloth are continuous not by reason of the number, but by reason of the thing numbered. Now number, as it exists in the thing numbered, is not the same for all; but is diverse for diverse things. Hence, others[4] assert that the unity of eternity as the principle of all duration is the cause of the unity of time. Thus all durations are one, in that view, in the light of their principle, but are many in the light of the diversity of things receiving duration from the influx of the first principle. On the other hand, others[5] assign primary matter as the reason why time is one; as it is the first subject of movement, the measure of which is time. Neither of these reasons, however, is sufficient; because things which are one in principle, or in subject, especially if distant, are not one absolutely, but accidentally.

Therefore the true reason why time is one, is to be found in the oneness of the first movement by which, since it is most simple, all other movements are measured, as it is said in *Metaphysics* x.[6] Therefore, time is referred to that movement, not only as a measure

---

1. 参见 St. Bonaventure, *In II Sent.*, d. ii. pt. I, a. 1, q. 2 (II, 60).
2. 参见 Themistius, according to Averroes, *In Phys.*, IV, comm. 132 (IV, 93v)—Cf. St. Thomas, *In II Sent.*, d. ii, q. 1, a. 2.
3. 参见 *Phys.*, IV, 12 (220b 8).
4. 参见 Alex. of Hales, *Summa Theol.*, I, no. 66 (I, 102).
5. 参见 St. Bonaventure, *In II Sent.*, d. ii, pt. I. a. 1, q. 2 (II, 59).
6. 参见 Aristotle, *Metaph.*, IX, 1 (1053a 8). Cf. *Phys.*, IV, 14 (223a 29 ; b 18); Averroes, *In Phys.*, IV, comm. 132 (IV, 93v); St. Albert, *In Phys.*, IV, tr. 3, ch. 17 (III, 340).

is to the thing measured, but also as accident is to subject; and thus receives its unity from it. Whereas to other movements it is compared only as the measure is to the thing measured. Hence, it is not multiplied by their multitude, because many things can be measured by one separate measure.

This being established, we must observe that a twofold opinion existed concerning spiritual substances[1]. Some said that all proceeded from God in a certain equality, as Origen said;[2] or at least many of them, as some others thought.[3] Others said that all spiritual substances proceeded from God in a certain degree and order. Dionysius seems to have thought so, when he said that among spiritual substances there are the first, the middle and the last, even in one order of angels.[4] Now according to the first opinion, it must be said that there are many æviternities, as there are many first and equal æviternal things. But according to the second opinion, it would be necessary to say that there is one æviternity only; because, since each thing is measured by the most simple element of its genus, as it is said in *Metaphysics* x,[5] it must be that the existence of all æviternal things should be measured by the existence of the first æviternal thing, which is all the more simple the more it is first. Therefore, because the second opinion is the truer, as will be shown later,[6] we concede at present that there is only one æviternity.

Reply Obj. 1. Æviternity is sometimes taken for age, that is, the period of a thing's duration; and thus we say many æviternities, meaning many ages.

Reply Obj. 2. Although the heavenly bodies and spiritual substances

---

1. spiritual substances：精神实体
2. 参见 *Peri Archon*, I, 8 (PG 11, 176).
3. 参见 Cf. below, q. 50, a. 4.
4. 参见 *De Cael. Hier.*, X, 3 (PG 3, 273).
5. 参见 Aristotle, *Metaph.*, IX, 1 (1052b 33).
6. 参见 Q. 47, a. 2; q. 51, a. 4.

differ in the genus of their nature, still they agree in having a changeless being, and are thus measured by æviternity.

Reply Obj. 3. Not all temporal things begin together; nevertheless there is one time for all of them, by reason of that which is first measured by time; and thus all aeviternal things have one aeviternity by reason of the first, even though all may not begin together.

Reply Obj. 4. For things to be measured by one, it is not necessary that the one should be the cause of all, but that it be more simple than the rest.

Question XI
THE UNITY OF GOD
(*In Four Articles*)

AFTER the foregoing, we consider the divine unity, concerning which there are four points of inquiry: (1) Whether *one* adds anything to *being?* (2) Whether *one* and *many* are opposed to each other? (3) Whether God is one? (4) Whether He is in the highest degree one?

First Article
WHETHER ONE ADDS ANYTHING TO BEING?

We proceed thus to the First Article: —

Objection 1. It seems that *one* adds something to *being*. For everything is in a determinate genus by addition to being, which encompasses all genera. But *one* is in a determinate genus, for it is the principle of number, which is a species of quantity. Therefore *one* adds something to *being*.

Obj. 2. Further, that which divides something common is by addition to it. But *being* is divided by *one* and by *many*. Therefore *one* adds something to *being*.

Obj. 3. Further, if *one* does not add to *being*, *one* and *being* must have the same meaning. But it would be nugatory[1] to call *being* by the name of *being*: therefore it would be equally so to call being *one*. Now this is false. Therefore *one* adds something to *being*.

---

1. nugatory：琐碎的；无价值的；不重要的

On the contrary, Dionysius says: *Nothing which exists is not in some way one*,[1] which would be false if *one* were an addition to *being*, in the sense of limiting it. Therefore *one* is not an addition to *being*.

I answer that, One does not add any reality to *being*, but is only the negation of division; for *one* means undivided *being*. This is the very reason why *one* is convertible with *being*. For every being is either simple or composite. But what is simple is undivided, both actually and potentially; whereas what is composite has not being while its parts are divided, but after they make up and compose it. Hence it is manifest that the being of anything consists in indivision; and hence it is that everything guards its unity as it guards its being.

Reply Obj. 1. Some, thinking that the *one* convertible with *being* is the same as the *one* which is the principle of number, were divided into contrary opinions. Pythagoras and Plato, seeing that the *one* convertible with *being* did not add any reality to *being*, but signified the substance of *being* as undivided, thought that the same applied to the *one* which is the principle of number.[2] And because number is composed of unities, they thought that numbers were the substances of all things. Avicenna, however, on the contrary, considering that the *one* which is the principle of number added a reality to the substance of being (otherwise number made of unities would not be a species of quantity), thought that the *one* convertible with *being* added a reality to the substance of beings; as *white* adds to *man*.[3] This, however, is manifestly false, inasmuch as each thing is *one* by its substance. For if a thing were *one* by anything else but by its substance, since this again would be *one*, supposing it were again *one* by another thing, we

1. 参见 *De Div. Nom.*, V, 2 (PG 3, 977).
2. 参见 Cf. Aristotle, *Metaph.*, I, 5 (987a 13; a 19); I, 6 (987b 23).— Cf. also St. Thomas, *In Metaph.*, I, lect. 7 and 8.
3. 参见 *Metaph.*, III, 3 (7gr).— Cf. also Averroes, *Destruct. Destruct.*, III (IX, 25ra).

should be driven on to infinity. Hence we must adhere to the former statement; therefore we must say that the *one* which is convertible with *being* does not add a reality to being; but that the *one* which is the principle of number does add a reality to *being*, belonging to the genus of quantity.

Reply Obj. 2. There is nothing to prevent a thing, which in one way is divided, from being in another way undivided, as what is divided in number may be undivided in species; thus it may be that a thing is in one way *one*, and in another way *many*. Still, if it is absolutely undivided, either because it is so according to what belongs to its essence (though it may be divided as regards what is outside its essence, as what is one in subject may have many accidents), or because it is undivided actually, and divided potentially (as what is *one* in the whole, and is *many* in its parts), in which case a thing will be *one* absolutely, and *many* accidentally. On the other hand, if it be undivided accidentally, and divided absolutely, as if it were divided in essence and undivided in idea or in principle or cause, it will be *many* absolutely, and *one* accidentally; as what are *many* in number, and *one* in species, or *one* in principle. This is the way in which being is divided by *one* and by *many*; as it were by *one* absolutely, and by *many* accidentally. For multitude itself would not be contained under *being* unless it were in some way contained under *one*. Thus Dionysius says that *there is no kind of multitude that is not in a way one. But what are many in their parts are one in their whole; and what are many in accidents are one in subject; and what are many in number are one in species; and what are many in species are one in genus; and what are many in processions are one in principle.*[1]

Reply Obj. 3. It does not follow that it is nugatory to say *being* is *one*; since *one* adds something to *being* logically.

---

1. 参见 *De Div. Nom.*, XIII, 2 (PG 3, 980).

Second Article

WHETHER ONE AND MANY ARE OPPOSED TO EACH OTHER?

We proceed thus to the Second Article: —

Objection 1. It seems that *one* and *many* are not mutually opposed. For no opposite is predicated of its opposite. But every *multitude* is in a certain way *one*, as appears from the preceding article. Therefore *one* is not opposed to *multitude*.

Obj. 2. Further, no opposite is constituted by its opposite. But *multitude* is constituted by *one*. Therefore it is not opposed to *multitude*

Obj. 3. Further, each thing has one opposite. But the opposite of *many* is *few*. Therefore, the opposite is not *one*.

Obj. 4. Further, if *one* is opposed to *multitude*, it is opposed as the undivided is to the divided, and is thus opposed to it as privation is to habit. But this appears to be incongruous; because it would follow that *one* comes after *multitude*, and is defined by it; whereas, on the contrary, *multitude* is defined by *one*. Hence there would be a vicious circle in the definition; which is inadmissible. Therefore *one* and *many* are not opposed.

On the contrary, Things which are opposed in idea are themselves opposed to each other. But the idea of *one* consists in indivisibility[1]; and the idea of *multitude* contains division. Therefore *one* and *many* are opposed to each other.

I answer that, *One* is opposed to *many*, but in various ways. The *one* which is the principle of number is opposed to *multitude* which is number as the measure is to the thing measured. For *one* implies the idea of a primary measure; and number is *multitude* measured by *one*,

---

1. indivisibility：不可分割性

as is clear from *Metaph*.X.[1] But the *one* which is convertible with *being* is opposed to *multitude* by way of privation; as the undivided is to the divided.

Reply Obj. 1. No privation entirely takes away the being of a thing, inasmuch as privation means *negation in the subject*, according to the Philosopher.[2] Nevertheless, every privation takes away some being; and so in being, by reason of its community, the privation of being has its foundation in being; which is not the case in privations of special forms, as of sight, or of whiteness, and the like. And what applies to being applies also to one and to good, which are convertible with being, for the privation of good is founded in some good; likewise the removal of unity is founded in some one thing. Hence it happens that multitude is some one thing, and evil is some good thing, and non-being is some kind of being. Nevertheless, opposite is not predicated of opposite, since one is absolute, and the other is relative; for what is relatively being (*i.e.*, in potency) is non-being absolutely, *i.e.*, actually; or what is being absolutely in the genus of substance, is non-being relatively as regards some accidental being. In the same way, what is relatively good is absolutely bad, or *vice versa*; likewise, what is absolutely *one* is relatively *many*, and *vice versa*.

Reply Obj. 2. A *whole* is twofold. In one sense it is homogeneous, composed of like parts; in another sense it is heterogeneous[3], composed of dissimilar parts. Now in every homogeneous whole, the whole is made up of parts having the form of the whole, as, for instance, every part of water is water; and such is the constitution of a continuous thing made up of its parts. In every heterogeneous whole, however, every part is wanting in the form belonging to the whole; as, for instance, no part of a house is a house, nor is any part of man a

---

1. 参见 Aristotle, *Metaph*., IX, 1 (1052b 18); 6 (1057a 3).
2. 参见 *Op. cit*., III, 2 (1004a 15);cf. Cat., X (12a 26).
3. heterogeneous：多种多样的；混杂的

man. Now multitude is such a kind of whole. Therefore, inasmuch as its part has not the form of the multitude, the latter is composed of unities, as a house is composed of not houses; not, indeed, as if unities constituted multitude so far as they are undivided, in which way they are opposed to multitude, but so far as they have being; as also the parts of a house make up the house by the fact that they are beings not by the fact that they are not houses.

Reply Obj. 3. *Many* is taken in two ways: absolutely, and in that sense it is opposed to *one*; in another way, as importing some kind of excess, in which sense it is opposed to *few*. Hence, in the first sense two are many; but not in the second sense.

Reply Obj. 4. *One* is opposed to *many* privatively, inasmuch as the idea of *many* involves division. Hence division must be prior to unity, not absolutely in itself, but according to our way of apprehension. For we apprehend simple things by composite things; and hence we define a point to be, *what has no part, or the beginning of a line. Multitude* also, in idea, follows on *one*; because we do not understand divided things to convey the idea of multitude except by the fact that we attribute unity to every member. Hence *one* is placed in the definition of *multitude*; but *multitude* is not placed in the definition of *one*. But division comes to be understood from the very negation of being: so what first comes to the intellect is being; secondly, that this being is not that being, and thus we apprehend division as a consequence; thirdly, comes the notion of one; fourthly, the notion of multitude.

Third Article
WHETHER GOD IS ONE?

We proceed thus to the Third Article: —

Objection 1. It seems that God is not one. For it is written, *For there be many gods and many lords* (*1 Cor.* viii. 5).

Obj. 2. Further, *one*, as the principle of number, cannot be predicated of God, since quantity is not predicated of God; likewise, neither can *one* which is convertible with *being* be predicated of God, because it imports privation, and every privation is an imperfection, which cannot apply to God. Therefore God is not one.

On the contrary, It is written, *Hear, O Israel, the Lord our God is one Lord* (*Deut.* vi. 4).

I answer that, It can be shown from three sources that God is one. First from His simplicity. For it is manifest that the reason why any singular thing is *this particular thing* is because it cannot be communicated to many, since that whereby Socrates is a man can be communicated to many, whereas what makes him this particular man is communicable only to one. Therefore, if Socrates were a man by what makes him to be this particular man, as there cannot be many Socrateses, so there could not in that way be many men. Now this belongs to God alone; for God Himself is His own nature, as was shown above.[1] Therefore, in the very same way God is God and this God. It is impossible therefore that there should be many gods.

Secondly, this is proved from the infinity of His perfection. For it was shown above that God comprehends in Himself the whole perfection of being.[2] If, then, many gods existed, they would necessarily differ from each other. Something, therefore, would belong to one which did not belong to another. And if this were a privation, one of them would not be absolutely perfect; but if a perfection, one of them would be without it. So it is impossible for many gods to exist. Hence also the ancient philosophers, constrained as it were by truth, when they asserted an infinite principle, asserted likewise that there was only one such principle.

Thirdly, this is shown from the unity of the world. For all things that exist are seen to be ordered to each other since some serve others.

---

1. 参见 Q. 3, a. 3.
2. 参见 Q. 4, a. 2

But things that are diverse do not come together in the same order unless they are ordered thereto by some one being. For many are reduced into one order by one better than by many: because one is the *per se* cause of one, and many are only the accidental cause of one, inasmuch as they are in some way one. Since, therefore, what is first is most perfect, and is so *per se* and not accidentally, it must be that the first which reduces all into one order should be only one. And this is God.

Reply Obj. 1. Gods are called many by the error of some who worshipped many deities, thinking as they did that the planets and other stars were gods, and also the particular parts of the world. Hence the Apostle adds: *Our God is one, etc.* (*1 Cor.* viii. 6).

Reply Obj. 2. One which is the principle of number is not predicated of God, but only of material things. For *one* which is the principle of number belongs to the *genus* of mathematicals, which are material in being, and abstracted from matter only in idea. But *one* which is convertible with being is something metaphysical and does not, in being, depend on matter. And although in God there is no privation, still, according to the mode of our apprehension, He is known to us by way only of privation and remotion. Thus there is no reason why certain privative terms should not be predicated of God, for instance, that He is *incorporeal*, and *infinite*; and in the same way it is said of God that He is *one*.

Fourth Article
WHETHER GOD IS SUPREMELY ONE?

We proceed thus to the Fourth Article: —

Objection 1. It seems that God is not supremely *one*. For *one* is so called from the privation of division. But privation cannot be greater or less. Therefore God is not more *one* than other things which are called *one*.

Obj. 2. Further, nothing seems to be more indivisible than what is actually and potentially indivisible; such as a point, and unity. But a thing is said to be more *one* according as it is indivisible. Therefore God is not more *one* than unity is *one* and a point is *one*.

Obj. 3. Further, what is essentially good is supremely good. Therefore, what is essentially *one* is supremely *one*. But every being is essentially *one*, as the Philosopher says.[1] Therefore, every being is supremely *one*; and therefore God is not *one* more than any other being is *one*.

On the contrary, Bernard says: *Among all things called one, the unity of the Divine Trinity*[2] *holds the first place*.[3]

I answer that, Since *one* is an undivided being, if anything is supremely *one* it must be supremely being and supremely undivided. Now both of these belong to God. For He is supremely being inasmuch as His being is not determined by any nature to which it is adjoined; since He is being itself, subsistent, absolutely undetermined. And He is supremely undivided inasmuch as He is divided neither actually nor potentially by any mode of division; since He is altogether simple, as was shown above.[4] Hence it is manifest that God is *one* in the supreme degree.

Reply Obj. 1. Although privation considered in itself is not susceptive of more or less, still according as its opposite is subject to more and less, privation also can be predicated according to more and less. Therefore, according as a thing is more or less or not at all divided or divisible, in that degree it is called more, or less, or supremely, *one*.

Reply Obj. 2. A point and unity, which is the principle of number, are not supremely being, inasmuch as they have being only in some

---

1. 参见 *Metaph.*, III, 2 (1003b 32).
2. the Divine Trinity：天主三位一体
3. 参见 *De Consider.*, V, 8 (PL 182, 799).
4. 参见 Q. 3, a. 7.

subject. Hence neither of them can be supremely *one*. For as a subject cannot be supremely *one* because of the diversity of accident and subject, so neither can an accident.

Reply Obj. 3. Although every being is *one* by its substance, still every substance is not equally the cause of unity; for the substance of some things is composite, and of others not.

Question XII
HOW GOD IS KNOWN BY US
(*In Thirteen Articles*)

AS hitherto we have considered God as He is in Himself, we now go on to consider how He is in our knowledge, that is, how He is known by creatures. Concerning this there are thirteen points of inquiry. (1) Whether any created intellect can see the essence of God[1]? (2) Whether the essence of God is seen by the intellect through any created species? (3) Whether the essence of God can be seen by the corporeal eye? (4) Whether any created intellectual substance is sufficient by its own natural powers to see the essence of God? (5) Whether the created intellect needs any created light in order to see the essence of God? (6) Whether, of those who see the essence of God, one sees it more perfectly than another? (7) Whether any created intellect can comprehend the essence of God? (8) Whether a created intellect, seeing the essence of God, knows all things in it? (9) Whether what is there known is known by any likenesses? (10) Whether the created intellect knows all at once what it sees in God? (11) Whether in the state of this life any man can see the essence of God? (12) Whether by natural reason we can know God in this life? (13) Whether there is in this life any knowledge of God through grace above the knowledge of natural reason?

---

1. the essence of God：天主的本性

First Article

WHETHER ANY CREATED INTELLECT CAN SEE THE ESSENCE OF GOD?

We proceed thus to the First Article: —

Objection 1. It seems that no created intellect can see the essence of God. For Chrysostom, commenting on *John* i. 18 (*No man hath seen God at any time*), *says: Not prophets only, but neither angels nor archangels have seen God. For how can a creature see what is uncreatable?*[1] Dionysius also, speaking of God, says: *Neither is there sense, nor image, nor opinion, nor reason, nor knowledge of Him.*[2]

Obj. 2. Further, everything infinite, as such, is unknown. But God is infinite, as was shown above.[3] Therefore in Himself He is unknown.

Obj. 3. Further, the created intellect knows only existing things For what falls first under the apprehension of the intellect is being. Now God is not something existing; but He is rather super-existence[4], as Dionysius says.[5] Therefore God is not intelligible; but above all intellect.

Obj. 4. Further, there must be some proportion between the knower and the known, since the known is the perfection of the knower. But no proportion exists between the created intellect and God, for there is an infinite distance between them. Therefore a created intellect cannot see the essence of God.

On the contrary, It is written: *We shall see Him as He is* (*1 John* iii. 2).

I answer that, Since everything is knowable according as it is actual, God, Who is pure act without any admixture of potentiality, is in

1. 参见 *In Ioann.*, hom. XV (PG 59,98).
2. 参见 *De Div. Nom.*, I,5 (PG 3,593).
3. 参见 Q. 7, a. 1.
4. super-existence：超性的存在
5. 参见 *De Div. Nom.*, IV, 3 (PG 3, 697).

Himself supremely knowable. But what is supremely knowable in itself may not be knowable to a particular intellect, because of the excess of the intelligible object above the intellect; as, for example, the sun, which is supremely visible, cannot be seen by the bat by reason of its excess of light.

Therefore, some who considered this held that no created intellect can see the essence of God.[1] This opinion, however, is not tenable. For the ultimate beatitude of man consists in the use of his highest function, which is the operation of the intellect. Hence, if we suppose that a created intellect could never see God, it would either never attain to beatitude, or its beatitude would consist in something else beside God; which is opposed to faith. For the ultimate perfection of the rational creature is to be found in that which is the source of its being; since a thing is perfect so far as it attains to its source. Further, the same opinion is also against reason. For there resides in every man a natural desire to know the cause of any effect which he sees. Thence arises wonder in men. But if the intellect of the rational creature could not attain to the first cause of things, the natural desire would remain vain.

Hence it must be granted absolutely that the blessed see the essence of God.

Reply Obj. 1. Both of these authorities speak of the vision of comprehension. Hence Dionysius premises immediately before the words cited, *He is universally to all incomprehensible*,[2] etc. Chrysostom, likewise, after the words quoted, says: *He says this of the most certain vision of the Father, which is such a perfect consideration and comprehension as the Father has of the Son.*[3]

Reply Obj. 2. The infinity of matter not made perfect by form, is

---

1. 参见 Amaury of Bene, (text in G. C. Capelle, *Amaury de Bène*, p. 105).
2. 参见 *De Div. Nom.*, I, 5 (PG 3, 593).
3. 参见 *In Ioann.*, hom. XV(PG 59, 99).

unknown in itself, because all knowledge is through form; whereas the infinity of the form not limited by matter is in itself supremely known. God is infinite in this way, and not in the first way: as appears from what was said above.[1]

Reply Obj. 3. God is not said to be not existing as if He did not exist at all, but because He exists above all that exists, inasmuch as He is His own being. Hence it does not follow that He cannot be known at all, but that He transcends all knowledge; which means that He is not comprehended.

Reply Obj. 4. Proportion is twofold. In one sense it means a certain relation of one quantity to another, according to which double, treble and equal are species of proportion. In another sense, every relation of one thing to another is called proportion. And in this sense there can be a proportion of the creature to God, inasmuch as it is related to Him as the effect to its cause, and as potentiality to act; and in this way a created intellect can be proportioned to know God.

Second Article
WHETHER THE ESSENCE OF GOD IS SEEN BY A CREATED INTELLECT THROUGH A LIKENESS?

We proceed thus to the Second Article: —

Objection 1. It seems that the essence of God is seen by the created intellect through some likeness. For it is written: *We know that when He shall appear, we shall be like to Him, and we shall see Him as He is* (*1 John* iii. 2).

Obj. 2. Further, Augustine says: *When we know God, some likeness of God comes to be in us.*[2]

Obj. 3. Further, the intellect in act is the actual intelligible; as

---

1. 参见 Q. 7, a. 1.
2. 参见 *De Trin.*, IX, 11 (PL 42, 969).

sense in act is the actual sensible. But this comes about inasmuch as the sense is informed with the likeness of the sensible thing, and the intellect with the likeness of the thing understood. Therefore, if God is seen actually by the created intellect, it must be that He is seen through some likeness.

On the contrary, Augustine says, that when the Apostle says, 'We see through a glass and in an enigma,' *by the terms 'glass' and 'enigma' certain likenesses are signified by him, which are accommodated to an understanding of God.*[1] But to see the essence of God is not an enigmatic or a reflected vision, but is, on the contrary, of an opposite kind. Therefore the divine essence is not seen, through likenesses.

I answer that, Two things are required both for sensible and for intellectual vision — viz., power of sight, and union of the thing seen with the sight. For vision is made actual only when the thing seen is in a certain way in the seer. Now in corporeal things it is clear that the thing seen cannot be by its essence in the seer, but only by its likeness; as the likeness of a stone is in the eye, whereby the vision is made actual, whereas the substance of the stone is not there. But if the source of the visual power and the thing seen were one and the same thing, it would necessarily follow that the seer would possess both the visual power, and the form whereby it sees, from that one same thing.

Now it is manifest both that God is the author of the intellectual power and that He can be seen by the intellect. And since the intellectual power of the creature is not the essence of God, it follows that it is some kind of participated likeness of Him Who is the first intellect. Hence also the intellectual power of the creature is called an intelligible light, as it were, derived from the first light, whether this be understood of the natural power, or of some superadded perfection of grace or of glory. Therefore, in order to see God, there is needed some

1. 参见 *Op. cit.*, XV, 9 (PL 42. 1069).

likeness of God on the part of the visual power, whereby the intellect is made capable of seeing God. But on the part of the thing seen, which must in some way be united to the seer, the essence of God cannot be seen through any created likeness. First, because, as Dionysius says, *by the likenesses of the inferior order of things, the superior can in no way be known*;[1] as by the likeness of a body the essence of an incorporeal thing cannot be known. Much less therefore can the essence of God be seen through any created species whatever. Secondly, because the essence of God is His very being, as was shown above,[2] which cannot be said of any created form. Hence, no created form can be the likeness representing the essence of God to the seer. Thirdly, because the divine essence is uncircumscribed, and contains in itself supereminently whatever can be signified or understood by a created intellect. Now this cannot in any way be represented by any created species, for every created form is determined according to some aspect of wisdom, or of power, or of being itself, or of some like thing. Hence, to say that God is seen through some likeness is to say that the divine essence is not seen at all; which is false.

Therefore it must be said that to see the essence of God there is required some likeness in the visual power, namely, the light of glory strengthening the intellect to see God, which is spoken of in the *Psalm* (xxxv. 10): *In Thy light we shall see light.* The essence of God, however, cannot be seen by any created likeness representing the divine essence as it is in itself.

Reply Obj. 1. That authority speaks of the likeness which is caused by participation in the light of glory.

Reply Obj. 2. Augustine there speaks of the knowledge of God here on earth.[3]

---

1. 参见 *De Div. Nom.*, I,1 (PG 3, 588).
2. 参见 Q. 3, a. 4.
3. 参见 *De Trin.*, IX, 11 (PL 42, 969).

Reply Obj. 3. The divine essence is being itself. Hence, as other intelligible forms which are not their own being are united to the intellect by means of some being whereby the intellect itself is informed and made in act, so the divine essence is united to the created intellect, as the object actually understood, making the intellect in act through itself.

Third Article

WHETHER THE ESSENCE OF GOD CAN BE SEEN WITH THE BODILY EYE?

We proceed thus to the Third Article: —

Objection 1. It seems that the essence of God can be seen by the bodily eye. For it is written (*Job* xix. 26): *In my flesh I shall see . . . God*, and (*ibid*. xlii. 5), *With the hearing of the ear I have heard Thee, but now my eye seeth Thee.*

Obj. 2. Further, Augustine says: *Those eyes* (*namely*, *of the glorified*) *will therefore have a greater power of sight, not so much to see more keenly, as some report of the sight of serpents or of eagles* (*for whatever acuteness of vision is possessed by these creatures, they can see only corporeal things*), *but to see even incorporeal things.*[1] Now whoever can see incorporeal things, can be raised up to see God. Therefore the glorified eye can see God.

Obj. 3. Further, God can be seen by man through a vision of the imagination. For it is written: *I saw the Lord sitting upon a throne, etc.* (*Isa.* vi. 1). But an imaginary vision originates from sense; for imagination is a movement produced by the sense in act.[2] Therefore God can be seen by a vision of sense.

On the contrary, Augustine says: *No one has ever seen God as He is either in this life, or in the angelic life, in the manner that visible things are seen by*

1. 参见 *De Civit. Dei*, XXII, 29 (PL 41, 799).
2. 参见 Aristotle, *De An.*, III, 3 (429a 1).

corporeal vision.[1]

I answer that, It is impossible for God to be seen by the sense of sight, or by any other sense or power of the sensitive part of the soul. For every such power is the act of a corporeal organ, as will be shown later.[2] Now act is proportioned to the being whose act it is. Hence no power of that kind can go beyond corporeal things. But God is incorporeal, as was shown above.[3] Hence, He cannot be seen by the sense or the imagination, but only by the intellect.

Reply Obj. 1. The words, *In my flesh I shall see God my Saviour*, do not mean that God will be seen with the eye of flesh, but that man existing in the flesh after the resurrection[4] will see God. Likewise the words *Now my eye seeth Thee*, are to be understood of the mind's eye, as the Apostle says: *May* He *give unto you the spirit of wisdom ... in the knowledge of Him*, that *the eyes of your heart* may be *enlightened* (*Ephes.* i. 17, 18).

Reply Obj. 2. Augustine speaks[5] as one inquiring, and conditionally. This appears from what preceded that remark: *Therefore they will have an altogether different power* [viz., glorified eyes], *if through it they shall see that incorporeal nature*; and afterwards he explains this, saying: *It is very credible that we shall so see the mundane bodies of the new heavens and the new earth, as to see most clearly God everywhere present and governing all corporeal things; not as we now see the invisible things of God as understood by what is made, but as when we see men among whom we live, living and exercising the functions of human life, we do not believe they live, but see it.* Hence it is evident that the glorified eyes will see God in the way that now our eyes see the life of another. But life is not seen with the bodily eye as a thing in itself visible, but as the accidental object[6] of the sense; which

1. 参见 *Epist.* CXLVII, 11 (PL 33, 609).
2. 参见 Q. 78, a. 1.
3. 参见 Q. 3, a. 1.
4. resurrection：复活
5. 参见 *De Civit. Dei*, XXII, 29 (PL 41,780).
6. the accidental object：偶然的或附带的对象

indeed is not known by sense, but at once, together with sense, by some other cognitive power. But that the divine presence is known by the intellect immediately on the sight of, and through corporeal things, happens from two causes — viz., from the perspicacity[1] of the intellect, and from the refulgence[2] of the divine glory infused into the body after its renovation.

Reply Obj. 3. The essence of God is not seen in a vision of the imagination, but the imagination receives some form representing God according to some mode of likeness; as in divine Scripture divine things are metaphorically described by means of sensible things.

Fourth Article
WHETHER ANY CREATED INTELLECT BY ITS NATURAL POWERS CAN SEE THE DIVINE ESSENCE?

We proceed thus to the Fourth Article: —

Objection 1. It seems that a created intellect can see the divine essence by its own natural power. For Dionysius says: *An angel is a pure mirror, most clear, receiving, if it is permissible to say so, the whole beauty of God.*[3] But the original is seen when its reflection is seen. Therefore, since an angel understands himself by his natural power, it seems that by his own natural power he understands the divine essence.

Obj. 2. Further, what is supremely visible is made less visible to us by reason of our defective bodily or intellectual sight. But the angelic intellect[4] has no defect. Therefore, since God is supremely intelligible[5] in Himself, it seems that in like manner He is supremely so to an

1. perspicacity：敏锐
2. refulgence：光辉；灿烂
3. 参见 *De Div. Nom.*, IV, 27 (PG 3, 724).
4. the angelic intellect：天使的智力
5. supremely intelligible：极其简单明了

angel. Therefore, if the angel can understand other intelligible things[1] by his own natural power, all the more can he understand God.

Obj. 3. Further, bodily sense cannot be raised up to understand incorporeal substance, since it is above its nature. Therefore, if to see the essence of God is above the nature of every created intellect, it follows that no created intellect can reach the vision of the essence of God at all. But this is false, as appears from what is said above. Therefore it seems that it is natural for a created intellect to see the divine essence.

On the contrary, It is written: *The grace of God is life everlasting* (*Rom*. vi. 23). But life everlasting consists in the vision of the divine essence according to the words: *This is eternal life, that they may know Thee the only true God*, etc. (*Jo*. xvii. 3). Therefore, to see the essence of God is possible to the created intellect by grace, and not by nature.

I answer that, It is impossible for any created intellect to see the essence of God by its own natural power. For knowledge takes place according as the thing known is in the knower. But the thing known is in the knower according to the mode of the knower. Hence the knowledge of every knower is according to the mode of its own nature. If therefore the mode of being of a given thing exceeds the mode of the knower, it must result that the knowledge of that thing is above the nature of the knower. Now the mode of being of things is manifold. For some things have being only in this individual matter; such are all bodies. There are other beings whose natures are themselves subsisting, not residing in matter at all, which, however, are not their own being, but receive it: and these are the incorporeal substances called angels. But to God alone does it belong to be His own subsistent being.

Therefore, what exists only in individual matter we know naturally,

1. intelligible things：可理解的事物

since our soul, through which we know, is the form of some particular matter. Now our soul possesses two cognitive powers. One is the act of a corporeal organ, which naturally knows things existing in individual matter; hence sense knows only the singular. But there is another kind of cognitive power in the soul, called the intellect; and this is not the act of any corporeal organ. Therefore the intellect naturally knows natures which exist only in individual matter; not indeed as they are in such individual matter, but according as they are abstracted therefrom by the consideration of the intellect. Hence it follows that through the intellect we can understand these things in a universal way; and this is beyond the power of sense. Now the angelic intellect naturally knows natures that are not in matter; but this is beyond the power of the intellect of the human soul in the state of its present life, united as it is to the body.

It follows, therefore, that to know self-subsistent being[1] is natural to the divine intellect alone, and that it is beyond the natural power of any created intellect; for no creature is its own being, since its being is participated. Therefore, a created intellect cannot see the essence of God unless God by His grace unites Himself to the created intellect, as an object made intelligible to it.

Reply Obj. 1. This mode of knowing God is natural to an angel — namely, to know Him by His own likeness refulgent in the angel himself. But to know God by any created likeness is not to know the essence of God, as was shown above. Hence it does not follow that an angel can know the essence of God by his own power.

Reply Obj. 2. The angelic intellect is not defective, if defect be taken to mean privation, as if it were without anything which it ought to have. But if defect be taken negatively, in that sense every creature is defective, when compared with God , since it does not possess the

1. self-subsistent being：自我存在

excellence which is in God.

Reply Obj. 3. The sense of sight, as being altogether material, cannot be raised up to anything immaterial[1]. But our intellect, or the angelic intellect, inasmuch as it is elevated above matter in its own nature, can be raised up above its own nature to a higher level by grace. An indication of this is that sight cannot in any way know in abstraction what it knows concretely; for in no way can it perceive a nature except as this one particular nature; whereas our intellect is able to consider in abstraction what it knows in concretion. For although it knows things which have a form residing in matter, still it resolves the composite into both elements, and considers the form separately by itself. Likewise, also, the intellect of an angel, although it naturally knows , the being concreted in any nature, still it is able to separate that being by its intellect; since it knows that the thing itself is one thing, and its being is another. Since therefore a created intellect is naturally capable of apprehending the concreted form and the concreted being in abstraction, by way of a certain resolution, it can by grace be raised up to know separate subsisting substance and separate subsisting being.

Fifth Article

WHETHER THE CREATED INTELLECT NEEDS ANY CREATED LIGHT IN ORDER TO SEE THE ESSENCE OF GOD?

We proceed thus to the Fifth Article: —

Objection 1. It seems that the created intellect does not need any created light in order to see the essence of God. For what is of itself lucid in sensible things does not require any other light in order to be seen. Therefore the same applies to intelligible things. Now God

---

1. immaterial：非物质的

is intelligible light [*lux*]. Therefore He is not seen by the means of any created light [*lumen*].

Obj. 2. Further, if God is seen through a medium, He is not seen in His essence. But if seen by any created light, He is seen through a medium. Therefore He is not seen in His essence.

Obj. 3. Further, what is created can be natural to some creature. Therefore, if the essence of God is seen through any created light, such a light could be made natural to some creature. And thus, that creature would not need any other light to see God; which is impossible. Therefore it is not necessary that every creature should require a superadded light in order to see the essence of God.

On the contrary, It is written: *In Thy light we shall see light* (*Ps.* xxxv. 10).

I answer that, Everything which is raised up to what exceeds its nature must be prepared by some disposition above its nature; as, for example, if air is to receive the form of fire, it must be prepared by some disposition for such a form. But when any created intellect sees the essence of God, the essence of God itself becomes the intelligible form of the intellect. Hence it is necessary that some supernatural disposition should be added to the intellect in order that it may be raised up to such a great height. Now since the natural power of the created intellect does not enable it to see the essence of God, as was shown above, it is necessary that its power of understanding should be increased by divine grace. Now this increase of the intellectual powers is called the illumination of the intellect, as we also call the intelligible itself by the name of light or illumination. And this is the light spoken of in the *Apocalypse* (xxi. 23): *The glory of God hath enlightened, it*— viz., the society of the blessed who see God. By this light the blessed are made *deiform* — that is, like to God, according to the saying: *When He shall appear we shall be like to Him, and we shall see Him as He is* (*1 John* iii. 2).

Reply Obj. 1. A created light is necessary to see the essence of God, not in order to make the essence of God intelligible, which is of itself intelligible, but in order to enable the intellect to understand in the same way as a habit makes a power more able to act. In the same way, corporeal light is necessary as regards external sight, inasmuch as it makes the medium actually transparent, and susceptible of color.

Reply Obj. 2. This light is required to see the divine essence, not as a likeness in which God is seen, but as a perfection of the intellect, strengthening it to see God. Therefore it may be said that this light is not a medium *in which* God is seen, but one *by which* He is seen; and such a medium does not take away the immediate vision of God.

Reply Obj. 3. The disposition to the form of fire can be natural only to the subject of that form. Hence the light of glory cannot be natural to a creature unless the creature were to have a divine nature; which is impossible. For by this light the rational creature is made deiform, as was said above.

Sixth Article
WHETHER OF THOSE WHO SEE THE ESSENCE OF GOD, ONE SEES MORE PERFECTLY THAN ANOTHER?

We proceed thus to the Sixth Article:—

Objection 1. It seems that of those who see the essence of God, one does not see more perfectly than another. For it is written (*1 John* iii. 2): *We shall see Him as He is*. But He is only in one way. Therefore He will be seen by all in one way only; and therefore He will not be seen more perfectly by one and less perfectly by another.

Obj. 2. Further, Augustine says that one person cannot understand one and the same thing more perfectly than another.[1] But all who see God in His essence have an understanding of the divine essence; for God is seen by the intellect and not by sense, as was shown above.

1. 参见 *Lib. 83 Quaest.*, q. 32 (PL 40, 22).

Therefore of those who see the divine essence, one does not see more clearly than another.

Obj. 3. Further, That anything be seen more perfectly than another can happen in two ways: either on the part of the visible object, or on the part of the visual power of the seer. On the part of the object, it may so happen because the object is received more perfectly in the seer, that is, according to a more perfect likeness; but this does not apply to the present question, for God is present to the intellect seeing His essence not through any likeness, but through His essence. It follows then that if one is to see Him more perfectly than another, this will happen according to a difference in intellectual power. Thus it follows too that the one whose intellectual power is the higher will see Him the more clearly; and this is incongruous, since equality with angels is promised to men as their beatitude.

On the contrary, Eternal life consists in the vision of God, according to *John* (xvii. 3): *This is eternal life, that they may know Thee the only true God*, etc. Therefore, if all see the essence of God equally in eternal life, all will be equal; the contrary to which is declared by the Apostle: *Star differs from star in glory* (*1 Cor.* xv. 41).

I answer that, Of those who see the essence of God, one sees Him more perfectly than another. This does not take place as if one had a more perfect likeness of God than another, since that vision will not be through any likeness. But it will take place because one intellect will have a greater power or faculty to see God than another. The faculty of seeing God, however, does not belong to the created intellect naturally but through the light of glory, which establishes the intellect in a kind of *deiformity*, as appears from what is said above. Hence the intellect which Has more of the light of glory will see God the more perfectly. But he will have a fuller participation of the light of glory who has more charity, because where there is the greater charity, there is the more desire, and desire in a certain manner makes the one desiring apt and prepared to receive the object desired. Hence he who possesses the more charity, will see God the more perfectly, and will be the more beatified.

Reply Obj. 1. In the words, *We shall see Him as He is*, the conjunction *as* determines the mode of vision on the part of the object seen, so that the meaning is, we shall see Him to be as He is, because we shall see His being, which is His essence. But it does not determine the mode of vision on the part of the one seeing; as if the meaning was that the mode of seeing God will be as perfect as is the mode of God's being.

Thus appears the answer to the Second Objection. For when it is said that one intellect does not understand one and the same thing better than another, this would be true if referred to the mode of the thing understood; for whoever understands it otherwise than it really is does not understand it truly. But if it is referred to the mode of understanding, then the statement is not true, for the understanding of one is more perfect than the understanding of another.

Reply Obj. 3. The diversity of seeing will not arise because of the object seen, for the same object will be presented to all — viz., the essence of God; nor will it arise from the diverse participation of the object through different likenesses; but it will arise because of the diverse faculty of the intellect, not, indeed, the natural faculty, but the glorified faculty, as was said.

Seventh Article
WHETHER THOSE WHO SEE THE ESSENCE OF GOD COMPREHEND HIM?

We proceed, thus to the Seventh Article: —

Objection 1. It seems that those who see the divine essence comprehend God. For the Apostle says (*Phil.* iii. 12): *But I follow after, if I may by any means comprehend.* But the Apostle did not follow in vain, for he himself said (*1 Cor.* ix. 26): *I . . . so run, not as at an uncertainty.*

Therefore he comprehended; and in the same way others also, whom he invites to do the same, saying: *So run that you may comprehend.*

Obj. 2. Further, Augustine says: *That is comprehended which is so seen as a whole, that nothing of it is hidden from the seer.*[1] But if God is seen in His essence, He is seen whole, and nothing of Him is hidden from the seer, since God is simple. Therefore, whoever sees His essence, comprehends Him.

Obj. 3. Further, if it be said that He is seen as a *whole*, but *not wholly*, it may be contrarily urged that *wholly* refers either to the mode of the seer or to the mode of the thing seen. But he who sees the essence of God sees Him wholly, if the mode of the thing seen is considered, since he sees Him as He is; so, too, he sees Him wholly if the mode of the seer be meant, since the intellect will with its full power see the divine essence. Therefore all who see the essence of God see Him wholly; therefore they comprehend Him.

On the contrary, It is written: *O most mighty*[2], *great, and powerful, the Lord*[3] *of hosts is Thy Name. Great in counsel, and incomprehensible in thought* (*Jer.* xxxii. 18, 19). Therefore, He cannot be comprehended.

I answer that, It is impossible for any created intellect to comprehend God; but *to attain to God with the mind in some degree is great beatitude*, as Augustine says.[4]

In proof of this we must consider that what is comprehended is perfectly known; and that is perfectly known which is known so far as it can be known. Thus, if anything which is capable of scientific demonstration is held only by an opinion resting on a probable proof, it is not comprehended. For instance, if anyone knows by scientific demonstration that a triangle has three angles equal to two right

---

1. 参见 *Epist.* CXLVIII, 9 (PL 33,606).
2. most mighty：至高者
3. the Lord：主；耶稣基督
4. 参见 *Serm.* CXVII, 3 (PL 38, 663).

angles, he comprehends that truth; whereas if anyone accepts it as a probable opinion because wise men or most men teach it, he does not comprehend the thing itself, because he does not attain to that perfect mode of knowledge of which it is intrinsically capable. But no created intellect can attain to that perfect mode of the knowledge of the divine intellect whereof it is intrinsically capable. Here is the proof. Everything is knowable according to its actuality. But God, Whose being is infinite, as was shown above,[1] is infinitely knowable. Now no created intellect can know God infinitely. For a created intellect knows the divine essence more or less perfectly in proportion as it receives a greater or lesser light of glory. Since therefore the created light of glory received into any created intellect cannot be infinite, it is clearly impossible for any created intellect to know God in an infinite degree. Hence it is impossible that it should comprehend God.

Reply Obj. 1. *Comprehension* is twofold: in one sense it is taken strictly and properly, according as something is included in the one comprehending; and thus in no way is God comprehended either by the intellect or by anything else; for since He is infinite, He cannot be included in any finite being, so that a finite being contain Him infinitely, as befits Him. It is in this sense that we now take *comprehension*. But in another sense *comprehension* is taken more largely as opposed to *non-attainment*[2]; for he who attains to anyone is said to comprehend him when he attains to him. And in this sense God is comprehended by the blessed, according to the words, *I held him, and I will not let him go* (*Cant.* iii. 4); in this sense also are to be understood the words quoted from the Apostle concerning comprehension. According to this meaning, *comprehension* is one of the three prerogatives of the soul, answering to hope, as vision answers to faith, and fruition answers to charity. For even among ourselves

1. 参见 Q. 7, a. 1.
2. non-attainment：未达到的目标

not everything seen is held or possessed, since things sometimes appear afar off, or they are not in our power of attainment. Neither, again, do we always enjoy what we possess, either because we find no pleasure in them, or because such things are not the ultimate end of our desire, so as to give it fulfillment and peace. But the blessed possess these three things in God, because they see Him, and in seeing Him, possess Him as present, having the power to see Him always; and possessing Him, they enjoy Him as the ultimate fulfillment of desire.

Reply Obj. 2. God is called incomprehensible not because anything of Him is not seen, but because He is not seen as perfectly as He is capable of being seen. Thus, when any demonstrable proposition is known by a probable reason only, it does not follow that any part of it is unknown, either the subject, or the predicate, or the composition; but as a whole it is not as perfectly known as it is capable of being known. Hence Augustine, in his definition of comprehension, says: *a whole is comprehended when it is seen in such a way that nothing of it is hidden from the seer, or when its boundaries can be completely viewed or traced*;[1] for the boundaries of a thing are said to be completely surveyed when the end of the knowledge of it is attained.

Reply Obj. 3. The word *wholly* denotes a mode of the object; not that the whole object does not come under knowledge, but that the mode of the object is not the mode of the one who knows. Therefore, he who sees God's essence sees in Him that He exists infinitely, and is infinitely knowable. Nevertheless, this infinite mode does not extend to enable the knower to know infinitely; thus, for instance, a person can have a probable opinion that a proposition is demonstrable, although he himself does not know it as demonstrated.

---

1. 参见 *Epist*. CXLVII, 9 (PL 33, 606).

Eighth Article

WHETHER THOSE WHO SEE THE ESSENCE OF GOD SEE ALL IN GOD?

We proceed thus to the Eighth Article: —

Objection 1. It seems that those who see the essence of God see all things in God. For Gregory says: *What do they not see, who see Him Who sees all things?*[1] But God sees all things. Therefore, those who see God see all things.

Obj. 2. Further, whoever sees a mirror, sees what is reflected in the mirror. But all actual or possible things shine forth in God as in a mirror; for He knows all things in Himself. Therefore, whoever sees God, sees all actual things, and also all possible things.

Obj. 3. Further, whoever understands the greater, can understand the least, as is said in *De Anima* iii.[2] But all that God does, or can do, is less than His essence. Therefore, whoever understands God, can understand all that God does or can do.

Obj. 4. Further, the rational creature naturally desires to know all things. Therefore, if in seeing God it does not know all things, its natural desire will not rest satisfied. Hence, in seeing God it will not be fully happy; which is incongruous. Therefore, he who sees God knows all things.

On the contrary, The angels see the essence of God, and yet they do not know all things. For, as Dionysius says, *the inferior angels are cleansed from ignorance by the superior angels.*[3] Also they are ignorant of future contingent things, and of secret thoughts; for this knowledge belongs to God alone. Therefore, whosoever sees the essence of God does not

---

1. 参见 *Dial.*, IV, 33 (PL 77, 376).
2. 参见 Aristotle, *De An.*, III, 4 (429b 3).
3. 参见 *De Cael.*, *Hier.*, VII, 3 (PG 3, 208).

know all things.

I answer that, A created intellect, in seeing the divine essence, does not see in it all that God does or can do. For it is manifest that things are seen in God according as they are in Him. But all things are in God as effects are in the power of their cause. Therefore all things are seen in God as an effect is seen in its cause. Now it is clear that the more perfectly a cause is seen, the more of its effects can be seen in it. For whoever has a lofty understanding, as soon as one demonstrative principle is put before him, can gather the knowledge of many conclusions; but this is beyond one of a weaker intellect, for he needs things to be explained to him separately. And so that intellect can know all the effects of a cause and the reasons for those effects in the cause itself which comprehends the cause wholly. Now no created intellect can comprehend God wholly, as was shown above. Therefore, no created intellect, in seeing God, can know all that God does or can do, for this would be to comprehend His power; but, among the things that God does or can do, any intellect can know the more, the more perfectly it sees God.

Reply Obj, 1. Gregory speaks concerning the sufficiency of the object, namely, God, Who in Himself sufficiently contains and shows forth all things; but it does not follow that whoever sees God knows all things, for he does not perfectly comprehend Him.

Reply Obj. 2. It is not necessary that whoever sees a mirror should see all that is in the mirror, unless his glance comprehends the mirror itself.

Reply Obj. 3. Although it is greater to see God than to see all things else, still it is a greater thing to see Him so that all things are known in Him, than to see Him in such a way that not all things, but fewer or more, are known in Him. For it has already been shown that the number of things known in God varies according as He is seen more or less perfectly.

Reply Obj. 4. The natural desire of a rational creature is to know everything that belongs to the perfection of the intellect, namely, the species and genera of things and their essences, and these everyone who sees the divine essence will see in God. But to know other singulars, their thoughts and their deeds, does not belong to the perfection of a created intellect nor does its natural desire go out to these things; neither, again, does it desire to know things that as yet do not exist, but which God can call into being. But if God alone were seen, Who is the fount and source of all being and of all truth He would so fill the natural desire for knowledge that nothing else would be desired, and the seer would be completely beatified. Hence Augustine says: *Unhappy the man who knoweth all these* [that is, all creatures] *and knoweth not Thee ! but happy whoso knoweth Thee although he know not these. And whoso knoweth both Thee and them is not the happier for them, but for Thee alone.*[1]

Ninth Article

WHETHER WHAT IS SEEN IN GOD, BY THOSE WHO SEE THE DIVINE ESSENCE, IS SEEN THROUGH ANY LIKENESS?

We proceed thus to the Ninth Article: —

Objection 1. It seems that what is seen in God by those who see the divine essence is seen by means of some likeness. For every kind of knowledge comes about by the knower being assimilated to the object known. For thus the intellect in act becomes the actual intelligible, and the sense in act becomes the actual sensible, inasmuch as it is informed by a likeness of the object, as the eye by the likeness of color. Therefore, if the intellect of one who sees the divine essence understands any creatures in God, it must be informed by their likenesses.

1. 参见 *Confess.*, V, 4 (PL 32, 708).

Obj. 2. Further, what we have seen, we keep in memory. But Paul, seeing the essence of God while in rapture, when he had ceased to see the divine essence, as Augustine says,[1] remembered many of the things he had seen in that rapture; hence he said: I have *heard secret words which it is not granted to man to utter* (*2 Cor.* xii. 4). Therefore it must be said that certain Likenesses of what he remembered remained in his mind; and in the same way, when he actually saw the essence of God, he had certain likenesses or species of what he actually saw in it.

On the contrary, A mirror and what is in it are seen by means of one species. But all things are seen in God as in an intelligible mirror. Therefore, if God Himself is not seen by any likeness but by His own essence, neither are the things seen in Him seen by any likenesses or species.

I answer that, Those who see the divine essence see what they see in God not by any likeness, but by the divine essence itself united to their intellect. For each thing is known in so far as its likeness is in the one who knows. Now this takes place in two ways. For as things which are like to one and the same thing are like to each other, a cognitive power can be assimilated to any knowable object in two ways. In one way, it is assimilated by the object itself, when it is directly informed by the likeness of the object; in which case the object is known in itself. In another way, when the cognitive power is informed by a species of something which resembles the object; and in this way the knowledge is not of the thing in itself, but of the thing in its likeness. For the knowledge of a man in himself differs from the knowledge of him in his image. Hence, to know things thus by their likeness in the one who knows, is to know them in themselves or in their own natures; whereas to know them by their likenesses pre-existing in God is to see them in God. Now there is a difference between these two kinds of knowledge.

---

1. 参见 *De Genesi ad Litt.*, XII, 28; 34 (PL 34, 478; 483) ; *Epist.* CXLVII, 13 (PL 33, 611)

Hence, according to the knowledge whereby things are known by those who see the essence of God, they are seen in God Himself not by any other likenesses but by the divine essence alone present to the intellect; by which also God Himself is seen.

Reply Obj. 1. The created intellect of one who sees God is assimilated to the things seen in God inasmuch as it is united to the divine essence, in which the likenesses of all things pre-exist.

Reply Obj. 2. There are some cognitive powers which can form other images from those first conceived: thus the imagination from the preconceived species of a mountain and of gold forms the likeness of a golden mountain; and the intellect, from the preconceived ideas of genus and difference, forms the idea of species. In like manner, from the likeness of an image we can form in our minds the likenesses of the original of the image. Thus Paul, or any other person who sees God, by the very vision of the divine essence, can form in himself the likenesses of the things seen in the divine essence; which remained in Paul even when he had ceased to see the essence of God. Still, this kind of vision, whereby things are seen by these species thus conceived, is not the same as that whereby things are seen in God.

Tenth Article
WHETHER THOSE WHO SEE THE ESSENCE OF GOD SEE ALL THEY SEE IN IT AT THE SAME TIME?

We proceed thus to the Tenth Article: —

Objection 1. It seems that those who see the essence of God do not see all they see in Him at one and the same time. For, according to the Philosopher: *It may happen that many things are known, but only one is understood.*[1] But what is seen in God, is understood; for God is seen by

1. 参见 *Top.*, II, 10(114b 34).

the intellect. Therefore, those who see God do not see many things in Him at the same time.

Obj. 2. Further, Augustine says, *God moves the spiritual creature according to time*[1]— that is, by intelligence and affection. But the spiritual creature[2] is the angel, who sees God. Therefore those who see God understand and are affected successively; for time means succession[3].

On the contrary, Augustine says: *Our thoughts will not be unstable, going to and fro from one thing to another; but we shall see all we know at one glance.*[4]

I answer that, What is seen in the Word is seen not successively, but at the same time. In proof whereof, the reason why we ourselves cannot know many things all at once is because we understand many things by means of diverse species. But our intellect cannot be actually informed by diverse species at the same time, so as to understand by them; as one body cannot bear different shapes simultaneously. Hence, when many things can be understood by one species, they are understood at the same time; as the diverse parts of a whole are understood successively, and not all at the same time, if each one is understood by its own species, whereas if all are understood under the one species of the whole, they are understood simultaneously. Now it was shown above that things seen in God are not seen singly by their own similitude, but all are seen by the one essence of God. Hence they are seen simultaneously, and not successively.

Reply Obj. 1. We understand one thing only when we understand by one species; but many things understood by one species are understood simultaneously, as in the species of a *man* we understand

---

1. 参见 *De Genesi ad Litt.*, VIII, 20; 22 (PL 34, 388; 389).
2. spiritual creature：精神受造物
3. succession：连续不断
4. 参见 *De Trin.*, XV, 16 (PL 42, 1079).

animal and *rational*, and in the species of a *house* we understand the *wall* and the *roof*.

Reply Obj. 2. As regards their natural knowledge, whereby they know things by the diverse species with which they are endowed, the angels do not know all things simultaneously, and thus, in understanding, they are moved according to time; but as regards the things which they see in God, they see all at the same time.

Eleventh Article

WHETHER ANYONE IN THIS LIFE CAN SEE THE ESSENCE OF GOD?

We proceed thus to the Eleventh Article: —

Objection 1. It seems that in this life one can see the divine essence. For Jacob said: *I have seen God face to face* (*Gen.* xxxii. 30). But to see Him face to face is to see His essence, as appears from the words: *We see now in a glass and in a dark manner, but then face to face* (*1 Cor.* xiii. 12). Therefore God can be seen in this life in His essence.

Obj. 2. Further, the Lord said of Moses: *I speak to him mouth to mouth, and plainly, and not by riddles and figures doth he see the Lord* (*Num.* xii. 8); but this is to see God in His essence. Therefore it is possible to see the essence of God in this life.

Obj. 3. Further, that wherein we know all other things, and whereby we judge of other things, is in itself known to us. But even now we know all things in God; for Augustine says: *If we both see that what you say is true, and we both see that what I say is true, where, I ask, do we see this? neither I in thee, nor thou in me; but both of us in that incommutable truth itself above our minds.*[1] He also says that, *We judge of all things according to the divine truth*[2] and that, *it is the business of reason to judge of these corporeal*

1. 参见 *Confess.*, XII, 25 (PL 32, 840).
2. 参见 *De Vera Relig.*, XXX; XXXI (PL 34, 146; 147).

things according to the incorporeal and eternal ideas; which, unless they were above the mind, could not be incommutable.[1] Therefore even in this life we see God Himself.

Obj. 4. Further, according to Augustine, those things that are in the soul by their essence are seen by intellectual vision.[2] But intellectual vision is of intelligible things, not by any likenesses, but by their very essences, as he also says there. Therefore, since God is in our soul by His essence, it follows that He is seen by us in His essence.

On the contrary. It is written, *Man shall not see Me, and live* (*Exod.* xxxiii. 20), and the *Gloss* upon this says: *In this mortal life God can be seen by certain images, but not by the likeness itself of His own nature.*[3]

I answer that, God cannot be seen in His essence by one who is merely man, except he be separated from this mortal life. The reason is, because, as was said above, the mode of knowledge follows the mode of the nature of the knower. But our soul, as long as we live in this life, has its being in corporeal matter; hence it knows naturally only what has a form in matter. or what can be known by such a form. Now it is evident that the divine essence cannot be known through the nature of material things. For it was shown above that the knowledge of God by means of any created likeness is not the vision of His essence. Hence it is impossible for the soul of man in this life to see the essence of God. This can be seen in the fact that the more our soul is abstracted from corporeal things, the more it is capable of receiving abstract intelligible things. Hence in dreams and alienations of the bodily senses, divine revelations and foresight of future events are perceived the more clearly. It is not possible, therefore, that the soul in this mortal life should be raised up to the highest of intelligible objects, that is, to the divine essence.

---

1. 参见 *De Trin.*, XII, 2 (PL 42, 999).
2. 参见 *De Genesi ad Litt.*, XII, 24; 31 (PL 34, 474; 479).
3. 参见 *Glossa ordin.* (I, 203B).4

Reply Obj. 1. According to Dionysius, *a man is said in the Scriptures to have seen God in the sense that certain figures were formed in the senses or imagination, according to some likeness representing something divine.*[1] So when Jacob says, *I have seen God face to face*, this does not mean the divine essence, but some figure representing God. And this is to be referred to some high mode of prophecy[2], so that God is seen to speak, though in an imaginary vision; as will later be explained in treating of the degrees of prophecy.[3] We may also say that Jacob[4] spoke thus to designate some exalted intellectual contemplation, above the ordinary state.

Reply Obj. 2. As God works miracles in corporeal things, so also He does supernatural wonders above the common order, raising the minds of some living in the flesh, but who forego the use of the senses, even up to the vision of His own essence; as Augustine says of Moses[5], the teacher of the Jews, and of Paul, the teacher of the Gentiles.[6] This will be treated more fully in the question on rapture.[7]

Reply Obj. 3. All things are said to be seen in God, and all things are judged in Him, because by the participation of His light we know and judge all things; for the very light of natural reason is a participation of the divine light; as likewise we are said to see and judge of sensible things in the sun, that is, by the sun's light. Hence Augustine says, *The lessons of instruction can be seen only if they be illumined by their own sun*,[8] namely, God. Just as therefore, in order to see a sensible thing it is not necessary to see the substance of the sun, so in like manner to see

1. 参见 *De Cael. Hier.*, IV, 3 (PG 3, 180).
2. prophecy：预言；预言书
3. 参见 *S.T.* II-II, q. 174, a. 3.
4. Jacob：雅各伯：旧约的记述的以色列先祖之一
5. Moses：梅瑟：旧约的先知，曾带领以色列民族逃离埃及
6. 参见 *De Genesi ad Litt.*, XII, 26; 27; 28; 34 (PL 34, 476; 477; 478; 482); *Epist.* CXLVII, 13 (PL 33, 610).
7. 参见 *S.T.* II-II, q. 175, a. 3, 4, 5 and 6.
8. 参见 *Solil.*, I, 8 (PL 32, 877).

something intelligible, it is not necessary to see the essence of God.

Reply Obj. 4. Intellectual vision is of the things which are in the soul by their essence, as intelligible things are in the intellect. And thus God is in the souls of the blessed; not thus is He in our soul, but by presence, essence, and power.

Twelfth Article
WHETHER GOD CAN BE KNOWN IN THIS LIFE BY NATURAL REASON?

We proceed thus to the Twelfth Article: —

Objection 1. It seems that by natural reason we cannot know God in this life. For Boethius says that *reason does not grasp a simple form.*[1] But God is a supremely simple form, as was shown above.[2] Therefore natural reason cannot attain to know Him.

Obj. 2. Further, the soul understands nothing by natural reason without an image.[3] But we cannot have an image of God, Who is incorporeal. Therefore we cannot know God by natural knowledge.

Obj. 3. Further, the knowledge of natural reason belongs to both good and evil, inasmuch as they have a common nature. But the knowledge of God belongs only to the good; for Augustine says: *The eye of the human mind is not fixed on that excellent light unless purified by the justice of faith.*[4] Therefore God cannot be known by natural reason.

On the contrary, It is written (*Rom.* i, 19), *That which is known of God,* namely, what can be known of God by natural reason, *is manifest in them.*

I answer that, Our natural knowledge begins from sense. Hence our natural knowledge can go as far as it can be led by sensible things.

---

1. 参见 *De Consol.*, V, prose 4 (PL 63, 847).
2. 参见 Q. 3, a. 7.
3. 参见 Aristotle, *De An.*, III, 7 (431a 16).
4. 参见 *De Trin.*, I, 2 (PL 42, 822).

But our intellect cannot be led by sense so far as to see the essence of God; because sensible creatures are effects of God which do not equal the power of God, their cause. Hence from the knowledge of sensible things the whole power of God cannot be known; nor therefore can His essence be seen. But because they are His effects and depend on their cause, we can be led from them so far as to know of God *whether He exists*, and to know of Him what must necessarily belong to Him, as the first cause of all things, exceeding all things caused by Him.

Hence, we know His relationship with creatures, that is, that He is the cause of all things; also that creatures differ from Him, inasmuch as He is not in any way part of what is caused by Him; and that His effects are removed from Him, not by reason of any defect on His part, but because He superexceeds them all.

Reply Obj. 1. Reason cannot reach a simple form, so as to know *what it is*; but it can know *whether it is.*

Reply Obj. 2. God is known by natural knowledge through the images of His effects.

Reply Obj. 3. Since the knowledge of God's essence is by grace, it belongs only to the good, but the knowledge of Him by natural reason can belong to both good and bad; and hence Augustine says, retracting what he had said before: *I do not approve what I said in prayer, 'God who wiliest that only the pure should know truth.'*[1] *For it can be answered that many who are not pure know many truths*,[2] that is, by natural reason.

Thirteenth Article
WHETHER BY GRACE A HIGHER KNOWLEDGE OF GOD CAN BE OBTAINED THAN BY NATURAL REASON?

We proceed thus to the Thirteenth Article:—

1. 参见 *Solil.*, I, 1 (PL 32, 870).
2. 参见 *Retract.*, I, 4 (PL 32, 589).

Objection 1. It seems that by grace a higher knowledge of God is not obtained than by natural reason. For Dionysius says that whoever is the better united to God in this life, is united to Him as to one entirely unknown.[1] He says the same of Moses, who nevertheless obtained a certain excellence by the knowledge conferred by grace. But to be united to God, while not knowing of Him *what He is*, comes about also by natural reason. Therefore God is not more known to us by grace than by natural reason.

Obj. 2. Further, we can acquire the knowledge of divine things by natural reason only through images; and the same applies to the knowledge given by grace. For Dionysius says that *it is impossible for the divine ray to shine upon us except as screened round about by the many colored sacred veils.*[2] Therefore we do know God more fully by grace than by natural reason.

Obj. 3. Further, our intellect adheres to God by the grace of faith. But faith does not seem to be knowledge; for Gregory says that *things not seen are the objects of faith, and not of knowledge.*[3] Therefore there is not given to us a more excellent knowledge of God by grace.

On the contrary, The Apostle says that *God hath revealed to us by His Spirit, what none of the princes of this world knew* (*1 Cor.* ii. 8, 10), namely, *the philosophers*, as the *Gloss* expounds.[4]

I answer that, We have a more perfect knowledge of God by grace than by natural reason. Which is proved thus. The knowledge which we have by natural reason requires two things: images derived from the sensible things, and a natural intelligible light enabling us to abstract intelligible conceptions from them.

Now in both of these, human knowledge is assisted by the revelation

---

1. 参见 *De Myst. Theol.*, I, 3 (PG 3, 1001).
2. 参见 *De Cael. Hier.*, I, 2 (PG 3, 121).
3. 参见 *In Evang.*, II, hom. 26 (PL 76, 1202).
4. 参见 *Glossa interl.*, super I Cor. II, 1o (VI, 36r).

of grace. For the intellect's natural light is strengthened by the infusion of gratuitous light, and sometimes also the images in the imagination are divinely formed, so as to express divine things better than do those which we receive naturally from sensible things, as appears in prophetic visions[1]; while sometimes sensible things, or even voices, are divinely formed to express some divine meaning; as in the Baptism[2], the Holy Ghost[3] was seen in the shape of a dove, and the voice of the Father was heard, *This is My beloved Son* (*Matt.* iii. 17).

Reply Obj. 1. Although by the revelation of grace in this life we do not know of God *what He is*, and thus are united to Him as to one unknown, still we know Him more fully according as many and more excellent of His effects are demonstrated to us, and according as we attribute to Him some things known by divine revelation, to which natural reason cannot reach, as, for instance, that God is Three and One.

Reply Obj. 2. From the images either naturally received from sense, or divinely formed in the imagination, we have so much the more excellent intellectual knowledge, the stronger the intelligible light is in man; and thus through the revelation given by the images a fuller knowledge is received by the infusion of the divine light.

Reply Obj. 3. Faith[4] is a kind of knowledge, inasmuch as the intellect is determined by faith to some knowable object. But this determination to one object does not proceed from the vision of the believer, but from the vision of Him Who is believed. Thus, as far as faith falls short of vision, it falls short of the nature which knowledge has when it is science; for science determines the intellect to one object by the vision and understanding of first principles.

1. prophetic visions：预言的异象
2. the Baptism：洗礼；圣洗
3. the Holy Ghost：圣神：三位一体的天主的第三位
4. Faith：宗教信仰，信德

Question XIII
THE NAMES OF GOD
(*In Twelve Articles*)

AFTER the consideration of those things which belong to the divine knowledge, we now proceed to the consideration of the divine names. For everything is named by us according to our knowledge of it.

Under this head, there are twelve points for inquiry. (1) Whether God can be named by us? (2) Whether any names applied to God are predicated of Him substantially? (3) Whether any names applied to God are said of Him properly, or are all to be taken metaphorically? (4) Whether any names applied to God are synonymous? (5) Whether some names are applied to God and to creatures univocally or equivocally? (6) Whether, supposing they are applied analogically, they are applied first to God or to creatures? (7) Whether any names are applicable to God from time? (8) Whether this name *God* is a name of nature, or of operation? (9) Whether this name *God* is a communicable name? (10) Whether it is taken univocally or equivocally as signifying God, by nature, by participation, and by opinion ? (11) Whether this name, *Who is*, is the supremely appropriate name of God? (12) Whether affirmative propositions can be formed about God?

First Article
WHETHER A NAME CAN BE GIVEN TO GOD ?

We proceed thus to the First Article: —

Objection 1. It seems that no name can be given to God. For

Dionysius says that, *Of Him there is neither name, nor can one be found of Him;*[1] and it is written: *What is His name, and what is the name of His Son, if thou knowest?* (*Prov.* xxx. 4).

Obj. 2. Further, every name is either abstract or concrete. But concrete names do not belong to God, since He is simple, nor do abstract names belong to Him, since they do not signify any perfect subsisting thing. Therefore no name can be said of God.

Obj. 3. Further, nouns signify substance with quality; verbs and participles signify substance with time; pronouns the same with demonstration or relation. But none of these can be applied to God, for He has no quality, or accident, or time; moreover, He cannot be felt, so as to be pointed out; nor can He be described by relation, inasmuch as relations serve to recall a thing mentioned before by nouns, participles or demonstrative pronouns. Therefore God cannot in any way be named by us.

On the contrary, It is written (*Exod.* xv. 3): *The Lord is a man of war, Almighty is His name.*

I answer that, Since, according to the Philosopher,[2] words are signs of ideas, and ideas the similitudes of things, it is evident that words function in the signification of things through the conception of the intellect. It follows therefore that we can give a name to anything in as far as we can understand it. Now it was shown above that in this life we cannot see the essence of God;[3] but we know God from creatures as their cause, and also by way of excellence and remotion. In this way therefore He can be named by us from creatures, yet not so that the name which signifies Him expresses the divine essence in itself in the way that the name *man* expresses the essence of man in himself, since it signifies the definition which manifests his essence. For the idea

1. 参见 *De Div. Nom.*, I, 5 (PG 3, 593).
2. 参见 *Perih.*, I (16a 3).
3. 参见 Q. 12, a. 11 and 12.

expressed by the name is the definition.

Reply Obj. 1. The reason why God has no name, or is said to be above being named, is because His essence is above all that we understand about God and signify in words.

Reply Obj. 2. Because we come to know and name God from creatures, the names we attribute to God signify what belongs to material creatures, of which the knowledge is natural to us, as was shown above.[1] And because in creatures of this kind what is perfect and subsistent is composite, whereas their form is not a complete subsisting thing, but rather is that whereby a thing is, hence it follows that all names used by us to signify a complete subsisting thing must have a concrete meaning, as befits composite things. On the other hand, names given to signify simple forms signify a thing not as subsisting, but as that whereby a thing is; as, for instance, whiteness signifies that whereby a thing is white. And since God is simple and subsisting, we attribute to Him simple and abstract names to signify. His simplicity, and concrete names to signify His subsistence and perfection; although both these kinds of names fail to express His mode of being, because our intellect does not know Him in this life as He is.

Reply Obj. 3. To signify substance with quality is to signify the *suppositum* with a nature or determined form in which it subsists. Hence, as some things are said of God in a concrete sense, to signify His subsistence and perfection, so likewise nouns are applied to God signifying substance with quality. Further, verbs and participles, which signify time, are applied to Him because His eternity includes all time. For as we can apprehend and signify simple subsistents only by way of composite things, so we can understand and express simple eternity only by way of temporal things, because our intellect has a natural

---

1. 参见 Q. 12, a. 4.

proportion to composite and temporal things. But demonstrative pronouns are applied to God as pointing to what is understood, not to what is sensed. For we can point to Him only as far as we understand Him. Thus, according as nouns, participles and demonstrative pronouns are applicable to God, so far can He be signified by relative pronouns.

Second Article

WHETHER ANY NAME CAN BE APPLIED TO GOD SUBSTANTIALLY?

We proceed thus to the Second Article: —

Objection 1. It seems that no name can be applied to God substantially. For Damascene says: *Everything said of God must not signify His substance, but rather show forth what He is not; or express some relation, or something following from His nature or operation.*[1]

Obj. 2. Further, Dionysius says: *You will find a chorus of holy doctors addressed to the end of distinguishing clearly and praiseworthily the divine processions in the denominations of God.*[2] This means that the names applied by the holy doctors in praising God are distinguished according to the divine processions themselves. But what expresses the procession of anything does not signify anything pertaining to its essence. Therefore the names said of God are not said of Him substantially.

Obj. 3. Further, a thing is named by us according as we understand it. But in this life God is not understood by us in His substance. Therefore neither is any name we can use applied substantially to God.

On the contrary, Augustine says: *For God to be is to be strong or wise, or*

---

1. 参见 *De Fide Orth.*, I, 9 (PG 94. 833).
2. 参见 *De Div. Nom.*, I, 4 (PG 3, 589).

whatever else we may say of that simplicity whereby His substance is signified.[1] Therefore all names of this kind signify the divine substance.

I answer that, Names which are said of God negatively or which signify His relation to creatures manifestly do not at all signify His substance, but rather express the distance of the creature from Him, or His relation to something else, or rather, the relation of creatures to Himself.

But as regards names of God said absolutely and affirmatively, as *good*, *wise*, and the like, various and many opinions have been held. For some have said that all such names, although they are applied to God affirmatively, nevertheless have been brought into use more to remove something from God than to posit something in Him. Hence they assert that when we say that God lives, we mean that God is not like an inanimate thing[2]; and the same in like manner applies to other names. This was taught by Rabbi Moses.[3] Others[4] say that these names applied to God signify His relationship towards creatures: thus in the words, *God is good*, we mean, God is the cause of goodness in things; and the same interpretation applies to other names.

Both of these opinions, however, seem to be untrue for three reasons. First, because in neither of them could a reason be assigned why some names more than others should be applied to God. For He is assuredly the cause of bodies in the same way as He is the cause of good things; therefore if the words *God is good* signified no more than, *God is the cause of good things*, it might in like manner be said that God is a body, inasmuch as He is the cause of bodies. So also to say that He is a body implies that He is not a mere potentiality, as is primary matter. Secondly, because it would follow that all names applied to God would

---

1. 参见 *De Trin.*,VI, 4 (PL 42, 927).
2. inanimate thing：无生命之物
3. 参见 *Guide*, I, 58 (p. 82).
4. 参见 Alain of Lille, *Theol. Reg.* XXI; XXVI (PL 210,631; 633).

be said of Him by way of being taken in a secondary sense, as healthy is secondarily said of medicine, because it signifies only the cause of health in the animal which primarily is called healthy. Thirdly, because this is against the intention of those who speak of God. For in saying that God lives, they assuredly mean more than to say that He is the cause of our life, or that He differs from inanimate bodies.

Therefore we must hold a different doctrine[1]— viz., that these names signify the divine substance, and are predicated substantially of God, although they fall short of representing Him. Which is proved thus. For these names express God, so far as our intellects know Him. Now since our intellect knows God from creatures, it knows Him as far as creatures represent Him. But it was shown above that God prepossesses in Himself all the perfections of creatures, being Himself absolutely and universally perfect.[2] Hence every creature represents Him, and is like Him, so far as it possesses some perfection: yet not so far as to represent Him as something of the same species or genus, but as the excelling source of whose form the effects fall short, although they derive some kind of likeness thereto, even as the forms of inferior bodies represent the power of the sun. This was explained above in treating of the divine perfection.[3] Therefore, the aforesaid names signify the divine substance, but in an imperfect manner, even as creatures represent it imperfectly. So when we say, *God is good*, the meaning is not, *God is the cause of goodness*, or, *God is not evil*; but the meaning is, *Whatever good we attribute to creatures pre-exists in God*, and in a higher way. Hence it does not follow that God is good because He causes goodness; but rather, on the contrary, He causes goodness in things because He is good. As Augustine says, *Because He is good, we*

1. doctrine：教义；教理
2. 参见 Q. 4, a. 2.
3. 参见 Q.4, a.3.

are.[1]

Reply Obj. 1. Damascene says that these names do not signify what God is because by none of these names is what He is perfectly expressed; but each one signifies Him in an imperfect manner, even as creatures represent Him imperfectly.

Reply Obj. 2. In the signification of names, that from which the name is derived is different sometimes from what it is intended to signify, as for instance this name *stone* [*lapis*] is imposed from the fact that it hurts the *foot* [*lædit pedem*]; yet it is not imposed to signify that which hurts the foot, but rather to signify a certain kind of body; otherwise everything that hurts the foot would be a stone. So we must say that such divine names are imposed from the divine processions; for as according to the diverse processions of their perfections, creatures are the representations of God, although in an imperfect manner, so likewise our intellect knows and names God according to each kind of procession. But nevertheless these names are not imposed to signify the processions themselves, as if when we say *God lives*, the sense were, *life proceeds from Him*, but to signify the principle itself of things, in so far as life pre-exists in Him, although it pre-exists in Him in a more eminent way than is understood or signified.

Reply Obj. 3. In this life, we cannot know the essence of God as it is in itself, but we know it according as it is represented in the perfections of creatures; and it is thus that the names imposed by us signify it.

Third Article
WHETHER ANY NAME CAN BE APPLIED TO GOD PROPERLY?

We proceed thus to the Third Article: —

---

1. 参见 *De Doc. Christ.*, I, 32 (PL 34, 32).

Objection 1. It seems that no name is applied properly to God. For all names which we apply to God are taken from creatures; as was explained above. But the names of creatures are applied to God metaphorically, as when we say, God is a stone, or a lion, or the like. Therefore names are applied to God in a metaphorical sense.

Obj. 2. Further, no name can be applied properly to anything if it should be more truly denied of it than given to it. But all such names as *good*, *wise*, and the like, are more truly denied of God than given to Him; as appears from what Dionysius says.[1] Therefore none of these names is said of God properly.

Obj. 3. Further, corporeal names are applied to God in a metaphorical sense only, since He is incorporeal. But all such names imply some kind of corporeal condition; for their meaning is bound up with time and composition and like corporeal conditions. Therefore all these names are applied to God in a metaphorical sense.

On the contrary, Ambrose says, *Some names there are which express evidently the property of the divinity, and some which express the clear truth of the divine majesty*[2]; *but others there are which are said of God metaphorically by way of similitude.*[3] Therefore not all names are applied to God in a metaphorical sense, but there are some which are said of Him properly.

I answer that, According to the preceding article, our knowledge of God is derived from the perfections which flow from Him to creatures; which perfections are in God in a more eminent way than in creatures. Now our intellect apprehends them as they are in creatures, and as it apprehends them thus does it signify them by names. Therefore, as to the names applied to God, there are two things to be considered — viz., the perfections themselves which they signify, such as goodness, life, and the like, and their mode of signification. As regards what

1. 参见 *De Cael. Hier.*, II, 3 (PG 3, 141).
2. the divine majesty：神圣的至高权威者，指天主
3. 参见 *De Fide*, II, Prol. (PL 16, 583).

is signified by these names, they belong properly to God, and more properly than they belong to creatures, and are applied primarily to Him. But as regards their mode of signification, they do not properly and strictly apply to God; for their mode of signification befits creatures.

Reply Obj. 1. There are some names which signify these perfections flowing from God to creatures in such a way that the imperfect way in which creatures receive the divine perfection is part of the very signification of the name itself, as *stone* signifies a material being; and names of this kind can be applied to God only in a metaphorical sense. Other names, however, express the perfections themselves absolutely, without any such mode of participation being part of their signification, as the words *being*, *good*, *living*, and the like; and such names can be applied to God properly.

Reply Obj. 2. Such names as these, as Dionysius shows, are denied of God for the reason that what the name signifies does not belong to Him in the ordinary sense of its signification, but in a more eminent way. Hence Dionysius says also that God is above all substance and all life.[1]

Reply Obj. 3. These names which are applied to God properly imply corporeal conditions, not in the thing signified, but as regards their mode of signification; whereas those which are applied to God metaphorically imply and mean a corporeal condition in the thing signified.

Fourth Article
WHETHER NAMES APPLIED TO GOD ARE SYNONYMOUS?

We proceed thus to the Fourth Article: —

---

1. 参见 *De Cael. Hier.*, II, 3 (PG 3, 141).

Objection 1. It seems that these names applied to God are synonymous names[1]. For synonymous names are those which mean exactly the same. But these names applied to God mean entirely the same thing in God; for the goodness of God is His essence, and likewise it is His wisdom. Therefore these names are entirely synonymous.

Obj. 2. Further, if it be said that these names signify one and the same thing in reality, but differ in idea, it can be objected that an idea to which no reality corresponds is an empty notion. Therefore if these ideas are many, and the thing is one, it seems also that all these ideas are empty notions.

Obj. 3. Further, a thing which is one in reality and in idea is more one than what is one in reality and many in idea. But God is supremely one. Therefore it seems that He is not one in reality and many in idea; and thus the names applied to God do not have different meanings. Hence they are synonymous.

On the contrary, All synonyms united with each other are redundant, as when we say, *vesture clothing*. Therefore if all names applied to God are synonymous, we cannot properly say *good God*, or the like; and yet it is written, *O most mighty, great and powerful, the Lord of hosts is Thy name* (*Jer.* xxxii. 18).

I answer that, These names spoken of God are not synonymous. This would be easy to understand, if we said that these names are used to remove or to express the relation of cause to creatures; for thus it would follow that there are different ideas as regards the diverse things denied of God, or as regards diverse effects connoted. But according to what was said above, namely, that these names signify the divine substance, although in an imperfect manner, it is also clear from what has been said that they have diverse meanings. For the idea signified

1. synonymous names: 同义的名称

by the name is the conception in the intellect of the thing signified by the name. But since our intellect knows God from creatures, in order to understand God it forms conceptions proportioned to the perfections flowing from God to creatures. These perfections pre-exist in God unitedly and simply, whereas in creatures they are received divided and multiplied. Just as, therefore, to the diverse perfections of creatures there corresponds one simple principle represented by the diverse perfections of creatures in a various and manifold manner, so also to the various and multiplied conceptions of our intellect there corresponds one altogether simple principle, imperfectly understood through these conceptions. Therefore, although the names applied to God signify one reality, still, because they signify that reality under many and diverse aspects, they are not synonymous.

Thus appears the solution of the First Objection, since synonymous names signify one thing under one aspect; for names which signify different aspects of one thing do not signify primarily and absolutely one thing, because a name signifies a thing only through the medium of the intellectual conception, as was said above.

Reply Obj. 2. The many aspects of these names are not useless and empty, for there corresponds to all of them one simple reality represented by them in a manifold and imperfect manner.

Reply Obj. 3. The perfect unity of God requires that what are manifold and divided in others should exist in Him simply and unitedly. Thus it comes about that He is one in reality, and yet multiple in idea, because our intellect apprehends Him in a manifold manner, as things represent Him.

Fifth Article
WHETHER WHAT IS SAID OF GOD AND OF CREATURES IS UNIVOCALLY PREDICATED OF THEM?

We proceed thus to the Fifth Article: —

Objection 1. It seems that the things attributed to God and creatures are univocal. For every equivocal term is reduced to the univocal, as many are reduced to one: for if the name *dog* be said equivocally of the barking dog and of the dogfish, it must be said of some univocally — viz., of all barking dogs; otherwise we proceed to infinitude. Now there are some univocal agents which agree with their effects in name and definition, as man generates man; and there are some agents which are equivocal, as the sun which causes heat, although, the sun is hot only in an equivocal sense. Therefore it seems that the first agent, to which all other agents are reduced, is a univocal agent: and thus what is said of God and creatures is predicated univocally.

Obj. 2. Further, no likeness is understood through equivocal names. Therefore, as creatures have a certain likeness to God, according to the text of *Genesis* (i. 26), *Let us make man to our image and likeness*, it seems that something can be said of God and creatures univocally.

Obj. 3. Further, measure is homogeneous with the thing measured, as is said in *Metaph.* x.[1] But God is the first measure of all beings. Therefore God is homogeneous with creatures; and thus a name may be applied univocally to God and to creatures.

On the contrary, Whatever is predicated of various things under the same name but not in the same sense is predicated equivocally. But no name belongs to God in the same sense that it belongs to creatures for instance, wisdom in creatures is a quality, but not in God. Now a changes in genus changes an essence, since the genus is part of the definition; and the same applies to other things. Therefore whatever is said of God and of creatures is predicated equivocally.

Further, God is more distant from creatures than any creatures are from each other. But the distance of some creatures makes any univocal predication of them impossible, as in the case of those things

1. 参见 Aristotle, *Metaph.*, IX, 1 (1053a 24).

which are not in the same genus. Therefore much less can anything be predicated univocally of God and creatures; and so only equivocal predication can be applied to them.

I answer that, Univocal predication is impossible between God and creatures. The reason of this is that every effect which is not a proportioned result of the power of the efficient cause receives the similitude of the agent not in its full degree, but in a measure that falls short; so that what is divided and multiplied in the effects resides in the agent simply, and in an unvaried manner. For example, the sun by the exercise of its one power produces manifold and various forms in these sublunary things[1]. In the same way, as was said above, all perfections existing in creatures divided and multiplied pre-exist in God unitedly. Hence, when any name expressing perfection is applied to a creature, it signifies that perfection as distinct from the others according to the nature of its definition; as, for instance, by this term *wise* applied to a man, we signify some perfection distinct from a man's essence, and distinct from his power and his being, and from all similar things. But when we apply *wise* to God, we do not mean to signify anything distinct from His essence or power or being. And thus when this term *wise* is applied to man, in some degree it circumscribes[2] and comprehends the thing signified; whereas this is not the case when it is applied to God, but it leaves the thing signified as uncomprehended and as exceeding the signification of the name. Hence it is evident that this term *wise* is not applied in the same way to God and to man. The same applies to other terms. Hence, no name is predicated univocally of God and of creatures.

Neither, on the other hand, are names applied to God and creatures

---

1. sublunary things: 次要的东西
2. circumscribe：划定；限制

in a purely equivocal sense, as some have said.[1] Because if that were so, it follows that from creatures nothing at all could be known or demonstrated about God; for the reasoning would always be exposed to the fallacy of equivocation[2]. Such a view is against the Philosopher, who proves many things about God, and also against what the Apostle says: *The invisible things of* God *are clearly seen being understood by the things that are made* (*Rom.* i. 20). Therefore it must be said that these names are said of God and creatures in an *analogous* sense, that is, according to proportion.

This can happen in two ways: either according as many things are proportioned to one (thus, for example *healthy* is predicated of medicine and urine in relation and in proportion to health of body, of which the latter is the sign and the former the cause), or according as one thing is proportioned to another (thus, *healthy* is said of medicine and an animal, since medicine is the cause of health in the animal body). And in this way some things are said of God and creatures analogically, and not in a purely equivocal nor in a purely univocal sense. For we can name God only from creatures. Hence, whatever is said of God and creatures is said according as there is some relation of the creature to God as to its principle and cause, wherein all the perfections of things pre-exist excellently. Now this mode of community is a mean between pure equivocation and simple univocation[3]. For in analogies the idea is not, as it is in univocals, one and the same; yet it is not totally diverse as in equivocals; but the name which is thus used in a multiple sense signifies various proportions to some one thing: *e.g.*, *healthy*, applied to urine, signifies the sign of animal health; but applied to medicine, it signifies the cause of the

1. 参见 Maimonides, *Guide*, I, 59 (p. 84); Averroes, *In Metaph*, XII. comm. 51 (VIII, 158r)
2. equivocation：模棱两可的话
3. univocation：意思明确的话

same health.

Reply Obj. 1. Although in predications all equivocals must be reduced to univocals, still in actions the non-univocal agent must precede the univocal agent. For the non-univocal agent is the universal cause of the whole species, as the sun is the cause of the generation of all men. But the univocal agent is not the universal efficient cause of the whole species (otherwise it would be the cause of itself, since it is contained in the species), but is a particular cause of this individual which it places under the species by way of participation. Therefore the universal cause of the whole species is not a univocal agent: and the universal cause comes before the particular cause. But this universal agent, while not univocal, nevertheless is not altogether equivocal (otherwise it could not produce its own likeness); but it can be called an analogical agent, just as in predications all univocal names are reduced to one first non-univocal analogical name, which is *being*.

Reply Obj. 2. The likeness of the creature to God is imperfect, for it does not represent the same thing even generically.[1]

Reply Obj. 3. God is not a measure proportioned to the things measured; hence it is not necessary that God and creatures should be in the same genus.

The arguments adduced in the contrary sense prove indeed that these names are not predicated univocally of God and creatures; yet they do not prove that they are predicated equivocally.

Sixth Article
WHETHER NAMES PREDICATED OF GOD ARE PREDICATED PRIMARILY OF CREATURES?

We proceed, thus to the Sixth Article: —

---

1. 参见 Q. 4, a. 3.

Objection 1. It seems that names are predicated primarily of creatures rather than of God. For we name anything accordingly as we know it, since *names*, as the Philosopher says,[1] *are signs of ideas*. But we know creatures before we know God. Therefore the names imposed by us are predicated primarily of creatures rather than of God.

Obj. 2. Further, Dionysius says that we name God from creatures.[2] But names transferred from creatures to God are said primarily of creatures rather than of God; as *lion*, *stone*, and the like. Therefore all names applied to God and creatures are applied primarily to creatures rather than to God.

Obj. 3. Further, all names applied to God and creatures in common *are applied to God as the cause of all creatures*, as Dionysius says.[3] But what is applied to anything through its cause is applied to it secondarily; for *healthy* is primarily predicated of animal rather than of medicine, which is the cause of health. Therefore these names are said primarily of creatures rather than of God.

On the contrary, It is written, *I bow my knees to the Father of our Lord Jesus Christ, of Whom all paternity in heaven and earth is named* (*Ephes.* iii 14, 15); and the same holds of the other names applied to God and creatures. Therefore these names are applied primarily to God rather than to creatures.

I answer that, In names predicated of many in an analogical sense, all are predicated through a relation to some one thing; and this one thing must be placed in the definition of them all. And since *the essence expressed by the name is the definition*, as the Philosopher says,[4] such a name must be applied primarily to that which is put in the definition of the other things, and secondarily to these others according as they

1. 参见 *Perih.*, I (16a 3).
2. 参见 *De Div. Nom.*, I, 6 (PG 3, 596)
3. 参见 *De Myst. Theol.*, I, 2 (PG 3, 1000).
4. 参见 Aristotle, *Metaph.*, III, 7 (1012a 23).

approach more or less to the first. Thus, for instance, *healthy* applied to animals comes into the definition of *healthy* applied to medicine, which is called healthy as being the cause of health in the animal; and also into the definition of *healthy* which is applied to urine, which is called healthy in so far as it is the sign of the animal's health.

So it is that all names applied metaphorically to God are applied to creatures primarily rather than to God, because when said of God they mean only similitudes to such creatures. For as *smiling* applied to a field means only that the field in the beauty of its flowering is like to the beauty of the human smile by proportionate likeness, so the name of *lion* applied to God means only that God manifests strength in His works, as a lion in his. Thus it is clear that applied to God the signification of these names can be defined only from what is said of creatures.

But to other names not applied to God in a metaphorical sense, the same rule would apply if they were spoken of God as the cause only, as some have supposed.[1] For when it is said, *God is good*, it would then only mean, *God is the cause of the creature's goodness*; and thus the name *good* applied to God would include in its meaning the creature's goodness. Hence *good* would apply primarily to creatures rather than God. But, as was shown above, these names are applied to God not as the cause only, but also essentially. For the words, *God is good*, or *wise*, signify not only that He is the cause of wisdom or goodness, but that these exist in Him in a more excellent way. Hence as regards what the name signifies, these names are applied primarily to God rather than to creatures, because these perfections flow from God to creatures; but as regards the imposition of the names, they are primarily applied by us to creatures which we know first. Hence they have a mode of signification which belongs to creatures, as was said above.

---

1. 参见 Alain of Lille, *Theol. Reg.*, XXI; XXVI (PL 210, 631 ; 633).

Reply Obj. 1. This objection refers to the imposition of the name: to that extent it is true.

Reply Obj. 2. The same rule does not apply to metaphorical and to other names, as was said above.

Reply Obj. 3. This objection would be valid if these names were applied to God only as cause, and not also essentially, for instance, as *healthy* is applied to medicine.

Seventh Article
WHETHER NAMES WHICH IMPLY RELATION TO CREATURES ARE PREDICATED OF GOD TEMPORALLY?

We proceed thus to the Seventh Article: —

Objection 1. It seems that names which imply relation to creatures are not predicated of God temporally. For all such names signify the divine substance, as is universally held. Hence also Ambrose says that this name *Lord* is a name of power,[1] which is the divine substance; and *Creator*[2] signifies the action of God, which is His essence. Now the divine substance is not temporal, but eternal. Therefore these names are not applied to God temporally, but eternally.

Obj. 2. Further, that to which something applies temporally can be described as made; for what is white temporally is made white. But to be made does not apply to God. Therefore nothing can be predicated of God temporally.

Obj. 3. Further, if any names are applied to God temporally because they imply relation to creatures, the same rule holds good of all things that imply relation to creatures. But some names implying relation to creatures are spoken of God from eternity; for from eternity He knew and loved the creature, according to the word: *I have loved thee with*

---

1. 参见 *De Fide*, I (PL 16, 553).
2. Creator：造物主；天主

an everlasting love (*Jer.* xxxi. 3). Therefore also other names implying relation to creatures, as *Lord* and *Creator*, are applied to God from eternity.

Obj. 4. Further, names of this kind signify relation. Therefore that relation must be something in God, or in the creature only. But it cannot be that it is something in the creature only, for in that case God would be called *Lord* from the opposite relation which is in creatures; and nothing is named from its opposite. Therefore the relation must be something in God. But nothing temporal can be in God, for He is above time. Therefore these names are not applied to God temporally.

Obj. 5. Further, a thing is called relative from relation; for instance, lord from lordship, and white from whiteness. Therefore if the relation of lordship is not really in God, but only in idea, it follows that God is not really Lord, which is plainly false.

Obj. 6. Further, in relative things which are not simultaneous in nature, one can exist without the other; as a knowable thing can exist without the knowledge of it, as the Philosopher says.[1] But relative things which are said of God and creatures are not simultaneous in nature. Therefore a relation can be predicated of God to the creature even without the existence of the creature; and thus these names, *Lord* and *Creator*, are predicated of God from eternity, and not temporally.

On the contrary, Augustine says, that this relative appellation *Lord* is applied to God temporally.[2]

I answer that, Some names which import relation to creatures are applied to God temporally, and not from eternity.

To see this we must learn that some have said that relation is not a reality, but only an idea.[3] But this is plainly seen to be false from

1. 参见 Aristotle, *Cat.*, VII (7b 30).
2. 参见 *De Trin.*, V, 16 (PL 42, 922).
3. 参见 Cf. Averroes, *In Metaph.*, XII, comm. 19 (VIII, 1441r).— Cf. also St. Thomas, *De Pot.*, q. 8, a. 2.

the very fact that things themselves have a mutual natural order and relation. Nevertheless it is necessary to know that, since a relation needs two extremes, there are three conditions that make a relation to be real or logical. Sometimes from both extremes it is an idea only, as when a mutual order or relation can be between things only in the apprehension of reason; as when we say that *the same is the same as itself*. For the reason, by apprehending one thing twice, regards it as two; and thus it apprehends a certain relation of a thing to itself. And the same applies to relations between *being* and *non-being* formed by reason, inasmuch as it apprehends *non-being* as an extreme. The same is true of those relations that follow upon an act of reason, as genus and species, and the like.

Now there are other relations which are realities as regards both extremes, as when a relation exists between two things according to some reality that belongs to both. This is clear of all relations consequent upon quantity, as great and small, double and half, and the like; for there is quantity in both extremes. The same applies to relations consequent upon action and passion, as motive power and the movable thing, father and son, and the like.

Again, sometimes a relation in one extreme may be a reality, while in the other extreme it is only an idea. This happens whenever two extremes are not of one order, as sense and science refer, respectively, to sensible things and to knowable things; which, inasmuch as they are realities existing in nature, are outside the order of sensible and intelligible existence. Therefore, in science and in sense a real relation exists, because they are ordered either to the knowledge or to the sensible perception of things; whereas the things looked at in themselves are outside this order. Hence in them there is no real relation to science and sense, but only in idea, inasmuch as the intellect apprehends them as terms of the relations of science and sense. Hence, the Philosopher says that they are called relative, not because they are related to other things, but because others are related to them.[1] Likewise, *on the right* is not applied to a column, unless it stands on the right side of animal; which relation is not really in the column, but in the animal.

Since, therefore, God is outside the whole order of creation, and all creatures are ordered to Him, and not conversely, it is manifest that creatures are really related to God Himself; whereas in God there is no real relation to creatures, but a relation only in idea, inasmuch as creatures are related to Him. Thus there is nothing to prevent such names, which import relation to the creature, from being predicated of God temporally, not by reason of any change in Him, but by reason of the change in the creature; as a column is on the right of an animal, without change in itself, but because the animal has moved.

Reply Obj. 1. Some relative names are imposed to signify the relational ordinations themselves, as *master* and *servant*, *father* and *son*, and the like; and these are called relatives *in being* [*secundum esse*]. But others are imposed to signify the things from which follow certain relations, as the *mover* and the *moved*, the *head* and the *being that has a head*, and the like; and these are called relatives *in name* [*secundum dici*]. Thus, there is the same twofold difference in divine names. For some signify the relation itself to the creature, as *Lord*, and these do not signify the divine substance directly, but indirectly, in so far as they presuppose the divine substance; as dominion presupposes power, which is the divine substance. Others signify the divine essence directly, and the corresponding relation consequently; as *Savior*, *Creator*, and the like, signify the action of God, which is His essence. Yet both kinds of names are said of God temporally so far as they imply a relation either principally or consequently, but not so far as they signify the essence, either directly or indirectly.

Reply Obj. 2. Just as relations applied to God temporally are in God

---

1. 参见 *Metaph.*, IV, 15 (1021a 29).

only in our idea, so, *to become, or to be made* are applied to God only in idea, with no change in Him; as when we say, *Lord, Thou art become our refuge* (*Ps.* lxxxix. 1).

Reply Obj. 3. The operation of the intellect and will is in the operator, and therefore names signifying relations following upon the action of the intellect or will are applied to God from eternity; whereas those following upon the actions proceeding, according to our mode of thinking, to external effects are applied to God temporally, as *Savior, Creator*, and the like.

Reply Obj. 4. Relations signified by such names as are applied to God temporally are in God only in idea; but the opposite relations in creatures are real. Nor is it incongruous that God should be denominated from relations really existing in things, provided that the opposite relations be at the same time understood by us as existing in God, so that God is spoken of relatively to the creature inasmuch as the creature is related to Him; just as the Philosopher says that the object is said to be knowable relatively because knowledge relates to it.[1]

Reply Obj. 5. Since God is related to the creature for the reason that the creature is related to Him: and since the relation of subjection is real in the creature, it follows that God is Lord not in idea only, but in reality; for He is called Lord according to the manner in which the creature is subject to Him.

Reply Obj. 6. To know whether relations are simultaneous by nature or otherwise, it is not necessary to consider the order of things to which they belong but the meaning of the relations themselves. For if one includes another in its idea, and *vice versa*, then they are simultaneous by nature: as double and half, father and son, and the like. But if one includes another in its idea, and not *vice versa*, they

1. 参见 *Metaph.*, IV, 15 (1021a 30).

are not simultaneous by nature. This is the way that science and its object are related, for the *knowable* expresses a possibility, and *science* expresses a possible habit, or an act. Hence the concept *knowable* according to its mode of signification is prior to *science*; but if the knowable object becomes actually known, then it is simultaneous with science in act; for the known object is nothing as such unless the knowledge of it exists. Hence, though God is prior to the creature, still, because the signification of Lord includes the idea of a servant and *vice versa*, these two relative terms, *Lord* and *servant*, are simultaneous by nature. Hence God was not *Lord* until He had a creature subject to Himself.

Eighth Article
WHETHER THIS NAME *GOD* NAMES A NATURE?

We proceed thus to the Eighth Article: —

Objection 1. It seems that this name, *God*, does not name a nature. For Damascene says that *God* (Θεός) *is so called from* θεεῖυ which means to take care of, *and to cherish all things*; *or from* χἴθειυ, *that is, to burn, for our God is a consuming fire*; *or from* θεᾶσθαι, *which means to consider all things.*[1] But all these names belong to operation. Therefore this name *God* signifies His operation and not His nature.

Obj. 2. Further, a thing is named by us as we know it. But the divine nature is unknown to us. Therefore this name *God* does not signify the divine nature.

On the contrary, Ambrose says that *God* names a nature.[2]

I answer that, Whence a name is imposed, and what the name signifies are not always the same thing. For just as we know substance from its properties and operations, so we sometimes name a substance

1. 参见 *De Fide Orth.*, I, 9 (PG 94, 835).
2. 参见 *De Fide*, I, 1 (PL 16, 553).

from some operation or property: *e.g.*, we name the substance of a stone from a particular action, namely, that it hurts the foot [*lædit pedem*]; but still this name is not meant to signify the particular action, but the stone's substance. On the other hand, when the things in question are known to us in themselves, such as heat, cold, whiteness, and the like, then they are not named from other things. Hence, as regards such things, the meaning of the name and its source are the same.

Because therefore God is not known to us in His nature, but is made known to us from His operations or His effects, it is from these that we can name Him, as was said above; hence this name *God* is a name of operation so far as relates to the source of its meaning. For this name is imposed from His universal providence over all things; since all who speak of God intend to name *God* that being which exercises providence over all. Hence Dionysius says: *The Deity*[1] *watches over all with perfect providence and goodness.*[2] But though taken from this operation, this name *God* is imposed to signify the divine nature.

Reply Obj. 1. All that Damascene says refers to providence,[3] which is the source of the signification of the name *God*.

Reply Obj. 2. We can name a thing according to the knowledge we have of its nature from its properties and effects. Hence because we can know what stone is in itself from its property, this name *stone* signifies the nature of stone in itself; for it signifies the definition of stone, by which we know what it is, *for the essence which the name signifies is the definition*, as is said in *Metaph.* iv.[4] Now from the divine effects we cannot know the divine nature in itself, so as to know what it is; but

---

1. Deity：天主；天主性
2. 参见 *De Div. Nom.*, XII, 2 (PG 3,969).
3. 参见 *De Fide Orth.*, I, 9 (PG 94, 836).
4. 参见 Aristotle, *Metaph.*, III, 7 (1012a 23).

only by way of eminence, causality, and negation, as was stated above.[1] So it remains that the name *God* signifies the divine nature. For this name was imposed to signify something existing above all things, the principle of all things, and removed from all things; for this is what those who name God intend to signify.

Ninth Article
WHETHER THIS NAME *GOD* IS COMMUNICABLE?

We proceed thus to the Ninth Article: —

Objection 1. It seems that this name *God* is communicable. For whosoever shares in the thing signified by a name shares in the name itself. But this name *God* signifies the divine nature, which is communicable to others, according to the words, *He hath given us great and precious promises, that by these we may be made partakers of the divine nature* (*2 Pet.* i. 4). Therefore this name *God* can be communicated to others.

Obj. 2. Further, only proper names are not communicable. Now this name *God* is not a proper, but an appellative noun; which appears from the fact that it has a plural, according to the text, *I have said, You are gods* (*Ps.* lxxxi. 6). Therefore this name *God* is communicable.

Obj. 3. Further, this name *God* comes from operation, as was explained. But other names given to God from His operations or effects are communicable ;as *good*, *wise*, and the like. Therefore this name *God* is communicable.

On the contrary, It is written: *They gave the incommunicable*[2] *name to wood and stones* (*Wis.* xiv. 21), in reference to the divine name. Therefore this name *God* is incommunicable.

I answer that, A name is communicable in two ways, properly, and

---

1. 参见 Q. 12, a. 12.
2. communicable：通用的；共享的

through likeness. It is properly communicable if its whole signification can be given to many; through likeness it is communicable according to some part of the signification of the name. For instance, this name *lion* is properly communicated to all beings of the same nature as *lion*; through likeness it is communicable to those who share in something of the lion's nature, as for instance courage, or strength, and such are called lions metaphorically. To know, however, what names are properly communicable, we must consider that every form existing in a singular subject, by which it is individuated[1], is common to many either in reality or at least in idea; as human nature is common to many in reality and in idea, whereas the nature of the sun is not common to many in reality, but only in idea. For the nature of the sun can be understood as existing in many subjects; and the reason is because the intellect understands the nature of every species by abstraction from the singular. Hence, to be in one singular subject or in many is outside the idea of the nature of the species. So, given the idea of a species, it can be understood as existing in many. But the singular, from the fact that it is singular, is divided off from all others. Hence every name imposed to signify any singular thing is incommunicable both in reality and idea: for the plurality of this individual thing cannot be conceived. Hence no name signifying any individual thing is properly communicable to many, but only by way of likeness; as a person can be called *Achilles* metaphorically, because he may possess something of the characteristics of Achilles, such as strength. On the other hand, forms which are individualed not by any *suppositum*, but by and of themselves, as being subsisting forms, if understood as they are in themselves, could not be communicable either in reality or in idea; but only perhaps by way of likeness, as was said of individuals. But since we are unable to understand simple

1. individuated：赋予个性的；个性化的

self-subsisting forms as they really are, and we understand them after the manner of composite things having forms in matter, therefore, as was said in the first article, we give them concrete names signifying a nature existing in some *suppositum*. Hence, so far as concerns names, the same situation applies to names we impose to signify the nature of composite things as to names given by us to signify simple subsisting natures.

Since, then, this name *God* is given to signify the divine nature, as was stated above, and since the divine nature cannot be multiplied as was shown above,[1] it follows that this name *God* is incommunicable in reality, but communicable in human opinion; just as in the same way this name *sun* would be communicable according to the opinion of those who say there are many suns. Therefore, it is written: *You served them who by nature are not gods* (*Gal.* iv. 8); and the *Gloss* adds, *Gods not in nature, but in human opinion*,[2] Nevertheless, this name *God* is communicable, not in its whole signification, but in some part of it by way of some likeness; so that they are called gods who share in divinity by likeness, according to the text, *I have said, You are gods* (*Ps.* lxxxi. 6).

But if any name were given to signify God not as to His nature but as to His *suppositum*, accordingly as He is considered as *this something*, that name would be absolutely incommunicable; as, for instance, perhaps the Tetragrammaton[3] among the Hebrews; and this is like giving to the sun a name which signifies this individual one.

Reply Obj. 1. The divine nature is communicable only according to the participation of some likeness.

Reply Obj. 2. This name *God* is an appellative name, and not a proper name, for it signifies the divine nature as residing in some one

---

1. 参见 Q. 11, a. 3.
2. 参见 Peter Lombard, *In Gal.*, super IV, 8 (PL 192, 139) ; cf. *Glossa interl.* (VI, 84v).
3. Tetragrammaton：天主之名；四个字母的神名

possessing it; although God Himself in reality is neither universal nor particular. For names do not follow upon the mode of being in things, but upon the mode of being that things have in our knowledge. And yet *God* is incommunicable in reality, as was said above concerning the name *sun*.

Reply Obj. 3. These names *good*, *wise*, and the like, are imposed from the perfections proceeding from God to creatures; but they are not meant to signify the divine nature, but rather the perfections themselves absolutely; and therefore even in reality they are communicable to many. But this name *God* is given to God from His own proper operation, which we experience continually, to signify the divine nature.

Tenth Article
WHETHER THIS NAME *GOD* IS APPLIED TO GOD UNIVOCALLY, BY NATURE, BY PARTICIPATION, AND ACCORDING TO OPINION?

We proceed thus to the Tenth Article: —

Objection 1. It seems that this name *God* is applied to God univocally by nature, by participation, and according to opinion. For where a diverse signification exists, there is no contradiction of affirmation and negation; for equivocation prevents contradiction. But a Catholic[1] who says: *An idol is not God*, contradicts a pagan who says: *An idol is God*. Therefore *God* in both instances is said univocally.

Obj. 2. Further, as an idol is God in opinion, and not in truth, so the enjoyment of carnal pleasures is called happiness in opinion, and not in truth. But this name *beatitude* is applied univocally to this opined happiness, and also to true happiness. Therefore this name *God* is also

1. Catholic：大公的；天主教徒；天主教的

applied univocally to the true God and to God according to opinion.

Obj. 3. Further, those names are called univocal which are one in meaning. Now when a Catholic says: *There is one God*, he understands by the name *God* an omnipotent[1] being, and one to be venerated above all things; while the pagan understands the same when he says: *An idol is God*. Therefore this name *God* is applied univocally to both.

On the contrary, That which is in the intellect is the likeness of what is in the thing, as is said in *Periherm.* i.[2] But the word *animal*, applied to a true animal and to a picture of one, is used equivocally. Therefore this name *God*, when applied to the true God and to God in opinion, is applied equivocally.

Further, No one can signify what he does not know. But the pagan does not know the divine nature. So when he says *an idol is God*, he does not signify the true Deity. On the other hand, a Catholic signifies the true Deity when he says there is one God. Therefore this name God is not applied univocally, but equivocally, to the true God and to God according to opinion.

I answer that, This name *God* in the three aforesaid significations is taken neither univocally nor equivocally, but analogically. This is apparent from this reason:— Univocal names have absolutely the same meaning, while equivocal names have absolutely diverse meanings; whereas in analogicals, a name taken in one signification must be placed in the definition of the same name taken in other significations; as, for instance, *being* which is applied to *substance* is placed in the definition of being as applied to *accident*; and *healthy* applied to animal is placed in the definition of healthy as applied to urine and medicine. For of health in the animal urine is the sign and medicine the cause.

The same applies to the question at issue. For this name *God*, as signifying the true God, includes the idea of God when it is used to

---

1. omnipotent：全能的；无所不能的
2. 参见 Aristotle, *Perih.*, I (16a 5).

signify God according to opinion or by participation. For when we name anyone god by participation, we understand by the name *god* some likeness of the true God. Likewise, when we call an idol *god*, by this name god we understand that something is signified which men think to be God. It is thus manifest that *God* has different meanings, but that one of them is present in the others. Hence it is manifestly said analogically.

Reply Obj. 1. The multiplicity of names does not depend on the predication of a name, but on its signification: for this name *man*, of whomsoever it is predicated, whether truly or falsely, is predicated in one sense. But it would be multiplied if by the name *man* we meant to signify diverse things; for instance, if one meant to signify by this name *man* what man really is, and another meant to signify by the same name a stone, or something else. Hence it is evident that a Catholic saying that an idol is not God contradicts the pagan asserting that it is God; because each of them uses this name *God* to signify the true God. For when the pagan says an idol is God, he does not use this name as meaning God in opinion, for he would then speak the truth, as also Catholics sometimes use the name in that sense, as in the Psalm, *All the gods of the Gentiles are demons* (*Ps.* xcv. 5).

The same remark applies to the second and third Objections. For those arguments proceed according to a diversity in the predication of a name, and not according to a diverse signification.

Reply Obj. 4. *Animal* applied to a true and a pictured animal is not said in a purely equivocal way: for the Philosopher takes equivocal names in a large sense, according to which they include analogous names,[1] because *being* as well, which is predicated analogically, is something said to be predicated equivocally of diverse predicaments.

Reply Obj. 5. Neither a Catholic nor a pagan knows the very nature

---

1. 参见 *Cat.*, I (1a 1).

of God as it is in itself; but each one knows it according to some idea of causality, or excellence, or remotion as was said above.[1] So a pagan can take this name *God* in the same way when he says *an idol is God*, as the Catholic does in saying *an idol is not God*. But if there were someone entirely ignorant of God, he could not even name Him; unless, perhaps, as we utter names the meaning of which we do not know.

Eleventh Article

WHETHER THIS NAME, *HE WHO IS*, IS THE MOST PROPER NAME OF GOD?

We proceed thus to the Eleventh Article: —

Objection 1. It seems that this name *HE WHO IS* is not the most proper name of God. For this name *God* is an incommunicable name. But this name, *HE WHO IS*[2], is not an incommunicable name. Therefore this name *HE WHO IS* is not the most proper name of God.

Obj. 2. Further, Dionysius says that *the name Good excellently manifests all the processions of God*.[3] But it especially belongs to God to be the universal source of all things. Therefore this name *GOOD* is supremely proper to God, and not this name *HE WHO IS*.

Obj. 3. Further, every divine name seems to imply relation to creatures, for God is known to us only through creatures. But this name *HE WHO IS* imports no relation to creatures. Therefore this name *HE WHO IS* is not the most proper name of God.

On the contrary, It is written that when Moses asked, *If they should say to me, What is His name? what shall I say to them?* the Lord answered him, *Thus shalt thou say to them, HE WHO IS hath sent me to you* (*Exod*.iii. 13, 14). Therefore this name, *HE WHO IS*, is the most proper name of

---

1. 参见 Q. 12, a. 12.
2. HE WHO IS.：祂是自有者。
3. 参见 *De Div. Nom.*, III, 1 (PG 3, 680).

God.

I answer that, This name, *HE WHO IS,* is the most proper name of God for three reasons:—

First, because of its signification. For it does not signify some form, but being itself. Hence, since the being of God is His very essence (which can be said of no other being),[1] it is clear that among other names this one most properly names God; for everything is named according to its essence.

Secondly, because of its universality. For all other names are either less universal, or, if convertible with it, add something above it at least in idea; hence in a certain way they inform and determine it. Now in this life our intellect cannot know the essence itself of God as it is in itself, but however it may determine what it understands about God, it falls short of what God is in Himself. Therefore the less determinate the names are, and the more universal and absolute they are, the more properly are they applied to God. Hence Damascene says that, HE WHO IS *is the principal of all names applied to God; for comprehending all in itself, it contains being itself as an infinite and indeterminate sea of substance.*[2] Now by any other name some mode of substance is expressed determinately, whereas this name HE WHO IS determines no mode of being, but is related indeterminately to all; and that is why it names the *infinite ocean of substance.*

Thirdly, from its consignification, for it signifies being *in the present*; and this above all properly applies to God, *whose being knows not past or future,* as Augustine says.[3]

Reply Obj. 1. This name HE WHO IS is the name of God more properly than this name *God,* both as regards its source, namely, being,

1. 参见 Q. 3, a. 4.
2. 参见 *De Fide Orth.*, I, 9 (PG 94, 836).
3. 参见 Cf. Peter Lombard, *Sent.*, I, viii, 1 (I, 58); St. Isidore, *Etymol.*, VII, 1 (PL 82, 261); Rhabanus Maurus, *In Exod.*, I, 6 (PL 108, 21).

and as regards the mode of signification and consignification, as was said above. But as regards the object intended to be signified by the name, this name *God* is more proper, as it is imposed to signify the divine nature; and still more proper is the name Tetragrammaton, imposed to signify the substance itself of God, incommunicable and, if one may so speak, singular.

Reply Obj. 2. This name *Good* is the principal name of God in so far as He is a cause, but not absolutely; for absolutely speaking, *being* is understood by us before *cause*.

Reply Obj. 3. It is not necessary that all the divine names should import relation to creatures; it suffices that they be imposed from some perfections flowing from God to creatures. Among these the first is being, from which comes this name, HE WHO IS.

Twelfth Article
WHETHER AFFIRMATIVE PROPOSITIONS CAN BE FORMED ABOUT GOD?

We proceed thus to the Twelfth Article: —

Objection 1. It seems that affirmative propositions cannot be formed about God. For Dionysius says that *negations about God are true*; *but affirmations are vague.*[1]

Obj. 2. Further, Boethius says that *a simple form cannot be a subject.*[2] But God is most absolutely a simple form, as was shown.[3] Therefore He cannot be a subject. But everything about which an affirmative proposition is made is taken as a subject. Therefore an affirmative proposition cannot be formed about God.

Obj. 3. Further, every intellect is false which understands a thing

1. 参见 *De Cael. Hier.*, II, 3 (PG 3, 140).
2. 参见 *De Trin.*, II (PL 64, 1250).
3. 参见 Q. 3, a. 7.

otherwise than as it is. But God has being without any composition, as was shown above.[1] Therefore, since every intellect which makes an affirmation understands something as composite, it seems that a true affirmative proposition about God cannot be made.

On the contrary, What is of faith cannot be false. But some affirmative propositions are of faith; as that God is Three and One , and that He is omnipotent. Therefore true affirmative propositions can be formed about God.

I answer that, Affirmative propositions can be truly formed about God. To prove this we must observe that in every true affirmative proposition the predicate and the subject must signify in some way the same thing in reality, and diverse things in idea. And this appears to be the case both in propositions which have an accidental predicate and in those which have a substantial predicate. For it is manifest that *man* and *white* are the same in subject, and diverse in idea; for the idea of man is one thing, and that of whiteness is another. The same applies when I say, *man is an animal*, since the same thing which is man is truly animal; for in the same *suppositum* there is both a sensible nature by reason of which he is called animal, and the rational nature by reason of which he is called man; hence, here again, predicate and subject are the same as to *suppositum*, but diverse as to idea. But in propositions where the same thing is predicated of itself, the same rule in some way applies, inasmuch as the intellect considers as the *suppositum* what it places in the subject; and what it places in the predicate it considers as the nature of the form existing in the *suppositum*, according to the saying that *predicates are taken formally, and subjects materially*. To this diversity in idea corresponds the plurality of predicate and subject, while the intellect signifies the identity of the thing by the composition itself.

---

1. 参见 Q. 3, a. 7.

God, however, as considered in Himself, is altogether one and simple, yet our intellect knows Him according to diverse conceptions because it cannot see Him as He is in Himself. Nevertheless, although it understands Him under diverse conceptions, it yet knows that absolutely one and the same reality corresponds to its conceptions. Therefore the plurality of predicate and subject represents the plurality of idea; and the intellect represents the unity by composition.

Reply Obj. 1. Dionysius says that affirmations about God are vague or, according to another translation, *incongruous*, inasmuch as no name can be applied to God according to its mode of signification,[1] as was said above.

Reply Obj. 2. Our intellect cannot apprehend simple subsisting forms as they really are in themselves; but it apprehends them after the manner of composite things in which there is something taken as subject and something that is inherent. Therefore it apprehends the simple form as a subject and attributes something else to it.

Reply Obj. 3. This proposition, *The intellect understanding anything otherwise than it is, is false*, can be taken in two senses, according as this adverb *otherwise* modifies the verb *to understand* from the standpoint of the thing understood, or from the standpoint of the one who understands. Taken as referring to the thing understood, the proposition is true, and the meaning is: Any intellect which understands that a thing is otherwise than it is, is false. But this does not hold in the present case, because our intellect, in forming a proposition about God, does not affirm that He is composite, but that He is simple. But taken as referring to the one who understands, the proposition is false. For our intellect understands in one way, and things are in another. Thus it is clear that our intellect understands material things below itself in an immaterial way; not

1. 参见 *De Cael. Hier.*, II,3 (PG 3,140).

that it understands them to be immaterial things: but its way of understanding is immaterial. Likewise, when it understands simple things above itself, it understands them according to its own way, which is composite; yet not so as to understand them to be composite things. And thus our intellect is not false in composing a judgment concerning God.

Question XIV
ON GOD'S KNOWLEDGE
(*In Sixteen Articles*)

HAVING considered what belongs to the divine substance, we have now to treat of what belongs to God's operation. And since one kind of operation is immanent, and another kind of operation proceeds to an exterior effect, we shall treat first of knowledge and of will[1] (for understanding abides in the intelligent agent, and will in the one who wills); and afterwards of the power of God, which is taken to be the principle of the divine operation as proceeding to an exterior effect.[2] Now because to understand is a kind of life, after treating of the divine knowledge, we must consider the divine life.[3] And as knowledge concerns truth, we shall have to consider truth[4] and falsehood.[5] Further, as everything known is in the knower, and the essences of things as existing in the knowledge of God are called *ideas*, to the consideration of knowledge there will have to be added a consideration of ideas.[6]

Concerning knowledge, there are sixteen points for inquiry: (1) Whether there is knowledge in God? (2) Whether God understands Himself? (3) Whether He comprehends Himself? (4) Whether His understanding is His substance? (5) Whether He understands other

---

1. 参见 Q. 19.
2. 参见 Q. 25.
3. 参见 Q. 18.
4. 参见 Q. 16.
5. 参见 Q. 17.
6. 参见 Q. 15.

things besides Himself? (6) Whether He has a proper knowledge of them? (7) Whether the knowledge of God is discursive? (8) Whether the knowledge of God is the cause of things? (9) Whether God has knowledge of non-existing things? (10) Whether He has knowledge of evil? (11) Whether He has knowledge of individual things? (12) Whether He knows the infinite? (13) Whether He knows future contingent things? (14) Whether He knows whatever is enunciable? (15) Whether the knowledge of God is variable? (16) Whether God has speculative or practical knowledge of things?

First Article
WHETHER THERE IS KNOWLEDGE IN GOD?

We proceed thus to the First Article: —

Objection 1. It seems that in God there is not knowledge [*scientia*]. For knowledge is a habit; and habit does not belong to God, since it is the mean between potentiality and act. Therefore knowledge is not in God.

Obj. 2. Further, since science is about conclusions, it is a kind of knowledge caused by something else, namely, the knowledge of principles. But nothing caused is in God; therefore science is not in God.

Obj. 3. Further, all knowledge is universal, or particular. But in God there is no universal or particular.[1] Therefore there is no knowledge in God.

On the contrary, The Apostle says, *O the depth of the riches of the wisdom and of the knowledge of God* (*Rom.* xi. 33).

I answer that, In God there exists the most perfect knowledge. To prove this, we must note that knowing beings are distinguished from

1. 参见 Q. 13, a. 9, ad 2.

non-knowing beings in that the latter possess only their own form; whereas the knowing being is naturally adapted to have also the form of some other thing, for the species of the thing known is in the knower. Hence it is manifest that the nature of a non-knowing being is more contracted and limited; whereas the nature of knowing beings has a greater amplitude and extension. That is why the Philosopher says that *the soul is in a sense all things*.[1] Now the contraction of a form comes through the matter. Hence, as we have said above, according as they are the more immaterial, forms approach more nearly to a kind of infinity.[2] Therefore it is clear that the immateriality[3] of a thing is the reason why it is cognitive, and that according to the mode of immateriality is the mode of cognition. Hence, it is said in *De Anima* ii. that plants do not know, because of their materiality.[4] But sense is cognitive because it can receive species free from matter; and the intellect is still further cognitive, because it is more *separated from matter and unmixed*, as is said in *De Anima* iii.[5] Since therefore God is in the highest degree of immateriality, as was stated above,[6] it follows that He occupies the highest place in knowledge.

Reply Obj. 1. Because perfections flowing from God to creatures exist in a higher state in God Himself,[7] whenever a name taken from any created perfection is attributed to God, there must be separated from its signification anything that belongs to the imperfect mode proper to creatures. Hence knowledge is not a quality in God, nor a habit; but substance and pure act.

Reply Obj. 2. Whatever is divided and multiplied in creatures

---

1. 参见 *De An.*, III, 8 (431b 21).
2. 参见 Q. 7, a. 2.
3. immateriality：无形之物；非物质
4. 参见 Aristotle, *De An.*, II, 12 (424a 32).
5. 参见 *Op. cit.*, III, 4 (429a 18; b5).
6. 参见 Q. 7, a. 1.
7. 参见 Q. 4, a. 2.

exists in God simply and unitedly as was said above.[1] Now man has different kinds of knowledge, according to the different objects of his knowledge. He has *understanding* as regards the knowledge of principles; he has *science* as regards knowledge of conclusions; he has *wisdom*, according as he knows the highest cause; he has *counsel* or *prudence*, according as he knows what is to be done. But God knows all these by one simple act of knowledge, as will be shown. Hence the simple knowledge of God can be named by all these names; in such a way, however, that there must be removed from each of them, so far as they are predicated of God, everything that savors of imperfection; and everything that expresses perfection is to be retained in them. Hence it is said, *With Him is wisdom and strength, He hath counsel and understanding* (*Job* xii. 13).

Reply Obj. 3. Knowledge is according to the mode of the one who knows, for the thing known is in the knower according to the mode of the knower. Now since the mode of the divine essence is higher than that of creatures, divine knowledge does not exist in God after the mode of created knowledge, so as to be universal or particular, or habitual, or potential, or existing according to any such mode.

Second Article
WHETHER GOD UNDERSTANDS HIMSELF?

We proceed thus to the Second Article: —

Objection 1. It seems that God does not understand Himself. For it is said in the *Book of Causes*, *Every knower who knows his own essence returns completely to his own essence.*[2] But God does not go out from His own essence, nor is He moved at all; thus He cannot return to His own essence. Therefore He does not know His own essence.

---

1. 参见 Q. 13, a. 4.
2. 参见 *De Causis*, XV (p. 173).

Obj. 2. Further, *to understand is a kind of passion and becoming*, as the Philosopher says;[1] and knowledge also is a kind of assimilation to the object known, and the thing known is the perfection of the knower. But nothing becomes, or suffers, or is made perfect by itself; *nor*, as Hilary says, *is a thing its own likeness*.[2] Therefore God does not know Himself.

Obj. 3. Further, we are like to God chiefly in our intellect, because we are in the image of God in our mind, as Augustine says.[3] But our intellect understands itself only as it understands other things, as is said in *De Animu* iii.[4] Therefore God understands Himself only so far perchance as He understands other things.

On the contrary, It is written: *The things that are of God no man knoweth, but the Spirit of God* (*I Cor.* ii. 11).

I answer that, God understands Himself through Himself. In proof whereof it must be known that, although in operations which pass to an external effect, the object of the operation, which is taken as the term, exists outside the operator, nevertheless, in operations that remain in the operator, the object signified as the term of operation resides in the operator; and according as it is in the operator is the operation actual. Hence the Philosopher says that *the sensible in act is the sense in act, and the intelligible in act is the intellect in act*.[5] For the reason why we actually feel or know a thing is because our intellect or sense is actually informed by the sensible or intelligible species. And because of this only, it follows that sense or intellect is distinct from the sensible or intelligible object, since both are in potentiality.

Since therefore God has nothing in Him of potentiality, but is pure act, His intellect and its object must be altogether the same; so

1. 参见 *De An.*, III, 4 (429b 24); 7 (431a 6).
2. 参见 *De Trin.*,III, 23 (PL 10, 92).
3. 参见 *De Genesi ad Litt.*, VII, 12 (PL 34, 347); *De Trin.*, XV, 1(PL 42, 1057).
4. 参见 Aristotle, *De An.*, III, 4 (430a 2).
5. 参见 *Op. cit.*, III, 2 (426a 16); 4 (430a 3).

that He neither is without the intelligible species, as is the case with our intellect when it understands potentially, nor does the intelligible species differ from the substance of the divine intellect, as it differs in our intellect when it understands actually; but the intelligible species itself is the divine intellect itself, and thus God understands Himself through Himself.

Reply Obj. 1. To return to its own essence means only that a thing subsists in itself. Inasmuch as the form perfects the matter by giving it being, it is in a certain way diffused in it; and it returns to itself inasmuch as it has being in itself. Therefore, those cognitive powers which are not subsisting, but are the acts of organs, do not know themselves, as in the case of each of the senses; whereas those cognitive powers which are subsisting know themselves, and this is why it is said in the *Book of Causes* that *whoever knows his essence returns to it.*[1] Now it supremely belongs to God to be self-subsisting. Hence, according to this mode of speaking, He supremely returns to His own essence and knows Himself.

Reply Obj. 2. Becoming and passion are taken equivocally when to *understand is described as a kind of becoming or passion, as is stated in De Anima* iii.[2] For to understand is not the motion that is an act of something imperfect passing from one state to another, but it is an act, existing in the agent itself, of something perfect. Likewise, that the intellect is perfected by the intelligible object, *i.e.*, is assimilated to it, this belongs to an intellect which is sometimes in potentiality; because the fact of its being in a state of potentiality makes it differ from the intelligible object and assimilates it thereto through the intelligible species, which is the likeness of the thing understood, and makes it to be perfected thereby, as potentiality is perfected by act. On the other hand, the divine intellect, which is in no way in potentiality, is not

1. 参见 *De Causis*, XV (p. 173).
2. 参见 Aristotle, *De An.*, III, 4 (429b 24); 7 (431a 6).

perfected by the intelligible object, nor is it assimilated thereto, but is its own perfection and its own intelligible object.

Reply Obj. 3. Its physical being does not belong to primary matter, which is a potentiality, unless it is reduced to act by a form. Now our possible intellect has the same relation to intelligible objects as primary matter has to physical things; for it is in potentiality as regards intelligible objects, just as primary matter is to physical things. Hence our possible intellect can be exercised concerning intelligible objects only so far as it is perfected by the intelligible species of something; and thus it understands itself by an intelligible species, in the same way that it understands other things: for it is manifest that by knowing the intelligible object it understands also its own act of understanding, and by this act knows the intellectual power. But God is as pure act both in the order of being, as also in the order of intelligible objects; therefore He understands Himself through Himself.

Third Article
WHETHER GOD COMPREHENDS HIMSELF?

We proceed thus to the Third Article: —

Objection 1. It seems that God does not comprehend Himself. For Augustine says, that *whatever comprehends itself is finite to itself.*[1] But God is in all ways infinite. Therefore He does not comprehend Himself.

Obj. 2. If it be said that God is infinite to us, and finite to Himself, it can be urged to the contrary, that everything in God is truer than it is in us. If therefore God is finite to Himself, but infinite to us, then God is more truly finite than infinite; which is against what was laid down above.[2] Therefore God does not comprehend Himself.

On the contrary, Augustine says, *Everything that understands itself,*

---

1. 参见 *Lib. 83 Quaest.*, q. 15 (PL 40, 15).
2. 参见 Q. 7, a. 1.

comprehends itself.[1] But God understands Himself. Therefore He comprehends Himself.

I answer that, God comprehends Himself perfectly, as can be thus proved. A thing is said to be comprehended when the end of the knowledge of it is attained, and this is accomplished when it is known as perfectly as it is knowable. Thus, a demonstrable proposition is comprehended when known by demonstration, not, however, when it is known by some probable argument. Now it is manifest that God knows Himself as perfectly as He is perfectly knowable. For everything is knowable according to the mode of its actuality, since a thing is not known according as it is in potentiality, but in so far as it is in actuality, as said in *Metaph.* ix.[2] Now the power of God in knowing is as great as His actuality in existing; because it is from the fact that He is in act and free from all matter and potentiality, that God is cognitive, as was shown above. Whence it is manifest that He knows Himself as much as He is knowable; and for that reason He perfectly comprehends Himself.

Reply Obj. 1. The strict meaning of *comprehension* signifies that one thing possesses and includes another; and in this sense everything comprehended is finite, as also is everything included in another. But God is not said to be comprehended by Himself in this sense, as if His intellect were another reality apart from Himself which contained and included Him; such ways of speaking are rather to be taken by way of negation. For just as God is said to be in Himself inasmuch as He is not contained by anything outside of Himself; so He is said to be comprehended by Himself inasmuch as nothing in Himself is hidden from Him. For Augustine says that *The whole is comprehended when seen, if it is seen in such a way that nothing of it is hidden from the seer.*[3]

1. 参见 *Lib. 83 Quaest.*, q. 15 (PL 40, 15).
2. 参见 Aristotle, *Metaph.*, VIII, 9 (1051a 31).
3. 参见 *Epist.* CXLVII, 9 (PL 33, 606).

Reply Obj. 2. When it is said, *God is finite to Himself*, this is to be understood according to a certain proportional likeness, because He has the same relation in not exceeding His intellect, as anything finite has in not exceeding a finite intellect. But God is not to be called finite to Himself in the sense that He understands Himself to be something finite.

Fourth Article
WHETHER THE ACT OF GOD'S INTELLECT IS HIS SUBSTANCE?

We proceed thus to the Fourth Article: —

Objection 1. It seems that the act of God's intellect is not His substance. For to understand is an operation. But an operation signifies something proceeding from the operator. Therefore the act of God's intellect is not His substance.

Obj. 2. Further, to understand one's act of understanding, is to understand something that is neither great nor chiefly understood, but secondary and accessory. If therefore God be His own act of understanding, His act of understanding will be as when we understand our act of understanding: and thus God's act of understanding will not be something great.

Obj. 3. Further, every act of understanding involves understanding something. When therefore God understands Himself, if He Himself is not distinct from this act of understanding, He understands that He understands, and that He understands that He understands Himself; and so on to infinity. Therefore the act of God's intellect is not His substance.

On the contrary, Augustine says, *In God to be is the same as to be wise.*[1] But to be wise is the same thing as to understand. Therefore in God

---

1. 参见 *De Trin.*, VII, 2; VI, 4 (PL 42, 936; 927).

to be is the same thing as to understand. But God's being is His substance, as was shown above.[1] Therefore the act of God's intellect is His substance.

I answer that, It must be said that the act of God's intellect is His substance. For if His act of understanding were other than His substance, then something else, as the Philosopher says,[2] would be the act and perfection of the divine substance, to which the divine substance would be related as potentiality is to act; which is altogether impossible, because the act of understanding is the perfection and act of the one understanding. Let us now consider how this is. As was laid down above, to understand is not an act passing to anything extrinsic, but it remains in the operator as his own act and perfection ;as being is the perfection of the one existing: for just as being follows on the form so in like manner to understand follows on the intelligible species. Now in God there is no form which is something other than His being, as was shown above.[3] Hence, as His essence itself is also His intelligible species, it necessarily follows that His act of understanding must be His essence and His being.

Thus it follows from all the foregoing that in God intellect, the object understood, the intelligible species, and His act of understanding are entirely one and the same. Hence, when God is said to be understanding, no multiplicity is attached to His substance.

Reply Obj. 1. To understand is not an operation proceeding out of the operator, but remaining in him.

Reply Obj. 2. When that act of understanding which is not subsistent is understood, something great is not understood; as when we understand our act of understanding; and so this cannot be likened to the act of the divine understanding which is subsistent.

1. 参见 Q. 3, a. 4.
2. 参见 *Metaph.*, XI, 9(1074b 18).
3. 参见 Q. 3, a. 4.

Thus appears the *Reply to Obj.* 3. For the act of divine understanding, which subsists in itself, belongs to its very self and is not another's; hence it need not proceed to infinity.

Fifth Article
WHETHER GOD KNOWS THINGS OTHER THAN HIMSELF?

We proceed thus to the Fifth Article: —

Objection 1. It seems that God does not know other things besides Himself. For all other things but God are outside of God. But Augustine says that *God does not behold anything out of Himself.*[1] Therefore He does not know things other than Himself.

Obj. 2. Further, the object understood is the perfection of the one who understands. If therefore God understands other things besides Himself, something else will be the perfection of God, and will be nobler than He; which is impossible.

Obj. 3. Further, the act of understanding is specified by the intelligible object, as is every other act from its own object. Hence the intellectual act is so much the nobler, the nobler the object understood. But God is His own intellectual act, as is clear from what has been said. If therefore God understands anything other than Himself, then God Himself is specified by something other than Himself; which cannot be. Therefore He does not understand things other than Himself.

On the contrary, It is written: *All things are naked and open to His eyes* (*Heb.* iv. 13).

I answer that, God necessarily knows things other than Himself. For it is manifest that He perfectly understands Himself; otherwise His being would not be perfect, since His being is His act of

---

1. 参见 *Lib. 83 Quaest.*, q. 46 (PL 40, 30).

understanding. Now if anything is perfectly known, it follows of necessity that its power is perfectly known. But the power of anything can be perfectly known only by knowing to what that power extends. Since, therefore, the divine power extends to other things by the very fact that it is the first effective cause of all things, as is clear from the aforesaid,[1] God must necessarily know things other than Himself. And this appears still more plainly if we add that the very being of the first efficient cause — viz., God — is His own act of understanding. Hence whatever effects pre-exist in God, as in the first cause, must be in His act of understanding, and they must be there in an intelligible way: for everything which is in another is in it according to the mode of that in which it is.

Now in order to know how God knows things other than Himself, we must consider that a thing is known in two ways: in itself, and in another. A thing is known *in itself* when it is known by the proper species adequate to the knowable object itself; as when the eye sees a man through the species of a man. A thing is seen *in another* through the species of that which contains it; as when a part is seen in the whole through the species of the whole, or when a man is seen in a mirror through the species of the mirror, or by any other way by which one thing is seen in another.

So we say that God sees Himself in Himself, because He sees Himself through His essence; and He sees other things, not in themselves, but in Himself, inasmuch as His essence contains the likeness of things other than Himself.

Reply Obj. 1. The passage of Augustine in which it is said that God *sees nothing outside Himself* is not to be taken in such a way, as if God saw nothing that was outside Himself, but in the sense that what is outside Himself He does not see except in Himself, as was explained

---

1. 参见 Q. 2, a. 3

above.

Reply Obj. 2. The object understood is a perfection of the one understanding, not by its substance, but by its species, according to which it is in the intellect as its form and perfection. For, as is said in *De Anima* iii,[1] *a stone is not in the soul, but its species.* Now those things which are other than God are understood by God inasmuch as the essence of God contains their species, as was explained above; and hence it does not follow that anything is the perfection of the divine intellect other than the divine essence.

*Reply Obj.*3. The intellectual act is not specified by what is understood in another, but by the principal object understood in which other things are understood. For the intellectual act is specified by its object inasmuch as the intelligible form is the principle of the intellectual operation, since every operation is specified by the form which is its principle of operation, as heating by heat. Hence the intellectual operation is specified by that intelligible form which makes the intellect to be in act. And this is the species of the principal thing understood, which in God is nothing but His own essence in which all the species of things are comprehended. Hence it does not follow that the divine intellectual act, or rather God Himself, is specified by anything other than the divine essence itself.

Sixth Article
WHETHER GOD KNOWS THINGS OTHER THAN HIMSELF BY PROPER KNOWLEDGE ?

We proceed thus to the Sixth Article: —

Objection 1. It seems that God does not know things other than Himself by proper knowledge. For, as was shown, God knows things

---

1. 参见 Aristotle, *De An.*, III, 8 (431b 29).

other than Himself according as they are in Him. But other things are in Him as in their common and universal first cause, and are therefore known by God as in their first and universal cause. This is to know them by general, and not by proper, knowledge. Therefore God knows things besides Himself by general, and not by proper, knowledge.

Obj. 2. Further, the created essence is as distant from the divine essence, as the divine essence is distant from the created essence. But the divine essence cannot be known through the created essence, as was said above.[1] Therefore neither can the created essence be known through the divine essence. Thus, as God knows only by His essence, it follows that He does not know what the creature is in its essence, so as to know *what it is*, which is to have a proper knowledge of it.

Obj. 3. Further, proper knowledge of a thing can come only through its proper likeness. But as God knows all things by His essence, it seems that He does not know each thing by its proper likeness; for one thing cannot be the proper likeness of many and diverse things. Therefore God has not a proper knowledge of things, but a general knowledge; for to know things otherwise than by their proper likeness is to have only a common knowledge of them.

On the contrary, To have a proper knowledge of things is to know them not only in general, but as they are distinct from each other. Now God knows things in that manner. Hence it is written that He reaches *even to the division of the soul and the spirit, of the joints also and the marrow, and is a discerner of the thoughts and intents of the heart; neither is there any creature invisible in His sight* (*Heb.* iv. 12, 13).

I answer that, Some have erred on this point, saying that God knows things other than Himself only in general, that is, only as beings.[2] For as fire, if it knew itself as the principle of heat, would know the nature of heat, and all things else in so far as they are hot; so God, through

---

1. 参见 Q. 12, a. 2.
2. 参见 Attributed to Averroes by St. Thomas. *In I Sent.*, d. xxxv, q. 1 a. 3.

knowing Himself as the source of being, knows the nature of being, and all other things in so far as they are beings.

But this cannot be. For to know a thing in general, and not in particular, is to have an imperfect knowledge of it. Hence our intellect, when it is reduced from potentiality to act, acquires first a universal and confused knowledge of things, before it knows them in particular; as proceeding from the imperfect to the perfect, as is clear from *Physics* i.[1] If therefore the knowledge of God regarding things other than Himself were only universal and not particular, it would follow that His understanding would not be absolutely perfect; therefore neither would His being. And this is against what was said above.[2] We must therefore say that God knows things other than Himself with a proper knowledge, not only in so far as being is common to them, but in so far as one is distinguished from the other.

In proof thereof we may observe that some, wishing to show that God knows many things by one means, bring forward some examples, as, for instance, that if the center knew itself, it would know all lines that proceed from the center;[3] or if light knew itself, it would know all colors.[4] Now although these examples are similar in part, namely, as regards universal causality, nevertheless they fail in this respect, that multitude and diversity are caused by the one universal principle, not as regards that which is the principle of distinction, but only as regards that in which they communicate. For the diversity of colors is not caused by the light only, but by the diverse disposition of the diaphanous medium[5] which receives it; and likewise, the diversity of the lines is caused by their diverse position. Hence it is that this kind

---

1. 参见 Aristotle, *Phys.*, I, 1 (184a 22).
2. 参见 Q. 4, a. 1.
3. 参见 Cf. Alex, of Hales, *Summa Theol.*, I, no. 166 (I, 249).
4. 参见 Cf. Pseudo-Dionysius, *De Div. Nom.*, VII, 2 (PG 3, 870).
5. diaphanous medium：透明介质

of diversity and multitude cannot be known in its principle by a proper knowledge, but only in a general way. In God, however, it is otherwise. For it was shown above that whatever perfection exists in any creature wholly pre-exists and is contained in God in an excelling manner.[1] Now not only what is common to creatures — viz. being — belongs to their perfection, but also what makes them distinguished from each other; as living and understanding, and the like, whereby living beings are distinguished from the nonliving, and the intelligent from the non-intelligent. Likewise, every form whereby each thing is constituted in its own species is a perfection. Hence it is that all things pre-exist in God, not only as regards what is common to all, but also as regards what distinguishes one thing from another. And therefore as God contains all perfections in Himself, the essence of God is compared to all other essences of things, not as the common to the proper, as unity is to numbers, or as the center [of a circle] to the radii, but as perfect acts to imperfect; as if I were to compare man to animal, or six, a perfect number, to the imperfect numbers contained under it. Now it is manifest that by a perfect act imperfect acts can be known not only in general but also by proper knowledge; thus, for example, whoever knows a man, knows an animal by proper knowledge, and whoever knows the number six, knows the number three also by proper knowledge.

Since therefore the essence of God contains in itself all the perfection contained in the essence of any other being, and far more, God can know all things in Himself with a proper knowledge. For the nature proper to each thing consists in some particular participation of the divine perfection. Now God could not be said to know Himself perfectly unless He knew all the ways in which His own perfection can be shared by others. Neither could He know the very nature of being

1. 参见 Q. 4, a. 2.

perfectly, unless He knew all the ways of being. Hence it is manifest that God knows all things with a proper knowledge, according as they are distinguished from each other.

Reply Obj. 1. Thus to know a thing as it is in the knower may be understood in two ways. In one way, according as this adverb *thus* imports the mode of knowledge on the part of the thing known; and in that sense it is false. For the knower does not always know the object known according to the being it has in the knower; since the eye does not know a stone according to the being it has in the eye, but by the species of the stone which is in it the eye knows the stone according to its being outside the eye. And even if any knower should know the object known according to the being it has in the knower, the knower nevertheless knows it according to its being outside the knower; thus the intellect knows a stone according to the intelligible being it has in the intellect, inasmuch as it knows that it understands; and yet it knows the being of a stone in its own nature. If however the adverb *thus* be understood to import the mode [of knowledge] on the part of the knower, in that sense it is true that only the knower has knowledge of the object known as it is in the knower; for the more perfectly the thing known is in the knower, the more perfect is the mode of knowledge.

We must say therefore that God knows not only that things are in Him, but, by the fact that they are in Him, He knows them in their own nature, and all the more perfectly, the more perfectly each one is in Him.

Reply Obj. 2. The created essence is compared to the essence of God as the imperfect to the perfect act. Therefore the created essence cannot sufficiently lead us to the knowledge of the divine essence, but rather the converse.

Reply Obj. 3. The same thing cannot be considered as the proportioned likeness of diverse things. But the divine essence *excels* all creatures. Hence it can be taken as the proper likeness of each thing according to the diverse ways in which diverse creatures participate in it and imitate it.

Seventh Article
WHETHER THE KNOWLEDGE OF GOD IS DISCURSIVE?

We proceed thus to the Seventh Article: —

Objection 1. It seems that the knowledge of God is discursive. For the knowledge of God is not habitual knowledge, but actual knowledge. Now the Philosopher says: *The habitual knowledge may regard many things at once; but actual understanding regards only one thing at a time.*[1] Therefore as God knows many things, Himself and others, as was shown above, it seems that He does not understand all at once, but proceeds from one to another.

Obj. 2. Further, to know the effect through its cause belongs to discursive knowledge. But God knows other things through Himself, as effects through their cause. Therefore His knowledge is discursive.

Obj. 3. Further, God knows each creature more perfectly than we know it. But we know the effects in their created causes; and thus we go discursively from causes to things caused. Therefore it seems that the same applies to God.

On the contrary, Augustine says, *God does not see all things in their particularity or separately, as if He looked first here and then there; but He sees all things together at once.*[2]

I answer that, In the divine knowledge there is no discursiveness; the proof of which is as follows. In our knowledge there is a twofold discursion. One is according to succession only, as when we have actually understood anything, we turn ourselves to understand something else; while the other mode of discursion is according to causality, as when through principles we arrive at the knowledge of conclusions. The first kind of discursion cannot belong to God. For many things, which we understand in succession if each is considered in

1. 参见 *Top*.. II. 10 (114b 34).
2. 参见 *De Trin.*, XV, 14 (PL 42, 1077).

itself, we understand simultaneously if we see them in some one thing; if, for instance, we understand the parts in the whole, or see different things in a mirror. Now God sees all things in one thing alone, which is Himself. Therefore God sees all things together, and not successively. Likewise the second mode of discursion cannot be applied to God. First, because this second mode of discursion presupposes the first, for whosoever proceeds from principles to conclusions does not consider both at once; secondly, because to advance thus is to proceed from the known to the unknown. Hence it is manifest that when the first is known, the second is still unknown ;and thus the second is known not in the first, but from the first. Now the term of discursive reasoning is attained when the second is seen in the first, by resolving the effects into their causes; and then the discursion ceases. Hence as God sees His effects in Himself as in their cause, His knowledge is not discursive.

Reply Obj. 1. Although the act of understanding is one in itself, nevertheless many things may be understood in something one, as was shown above.

Reply Obj. 2. God does not know first a cause and then, through it, its hitherto supposedly unknown effects; He knows the effects in the cause, and hence His knowledge is not discursive, as was shown above.

Reply Obj. 3. It is true that God sees the effects of created causes in the causes themselves, much better than we can; but still not in such a manner that the knowledge of the effects is caused in Him by the knowledge of the created causes, as is the case with us; and hence His knowledge is not discursive.

Eighth Article
WHETHER THE KNOWLEDGE OF GOD IS THE CAUSE OF THINGS?

We proceed thus to the Eighth, Article: —

Objection 1. It seems that the knowledge of God is not the cause of things. For Origen says (on *Rom.* viii. 30): *A thing will not happen, because God knows it as future, but because it is future, it is on that account known by God before it exists.*[1]

Obj. 2. Further, given the cause, the effect follows. But the knowledge of God is eternal. Therefore if the knowledge of God is the cause of created things, it seems that creatures are eternal.

Obj. 3. Further, *The knowable thing is prior to knowledge, and is its measure,* as the Philosopher says.[2] But what is posterior and measured cannot be a cause. Therefore the knowledge of God is not the cause of things.

On the contrary, Augustine says, *Not because they are, does God know all creatures spiritual and temporal, but because He knows them, therefore they are.*[3]

I answer that, The knowledge of God is the cause of things. For the knowledge of God is to all creatures what the knowledge of the artificer is to things made by his art. Now the knowledge of the artificer is the cause of the things made by his art from the fact that the artificer works through his intellect. Hence the form in the intellect must be the principle of action; as heat is the principle of heating. Nevertheless, we must observe that a natural form, being a form that remains in that to which it gives being, denotes a principle of action according only as it has an inclination to an effect; and likewise, the intelligible form does not denote a principle of action in so far as it resides in the one who understands unless there is added to it the inclination to an effect, which inclination is through the will. For since the intelligible form has a relation to contraries (inasmuch as the same knowledge relates to contraries), it would not produce a determinate effect unless it were determined to one thing by the appetite, as the Philosopher says.[4] Now it is manifest that God causes things by His intellect, since His being is

1. 参见 *In Rom.*, VII, super VIII, 30 (PG 14, 1126).
2. 参见 Aristotle, *Metaph.*, IX, 1 (1053a 33).
3. 参见 *De Trin.*, XV, 13 (PL 42,1076) ; VI, 10 (PL 42,931).
4. 参见 Aristotle, *Metaph.*, VIII, 5 (1048a 11).

His act of understanding; and hence His knowledge must be the cause of things, in so far as His will is joined to it. Hence the knowledge of God as the cause of things is usually called the *knowledge of approbation*.

Reply Obj. 1. Origen[1] spoke in reference to that aspect of knowledge to which the idea of causality does not belong unless the will is joined to it, as is said above.

But when he says that the reason why God foreknows some things is because they are future, this must be understood according to the cause of consequence, and not according to the cause of being. For if things are in the future, it follows that God foreknows them; but the futurity of things is not the cause why God knows them.

Reply Obj. 2. The knowledge of God is the cause of things according as things are in His knowledge. But that things should be eternal was not in the knowledge of God; hence, although the knowledge of God is eternal, it does not follow that creatures are eternal.

Reply Obj. 3. Natural things are midway between the knowledge of God and our knowledge: for we receive knowledge from natural things, of which God is the cause by His knowledge. Hence, just as the natural things that can be known by us are prior to our knowledge, and are its measure, so the knowledge of God is prior to them, and is their measure; as, for instance, a house is midway between the knowledge of the builder who made it, and the knowledge of the one who gathers his knowledge of the house from the house already built.

Ninth Article
WHETHER GOD HAS KNOWLEDGE OF THINGS THAT ARE NOT?

We proceed thus to the Ninth Article: —

1. 参见 *In Rom.*, VII, super VIII, 30 (PG 14, 1126).

Objection 1. It seems that God has not knowledge of things that are not. For the knowledge of God is of true things. But *truth* and *being* are convertible terms. Therefore the knowledge of God is not of things that are not.

Obj. 2. Further, knowledge requires likeness between the knower and the thing known. But those things that are not cannot have any likeness to God, Who is very being. Therefore what is not, cannot be known by God.

Obj. 3. Further, the knowledge of God is the cause of what is known by Him. But it is not the cause of things that are not, because a thing that is not has no cause. Therefore God has no knowledge of things that are not.

On the contrary, The Apostle says: *Who . . . calleth those things that are not as those that are* (*Rom.* iv. 17).

I answer that, God knows all things whatsoever that in any way are. Now it is possible that things that are not absolutely should be in a certain sense. For, absolutely speaking, those things are which are actual; whereas things, which are not actual, are in the power either of God Himself or of a creature, whether in active power, or passive; whether in the power of thought or of imagination, or of any other kind whatsoever. Whatever therefore can be made, or thought, or said by the creature, as also whatever He Himself can do, all are known to God, although they are not actual. And to this extent it can be said that He has knowledge even of things that are not.

Now, among the things that are not actual, a certain difference is to be noted. For though some of them may not be in act now, still they have been, or they will be; and God is said to know all these with the *knowledge of vision:* for since God's act of understanding, which is His being, is measured by eternity, and since eternity is without succession, comprehending all time, the present glance of God extends over all time, and to all things which exist in any time, as to objects present to Him. But there are other things in God's power, or the creature's, which nevertheless are not, nor will be, nor have been; and as regards these He is said to have the knowledge, not of vision, but of *simple intelligence*. This is so called because the things we see around us have distinct being outside the seer.

Reply Obj. 1. Those things that are not actual are true in so far as they are in potentiality, for it is true that they are in potentiality; and as such they are known by God.

Reply Obj. 2. Since God is very being, everything is in so far as it participates in the likeness of God; as everything is hot in so far as it participates in heat. So, things in potentiality are known by God, even though they are not in act.

Reply Obj. 3. The knowledge of God is the cause of things when the will is joined to it. Hence it is not necessary that whatever God knows should be, or have been or is to be; but this is necessary only as regards what He wills to be, or permits to be. Further, it is not in the knowledge of God that these things be, but that they be possible.

Tenth Article
WHETHER GOD KNOWS EVIL THINGS?

We proceed thus to the Tenth Article: —

Objection 1. It seems that God does not know evil things. For the Philosopher says that the intellect which is not in potentiality does not know privation.[1] But *evil is the privation of good*[2], as Augustine says.[3] Therefore, as the intellect of God is never in potentiality, but always in act, as is clear from the foregoing, it seems that God does not know evil things.

Obj. 2. Further, all knowledge is either the cause of the thing known,

---

1. 参见 *De An.*, III, 6 (430b 23).
2. Evil is the privation of good.：恶是善的欠缺。
3. 参见 *Confess.* III, 7 (PL 32, 688).

or is caused by it. But the knowledge of God is not the cause of evil, nor is it caused by evil. Therefore God does not know evil things.

Obj. 3. Further, everything known is known either by its likeness, or by its opposite. But whatever God knows, He knows through His essence, as is clear from the foregoing. Now neither is the divine essence the likeness of evil, nor is evil its contrary; for the divine essence has no contrary,as Augustine says.[1] Therefore God does not know evil things.

Obj. 4. Further, what is known through another, and not through itself, is imperfectly known. But evil is not known by God through itself, otherwise evil would be in God; for the thing known must be in the knower. Therefore if evil is known through something else, namely, through good, it will be known by Him imperfectly; which cannot be for the knowledge of God is not imperfect. Therefore God does not know evil things.

On the contrary, It is written (*Prov.* xv. 11), *Hell and destruction are before God.*

I answer that, Whoever knows a thing perfectly must know all that can occur to it. Now there are some good things to which corruption by evil may occur. Hence God would not know good things perfectly, unless He also knew evil things. Now a thing is knowable in the degree in which it is; hence, since this is the essence of evil that it is the privation of good, by the very fact that God knows good things, He also knows evil things; as by light darkness is known. Hence Dionysius says: *God through Himself receives the vision of darkness, not otherwise seeing darkness except through light.*[2]

Reply Obj. 1. The saying of the Philosopher must be understood as meaning that the intellect which is not in potentiality does not know privation by a privation existing in it; and this agrees with what he had

1. 参见 *De Civit. Dei*, XII, 2 (PL 41,350).
2. 参见 *De Div. Nom.*, VII, 2 (PG 3, 869).

said previously, that a point and every indivisible thing are known by privation of division. This is because simple and indivisible forms are in our intellect, not actually, but only potentially; for were they in our intellect actually, they would not be known by privation. It is thus that simple things are known by separate substances. God therefore knows evil, not by a privation existing in Himself, but by its opposite, the good.

Reply Obj. 2. The knowledge of God is not the cause of evil; it is the cause of the good whereby evil is known.

Reply Obj. 3. Although evil is not opposed to the divine essence, which is not corruptible by evil, it is opposed to the effects of God, which He knows by His essence; and knowing them, He knows the opposite evils.

Reply Obj. 4. To know a thing by something else only, belongs to imperfect knowledge, if that thing is knowable in itself; but evil is not knowable in itself because the very nature of evil consists in the privation of good; therefore evil can neither be defined nor known except by good.

Eleventh Article
WHETHER GOD KNOWS SINGULAR THINGS ?

We proceed thus to the Eleventh Article: —

Objection 1. It seems that God does not know singular things. For the divine intellect is more immaterial than the human intellect. Now the human intellect, by reason of its immateriality, does not know singular things; but as the Philosopher says, *reason has to do with universals, sense with singular things.*[1] Therefore God does not know singular things.

Obj. 2. Further, in us those powers alone know the singular, which

---

1. 参见 *De An.*, II, 5 (417b 22).

receive the species not abstracted from material conditions. But in God things are in the highest degree abstracted from all materiality. Therefore God does not know singular things.

Obj. 3. Further, all knowledge comes about through some likeness. But the likeness of singular things, in so far as they are singular, does not seem to be in God; for the principle of singularity[1] is matter, which, since it is in potentiality only, is altogether unlike God, Who is pure act. Therefore God cannot know singular things.

On the contrary, It is written (*Prov.* xvi, 2), *All the ways of a man are open to His eyes.*

I answer that, God knows singular things. For all perfections found in creatures pre-exist in God in a higher way, as is clear from the foregoing.[2] Now to know singular things is part of our perfection Hence God must know singular things. Even the Philosopher considers it incongruous that anything known by us should be unknown to God; and thus against Empedocles he argues that *God would be most ignorant if He did not know discord.*[3] Now the perfections which are found divided among inferior beings exist simply and unitedly in God; hence, although by one power we know the universal and immaterial, and by another we know singular and material things, nevertheless God knows both by His simple intellect.

Now some, wishing to show how this can be, said that God knows singular things through universal causes.[4] For nothing exists in any singular thing that does not arise from some universal cause. They give the example of an astronomer who knows all the universal movements of the heavens, and can thence foretell all eclipses that are to come. This, however, is not enough; for from universal causes singular things

1. singularity：个别性
2. 参见 Q. 4, a. 2.
3. 参见 *De An.*, I, 5 (410b 4); *Metaph.*, II, 4 (1000b 3).
4. 参见 Cf. Avicenna, *Metaph.*, VIII, 6 (1oorb).

acquire certain forms and powers which, however they may be joined together, are not individuated except by individual matter. Hence he who knows Socrates because he is white, or because he is the son of Sophroniscus, or because of something of that kind, would not know him in so far as he is this particular man. Hence, following the above explanation, God would not know singular things in their singularity.

On the other hand, others have said that God knows singular things by the application of universal causes to particular effects.[1] But this will not hold; for no one can apply a thing to another unless he first knows that other thing. Hence the said application cannot be the reason of knowing the particular; it rather presupposes the knowledge of singular things.

Therefore we must propose another explanation. Since God is the cause of things by His knowledge, as was stated above, His knowledge extends as far as His causality extends. Hence, as the active power of God extends not only to forms, which are the source of universality, but also to matter, as we shall prove further on, the knowledge of God must extend to singular things, which are individuated by matter.[2] For since He knows things other than Himself by His essence, as being the likeness of things, or as their active principle, His essence must be the sufficing principle of knowing all things made by Him, not only in the universal, but also in the singular. The same would apply to the knowledge of the artificer, if it were productive of the whole thing, and not only of the form.

Reply Obj. 1. Our intellect abstracts the intelligible species from the individuating principles; hence the intelligible species in our intellect cannot be the likeness of the individual principles, and on that account our intellect does not know the singular. But the intelligible species in the divine intellect, which is the essence of God, is immaterial not by

---

1. 参见 Cf. Averroes, *Destruct. Destruct.*, XI (IX, 47rb).
2. 参见 Q. 44, a. 2.

abstraction, but of itself, being the principle of all the principles which enter into the composition of the thing, whether these be principles of the species or principles of the individual; hence by it God knows not only universals, but also singular things.

Reply Obj. 2. Although the species in the divine intellect has no material conditions in its being like the species received in the imagination and sense, yet it extends to both immaterial and material things through its power.

Reply Obj. 3. Although matter, because of its potentiality, recedes from likeness to God, yet, even in so far as it has being in this wise, it retains a certain likeness to the divine being.

Twelfth Article
WHETHER GOD CAN KNOW INFINITE THINGS ?

We proceed thus to the Twelfth Article: —

Objection 1. It seems that God cannot know infinite things. For the infinite, as such, is unknown, since the infinite is that which, *to those who measure it, leaves always something more to be measured*, as the Philosopher says.[1] Moreover, Augustine says that *whatever is comprehended by knowledge is bounded by the comprehension of the knower*.[2] Now infinite things have no boundary. Therefore they cannot be comprehended by the knowledge of God.

Obj. 2. Further, if it be said that things infinite in themselves are finite in God's knowledge, against this it may be urged that the essence of the infinite is that it is untraversable[3], and of the finite that it is traversable, as is said in *Physics* iii.[4] But the infinite is not traversable either by the

1. 参见 *Phys.*, III, 6 (207a 7).
2. 参见 *De Civit. Dei*, XII, 18 (PL 41, 368).
3. untraversable：不可穿越的
4. 参见 Aristotle, *Phys.*, III, 4 (204a 3).

finite or by the infinite, as is proved in *Physics* vi.[1] Therefore the infinite cannot be bounded by the finite, nor even by the infinite; and so the infinite cannot be finite in God's knowledge, which is infinite.

Obj. 3. Further, the knowledge of God is the measure of what is known. But it is contrary to the essence of the infinite that it be measured. Therefore infinite things cannot be known by God.

On the contrary, Augustine says, *Although we cannot number the infinite, nevertheless it can be comprehended by Him whose knowledge has no number.*[2]

I answer that, Since God knows not only things actual but also things possible to Himself or to created things, as was shown above, and since these must be infinite, it must be held that He knows infinite things. Although the *knowledge of vision*, which has relation only to things that are, or will be, or have been, is not of infinite things, as some say,[3] for we do not hold that the world is eternal, nor that generation and movement will go on for ever, so that individuals be infinitely multiplied; yet, if we consider more attentively, we must hold that God knows infinite things even by the knowledge of vision. For God knows even the thoughts and affections of hearts, which will be multiplied to infinity since rational creatures will endure forever.

The reason of this is to be found in the fact that the knowledge of every knower is measured by the mode of the form which is the principle of knowledge. For the sensible species in the sense is the likeness of only one individual thing, and can give the knowledge of only one individual. But the intelligible species in our intellect is the likeness of the thing as regards its specific nature, which is participable by infinite particulars. Hence our intellect by the intelligible species of man in a certain way knows infinite men, not however as distinguished from each other, but as communicating in the nature of the species;

---

1. 参见 *Op. cit.*, VI, 7 (238b 17).
2. 参见 *De Civit. Dei*, XII, 18 (PL 41, 368).
3. 参见 Cf. q. 7, a. 4; q. 46, a. 2, ad 8.

and the reason is because the intelligible species of our intellect is the likeness of man, not as to the individual principles, but as to the principles of the species. On the other hand, the divine essence, whereby the divine intellect understands, is a sufficing likeness of all things that are , or can be, not only as regards the universal principles, but also as regards the principles proper to each one, as was shown above. Hence it follows that the knowledge of God extends to infinite things, even according as they are distinct from each other.

Reply Obj. 1. *The idea of the infinite pertains to quantity*, as the Philosopher says.[1] But the idea of quantity implies an order of parts. Therefore to know the infinite according to the mode of the infinite is to know part after part; and in this way the infinite cannot be known; for whatever quantity of parts be taken, there will always remain something else outside. But God does not know the infinite, or infinite things, as if He enumerated part after part; since He knows all things simultaneously and not successively, as was said above. Hence there is nothing to prevent Him from knowing infinite things.

Reply Obj. 2. Transition imports a certain succession of parts; and hence it is that the infinite cannot be traversed by the finite, nor by the infinite. But equality suffices for comprehension, because that is said to be comprehended which has nothing outside the comprehender. Hence, it is not against the idea of the infinite to be comprehended by the infinite. And so, what is infinite in itself can be called finite to the knowledge of God as comprehended; but not as if it were traversable.

Reply Obj. 3. The knowledge of God is the measure of things, not quantitatively, for the infinite is not subject to this kind of measure, but because it measures the essence and truth of things. For everything has truth of nature according to the degree in which it imitates the knowledge of God, as the thing made by art agrees with the art.

1. 参见 *Phys.*, I, 2 (185a 33).

Granted, however, an actually infinite number of things (for instance, an infinitude of men, or an infinitude in continuous quantity, as an infinite air, as some of the ancients held),[1] yet it is manifest that these would have a determinate and finite being, because their being would be limited to certain determinate natures. Hence they would be measurable as regards the knowledge of God.

Thirteenth Article

WHETHER THE KNOWLEDGE OF GOD IS OF FUTURE CONTINGENT THINGS?

We proceed thus to the Thirteenth Article: —

Objection 1. It seems that the knowledge of God is not of future contingent[2] things. For from a necessary cause proceeds a necessary effect. But the knowledge of God is the cause of things known, as was said above. Since therefore that knowledge is necessary, what He knows must also be necessary. Therefore the knowledge of God is not of contingent things.

Obj. 2. Further, every conditional proposition, of which the antecedent is absolutely necessary, must have an absolutely necessary consequent. For the antecedent is to the consequent as principles are to the conclusion: and from necessary principles only a necessary conclusion can follow, as is proved in *Poster*, i.[3] But this is a true conditional proposition, *If God knew that this thing will be*, *it will be*,[4]

---

1. 参见 Attributed to Anaximenes and Diogenes by Aristotle, *Phys.*, III, 4 (203a 18); *Metaph.*, I, 3 (984a 5).
2. contingent：可能发生的
3. 参见 Aristotle, *Post. Anal.*, I, 6 (75a 4).
4. 参见 Cf. St. Anselm, *De Concord. Praesc. cum Lib. Arb.*, q. I, 1 (PL 158, 509); St. Augustine, *De Civit. Dei*, V, 9; XI, 21 (PL 41, 148; 334); *De Lib. Arb.*, III, 4 (PL 32, 1276); Boethius, *De Consol.*, V, prose 3; prose 6 (PL 63, 840; 860); Peter Lombard, *Sent.*, I, xxxviii, 2 (I, 244).

for the knowledge of God is only of true things. Now, the antecedent of this conditioned proposition is absolutely necessary, because it is eternal, and because it is signified as past. Therefore the consequent is also absolutely necessary. Therefore whatever God knows is necessary; and so the knowledge of God is not of contingent things.

Obj. 3. Further, everything known by God must necessarily be, because even what we ourselves know must necessarily be; and, of course, the knowledge of God is much more certain than ours. But no future contingent thing must necessarily be. Therefore no contingent future thing is known by God.

On the contrary, It is written (*Ps.* xxxii. 15), *He Who hath made the hearts of every one of them, Who understandeth all their works*, that is, of men. Now the works of men are contingent, being subject to free choice. Therefore God knows future contingent things.

I answer that, Since, as was shown above, God knows all things, not only things actual but also things possible to Him and to the creature, and since some of these are future contingent to us, it follows that God knows future contingent things.

In evidence of this, we must observe that a contingent thing can be considered in two ways. First, in itself, in so far as it is already in act, and in this sense it is not considered as future, but as present; neither is it considered as contingent to one of two terms, but as determined to one; and because of this it can be infallibly[1] the object of certain knowledge, for instance to the sense of sight, as when I see that Socrates is sitting down. In another way, a contingent thing can be considered as it is in its cause, and in this way it is considered as future, and as a contingent thing not yet determined to one; for a contingent cause has relation to opposite things: and in this sense a contingent thing is not subject to any certain knowledge. Hence,

---

1. infallibly：绝无错误的

whoever knows a contingent effect in its cause only, has merely a conjectural knowledge of it. Now God knows all contingent things not only as they are in their causes, but also as each one of them is actually in itself. And although contingent things become actual successively, nevertheless God knows contingent things not successively, as they are in their own being, as we do, but simultaneously. The reason is because His knowledge is measured by eternity, as is also His being; and eternity, being simultaneously whole, comprises all time, as was said above.[1] Hence, all things that are in time are present to God from eternity, not only because He has the essences of things present within Him, as some say,[2] but because His glance is carried from eternity over all things as they are in their presentiality[3]. Hence it is manifest that contingent things are infallibly known by God, inasmuch as they are subject to the divine sight in their presentiality; and yet they are future contingent things in relation to their own causes.

Reply Obj. 1. Although the supreme cause is necessary, the effect may be contingent by reason of the proximate[4] contingent cause; just as the germination of a plant is contingent by reason of the proximate contingent cause, although the movement of the sun, which is the first cause, is necessary. So, likewise, things known by God are contingent because of their proximate causes, while the knowledge of God, which is the first cause, is necessary.

Reply Obj. 2. Some say that this antecedent, *God knew this contingent to be future*, is not necessary, but contingent; because, although it is past, still it imports a relation to the future.[5] This, however, does not remove necessity from it, for whatever has had relation to the future, must

---

1. 参见 Q. 10, a. 2, ad 4.
2. 参见 Avicenna, *Metaph.*, VIII, 6 (100rb).
3. presentiality：预感
4. proximate：临近的，直接的
5. 参见 St. Bonaventure, *In I Sent.*, d. xxxviii, a. 2, q. 2 (I, 678); St. Albert, *In I Sent.*, d. xxxviii, a. 4 (XXVI, 290).

have had it, even though the future sometimes is not realized. On the other hand, some say that this antecedent is contingent because it is a compound of the necessary and the contingent;[1] as this saying is contingent, *Socrates is a white man*. But this also is to no purpose; for when we say, *God knew this contingent to be future*, contingent is used here only as the matter of the proposition, and not as its principal part. Hence its contingency or necessity has no reference to the necessity or contingency of the proposition, or to its being true or false. For it may be just as true that I said a man is an ass, as that I said Socrates runs, or God is: and the same applies to necessary and contingent.

Hence it must be said that this antecedent is absolutely necessary. Nor does it follow, as some say, that the consequent is absolutely necessary because the antecedent is the remote cause of the consequent, which is contingent by reason of the proximate cause[2].[3] But this is to no purpose. For the conditional would be false were its antecedent the remote necessary cause, and the consequent a contingent effect; as, for example, if I said, *if the sun moves, the grass will grow*.

Therefore we must reply otherwise: when the antecedent contains anything belonging to an act of the soul, the consequent must be taken, not as it is in itself, but as it is in the soul; for the being of a thing in itself is other than the being of a thing in the soul. For example, when I say, *What the soul understands is immaterial*, the meaning is that it is immaterial as it is in the intellect, not as it is in itself. Likewise if I say, *If God knew anything, it will be*, the consequent must be understood as it is subject to the divine knowledge, that is, as it is in its presentiality.

1. 参见 Robert Grosseteste, *De Lib. Arb.*, VI (p. 170).
2. the proximate cause：直接原因，近因
3. 参见 Alex of Hales, *Summa Theol.*, I, no. 171 (I, 255); no. 184 (I, 270); Alain of Lille, *Theol. Reg.* . LXVI (PL 210, 653).

And thus it is necessary, as is also the antecedent; *for everything that is, while it is, must necessarily be*, as the Philosopher says in *Periherm*. i.[1]

Reply Obj. 3. Things reduced to actuality in time are known by us successively in time, but by God they are known in eternity, which is above time. Whence to us they cannot be certain, since we know future contingent things only as contingent futures; but they are certain to God alone, Whose understanding is in eternity above time. Just as he who goes along the road does not see those who come after him; whereas he who sees the whole road from a height sees at once all those traveling on it. Hence, what is known by us must be necessary, even as it is in itself; for what is in itself a future contingent cannot be known by us. But what is known by God must be necessary according to the mode in which it is subject to the divine knowledge, as we have already stated, but not absolutely as considered in its proper causes. Hence also this proposition, *Everything known by God must necessarily be*, is usually distinguished,[2] for it may refer to the thing or to the saying. If it refers to the thing, it is divided and false; for the sense is, *Everything which God knows is necessary*. If understood of the saying, it is composite and true, for the sense is, *This proposition, 'that which is known by God is' is necessary*.

Now some urge an objection and say that this distinction holds good with regard to forms that are separable from a subject.[3] Thus if I said, *It is possible for a white thing to be black*, it is false as applied to the saying, and true as applied to the thing: for a thing which is white can become black; whereas this saying, *a white thing is black*, can never be true. But in forms that are inseparable from a subject, this distinction does not hold: for instance, if I said, *A black crow can be white*; for in

1. 参见 Aristotle, *Perih*., I, 9 (19a 23).
2. 参见 Cf. Wm. of Sherwood, *Introd. in Logicam* (p. 89); St. Albert, *In Prior. Anal*., I, tr. 4, ch. 16 (I, 562).
3. 参见 Cf. St. Thomas, *In I Sent*., d. xxxviii, q. 1, a. 5, ad 5-6; *De Ver*., II, 12, ad 4.

both senses it is false. Now to be known by God is inseparable from a thing; for what is known by God cannot be not known. This objection, however, would hold if these words *that which is known* implied any disposition inherent in the subject; but since they import an act of the knower, something can be attributed to the known thing in itself (even if it always be known) which is not attributed to it in so far as it falls under an act of knowledge. Thus, material being is attributed to a stone in itself, which is not attributed to it inasmuch as it is intelligible.

Fourteenth Article
WHETHER GOD KNOWS WHATEVER IS ENUNCIABLE?

We proceed thus to the Fourteenth Article: —

Objection 1. It seems that God does not know whatever is enunciable[1]. For to know it belongs to our intellect as it composes and divides. But in the divine intellect there is no composition. Therefore God does not know whatever is enunciable.

Obj. 2. Further, every kind of knowledge takes place through some likeness. But in God there is no likeness of enunciables, since He is altogether simple[2]. Therefore God does not know enunciables.

On the contrary, It is written: *The Lord knoweth the thoughts of men* (*Ps.* xciii. 11). But what can be enunciated is contained in the thoughts of men. Therefore God knows what can be enunciated.

I answer that, Since it is in the power of our intellect to form enunciations, and since God knows whatever is in His own power or in that of creatures, as was said above, it follows of necessity that God knows all enunciations that can be formed.

Now just as He knows material things immaterially, and composite things simply, so likewise He knows what can be enunciated, not

1. enunciable：可陈述的
2. altogether simple：完全单纯

after its own manner, as if in His intellect there were composition or division of enunciations ,but He knows each thing by simple intelligence, by understanding the essence of each thing; as if we, by the very fact that we understand what man is, were to understand all that can be predicated of man. This, however, does not happen in the case of our intellect, which proceeds from one thing to another, since the intelligible species represents one thing in such a way as not to represent another. Hence, when we understand what man is, we do not forthwith understand other things which belong to him, but we understand them one by one, according to a certain succession. On this account, the things we understand as separated we must reduce to one by way of composition or division, by forming an enunciation. Now the species of the divine intellect, which is God's essence, suffices to manifest all things. Hence, by understanding His essence, God knows the essences of all things, and also whatever can be added to them.

Reply Obj. 1. This objection would be true if God knew enunciations according to their own limitations.

Reply Obj. 2. Composition in an enunciation signifies some sort of being in a thing; and so God, by His being, which is His essence, is the likeness of everything signified by enunciations.

Fifteenth Article
WHETHER THE KNOWLEDGE OF GOD IS VARIABLE?

We proceed thus to the Fifteenth Article: —

Objection 1. It seems that the knowledge of God is variable. For knowledge is related to what is knowable. But whatever imports relation to the creature is applied to God from time, and varies according to the variation of creatures. Therefore, the knowledge of God is variable according to the variation of creatures.

Obj. 2. Further, whatever God can make He can know. But God can make more things than He does. Therefore, He can know more than He knows. Thus, His knowledge can vary according to increase and diminution[1].

Obj. 3. Further, God knew that Christ would be born. But He does not know now that Christ will be born, because Christ is not to be born in the future. Therefore God does not know everything He once knew; and thus the knowledge of God is variable.

On the contrary, It is said, that in God *there is no change nor shadow of alteration* (*Jas.* i. 17).

I answer that, Since the knowledge of God is His substance, as is clear from the foregoing, just as His substance is altogether immutable, as was shown above,[2] so His knowledge likewise must be altogether invariable.

Reply Obj. 1. *Lord*, *Creator*, and the like, import relations to creatures in so far as they are in themselves. But the knowledge of God imports relation to creatures in so far as they are in God; because everything is actually understood according as it is in the one who understands. Now created things are in God in an invariable manner; while they exist variably in themselves. — Or we may say that *Lord*, *Creator*, and the like, import the relations consequent upon the acts which are understood as terminating in the creatures themselves as they are in themselves; and thus these relations are attributed to God variously, according to the variation of creatures. But *knowledge* and *love*, and the like, import relations consequent upon the acts which are understood to be in God; and therefore these are predicated of God in an invariable manner.

Reply Obj. 2. God knows also what He can make, and does not make. Hence from the fact that He can make more than He makes, it does not follow that He can know more than He knows, unless this

1. diminution：减少，缩减
2. 参见 Q. 9, a. 1.

be referred to the *knowledge of vision*, according to which He is said to know those things which actually exist in some period of time. But from the fact that He knows that some things can be which are not, or that some things can not-be which are, it does not follow that His knowledge is variable, but rather that He knows the variability[1] of things. If, however, anything existed which God did not previously know, and afterwards knew, then His knowledge would be variable. But this is impossible, for whatever is, or can be in any period of time, is known by God in His eternity. Therefore, from the fact that a thing is said to exist in some period of time, we must say that it is known by God from all eternity. Therefore it cannot be granted that God can know more than He knows; because such a proposition implies that first of all He did not know, and then afterwards knew.

Reply Obj. 3. The ancient Nominalists[2] said that it was the same thing to say *Christ is born* and *will be born*, and *was born*; because the same thing is signified by these three — viz., the nativity of Christ.[3] Therefore it follows, they said, that whatever God knew, He knows; because now He knows that Christ is born, which means the same thing as that Christ will be born. This opinion, however, is false, both because the diversity in the parts of a sentence causes a diversity in enunciations, and because it would follow that a proposition which is true once would always be true; which is contrary to what the Philosopher lays down when he says that this sentence, *Socrates sits*, is true when he is sitting, and false when he stands up.[4] Therefore, it must be conceded that this proposition, *Whatever God knew He knows*, is not true if referred to what is enunciated. But because of this, it does

1. variability：变化性；易变；变化的倾向
2. Nominalists：唯名论者
3. 参见 Cf. Abelard, *Introd. ad Theol.*, III, 5 (PL 178, 1102); Peter Lombard, *Sent.*, I, xli, 3 (I, 258)
4. 参见 *Cat.*, V (4a 23).

not follow that the knowledge of God is variable. For as it is without variation in the divine knowledge that God knows one and the same thing sometime to be, and sometime not, so it is without variation in the divine knowledge that God knows that an enunciation is sometime true, and sometime false. The knowledge of God, however, would be variable if He knew enunciations according to their own limitations, by composition and division, as occurs in our intellect. Hence our knowledge varies either as regards truth and falsity, for example, if when a thing is changed we retained the same opinion about it; or as regards diverse opinions, as if we first thought that someone was sitting, and afterwards thought that he was not sitting; neither of which can be in God.

Sixteenth Article
WHETHER GOD HAS A SPECULATIVE KNOWLEDGE OF THINGS?

We proceed thus to the Sixteenth Article: —

Objection 1. It seems that God has not a speculative[1] knowledge of things. For the knowledge of God is the cause of things, as was shown above. But speculative knowledge is not the cause of the things known. Therefore the knowledge of God is not speculative.

Obj. 2. Further, speculative knowledge comes by abstraction from things; which does not belong to the divine knowledge. Therefore the knowledge of God is not speculative.

On the contrary, Whatever is the more excellent must be attributed to God. But *speculative knowledge is more excellent than practical knowledge*, as the Philosopher says in the beginning of the *Metaphysics*.[2] Therefore God has a speculative knowledge of things.

---

1. speculative：观看的；鉴赏的
2. 参见 *Metaph.*, I, 1 (982a 1).

I answer that, Some knowledge is speculative only, some is practical only, and some is partly speculative and partly practical. In proof whereof it must be observed that knowledge can be called speculative in three ways: first, in relation to the things known, which are not operable by the knower; such is the knowledge of man about natural or divine things. Secondly, as regards the manner of knowing — as, for instance, if a builder were to consider a house by defining and dividing, and considering what belongs to it in general: for this is to consider operable things in a speculative manner, and not as they are operable; for *operable* means the application of form to matter, and not the resolution of the composite into its universal formal principles. Thirdly, as regards the end; *for the practical intellect differs from the speculative by its end*, as the Philosopher says.[1] For the practical intellect is ordered to the end of operation; whereas the end of the speculative intellect is the consideration of truth. Hence if a builder were to consider how a house can be made, but without ordering this to the end of operation, but only towards knowledge, this would be only a speculative consideration as regards the end, although it concerns an operable thing. Therefore, knowledge which is speculative by reason of the thing itself known is merely speculative. But that which is speculative either in its mode or as to its end is partly speculative and partly practical: and when it is ordained to an operative end it is strictly practical.

In accordance with this, therefore, it must be said that God has of Himself a speculative knowledge only; for He Himself is not operable.

But of all other things He has both speculative and practical knowledge. He has speculative knowledge as regards the mode; for whatever we know speculatively in things by defining and dividing, God knows all this much more perfectly.

---

1. 参见 *De An.*, III, 10 (433a 14).

Now of things which He can make, but does not make at any time, He has not a practical knowledge, according as knowledge is called practical from the end. In this sense He has a practical knowledge of what He makes in some period of time. And, as regards evil things, although they are not operable by Him, yet they fall under His practical knowledge, as also do good things, inasmuch as He permits, or impedes, or directs them; just as sicknesses fall under the practical knowledge of the physician, inasmuch as he cures them by his art.

Reply Obj. 1. The knowledge of God is a cause, not indeed of Himself, but of other things. He is actually the cause of some, that is, of things that come to be in some period of time; He is virtually the cause of others, that is, of things which He can make, and which nevertheless are never made.

Reply Obj. 2. The fact that knowledge is derived from things known does not belong to speculative knowledge essentially, but only accidentally in so far as it is human.

In answer to what is objected to the contrary, we must say that perfect knowledge of operable things is obtainable only if they are known in so far as they are operable. Therefore, since the knowledge of God is in every way perfect, He must know what is operable by Him precisely insofar as it is operable, and not only insofar as it is speculative. Nevertheless this does not impair the nobility of His speculative knowledge, for He sees all things other than Himself in Himself, and He knows Himself speculatively; and so in the speculative knowledge of Himself, He possesses both speculative and practical knowledge of all other things.

Question XV
ON IDEAS
(*In Three Articles*)

AFTER considering the knowledge of God, it remains to consider ideas. And about this there are three points of inquiry: (1) Whether there are ideas? (2) Whether they are many, or one only? (3) Whether there are ideas of all things known by God?

First Article
WHETHER THERE ARE IDEAS?

We proceed thus to the First Article: —

Objection 1. It seems that there are no ideas. For Dionysius says that God does not know things by ideas.[1] But ideas are for nothing else except that things may be known through them. Therefore there are no ideas.

Obj. 2. Further, God knows all things in Himself, as has been already said.[2] But He does not know Himself through an idea; neither therefore other things.

Obj. 3. Further, an idea is considered to be the principle of knowledge and action. But the divine essence is a sufficient principle of knowing and effecting all things. It is not therefore necessary to posit ideas.

On the contrary, Augustine says, *Such is the power inherent in ideas, that*

1. 参见 *De Div. Nom.*, VII, 2 (PG 3, 868).
2. 参见 Q. 14, a. 5.

no one can be wise unless they be understood.[1]

I answer that, It is necessary to posit ideas in the divine mind. For the Greek word 'Ιδέα is in Latin *Forma*. Hence by ideas are understood the forms of things, existing apart from the things themselves. Now the form of anything, existing apart from the thing itself, can be for one of two ends; either to be the exemplar of that of which it is called the form, or to be the principle of the knowledge of that thing, according as the forms of knowable things are said to be in him who knows them. In either case we must posit ideas, as is clear for the following reason:

In all things not generated by chance, the form must be the end of any generation whatsoever. But an agent does not act for the sake of the form, except in so far as the likeness of the form is in the agent; which may happen in two ways. For in some agents the form of the thing-to-be-made pre-exists according to its natural being, as in those that act by their nature; as a man generates a man, or fire generates fire. Whereas in other agents the form of the thing-to-be-made pre-exists according to intelligible being, as in those that act by the intellect; and thus the likeness of a house pre-exists in the mind of the builder. And this may be called the idea of the house, since the builder intends to build his house like the form conceived in his mind.

Since, then, the world was not made by chance, but by God acting by His intellect, as will appear later,[2] there must exist in the divine mind a form to the likeness of which the world was made. And in this the notion of an idea consists.

Reply Obj. 1. God does not understand things according to an idea existing outside Himself. Thus Aristotle likewise rejects the opinion of Plato, who held that Ideas existed of themselves, and not in the

1. 参见 *Lib. 83 Quaest.*, q. 46 (PL 40, 29).
2. 参见 Q. 47, a. 1.

intellect.[1]

Reply Obj. 2. Although God knows Himself and all else by His own essence, yet His essence is the operative principle of all things, except of Himself. It has therefore the nature of an idea with respect to other things; though not with respect to God Himself.

Reply Obj. 3. God is the likeness of all things according to His essence; therefore an idea in God is nothing other than His essence.

Second Article
WHETHER THERE ARE MANY IDEAS?

We proceed thus to the Second Article: —

Objection 1. It seems that there are not many ideas. For an idea in God is His essence. But God's essence is one only. Therefore there is only one idea.

Obj. 2. Further, as the idea is the principle of knowing and operating, so are art and wisdom. But in God there are not several arts or wisdoms. Therefore in Him there is no plurality of ideas.

Obj. 3. Further, if it be said that ideas are multiplied according to their relations to different creatures, it may be argued on the contrary that the plurality of ideas is eternal. If, then, ideas are many, but creatures temporal, then the temporal must be the cause of the eternal.

Obj. 4. Further, these relations are either real in creatures only, or in God also. If in creatures only, since creatures are not from eternity, the plurality of ideas cannot be from eternity, if ideas are multiplied only according to these relations. But if they are real in God, it follows that there is a real plurality in God other than the plurality of Persons: and this is against the teaching of Damascene, who says that in God all things are one, except *ingenerability*, *generation*, *and procession*.[2] Ideas

1. 参见 *Metaph.*, II, 2 (997b 6); VI, 6 (1031b 5).
2. 参见 *De Fide Orth.*, I, 10(PG 94, 837).

therefore are not many.

On the contrary, Augustine says, *Ideas are certain original forms or permanent and immutable models of things which are contained by the divine intelligence. They are immutable because they themselves have not been formed; and that is why they are eternal and always the same. But though they themselves neither come to be nor perish, yet it is according to them that everything, which can come to be or pass away or which actually comes to be and passes away, is said to be formed.*[1]

I answer that, It must necessarily be held that ideas are many. In proof of which it is to be considered that in every effect the ultimate end is the proper intention of the principal agent, as the order of an army is the proper intention of the general. Now that which is best in things is the good of the order of the universe, as the Philosopher clearly teaches in *Metaph.* xii.[2] Therefore, the order of the universe is properly intended by God, and is not the accidental result of a succession of agents, as has been supposed by those who have taught that God created only the first creature, and that this creature created a second creature, and so on, until this great multitude of beings was produced.[3] According to this opinion, God would have an idea of the first created thing alone; whereas, if the very order of the universe was itself created by Him immediately, and intended by Him, He must have the idea of the order of the universe. Now there cannot be an idea of any whole, unless particular ideas are had of those parts of which the whole is made; just as a builder could not conceive the idea of a house unless he had the idea of each of its parts. So, then, it must needs be that in the divine mind there are the proper ideas of all things. Hence Augustine says *that each thing was created by God according*

---

1. 参见 *Lib. 83 Quaest.*, q. 46 (PL 40, 30).
2. 参见 *Metaph.*, XI, 10 (1075a 13).
3. 参见 Cf. below,q. 45, a. 5.

to the idea proper to it;[1] from which it follows that in the divine mind there are many ideas.

Now it can easily be seen how this is not repugnant to the simplicity of God, if we consider that the idea of the thing to be produced is in the mind of the producer as that which is understood, and not as the likeness whereby he understands, which is a form that makes the intellect in act. For the form of the house in the mind of the builder is something understood by him, to the likeness of which he forms the house in matter. Now, it is not repugnant to the simplicity of the divine mind that it understand many things; though it would be repugnant to its simplicity were God's understanding to be informed by a plurality of likenesses. Hence many ideas exist in the divine mind as that which is understood by it; as can be proved thus. Inasmuch as God knows His own essence perfectly, He knows it according to every mode in which it can be known. Now it can be known not only as it is in itself, but as it can be participated in by creatures according to some kind of likeness. But every creature has its own proper species, according to which it participates in some way in the likeness of the divine essence. Therefore, as God knows His essence as so imitable by such a creature, He knows it as the particular model and idea of that creature: and in like manner as regards other creatures. So it is clear that God understands many models proper to many things; and these are many ideas.

Reply Obj. 1. The divine essence is not called an idea in so far as it is that essence, but only in so far as it is the likeness or model of this or that thing. Hence ideas are said to be many, inasmuch as many models are understood through the self-same essence.

Reply Obj. 2. By wisdom and art we signify *that by which* God understands; but by an idea, *that which* God understands. For God by

1. 参见 *Lib. 83 Quaest.*, q. 46 (PL 40, 30).

one principle understands many things, and that not only according as they are in themselves, but also according as they are understood; and this is to understand the several models of things. In the same way, an architect is said to understand a house, when he understands the form of the house in matter. But if he understands the form of a house, as devised by himself, from the fact that he understands that he understands it, he thereby understands the model or the idea of the house. Now not only does God understand many things by His essence, but He also understands that He understands many things by His essence. And this means that He understands the several models of things; or that many ideas are in His intellect as understood by Him.

Reply Obj. 3. Such relations, whereby ideas are multiplied, are caused not by the things themselves, but by the divine intellect comparing its own essence with these things.

Reply Obj. 4. Relations multiplying ideas do not exist in created things, but in God. Yet they are not real relations, such as those whereby the Persons are distinguished, but relations understood by God.

Third Article

WHETHER THERE ARE IDEAS OF ALL THINGS THAT GOD KNOWS?

We proceed thus to the Third Article: —

Objection 1. It seems that there are not ideas in God of all things that He knows. For the idea of evil is not in God; since it would follow that evil was in Him. But evil things are known by God. Therefore there are not ideas of all things that God knows.

Obj. 2. Further, God knows things that neither are, nor will be, nor have been, as has been said above.[1] But of such things there are no

---

1. 参见 Q. 14, a. 9.

ideas, since, as Dionysius says: *Acts of the divine will are the determining and effective models of things.*[1] Therefore in God there are not ideas of all things known by Him.

Obj. 3. Further, God knows primary matter, of which there can be no idea, since it has no form. Hence the same conclusion.

Obj. 4. Further, it is certain that God knows not only species, but also genera, singulars, and accidents. But there are no ideas of these, according to Plato's teaching, who first taught ideas, as Augustine says.[2] Therefore there are not ideas in God of all things known by Him.

On the contrary, Ideas are exemplars existing in the divine mind, as is clear from Augustine.[3] But God has the proper exemplars of all the things that He knows; and therefore He has ideas of all things known by Him.

I answer that, As ideas, according to Plato,[4] were the principles of the knowledge of things and of their generation, an idea, as existing in the mind of God, has this twofold office. So far as the idea is the principle of the making of things, it may be called an *exemplar*, and belongs to practical knowledge. But so far as it is a principle of knowledge, it is properly called a *likeness*, and may belong to speculative knowledge also. As an exemplar, therefore, it is related to everything made by God in any period of time; whereas as a principle of knowledge it is related to all things known by God, even though they never come to be in time; and to all things that He knows according to their proper likeness, in so far as they are known by Him in a speculative manner.

Reply Obj. 1. Evil is known by God, not through its own likeness,

---

1. 参见 *De Div. Nom.*, V, 8 (PG 3, 845).
2. 参见 *Lib. 83 Quaest.*, q. 46 (PL 40, 29).
3. 同上 (PL 40, 30).
4. 参见 Cf. below, q. 84,a. 4.— Cf. also Aristotle, *Metaph.*, Iα, 9 (991b 3).

but through the likeness of good. Evil, therefore, has no idea in God, neither in so far as an idea is an *exemplar*, nor so far as it is a *likeness*.

Reply Obj. 2. God has no practical knowledge, except virtually, of things which neither are, nor will be, nor have been. Hence, with respect to these there is no idea in God in so far as idea signifies an *exemplar*, but only in so far as it signifies a *likeness*.

Reply Obj. 3. Plato is said by some to have considered matter as not created ;[1] and therefore he held, not that there was an idea of matter, but that an idea was a co-cause with matter. Since, however, we hold matter to be created by God, though not apart from form, matter has its idea in God, but not apart from the idea of the composite; for matter in itself can neither exist, nor be known.

Reply Obj. 4. Genus can have no idea apart from the idea of species, in so far as idea denotes an *exemplar*; for genus cannot exist except in some species. The same is the case with those accidents that inseparably accompany their subject; for these come into being along with their subject. But accidents which are added to the subject have their special idea. For an architect produces through the form of the house all the accidents that originally accompany it; whereas those that are superadded[2] to the house when completed, such as decorations, or any other such thing, are produced through some other form. Now individual things, according to Plato, have no other idea than that of the species,[3] both because singular things are individuated by matter, which, as some say, he held to be uncreated and a cocause with the idea; and because the intention of nature aims at the species, and produces individuals only that

1. 参见 Cf. Chalcidius, *In Timaeum*, CCXLVIII (p. 245).— Cf. also Peter Lombard, *Sent.* II, i, 1 (I, 306-307).
2. superadd：加上；再添加
3. 参见 Cf. Aristotle, *Metaph.*, I, 9 (990b 29).

in them the species may be preserved. However, divine providence extends not merely to species, but to individuals, as will be shown later.[1]

1. 参见 Q. 22, a. 2.

Question XVI
ON TRUTH
(*In Eight Articles*)

SINCE knowledge is of what is true, after the consideration of the knowledge of God, we must inquire concerning truth. About this there are eight points of inquiry: (1) Whether truth resides in the thing, or only in the intellect? (2) Whether it resides only in the intellect composing and dividing? (3) On the comparison of the true with being. (4) On the comparison of the true with the good. (5) Whether God is truth? (6) Whether all things are true by one truth, or by many? (7) On the eternity of truth. (8) On the unchangeableness of truth.

First Article
WHETHER TRUTH RESIDES ONLY IN THE INTELLECT?

We proceed thus to the First Article: —

Objection 1. It seems that truth does not reside only in the intellect, but rather in things. For Augustine condemns this definition of truth, *That is true which is seen*;[1] since it would follow that stones hidden in the bosom of the earth would not be true stones, as they are not seen. He also condemns the following, *That is true which is as it appears to the knower, who is willing and able to know*; for hence it would follow that nothing would be true, unless someone could know it. Therefore he

1. 参见 *Solil.*, II,5 (PL 32, 888).

defines truth thus: *The true is which is*[1]. It seems, then, that truth resides in things, and not in the intellect.

*Obj.*2. Further, whatever is true, is true by reason of truth. If, then, truth is only in the intellect, nothing will be true except in so far as it is understood. But this is the error of the ancient philosophers, who said that whatever seems to be true is so.[2] Consequently contradictories can be true at the same time, since contradictories seem to be true as seen by different persons at the same time.

Obj. 3. Further, *that because of which a thing is so, is itself more so*, as is evident from the Philosopher.[3] But *it is from the fact that a thing is or is not, that our thought or word is true or false*, as the Philosopher teaches.[4] Therefore truth resides rather in things than in the intellect.

On the contrary, The Philosopher says, *The true and the false reside not in things, but in the intellect.*[5]

I answer that, As *good* names that towards which the appetite tends, so *the true* names that towards which the intellect tends. Now there is this difference between the appetite and the intellect, or any knowledge whatsoever, that knowledge is according as the thing known is in the knower, while appetite is according as the desirer tends towards the thing desired. Thus the term of the appetite, namely good, is in the desirable thing, and the term of the intellect, namely the true, is in the intellect itself. Now as good exists in a thing so far as that thing is related to the appetite — and hence the aspect of goodness passes on from the desirable thing to the appetite, in so far as the appetite is called good if its object is good; so, since the true is in the intellect in

---

1. The true is which is.：凡存在的都是真的。
2. 参见 Attributed to Democritus and Protagoras by Aristotle, *De An.*, I, 2 (404a 28) ; *Metaph.*, III, 5 (1009a 8).
3. 参见 Aristotle, *Post. Anal.*, I, 2 (72a 29).
4. 参见 *Cat.*, V (4b 8).
5. 参见 *Metaph.*, V, 4 (1027b 25).

so far as the intellect is conformed to the thing understood, the aspect of the true must needs pass from the intellect to the thing understood, so that also the thing understood is said to be true in so far as it has some relation to the intellect.

Now a thing understood may be in relation to an intellect either essentially or accidentally. It is related essentially to an intellect on which it depends as regards its being, but accidentally to an intellect by which it is knowable; even as we may say that a house is related essentially to the intellect of the architect, but accidentally to the intellect upon which it does not depend. Now we do not judge of a thing by what is in it accidentally, but by what is in it essentially. Hence, everything is said to be true absolutely, in so far as it is related to the intellect on which it depends; and thus it is that artificial things are said to be true as being related to our intellect. For a house is said to be true that fulfills the likeness of the form in the architect's mind; and words are said to be true so far as they are the signs of truth in the intellect. In the same way, natural things are said to be true in so far as they express the likeness of the species that are in the divine mind. For a stone is called true, which possesses the nature proper to a stone, according to the preconception in the divine intellect. Thus, then, truth resides primarily in the intellect, and secondarily in things according as they are related to the intellect as their source.

Consequently, there are various definitions of truth. Augustine says, *Truth is that whereby is made manifest that which is*;[1] and Hilary says that *Truth makes being clear and evident*:[2] and this pertains to truth according as it is in the intellect. As to the truth of things in so far as they are related to the intellect, we have Augustine's definition, *Truth*

1. 参见 *De Vera Relig.*, XXXVI (PL 34, 151).
2. 参见 *De Trin.*, V (PL 10, 131).

is a supreme likeness, without any unlikeness, to its source;[1] also Anselm's definition, *Truth is rightness, perceptible by the mind alone*;[2] for that is right which is in accordance with its source; also Avicenna's definition, *The truth of each thing is a property of the being which has been given to it*.[3] The definition that *Truth is the equation of thought and thing* is applicable to it under either aspect.

Reply Obj. 1. Augustine is speaking about the truth of things, and from the notion of this truth excludes relation to our intellect; for what is accidental is excluded from every definition.

Reply Obj. 2. The ancient philosophers held that the species of natural things did not proceed from any intellect, but came about by chance.[4] But as they saw that truth implies relation to intellect, they were compelled to base the truth of things on their relation to our intellect. From this fact there followed the various awkward consequences that the Philosopher attacks.[5] Such consequences, however, do not follow, if we say that the truth of things consists in their relation to the divine intellect.

Reply Obj. 3. Although the truth of our intellect is caused by the thing, yet it is not necessary that the essence of truth should be there primarily, any more than that the essence of health should be primarily in medicine, rather than in the animal: for it is the power of medicine, and not its health, that is the cause of health, since the agent is not univocal. In the same way, the being of the thing, not its truth, is the cause of truth in the intellect. Hence the Philosopher says that an opinion or a statement is true *from the fact that a thing is, not from the fact that a thing is true*.[6]

---

1. 参见 *De Vera Relig.* XXXVI (PL 34, 152).
2. 参见 *De Ver.*, XI (PL 158, 480).
3. 参见 *Metaph.*, VIII, 6 (100r).
4. 参见 Cf. below, q. 22, a. 2.
5. 参见 *Metaph.*, III, 5 (1009a 6); 6 (1011a 3).
6. 参见 *Cat.*, V (4b 8).

Second Article

WHETHER TRUTH RESIDES ONLY IN THE INTELLECT COMPOSING AND DIVIDING?

We proceed thus to the Second Article: —

Objection 1. It seems that truth does not reside only in the intellect composing and dividing. For the Philosopher says that *as the senses are always true as regards their proper sensible objects, so is the intellect as regards what a thing is.*[1] Now composition and division are neither in the senses nor in the intellect knowing *what a thing is.* Therefore truth does not reside only in the intellect composing and dividing.

Obj. 2. Further, Isaac says in his book *On Definitions* that truth is the equation of thought and thing.[2] Now just as the intellect which forms judgments can be equated to things, so also can the intellect that simply apprehends essences; and this is true likewise of sense apprehending a thing as it is. Therefore truth does not reside only in the intellect composing and dividing.

On the contrary, the Philosopher says that *with regard to simple things and what a thing is, truth is not found either in the intellect or in things.*[3]

I answer that, As was stated before, truth resides, in its primary aspect, in the intellect. Now since everything is true according as it has the form proper to its nature, the intellect, in so far as it is knowing, must be true according as it has the likeness of the thing known, which is its form as a knowing power. For this reason truth is defined by the conformity of intellect and thing; and hence to know this

1. 参见 *De An.*, III, 6 (430b 27).
2. 参见 Cf. J. T. Muckle, "Isaac Israeli's Definition of Truth" (*Archives d'hist. doct. et litt. du moyen age*, viii, 1933, pp. 5-8).
3. 参见 *Metaph.*, V, 4 (1027b 27).

conformity[1] is to know truth. But in no way does sense know this. For although sight has the likeness of a visible thing, yet it does not know the comparison which exists between the thing seen and that which it itself is apprehending concerning it. But the intellect can know its own conformity with the intelligible thing; yet it does not apprehend it by knowing of a thing *what a thing is*. When, however, it judges that a thing corresponds to the form which it apprehends about that thing, then it first knows and expresses truth. This it does by composing and dividing: for in every proposition it either applies to, or removes from, the thing signified by the subject some form signified by the predicate. This clearly shows that the sense is true in regard to a given thing, as is also the intellect, in knowing *what a thing is*; but it does not thereby know or affirm truth. This is, in like manner, the case with propositions or terms. Truth, therefore, may be in the sense, or in the intellect knowing *what a thing is*, as in something that is true; yet not as the thing known is in the knower, which is implied by the word *truth*; for the perfection of the intellect is truth *as known*. Therefore, properly speaking, truth resides in the intellect composing and dividing; and not in the sense, nor in the intellect knowing *what a thing is*.

And thus the Objections given are solved.

Third Article
WHETHER THE TRUE AND BEING ARE CONVERTIBLE TERMS ?

We proceed thus to the Third Article: —

Objection 1. It seems that the true and being are not convertible terms. For the true resides properly in the intellect, as has been stated, while being is properly in things. Therefore they are not convertible.

---

1. conformity：一致性

Obj. 2. Further, that which extends to being and non-being is not convertible with being. But the true extends to being and non-being; for it is true that what is, is, and that what is not, is not. Therefore the true and being are not convertible.

Obj. 3. Further, things which stand to each other in order of priority and posteriority seem not to be convertible. But the true appears to be prior to being; for being is not understood except under the aspect of the true. Therefore it seems they are not convertible.

On the contrary, the Philosopher says that there is the same disposition of things in being and in truth.[1]

I answer that, As *good* has the nature of what is desirable, so *the true* is related to knowledge. Now everything is knowable in as far as it has being. Therefore it is said in *De Anima* iii. that *the soul is in some manner all things*,[2] through the senses and the intellect. And therefore, as good is convertible with being, so is the true. But as good adds to being the notion of the desirable, so the true adds a relation to the intellect.

Reply Obj. 1. The true resides in things and in the intellect, as was said before. But the true that is in things is substantially convertible with being, while the true that is in the intellect is convertible with being, as that which manifests is convertible with the manifested; for this belongs to the nature of truth, as has been said already. It may, however, be said, that being also is in things and in the intellect, as is the true; even though truth is primarily in the intellect, while being is primarily in things. This is so because truth and being differ in idea.

Reply Obj. 2. Non-being has nothing in itself whereby it can be known; but it is known in so far as the intellect renders it knowable. Hence the true is based on being, inasmuch as non-being is a certain logical being (apprehended, that is, by reason).

Reply Obj. 3. When it is said that being cannot be apprehended

1. 参见 *Op. cit.*, Ia, 1 (993b 30).
2. 参见 *De An.*, III, 8 (431b 21).

except under the notion of the true, this can be understood in two ways. In the one way, so as to mean that being is not apprehended without the idea of the true following upon the apprehension of being; and this is true. In the other way, so as to mean that being cannot be apprehended unless the notion of the true be also apprehended; and this is false. But the true cannot be apprehended unless the notion of being be also apprehended; since being is included in the notion of the true. The case is the same if we were to compare the intelligible object with being. For being cannot be understood except because being is intelligible. Yet being can be understood while its intelligibility is not understood. Similarly, being understood by the intellect is true; yet the true is not understood by understanding being.

Fourth Article
WHETHER GOOD IS LOGICALLY PRIOR TO THE TRUE?

We proceed thus to the Fourth Article: —

Objection 1. It seems that good is logically prior to the true. For what is more universal is logically prior, as is evident from *Physics* i.[1] But the good is more universal than the true, since the true is a kind of good, namely, of the intellect. Therefore the good is logically prior to the true.

Obj. 2. Further, good is in things, but the true in the intellect composing and dividing, as was said before. But that which is in things is prior to that which is in the intellect. Therefore good is logically prior to the true.

Obj. 3. Further, truth is a species of virtue, as is clear from *Ethics* iv.[2] But virtue is included under good, since, as Augustine says, it is a good

---

1. 参见 Aristotle, *Phys.*, I, 5 (189a 5).
2. 参见 Aristotle, *Eth.*, IV, 7 (1127a 29).

quality of the mind.[1] Therefore the good is prior to the true.

On the contrary, What is in more things is prior logically. But the true is in some things wherein good is not, as, for instance, in mathematics. Therefore the true is prior to good.

I answer that, Although the good and the true are convertible with being, as to suppositum[2], yet they differ logically. And in this manner the true, speaking absolutely, is prior to good, as appears from two reasons. First, because the true is more closely related to being which is itself prior to the good. For the true regards being itself absolutely and immediately, while the nature of good follows being in so far as being is in some way perfect; for thus it is desirable. Secondly, it is evident from the fact that knowledge naturally precedes appetite. Hence, since the true is related to knowledge, and the good to the appetite, the true must be prior in nature to the good.

Reply Obj. 1. The will and the intellect mutually include one another: for the intellect understands the will, and the will wills the intellect to understand. So then, among the things related to the object of the will, are comprised also those that belong to the intellect; and conversely. Whence, in the order of desirable things, good stands as the universal and the true as the particular; whereas in the order of intelligible things the converse is the case. From the fact, then, that the true is a kind of good, it follows that the good is prior in the order of desirable things; but not that it is absolutely prior.

Reply Obj. 2. A thing is prior logically in so far as it is prior in the apprehension of the intellect. Now the intellect first apprehends being itself; secondly, it apprehends that it understands being; and thirdly, it apprehends that it desires being. Hence the notion of being is first, that of truth second, and the notion of good third, even though the good is in things.

---

1. 参见 *De Lib. Arb.*, II, 19 (PL 32, 1267).
2. suppositum：实存

Reply Obj. 3. The virtue which is called *truth* is not truth in general, but a certain kind of truth according to which man shows himself in deed and word as he really is. But truth as applied to *life* is used in a particular sense, inasmuch as a man fulfills in his life that to which he is ordained by the divine intellect; much as it has been said that truth exists in all other things. Furthermore, the truth of *justice* is found in man as he fulfills his duty to his neighbor, as ordained by law. Hence we cannot argue from these particular truths to truth in general.

Fifth Article
WHETHER GOD IS TRUTH?

We proceed thus to the Fifth Article: —

Objection 1. It seems that God is not truth. For truth consists in the intellect composing and dividing. But in God there is no composition and division. Therefore in God there is no truth.

Obj. 2. Further, truth, according to Augustine, is a *likeness to the source.*[1] But in God there is no likeness to a source. Therefore in God there is no truth.

Obj. 3. Further, whatever is said of God, is said of Him as of the first cause of all things. Thus the being of God is the cause of all being, and His goodness the cause of all good. If therefore there is truth in God, all truth will be from Him. But it is true that someone sins. Therefore this will be from God; which is evidently false.

On the contrary, Our Lord says, *I am the Way, the Truth and the Life* (*Jo.* xiv. 6).

I answer that, As was said above, truth is found in the intellect according as it apprehends a thing as it is; and in things according as they have being conformable[2] to an intellect. This is to the greatest degree found in God. For His being is not only conformed

---

1. 参见 *De Vera Relig.*, XXXVI (PL 34, 152).
2. conformable：适合的；一致的

to His intellect, but it is the very act of His intellect; and His act of understanding is the measure and cause of every other being and of every other intellect; and He Himself is His own being and act of understanding. Whence it follows not only that truth is in Him, but that He is the highest and first truth itself.

Reply Obj. 1. Although in the divine intellect there is neither composition nor division, yet in His simple act of intelligence He judges of all things and knows all propositions; and thus there is truth in His intellect.

Reply Obj. 2. The truth of our intellect is according to its conformity with its source, that is to say, the things from which it receives knowledge. The truth also of things is according to their conformity with their source, namely, the divine intellect. Now this cannot be said properly speaking, of divine truth; unless perhaps in so far as truth is appropriated to the Son, Who has a source. But if we speak of divine truth in its essence, we cannot understand what Augustine has said unless the affirmative proposition be resolved into the negative one, as when one says: *the Father is of Himself, because He is not from another*. Similarly, the divine truth can be called *a likeness of its source*, inasmuch as His being is not unlike His intellect.

Reply Obj. 3. Non-being and privation have no truth of themselves, but only in the apprehension of the intellect. Now all apprehension of the intellect is from God. Hence all the truth that exists in the statement,—*that this person commits fornication is true*, is entirely from God. But to argue, *Therefore that this person fornicates is from God*, is a fallacy of accident.

Sixth Article
WHETHER THERE IS ONLY ONE TRUTH ACCORDING TO WHICH ALL THINGS ARE TRUE?

We proceed thus to the Sixth Article:—

Objection 1. It seems that there is only one truth according to which all things are true. For according to Augustine, *nothing is greater than the mind of man, except God.*[1] Now truth is greater than the mind of man; otherwise the mind would be the judge of truth: whereas in fact it judges all things according to truth, and not according to its own measure. Therefore God alone is truth. Therefore there is no other truth but God.

Obj. 2. Further, Anselm says that, *as is the relation of time to temporal things, so is that of truth to true things.*[2] But there is only one time for all temporal things. Therefore there is only one truth, by which all things are true.

On the contrary, it is written (*Ps.* xi. 2), *Truths are decayed from among the children of men.*

I answer that, In a sense there is one truth whereby all things are true, and in a sense not. In proof of which we must consider that when anything is predicated of many things univocally, it is found in each of them according to its proper nature; as animal is found in each species of animal. But when anything is predicated of many things analogically, it is found in only one of them according to its proper nature, and from this one the rest are denominated. So healthiness is predicated of animal, of urine, and of medicine; not that health is not only in the animal, but from the health of the animal, medicine is called healthy, in so far as it is the cause of health, and urine is called healthy, in so far as it indicates health. And although health is neither in medicine nor in urine, yet in either there is something whereby the one causes, and the other indicates health.

Now we have said that truth resides primarily in the intellect, and secondarily in things, according as they are related to the divine intellect. If therefore we speak of truth as it exists in the intellect,

---

1. 参见 *De Trin.*, XV, 1 (PL 42, 1057).
2. 参见 *De Ver.*, XIV (PL 158, 484).

according to its proper nature, then are there many truths in many created intellects; and even in one and the same intellect, according to the number of things known. Whence the *Gloss* on *Ps*. xi. 2 (*Truths are decayed from among the children of men*) says: *As from one man's face many likenesses are reflected in a mirror, so many truths are reflected from the one divine truth.*[1] But if we speak of truth as it is in things, then all things are true by one primary truth, to which each one is assimilated according to its own entity. And thus, although the essences or forms of things are many, yet the truth of the divine intellect is one, in conformity to which all things are said to be true.

Reply Obj. 1. The soul does not judge of all things according to any kind of truth, but according to the first truth, inasmuch as it is reflected in the soul, as in a mirror, by reason of the first principles of the understanding. It follows, therefore, that the first truth is greater than the soul. And yet, even created truth, which resides in our intellect, is greater than the soul, not absolutely, but to the extent that it is the perfection of the intellect; even as science may also be said to be greater than the soul. Yet it remains true that nothing subsisting is greater than the rational soul, except God.

Reply Obj. 2. The saying of Anselm is correct in so far as things are said to be true by their relation to the divine intellect.

Seventh Article
WHETHER CREATED TRUTH IS ETERNAL?

We proceed thus to the Seventh Article: —

Objection 1. It seems that created truth is eternal. For Augustine says, *Nothing is more eternal than the nature of a circle, and that two added to three*

1. 参见 Peter Lombard, *In Psalm.*, super XI, 2 (PL 191, 155); cf *Glossa interl.* (III. 102r).—Cf. also St. Augustine, *Enarr. in Psalm.*, super XI, 2 (PL 36, 158).

make five.[1] But the truth of these is a created truth. Therefore created truth is eternal.

Obj. 2. Further, that which is always, is eternal. But universals are always and everywhere; therefore they are eternal. So therefore is truth, which is the most universal.

Obj. 3. Further, it was always true that what is true in the present was to be in the future. But as the truth of a proposition regarding the present is a created truth, so is that of a proposition regarding the future. Therefore some created truth is eternal.

Obj. 4. Further, all that is without beginning and end is eternal. But the truth of enunciations is without beginning and end. For if their truth had a beginning, then since it was not previously, it was true that truth was not, and true, of course, by reason of truth; so that truth was before it began to be. Similarly, if it be asserted that truth has an end, it follows that it is after it has ceased to be, for it will still be true that truth is not. Therefore truth is eternal.

On the contrary, God alone is eternal, as was laid down before.[2]

I answer that, The truth of enunciations is nothing other than the truth of the intellect. For an enunciation resides in the intellect, and in speech. Now according as it is in the intellect, it has truth of itself, but according as it is in speech, it is called enunciable[3] truth,according as it signifies some truth of the intellect, and not because of any truth residing in the enunciation, as though in a subject. Thus urine is called healthy, not from any health within it but from the health of an animal which it indicates. In like manner, it has been already said that things are called true from the truth of the intellect. Hence, if no intellect were eternal, no truth would be eternal. Now because only the divine intellect is eternal, in it alone

---

1. 参见 *De Lib. Arb.*, II, 8 (PL 32, 1251); *Solil.*, II, 19 (PL 32, 901).
2. 参见 Q. 10, a. 3.
3. enunciable：可陈述的

truth has eternity. Nor does it follow from this that anything else but God is eternal, since the truth of the divine intellect is God Himself, as has already been shown.

Reply Obj. 1. The nature of a circle, and the fact that two and three make five, have eternity in the mind of God.

Reply Obj. 2. That something is always and everywhere can be understood in two ways. In one way, as having in itself the power to extend to all time and to all places, as it belongs to God to be everywhere and always. In the other way, as not having in itself determination to any place or time; as primary matter is said to be one, not because it has one form, as man is one by the unity of one form, but by the absence of all distinguishing forms. In this manner, all universals are said to be everywhere and always, in so far as universals abstract from place and time. It does not, however, follow from this that they are eternal, except in an intellect, if one exists that is eternal.

Reply Obj. 3. What is now was to be, before it was, because its future lay in its cause. Hence, if the cause were removed, that thing's coming to be would not be future. But the first cause is alone eternal. Hence it does not follow that it was always true that what now is would be, except in so far as its future being was in the sempiternal cause; and God alone is such a cause.

Reply Obj. 4. Because our intellect is not eternal, neither is the truth of enunciable propositions, which are formed by us, eternal, but it had a beginning in time. Now before such truth existed, it was not true to say that such a truth did exist, except by reason of the divine intellect, wherein alone truth is eternal. But it is true now to say that that truth did not then exist: and this is true only by reason of the truth that is now in our intellect, and not by reason of any truth in the things. For this is truth concerning non-being, and non-being has no truth of itself, but only so far as our intellect apprehends it. Hence it is true to say that truth did not exist, in so far as we apprehend its non-being as preceding its being.

Eighth Article
WHETHER TRUTH IS IMMUTABLE?

We proceed thus to the Eighth Article: —

Objection 1. It seems that truth is immutable[1]. For Augustine says that *Truth and mind do not rank as equals, otherwise truth would be mutable, as the mind is.*[2]

Obj. 2. Further, what survives all change is immutable; as primary matter is unbegotten and incorruptible, since it survives all generation and corruption. But truth survives all change; for after every change it is true to say that a thing is, or is not. Therefore, truth is immutable.

Obj. 3. Further, if the truth of an enunciation changes, it changes especially with the changing of the thing. But it does not thus change. For truth, according to Anselm, *is a certain rightness*, in so far as a thing answers to that which is in the divine mind concerning it.[3] But this proposition, *Socrates sits*, receiver from the divine mind the signification that Socrates does sit; and it has the same signification even though he does not sit. Therefore the truth of the proposition in no way changes.

Obj. 4. Further, where there is the same cause, there is the same effect. But the same thing is the cause of the truth of the three propositions, *Socrates sits*, *will sit*, *sat*. Therefore the truth of each is the same. But one or other of these must be the true one. Therefore the truth of these propositions remains immutable; and for the same reason that of any other proposition.

On the contrary, It is written (*Ps.* xi. 2), *Truths are decayed from among the children of men.*

---

1. immutable：不可改变的
2. 参见 *De Lib. Arb.*, II, 12 (PL 32, 1259).
3. 参见 *De Ver.*, VII ; X (PL 158, 475; 478).

I answer that, Truth, properly speaking, resides only in the intellect, as was said before; but things are called true in virtue of the truth residing in an intellect. Hence the mutability of truth must be regarded from the point of view of the intellect, the truth of which consists in its conformity to the things understood. Now this conformity may vary in two ways, even as any other likeness, through change in one of the two extremes. Hence, in one way, truth varies on the part of the intellect, from the fact that a change of opinion occurs about a thing which in itself has not changed, and, in another way, when the thing is changed, but not the opinion. In either way there can be a change from true to false. If, then, there is an intellect wherein there can be no alternation of opinions, and the knowledge of which nothing can escape, in this is immutable truth. Now such is the divine intellect, as is clear from what has been said before.[1] Hence the truth of the divine intellect is immutable. But the truth of our intellect is mutable, not because it is itself the subject of change, but in so far as our intellect changes from truth to falsity; for thus forms may be called mutable. But the truth of the divine intellect is that according to which natural things are said to be true, and this is altogether immutable.

Reply Obj. 1. Augustine is speaking of divine truth.

Reply Obj. 2. The true and being are convertible terms. Hence, just as being is not generated nor corrupted of itself, but accidentally, in so far as this being or that is corrupted or generated, as is said in *Physics* i.,[2] so does truth change, not so as that no truth remains, but because that particular truth does not remain which existed previously.

Reply Obj. 3. A proposition not only has truth, as other things are said to have it, namely, in so far as they correspond to that which is the design of the divine intellect concerning them, but it is said to have truth in a special way, in so far as it indicates the truth of the intellect,

---

1. 参见 Q. 14, a. 15.
2. 参见 Aristotle, *Phys.*, I, 8(191b 17).

which consists in the conformity of the intellect with a thing. When this disappears, the truth of an opinion changes, and consequently the truth of the proposition. So therefore this proposition, *Socrates sits*, is true, as long as he is sitting, both with the truth of the thing, in so far as the expression is significative, and with the truth of signification, in so far as it signifies a true opinion. When Socrates rises, the first truth remains, but the second is changed.

Reply Obj. 4. The sitting of Socrates, which is the cause of the truth of the proposition, *Socrates sits*, has not the same status when Socrates sits, after he sits, and before he sits. Hence the truth which results varies, and is variously signified by these propositions concerning present, past, or future. Thus it does not follow, though one of the three propositions is true, that the same truth remains invariable.

Question XVII
CONCERNING FALSITY
(*In Four Articles*)

We next consider falsity[1]. About this, four points of inquiry arise: (1) Whether falsity exists in things? (2) Whether it exists in the sense? (3) Whether it exists in the intellect? (4) Concerning the opposition of the true and the false.

First Article
WHETHER FALSITY EXISTS IN THINGS?

We proceed thus to the First Article: —

Objection 1. It appears that falsity does not exist in things. For Augustine says, *If the true is that which is, it will be concluded that the false exists nowhere; whatever reason may appear to the contrary.*[2]

Obj. 2. Further, false is derived from *fallere* [to deceive]. But things do not deceive; for, as Augustine says, they show nothing but their own species.[3] Therefore the false is not found in things.

Obj. 3. Further, the true is said to exist in things by conformity to the divine intellect, as was stated above.[4] But everything, in so far as it exists, imitates God. Therefore everything is true without admixture[5]

---

1. falsity：虚伪；谎言；错误
2. 参见 *Solil.*, II, 8 (PL 32, 892).
3. 参见 *De Vera Relig.*, XXXVI (PL 34, 152).
4. 参见 Q. 16, a. 1.
5. admixture：混合物；添加剂

of falsity; and thus nothing is false.

On the contrary, Augustine says: *Every body is a true body and a false unity:* for it imitates unity without being unity.[1] But everything imitates the divine unity, yet falls short of it. Therefore in all things falsity exists.

I answer that, Since true and false are opposed, and since opposites stand in relation to the same thing, we must needs seek falsity where primarily we find truth, that is to say, in the intellect. Now, in things, neither truth nor falsity exists, except in relation to the intellect. And since every thing is denominated absolutely by what belongs to it essentially, but is denominated relatively by what belongs to it accidentally, a thing may be called false absolutely when compared with the intellect on which it depends, and to which it is related essentially; but it may be called false relatively as ordered to another intellect, to which it is related accidentally.

Now natural things depend on the divine intellect, as artificial things on the human. Therefore, artificial things are said to be false absolutely and in themselves, in so far as they fall short of the form of the art; whence a craftsman is said to produce a false work, if it falls short of the proper operation of his art. In things that depend on God, falseness cannot be found, in so far as they are compared with the divine intellect; since whatever takes place in things proceeds from the ordinance[2] of that intellect, unless perhaps in the case of voluntary agents only, who have it in their power to withdraw themselves from what is so ordained; wherein consists the evil of sin. Thus sins themselves are called untruths and lies in the Scriptures, according to the words of the text, *Why do you love vanity, and seek after lying?* (*Ps.* iv. 3); as on the other hand virtuous deeds are called the *truth of life* as being obedient to the order of the divine intellect. Thus it is said, *He*

---

1. 参见 *De Vera Relig.*, XXXIV (PL 34, 150).
2. ordinance：条例；法令

that doth truth, cometh to the light (*Jo.* iii. 21).

But in relation to our intellect, natural things, which are compared thereto accidentally, can be called false, not absolutely, but relatively; and that in two ways. In one way, according to the thing signified, and thus a thing is said to be false which is signified or represented by false speech or thought. In this manner, anything can be said to be false as regards any quality not possessed by it; as if we should say that a diameter is a false commensurable thing, as the Philosopher says.[1] So, too, Augustine says: *The tragedian*[2] *is false Hector.*[3] So too, on the contrary, anything can be called true, in regard to that which belongs to it. In another way, a thing can be called false, by way of cause —and thus a thing is said to be false that naturally begets a false opinion. And because it is innate in us to judge of things by external appearances, since our knowledge takes its rise from sense, which principally and essentially deals with external accidents, therefore those external accidents which resemble things other than themselves are said to be false with respect to those things; thus gall is false honey, and tin, false silver. Regarding this, Augustine says: We call those things false that appear to our apprehension like the true;[4] and the Philosopher says: *Things are called false that are naturally apt to appear such as they are not, or what they are not.*[5] In this sense a man is called false as delighting in false opinions or words, and not because he can invent them; for in that way many wise and learned persons might be called false, as is stated in *Metaph.* v.[6]

Reply Obj. 1. A thing compared with the intellect is said to be true in respect to what it is, and false in respect to what it is not. Hence, *The*

---

1. 参见 *Metaph.*, IV, 29 (1024b 19).
2. tragedian：悲剧演员
3. 参见 *Solil.*, II, 10 (PL 32, 893).
4. 参见 *Op. cit.*, II, 6 (PL 32, 889).
5. 参见 *Metaph.*, IV, 29 (1024b 21).
6. 同上 (1025a 2).

true tragedian is a false Hector, as stated in *Soliloq*. ii.[1] As, therefore, in things that are there is found a certain non-being, so in things that are is found a certain character of falseness.

Reply Obj. 2. Things do not deceive by their own nature, but by accident. For they give occasion to falsity by the likeness they bear to things which they actually are not.

Reply Obj. 3. Things are said to be false, not as compared with the divine intellect, in which case they would be false absolutely, but as compared with our intellect; and thus they are false only relatively.

To the argument which is urged on the contrary: A defective likeness or representation does not involve the character of falsity except in so far as it gives occasion to false opinion. Hence a thing is not always said to be false because it resembles another thing, but only when the resemblance is such as naturally to produce a false opinion, not in some cases, but in general.

Second Article
WHETHER THERE IS FALSITY IN THE SENSES ?

We proceed thus to the Second Article: —

Objection 1. It seems that falsity is not in the senses. For Augustine says: *If all the bodily senses report as they are affected, I do not know what more we can require from them.*[2] Thus it seems that we are not deceived by the senses. Therefore falsity is not in them.

Obj. 2. Further, the Philosopher says that falsity is not proper to the senses, but to the imagination.[3]

Obj. 3. Further, in concepts there is neither true nor false, but in judgments only. But affirmation and negation do not belong to the

1. 参见 *Solil*., II,10 (PL 32, 893).
2. 参见 *De Vera Relig*., XXXIII (PL 34, 149).
3. 参见 *Metaph*., III, 5 (1010b 2).

senses. Therefore in the senses there is no falsity.

On the contrary, Augustine says, *It appears that the senses entrap us into error by their deceptive similitudes.*[1]

I answer that, Falsity is not to be sought in the senses except as truth is in them. Now truth is not in them in such a way that the senses know truth, but in so far as they have a true apprehension of sensible things, as was said above.[2] This takes place through the senses apprehending things as they are; and hence it happens that falsity exists in the senses through their apprehending or judging things to be otherwise than they really are.

Now the knowledge of things by the senses is in proportion to the existence of their likeness in the senses; and the likeness of a thing can exist in the senses in three ways. In the first way, primarily and essentially, as in sight there is the likeness of colors and of other sensible objects proper to it. Secondly, essentially, though not primarily; as in sight there is the likeness of figure or bodily shape, and of other sensible objects common to more than one sense. Thirdly, neither primarily nor essentially, but accidentally; as in sight, there is the likeness of a man, not as man, but in so far as it happens to the colored object to be a man.

Sense, then, has no false knowledge about its proper objects, except accidentally and rarely, and then because of an indisposition[3] in the organ it does not receive the sensible form rightly; just as other passive subjects because of their indisposition receive defectively the impressions of the agent. Hence, for instance, it happens that because of an unhealthy tongue sweet seems bitter to a sick person. But as to common objects of sense, and accidental objects, even a rightly disposed sense may have a false judgment, because the sense is

---

1. 参见 *Solil.*, II, 6 (PL 32, 890).
2. 参见 Q. 16, a. 2.
3. indisposition：微恙；不愿意；嫌恶

referred to them not directly, but accidentally, or as a consequence of being related to other objects.

Reply Obj. 1. The affection of sense is its sensation itself. Hence, from the fact that sense reports as it is affected, it follows that we are not deceived in the judgment by which we judge that we are sensing something. Since, however, sense is sometimes affected otherwise than is the thing, it follows that it sometimes reports that thing otherwise than as it is; and thus we are deceived by sense about the thing, not about the fact of sensation.

Reply Obj. 2. Falsity is said not to be proper to sense, since sense is not deceived as to its proper object. Hence in another translation the text reads more plainly, *Sense, about its proper object, is never false.*[1] Falsity is attributed to the imagination, however, as it represents the likeness of something even in its absence. Hence, when anyone perceives the likeness of a thing as if it were the thing itself, falsity results from such an apprehension; and for this reason the Philosopher says that *shadows, pictures and dreams* are said to be false inasmuch as they convey the likeness of things without the substance.[2]

Reply Obj. 3. This argument proves that the false is not in the sense as in that which knows the true and the false.

Third Article
WHETHER FALSITY IS IN THE INTELLECT?

We proceed thus to the Third Article: —

Objection 1. It seems that falsity is not in the intellect. For Augustine says, *Everyone who is deceived understands not that in which he is deceived.*[3] But falsity is said to exist in any knowledge in so far as we are deceived

---

1. 参见 Cf. B. Geyer, in *Phil. Jahrbuch*, XXX (1917), P. 406.
2. 参见 *Metaph.*, IV, 29 (1024b 23).
3. 参见 *Lib. 83 Quaest.*, q. 32 (PL 40, 22).

therein. Therefore falsity does not exist in the intellect.

Obj. 2. Further, the Philosopher says that *the intellect is always right.*[1] Therefore there is no falsity in the intellect.

On the contrary, It is said in *De anima* iii. that *where there is composition of objects understood, there there is truth and falsehood.*[2] But such composition is in the intellect. Therefore truth and falsehood exist in the intellect.

I answer that, Just as a thing has being by its proper form, so the knowing power has knowledge by the likeness of the thing known. Hence, as natural things do not fall short of the being that belongs to them by their form, but may fall short of accidental or consequent qualities, even as a man may fail to possess two feet, but not fail to be a man; so the power of knowing cannot fail in the knowledge of the thing with the likeness of which it is informed, but may fail with regard to something consequent upon that form, or accidental thereto. For it has been said that sight is not deceived in its proper sensible, but about common sensibles that are consequent upon that proper object, or about accidental objects of sense. Now as the sense is directly informed by the likeness of its proper object, so is the intellect by the likeness of the essence of a thing. Hence the intellect is not deceived about the essence of a thing, as neither the sense about its proper object. But in affirming and denying, the intellect may be deceived by attributing to the thing, of which it understands the essence, something which is not consequent upon it, or is opposed to it. For the intellect is in the same position as regards judging of such things, as sense is as to judging of common, or accidental, sensible objects. There is, however, this difference, as was before mentioned regarding truth, that falsity can exist in the intellect not merely because the knowledge of the intellect is false, but because the intellect is conscious of that false knowledge,

1. 参见 *De An.*, III, 10 (433a 26).
2. 参见 *Op. cit.*, III, 6 (430a 27).

as it is conscious of truth;[1] whereas in sense falsity does not exist as known, as was stated above.

But because falsity of the intellect is concerned essentially only with the composition of the intellect, falsity can occur accidentally also in that operation of the intellect whereby it knows the essence of a thing in so far as a composition of the intellect is involved in it. This can take place in two ways. In one way, by the intellect applying to one thing the definition proper to another; as that of a circle to a man. Therefore the definition of one thing is false of another. In another way, by composing a definition of parts which are mutually repugnant. For thus the definition is not only false of the thing, but false in itself. A definition such as 'a four-footed rational animal' would be of this kind, and the intellect false in making it; for such a statement as 'some rational animals are four-footed' is false in itself. For this reason the intellect cannot be false in its knowledge of simple essences; but it is either true, or it understands nothing at all.

Reply Obj. 1. Because the essence of a thing is the proper object of the intellect, we are properly said to understand a thing when we reduce it to its essence, and judge of it thereby; as takes place in demonstrations, in which there is no falsity. In this sense Augustine's words must be understood, *that he who is deceived understands not that wherein he is deceived*; and not in the sense that no one is ever deceived in any operation of the intellect.

Reply Obj. 2. The intellect is always right as regards first principles, since it is not deceived about them for the same reason that it is not deceived about *what a thing is.* For self-known principles are such as are known as soon as the terms are understood, from the fact that the predicate is contained in the definition of the subject.

---

1. 参见 Q. 16, a. 2.

Fourth Article
WHETHER TRUE AND FALSE ARE CONTRARIES?

We proceed thus to the Fourth Article: —

Objection 1. It seems that true and false are not contraries. For true and false are opposed as that which is to that which is not; for *the true*, as Augustine says, *is that which is.*[1] But that which is and that which is not are not opposed as contraries. Therefore true and false are not contraries.

Obj. 2. Further, one of two contraries is not in the other. But falsity is in truth, because, as Augustine says, *A tragedian would not be a false Hector, if he were not a true tragedian.*[2] Therefore true and false are not contraries.

Obj. 3. Further, in God there is no contrariety, for *nothing is contrary to the Divine Substance*, as Augustine says.[3] But falsity is opposed to God, for an idol is called a lie in Scripture. *They have laid hold on lying* (*Jer.* viii. 5), that is to say, *an idol*, as the *Gloss* says.[4] Therefore true and false are not contraries.

On the contrary, The Philosopher says that a false opinion is contrary to a true one.[5]

I answer that, True and false are opposed as contraries, and not, as some have said, as affirmation and negation.[6] In proof of which it must be considered that negation neither asserts anything nor determines for itself any subject. It can therefore be said of being as of non-being.

---

1. 参见 *Solil.*, II, 5 (PL 32, 889).
2. 参见 *Op. cit.*, II, 10 (PL 32, 893).
3. 参见 *De Civit. Dei*,XII, 2 (PL 41, 350).
4. 参见 *Glossa interl.*, super *Jeremiah*, VIII, 5 (IV, 123V).— Cf. St. Jerome, *In Jerem.*, super VIII, 5 (PL 24, 765).
5. 参见 *Perih.*, II, 14 (23b 35).
6. 参见 Cf. Alex. of Hales, *Summa Theol.*, I, no. 101 (1,159).

for instance, not-seeing or not-sitting. But though privation asserts nothing, it determines a subject, for it is *negation in a subject*, as is stated in *Metaph.* iv.;[1] for blindness is not said except of one whose nature it is to see. Contraries, however, both assert something and determine a subject, for blackness is a species of color. Now falsity asserts something, for a thing is false, as the Philosopher says,[2] inasmuch as *something is said or seems to be something that it is not, or not to be what it really is.* For as truth implies an adequate apprehension of a thing, so falsity implies the contrary. Hence it is clear that true and false are contraries.

Reply Obj. 1. What is in things is the truth of the thing; but what is apprehended is the truth of the intellect, wherein truth primarily resides. Hence the false is that which is not as apprehended. But to apprehend being and non-being implies contrariety; for, as the Philosopher proves, the contrary of the statement *good is good* is, *good is not good.*[3]

Reply Obj. 2. Falsity is not founded in the truth which is contrary to it, just as evil is not founded in the good which is contrary to it, but in that which is its proper subject. This happens in both cases because *true* and *good* are universals and convertible with being. Hence, as every privation is founded in a subject that is a being, so every evil is founded in some good, and every falsity in some truth.

Reply Obj. 3. Because contraries, and opposites by way of privation, are by nature about one and the same thing, therefore there is nothing contrary to God, considered in Himself, either with respect to His goodness or His truth; for in His intellect there can be nothing false. But in our apprehension of Him, God has a contrary, for the false opinion concerning Him is contrary to the true. So idols are

---

1. 参见 Aristotle, *Metaph.*, III, 2 (1004a 15) ; IV, 22 (1022a 26).
2. 参见 *Op. cit.*, III. 7 (1011b 26).
3. 参见 *Perih.*, II, 14 (23b 35).

called lies which are opposed to the divine truth, inasmuch as the false opinion concerning them is contrary to the true opinion of the divine unity.

Question XVIII
THE LIFE OF GOD
(*In Four Articles*)

SINCE to understand belongs to living beings, after considering the divine knowledge and intellect, we must consider the divine life. About this, four points of inquiry arise: (1) To whom does it belong to live? (2) What is life? (3) Whether life is properly attributed to God? (4) Whether all things in God are life?

First Article
WHETHER TO LIVE BELONGS TO ALL NATURAL THINGS?

We proceed thus to the First Article: —

Objection 1. It seems that to live belongs to all natural things. For the Philosopher says that *movement is like a kind of life possessed by all things existing in nature.*[1] But all natural things participate in movement. Therefore all natural things partake in life.

Obj. 2. Further, plants are said to live, inasmuch as they have in themselves a principle of movement, of growth and decay. But local movement is naturally more perfect than, and prior to, movement of growth and decay, as the Philosopher shows.[2] Since, then, all natural bodies have in themselves some principle of local movement, it seems that all natural bodies live.

Obj. 3. Further, among natural bodies the elements are the less

1. 参见 *Phys.*, VIII, 1 (250b 14).
2. 参见 *Op. cit.*, VIII, 7 (260a 28).

perfect. Yet life is attributed to them, for we speak of 'living waters.' Much more, therefore, have other natural bodies life.

On the contrary, Dionysius says that *The last echo of life is heard in the plants*;[1] whereby it is inferred that their life is life in its lowest degree. But inanimate bodies are inferior to plants. Therefore they have not life.

I answer that, We can gather to what things life belongs, and to what it does not, from such things as manifestly possess life. Now life manifestly belongs to animals, for it is said in *De Vegetab.* i. that in animals life is manifest.[2] We must, therefore, distinguish living from lifeless things by comparing them to that by reason of which animals are said to live: and this it is in which life is manifested first and remains last. We say then that an animal begins to live when it begins to move of itself: and as long as such movement appears in it, so long is it considered to be alive. When it no longer has any movement of itself, but is moved only by another power, then its life is said to fail, and the animal to be dead. Whereby it is clear that those beings are properly called living that move themselves by some kind of movement whether it be movement properly so called, as *the act of the imperfect* (*i.e.*, of a thing which exists in potentiality) is called movement; or movement in a more general sense, as when said of *the act of the perfect*, *as understanding* and *sensing* are called movements, as is said in *De Anima*, iii.[3] Accordingly, all things are said to be alive that determine themselves to movement or to operation of any kind: whereas those things that cannot by their nature do so cannot be called living, unless by some likeness.

Reply Obj. 1. These words of the Philosopher may be understood either of the first movement, namely, that of the celestial bodies, or of

1. 参见 *De Div. Nom.*, VI, 1 (PG 3, 856).
2. 参见 Aristotle, *De Plantis*, I, 1 (815a 10).
3. 参见 Aristotle, *De An.*, III, 7 (431a 6); I, 4 (408b 6).

movement in its general sense. In either way movement is called the life, as it were, of natural bodies only metaphorically and not properly. The movement of the heavens is in the universe of corporeal natures as the movement of the heart, whereby life is preserved, is in animals. Similarly also every natural movement in respect to natural things has a certain likeness to the operations of life. Hence, if the whole corporeal universe were one animal, so that its movement came from an interior moving principle, as some in fact have held, in that case movement would really be the life of all natural bodies.

Reply Obj. 2. To bodies, whether heavy or light, movement does not belong, except in so far as they are displaced from their natural conditions, and are out of their proper place; for when they are in the place that is proper and natural to them, then they are at rest. Plants and other living things move with vital movement, in accordance with the disposition of their nature, but not by approaching thereto, or by receding from it, for in so far as they recede from such movement, so far do they recede from their natural disposition[1]. Furthermore, *heavy and light bodies are moved by an extrinsic mover*[2], *either generating them and giving them form, or removing obstacles from their way*, as is said in *Physics* viii.[3] They do not therefore move themselves, as do living bodies.

Reply Obj. 3. Waters are called living that have a continuous current[4]: for standing waters, that are not connected with a continually flowing source, are called dead, as in cisterns and ponds. This is merely a similitude, inasmuch as the movement they are seen to possess makes them look as if they were alive. Yet they do not have life in its real nature, since this movement of theirs is not from themselves but from the cause that generates them; as is the case with the movement of

---

1. disposition：天性；安排
2. extrinsic mover：外在的推动者
3. 参见 Aristotle, *Phys.*, VIII, 4 (255b 35).
4. continuous current：连续流动；直流

other heavy and light bodies.

Second Article
WHETHER LIFE IS AN OPERATION ?

We proceed thus to the Second Article: —

Objection 1. It seems that life is an operation. For nothing is divided except into parts of the same genus. But life is divided by certain operations, as is clear from the Philosopher[1] who distinguishes four kinds of life, namely, nourishment, sensation, local movement and understanding. Therefore life is an operation.

Obj. 2. Further, the active life is said to be different from the contemplative. But the contemplative is only distinguished from the active by certain operations. Therefore life is an operation.

Obj. 3. Further, to know God is an operation. But this is life, as is clear from the words of *John* xvii. 3, *Now this is eternal life, that they may know Thee, the only true God.* Therefore life is an operation.

On the contrary, The Philosopher says: *In living things to live is to be.*[2]

I answer that, As is clear from what has been said, our intellect, which knows the essence of a thing as its proper object, derives knowledge from sense, of which the proper objects are external accidents.[3] Hence it is that from external appearances we come to the knowledge of the essence of things. And because we name a thing in accordance with our knowledge of it, as is clear from what has already been said,[4] so from external properties names are often imposed to signify essences. Hence such names are sometimes taken strictly to denote the essence itself, the signification of which is their principal

---

1. 参见 *De An.*, II, 2 (413a 22).
2. 参见 *Op. cit.*, II, 4 (415b 13).
3. 参见 Q. 17, a. 1 and 3.
4. 参见 Q. 13, a. 1.

object; but sometimes, and less strictly, to denote the properties by reason of which they are imposed. And so we see that the word *body* is used to denote a particular genus of substances from the fact of their possessing three dimensions; and so it is sometimes taken to denote the dimensions themselves, in which sense body is said to be a species of quantity.

The same must be said of life. The name is given from a certain external appearance, namely, self-movement, yet not precisely to signify this, but rather a substance to which self-movement, or the application of itself to any kind of operation, belongs naturally. *To live*, accordingly, is nothing else than for a substance with such a nature *to be*; and *life* signifies this very fact, but abstractly, as *running* abstractly signifies *to run*. Hence *living* is not an accidental, but a substantial, predicate. Sometimes, however, life is used less properly for the operations from which its name is taken; and thus the Philosopher says that *to live is principally to sense or to understand.*[1]

Reply Obj. 1. The Philosopher here takes *to live* to mean an operation of life. Or it would be better to say that sensation and intelligence, and the like, are sometimes taken for the operations, sometimes for the being itself of those who are operating in this way. For he says that to be is to sense or to understand[2] — in other words, to have a nature capable of sensation or understanding. It is in this way that he distinguishes life by the four operations mentioned. For in this lower world there are four kinds of living things. It is the nature of some to be capable of nothing more than taking nourishment, and, as a consequence, of growing and generating. Others are able, in addition, to sense, as we see in the case of shellfish and other animals without movement. Others have the further power of moving from place to place, as perfect animals, such as quadrupeds, and birds, and so on.

1. 参见 *Eth.*, IX, 9 (1170a 18).
2. 同上 (1170a 33)

Others, as man, have the still higher perfection of understanding.

Reply Obj. 2. By vital operations are meant those whose principles are within the operator, and in virtue of which the operator produces such operations of itself. It happens, however, that there exist in men not merely such natural principles of certain operations as are their natural powers, but something over and above these, namely, habits inclining them in the manner of a nature to particular kinds of operations and rendering those operations pleasurable. Thus, as by a similitude, any kind of work in which a man takes delight, so that his bent is towards it, his time spent in it, and his whole life ordered with a view to it, is said to be the life of that man. Hence some are said to lead a life of self-indulgence, others a life of virtue. It is in this way that the contemplative life[1] is distinguished from the active; and in this manner likewise to know God is said to be life eternal.

Wherefore the Reply to the third objection is clear.

Third Article
WHETHER LIFE IS PROPERLY ATTRIBUTED TO GOD?

We proceed thus to the Third Article: —

Objection 1. It seems that life is not properly attributed to God For things are said to live inasmuch as they move themselves, as was previously stated. But movement does not belong to God. Neither therefore does life.

Obj. 2. Further, in all living things we must needs suppose some principle of life. Hence it is said by the Philosopher that *the soul is the cause and principle of the living body.*[2] But God has no principle. Therefore life cannot be attributed to Him.

Obj. 3. Further, the principle of life in the living things around us is

1. the contemplative life：默观生活
2. 参见 *De An.*, II, 4 (415b 8).

the vegetative soul. But this exists only in corporeal things. Therefore life cannot be attributed to incorporeal things.

On the contrary, It is said (*Ps.* lxxxiii. 3): *My heart and my flesh have rejoiced in the living God.*

I answer that, Life is most properly in God. In proof of which it must be, considered that since a thing is said to live in so far as it operates of itself and not as moved by another, the more perfectly this power is found in anything, the more perfect is the life of that thing. In things that move and are moved three things are distinguished in order. In the first place, the end moves the agent: and the principal agent is that which acts through its own form (sometimes it does so through some instrument that acts by virtue, not of its own form, but of the principal agent, and does no more than execute the action). Accordingly, there are things that move themselves, not in relation to any form or end naturally inherent in them, but only with relation to the execution of the movement: the form by which they act, and the end of the action are determined for them by their nature. Of this kind are plants, which move themselves according to their inherent nature, with regard only to executing the movements of growth and decay.

Other things have self-movement in a higher degree, that is, not only with relation to the execution of the movement, but even with relation to the form which is the principle of movement, which they acquire by themselves. Of this kind are animals, in which the principle of movement is not a naturally implanted form, but one received through sense. Hence the more perfect their sense, the more perfect is their power of self-movement. Such as have only the sense of touch, as shellfish, move only with the motion of expansion and contraction; and thus their movement hardly exceeds that of plants. Whereas such as have the power of sense in perfection, so as to recognize not only what is joined to them or touches them, but also objects apart from themselves, can move themselves to a distance by progressive movement.

Yet although animals of the latter kind receive through sense the form that is the principle of their movement, nevertheless they cannot of themselves propose to themselves the end of their operation or their movement, for this has been implanted in them by nature; and by natural instinct they are moved to any action through the form apprehended by sense. Hence such animals as move themselves in relation to an end that they themselves propose are superior to these. This can be done only by reason and intellect, whose province it is to know the proportion between the end and the means to that end, and duly co-ordinate them. Hence a more perfect degree of life is that of intelligent beings, for their power of self-movement is more perfect. This is shown by the fact that in one and the same man the intellectual power moves the sensitive powers; and these by their command move the organs of movement. Just as also in the arts we see that the art of using a ship, *i.e.*, the art of navigation, rules the art of ship-designing; and this in its turn rules the art that is only concerned with preparing the material for the ship.

But although our intellect moves itself to some things, yet others are set for it by nature, as are first principles, which it must accept, and the last end, which it cannot but will. Hence, although with respect to some things it moves itself, yet with regard to other things it must be moved by another. Hence, that being whose act of understanding is its very nature, and which, in what it naturally possesses, is not determined by another, must have life in the most perfect degree. Such is God; and hence in Him principally is life. From this the Philosopher concludes, after showing God to be intelligent, that God has life most perfect and eternal, since His intellect is most perfect and always in act.[1]

Reply Obj. 1. As is stated in *Metaph.* ix.,[2] action is twofold. Actions of

1. 参见 *Metaph.*, XI, 7 (1072b 27).
2. 参见 *Op. cit.*, VIII, 8 (1050a 22).

one kind pass out to external matter, as to heat or to cut, while actions of the other kind remain in the agent, as to understand, to sense, and to will. The difference between them is this, that the former action is the perfection, not of the agent that moves, but of the thing moved; whereas the latter action is the perfection of the agent. Hence, because movement is an act of the thing in movement, the latter action, in so far as it is the act of the operator, is called its movement, on the basis of the similitude that as movement is an act of the thing moved, so an action of this kind is the act of the agent. And although movement is an act of the imperfect, that is, of what is in potentiality, this kind of action is an act of the perfect, that is to say, of what is in act, as is stated in *De anima* iii.[1] In the sense, therefore, in which understanding is movement, that which understands itself is said to move itself. It is in this sense that Plato also taught that God moves Himself,[2] and not in the sense in which movement is an act of the imperfect.

Reply Obj. 2. As God is His own being and understanding, so He is His own life; and therefore He so lives that He has no principle of life.

Reply Obj. 3. Life in this lower world is bestowed on a corruptible nature, that needs generation to preserve the species, and nourishment to preserve the individual. For this reason life is not found here below apart from a vegetative soul: but this does not hold good among incorruptible beings.

Fourth Article
WHETHER ALL THINGS ARE LIFE IN GOD?

We proceed thus to the Fourth Article: —

Objection 1. It seems that not all things are life in God. For it is said (*Acts* xvii. 28), *In Him we live, and move, and are.* But not all things in

---

1. 参见 Aristotle, *De An.*, III, 7 (431a 6).
2. 参见 Cf. above, q. 9, a. 1, ad 1.

God are movement. Therefore not all things are life in Him.

Obj. 2. Further, all things are in God as in their first exemplar. But all likenesses of an exemplar should be modeled after it. Since, then, not all things have life in themselves, it seems that not all things are life in God.

Obj. 3. Further, as Augustine says,[1] a living substance is better than a substance that does not live. If, therefore, things which in themselves have not life are life in God, it seems that things exist more truly in God than in themselves. But this appears to be false, since in themselves they exist actually, but in God potentially.

Obj. 4. Further, just as good things and things made in time are known by God, so are evils and things that God can make, but that never will be made. If, therefore, all things are life in God, inasmuch as known by Him, it seems that even evils and things that will never be made are life in God, as known by Him, and this appears inadmissible[2].

On the contrary (*Jo.* i. 3, 4), It is said, *What was made, in Him was life.* But all things were made, except God. Therefore all things are life in God.

I answer that, In God to live is to understand, as was before stated. But in God intellect, the thing understood, and the act of understanding are one and the same. Hence whatever is in God as understood is the very living or life of God. Now, therefore, since all things that have been made by God are in Him as things understood, it follows that all things in Him are the divine life itself.

Reply Obj. 1. Creatures are said to be in God in a two-fold sense. In one way, so far as they are contained and preserved by the divine power; even as we say that things that are in our power are in us. And thus creatures are said to be in God, even according to their existence

1. 参见 *De Vera Relig.*, XXIX (PL 34, 145).
2. inadmissible：不能允许的；不可接受的

in their own natures. In this sense we must understand the words of the Apostle when he says, *In Him we live, and move, and are*; since our living, being and moving are themselves caused by God. In another sense, things are said to be in God as in Him who knows them; in which sense they are in God through their proper likenesses, which are nothing other in God than the divine essence. Hence things as they are in this way in God are the divine essence. And since the divine essence is life but not movement, it follows that things existing in God in this manner are not movement, but life.

Reply Obj. 2. The thing modeled must be like the exemplar according to the form, not the mode of being. For sometimes the form has being of another kind in the exemplar from that which it has in the thing modeled. Thus the form of a house has immaterial and intelligible being in the mind of the architect; but in the house that exists outside his mind, material and sensible being. Hence the likenesses of these things, which do not have life in themselves, are life in the divine mind, as having a divine being in that mind.

Reply Obj. 3. If form only, and not matter, belonged to natural things, then in all respects natural things would exist more truly in the divine mind, by the ideas of them, than in themselves. For which reason, in fact, Plato held that the *separate* man was the true man,[1] and that man, as he exists in matter, is man only by participation. But since matter enters into the being of natural things, we must say that natural things have a truer being absolutely in the divine mind than in themselves, because in that mind they have an uncreated being, but in themselves a created being. But to be this particular being, namely, a man or a horse, this they have more truly in their own nature than in the divine mind, because it belongs to human nature to be material, which, as existing in the divine mind, it is not. Even so a house has

1. 参见 Cf. St. Augustine, *Epist.* III (PL 33, 64); *Epist.* CXVIII, 3 (PL 33, 441). — Cf. also Aristotle, *Metaph.*, I, 6 (987b 7).

nobler being in the architect's mind than in matter; yet a material house is called a house more truly than the one which exists in the mind, since the former is actual, the latter only potential.

Reply Obj. 4. Although evils are in God's knowledge, as being comprehended by that knowledge, yet they are not in God as created by Him, or preserved by Him, or as having a likeness in Him. For they are known by God through the likenesses of good things. Hence it cannot be said that evils are life in God. Those things that at no time exist may be called life in God in so far as life means understanding only, and inasmuch as they are understood by God; but not in so far as life implies a source of operation.

Question XIX
THE WILL OF GOD
(*In Twelve Articles*)

AFTER considering the things belonging to the divine knowledge, we consider what belongs to the divine will. The first consideration is about the divine will itself; the second, about what belongs to His will absolutely;[1] the third, about what belongs to the intellect in relation to His will.[2] About His will itself there are twelve points of inquiry: (1) Whether there is will in God? (2) Whether God wills things other than Himself? (3) Whether whatever God wills, He wills necessarily? (4) Whether the will of God is the cause of things? (5) Whether any cause can be assigned to the divine will? (6) Whether the divine will is always fulfilled? (7) Whether the will of God is mutable? (8) Whether the will of God imposes necessity on the things willed? (9) Whether God wills evil? (10) Whether God has free choice? (11) Whether the *will of sign* is distinguished in God? (12) Whether five signs of will are rightly held of the divine will?

First Article
WHETHER THERE IS WILL IN GOD?

We proceed thus to the First Article: —

Objection 1. It seems that there is no will in God. For the object of will is the end and the good. But we cannot assign any end to God.

---

1. 参见 Q. 20.
2. 参见 Q. 22.

Therefore there is no will in God.

Obj. 2. Further, will is a kind of appetite. But appetite, since it is directed to things not possessed, implies imperfection, which cannot be imputed to God. Therefore there is no will in God.

Obj. 3. Further, according to the Philosopher, the will is a moved mover.[1] But God is the first mover, Himself unmoved, as is proved in *Physics* viii.[2] Therefore there is no will in God.

On the contrary, The Apostle says (*Rom.* xii. 2): *That you may prove what is the will of God.*

I answer that, There is will in God, just as there is intellect: since will follows upon intellect. For as natural things have actual being by their form, so the intellect is actually knowing by its intelligible form. Now everything has this disposition towards its natural form, that when it does not have it, it tends towards it; and when it has it, it is at rest therein. It is the same with every natural perfection, which is a natural good. This disposition to good in things without knowledge is called *natural appetite*[3]. Whence also intellectual natures have a like disposition to good as apprehended through an intelligible form, so as to rest therein when possessed, and when not possessed to seek to possess it; both of which pertain to the will. Hence in every intellectual being there is will, just as in every sensible being there is animal appetite. And so there must be will in God, since there is intellect in Him. And as His knowing is His own being, so is His willing.

Reply Obj. 1. Although nothing apart from God is His end, yet He Himself is the end with respect to all things made by Him. And He is the end by His essence, for by His essence He is good, as was shown above:[4] for the end has the aspect of good.

---

1. 参见 *De An.*, III, 10 (433b 16).
2. 参见 Aristotle, *Phys.*, VIII, 6 (258b 10)
3. natural appetite：自然欲望
4. 参见 Q. 6, a. 3.

Reply Obj. 2. Will in us belongs to the appetitive part, which, although named from appetite, has not for its only act to seek what it does not possess, but also to love and delight in what it does possess. In this respect will is said to be in God, as always possessing the good which is its object; since, as we have already said, it is not in essence distinct from this good.

Reply Obj. 3. A will, of which the principal object is a good outside itself, must be moved by another: but the object of the divine will is His goodness, which is His essence. Hence, since the will of God is His essence, it is not moved by another than itself, but by itself alone (in the same sense, of course, in which understanding and willing are said to be movements). This is what Plato meant when he said that the first mover moves himself.[1]

Second Article
WHETHER GOD WILLS THINGS OTHER THAN HIMSELF ?

We proceed thus to the Second Article: —

Objection 1. It seems that God does not will things other than Himself. For the divine will is the divine being. But God is not other than Himself. Therefore He does not will things other than Himself.

Obj. 2. Further, the object willed moves the one who wills, as the appetible the appetite, as is stated in *De anima* iii.[2] If, therefore, God wills anything apart from Himself, His will must be moved by another; which is impossible.

Obj. 3. Further, if what is willed suffices the one who wills, he seeks nothing beyond it. But His own goodness suffices God, and completely satisfies His will. Therefore God does not will anything other than Himself.

---

1. 参见 Cf. above, q. 9, a. 1, ad. 1.
2. 参见 Aristotle, *De An.*, III, 10 (433b 17).

Obj. 4. Further, acts of the will are multiplied according to the number of their objects. If, therefore, God wills Himself and things other than Himself, it follows that the act of His will is manifold[1], and consequently His being, which is His will. But this is impossible. Therefore God does not will things other than Himself.

On the contrary, The Apostle says (*1 Thess.* iv. 3): *This is the will of God, your sanctification.*

I answer that, God wills not only Himself, but also things other than Himself. This is clear from the comparison made above. For natural things have a natural inclination not only towards their own proper good, to acquire it if not possessed, and, if possessed, to rest therein; but also to diffuse their own good among others so far as possible. Hence we see that every agent, in so far as it is perfect and in act, produces its like. It pertains, therefore, to the nature of the will to communicate as far as possible to others the good possessed; and especially does this pertain to the divine will, from which all perfection is derived in some kind of likeness. Hence, if natural things, in so far as they are perfect, communicate their good to others, much more does it pertain to the divine will to communicate by likeness its own good to others as much as is possible. Thus, then, He wills both Himself to be, and other things to be; but Himself as the end, and other things as ordained to that end, inasmuch as it befits the divine goodness that other things should be partakers therein.

Reply Obj. 1. Although in God to will is really the same as to be, yet they differ logically, according to the different ways of understanding them and signifying them, as is clear from what has been already said.[2] For when we say that God exists, no relation to any other thing is implied, as we do imply when we say that God wills. Therefore, although He is not anything other than Himself, yet He does will

1. manifold：多样的；各种各样的
2. 参见 Q. 13, a. 4.

things other than Himself.

Reply Obj. 2. In things willed for the sake of the end, the whole reason for our being moved is the end; and this it is that moves the will, as most clearly appears in things willed only for the sake of the end. He who wills to take a bitter draught, in doing so wills nothing else than health; and this alone moves his will. It is different with one who takes a draught that is pleasant, which anyone may will to do, not only for the sake of health, but also for its own sake. Hence, although God wills things other than Himself only for the sake of the end, which is His own goodness, it does not follow that anything else moves His will, except His goodness. So, as He understands things other than Himself by understanding His own essence, so He wills things other than Himself by willing His own goodness.

Reply Obj. 3. From the fact that His own goodness suffices the divine will, it does not follow that it wills nothing other than itself, but rather that it wills nothing except by reason of its goodness. Thus, too, the divine intellect: although its perfection consists in its knowledge of the divine essence, yet in that essence it knows other things.

Reply Obj. 4. As the divine knowing is one, as seeing the many only in the one, in the same way the divine willing is one and simple, as willing the many only through the one, that is, through its own goodness.

Third Article
WHETHER WHATEVER GOD WILLS HE WILLS NECESSARILY?

We proceed thus to the Third Article: —

Objection 1. It seems that whatever God wills He wills necessarily. For everything eternal is necessary. But whatever God wills, He wills from eternity, for otherwise His will would be mutable. Therefore whatever He wills, He wills necessarily.

Obj. 2. Further, God wills things other than Himself inasmuch as He wills His own goodness. Now God wills His own goodness necessarily. Therefore He wills things other than Himself necessarily.

Obj. 3. Further, whatever belongs to the nature of God is necessary, for God is of Himself necessary being, and the source of all necessity, as was above shown.[1] But it belongs to His nature to will whatever He wills; since in God there can be nothing over and above His nature, as is stated in *Metaph.* v.[2] Therefore whatever He wills, He wills necessarily.

Obj. 4. Further, being that is not necessary, and being that is possible not to be, are one and the same thing. If, therefore, God does not necessarily will a thing that He wills, it is also possible for Him not to will it, and therefore possible for Him to will what He does not will. And so the divine will is contingent, with respect to choosing determinately among these things; and also imperfect, since everything contingent is imperfect and mutable.

Obj. 5. Further, on the part of that which is indifferent to one or the other of two things, no action results unless it is inclined to one or the other by some other being, as the Commentator says on *Physics* ii.[3] If, then, the will of God is indifferent with regard to anything, it follows that His determination to a given effect comes from another; and thus He has some cause prior to Himself.

Obj. 6. Further, whatever God knows He knows necessarily. But as the divine knowledge is His essence, so is the divine will. Therefore whatever God wills He wills necessarily.

On the contrary, The Apostle says (*Ephes* i. 11): *Who worketh all things according to the counsel of His will.* Now, what we work according to the counsel of the will, we do not will necessarily. Therefore God does not

1. 参见 Q. 2,a. 3.
2. 参见 Aristotle, *Metaph.*, IV, 5 (1015b 15)
3. 参见 *Phys.*, II, comm. 48 (IV, 31V).

will necessarily whatever He wills.

I answer that, There are two ways in which a thing is said to be necessary, namely, absolutely, and by supposition. We judge a thing to be absolutely necessary from the relation of the terms, as when the predicate forms part of the definition of the subject: thus it is necessary that man is an animal; or as when the subject forms part of the notion of the predicate: thus it is necessary that a number must be odd or even. In this way it is not necessary that Socrates sits: hence it is not necessary absolutely, but it may be so by supposition; for, granted that he is sitting, he must necessarily sit, as long as he is sitting.

Accordingly, as to things willed by God, we must observe that He wills something of absolute necessity; but this is not true of all that He wills. For the divine will has a necessary relation to the divine goodness, since that is its proper object. Hence God wills the being of His own goodness necessarily, even as we will our own happiness necessarily, and as any other power has a necessary relation to its proper and principal object, for instance the sight to color, since it is of its nature to tend to it. But God wills things other than Himself in so far as they are ordered to His own goodness as their end. Now in willing an end we do not necessarily will things that conduce to it, unless they are such that the end cannot be attained without them; as, we will to take food to preserve life, or to take a ship in order to cross the sea. But we do not will necessarily those things without which the end is attainable, such as a horse for a stroll, since we can take a stroll without a horse. The same applies to other means. Hence, since the goodness of God is perfect and can exist without other things, inasmuch as no perfection can accrue to Him from them, it follows that for Him to will things other than Himself is not absolutely necessary. Yet it can be necessary by supposition, for supposing that He wills a thing, then He is unable not to will it, as His will cannot change.

Reply Obj. 1. From the fact that God wills from eternity whatever

He wills, it does not follow that He wills it necessarily, except by supposition.

Reply Obj. 2. Although God wills necessarily His own goodness, He does not necessarily will things willed because of His goodness; for it can exist without other things.

Reply Obj. 3. It is not natural to God to will any of those other things that He does not will necessarily; and yet it is not unnatural or contrary to His nature, but voluntary.

Reply Obj. 4. Sometimes a necessary cause has a non-necessary relation to an effect, owing to a deficiency in the effect, and not in the cause. Thus, the sun's power has a non-necessary relation to some contingent events on this earth owing to a defect, not in the solar power, but in the effect that proceeds not necessarily from the cause. In the same way, that God does not necessarily will some of the things that He wills, does not result from defect in the divine will, but from a defect belonging to the nature of the thing willed, namely, that the perfect goodness of God can be without it; and such defect accompanies every created good.

Reply Obj. 5. A naturally contingent cause must be determined to act by some external being. The divine will, however, which by its nature is necessary, determines itself to will things to which it has no necessary relation.

Reply Obj. 6. Just as the divine being is necessary of itself, so is the divine willing and the divine knowing; but the divine knowing has a necessary relation to the thing known; not the divine willing, however, to the thing willed. The reason for this is that knowledge is of things as they exist in the knower; but the will is related to things as they exist in themselves. Since, then, all other things have a necessary being inasmuch as they exist in God, but no absolute necessity to be necessary in themselves, in so far as they exist in themselves, it follows that God knows necessarily whatever He knows, but does not will necessarily whatever He wills.

Fourth Article

WHETHER THE WILL OF GOD IS THE CAUSE OF THINGS?

We proceed thus to the Fourth Article: —

Objection 1. It seems that the will of God is not the cause of things. For Dionysius says: *As our sun, not by reasoning nor by choice, but by its very being, enlightens all things that can participate in its light, so the divine good by its very essence pours the rays of its goodness upon everything that exists.*[1] But every voluntary agent acts by reasoning and choice. Therefore God does not act by will; and so His will is not the cause of things.

Obj. 2. Further, the first in any order is that which is essentially so; thus in the order of burning things, that comes first which is fire by its essence. But God is the first agent. Therefore He acts by His essence; and that is His nature. He acts then by nature, and not by will. Therefore the divine will is not the cause of things.

Obj. 3. Further, whatever is the cause of anything, because it itself is such a thing, is a cause by nature, and not by will. For fire is the cause of heat, as being itself hot; whereas an architect is the cause of a house, because he wills to build it. Now Augustine says, *Because God is good, we exist.*[2] Therefore God is the cause of things by His nature, and not by His will.

Obj. 4. Further, of one thing there is one cause. But the cause of created things is the knowledge of God, as was said before.[3] Therefore the will of God cannot be considered the cause of things.

On the contrary, It is said (*Wis.* xi. 26), *How could anything endure, if Thou wouldst not?*

I answer that, We must hold that the will of God is the cause of things, and that He acts by the will, and not, as some have supposed,

1. 参见 *De Div. Nom.*, IV, 1 (PG 3, 693).
2. 参见 *De Doct. Christ.*, I, 32 (PL 34, 32).
3. 参见 Q. 14, a. 8.

by a necessity of His nature.

This can be shown in three ways: First, from the order itself of agent causes. Since both *intellect and nature* act for an end, as is proved in *Physics* ii.,[1] the natural agent must have the end and the necessary means predetermined for it by some higher intellect; as, the end and definite movement is predetermined for the arrow by the archer. Hence the intellectual and voluntary agent must precede the agent that acts by nature. Hence, since God is first in the order of agents, He must act by intellect and will.

This is shown, secondly, from the character of a natural agent, to which it belongs to produce one and the same effect; for nature operates in one and the same way, unless it be prevented. This is because the nature of the act is according to the nature of the agent, and hence as long as it has that nature, its acts will be in accordance with that nature; for every natural agent has a determinate being. Since, then, the divine being is undetermined, and contains in Himself the full perfection of being, it cannot be that He acts by a necessity of His nature, unless He were to cause something undetermined and indefinite in being; and that this is impossible has been already shown.[2] He does not, therefore, act by a necessity of His nature, but determined effects proceed from His own infinite perfection according to the determination of His will and intellect.

Thirdly, it is shown by the relation of effects to their cause. For effects proceed from the agent that causes them in so far as they pre-exist in the agent; since every agent produces its like. Now effects pre-exist in their cause after the mode of the cause. Therefore, since the divine being is His own intellect, effects pre-exist in Him after the mode of intellect, and therefore proceed from Him after the same mode. Consequently, they proceed from Him after the mode of will,

---

1. 参见 Aristotle, *Phys.*, II, 5 (196b 21).
2. 参见 Q. 7, a. 2.

for His inclination to put in act what His intellect has conceived pertains to the will. Therefore the will of God is the cause of things.

Reply Obj. 1. Dionysius in these words does not intend to exclude election from God absolutely, but only in a certain sense, in so far, that is, as He communicates His goodness not merely to certain beings, but to all: whereas election implies a certain distinction.

Reply Obj. 2. Because the essence of God is His intellect and will, from the fact of His acting by His essence it follows that He acts after the mode of intellect and will.

Reply Obj. 3. Good is the object of the will. The words, therefore, *Because God is good, we exist*, are true inasmuch as His Goodness is the reason of His willing all other things, as was said before.

Reply Obj. 4. Even in us the cause of one and the same effect is knowledge as directing it, whereby the form of the thing to be done is conceived, and will as commanding it, since the form as it is only in the intellect is not determined to exist or not to exist actually, except by the will. Hence, the speculative intellect has nothing to say as to operation. But the power of the agent is cause, as executing the effect, since it denotes the immediate principle of operation. But in God all these things are one.

Fifth Article
WHETHER ANY CAUSE CAN BE ASSIGNED TO THE DIVINE WILL?

We proceed thus to the Fifth Article: —

Objection 1. It seems that some cause can be assigned to the divine will. For Augustine says: *Who would venture to say that God made all things irrationally*?[1] But to a voluntary agent, the reason for acting is also the

1. 参见 *Lib.* 83 *Quoest.*, q. 46 (PL 40, 30).

cause of willing. Therefore the will of God has some cause.

Obj. 2. Further, in things made by one who wills to make them, and whose will is influenced by no cause, there can be no cause assigned except the will of him who wills. But the will of God is the cause of all things, as has been already shown. If, then, there is no cause of His will, in the whole realm of natural things we cannot seek any cause, except the divine will alone. Thus all the sciences would be in vain, since science seeks to assign causes to effects. This seems inadmissible, and therefore we must assign some cause to the divine will.

Obj. 3. Further, what is done by the one who wills, because of no cause, depends absolutely on his will. If, therefore, the will of God has no cause, it follows that all things made depend absolutely on His will, and have no other cause. But this also is not admissible.

On the contrary, Augustine says: *Every efficient cause is greater than the thing effected. But nothing is greater than the will of God. We must not then seek for a cause of it.*[1]

I answer that, In no wise has the will of God a cause. In proof of which we must consider that, since the will follows from the intellect, the cause explaining the willing of one who wills is the same as the cause explaining the knowing of one who knows. The case with the intellect is this: that if the principle and its conclusion are understood separately from each other, the understanding of the principle is the cause that the conclusion is known. But if the intellect perceive the conclusion in the principle itself, apprehending both the one and the other at the same glance, in this case the knowledge of the conclusion would not be caused by understanding the principles, since a thing cannot be its own cause; and yet, it would be true that the intellect would understand the principles to be the cause of the conclusion. It is the same with the will, with respect to which the end stands in

1. 参见 *Op. cit.*, q. 28 (PL 40, 18).

the same relation to the means as principles to the conclusions in the intellect.

Hence, if anyone in one act wills an end, and in another act the means to that end, his willing the end will be the cause of his willing the means. This cannot be the case if in one act he wills both end and means; for a thing cannot be its own cause. Yet it will be true to say that he wills to order to the end the means to the end. Now as God by one act understands all things in His essence, so by one act He wills all things in His goodness. Hence, as in God to understand the cause is not the cause of His understanding the effect (for He understands the effect in the cause), so, in Him, to will an end is not the cause of His willing the means; yet He wills the ordering of the means to the end. Therefore He wills this to be as means to that; but He does not will this because of that.

Reply Obj. 1. The will of God is reasonable, not because anything is to God a cause of willing, but in so far as He wills one thing to be because of another.

Reply Obj. 2. Since God wills effects to proceed from definite causes, for the preservation of order in the universe, it is not unreasonable to seek for causes secondary to the divine will. It would, however, be unreasonable to do so, if such were considered as primary, and not as dependent on the will of God. In this sense Augustine says: *Philosophers in their vanity have thought fit to attribute contingent effects to other causes, being utterly unable to perceive the cause that is above all others, the will of God.*[1]

Reply Obj. 3. Since God wills that effects be because of their causes, all effects that presuppose some other effect do not depend solely on the will of God, but on something else besides: but the first effect depends on the divine will alone. Thus, for example, we may say that

---

1. 参见 *De Trin.*, III, 2 (PL 42, 871).

God willed man to have hands to serve his intellect by their work, and an intellect, that he might be man; and willed him to be man that he might enjoy Him, or for the completion of the universe. But this cannot be reduced to further created secondary ends. Hence such things depend on the simple will of God; but the others on the order of other causes.

Sixth Article
WHETHER THE WILL OF GOD IS ALWAYS FULFILLED?

We proceed thus to the Sixth Article: —

Objection 1. It seems that the will of God is not always fulfilled. For the Apostle says (*1 Tim.* ii. 4): *God will have all men to be saved, and to come to the knowledge of the truth.* But this does not happen. Therefore the will of God is not always fulfilled.

Obj. 2. Further, as is the relation of knowledge to truth, so is that of the will to good. Now God knows all truth. Therefore He wills all good. But not all good actually exists; for much more good might exist. Therefore the will of God is not always fulfilled.

Obj. 3. Further, since the will of God is the first cause, it does not exclude intermediate causes. But the effect of a first cause may be hindered by a defect of a secondary cause; as the effect of the locomotive power of the body may be hindered by the incapacity of a leg. Therefore the effect of the divine will may be hindered by a defect of the secondary causes. The will of God, therefore, is not always fulfilled.

On the contrary, It is said (*Ps.* cxiii, 11): *God hath done all things, whatsoever He would.*

I answer that, The will of God must needs always be fulfilled. In proof of which we must consider that, since an effect is conformed to the agent according to its form, the rule is the same with agent causes as with formal causes. The rule in forms is this: that although a thing may fall short of any particular form, it cannot fall short of the universal form. For though a thing may fail to be a man or a living being, for example, yet it cannot fail to be a being. Hence the same must happen in agent causes. Something may escape the order of any particular agent cause, but not the order of the universal cause under which all particular causes are included; and if any particular cause fails of its effect, this is because of the hindrance of some other particular cause, which is included within the order of the universal cause. Therefore, an effect cannot possibly escape the order of the universal cause. This is clearly seen also in corporeal things. For it may happen that a star is hindered from producing its effects; yet whatever effect does result within the realm of corporeal things, as a consequence of this hindrance of a corporeal cause, must be referred through intermediate causes to the universal influence of the first heavens.

Since, then, the will of God is the universal cause of all things, it is impossible that the divine will should not produce its effect. Hence that which seems to depart from the divine will in one order, returns into it in another; as does the sinner, who by sin falls away from the divine will as much as lies in him, yet falls back into the order of that will, when by its justice he is punished.

Reply Obj. 1. The words of the Apostle, *God will have all men to be saved*, etc., can be understood in three ways. First, by a restricted application, in which case they would mean, as Augustine says, *God wills all men to be saved that are saved, not because there is no man whom He does not wish saved, but because there is no man saved whose salvation He does not will.*[1] Secondly, they can be understood as applying to every class of individuals, not to every individual of each class; in which case they mean that God wills some men of every class and condition to

1. 参见 *Enchir.*, 103 (PL 40, 280).

be saved, males and females, Jews and Gentiles[1], great and small, but not all of every condition. Thirdly, according to Damascene, they are understood of the antecedent will of God; not of the consequent will.[2] This distinction must not be taken as applying to the divine will itself, in which there is nothing antecedent or consequent, but to the things willed.

To understand this we must consider that everything, in so far as it is good, is willed by God. A thing taken in its primary sense, and absolutely considered, may be good or evil, and yet, when some additional circumstances are taken into account, by a consequent consideration may be changed into the contrary. Thus that a man should live is good; and that a man should be killed is evil, absolutely considered. But if in a particular case we add that a man is a murderer or dangerous to society, to kill him is a good; that he live is an evil. Hence it may be said of a just judge, that antecedently he wills all men to live; but consequently wills the murderer to be hanged. In the same way, God antecedently[3] wills all men to be saved, but consequently wills some to he damned, as His justice exacts. Nor do we will absolutely what we will antecedently, but rather we will it in a qualified manner; for the will is directed to things as they are in themselves, and in themselves they exist under particular conditions. Hence we will a thing absolutely inasmuch as we will it when all particular circumstances are considered; and this is what is meant by willing consequently. Thus it may be said that a just judge wills absolutely the hanging of a murderer, but in a qualified manner he would will him to live, namely inasmuch as he is a man. Such a qualified will may be called a velleity rather than an absolute will. Thus it is clear that whatever God wills absolutely takes place; although what He wills

1. Gentiles：异教徒；非犹太人；外邦人
2. 参见 *De Fide Orth.*, II, 29 (PG 94, 968).
3. antecedently：在先地；先行地

antecedently may not take place.

Reply Obj. 2. An act of the cognitive power takes place according as the thing known is in the knower; while an act cf the appetitive power is directed to things as they exist in themselves. But all that can have the nature of being and truth is virtually in God, though it does not all exist in created things. Therefore God knows all truth, but does not will all good, except in so far as He wills Himself, in Whom all good exists virtually.

Reply Obj. 3. A first cause can be hindered in its effect by deficiency in the secondary cause, when it is not the universal first cause, including under itself all causes; for then the effect could in no way escape the order of this cause. And thus it is with the will of God, as was said above.

Seventh Article
WHETHER THE WILL OF GOD IS CHANGEABLE?

We proceed thus to the Seventh Article: —

Objection 1. It seems that the will of God is changeable. For the Lord says (*Gen.* vi. 7): *It repenteth*[1] *Me that I have made man.* But whoever repents of what he has done, has a changeable will. Therefore God has a changeable will.

Obj. 2. Further, it is said in the person of the Lord: *I will speak against a nation and against a kingdom, to root out, and to pull down, and to destroy it; but if that nation shall repent of its evil, I also will repent of the evil that I have thought to do to them* (*Jer.* xviii. 7, 8). Therefore God has a changeable will.

Obj. 3. Further, whatever God does, He does voluntarily. But God does not always do the same thing, for at one time He ordered the law

---

1. repenteth：后悔；悔改

to be observed, and at another time forbade it. Therefore He has a changeable will.

Obj. 4. Further, God does not will of necessity what He wills, as was said before. Therefore He can both will and not will the same thing. But whatever can incline to either of two opposites is changeable; as that which can exist and not exist is changeable substantially, and that which can exist in a place or not in that place is changeable locally. Therefore God is changeable as regards His will.

On the contrary, It is said: *God is not as a man, that He should lie, nor as the son of man, that He should be changed* (*Num.* xxiii. 19).

I answer that, The will of God is entirely unchangeable. On this point we must consider that to change the will is one thing; to will that certain things should be changed is another. For it is possible to will a thing to be done now and its contrary afterwards, and yet for the will to remain permanently the same; whereas the will would be changed if one should begin to will what before he had not willed, or cease to will what he had willed before. This cannot happen, unless we presuppose change either in the knowledge or in the disposition of the substance of the one who wills. For since the will is concerned with the good a man may in two ways begin to will a thing. In one way, when that thing begins to be good for him, and this does not take place without a change in him. Thus when the cold weather begins, it becomes good to sit by the fire; though it was not so before. In another way, when he knows for the first time that a thing is good for him, though he did not know it before. For, after all, we take counsel in order to know what is good for us. Now it has already been shown that both the substance of God and His knowledge are entirely unchangeable.[1] Therefore His will must be entirely unchangeable.

Reply Obj. 1. These words of the Lord are to be understood

---

1. 参见 Q. 9, a. 1; q. 14, a. 15.

metaphorically, and according to the likeness of our nature. For when we repent, we destroy what we have made; although we may even do so without change of will, as, when a man wills to make a thing, at the same time intending to destroy it later. Therefore, God is said to have repented by way of comparison with our mode of acting, in so far as by the deluge He removed from the face of the earth man whom He had previously made.

Reply Obj. 2. The will of God, as it is the first and universal cause, does not exclude intermediate causes that have power to produce certain effects. Since, however, all intermediate causes are inferior in power to the first cause, there are many things in the divine power, knowledge and will that are not included in the order of inferior causes. Thus in the case of the raising of Lazarus, one who looked only at inferior causes could have said: *Lazarus will not rise again*; but looking at the divine first cause, he could have said: *Lazarus will rise again*. And God wills both: that is, that a thing shall happen in the order of the inferior cause, but that it shall not happen in the order of the higher cause; or He may will conversely. We may say, then, that God sometimes declares that a thing shall happen according as it falls under the order of inferior causes (for example, the dispositions of nature or the merits of men[1]), which yet does not happen, as not being in the designs of the divine and higher cause. Thus He foretold to Ezechias: *Take order with thy house, for thou shalt die, and not live* (*Isa.* xxxviii. 1). Yet this did not take place, since from eternity it was otherwise disposed in the divine knowledge and will, which is unchangeable. Hence Gregory says: *The sentence of God changes, but not His counsel*[2] — that is to say, the counsel of His will. When therefore He says, *I also will repent*,His words must be understood metaphorically[3].

1. merits of men：人的功绩
2. 参见 *Moral.*, XVI, 10 (PL 75, 1127).
3. metaphorically：比喻地；隐喻地

For men seem to repent, when they do not fulfill what they have threatened.

Reply Obj. 3. It does not follow from this argument that God has a will that changes, but that He wills that things should change.

Reply Obj. 4. Although God's willing a thing is not by absolute necessity, yet it is necessary by supposition, because of the unchangeableness[1] of the divine will, as has been said above.

Eighth Article
WHETHER THE WILL OF GOD IMPOSES NECESSITY ON THE THINGS WILLED?

We proceed thus to the Eighth Article: —

Objection 1. It seems that the will of God imposes necessity on the things willed. For Augustine says: *No one is saved, except whom God has willed to be saved. He must therefore be asked to will it; for if He wills it, it must necessarily be.*[2]

Obj. 2. Further, every cause that cannot be hindered produces its effect necessarily, because, as the Philosopher says, *nature always works in the same way, if there is nothing to hinder it.*[3] But the will of God cannot be hindered. For the Apostle says (*Rom.* ix. 19): *Who resisteth His will?* Therefore the will of God imposes necessity on the things willed.

Obj. 3. Further, whatever is necessary by its antecedent cause is necessary absolutely; it is thus necessary that animals should die, being compounded of contrary elements. Now things created by God are related to the divine will as to an antecedent cause, whereby they have necessity. For this conditional proposition is true: *if God wills a thing, it comes to pass:* and every true conditional proposition is necessary. It

1. unchangeableness：不变
2. 参见 *Enchir.*, 103 (PL 40, 280).
3. 参见 Aristotle, *Phys.* II, 8 (199b 18).

follows therefore that all that God wills is necessary absolutely.

On the contrary, All good things that exist God wills to be. If therefore His will imposes necessity on the things willed, it follows that all good happens of necessity; and thus there is an end of free choice, counsel, and all other such things.

I answer that, The divine will imposes necessity on some things willed, but not on all. The reason of this some have chosen to assign to intermediate causes, holding that what God produces by necessary causes is necessary, and what He produces by contingent causes contingent.

This does not seem to be a sufficient explanation, for two reasons. First, because the effect of a first cause is contingent because of the secondary cause, from the fact that the effect of the first cause is hindered by deficiency in the second cause, as the sun's power is hindered by a defect in the plant. But no defect of a secondary cause can hinder God's will from producing its effect. Secondly, because if the distinction between the contingent and the necessary is to be referred only to secondary causes, this must mean that the distinction itself escapes the divine intention and will; which is inadmissible.

It is better therefore to say that this happens because of the efficacy of the divine will. For when a cause is efficacious to act, the effect follows upon the cause, not only as to the thing done, but also as to its manner of being done or of being. Thus from defect of active power in the seed it may happen that a child is born unlike its father in accidental points, which belong to its manner of being. Since then the divine will is perfectly efficacious[1], it follows not only that things are done, which God wills to be done, but also that they are done in the way that He wills. Now God wills some things to be done necessarily, some contingently, so that there be a right order in things for the

1. efficacious：措施有效的

perfection of the universe. Therefore to some effects He has attached unfailing necessary causes, from which the effects follow necessarily; but to others defectible and contingent causes, from which effects arise contingently. Hence it is not because the proximate causes[1] are contingent that the effects willed by God happen contingently; but God has prepared contingent causes[2] for them because He has willed that they should happen contingently.

Reply Obj. 1. By the words of Augustine we must understand a necessity in things willed by God that is not absolute, but conditional. For the conditional proposition that *if God wills a thing, it must necessarily be*, is necessarily true.

Reply Obj. 2. From the very fact that nothing resists the divine will, it follows not only that those things happen that God wills to happen, but that they happen necessarily or contingently according to His will

Reply Obj. 3. Consequents have necessity from their antecedents according to the mode of the antecedents. Hence things effected by the divine will have that kind of necessity that God wills them to have, either absolute or conditional. Not all things, therefore, are necessary absolutely.

Ninth Article
WHETHER GOD WILLS EVILS?

We proceed thus to the Ninth Article: —

Objection 1. It seems that God wills evils. For every good that exists, God wills. But it is a good that evil should exist. For Augustine says: *Although evil in so far as it is evil is not a good, yet it is good that not only good things should exist, but also evil things.*[3] Therefore God wills evil things.

---

1. proximate cause：直接原因；近因
2. contingent cause：偶然原因
3. 参见 *Enchir.*, XCVI (PL 40, 276).

Obj. 2. Further, Dionysius says: *Evil would conduce to the perfection of everything, i.e.*, the universe.[1] And Augustine says: *Out of all things is built up the admirable beauty of the universe, wherein even that which is called evil, properly ordered and disposed, commends the good the more evidently, so that the good be more pleasing and praiseworthy when contrasted with evil.*[2] But God wills all that pertains to the perfection and beauty of the universe, for this is what God desires above all things in His creatures. Therefore God wills evils.

Obj. 3. Further, that evil should exist, and should not exist, are contradictory opposites. But God does not will that evil should not exist; otherwise, since various evils do exist, God's will would not always be fulfilled. Therefore God wills that evils should exist.

On the contrary, Augustine says: *No wise man is the cause of another man becoming worse. Now God surpasses all men in wisdom. Much less therefore is God the cause of man becoming worse: and when He is said to be the cause of a thing, He is said to will it.*[3] Therefore it is not by God's will that man becomes worse. Now it is clear that every evil makes a thing worse. Therefore God does not will evils.

I answer that, Since the good and the appetible[4] are the same in nature, as was said before,[5] and since evil is opposed to good, it is impossible that any evil, as such, should be sought for by the appetite, either natural, or animal, or by the intellectual appetite which is the will. Nevertheless evil may be sought accidentally, so far as it accompanies a good, as appears in each of the appetites. For a natural agent does not intend privation or corruption; he intends the form to which is yet annexed the privation of some other form, and the generation of one

---

1. 参见 *De Div. Nom.*, IV, 19 (PG 3 717).
2. 参见 *Enchir.*, X (PL 40, 236).
3. 参见 *Lib.* 83 Quaest., q. 3 (PL 40, 11).
4. appetible：值得欲求的
5. 参见 Q. 5, a. 1.

thing, which yet implies the corruption of another. For when a lion kills a stag, his object is food, which yet is accompanied by the killing of the animal. Similarly the fornicator has merely pleasure for his object, which is yet accompanied by the deformity of sin.

Now the evil that accompanies one good is the privation of another good. Never therefore would evil be sought after, not even accidentally, unless the good that accompanies the evil were more desired than the good of which the evil is the privation. Now God wills no good more than He wills His own goodness; yet He wills one good more than another. Hence He in no way wills the evil of sin, which is the privation of right order towards the divine good. The evil of natural defect, or of punishment, He does will, by willing the good to which such evils are attached. Thus, in willing justice He wills punishment; and in willing the preservation of the order of nature, He wills some things to be naturally corrupted.

Reply Obj. 1. Some have said that although God does not will evil, yet He wills that evil should be or be done, because, although evil is not a good, yet it is good that evil should be or be done.[1] This they said because things evil in themselves are ordered to some good end; and this order they thought was expressed in the words *that evil should be* or *be done*. This, however, is not correct; since evil is not of itself ordered to good, but accidentally. For it is outside the intention of the sinner that any good should follow from his sin; as it was outside the intention of tyrants that the patience of the martyrs should shine forth from all their persecutions. It cannot therefore be said that such an ordering to good is implied in the statement that it is a good thing that evil should be or be done, since nothing is judged by that which pertains to it accidentally, but by that which belongs to it essentially.

Reply Obj. 2. Evil does not contribute towards the perfection

1. 参见 Hugh of St. Victor, *De Sacram.*, I, iv, 13 (PL 176, 239) ; *Summa Sent.*, I, 13 (PL 176, 66). — Cf. Peter Lombard, *Sent.*, I, xlvi, 3 (I, 280).

and beauty of the universe, except accidentally, as was said above. Therefore, in saying that *evil would conduce to the perfection of the universe*, Dionysius draws this conclusion as the consequence of false premises.

Reply Obj. 3. The statements that evil comes to be and that it does not come to be are opposed as contradictories; yet the statements that anyone wills evil to be and that he wills it not to be, are not so opposed, since either is affirmative. God therefore neither wills evil to be done, nor wills it not to be done; but He wills to permit evil to be done, and this is a good.

Tenth Article
WHETHER GOD HAS FREE CHOICE ?

We proceed thus to the Tenth Article: —

Objection 1. It seems that God has not free choice. For Jerome says, in a homily on the prodigal son: *God alone it is Who is not liable to sin, nor can be liable: all others, as having free choice, can be inclined to either side.*[1]

Obj. 2. Further, free choice is a faculty of the reason and will, by which good and evil are chosen. But God does not will evil, as has been said. Therefore there is not free choice in God.

On the contrary, Ambrose says: *The Holy Spirit divideth unto each one as He will, namely, according to the free choice of the will, not in obedience to necessity.*[2]

I answer that, We have free choice with respect to what we do not will of necessity, or by natural instinct. That we will to be happy does not pertain to free choice but to natural instinct. Hence other animals, that are moved to act by natural instinct, are not said to be moved by free choice. Since then God wills His own goodness necessarily, but other things not necessarily, as was shown above, He has free choice

1. 参见 *Epist*, XXI (PL 22, 393).
2. 参见 *De Fide*, II, 6 (PL 16, 592).

with respect to what He does not will necessarily.

Reply Obj. 1. Jerome seems to deny free choice to God, not absolutely, but not as regards the turning to sin.

Reply Obj. 2. Since the evil of sin consists in turning away from the divine goodness, by which God wills all things, as was above shown, it is manifestly impossible for Him to will the evil of sin; yet He can choose one of two opposites, inasmuch as He can will a thing to be or not to be. In the same way we ourselves can, without sin, will to sit down and not will to sit down.

Eleventh Article

WHETHER THE WILL OF SIGN IS TO BE DISTINGUISHED IN GOD?

We proceed thus to the Eleventh Article: —

Objection 1. It seems that the will of sign is not to be distinguished in God. For as the will of God is the cause of things, so is His wisdom. But there are no signs of the divine wisdom. Therefore, neither ought there to be signs of the divine will.

Obj. 2. Further, every sign that is not in agreement with what it signifies is false. If therefore the signs of the divine will are not in agreement with that will, they are false. But if they do agree, they are superfluous. No signs therefore of the divine will are to be recognized.

On the contrary, The will of God is one, since it is the very essence of God. Yet sometimes it is spoken of as many, as in the words of *Ps.* cx. 2: *Great are the works of the Lord, sought out according to all His wills*. Therefore, sometimes the sign must be taken for the will.

I answer that, Some things are said of God in their strict sense, others by metaphor, as appears from what has been said before.[1]

---

1. 参见 Q. 13, a. 3.

When certain human passions are predicated of the Godhead[1] metaphorically, this is done because of a likeness in the effect. Hence a thing that is in us a sign of some passion is signified metaphorically in God under the name of that passion. Thus with us it is usual for an angry man to punish, so that punishment becomes an expression of anger. Therefore punishment itself is signified by the name of anger, when anger is attributed to God. In the same way, what is usually with us an expression of will is sometimes metaphorically called will in God; just as when anyone lays down a precept, it is a sign that he wishes that precept obeyed. Hence a divine precept is sometimes called by metaphor the will of God, as in the words: *Thy will be done on earth, as it is in heaven* (*Matt.* vi. 10). There is, however, this difference between will and anger, that anger is never attributed to God properly, since in its primary meaning it includes passion; whereas will is attributed to Him properly. Therefore in God there are distinguished will in its proper sense and will as attributed to Him by metaphor. Will in its proper sense is called the *will of good pleasure*, and will metaphorically taken is the *will of sign*, inasmuch as the sign itself of will is called will.

Reply Obj. 1. Knowledge is not the cause of a thing being done, unless through the will. For we do not put into act what we know, unless we will to do so. Accordingly, signs are not attributed to knowledge, but to will.

Reply Obj. 2. Signs of will are called divine wills, not as being signs that God wills anything, but because what in us are the usual signs of our will, are called *divine wills* in God. Thus punishment is not a sign that there is anger in God; but it is called anger in Him, from the fact that it is a sign of anger in ourselves.

---

1. Godhead：天主；天主性

Twelfth Article

WHETHER FIVE SIGNS OF WILL ARE RIGHTLY HELD OF THE DIVINE WILL?

We proceed thus to the Twelfth Article: —

Objection 1. It seems that five signs of will — namely, *prohibition*, *precept*, *counsel*, *operation*, and *permission* — are not rightly held of the divine will. For the same things that God bids us do by His precept or counsel,these He sometimes operates in us; and the same things that He prohibits, these He sometimes permits. They ought not therefore to be enumerated as distinct.

Obj. 2. Further, God works nothing unless He will it, as the Scripture says (*Wis.* xi. 26). But the will of sign is distinct from the will of good pleasure. Therefore operation ought not to be comprehended in the will of sign.

Obj. 3. Further, operation and permission pertain to all creatures in common, since God works in them all, and permits some action in them all. But precept, counsel and prohibition pertain to rational creatures only. Therefore they do not come rightly under one division, not being of one order.

Obj. 4. Further, evil happens in more ways than does good, since *good happens in one way, but evil in all kinds of ways*, as is declared by the Philosopher,[1] and Dionysius.[2] It is not right therefore to propose one sign only in the case of evil — namely, prohibition — and two — namely, counsel and precept — in the case of good.

I answer that, These signs are so called because by them we are accustomed to show that we will something. A man may show that he wills something, either by himself or by means of another. He may show it by himself, by doing something either directly or indirectly

1. 参见 *Eth.*, II, 6 (1106b 35).
2. 参见 *De Div. Nom.*, IV, 30 (PG 3, 729).

and accidentally. He shows it directly when he works in his own person; in that way the sign of his will is said to be *operation*. He shows it indirectly, by not hindering the doing of a thing; for *what removes an impediment is called an accidental mover.*[1] In this the sign is called *permission*. He declares his will by means of another when he orders another to perform a work, either by insisting upon it as necessary by *precept*, and by *prohibiting* its contrary; or by persuasion, which is a part of *counsel*.

Since the will of man makes itself known in these ways, the same five are sometimes named divine wills, in the sense of being signs of that will. That *precept*, *counsel* and *prohibition* are called the will of God is clear from the words of *Matt*. vi. 10: *Thy will be done on earth as it is in heaven*. That *permission* and *operation* are called the will of God is clear from Augustine, who says: *Nothing is done, unless the Almighty wills it to be done, either by permitting it, or by actually doing it.*[2]

Or it may be said that permission and operation refer to present time, permission being with respect to evil, operation with regard to good. While as to future time, prohibition is in respect to evil, precept to good that is necessary, and counsel to good that is of supererogation[3].

Reply Obj. 1. There is nothing to prevent anyone declaring his will about the same matter in different ways; thus we find many names that mean the same thing. Hence there is no reason why the same thing should not be the subject of precept, operation, counsel, prohibition or permission.

Reply Obj. 2. As God may by metaphor be said to will what by His will, properly understood, He wills not, so He may by metaphor be said to will what He does, properly speaking, will. Hence there is

1. 参见 Aristotle. *Phys*., VIII, 4 (255b 24).
2. 参见 *Enchir*., XCV (PL 40, 276).
3. supererogation：额外的努力；职责以外的工作

nothing to prevent the same thing from being the object of the will of good pleasure and of the will of sign. But operation is always the same as the will of good pleasure, while precept and counsel are not, both because the former regards the present, and the two latter the future, and because the former is of itself the effect of the will, while the latter is the effect as fulfilled by means of another.

Reply Obj. 3. Rational creatures are masters of their own acts; and for this reason certain special signs of the divine will are proposed for them, inasmuch as God ordains rational creatures to act voluntarily and of themselves. Other creatures act only as moved by the divine operation; therefore only operation and permission are concerned with these.

Reply Obj. 4. All evil of sin, though happening in many ways, agrees in being out of harmony with the divine will. Hence with regard to evil, only one sign is proposed, that of prohibition. On the other hand, good stands in various relations to the divine goodness, since there are good deeds without which we cannot attain to the fruition of that goodness, and these are the subject of precept; and there are other goods by which we attain to it more perfectly, and these are the subject of counsel. Or it may be said that counsel is concerned not only with the obtaining of greater good, but also with the avoiding of lesser evils.

Question XX
GOD'S LOVE
(*In Four Articles*)

WE next consider those things that pertain absolutely to the will of God. In the appetitive part of the human soul there are found both the passions of the soul, as joy, love, and the like; and the habits of the moral virtues, as justice, fortitude, and the like. Hence we shall first consider the love of God, and secondly his justice and mercy. About the first there are four points of inquiry: (1) Whether love exists in God? (2) Whether He loves all things? (3) Whether He loves one thing more than another? (4) Whether He loves better things more?

First Article
WHETHER LOVE EXISTS IN GOD?

We proceed thus to the First Article:—

Objection 1. It seems that love does not exist in God. For in God there are no passions. Now love is a passion. Therefore love is not in God.

Obj. 2. Further, love, anger, sorrow, and the like, are mutually divided against one another. But sorrow and anger are not attributed to God, unless by metaphor. Therefore neither is love attributed to Him.

Obj. 3. Further, Dionysius says: *Love is a uniting and binding force.*[1] But

---

1. 参见 *De Div. Nom.*, IV, 15 (PG 3, 713).

this cannot take place in God, since He is simple. Therefore love does not exist in God.

On the contrary, It is written: *God is love* (*1 John* iv. 16).

I answer that, We must needs assert that in God there is love, because love is the first movement of the will and of every appetitive power. For since the acts of the will and of every appetitive power tend towards good and evil as to their proper objects, and since good is essentially and especially the object of the will and the appetite, whereas evil is only the object secondarily and indirectly (as opposed to good): it follows that the acts of the will and appetite that regard good must naturally be prior to those that regard evil; thus, for instance, joy is prior to sorrow, love to hate. For what exists of itself is always prior to that which exists through another.

Again, the more universal is naturally prior to what is less so. Hence the intellect is first directed to universal truth, and in the second place to particular and special truths. Now there are certain acts of will and appetite that regard good under some special condition, as joy and delight regard good present and possessed; whereas desire and hope regard good not as yet possessed. Love, however, regards good universally; whether possessed or not. Hence love is naturally the first act of will and appetite; for which reason all the other appetitive movements presuppose love as their root and origin. For nobody desires anything nor rejoices in anything, except as a good that is loved; nor is anything an object of hate except as opposed to the object of love. Similarly, it is clear that sorrow, and other things like to it, refer to love as to their first principle. Hence, in whomsoever there is will and appetite, there must also be love: since if the first is wanting, all that follows is also wanting. Now it has been shown that will is in God.[1] Hence we must attribute love to Him.

---

1. 参见 Q. 19, a. 1.

Reply Obj. 1. The cognitive power does not move except through the medium of the appetitive: and just as in ourselves the universal reason moves through the medium of the particular reason, as is stated in *De anima* iii.,[1] so in ourselves the intellectual appetite, which is called the will, moves through the medium of the sensitive appetite. Hence, in us the sensitive appetite is the proximate motive-power of our bodies. Some bodily change therefore always accompanies an act of the sensitive appetite, and this change affects especially the heart, which is the first source of movement in animals. Therefore acts of the sensitive appetite, inasmuch as they have annexed to them some bodily change, are called passions; whereas acts of the will are not so called. Love, therefore, and joy and delight are passions, in so far as they denote acts of the sensitive appetite; but in so far as they denote acts of the intellective appetite, they are not passions. It is in this latter sense that they are in God. Hence the Philosopher says: *God rejoices by an operation that is one and simple.*[2] And for the same reason He loves without passion.

Reply Obj. 2. In the passions of the sensitive appetite there may be distinguished a certain material element — namely, the bodily change — and a certain formal element, which is on the part of the appetite. Thus in anger, as the Philosopher says,[3] the material element is the surging of the blood about the heart; but the formal, the appetite for revenge. Again, as regards the formal element of some passions, a certain imperfection is implied, as in desire, which is of the good we have not, and in sorrow, which is about the evil we have. This applies also to anger, which supposes sorrow. Certain other passions, however, as love and joy, imply no imperfection. Since therefore none of these can be attributed to God on their material side, as has been said,

1. 参见 *De An.*, III, 11 (434a 20).
2. 参见 *Eth.*, VII, 14 (1154b 26).
3. 参见 Aristotle, *De An.*, I, 1 (403a 30).

neither can those that even on their formal side imply imperfection be attributed to Him; except metaphorically, and from likeness of effects, as has already been shown.[1] On the other hand, those that do not imply imperfection, such as love and joy, can be properly predicated of God, though without attributing passion to Him, as was said before.

Reply Obj. 3. An act of love always tends towards two things: to the good that one wills, and to the person for whom one wills it: since to love a person is to will good for that person. Hence, inasmuch as we love ourselves, we will good for ourselves; and, so far as possible, union with that good. In this sense, love is called a unitive force even in God, yet without implying composition; for the good that He wills for Himself is none other than Himself, Who is good by His essence, as was shown above.[2] And by the fact that anyone loves another, he wills good to that other. Thus he puts the other, as it were, in the place of himself, and regards the good done to him as done to himself. So far love is a binding force, since it joins another to ourselves, and refers his good to our own. And in this way too the divine love is a binding force, inasmuch as God wills good to others; yet without implying any composition in God.

Second Article
WHETHER GOD LOVES ALL THINGS ?

We proceed thus to the Second Article: —

Objection 1. It seems that God does not love all things. For according to Dionysius, love places the lover outside himself, and causes him to pass, as it were, into the object of his love.[3] But it is not admissible to say that God is placed outside of Himself, and passes into other things.

---

1. 参见 Q. 3, a. 2, ad 2 ; q. 19, a. 11.
2. 参见 Q. 6, a. 3.
3. 参见 *De Div. Nom.*, IV, 13 (PG 3, 712).

Therefore it is inadmissible to say that God loves things other than himself.

Obj. 2. Further, the love of God is eternal. But things apart from God are not from eternity; except in God. Therefore God does not love anything, except as it exists in Himself. But as existing in Him, it is no other than Himself. Therefore God does not love things other than Himself.

Obj. 3. Further, love is twofold — the love, namely, of desire, and the love of friendship. Now God does not love irrational creatures with the love of desire, since He needs no creature outside Himself. Nor with the love of friendship, since there can be no friendship with irrational creatures, as the Philosopher shows.[1] Therefore God does not love all things.

Obj. 4. Further, it is written (*Ps.* v. 7): *Thou hatest all the workers of iniquity*. Now nothing is at the same time hated and loved. Therefore God does not love all things.

On the contrary, It is said (*Wis.* xi. 25): *Thou lovest all things that are, and hatest none of the things which Thou hast made.*

I answer that, God loves all existing things. For all existing things, in so far as they exist, are good, since the being of a thing is itself a good; as is likewise whatever perfection it possesses. Now it has been shown above that God's will is the cause of all things.[2] It must needs be, therefore, that a thing has some being, or any kind of good, only inasmuch as it is willed by God. To every existing thing, then, God wills some good. Hence, since to love anything is nothing else than to will good to that thing, it is manifest that God loves everything that exists. Yet not as we love. Because, since our will is not the cause of the goodness of things, but is moved by it as by its object, our love, whereby we will good to anything, is not the cause of its goodness; but

1. 参见 *Eth.*, VIII. 2 (1155b 27).
2. 参见 Q. 19, a. 4.

conversely its goodness, whether real or imaginary, calls forth our love, by which we will that it should preserve the good it has, and receive besides the good it has not, and to this end we direct our actions: whereas the love of God infuses and creates goodness in things.

Reply Obj. 1. A lover is placed outside himself, and made to pass into the object of his love, inasmuch as he wills good to the beloved, and works for that good by his providence even as he works for his own. Hence Dionysius says: *On behalf of the truth we must make bold to say even this, that He Himself, the cause of all things, by His abounding love and goodness, is placed outside Himself by His providence over all existing things.*[1]

Reply Obj. 2. Although creatures have not existed from eternity, except in God, yet because they have been in Him from eternity, God has known them eternally in their proper natures, and for that reason has loved them; even as we, by the likenesses of things within us, know things existing in themselves.

Reply Obj. 3. Friendship cannot exist except towards rational creatures, who are capable of returning love and of communicating with one another in the various works of life, and who may fare well or ill, according to the changes of fortune and happiness; even as towards them is benevolence, properly speaking, exercised. But irrational creatures cannot attain to loving God, nor to any share in the intellectual and beatific life that He lives. Strictly speaking, therefore, God does not love irrational[2] creatures with the love of friendship, but as it were with the love of desire, in so far as He orders them to rational creatures, and even to Himself. Yet this is not because He stands in need of them, but only because of His goodness, and of the services they render to us. For we can desire a thing for others as well as for ourselves.

Reply Obj. 4. Nothing prevents one and the same thing from being

---

1. 参见 *De Div. Nom.*, IV, 13 (PG 3,712).
2. irrational：无理性的；不合理的

loved under one aspect, while it is hated under another. God loves sinners in so far as they are existing natures; for thus they both are and are from Him. In so far as they are sinners, they are not, and they fail of being; and this is not in them from God. Hence under this aspect, they are hated by Him.

Third Article
WHETHER GOD LOVES ALL THINGS EQUALLY?

We proceed thus to the Third Article: —

Objection 1. It seems that God loves all things equally. For it is said: *He hath equally care of all* (*Wis.* vi. 8). But God's providence over things comes from the love wherewith He loves them. Therefore He loves all things equally.

Obj. 2. Further, the love of God is His essence. But God's essence does not admit of degree; neither therefore does His love. He does not therefore love some things more than others.

Obj. 3. Further, as God's love extends to created things, so do His knowledge and will extend. But God is not said to know some things more than others; nor to will one thing more than another. Neither therefore does He love some things more than others.

On the contrary, Augustine says: *God loves all things that He has made, and among them rational creatures more, and of these especially those who are members of His only-begotten Son; and much more than all, His only-begotten Son Himself.*[1]

I answer that, Since to love a thing is to will it good, anything may be loved more or less in a twofold way. In one way on the part of the act of the will itself, which is more or less intense. In this way, God does not love some things more than others, because He loves all things by

---

1. 参见 *Tract.* CX, super *Ioann.*, XVII, 23 (PL 35, 1924).

an act of the will that is one, simple, and always the same. In another way, on the part of the good itself that a person wills for the one whom he loves. In this way we are said to love that being more than another, for whom we will a greater good, even though our will is not more intense. In this way we must needs say that God loves some things more than others. For since God's love is the cause of goodness in things, as has been said, no one thing would be better than another, if God did not will greater good for one than for another.

Reply Obj. 1. God is said to have equally care of all, not because by His care He deals out equal good to all, but because He administers all things with a like wisdom and goodness.

Reply Obj. 2. This argument is based on the intensity of love on the part of the act of the will, which is the divine essence. But the good that God wills for His creatures is not the divine essence. Therefore there is no reason why it may not vary in degree.

Reply Obj. 3. To understand and to will signify only acts, and do not include in their meaning objects from the diversity of which God may be said to know or will more or less; as has been said with respect to God's love.

Fourth Article
WHETHER GOD ALWAYS LOVES BETTER THINGS MORE?

We proceed thus to the Fourth Article: —

Objection 1. It seems that God does not always love better things more. For it is manifest that Christ is better than the whole human race, being God and man. But God loved the human race more than He loved Christ; for it is said: *He spared not His own Son, but delivered Him up for us all* (*Rom*, viii. 32). Therefore God does not always love better things more.

Obj. 2. Further, an angel is better than a man. Hence it is said of man: *Thou hast made him a little less than the angels* (*Ps.* viii. 6). But God loved men more than He loved the angels, for it is said: *Nowhere doth He take hold of the angels, but of the seed of Abraham He taketh hold* (*Heb.* ii. 16). Therefore God does not always love the better things more.

Obj. 3. Further, Peter was better than John, since he loved Christ more. Hence the Lord, knowing this to be true, asked Peter, saying: '*Simon, son of John, lovest thou Me more than these?*' (*Jo.* xxi. 15). Yet Christ loved John more than He loved Peter. For as Augustine says, commenting on the words, 'Simon, son of John, lovest thou Me?' *By this very mark is John distinguished from the other disciples, not that He loved him only, but that He loved him more than the rest.*[1] Therefore God does not always love better things more.

Obj. 4. Further, the innocent man is better than the repentant, since repentance is, as Jerome says, *a second plank after shipwreck.*[2] But God loves the penitent more than the innocent; since He rejoices over him the more. For it is said: *I say to you that there shall be joy in heaven upon one sinner that doth penance, more than upon ninety-nine just who need not penance* (*Luke* xv. 7). Therefore God does not always love better things more.

Obj. 5. Further, the just man who is merely foreknown is better than the predestined sinner. Now God loves the predestined sinner more, since He wills for him a greater good, namely, life eternal. Therefore God does not always love better things more.

On the contrary, Everything loves what is like it, as appears from what is written (*Ecclus.* xiii. 19): *Every beast loveth its like.* Now the more like God a thing is, the better it is. Therefore, better things are more loved by God.

I answer that, It must be said, according to what has gone before, that God loves better things more. For it has been shown that God's loving one thing more than another is nothing else than His willing for that thing a greater good: because God's will is the cause of goodness in things, and the reason why some things are better than others is

1. 参见 *Tract.* CXXIV (PL 35, 1971).
2. 参见 *In Isaiam*, II, super III, 8 (PL 24, 66).

that God wills for them a greater good. Hence it follows that He loves better things more.

Reply Obj. 1. God loves Christ not only more than He loves the whole human race, but more than He loves the entire created universe: because He willed for Him the greater good in giving Him *a name that is above all names* (*Phil.* ii. 9); so that by God's will Christ was true God. Nor did anything of His excellence diminish when God delivered Him up to death for the salvation of the human race; rather did He become thereby a glorious conqueror: *The government was placed upon His shoulder*, according to *Isa.* ix. 6.

Reply Obj. 2. God loves the human nature assumed by the Word of God in the person of Christ more than He loves all the angels; for that nature is better, especially on the ground of union with the Godhead. But speaking of human nature in general, and comparing it with the angelic, the two are found equal in the order of grace and of glory, since according to *Apoc.* xxi. 17, *the measure of a man and of an angel* is the same: yet so that, in this respect, some angels are found nobler than some men, and some men nobler than some angels. But as to the condition of their natures, an angel is better than a man. God therefore did not assume human nature because, absolutely speaking, He loved man more, but because the needs of man were greater; just as the master of a house may give some costly delicacy to a sick servant, that he does not give to his own son who is well.

Reply Obj. 3. This doubt concerning Peter and John has been solved in various ways. Augustine interprets it mystically, and says that the active life, signified by Peter, loves God more than the contemplative, signified by John, because the former is more conscious of the miseries of this present life, and therefore the more ardently desires to be freed from them, and reach God.[1] But God, he says, loves the contemplative

1. 参见 *Tract.* CXXIV, super *Ioann.*, XXI, 20 (PL 35, 1974).

life more, since He preserves it longer. For it does not end, as the active life does, with the ending of the life of the body.

Some, on the other hand, say that Peter loved Christ more in His members, and therefore was loved more by Christ also, for which reason He gave him the care of the Church,[1] but that John loved Christ more in Himself, and so was loved more by Him; on which account Christ commended His mother to his care. Still others say that it is uncertain which of them loved Christ more with the love of charity, and uncertain also which of them God loved more and ordained to a greater degree of glory in eternal life.[2] Peter is said to have loved more, in regard to a certain promptness and fervor, whereas John was more loved, with respect to certain marks of familiarity which Christ showed to him rather than to others, because of his youth and purity. And there are others who say that Christ loved Peter more, from his more excellent gift of charity; but John more, from his gifts of intellect.[3] Hence, absolutely speaking, Peter was the better and the more beloved; but, in a certain sense, John was the better, and was loved the more.

However, it seems presumptuous to pass judgment on these matters, since *the Lord* and no other *is the weigher of spirits* (*Prov.* xvi. 2).

Reply Obj. 4. The penitent and the innocent are related as exceeding and exceeded. For whether innocent or penitent, those are the better and the better loved who have more grace. Now, other things being equal, innocence is the nobler thing and the more beloved. Yet God is said to rejoice more over the penitent than over the innocent, because often penitents rise from sin more cautious, humble, and fervent. Hence Gregory commenting on these words says that, *In battle, the general loves the soldier who after flight returns and bravely pursues the enemy,*

---

1. 参见 St. Albert, *In III Sent.*, d. xxxi, a. 12 (XXVIII, 593).
2. 参见 Cf. St. Bernard, *Serm. de Diversis*, XXIX (PL 183, 622).
3. 参见 Cf. St. Albert, *Enarr. in Ioann.* (XXIV, 13).

more than him who has never fled, but has never done a brave deed.[1]

Or it may be answered that an equal gift of grace is greater in relation to a penitent sinner who merited punishment than to an innocent person who did not merit it; just as a hundred pieces of gold are a greater gift to a poor man than to a king.

Reply Obj. 5. Since God's will is the cause of goodness in things, the goodness of one who is loved by God is to be reckoned according to the time when some good is to be given to him by the divine goodness. According therefore to that time when a greater good is to be given by the divine will to the predestined sinner, the sinner is the better; although at another time he may be worse than the innocent man; for there is even a time when he is neither good nor bad.

1. 参见 *In Evang.*, II, hom. 34 (PL 76, 1248).

Question XXI
THE JUSTICE AND MERCY OF GOD
(*In Four Articles*)

AFTER considering the divine love, we must treat of God's justice and mercy. Under this head there are four points of inquiry: (1) Whether there is justice in God? (2) Whether His justice can be called truth? (3) Whether there is mercy in God? (4) Whether in every work of God there are justice and mercy?

First Article
WHETHER THERE IS JUSTICE IN GOD?

We proceed thus to the First Article: —

Objection 1. It seems that there is no justice in God. For justice and temperance are divided as members of the same class. But temperance does not exist in God: neither therefore does justice.

Obj. 2. Further, he who does whatsoever he wills and pleases does not work according to justice. But, as the Apostle says: *God worketh all things according to the counsel of his will* (*Ephes.* i. 11). Therefore justice cannot be attributed to Him.

Obj. 3. Further, the act of justice is to pay what is due. But God is no man's debtor. Therefore justice does not belong to God.

Obj. 4. Further, whatever is in God is His essence. But justice cannot belong to the divine essence. For Boethius says: *Good refers to the essence; justice to the act.*[1] Therefore justice does not belong to God.

---

1. 参见 *De Hebdom.* (PL 64, 1314).

On the contrary, It is said (*Ps*. x. 8): *The Lord is just, and hath loved justice.*

I answer that, There are two kinds of justice. The one consists in mutual giving and receiving, as in buying and selling, and other kinds of communication and exchange. This justice the Philosopher calls *commutative justice*[1], which directs exchange and the communication of business.[2] This does not belong to God, since, as the Apostle says: *Who hath first given to Him, and recompense shall be made him?* (*Rom*. xi. 35). The other kind of justice consists in distribution, and is called *distributive justice*[3], whereby a ruler or a steward gives to each what his rank deserves. As, then, the proper order displayed in ruling a family or any kind of multitude evinces justice of this kind in the ruler, so the order of the universe, which is seen both in effects of nature and in effects of will, shows forth the justice of God. Hence Dionysius says: *We must needs see that God is truly just, in seeing how He gives to all existing things what is proper to the condition of each; and preserves the nature of each one in the order and with the powers that properly belong to it.*[4]

Reply Obj. 1. Certain of the moral virtues are concerned with the passions, as temperance with concupiscence, fortitude with fear and temerity, meekness with anger. Such virtues as these can be attributed to God only metaphorically, since, as was stated above, in God there are no passions,[5] nor a sensitive appetite, which is, as the Philosopher says, the subject of those virtues.[6] On the other hand, certain moral virtues are concerned with works of giving and expending: such are justice, liberality and magnificence; and these reside not in the sensitive power, but in the will. Hence, there is nothing to prevent our

1. commutative justice：交换正义
2. 参见 *Eth*., V, 4 (1131b 25).
3. distributive justice：分配正义
4. 参见 *De Div. Nom*., VIII, 7 (PG 3, 896).
5. 参见 Q. 20, a. 1, ad 1.
6. 参见 *Eth*. III, 10 (1117b 24).

attributing these virtues to God; although not in reference to civil matters, but in such acts as befit Him. For, as the Philosopher says, it would be absurd to praise God for His political virtues.[1]

Reply Obj. 2. Since the apprehended good is the object of the will, it is impossible for God to will anything but what His wisdom approves. For wisdom is, as it were, His law of justice, in accordance with which His will is right and just. Hence, what He does according to His will He does justly; as we do justly what we do according to law. But whereas law comes to us from some higher power, God is a law unto Himself.

Reply Obj. 3. To each one is due what is his own. Now that which is ordered to a man is what is said to be his own. Thus, the master owns the servant, and not conversely, for that is free which is its own master. In the word *debt*, therefore, there is implied a certain exigency[2] or necessity on the part of one being towards another being to which it is ordered. Now a twofold order has to be considered in things: the one, whereby one created thing is ordained to another, as the parts to the whole, accident to substance, and all things whatsoever to their end; the other, whereby all created things are ordered to God. Thus in the divine operations, a debt may be regarded in two ways, as due either to God, or to creatures; and in either way God pays what is due. *God has a debt to Himself* that there should be fulfilled in creatures what His will and wisdom contain, and what manifests His goodness. In this respect God's justice regards what befits Him; inasmuch as He renders to Himself what is due to Himself. *There is also a debt to each creature* that it should possess what is ordered to it; thus it is due to man to have hands, and that other animals should serve him. Thus also God carries out justice, when He gives to each thing what is due it according to its nature and condition. This debt, however, is derived from the first;

---

1. 参见 *Op. cit.*, X, 8 (1178b 10).
2. exigency：紧急；紧急事件

since what is due each thing is due to it as ordered to it according to the divine wisdom. And although God in this way pays each thing its due, yet He Himself is not the debtor, since He is not ordered to other things, but rather other things to Him. Justice, therefore, in God is sometimes spoken of as the fitting accompaniment[1] of His goodness; sometimes as the reward of merit. Anselm touches on both views where he says: *When Thou dost punish the wicked, it is just, since it agrees with their deserts; and when Thou dost spare the wicked, it is also just, since it befits Thy goodness.*[2]

Reply Obj. 4. Although justice refers to an act, this does not prevent its being the essence of God; since even that which is of the essence of a thing may be a principle of action. But good does not always refer to an act, since a thing is called good not merely with respect to its acts, but also with respect to the perfection in its essence. For this reason it is said that the good is related to the just as the general to the special.

Second Article
WHETHER THE JUSTICE OF GOD IS TRUTH?

We proceed thus to the Second Article: —

Objection 1. It seems that the justice of God is not truth. For justice resides in the will, since, as Anselm says, it is *the rectitude of the will*;[3] whereas truth resides in the intellect, as the Philosopher says, *Metaph*. vi.[4] and *Ethics* vi.[5] Therefore justice does not pertain to truth.

Obj. 2. Further, according to the Philosopher, truth is a virtue

1. accompaniment：陪伴物；附属品
2. 参见 *Proslog.*, X (PL 158, 233).
3. 参见 *De Ver.*, XII (PL 158, 482).
4. 参见 *Metaph.*, V, 4 (1027b 27).
5. 参见 *Eth.*, VI, 2 (1139a 27).

distinct from justice.[1] Truth therefore does not pertain to the nature of justice.

On the contrary, It is said (*Ps.* lxxxiv. 11): *Mercy and truth have met each other:* where truth stands for justice.

I answer that, Truth consists in the equation of intellect and thing, as was said above.[2] Now the intellect that is the cause of the thing is related to it as its rule and measure: whereas the converse is the case with the intellect that receives its knowledge from things. When, therefore, things are the measure and rule of the intellect, truth consists in the equation of the intellect to the thing; as happens in ourselves. For according as a thing is, or is not, our thoughts or our words about it are true or false. But when the intellect is the rule or measure of things, truth consists in the equation of things to the intellect; just as the work of an artist is said to be true when it is in accordance with his art.

Now as works of art are related to the art, so are works of justice related to the law with which they accord. Therefore, God's justice, which has established in things the order conforming to the rule of His wisdom, which is the law of His justice, is fittingly called truth. Thus we too speak of the truth of justice in human affairs.

Reply Obj. 1. Justice, as to the law that governs, resides in the reason or intellect; but as to the command whereby our actions are governed according to the law, it resides in the will.

Reply Obj. 2. The truth of which the Philosopher is speaking in this passage, is that virtue whereby a man shows himself in word and deed such as he really is. Thus it consists in the conformity of the sign with the thing signified; and not in that of the effect with its cause and rule: as has been said regarding the truth of justice.

---

1. 参见 *Op cit.*, IV, 7 (1127a 34).
2. 参见 Q. 16, a. 1.

Third Article

WHETHER MERCY CAN BE ATTRIBUTED TO GOD ?

We proceed thus to the Third Article: —

Objection 1. It seems that mercy cannot be attributed to God. For mercy is a kind of sorrow, as Damascene says.[1] But there is no sorrow in God; and therefore there is no mercy in Him.

Obj. 2. Further, mercy is a relaxation of justice. But God cannot remit what pertains to His justice. For it is said (2 Tim. ii. 13): *If we believe not, He continueth faithful: He cannot deny Himself.* But he would deny Himself, as the *Gloss* says, if He should deny His words.[2] Therefore mercy is not becoming to God.

On the contrary, It is said (*Ps.* cx. 4): *He is a merciful and gracious Lord.*

I answer that, Mercy is especially to be attributed to God, provided it be considered in its effect, but not as an affection of passion. In proof of which it must be observed that a person is said to be merciful [*misericors*] as being, so to speak, sorrowful at heart [*miserum cor*]; in other words, as being affected with sorrow at the misery of another as though it were his own. Hence it follows that he endeavors to dispel the misery of this other, as if it were his; and this is the effect of mercy. To sorrow, therefore, over the misery of others does not belong to God; but it does most properly belong to Him to dispel that misery, whatever be the defect we call misery. Now defects are not removed, except by the perfection of some kind of goodness; and the primary source of goodness is God, as was shown above.[3]

It must, however, be considered that to bestow perfections on things pertains not only to the divine goodness, but also to the divine justice,

---

1. 参见 *De Fide Orth.*, II, 14 (PG 94, 932).
2. 参见 *Glossa interl.* (VI, 125r); Peter Lombard, *In II Tim.*, super II, 13 (PL 192, 370).
3. 参见 Q. 6, a. 4.

liberality and mercy; yet under different aspects. The communicating of perfections, absolutely considered, pertains to goodness, as was shown above;[1] in so far as perfections are given to things according to what is due them, it is a work of justice, as has been already said; in so far as God does not bestow them for His own use, but only because of His goodness, it belongs to liberality; in so far as perfections given to things by God expel defects, it belongs to mercy.

Reply Obj. 1. This argument is based on mercy regarded as an affection of passion.

Reply Obj. 2. God acts mercifully, not indeed by going against His justice, but by doing something more than justice. Thus a man who pays another two hundred pieces of money, though owing him only one hundred, does nothing against justice, but acts liberally or mercifully. The case is the same with one who pardons an offense committed against him; for in remitting it he may be said to bestow a gift. Hence the Apostle calls remission a forgiving: *Forgive one another, as Christ has forgiven you* (*Ephes.* iv. 32). Hence it is clear that mercy does not destroy justice, but in a sense is the fulness thereof. And thus it is said: *Mercy exalteth itself above judgment* (*Jas.* ii. 13).

Fourth Article
WHETHER IN EVERY WORK OF GOD THERE ARE MERCY AND JUSTICE?

We proceed thus to the Fourth Article: —

Objection 1. It seems that not in every work of God are mercy and justice. For some works of God are attributed to mercy, as the justification of the sinners; and others to justice, as the damnation of the wicked. Hence it is said: *Judgment without mercy to him that hath not*

---

1. 参见 Q. 6, a. 1.

done mercy (*Jas.* ii. 13). Therefore not in every work of God do mercy and justice appear.

Obj. 2. Further, the Apostle attributes the conversion of the Jews to justice and truth, but that of the Gentiles to mercy (*Rom.* xv. 8). Therefore not in every work of God are there justice and mercy.

Obj. 3. Further, many just persons are afflicted in this world; which is unjust. Therefore not in every work of God are there justice and mercy.

Obj. 4. Further, it is the part of justice to pay what is due, but of mercy to relieve misery. Thus both justice and mercy presuppose something in their works: whereas creation presupposes nothing. Therefore in creation neither mercy nor justice is found.

On the contrary, It is said (*Ps.* xxiv. 10): *All the ways of the Lord are mercy and truth.*

I answer that, Mercy and truth are necessarily found in all God's works, provided mercy be taken to mean the removal of any kind of defect. Not every defect, however, can properly be called a misery, but only defect in a rational nature whose lot is to be happy; for misery is opposed to happiness. For this necessity there is a reason, because since a debt paid according to the divine justice is one due either to God, or to some creature, neither the one nor the other can be lacking in any work of God: for God can do nothing that is not in accord with His wisdom and goodness. It is in this sense, as we have said, that anything is said to be a debt on the part of God. Likewise, whatever is done by Him in created things, is done according to proper order and proportion; wherein consists the nature of justice. Thus justice must exist in all God's works.

Now the work of divine justice always presupposes the work of mercy; and is founded thereupon. For nothing is due to creatures, except on the supposition of something already existing or already known in them. Again, if this is due to a creature, it must be due because of something that precedes. And since we cannot go on to infinity, we must come to something that depends only on the goodness of the divine will — which is the ultimate end. We may say, for instance, that to possess hands is due to man because of his rational soul; and his rational soul is due to him that he may be man; and his being man is for the sake of the divine goodness. So in every work of God, viewed at its primary source, there appears mercy. In all that follows, the power of mercy remains, and works indeed with even greater force; as the influence of the first cause is more intense than that of second causes. For this reason does God out of the abundance of His goodness bestow upon creatures what is due them more bountifully than is proportionate to their deserts: since less would suffice for preserving the order of justice than what the divine goodness confers; because between creatures and God's goodness there can be no proportion.

Reply Obj. 1. Certain works are attributed to justice, and certain others to mercy, because in some justice appears more forcibly and in others mercy. Yet even in the damnation of the reprobate mercy is seen, which, though it does not totally remit, yet somewhat alleviates, in punishing short of what is deserved.

In the justification of the sinner justice is seen, when God remits sins because of love, though He Himself has mercifully infused that love. So we read of Magdalen: *Many sins are forgiven her, because she hath loved much* (*Luke* vii. 47).

Reply Obj. 2. God's justice and mercy appear both in the conversion of the Jews and of the Gentiles. But an aspect of justice appears in the conversion of the Jews which is not seen in the conversion of the Gentiles, inasmuch as the Jews were saved because of the promises made to their fathers.

Reply Obj. 3. Justice and mercy appear in the punishment of the just in this world, since by afflictions lesser faults are cleansed in them, and they are the more raised up from earthly affections to God. As to this Gregory says: *The evils that press on us in this world force us to go to God.*[1]

---

1. 参见 *Moral.*, XXVI, 13 (PL 76, 360).

Reply Obj. 4. Although creation presupposes nothing in the universe, yet it does presuppose something in the knowledge of God. In this way too the idea of justice is preserved in creation, inasmuch as things are brought into being in a manner that accords with the divine wisdom and goodness. And the idea of mercy is also preserved in the transition of creatures from non-being to being.

Question XXII
THE PROVIDENCE[1] OF GOD
(*In Four Articles*)

HAVING considered all that relates to the will absolutely, we must now proceed to those things which have relation to both the intellect and the will, namely providence, in relation to all created things; predestination and reprobation, and all that is connected with them, in relation especially to man as ordered to his eternal salvation.[2] For in the science of morals, after the moral virtues themselves, comes the consideration of prudence, to which providence would seem to belong. Concerning God's providence there are four points of inquiry: (1) Whether providence is suitably assigned to God? (2) Whether everything comes under divine providence? (3) Whether divine providence is immediately concerned with all things? (4) Whether divine providence imposes any necessity upon what it foresees?

First Article
WHETHER PROVIDENCE CAN SUITABLY BE ATTRIBUTED TO GOD?

We proceed thus to the First Article: —

Objection 1. It seems that providence is not becoming to God. For providence, according to Tully, is a part of prudence.[3] But since,

---

1. providence：天道；天意；眷顾，这里指照顾
2. 参见 Q. 23.
3. 参见 *De Invent.*, II, 53 (P. 147^b).

according to the Philosopher, prudence gives good counsel,[1] it cannot belong to God, Who never has any doubt for which He should take counsel. Therefore providence cannot belong to God.

Obj. 2. Further, whatever is in God is eternal. But providence is not anything eternal, *for it is concerned with existing things* that are not eternal, according to Damascene.[2] Therefore there is no providence in God.

Obj. 3. Further, there is nothing composite in God. But providence seems to be something composite, because it includes both the intellect and the will. Therefore providence is not in God.

On the contrary, It is said (*Wis.* xiv. 3): *But Thou, Father, governeth all things by providence.*

I answer that, It is necessary to attribute providence to God. For all the good that is in things has been created by God, as was shown above.[3] Good is found in things not only as regards their substance, but also as regards their order towards an end and especially their last end, which, as was said above, is the divine goodness.[4] This good of order existing in created things is itself created by God. Now God is the cause of things by His intellect, and therefore it is necessary that the exemplar of every effect should pre-exist in Him, as is clear from what has gone before.[5] Hence, the exemplar of the order of things towards their end must necessarily pre-exist in the divine mind: and the exemplar of things ordered towards an end is, properly speaking, providence. For providence is the chief part of prudence, to which two other parts are directed — namely, remembrance of the past, and understanding of the present; inasmuch as from the remembrance of

---

1. 参见 *Eth.*,VI, 5 (1140a 26).
2. 参见 *De Fide Orth.*, II, 29 (PG 94, 964).
3. 参见 Q. 6, a. 4.
4. 参见 Q. 21, a. 4.
5. 参见 Q. 19, a. 4.

what is past and the understanding of what is present, we gather how to provide for the future. Now it belongs to prudence, according to the Philosopher, *to direct other things towards an end*,[1] whether in regard to oneself — as for instance, a man is said to be prudent, who orders well his acts towards the end of life — or in regard to others subject to him, in a family, city, or kingdom; in which sense it is said (*Matt.* xxiv. 45): a *faithful and wise servant*, *whom his lord hath appointed over his family*. In this second way prudence or providence may suitably be attributed to God. For in God Himself there can be nothing ordinable towards an end, since He is the last end. Hence, the very exemplar of the order of things towards an end is in God called providence. Whence Boethius says that *Providence is the divine reason itself which*, *seated in the Supreme Ruler*, *disposes all things*;[2] which disposition may refer either to the exemplar of the order of things towards an end, or to the exemplar of the order of parts in the whole.

Reply Obj. 1. According to the Philosopher, *Prudence*, *strictly speaking*, *commands all that 'eubulia' has rightly counselled and 'synesis' rightly judged*.[3] Whence, though to take counsel may not be fitting to God, insofar as counsel is an inquiry into matters that are doubtful, nevertheless to give a command as to the ordering of things towards an end, the right reason of which He possesses, does belong to God, according to *Ps.* cxlviii. 6: *He hath made a decree*, *and it shall not pass away*. In this manner both prudence and providence belong to God. At the same time, it may also be said that the very exemplar of things to be done is called counsel in God; not because of any inquiry necessitated, but from the certitude of the knowledge, to which those who take counsel come by inquiry. Whence it is said: *Who worketh all things according to the counsel of His will* (*Ephes.* i. 11).

---

1. 参见 *Eth.*, VI, 12 (1144a 8).
2. 参见 *De Consol.*, IV, prose 6 (PL 63, 814).
3. 参见 *Eth.*, VI, 9 (1142b 31) ; 10 (1143b 8).

Reply Obj. 2. Two things pertain to the care of providence — namely, the *exemplar of order*, which is called providence and disposition; and the *execution of order*, which is termed government. Of these, the first is eternal, and the second is temporal.

Reply Obj. 3. Providence resides in the intellect; but it presupposes the act of willing the end. For no one gives a precept about things done for an end, unless he wills that end. Hence likewise prudence presupposes the moral virtues, by means of which the appetitive power is directed towards good, as the Philosopher says.[1] But even supposing that providence were equally related to the divine will and intellect, this would not affect the divine simplicity, since in God both the will and intellect are one and the same thing, as we have said above.[2]

Second Article
WHETHER EVERYTHING IS SUBJECT TO THE PROVIDENCE OF GOD?

We proceed thus to the Second Article: —

Objection 1. It seems that not everything is subject to divine providence. For nothing foreseen can happen by chance. If then everything has been foreseen by God, nothing will happen by chance. And thus chance and fortune disappear; which is against common opinion.

Obj. 2. Further, a wise provider excludes any defect or evil, as far as he can, from those over whom he has a care. But we see many evils existing in things. Either, then, God cannot hinder these, and thus is not omnipotent; or else He does not have care for everything.

Obj. 3. Further, whatever happens of necessity does not require providence or prudence. Hence, according to the Philosopher: *Prudence*

1. 参见 Aristotle, *Eth.*, VI, 13 (1144b 32).
2. 参见 Q. 19, a. 1; a. 4, ad 2.

is the right reason of contingent things concerning which there is counsel and choice.[1] Since, then, many things happen from necessity, everything cannot be subject to providence.

Obj. 4. Further, whatsoever is left to itself cannot be subject to the providence of a governor. But men are left to themselves by God, in accordance with the words: *God made man from the beginning, and left him in the hand of his own counsel* (*Ecclus.* xv. 14). And particularly in reference to the wicked: *I let them go according to the desires of their heart* (*Ps.* lxxx. 13). Everything, therefore, cannot be subject to divine providence.

Obj. 5. Further, the Apostle says (*1 Cor.* ix. 9): *God doth not care for oxen*; and we may say the same of other irrational creatures. Thus everything cannot be under the care of divine providence.

On the contrary, It is said of divine wisdom: *She reacheth from end to end mightily, and ordereth all things sweetly* (*Wis.* viii. 1).

I answer that, Certain persons totally denied the existence of providence, as Democritus and the Epicureans,[2] maintaining that the world was made by chance. Others taught that incorruptible substances[3] only were subject to providence, while corruptible substances were not in their individual being, but only according to their species; for in this respect they are incorruptible.[4] They are represented as saying (*Job* xxii. 14): *The clouds are His covert; and He doth not consider our things; and He walketh about the poles of heaven.* Rabbi Moses, however, excluded men from the generality of corruptible things, because of the excellence of the intellect which they possess, but in reference to all else that suffers corruption he adhered to the

---

1. 参见 *Eth.*, VI, 5 (1140a 35); 7 (1141b 9) ; 13 (1144b 27).
2. 参见 Cf. Nemesius, *De Nat. Hom.*, XLIV (PG 40, 795).
3. incorruptible substances：不朽坏的物质
4. 参见 St. Thomas himself (*In I Sent.*, d. xxxix, q. 2, a. 2), this; Cf. Maimonides, *Guide*, III, 17 (p. 282); Averroes, *In Metaph.*, XII, comm. 52 (VIII, 158v).

opinion of the others.[1]

We must say, however, that all things are subject to divine providence, not only in general, but even in their own individual being. This is made evident thus. For since every agent acts for an end, the ordering of effects towards that end extends as far as the causality of the first agent extends. Whence it happens that in the effects of an agent something takes place which has no reference towards the end, because the effect comes from some other cause outside the intention of the agent. But the causality of God, Who is the first agent, extends to all beings not only as to the constituent principles of species, but also as to the individualizing principles; not only of things incorruptible, but also of things corruptible. Hence all things that exist in whatsoever manner are necessarily directed by God towards the end; as the Apostle says: *Those things that are of God are well ordered* (*Rom.* xiii. 1). Since, therefore, the providence of God is nothing other than the notion of the order of things towards an end, as we have said, it necessarily follows that all things, inasmuch as they participate being, must to that extent be subject to divine providence. It has also been shown that God knows all things, both universal and particular.[2] And since His knowledge may be compared to the things themselves as the knowledge of art to the objects of art, as was said above,[3] all things must of necessity come under His ordering; as all things wrought by an art are subject to the ordering of that art.

Reply Obj. 1. There is a difference between universal and particular causes. A thing can escape the order of a particular cause, but not the order of a universal cause. For nothing escapes the order of a particular cause, except through the intervention and hindrance of

1. 参见 *Guide*, III, 17 (p. 286).
2. 参见 Q. 14, a. 11.
3. 参见 Q. 14, a. 8.

some other particular cause; as, for instance, wood may be prevented from burning by the action of water. Since, then, all particular causes are included under the universal cause, it is impossible that any effect should escape the range of the universal cause. So far then as an effect escapes the order of a particular cause, it is said to be by chance or fortuitous in respect to that cause; but if we regard the universal cause, outside whose range no effect can happen, it is said to be foreseen. Thus, for instance, the meeting of two servants, although to them it appears a chance circumstance, has been fully foreseen by their master, who has purposely sent them to meet at the one place, in such a way that the one has no knowledge of the other.

Reply Obj. 2. It is otherwise with one who is in charge of a particular thing, and one whose providence is universal, because a particular provider excludes all defects from what is subject to his care as far as he can; whereas one who provides universally allows some little defect to remain, lest the good of the whole should be hindered. Hence, corruption and defects in natural things are said to be contrary to some particular nature, yet they are in keeping with the plan of universal nature, inasmuch as the defect in one thing yields to the good of another, or even to the universal good: for the corruption of one is the generation of another, and through this it is that a species is kept in existence. Since God, then, provides universally for all being, it belongs to His providence to permit certain defects in particular effects, that the perfect good of the universe may not be hindered; for if all evil were prevented, much good would be absent from the universe. A lion would cease to live, if there were no slaying of animals; and there would be no patience of martyrs if there were no tyrannical persecution[1]. Thus Augustine says: *Almighty God would in no wise permit evil to exist in His works, unless He were so almighty and so good as to produce*

---

1. tyrannical persecution：专制迫害

good even from evil.[1] It would appear that it was because of these two arguments to which we have just replied, that some were persuaded to consider corruptible things — *i.e.*, things in which chance and evil are found — as removed from the care of divine providence.

Reply Obj. 3. Man is not the author of nature; but he uses natural things for his own purposes in his works of art and virtue. Hence human providence does not reach to that which takes place in nature from necessity; but divine providence extends thus far, since God is the author of nature. Apparently it was this argument that moved those who withdrew the course of nature from the care of divine providence, attributing it rather to the necessity of matter, as did Democritus, and others of the ancients.[2]

Reply Obj. 4. When it is said that God left man to himself, this does not mean that man is exempt from divine providence, but merely that he has not a prefixed operating power determined to only the one effect; as in the case of natural things, which are only acted upon as though directed by another towards an end: for they do not act of themselves, as if they directed themselves towards an end, like rational creatures, through the possession of free choice, by which these are able to take counsel and make choices. Hence it is significantly said: *In the hand of his own counsel.* But since the very act of free choice is traced to God as to a cause, it necessarily follows that everything happening from the exercise of free choice must be subject to divine providence. For human providence is included under the providence of God as a particular cause under a universal cause. God, however, extends His providence over the just in a certain more excellent way than over the wicked, inasmuch as He prevents anything happening which would impede their final salvation. For *to them that love God, all things work together unto good* (*Rom.* viii. 28). But from the fact that He does not

1. 参见 *Enchir.*, XI (PL 40, 236).。
2. 参见 Cf. Aristotle, *Metaph.*, I, 3 (983b 7); 4 (985b 5).

restrain the wicked from the evil of sin, He is said to abandon them. This does not mean that He altogether withdraws His providence from them; otherwise they would return to nothing, if they were not preserved in existence by His providence. This was the reason that had weight with Tully, who withdrew human affairs, concerning which we take counsel, from the care of divine providence.[1]

Reply Obj. 5. Since a rational creature has, through its free choice, control over its actions, as was said above,[2] it is subject to divine providence in an especial manner: something is imputed to it as a fault, or as a merit, and accordingly there is given to it something by way of punishment or reward. In this way the Apostle withdraws oxen from the care of God: not, however, that individual irrational creatures escape the care of divine providence, as was the opinion of the Rabbi Moses.[3]

Third Article
WHETHER GOD HAS IMMEDIATE PROVIDENCE OVER EVERYTHING?

We proceed thus to the Third Article: —

Objection 1. It seems that God has not immediate providence over all things. For whatever pertains to dignity must be attributed to God. But it belongs to the dignity of a king that he should have ministers, through whose mediation he provides for his subjects. Therefore much less has God Himself immediate providence over all things.

Obj. 2. Further, it belongs to providence to order all things to an end. Now the end of everything is its perfection and its good. But it pertains to every cause to bring its effect to good; and therefore every

---

1. 参见 *De Divinat.*, II, 5 (p. 69).
2. 参见 Ad 4, and q. 19, a. 10.
3. 参见 *Guide*, III, 17 (p. 286).

agent cause is a cause of the effect over which it has providence. If therefore God were to have immediate providence over all things, all secondary causes would be withdrawn.

Obj. 3. Further, Augustine says that, *It is better to be ignorant of some things than to know them, for example, ignoble things*;[1] and the Philosopher says the same.[2] But whatever is better must be attributed to God. Therefore He has not immediate providence over ignoble and wicked things.

On the contrary, It is said (Job xxxiv. 13): *What other hath He appointed over the earth? or whom hath He set over the world which He made?* On which passage Gregory says: *Himself He ruleth the world which He Himself hath made.*[3]

I answer that, Two things belong to providence — namely, the exemplar of the order of things foreordained towards an end, and the execution of this order, which is called government. As regards the first of these, God has immediate providence over everything, because he has in His intellect the exemplars of everything, even the smallest; and whatsoever causes He assigns to certain effects, He gives them the power to produce those effects. Whence it must be that He has pre-comprehended the order of those effects in His mind. As to the second, there are certain intermediaries of God's providence, for He governs things inferior by superior, not because of any defect in His power, but by reason of the abundance of His goodness; so that the dignity of causality is imparted even to creatures. Thus Plato's opinion, as narrated by Gregory of Nyssa, is removed.[4] He taught a threefold providence. First, one which belongs to the supreme Deity, Who first and foremost has provision over spiritual things, and thus

1. 参见 *Enchir.*, XVII (PL 40, 239).
2. 参见 *Metaph.*, XI, 10 (1074b 32).
3. 参见 *Moral.*, XXIV, 20 (PL 76, 314).
4. 参见 Cf. Nemesius, *De Nat. Hom.*, XLIV (PG 40, 794).

over the whole world as regards genus, species, and universal causes. The second providence, which is over the individuals of all that can be generated and corrupted, he attributed to the divinities who circulate in the heavens; that is, certain separate substances, which move corporeal things in a circular motion. The third providence, which is over human affairs, he assigned to demons, whom the Platonic philosophers placed between us and the gods, as Augustine tells us.[1]

Reply Obj. 1. It pertains to a king's dignity to have ministers who execute his providence. But the fact that he does not know the plans of what is done by them arises from a deficiency in himself. For every operative science is the more perfect, the more it considers the particular things where action takes place.

Reply Obj. 2. God's immediate provision over everything does not exclude the action of secondary causes, which are the executors of His order, as was said above.[2]

Reply Obj. 3. It is better for us not to know evil and ignoble things, insofar as by them we are impeded in our knowledge of what is better and higher (for we cannot understand many things simultaneously), and insofar as the thought of evil sometimes perverts the will towards evil. This does not hold true of God, Who sees everything simultaneously at one glance, and Whose will cannot turn in the direction of evil.

Fourth Article
WHETHER PROVIDENCE IMPOSES ANY NECESSITY ON WHAT IT FORESEES?

We proceed thus to the Fourth Article: —

Objection 1. It seems that divine providence imposes necessity upon

1. 参见 *De Civit. Dei*, IX 1 (PL 41, 257); VIII, 14 (PL 41, 238).
2. 参见 Q. 19, a. 5 and 8.

what it foresees. For every effect that has an essential cause (present or past) which it necessarily follows, comes to be of necessity; as the Philosopher proves.[1] But the providence of God, since it is eternal, precedes its effect, and the effect flows from it of necessity; for divine providence cannot be frustrated. Therefore divine providence imposes a necessity upon what it foresees.

Obj. 2. Further, every provider makes his work as stable as he can, lest it should fail. But God is most powerful. Therefore He assigns the stability of necessity to things whose providence He is.

Obj. 3. Further, Boethius says: *Fate from the immutable source of providence binds together human acts and fortunes by the indissoluble connexion*[2] *of causes.*[3] It seems therefore that providence imposes necessity upon what it foresees.

On the contrary, Dionysius says that *to corrupt nature is not the work of providence.*[4] But it is in the nature of some things to be contingent. Divine providence does not therefore impose any necessity upon things so as to destroy their contingency.

I answer that, Divine providence imposes necessity upon some things; not upon all, as some believed.[5] For to providence it belongs to order things towards an end. Now after the divine goodness, which is an extrinsic end to all things, the principal good in things themselves is the perfection of the universe; which would not be, were not all grades of being found in things. Whence it pertains to divine providence to produce every grade of being. And thus for some things it has prepared necessary causes, so that they happen of necessity; for others contingent causes, that they may happen by contingency,

---

1. 参见 *Metaph.*, V, 3 (1027a 30).
2. indissoluble connexion：不解之缘
3. 参见 *De Consol.*, IV, prose 6 (PL 63, 817).
4. 参见 *De Div. Nom.*, IV, 33 (PG 3, 733).
5. 参见 The Stoics: cf. Nemesius, *De Nat. Hom.*, XXXVII (PG 40, 752).

according to the disposition of their proximate causes.

Reply Obj. 1. The effect of divine providence is not only that things should happen *somehow*; but that they should happen either by necessity or by contingency. Therefore whatsoever divine providence ordains to happen infallibly and of necessity, happens infallibly and of necessity; and what the divine providence plans to happen contingently, happens contingently.

Reply Obj. 2. The order of divine providence is unchangeable and certain, so far as all things foreseen happen as they have been foreseen, whether from necessity or from contingency.

Reply Obj. 3. The indissolubility[1] and unchangeableness, of which Boethius speaks, pertain to the certainty of providence, which does not fail to produce its effect, and that in the way foreseen; but they do not pertain to the necessity of the effects. We must remember that, properly speaking, *necessary* and *contingent* are consequent upon being as such. Hence the mode both of necessity and of contingency falls under the foresight of God, Who provides universally for all being; not under the foresight of causes that provide only for some particular order of things.

1. indissolubility：永续性；不溶性

Question XXIII
PREDESTINATION
(*In Eight Articles*)

AFTER the consideration of divine providence, we must treat of predestination[1] and the book of life. Concerning predestination there are eight points of inquiry: (1) Whether predestination is suitably attributed to God? (2) What is predestination, and whether it places anything in the predestined? (3) Whether to God belongs the reprobation of some men? (4) On the comparison of predestination to election; whether, that is to say, the predestined are elected? (5) Whether merits are the cause or reason of predestination, or reprobation, or election? (6) Of the certainty of predestination; whether the predestined will infallibly be saved? (7) Whether the number of the predestined is certain? (8) Whether predestination can be furthered by the prayers of the saints?

First Article
WHETHER MEN ARE PREDESTINED BY GOD?

We proceed thus to the First Article: —

Objection 1. It seems that men are not predestined by God, for Damascene says: *It must be borne in mind that God foreknows, but does not predetermine, everything; since He foreknows all that is in us, but does not predetermine it.*[2] But human merit and demerit are in us, inasmuch as

---

1. predestination：命运；预先注定
2. 参见 *De Fide Orth.*, II, 30 (PG 94, 972).

we are the masters of our own acts by free choice. All that pertains therefore to merit or demerit is not predestined by God; and thus man's predestination is done away.

Obj. 2. Further, all creatures are directed to their ends by divine providence, as was said above.[1] But other creatures are not said to be predestined by God. Therefore, neither are men.

Obj. 3. Further, the angels are capable of beatitude, as well as men. But predestination does not befit angels, since in them there never was any unhappiness [*miseria*]; for predestination, as Augustine says,[2] is *a work aimed at showing mercy.* Therefore men are not predestined.

Obj. 4. Further, the benefits God confers upon men are revealed by the Holy Ghost to holy men, according to the saying of the Apostle (*1 Cor.* ii. 12): *Now we have received not the spirit of this world, but the Spirit that is of God: that we may know the things that are given us from God.* Therefore if man were predestined by God, since predestination is a benefit from God, predestination would be made known to all predestined; which is clearly false.

On the contrary, It is written (*Rom.* viii. 30): *Whom He predestined, them He also called.*

I answer that, It is fitting that God should predestine men. For all things are subject to His providence, as was shown above.[3] Now it belongs to providence to direct things towards their end, as was also said.[4] The end towards which created things are directed by God is twofold: one which exceeds all proportion and ability of created nature; and this end is life eternal, consisting in the vision of God

---

1. 参见 Q. 22, a. 1 and 2.
2. 参见 Cf. *De Divers. Quaest. ad Simplic.*, I, 2 (PL 40, 115); *Contra duas Epist. Pelag.*, II, 9 (PL 44, 586); *De Praedest. Sanct.*, III; VI; XVII (PL 44, 965, 969; 985).
3. 参见 Q. 22, a. 2.
4. 参见 Q. 22, a. 1.

which is above the nature of every creature, as was shown above.[1] The other end, however, is proportionate to created nature, to which end created being can attain according to the power of its nature. Now if a thing cannot attain to something by the power of its nature, it must be directed thereto by another; thus, an arrow is directed by the archer towards a mark. Hence, properly speaking, a rational creature, capable of eternal life, is led towards it, directed, as it were, by God. The exemplar of that direction pre-exists in God; just as in Him is the exemplar of the order of all things towards an end, which we declared above to be providence.[2] Now the exemplar in the mind of the doer of something to be done is a kind of pre-existence in him of the thing to be done. Hence the exemplar of the aforesaid direction of a rational creature towards the end of life eternal is called predestination. For to destine is to direct or send. Thus it is clear that predestination, as regards its objects, is a part of providence.

Reply Obj. 1. Damascene calls predestination an imposition of necessity, after the manner of natural things which are predetermined towards one end. This is clear from his adding: *He does not will malice, nor does He compel virtue.* Whence predestination is not excluded by him.

Reply Obj. 2. Irrational creatures have not the capacity for that end which exceeds the ability of human nature. Whence they cannot properly be said to be predestined; although improperly the term is used in respect of any other end.

Reply Obj. 3. Predestination applies to angels, just as it does to men, although they have never been unhappy. For movement does not take its nature from the term *wherefrom*, but from the term *whereto*. Because it matters nothing, in respect of the notion of making white, whether he who is made white was before black, yellow, or red. Likewise, it matters nothing in respect of the notion of predestination whether one

1. 参见 Q. 12, a. 4.
2. 参见 Q. 22, a. 1.

is predestined to life eternal from the state of misery or not. Although it may be said that every conferring of good above that which is due pertains to mercy; as was shown previously.[1]

Reply Obj. 4. Even if by a special privilege their predestination were revealed to some, it is not fitting that it should be revealed to everyone; because, if so, those who were not predestined would despair; and security would beget negligence in the predestined.

Second Article
WHETHER PREDESTINATION PLACES ANYTHING IN THE PREDESTINED?

We proceed thus to the Second Article: —

Objection 1. It seems that predestination does place something in the predestined. For every action of itself causes passion. If therefore predestination is action in God, predestination must be passion in the predestined.

Obj. 2. Further, Origen says on the text, *He who was predestined*, etc. (*Rom.* i. 4): *Predestination is of one who is not*; *destination*, *of one who is.*[2] And Augustine says: *What is predestination but the destination of one who is?*[3] Therefore predestination is only of one who actually exists; and it thus places something in the predestined.

Obj. 3. Further, preparation is something in the thing prepared. But predestination is the preparation of God's benefits, as Augustine says.[4] Therefore predestination is something in the predestined.

Obj. 4. Further, nothing temporal enters into the definition of eternity. But grace, which is something temporal, is found in the

---

1. 参见 Q. 21, a. 3, ad 2; a. 4.
2. 参见 *In Rom.*, I (PG 14, 849).
3. 参见 *De Divers. Quaest. ad Simplic.*, I, 2 (PL 40, 114).
4. 参见 Cf. *De Dono Persev.*, XIV (PL 45, 1014).

definition of predestination. For predestination is the preparation of grace in the present, and of glory in the future.[1] Therefore predestination is not anything eternal. So it must needs be that it is in the predestined, and not in God; for whatever is in God is eternal.

On the contrary, Augustine says that *predestination is the foreknowledge of God's benefits.*[2] But foreknowledge is not in the things foreknown, but in the person who foreknows them. Therefore, predestination is in the one who predestines, and not in the predestined.

I answer that, Predestination is not anything in the predestined, but only in the person who predestines. We have said above that predestination is a part of providence. Now providence is not anything in the things provided for, but is an exemplar in the mind of the provider, as was proved above.[3] But the execution of providence, which is called government, is in a passive way in the thing governed, and in an active way in the governor. Whence it is clear that predestination is a kind of exemplar of the ordering of some persons towards eternal salvation, existing in the divine mind. The execution, however, of this order is in a passive way in the predestined, but actively in God. The execution of predestination is *calling* and *magnification*; according to the Apostle (*Rom.* viii. 30): *Whom He predestinated, them He also called*; *and whom He called, them He also magnified* [Vulg., *justified*].

Reply Obj. 1. Actions passing out to external matter of themselves produce passion — for example, the actions of warming and cutting; but not so actions remaining in the agent, as understanding and willing, as was said above.[4] Predestination is an action of this latter class. Therefore, it does not put anything in the predestined. But its execution, which passes out to external things, posits an effect in them.

---

1. 参见 Cf. Peter Lombard, *Sent.*, I, xl, 2 (I, 251).
2. 参见 *De Dono Persev.*, XIV (PL 45, 1014).
3. 参见 Q. 22, a. 1.
4. 参见 Q. 14, a. 2; q. 18, a. 3, ad 1.

Reply Obj. 2. Destination sometimes denotes a real mission of someone to a given end; thus, destination can be said only of someone actually existing. It is taken, however, in another sense for a mission which a person conceives in the mind; and in this manner we are said to destine a thing which we firmly resolve in our mind. In this latter way it is said that Eleazar *determined not to do any unlawful things for the love of life* (*2 Mac.* vi. 20). Thus destination can be of a thing which does not exist. Predestination, however, by reason of the antecedent nature it implies, can be attributed to a thing which does not actually exist, however its destination may be understood.

Reply Obj. 3. Preparation is twofold: of the patient in respect to passion, and this is in the thing prepared; and of the agent, to action, and this is in the agent. Such a preparation is predestination, in so far as an agent is said to prepare itself by intellect to act, according as it preconceives the idea of what is to be done. Thus, God from all eternity prepared the work of salvation by predestination, in conceiving the idea of the direction of some towards salvation.

Reply Obj. 4. Grace does not come into the definition of predestination, as something belonging to its essence, but inasmuch as predestination implies a relation to grace, as of cause to effect, and of act to its object. Whence it does not follow that predestination is anything temporal.

Third Article
WHETHER GOD REPROBATES ANY MAN?

We proceed thus to the Third Article: —

Objection 1. It seems that God reprobates no man. For nobody reprobates what he loves. But God loves every man, according to the words (*Wis.* xi. 25): *Thou lovest all things that are, and Thou hatest none of the things Thou hast made.* Therefore God reprobates no man.

Obj. 2. Further, if God reprobates any man, it would be necessary for reprobation to have the same relation to the reprobate as predestination has to the predestined. But predestination is the cause of the salvation of the predestined. Therefore reprobation will likewise be the cause of the loss of the reprobate. But this is false. For it is said (*Osee* xiii. 9): *Destruction is thy own, O Israel; Thy help is only in Me.* God does not, then, reprobate any man.

Obj. 3. Further, to no one ought anything to be imputed which he cannot avoid. But if God reprobates anyone, that one must perish. For it is said (*Eccles.* vii. 14): *Consider the works of God, that no man can correct whom He hath despised.* Therefore it could not be imputed to any man, were he to perish. But this is false. Therefore God does not reprobate anyone.

On the contrary, It is said (*Malach.* i. 2, 3): *I have loved Jacob, but have hated Esau.*

I answer that, God does reprobate some persons. For it was said above that predestination is a part of providence. To providence, however, it belongs to permit certain defects in those things which are subject to providence, as was said above.[1] Thus, as men are ordained to eternal life through the providence of God, it likewise is part of that providence to permit some to fall away from that end; this is called *reprobation*. Thus, as predestination is a part of providence, in regard to those divinely ordained to eternal salvation, so reprobation is a part of providence in regard to those who turn aside from that end. Hence reprobation implies not only foreknowledge, but also something more, as does providence, as was said above.[2] Therefore, as predestination includes the will to confer grace and glory, so also reprobation includes the will to permit a person to fall into sin, and to impose the punishment of damnation because of that sin.

---

1. 参见 Q. 22, a. 2, ad 2.
2. 参见 Q. 22, a. 1, ad 3.

Reply Obj. 1. God loves all men and all creatures, inasmuch as He wishes them all some good; but He does not wish every good to them all. So far, therefore, as He does not wish for some this particular good — namely, eternal life — He is said to hate or reprobate them.

Reply Obj. 2. Reprobation differs in its causality from predestination. This latter is the cause both of what is expected in the future life by the predestined — namely, glory — and of what is received in this life — namely, grace. Reprobation, however, is not the cause of what is in the present — namely, sin; but it is the cause of abandonment by God. It is the cause, however, of what is assigned in the future — namely, eternal punishment. But guilt proceeds from the free choice of the person who is reprobated and deserted by grace. In this way the word of the prophet is true — namely, *Destruction is thy own, O Israel.*

Reply Obj. 3. Reprobation by God does not take anything away from the power of the person reprobated. Hence, when it is said that the reprobated cannot obtain grace, this must not be understood as implying absolute impossibility, but only conditional impossibility; just as it was said above that the predestined must necessarily be saved, yet by a conditional necessity, which does not do away with the liberty of choice.[1] Whence, although anyone reprobated by God cannot acquire grace, nevertheless, that he falls into this or that particular sin comes from the use of his free desire. Hence it is rightly imputed to him as guilt.

Fourth Article
WHETHER THE PREDESTINED ARE ELECTED BY GOD?

We proceed thus to the Fourth Article: —

Objection 1. It seems that the predestined are not elected by God.

---

1. 参见 Q. 19, a. 3.

For Dionysius says that as the corporeal sun sends his rays upon all without selection, so does God His goodness.[1] But the goodness of God is communicated to some in an especial manner through a participation of grace and glory. Therefore God communicates His grace and glory without election; and this belongs to predestination.

Obj. 2. Further, election is of things that exist. But predestination from all eternity is also of things which do not exist. Therefore, some are predestined without election.

Obj. 3. Further, election implies some discrimination. Now *God wills all men to be saved* (*1 Tim.* ii. 4). Therefore predestination, which ordains men towards eternal salvation, is without election.

On the contrary, It is said (*Ephes.* i. 4): *He chose us in Him before the foundation of the world.*

I answer that, Predestination logically presupposes election; and election presupposes love. The reason for this is that predestination, as was stated above, is a part of providence. Now providence, as also prudence, is the plan existing in the intellect directing the ordering of some things towards an end; as was proved above.[2] But nothing is directed towards an end unless the will for that end already exists. Whence the predestination of some to eternal salvation logically presupposes that God wills their salvation; and to this belong both election and love: — love, inasmuch as He wills them this particular good of eternal salvation; since to love is to wish well to anyone, as was stated above:[3] — election, inasmuch as He wills this good to some in preference to others; since He reprobates some, as was stated above. Election and love, however, are diversely ordered in God, and in ourselves: because in us the will in loving does not cause good, but we are incited to love by a good which already exists; and therefore

1. 参见 *De Div. Nom.* IV, 1 (PG 3, 693).
2. 参见 Q. 22, a. 1.
3. 参见 Q. 20, a. 2 and 3.

we choose someone to love, and so election in us precedes love. In God, however, it is the reverse. For His will, by which in loving He wishes good to someone, is the cause of that good possessed by some in preference to others. Thus it is clear that, logically, love precedes election, and election precedes predestination. Whence all the predestinate are objects of election and love.

Reply Obj. 1. If the communication of the divine goodness in general be considered, God communicates His goodness without election, inasmuch as there is nothing which does not in some way share in His goodness, as we said above.[1] But if we consider the communication of this or that particular good, He does not allot it without election; since He gives certain goods to some men, which He does not give to others. Thus in the conferring of grace and glory election is implied.

Reply Obj. 2. When the will of the person choosing is incited to choice by the good already existing in things, the choice must needs be of those things which already exist, as happens in our choice. In God it is otherwise, as was said above.[2] Thus, as Augustine says: *Those are chosen by God, who do not exist; yet He does not err in His choice.*[3]

Reply Obj. 3. God wills all men to be saved by His antecedent will, which is to will, not absolutely, but relatively; and not by His consequent will, which is to will absolutely.

Fifth Article
WHETHER THE FOREKNOWLEDGE OF MERITS IS THE CAUSE OF PREDESTINATION?

We proceed thus to the Fifth Article: —

Objection 1. It seems that foreknowledge of merits is the cause of

---

1. 参见 Q. 6, a. 4.
2. 参见 Q. 20, a. 2.
3. 参见 *Serm.* XXVI, 4 (PL 38, 173).

predestination. For the Apostle says (*Rom.* viii. 29): *Whom He foreknew, He also predestinated.* Again, the *Gloss* of Ambrose on *Rom.* ix. 15 (*I will have mercy upon whom I will have mercy*) says: *I will give mercy to him who, I foresee, will turn to Me with his whole heart.*[1] Therefore it seems the foreknowledge of merits is the case of predestination.

Obj. 2. Further, divine predestination includes the divine will, which cannot be irrational; since predestination is *a work aimed at showing mercy*, as Augustine says.[2] But there can be no other reason for predestination than the foreknowledge of merits. Therefore it must be the cause or reason of predestination.

Obj. 3. Further, *There is no injustice in God* (*Rom.* ix. 14). Now it would seem unjust that unequal things be given to equals. But all men are equal as regards both nature and original sin; and inequality in them arises from the merits or demerits of their actions. Therefore God does not prepare unequal things for men by predestinating and reprobating, unless through the foreknowledge of their merits and demerits.

On the contrary, The Apostle says (*Tit.* iii. 5): *Not by the works of justice which we have done, but according to His mercy He saved us.* But as He saved us, so He predestined that we should be saved. Therefore, foreknowledge of merits is not the cause or reason of predestination.

I answer that, Since predestination includes will, as was said above, the reason of predestination must be sought in the same way as was the reason of the will of God. Now it was shown above[3] that we cannot assign any cause of the divine will on the part of the act of willing; but a reason can be found on the part of the things willed, inasmuch as God wills one thing because of something else. Therefore nobody has

---

1. 参见 *In Rom.*, super IX, 15 (PL 17, 142). — Cf. *Glossa ordin.*, super *Rom* IX, 15 (VI, 21E).
2. 参见 Cf. *De Divers. Quaest. ad Simplic.*, I, 2 (PL 40, 115); *Contra duas Epist Pelag.*, II, 9 (PL 44, 586); *De Praedest. Sanct.*, III; VI; XVII (PL 44, 965. 969; 985).
3. 参见 Q. 19, a. 5.

been so insane as to say that merit is the cause of divine predestination as regards the act of the predestinator. But the question is rather this, whether, as regards the effect, predestination has any cause; or, what comes to the same thing, whether God pre-ordained that He would give the effect of predestination to anyone because of any merits.

Accordingly, there were some who said that the effect of predestination was pre-ordained for some because of pre-existing merits in a former life. This was the opinion of Origen, who thought that the souls of men were created in the beginning, and, according to the diversity of their works, different states were assigned to them in this world when united to the body.[1] The Apostle, however, discards this opinion when he says (*Rom.* ix. 11, 12): *For when they were not yet born, nor had done any good or evil, . . . not of works, but of Him that calleth, it was said to her: The elder shall serve the younger.*

Others said that pre-existing merits in this life are the reason and cause of the effect of predestination. For the Pelagians taught that the beginning of doing well came from us, and the consummation from God;[2] so that it came about that the effect of predestination was granted to one, and not to another, because the one made a beginning by preparing, whereas the other did not. But against this we have the saying of the Apostle (*2 Cor.* iii. 5), that *we are not sufficient to think anything of ourselves as of ourselves.* Now no principle of action can be found which is prior to the act of thinking. Therefore it cannot be said that anything begun in us can be the reason of the effect of predestination.

And so others said that merits following the effect of predestination are the reason for predestination.[3] By this they mean us to understand that God gives grace to a person, and has pre-ordained that He will

1. 参见 *Peri Archon*, I, 6 (PG 11, 166).
2. 参见 Cf. Denzinger, no. 105 (p. 48).
3. 参见 Cf. *Glossa ordin.*, super *Rom.* IX, 5 (VI, 21E).

give it, because He knows beforehand that he will make good use of that grace; as if a king were to give a horse to a soldier because he knows he will make good use of it. But these seem to have drawn a distinction between that which flows from grace, and that which flows from free choice, as if the same thing cannot come from both. It is, however, manifest that what is of grace is the effect of predestination; and this cannot be considered as the reason for predestination, since it is included within predestination. Therefore, if anything else in us be the reason of predestination, it will be outside the effect of predestination. Now there is no distinction between what flows from free choice and what is of predestination; as there is no distinction between what flows from a secondary cause and from a first cause. For the providence of God produces effects through the operation of secondary causes, as was above shown[1]. Therefore, that which flows from free choice is also of predestination.

We must say, therefore, that the effect of predestination may be considered in a twofold light. In one way, in particular, and thus there is no reason why one effect of predestination should not be the reason and cause of another; a subsequent effect being the reason of a previous effect, as its final cause, and the previous effect being the reason of the subsequent as its meritorious cause, which plays the part of the disposition of the matter. Thus we might say that God preordained to give glory because of merit, and that He preordained to give grace to merit glory. In another way, the effect of predestination may be considered in general. Thus understood, it is impossible that the whole effect of predestination in general should have any cause as coming from us; because whatsoever is in man disposing him towards salvation is all included under the effect of predestination; even the preparation for grace. For neither does this preparation for

1. 参见 Q. 22, a. 3.

grace happen otherwise than by divine help, according to the prophet Jeremias (*Lam.* v. 21): *Convert us, O Lord, to Thee, and we shall be converted.* Yet predestination has in this way, in regard to its effect, the goodness of God for its reason; towards which the whole effect of predestination is directed as to an end, and from which it proceeds as from its first moving principle.

Reply Obj. 1. The use of grace foreknown by God is not the cause of conferring grace, except after the manner of a final cause; as was explained above.

Reply Obj. 2. Predestination has its foundation in the goodness of God as regards its effects in general. Considered in its particular effects, however, one effect is the reason of another; as we have already stated.

Reply Obj. 3. The reason for the predestination of some, and reprobation of others, must be sought in the goodness of God. Thus God is said to have made all things through His goodness, so that the divine goodness might be represented in things. Now it is necessary that God's goodness, which in itself is one and simple, should be manifested in many ways in His creation; because creatures in themselves cannot attain to the simplicity of God. Thus it is that for the completion of the universe there are required diverse grades of being, of which some hold a high and some a low place in the universe. That this multiformity of grades may be preserved in things, God allows some evils, lest many good things should be hindered, as was said above.[1] Let us then consider the whole of the human race as we consider the whole universe. God has willed to manifest His goodness in men: in respect to those whom He predestines, by means of His mercy, in sparing them; and in respect of others, whom he reprobates, by means of His justice, in punishing

1. 参见 Q. 22, a. 2.

them. This is the reason why God elects some and rejects others. To this the Apostle refers, saying (*Rom.* ix. 22, 23): *What if God, willing to show His wrath* (that is, the vengeance of His justice), *and to make His power known, endured* (that is, permitted) *with much patience vessels of wrath, fitted for destruction; that He might show the riches of His glory on the vessels of mercy, which He hath prepared unto glory* (*Rom.* ix. 22, 23): and (*2 Tim.* ii. 20): *But in a great house there are not only vessels of gold and silver; but also of wood and of earth; and some, indeed, unto honor, but some unto dishonor.* Yet why He chooses some for glory, and reprobates others, has no reason, except the divine will. Whence Augustine says: *Why He draws one, and another He draws not, seek not to judge, if thou dost not wish to err.*[1] Thus too, in the things of nature, since primary matter is altogether uniform, a reason can be assigned as to why one part of it was fashioned by God from the beginning under the form of fire, another under the form of earth, namely, so that there might be a diversity of species in the things of nature. Yet why this particular part of matter is under this particular form, and that under another, depends upon the simple will of God; just as from the simple will of the artificer it depends that this stone is in this part of the wall, and that in another; although the plan requires that some stone should be in this place, and some other in that place. Neither on this account can there be said to be injustice in God, if He prepares unequal lots for not unequal things. This would be altogether contrary to the notion of justice, if the effect of predestination were granted as a debt, and not gratuitously[2]. In things which are given gratuitously a person can give more or less, just as he pleases (provided he deprives nobody of his due) without any infringement of justice. This is what the master of the house said: *Take what is thine, and go thy way. Is it not lawful for me to do what I will?* (*Matt.* xx. 14, 15).

---

1. 参见 *Tract.* XXVI, super *Ioann.*, VI, 44 (PL 35, 1607).
2. gratuitously：不必要地；无偿地

Sixth Article
WHETHER PREDESTINATION IS CERTAIN?

We proceed thus to the Sixth Article: —

Objection 1. It seems that predestination is not certain. Because on the words *Hold fast that which thou hast, that no one take thy crown* (*Apoc.* iii. 11), Augustine says: *Another will not receive it, unless this one were to lose it.*[1] Hence the crown which is the effect of predestination can be both acquired and lost. Therefore predestination cannot be certain.

Obj. 2. Further, granted what is possible, nothing impossible follows. But it is possible that one predestined — *e.g.*, Peter — may sin and then be killed. But if this were so, it would follow that the effect of predestination would be thwarted. This, then, is not impossible. Therefore predestination is not certain.

Obj. 3. Further, whatever God could do in the past, He can do now. But He could have not predestined whom He hath predestined. Therefore now He is able not to predestine him. Therefore predestination is not certain.

On the contrary, the *Gloss* on *Rom.* viii. 29 (*Whom He foreknew, He also predestinated*) says: *Predestination is the foreknowledge and preparation of the benefits of God, by which whosoever are freed will most certainly be freed.*[2]

I answer that, Predestination achieves its effect most certainly and infallibly, and yet it does not impose any necessity, such that its effect should take place from necessity. For it was said above that predestination is a part of providence. But not all things subject to providence are necessary; for some things happen from contingency, according to the disposition of the proximate causes which divine providence has ordained for such effects. Yet the order of providence

---

1. 参见 *De Corrept. et Grat.*, XIII (PL 44, 940).
2. 参见 *Glossa ordin.*, super *Rom.* VIII, 29 (VI, 19F); Peter Lombard, *In Rom.*, VIII, 29 (PL 191, 1449).

is infallible, as was shown above.[1] So also is the order of predestination certain; and yet free choice, from which the effect of predestination has its contingency is not destroyed. Moreover all that has been said about the divine knowledge and will must also be taken into consideration;[2] since they do not destroy contingency in things, although they themselves are most certain and infallible.

Reply Obj. 1. The crown may be said to belong to a person in two ways: first, by God's predestination, and thus no one loses his crown; secondly, by the merit of grace (for what we merit, in a certain way is ours), and thus anyone may lose his crown by mortal sin. Another person receives that crown thus lost, inasmuch as he takes the former's place. For God does not permit some to fall, without raising others, according to Job xxxiv. 24: *He shall break in pieces many and innumerable, and make others to stand in their stead.* Thus men have been substituted in the place of the fallen angels; and the Gentiles in that of the Jews. He who is substituted for another in the state of grace receives also the crown of the fallen in this respect, namely, that in eternal life he will enjoy the good the other has done; for in eternal life he will enjoy the good done by others as well as by himself.

Reply Obj. 2. Although it is possible for one who is predestinated, considered in himself, to die in mortal sin; yet it is not possible, if it be supposed, as in fact it is supposed, that he is predestinated. Whence it does not follow that predestination can fall short of its effect.

Reply Obj. 3. Predestination includes the divine will. Hence, just as we said above[3] that God's willing of any created thing is necessary on the supposition that He so wills, because of the immutability of the divine will, but not necessary absolutely; so we must now say the same thing of predestination. Therefore, one ought not to say that God is

1. 参见 Q. 22, a. 4.
2. 参见 Q. 14, a. 13; q. 19, a. 4 and 8.
3. 参见 Q. 19, a. 3.

able not to predestinate one whom He has predestinated, taking it in a composite sense; though, absolutely speaking, God can predestinate or not. But in this way the certainty of predestination is not destroyed.

Seventh Article
WHETHER THE NUMBER OF THE PREDESTINED IS CERTAIN ?

We proceed thus to the Seventh Article: —

Objection 1. It seems that the number of the predestined is not certain. For a number to which an addition can be made is not certain. But there can be an addition to the number of the predestined, as it seems; for it is written (*Deut.* i. 11): *The Lord God adds to this number many thousands*, and the *Gloss* adds, *fixed by God, who knows those who belong to Him.*[1] Therefore the number of the predestined is not certain.

Obj. 2. Further, no reason can be assigned why God pre-ordains to salvation one number of men more than another. But nothing is arranged by God without a reason. Therefore the number to be saved pre-ordained by God cannot be certain.

Obj. 3. Further, the operations of God are more perfect than those of nature. But in the works of nature, good is found in the majority of things, defect and evil in the minority. If, then, the number of the saved were fixed by God at a certain figure, there would be more saved than lost. Yet the contrary follows from *Matt.* vii. 13, 14: *For wide is the gate, and broad the way that leadeth to destruction, and many there are who go in thereat. How narrow is the gate, and strait is the way that leadeth to life; and few there are that ind it!* Therefore the number of those preordained by God to be saved is not certain.

On the contrary, Augustine says: *The number of the predestined is certain,*

---

1. 参见 *Glossa ordin.*, super *Deut.*, I, 11 (I, 330B).

and can neither be increased nor diminished.[1]

I answer that, The number of the predestined is certain. Some have said that it was formally, but not materially certain;[2] as if we were to say that it was certain that a hundred or a thousand would be saved, not however these or those individuals. But this destroys the certainty of predestination, of which we spoke above. Therefore we must say that to God the number of the predestined is certain, not only formally, but also materially.

It must, however, be observed that the number of the predestined is said to be certain to God, not only by reason of His knowledge, because, that is to say, He knows how many will be saved (for in this way the number of drops of rain and the sands of the sea are certain to God); but by reason of His election and determination. For the further evidence of which we must remember that every agent intends to make something finite, as is clear from what has been said above when we treated of the infinite.[3] Now whosoever intends some definite measure in his effect thinks out some definite number in the essential parts, which are by their very nature required for the perfection of the whole. For of those things which are required, not principally, but only because of something else, he does not select any definite number *per se*; but he accepts and uses them in such numbers as are necessary because of that other thing. For instance, a builder thinks out the definite measurements of a house, and also the definite number of rooms which he wishes to make in the house; and definite measurements of the walls and the roof; he does not, however, select a definite number of stones, but accepts and uses just so many as are sufficient for the required measurements of the wall. This we must also suppose to be the situation of God in regard to the whole universe,

1. 参见 *De Corrept. et Grat.*, XIII (PL 44, 940).
2. 参见 Cf. *De Ver.*, q. 6, a. 4, — Cf. also St. Albert, *In I Sent.*, d. xl, a. 11 (XXVI, 319).
3. 参见 Q. 7, a. 2, 3 and 4.

which is His effect. For He pre-ordained the measurements of the whole of the universe, and what number would befit the essential parts of that universe — that is to say, which have in some way been ordained in perpetuity: how many spheres, how many stars, how many elements, and how many species. Individuals, however, which undergo corruption, are not ordained as it were chiefly for the good of the universe, but in a secondary way, inasmuch as the good of the species is preserved through them. Whence, although God knows the total number of individuals, yet the number of oxen, flies, and such-like, is not in itself pre-ordained by God; but divine providence produces just so many as are sufficient for the preservation of the species.

Now of all creatures, the rational creature chiefly is ordained for the good of the universe, being as such incorruptible; and more especially that rational creature which attains to eternal happiness, since it reaches the ultimate end more immediately. Hence, the number of the predestined is certain to God, not only by way of knowledge, but also by way of an original pre-ordination. The same situation does not entirely obtain in the case of the number of the reprobate, who would seem to be pre-ordained by God for the good of the elect, in whose regard *all things work together unto good* (*Rom.* viii. 28). Concerning the number of all the predestined, some[1] say that so many men will be saved as angels fell; some,[2] so many as there were angels left; others,[3] as many as the number of angels who fell, added to that of all the angels created by God. It is, however, better to say that, *to God alone is known the number for whom is reserved eternal happiness.*

Reply Obj. 1. These words of *Deuteronomy* must be taken as applied

---

1. 参见 St. Augustine, *Enchir.*, XXIX; LXII (PL 40, 246; 261); *De Civit. Dei*, XXII, 1 (PL 41, 751); St. Isidore, *Sent.*, I, 10 (PL 83, 556).
2. 参见 Peter Lombard, *Sent.*, II, ix, 7 (I, 350). — Cf. St. Gregory the Great, *In Evang.*, II, hom. 34 (PL 76, 1252); *Moral.*, XXXI, 49 (PL 76, 628).
3. 参见 Cf. G. Bareille, "Anges. II" (*Dict, de théol. cath.*, I, 1909, col. 1206).

to those who are marked out by God beforehand in respect to righteousness in the present life. For their number is increased and diminished; but not the number of the predestined.

Reply Obj. 2. The reason of the quantity of any one part must be judged from the proportion of that part to the whole. Thus in God the reason why He has made so many stars, or so many species of things, or predestined so many, is according to the proportion of the principal parts to the good of the whole universe.

Reply Obj. 3. The good that is proportionate to the common state of nature is to be found in the majority, and is wanting in a small number of cases. The good that exceeds the common state of nature is to be found in the minority, and is wanting in the majority. Thus it is clear that the majority of men have a sufficient knowledge for the guidance of life; and there are a few who have not this knowledge and who are said to be half-witted[1] or foolish; but they who attain to a profound knowledge of things intelligible are a very small minority in comparison with the rest. Since eternal happiness, consisting as it does in the vision of God, exceeds the common state of nature, and especially in so far as this is deprived of grace through the corruption of original sin, those who are saved are in the minority. In this especially, however, appears the mercy of God, that He has chosen some for that salvation, from which very many in accordance with the common course and tendency of nature fall short.

Eighth Article
WHETHER PREDESTINATION CAN BE FURTHERED BY THE PRAYERS OF THE SAINTS?

We proceed thus to the Eighth Article: —

---

1. half-witted：愚笨的

Objection 1. It seems that predestination cannot be furthered by the prayers of the saints. For nothing eternal can be aided by anything temporal; and in consequence nothing temporal can help towards making something eternal. But predestination is eternal. Therefore, since the prayers of the saints are temporal, they cannot so help as to cause anyone to become predestined. Predestination therefore is not furthered by the prayers of the saints.

Obj. 2. Further, as there is no need of advice except because of defective knowledge, so there is no need of help except through defective power. But neither of these things can be said of God when He predestines. Whence it is said: *Who hath helped the Spirit of the Lord? Or who hath been His counsellor?* (*Rom.* xi. 34). Therefore predestination cannot be furthered by the prayers of the saints.

Obj. 3. Further, if a thing can be helped, it can also be hindered. But predestination cannot be hindered by anything. Therefore it cannot be furthered by anything.

On the contrary, It is said that *Isaac besought the Lord for his wife because she was barren*; *and He heard Him and made Rebecca to conceive* (*Gen.* xxv. 21). But from that conception Jacob was born, and he was predestined. Now his predestination would not have been accomplished if he had never been born. Therefore predestination can be furthered by the prayers of the saints.

I answer that, Concerning this question, there have been different errors. Some,[1] looking to the certainty of divine predestination, said that prayers were superfluous, as also anything else done to attain salvation; because whether these things were done or not, the predestined would attain, and the reprobate would not attain, eternal salvation. But against this opinion are all the warnings of Holy

---

1. 参见 Attributed to the Epicureans by St. Thomas, *De Ver.*, q. 6, a. 6.—Cf. Epicurus' fragment cited by Nemesius, *De Nat. Hom.*, XLIV (PG 40, 796).

Scripture, exhorting us to prayer and other good works.

Others[1] have declared that the divine predestination is altered through prayer. This is said to have been the opinion of the Egyptians, who thought that the divine ordination, which they called *fate*, could be frustrated by certain sacrifices and prayers. Against this also is the authority of Scripture. For it is said: *But the triumpher in Israel will not spare and will not be moved to repentance* (*1 Kings* xv. 29); and that *the gifts and the calling of God are without repentance* (*Rom.* xi. 29).

We must therefore propose a different explanation, namely, that in predestination two things are to be considered — the divine preordination, and its effect. As regards the former, in no possible way can predestination be furthered by the prayers of the saints. For it is not due to their prayers that anyone is predestined by God. As regards the latter, predestination is said to be helped by the prayers of the saints and by other good works; because providence, of which predestination is a part, does not do away with secondary causes, but so exercizes providence over effects that the very order of secondary causes falls under providence. So, just as God so exercized providence over natural effects, that natural causes are ordained to bring about these natural effects, without which those effects would not happen; so the salvation of a particular person is predestined by God in such a way, that whatever helps that person towards salvation falls under the order of predestination; whether it be one's own prayers, or those of another, or other good works, and the like, without which one would not attain to salvation. Whence, the predestined must strive after good works and prayer; because through these means the effect of predestination is most certainly fulfilled. For this reason it is said: *Labor the more that by good works you may make sure your calling and election* (*2 Pet.* i. 10).

---

1. 参见 Cf. Nemesius, *op. cit.*, XXXVI (PG 40, 746).— Cf. below, q. 116, a. 3.

Reply Obj. 1. This argument shows that predestination is not furthered by the prayers of the saints, as regards the divine preordination[1].

Reply Obj. 2. One is said to be helped by another in two ways. In one way, inasmuch as he receives power from him; and to be helped thus belongs to the weak. But this cannot be said of God, and it is thus we are to understand the words, *Who hath helped the Spirit of the Lord?* In another way one is said to be helped by a person through whom he carries out his work, as a master through a servant. In this way, God is helped by us, inasmuch as we execute His orders, according to *1 Cor.* iii. 9: *We are God's coadjutors.* Nor is this because of any defect in the power of God, but because He employs intermediary causes, in order that the beauty of order may be preserved in the universe, and also that He may communicate to creatures the dignity of causality.

Reply Obj. 3. Secondary causes cannot escape the order of the first universal cause, as has been said above.[2] Indeed, they execute that order. Therefore, predestination can be furthered by creatures, but it cannot be impeded by them.

---

1. preordination：预定；预先注定命运
2. 参见 Q. 19, a. 6; q. 22, a. 2, ad 1.

Question XXIV
THE BOOK OF LIFE
(*In Three Articles*)

WE must now consider the book of life, concerning which there are three points of inquiry: (1) What is the book of life? (2) Of what life is it the book? (3) Whether anyone can be blotted out of the book of life?

First Article
WHETHER THE BOOK OF LIFE IS THE SAME AS PREDESTINATION?

We proceed thus to the First Article: —

Objection 1. It seems that the book of life is not the same thing as predestination. For it is said, *All these things are the book of life* (*Ecclus* xxiv. 32) — *i.e. the Old and New Testament*, according to the *Gloss*. This, however, is not predestination. Therefore, the book of life is not predestination.

Obj. 2. Further, Augustine says that *the book of life is a certain divine energy, by which it happens that the good or evil works of each one are recalled to his memory*.[2] But divine energy belongs, seemingly, not to predestination, but rather to divine power. Therefore the book of life is not the same thing as predestination.

Obj. 3. Further, reprobation is opposed to predestination. So, if the book of life were the same as predestination, there should also be a

1. 参见 *Glossa interl.*, super *Ecclus*. XXIV, 32 (III, 412V).
2. 参见 *De Civit. Dei*, XX, 14 (PL 41, 680).

book of death, as there is a book of life.

On the contrary, It is said, in the *Gloss* upon *Ps*. lxviii. 29 (*Let them be blotted out of the book of the living*), *This book is the knowledge of God, by which He hath predestined to life those whom He foreknew.*[1]

I answer that, The book of life is in God taken in a metaphorical sense, according to a likeness with human affairs. For it is usual among men that they who are chosen for any office should be inscribed in a book; as, for instance, soldiers, or counsellors, who formerly were called *conscript fathers*. Now it is clear from the preceding that all the predestined are elected by God to possess eternal life.[2] Now this conscription of the predestined is called the book of life. Furthermore, a thing is said to be written metaphorically upon the mind of anyone when it is firmly held in the memory, according to *Prov*. (iii. 3): *Forget not My law, and let thy heart keep My commandments*; and further on, *Write them in the tables of thy heart*. For things are written down in material books to help the memory. Whence, the knowledge of God, by which He firmly holds in mind that He has predestined some to eternal life, is called the book of life. For as the writing in a book is the sign of things to be done, so the knowledge of God is a sign in Him of those who are to be brought to eternal life, according to *2 Tim*. ii. 19: *The sure foundation of God standeth firm, having this seal*; *the Lord knoweth who are His*.

Reply Obj, 1. The book of life may be understood in two senses. In one sense, as the inscription of those who are chosen to life; and thus we now speak of the book of life. In another sense, the inscription of those things which lead us to life may be called the book of life; and this also is twofold. It may refer to the things to be done, and thus the Old and New Testaments are called a book of life; or it may refer to

---

1. 参见 *Glossa ordin.*, super *Ps*. LXVIII, 29 (III, 182F); Peter Lombard, *In Psalm.*, super LXVIII, 29 (PL 191, 639).
2. 参见 Q. 23, a. 4.

things already done, and thus that divine energy by which the deeds of each one will be recalled to his memory is spoken of as the book of life. We may in like manner speak of the book of war, whether it contains the names of those chosen for military service, or treats of the art of warfare, or relates the deeds of soldiers.

Hence the solution of the *Second Objection* is clear.

Reply Obj. 3. It is the custom to inscribe, not those who are rejected, but those who are chosen. Whence there is no book of death corresponding to reprobation, as does the book of life to predestination.

Reply Obj. 4. The book of life differs logically from predestination, for it implies the knowledge of predestination; as is also made clear from the *Gloss* quoted above.

Second Article
WHETHER THE BOOK OF LIFE REGARDS ONLY THE LIFE OF GLORY OF THE PREDESTINED ?

We proceed thus to the Second Article: —

Objection 1. It seems that the book of life does not regard only the life of glory of the predestined. For the book of life is the knowledge of life. But God, through His own life, knows all other life. Therefore the book of life is so called in relation to divine life; and not only in relation to the life of the predestined.

Obj. 2. Further, as the life of glory comes from God, so also does the life of nature. Therefore, if the knowledge of the life of glory is called the book of life, so also should the knowledge of the life of nature be so called.

Obj. 3. Further, some are chosen to the life of grace who are not chosen to the life of glory; as is clear from what is said: *Have not I chosen you twelve, and one of you is a devil?* (*Jo.* vi. 71). But the book of life is the inscription of the divine election, as was stated above. Therefore, it applies also to the life of grace.

On the contrary, The book of life is the knowledge of predestination, as was stated above. But predestination does not regard the life of grace, except so far as it is directed to glory; for those are not predestined who have grace and yet fail to obtain glory. The book of life therefore is so called only in relation to the life of glory.

I answer that, The book of life, as was stated above, signifies a conscription or a knowledge of those chosen to life. Now a man is elected to something which does not belong to him by nature. Furthermore, that to which a man is elected has the nature of an end. For a soldier is not elected or inscribed merely to put on armor, but to fight; since this is the proper duty to which military service is directed. But the life of glory is an end exceeding human nature, as was said above.[1] Therefore, strictly speaking, the book of life regards the life of glory.

Reply Obj. 1. The divine life, even considered as a life of glory, is natural to God; hence, there is no election in reference to it, and in consequence no book of life. For we do not say that anyone is chosen to possess the power of sense or any of the things that are consequent on nature.

From this we gather the *Reply* to the *Second Objection.* For there is no election, nor a book of life, as regards the life of nature.

Reply Obj. 3. The life of grace has the nature, not of an end, but of something that is a means towards an end. Hence, no one is said to be chosen to the life of grace, except insofar as the life of grace is directed to glory. For this reason, those who, possessing grace, fail to obtain glory, are not said to be chosen absolutely, but relatively. Likewise, they are not said to be written in the book of life absolutely, but relatively; that is to say, it is in the ordination and knowledge of God

---

1. 参见 Q. 12, a. 4; q. 23, a. 1.

that they are to have some relation to eternal life, according to their participation in grace.

Third Article
WHETHER ANYONE MAY BE BLOTTED OUT OF THE BOOK OF LIFE?

We proceed thus to the Third Article: —

Objection 1. It seems that no one can be blotted out of the book of life. For Augustine says: *God's foreknowledge, which cannot be deceived, is the book of life.*[1] But nothing can be taken away from the foreknowledge of God, nor from predestination. Therefore neither can anyone be blotted out from the book of life.

Obj. 2. Further, whatever is in a thing, is in it according to the disposition of that thing. But the book of life is something eternal and immutable. Therefore whatsoever is written therein, is there not in a temporary way, but unchangeably and indelibly.

Obj. 3. Further, blotting out is the contrary of inscription. But nobody can be written a second time in the book of life. Neither therefore can he be blotted out.

On the contrary, It is said, *Let them be blotted out from the book of the living* (*Ps.* lxviii. 29).

I answer that, Some have said that none could be blotted out of the book of life as a matter of fact, but only in the opinion of men. For it is customary in the Scriptures to say that something is done when it becomes known. Thus some are said to be written in the book of life, inasmuch as men think they are written therein, because of the present righteousness they see in them; but when it becomes evident, either in this world or in the next, that they have fallen from that state of

---

1. 参见 *De Civit. Dei.*, XX, 15 (PL 41, 681).

righteousness, they are then said to be blotted out. And thus the *Gloss* explains the passage: *Let them be blotted out of the book of the living.*[1]

But not to be blotted out of the book of life is placed among the rewards of the just, according to the text, *He that shall overcome, shall thus be clothed in white garments, and I will not blot his name out of the book of life* (*Apoc.* iii. 5); and what is promised to holy men, is not merely something in the opinion of men. For this reason, it can therefore be said that to be blotted out, and not blotted out, of the book of life is to be referred not merely to the opinion of man, but also to the reality of the fact. For the book of life is the inscription of those ordained to eternal life, to which one is directed from two sources, namely, from predestination, which never fails, and from grace; for whoever has grace, by this very fact is worthy for eternal life This direction of grace sometimes fails, because some are directed, by possessing grace, to obtain eternal life, yet they fail to obtain it through mortal sin. Those, therefore, who are ordained to possess eternal life through divine predestination are written down in the book of life absolutely, because they are written therein to have eternal life in reality. Such are never blotted out from the book of life. Those, however, who are ordained to eternal life, not through the divine predestination, but only through grace, are said to be written in the book of life not absolutely, but relatively; for they are written therein to have eternal life not in itself, but only in its cause. Yet, though such men can be said to be blotted out of the book of life, this blotting out must not be referred to God, as if God foreknew a thing, and afterwards knew it not; but rather to the thing known: in other words, God knows that one is first ordained to eternal life, and afterwards not ordained to it, when he falls from grace.

Reply Obj. 1. The act of blotting out does not refer to the book of life

---

1. 参见 *Glossa ordin.*, super *Ps.* LXVIII, 29 (III, 182F); Peter Lombard, *In Psalm.*, super LXVIII, 29 (PL 191, 639).

as regards God's foreknowledge, as if in God there were any change; but as regards things foreknown, which can change.

Reply Obj. 2. Although things are immutable in God, yet in themselves they are mutable. To this it is that the blotting out of the book of life refers.

Reply Obj. 3. Just as one can be said to be blotted out of the book of life, so one is said to be written therein anew. This is true either according to the opinion of men, or according as he begins anew to be ordered towards eternal life by means of grace. What is more, this fact, too, is comprehended by the divine knowledge, but not anew.

Question XXV
THE POWER OF GOD
(*In Six Articles*)

AFTER considering the divine knowledge and will, and what pertains to them, it remains for us to consider the power of God. About this are six points of inquiry: (1) Whether there is power in God? (2) Whether His power is infinite? (3) Whether He is omnipotent? (4) Whether He could make the past not to have been? (5) Whether He could do what He does not, or not do what He does? (6) Whether what He makes He could make better?

First Article
WHETHER THERE IS POWER IN GOD?

We proceed thus to the First Article: —

Objection 1. It seems that power is not in God. For as primary matter is to power, so God, who is the first agent, is to act. But primary matter, considered in itself, is devoid of all act. Therefore, the first agent — namely, God — is devoid of power.

Obj. 2. Further, according to the Philosopher, better than every power is its act.[1] For form is better than matter, and action than active power, since it is its end. But nothing is better than what is in God; because whatsoever is in God, is God, as was shown above.[2] Therefore, there is no power in God.

---

1. 参见 *Metaph.*, VIII, 9 (1051a 4).
2. 参见 Q. 3, a. 3.

Obj. 3. Further, power is the principle of operation. But the divine power is God's essence, since there is nothing accidental in God. But of the essence of God there is no principle. Therefore there is no power in God.

Obj. 4. Further, it was shown above that God's knowledge and will are the cause of things.[1] But *cause* and *principle* are identical. We ought not, therefore, to assign power to God but only knowledge and will.

On the contrary, It is said: *Thou art mighty, O Lord, and Thy truth is round about Thee* (*Ps*. lxxxviii. 9).

I answer that, Power is twofold — namely, passive, which exists not at all in God; and active, which we must assign to Him in the highest degree. For it is manifest that everything, according as it is in act and is perfect, is the active principle of something; whereas everything is passive according as it is deficient and imperfect. Now it was shown above that God is pure act, absolutely and universally perfect, and completely without any imperfection.[2] Whence it most fittingly belongs to Him to be an active principle, and in no way whatsoever to be passive. On the other hand, the nature of active principle belongs to active power. For active power is the principle of acting upon something else; whereas passive power is the principle of being acted upon by something else, as the Philosopher says.[3] It remains, therefore, that in God there is active power in the highest degree.

Reply Obj. 1. Active power is not contrary to act, but is founded upon it, for everything acts according as it is actual; but passive power is contrary to act, for a thing is passive according as it is potential. Whence this potentiality is excluded from God, but not active power.

---

1. 参见 Q. 14, a. 8; q. 19, a. 4.
2. 参见 Q. 3, a. 1 and 2; q. 4, a. 1 and 2.
3. 参见 *Metaph*., IV, 12 (1019a 19).

Reply Obj. 2. Whenever act is distinct from power, act must be nobler than power. But God's action is not distinct from His power, for both are His divine essence; since neither is His being distinct from His essence. Hence it does not follow that there should be anything in God nobler than His power.

Reply Obj. 3. In creatures, power is the principle not only of action, but likewise of the effect of action. So in God the idea of power is retained in so far as it is the principle of an effect, not, however, so far as it is a principle of action, for this is the divine essence itself; except, perchance, according to our manner of understanding, inasmuch as the divine essence, which precontains in itself all perfection that exists in created things, can be understood either under the notion of action, or under that of power; just as it is also understood under the notion of a *suppositum* possessing nature, and under that of nature. Accordingly the nature of power is retained in God in so far as it is the principle of an effect.

Reply Obj. 4. Power is predicated of God not as something really distinct from His knowledge and will, but as differing from them logically; inasmuch (namely) as power implies the notion of a principle putting into execution what the will commands and what knowledge directs; which three things in God are identified. — Or we may say that the knowledge or will of God, according as it is an effective principle, has the notion of power contained in it. Hence the consideration of the knowledge and will of God precedes the consideration of His power as the cause precedes operation and the effect.

Second Article
WHETHER THE POWER OF GOD IS INFINITE ?

We proceed thus to the Second Article: —

Objection 1. It seems that the power of God is not infinite. For everything that is infinite is imperfect according to the Philosopher.[1] But the power of God is far from imperfect. Therefore it is not infinite.

Obj. 2. Further, every power is made known by its effect; otherwise it would be in vain. If, then, the power of God were infinite, it could produce an infinite effect, but this is impossible.

Obj. 3. Further, the Philosopher proves that if the power of any corporeal thing were infinite, it would cause movement instantaneously.[2] God, however, does not cause instantaneous movement[3], but *moves the spiritual creature in time, and the corporeal creature in place and time*, as Augustine says.[4] Therefore, His power is not infinite.

On the contrary, Hilary says, that *God's power is immeasurable. He is the living mighty One.*[5] Now everything that is immeasurable is infinite. Therefore the power of God is infinite.

I answer that, As was stated above, active power exists in God according to the measure in which He is actual. Now His being is infinite, inasmuch as it is not limited by anything that receives it, as is clear from what was said when we discussed the infinity of the divine essence.[6] Therefore, it is necessary that the active power of God should be infinite. For in every agent we find that the more perfectly an agent has the form by which it acts, the greater its power to act. For instance, the hotter a thing is, the greater power has it to give heat; and it would have infinite power to give heat, were its own heat infinite. Whence, since the divine essence, through which God acts, is infinite, as was shown above,[7] it follows that His power likewise is infinite.

---

1. 参见 *Phys.*, III, 6 (207a 7).
2. 参见 *Op. cit.*, VIII, 10 (266a 31).
3. instantaneous movement：瞬间运动
4. 参见 *De Genesi ad Litt.*, VIII, 20; 22 (PL 34, 388; 389).
5. 参见 *De Trin.*, VIII, 24 (PL 10, 253).
6. 参见 Q. 7, a. 1.
7. 同上

Reply Obj. 1. The Philosopher is here speaking of an infinity belonging to matter not limited by any form; and such infinity belongs to quantity. But the divine essence is not infinite in this way, as was shown above, and consequently neither is God's power. It does not follow, therefore, that it is imperfect.

Reply Obj. 2. The power of a univocal agent is wholly manifested in its effect. The generative power of man, for example, is not able to do more than beget man. But the power of a non-univocal agent does not wholly manifest itself in the production of its effect: as, for example, the power of the sun does not wholly manifest itself in the production of an animal generated from putrefaction[1]. Now it is clear that God is not a univocal agent. For nothing agrees with Him either in species or in genus, as was shown above.[2] Whence it follows that His effect is always less than His power. It is not necessary, therefore, that the infinite power of God should be manifested in the production of an infinite effect. Yet even if it were to produce no effect, the power of God would not be in vain; because a thing is in vain if it is ordained towards an end to which it does not attain. But the power of God is not ordered toward its effect as towards an end; rather, it is the end of the effect produced by it.

Reply Obj. 3. The Philosopher proves that *if a body had infinite power, it would move in null time.*[3] And yet he shows that the power of the mover of heaven is infinite, because he can move in an infinite time.[4] It remains, therefore, according to Aristotle's intention, that the infinite power of a body, if such existed, would move in null time; not, however, the power of an incorporeal mover. The reason for this is that one body moving another is a univocal agent; wherefore it follows that

1. putrefaction：腐败；腐败物
2. 参见 Q. 3, a. 5; q. 4, a. 3.
3. 参见 *Phys.*, VIII, 10 (266a 29).
4. 同上 (267b 24).

the whole power of the agent is made manifest in its motion. Since then the greater the power of a moving body, the more quickly does it move, the necessary conclusion is that, if its power were infinite, it would move with a speed incommensurably faster; and this is to move in null time. An incorporeal mover, however, is not a univocal agent; whence it is not necessary that the whole of its power should be manifested in motion, which would in fact be a motion in null time; especially since an incorporeal mover moves in accordance with the disposition of his will.

Third Article
WHETHER GOD IS OMNIPOTENT?

We proceed thus to the Third Article: —

Objection 1. It seems that God is not omnipotent. For movement and passiveness belong to everything. But this is impossible for God, since He is immovable, as was said above.[1] Therefore He is not omnipotent.

Obj. 2. Further, sin is an act of some kind. But God cannot sin, nor *deny Himself*, as it is said *2 Tim*. ii. 13. Therefore He is not omnipotent.

Obj. 3. Further, it is said of God that He manifests His omnipotence *especially by sparing and having mercy*. Therefore the greatest act possible to the divine power is to spare and have mercy. There are things much greater, however, than sparing and having mercy; for example, to create another world, and the like. Therefore God is not omnipotent.

Obj. 4. Further, upon the text, *God hath made foolish the wisdom of this world* (*1 Cor*. i. 20), the *Gloss* says: *God hath made the wisdom of this world foolish* by showing those things to be possible which it judges to

1. 参见 Q. 2, a. 3; q. 9, a. 1.

be impossible.[1] Whence it seems that nothing is to be judged possible or impossible in reference to inferior causes, as the wisdom of this world judges them; but in reference to the divine power. If God, then, were omnipotent, all things would be possible; nothing, therefore, impossible. But if we take away the impossible, then we destroy also the necessary; for what necessarily exists cannot possibly not exist. Therefore, there would be nothing at all that is necessary in things if God were omnipotent. But this is an impossibility. Therefore God is not omnipotent.

On the contrary, It is said: *No word shall be impossible with God* (*Luke* i. 37).

I answer that, All confess that God is omnipotent; but it seems difficult to explain in what His omnipotence precisely consists. For there may be a doubt as to the precise meaning of the word "all" when we say that God can do all things. If, however, we consider the matter aright, since power is said in reference to possible things, this phrase, *God can do all things*, is rightly understood to mean that God can do all things that are possible; and for this reason He is said to be omnipotent. Now according to the Philosopher a thing is said to be possible in two ways.[2] First, in relation to some power; thus whatever is subject to human power is said to be possible to man. Now God cannot be said to be omnipotent through being able to do all things that are possible to created nature; for the divine power extends farther than that. If, however, we were to say that God is omnipotent because He can do all things that are possible to His power, there would be a vicious circle in explaining the nature of His power. For this would be saying nothing else but that God is omnipotent because He can do all that He is able to do.

---

1. 参见 *Glossa ordin.*, *super I Cor.* I, 20 (VI, 34E). — Cf. St. Ambrose, *In I Cor.*, super I, 20 (PL 17, 199).
2. 参见 *Metaph.*, IV, 12 (1019b 34).

It remains, therefore, that God is called omnipotent because he can do all things that are possible absolutely; which is the second way of saying a thing is possible. For a thing is said to be possible or impossible absolutely, according to the relation in which the very terms stand to one another: possible, if the predicate is not incompatible with the subject, as that Socrates sits; and absolutely impossible when the predicate is altogether incompatible with the subject, as, for instance, that a man is an ass.

It must, however, be remembered that since every agent produces an effect like itself, to each active power there corresponds a thing possible as its proper object according to the nature of that act on which its active power is founded; for instance, the power of giving warmth is related, as to its proper object, to the being capable of being warmed. The divine being, however, upon which the nature of power in God is founded, is infinite; it is not limited to any class of being, but possesses within itself the perfection of all being. Whence, whatsoever has or can have the nature of being is numbered among the absolute possibles, in respect of which God is called omnipotent.

Now nothing is opposed to the notion of being except non-being. Therefore, that which at the same time implies being and non-being is repugnant to the notion of an absolute possible, which is subject to the divine omnipotence. For such cannot come under the divine omnipotence; not indeed because of any defect in the power of God, but because it has not the nature of a feasible or possible thing. Therefore, everything that does not imply a contradiction in terms is numbered among those possibles in respect of which God is called omnipotent; whereas whatever implies contradiction does not come within the scope of divine omnipotence, because it cannot have the aspect of possibility. Hence it is more appropriate to say that such things cannot be done, than that God cannot do them. Nor is this contrary to the word of the angel, saying: *No word shall be impossible with God* (*Luke* i. 37). For whatever implies a contradiction cannot be a word, because no intellect can possibly conceive such a thing.

Reply Obj. 1. God is said to be omnipotent in respect to active power, not to passive power, as was shown above. Whence the fact that He is immovable or impassible[1] is not repugnant to His omnipotence.

Reply Obj. 2. To sin is to fall short of a perfect action; hence to be able to sin is to be able to fall short in action, which is repugnant to omnipotence. Therefore it is that God cannot sin, because of His omnipotence. Now it is true that the Philosopher says that *God can deliberately do what is evil.*[2] But this must be understood either on a condition, the antecedent of which is impossible — as, for instance, if we were to say that God can do evil things if He will. For there is no reason why a conditional proposition should not be true, though both the antecedent and consequent are impossible: as if one were to say: *If man is an ass, he has four feet.* Or he may be understood to mean that God can do some things which now seem to be evil: which, however, if He did them, would then be good. Or he is, perhaps, speaking after the common manner of the pagans, who thought that men became gods, like Jupiter or Mercury.

Reply Obj. 3. God's omnipotence is particularly shown in sharing and having mercy, because in this it is made manifest that God has supreme power, namely, that He freely forgives sins. For it is not for one who is bound by laws of a superior to forgive sins of his own free choice. Or, it is thus shown because by sparing and having mercy upon men, He leads them to the participation of an infinite good; which is the ultimate effect of the divine power. Or it is thus shown because, as was said above, the effect of the divine mercy is the foundation of all the divine works.[3] For nothing is due anyone, except because of something already given him gratuitously by God. In this way

1. impassible：不觉痛苦的；不能伤害的
2. 参见 *Top.*, IV, 5 (126a 34).
3. 参见 Q. 21, a. 4.

the divine omnipotence is particularly made manifest, because to it pertains the first foundation of all good things.

Reply Obj. 4. The absolute possible is not so called in reference either to higher causes, or to inferior causes, but in reference to itself. But that which is called possible in reference to some power is named possible in reference to its proximate cause. Hence those things which it belongs to God alone to do immediately — as, for example, to create, to justify, and the like — are said to be possible in reference to a higher cause. Those things, however, which are such as to be done by inferior causes, are said to be possible in reference to those inferior causes. For it is according to the condition of the proximate cause that the effect has contingency or necessity, as was shown above.[1] Thus it is that the wisdom of the world is deemed foolish, because what is impossible to nature it judges to be impossible to God. So it is clear that the omnipotence of God does not take away from things their impossibility and necessity.

Fourth Article
WHETHER GOD CAN MAKE THE PAST NOT TO HAVE BEEN ?

We proceed thus to the Fourth Article: —

Objection. 1. It seems that God can make the past not to have been. For what is impossible in itself is much more impossible than that which is impossible accidentally. But God can do what is impossible in itself, as to give sight to the blind, or to raise the dead. Therefore, all the more can He do what is impossible accidentally. Now for the past not to have been is impossible accidentally: thus, for Socrates not to be running is accidentally impossible, from the fact that his running is a thing of the past. Therefore God can make the past not to have been.

---

1. 参见 Q. 14, a. 13, ad 1.

Obj. 2. Further, what God could do, He can do now, since His power is not lessened. But God could have effected, before Socrates ran, that he should not run. Therefore, after Socrates has run, God could bring it about that he had not run.

Obj. 3. Further, charity is a more excellent virtue than virginity. But God can restore charity that is lost; therefore also lost virginity. Therefore He can bring it about that a person who has lost her virginity did not lose it.

On the contrary, Jerome says: *Although God can do all things, He cannot bring it about that a woman who was seduced was not seduced.*[1] Therefore, for the same reason, He cannot bring it about that anything else which is past should not have been.

I answer that, As was said above, nothing that implies a contradiction falls under the scope of God's omnipotence.[2] Now that the past should not have been implies a contradiction. For just as it implies a contradiction to say that Socrates is sitting and not sitting, so does it to say that he sat and did not sit. But to say that he did sit is to say that it happened in the past. To say that he did not sit is to say that it did not happen. Whence, that the past should not have been, does not come under the scope of divine power. This is what Augustine means when he says: *Whosoever says, If God is almighty, let Him make what is done as if it were not done, does not see that this is to say: If God is almighty let Him effect that what is true, by the very fact that it is true, be false.*[3] And the Philosopher says: *Of this one thing alone is God deprived — namely, to make undone the things that have been done.*[4]

Reply Obj. 1. Although it is accidentally impossible for the past not to have been, if one considers the past thing itself (as, for instance, the

---

1. 参见 *Epist.* XXII (PL 22, 397).
2. 参见 A. 3; q. 7, a. 2, ad 1.
3. 参见 *Contra Faust.*, XXV, 5 (PL 42, 481).
4. 参见 *Eth.*, VI, 2 (1139b 10).

running of Socrates), nevertheless, if the past thing is considered as past, that it should not have been is impossible, not only in itself, but absolutely, since it implies a contradiction. Thus, it is more impossible than the raising of the dead, in which there is nothing contradictory, because this is reckoned impossible in reference to some power, that is to say, some natural power; for such impossible things do come beneath the scope of divine power.

Reply Obj. 2. As God, in accordance with the perfection of the divine power, can do all things, and yet some things are not subject to His power, because they fall short of being possible; so, also, if we consider the immutability of the divine power, whatever God could do, He can do now. Some things, however, were at one time in the realm of possibility, while they were yet to be done, which now fall short of being possible, since they have been done. So God is said not to be able to do them because they themselves cannot be done.

Reply Obj. 3. God can remove all corruption of the mind and body from a woman who has been seduced; but the fact that she had been seduced cannot be removed from her. In the same way, it is impossible that the fact of having sinned and lost charity can be removed from the sinner.

Fifth Article
WHETHER GOD CAN DO WHAT HE DOES NOT?

We proceed thus to the Fifth Article: —

Objection 1. It seems that God can do only what He does. For God cannot do what He has not foreknown and pre-ordained that He would do. But He neither foreknew nor pre-ordained that He would do anything except what He does. Therefore He can do only what He does.

Obj. 2. Further, God can do only what ought to be done and what is just. But God is not bound to do what He does not; nor is it just that

He should do what He does not. Therefore He can do only what He does.

Obj. 3. Further, God cannot do anything that is not good and befitting creation. But it is not good for creatures nor befitting them to be otherwise than as they are. Therefore God can do only what He does.

On the contrary, It is said: *Thinkest thou that I cannot ask My Father, and He will give Me presently more than twelve legions of angels?* (*Matt.* xxvi. 53). But He neither asked for them, nor did His Father show them to refute the Jews. Therefore God can do what He does not.

I answer that, In this matter certain persons erred in two ways. Some[1] laid it down that God acts from natural necessity in such way that, just as from the action of natural things nothing else can happen beyond what actually takes place — as, for instance, from the seed of man, a man must come, and from that of an olive, an olive; so from the divine operation there could not come forth other things, nor another order of things, than that which now is. But we showed above that God does not act from natural necessity, but that His will is the cause of all things;[2] we showed also that the divine will is not naturally and from any necessity determined to these creatures. Whence in no way is the present scheme of things produced by God with such necessity that other things could not come to be.

Others,[3] however, said that the divine power is restricted to this present scheme of things because of the order of the divine wisdom and justice, without which God does nothing. But since the power of God, which is His essence, is nothing else but His wisdom, it can

---

1. 参见 Cf. Maimonides, *Guide*, II, 20 (p. 189). — Cf. also St. Thomas, *De Pot.*, q. 3, a. 4.
2. 参见 Q. 19, a. 3.
3. 参见 Peter Abelard, *Introd. ad Theol.*, III, 5 (PL 178, 1093). — Cf. St. Thomas, *De Pot.*, I, 5. — Cf. also St. Albert, *In I Sent.*, d. xliv, a. 2 (XXVI, 391).

indeed be fittingly said that there is nothing in the divine power which is not in the order conceived by the divine wisdom; for the divine wisdom comprehends the power of God in its entirety. However, the order established in creation by divine wisdom (in which the notion of His justice consists, as was said above[1]), is not so equal to the divine wisdom that the divine wisdom should be restricted to it. For it is clear that the whole nature of the order which a wise man puts into the things made by him is taken from their end. So, when the end is proportionate to the things made for that end, the wisdom of the maker is restricted to a definite order. But the divine goodness is an end exceeding created things beyond all proportion. Therefore, the divine wisdom is not so restricted to any particular order that no other scheme of things could proceed from it. Hence we must say absolutely that God can do other things than those He has done.

Reply Obj. 1. In ourselves, in whom power and essence are distinct from will and intellect, and in whom intellect is distinct from wisdom, and will from justice, something can reside in our power which cannot reside in a just will or in a wise intellect. But in God, power, essence, will, intellect, wisdom and justice are one and the same. Whence, there can be found nothing in the divine power which cannot also be found in His just will or in His wise intellect. Now, because His will cannot be determined from necessity to this or that order of things, except upon supposition, as was said above;[2] and because the wisdom and justice of God are likewise restricted not to this present order, as was shown above; for this reason, nothing prevents there being something in the divine power which He does not will, and which is not included in the order that He has established in things. Furthermore, because power is considered as *executing*, will as *commanding*, and intellect and wisdom as *directing*,

1. 参见 Q. 21, a. 2 and 4.
2. 参见 Q. 19, a. 3.

what is attributed to His power considered in itself God is said to be able to do in accordance with His *absolute power*. Of such a kind is everything which verifies the nature of being, as was said above. On the other hand, what is attributed to the divine power, according as it carries into execution the command of a just will, God is said to be able to do by His *ordained power*. In this manner, we must say that by His absolute power God can do other things than those He has foreknown and pre-ordained to do. But it could not happen that He should do anything which He has not foreknown and not pre-ordained that He would do. For His doing is subject to His foreknowledge and preordination, though His power, which is His nature, is not. For God does things because He so wills; yet He is able to do so, not because He so wills, but because He is such in His nature.

Reply Obj. 2. God is bound to nobody but Himself. Hence, when it is said that God can do only what He ought, nothing else is meant by this than that God can do nothing but what is for Him fitting and just. But these words *fitting* and *just* may be understood in two ways: one, in direct connection with the verb *is*; and thus they would be restricted to signifying the present order of things. They would therefore refer to His power under this restriction. In that case, what is said in the objection is false, for its meaning is that God can do nothing except what is now fitting and just. If, however, *fitting* and *just* are joined directly with the verb *can* (which has the effect of extending their application), and then secondly with *is*, the result will be a present signified in a confused and general way. The proposition would then be true, and its meaning would be: *God cannot do anything except that which, if He did it, would be suitable and just.*

Reply Obj. 3. Although the present order of things is restricted to what now exists, the divine power and wisdom are not thus restricted. Whence, although no other order would be suitable and good for the things which now exist, yet God can make other things and impose upon them another order.

Sixth Article
WHETHER GOD CAN DO BETTER THAN WHAT HE DOES ?

We proceed thus to the Sixth Article: —

Objection 1. It seems that God cannot do better than He does. For whatever God does, He does in a most powerful and wise way. But a thing is so much the better done as it is more powerfully and wisely done. Therefore God cannot do anything better than He does.

Obj. 2. Further, Augustine argues thus: *If God could, but would not, beget a Son His equal, He would have been envious.*[1] For the same reason, if God could have made better things than He has done, but was not willing so to do, He would have been envious. But envy is far removed from God. Therefore God has made everything perfect. He cannot therefore make anything better than He has done.

Obj. 3. Further, what is very good and the best of all cannot be bettered; because nothing is better than the best. But as Augustine says, *each thing that God has made is good, and, taken all together they are very good; because in them all consists the wondrous beauty of the universe.*[2] Therefore the good in the universe could not be made better by God.

Obj. 4. Further, Christ as man is full of grace and truth, and possesses the Spirit without measure; and so He cannot be better. Again, created happiness is described as the highest good, and thus could not be better. And the Blessed Virgin Mary is raised above all the choirs of angels, and so cannot be better than she is. God cannot therefore make all things better than He has made them.

On the contrary, It is said (*Ephes.* iii. 20): *God is able to do all things more*

---

1. 参见 *Contra Maximin.*, II, 7 (PL 42, 762).
2. 参见 *Enchir.*, X (PL 40, 236).

abundantly than we desire or understand.

I answer that, The goodness of anything is twofold. One belongs to its essence: — thus, for instance, to be rational belongs to the essence of man. As regards this good, God cannot make a thing better than it is itself, although He can make another thing better than it. In the same way, He cannot make the number four greater than it is, because if it were greater it would no longer be four, but another number. For the addition of a substantial difference in definitions is after the manner of the addition of unity in numbers.[1] Another kind of goodness is that which is over and above the essence; thus, the good of a man is to be virtuous or wise. As regards this kind of goodness, God can make better the things He has made. Absolutely speaking, however, God can make something else better than each thing made by Him.

Reply Obj. 1. When it is said that God can make better things than He does, if *better* is taken substantively, this proposition is true. For He can always make something else better than any individual thing: and He can make the same thing in one way better than it is, and in another way not; as was explained above. If, however, *better* is taken as an adverb, referring to the mode of God's activity, then God cannot make anything better than He makes it, because He cannot make it from greater wisdom and goodness. Finally, if it implies the mode of being in the things that God has made, then He can make something better; because He can give to things made by Him a better manner of being as regards accidents, although not as regards the substance.

Reply Obj. 2. It is of the nature of a son that he should be equal to his father, when he comes to maturity. But it is not of the nature of anything created that it should be better than it was made by God. Hence the comparison fails.

---

1. 参见 Aristotle, *Metaph.*, VII, 3 (1044a 1).

Reply Obj. 3. Given the things which actually exist, the universe cannot be better, for the order which God has established in things, and in which the good of the universe consists, most befits things. For if any one thing were bettered, the proportion of order would be destroyed; just as if one string were stretched more than it ought to be, the melody of the harp would be destroyed. Yet God could make other things, or add something to the present creation; and then there would be another and a better universe.

Reply Obj. 4. An infinite dignity, resulting from the infinite good which is God, is in a way possessed by the humanity of Christ because it is united to God; by created beatitude because it is the enjoyment of God; and by the Blessed Virgin[1] because she is the mother of God[2]. From this point of view, nothing better than these can be made; just as there cannot be anything better than God.

---

1. the Blessed Virgin：荣福童贞女，指圣母玛利亚
2. the mother of God：天主之母，指圣母玛利亚

Question XXVI
THE DIVINE BEATITUDE
(*In Four Articles*)

AFTER considering all that pertains to the unity of the divine essence, we must turn to the divine beatitude. Concerning this, there are four points of inquiry: (1) Whether beatitude belongs to God? (2) In relation to what is God called blessed? Whether in relation to His act of intellect? (3) Whether He is essentially the beatitude of each of the blessed? (4) Whether every beatitude is included in the divine beatitude?

First Article
WHETHER BEATITUDE BELONGS TO GOD?

We proceed thus to the First Article: —

Objection 1. It seems that beatitude does not belong to God. For beatitude, according to Boethius, *is a state made perfect by the aggregation of all good things.*[1] But an aggregation of goods has no place in God; nor has composition. Therefore beatitude does not belong to God.

Obj. 2. Further, beatitude or happiness is *the reward of virtue*, according to the Philosopher.[2] But reward does not befit God; as neither does merit. Therefore neither does beatitude.

On the contrary, The Apostle says: *Which in His times He shall show, who is the Blessed and only Mighty, the King of Kings and Lord of Lords* (*1 Tim.* vi.

---

1. 参见 *De Consol.*, III, prose 2 (PL 63, 724).
2. 参见 *Eth.*, I, 9 (1099b 16).

15).

I answer that, Beatitude belongs to God in a supreme way. For nothing else is understood by the term *beatitude* than the perfect good of an intellectual nature which is capable of knowing that it has a plenitude of the good it possesses, and which is properly the subject of good and evil and hence master of its own actions. Both of these attributes belong in a most excellent manner to God — namely, to be perfect, and to possess intelligence. Whence beatitude belongs to God in the highest degree.

Reply Obj. 1. An aggregation of goods is in God, not after the manner of composition, but that of simplicity; for those things which in creatures are manifold pre-exist in God in simplicity and unity, as was said above.[1]

Reply Obj. 2. To be the reward of virtue is accidental to beatitude or happiness, arising from the fact that some one attains to it; even as to be the term of generation belongs accidentally to a being, so far as it passes from potentiality to act. As, then, God has being, though not begotten, so He has beatitude, although not acquired by merit.

Second Article

WHETHER GOD IS CALLED BLESSED ACCORDING TO HIS INTELLECT ?

We proceed thus to the Second Article: —

Objection 1. It seems that God is not called blessed according to His intellect. For beatitude is the highest good. But good is said to be in God according to His essence, because good has reference to being which is according to essence, according to Boethius.[2] Therefore beatitude also is said to be in God according to His essence, and not to

---

1. 参见 Q. 4, a. 2 ; q. 13, a. 4.
2. 参见 *De Hebdom.* (PL 64, 1314).

His intellect.

Obj. 2. Further, beatitude has the nature of an end Now the end is the object of the will, as is also the good. Therefore beatitude is said to be in God with reference to His will, and not with reference to His intellect.

On the contrary, Gregory says: *He is in glory, Who, while He rejoices in Himself, needs not further praise.*[1] To be in glory, however, is the same as to be blessed. Therefore, since we enjoy God through our intellect, because *vision is the whole of the reward*, as Augustine says,[2] it would seem that beatitude is said to be in God according to His intellect.

I answer that, Beatitude, as was stated above, is the perfect good of an intellectual nature. Thus it is that, as everything desires the perfection of its nature, so an intellectual nature desires naturally to be happy. Now that which is most perfect in any intellectual nature is the intellectual operation, by which in some sense it grasps everything. Whence the beatitude of every created intellectual nature consists in understanding. Now, in God, to be and to understand are one and the same thing, differing only in the manner of our understanding them. Beatitude must therefore be attributed to God according to His intellect; as also to the blessed, who are called blessed by reason of their likeness to His blessedness.

Reply Obj. 1. This argument proves that beatitude belongs to God essentially; it does not prove that beatitude pertains to Him under the aspect of His essence, but rather under the aspect of His intellect.

Reply Obj. 2. Since beatitude is a good, it is the object of the will. Now the object is presupposed to the act of a power. Hence, in our manner of understanding, divine beatitude precedes the act of the will at rest in beatitude. This cannot be other than the act of the intellect, and thus beatitude is to be found in an act of the intellect.

---

1. 参见 *Moral.*, XXXIII, 6 (PL 76, 639).
2. 参见 *Enarr. in Psalm.*, super XC, 16 (PL 37, 1170) ; *De Trin.*, I, 9 (PL 42, 833).

Third Article

WHETHER GOD IS THE BEATITUDE OF EACH OF THE BLESSED?

We proceed thus to the Third Article: —

Objection 1. It seems that God is the beatitude of each of the blessed[1]. For God is the highest good, as was said above.[2] But it is quite impossible that there should be many highest goods, as also is clear from what has been said above.[3] Therefore, since it is of the essence of beatitude that it should be the highest good, it seems that beatitude is nothing else but God Himself.

Obj. 2. Further, beatitude is the last end of the rational nature. But to be the last end of the rational nature belongs only to God. Therefore the beatitude of all blessed persons is God alone.

On the contrary, The beatitude of one is greater than that of another, according to *1 Cor.* xv. 41: *Star differeth from star in glory*. But nothing is greater than God. Therefore beatitude is something other than God.

I answer that, The beatitude of an intellectual nature consists in an act of the intellect. In this we may consider two things — namely, the object of the act, which is the thing understood; and the act itself, which is to understand. If, then, beatitude be considered on the side of the object, God is the only beatitude; for everyone is blessed from this sole fact, that he understands God. For as Augustine says: *Blessed is he who knoweth Thee, though he know nought else.*[4] But as regards the act of understanding, beatitude is a created thing in beatified creatures. In God, however, even in this respect beatitude is something uncreated.

---

1. the blessed：有福之人
2. 参见 Q. 6, a. 2 and 4.
3. 参见 Q. 11, a. 3.
4. 参见 *Confess.*, V, 4 (PL 32, 708).

Reply Obj. 1. Beatitude, as regards its object, is the highest good absolutely; but as regards its act, in beatified creatures, it is not the supreme good absolutely, but in the genus of goods which a creature can participate.

Reply Obj. 2. End is twofold, namely, *objective* and *subjective*, as the Philosopher says, namely, the *reality itself* and *its use*.[1] Thus, to a miser the end is money, and its acquisition. Accordingly, the last end of a rational creature is God, considered as the reality itself of the end; but created beatitude is the end, considered as the use, or rather the fruition, of that reality.

Fourth Article
WHETHER EVERY BEATITUDE IS INCLUDED IN THE BEATITUDE OF GOD?

We proceed thus to the Fourth Article: —

Objection 1. It seems that the divine beatitude does not embrace all other beatitudes. For there are some false beatitudes. But nothing false can be in God. Therefore the divine beatitude does not embrace every beatitude.

Obj. 2. Further, a certain beatitude, according to some, consists in corporeal things, *e.g.*, in pleasure, riches, and the like. Now none of these have to do with God, since He is incorporeal. Therefore His beatitude does not embrace every beatitude.

On the contrary, Beatitude is a certain perfection. But the divine perfection embraces every perfection, as was shown above.[2] Therefore the divine beatitude embraces every beatitude.

I answer that, Whatever is desirable in whatsoever beatitude, whether true or false, all pre-exists in a more eminent way in the divine

---

1. 参见 *De An.*, II, 4 (415b 20).
2. 参见 Q. 4, a. 2.

beatitude. As to contemplative happiness, God possesses a continual and most certain contemplation of Himself and of all things else; and as to that which is active, He has the governance of the whole universe. As to earthly happiness, which consists in pleasure, riches, power, dignity, and fame, according to Boethius,[1] He possesses joy in Himself and all things else for His pleasure; instead of riches, He has that complete self-sufficiency, which is promised by riches; in place of power, He has omnipotence; for dignities, the governance of all things; and in place of fame, He possesses the admiration of all creatures.

Reply Obj. 1. A particular kind of beatitude is false according as it falls short of the essence of true beatitude; and thus it is not in God. But whatever semblance it has, howsoever slight, of beatitude, the whole of it pre-exists in the divine beatitude.

Reply Obj. 2. The good that exists in corporeal things in a corporeal manner is also in God, but in a spiritual manner.

We have now spoken enough concerning what pertains to the unity of the divine essence.

---

1. 参见 *De Consol.*, III, prose 2 (PL 63, 724).

TREATISE ON THE TRINITY

Question XXVII
THE PROCESSION OF THE DIVINE PERSONS
(*In Five Articles*)

HAVING considered what belongs to the unity of the divine essence, it remains to treat of what belongs to the Trinity of the persons in God. And because the divine Persons[1] are distinguished from each other according to the relation of orgin, the orider of doctrine leads us to consider, first, the question of origin or procession; secondly, the relations of origin;[2] thirdly, the persons.[3]

Concerning procession there are five points of inquiry:

(1) Whether there is procession in God? (2) Whether any procession in God can be called generation? (3) Whether there can be any other procession in God besides generation? (4) Whether that other procession can be called generation? (5) Whether there are more than two processions in God?

First Article
WHETHER THERE IS PROCESSION IN GOD?

We proceed thus to the First Article: —

Objection 1. It would seem that there cannot be any procession in

---

1. the divine Persons：神圣位格，指三位一体的天主的三个位格，即圣父、圣子、圣神
2. 参见 Q. 28.
3. 参见 Q. 29.

God. For procession signifies outward movement. But in God there is no movable subject, nor anything extraneous. Therefore neither is there procession in God.

Obj. 2. Further, everything which proceeds differs from that whence it proceeds. But in God there is no diversity, but supreme simplicity. Therefore in God there is no procession.

Obj. 3. Further, to proceed from another seems to be against the nature of the first principle. But God is the first principle, as was shown above.[1] Therefore in God there is no procession.

On the contrary, Our Lord says, *From God I proceeded* (*Jo.* viii. 42).

I answer that, Divine Scripture[2] uses, in relation to God, names which signify procession. This procession has been variously understood. Some have understood it in the sense of an effect proceeding from its cause. So Arius took it, saying that the Son proceeds from the Father as His primary creature, and that the Holy Ghost proceeds from the Father and the Son as the creature of both.[3] In this sense, neither the Son nor the Holy Ghost would be true God; and this is contrary to what is said of the Son, *That ... we may be in His true Son. This is the true God* (*1 John* v. 20). Of the Holy Ghost it is also said, *Know you not that your members are the temple of the Holy Ghost?* (*1 Cor.* vi. 19). Now, to have a temple is God's prerogative. Others take this procession to mean the cause proceeding to the effect, as moving it, or impressing its own likeness on it; in which sense it was understood by Sabellius, who said that God the Father is called Son in assuming flesh from the Virgin, and that the Father also is called Holy Ghost in sanctifying the rational creature, and moving it to life.[4] The words of the Lord contradict such a meaning, when He speaks of Himself, *The*

---

1. 参见 Q. 2, a. 3.
2. Divine Scripture：圣经
3. 参见 Cf. St. Augustine, *De Haercs.*, 49 (PL 42, 39).
4. 参见 *Op. cit.*, 41 (PL 42, 32).

Son cannot of Himself do anything (*Jo.* v. 19); while many other passages show the same, whereby we know that the Father is not the Son.

Careful examination shows that both of these opinions take procession as meaning an outward act; hence neither of them affirms procession as existing in God Himself. But procession always supposes action; and as there is an outward procession corresponding to the act tending to external matter, so there must be an inward procession corresponding to the act remaining within the agent. This applies most conspicuously[1] to the intellect, the action of which remains in the intelligent agent. For whenever we understand, by the very fact of understanding there proceeds something within us, which is a conception of the thing understood, a conception issuing from our intellectual power and proceeding from our knowledge of that thing. This conception is signified by the spoken word; and it is called the word of the heart signified by the word of the voice.

As God is above all things, we should understand what is said of God, not according to the mode of the lowest creatures, namely bodies, but from the likeness of the highest creatures, the intellectual substances; although even the likenesses derived from these fall short in the representation of divine objects. Procession, therefore, is not to be understood from what it is in bodies, either according to local movement, or by way of a cause proceeding forth to its exterior effect; as, for instance, like heat proceeding from the agent to the thing made hot. Rather it is to be understood by way of an intelligible emanation, for example, of the intelligible word which proceeds from the speaker, yet remains in him. In that sense the Catholic Faith[2] understands procession as existing in God.

Reply Obj. 1. This objection comes from the idea of procession in the sense of local motion, or of an action tending to external matter, or to

1. conspicuously：显眼的；明显的
2. the Catholic Faith：天主教的信仰

an exterior effect; which kind of procession does not exist in God, as we have explained.

Reply Obj. 2. Whatever proceeds by way of outward procession is necessarily distinct from the source whence it proceeds, whereas whatever proceeds within by an intelligible procession is not necessarily distinct; indeed, the more perfectly it proceeds, the more closely it is one with the source whence it proceeds. For it is clear that the more a thing is understood, the more closely is the intellectual conception joined and united to the intelligent agent; since the intellect by the very act of understanding is made one with the object understood. Hence, as the divine understanding is the very supreme perfection of God,[1] the divine Word is of necessity perfectly one with the source whence He proceeds, without any diversity.

Reply Obj. 3. To proceed from a principle, so as to be something outside and distinct from that principle, is irreconcilable[2] with the idea of a first principle; whereas an intimate and non-diverse procession by way of an intelligible act is included in the idea of a first principle. For when we call the builder the principle of the house, in the idea of such a principle is included that of his art; and it would be included in the idea of the first principle, were the builder the first principle of the house. God, Who is the first principle of all things, may be compared to created things as the artisan is to the works of his art.

Second Article
WHETHER ANY PROCESSION IN GOD CAN BE CALLED GENERATION?

We proceed thus to the Second Article: —

Objection 1. It would seem that no procession in God can be called

---

1. 参见 Q. 14, a. 1.
2. irreconcilable：不可调和的；不相容的

generation. For generation is change from non-being to being, and is opposed to corruption; while matter is the subject of both. Nothing of all this belongs to God. Therefore generation cannot exist in God.

Obj. 2. Further, procession exists in God, according to an intelligible mode, as above explained. But such a process is not called generation in us; therefore neither is it to be so called in God.

Obj. 3. Further, anything that is generated derives being from its generator. Therefore such being is derived being. But no derived being can be self-subsistent. Therefore, since the divine being is self-subsisting,[1] it follows that no generated being can be the divine being. Therefore there is no generation in God.

On the contrary, It is said (*Ps.* ii. 7): *This day have I begotten Thee.*

I answer that, The procession of the Word in God is called generation. In proof whereof we must observe that generation has a twofold meaning: one common to everything subject to generation and corruption; in which sense generation is nothing but change from non-being to being. In another sense, it is proper and belongs to living things; in which sense it signifies the origin of a living being from a conjoined living principle. And this is properly called birth. Not everything of that kind, however, is called begotten, but, strictly speaking, only what proceeds by way of likeness. Hence a hair has not the aspect of generation and of sonship, but only that has which proceeds by way of likeness. Nor will any likeness suffice; for a worm which is generated from animals has not the aspect of generation and sonship, although it has a generic likeness; for this kind of generation requires that there should be a procession by way of likeness in the same specific nature, as a man proceeds from a man, and a horse from a horse. So in living things, which proceed from potential to actual life, such as men and animals, generation includes both these

1. 参见 Q. 3, a. 4.

kinds of generation. But if there is a being whose life does not proceed from potentiality to act, procession (if found in such a being) excludes entirely the first kind of generation; whereas it may have that kind of generation which belongs to living things. So in this manner the procession of the Word in God is generation; for He proceeds by way of intelligible action, which is a vital operation: — from a conjoined principle (as above described): — by way of likeness, because the conception of the intellect is a likeness of the object conceived: — and exists in the same nature, because in God the act of understanding and His being are the same, as was shown above.[1] Hence the procession of the Word in God is called generation; and the Word Himself proceeding is called the Son.

Reply Obj. 1. This objection is based on the idea of generation in the first sense, implying the issuing forth from potentiality to act; in which sense it is not found in God.

Reply Obj. 2. The act of understanding in ourselves is not the substance itself of the intellect. Hence the word which proceeds within us by intelligible operation is not of the same nature as the source whence it proceeds; so the idea of generation cannot be properly and fully applied to it. But the divine act of understanding is the very substance itself of the one who understands.[2] The Word proceeding, therefore, proceeds as subsisting in the same nature, and so is properly called begotten, and Son. Hence Scripture employs terms which denote generation of living things in order to signify the procession of the divine wisdom, namely, conception and birth; as is declared in the person of the divine wisdom, *The depths were not as yet, and I was already conceived; before the hills, I was brought forth* (*Prov.* viii. 24). In our way of understanding we use the word *conception* in order to signify that in the word of our intellect is found the likeness of the thing understood,

1. 参见 Q. 14, a. 4.
2. 同上

although there be no identity of nature.

Reply Obj. 3. Not everything derived from another has existence in another subject; otherwise we could not say that the whole substance of created being comes from God, since there is no subject that could receive the whole substance. So, then, what is generated in God receives being from the generator, not as though that being were received into matter or into a subject (which would conflict with the divine self-subsistence); but when we speak of His being as received, we mean that He Who proceeds receives divine being from another, not, however, as if He were other from the divine nature. For in the perfection itself of the divine being are contained both the Word intelligibly proceeding and the principle of the Word, with whatever belongs to His perfection.[1]

Third Article
WHETHER ANY OTHER PROCESSION EXISTS IN GOD BESIDES THAT OF THE WORD?

We proceed thus to the Third Article: —

Objection 1. It would seem that no other procession exists in God besides the generation of the Word. Because, for whatever reason we admit another procession, we should be led to admit yet another, and so on to infinitude; which cannot be. Therefore we must stop at the first, and hold that there exists only one procession in God.

Obj. 2. Further, every nature possesses but one mode of self-communication[2]; because operations derive unity and diversity from their termini. But procession in God is only by way of communication of the divine nature. Therefore, as there is only one divine nature,[3] it

1. 参见 Q. 4, a. 2.
2. self-communication：自我沟通
3. 参见 Q. 11, a. 3 and 4.

follows that only one procession exists in God.

Obj. 3. Further, if any other procession but the intelligible procession of the Word existed in God, it could only be the procession of love, which is by the operation of the will. But such a procession is identified with the intelligible procession of the intellect, inasmuch as in God the will is the same as His intellect.[1] Therefore in God there is no other procession but the procession of the Word.

On the contrary, The Holy Ghost proceeds from the Father (*Jo.* xv. 26); and He is distinct from the Son, according to the words, *I will ask My Father, and He will give you another Paraclete* (*Jo.* xiv. 16). Therefore in God another procession exists besides the procession of the Word.

I answer that, There are two processions in God, the procession of the Word, and another.

In evidence whereof we must observe that procession exists in God only according to an action which does not tend to anything external, but remains in the agent itself. Such action in an intellectual nature is that of the intellect and of the will. The procession of the Word is by way of an intelligible operation. The operation of the will within ourselves involves also another procession, that of love, whereby the object loved is in the one who loves; just as, by the conception of the word, the object expressed or understood is in the intelligent agent. Hence, besides the procession of the Word in God, there exists in Him another procession called the procession of love.

Reply Obj. 1. There is no need to go on to infinity in the divine processions; for the procession which is accomplished within the agent in an intellectual nature terminates in the procession of the will.

Reply Obj. 2. All that exists in God, is God;[2] whereas the same does not apply to others. Therefore the divine nature is communicated by every procession which is not outward; and this does not apply to other

1. 参见 Q. 19, a. 1.
2. 参见 Q. 3, a. 3 and 4.

natures.

Reply Obj. 3. Though will and intellect are not diverse in God, nevertheless the nature of will and intellect requires that the processions belonging to each of them exist in a certain order. For the procession of love occurs in due order as regards the procession of the Word, since nothing can be loved by the will unless it is conceived in the intellect. So, as there exists a certain order of the Word to the principle whence He proceeds (although in God the substance of the intellect and its conception are the same) , so, although in God the will and the intellect are the same, still, inasmuch as love requires by its very nature that it proceed only from the conception of the intellect, there is a distinction of order between the procession of love and the procession of the Word in God.

Fourth Article
WHETHER THE PROCESSION OF LOVE IN GOD IS GENERATION?

We proceed thus to the Fourth Article: —

Objection 1. It would seem that the procession of love in God is generation. For what proceeds by way of likeness of nature among living things is said to be generated and born. But what proceeds in God by way of love proceeds in the likeness of nature; otherwise it would be extraneous to the divine nature, and would thus be an external procession. Therefore what proceeds in God by way of love proceeds as generated and born.

Obj. 2. Further, as likeness is of the nature of the word, so it is of the nature of love. Hence it is said that *every beast loves its like* (*Ecclus.* xiii. 19). Therefore, if the Word is begotten and born by way of likeness, it seems becoming that love should proceed by way of generation.

Obj. 3. Further, what is not in any species is not in the genus. So if there is a procession of love in God, there ought to be some special name besides this common name of procession. But no other name is applicable but generation. Therefore the procession of love in God is generation.

On the contrary, Were this true, it would follow that the Holy Ghost, Who proceeds as love, would proceed as begotten; which is against the statement of Athanasius: *The Holy Ghost is from the Father and the Son, not made, nor begotten, but proceeding.*[1]

I answer that, The procession of love in God ought not to be called generation. In evidence whereof we must consider that the intellect and the will differ in this, that the intellect is made actual by the thing understood residing in the intellect according to its own likeness; whereas the will is made actual, not by any likeness of the thing willed within it, but by its having a certain inclination to the thing willed. Thus the procession of the intellect is by way of likeness, and is called generation, because every generator begets its own like; whereas the procession of the will is not by way of likeness, but is rather by way of impulse and movement towards some thing.

So what proceeds in God by way of love does not proceed as begotten, or as son, but proceeds rather as spirit; which name expresses a certain vital movement and impulse, according as anyone is described as moved or impelled by love to perform an action.

Reply Obj. 1. All that exists in God is one with the divine nature. Hence the proper notion of this or that procession, by which one procession is distinguished from another, cannot be on the part of this unity; but the proper notion of this or that procession must be taken from the order of one procession to another, which order is derived from the nature of will and intellect. Hence, each procession in God takes its name from the proper notion of will and intellect; the name being imposed to signify what its nature really is; and so it is that the Person proceeding as love receives the divine nature, but is not said to

1. 参见 Cf. Pseudo-Athanasius, *Symb.* "*Quicumque*" (Denzinger, no. 39).

be born.

Reply Obj. 2. Likeness belongs in a different way to the word and to love. It belongs to the word as being the likeness of the thing understood, as the thing generated is the likeness of the generator; but it belongs to love, not as though love itself were a likeness, but because likeness is the principle of loving. Thus it does not follow that love is begotten, but that the one begotten is the principle of love.

Reply Obj. 3. We can name God only from creatures.[1] But because in creatures generation is the only principle of the communication of nature, procession in God has no proper or special name, except that of generation. Hence the procession which is not generation has remained without a special name; but it can be called spiration, since it is the procession of the Spirit.

Fifth Article

WHETHER THERE ARE MORE THAN TWO PROCESSIONS IN GOD?

We proceed thus to the Fifth Article: —

Objection 1. It would seem that there are more than two processions in God. As knowledge and will are attributed to God, so is power. Therefore, if two processions exist in God, namely, according to intellect and will, it seems that there must also be a third procession according to power.

Obj. 2. Further, goodness seems to be the greatest principle of procession, since goodness is diffusive of itself.[2] Therefore there must be a procession of goodness in God.

Obj. 3. Further, in God there is greater power of fecundity than in us. But in us there is not only one procession of the word, but

---

1. 参见 Q. 13, a. 1.
2. 参见 Cf. Pseudo-Dionysius, *De Div. Nom.*, IV, 20 (PG 3, 720).

many; for in us from one word proceeds another; and also from one love proceeds another. Therefore in God there are more than two processions.

On the contrary, In God there are not more than two who proceed — the Son and the Holy Ghost. Therefore there are in Him but two processions.

I answer that, The divine processions can be derived only from the actions which remain within the agent. In a nature which is intellectual and divine these acts are only two, the acts of understanding and willing. For the act of sensation, which also appears to be an operation within the agent, takes place outside the intellectual nature, and it cannot be reckoned as wholly removed from the sphere of external actions; for the act of sensation is perfected by the action of the sensible thing upon sense. It follows that no other procession is possible in God but the procession of the Word, and of Love.

Reply Obj. 1. Power is the principle whereby one thing acts on another. Hence it is that external action points to power. In this sense the divine power does not imply the procession of a divine person, but is indicated by the procession therefrom of creatures.

Reply Obj. 2. As Boethius says, goodness belongs to the essence and not to operation, unless perhaps considered as the object of the will.[1]

Thus, since the divine processions must be denominated from certain actions, no other processions can be understood in God according to goodness and the like attributes except those of the Word and of Love, according as God understands and loves His own essence, truth and goodness.

Reply Obj. 3. As was above explained, God understands all things by one simple act; and by one act also He wills all things.[2] Hence there

1. 参见 *De Hebdom.* (PL 64, 1314).
2. 参见 Q. 14, a. 7; q. 19, a. 5.

cannot exist in Him a procession of Word from Word, nor of Love from Love: for there is in Him only one perfect Word, and one perfect Love. Thereby is manifested His perfect fecundity.

Question XXVIII
THE DIVINE RELATIONS
(*In Four Articles*)

THE divine relations are next to be considered, in four points of inquiry: (1) Whether there are real relations in God? (2) Whether these relations are the divine essence itself, or are extrinsic to it? (3) Whether in God there can be several relations really distinct from each other? (4) The number of these relations.

First Article
WHETHER THERE ARE REAL RELATIONS IN GOD?

We proceed thus to the First Article: —

Objection 1. It would seem that there are no real relations in God. For Boethius says, *All possible predicaments used as regards the Godhead refer to the substance; for nothing can be predicated relatively.*[1] But whatever really exists in God can be predicated of Him. Therefore no real relation exists in God.

Obj. 2. Further, Boethius says that, *Relation in the Trinity of the Father to the Son, and of both to the Holy Ghost, is the relation of the same to the same.*[2] But a relation of this kind is only a logical one, for every real relation requires and implies two terms in reality. Therefore, the divine relations are not real relations, but are formed only by the mind.

Obj. 3. Further, the relation of paternity is the relation of a principle.

---

1. 参见 *De Trin.*, IV (PL 64, 1253).
2. 参见 *Op. cit.*, VI (PL 64, 1255).

But to say that God is the principle of creatures does not signify any real relation, but only a logical one. Therefore paternity in God is not a real relation, and the same applies for the same reason to the other relations in God.

Obj. 4. Further, the divine generation proceeds by way of an intelligible word. But the relations following upon the operation of the intellect are logical relations. Therefore paternity and filiation in God[1], consequent upon generation, are only logical relations.

On the contrary, The Father is denominated only from paternity; and the Son only from filiation. Therefore, if no real paternity or filiation existed in God, it would follow that God is not really Father or Son, but only in our manner of understanding; and this is the Sabellian heresy.

I answer that, Relations exist in God really. In proof of this we may consider that in relations alone is there found something which is only in the apprehension and not in reality. This is not found in any other genus, since other genera as quantity and quality, in their strict and proper meaning, signify something inherent in a subject. But relation in its own proper meaning signifies only what refers to another. Such relation to another exists sometimes in the nature of things, as in those things which by their own very nature are ordered to each other and have a mutual inclination. Such relations are necessarily real relations, as in a heavy body is found an inclination and order to the center of the universe; and hence there exists in the heavy body a certain relation in regard to the center, and the same applies to other things. Sometimes, however, this reference to another, signified by relation, is to be found only in the apprehension of the reason comparing one thing to another, and this is a logical relation only; as, for instance, when reason compares man to animal as the species to the genus. But

1. filiation in God：天主内的父子关系

when something proceeds from a principle of the same nature, then both the one proceeding and the source of procession communicate in the same order; and then they have real relations to each other. Therefore, as the divine processions are in the identity of the same nature, as was above explained,[1] these relations, which are according to the divine processions, are necessarily real relations.

Reply Obj. 1. Relationship is not predicated of God according to its proper and formal meaning, that is to say, in so far as its proper meaning denotes reference to that in which relation is inherent, but only as denoting reference to another. Nevertheless, Boëthius did not wish to exclude relation in God; but he wished to show that it was not to be predicated of Him as regards the mode of inherence in Himself in the strict meaning of relation, but rather by way of relation to another.

Reply Obj. 2. The relation signified by the term *the same* is a logical relation only if it is taken in regard to absolutely the same thing; because such a relation can exist only in a certain order observed by reason as regards the order of anything to itself, according to some two aspects thereof. The case is otherwise, however, when things are called the same, not numerically, but generically or specifically. Thus Boethius likens the divine relations to a relation of identity, not in every respect, but only as regards the fact that the substance is not diversified by these relations, as neither is it by a relation of identity.

Reply Obj. 3. As the creature proceeds from God in diversity of nature, God is outside the order of the whole creation, nor does any relation to the creature arise from His nature; for He does not produce the creature by necessity of His nature, but by His intellect and will, as was above explained.[2] Therefore, there is no real relation, in God to the creature, whereas in creatures there is a real relation to God;

---

1. 参见 Q. 27, a. 3, ad 2.
2. 参见 Q. 14, a. 8; q. 19, a. 4.

because creatures are contained under the divine order, and their very nature entails dependence on God. On the other hand, the divine processions are in one and the same nature. Hence no parallel exists.

Reply Obj. 4. Relations which result in the things understood from the operation of the intellect alone are logical relations only, inasmuch as reason observes them as existing between two understood things. Those relations, however, which follow the operation of the intellect, and which exist between the word intellectually proceeding and the source whence it proceeds, are not logical relations only, but real relations, inasmuch as the intellect itself or reason is a real thing and really related to that which proceeds from it intelligibly; as a corporeal thing is related to that which proceeds from it corporeally. Thus paternity and filiation are real relations in God.

Second Article
WHETHER RELATION IN GOD IS THE SAME AS HIS ESSENCE?

We proceed thus to the Second Article: —

Objection 1. It would seem that relation in God is not the same as the divine essence. For Augustine says that *not all that is said of God is said of His substance, for we say some things relatively, as Father in respect of the Son: but such things do not refer to the substance.*[1] Therefore relation is not the divine essence.

Obj. 2. Further, Augustine says that *every relative expression is something besides the relation expressed, as master is a man, and slave is a man.*[2] Therefore, if relations exist in God, there must be something else besides relation in God. This can only be His essence. Therefore essence differs from relation.

Obj. 3. Further, the being of relation is the being referred to another,

1. 参见 *De Trin.*, V, 5 (PL 42, 914).
2. 参见 *Op. cit.*, VII, 1 (PL 42, 935).

as the Philosopher says.[1] So if relation is the divine essence, it follows that the being of the divine essence is itself a relation to something else; whereas this is repugnant to the perfection of the divine being, which is supremely absolute and self-subsisting.[2] Therefore relation is not the divine essence.

On the contrary, Everything which is not the divine essence is a creature. But relation really belongs to God. If therefore it is not the divine essence, it is a creature, and it cannot claim the adoration of latria, contrary to what is sung in the Preface: *Let us adore the distinction of the Persons, and the equality of their Majesty.*

I answer that, It is reported that Gilbert de la Porrée erred on this point,[3] but revoked his error later at the council of Rheims.[4] For he said that the divine relations are assistant, or externally affixed.

To perceive the error here expressed, we must consider that in each of the nine genera of accidents there are two points for remark. One is the nature belonging to each one of them considered as an accident, and this is, in the case of all of them, that their being is to inhere in a subject; for the being of an accident is to inhere. The other point of remark is the proper nature of each one of these genera. In the genera, apart from that of *relation*, as in quantity and quality, even the true notion of the genus itself is derived from a relation to a subject; for quantity is called the measure of substance, and quality is the disposition of substance. But the true notion of relation is not taken from its respect to that in which it is, but from its respect to something outside. So, even in creatures, relations are found as such to be *assistant*, and not intrinsically affixed; for they signify, as it were, a respect which affects the thing related, inasmuch as it tends from

---

1. 参见 Aristotle, *Cat.*, VII (8a 39).
2. 参见 Q. 3, a. 4.
3. 参见 *In De Trin.* (PL 64, 1292); *In De Praedicat. trium Pers.* (PL 64, 1309).
4. 参见 Cf. St. Bernard, *In Cant., serm.* LXXX (PL 183, 1170).

that thing to something else; whereas, if relation is considered as an accident, it inheres in a subject, and has an accidental being in it. Gilbert de la Porrée considered relation in the former mode only.

Now whatever has an accidental being in creatures, when considered as transferred to God, has a substantial being; for there is no accident in God since everything in Him is His essence. So, in so far as relation has an accidental being in creatures, relation really existing in God has the being of the divine essence in no way distinct therefrom. But in so far as relation implies respect to something else, no respect to the essence is signified, but rather to its opposite term.

Thus it is manifest that relation really existing in God is really the same as His essence, and differs only in its mode of intelligibility; as in relation is meant that regard to its opposite which is not expressed in the name of essence. Thus it is clear that in God relation and essence do not differ in being from each other, but are one and the same.

Reply Obj. 1. These words of Augustine do not imply that paternity or any other relation in God is not in its very being the same as the divine essence; they imply that, as existing in Him to Whom it is applied, it is not predicated under the mode of substance but as a relation. So there are said to be two predicaments only in God, since other predicaments signify relation to that of which they are spoken, both in their generic and in their specific nature; but nothing that exists in God can have any relation to that wherein it exists, or of whom it is spoken, except the relation of identity, and this by reason of God's supreme simplicity.

Reply Obj. 2. As the relation which exists in creatures involves not only a regard to another, but also something absolute, so the same applies to God; yet not in the same way. What is contained in the creature, above and beyond what is contained in the meaning of relation, is something else besides that relation; whereas in God there is no distinction, but both are one and the same reality; and this is not perfectly expressed by the word *relation*, as if it were comprehended in the ordinary meaning of that term. For it was above explained, in treating of the divine names, that more is contained in the perfection of the divine essence than can be signified by any name.[1] Hence it does not follow that in God there exists anything besides relation really other than it; but only in the various names imposed by us.

Reply Obj. 3. If the divine perfection contained only what is signified by relative names, it would follow that it is imperfect, being thus related to something else; as in the same way, if nothing more were contained in it than what is signified by the word *wisdom*, it would not in that case be anything subsistent. But as the perfection of the divine essence is greater than can be included in any name, it does not follow, if a relative term or any other name applied to God signifies something imperfect, that the divine essence is in any way imperfect; for the divine essence comprehends within itself the perfection of every genus.[2]

Third Article
WHETHER THE RELATIONS IN GOD ARE REALLY DISTINGUISHED FROM EACH OTHER?

We proceed thus to the Third Article: —

Objection 1. It would seem that the divine relations are not really distinguished from each other. For things which are identified with the same thing are identified with each other. But every relation in God is really the same as the divine essence. Therefore the relations are not really distinguished from each other.

Obj. 2. Further, as paternity and filiation are by name distinguished from the divine essence, so likewise are goodness and power. But this kind of distinction does not make any real distinction of the

1. 参见 Q. 13, a. 2.
2. 参见 Q. 4, a. 2.

divine goodness and power. Therefore neither does it make any real distinction of paternity and filiation.

Obj. 3. Further, in God there is no real distinction but that of origin. But one relation does not seem to arise from another. Therefore the relations are not really distinguished from each other.

On the contrary, Boethius says that in God *the substance contains the unity; and relation multiplies the trinity.*[1] Therefore, if the relations were not really distinguished from each other, there would be no real trinity in God, but only a logical trinity, which is the error of Sabellius.[2]

I answer that, The attribution of anything to another involves the attribution likewise of whatever is contained in it. So when *man* is attributed to anyone, a rational nature is likewise attributed to him. The idea of relation, however, necessarily means the reference of one to another, according as one is relatively opposed to another. So as in God there is a real relation, there must also be a real opposition. The very nature of relative opposition includes distinction. Hence, there must be real distinction in God, not, indeed, according to that which is absolute — namely, essence, wherein there is supreme unity and simplicity — but according to that which is relative.

Reply Obj. 1. According to the Philosopher, this argument (namely, that whatever things are identified with the same thing are identified with each other) holds if the identity be real and logical (as, for instance, a tunic and a garment), but not if they differ logically.[3] Hence in the same place he says that although action is the same as motion, and likewise passion, still it does not follow that action and passion are the same; because action implies reference as of something *from which* there is motion in the thing moved, whereas passion implies reference as of something *which is from* another. Likewise, although paternity

1. 参见 *De Trin.*, VI (PL 64, 1255).
2. 参见 Cf. St. Augustine, *De Haeres.*, 41 (PL 42, 32).
3. 参见 *Phys.*, III, 3 (202b 13).

like filiation, is really the same as the divine essence, nevertheless, these two in their own proper notions and definitions import opposite relations. Hence they are distinguished from each other.

Reply Obj. 2. Power and goodness do not signify any opposition in their respective natures; and hence there is no parallel argument.

Reply Obj. 3. Although relations, properly speaking, do not arise or proceed from each other, nevertheless, they are considered as opposed according to the procession of one from another.

Fourth Article

WHETHER IN GOD THERE ARE ONLY FOUR REAL RELATIONS — PATERNITY, FILIATION, SPIRATION AND PROCESSION?

We proceed thus to the Fourth Article: —

Objection 1. It would seem that in God there are not only four real relations — paternity, filiation, spiration and procession. For it must be observed that in God there exist the relations of the intelligent agent to the object understood, and of the one willing to the object willed; which are real relations not comprised under those above enumerated. Therefore there are not only four real relations in God.

Obj. 2. Further, real relations in God are understood as coming from the intelligible procession of the Word. But intelligible relations are infinitely multiplied, as Avicenna says.[1] Therefore in God there exists an infinite series of real relations.

Obj. 3. Further, ideas in God are eternal,[2] and are distinguished from each other only by reason of their relation to things, as was above stated. Therefore in God there are many more eternal relations.

Obj. 4. Further, equality, and likeness, and identity are relations: and

1. 参见 *Metaph.*, III, 10 (83va).
2. 参见 Q. 15, a. 2.

they are in God from eternity. Therefore several more relations are eternal in God than the above named.

Obj. 5. Further, it may on the contrary be said that there are fewer relations in God than those named above. For, according to the Philosopher, *The way from Athens to Thebes is the same as from Thebes to Athens.*[1] By the same way of reasoning there is the same relation from the Father to the Son (that of paternity) and from the Son to the Father (that of filiation); and thus there are not four relations in God.

I answer that, According to the Philosopher, every relation is based either on quantity, as double and half, or on action and passion, as the doer and the deed, the father and the son, the master and the servant, and the like.[2] Now as there is no quantity in God, for He is great without quantity, as Augustine says,[3] it follows that a real relation in God can be based only on action. Such relations are not based on the actions of God according to any extrinsic procession, since the relations of God to creatures are not real in Him.[4] Hence, it follows that real relations in God can be understood only in regard to those actions according to which there are internal, and not external, processions in God. These processions are only two, as was above explained,[5] one derived from the action of the intellect, the procession of the Word, and the other from the action of the will, the procession of Love. In respect of each of these processions two opposite relations arise, one of which is the relation of the person proceeding from the principle, the other is the relation of the principle Himself. The procession of the Word is called generation in the proper sense of the term, whereby it is applied to living things. Now the relation of the

---

1. 参见 *Phys.*, III, 3 (202b 13).
2. 参见 *Metaph.*, IV, 15 (1020b 26).
3. 参见 *Contra Epist. Manich.*, XV (PL 42, 184).
4. 参见 Q. 13, a. 7.
5. 参见 Q. 27, a. 5.

principle of generation in perfect living beings is called *paternity*; and the relation of the one proceeding from the principle is called *filiation*. But the procession of Love has no proper name of its own,[1] and so neither have the ensuing relations a proper name of their own. The relation of the principle of this procession is called *spiration*, and the relation of the person proceeding is called *procession*; although these two names belong to the processions or origins themselves, and not to the relations.

Reply Obj. 1. In those things in which there is a difference between the intellect and its object, and the will and its object, there can be a real relation both of science to its object, and of the one willing to the object willed. In God, however, the intellect and its object are one and the same, because by understanding Himself, God understands all other things; and the same applies to His will and the object that He wills. Hence it follows that in God these relations are not real; as neither is the relation of a thing to itself. Nevertheless, the relation to the Word is a real relation, because the Word is understood as proceeding by an intelligible action, and not as a thing understood. For when we understand a stone, that which the intellect conceives of the thing understood is called the word.

Reply Obj. 2. Intelligible relations in ourselves are infinitely multiplied, because a man understands a stone by one act, and by another act understands that he understands the stone, and again by another, understands that he understands this; thus the acts of understanding are infinitely multiplied, and consequently also the relations understood. This does not apply to God, inasmuch as He understands all things by one act alone.

Reply Obj. 3. Ideal relations exist in God as understood by Him. Hence it does not follow from their plurality that there are many

---

1. 参见 Q. 27, a. 4.

relations in God, but that God knows these many relations.

Reply Obj. 4. Equality and likeness in God are not real relations, but only logical relations, as will later be shown.[1]

Reply Obj. 5. The way from one term to another and conversely is the same; nevertheless, the mutual relations are not the same. Hence, we cannot conclude that the relation of the father to the son is the same as that of the son to the father; but we could conclude this of something absolute, if there were such between them.

1. 参见 Q. 42, a. 1, ad 1.

Question XXIX
THE DIVINE PERSONS
(*In Four Articles*)

HAVING premised what have appeared necessary notions concerning the processions and the relations, we must now approach the subject of the Persons.

First, we shall consider the persons absolutely, and then comparatively as regards each other.[1] We must consider the Persons absolutely first in general, and then singly.[2]

The general consideration of the Persons appears to involve four points: (1) The signification of this name *person*; (2) the number of the Persons;[3] (3) what is involved in the number of the Persons, or is opposed thereto; as diversity, and similitude, and the like;[4] (4) what belongs to our knowledge of the Persons.[5]

Four subjects of inquiry are comprised in the first point: (1) The definition of *person*. (2) The comparison of person to essence, subsistence, and hypostasis[6]. (3) Whether the name *person* is becoming to God? (4) What does it signify in Him?

First Article

---

1. 参见 Q. 39.
2. 参见 Q. 33.
3. 参见 Q. 30.
4. 参见 Q. 31.
5. 参见 Q. 32.
6. hypostasis：根本原理；本质；第一自立体

THE DEFINITION OF *PERSON.*

We proceed thus to the First Article: —

Objection 1. It would seem that the definition of person given by Boethius is insufficient — that is, *a person is an individual substance of a rational nature.*[1] For nothing singular can be subject to definition. But *person* signifies something singular. Therefore person is improperly defined.

Obj. 2. Further, substance, as placed above in the definition of person, is either first substance or second substance. If it is the former, the word *individual* is superfluous, because first substance is individual substance; if it stands for second substance, the added word *individual* is false, for there is a contradiction in terms, since second substances are called *genera* or *species.* Therefore this definition is incorrect.

Obj. 3. Further, a term of intention must not be included in the definition of a thing. For to define a man as *a species of animal* would not be a correct definition, since *man* is the name of a thing, and *species* is a name of an intention. Therefore, since person is the name of a thing (for it signifies a substance of a rational nature), the word *individual* which is an intentional name comes improperly into the definition.

Obj. 4. Further, *Nature is the principle of motion and rest, in those things in which it is essentially, and not accidentally*, as Aristotle says.[2] But *person* is found in immovable things, as in God, and in the angels. Therefore the word *nature* ought not to enter into the definition of person, but the word should rather be *essence.*

Obj. 5. Further, the separated soul is an individual substance of a rational nature; but it is not a person. Therefore person is not properly defined as above.

I answer that, Although universal and particular exist in every genus, nevertheless, in a certain special way the individual belongs to

---

1. 参见 *De Duab. Nat.*, III (PL 64, 1343).
2. 参见 *Phys.*, II, 1 (192b 21).

the genus of substance. For substance is individuated through itself, whereas the accidents are individuated by the subject, which is the substance. For this particular whiteness is called *this* because it exists in this particular subject. And so it is reasonable that the individuals of the genus substance should have a special name of their own; for they are called *hypostases*,[1] or first substances.

Further still, in a more special and perfect way, the particular and the individual are found in rational substances, which have dominion over their own actions, and which are not only made to act, as are others, but act of themselves; for actions belong to singulars. Therefore, individuals of a rational nature even have a special name among other substances; and this name is *person*.

Thus the term *individual substance* is placed in the definition of person, as signifying the singular in the genus of substance; and the term *rational nature* is added, as signifying the singular in the class of rational substances.

Reply Obj. 1. Although this or that singular may not be definable, yet what belongs to the general idea of singularity can be defined; and so the Philosopher gives a definition of first substance.[2] This is also the way in which Boethius defines person.

Reply Obj. 2. In the opinion of some, the term *substance* in the definition of person stands for first substance, which is the hypostasis;[3] nor is the term *individual* superfluously added, inasmuch as by the name of hypostasis or first substance the idea of universality and of part is excluded. For we do not say that man-in-general is an hypostasis, nor that the hand is, since it is only a part. But when *individual* is added, the idea of assumptibility is excluded from person;

1. 参见 Cf. Boethius, *De Duab. Nat.*, III (PL 64, 1344).
2. 参见 *Cat.*, V (2a 11).
3. 参见 Richard of St.Victor, *De Trin.*, IV, 4 ; 20 (PL 196, 932 ; 943); Alex. of Hales, *Summa Theol.*, II, no. 387 (I, 571).

for the human nature in Christ is not a person, since it is assumed by a greater — that is, by the Word of God. It is, however, better to say that substance is here taken in a general sense, as divided into first and second, and that when *individual* is added, it is restricted to first substance.

Reply Obj. 3. Since substantial differences are unknown to us, or at least unnamed by us, it is sometimes necessary to use accidental differences in their place; as, for example, we may say that fire is a simple, hot, and dry body: for proper accidents are the effects of substantial forms, and make them known. Likewise, terms expressive of intention can be used in defining realities if used to signify things which are unnamed. And so the term *individual* is placed in the definition of person to signify the mode of subsistence which belongs to particular substances.

Reply Obj. 4. According to the Philosopher, the term *nature* was first used to signify *the generation of living things*, which is called nativity.[1] And because this kind of generation comes from an intrinsic principle, this term is extended to signify *the intrinsic principle of any kind of movement.* In this sense he defines *nature.*[2] And since this kind of principle is either formal or material, both matter and form are commonly called nature. And as the essence of anything is completed by the form, for this reason the essence of anything, signified by the definition, is commonly called nature. And here nature is taken in that sense. Hence Boethius says that *nature is the specific difference giving its form to each thing*;[3] for the specific difference completes the definition, and is derived from the proper form of a thing. So in the definition of *person*, which means the singular in a determined *genus*, it was more correct for Boethius to use the term *nature*

1. 参见 *Metaph.*, IV, 4 (1014b 16).
2. 参见 Aristotle, *Phys.*, II, 1 (192b 14).
3. 参见 *De Duab. Nat.*, I (PL 64, 1432).

than *essence*, because the latter is taken from being, which is most common.

Reply Obj. 5. The soul is a part of the human species; and so, although it may exist in a separate state, yet since it retains its nature of unibility, it cannot be called an individual substance, which is the hypostasis or first substance, as neither can the hand, nor any other part of man. Hence neither the definition nor the name of person belongs to it.

Second Article

WHETHER *PERSON* IS THE SAME AS HYPOSTASIS, SUBSISTENCE, AND ESSENCE?

We proceed thus to the Second Article: —

Objection 1. It would seem that *person* is the same as *hypostasis*, *subsistence*, and *essence*. For Boethius says that *the Greeks called the individual substance of a rational nature by the name hypostasis.*[1] But this with us signifies *person*. Therefore *person* is altogether the same as *hypostasis*.

Obj. 2. Further, as we say there are three persons in God, so we say there are three subsistences in God; which implies that *person* and *subsistence* have the same meaning. Therefore *person* and *subsistence* mean the same.

Obj. 3. Further, Boethius says that οὐσία, which means essence, signifies a being composed of matter and form.[2] Now, that which is composed of matter and form is the individual substance called *hypostasis* and *person*. Therefore all the aforesaid names seem to have the same meaning.

Obj. 4. *On the contrary*, Boethius says that *genera and species only subsist*;

---

1. 参见 *Op. cit.*, III (PL 64, 1344).
2. 参见 *In Cat. Arist.*, I (PL 64, 184).

whereas individuals not only subsist, but also substand.[1] But subsistences are so called from subsisting, as substance or hypostasis is so called from substanding. Therefore, since genera and species are not hypostases or persons, these are not the same as subsistences.

Obj. 5. Further, Boethius says that matter is called hypostasis, and form is called οὐσίωσις — that is, subsistence.[2] But neither form nor matter can be called person. Therefore person differs from the others.

I answer that, According to the Philosopher, substance is twofold.[3] In one sense, it means *the quiddity of a thing*, signified by the definition, and thus we say that the definition signifies the substance of a thing; in which sense substance is called by the Greeks οὐσία, which we may call *essence*. In another sense, substance means a *subject* or *suppositum*, which subsists in the genus of substance. To this, taken in a general sense, can be applied a name expressive of an intention; and thus it is called the *suppositum*. It is also called by three names signifying a reality — that is, *a thing of nature*, *subsistence*, and *hypostasis*, according to a threefold consideration of the substance thus named. For, as it exists in itself and not in another, it is called *subsistence*; for we say that those things subsist which exist in themselves, and not in another. As it underlies some common nature, it is called *a thing of nature*; as, for instance, this particular man is a reality of a human nature. As it underlies the accidents, it is called *hypostasis* or *substance*. What these three names signify in common in the whole genus of substances, this name *person* signifies in the genus of rational substances.

Reply Obj. 1. Among the Greeks, the term *hypostasis*, taken in the

1. 参见 *De Duab. Nat.*, III (PL 64, 1344).
2. 参见 *In Cat. Arist.*, I, De subst. (PL 64, 182). — Cf. St. Albert, *Sent.*, I, d. xxiii, a. 4, arg. 1 (XXV, 591).
3. 参见 *Metaph.*, IV, 8 (1017b 23).

strict interpretation of the term, signifies any individual of the genus substance; but in the usual way of speaking, it means the individual of a rational nature, by reason of the excellence of that nature.

Reply Obj. 2. As we speak in the plural of *three persons* in God, and *three subsistences*, so the Greeks say *three hypostases*. But because the word *substance*, which, properly speaking, corresponds in meaning to *hypostasis*, is used among us in an equivocal sense (since it sometimes means the essence, and sometimes the hypostasis), in order to avoid any occasion of error, it was thought preferable to use *subsistence* for hypostasis, rather than *substance*.

Reply Obj. 3. Strictly speaking, the essence is what is expressed by the definition. Now, the definition comprises the principles of the species, but not the individual principles. Hence in things composed of matter and form, the essence signifies not only the form, nor only the matter, but what is composed of matter and the common form, as the principles of the species. But what is composed of this matter and this form has the nature of hypostasis and person. For soul, flesh, and bone belong to the nature of man; whereas this soul, this flesh, and this bone belong to the nature of this man. Therefore hypostasis and person add the individual principles to the notion of essence; nor are these identified with the essence in things composed of matter and form, as we said above when considering the divine simplicity.[1]

Reply Obj. 4. Boethius says that genera and species subsist,[2] inasmuch as it belongs to some individual things to subsist; for which the reason is that they belong to genera and species comprised in the predicament of substance, and not because species and genera themselves subsist, except in the opinion of Plato, who asserted that the species of things subsisted separately from singular things.

---

1. 参见 Q. 3, a. 4.
2. 参见 *In Porphyrium*, I (PL 64, 85).

To substand, however, belongs to the same individual things[1] in relation to the accidents, which are outside the essence of genera and species.

Reply Obj. 5. The individual composed of matter and form substands in relation to accident from the very nature of matter. Hence Boethius says: *A simple form cannot be a subject.*[2] Its self-subsistence, however, is derived from the nature of its form, which does not enter an already subsisting thing, but gives actual existence to the matter, and so enables the individual to subsist. On this account, therefore, he ascribes hypostasis to matter, and οὐσίωσις, or subsistence, to the form, because the matter is the principle of substanding, and the form is the principle of subsisting.

Third Article
WHETHER THE NAME *PERSON* SHOULD BE SAID OF GOD?

We proceed thus to the Third Article: —

Objection 1. It would seem that the name *person* should not be said of God. For Dionysius says: *No one should ever dare to say or think anything of the supersubstantial and hidden Divinity, beyond what has been divinely expressed to us by the sacred writings.*[3] But the name *person* is not expressed to us in the sacred text of the Old or New Testament. Therefore *person* is not to be applied to God.

Obj. 2. Further, Boethius says: *The term person seems to be taken from the masks which represented men in comedies and tragedies. For 'person' comes from 'sounding through'* [personando], *since a greater volume of sound is produced through the cavity in the mask. These 'persons' or masks the Greeks called* πρόσωπα, *as they were placed on the face and covered*

---

1. 参见 Cf. *ibid.*
2. 参见 *De Trin.*, II, 2 (PL 64, 1250).
3. 参见 *De Div. Nom.* I, 1(PG 3, 588).

the features from the eyes of the spectators.[1] This, however, can apply to God only in a metaphorical sense. Therefore the term *person* is only applied to God metaphorically.

Obj. 3. Further, every person is a hypostasis. But the term *hypostasis* does not apply to God, since, as Boethius says,[2] it signifies what is the subject of accidents, which do not exist in God. Jerome also says that, *in this term hypostasis, poison lurks in honey.*[3] Therefore the term *person* should not be said of God.

Obj. 4. Further, if a definition is denied of anything, the thing defined is also denied of it. But the definition of *person*, as given above, does not apply to God. Both because reason implies a discursive knowledge, which does not apply to God, as we proved above;[4] and thus God cannot be said to have *a rational nature.* And also because God cannot be called an *individual* substance, since the principle of individuation is matter; while God is immaterial. Nor is He the subject of accidents, so as to be called a *substance.* Therefore the term *person* ought not to be attributed to God.

On the contrary, In the Creed of Athanasius we say: *One is the person of the Father, another of the Son, another of the Holy Ghost.*[5]

I answer that, Person signifies what is most perfect in all nature — that is, a subsistent individual of a rational nature. Hence, since everything that is perfect must be attributed to God, inasmuch as His essence contains every perfection, this name *person* is fittingly applied to God; not, however, as it is applied to creatures, but in a more excellent way. The same is true also of other names, which we attribute to God although we have imposed them on creatures; as we showed

---

1. 参见 *De Duab. Nat.*, III (PL 64, 1344).
2. 同上
3. 参见 *Epist.* XV (PL 22, 357).
4. 参见 Q. 14, a. 7.
5. 参见 *Symb.* "*Quicumque*" (Denzinger, no. 39).

above when treating of the names of God.[1]

Reply Obj. 1. Although the term *person* is not found applied to God in Scripture, either in the Old or New Testament, nevertheless what the term signifies is found to be affirmed of God in many places of Scripture; as that He is the supreme self-subsisting being, and the most perfectly intelligent being. If we could speak of God only in the very terms themselves of Scripture, it would follow that no one could speak about God in any but the original language of the Old or New Testament. The urgency of confuting heretics made it necessary to find new words to express the ancient faith about God. Nor is such a kind of novelty to be shunned, since it is by no means profane, for it does not lead us astray from the sense of Scripture. Now what the Apostle warns us to avoid is *profane novelties of words* (*1 Tim.* vi. 20).

Reply Obj. 2. Although this name *person* may not belong to God as regards the origin of the term, nevertheless it most excellently belongs to God in its objective meaning. For as famous men were represented in comedies and tragedies, the name *person* was given to signify those who held high dignity. Hence, those who held high rank in the Church came to be called *persons.* Hence some define person as a *hypostasis distinct by reason of dignity.*[2] And because subsistence in a rational nature is of high dignity, therefore every individual of a rational nature is called a *person.* Now the dignity of the divine nature excels every other dignity; and thus the name *person* pre-eminently belongs to God.

Reply Obj. 3. The name *hypostasis* does not apply to God as regards its source of origin, since He does not underlie accidents; but it applies to Him in its objective sense, for it is imposed to signify a subsisting reality. Jerome said that *poison lurks in this term*, because before it was

1. 参见 Q. 13, a. 3.
2. 参见 Alain of Lille, *Theol. Reg.*, XXXII (PL 210, 637).

fully understood by the Latins, the heretics used the term person to deceive the simple, to make people profess many essences as they profess several hypostases, inasmuch as the term *substance*, which corresponds to hypostasis in Greek, is commonly taken among us to mean essence.

Reply Obj. 4. It may be said that God has a *rational nature*, if reason be taken to mean, not discursive thought, but, in a general sense, an intelligent nature. But God cannot be called an *individual* in the sense in which matter is the principle of individuation, but only in the sense in which *individual* implies incommunicability. *Substance* can be applied to God in the sense of signifying self-subsistence. There are some, however, who say that the definition of Boethius, quoted above, is not a definition of person in the sense we use when speaking of persons in God.[1] Therefore Richard of St. Victor amends this definition by adding that *person* in God is *the incommunicable existence of the divine nature.*[2]

Fourth Article
WHETHER THIS NAME *PERSON* SIGNIFIES RELATION?

We proceed thus to the Fourth Article: —

Objection 1. It would seem that this word *person*, as applied to God, does not signify relation, but substance. For Augustine says: *When we speak of the person of the Father, we mean nothing else but the substance of the Father, for person is said in regard to Himself, and not in regard to the Son.*[3]

Obj. 2. Further, the interrogation *What?* refers to the essence. But, as Augustine says: *When we say there are three who bear witness in heaven, the Father, the Word, and the Holy Ghost, and it is asked, Three what? the answer*

---

1. 参见 Richard of St. Victor, *De Trin.*, IV, 21 (PL 196, 945).
2. 同上
3. 参见 *De Trin.*, VII, 6 (PL 42, 943).

is, *Three persons.*[1] Therefore *person* signifies the essence.

Obj. 3. According to the Philosopher, the meaning of a term is its definition.[2] But the definition of *person* is this: *The individual substance of a rational nature*, as was stated above. Therefore *person* signifies a substance.

Obj. 4. Further, *person* in men and angels does not signify relation, but something absolute. Therefore, if in God it signified relation, it would bear an equivocal meaning in God, in man, and in angels.

On the contrary, Boethius says that *every term that refers to the Persons signifies relation.*[3] But no term belongs to person more strictly than *person* itself. Therefore this term *person* signifies relation.

I answer that, A difficulty arises concerning the meaning of this term *person* in God,[4] from the fact that it is predicated in the plural of the Three in contrast to the nature of the names belonging to the essence; nor is it in itself said relatively, as are the terms which express relation.

Hence some[5] have thought that this term *person* of itself expresses absolutely the divine essence, as does this name *God* and this name *Wise*; but that to meet heretical attack, it was ordained by conciliar decree that it could be taken in a relative sense, and especially in the plural, or with the addition of a distinguishing adjective; as when we say, *Three persons*, or, *one is the person of the Father*, *another of the Son*, etc. Taken in the singular, however, it may be either absolute or relative. But this does not seem to be a satisfactory explanation, for, if this term *person*, by force of its own signification, expresses only the divine

---

1. 参见 *Op. cit.*, VII, 4; 5; V, 9 (PL 42, 940; 943; 913).
2. 参见 *Metaph.*, III, 7 (1012a 23).
3. 参见 *De Trin.*, VI (PL 64, 1254).
4. 参 见 For the different opinions, cf. Richard Fishacre, *In I Sent.*, d. xxv (ed. M. Bergeron, in *Études d'hist. litt. et doctr. du xiii siècle,* II, Ottawa, 1932, p. 149).
5. 参见 St. Augustine, *De Trin.*, VII, 5 (PL 42, 943) ; anonymous author of *Sum. Sent.*, I, 9 (PL 176, 56).

essence, it follows that insofar as we speak of *three persons*, the heretics, so far from being silenced, would have had still more reason to argue. Seeing this, others[1] maintained that this term *person* in God signifies both the essence and the relation. Some of these[2] said that it signifies directly the essence, and relation indirectly, for *person* means as it were *by itself one* [*per se una*], and unity belongs to the essence. And what is *by itself* implies relation indirectly; for the Father is understood to exist *by Himself*, as relatively distinct from the Son. Others,[3] however, said, on the contrary, that *person* signifies relation directly, and essence indirectly; for in the definition of *person* nature is included indirectly. These come nearer to the truth.

To determine the question, we must consider that something may be included in the meaning of a less common term, which yet is not included in the more common term; as *rational* is included in the meaning of *man*, and not in the meaning of *animal*. So that it is one thing to ask the meaning of the term *animal*, and another to ask its meaning when the animal in question is *man*. So, too, it is one thing to ask the meaning of this term *person* in general, and another to ask the meaning of *person* as applied to God. For *person* in general signifies the individual substance of a rational nature. But the individual in itself is undivided, but is distinct from others. Therefore *person* in any nature signifies what is distinct in that nature: thus in human nature it signifies this flesh, these bones, and this soul, which are the individuating principles of a man, and which, though not belonging to *person* in general, nevertheless do belong to the meaning of a human person. Now distinction in God is only by relation of origin, as was

---

1. 参见 Peter Lombard, *Sent.*, I, xxv, 2 (I, 159).
2. 参见 Simon of Tournai; cf. the text edited by M. Schmaus, in *Recherches de théol. ancien. et méd.*, IV, 1932, p. 62.
3. 参见 William of Auxerre, *Summa Aurea*, I, tr. 6, ch. 3 (fol. 11a).

stated above.[1] But relation in God is not as an accident in a subject, but is the divine essence itself; and so it is subsistent, for the divine essence is subsistent. Therefore, as the Godhead is God, so the divine paternity is God the Father, Who is a divine person. Therefore a divine person signifies a relation as subsisting.

And this is to signify relation by way of substance, which is a hypostasis subsisting in the divine nature; although it remains that that which subsists in the divine nature is the divine nature itself. Thus it is true to say that the name *person* signifies relation directly, and the essence indirectly; not, however, the relation as such, but as expressed by way of a hypostasis. So likewise it signifies directly the essence, and indirectly the relation, inasmuch as the essence is the same as the hypostasis. Now in God the hypostasis is expressed as distinct by the relation; and thus relation, signified as a relation, enters into the notion of the person indirectly.

Thus we can also say that this signification of the term *person* was not clearly perceived before it was attacked by heretics. Hence, this term *person* was used just as any other absolute term. But afterwards it was applied to express relation, as it lent itself to that signification so that *person* means relation not only by use and custom, according to the first opinion, but also by force of its own proper signification.

Reply Obj. 1. The term *person* is said in relation to itself, not to another; for it signifies relation, not as such, but by way of a substance which is a hypostasis. In that sense Augustine says that it signifies the essence, inasmuch as in God essence is the same as hypostasis, because in God what He is and that whereby He is are the same.

Reply Obj. 2. The term *what* sometimes refers to the nature expressed by the definition, as when we ask: What is man? and we answer: A mortal rational animal. Sometimes it refers to the *suppositum*, as when

---

1. 参见 Q. 28, a. 3.

we ask: What swims in the sea? and answer: A fish. So to those who have this understanding of the question, Three what? we answer: Three persons.

Reply Obj. 3. In God, the individual — *i. e.*, distinct and incommunicable substance — includes the idea of relation, as was above explained.

Reply Obj. 4. The different meaning of the less common term does not produce equivocation in the more common. Although a horse and an ass have their own proper definitions, nevertheless they agree univocally in animal, because the common definition of animal applies to both. So it does not follow that, although relation is contained in the signification of divine person, but not in that of an angelic or of a human person, the term *person* is used in an equivocal sense. Though neither is it used univocally, since nothing can be said univocally of God and creatures, as was shown above.[1]

---

1. 参见 Q. 13, a. 5.

Question XXX
THE PLURALITY[1] OF PERSONS IN GOD
(*In Four Articles*)

WE are now led to consider the plurality of the persons; about which there are four points of inquiry: (1) Whether there are many persons in God? (2) How many are they? (3) What numeral terms signify in God? (4) The community of the term *person*.

First Article
WHETHER THERE ARE MANY PERSONS IN GOD?

We proceed thus to the First Article: —

Objection 1. It would seem that there are not many persons in God. For person is *the individual substance of a rational nature*. If then there are many persons in God, there must be many substances; which appears to be heretical.

Obj. 2. Further, plurality of absolute properties does not make a distinction of persons, either in God, or in ourselves. Much less therefore is this effected by a plurality of relations. But in God there is no plurality but of relations.[2] Therefore there cannot be many persons in God.

Obj. 3. Further, Boethius says of God that *this is truly one which has no number*.[3] But plurality implies number. Therefore there are not many persons in God.

---

1. Plurality：多元性
2. 参见 Q. 28, a. 3.
3. 参见 *De Trin.*, III (PL 64, 1251).

Obj. 4. Further, where number is, there is whole and part. Thus, if in God a number of persons exists, there must be whole and part in God; which is inconsistent with the divine simplicity.

On the contrary, Athanasius says: *One is the person of the Father, another of the Son, another of the Holy Ghost.*[1] Therefore the Father, and the Son, and the Holy Ghost are many persons.

I answer that, It follows from what precedes that there are many persons in God. For it was shown above that this term *person* signifies in God a relation as subsisting in the divine nature.[2] It was also established that there are many real relations in God.[3] Hence it follows that there are many realities subsistent in the divine nature; which means that there are many persons in God.

Reply Obj. 1. The definition of *person* includes *substance*, not as meaning the essence, but the *suppositum*, which is made clear by the addition of the term *individual*. To signify substance thus understood, the Greeks use the name *hypostasis*. So, as we say *three persons*, they say *three hypostases*. We are not, however, accustomed to say three substances, lest we be understood to mean three essences or natures, by reason of the equivocal signification of the term.

Reply Obj. 2. The absolute properties in God, such as goodness and wisdom, are not mutually opposed; and hence, neither are they really distinguished from each other. Therefore, although they subsist, nevertheless they are not many subsistent realities — that is, many persons. But the absolute properties in creatures do not subsist, although they are really distinguished from each other, as whiteness and sweetness; on the other hand, the relative properties in God both subsist, and are really distinguished from each other.[4] Hence the

---

1. 参见 Cf. *Symb. "Quicumque"* (Denzinger, no. 39).
2. 参见 Q. 29, a. 4.
3. 参见 Q. 28, a. 1, 3 and 4.
4. 参见 Q. 28, a. 3; q. 29, a. 4.

plurality of such properties suffices for the plurality of persons in God.

Reply Obj. 3. The supreme unity and simplicity of God exclude every kind of plurality taken absolutely, but not plurality of relations; for relations are predicated relatively, and thus they do not imply composition in that of which they are predicated, as Boethius teaches in the same book.[1]

Reply Obj. 4. Number is twofold, simple or absolute, as two, three and four; and number as existing in things numbered, as two men and two horses. So, if number in God is taken absolutely or abstractedly, there is nothing to prevent whole and part from being in Him; and thus number in Him is only in our way of understanding, for number regarded apart from things numbered exists only in the intellect. But if number be taken as it is in the things numbered, in that sense, as existing in creatures, one is part of two, and two of three, as one man is part of two men, and two of three. This however does not apply to God, because the Father is of the same magnitude as the whole Trinity, as we shall show further on.[2]

Second Article
WHETHER THERE ARE MORE THAN THREE PERSONS IN GOD?

We proceed thus to the Second Article: —

Objection 1. It would seem that there are more than three persons in God. For the plurality of persons in God arises from the plurality of the relative properties, as was stated above. But there are four relations in God, as was stated above,[3] namely paternity, filiation, common spiration and procession. Therefore there are four persons in God.

---

1. 参见 *De Trin.*, VI (PL 64, 1354).
2. 参见 Q. 42, a. 4, ad 3.
3. 参见 Q. 28, a. 4.

Obj. 2. The nature of God does not differ from His will more than from His intellect. But in God, one person proceeds from the will, as Love; and another proceeds from His nature, as Son. Therefore another proceeds from His intellect, as Word, besides the one Who proceeds from His nature, as Son. Thus again it follows that there are not only three persons in God.

Obj. 3. Further, the more perfect a creature is, the more intrinsic are its operations; as a man has understanding and will beyond other animals. But God infinitely excels every creature. Therefore in God not only is there a person proceeding from the will, and another from the intellect, but also in an infinite number of ways. Therefore there is an infinite number of persons in God.

Obj. 4. Further, it is from the infinite goodness of the Father that He communicates Himself infinitely in the production of a divine person. But also in the Holy Ghost there is infinite goodness. Therefore the Holy Ghost produces a divine person; and that person another; and so to infinity.

Obj. 5. Further, everything within a determinate number is measured, for number is a measure. But the divine persons are immense, as we say in the Creed of Athanasius: *The Father is immense, the Son is immense, the Holy Ghost is immense.*[1] Therefore the persons are not contained within the number three.

On the contrary, It is said: *There are three who bear witness in heaven, the Father, the Word, and the Holy Ghost* (1 *John* v. 7). To those who ask, *Three what?* we answer, with Augustine, *Three persons.*[2] Therefore there are but three persons in God.

I answer that, As was explained above, there can be only three persons in God. For it was shown above that the many persons are the many subsisting relations really distinct from each other. But a real distinction between the divine relations can come only from relative opposition. Therefore two opposite relations must needs refer to two persons: and

---

1. 参见 Cf. *Symb. "Quicumque"* (Denzinger, no. 39).
2. 参见 *De Trin.*, VII, 4; 6; V, 9 (PL 42, 940; 943; 913).

if any relations are not opposite, they must needs belong to the same person. Since then paternity and filiation are opposite relations, they belong necessarily to two persons. Therefore the subsisting paternity is the person of the Father and the subsisting filiation is the person of the Son. The other two relations are not opposed to either of these, but they are opposed to each other; therefore these two cannot belong to one person. Hence either one of them must belong to both of the aforesaid persons, or one must belong to one person, and the other to the other. Now, procession cannot belong to the Father and the Son, or to either of them; for thus it would follow that the procession of the intellect, which in God is generation (wherefrom paternity and filiation are derived), would issue from the procession of love (whence spiration and procession are derived); and thus the person generating and the person generated would proceed from the person spirating. This is against what was laid down above.[1] We must consequently admit that spiration belongs to the person of the Father and to the person of the Son, inasmuch as it has no relative opposition either to paternity or to filiation; and consequently that procession belongs to the other person who is called the person of the Holy Ghost, who proceeds by way of love, as was above explained.[2] Therefore only three persons exist in God, the Father[3], the Son[4], and the Holy Ghost[5].

Reply Obj. 1. Although there are four relations in God, one of them, spiration, is not separated from the person of the Father and of the Son, but belongs to both; and thus, although it is a relation, it is not called a property, because it does not belong to only one person, nor is it a personal relation — *i.e.*, constituting a person. The three relations —

---

1. 参见 Q. 27, a. 3, ad 3.
2. 参见 Q. 27, a. 4.
3. the Father：天父，三位一体的天主的第一位
4. the Son：圣子，三位一体的天主的第二位，即耶稣基督
5. the Holy Ghost：圣神，三位一体的天主的第三位

paternity, filiation, and procession — are called personal properties, constituting as it were the persons; for paternity is the person of the Father, filiation is the person of the Son, procession is the person of the Holy Ghost proceeding.

Reply Obj. 2. That which proceeds by way of intellect, as a word, proceeds according to likeness, as does also that which proceeds by way of nature. Hence, as was explained above, the procession of the divine Word is the very same as generation by way of nature.[1] But love, as such, does not proceed as the likeness of that whence it proceeds, even though in God love is coessential as being divine; and therefore the procession of love is not called generation in God.

Reply Obj. 3. As man is more perfect than other animals, he has a greater number of intrinsic operations than other animals, because his perfection is something composite. Hence the angels, who are more perfect and more simple, have fewer intrinsic operations than man, for they have no imagination, sensation, or the like. In God, however, there exists only one real operation — that is, His essence. How there are in Him two processions was above explained.[2]

Reply Obj. 4. This argument would hold if the Holy Ghost possessed another goodness apart from the goodness of the Father; for then if the Father produced a divine person by His goodness, the Holy Ghost also would do so. But the Father and the Holy Ghost have one and the same goodness. Nor is there any distinction between them except by the personal relations. So goodness belongs to the Holy Ghost, as derived from another; and it belongs to the Father, as the principle of its communication to another. The opposition of relation does not allow the relation of the Holy Ghost to be joined with the relation which is the principle of another divine person; because He Himself proceeds from the other persons who are in God.

---

1. 参见 Q. 27, a. 2; q. 28, a. 4.
2. 参见 Q. 27, a 3 and 5.

Reply Obj. 5. A determinate number, if taken as a simple number, existing in the intellect only, is measured by *one*. But when we speak of a number of things as applied to the persons in God, the notion of measure has no place, because the magnitude of the three persons is the same, and the same is not measured by the same.

Third Article
WHETHER NUMERAL TERMS DENOTE ANYTHING REAL IN GOD?

We proceed thus to the Third Article: —

Objection 1. It would seem that numeral terms denote something real in God. For the divine unity is the divine essence. But every number is unity repeated. Therefore every numeral term in God signifies the essence; and therefore it denotes something real in God.

Obj. 2. Further, whatever is said of God and of creatures belongs to God in a more eminent manner[1] than to creatures. But numeral terms denote something real in creatures; therefore much more so in God.

Obj. 3. Further, if numeral terms do not denote anything real in God, and are introduced simply in a negative and removing sense, as plurality is employed to remove unity, and unity to remove plurality, it follows that a vicious circle results, confusing the intellect and obscuring the truth; and this ought not to be. Therefore it must be said that numeral terms denote something real in God.

On the contrary, Hilary says: *If we admit companionship* — that is, plurality — *we exclude the idea of oneness and of solitude;*[2] and Ambrose says: *When we say one God, unity excludes a plurality of gods; it does not imply quantity in God.*[3] Hence we see that these terms are applied to God in order to

1. eminent manner：杰出的方式
2. 参见 *De Trin.*, IV (PL 10, 111).
3. 参见 *De Fide*, I, 2 (PL 16, 555).

remove something, and not to denote anything positive.

I answer that, The Master of the *Sentences* considers that numeral terms do not denote anything positive in God, but have only a negative meaning.[1] Others, homever, assert the contrary.[2]

In order to resolve this point, we may observe that all plurality is a consequence of some division. Now division is twofold. One is material, and is division of the continuous; from this results number, which is a species of quantity. Number in this sense is found only in material things, which have quantity. The other kind of division is called formal, and is effected by opposite or diverse forms; and this kind of division results in a multitude, which does not belong to a genus, but is transcendental in the sense in which being is divided by one and by many. Only this kind of multitude is found in immaterial things.

Some,[3] considering only that multitude which is a species of discrete quantity, and seeing that such quantity has no place in God, asserted that numeral terms do not denote anything real in God, but remove something from Him. Others, considering the same kind of multitude, said that as knowledge exists in God according to the strict sense of the word, but not according to the genus to which it belongs (as in God there is no such thing as a quality), so number exists in God in the proper sense of number, but not according to the genus to which it belongs, which is quantity.

But our view of the problem is that numeral terms predicated of God are not derived from number which is a species of quantity, for in that sense they could bear only a metaphorical sense in God, like other corporeal properties, such as length, breadth, and the like;

---

1. 参见 Peter Lombard, *Sent.*, I, xxiv, 1 (I, 153).
2. 参见 A common opinion at Paris, according to St. Bonaventure, *In I Sent.* d. xxiv, a. 2, q. 1, concl. (I, 426).
3. 参见 Peter Lombard, *Sent.*, I, xxiv, 1 (I, 154).

but that they are taken from multitude in a transcendental sense. Now multitude so understood has relation to the many of which it is predicated, as *one* convertible with *being* is related to being; which kind of oneness does not add anything to being, except only a negation of division, as we saw when treating of the divine unity.[1] For *one* signifies undivided being. So, of whatever we say *one*, we signify its undivided reality: thus, for instance, *one* applied to man signifies the undivided nature or substance of a man. In the same way, when we speak of many things, multitude in this latter sense points to those things as being each undivided in itself. But number, if taken as a species of quantity, denotes an accident added to being; as also does *one* which is the principle of that number.

Therefore numeral terms in God signify the things of which they are said, and beyond this they add only negation, as was stated. In this respect the Master of the *Sentences* was right. So when we say, the essence is one, the term *one* signifies the essence undivided; and when we say the person is *one*, it signifies the person undivided; and when we say the persons are *many*, we signify the persons and their individual undividedness; for it is of the very nature of multitude that it should be composed of units.

Reply Obj. 1. One, as it is a transcendental, is wider and more general than substance and relation; so likewise is multitude. Hence in God, *one* may mean both substance and relation, according to the context. Still, the very signification of such names adds a negation of division, beyond substance and relation; as was explained above.

Reply Obj. 2. Multitude, which denotes something real in creatures, is a species of quantity, and cannot be used when speaking of God unlike transcendental multitude, which adds only indivision to those of which it is predicated. Such a kind of multitude is applicable to God.

1. 参见 Q. 11, a. 1.

Reply Obj. 3. *One* does not exclude multitude, but division, which logically precedes one or multitude. Multitude does not remove unity, but division from each of the individuals which compose the multitude. This was explained when we treated of the divine unity.[1]

It must be observed, nevertheless, that the arguments to the contrary do not sufficiently prove the point advanced. For although the idea of solitude is excluded by plurality, and the plurality of gods by unity, it does not follow that these terms express this signification alone. For blackness is excluded by whiteness; nevertheless, the term whiteness does not signify the mere exclusion of blackness.

Fourth Article

WHETHER THIS TERM *PERSON* CAN BE COMMON TO THE THREE PERSONS?

We proceed thus to the Fourth Article: —

Objection 1. It would seem that this term *person* cannot be common to the three persons. For nothing is common to the three persons but the essence. But this term *person* does not signify the essence directly. Therefore, it is not common to all three.

Obj. 2. Further, the common is the opposite to the incommunicable[2]. But the very meaning of person is that it is incommunicable; as appears from the definition given by Richard of St. Victor.[3] Therefore, this term *person* is not common to all the three persons.

Obj. 3. Further, if the name *person* is common to the three, it is common either really, or logically. But it is not so really, otherwise the three persons would be one person; nor again is it so logically, otherwise *person* would be a universal. But in God there is neither

1. 参见 Q. 11, a. 2, ad 4.
2. incommunicable：不能传达的
3. 参见 Q. 29, a. 3, ad 4.

universal nor particular, neither genus nor species, as we proved above.[1] Therefore this term *person* is not common to the three.

On the contrary, Augustine says that when we ask, *Three what?* we say, *Three persons*, because what a person is, is common to them.[2]

I answer that, The very mode of expression itself shows that this term *person* is common to the three when we say *three persons*; just as when we say *three men* we show that *man* is common to the three. Now it is clear that this is not community of a real thing, as if one essence were common to the three; otherwise there would be only one person among the three, just as there is one essence.

What is meant by such a community has been variously determined by those who have examined the subject. Some[3] have called it a community of exclusion, because the definition of *person* contains the word *incommunicable*. Others[4] thought it to be a community of intention, as the definition of person contains the word *individual*; as we say that to be a *species* is common to horse and ox. Both of these explanations, however, are excluded by the fact that *person* is not a name of exclusion nor of intention, but the name of a reality.

We must therefore affirm that even in human affairs this name *person* is common by a community of idea, not as genus or species, but as a vague individual thing. The names of genera and species, as man or animal, are given to signify the common natures themselves, but not the intentions of those common natures, signified by the terms *genus* or *species*. The vague individual thing, *as some man*, signifies the common nature with the determinate mode of existence of singular things — that is, something self-subsisting, as distinct from others. But the name of a designated singular thing signifies that which distinguishes the

---

1. 参见 Q. 3. a. 5.
2. 参见 *De Trin.*,VII, 4; 6; V, 9 (PL 42, 940; 943; 913).
3. 参见 William of Auxerre, *Summa Aurea*, I, tr. 6, ch. 2 (fol. 10c).
4. 参见 Cf. Alex. of Hales, *Summa Theol.*, II, no. 389 (I, 573).

determinate thing; as the name Socrates signifies this flesh and this bone. But there is this difference — that the term *some man* signifies the nature, or the individual on the part of its nature, with the mode of existence of singular things; while this name *person* is not given to signify the individual on the part of the nature, but the subsistent reality in that nature. Now this is common in idea to the divine persons, that each of them subsists distinctly from the others in the divine nature. Thus this name *person* is common in idea to the three divine persons.

Reply Obj. 1. This argument is founded on a real community.

Reply Obj. 2. Although person is incommunicable, yet the mode itself of incommunicable existence can be common to many.

Reply Obj. 3. Although this community is logical and not real, yet it does not follow that in God there is universal or particular, or genus, or species; both because neither in human affairs is the community of person the same as community of genus or species, and because the divine persons have one being, whereas genus and species and every other universal are predicated of many which differ in being.

Question XXXI
WHAT BELONGS TO THE UNITY OR PLURALITY IN GOD
(*In Four Articles*)

WE now consider what belongs to the unity or plurality in God; which gives rise to four points of inquiry: (1) Concerning the term *Trinity*. (2) Whether we can say that the Son is other than the Father? (3) Whether an exclusive term, which seems to exclude otherness, can be joined to an essential name in God? (4) Whether it can be joined to a personal term?

First Article
WHETHER THERE IS A TRINITY IN GOD?

We proceed thus to the First Article: —

Objection 1. It would seem there is not a trinity in God. For every name in God signifies substance or relation. But this name *trinity* does not signify the substance; otherwise it would be predicated of each one of the persons: nor does it signify relation; for it is not said as a relative name. Therefore the name *Trinity* is not to be applied to God.

Obj. 2. Further, this name *trinity* is a collective term, since it signifies multitude. But such a name does not apply to God; as the unity of a collective name is the least of unities, whereas in God there exists the greatest possible unity. Therefore this name *trinity* does not apply to God.

Obj. 3. Further, every triple is threefold. But in God there is not triplicity, since triplicity is a kind of inequality. Therefore neither is there a trinity in God.

Obj. 4. Further, all that exists in God exists in the unity of the divine essence, because God is His own essence. Therefore, if a Trinity exists in God, it exists in the unity of the divine essence; and thus in God there would be three essential unities; which is heresy.

Obj. 5. Further, in all that is said of God, the concrete is predicated of the abstract; for Deity is God and paternity is the Father. But the Trinity cannot be called triple; otherwise there would be nine realities in God; which, of course, is erroneous. Therefore the name trinity is not to be applied to God.

On the contrary, Athanasius says: *Unity in Trinity, and Trinity in Unity is to be revered.*[1]

I answer that, The name *Trinity* in God signifies the determinate number of persons. And so the plurality of persons in God requires that we should use the name trinity; because what is indeterminately signified by plurality, is signified by trinity in a determinate manner.

Reply Obj. 1. In its etymological[2] sense, this name *Trinity* seems to signify the one essence of the three persons, according as trinity may mean three-in-one. But in the strict meaning of the term, it rather signifies the number of persons of one essence; and on this account we cannot say that the Father is the Trinity, as He is not three persons. Yet it does not mean the relations themselves of the Persons, but rather the number of persons related to each other; and hence it is that the name in itself is not used as a relative name.

Reply Obj. 2. Two things are implied in a collective term, plurality of the *supposita*, and a unity of some kind of order. For *people* is a multitude of men comprehended under a certain order. As to the first point, this name *trinity* is like collective names; but as to the second, it differs from them, because in the divine Trinity not only is there unity

1. 参见 Cf. *Symb. "Quicumque"* (Denzinger, no. 39).
2. etymological：语源的；根据语源学的

of order, but with this there also is unity of essence.

Reply Obj. 3. *Trinity* is taken in an absolute sense, for it signifies the threefold number of persons. *Triplicity* signifies a proportion of inequality; for it is a species of unequal proportion, according to Boethius.[1] Therefore in God there is not triplicity, but Trinity.

Reply Obj. 4. In the divine Trinity is to be understood both number and the persons numbered. So when we say, *Trinity in Unity*, we do not place number in the unity of the essence, as if we meant three times one; but we place the Persons numbered in the unity of nature, just as the *supposita* of a nature are said to exist in that nature. On the other hand, we say *Unity in Trinity*, meaning that the nature is in its *supposita*.

Reply Obj. 5. When we say, the *Trinity is threefold*, by reason of the number implied, we signify the multiplication of that number by itself; since the word threefold implies a distinction in the *supposita* of which it is spoken. Therefore it cannot be said that the Trinity is threefold, otherwise it follows that, if the Trinity be threefold, there would be three *supposita* of the Trinity; as when we say, *God is triune*, it follows that there are three *supposita* of the Godhead.

Second Article
WHETHER THE SON IS OTHER THAN THE FATHER?

We proceed thus to the Second Article: —

Objection 1. It seems that the Son is not other than the Father. For *other* is a relative term implying diversity of substance. If, then, the Son is other than the Father, He must be different from the Father; which is contrary to what Augustine says, namely, that when we speak of three persons, *we do not mean to imply diversity.*[2]

Obj. 2. Further, whosoever are other from one another, differ in

---

1. 参见 *Arithm.*, I, 23 (PL 63, 1101).
2. 参见 *De Trin.*, VII, 4 (PL 42, 940).

some way from one another. Therefore, if the Son is other than the Father, it follows that He differs from the Father; which is against what Ambrose says, that *the Father and the Son are one in Godhead; nor is there any difference in substance between them, nor any diversity.*[1]

Obj. 3. Further, the term alien is taken from *alius* [other]. But the Father is not alien from the Son, for Hilary says that *in the divine persons there is nothing diverse, nothing alien, nothing separable.*[2] Therefore the Son is not other than the Father.

Obj. 4. Further, the terms *other person* and *other thing* [*alius et aliud*] have the same meaning, differing only in gender. So if the Son is another person from the Father, it follows that the Son is a thing apart from the Father.

On the contrary, Augustine says: *There is one essence of the Father and Son and Holy Ghost, in which the Father is not one thing, the Son another, and the Holy Ghost another; although the Father is one person, the Son another, and the Holy Ghost another.*[3]

I answer that, Since, as Jerome remarks, a heresy arises from words wrongly used,[4] when we speak of the Trinity we must proceed with care and with befitting modesty; because, as Augustine says, *nowhere is error more harmful, the quest more toilsome, the finding more fruitful,*[5] Now, in treating of the Trinity, we must beware of two opposite errors, and proceed cautiously between them — namely, the error of Arius, who posited a Trinity of substances with the Trinity of persons,[6] and the error of Sabellius, who posited a unity of person with the unity of essence.[7]

---

1. 参见 *De Fide*, I ,2 (PL 16, 555).
2. 参见 *De Trin.*, VII (PL 10, 233).
3. 参见 Cf. Fulgentius, *De Fide ad Petrum*, I (PL 65, 674).
4. 参见 Cf. Peter Lombard, *Sent.*, IV, xiii, 2 (II, 818).
5. 参见 *De Trin.*, I, 3 (PL 42, 822).
6. 参见 Cf. St. Augustine, *De Haeres.*, 49 (PL 42, 39).
7. 参见 Cf. *op. cit.*, 41 (PL 42, 32).

Thus, to avoid the error of Arius we must shun the use of the terms diversity and difference in God, lest we take away the unity of essence; we may, however, use the term *distinction* because of the relative opposition. Hence, whenever we find the terms *diversity* or *difference* of Persons used in an authentic work, these terms *diversity* or *difference* are taken to mean *distinction*. But lest the simplicity and singleness of the divine essence be taken away, the terms *separation* and *division*, which belong to the parts of a whole, are to be avoided. Lest equality be taken away, we avoid the use of the term *disparity*. And lest we remove *likeness*, we avoid the terms *alien* and *discrepant*. For Ambrose says that *in the Father and the Son there is no discrepancy, but one Godhead*;[1] and according to Hilary, as quoted above, *in God there is nothing alien, nothing separable.*[2]

To avoid the heresy of Sabellius, on the other hand, we must shun the term *singularity*, lest we take away the communicability of the divine essence. Hence Hilary says: *It is sacrilege to assert that the Father and the Son are separate in Godhead.*[3] We must avoid the term *only* [*unici*] lest we take away the number of persons. Hence Hilary says in the same book: *We exclude from God the idea of singularity or uniqueness.*[4] Nevertheless, we can say *the only Son*, for in God there is no plurality of Sons. Yet, we do not say *the only God*, for Deity is common to many. We avoid the term *confused*, lest we take away from the Persons the order of their nature. Hence Ambrose says: *What is one is not confused, and there is no multiplicity where there is no difference.*[5] The term *solitary* is also to be avoided, lest we take away the society of the three persons; for, as Hilary says, *We confess neither a solitary God nor a God with diversity.*[6]

---

1. 参见 *De Fide*, I, 2 (PL 16, 555).
2. 参见 *De Trin.*, VII (PL 10, 233).
3. 同上
4. 参见 *Ibid.* (PL 10, 231).
5. 参见 *De Fide*, I, 2 (PL 16, 555).
6. 参见 *De Trin.*, IV(PL 10, 111).

This term *other* [*alius*], however, in the masculine gender, means only a distinction of *suppositum*; and hence we can properly say that *the Son is other than the Father*, because He is another *suppositum* of the divine nature; just as He is another person and another hypostasis.

Reply Obj. 1. *Other*, being like the name of a particular thing, refers to the *suppositum*; and so, there is sufficient reason for using it, where there is a distinct substance in the sense of hypostasis or person. But diversity requires a distinct substance in the sense of essence. Thus we cannot say that the Son is diverse from the Father, although He is *other*.

Reply Obj. 2. *Difference* implies distinction of form. There is one form only in God, as appears from the text, *Who, when He was in the form of God* (*Phil.* ii. 6). Therefore, the term *difference* does not properly apply to God, as appears from the authority quoted. Yet Damascene employs the term *difference* in the divine persons, as meaning that the relative property is signified by way of form. Hence he says that the hypostases do not differ from each other in substance, but according to determinate properties.[1] But *difference* is taken for *distinction*, as was above stated.

Reply Obj. 3. The term *alien* [*alienum*] means what is extraneous and dissimilar; which is not expressed by the term *other* [*alius*]; and therefore we say that the Son is *other* than the Father, but not that He is anything *alien*.

Reply Obj. 4. The neuter gender is formless, whereas the masculine is formed and distinct; and so is the feminine. So the common essence is properly and aptly expressed by the neuter gender; but by the masculine and feminine is expressed the determined subject in the common nature. Hence also in human affairs, if we ask, *Who* is this man? we answer, *Socrates*, which is the name of the *suppositum*; whereas, if we ask, *What* is he? we reply, *A rational and mortal*

---

1. 参见 *De Fide Orth.*, III, 5 (PG 94, 1000).

animal. So, because in God distinction is by the persons, and not by the essence, we say that the Father is other than the Son, but not something else; while conversely we say that they are one thing, but not one person.

Third Article
WHETHER THE EXCLUSIVE WORD *ALONE* SHOULD BE ADDED TO AN ESSENTIAL TERM IN GOD?

We proceed thus to the Third Article: —

Objection 1. It would seem that the exclusive word *alone* [*solus*] is not to be added to an essential term in God. For, according to the Philosopher, *He is alone who is not with another.*[1] But God is with the angels and the souls of the saints. Therefore we cannot say that God is alone.

Obj. 2. Further, whatever is joined to an essential term in God can be predicated of every person *per se*, and of all the persons together; for, as we can properly say that God is wise, we can say the Father is a wise God, and the Trinity is a wise God. But Augustine says: *We must consider the opinion that the Father is not true God alone.*[2] Therefore God cannot be said to be alone.

Obj. 3. Further, if this expression *alone* is joined to an essential term it would be so joined as regards either the personal predicate or the essential predicate. But it cannot be the former, as it is false to say, *God alone is Father*, since man also is a father; nor, again, can it be applied as regards the latter, for, if this saying were true, *God alone creates*, it would follow that the *Father alone creates*, as whatever is said of God can be said of the Father; and it would be false, as the Son also creates. Therefore this expression *alone* cannot be joined to an essential term in

1. 参见 *Soph. Elench.*, XXII (178a 39).
2. 参见 *De Trin.*, VI, 9 (PL 42, 930).

God.

On the contrary, It is said, *To the King of ages, immortal, invisible, the only God* (1 *Tim*. i. 17).

I answer that, This term *alone* can be taken as a categorematical term[1], or as a syncategorematical term[2]. A categorematical term is one which ascribes absolutely its meaning to a given *suppositum*; as, for instance, *white* to man, as when we say *a white man*. If the term *alone* is taken in this sense, it cannot in any way be joined to any term in God; for it would mean solitude in the term to which it is joined; and it would follow that God was solitary, against what is above stated. A syncategorematical term signifies the order of the predicate to the subject, as this expression, *every one* or *no one*; and likewise the term *alone*, as excluding every other *suppositum* from the predicate. Thus, when we say, *Socrates alone writes*, we do not mean that Socrates is solitary, but that he has no companion in writing, though many others may be with him. In this way, nothing prevents the term *alone* being joined to any essential term in God, as excluding the predicate from all things but God; as if we said, *God alone is eternal*, because nothing but God is eternal.

Reply Obj. 1. Although the angels and the souls of the saints are always with God, nevertheless, if a plurality of persons did not exist in God, He would be alone or solitary. For solitude is not removed by association with anything that is extraneous in nature; and thus one is said to be alone in a garden, though many plants and animals are with him in the garden. Likewise, God would be alone or solitary, though angels and men were with Him, supposing that several persons were not within Him. Therefore the society of angels and of souls does not take away absolute solitude from God; much less does it remove respective solitude, in reference to a predicate.

---

1. categorematical term：绝对术语
2. syncategorematical term：相对术语

Reply Obj. 2. This expression *alone*, properly speaking, does not affect the predicate, which is taken formally, for it refers to the *suppositum*, as excluding any other suppositum from the one which it qualifies. But the adverb *only*, being exclusive, can be applied either to subject or to predicate. For we can say, *Only Socrates* — that is, no one else — *runs*; and, *Socrates only runs* — that is, he does nothing else. Hence it is not properly said that the Father is God alone, or the Trinity is God alone, unless some implied meaning be assumed in the predicate, as, for instance, *The Trinity is God, Who alone is God.* In that sense it can be true to say that the Father is that God who alone is God, if the relative be referred to the predicate, and not to the *suppositum.* So, when Augustine says that the Father is not God alone, but that the Trinity is God alone, he speaks expositively, as he might explain the words, '*To the King of ages, invisible, the only God,*' as applying not to the Father, but to the Trinity alone.

Reply Obj. 3. The term *alone* can be joined to an essential term in both ways. For this proposition, *God alone is Father*, can mean two things, because the *Father* can signify the person of the Father, and then it is true, for no man is that person; or it can signify only the relation, and thus it is false, because the relation of paternity is found also in others, though not in a univocal sense. Likewise it is true to say God alone creates; nor does it follow, *therefore the Father alone creates*, because, as logicians say, an exclusive expression so fixes the term to which it is joined that what is said exclusively of that term cannot be said exclusively of an individual contained in that term: for instance, from the proposition, *Man alone is a mortal rational animal*, we cannot conclude, *therefore Socrates alone is such.*

Fourth Article
WHETHER AN EXCLUSIVE EXPRESSION CAN BE JOINED TO THE PERSONAL TERM?

We proceed thus to the Fourth Article: —

Objection 1. It would seem that an exclusive expression can be joined to a personal term, even though the predicate is common. For our Lord, speaking to the Father, said: *That they may know Thee, the only true God* (*Jo.* xvii. 3). Therefore the Father alone is true God.

Obj. 2. Further, He said: *No one knows the Son but the Father* (*Matt.* xi. 27); which means that the Father alone knows the Son. But to know the Son is common. Therefore the same conclusion follows.

Obj. 3. Further, an exclusive expression does not exclude what enters into the concept of the term to which it is joined. Hence it does not exclude the part, nor the universal; for it does not follow that if we say *Socrates alone is white*, therefore *his hand is not white*, or that *man is not white*. But one person is in the concept of another; as the Father is in the concept of the Son; and conversely. Therefore, when we say, The Father alone is God, we do not exclude the Son, nor the Holy Ghost; so that such a mode of speaking is true.

Obj. 4. Further, the Church sings: *Thou alone art Most High, O Jesus Christ.*[1]

On the contrary, This proposition *The Father alone is God* includes two assertions — namely, that the Father is God, and that no other besides the Father is God. But this second proposition is false, for the Son who is God, is other than the Father. Therefore this is false, The Father alone is God; and the same can be said of similar expressions.

I answer that, When we say, *The Father alone is God*, such a proposition can be taken in several senses. If *alone* means solitude in the Father, it is false in a categorematical sense; but if taken in a syncategorematical sense, it can again be understood in several ways. For if it excludes [all others] from the form of the subject, it is true; so that the sense is, *the Father alone is God* — that is, *He who, with no other is the Father, is God.* In this way Augustine explains the point when

---

1. In the *Gloria* of the Mass.：这句话在天主教弥撒礼仪的“光荣颂”里

he says: *We say the Father alone, not because He is separate from the Son, or from the Holy Ghost, but because they are not the Father together with Him.*[1] This, however, is not the usual way of speaking, unless we understand another implication, as though we said *He who alone is called the Father is God.* But in the strict sense, the exclusion affects the predicate. And thus the proposition is false if it excludes *another* in the masculine gender, but it is true if it excludes it in the neuter; because the Son is another person than the Father, but not another thing; and the same applies to the Holy Ghost. But because this expression *alone* refers, properly speaking, to the subject, it tends to exclude another Person rather than other things. Hence such a way of speaking is not to be taken too literally, but it should be respectfully expounded, whenever we find it in an authentic work.

Reply Obj. 1. When we say, *Thee the only true God*, we do not understand it as referring to the person of the Father, but to the whole Trinity, as Augustine expounds.[2] Or, if understood of the person of the Father, the other persons are not excluded by reason of the unity of essence; for *only* excludes *another* thing, as was above explained.

The same Reply can be given to *Obj.* 2. For an essential term applied to the Father does not exclude the Son or the Holy Ghost, by reason of the unity of essence. Hence we must understand that in the text quoted the term *no one* [*nemo*] is not the same *as no man* [*nullus homo*] which the word itself would seem to signify (for the person of the Father could not be excepted), but is taken according to the usual way of speaking, in a distributive sense, to mean any rational nature.

Reply Obj. 3. The exclusive expression does not exclude what enters into the concept of the term to which it is adjoined, if they do not differ in *suppositum*, as part and universal. But the Son differs in *suppositum* from the Father; and so there is no parity.

---

1. 参见 *De Trin.*, VI, 7 (PL 42, 929).
2. 参见 *Op. cit.*, VI, 9 (PL 42, 930).

Reply Obj. 4. We do not say absolutely that the Son alone is Most High; but that He alone is Most High *with the Holy Ghost*, *in the glory of God the Father.*

Question XXXII
THE KNOWLEDGE OF THE DIVINE PERSONS
(*In Four Articles*)

WE proceed to inquire concerning the knowledge of the divine persons; and this involves four points of inquiry: (1) Whether the divine persons can be known by natural reason? (2) Whether notions are to be attributed to the divine persons? (3) The number of the notions. (4) Whether we may have various contrary opinions concerning these notions?

First Article
WHETHER THE TRINITY OF THE DIVINE PERSONS CAN BE KNOWN BY NATURAL REASON ?

We proceed thus to the First Article: —

Objection 1. It would seem that the trinity of the divine persons can be known by natural reason. For philosophers came to the knowledge of God not otherwise than by natural reason.[1] Now we find that they have said many things about the trinity of persons. For Aristotle says: *Through this number* — namely, three — *we bring ourselves to acknowledge the greatness of one God, surpassing all things created.*[2] And Augustine says: *I have read in their works*, that is, in the books of the Platonists, *not in so*

---

1. 参见 Cf. R. Arnou, "Platonisme des Pères" (*Dict. de thèol. cath.*, XII, 2, 1935, coll. 2322–2327).
2. 参见 *De Caelo*, I, 1 (268a 13).

many words, but enforced by many and various reasons, that in the beginning was the Word, and the Word was with God, and the Word was God,[1] and so on; in which passage the distinction of persons is laid down. We read, moreover, in the *Gloss* on *Rom.* i. and *Exod.* viii. that the magicians of Pharaoh failed in the third sign[2] — that is, as regards knowledge of a third person — *i.e.*, of the Holy Ghost, and thus it is clear that they knew at least two persons. Likewise Trismegistus says: *The monad begot a monad, and reflected upon itself its own desire.*[3] By which words the generation of the Son and the procession of the Holy Ghost seem to be indicated. Therefore knowledge of the divine persons can be obtained by natural reason.

Obj. 2. Further, Richard of St. Victor says: *I believe without doubt that not only probable but even necessary arguments can be found for any explanation of the truth.*[4] So even to prove the Trinity some have brought forward an argument based on the infinite goodness of God, which communicates itself infinitely in the procession of the divine persons;[5] while some are moved by the consideration that *no good thing can be joyfully possessed without partnership.*[6] Augustine, on the other hand, proceeds to prove the trinity of persons by the procession of the word and of love in our own mind;[7] and we have followed him in this.[8] Therefore the trinity of persons can be known by natural reason.

---

1. 参见 *Confess.*, VII, 9 (PL 32, 740).
2. 参见 *Glossa ordin.*, super *Exod.* VIII, 19 (I, 140E). — Cf. St. Isidore, *Quaest. in Vet. Test., In Exod.*, XIV, super VIII, 19 (PL 83, 293). — Cf. also St. Augustine, *Epist.* LV., ch. 16 (PL 33, 219).
3. 参见 Pseudo-Hermes Trismegistus, *Lib.* 24 *Philosoph.*, prop. 1 (p. 31).
4. 参见 *De Trin.* (PL 196, 892).
5. 参见 Alexander of Hales, *Summa Theol.*, I, no. 295 (I, 414); St. Bonaventure, *Itin. Mentis in Deum*, VI (V, 310).
6. 参见 Richard of St. Victor, *De Trin.*, III, 3 (PL 196, 917).
7. 参见 *De Trin.*, IX, 4 (PL 42, 963).
8. 参见 Q. 27, a. 1 and 3.

Obj. 3. Further, it seems to be superfluous to teach what cannot be known by natural reason. But it may not be said that the divine teaching on the Trinity is superfluous. Therefore the trinity of persons can be known by natural reason.

On the contrary, Hilary says, *Let man not think to reach the sacred mystery of generation by his own mind.*[1] And Ambrose says, *It is impossible to know the secret of generation. The mind fails, the voice is silent.*[2] But the trinity of the divine persons is distinguished by origin of generation and procession.[3] Since, therefore, man cannot know, and with his understanding attain to, that for which no necessary argument can be given, it follows that the trinity of persons cannot be known by reason.

I answer that, It is impossible to attain to the knowledge of the Trinity by natural reason. For, as was above explained,[4] man cannot obtain a knowledge of God by natural reason except from creatures. Now creatures lead us to the knowledge of God, as effects do to their cause. Accordingly, by natural reason we can know of God only that which of necessity belongs to Him as the cause [*principium*] of all things, and we have used this as a fundamental principle in treating of God.[5] Now, the creative power of God is common to the whole Trinity; and hence it belongs to the unity of the essence, and not to the distinction of the persons. Therefore, by natural reason we can know what belongs to the unity of the essence, but not what belongs to the distinction of the persons.

Whoever, then, tries to prove the trinity of persons by natural reason, detracts from faith in two ways. First, as regards the dignity of faith itself, which consists in its being concerned with invisible

---

1. 参见 *De Trin.*, II (PL 10, 58).
2. 参见 *De Fide*, I, 10 (PL 16, 566).
3. 参见 Q. 12, a. 12
4. 参见 Q. 12, a. 4, 11 and 12
5. 参见 Q. 12, a. 12.

things that exceed human reason; wherefore the Apostle says that *faith is of things that appear not* (*Heb.* xi. 1), and the same Apostle says also, *We speak wisdom among the perfect, but not the wisdom of this world, nor of the princes of this world; but we speak the wisdom of God in a mystery which is hidden* (1 *Cor.* ii. 6, 7). Secondly, as regards the utility of drawing others to the faith. For when anyone in the endeavor to prove what belongs to faith brings forward arguments which are not cogent[1], he falls under the ridicule of the unbelievers: since they suppose that we base ourselves upon such arguments, and that we believe on their account.

Therefore, we must not attempt to prove what is of faith, except by authority alone, to those who receive the authority; while as regards others, it suffices to prove that what faith teaches is not impossible. Hence it is said by Dionysius: *Whoever wholly resists Scripture, is far off from our philosophy; whereas if he regards the truth of the sacred writings we are agreed in following the same rule.*[2]

Reply Obj. 1. The philosophers did not know the mystery of the trinity of the divine persons by its proper attributes, namely, paternity, filiation, and procession; according to the Apostle's words, *We speak the wisdom of God which none of the princes of the world* — *i.e.*, "the philosophers," according to the *Gloss*[3] — *knew* (1 *Cor.* ii. 6). Nevertheless, they knew some of the essential attributes appropriated to the persons, as power to the Father, wisdom to the Son, goodness to the Holy Ghost; as will later on appear.[4] So, when Aristotle said, *By this number*, etc.,[5] we must not take it as if he affirmed a threefold number in God, but that he wished to say that the ancients used the

1. cogent：令人信服的；强有力的
2. 参见 *De Div. Norm.*, II, 2 (PG 3, 640).
3. 参见 *Glossa interl.* (VI, 36r); Peter Lombard, *In I Cor.* (PL 191, 1548).
4. 参见 Q. 39, a. 7.
5. 参见 *De Caelo*, I, 1 (268a 13).

threefold number in their sacrifices and prayers because of some perfection residing in the number three. In the Platonic books also we find, *In the beginning was the word*,[1] not as meaning the Person begotten in God, but as meaning the ideal model whereby God made all things, and which is appropriated to the Son. And even though it be said that they knew these were appropriated to the three persons, yet they are said to have failed in the third sign — that is, in the knowledge of the third person, because they deviated from the goodness appropriated to the Holy Ghost, in that, knowing God, *they did not glorify Him as God* (*Rom.* i. 21); or because the Platonists, asserting the existence of one Primal Being whom they also declared to be the father of the universe,[2] then maintained the existence of another substance beneath him, which they called *mind*[3] or the *paternal intellect*,[4] containing the models of all things, as Macrobius relates.[5] They did not, however, assert the existence of a third separate substance which might correspond to the Holy Ghost. Now we do not thus assert that the Father and the Son differ in substance, which was the error of Origen and Arius, who in this followed the Platonists.[6] When Trismegistus says, *Monad begot monad*, etc.,[7] this does not refer to the generation of the Son, or to the procession of the Holy Ghost, but to the production of the world. For one God produced one world by reason of His love for Himself.

Reply Obj. 2. Reasoning may be brought forward for anything in a twofold way: firstly, for the purpose of furnishing sufficient proof

---

1. 参见 Cf. St. Augustine, *Confess.*, VII, 9 (PL 32, 740).
2. 参见 Macrobius, *In Somn. Scipion.*, I, 14 (p. 539).
3. 参见 *Op. cit.*, I, 2 (p. 482); 14 (p. 540).
4. 参见 St. Albert, *Metaph.*, I, tr. 4, ch. 12 (VI, 82); *De 15 Problem.*, problem. I (p. 34).
5. 参见 *In Somn. Scipion.*, I, 2 (p. 482).
6. 参见 Cf. St. Jerome, *Epist.* LXXXIV, 1 (PL 22, 746).
7. 参见 Pseudo-Hermes Trismegistus, *Lib. 24 Philosoph.*, prop. 1 (p. 31).

of some principle, as in natural science, where sufficient proof can be brought to show that the movement of the heavens is always of a uniform velocity. Reasoning is employed in another way, not as furnishing a sufficient proof of a principle, but as showing how the remaining effects are in harmony with an already posited principle; as in astronomy the theory of eccentrics and epicycles is considered as established, because thereby the sensible appearances of the heavenly movements can be explained; not, however, as if this proof were sufficient, since some other theory might explain them. In the first way we can prove that *God is one*, and the like. In the second way, arguments may be said to manifest the Trinity; that is to say, given the doctrine of the Trinity, we find arguments in harmony with it. We must not, however, think that the trinity of persons is adequately proved by such reasons. This becomes evident when we consider each point; for the infinite goodnpss of God is manifested also in creation, because to produce from nothing is an act of infinite power. For if God communicates Himself by His infinite goodness, it is not necessary that an infinite effect should proceed from God: but that, according to its own mode and capacity, the effect should receive the divine goodness. Likewise, when it is said that the joyous possession of good requires partnership, this holds in the case of a person not having perfect goodness: hence he needs to share in the good of someone of his fellows, in order to have the goodness of complete happiness. Nor is the divine image in the intellect an adequate proof about anything in God, since intellect is not in God and ourselves univocally. Hence, Augustine says that by faith we arrive at knowledge, and not conversely.[1]

Reply Obj. 3. There are two reasons why the knowledge of the divine persons was necessary for us. It was necessary for the right idea of

1. 参见 *Tract.* XXVI, super *Ioann.*, VI, 64 (PL 35, 1618).

creation. The fact of saying that God made all things by His Word excludes the error of those who say that God produced things by necessity. When we say that in Him there is a procession of love, we show that God produced creatures not because He needed them, nor because of any other extrinsic reason, but because of the love of His own goodness. So Moses, when he had said, *In the beginning God created heaven and earth*, subjoined, *God said, Let there be light*, to manifest the divine Word; and then said, *God saw the light that it was good* (*Gen.* i. 1, 3, 4), to show the proof of the divine love. The same is also found in the other works of creation.

In another way, and chiefly, that we may think rightly concerning the salvation of the human race, accomplished by the Incarnate Son, and by the gift of the Holy Ghost.

Second Article
WHETHER THERE ARE NOTIONS IN GOD?

We proceed thus to the Second Article: —

Objection 1. It would seem that in God there are no notions. For Dionysius says: *We must not dare to say anything of God but what is taught to us by the Holy Scripture.*[1] But Holy Scripture does not say anything concerning notions. Therefore there are none in God.

Obj. 2. Further, all that exists in God belongs to the unity of the essence or the trinity of the persons. But the notions do not belong to the unity of the essence, nor to the trinity of the persons; for neither can what belongs to the essence be predicated of the notions: for instance, we do not say that paternity is wise or creates; nor can what belongs to the persons be so predicated: for example, we do not say that paternity begets, nor that filiation is begotten. Therefore notions

1. 参见 *De Div. Nom.*, I, 1; 2 (PG 3, 588).

are not found in God.

Obj. 3. Further, we do not require to presuppose any abstract notions as principles of knowing things which are devoid of composition: for they are known of themselves. But the divine persons are supremely simple. Therefore we are not to suppose any notions in God.

On the contrary, Damascene says: *We recognize the difference of the hypostases* (*i.e.*, *persons*), in the *three properties*; *i.e.*, *in the paternal*, *the filial*, *and the processional.*[1] Therefore we must admit properties and notions in God.

I answer that, Prepositinus, considering the simplicity of the persons, said that in God there were no properties or notions; and so wherever they occur, he explains them as being abstract terms standing for the concrete.[2] For as we are accustomed to say, *I beseech your kindness* — *i.e.*, *you who are kind* — so, when we speak of paternity in God, we mean God the Father.

But, as was shown above, the use of concrete and abstract names in God is not in any way repugnant to the divine simplicity,[3] for we always name a thing as we understand it. Now, our intellect cannot attain to the very simplicity of the divine essence, considered in itself, and therefore our intellect apprehends and names divine things in its own way, that is, according to what is found in sensible things whence its knowledge is derived. What happens in the case of sensible things is this: we use abstract terms to signify simple forms; and to signify subsistent beings we use concrete terms. In the same way, likewise, we signify divine things, as was above stated, by abstract names in order to express their simplicity;[4]

1. 参见 *De Fide Orth.*, III, 5 (PG 94, 1000).
2. 参见 Cf. the reference in the Ottawa edition of *Sum. Theol.*, I, q. 32, a. 2 (col. 211a 8).
3. 参见 Q. 3, a. 3, ad 1.
4. 同上

whereas, to express their subsistence and completeness, we use concrete names.

But essential names must not be the only ones used in the abstract and in the concrete, as when we say *Deity* and *God*, or *wisdom* and *wise*; but the same must apply to the personal names, so that we may say paternity and Father.

Two chief motives for this can be cited. The first arises from the issue posed by heretics. For since we confess the Father, the Son and the Holy Ghost to be one God and three persons, to those who ask: *Whereby are They one God? and whereby are they three persons?* as we answer that they are one in essence or deity, so there must also be some abstract terms whereby we may answer that the persons are distinguished; and these are the properties or notions signified by an abstract term, as paternity and filiation. Therefore the divine essence is signified as *What*; and the person as *Who*; and the property as *Whereby*.

The second motive: one Person in God is related to two Persons — namely, the person of the Father to the person of the Son and to the person of the Holy Ghost. This is not, however, by one relation; otherwise it would follow that the Son also and the Holy Ghost would be related to the Father by one and the same relation. Hence, since relation alone multiplies the Trinity, it would follow that the Son and the Holy Ghost would not be two persons. Nor can it be said with Prepositinus[1] that, just as God is related in one way to creatures, although creatures are related to Him in divers ways, so the Father is related by one relation to the Son and to the Holy Ghost, although these two persons are related to the Father by two relations. For, since the specific nature of the relative is that it refers to another, it must be said that two relations are not specifically different if but one

1. 参见 Cf. above, note 30 of the present article.

opposite relation corresponds to them. For the relations of lord and father must differ specifically according to the difference of filiation and servitude. Now, all creatures are related to God as His creatures by one specific relation. But the Son and the Holy Ghost are not related to the Father by one and the same kind of relation. Hence there is no parity.

Further, in God there is no need to admit any real relation to the creature;[1] but there is no reason against multiplying logical relations in God. But in the Father there must be a real relation to the Son and to the Holy Ghost. Hence, corresponding to the two relations of the Son and of the Holy Ghost, whereby they are related to the Father, we must understand two relations in the Father, whereby He is related to the Son and to the Holy Ghost. Hence, since there is only one Person of the Father, it is necessary that the relations should be separately signified in the abstract; and these are what we mean by properties and notions.

Reply Obj. 1. Although the notions are not mentioned in Holy Scripture, yet the persons are mentioned, comprising the idea of notions, as the abstract is contained in the concrete.

Reply Obj. 2. In God the notions have their significance not after the manner of realities, but by way of certain ideas whereby the persons are known; although in God these notions or relations are real, as was stated above.[2] Therefore, whatever has order to any essential or personal act, cannot be applied to the notions; for this is against their mode of signification. Hence we cannot say that paternity begets, or creates, or is wise, or is intelligent. Essential names, however, which are not ordered to any act, but simply remove creaturely conditions from God, can be predicated of the notions; for we can say that paternity is eternal, or immense, or the like. So, too, because of the

1. 参见 Q. 28, a. 1, ad 3.
2. 参见 Q. 28, a. 1.

identity in God, substantive terms, whether personal or essential, can be predicated of the notions; for we can say that paternity is God, and that paternity is the Father.

Reply Obj. 3. Although the persons are simple, still, without prejudice to their simplicity, the proper natures of the persons can be abstractly signified, as was above explained.

Third Article
WHETHER THERE ARE FIVE NOTIONS?

We proceed thus to the Third Article: —

Objection 1. It would seem that there are not five notions. For the notions proper to the persons are the relations whereby they are distinguished from each other. But the relations in God are only four.[1] Therefore the notions are only four in number.

Obj. 2. Further, because there is only one essence in God, He is called one God; and because in Him there are three persons, He is called the Triune God. Therefore, if in God there are five notions, He may be called quinary; which cannot be allowed.

Obj. 3. Further, if there are five notions for the three persons in God, there must be in some one person two or more notions, as in the person of the Father there is innascibility, paternity and common spiration. Either these three notions differ really, or not. If they differ really, it follows that the person of the Father is composed of several realities. But if they differ only logically, it follows that one of them can be predicated of another, so that we can say that, just as the divine goodness is the same as the divine wisdom by reason of their identity in reality, so common spiration is paternity; which is not to be admitted. Therefore there are not five notions.

---

1. 参见 Q. 28, a. 4.

Obj. 4. *On the contrary.* It seems that there are more than five. For the Father is *from no one*, and hence the notion of *innascibility*; so from the Holy Ghost *no other person proceeds.* It would thus seem that the notions total six.

Obj. 5. Further, as the Father and the Son are the common origin of the Holy Ghost, so it is common to the Son and the Holy Ghost to proceed from the Father. Therefore, as one notion is common to the Father and the Son, so there ought to be one notion common to the Son and to the Holy Ghost.

I answer that, A notion is the proper idea whereby we know a divine Person. Now the divine persons are multiplied by reason of their origin: and origin includes the idea of *someone from whom another comes*, and of *someone that comes from another*; and in these two ways a person can be known. Therefore the Person of the Father cannot be known by the fact that He is from another, but by the fact that He is from no one; and thus the notion that belongs to Him is called *innascibility.*[1] As the source of another, He can be known in two ways, because as the Son is from Him, the Father is known by the notion of *paternity*; and as the Holy Ghost is from Him, He is known by the notion of *common spiration*[2]. The Son can be known as begotten by another, and thus He is known by *filiation*; and also by another person proceeding from Him, the Holy Ghost, and thus He is known in the same way as the Father is known, by *common spiration.* The Holy Ghost can be known by the fact that He is from another, or from others, and thus He is known by *procession*; but not by the fact that another is from Him, as no divine person proceeds from Him.

Therefore there are five notions in God: *innascibility*, *paternity*[3],

1. innascibility：无起源性；非产生性
2. common spiraion：共同发出；共发
3. paternity：父性

filiation[1], *common spiration*, and *procession*. Of these only four are relations, for *innascibility* is not a relation, except by reduction, as will appear later.[2] Four only are properties. For *common spiration* is not a property, because it belongs to two persons. Three are personal notions — *i.e.*, constituting persons, namely, *paternity*, *filiation*, and *procession*. *Common spiration* and *innascibility* are called notions of Persons, but not personal notions, as we shall explain further on.[3]

Reply Obj. 1. Besides the four relations, another notion must be admitted, as was above explained.

Reply Obj. 2. The divine essence is signified as a reality, and likewise the persons are signified as realities; whereas the notions are signified as ideas which make known the persons. Therefore, although God is one by unity of essence, and triune by trinity of persons, nevertheless, He is not quinary by the five notions.

Reply Obj. 3. Since the real plurality in God is founded only on relative opposition, the several properties of one Person, as they are not relatively opposed to each other, do not differ really. Nor again are they predicated of each other, because they are different ideas of the persons. In the same way, we do not say that the attribute of power is the attribute of knowledge, although we do say that His knowledge is His power.

Reply Obj. 4. Since Person implies dignity, as was stated above,[4] we cannot derive a notion of the Holy Ghost from the fact that no person is from Him. For this does not belong to His dignity, as it belongs to the authority of the Father that He is from no one.

Reply Obj. 5. The Son and the Holy Ghost do not agree in one special mode of existence derived from the Father; as the Father and

---

1. filiation：子性
2. 参见 Q. 33, a. 4, ad 3.
3. 参见 Q. 40, a. 1, ad 1.
4. 参见 Q. 29, a. 3, ad 2.

the Son agree in one special mode of producing the Holy Ghost. But the principle on which a notion is based must be something special. Thus no parity of reasoning exists.

Fourth Article

WHETHER WE MAY HAVE VARIOUS CONTRARY OPINIONS ABOUT THE NOTIONS?

We proceed thus to the Fourth Article: —

Objection 1. It would seem that we may not have various contrary opinions of the notions: For Augustine says: *No error is more dangerous than any as regards the Trinity;*[1] to which mystery the notions assuredly belong. But contrary opinions must be in some way erroneous. Therefore it is not right to have contrary opinions of the notions.

Obj. 2. Further, the persons are known by the notions. But contrary opinions concerning the persons are not permissible. Therefore neither can there be any such about the notions.

On the contrary, The notions are not articles of faith. Therefore different opinions of the notions are permissible.

I answer that, Anything is of faith in two ways. *Directly*, and such are truths that come to us principally as divinely taught, as the trinity and unity of God, the Incarnation of the Son, and the like; and concerning these truths a false opinion of itself involves heresy, especially if it be held obstinately. A thing is of faith *indirectly*, if the denial of it involves as a consequence something against faith, as, for instance, if anyone said that Samuel was not the son of Elcana; for it follows that the divine Scripture would be false. Concerning such things anyone may have a false opinion without danger of heresy, before the matter has been considered or settled as involving consequences against faith, and

---

1. 参见 *De Trin.*, I, 3 (PL 42, 822).

particularly if no obstinacy be shown; whereas when it is manifest, and especially if the Church has decided that consequences follow against faith, then the error cannot be free from heresy. For this reason, many things are now considered as heretical which were formerly not so considered, as their consequences are now more manifest.

So we must conclude that we may, without danger of heresy, entertain contrary opinions about the notions, if we do not mean to uphold anything at variance with faith. If, however, anyone should entertain a false opinion of the notions, knowing or thinking that consequences against the faith would follow, he would lapse into heresy.

By what has been said all the objections may be solved.

Question XXXIII
THE PERSON OF THE FATHER
(*In Four Articles*)

WE now consider the persons singly; and first, the Person of the Father, concerning Whom there are four points of inquiry: (1) Whether the Father is the Principle? (2) Whether the person of the Father is properly signified by this name *Father*? (3) Whether *Father* in God is said personally before it is said essentially? (4) Whether it belongs to the Father alone to be unbegotten?

First Article
WHETHER IT BELONGS TO THE FATHER TO BE THE PRINCIPLE?

We proceed thus to the First Article: —

Objection 1. It would seem that the Father cannot be called the principle of the Son, or of the Holy Ghost. For principle and cause are the same, according to the philosopher.[1] But we do not say that the Father is the cause of the Son. Therefore we must not say that He is the principle of the Son.

Obj. 2. Further, a principle is so called in relation to the thing principled. So if the Father is the principle of the Son, it follows that the Son is a person principled, and is therefore created; which appears false.

---

1. 参见 *Metaph.*, III, 2 (1003b 24).

Obj. 3. Further, the term *principle* is taken from *priority.* But in God there is no *before* and *after*, as Athanasius says.[1] Therefore, in speaking of God, we ought not to use the term *principle.*

On the contrary, Augustine says, *The Father is the Principle of the whole Deity.*[2]

I answer that, The term *principle* signifies only that whence another proceeds, since anything whence something proceeds in any way we call a principle; and conversely. As the Father then is the one whence another proceeds, it follows that the Father is a principle.

Reply Obj. 1. The Greeks use the words *cause* and *principle* indifferently, when speaking of God; whereas the Latin Doctors do not use the word *cause*, but only *principle.* The reason is because *principle* is a wider term than *cause*, just as *cause* is more common than *element.* For the first term of a thing, as also the first part, is called the principle, but not the cause. Now the wider a term is, the more suitable it is to use as regards God,[3] because the more special terms are, the more determinately they express the mode adapted to the creature. Hence this term *cause* seems to mean diversity of substance and dependence of one on another; which is not implied in the term *principle.* For in all kinds of causes there is always to be found between the cause and the effect a distance of perfection or of power: whereas we use the term *principle* even in things which have no such difference, but have only a certain order to each other; as when we say that a point is the principle of a line, or also when we say that the first part of a line is the principle of a line.

Reply Obj. 2. It is the custom with the Greeks to say that the Son and the Holy Ghost are principled. This is not, however, the custom with our Doctors; because, although we attribute to the Father something of authority by reason of His being the principle, still we do not attribute

---

1. 参见 Cf *Symb.* "*Quicumque*" (Denzinger, no. 39).
2. 参见 *De Trin.*, IV, 20 (PL 42, 908).
3. 参见 Q. 13, a. 11.

any kind of subjection or inferiority to the Son, or to the Holy Ghost, to avoid any occasion of error. In this way, Hilary says: *By authority of the Giver, the Father is the greater; nevertheless, the Son is not less, to Whom oneness of nature is given.*[1]

Reply Obj. 3. Although this term principle, as regards its derivation, seems to be taken from priority, still it does not signify priority, but origin. For what a term signifies, and the reason why it was imposed, are not the same thing, as was stated above.[2]

Second Article

WHETHER THIS NAME FATHER IS PROPERLY THE NAME OF A DIVINE PERSON ?

We proceed thus to the Second Article: —

Objection 1. It would seem that this name *Father* is not properly the name of a divine person. For the name *Father* signifies relation, but *person* is an individual substance. Therefore this name *Father* is not properly a name signifying a Person.

Obj. 2. Further, a begetter is more common than father, for every father begets; but it is not so conversely. But a more common term is more properly applied to God, as was stated above. Therefore the more proper name of the divine person is *begetter* and *genitor* than Father.

Obj. 3. Further, a metaphorical term cannot be the proper name of anyone. But the word of our intellect is metaphorically called begotten, or off-spring; and consequently he to whom the word belongs is metaphorically called father. Therefore the principle of the Word in God is not properly called Father.

Obj. 4. Further, everything which is said properly of God is said of God first before creatures. But generation appears to apply to creatures

1. 参见 *De Trin.*, IX (PL 10, 325).
2. 参见 Q. 13, a. 3, ad 2; a. 8.

before God, because generation seems to be truer when the one who proceeds is distinct, not only by relation but also by essence, from the one whence it proceeds. Therefore the name *Father* taken from generation does not seem to be the proper name of any divine person.

On the contrary, It is said (*Ps.* lxxxviii. 27): *He shall cry out to me: Thou art my Father.*

I answer that, The proper name of any person signifies that whereby the person is distinguished from all other persons. For as body and soul belong to the nature of man, so to the concept of this particular man belong *this soul and this body*, as it is said in *Metaph.* vii.;[1] and by these is this particular man distinguished from all other men. Now it is paternity which distinguishes the person of the Father from all the other persons. Hence this name *Father*, whereby paternity is signified, is the proper name of the person of the Father.

Reply Obj. 1. Among us relation is not a subsisting person. So this name *father* among us does not signify a person, but the relation of a person. In God, however, it is not so, as some wrongly thought; for in God the relation signified by the name *Father* is a subsisting person. Hence, as was above explained, this name *person* in God signifies a relation subsisting in the divine nature.[2]

Reply Obj. 2. According to the Philosopher, a thing is denominated chiefly by its perfection, and by its end.[3] Now generation signifies something in process of being made, whereas paternity signifies that the generation is something completed; and therefore the name *Father* is more expressive as regards the divine person than genitor or begetter.

Reply Obj. 3. In human nature the word is not something subsistent, and hence it is not properly called begotten or son. But the divine

1. 参见 *Metaph.*,VI, 11 (1037a 9).
2. 参见 Q. 29, a. 4.
3. 参见 *De An.*, II, 4 (416b 23).

Word is something subsistent in the divine nature; and hence He is properly and not metaphorically called Son, and His principle is called Father.

Reply Obj. 4. The terms *generation* and *paternity*, like the other terms properly applied to God, are said of God before creatures as regards the thing signified, but not as regards the mode of signification. Hence also the Apostle says, *I bend my knee to the Father of my Lord Jesus Christ, from whom all paternity in heaven and on earth is named* (*Ephes.* iii. 14). This is explained thus. It is manifest that generation receives its species from its terminus[1], which is the form of the thing generated; and the nearer this terminus is to the form of the generator, the truer and more perfect is the generation; as univocal generation is more perfect than non-univocal, for it belongs to the essence of a generator to generate what is like itself in form. Hence the very fact that in the divine generation the form of the Begetter[2] and Begotten[3] is numerically the same, whereas in creatures it is not the same numerically, but only specifically, shows that generation, and consequently paternity, is applied to God before creatures. Hence the very fact that in God a distinction exists of the Begotten from the Begetter as regards only relation belongs to the truth of the divine generation and paternity.

Third Article

WHETHER THIS NAME *FATHER* IS APPLIED TO GOD WITH PRIORITY AS A PERSONAL NAME?

We proceed thus to the Third Article: —

Objection 1. It would seem that this name *Father* is not applied to God with priority as a personal name. For in the intellect, the common

---

1. terminus：终点
2. the Begetter：产生者，指天父
3. the Begotten：受生者，指圣子耶稣基督

precedes the proper. But this name *Father*, as a personal name, belongs to the person of the Father, and taken in an essential sense it is common to the whole Trinity; for we say *Our Father* to the whole Trinity. Therefore Father comes first as an essential name before its personal sense.

Obj. 2. Further, in things of which the concept is the same there is no priority of predication. But paternity and filiation seem to be of the same nature, according as a divine person is Father of the Son, and the whole Trinity is our (that is, the creature's) Father; since, according to Basil,[1] to receive is common to the creature and to the Son. Therefore *Father* in God is not taken as an essential name before it is taken personally.

Obj. 3. Further, it is not possible to compare things which have not a common concept. But the Son is compared to the creature by reason of filiation or generation, according to *Col.* i. 15: *Who is the image of the invisible God, the first-born of every creature.* Therefore paternity taken in a personal sense is not prior to, but has the same concept as, paternity taken essentially.

On the contrary, The eternal comes before the temporal. But God is the Father of the Son from eternity; while He is Father of the creature in time. Therefore paternity in God is taken in a personal sense in relation to the Son before it is so taken in relation to the creature.

I answer that, A name is applied to that wherein is perfectly contained its whole signification before it is applied to that which only partially contains it; for the latter bears the name by reason of a kind of a likeness to that which answers perfectly to the signification of the name, since all imperfect things are taken from perfect things. Hence this name *lion* is applied first to the animal containing the whole nature of a lion, and which is properly so called, before it is applied to

1. 参见 *Hom.* XV, *De Fide* (PG 31, 468).

a man who shows something of a lion's nature, as boldness or strength, or the like. For of man it is said by way of likeness.

Now it is manifest from the foregoing that the perfect idea of paternity and filiation is to be found in God the Father, and in God the Son, because the nature and glory of the Father and the Son is one.[1] But in the creature, filiation is found in relation to God, not in a perfect manner, since the Creator and the creature have not the same nature, but by way of a certain likeness, which is the more perfect the nearer we approach to the true nature of filiation. For God is called the Father of some creatures by reason only of a *trace*, for instance of irrational creatures, according to *Job* xxxviii. 28: *Who is the father of the rain? or who begot the drops of dew?* Of some, namely, the rational creature, He is the Father by reason of the likeness of His image, according to *Deut.* xxxii. 6: *Is He not thy Father, who possessed, and made, and created thee?* And of others He is the Father by the likeness of grace, and these are also called adoptive sons, as ordained to the heritage of eternal glory by the gift of grace which they have received, according to *Rom.* viii. 16, 17: *The Spirit Himself gives testimony to our spirit that we are the sons of God; and if sons, heirs also.* Lastly, He is the Father of others by the likeness of glory, inasmuch as they have already obtained possession of the heritage of glory, according to *Rom.* v. 2: *We glory in the hope of the glory of the sons of God.* Therefore it is plain that *paternity* is applied to God with priority as signifying the relation of one Person to another Person, before it signifies the relation of God to creatures.

Reply Obj. 1. Common terms, taken absolutely, come before proper terms according to the order of our intellect because they are included in the understanding of proper terms; but not conversely. For in the concept of the person of the Father, God is understood; but not

1. 参见 Q. 27, a. 2 ; q. 28, a. 4.

conversely. But common terms which signify relation to the creature come after proper terms which signify personal relations, because the person proceeding in God proceeds as the principle of the production of creatures. For as the word conceived in the mind of the artist is understood to proceed from the artist prior to the procession of the work of art, which is produced to the likeness of the word conceived in the artist's mind, so the Son proceeds from the Father before the creature, to which the name of filiation is applied according as it participates in the likeness of the Son. This is clear from the words of *Row*. viii. 29: *Whom He foreknew and predestined to be made conformable to the image of His Son.*

Reply Obj. 2. *To receive* is said to be common to the creature and to the Son not in a univocal sense, but according to a certain remote likeness whereby He is called the First Born of creatures. Hence the authority quoted subjoins: *That He may be the First Born among many brethren* (*Rom*. viii. 20), after saying that some were conformed to the image of the Son of God. But the Son of God possesses a position of singularity above others, in having by nature what He receives, as Basil also declares;[1] hence He is called the only begotten (*Jo*. i. 18): *The only begotten Who is in the bosom of the Father, He hath declared unto us.*

From this appears the *Reply to Obj*. 3.

Fourth Article
WHETHER IT IS PROPER TO THE FATHER TO BE UNBEGOTTEN?

We proceed thus to the Fourth Article: —

Objection 1. It would seem that it is not proper to the Father to be unbegotten. For every property supposes something in that of which it

1. 参见 *Hom*. XV, *De Fide* (PG 31, 468).

is the property. But *unbegotten* supposes nothing in the Father; it only removes something. Therefore it does not signify a property of the Father.

Obj. 2. Further, *Unbegotten* is taken either in a privative, or in a negative, sense. If in a negative sense, then whatever is not begotten can be called unbegotten. But the Holy Ghost is not begotten; neither is the divine essence. Therefore to be unbegotten belongs also to the essence; thus it is not proper to the Father. But if it be taken in a privative sense, since every privation signifies imperfection in the thing which is the subject of privation, it follows that the Person of the Father is imperfect; which cannot be.

Obj. 3. Further, in God, *unbegotten* does not signify relation, for it is not used relatively. Therefore it signifies substance; therefore unbegotten and begotten differ in substance. But the Son, Who is begotten, does not differ from the Father in substance. Therefore the Father ought not to be called unbegotten.

Obj. 4. Further, property means what belongs to one alone. Since, then, there are more than one in God proceeding from another, there is nothing to prevent several not receiving their being from another. Therefore the Father is not alone unbegotten.

Obj. 5. Further, as the Father is the principle of the person begotten, so is He of the person proceeding. So if by reason of His opposition to the person begotten, it is proper to the Father to be unbegotten, it follows that it is proper to Him also to be unproceeding.

On the contrary, Hilary says: *One is from one — that is, the Begotten is from the Unbegotten*[1] *— namely, by the property in each one respectively of innascibility and origin.*[2]

I answer that, As in creatures there exist a first and a secondary principle, so also in the divine Persons, in Whom there is no before or

1. the Unbegotten：非受生者，指天父
2. 参见 *Dr Trin.*, IV (PL 10, 120).

after, is found the principle not from a principle, Who is the Father; and the principle from a principle, Who is the Son.

Now in created things a first principle is known in two ways. In one way, as the first *principle*, by reason of its having a relation to what proceeds from itself; in another way, inasmuch as it is a *first* principle by reason of its not being from another. So, too, the Father is known both by paternity and by common spiration in relation to the persons proceeding from Himself. But as the principle, not from a principle, He is known by the fact that He is not from another; and this belongs to the property of innascibility, signified by this word *unbegotten*.

Reply Obj. 1. Some there are who say that innascibility, signified by the term *unbegotten*, as a property of the Father, is not a negative term only, but either that it means both these things together — namely, *that the Father is from no one, and that He is the principle of others*; or that it means *universal authority*, or also His *plenitude as the source of all*.[1] This, however, does not seem true, because thus innascibility would not be a property distinct from paternity and spiration, but would include them as the proper is included in the common. For *source* and *authority* signify in God nothing but a principle of origin. We must therefore say with Augustine that *unbegotten* signifies the negation of passive generation.[2] For he says that *unbegotten has the same meaning as* '*not a son.*' Nor does it follow that *unbegotten* is thus not the proper notion of the Father; for primary and simple things are made known by negations; as, for instance, a point is defined as that which has no part.

Reply Obj. 2. *Unbegotten* is taken sometimes in a negative sense only and in that sense Jerome says that *the Holy Ghost is unbegotten* — that is, He is not begotten.[3] Then, *unbegotten* may also be taken in a kind of

1. 参见 For a statement of these opinions, cf. William of Auxerre, *Summa Aurea*, I , tr. 8, ch. 5 (fol. 16va).
2. 参见 *De Trin.*, V, 17 (PL 42, 916).
3. 参见 Cf . Peter Lombard, *Sent.*, I, xiii, 4 (I, 89).

privative sense, though not as implying any imperfection. For privation can be taken in many ways. In one way, when a thing has not what naturally belongs to another, even though it is not of its own nature to have it; as, for instance, if a stone were to be called a dead thing, as not possessing life, which naturally belongs to some other things. In another sense, privation is so called when something has not what naturally belongs to some members of its genus; as for instance, when a mole is called blind. In a third sense, privation means the absence of that which something ought to have; in which sense, privation signifies an imperfection. In this sense, *unbegotten* is not attributed to the Father as a privation, but it may be so attributed in the second sense, meaning that a certain person of the divine nature is not begotten, while some person of the same nature is begotten. In this sense, however, the term *unbegotten* can be applied also to the Holy Ghost. Hence to consider it as a term proper to the Father alone, it must be further understood that the name *unbegotten* belongs to a divine person as the principle of another person; so that it be thus understood to mean negation in the genus of principle taken personally in God. Or, in other words, we must understand in the term *unbegotten* that He is not in any way derived from another, and not only that He is not from another only by way of generation. In this sense, the term *unbegotten* does not belong at all to the Holy Ghost, Who is from another by procession, as a subsisting person; nor does it belong to the divine essence, of which it may be said that it is in the Son or in the Holy Ghost from another — namely, from the Father.

Reply Obj. 3. According to Damascene, *unbegotten* in one sense signifies the same as *uncreated*;[1] and thus it applies to substance, for thereby does created substance differ from the uncreated. In another sense, it signifies *what is not begotten*, and in this sense it is a relative

---

1. 参见 *De Fide Orth.*, I, 8 (PG 94, 817).

term; just as negation is reduced to the genus of affirmation, as *not man* is reduced to the genus of substance, and *not white* to the genus of quality. Hence, since *begotten* implies relation in God, *unbegotten* also belongs to relation. Thus it does not follow that the Father unbegotten is substantially distinguished from the Son begotten, but only by relation; that is, as the relation of Son is denied of the Father.

Reply Obj. 4. In every genus there must be something first; so in the divine nature there must be some one principle which is not from another, and which we call *unbegotten*. To admit two innascibles[1] is to suppose the existence of two Gods, and two divine natures. Hence Hilary says: *As there is one God, so there cannot be two innascibles.*[2] And this especially because, did two innascibles exist, one would not be from the other, and they would not be distinguished by relative opposition: therefore they would be distinguished from each other by diversity of nature.

Reply Obj. 5. The property of the Father, whereby He is not from another, is more clearly signified by the removal of the nativity of the Son, than by the removal of the procession of the Holy Ghost; both because the procession of the Holy Ghost has no special name, as was stated above,[3] and because even in the order of nature it presupposes the generation of the Son. Hence, once it is denied of the Father that He is begotten, although He is the principle of generation, it follows, as a consequence, that He does not proceed by the procession of the Holy Ghost, because the Holy Ghost is not the principle of generation, but proceeds from the person begotten.

---

1. innascibles：非出生者，无起源者
2. 参见 *De Synod.* (PL 10, 521).
3. 参见 Q. 27, a. 4, ad 3.

Question XXXIV
THE PERSON OF THE SON
(*In Three Articles*)

WE next consider the person of the Son. Three names are attributed to the Son — namely, *Son*, *Word*, and *Image*. The idea of Son is gathered from the idea of Father. Hence it remains for us to consider Word and Image.

Concerning Word there are three points of inquiry: (1) Whether *Word* is an essential term in God, or a personal term? (2) Whether it is the proper name of the Son? (3) Whether in the name of Word is expressed relation to creatures?

First Article
WHETHER *WORD* IN GOD IS A PERSONAL NAME?

We proceed thus to the First Article: —

Objection 1. It would seem that Word in God is not a personal name. For personal names are applied to God in a proper sense, as *Father* and *Son*. But *Word is applied to God metaphorically*, as Origen says on (*Jo*. i. 1): *In the beginning was the Word.*[1] Therefore Word is not a personal name in God.

Obj. 2. Further, according to Augustine, *The Word is knowledge with love*;[2] and according to Anselm, *To speak is to the Supreme Spirit nothing*

---

1. 参见 *In Ioann.*, I (PG 14, 59).
2. 参见 *De Trin.*, IX, 10 (PL 42, 969).

but to see by thought.[1] But knowledge, thought, and sight are essential terms in God. Therefore Word is not a personal term in God.

Obj. 3. Further, it is essential to a word to be spoken. But, according to Anselm, as the Father is intelligent, the Son intelligent, and the Holy Ghost intelligent,[2] so the Father speaks, the Son speaks, and the Holy Ghost speaks; and likewise, each one of them is spoken. Therefore, the name Word is used as an essential term in God, and not in a personal sense.

Obj. 4. Further, no divine person is made. But the Word of God is something made. For it is said, *Fire, hail, snow, ice, the storms which do His Word* (*Ps.* cxlviii. 8). Therefore the Word[3] is not a personal name in God.

On the contrary, Augustine says: *As the Son is related to the Father, so also is the Word to Him Whose Word He is.*[4] But Son is a personal name, since it is said relatively. Therefore so also is *Word.*

I answer that, The name *Word* in God, if taken in its proper sense, is a personal name, and in no way an essential name.

To see how this is true, we must know that our own word, taken in its proper sense, has a threefold meaning; while in a fourth sense it is taken improperly or figuratively. The clearest and most common sense is that in which *word* is said of what is spoken by the voice; and this proceeds from an interior source as regards two things found in the exterior word — that is, the vocal sound itself, and the signification of the sound. For, according to the Philosopher, vocal sound signifies the concept of the intellect;[5] or, according to another text, the vocal sound proceeds from the signification or the imagination, as is stated

1. 参见 *Monolog.*, LXIII (PL 158, 208).
2. 参见 *Op. cit.*, LIX (PL 158, 205).
3. the Word：圣言，指耶稣基督
4. 参见 *De Trin.*, VII, 2 (PL 42, 936).
5. 参见 *Perih.*, I, 1 (16a 3).

in *De Anima*, ii.[1] The vocal sound which has no signification cannot be called a word: wherefore the exterior vocal sound is called a word from the fact that it signifies the interior concept of the mind. Therefore it follows that, first and chiefly, the interior concept of the mind is called a word; secondarily, the vocal sound itself, signifying the interior concept, is so called; and thirdly, the imagination of the vocal sound is called a word. Damascene expresses these three kinds of words, saying that *word* is called *the natural movement of the intellect, whereby it is moved, and understands, and thinks, as a light and a luminous beam*;[2] which is the first kind. *Again*, he says, *the word is what is not pronounced by a vocal word, but is uttered in the heart*; which is the third kind. *Again* also, *the word is the angel*, that is, the messenger of *intelligence*; which is the second kind.

Word is also used in a fourth way figuratively for that which is signified or effected by a word; thus we are wont to say, *this is the word I have said, or which the king has commanded*, alluding to some deed signified by the word either by way of assertion or of command.

Now *word* is taken strictly in God, as signifying the concept of the intellect. Hence Augustine says: *Whoever can understand the word, not only before it is sounded, but also before thought has clothed it with imaginary sound, can already see some likeness of that Word of Whom it is said: In the beginning was the Word.*[3] The concept itself of the heart has of its own nature to proceed from something other than itself — namely, from the knowledge of the one conceiving. Hence *Word*, according as we use the term strictly of God, signifies something proceeding from another; which belongs to the nature of personal terms in God, inasmuch as the divine persons are distinguished by origin.[4] Hence the term *Word*,

---

1. 参见 Aristotle. *De An.*, II, 8 (420b 32).
2. 参见 *De Fide Orth.*, I, 13 (PG 94, 857).
3. 参见 *De Trin.*, XV, 10 (PL 42, 1071).
4. 参见 Q. 27, introd.; q. 32, a. 3.

according as we use the term strictly of God, is to be taken as said not essentially, but personally.

Reply Obj. 1. The Arians, who sprang from Origen.[1] declared that the Son differed in substance from the Father. Hence, they endeavored to maintain that when the Son of God is called the Word, this is not to be understood in a strict sense, lest the idea of the Word proceeding should compel them to confess that the Son of God is of the same substance as the Father. For the interior word proceeds in such a manner from the one who expressed it, as to remain within him. But supposing Word to be said metaphorically of God, we must still assert the Word in God in its strict sense. For if a thing be called a word metaphorically, this can only be by reason of some manifestation[2]; either it makes something manifest as a word, or it is manifested by a word. If manifested by a word, there must exist a word whereby it is manifested. If it is called a word because it exteriorly manifests, the things which it exteriorly manifests cannot be called words except in as far as they signify the interior concept of the mind, which anyone may manifest also by exterior signs. Therefore, although Word may be sometimes said of God metaphorically, nevertheless, we must also admit Word in the proper sense, and which is said personally.

Reply Obj. 2. Nothing belonging to the intellect can be applied to God personally, except word alone; for word alone signifies that which emanates from another. For what the intellect forms in its conception is the word. Now, the intellect itself, according as it is made actual by the intelligible species, is considered absolutely; likewise the act of understanding which is to the actual intellect what being [*esse*] is to actual being [*ens in actu*]; since the act of understanding does not signify an act going out from the intelligent agent, but an act remaining in the agent. Therefore when we say that the word is

1. 参见 Cf. Origen, *In Ioann.*, II (PG 14, 109).
2. manifestation：显现；显示

knowledge, the term knowledge does not mean the act of a knowing intellect, or any one of its habits, but stands for what the intellect conceives by knowing. Hence also Augustine says that the Word is *begotten wisdom*;[1] for it is nothing but the concept of the Wise One; and in the same way It can be called *begotten knowledge*. Thus can also be explained how to *speak* is in God *to see by thought*, inasmuch as the Word is conceived by the gaze of the divine thought. Still the term *thought* does not properly apply to the Word of God. For Augustine says: *Therefore do we speak of the Word of God, and not of the Thought of God, lest we believe that in God there is something unstable, now assuming the form of Word, now putting off that form and remaining latent and as it were formless.*[2] For thought consists properly in the search after truth, and this has no place in God. But when the intellect attains to the form of truth, it does not think, but perfectly contemplates the truth. Hence Anselm takes *thought* in an improper sense for *contemplation*.[3]

Reply Obj. 3. As, properly speaking, Word in God is said personally, and not essentially, so likewise is *to speak*. Hence, as the Word is not common to the Father, Son, and Holy Ghost, so it is not true that the Father, Son, and Holy Ghost are one speaker. So Augustine says: *He who speaks in that coeternal Word is understood as not alone in God.*[4] On the other hand, *to be spoken* belongs to each Person, for not only is the word spoken, but also the reality understood or signified by the word. Therefore in this manner to one person alone in God does it belong to be spoken in the same way as a word is spoken; whereas in the way whereby a reality is spoken as being understood in the word, it belongs to each Person to be spoken. For the Father, by understanding Himself, the Son, and the Holy Ghost, and all other things comprised in this

1. 参见 *De Trin.*, VII, 2 (PL 42, 936).
2. 参见 *Op. cit.*, XV, 16 (PL 42, 1079).
3. contemplation：静观；默观
4. 参见 *De Trin.*, VII, 1 (PL 42, 933).

knowledge, conceives the Word; so that thus the whole Trinity is *spoken* in the Word, and likewise also all creatures, just as the intellect of a man by the word he conceives in the act of understanding a stone, speaks a stone.

Anselm took the term *speak* improperly for the act of understanding; whereas they really differ from each other. For to *understand* means only the relation of the intelligent agent to the thing understood, in which relation no idea of origin is conveyed, but only a certain information of our intellect, inasmuch as our intellect is made actual by the form of the thing understood. In God, however, to understand means complete identity, because in God the intellect and the thing understood are altogether the same, as was proved above.[1] But to *speak* means chiefly the relation to the word conceived; for *to speak* is nothing but to utter a word. But by means of the word, to speak implies a relation to the thing understood which is manifested in the word uttered to the one who understands. Thus, only the Person who utters the Word is *speaker* in God, although each Person understands and is understood, and consequently is spoken by the Word.

Reply Obj. 4. The term *word* is there taken figuratively, according as the thing signified or effected by word is called word. For thus creatures are said to do the word of God, as executing any effect, whereto they are ordained from the conceived Word of the divine wisdom; as anyone is said to do the word of the king when he does the work to which he is appointed by the king's word.

Second Article
WHETHER *WORD* IS THE SON'S PROPER NAME?

We proceed thus to the Second Article: —

---

1. 参见 Q. 14, a. 2 and 4.

Objection 1. It would seem that *Word* is not the proper name of the Son. For the Son is a subsisting person in God. But word does not signify a subsisting thing, as appears in ourselves. Therefore *Word* cannot be the proper name of the person of the Son.

Obj. 2. Further, the word proceeds from the speaker by being uttered. Therefore if the Son is properly the Word, He proceeds from the Father by way only of utterance; which is the heresy[1] of Valentine, as appears from Augustine.[2]

Obj. 3. Further, every proper name of a person signifies some property of that person. Therefore, if the Word is the Son's proper name, it signifies some property of His; and thus there will be several more properties in God than those above mentioned.[3]

Obj. 4. Further, Whoever understands conceives a word in the act of understanding. But the Son understands. Therefore some word belongs to the Son: and consequently to be Word is not proper to the Son.

Obj. 5. Further, it is said of the Son (*Heb*, i. 3): *Bearing all things by the word of His power*; whence Basil infers that the Holy Ghost is the son's Word.[4] Therefore to be Word is not proper to the Son.

On the contrary, Augustine says: *By* Word *we understand the Son alone.*[5]

I answer that, *Word*, said of God in its proper sense, is used personally, and is the proper name of the person of the Son. For it signifies an emanation of the intellect, and the person Who proceeds in God by way of an emanation of the intellect is called the Son; and this procession is called generation, as we have shown above.[6] Hence it follows that the Son alone is properly called Word in God.

---

1. heresy：异端邪说；异教
2. 参见 *De Haeres.*, 11 (PL 42, 28).
3. 参见 Q. 32, a. 3.
4. 参见 *Contra Eunom.*, V (PG 29, 732).
5. 参见 *De Trin.*, VI, 2 (PL 42, 925).
6. 参见 Q. 27, a. 2.

Reply Obj. 1. *To be* and *to understand* are not the same in us. Hence that which in us has intelligible being does not belong to our nature. But in God *to be* and to *understand* are one and the same: hence the Word of God is not an accident in Him, or an effect of His, but belongs to His very nature. It must therefore needs be something subsistent, for whatever is in the nature of God subsists; and so Damascene says that *the Word of God is substantial and has a hypostatic being; but other words* (as our own) *are forces of the soul.*[1]

Reply Obj. 2. The error of Valentine was condemned, not as the Arians pretended (according to the testimony of Hilary[2]), because he asserted that the Son was born by being uttered; but because of the different mode of utterance proposed by its author, as appears from Augustine.[3]

Reply Obj. 3. In the term *Word* the same property is comprised as in the term Son. Hence Augustine says: *Word and Son express the same.*[4] For the Son's nativity, which is His personal property, is signified by different names, which are attributed to the Son to express His perfection in various ways. To show that He is of the same nature as the Father, He is called the Son; to show that He is co-eternal, He is called the Splendor; to show that He is altogether like, He is called the Image; to show that He is begotten immaterially, He is called the Word. All these truths cannot be expressed by only one name.

Reply Obj. 4. To be intelligent belongs to the Son in the same way as it belongs to Him to be God, since to understand is said of God essentially, as was stated above. Now the Son is God begotten, and not God begetting; and hence He is intelligent, not as producing a Word, but as the Word proceeding; inasmuch as in God the Word proceeding

---

1. 参见 *De Fide Orth.*, I, 13 (PG 94, 857).
2. 参见 *De Trin.*, VI (PL 10, 162).
3. 参见 *De Haeres.*, 11 (PL 42, 28).
4. 参见 *De Trin.*, VII, 2 (PL 42, 936).

does not differ really from the divine intellect, but is distinguished from the principle of the Word only by relation.

Reply Obj. 5. When it is said of the Son, *Bearing all things by the word of His power*, *word* is taken figuratively for the effect of the Word. Hence the *Gloss* says that *word* is here taken to mean command;[1] inasmuch as by the effect of the power of the Word things are kept in being, just as by the effect of the power of the Word things are brought into being. As for Basil, he is speaking improperly and figuratively in applying Word to the Holy Ghost. His meaning is that everything which manifests a person may be called his word; and so in that way the Holy Ghost may be called the Son's Word, because He manifests the Son.

Third Article
WHETHER THE NAME *WORD* IMPLIES RELATION TO CREATURES?

We proceed thus to the Third Article: —

Objection 1. It would seem that the name *Word* does not imply relation to creatures. For every name that connotes some effect in creatures is said of God essentially. But Word is not said essentially, but personally. Therefore Word does not imply relation to creatures.

Obj. 2. Further, whatever implies relation to creatures is said of God in time; as *Lord* and *Creator*. But Word is said of God from eternity. Therefore it does not imply relation to the creature.

Obj. 3. Further, Word implies relation to the source whence it proceeds. Therefore if it implies relation to the creature, it follows that the Word proceeds from the creature.

Obj. 4. Further, Ideas are many according to the various relations to creatures. Therefore, if Word implies relation to creatures, it follows

1. 参见 *Glossa interl.*, super *Hebr.* I, 3 (VI, 134r); Peter Lombard, *In Hebr.*, super I, 3 (PL 192, 406).

that in God there is not one Word only, but many.

Obj. 5. Further, if Word implies relation to the creature, this can be only because creatures are known by God. But God does not know beings only; He knows also non-beings. Therefore in the Word are implied relations to non-beings; which appears to be false.

On the contrary, Augustine says, that *the name Word signifies not only relation to the Father, but also relation to those beings which are made through the Word, by His operative power.*[1]

I answer that, *Word* expresses relation to creatures. For God, by knowing Himself, knows every creature. Now the word conceived in the mind is representative of everything that is actually understood. Hence there are in ourselves different words for the different things which we understand. But because God, by one act, understands Himself and all things, His one only Word is expressive not only of the Father, but of all creatures. And as the knowledge of God is only cognitive as regards God, whereas, as regards creatures, it is both cognitive and operative, so the Word of God is only expressive of what is in God the Father, but is both expressive and operative of creatures. And so it is said (*Ps*, xxxii. 9): *He spake, and they were made*; because in the Word is expressed the operative idea of what God makes.

Reply Obj. 1. The nature is also included indirectly in the name of the person; for a person is an individual substance of a rational nature. Therefore, the name of a divine person, as regards the personal relation, does not express relation to the creature; but the relation is expressed in the name which belongs to the nature. Yet there is nothing to prevent the person from expressing relation to creatures, so far as the essence is included in its meaning: for as it properly belongs to the Son to be the Son, so it properly belongs to Him to be God begotten, or the Creator begotten; and in this way the name Word expresses relation to creatures.

1. 参见 *Lib. 83 quaest.*, q. 63 (PL 40, 54).

Reply Obj. 2. Since relations result from actions, some names express that relation of God to creatures, which follows on the action of God passing into some exterior effect; as *to create* and *to govern*. Such names are applied to God in time. But others express a relation which follows from an action which does not pass into an exterior effect, but abides in the agent, as to know and to will. Such names are not applied to God in time; and this kind of relation to creatures is implied in the name *Word*. Nor is it true that all names which express the relation of God to creatures are applied to Him in time; but only those names are applied in time which express relation following on the action of God passing into exterior effect.

Reply Obj. 3. Creatures are known to God, not by a knowledge derived from the creatures themselves, but by His own essence. Hence it is not necessary that the Word should proceed from creatures, even though the Word is expressive of creatures.

Reply Obj. 4. The name *Idea* is imposed chiefly to signify relation to creatures; it is therefore used in the plural in God, and not said personally. But the name *Word* is imposed chiefly to signify relation to the speaker, and consequently, relation to creatures, inasmuch as God, by understanding Himself, understands all creatures; and so there is only one Word in God, and that a personal one.

Reply Obj. 5. In the way in which the knowledge of God is of non-beings, so is the Word of God; because the Word of God contains no less than does the knowledge of God, as Augustine says.[1] It remains, however, that the Word is of beings as expressing and making them; whereas it is of non-beings as expressing and manifesting them.

---

1. 参见 *De Trin.*, XV, 14 (PL 42, 1076).

Question XXXV
THE IMAGE
(*In Two Articles*)

WE next inquire concerning the Image: about which there are two points of inquiry: (1) Whether Image in God is said personally? (2) Whether this name belongs to the Son alone?

First Article
WHETHER IMAGE IN GOD IS SAID PERSONALLY?

We proceed thus to the First Article: —

Objection 1. It would seem that image is not said personally of God. For Augustine says, *The Godhead of the Holy Trinity and the Image whereunto man is made are one.*[1] Therefore Image is said of God essentially, and not personally.

Obj. 2. Further, Hilary says: *An image is a like species of that which it represents.*[2] But species or form is said of God essentially. Therefore so also is Image.

Obj. 3. Further, Image is derived from imitation, which implies *before* and *after*. But in the divine persons there is no *before* and *after*. Therefore Image cannot be a personal name in God.

On the contrary, Augustine says: *What is more absurd than to say that an image is referred to itself?*[3] Therefore Image in God is said relatively, and

---

1. 参见 Cf. Fulgentius, *De Fide ad Petrum*, I (PL 65, 674).
2. 参见 *De Synod.* (PL 10, 490).
3. 参见 *De Trin.*, VII, 1 (PL 42, 934).

is thus a personal name.

I answer that, The idea of Image includes likeness. Still, not any kind of likeness suffices for the nature of image, but only likeness of species, or at least of some specific sign. In corporeal things the specific sign seems to be especially the figure. For we see that the species of different animals are of different figures; but not of different colors. Hence if the color of anything is depicted on a wall, this is not called an image unless the figure is likewise depicted. But neither the likeness of species nor that of figure is enough for an image, for it requires also the idea of origin; because, as Augustine says. *One egg is not the image of another, because it is not derived from it.*[1] Therefore, for a true image it is required that one thing proceed from another like to it in species, or at least in specific sign. Now in God, whatever implies procession or origin, belongs to the persons. Hence the name *Image* is a personal name.

Reply Obj. 1. Image, properly speaking, means whatever proceeds forth in likeness to another. That to the likeness of which anything proceeds, is properly speaking called the exemplar, and is improperly called the image. Nevertheless Augustine uses the name of Image in this sense when he says that the divine nature of the Holy Trinity is the Image to which man was made.[2]

Reply Obj. 2. *Species*, as mentioned by Hilary in the definition of image, means the form derived from one thing to another. In this sense, image is said to be the species of anything, just as that which is assimilated to anything is called its form, inasmuch as it has a like form.

Reply Obj. 3. Imitation in God does not signify posteriority, but only assimilation.

---

1. 参见 *Lib. 83 Quaest.*, q. 74 (PL 40, 86).
2. 参见 Cf. Fulgentius, *De Fide ad Petrum*, I (PL 65, 674).

Second Article

WHETHER THE NAME *IMAGE* IS PROPER TO THE SON?

We proceed thus to the Second Article: —

Objection 1. It would seem that the name Image is not proper to the Son, because, as Damascene says, *The Holy Ghost is the Image of the Son.*[1] Therefore Image does not belong to the Son alone.

Obj. 2. Further, Likeness and derivation belong to the nature of an image, as Augustine says.[2] But this befits the Holy Ghost, Who proceeds from another by way of likeness. Therefore the Holy Ghost is an Image, and so to be an Image does not belong to the Son alone.

Obj. 3. Further, man too is called the image of God[3], according to 1 *Cor.* xi. 7, *The man ought not to cover his head, for he is the image and the glory of God.* Therefore Image is not proper to the Son.

On the contrary, Augustine says: *The Son alone is the Image of the Father.*[4]

I answer that, The Greek Doctors commonly say that the Holy Ghost is the Image both of the Father and of the Son,[5] but the Latin Doctors at tribute the name Image to the Son alone.[6] For it is not found in the canonical Scripture except as applied to the Son; as in the words, *Who is the Image of the invisible God, the firstborn of creatures* (*Col.* i. 15); and again: *Who being the brightness of His glory, and the figure of His substance* (*Heb.* i . 3).

---

1. 参见 *De Fide Orth.*, I, 13 (PG 94, 856).
2. 参见 *Lib. 83 Quaest.*, q.74 (PL 40, 86).
3. the image of God：天主的肖像，指人。根据《圣经》记载，人是天主按照自己的肖像创造的，人是唯一的有灵魂的受造物。
4. 参见 *De Trin.*, VI, 2 (PL 42, 925).
5. 参见 Cf. St. Thomas, *Contra Errores Graecorum*, X.
6. 参见 Cf. St. Thomas, *ibid.*

Some[1] explain this by the fact that the Son agrees with the Father, not in nature only, but also in the notion of principle; whereas the Holy Ghost agrees neither with the Son, nor with the Father in any notion. This, however, does not seem to suffice. For, just as it is not by reason of the relations that we consider either equality or inequality in God, as Augustine says,[2] so neither [by reason thereof do we consider] the likeness which is essential to the notion of image. Hence others[3] say that the Holy Ghost cannot be called the Image of the Son, because there cannot be an image of an image; nor the image of the Father, because the image is immediately related to that of which it is the image: and the Holy Ghost is related to the Father through the Son; nor again is He the Image of the Father and the Son, because then there would be one image of two; which is impossible. Hence it follows that the Holy Ghost is in no way an Image. But this argument is worthless, for the Father and the Son are one principle of the Holy Ghost, as we shall explain further on.[4] Hence, in this sense, there is nothing to prevent there being one Image of the Father and of the Son, inasmuch as they are one; since even man is one image of the whole Trinity.

Therefore we must explain the matter otherwise. For, although by His procession the Holy Ghost receives the nature of the Father, as does the Son, nevertheless He is not said to be *born*; so, in like manner, although He receives the likeness of the Father, He is not called the Image; because the Son proceeds as Word, and it is essential to a word to be of like species with the being from which it proceeds, whereas

---

1. 参见 Richard of St. Victor, *De Trin.*, VI, 11; 20 (PL 196, 975; 984); Alex. of Hales, *Summa Theol.*, II, no. 418 (I, 609); St. Bonaventure, *In IV Sent.*, d. xxxi, pt. II, a. 1, q. 2 (II, 542).
2. 参见 *Contra Maximin.*, II, 14; 18 (PL 42, 775; 786); *De Trin.* V, 6 (PL 42, 914).
3. 参见 Rupertus, *De Trin.*, II, 2 (PL 167, 248). — Cf. Alex. of Hales, *Summa Theol.*, II, no. 418 (I, 609).
4. 参见 Q. 36, a. 4.

this does not essentially belong to love, even though it may belong to that love which is the Holy Ghost, inasmuch as He is the divine love.

Reply Obj. 1. Damascene and the other Greek Doctors commonly employ the term image as meaning a perfect likeness.

Reply Obj. 2. Although the Holy Ghost is like to the Father and the Son, still it does not follow that He is the Image, as was above explained.

Reply Obj. 3. The image of a thing may be found in something in two ways. In one way, it is found in something of the same specific nature; as the image of the king is found in his son. In another way, it is found in something of a different nature, as the king's image on the coin. In the first sense, the Son is the Image of the Father; in the second sense, man is called the image of God. And so, in order to express the imperfect character of the divine image in man, man is not simply called the image, but *to the image*; whereby is expressed a certain movement of one tending to perfection. But it cannot be said that the Son of God is *to the image*, because He is the perfect Image of the Father.

Question XXXVI
THE PERSON OF THE HOLY GHOST
(*In Four Articles*)

WE now proceed to treat of what belongs to the person of the Holy Ghost, Who is called not only the Holy Ghost, but also the Love and Gift of God. Concerning the name *Holy Ghost*, there are four points of treatment: (1) Whether this Name, *Holy Ghost*, is the proper name of a divine Person? (2) Whether that divine person, Who is called the Holy Ghost, proceeds from the Father and the Son? (3) Whether He proceeds from the Father through the Son? (4) Whether the Father and the Son are one principle of the Holy Ghost?

First Article
WHETHER THIS NAME, *HOLY GHOST*, IS THE PROPER NAME OF A DIVINE PERSON?

We proceed thus to the First Article: —

Objection 1. It would seem that this name *Holy Ghost* is not the proper name of a divine person. For no name which is common to the three persons is the proper name of any one person. But this name of *Holy Ghost* is common to the three persons; for Hilary[1] shows that the *Spirit of God* sometimes means the Father, as in the words of *Isaias* (lxi. 1): *The Spirit of the Lord is upon me* (*Luke* iv. 18); sometimes the Son, as when the Son says: *In the Spirit of God I cast out devils* (*Matt.* xii. 28), showing

---

1. 参见 *De Trin.*, VIII, 8 (PL 10, 253).

that He cast out devils by His own natural power; and that sometimes it means the Holy Ghost, as in the words of *Joel* (ii. 28): *I will pour out of My Spirit over all flesh* (cf. *Acts* ii. 17). Therefore this name *Holy Ghost* is not the proper name of a divine person.

Obj. 2. Further, the names of the divine persons are relative terms, as Boethius says.[1] But this name *Holy Ghost* is not a relative term. Therefore this name is not the proper name of a divine Person.

Obj. 3. Further, because the Son is the name of a divine Person He cannot be called the Son of this one or of that. But the spirit is spoken of as of this or that man, as appears in the words, *The Lord said to Moses, I will take of thy spirit and will give to them* (*Num.* xi. 17); and also, *The spirit of Elias rested upon Eliseus* (*4 Kings* ii. 15). Therefore *Holy Ghost* does not seem to be the proper name of a divine Person.

On the contrary, It is said (*1 John* v. 7): *There are three who bear witness in heaven, the Father, the Word, and the Holy Ghost.* As Augustine says: *When we ask, Three what? we say, Three persons.*[2] Therefore the Holy Ghost is the name of a divine person.

I answer that, While there are two processions in God, one of these, the procession of love, has no proper name of its own, as was stated above.[3] Hence the relations also which follow from this procession are without a name.[4] For this reason, the Person proceeding in that manner has not a proper name. But as some names are accommodated by the usual mode of speaking to signify the aforesaid relations, as when we use the names of procession and spiration, which in the strict sense more fittingly signify the notional acts than the relations; so to signify the divine Person, Who proceeds by way of love, this name *Holy Ghost* is by the use of scriptural speech accommodated to Him

1. 参见 *De Trin.*, V (PL 64, 1254).
2. 参见 *De Trin.*, VII, 4; 6; V, 9 (PL 42, 940; 943; 918).
3. 参见 Q. 27, a. 4, ad 3.
4. 参见 Q. 28, a. 4.

The appropriateness of this name may be shown in two ways. Firstly, from the fact that the Person Who is called *Holy Ghost* has something in common with the other Persons. For, as Augustine says, *Because the Holy Ghost is common to both, He Himself is called that properly which both are called in common. For the Father is a spirit, and the Son is a spirit; and the Father is holy, and the Son is holy.*[1] Secondly, from the proper signification of the name. For the name spirit [*spiritus*] in corporeal things seems to signify impulse and motion; for we call the breath and the wind by the term spirit. Now it is a property of love to move and impel the will of the lover towards the object loved. Further, holiness is attributed to whatever is ordered to God. Therefore because the divine person proceeds by way of the love whereby God is loved, that person is most properly named *The Holy Ghost* [*Spiritus Sanctus*].

Reply Obj. 1. The expression Holy Spirit [*Spiritus Sanctus*], if taken as two words, is applicable to the whole Trinity: because by *spirit* the immateriality of the divine substance is signified; while corporeal spirit is invisible, and has but little matter. Hence we apply this term to all immaterial and invisible substances. And by adding the word *holy* we signify the purity of divine goodness. But if Holy Spirit be taken as one word, it is thus that the expression, in the usage of the Church, is accommodated to signify one of the three persons, the one who proceeds by way of love, for the reason above explained.

Reply Obj. 2. Although this name *Holy Ghost* does not indicate a relation, still it takes the place of a relative term, inasmuch as it is accommodated to signify a Person distinct from the others by relation only. Yet this name may be understood as including a relation, if we understand the Holy Spirit as meaning (so to say) one *who is spirated.*

Reply Obj. 3. In the name *Son* we understand only that relation to its principle of that which is from a principle; but in the name *Father* we

---

1. 参见 *De Trin.*, XV, 19; V, 11 (PL 42, 1086; 919).

understand the relation of principle, and likewise in the name *Spirit*, inasmuch as it implies a moving power. But to no creature does it belong to be a principle in relation to any divine person; but rather the reverse. Therefore we can say *our Father*, and *our Spirit*; but we cannot say *our Son*.

Second Article
WHETHER THE HOLY GHOST PROCEEDS FROM THE SON?

We proceed thus to the Second Article: —

Objection 1. It would seem that the Holy Ghost does not proceed from the Son. For as Dionysius says, *We must not dare to say anything concerning the substantial Divinity except what has been divinely expressed to us by the sacred writings*[1] But in the Sacred Scripture we are not told that the Holy Ghost proceeds from the Son, but only that He proceeds from the Father; as appears from *Jo.* xv. 26: *The Spirit of truth, Who proceeds from the Father.* Therefore the Holy Ghost does not proceed from the Son.

Obj. 2. Further, In the creed of the council of Constantinople we read: *We believe in the Holy Ghost, the Lord and Lifegiver*[2], *Who proceeds from the Father, and Who with the Father and the Son is to be adored and glorified.*[3] Therefore it should not be added in our Creed that the Holy Ghost proceeds from the Son, and those who added such a thing appear to be worthy of anathema.

Obj. 3. Further, Damascene says: *We say that the Holy Ghost is from the Father, and we name Him the Spirit of the Father; but we do not say that the Holy Ghost is from the Son, yet we name Him the Spirit of the Son.*[4] Therefore

---

1. 参见 *De Div. Nom*, I, 1; 2 (PG 3, 588).
2. the Lifegiver：赋予生命者，指三位一体的第三位，即圣神
3. 参见 *Symb. Nicaeno-Constantinopolitanum* (Denzinger, no. 86).
4. 参见 *De Fide Orth.*, I, 8 (PG 94, 832).

the Holy Ghost does not proceed from the Son.

Obj. 4. Further, Nothing proceeds from that wherein it rests. But the Holy Ghost rests in the Son, for it is said in the legend of St. Andrew: *Peace be to you and to all who believe in the one God the Father, and in His only Son our Lord Jesus Christ, and in the one Holy Ghost proceeding from the Father, and abiding in the Son.*[1] Therefore the Holy Ghost does not proceed from the Son.

Obj. 5. Further, the Son proceeds as the Word. But our breath [*spiritus*] does not seem to proceed in ourselves from our word. Therefore the Holy Ghost does not proceed from the Son.

Obj. 6. Further, the Holy Ghost proceeds perfectly from the Father. Therefore it is superfluous to say that He proceeds from the Son.

Obj. 7. Further, *the actual and the possible do not differ in things perpetual*,[2] and much less so in God. But it is possible for the Holy Ghost to be distinguished from the Son, even if He did not proceed from Him. For Anselm says: *The Son and the Holy Ghost have their being front the Father. but each in a different way; one by Birth, the other by Procession, so that they are thus distinct from one another.*[3] And further on he says: *For even if for no other reason were the Son and the Holy Spirit distinct, this alone would suffice.*[4] Therefore the Holy Spirit is distinct from the Son, without proceeding from Him.

On the contrary, Athanasius says: *The Holy Ghost is from the Father and the Son; not made, nor created, nor begotten, but proceeding.*[5]

I answer that, It must be said that the Holy Ghost is from the Son. For if He were not from Him, He could in no wise be personally distinguished from Him; as appears from what has been said above.[6]

---

1. 参见 *Acta S. Andr.* (PG 2, 1217).
2. 参见 Aristotle, *Phys.*, III, 4 (203b 30).
3. 参见 *De Process. Spir. Sancti*, IV (PL 158, 292).
4. 同上
5. 参见 Cf. *Symb.* "*Quicumque*" (Denzinger, no. 39).
6. 参见 Q. 28, a. 3; q. 30, a. 2.

For it cannot be said that the divine Persons are distinguished from each other in any absolute sense, for it would then follow that there would not be one essence of the three persons: since everything that is spoken of God in an absolute sense belongs to the unity of essence. Therefore it must be said that the divine persons are distinguished from each other only by the relations. Now the relations cannot distinguish the persons except according as they are opposite relations, which appears from the fact that the Father has two relations, by one of which He is related to the Son, and by the other to the Holy Ghost; but these are not opposite relations, and therefore they do not make two persons, but belong only to the one person of the Father. If therefore in the Son and the Holy Ghost there were only two relations, whereby each of them were related to the Father, these relations would not be opposite to each other, as neither would be the two relations whereby the Father is related to them. Hence, just as the person of the Father is one, so it would follow that the person of the Son and of the Holy Ghost would be one, having two relations opposed to the two relations of the Father. But this is heretical, since it destroys the Faith in the Trinity. Therefore the Son and the Holy Ghost must be related to each other by opposite relations. Now there cannot be in God any relations opposed to each other, except relations of origin, as was proved above.[1] But opposite relations of origin are to be understood as of a *principle*, and of what is *from the principle*. Therefore we must conclude that it is necessary to say that either the Son is from the Holy Ghost, which no one says; or that the Holy Ghost is from the Son, as we confess.

Furthermore, the nature of the procession of each one agrees with this conclusion. For it was said above, that the Son proceeds by way of the intellect as Word, and the Holy Ghost by way of the will as Love[2]

1. 参见 Q. 28, a. 4.
2. 参见 Q. 27, a. 2 and 4; q. 28, a. 4.

Now love must proceed from a word. For we do not love anything unless we apprehend it by a mental conception. Hence also in this way it is manifest that the Holy Ghost proceeds from the Son.

We derive a knowledge of the same truth from the very order of nature itself. For we nowhere find that several things proceed from one without order, except in those which differ only by their matter; as, for instance, one smith produces many knives distinct from each other materially, with no order to each other; whereas in things in which there is not a material distinction alone, we always find that some order exists in the multitude produced. Hence in the order of produced creatures even the beauty of the divine wisdom is displayed. So if from the one Person of the Father two persons proceed, namely, the Son and the Holy Ghost, there must be some order between them. Nor can any other be assigned except the order of their nature, whereby one is from the other. Therefore, it cannot be said that the Son and the Holy Ghost so proceed from the Father that neither of them proceeds from the other, unless we admit in them a material distinction; which is impossible.

Hence even the Greeks themselves recognize that the procession of the Holy Ghost has some order to the Son. For they grant that the Holy Ghost is the Spirit *of the Son*; and that He is from the Father *through the Son*. Some of them are said also to concede that *He is from the Son*; or that He *flows from the Son*, but not that He proceeds; which seems to come from ignorance or obstinacy. For a just consideration of the truth will convince anyone that the word *procession* is the most common among all that denote origin of any kind. For we use the word to describe any kind of origin; as when we say that a line proceeds from a point, a ray from the sun, a stream from a source, and likewise in everything else. Hence, granted that the Holy Ghost originates in any way from the Son, we can conclude that the Holy Ghost proceeds from the Son.

Reply Obj. 1. We ought not to say about God anything which is not found in Holy Scripture either explicitly or implicitly. But although we do not find it verbally expressed in Holy Scripture that the Holy Ghost proceeds from the Son, still we do find it in the sense of Scripture, especially where the Son says, speaking of the Holy Ghost, *He will glorify Me, because He shall receive of Mine* (*Jo*. xvi. 14). It is also a rule of Holy Scripture that whatever is said of the Father applies to the Son, even though there be added an exclusive term; except only as regards what belongs to the opposite relations, whereby the Father and the Son are distinguished from each other. For when the Lord says, *No one knoweth the Son, but the Father*, the idea of the Son knowing Himself is not excluded. So therefore when we say that the Holy Ghost proceeds from the Father, even though it be added that He proceeds from the Father alone, the Son would not thereby be at all excluded; because as regards being the principle of the Holy Ghost, the Father and the Son are not opposed to each other, but only as regards the fact that one is the Father, and the other is the Son.

Reply Obj. 2. In every council of the Church a symbol of faith has been drawn up to meet some prevalent error condemned in the council at that time. Hence subsequent councils are not to be described as making a new symbol of faith; but what was implicitly contained in the first symbol was explained by some additions directed against rising heresies. Hence in the decision of the council of Chalcedon, it is declared that those who were congregated together in the council of Constantinople[1] handed down the doctrine about the Holy Ghost. This did not imply that there was anything wanting in the doctrine of their predecessors who had gathered together at Nicæa; what they were doing rather was to explain, against the heretics, what those fathers had understood on the matter.[2] Therefore, because at the time

---

1. the council of Constantinople：君士坦丁堡大公会议，天主教大公会议之一
2. 参见 Council of Chalcedon, V; ed. Mansi, VII, 111.

of the ancient councils the error of those who said that the Holy Ghost did not proceed from the Son had not yet arisen, it was not necessary to make any explicit declaration on that point; whereas, later on, when certain errors rose up, in another council assembled in the west, the matter was explicitly defined by the authority of the Roman Pontiff[1], by whose authority also the ancient councils were summoned and confirmed. Nevertheless the truth was contained implicitly in the belief that the Holy Ghost proceeds from the Father.

Reply Obj. 3. The Nestorians[2] were the first to introduce the error that the Holy Ghost did not proceed from the Son, as appears in a Nestorian creed condemned in the council of Ephesus.[3] This error was embraced by Theodoric the Nestorian,[4] and several others after him, among whom was also Damascene.[5] Hence, in that point his opinion is not to be held. Yet some may be inclined to say that, while Damascene did not confess that the Holy Ghost was from the Son, neither do those words of his express a denial thereof.

Reply Obj. 4. When the Holy Ghost is said to rest or abide in the Son, it does not mean that He does not proceed from Him; for the Son also is said to abide in the Father, although He proceeds from the Father. Then, too, the Holy Ghost is said to rest in the Son as the love of the lover abides in the beloved; or in reference to the human nature of Christ, by reason of what is written: *On whom thou shalt see the Spirit descending and remaining upon Him, He it is who baptizes* (*Jo.* i. 33).

Reply Obj. 5. The Word in God is not taken according to the likeness of the vocal word, from which the breath [*spiritus*] does not proceed; for it would then be only metaphorical; but according to the likeness of the

---

1. the Roman Pontiff：罗马教宗
2. the Nestorians：奈斯多利派人士。奈斯多利派是第五世纪出现的一个天主教异端教派，636 年，即唐贞观九年传入中国，被称为“景教”。
3. 参见 Council of Ephesus, VI; ed. Mansi, IV, 1347.
4. 参见 *Epist.* CLXXI (PG 83, 1484).
5. 参见 *De Fide Orth.*, I, 8 (PG 94, 832).

mental word from which love proceeds.

Reply Obj. 6. For the reason that the Holy Ghost proceeds from the Father perfectly, not only is it not superfluous to say He proceeds from the Son, but rather it is absolutely necessary. For one power belongs to the Father and the Son, and whatever is from the Father must be from the Son, unless it be opposed to the property of filiation; for the Son is not from Himself, although He is from the Father.

Reply Obj. 7. The Holy Ghost is distinguished personally from the Son, inasmuch as the origin of the one is distinguished from the origin of the other; but the difference itself of origin comes from the fact that the Son is only from the Father, whereas the Holy Ghost is from the Father and the Son. Otherwise the processions would not be distinguished from each other, as was explained above.

Third Article
WHETHER THE HOLY GHOST PROCEEDS FROM THE FATHER THROUGH THE SON?

We proceed thus to the Third Article: —

Objection 1. It would seem that the Holy Ghost does not proceed from the Father through the Son. For whatever proceeds from one through another, does not proceed immediately. Therefore, if the Holy Ghost proceeds from the Father through the Son, He does not proceed immediately from the Father; which seems to be unfitting.

Obj. 2. Further, if the Holy Ghost proceeds from the Father through the Son, He does not proceed from the Son except because of the Father. But *whatever causes a thing to be such is yet more so.* Therefore He proceeds more from the Father than from the Son.

Obj. 3. Further, the Son has His being by generation. Therefore if the Holy Ghost is from the Father through the Son, it follows that the Son is first generated and afterwards the Holy Ghost proceeds; and thus the procession of the Holy Ghost is not eternal, which is heretical.

Obj. 4. Further, when anyone acts through another, the same may be said conversely. For as we say that the king acts through the bailiff, so it can be said conversely that the bailiff acts through the king. But we can never say that the Son spirates the Holy Ghost through the Father. Therefore it can never be said that the Father spirates the Holy Ghost through the Son.

On the contrary, Hilary says: *Keep me, I pray, in this expression of my faith, that I may ever possess the Father, namely, Thyself: that I may adore Thy Son together with Thee: and that I may deserve Thy Holy Spirit, Who is through Thy Only Begotten.*[1]

I answer that, Whenever one is said to act through another, this preposition *through* points out, in what is covered by it, some cause or principle of that act. But since action is a mean between the agent and the thing done, sometimes that which is covered by the preposition *through* is the cause of the action, as proceeding from the agent; and in that case it is the cause of why the agent acts, whether it be a final cause or a formal cause, whether it be effective or motive. It is a final cause when we say, for instance, that the artisan works through love of gain. It is a formal cause when we say that he works through his art. It is a motive cause when we say that he works through the command of another. Sometimes, however, that which is covered by this preposition *through* is the cause of the action regarded as terminated in the thing done; as, for instance, when we say, the artisan acts through the hammer. For this does not mean that the hammer is a cause causing the artisan to act, but that it is a cause causing the thing made to proceed from the artisan; and this character it has from the artisan. This is why it is sometimes said that this preposition *through* sometimes denotes direct authority, as when we say, the king works through the bailiff[2]; and sometimes indirect authority, as when we say, the bailiff

1. 参见 *De Trin.*, XII (PL 10, 471).
2. bailiff：法警；法律执行者

works through the king.

Therefore, because the Son receives from the Father that the Holy Ghost proceed from Him, it can be said that the Father spirates the Holy Ghost through the Son, or that the Holy Ghost proceeds from the Father through the Son. The meaning is the same.

Reply Obj. 1. In every action, two things are to be considered: the *suppositum* acting, and the power whereby it acts; as, for instance, fire heats through heat. So if we consider in the Father and the Son the power whereby they spirate the Holy Ghost, there is no mean, for this is one and the same power. But if we consider the persons themselves spirating, then, as the Holy Ghost proceeds both from the Father and from the Son, the Holy Ghost proceeds from the Father immediately as from Him, and mediately, as from the Son; and thus He is said to proceed from the Father through the Son. So, too, Abel proceeded immediately from Adam, inasmuch as Adam was his father; and mediately, as Eve was his mother, who proceeded from Adam; although, indeed, this example of a material procession is inept to signify the immaterial procession of the divine Persons.

Reply Obj. 2. If the Son received from the Father a numerically distinct power for the spiration of the Holy Ghost, it would follow that He would be a secondary and instrumental cause, and thus the Holy Ghost would proceed more from the Father than from the Son; whereas, on the contrary, the same spirative power belongs to the Father and to the Son; and therefore the Holy Ghost proceeds equally from both, although sometimes He is said to proceed principally or properly from the Father, because the Son has this power from the Father.

Reply Obj. 3. As the begetting of the Son is coeternal with the begetter (and hence the Father does not exist before begetting the Son), so the procession of the Holy Ghost is coeternal with His principle. Hence, the Son was not begotten before the Holy Ghost proceeded; but each of the operations is eternal.

Reply Obj. 4. When anyone is said to work through anything, the converse proposition is not always true. For we do not say that the hammer works through the workman; whereas we can say that the bailiff acts through the king. For it is the bailiff's place to act, since he is master of his own act, but it is not the hammer's place to act, but only to be made to act; and hence it is used only as an instrument. The bailiff, however, is said to act through the king, although this preposition *through* denotes a medium; for the more a *suppositum* is prior in action, so much the more is its power immediate as regards the effect, inasmuch as the power of the first cause unites the second cause to its effect. Hence first principles are said to be immediate in the demonstrative sciences. Therefore, in so far as the bailiff is intermediate in the order of acting causes, the king is said to work through the bailiff; but according to the order of powers, the bailiff is said to act through the king, for it is the power of the king that gives the bailiff's action its effect. Now there is no order of power between Father and Son, but only order of *supposita*; and hence we say that the Father spirates through the Son, and not conversely.

Fourth Article
WHETHER THE FATHER AND THE SON ARE ONE PRINCIPLE OF THE HOLY GHOST?

We proceed thus to the Fourth Article: —

Objection 1. It would seem that the Father and the Son are not one principle of the Holy Ghost. For the Holy Ghost does not proceed from the Father and the Son according as they are one: not as they are one in nature, for the Holy Ghost would in that way proceed from Himself, as He is one in nature with Them; nor again inasmuch as they are united in any one property, for it is clear that one property cannot belong to two subjects. Therefore, the Holy Ghost proceeds from the Father and the Son as distinct from one another. Therefore the Father and the Son are not one principle of the Holy Ghost.

Obj. 2. Further, in this proposition *the Father and the Son are one principle of the Holy Ghost*, we do not designate personal unity, because in that case the Father and the Son would be one person. Nor again do we designate the unity of property, because, if one property were the reason of the Father and the Son being one principle of the Holy Ghost, similarly, because of His two properties the Father would be two principles of the Son and of the Holy Ghost; which cannot be admitted. Therefore the Father and the Son are not one principle of the Holy Ghost.

Obj. 3. Further, the Son is not one with the Father more than is the Holy Ghost. But the Holy Ghost and the Father are not one principle as regards any divine person. Therefore neither are the Father and the Son.

Obj. 4. Further, if the Father and the Son are one principle of the Holy Ghost, this *one* is either the Father or it is not the Father. But we cannot assert either of these positions because if the one is the Father, it follows that the Son is the Father; and if the one is not the Father, it follows that the Father is not the Father. Therefore, we cannot say that the Father and the Son are one principle of the Holy Ghost.

Obj. 5. Further, if the Father and the Son are one principle of the Holy Ghost, it seems necessary to say, conversely, that the one principle of the Holy Ghost is the Father and the Son. But this seems to be false, for this term *principle* stands either for the person of the Father, or for the person of the Son; and in either sense it is false. Therefore this proposition also is false, that the Father and the Son are one principle of the Holy Ghost.

Obj. 6. Further, unity in substance makes identity. So if the Father and the Son are the one principle of the Holy Ghost, it follows that they are the same principle; which is denied by many. Therefore we cannot grant that the Father and the Son are one principle of the Holy Ghost.

Obj. 7. Further, the Father, Son and Holy Ghost are called one Creator, because they are the one principle of the creature. But the Father and the Son are not one, but two Spirators, as many assert;[1] and this agrees also with what Hilary says, *that the Holy Ghost is to be confessed as proceeding from Father and Son as authors.*[2] Therefore the Father and the Son are not one principle of the Holy Ghost.

On the contrary, Augustine says that the Father and the Son are not two principles, but one principle of the Holy Ghost.[3]

I answer that, The Father and the Son are in everything one, wherever there is no distinction between them of opposite relation. Hence, since there is no relative opposition between them as the principle of the Holy Ghost, it follows that the Father and the Son are one principle of the Holy Ghost.

Some, however, assert that this proposition is incorrect: *The Father and the Son are one principle of the Holy Ghost*, because, they declare, since the term *principle* in the singular does not signify *person*, but *property*, it must be taken as an adjective;[4] and since an adjective cannot be modified by another adjective, it cannot properly be said that the Father and the Son are one principle of the Holy Ghost unless *one* be taken as an adverb, so that the meaning should be: They are one principle — that is, in one and the same way. But then it might be equally right to say that the Father is two principles of the Son and of the Holy Ghost — namely, in two ways. Therefore, we must say that, although this term *principle* signifies a property, it does so after the manner of a substantive, as do the terms *father* and *son* even in things created. Hence it takes its number from the form that it signifies, like

---

1. 参见 Cf. below, the note to the reply to this obj.
2. 参见 *De Trin.*, II (PL 10, 69).
3. 参见 Cf. *De Trin.*, V, 14 (PL 42, 921).
4. 参见 Alain of Lille, *Theol. Reg.*, LI (PL 210, 644). — Cf. William of Auxerre, *Summa Aurea*, I, tr. 8, ch. 6 (fol. 17va).

other substantives. Therefore, as the Father and the Son are one God, by reason of the unity of the form that is signified by this term *God*, so they are one principle of the Holy Ghost by reason of the unity of the property that is signified in this term *principle*.

Reply Obj. 1. If we consider the spirative power, the Holy Ghost proceeds from the Father and the Son as they are one in the spirative power, which in a certain way signifies the nature with the property, as we shall see later.[1] Nor is there any reason against one property being in two *supposita* that possess one common nature. But if we consider the *supposita* of the spiration, then we may say that the Holy Ghost proceeds from the Father and the Son, as distinct; for He proceeds from them as the unitive love of both.

Reply Obj. 2. In the proposition *the Father and the Son are one principle of the Holy Ghost*, one property is designated which is the form signified by the term. But it does not therefore follow that by reason of the several properties the Father can be called several principles, for this would imply in Him a plurality of subjects.

Reply Obj. 3. It is not by reason of relative properties that we speak of likeness or unlikeness in God, but by reason of the essence. Hence, as the Father is not more like to Himself than He is to the Son, so likewise neither is the Son more like to the Father than is the Holy Ghost.

Reply Obj. 4. These two propositions, *The Father and the Son are one principle which is the Father*, or, *one principle which is not the Father*, are not mutually contradictory; and hence it is not necessary to assert one or the other of them. For when we say the Father and the Son are one principle, this term *principle* has not determinate supposition; but it rather stands indeterminately for two persons together. Hence there is a fallacy of *figure of speech*, as the argument concludes from

---

1. 参见 Q. 41, a 5.

indeterminate supposition to determinate.

Reply Obj. 5. This proposition is also true: — *The one principle of the Holy Ghost is the Father and the Son*; because the word *principle* does not stand for one person only, but indistinctly for the two persons, as was above explained.

Reply Obj. 6. There is no reason against saying that the Father and the Son are the same principle, for the term *principle* stands confusedly and indistinctly for the two Persons together.

Reply Obj. 7. Some say that, although the Father and the Son are one principle of the Holy Ghost, there are two spirators, by reason of the distinction of *supposita*, as also there are two spirating, because acts refer to *supposita*.[1] Yet this does not hold good as to the name *Creator*, because the Holy Ghost proceeds from the Father and the Son as from two distinct persons, as was above explained; whereas the creature proceeds from the three persons, not as distinct persons, but as united in essence. But it seems better to say that, because *spirating* is an adjective, and *spirator* a substantive, we can say that the Father and the Son are two spirating, by reason of the plurality of the *supposita*, but not two spirators by reason of the one spiration. For adjectival terms derive their number from the *supposita*, but substantives from themselves, according to the form signified. As to what Hilary says, that *the Holy Ghost is from the Father and the Son as His authors*, this is to be explained in the sense that the substantive here stands for the adjective.

---

1. 参见 Alex. of Hales, *Summa Theol.*, II, no. 493 (I, 695); St. Bonaventure, *In I Sent.*, d. xxix, a. 2, q. 2 (I, 515); St. Albert, *In I Sent.*, d. xxix, a. 5 (XXVI, 9); St. Thomas, *In I Sent.*, d. xi, q. 1, a. 4.

Question XXXVII
THE NAME OF THE HOLY GHOST: LOVE
(*In Two Articles*)

WE now inquire concerning the name *Love*, on which arise two points for consideration: (1) Whether it is the proper name of the Holy Ghost? (2) Whether the Father and the Son love each other by the Holy Ghost?

First Article
WHETHER *LOVE* IS THE PROPER NAME OF THE HOLY GHOST?

We proceed thus to the First Article: —

Objection 1. It would seem that *Love* is not the proper name of the Holy Ghost. For Augustine says: *As the Father, Son and Holy Ghost are called Wisdom, and are not three Wisdoms, but one; I know not why the Father, Son, and Holy Ghost should not be called Charity, and all together one Charity.*[1] But no name, which is predicated in the singular of each person and of all together is a proper name of a person. Therefore this name, *Love*, is not the proper name of the Holy Ghost.

Obj. 2. Further, the Holy Ghost is a subsisting person, but love is not used to signify a subsisting person, but rather an action passing from the lover to the beloved. Therefore Love is not the proper name of the Holy Ghost.

---

1. 参见 *De Trin.*, XV, 17 (PL 42, 1081).

Obj. 3. Further, Love is the bond between lovers, for, as Dionysius says, *Love is a unitive force.*[1] But a bond is a medium between what it joins together, not something proceeding from them. Therefore, since the Holy Ghost proceeds from the Father and the Son, as was shown above,[2] it seems that He is not the Love or bond of the Father and the Son.

Obj. 4. Further, Love belongs to every lover. But the Holy Ghost is a lover: therefore He has love. So if the Holy Ghost is Love, He must be love of love, and spirit from spirit; which is not admissible.

On the contrary, Gregory says: *The Holy Ghost Himself is Love.*[3]

I answer that, The name *Love* in God can be taken essentially and personally. If taken personally it is the proper name of the Holy Ghost, just as *Word* is the proper name of the Son.

To see this, we must know, as was shown above,[4] that there are two processions in God, one by way of the intellect, which is the procession of the Word, and another by way of the will, which is the procession of Love. Hence, inasmuch as the former is the more known to us, we have been able to apply more suitable names to express our various considerations about that procession, but not about the procession of the will. Hence, we are obliged to employ circumlocution as regards the person Who proceeds, and the relations following from this procession which are called *procession* and *spiration*, as was stated above,[5] even though they are names expressing origin rather than relation, if taken strictly. Nevertheless we must consider them in respect of each procession simply. For just as, when a thing is understood by anyone, there results in the one who understands

---

1. 参见 *De Div. Nom.*, IV, 15 (PG 3, 713).
2. 参见 Q. 36, a. 2.
3. 参见 *In Evang.*, II, hom. 30 (PL 76, 1220).
4. 参见 Q. 27, a. 1, 3 and 5.
5. 参见 Q. 28, a. 4.

a conception of the thing understood, which conception we call a *word*; so when anyone loves some thing, a certain impression results, so to speak, of the thing loved in the affection of the lover, by reason of which the object loved is said to be in the lover, just as the thing understood is in the one who understands. So, it follows that when anyone understands and loves himself, he is in himself not only by real identity, but also as the thing understood is in the one who understands, and the thing loved is in the lover.

As regards the intellect, however, words have been found to describe the mutual relation of the one who understands to the thing understood, as appears in the word *to understand*; and other words have also been found to express the procession of the intellectual conception[1] — namely, *to speak*, and *word*. Hence in God, *to understand* is applied only to the essence, because it does not express relation to the Word that proceeds; whereas *Word* is said personally, because it signifies what proceeds, while the term *to speak* is a notional term as expressing the relation of the principle of the Word to the Word Himself. On the other hand, on the part of the will, with the exception of the words *dilection*[2] and *love*, which express the relation of the lover to the thing loved, there are no other terms in use to express the relation of the impression or affection of the thing loved, produced in the lover by the fact that he loves, to the principle of that impression, or *vice versa*. And therefore, because of the poverty of our vocabulary, we express these relations by the words *love* and *dilection*: just as if we were to call the Word *intelligence conceived*, or *wisdom begotten*.

It follows that so far as love means only the relation of the lover to the thing loved, *love* and *to love* are said of the essence, as *understanding* and *to understand*; but, on the other hand, so far as these words are used

1. intellectual conception：理智领悟或理智孕育，指言语
2. dilection：爱慕，来自拉丁文 diligere

to express the relation to its principle of what proceeds by way of love, and *vice versa*, so that by *love* is understood the *love proceeding*, and by *to love* is understood *the spiration of the love proceeding*, in that sense *love* is the name of the person, and *to love* is a notional term, as *to speak* and *to beget*.

Reply Obj. 1. Augustine is there speaking of charity as it means the divine essence, as was said above.

Reply Obj. 2. Although to understand, to will, and to love signify actions passing on to their objects, nevertheless they are actions that remain in their agents, as was stated above;[1] yet they remain in such a way that in the agent itself they express a certain relation to their objects. Hence, love also in ourselves is something that abides in the lover, and the word of the heart is something abiding in the speaker; yet they so abide that they maintain a relation to the thing expressed by the word, or loved. But in God, in Whom there is nothing accidental, there is more than this, because both Word and Love are subsistent. Therefore, when we say that the Holy Ghost is the Love of the Father for the Son, or for something else, we do not mean anything that passes into another, but only the relation of love to the beloved; as also in the Word is implied the relation of the Word to the thing expressed by the Word.

Reply Obj. 3. The Holy Ghost is said to be the bond of the Father and Son, inasmuch as He is Love; because, since the Father loves Himself and the Son with one Love, and conversely, there is expressed in the Holy Ghost, as Love, the relation of the Father to the Son, and conversely, as that of the lover to the beloved. But from the fact that the Father and the Son mutually love one another, it necessarily follows that this mutual Love, the Holy Ghost, proceeds from both. As regards origin, therefore, the Holy Ghost is not the medium, but the third

---

1. 参见 Q. 14, a. 2.

person in the Trinity; whereas as regards the aforesaid relation, He is the bond between the two persons, as proceeding from both.

Reply Obj. 4. Just as it does not belong to the Son, though He understands, to produce a word, for to understand belongs to Him as to the Word proceeding; so in like manner, although the Holy Ghost loves, taking Love as an essential term, still it does not belong to Him to spirate love, which is to take love as a notional term; because He loves essentially as love proceeding, but not as the one whence love proceeds.

Second Article
WHETHER THE FATHER AND THE SON LOVE EACH OTHER BY THE HOLY GHOST?

We proceed thus to the Second Article: —

Objection 1. It would seem that the Father and the Son do not love each other by the Holy Ghost. For Augustine proves that the Father is not wise by the Wisdom begotten.[1] But as the Son is Wisdom begotten, so the Holy Ghost is the Love proceeding, as was explained above. Therefore the Father and the Son do not love each other by the Love proceeding Who is the Holy Ghost.

Obj. 2. Further, in the proposition, *The Father and the Son love each other by the Holy Ghost*, this word *love* is to be taken either essentially or notionally. But it cannot be true if taken essentially, because in the same way we might say that *the Father understands by the Son*; nor, again, if it is taken notionally, for then, in like manner, it might be said that *the Father and the Son spirate by the Holy Ghost*, or *that the Father generates by the Son*. Therefore in no way is this proposition true: *The Father and the Son love each other by the Holy Ghost.*

---

1. 参见 *De Trin.*, VII, 1 (PL 42, 933).

Obj. 3. Further, by the same love the Father loves the Son, and Himself, and us. But the Father does not love Himself by the Holy Ghost; for no notional act is reflected back on the principle of the act, since it cannot be said that the *Father begets Himself*, or that He *spirates Himself*. Therefore, neither can it be said that *He loves Himself by the Holy Ghost*, if *to love* is taken in a notional sense. Again, the love wherewith He loves us does not seem to be the Holy Ghost, because it implies a relation to creatures, and this belongs to the essence. Therefore this also is false: *The Father loves the Son by the Holy Ghost.*

On the contrary, Augustine says: *The Holy Ghost is He whereby the Begotten is loved by the one begetting and loves His Begetter.*[1]

I answer that, A difficulty about this question is raised by the fact that when we say, *the Father loves the Son by the Holy Ghost*, since the ablative is construed as denoting a cause, it seems to mean that the Holy Ghost is the principle of love to the Father and the Son; which cannot be admitted.

In view of this difficulty some[2] have held that it is false that *the Father and the Son love each other by the Holy Ghost*; and they add that it was retracted by Augustine when he retracted its equivalent to the effect that *the Father is wise by the Wisdom begotten.*[3] Others[4] say that the proposition is inaccurate and ought to be interpreted to mean that *the Father loves the Son by the Holy Ghost* — that is, *by His essential Love*, which is appropriated to the Holy Ghost. Others[5] further say that this ablative should be construed as importing a sign, so that it means, *the Holy Ghost is the sign that the Father loves the Son*, inasmuch as the Holy Ghost as Love proceeds from them both. Others,[6] again, say that this ablative

1. 参见 *Op. cit.*, VI, 5 (PL 42, 928).
2. 参见 Cf. Peter of Poitiers, *Sent.*, I, 21 (PL 211, 872).
3. 参见 *Retract.*, I, 26 (PL 32, 625).
4. 参见 Cf. Alex. of Hales, *Summa Theol.*, II, no. 460 (I. 657).
5. 参见 Simon of Tournai, *Sent.*, I (p. 297).
6. 参见 William of Auxerre, *Summa Aurea*, I, tr. 8, ch. 7 (fol. r8rb).

must be construed as importing the relation of formal cause, because the Holy Ghost is the love whereby the Father and the Son formally love each other. Others,[1] finally, say that it should be construed as expressing the relation of a formal effect; and these approach nearer to the truth.

To make the matter clear, we must consider that, since things are commonly denominated from their forms, as *white* from whiteness, and man from humanity, everything whence anything is denominated, in this particular respect stands to that thing in the relation of form. So when I say, *this man is clothed with a garment*, the ablative is to be construed as having relation to the formal cause, although the garment is not the form. Now it may happen that a thing may be named from that which proceeds from it, not only as an agent is named from its action, but also as it is named from the term itself of the action — that is, the effect, when the effect itself is included in the idea of the action. For we say that fire warms by heating, although heating is not the heat which is the form of the fire, but is an action proceeding from the fire; and we say that a tree flowers with flowers, although flowers are not tree's form, but the effect proceeding from the form.

In this way, therefore, we must say that since in God *to love* is taken in two ways, essentially and notionally, when it is taken essentially, it means that the Father and the Son love each other not by the Holy Ghost, but by their essence. Hence Augustine says: *Who dares to say that the Father loves neither Himself, nor the Son, nor the Holy Ghost, except by the Holy Ghost.*[2] The opinions first quoted are to be taken in this sense. But when the term *to love* is taken in a notional sense, it means nothing else than *to spirate love*; just as *to speak* is to *produce a word*, and to flower is

1. 参见 Cf. Richard of St. Victor, *Quomodo Spiritus Sanctus est Amor Patris et Filii?* (PL 196, 1011). — Cf. also St. Bonaventure, *In I Sent.*, d. xxxii, a. 1, q. 2 (I, 560, n. 7).
2. 参见 *De Trin.*, XV, 7 (PL 42, 1065).

to produce flowers. Just as, therefore, we say that a tree flowers by its flower, so do we say that by the Word, or the Son, the Father speaks Himself and His creatures; and that the Father and the Son love each other and us by the Holy Ghost, or by Love proceeding.

Reply Obj. 1. To be wise or intelligent is taken only essentially in God; and therefore we cannot say that *the Father is wise or intelligent by the Son.* But to love is taken not only essentially, but also in a notional sense; and in this way we can say that the Father and the Son love each other by the Holy Ghost, as was above explained.

Reply Obj. 2. When the idea of an action includes a determined effect, the principle of the action may be denominated both from the action and from the effect; so we can say, for instance, that a tree flowers by its flowering and by its flowers. When, however, the idea of an action does not include a determined effect, then, in that case, the principle of the action cannot be denominated from the effect, but only from the action. For we do not say that the tree produces the flower by the flower, but by the production of the flower. So when we say *spirates* or *begets*, this expresses only a notional act. Hence we cannot say that the Father spirates by the Holy Ghost, or begets by the Son. But we can say that the Father speaks by the Word as by the Person proceeding, and speaks by the speaking as by a notional act; for *to speak* implies a determinate person proceeding, since *to speak* means to produce a word. In the same way, to love, taken in a notional sense, means to produce love; and so it can be said that the Father loves the Son by the Holy Ghost, as by the person proceeding, and by Love itself as a notional act.

Reply Obj. 3. The Father loves not only the Son, but also Himself and us, by the Holy Ghost; because, as was above explained, to love, taken in a notional sense, implies not only the production of a divine person, but also the person produced by way of love, which love has relation to the thing loved. Hence, as the Father speaks Himself and every creature by His begotten Word, inasmuch as the Word *begotten* adequately represents the Father and every creature, so He loves Himself and every creature by the Holy Ghost, inasmuch as the Holy Ghost proceeds as the love of the primal goodness whereby the Father loves Himself and every creature. Thus it is evident that relation to the creature is implied both in the Word and in the proceeding Love, as it were in a secondary way, inasmuch as the divine truth and goodness are a principle of understanding and loving all creatures.

Question XXXVIII
THE NAME OF THE HOLY GHOST AS *GIFT*
(*In Two Articles*)

THERE now follows the consideration of the Gift, concerning which there are two points of inquiry: (1) Whether *Gift* can be a personal name? (2) Whether it is the proper name of the Holy Ghost?

First Article
WHETHER GIFT IS A PERSONAL NAME?

We proceed thus to the First Article: —

Objection 1. It would seem that *Gift* is not a personal name. For every personal name implies a distinction in God. But the name of *Gift* does not imply a distinction in God; for Augustine says that *the Holy Ghost is so given as God's Gift, that He also gives Himself as God.*[1] Therefore *Gift* is not a personal name.

Obj. 2. Further, no personal name belongs to the divine essence. But the divine essence is the Gift[2] which the Father gives to the Son, as Hilary says.[3] Therefore *Gift* is not a personal name.

Obj. 3. Further, according to Damascene, there is no subjection nor service in the divine persons.[4] But gift implies a subjection both as regards him to whom it is given, and as regards him by whom it is

---

1. 参见 *De Trin.*, XV, 19 (PL 42, 1086).
2. the Gift：恩惠，天主圣神的另一个名称
3. 参见 *De Trin.*, IX (PL 10, 325).
4. 参见 *De Fide Orth.*, III, 21 (PG 94, 1085).

given. Therefore *Gift* is not a personal name.

Obj. 4. Further, *Gift* implies relation to the creature, and it thus seems to be said of God in time. But personal names are said of God from eternity; as *Father*, and *Son*. Therefore *Gift* is not a personal name.

On the contrary, Augustine says: *As the body of flesh is nothing but flesh, so the gift of the Holy Ghost is nothing but the Holy Ghost.*[1] But *Holy Ghost* is a personal name; so also therefore is *Gift*.

I answer that, The term *gift* implies an aptitude for being given. Now what is given has an aptitude or relation both to the giver and to that to which it is given. For it would not be given by anyone, unless it was his to give; and it is given to someone to be his. But a divine person is said to belong to another either by origin, as the Son belongs to the Father, or as possessed by another. But we are said to possess what we can freely use or enjoy as we please: and in this way a divine person cannot be possessed, except by a rational creature united to God. Other creatures can be moved by a divine person, not, however, in such a way as to be able to enjoy the divine person, and to use the effect thereof. The rational creature does sometimes attain thereto; as when it is made partaker of the divine Word and of the Love proceeding, so as freely to know God truly and to love God rightly. Hence the rational creature alone can possess a divine person. Nevertheless, in order that it may possess Him in this manner, its own power avails nothing: hence this must be given it from above, for that is said to be given to us which we have from another source. Thus a divine person can be *given*, and can be a *gift*.

Reply Obj. 1. The name *Gift* implies a personal distinction in so far as gift implies something belonging to another through its origin. Nevertheless, the Holy Ghost gives Himself, inasmuch as He is

1. 参见 *De Trin.*, XV, 19 (PL 42, 1086).

His own, and can use or rather enjoy Himself; just as a freeman is said to belong to himself. This is what Augustine says: *What is more yours than yourself?*[1] Or we might say, and more fittingly, that a gift must belong in a way to the giver. But the phrase, *this is this one's*, can be understood in several senses. In one way it means identity, as Augustine says;[2] and in that sense *gift* is the same as *the giver*, but not the same as the one to whom it is given. The Holy Ghost gives Himself in that sense. In another sense, a thing is another's as a possession, or as a slave; and in that sense gift is essentially distinct from the giver, and the gift of God so taken is a created thing. In a third sense *this is this* one's through its origin only; and in this sense the Son is the Father's, and the Holy Ghost belongs to both. Therefore, so far as gift in this way signifies the possession of the giver, it is personally distinguished from the giver, and is a personal name.

Reply Obj. 2. The divine essence is the Father's gift in the first sense, as being the Father's by way of identity.

Reply Obj. 3. Gift as a personal name in God does not imply subjection, but only origin, as regards the giver; but as regards the one to whom it is given, it implies a free use, or enjoyment, as was above explained.

Reply Obj. 4. Gift is not so called from being actually given, but from its aptitude to be given. Hence the divine person is called Gift from eternity, although He is given in time. Nor does it follow that it is an essential name because it implies relation to the creature; but it is necessary that it should include something essential in its meaning, as the essence is included in the idea of person, as was stated above.[3]

---

1. 参见 *Tract.* XXIX, super *Ioann.*, VII, 16 (PL 35, 1629).
2. 同上
3. 参见 Q. 34, a. 3, ad. 1.

Second Article

WHETHER *GIFT* IS THE PROPER NAME OF THE HOLY GHOST?

We proceed thus to the Second Article: —

Objection 1. It would seem that *Gift* is not the proper name of the Holy Ghost. For the name Gift comes from being given. But, as Isaias says, *A Son is given to us* (ix. 6). Therefore to be Gift belongs to the Son, as well as to the Holy Ghost.

Obj. 2. Further, every proper name of a person signifies a property. But this name Gift does not signify a property of the Holy Ghost. Therefore *Gift* is not a proper name of the Holy Ghost.

Obj. 3. Further, the Holy Ghost can be called the spirit of a man, whereas He cannot be called the gift of any man, but *God's Gift* only. Therefore Gift is not the proper name of the Holy Ghost.

On the contrary, Augustine says: *As 'to be born' is, for the Son, to be from the Father, so, for the Holy Ghost, 'to be the Gift of God' is to proceed from Father and Son.*[1] But the Holy Ghost receives His proper name from the fact that He proceeds from Father and Son. Therefore *Gift* is the proper name of the Holy Ghost.

I answer that, *Gift*, taken personally in God, is the proper name of the Holy Ghost.

In proof of this we must know that a gift is properly an unreturnable giving, as Aristotle says,[2] — *i.e.*, a thing which is not given with the intention of a return; and it thus contains the idea of a gratuitous giving. Now, the reason for gratuitous giving is love, since therefore do we give something to anyone gratuitously inasmuch as we wish him well. So what we first give him is the love whereby we wish him well.

1. 参见 *De Trin.*, IV, 20 (PL 42, 908).
2. 参见 *Top.*, IV, 4 (125a 18).

Hence it is manifest that love has the nature of a first gift, through which all free gifts are given. So, since the Holy Ghost proceeds as love, as was stated above,[1] He proceeds as the first gift. Hence Augustine says: *By the gift, which is the Holy Ghost, many particular gifts are portioned out to the members of Christ.*[2]

Reply Obj. 1. Because the Son proceeds as a word, whose nature it is to be the likeness of its principle, He is properly called the Image, even though the Holy Ghost is also like the Father; so also, because the Holy Ghost proceeds from the Father as love, He is properly called Gift, although the Son, too, is given. For that the Son is given is from the Father's love, according to the words, *God so loved the world, as to give His only begotten Son* (*Jo.* iii. 16).

Reply Obj. 2. The name Gift involves the idea of belonging to the Giver through its origin; and thus it expresses the property of the origin of the Holy Ghost — that is, His procession.

Reply Obj. 3. Before a gift is given, it belongs only to the giver; but when it is given, it is his to whom it is given. Therefore, because *Gift* does not signify the actual giving, it cannot be called a gift of man, but the Gift of God giving. When, however, it has been given, then it is the spirit of man, or a gift bestowed on man.

---

1. 参见 Q. 27, a. 4; q. 37, a. 1.
2. 参见 *De Trin.*, XV, 19 (PL 42, 1084).

Question XXXIX
THE PERSONS IN REFERENCE TO THE ESSENCE
(*In Eight Articles*)

HAVING considered what belongs to the divine persons absolutely, we next treat of what concerns the persons in reference to the essence, to the properties,[1] and to the notional acts;[2] and of the comparison of these with each other.[3]

As regards the first of these, there are eight points of inquiry: (1) Whether the essence in God is the same as the person? (2) Whether we should say that the three persons are of one essence? (3) Whether essential names should be predicated of the persons in the plural, or in the singular? (4) Whether notional adjectives, or verbs, or participles, can be predicated of the essential names taken in a concrete sense? (5) Whether the same can be predicated of essential names taken in the abstract? (6) Whether the names of the persons can be predicated of concrete essential names? (7) Whether essential attributes can be appropriated to the persons? (8) Which attributes should be appropriated to each person?

First Article
WHETHER IN GOD THE ESSENCE IS THE SAME AS THE PERSON?

We proceed thus to the First Article: —

---

1. 参见 Q. 40.
2. 参见 Q. 41.
3. 参见 Q. 42.

Objection 1. It would seem that in God the essence is not the same as person. For whenever essence is the same as person or *suppositum*[1], there can be only one *suppositum* of one nature, as is clear in the case of all separate substances. For in those things which are really one and the same, one cannot be multiplied apart from the other. But in God there is one essence and three persons, as is clear from what was above explained.[2] Therefore essence is not the same as person.

Obj. 2. Further, simultaneous affirmation and negation of the same things in the same respect cannot be true. But affirmation and negation are true of essence and of person. For person is distinct, whereas essence is not. Therefore person and essence are not the same.

Obj. 3. Further, nothing can be subject to itself. But person is subject to essence; whence it is called *suppositum* or *hypostasis*[3]. Therefore person is not the same as essence.

On the contrary, Augustine says: *When we say the person of the Father, we mean nothing else but the substance of the Father.*[4]

I answer that, The truth of this question is quite clear if we consider the divine simplicity. For it was shown above that the divine simplicity requires that in God essence is the same as *suppositum*, which in intellectual substances is nothing else than person.[5] But a difficulty seems to arise from the fact that while the divine persons are multiplied, the essence nevertheless retains its unity. And because, as Boethius says, *relation multiplies the Trinity of persons*,[6] some have thought that in God essence and person differ, because they held the relations to be *adjacent*. In the relations, they thus considered only

---

1. suppositum：基体，被置于下者
2. 参见 Q. 28, a. 3; q. 30, a. 2.
3. hypostasis：根本原理；本质；原质
4. 参见 *De Trin.*, VII, 6 (PL 42, 943).
5. 参见 Q. 3, a. 3.
6. 参见 *De Trin.*, VI (PL 64, 1255).

the idea of *reference to another*, and not the relations as realities. But as it was shown above, in creatures relations are accidental, whereas in God they are the divine essence itself.[1] Thence it follows that in God essence is not really distinct from person, and yet that the persons are really distinguished from each other. For person, as was above stated, signifies relation as subsisting in the divine nature.[2] But relation, as referred to the essence, does not differ from it really, but only in our way of thinking; while as referred to an opposite relation, it has a real distinction by virtue of that opposition. Thus there are one essence and three persons.

Reply Obj. 1. There cannot be a distinction among *supposita* in creatures by means of relations, but only by essential principles; because in creatures relations are not subsistent. But in God relations are subsistent, and so by reason of the opposition between them they distinguish the *supposita*; and yet the essence is not distinguished, because the relations themselves are not distinguished from each other so far as they are really identified with the essence.

Obj. 2. As essence and person in God differ in our way of thinking, it follows that something can be denied of the one and affirmed of the other; and therefore, when we suppose the one, we need not suppose the other.

Obj. 3. Divine things are named by us after the way of created things, as was above explained.[3] And since created natures are individuated by matter which is the subject of the specific nature, it follows that individuals are called *subjects*, *supposita*, or *hypostases*. So the divine persons are named *supposita* or *hypostases*, but not as if there really existed any real *supposition* or *subjection*.

---

1. 参见 Q. 28, a. 2.
2. 参见 Q. 29, a. 4.
3. 参见 Q. 13, a. 1, ad 2; a. 3.

Second Article

WHETHER IT MUST BE SAID THAT THE THREE PERSONS ARE OF ONE ESSENCE?

We proceed thus to the Second Article: —

Objection 1. It would seem not right to say that the three persons are of one essence. For Hilary says that the Father, Son and Holy Ghost *are indeed three by substance, but one in harmony.*[1] But the substance of God is His essence. Therefore the three persons are not of one essence.

Obj. 2. Further, nothing is to be affirmed of God except what can be confirmed by the authority of Holy Scripture, as appears from Dionysius.[2] Now Holy Scripture never says that the Father, Son and Holy Ghost are of one essence: Therefore this should not be asserted.

Obj. 3. Further, the divine nature is the same as the divine essence. It suffices therefore to say that the three persons are of one nature.

Obj. 4. Further, it is not usual to say that the person is of the essence; but rather that the essence is of the person. Therefore it does not seem fitting to say that the three persons are of one essence.

Obj. 5. Further, Augustine says that we do not say that the three persons are *from one essence*, lest we should seem to imply that the essence and the persons are not the same reality in God.[3] But prepositions which imply transition denote the oblique case. Therefore it is equally wrong to say that the three persons are *of one essence.*

Obj. 6. Further, nothing should be said of God which can be occasion of error. Now, to say that the three persons are of one essence or substance furnishes occasion of error. For, as Hilary says: *One substance predicated of the Father and the Son signifies either one subsistent*

---

1. 参见 *De Synod.* (PL 10, 503).
2. 参见 *De Div. Nom.*, I, 2 (PG 3, 588).
3. 参见 *De Trin.*, VII, 6 (PL 42, 945).

with two denominations; or one substance divided into two imperfect substances; or a third prior substance taken and assumed by the other two.[1] Therefore it must not be said that the three persons are of one substance.

On the contrary, Augustine says that the word ὁμοούσιου, which the Council of Nicæa adopted against the Arians, means that the three persons are of one essence.[2]

I answer that, As was above explained, divine things are named by our intellect, not as they really are in themselves, for in that way our intellect does not know them, but in a way that belongs to created things.[3] And since among sensible things, whence the intellect derives its knowledge, the nature of the species is made individual by matter (and thus the nature is as the form, and the individual is the *suppositum* of the form), so also in God, according to our mode of signification, the essence is taken as the form of the three persons. Now in creatures we say that every form belongs to that being whose form it is; as the health and beauty of a man belongs to the man. But we do not say of that which has a form, that it belongs to the form, unless some adjective qualifies the form; as when we say: *That woman is of a handsome figure*, or: *This man is of perfect virtue*. In like manner, as in God the persons are multiplied, and the essence is not multiplied, we speak of one essence of the three persons, and three persons of the one essence, provided that these genitives be understood as designating the form.

Reply Obj. 1. Substance is here taken for the *hypostasis*, and not for the essence.

Reply Obj. 2. Although we may not find it declared in Holy Scripture in so many words that the three persons are of one essence, nevertheless we find it so stated as regards the meaning; for instance,

---

1. 参见 *De Synod.* (PL 10, 526).
2. 参见 *Contra Maximin.*, III, 14 (PL 42, 772); *Contra Serm. Arian.*, XXXVI(PL 42, 707).
3. 参见 Q. 13, a. 1, ad 2; a. 3.

I and the Father are one (*Jo.* x. 30), and *I am in the Father, and the Father in Me* (*Jo.* x. 38; xiv. 10); and there are many other texts of the same import.

Reply Obj. 3. Because *nature* designates the principle of action, while *essence* comes from being [*essendo*], things may be said to be of one nature which agree in some action, as all things which give heat; but only those things can be said to be of *one essence* which have one being. So the divine unity is better described by saying that the three persons are *of one essence* than by saying they are *of one nature.*

Reply Obj. 4. Form, in the absolute sense, is wont to be designated as belonging to that of which it is the form, as we say *the virtue of Peter.* On the other hand, the thing having form is not wont to be designated as belonging to the form, except when we wish to qualify or designate the form. In which case two genitives are required, one signifying the form, and the other signifying the determination of the form, as, for instance, when we say, *Peter is of great virtue*, or else one genitive must have the force of two, as, for instance, *he is a man of blood* — that is, he is a man who sheds much blood. So, because the divine essence is signified as a form in relation to the person, it may properly be said that the essence is of the person; but we cannot say the converse, unless we add some term to designate the essence, as, for instance, the Father is a person of the *divine essence*, or, the three persons are *of one essence.*

Reply Obj. 5. The preposition *from* or *out of* does not designate the relation of a formal cause, but rather the relation of an efficient or material cause; which causes are in all cases distinguished from those things of which they are the causes. For nothing can be its own matter, nor its own active principle. Yet a thing may be its own form, as appears in all immaterial things. So, when we say, *three persons of one essence*, taking essence as having the relation of form, we do not mean that essence is a different reality from person, which we should mean if we said, *three persons from the same essence.*

Reply Obj. 6. As Hilary says: *It would be prejudicial to holy things, if we had to do away with them, just because some do not think them holy. So if some misunderstand ὁμοούσιον, what is that to me, if I understand it rightly?*[1]. . . *The oneness of nature does not result from division, or from union, or from community of possession, but from one nature being proper to both Father and Son.*[2]

Third Article
WHETHER ESSENTIAL NAMES SHOULD BE PREDICATED IN THE SINGULAR OF THE THREE PERSONS?

We proceed thus to the Third Article: —

Objection 1. It would seem that essential names, as the name *God*, should not be predicated in the singular of the three persons, but in the plural. For as *man* signifies *one that has humanity*, so *God* signifies *one that has Godhead*. But the three persons are three who have Godhead. Therefore the three persons are *three Gods*.

Obj. 2. Further, in *Gen*. i. 1, where it is said, *In the beginning God created heaven and earth*, the Hebrew original has *Elohim*, which may be rendered *Gods* or *Judges*: and this word is used because of the plurality of persons. Therefore the three persons are *many Gods*, and not *one* God.

Obj. 3. Further, this word *thing*, when it is said absolutely, seems to belong to substance. But it is predicated of the three persons in the plural. For Augustine says: *The things that are the objects of our future glory are the Father, Son and Holy Ghost.*[3] Therefore other essential names can be predicated in the plural of the three persons.

Obj. 4. Further, as this name *God* signifies *a being who has Deity*, so

1. 参见 *De Synod.* (PL 10, 538).
2. 同上 (PL 10, 527).
3. 参见 *De Doc. Christ.*, I, 5 (PL 34, 21).

also this name *person* signifies a being subsisting in an intellectual nature. But we say that there are three persons. So for the same reason we can say there are *three Gods*.

On the contrary, It is said (*Deut.* vi. 4): *Hear, O Israel, the Lord thy God is one God.*

I answer that, Some essential names signify the essence after the manner of substantives; while others signify it after the manner of adjectives. Those which signify it as substantives are predicated of the three persons in the singular only, and not in the plural. Those which signify the essence as adjectives are predicated of the three persons in the plural. The reason for this is that substantives signify something by way of substance, while adjectives signify something by way of accident, which inheres in a subject. Now just as substance has existence of itself, so also it has of itself unity or multitude; wherefore the singularity or plurality of a substantive name depends upon the form signified by the name. But as accidents have their being in a subject, so they have unity or plurality from their subject; and therefore the singularity and plurality of adjectives depends upon their *supposita*. In creatures, however, one form does not exist in several *supposita* except by unity of order, as the form of an ordered multitude. So if the names signifying such a form are substantives, they are predicated of many in the singular; but not if they are adjectives. For we say that many men are a college, or an army, or a people; but we say that many men are collegians. Now in God the divine essence is signified by way of a form, as was above explained. This form is simple and supremely one, as was shown above.[1] So, names which signify the divine essence in a substantive manner are predicated of the three persons in the singular, and not in the plural. This, then, is the reason why we say that Socrates, Plato and Cicero are *three men*; whereas we

1. 参见 Q. 3, a. 7; q. 11, a. 4.

do not say the Father, Son and Holy Ghost are *three Gods*, but *one God*; for in the three *supposita* of human nature there are three humanities, whereas in the three divine Persons there is but one divine essence. On the other hand, the names which signify the essence in an adjectival manner are predicated of the three persons in the plural by reason of the plurality of *supposita*. For we say that there are three *existent* or three *wise* beings, or three *eternal*, *uncreated* and *immense* being, if these terms are understood in an adjectival sense. But if taken in a substantive sense, we say *one uncreated*, *immense*, *eternal being*, as Athanasius declares.[1]

Reply Obj. 1. Though the name *God* signifies a being having Godhead, nevertheless the mode of signification is different. For the name *God* is used substantively, whereas *having Godhead* is used adjectively. Consequently, although there are *three having Godhead*, it does not follow that there are three Gods.

Reply Obj. 2. Various languages have diverse modes of expression. So, as by reason of the plurality of *supposita* the Greeks said *three hypostases*, so also in Hebrew *Elohim* is in the plural. We, however, do not apply the plural either to *God* or to *substance*, lest plurality be referred to the substance.

Reply Obj. 3. This word *thing* is one of the transcendentals. Whence, so far as it is referred to relation, it is predicated of God in the plural; whereas, so far as it is referred to the substance, it is predicated in the singular. So Augustine says, in the passage quoted, that *the same Trinity is a certain supreme thing*.

Reply Obj. 4. The form signified by the name *person* is not essence or nature, but personality. So, as there are three personalities — that is, three personal properties in the Father, Son and Holy Ghost — it is predicated of the three, not in the singular, but in the plural.

1. 参见 Cf. *Symb. "Quicumque"* (Denzinger, no. 39).

Fourth Article

WHETHER THE CONCRETE ESSENTIAL NAMES CAN STAND FOR THE PERSON?

We proceed thus to the Fourth Article: —

Objection 1. It would seem that the concrete essential names cannot stand for the person, so that we could truly say *God begot God.* For, as the logicians say, *a singular term signifies what it stands for.*[1] But this name *God* seems to be a singular term, for it cannot be predicated in the plural, as above explained. Therefore, since it signifies the essence, it stands for essence, and not for person.

Obj. 2. Further, a term in the subject is not restricted by the predicate term as to its signification, but only as to the time co-signified in the predicate. But when I say, *God creates*, this name *God* stands for the essence. So when we say *God begot*, this term *God* cannot by reason of the notional predicate stand for person.

Obj. 3. Further, if this be true, *God begot*, because the Father generates, for the same reason this is true, *God does not beget*, because the Son does not beget. Therefore there is God who begets, and there is God who does not beget; and thus it follows that there are two Gods.

Obj. 4. Further, if *God begot God*, He begot either the God He is, or another God. But He did not beget the God He is, for, as Augustine says, *nothing begets itself.*[2] Neither did He beget another God, as there is only one God. Therefore it is false to say, *God begot God.*

Obj. 5. Further, if *God begot God*, He begot either the God who is the Father, or the God who is not the Father. If the God who is the Father, then God the Father was begotten. If the God who is not the

1. 参见 Peter of Spain, *Summulae Logicales*, tr. IX (unnumbered fol. 225).
2. 参见 *De Trin.*, I, 1 (PL 42, 820).

Father, then there is a God who is not God the Father: which is false. Therefore it cannot be said that *God begot God.*

On the contrary, In the Creed it is said, *God of God.*[1]

I answer that, Some[2] have said that *this name God and the like, properly according to their nature, stand for the essence, but by reason of some notional adjunct are made to stand for the Person.* This opinion apparently arose from considering the divine simplicity, which requires that in God He *who possesses* and *what is possessed* be the same. So He-who-possesses-Godhead, which is signified by the name God, is the same as Godhead.

But when we consider the proper way of expressing ourselves the mode of signification must be considered no less than the thing signified. Hence, as this name *God* signifies the divine essence as in Him Who possesses it, just as the name *man* signifies humanity in a subject, others[3] more truly have said that this name *God*, from its mode of signification, can, in its proper sense, stand for person, as does the name *man*. So this name *God* sometimes stands for the essence, as when we say *God creates*; because this predicate belongs to the subject by reason of the form signified — that is, the Godhead. But sometimes it stands for the person, either for only one, as when we say *God begets*, or for two, as when we say, *God spirates*, or for three, as when it is said: *To the King of ages, immortal, invisible, the only God*, etc. (1 *Tim.* i. 17).

Reply Obj. 1. Although this name *God* agrees with singular terms in that the form signified is not multiplied, nevertheless it agrees also with general terms so far as the form signified is to be found

1. 参见 *Symb. Nycaenum* (Denzinger, no. 54).
2. 参见 Gilbert de la Porrée, *In De Praedicat. trium Pers.* (PL 64, 1310). — Cf. Alex. of Hales, *Summa Theol.*, II, no. 357 (I. 535).
3. 参 见 Alain of Lille, *Theol. Reg.*, XXIV (PL 210, 632); XXXII (PL 210, 636); William of Auxerre, *Summa Aurea* II, tr. 4, ch. 4 (fol. 6a).

in several *supposita*. So it need not always stand for the essence it signifies.

Reply Obj. 2. This holds good against those who used to say that the name *God* does not naturally stand for person.

Reply Obj. 3. The name *God* stands for the person in a different way from that in which this name *man* does; for since the form signified by the name *man* — that is, humanity — is really divided among its different subjects, of itself it stands for the person, even if there is nothing added determining it to the person — that is, to a distinct subject. The unity or community of the human nature, however, is not a reality, but is only in the consideration of the mind. Hence this term *man* does not stand for the common nature, unless this is required by some addition, as when we say, *man is a species*. But the form signified by the name *God* — that is, the divine essence — is really one and common. And so, it stands of itself for the common nature, but by some addition it may be restricted so as to stand for the person. Hence, when we say, *God generates*, by reason of the notional act this name *God* stands for the person of the Father. But when we say, *God does not generate*, there is no addition to determine this name to the person of the Son, and hence the phrase means that generation is repugnant to the divine nature. If, however, something be added belonging to the person of the Son, that way of speaking will be true; as when we say, for instance, *God begotten does not beget*. Consequently, it does not follow that there exists a *God generator*, and a *God not generator*, unless there be an addition pertaining to the persons; as, for instance, if we were to say, *the Father is God the generator*, and *the Son is God the non-generator*: and so it does not follow that there are many Gods; for the Father and the Son are one God, as was said above.

Reply Obj. 4. This is false, *the Father begot the God He Himself is*, because the word *Himself*, as a reciprocal term, refers to the same *suppositum*. Nor is this contrary to what Augustine says, namely, that

God the Father begot another self [*alterum se*] ,[1] for the word *se* is either in the ablative case, and then it means He *begot another from Himself*, or it indicates a single relation, and thus points to identity of nature. This is, however, either an improper or an emphatic way of speaking, so that it would really mean, *He begot another most like to Himself*. Likewise also it is false to say, *He begot another God*, because although the Son is another than the Father, as was above explained,[2] nevertheless it cannot be said that He is *another God*; for this adjective *another* would be understood to apply to the substantive *God*, and thus the meaning would be that there is a distinction of Godhead. Yet this proposition *He begot another God* is tolerated by some, provided that *another* be taken as a substantive, and *God* be construed in apposition with it.[3] This, however, is an inexact way of speaking, and to be avoided, for fear of giving occasion to error.

Reply Obj. 5. To say, *God begot God Who is God the Father*, is wrong. For since *Father* is construed in apposition to *God*, the term *God* is restricted to the person of the Father; so that it would mean, *He begot God, Who is Himself the Father*; and then the Father would be spoken of as begotten, which is false. Therefore the negative of this proposition is true, *He begot God Who is not God the Father*. If, however, we understand these words not to be in apposition, and require something to be added, then, on the contrary, the affirmative proposition is true, and the negative is false; so that the meaning would be, *He begot God Who is God Who is the Father*. Such a rendering, however, appears to be forced, so that it is better to say simply that the affirmative proposition is false, and the negative is true.

Yet Prepositinus said that both the negative and the affirmative are false, because the relative *Who* in the affirmative proposition can be

---

1. 参见 *Epist.* CLXX (PL 33, 749).
2. 参见 Q. 31, a. 2.
3. 参见 William of Auxerre, *Summa Aurea*, I, tr. 4, ch. 4 (fol. 5d).

referred to the *suppositum*, whereas in the negative it denotes both the thing signified and the *suppositum*. Whence, in the affirmative the sense is that *to be God the Father* is befitting to the person of the Son; and in the negative the sense is that *to be God the Father* is to be removed from the Son's divinity as well as from His personality. This, however, appears to be irrational, since, according to the Philosopher, what can receive affirmation, can also receive negation.[1]

Fifth Article
WHETHER ABSTRACT ESSENTIAL NAMES CAN STAND FOR THE PERSON?

We proceed thus to the Fifth Article: —

Objection 1. It would seem that abstract essential names can stand for the person, so that this proposition is true, *Essence begets essence.* For Augustine says: *The Father and the Son are one Wisdom, because they are one essence; and taken singly Wisdom is from Wisdom, as essence from essence.*[2]

Obj. 2. Further, generation or corruption in ourselves implies generation or corruption of what is within us. But the Son is generated. Therefore since the divine essence is in the Son, it seems that the divine essence is generated.

Obj. 3. Further, God and the divine essence are the same, as is clear from what is above explained.[3] But, as was shown, it is true to say that *God begets God.* Therefore this is also true: *Essence begets essence.*

Obj. 4. Further, a predicate can stand for that of which it is predicated. But the Father is the divine essence; therefore essence can stand for the person of the Father. Thus the essence begets.

---

1. 参见 *Perih.*, VI (17a 30).
2. 参见 *De Trin.*, VII, 2 (PL 42, 936).
3. 参见 Q. 3, a. 3.

Obj. 5. Further, the essence is *a thing begetting*, because the essence is the Father who is begetting. Therefore if the essence is not begetting the essence will be *a thing begetting*, and *not begetting*: which cannot be.

Obj. 6. Further, Augustine says: *The Father is the principle of the whole Godhead.*[1] But He is principle only by begetting or spirating. Therefore the Father begets or spirates the Godhead.

On the contrary, Augustine says: *Nothing begets itself.*[2] But if the essence begets the essence, it begets itself only, since nothing exists in God as distinguished from the divine essence. Therefore the essence does not beget the essence.

I answer that, Concerning this question, the abbot Joachim erred in asserting that as we can say *God begot God*, so we can say *Essence begot essence.*[3] For he held that, by reason of the divine simplicity, God is nothing else but the divine essence. In this he was deceived. For if we wish to express ourselves correctly, we must take into account not only the thing which is signified, but also the mode of its signification, as was stated above. Now although *God* is really the same as *Godhead*, nevertheless the mode of signification is not in each case the same. For since the name *God* signifies the divine essence as existing in Him that possesses it, from its mode of signification it can of its own nature stand for person. Thus the things which properly belong to the persons can be predicated of the name *God*, as, for instance, we can say *God is begotten* or *is Begetter*, as was explained above. The name *essence*, however, in its mode of signification, cannot stand for Person, because it signifies the essence as an abstract form. Consequently, what properly belongs to the persons, distinguishing them from each other, cannot be attributed to the essence. For that would mean distinction in the divine essence, in the same way as there exists distinction in the

1. 参见 *De Trin.*, IV, 20 (PL 42, 908).
2. 参见 *Op. cit.*, I, 1 (PL 42, 820).
3. 参见 Cf. *Decretal. Gregor.* IX, bk. I, tit. 1. ch. 2 (II, 6).

supposita.

Reply Obj. 1. To express unity of essence and of person, the holy Doctors have sometimes expressed themselves with greater emphasis than the strict propriety of terms allows. Hence, instead of pressing such expressions, we should rather explain them: thus, for instance, abstract names should be explained by concrete names, or even by personal names; as when we find *essence from essence*, or *wisdom from wisdom*, we should take the sense to be: the Son, who is essence and wisdom, is from the Father, who is essence and wisdom. Nevertheless, as regards these abstract names a certain order should be observed, for what belongs to action is more nearly allied to the persons because actions belong to *supposita*. So *nature from nature*, and *wisdom from wisdom* are less inexact than *essence from essence.*

Reply Obj. 2. In creatures, the one generated does not receive the same nature numerically as the generator, but another nature, numerically distinct, which commences to exist in it anew by generation, and ceases to exist by corruption; and so it is generated and corrupted accidentally. But God begotten receives the same nature numerically as the begetter possesses. So the divine nature in the Son is not begotten either essentially or accidentally.

Reply Obj. 3. Although God and the divine essence are really the same, nevertheless, because of their different mode of signification, we must speak in a different way about each of them.

Reply Obj. 4. The divine essence is predicated of the Father by identity, by reason of the divine simplicity; yet it does not follow that it can stand for the Father, since its mode of signification is different. This objection would hold good as regards terms among which one is predicated of another as the universal of the particular.

Reply Obj. 5. The difference between substantive and adjectival names consists in this, that the former carry their subject with them, whereas the latter do not, but add the thing signified to the substantive. Whence logicians are wont to say that substantive names *stand*, but adjectival names do not stand, they *join*.[1] Therefore substantive personal names can be predicated of the essence, because they are really the same; nor does it follow that a personal property makes a distinct essence: it belongs to the *suppositum* expressed by the substantive name. But notional and personal adjectives cannot be predicated of the essence unless we add some substantive. And so, we cannot say that the *essence is begetting*; yet we can say that the *essence is a thing begetting*, or that it is *God begetting*, if *thing* and *God* stand for person, but not if they stand for essence. Consequently, there exists no contradiction in saying that *essence is a thing begetting* and *a thing not begetting*; because in the first case *thing* stands for person, and in the second it stands for the essence.

Reply Obj. 6. So far as Godhead is one in several *supposita*, it agrees in a certain degree with the form of a collective term. So when we say, *the Father is the principle of the whole Godhead*, the term Godhead can be taken for all the persons together, inasmuch as He is the principle in all the divine persons. Nor does it follow that He is His own principle; just as one of the people may be called the ruler of the whole people without being ruler of himself. We may also say that the Father is the principle of the whole Godhead, not as generating or spirating it, but as communicating it by generation and spiration.

Sixth Article
WHETHER THE PERSONS CAN BE PREDICATED OF THE ESSENTIAL NAMES?

We proceed thus to the Sixth Article: —

Objection 1. It would seem that the persons cannot be predicated of the concrete essential names, so that we can say for instance, *God is*

1. 参见 Peter of Spain, *Summulae Logicales*, tr. VII (unnumbered fol. 203v).

three persons; or, *God is the Trinity*. For it is false to say, *man is every man*, because it cannot be verified as regards any individual. For neither Socrates, nor Plato, nor anyone else is every man. In the same way, this proposition, *God is the Trinity*, cannot be verified of any one of the *supposita* of the divine nature. For the Father is not the Trinity; nor is the Son; nor is the Holy Ghost. So to say, *God is the Trinity*, is false.

Obj. 2. Further, the lower is not predicated of the higher except by accidental predication, as when I say, *animal is man*; for it is accidental to animal to be man. But this name *God*, as regards the three persons, is as a general term to inferior terms, as Damascene says.[1] Therefore, it seems that the names of the persons cannot be predicated of this name *God*, except accidentally.

On the contrary, Augustine says, in his sermon on Faith, *We believe that one God is one divinely named Trinity*.[2]

I answer that, As above explained, although adjectival terms, whether personal or notional, cannot be predicated of the essence, nevertheless substantive terms can be so predicated, owing to the real identity of essence and person. The divine essence, however, is not only really the same as one person, but it is really the same as the three persons. Whence, one person, and two, and three, can be predicated of the essence; as if we were to say, *The essence is the Father and the Son and the Holy Ghost*. And because this name *God* can of itself stand for the essence, as was above explained, hence, just as it is true to say, *The essence is the three persons*, so likewise it is true to say, *God is the three persons*.

Reply Obj. 1. As above explained, this term *man* can of itself stand for a person, whereas an addition is required for it to stand for universal human nature. So it is false to say, *Man is every man*, because it cannot

1. 参见 *De Fide Orth*., III, 4 (PG 94, 997).
2. 参见 *Sermo* CCXXXIII (PL 39, 2175). — Cf. Fulgentius, *De Fide ad Petrum*, I (PL 65, 673).

be verified of any individual human subject. On the contrary, this name *God* can of itself be taken for the divine essence. So, although to say of any of the *supposita* of the divine nature, *God is the Trinity*, is untrue, nevertheless it is ture of the divine essence. This was denied by Porretanus because he did not take note of this distinction.[1]

Reply Obj. 2. When we say, *God or the divine essence is the Father*, the predication is one of identity, and not of the lower in regard to a higher, because in God there is no universal and singular. Hence, as this proposition, *The Father is God* is an identity, so is this proposition *God is the Father*: it is not an accidental predication of a lower in relation to a higher.

Seventh Article
WHETHER THE ESSENTIAL NAMES SHOULD BE APPROPRIATED TO THE PERSONS?

We proceed thus to the Seventh Article: —

Objection 1. It would seem that the essential names should not be appropriated to the persons. For whatever might verge on error in faith should be avoided in the treatment of divine things; for, as Jerome says, *careless words involve risk of heresy.*[2] But to appropriate to any one person the names which are common to the three persons may verge on error in faith; for it may be supposed either that such belong only to the person to whom they are appropriated, or that they belong to Him in a fuller degree than to the others. Therefore the essential attributes should not be appropriated to the persons.

Obj. 2. Further, the essential attributes expressed in the abstract signify in the manner of a form. But one person is not as a form to another, since a form is not distinguished in subject from that of

---

1. 参见 *In De Trin.* (PL 64, 1311).
2. 参见 Cf. Peter Lombard, *Sent.*, IV, xiii, 2 (II, 818).

which it is the form. Therefore, the essential attributes, especially when expressed in the abstract, are not to be appropriated to the persons.

Obj. 3. Further, property is prior to the appropriated, for property is included in the idea of the appropriated. But the essential attributes, in our way of understanding, are prior to the persons as the common is prior to the proper. Therefore the essential attributes are not to be appropriated to the persons.

On the contrary, The Apostle says: *Christ the power of God and the wisdom of God* (1 *Cor.* i. 24).

I answer that, For the manifestation of our faith it is fitting that the essential attributes should be appropriated to the persons. For although the trinity of persons cannot be proved by demonstration, as was explained above,[1] nevertheless it is fitting that it be declared by things which are more known to us. Now the essential attributes of God are more clear to us in their nature than the personal properties, because we can arrive with certainty at a knowledge of the essential attributes of God, basing ourselves on the creatures from which our knowledge begins. But we cannot thus reach a knowledge of the personal properties, as was above explained.[2] As, therefore, we make use of the likeness of the trace or image found in creatures for the manifestation of the divine persons, so also do we make use of the essential attributes. And such a manifestation of the divine persons by the use of the essential attributes is called *appropriation*[3].

The divine persons, however, can be manifested in a twofold manner by the essential attributes. In one way by likeness, and thus the things which belong to the intellect are appropriated to

---

1. 参见 Q. 32, a. 1.
2. 同上 ad 1.
3. appropriation：归名；转拨；挪用

the Son, Who proceeds by way of intellect as Word. In another way by unlikeness; as power is appropriated to the Father, as Augustine says,[1] because among us fathers by reason of old age are sometimes feeble; and nothing of the kind must be imagined of God.

Reply Obj. 1. The essential attributes are not appropriated to the persons as if they exclusively belonged to them, but in order to make the persons manifest by way of likeness or unlikeness, as was explained above. So, no error in faith can arise, but rather manifestation of the truth.

Reply Obj. 2. If the essential attributes were appropriated to the persons as exclusively belonging to each of them, then it would follow that one person would be as a form in relation to another; which Augustine altogether repudiates[2], [3] showing that the Father is not wise by the wisdom begotten by Him, as though only the Son were Wisdom (which would thus mean that the Father and the Son together only can be called wise, but not the Father without the Son). But the Son is called the Wisdom of the Father, because He is Wisdom from the Father Who is Wisdom. For each of them is of Himself Wisdom; and both together are one Wisdom. Whence the Father is not wise by the wisdom begotten by Him, but by the wisdom which is His own essence.

Reply Obj. 3. Although an essential attribute is, in its proper concept, prior to person according to our way of understanding, nevertheless, so far as it is appropriated, there is nothing to prevent the personal property from being prior to that which is appropriated. Thus color is posterior to body considered as body, but is naturally prior to *white body*, considered as white.

---

1. 参见 Cf. Hugh of St. Victor, *De Sacram.* I, pt. 2, ch. 8 (PL 176, 209).
2. repudiate：拒绝接受；否认
3. 参见 *De Trin.*, VII, 1; VI, 2 (PL 42, 933; 925).

Eighth Article

WHETHER THE ESSENTIAL ATTRIBUTES ARE APPROPRIATED TO THE PERSONS IN A FITTING MANNER BY THE HOLY DOCTORS?

We proceed thus to the Eighth Article: —

Objection 1. It would seem that the essential attributes are appropriated to the persons unfittingly by the holy doctors. For Hilary says: *Eternity is in the Father, the species is in the Image; and use is in the Gift.*[1] In these words he designates three names proper to the persons: the name of the *Father*, the name *Image* proper to the Son,[2] and the name *Bounty* or *Gift*, which is proper to the Holy Ghost.[3] He also designates three appropriated terms. For he appropriates *eternity* to the Father, *species* to the Son, and *use* to the Holy Ghost. This he does apparently without reason. For *eternity* implies duration of being; *species*, the principle of being; and *use* belongs to the operation. But essence and operation are not found to be appropriated to any person. Therefore the above terms are not fittingly appropriated to the persons.

Obj. 2. Further, Augustine says: *Unity is in the Father, equality in the Son, and in the Holy Ghost is the concord of equality and unity.*[4] This does not, however, seem fitting, because one person does not receive formal denomination from what is appropriated to another. For the Father is not wise by the wisdom begotten, as was above explained.[5] But, as he subjoins, *All these three are one by the Father; all are equal by the Son,*

1. 参见 *De Trin.*, II (PL 10, 51).
2. 参见 Q. 35, a. 2.
3. 参见 Q. 38, a. 2.
4. 参见 *De Doc. Christ.*, I, 5 (PL 34, 21).
5. 参见 A. 7, ad 2; q. 37, a. 2.

and all united by the Holy Ghost. The above, therefore, are not fittingly appropriated to the Persons.

Obj. 3. Further, according to Augustine, to the Father is attributed *power*, to the Son *wisdom*, to the Holy Ghost *goodness.*[1] Nor does this seem fitting; for *strength* is part of power, whereas strength is found to be appropriated to the Son, according to the text, *Christ the strength* [Douay, *power*] *of God* (1 *Cor.* i. 24). So it is likewise appropriated to the Holy Ghost, according to the words, *strength* [Douay, *virtue*] *came out from Him and healed all* (*Luke* vi. 19). Therefore power should not be appropriated to the Father.

Obj. 4. Likewise Augustine says:[2] *What the Apostle says, "From Him, and by Him, and in Him," is not to be taken in a confused sense. "From Him" refers to the Father, "by Him" to the Son, "in Him" to the Holy Ghost.*[3] This, however, seems to be incorrectly said; for the words *in Him* seem to imply the relation of final cause, which is first among the causes. Therefore this relation of cause should be appropriated to the Father, Who is *the principle from no principle.*

Obj. 5. Likewise, Truth is appropriated to the Son, according to *Jo.* xiv. 6, *I am the Way, the Truth, and the Life.* So, too, is *the book of life*, according to *Ps.* xxxix. 9, *In the beginning of the book it is written of Me*, where the Gloss observes *that is, with the Father Who is My head.*[4] Also proper to the Son is the expression *Who is*; because on the text of Isaias, *Behold I go to the Gentiles* (lxv. 1), the *Gloss* adds, *The Son speaks Who said to Moses, I am Who am.*[5]

Yet these appear to belong to the Son, and are not appropriated. For *truth*, according to Augustine, *is the supreme likeness of the principle*

---

1. 参见 Cf. Hugh of St. Victor, *De Sacram.*, I, pt. 2, ch. 6 (PL 176, 208).
2. 参见 *De Trin.*, VI, 10 (PL 42, 932).
3. 参见 *Contra Maximin.*, II, 23 (PL 42, 800).
4. 参见 *Glossa ordin.*, super *Ps.* XXXIX, 8 (III, 143 B); Peter Lombard, *In Psalm.*, super XXXIX, 8 (PL 191, 403).
5. 参见 *Glossa interl.* (IV, 104r).

without any unlikeness.[1] So it seems that it properly belongs to the Son, Who has a principle. Also the *book of life* seems to be proper to the Son, as signifying *a thing from another*; for every book is written by someone. This also, *Who is*, appears to be proper to the Son; because, if when it was said to Moses, *I am Who am*, the Trinity spoke, then Moses could have said, *He Who is the Father, Son, and Holy Ghost sent me to you*; so also he could have said further, *He Who is the Father and the Son and the Holy Ghost sent me to you*, pointing out a certain person. This, however, is false; because no person is Father-Son-and-Holy Ghost. Therefore it cannot be common to the Trinity, but is proper to the Son.

I answer that, Our intellect, which is led to the knowledge of God from creatures, must consider God according to the mode derived from creatures. In considering any creature four points present themselves to us in due order. First, the thing itself taken absolutely is considered as a being. Secondly, it is considered as one. Thirdly, its intrinsic power of operation and causality is considered. The fourth point of consideration embraces its relation to its effects. Hence this fourfold consideration comes to our mind in reference to God.

It is according to the first point of consideration, whereby we consider God absolutely in His being, that the appropriation mentioned by Hilary applies; according to which *eternity* is appropriated to the Father, *species* to the Son, *use* to the Holy Ghost. For *eternity*, as meaning *a being* without a principle, has a likeness to the property of the Father, Who is *a principle without a principle.* Species or beauty has a likeness to the property of the Son. For beauty includes three conditions: *integrity* or *perfection*, since those things which are impaired are by that very fact ugly; due *proportion* or *harmony*; and lastly, *brightness*, or *clarity*, whence things are called beautiful which

1. 参见 *De Vera Relig.*, XXXVI (PL 34, 152).

have a bright color.

The first of these has a likeness to the property of the Son, because as Son He has in Himself truly and perfectly the nature of the Father To insinuate this, Augustine says in his explanation: *Where — that is, in the Son — there is supreme and primal life*, etc.[1]

The second agrees with the Son's property, inasmuch as He is the express Image of the Father. Hence we see that an image is said to be beautiful, if it perfectly represents even an ugly thing. This is indicated by Augustine when he says, *Where there exists wondrous proportion and primal equality*, etc.[2]

The third agrees with the property of the Son as the Word, which is the light and splendor of the intellect, as Damascene says.[3] Augustine alludes to the same when he says: *As the perfect Word, not wanting in anything, and, so to speak, the art of the omnipotent God*, etc.[4]

Use has a likeness to the property of the Holy Ghost, provided that *use* be taken in a wide sense, as including also the sense of *to enjoy*. Thus understood, *to use* is to employ something at the beck of the will, and *to enjoy* means to use joyfully, as Augustine says.[5] So *use*, whereby the Father and the Son enjoy each other, agrees with the property of the Holy Ghost, as Love. This is what Augustine says: *That love, that delectation, that felicity or beatitude, is called use by him.*[6] But the *use* by which we enjoy God is likened to the property of the Holy Ghost as the Gift ; and Augustine points to this when he says: *In the Trinity, the Holy Ghost, the sweetness of the Begetter and the Begotten, pours out upon us mere creatures His immense bounty and wealth.*[7] Thus it is

---

1. 参见 *De Trin.*, VI, 10 (PL 42, 931).
2. 同上
3. 参见 *De Fide Orth.*, I, 13 (PG 94, 857).
4. 参见 *De Trin.*, VI, 10 (PL 42, 931).
5. 参见 *Op. cit.*, X, 11 (PL 42, 982).
6. 参见 *Op. cit.*, VI, 10 (PL 42, 932).
7. 同上

clear how *eternity*, *species* and *use* are attributed or appropriated to the persons, but not essence or operation; because, being common, they have nothing in their concept to liken them to the properties of the Persons.

The second consideration of God regards Him as *one*. From this point of view, Augustine appropriates *unity* to the Father, *equality* to the Son, *concord* or *union* to the Holy Ghost.[1] It is manifest that these three express unity, but in different ways. For *unity* is said absolutely, as it does not presuppose anything else; and for this reason it is appropriated to the Father, to Whom any other person is not presupposed. For He is the *principle without a principle. Equality* implies unity in relation to another; for that is equal which has the same quantity as another. So equality is appropriated to the Son, Who is the *principle from a principle. Union* implies the unity of two; and is therefore appropriated to the Holy Ghost, inasmuch as He proceeds from two. And in this sense we can understand what Augustine means when he says that *The Three are one by reason of the Father*; *They are equal by reason of the Son*; *and are united by reason of the Holy Ghost*. For it is clear that we trace a thing back to that in which we find it first: just as in this lower world we attribute life to the vegetative soul, because therein we first find the nature of life in this sublunary world[2]. Now, *unity* is perceived at once in the person of the Father, even if, by an impossible hypothesis, the other persons were removed. So the other persons derive their unity from the Father. But if the other persons be removed, we do not find equality in the Father, but we find it as soon as we suppose the Son. So, all are equal by reason of the Son, not as if the Son were the principle of equality in the Father, but that, without the Son equal to the Father, the Father could not be called equal; because His equality is first considered in regard to the Son: for that

1. 参见 *De Doc Christ.*, I, 5 (PL 34, 21).
2. sublunary world：地上的或世俗的世界

the Holy Ghost is equal to the Father, is also from the Son. Likewise, if the Holy Ghost, Who is the union of the two, be excluded, we cannot understand the oneness of the union between the Father and the Son. So all are connected by reason of the Holy Ghost; because, given the Holy Ghost, we find whence the Father and the Son are said to be united.

According to the third consideration, which brings before us the adequate power of God in the sphere of causality, there is said to be a third kind of appropriation, namely of *power*, *wisdom* and *goodness*.[1] This kind of appropriation is made both by reason of likeness as regards what exists in the divine persons, and by reason of unlikeness if we consider what is in creatures. For *power* has the nature of a principle, and so it has a likeness to the heavenly Father, Who is the principle of the whole Godhead. But in an earthly father power is wanting sometimes by reason of old age. *Wisdom* has likeness to the heavenly Son, as the Word, for a word is nothing but the concept of wisdom. In an earthly son this is sometimes absent by reason of lack of years. *Goodness*, as the nature and object of love, has likeness to the Holy Ghost, Who is Love; but seems repugnant to the earthly spirit, which often implies a certain violent impulse, according to *Isaias* xxv. 4: *The spirit of the strong is as a blast beating on the wall. Strength* is appropriated to the Son and to the Holy Ghost, not as denoting the power itself of a thing, but as sometimes used to express that which proceeds from power; for instance, we say that a strong deed performed by an agent is the strength of that agent.

According to the fourth consideration, *i.e.*, God's relation to His effects, there arises appropriation of the expression *from Whom*, *by Whom*, and *in Whom*. For this preposition *from* [*ex*] sometimes implies a certain relation of the material cause, which has no place in God.

---

1. 参见 Cf. Hugh of St. Victor, *De Sacram.*, I, pt. 2, ch. 6 (PL 176, 208).

Sometimes it expresses the relation of the efficient cause, which can be applied to God by reason of His active power; hence it is appropriated to the Father in the same way as power. The preposition *by* [*per*] sometimes designates an intermediate cause; and thus we may say that a smith works *by* a hammer. Hence the word *by* is not always appropriated to the Son, but belongs to the Son properly and strictly, according to the text, *All things were made by Him* (*Jo.* i. 3); not that the Son is an instrument, but because He is *the principle from a principle.* Sometimes it designates the relation of a form *by* which an agent works; and thus we say that an artificer works *by* his art. Hence, as wisdom and art are appropriated to the Son, so also is the expression *by Whom.* The preposition *in* strictly denotes the relation of one containing. Now, God contains things in two ways: in one way, by their likenesses; thus things are said to be in God, as existing in His knowledge. In this sense the expression *in Him* should be appropriated to the Son. In another sense, things are contained in God inasmuch as by His goodness He preserves and governs them, by guiding them to a fitting end; and in this sense the expression *in Him* is appropriated to the Holy Ghost, as likewise is *goodness.* Nor need the relation of the final cause (though it be the first of causes) be appropriated to the Father, Who is *the principle without a principle*; because the divine persons, of Whom the Father is the principle, do not proceed from Him as towards an end, since each of Them is the last end; but They proceed by a natural procession, which seems more to belong to the nature of a natural power.

Regarding the other points of inquiry, we can say that since *truth* belongs to the intellect, as was stated above,[1] it is appropriated to the Son, without, however, being a property of His. For truth can be considered as existing in the intellect or in the thing itself.[2] Hence,

---

1. 参见 Q. 16, a. 1.
2. 同上

as intellect and thing, in their essential meaning, are referred to the essence, and not to the persons, so the same is to be said of truth. The definition quoted from Augustine belongs to truth as appropriated to the Son. The *book of life* directly means knowledge; but indirectly it means life. For, as was explained above, it is God's knowledge regarding those who are to possess eternal life.[1] Consequently, it is appropriated to the Son, even though life is appropriated to the Holy Ghost, as implying a certain kind of interior movement. In this sense, *the book of life* agrees with the property of the Holy Ghost as Love. To be written by another is not of the essence of a book considered as such; but this belongs, to it only as a work produced. So this does not imply origin; nor is it personal, but an appropriation to a person. The expression *Who is* is appropriated to the person of the Son, not by reason of itself, but by reason of an addition, inasmuch as, in God's word to Moses, was prefigured the delivery of the human race accomplished by the Son. Yet, when the word *Who* is taken in a relative sense, it may sometimes relate to the person of the Son, and in that sense it would be taken personally; as, for instance, were we to say, *The Son is the begotten* "*Who is,*" *for God begotten* is also taken personally. But taken indefinitely, it is an essential term. And although the pronoun *this* [*iste*] seems grammatically to point to a particular person, nevertheless, everything that we can point to can be grammatically treated as a person, although in its own nature it is not a person; as we may say, *this stone*, and *this ass*. So, speaking in a grammatical sense, so far as the name *God* signifies and stands for the divine essence, the latter may be designated by the pronoun *this*, according to *Exod.* xv 2: *This is my God, and I will glorify Him.*

1. 参见 Q. 24, a. 1.

Question XL
THE PERSONS AS COMPARED TO THE RELATIONS OR PROPERTIES
(*In Four Articles*)

WE now consider the persons in connection with the relations, or properties; and there are four points of inquiry: (1) Whether relation is the same as person? (2) Whether the relations distinguish and constitute the persons? (3) Whether, if the intellect abstracted the relations from the persons, the hypostases would remain distinct? (4) Whether the relations, according to our mode of understanding, presuppose the acts of the persons, or contrariwise?

First Article
WHETHER RELATION IS THE SAME AS PERSON?

We proceed thus to the First Article: —

Objection 1. It would seem that in God relation is not the same as person. For when things are identical, if one is multiplied, the other is multiplied. But in one person there are several relations; as in the person of the Father there is paternity and common spiration. Again, one relation exists in two persons, as common spiration in the Father and in the Son. Therefore relation is not the same as person.

Obj. 2. Further, according to the Philosopher, nothing is contained by itself.[1] But relation is in the person. Nor can it be said that this occurs

1. 参见 *Phys.*, IV, 3 (210a, 25).

because they are identical, for otherwise relation would be also in the essence. Therefore relation, or property, is not the same as person in God.

Obj. 3. Further, when several things are identical, what is predicated of one is predicated of the others. But all that is predicated of a Person is not predicated of His property. For we say that the Father begets, but not that the paternitv is begetting. Therefore property is not the same as person in God.

On the contrary, in God *what is* and *whereby it is* are the same, according to Boethius.[1] But the Father is Father by paternity. Therefore He is the same as paternity. In the same way, the other properties are the same as the persons.

I answer that, Different opinions have been held on this point. Some[2] have said that the properties are not the persons, nor in the persons; and these have thought thus owing to the mode of signification of the relations. which do not signify existence *in* something, but rather existence *towards* something. Whence, they styled the relations *assistant*, as was above explained.[3] But since relation, considered as really existing in God, is the divine essence Itself, and the essence is the same as person, as appears from what was said above,[4] relation must necessarily be the same as person.

Others,[5] therefore, considering this identity, said that the properties were indeed the persons, but not *in* the persons; for, they said, there are no properties in God except in our way of speaking, as was stated above.[6] We must, however, say that there are properties in God, as we have shown.[7] These are designated by abstract terms, being, as it were,

---

1. 参见 *De Hebdom.* (PL 64, 1311).
2. 参见 On these cf. St. Thomas, *De Pot.*, q. 8, a. 2.
3. 参见 Q. 28, a. 2.
4. 参见 Q. 39, a. 1.
5. 参见 Prepositinus: cf. above, q. 32, a. 2; note 30.
6. 参见 Q. 32, a. 2.
7. 同上

forms of the persons. So, since the nature of a form requires it to be *in* that of which it is the form, we must say that the properties are in the persons, and yet that they are the persons; as we say that the essence is in God, and yet is God.

Reply Obj. 1. Person and property are really the same, but differ in concept. Consequently, it does not follow that if one is multiplied, the other must also be multiplied. We must, however, consider that in God, by reason of the divine simplicity, a twofold real identity exists as regards what in creatures are distinct. For, since the divine simplicity excludes the composition of matter and form, it follows that in God the abstract is the same as the concrete, as *Godhead* and *God.* And as the divine simplicity excludes the composition of subject and accident, it follows that whatever is attributed to God is His essence Itself; and so, wisdom and power are the same in God, because they are both in the divine essence. According to this twofold identity, property in God is the same as person. For personal properties are the same as the persons because the abstract and the concrete are the same in God. For they are the subsisting persons themselves, as paternity is the Father Himself, and filiation is the Son, and procession is the Holy Ghost. But the non-personal properties are the same as the persons according to the other notion of identity, whereby whatever is attributed to God is His own essence. Thus, common spiration is the same as the person of the Father, and the person of the Son; not that it is one self-subsisting person, but that, as there is one essence in the two persons, so also there is one property in the two persons, as was above explained.[1]

Reply Obj. 2. The properties are said to be in the essence by identity only; but in the persons they exist by identity, not merely in reality, but also in the mode of signification; as the form exists in its subject. Thus the properties determine and distinguish the persons, but not the

---

1. 参见 Q. 30, a. 2.

essence.

Reply Obj. 3. Notional participles and verbs signify the notional acts: and acts belong to a *suppositum*. Now, properties are not designated as *supposita*, but as forms of *supposita*. And so their mode of signification prevents notional participles and verbs from being predicated of the properties.

Second Article
WHETHER THE PERSONS ARE DISTINGUISHED BY THE RELATIONS?

We proceed thus to the Second Article: —

Objection 1. It would seem that the persons are not distinguished by the relations. For simple things are distinct by themselves. But the persons are supremely simple. Therefore they are distinguished by themselves, and not by the relation.

Obj. 2. Further, a form is distinguished only according to its genus. For white is distinguished from black only according to quality. But *hypostasis* signifies an individual in the genus of substance. Therefore the hypostases cannot be distinguished by relations.

Obj. 3. Further, what is absolute comes before what is relative. But the distinction of the divine persons is the primary distinction. Therefore the divine persons are not distinguished by the relations.

Obj. 4. Further, whatever presupposes distinction cannot be the first principle of distinction. But relation presupposes distinction, since distinction comes into its definition; for a relation is essentially what is towards *another*. Therefore the first distinctive principle in God cannot be relation.

On the contrary, Boethius says: *Relation alone multiplies the Trinity of the divine persons.*[1]

---

1. 参见 *De Trin.*, VI (PL 64, 1255).

I answer that, In whatever multitude we find something common to all, it is necessary to seek a principle of distinction. So, as the three persons agree in the unity of essence, we must seek the principle of distinction whereby they are several. Now, there are two principles of difference among the divine persons, and these are *origin* and *relation.* Although these do not differ really, yet they differ in the mode of signification; for *origin* is signified by way of act, as *generation*, and *relation* by way of form, as *paternity*.

Some, then, considering that relation follows upon act, have said that the divine hypostases are distinguished by origin, so that we may say that the Father is distinguished from the Son, inasmuch as the former begets and the latter is begotten.[1] Further, that the relations, or the properties, make known the distinctions of the hypostases or persons as resulting therefrom; just as also in creatures the properties manifest the distinctions of individuals, which distinctions are caused by material principles.

This opinion, however, cannot stand — for two reasons. First, because, in order that two things be understood as distinct, their distinction must be understood as resulting from something intrinsic to both; thus, in things created it results from their matter or their form. Now the origin of a thing does not designate anything intrinsic, but means the way from something, or to something; as generation is signified as the way to the thing generated, and as proceeding from the generator. Hence it is not possible that what is generated and the generator should be distinguished by generation alone; but in the generator and in the thing generated we must presuppose whatever makes them to be distinguished from each other. In a divine person there is nothing to presuppose but essence and relation or property. Whence, since the

1. 参见 Cf. *De Pot.*, q. 8, a. 3, *obj.* 3 where Richard of St. Victor is mentioned (*De Trin.*, IV, 15 [PL 196, 939]). — Cf. also St. Bonaventure, *In I Sent.*, d. xxvi, a. 1, q. 2, arg. 3; q. 3, arg. 3 (I, 455; 456).

persons agree in essence, it remains that the persons are distinguished from each other by the relations.

Secondly, because the distinction of the divine persons is not to be understood as though something common is divided among them, for the common essence remains undivided; but the distinguishing principles themselves must constitute the things which are distinct. Now this is the way that the relations or the properties distinguish or constitute the hypostases or persons, inasmuch as they are themselves the subsisting persons; as paternity is the Father, and filiation is the Son, because in God the abstract and the concrete do not differ. But it is against the nature of origin that it should constitute a hypostasis or person. For origin, taken in an active sense, is signified as proceeding from a subsisting person, so that it presupposes the latter; while in a passive sense, origin, as *nativity*, signifies the way to a subsisting person, and as not yet constituting the person.

It is therefore better to say that the persons or hypostases are distinguished rather by relations than by origin. For, although they are distinguished in both ways, nevertheless in our mode of understanding they are distinguished chiefly and primarily by relations. Hence this name *Father* signifies not only a property, but also the hypostasis; whereas this name *Begetter* or *Begetting* signifies property only. For this name *Father* signifies the relation which is distinctive and constitutive of the hypostasis; and this name *Begetter* or *Begotten* signifies the origin, which is not distinctive and constitutive of the hypostasis.

Reply Obj. 1. The persons are the subsisting relations themselves. Hence it is not against the simplicity of the divine persons for them to be distinguished by the relations.

Reply Obj. 2. The divine persons are not distinguished as regards the being in which they subsist, nor in anything absolute, but only according to something relative. Hence relation suffices for their distinction.

Reply Obj. 3. The more prior a distinction is, the nearer it approaches to unity; and so it must be the least possible distinction. So the distinction of the persons must be by that which distinguishes the least possible; and this is by relation.

Reply Obj. 4. When relation is an accident, it presupposes the distinction of subjects; but when the relation is subsistent, it does not presuppose, but brings about, distinction. For when it is said that relation is by nature *to be with reference to another*, the word *another* signifies the correlative which is not prior, but simultaneous in the order of nature.

Third Article
WHETHER THE HYPOSTASES REMAIN IF THE RELATIONS ARE ABSTRACTED BY THE INTELLECT FROM THE PERSONS?

We proceed thus to the Third Article: —

Objection 1. It would seem that the hypostases remain if the properties or relations are abstracted by the intellect from the persons. For that to which something is added may be understood when the addition is taken away; just as man is something added to animal which can be understood if rational be taken away. But *person* is something added to hypostasis, for a person is *a hypostasis distinguished by a property of dignity.* Therefore, if a personal property be taken away from a person, the hypostasis remains.

Obj. 2. Further, that the Father is Father, and that He is someone, are not due to the same reason. For as He is the Father by paternity, to suppose that He is some one by paternity would mean that the Son, in Whom there is no paternity, would not be *someone.* So when paternity is abstracted by the intellect from the Father, He still remains *someone* — that is, a hypostasis. Therefore, if property be removed from person, the hypostasis remains.

Obj. 3. Further, Augustine says: *Unbegotten is not the same as Father; for if the Father had not begotten the Son, nothing would prevent Him from being called unbegotten.*[1] But if He had not begotten the Son, there would be no paternity in Him. Therefore, if paternity be removed, there still remains the hypostasis of the Father as unbegotten.

On the contrary, Hilary says: *The Son has nothing else than birth.*[2] But He is Son by *birth*. Therefore, if filiation be removed, the Son's hypostasis no longer remains; and the same holds as regards the other persons.

I answer that, Abstraction by the intellect is twofold. One takes place when the universal is abstracted from the particular, as animal is abstracted from man; the other, when form is abstracted from matter, as the form of a circle is abstracted by the intellect from all sensible matter. The difference between these two abstractions consists in the fact that in the abstraction of the universal from the particular, that from which the abstraction is made does not remain; for when the difference of rationality is removed from man, the man no longer remains in the intellect, but animal alone remains. But in abstraction in terms of form and matter, both the form and the matter remain in the intellect; as, for instance, if we abstract the form of a circle from brass, there remain in our intellect separately both the understanding of a circle and the understanding of brass.

Now, although there is really no universal or particular in God, nor form and matter, nevertheless, as regards the mode of signification, there is a certain likeness of these things in God. And in accord with this mode Damascene says that *substance is common and hypostasis is particular.*[3] So, if we speak of the abstraction of the universal from the particular, the common universal essence remains in the intellect if the properties are removed; but not the hypostasis of the Father, which is, as it were, a particular. But, as regards the abstraction of form from matter, if the non-personal properties are removed, then the concept of the hvpostases and persons remains:

1. 参见 *De Trin.*, V, 6 (PL 42, 914).
2. 参见 *De Trin.*, IV (PL 10, 103).
3. 参见 *De Fide Orth.*, III, 6 (PG 94, 1001).

as, for instance, if the fact that the Father is unbegotten or spirating be abstracted by the intellect from the Father, the Father's hypostasis or person remains. If, however, the personal property be abstracted by the intellect, the concept of the hypostasis no longer remains. For the personal properties are not to be understood as added to the divine hypostases, as a form is added to a pre-existing subject: but they carry with them their own *supposita*, inasmuch as they are themselves subsisting persons: thus, paternity is the Father Himself. For hypostasis signifies something distinct in God, since a hypostasis is an individual substance. So, as it is relation that distinguishes and constitutes the hypostases, as was above explained, it follows that if the personal relations are abstracted by the intellect, the hypostases no longer remain.

Some, however, think, as was noted above, that the divine hypostases are not distinguished by the relations, but only by origin; so that the Father is a hypostasis by the fact that He is not from another, and the Son is a hypostasis as being from another by generation. But it is the consequent relations, which are to be regarded as properties of dignity, that constitute the notion of person, and are thus called *personal* properties. Hence, the argument concludes, if these relations are abstracted by the intellect, the hypostases, but not the persons, remain. But this is impossible, for two reasons: first, because the relations distinguish and constitute the hypostases, as was shown above; secondly, because every hypostasis of a rational nature is a person, as appears from the definition of Boethius that *person is the individual substance of a rational nature.*[1] Hence, to have hypostasis and not person, it would be necessary to abstract the rationality from the nature, but not the property from the person.

Reply Obj. 1. Person does not add to hypostasis a distinguishing property absolutely, but 'a distinguishing property of dignity,' all

1. 参见 *De Duab. Nat.*, III (PL 64, 1343).

of which must be taken as the difference. Now, this distinguishing property is one of dignity precisely because it is understood as subsisting in a rational nature. Hence, if the distinguishing property be removed from the person, the hypostasis no longer remains, whereas it would remain were the rationality of the nature removed; for both person and hypostasis are individual substances. Consequently, in God the distinguishing relation belongs essentially to both.

Reply Obj. 2. By paternity the Father is not only Father, but He is a person, and He is *someone*, or a hypostasis. It does not follow, however, that the Son is not *someone* or a hypostasis, just as it does not follow that He is not a person.

Reply Obj. 3. Augustine does not mean to say that the hypostasis of the Father would remain as unbegotten, if His paternity were removed, as if innascibility constituted and distinguished the hypostasis of the Father; for this would be impossible, since *being unbegotten* asserts nothing positive but is only a negation, as he himself says.[1] But he speaks in a general sense, for not every unbegotten being is the Father. So, if paternity be removed, the hypostasis of the Father does not remain in God, as distinguished from the other persons, but only as distinguished from creatures; which is how the Jews understand it.

Fourth Article
WHETHER THE PROPERTIES PRESUPPOSE THE NOTIONAL ACTS?

We proceed thus to the Fourth Article: —

Objection 1. It would seem that the notional acts are understood before the properties. For the Master of the *Sentences* says that, *the Father always is, because He is ever begetting the Son.*[2] So it seems that

1. 参见 *De Trin.*, V, 6 (PL 42, 915).
2. 参见 *Sent.*, I, xxvii, 1 (I, 171).

generation precedes paternity according to the order of the intellect.

Obj. 2. Further, in the order of the intellect every relation presupposes that on which it is founded; as equality presupposes quantity. But paternity is a relation founded on the action of generation. Therefore paternity presupposes generation.

Obj. 3. Further, Active generation is to paternity as nativity is to filiation. But filiation presupposes nativity; for the Son is so called because He is born. Therefore paternity also presupposes generation.

On the contrary, Generation is the operation of the person of the Father. But paternity constitutes the person of the Father. Therefore, according to the order of the intellect, paternity is prior to generation.

I answer that, According to the opinion that the properties do not distinguish and constitute the hypostases in God, but only manifest them as already distinct and constituted,[1] we must say absolutely that the relations in our mode of understanding follow upon the notional acts, so that we can say, without qualifying the phrase, that *because He begets, He is the Father.* A distinction, however, is needed if we suppose that the relations distinguish and constitute the divine hypostases. For origin has in God an active and passive signification — active, as generation is attributed to the Father, and spiration, taken for the notional act, is attributed to the Father and the Son; passive, as nativity is attributed to the Son, and procession to the Holy Ghost. For, according to the order of the intellect, origins, in the passive sense, precede absolutely the properties (even the personal properties) of the persons proceeding; because origin, as passively understood, signifies the way to a person constituted by the property. In the same way, origin, signified actively, is prior in the intellect to the non-personal relation of the person originating; just as the notional act of spiration precedes, in the intellect, the unnamed relative property common to

---

1. 参见 Richard of St. Victor, *De Trin.*, IV, 15 (PL 196, 939).

the Father and the Son. Now, the personal property of the Father can be considered in a twofold sense: first, as a relation, and thus again, according to the intellect, it presupposes the notional act, for relation, as such, is founded upon an act; secondly, according as it constitutes the person, and thus the notional act presupposes the relation, just as an action presupposes a person acting.

Reply Obj. 1. When the Master says that *because He begets, He is Father,*[1] the term *Father* is taken as meaning relation only, but not as signifying the subsisting person; for then it would be necessary to say conversely that because He is Father He begets.

Reply Obj. 2. This objection is based on paternity as a relation, but not as constituting a person.

Reply Obj. 3. Nativity is the way to the person of the Son, and so, according to the intellect, it precedes filiation, even as constituting the person of the Son. But active generation signifies a proceeding from the person of the Father, and therefore it presupposes the personal property of the Father.

---

1. 参见 Peter Lombard, *Sent.*, I, xxvii, 1 (I, 171).

Question XLI
THE PERSONS IN REFERENCE TO THE NOTIONAL ACTS[1]
(*In Six Articles*)

WE now consider the persons in reference to the notional acts, concerning which six points of inquiry arise: (1) Whether the notional acts are to be attributed to the persons? (2) Whether these acts are necessary or voluntary? (3) Whether, as regards these acts, a person proceeds from nothing or from something? (4) Whether in God there exists a power as regards the notional acts? (5) What this power means? (6) Whether many persons can be the term of one notional act?

First Article
WHETHER THE NOTIONAL ACTS ARE TO BE ATTRIBUTED TO THE PERSONS?

We proceed thus to the First Article: —

Objection 1. It would seem that the notional acts are not to be attributed to the persons. For Boëthius says: *Whatever is predicated of God, of whatever genus it be, becomes the divine substance, except what pertains to the relation.* But action is one of the ten *genera*. Therefore, any action attributed to God belongs to His essence, and not to a notion.

Obj. 2. Further, Augustine says that everything which is said of God,

1. notional acts：表意活动

is said of Him either substantially or relatively.[1] But whatever belongs to the substance is signified by the essential attributes; and whatever belongs to the relations, by the names of the persons, or by the names of the properties. Therefore, in addition to these, notional acts are not to be attributed to the persons.

Obj. 3. Further, the nature of action is of itself to cause passion. But we do not place passions in God. Therefore neither are notional acts to be placed in God.

On the contrary, Augustine says: *It is a property of the Father to beget the Son*.[2] But to beget is an act. Therefore notional acts are to be placed in God.

I answer that, In the divine persons distinction is founded on origin. But origin can be properly designated only by certain acts. Therefore, to signify the order of origin in the divine persons, we must attribute notional acts to the persons.

Reply Obj. 1. Every origin is designated by an act. In God there is a twofold order of origin: one, inasmuch as the creature proceeds from Him, and this is common to the three persons; and so those actions which are attributed to God to designate the procession of creatures from Him belong to His essence. The other order of origin in God regards the procession of person from person. Hence, the acts which designate the order of this origin are called notional, because the notions of the persons are the mutual relations of the persons, as is clear from what was above explained.[3]

Reply Obj. 2. The notional acts differ from the relations of the persons only in their mode of signification; in reality they are altogether the same. Whence the Master says that *generation and nativity are by other names* called *paternity and filiation*.[4] To see this,

---

1. 参见 *De Trin.*, V, 4; 5 (PL 42, 913; 914).
2. 参见 Cf. Fulgentius, *De Fide ad Petrum*, II (PL 65, 675).
3. 参见 Q. 32, a. 2.
4. 参见 Peter Lombard, *Sent.*, I, xxvi, 2 (I, 165).

we must consider that the origin of one thing from another is firstly inferred from movement; for it is clear that, if anything be changed from its disposition through motion, this arises from some cause. Hence action, in its primary sense, means origin of motion. For just as motion, as existing in the subject receiving it, is called *passion*, so the origin of motion itself, as beginning from another and terminating in what is moved, is called *action*. Hence, if we take away motion, action implies nothing more than order of origin, in so far as action proceeds from some cause or principle to what is from that principle. Consequently, since in God there is no motion, the personal action of the one producing a person is nothing other than the reference of the principle to the person who is from the principle; which references are the relations or the notions. Nevertheless, we cannot speak of divine and intelligible things except after the manner of the sensible things from which we derive our knowledge, and wherein actions and passions, so far as these imply movement, differ from the relations which result from action and passion. For this reason, it is necessary to signify the references of the persons separately after the manner of act and after the manner of relations. Thus it is evident that they are really the same, differing only in their mode of signification.

Reply Obj. 3. Action, so far as it means origin of motion, naturally involves passion; but action in this sense is not attributed to God. Hence, passions are attributed to Him only from a grammatical standpoint, and in accordance with our manner of speaking: as we attribute *to beget* to the Father, and to the Son to be begotten.

Second Article
WHETHER THE NOTIONAL ACTS ARE VOLUNTARY?

WE *proceed thus to the Second Article:* —

Objection 1. It would seem that the notional acts are voluntary. For

Hilary says: *Not by natural necessity was the Father led to beget the Son.*[1]

Obj. 2. Further, the Apostle says, *He transferred us to the kingdom of the Son of His love* (*Col.* i. 13). But love belongs to the will. Therefore the Son was begotten of the Father by will.

Obj. 3. Further, nothing is more voluntary than love. But the Holy Ghost proceeds as Love from the Father and the Son. Therefore He proceeds voluntarily.

Obj. 4. Further, the Son proceeds according to the mode of the intellect, as the Word. But every word proceeds by the will from a speaker. Therefore the Son proceeds from the Father by will, and not by nature.

Obj. 5. Further, what is not voluntary is necessary. Therefore, if the Father begot the Son, but not by the will, it seems to follow that He begot Him by necessity; and this is against what Augustine says.[2]

On the contrary, Augustine says, in the same book, that *the Father begot the Son neither by will, nor by necessity.*[3]

I answer that, When anything is said to be, or to be made by the will, this can be understood in two senses. In one sense, the ablative designates only concomitance, as I can say that I am a man by my will — that is, I will to be a man; and in this way it can be said that the Father begot the Son by will; just as it can also be said that He is God by will, because He wills to be God, and wills to beget the Son. In the other sense, the ablative signifies the relation of a principle, as when it is said that the workman works by his will because the will is the principle of his work. In this sense it must be said that God the Father did not beget the Son by His will, but that He produced the creature by His will. Whence in the book *De Synodis*, it is said: *If anyone say that the Son was made by the Will of God, as a creature is said to be made, let him*

---

1. 参见 *De Synod.* (PL 10, 520).
2. 参见 Pseudo-Augustine, *Dial. 65 Quaest.*, q. 7 (PL 40, 736).
3. 同上

be anathema.[1]

The reason for this is that *will* and *nature* differ in their manner of causing in that nature is determined to one effect, while the will is not. This is so because the effect is assimilated to the form of the agent, whereby the agent acts. Now it is manifest that of one thing there is only one natural form through which the thing has being. Hence, such as its being is, such will be its actions. But the form whereby the will acts is not one only; it is many, according to the number of ideas understood. Hence, what is done by the will is not such as is the agent, but such as the agent wills and knows it to be. So the will is the principle of those things which can be this way or that way; whereas of those things which can be only in one way, the principle is nature.

What, however, can exist in different ways is far removed from the divine nature, whereas it belongs to the nature of a created being; because God is of Himself a necessary being, whereas a creature is made from nothing. And so, the Arians, wishing to prove the Son to be a creature, said that the Father begot the Son by will, taking will in the sense of principle.[2] But we, on the contrary, must assert that the Father begot the Son, not by will, but by nature. Wherefore Hilary says: *The will of God gave to all creatures their substance: but perfect birth gave the Son a nature derived from a substance impassible and unborn. All things created are such as God willed them to be; but the Son, born of God, subsists in the perfect likeness of God.*[3]

Reply Obj. 1. This pronouncement is directed against those who did not admit even the concomitance of the Father's will in the generation of the Son,[4] for they said that the Father so begot the Son by nature

1. 参见 Hilary, *De Synod.* (PL 10, 520).
2. 参见 Cf. *ibid.*
3. 同上
4. 同上

that the will to beget was absent; just as we ourselves suffer many things against our will from natural necessity — as, for instance, death, old age, and like ills. This appears from what precedes and from what follows in the quotation; for we read thus: *Not against His will, nor, as it were, forced, nor as if He were led by natural necessity did the Father beget the Son.*[1]

Reply Obj. 2. The Apostle calls Christ the Son of the love of God, inasmuch as He is superabundantly loved by God; not, however, as if love were the principle of the Son's generation.

Reply Obj. 3. The will itself, as a certain nature, wills something naturally. Thus, man's will naturally tends to happiness. So, too, God naturally wills and loves Himself; whereas in regard to things other than Himself, the will of God is, in a way, undetermined in itself, as was explained above.[2] Now, the Holy Ghost proceeds as Love, inasmuch as God loves Himself; and hence He proceeds naturally, although He proceeds according to the mode of the will.

Reply Obj. 4. Even as regards intellectual conceptions there is a reduction to those first principles which are naturally understood. But God naturally understands Himself, and thus the conception of the divine Word is natural.

Reply Obj. 5. A thing is said to be necessary *of itself* and *by reason of another.* Taken in the latter sense, it has a twofold meaning: first, as by an efficient and compelling cause, and thus necessary means what is violent; secondly, as by a final cause, when a thing is said to be necessary as the means to an end, in so far as without it the end could not be attained, or, at least, so well attained. In neither of these ways is the divine generation necessary, because God is not the means to an end, nor is He subject to compulsion. On the other hand, a thing is said to be necessary *of itself* if it cannot not be: in this sense, it is

1. 参见 Hilary, *De Synod.* (PL 10, 520).
2. 参见 Q. 19, a. 3.

necessary for God to be, and in the same sense it is necessary that the Father beget the Son.

Third Article
WHETHER THE NOTIONAL ACTS PROCEED FROM SOMETHING?

We proceed thus to the Third Article: —

Objection 1. It would seem that the notional acts do not proceed from anything. For if the Father begets the Son from something, this will be either from Himself or from something else. If from something else, since that whence a thing is generated exists in what is generated, it follows that something different from the Father exists in the Son, and this contradicts what is laid down by Hilary, namely, that *In them nothing diverse or different exists.*[1] If the Father begets the Son from Himself, since again that whence a thing is generated, if it be something permanent, receives as predicate the thing generated therefrom — just as we say, *The man is white*, since the man remains, when from not white he is made white — it follows either that the Father does not remain after the Son is begotten, or that the Father is the Son; which is false. Therefore the Father does not beget the Son from something, but from nothing.

Obj. 2. Further, that whence anything is generated is the principle of what is generated. So if the Father generates the Son from His own essence or nature, it follows that the essence or nature of the Father is the principle of the Son. Now it is not a material principle, because in God nothing material exists; and therefore it is a sort of active principle, as the begetter is the principle of the one begotten. Thus it follows that the essence generates, which was disproved above.[2]

---

1. 参见 *De Trin.*, VII (PL 10. 232).
2. 参见 Q. 39, a. 5.

Obj. 3. Further, Augustine says that the three persons are not from the same essence; because the essence is not another thing from the person.[1] But the person of the Son is not another thing from the Father's essence. Therefore the Son is not from the Father's essence.

Obj. 4. Further, every creature is from nothing. But in Scripture the Son is called a creature. For it is said (*Ecclus.* xxiv. 5) in the person of the Wisdom begotten, *I came out of the mouth of the Most High*[2], *the first-born before all creatures:* and further on (*verse* 14) it is said by the same Wisdom, *From the beginning, and before the world was I created.* Therefore the Son was not begotten from something, but from nothing. Likewise we can object concerning the Holy Ghost, by reason of what is said (*Zach.* xii. 1): *Thus saith the Lord Who stretcheth forth the heavens, and layeth the foundations of the earth, and formeth the spirit of man within him*; and elsewhere (*Amos* iv. 13), according to another version [Septuagint] *I Who form the earth, and create the spirit.*

On the contrary, Augustine says: *God the Father, of His nature, without beginning, begot the Son equal to Himself.*[3]

I answer that, The Son was not begotten from nothing, but from the Father's substance. For it was shown above that paternity, filiation and nativity really and properly exist in God.[4] Now, this is the difference be tween true *generation*, whereby one proceeds from another as a son, and *making*, that the maker makes something out of external matter, as a carpenter makes a bench out of wood, whereas a man begets a son from himself. Now, as a created workman makes a thing out of matter, so God makes things out of nothing, as will be shown later on.[5] This does not mean that *nothing* enters into the substance of the

---

1. 参见 *De Trin.*, VII, 6 (PL 42, 945).
2. the Most High：至高者，指天主
3. 参见 Cf. Fulgentius, *De Fide ad Petrum*, II (PL 65, 676).
4. 参见 Q. 27, a. 2; q. 33, a. 2 and 3.
5. 参见 Q. 45, a. 2.

thing made; it means that the whole substance of a thing is produced by Him without anything else whatever presupposed. So, were the Son to proceed from the Father as out of nothing, then the Son would be to the Father what the thing made is to the maker. As is evident, the name *filiation* would not apply to such a procedure except by a kind of likeness. Thus, if the Son of God proceeds from the Father out of nothing, He could not be properly and truly called the Son; whereas the contrary is stated (*1 John* v. 20): *That we may be in His true Son Jesus Christ*. Therefore the true Son of God is not from nothing; nor is He made, but begotten.

That certain creatures made by God out of nothing are called sons of God is to be taken in a metaphorical sense, according to a certain likeness of assimilation to Him Who is the true Son. Whence, as He is the only true and natural Son of God, He is called the *only begotten*, according to *Jo.* i. 18, *The only begotten Son, Who is in the bosom of the Father, He hath declared Him*. And in so far as others are entitled sons of adoption by their likeness to Him, He is called (as it were, metaphorically) the *first begotten*, according to *Rom.* viii. 29: *Whom He foreknew He also predestinated to be made conformable to the image of His Son, that He might be the first born of many brethren.*

Therefore, it remains that the Son of God is begotten of the substance of the Father, but not in the same way as man is born of man. For a part of the human substance in generation passes into the substance of the one begotten, whereas the divine nature cannot be parted. Whence it necessarily follows that the Father, in begetting the Son, does not transmit any part of His nature; He rather communicates His whole nature to Him, and the only distinction that remains is according to origin, as was explained above.[1]

Reply Obj. 1. When we say that the Son was born of the Father, the

---

1. 参见 Q. 40, a. 2.

preposition *of* designates a consubstantial generating principle, but not a material principle. For that which is produced from matter is made by a change of form in that from which it is produced. But the divine essence is unchangeable, and is not susceptive of another form.

Reply Obj. 2. When we say the Son is begotten of the essence of the Father, this denotes, as the Master of the *Sentences* explains,[1] the relation of a kind of active principle. According to him, *The Son is begotten of the essence of the Father* is to be taken as meaning that *He is begotten of the Father Who is essence.* For Augustine says: *When I say of the Father Who is essence, it is the same as if I said more explicitly, of the essence of the Father.*[2]

This, however, is not enough to explain the real meaning of the words. For we can say that the creature is from God Who is essence; but not that it is from the essence of God. So we may explain them otherwise, by observing that the preposition *of* [*de*] always denotes consubstantiality[3]. So we do not say that a house is *of* [*de*] the builder, since he is not the consubstantial cause. We can say, however, that something is *of* another, if this is its consubstantial principle, no matter in what way it is so: whether it be an active principle, as the son is said to be *of* the father; or a material principle, as a knife is *of* iron; or a formal principle, but in those things only in which the forms are subsisting, and not accidental to another (for we can say that an angel is *of* an intellectual nature). In this way, then, we say that the Son is begotten *of* the essence of the Father, inasmuch as the essence of the Father, communicated by generation, subsists in the Son.

Reply Obj. 3. When we say that the Son is begotten *of* the essence of the Father, a term is added which saves the distinction. But when we say that the three persons are *of* the divine essence, there is nothing expressed to warrant the distinction signified by the preposition so

---

1. 参见 Peter Lombard, *Sent.*, I, v, 2 (I, 49).
2. 参见 *De Trin.*,XV, 13 (PL 42, 1076).
3. consubstantiality：同体；同质

there is no parity of argument.

Reply Obj. 4. When we say *Wisdom was created*, this may be understood not of Wisdom which is the Son of God, but of created wisdom given by God to creatures: for it is said, *He created her* (namely, Wisdom) *in the Holy Ghost, and He poured her out over all His works* (*Ecclus.* i. 9, 10). Nor is it inconsistent for Scripture in one text to speak of the Wisdom begotten and wisdom created, for created wisdom is a kind of participation of the uncreated Wisdom. The saying may also be referred to the created nature assumed by the Son, so that the sense be, *From the beginning and before the world was I made* — that is, I was foreseen as united to the creature. Or the fact that wisdom is called both created and begotten suggests to us the mode of the divine generation; for in generation, what is generated receives the nature of the generator, and this pertains to perfection. whereas in creation the Creator is not changed, but the creature does not receive the Creator's nature. Thus the Son is called both created and begotten, in order that from the idea of creation the immutability[1] of the Father may be understood, and from generation the unity of nature in the Father and the Son. In this way Hilary expounds the sense of this text of Scripture.[2] The other passages quoted do not refer to the Holy Ghost, but to the created spirit, which is sometimes called wind, sometimes air, sometimes the breath of man, sometimes also the soul, or any other invisible substance.

Fourth Article
WHETHER IN GOD THERE IS A POWER IN RELATION TO THE NOTIONAL ACTS?

We proceed thus to the Fourth Article: —

---

1. immutability：不变；永恒性
2. 参见 *De Synod.* (PL 10, 494).

Objection 1. It would seem that in God there is no power in relation to the notional acts. For every kind of power is either active or passive; neither of which can be here applied, for there is nothing in God which we call passive power, as was above explained;[1] nor can active power belong to one person as regards another, since the divine persons were not made, as was stated above. Therefore in God there is no power in relation to the notional acts.

Obj. 2. Further, the object of power is what is possible. But the divine persons are not regarded as possible, but as necessary. Therefore, as regards the notional acts, whereby the divine persons proceed, there cannot be power in God.

Obj. 3. Further, the Son proceeds as the word, which is a conception of the intellect; and the Holy Ghost proceeds as love, which belongs to the will. But in God power is predicated as regards effects, and not as regards knowing and willing, as was stated above.[2] Therefore, in God power ought not to be predicated in reference to the notional acts.

On the contrary, Augustine says: *If God the Father could not beget a co-equal Son, where is the omnipotence of God the Father?*[3] Power therefore exists in God regarding the notional acts.

I answer that, As the notional acts are posited in God, so there must be posited a power in God regarding these acts; since power means only the principle of some act. So, as we understand the Father to be the principle of generation, and the Father and the Son to be the principle of spiration, we must attribute the power of generating to the Father, and the power of spiration to the Father and the Son; for the power of generation means that whereby the generator generates. Now every generator generates by something. Therefore in every generator

1. 参见 Q. 25, a. 1.
2. 参见 Q. 25, a. 1, ad 3 and 4.
3. 参见 *Contra Maximin.*, Ill, 7 (PL 42, 762).

we must posit the power of generating, and in the spirator the power of spirating.

Reply Obj. 1. As a person, according to the notional acts, does not proceed as if made, so the power in God as regards the notional acts has no reference to a person as if made, but only as regards the person as proceeding.

Reply Obj. 2. Possible, as opposed to what is necessary, is a consequence of a passive power, which does not exist in God. Hence, in God there is no such thing as possibility in this sense, but only in the sense of possible as contained in what is necessary; and in this latter sense it can be said that as it is possible for God to be, so also is it possible that the Son should be generated.

Reply Obj. 3. Power signifies a principle, and a principle implies distinction from that of which it is the principle. Now there is a double distinction in things said of God: one is a real distinction, the other is a distinction of reason only. By a real distinction, God by His essence is distinct from those things of which He is the principle by creation: just as one person is distinct from the other of which He is principle by a notional act. But in God the distinction of action and agent is one of reason only, otherwise action would be an accident in God. And therefore with regard to those actions in respect of which certain things proceed which are distinct from God, either personally or essentially, we may ascribe power to God in its proper sense of principle. And just as we ascribe to God the power of creating, so we may ascribe the power of begetting and of spirating. But *to understand* and *to will* are not such actions as to designate the procession of something distinct from God, either essentially or personally. Therefore, with regard to these actions we cannot ascribe power to God in its proper sense, but only after our way of understanding and speaking: inasmuch as we designate by different terms the intellect and the act of understanding in God, whereas in God the act of understanding is His very essence which has no principle.

Fifth Article

WHETHER THE POWER OF BEGETTING SIGNIFIES A RELATION, AND NOT THE ESSENCE?

We proceed thus to the Fifth Article: —

Objection 1. It would seem that the power of begetting, or of spirating, signifies relation and not the essence. For power signifies a principle, as appears from its definition: for active power is the principle of action, as we see from *Metaph.* v.[1] But in God, principle in regard to Person is said notionally. Therefore, in God, power does not signify essence but relation.

Obj. 2. Further, in God, to be able to act [*posse*] and *to act* are not distinct. But in God, begetting signifies relation. Therefore, the same applies to the power of begetting.

Obj. 3. Further, terms signifying the essence in God are common to the three persons. But the power of begetting is not common to the three persons, but proper to the Father. Therefore it does not signify the essence.

On the contrary, As God has the power to beget the Son, so also He wills to beget Him. But the will to beget signifies the essence. Therefore, also, the power to beget.

I answer that, Some have said that the power to beget signifies relation in God.[2] But this is not possible. For in every agent, that is properly called power, by which the agent acts. Now, everything that produces something by its action produces something like itself as to the form by which it acts; just as man begotten is like his begetter in his human nature, in virtue of which the father has the power to beget

---

1. 参见 Aristotle, *Metaph.*, IV, 2 (1019a 15).
2. 参见 Attributed to "the moderns" by St. Bonaventure, *In I Sent.*, d. vii, a. 1, q. 1 (I, 136).

a man. In every begetter, therefore, that is the power of begetting in which the begotten is like the begetter. Now the Son of God is like the Father, Who begets Him, in the divine nature. Therefore the divine nature in the Father is in Him the power of begetting. And so Hilary says: *The birth of God cannot but contain that nature from which it proceeded; for He cannot subsist other than God, Who subsists from no other source than God.*[1]

We must therefore conclude that the power of begetting signifies principally the divine essence, as the Master says,[2] and not the relation only. Nor does it signify the essence as identified with the relation, so as to signify both equally. For although paternity is signified as the form of the Father, nevertheless it is a personal property, being in respect to the person of the Father what the individual form is to the individual creature. Now the individual form in things created constitutes the person begetting, but it is not that by which the begetter begets, otherwise Socrates would beget Socrates. Hence, neither can paternity be understood as that by which the Father begets, but rather as constituting the person of the begetter, for otherwise the Father would beget the Father. But that by which the Father begets is the divine nature, in which the Son is like to Him. And in this sense Damascene says that generation is the *work of nature*, not of nature as generating, but of nature as being that by which the generator generates.[3] And therefore the power of begetting signifies the divine nature directly, but the relation indirectly.

Reply Obj. 1. Power does not signify the relation itself of a principle, for thus it would be in the genus of relation; but it signifies that which is a principle; not, indeed, in the sense in which we call the

1. 参见 *De Trin.*, V (PL 10, 155).
2. 参见 Peter Lombard, *Sent.*, I, vii, 2 (I, 56).
3. 参见 *De Fide Orth.*, I, 8 (PG 94, 812).

agent a principle, but in the sense in which that by which the agent acts is called a principle. Now the agent is distinct from that which it makes, and the generator from that which it generates; but that by which the generator generates is common to generated and generator, and so much the more perfectly as the generation is more perfect. Since, therefore, the divine generation is most perfect, that by which the Begetter begets is common to Begotten and Begetter by a community of identity, and not only of species, as in things created. Therefore, from the fact that we say that the divine essence *is the principle by which the Begetter begets*, it does not follow that the divine essence is distinct; which would follow if we were to say that the divine essence begets.

Reply Obj. 2. In God, the power of begetting is the same as the act of begetting, just as the divine essence is the same in reality as the act of begetting or paternity; although there is a distinction of reason.

Reply Obj. 3. When I speak of the *power of begetting*, power is signified directly, generation indirectly: just as if I were to say, the *essence of the Father*. Hence, as concerns the essence signified, the power of begetting is common to the three persons: but as concerns the notion that is connoted, it is proper to the person of the Father.

Sixth Article
WHETHER SEVERAL PERSONS CAN BE THE TERM OF ONE NOTIONAL ACT?

Objection 1. It would seem that a notional act can be directed to many Persons, so that there may be many Persons begotten or spirated in God. For whoever has the power of begetting can beget. But the Son has the power of begetting. Therefore He can beget. But He cannot beget Himself: therefore He can beget another son. Therefore there can be many Sons in God.

Obj. 2. Further, Augustine says: *The Son did not beget a Creator: not that*

He could not, but that it was not befitting.[1]

Obj. 3. Further, God the Father has greater power to beget than has a created father. But a man can beget several sons. Therefore God can also: the more so that the power of the Father is not diminished after begetting the Son.

On the contrary, In God *that which is possible,* and *that which is* do not differ. If, therefore, in God it were possible for many Sons to be, there would be many Sons. And thus there would be more than three Persons in God; which is heretical.

I answer that, As Athanasius says, in God there is only *one Father, one Son, one Holy Ghost.*[2] Four reasons may be given for this.

The first reason is in regard to the relations by which alone are the Persons distinct. For since the divine Persons are the relations themselves as subsistent, there could not be several Fathers, or several Sons in God, unless there were more than one paternity, or more than one filiation. And this, indeed, would not be possible except according to a material distinction, since forms of one species are not multiplied except according to matter, which is not in God. Hence, there can be but one subsistent filiation in God; just as there could be but one subsistent whiteness.

The second reason is taken from the manner of the processions. For God understands and wills all things by one simple act. Therefore there can be but one person proceeding after the manner of word, which person is the Son; and but one person proceeding after the manner of love, which person is the Holy Ghost.

The third reason is taken from the manner in which the persons proceed. For the persons proceed naturally, as we have said, and nature is determined to one mode of action.

The fourth reason is taken from the perfection of the divine

1. 参见 *Contra Maximin.*, II, 12 (PL 42, 768).
2. 参见 Cf. *Symb. "Quicumque"* (Denzinger, no. 39).

persons. For this reason is the Son perfect, because the entire divine filiation is contained in Him, and because there is but one Son. The same must be said in regard to the other persons.

Reply Obj. 1. We can grant, without distinction, that the Son has the same power as the Father; but we cannot grant that the Son has the power *generandi* [of begetting] thus taking *generandi*[1] as the gerund of the active verb, so that the sense would be that the Son has the *power to beget.* Just as, although Father and Son have the same being, it does not follow that the Son is the Father, by reason of the notional term added. But if the word *generandi* is taken as the gerundive of the passive verb, the power *generandi* is in the Son — that is, the power *of being begotten.* The same is to be said if it be taken as the gerundive of an impersonal verb, so that the sense be *the power* of generation — that is, a power by which it is generated by some person.

Reply Obj. 2. Augustine does not mean to say by those words that the Son could beget a Son, but that if He did not, it was not because He could not, as we shall see later on.[2]

Reply Obj. 3. The immateriality and perfection of God require that there cannot be several Sons in God, as we have explained. Therefore that there are not several Sons is not due to any lack of begetting power in the Father.

---

1. generandi：生育能力
2. 参见 Q. 42, a. 6, ad 3.

Question XLII
EQUALITY AND LIKENESS AMONG THE DIVINE PERSONS
(*In Six Articles*)

WE now have to consider the persons as compared to one another: first, with regard to equality and likeness; secondly, with regard to mission. Concerning the first there are six points of inquiry.

(1) Whether there is equality among the divine persons? (2) Whether the person who proceeds is equal to the one from Whom He proceeds in eternity? (3) Whether there is any order among the divine persons? (4) Whether the divine persons are equal in greatness? (5) Whether one divine person is in another? (6) Whether they are equal in power?

First Article
WHETHER THERE IS EQUALITY IN GOD?

We proceed thus to the First Article: —

Objection 1. It would seem that equality is not becoming to the divine persons. For equality is in relation to things which are one in quantity, as the Philosopher says.[1] But in the divine persons there is no quantity, neither continuous intrinsic quantity, which we call size, nor continuous extrinsic quantity, which we call place and time. Nor can there be equality by reason of discrete quantity, because two persons

1. 参见 *Metaph.*, IV, 15 (1021a 12).

are more than one. Therefore equality is not becoming to the divine persons.

Obj. 2. Further, the divine persons are of one essence, as we have said.[1] Now essence is signified by way of form. But agreement in form makes things to be alike, not to be equal. Therefore, we may speak of likeness in the divine persons, but not of equality.

Obj. 3. Further, things wherein there is to be found equality are equal to one another, for equality is reciprocal. But the divine persons cannot be said to be equal to one another. For as Augustine says: *If an image answers perfectly to that where of it is the image, it may be said to be equal to it; but that which it represents cannot be said to be equal to the image.*[2] But the Son is the image of the Father; and so the Father is not equal to the Son. Therefore equality is not to be found among the divine persons.

Obj. 4. Further, equality is a relation. But no relation is common to the three persons, for the persons are distinct by reason of the relations. Therefore equality is not becoming to the divine persons.

On the contrary, Athanasius says that *the three persons are co-eternal and co-equal to one another.*[3]

I answer that, We must needs admit equality among the divine persons. For, according to the Philosopher, equality signifies the negation of greater or less,[4] Now we cannot admit anything greater or less in the divine persons; for as Boethius says: *They must needs admit a difference* — namely, of Godhead — *who speak of either increase or decrease, as do the Arians, who sunder the Trinity by distinguishing degrees of merits, and thus produce a plurality.*[5] Now the reason for this is that unequal things

1. 参见 Q. 39, a. 2.
2. 参见 *De Trin.*, VI, 10 (PL 42, 931).
3. 参见 Cf. *Symb. "Quicumque"*(Denzinger, no. 39).
4. 参见 *Metaph.*, IX, 5 (1056a 22).
5. 参见 *De Trin.*, I (PL 64, 1249).

cannot have the same numerical quantity. But quantity, in God, is nothing else than His essence. Therefore it follows, that if there were any inequality in the divine persons, they would not have the same essence; and thus the three persons would not be one God. Which is impossible. We must therefore admit equality among the divine persons.

Reply Obj. 1. Quantity is twofold. There is quantity of *bulk* or dimensive quantity, which is to be found only in corporeal things, and has, therefore, no place in God. There is also quantity of *virtue*, which is measured according to the perfection of some nature or form: to this sort of quantity we allude when we speak of something as being more, or less, hot, inasmuch as it is more, or less, perfect in heat. Now this virtual quantity is measured firstly by its source — that is, by the very perfection of the form or nature: such is the greatness of spiritual things; just as we speak of great heat because of its intensity and perfection. And so Augustine says that *in things which are great, but not in bulk, to be greater is to be better,*[1] for the more perfect a thing is, the better it is. Secondly, virtual quantity is measured by the effects of the form. Now the first effect of form is being, for everything has being by reason of its form. The second effect is operation, for every agent acts through its form. Consequently, virtual quantity is measured both in regard to being and in regard to action: in regard to being, inasmuch as things of a more perfect nature are of longer duration; and in regard to action, inasmuch as things of a more perfect nature are more powerful to act. And so, as Augustine says, *We understand equality to be in the Father, Son and Holy Ghost, inasmuch as no one of them either precedes in eternity, or excels in greatness, or surpasses in power.*[2]

Reply Obj. 2. Where we have equality in respect of virtual quantity, equality includes likeness and something besides, because it excludes excess. For whatever things have a common form may be said to be

1. 参见 *De Trin.*, VI, 8 (PL 42, 929).
2. 参见 Cf. Fulgentius, *De Fide Ad Petrum*, I (PL 65, 674).

alike, even if they do not participate in that form equally, just as the air may be said to be like fire in heat; but they cannot be said to be equal, if one participates in the form more perfectly than another. And because the Father and the Son not only have one nature, but also possess it with perfect equality, therefore we say not only that the Son is like to the Father, in order to exclude the error of Eunomius,[1] but also that He is equal to the Father to exclude the error of Arius.[2]

Reply Obj. 3. Equality and likeness in God may be designated in two ways — namely, by nouns and by verbs. When designated by nouns, equality in the divine persons is mutual, and so is likeness; for the Son is equal and like to the Father, and conversely. This is because the divine essence is not more the Father's than the Son's. Therefore, just as the Son has the greatness of the Father, and is therefore equal to the Father, so the Father has the greatness of the Son, and is therefore equal to the Son. But in reference to creatures, as Dionysius says, *Equality and likeness are not mutual.*[3] For effects are said to be like their causes, inasmuch as they have the form of their causes; but not conversely, for the form is principally in the cause, and secondarily in the effect.

But verbs signify equality with movement. And although movement is not in God, there is something which receives. Since, therefore, the Son receives from the Father that whereby He is equal to the Father, and not conversely, for this reason we say that the Son is equalled to the Father, but not conversely.

Reply Obj. 4. In the divine persons there is nothing for us to consider but the essence which the persons have in common and the relations in which they are distinct. Now equality implies both — namely, distinction of persons, for nothing can be said to be equal to itself, and also unity of essence, since the persons are equal to one another

---

1. 参见 Cf. St. Augustine, *De Haeres.*, 54 (PL 42, 40).
2. 参见 *Op. cit.*, 49 (PL 42, 39).
3. 参见 *De Div, Nom.*, IX, 6 (PG 3, 913).

for the reason that they are of the same greatness and essence. Now it is clear that the relation of a thing to itself is not a real relation. Nor, again, is one relation referred to another by a further relation. For when we say that paternity is opposed to filiation, the opposition is not a relation mediating between paternity and filiation. For in both these ways relation would be multiplied indefinitely. Therefore equality and likeness in the divine persons is not a real relation distinct from the personal relations; but in its concept it includes both the relations which distinguish the persons, and the unity of essence. For this reason the Master of the *Sentences* says that in these *it is only the terms that are relative.*[1]

Second Article

WHETHER THE PERSON PROCEEDING IS CO-ETERNAL WITH HIS PRINCIPLE, AS THE SON WITH THE FATHER?

We proceed thus to the Second Article: —

Objection 1. It would seem that the person proceeding is not co-eternal with His principle, as the Son with the Father. For Arius gives twelve modes of generation.[2] The first mode is like the issue of a line from a point; wherein is wanting equality of simplicity. The second is like the emission of rays from the sun; wherein is absent equality of nature. The third is like the mark or impression made by a seal; wherein is wanting consubstantiality and executive power. The fourth is the infusion of a good will from God; wherein consubstantiality is also wanting. The fifth is the emanation of an accident from its subject; but the accident has no subsistence. The sixth is the abstraction of a species from matter, as sense receives the species from the sensible object; wherein is wanting equality of spiritual simplicity. The seventh is the exciting of the will by knowledge, which excitation is merely

1. 参见 Peter Lombard, *Sent.*, I, xxxi, 1 (I, 190).
2. 参见 Cf. Candidus Arianus, *De Gener.* Div. (PL 8, 1015).

temporal. The eighth is transformation, as an image is made of brass, which transformation is material. The ninth is motion from a mover; and here again we have effect and cause. The tenth is the eduction of species from genera; but this mode has no place in God, for the Father is not predicated of the Son as the genus of a species. The eleventh is the realization of an idea [*ideatio*], as an external coffer arises from the one in the mind. The twelfth is birth, as a man is begotten of his father; which implies priority and posteriority of time. Thus it is clear that equality of nature or of time is absent in every mode whereby one thing is from another. So if the Son is from the Father, we must say that He is less than the Father, or later than the Father, or both.

Obj. 2. Further, everything that comes from another has a principle. But nothing eternal has a principle. Therefore the Son is not eternal; nor is the Holy Ghost.

Obj. 3. Further, everything which is corrupted ceases to be. Hence everything generated begins to be, for the end of generation is existence. But the Son is generated by the Father. Therefore He begins to exist, and is not co-eternal with the Father.

Obj. 4. Further, if the Son be begotten by the Father, either He is always being begotten, or there is some moment in which He is begotten. If He is always being begotten, since, during the process of generation, a thing must be imperfect, as appears in successive things, which are always in process of becoming, as time and motion, it follows that the Son must be always imperfect; which cannot be admitted. Thus there is a moment to be assigned for the begetting of the Son, and before that moment the Son did not exist.

On the contrary, Athanasius declares that *all the three persons are coeternal with each other.*[1]

I answer that, We must say that the Son is co-eternal with the Father.

---

1. 参见 Cf. *Symb. "Quicumque"* (Denzinger, no. 39).

In proof of which we must consider that for a thing which proceeds from a principle to be posterior to its principle may be due to two reasons: one on the part of the agent, and the other on the part of the action. On the part of the agent, this happens differently as regards voluntary agents and natural agents. In voluntary agents, because of the choice of time; for as a free agent can choose the form it gives to the effect, as was stated above,[1] so it can choose the time in which to produce its effect. In natural agents, however, this happens because an agent does not have the perfection of its natural power, from the very first, but obtains it after a certain time; as, for instance, a man is not able to generate from the very first. Considered on the part of action, anything derived from a principle cannot exist simultaneously with its principle when the action is successive. So, given that an agent, as soon as it exists, begins to act thus, the effect would not exist in the same instant, but in the instant of the action's termination. Now it is manifest, according to what has been said, that the Father does not beget the Son by will, but by nature;[2] and also that the Father's nature was perfect from eternity; and again that the action whereby the Father produces the Son is not successive, because thus the Son would be successively generated, and His generation would be material and accompanied by movement, which is quite impossible. Therefore we conclude that the Son existed whensoever the Father existed; and thus the Son is co-eternal with the Father, and likewise the Holy Ghost is co-eternal with both.

Reply Obj. 1. As Augustine says, no mode of the procession of any creature perfectly represents the divine generation.[3] Hence we need to gather a likeness of it from many of these modes, so that what is wanting in one may be somewhat supplied from another; and thus it is

---

1. 参见 Q. 41, a. 2.
2. 同上
3. 参见 *Serm.* CXVII, 6; 10 (PL 38, 666; 669).

declared in the council of Ephesus: *Let Splendor tell thee that the co-eternal Son existed always with the Father; let the Word announce the impassibility*[1] *of His Birth; let the name of the Son insinuate His consubstantiality.*[2] Yet, above them all, the procession of the word from the intellect represents it more exactly; for the intellectual word is not posterior to its source except in an intellect passing from potentiality to act; and this cannot be said of God.

Reply Obj. 2. Eternity excludes a principle of duration, but not a principle of origin.

Reply Obj. 3. Every corruption is a change; and so all that corrupts begins not to exist and ceases to be. The divine generation, however, is not a change, as was stated above.[3] Hence the Son is ever being begotten, and the Father is always begetting.

Reply Obj. 4. In time there is something indivisible — namely, the instant; and there is something else which endures — namely, time. But in eternity the indivisible *now* stands ever still, as we have said above.[4] But the generation of the Son is not in the *now* of time, or in time, but in eternity. And so, to express the presentiality[5] and permanence[6] of eternity, we can say that *He is ever being born*, as Origen said.[7] But as Gregory and Augustine say, it is better to say *ever born*, so that *ever* may denote the permanence of eternity, and *born* the perfection of the Begotten.[8] Thus, therefore, neither is the Son imperfect, nor *was there a time when He was not*, as Arius said.[9]

---

1. impassibility：不觉痛苦；无感情
2. 参见 Cf. the *Acta* of the Council, pt. III, ch. 10; ed Mansi, V, 214.
3. 参见 Q. 27, a. 2.
4. 参见 Q. 10, a. 2, ad 1; a. 4, ad 2.
5. presentiality：现在
6. permanence：常存；持久
7. 参见 *In Ierem.*, hom. IX (PG 13, 357).
8. 参见 St. Gregory, *Moral.*, XXIX, 1 (PL 76, 477); St. Augustine, *Lib. 83 Quaest.*, q. 37 (PL 40, 27).
9. 参见 Cf. Athanasius, *Contra Arianos*, I (PG 26, 19).

Third Article

WHETHER IN THE DIVINE PERSONS THERE EXISTS AN ORDER OF NATURE?

We proceed thus to the Third Article: —

Objection 1. It would seem that among the divine persons there does not exist an order of nature. For whatever exists in God is the essence, or a person, or a notion. But the order of nature does not signify the essence, nor any of the persons, or notions. Therefore there is no order of nature in God.

Obj. 2. Further, wherever order of nature exists, there one comes before another, at least, according to nature and intellect. But in the divine persons there exists neither priority nor posteriority[1], as was declared by Athanasius.[2] Therefore, in the divine persons there is no order of nature.

Obj. 3. Further, wherever order exists, distinction also exists. But there is no distinction in the divine nature. Therefore it is not subject to order and order of nature does not exist in it.

Obj. 4. Further, the divine nature is the divine essence. But there is no order of essence in God. Therefore neither is there of nature.

On the contrary, Where plurality exists without order, confusion exists. But in the divine persons there is no confusion, as Athanasius says.[3] Therefore in God order exists.

I answer that, Order always has reference to some principle. Therefore, since there are many kinds of principle — namely, according to site, as a point; according to intellect, as the principle of demonstration; and according to each individual cause — so are there many kinds of order.

---

1. posteriority：后天性；在后
2. 参见 Cf. *Symb.* "*Quicumque*" (Denzinger, no. 39).
3. 同上

Now, as we have stated,[1] principle is said to exist in God according to origin without priority; so there must likewise be order according to origin without priority; and this is called *the order of nature:* in the words of Augustine: *Not whereby one is prior to another, but whereby one is from another.*[2]

Reply Obj. 1. The order of nature signifies the notion of origin in general, not a special kind of origin.

Reply Obj. 2. In created things, even when what is derived from a principle is coeval in duration with its principle, the principle still comes first in the order of nature and reason, if our consideration bears on that which is the principle. If, however, we consider the relations of cause and effect, or of the principle and the thing proceeding therefrom, it is clear that the things so related are simultaneous in the order of nature and reason, inasmuch as the one enters the definition of the other. But in God the relations themselves are the persons subsisting in one nature. So, neither on the part of the nature, nor on the part of the relations, can one person be prior to another, not even in the order of nature and reason.

Reply Obj. 3. The order of nature means, not the ordering of nature itself, but the existence of order in the divine Persons according to natural origin.

Reply Obj. 4. Nature in a certain way implies the idea of a principle, but essence does not; and so the order of origin is more correctly called the order of nature than the order of essence.

Fourth Article
WHETHER THE SON IS EQUAL TO THE FATHER IN GREATNESS?

We proceed thus to the Fourth Article: —

1. 参见 Q. 33, a. 1, ad 3.
2. 参见 *Contra Maximin.*, II, 14 (PL 42, 775).

Objection 1. It would seem that the Son is not equal to the Father in greatness. For He Himself said (*Jo.* xiv. 28): *The Father is greater than I*; and the Apostle says (*1 Cor.* xv. 28): *The Son Himself shall be subject to Him that put all things under Him.*

Obj. 2. Further, Paternity is part of the Father's dignity. But paternity does not belong to the Son. Therefore the Son does not possess all the Father's dignity; and so He is not equal in greatness to the Father.

Obj. 3. Further, wherever there exist a whole and a part, many parts are more than one only, or than fewer parts; as three men are more than two, or than one. But in God there seems to exist a universal whole, and a part; for under relation or notion, several notions are included. Therefore, since in the Father there are three notions, while in the Son there are only two, the Son is evidently not equal to the Father.

On the contrary, It is said (*Phil.* ii. 6): *He thought it not robbery to be equal with God.*

I answer that, The Son is necessarily equal to the Father in greatness. For the greatness of God is nothing but the perfection of His nature. Now it belongs to the very nature of paternity and filiation that the Son by generation should attain to the possession of the perfection of the nature which is in the Father, in the same way as it is in the Father Himself. But since in men generation is a certain kind of transmutation[1] of one proceeding from potentiality to act, it follows that a man is not equal at first to the father who begets him, but attains to equality by due growth, unless owing to a defect in the principle of generation it should happen otherwise. Now from what precedes it is evident that in God there really and properly exist paternity and filiation.[2] Nor can we say that the power of generation in

1. transmutation：变化；变形；演变
2. 参见 Q. 27, a. 2; q. 33, a. 2, ad 3 and 4; a. 3.

the Father was defective, or that the Son of God arrived at perfection in a successive manner and by change. Therefore we must say that the Son was eternally equal to the Father in greatness. Hence, Hilary says: *Remove bodily weakness, remove the beginning of conception, remove pain and all human shortcomings, then every son, by reason of his natural nativity, is the father's equal, because he has a like nature.*[1]

Reply Obj. 1. These words are to be understood of Christ's human nature, wherein He is less than the Father, and subject to Him; but in His divine nature He is equal to the Father. This is expressed by Athanasius: *Equal to the Father in His Godhead; less than the Father in humanity*;[2] and by Hilary: *By the fact of giving, the Father is greater; but He is not less to Whom the same being is given*;[3] and the same Hilary says: *The Son subjects Himself by His inborn piety* — that is, by His recognition of paternal authority; whereas *creatures are subject by their created weakness.*[4]

Reply Obj. 2. Equality is measured by greatness. In God greatness signifies the perfection of nature, as was above explained, and belongs to the essence. Thus equality and likeness in God have reference to the essence; nor can there be inequality[5] or dissimilitude[6] arising from the distinction of the relations. Therefore Augustine says: *The question of origin is, Who is from whom? but the question of equality is, Of what kind, or how great, is he?*[7] Therefore, paternity is the Father's dignity, as also the Father's essence, since dignity is something absolute, and pertains to the essence. Since, therefore, the same essence, which in the Father is paternity, in the Son is filiation, so the same dignity which, in the

1. 参见 *De Synod.* (PL 10, 528).
2. 参见 Cf. *Symb. "Quicumque"* (Denzinger, no. 40).
3. 参见 *De Trin.*, IX (PL 10, 325).
4. 参见 *De Synod.* (PL 10, 532).
5. inequality：不平等；不均等
6. dissimilitude：不同；相异点
7. 参见 *Contra Maximin.*, II 18 (PL 42, 786).

Father is paternity, in the Son is filiation. It is thus true to say that the Son possesses whatever dignity the Father has; but we cannot argue: *the Father has paternity, therefore the Son has paternity*, for there is a transition from substance to relation. For the Father and the Son have the same essence and dignity, which exist in the Father by the relation of giver, and in the Son by the relation of receiver.

Reply Obj. 3. In God relation is not a universal whole, although it is predicated of several relations, because all the relations are one in essence and being; which is irreconcilable with the idea of universal, the parts of which are distinguished in being. Person, likewise, is not a universal term in God, as we have seen above.[1] Therefore, all the relations together are not something greater than only one, nor are all the persons something greater than only one; because the whole perfection of the divine nature exists in each person.

Fifth Article
WHETHER THE SON IS IN THE FATHER, AND CONVERSELY?

We proceed thus to the Fifth Article: —

Objection 1. It would seem that the Son and the Father are not in each other. For the Philosopher gives eight modes of one thing existing in another,[2] according to none of which is the Son in the Father, or conversely; as is patent to anyone who examines each mode. Therefore the Son and the Father are not in each other.

Obj. 2. Further, nothing that has come out from another is within it. But the Son from eternity came out from the Father, according to Micheas v. 2 : *His going forth is from the beginning, from the days of eternity.* Therefore the Son is not in the Father.

Obj. 3. Further, one of two opposites cannot be in the other. But the

---

1. 参见 Q. 30, a. 4, ad 3.
2. 参见 *Phys.*, IV, 3 (210a 14).

Son and the Father are relatively opposed. Therefore one cannot be in the other.

On the contrary, It is said (*Jo.* xiv. 10): *I am in the Father, and the Father is in Me.*

I answer that, There are three points of consideration as regards the Father and the Son: the essence, the relation, and the origin; and according to each the Son and the Father are in each other. The Father is in the Son by His essence, for the Father is His own essence, and communicates His essence to the Son not by any change on His part. Hence it follows that, as the Father's essence is in the Son, the Father Himself is in the Son; likewise, since the Son is His own essence, it follows that He Himself is in the Father in Whom is His essence. This is what is said by Hilary: *The unchangeable God, so to speak, follows His own nature in begetting an unchangeable God. So we understand the nature of God to subsist in Him, for He is God in God.*[1] It is also manifest that, as regards the relations, each of two relative opposites is in the concept of the other. Regarding origin, furthermore, it is clear that the procession of the intelligible word is not outside the intellect, inasmuch as it remains in the utterer of the word; and likewise what is expressed by the word is contained in it. And the same applies to the Holy Ghost.

Reply Obj. 1. What is contained in creatures does not sufficiently represent what exists in God; so according to none of the ways enumerated by the Philosopher are the Son and the Father in each other. The way that most approaches to it is to be found in that whereby something exists in its originating principle, except that the unity of essence between the principle and that which proceeds from it is wanting in created things.

Reply Obj. 2. The Son's going forth from the Father is by way of

1. 参见 *De Trin.*, V (PL 10, 155).

the interior procession whereby the word emerges from the heart and remains therein. Hence this going forth in God is only by the distinction of the relations, not by any kind of essential separation.

Reply Obj. 3. The Father and the Son are relatively opposed, but not essentially; however, as was above explained, among relative opposites one is in the other.

Sixth Article
WHETHER THE SON IS EQUAL TO THE FATHER IN POWER?

We proceed thus to the Sixth Article: —

Objection 1. It would seem that the Son is not equal to the Father in power. For it is said (*Jo.* v. 19): *The Son cannot do anything of Himself but what He seeth the Father doing.* But the Father can act of Himself. Therefore the Father's power is greater than the Son's.

Obj. 2. Further, greater is the power of him who commands and teaches than of him who obeys and hears. But the Father commands the Son according to *Jo.* xiv. 31: *As the Father gave Me commandment, so do I.* The Father also teaches the Son: *The Father loveth the Son, and showeth Him all things that Himself doth* (*Jo.* v. 20). Also, the Son hears: *As I hear, so I judge* (*Jo.* v. 30). Therefore, the Father has greater power than the Son.

Obj. 3. Further, it belongs to the Father's omnipotence to be able to beget a Son equal to Himself. For Augustine says: *Were He unable to beget one equal to Himself, where would be the omnipotence of God the Father?*[1] But the Son cannot beget a Son, as was proved above.[2] Therefore the Son cannot do all that belongs to the Father's omnipotence; and hence He is not equal to Him in power.

On the contrary, It is said (*Jo.* v. 19): *Whatsoever things the Father doth,*

1. 参见 *Contra Maximin.*, II, 7 (PL 42, 762).
2. 参见 Q. 41, a. 6, ad 1 and 2.

these the Son also doth in like manner.

I answer that, The Son is necessarily equal to the Father in power. Power of action is a consequence of perfection of nature. In creatures, for instance, we see that the more perfect the nature, the greater power there is for action. Now it was shown above that the very notion of the divine paternity and filiation requires that the Son should be the Father's equal in greatness — that is, in perfection of nature. Hence it follows that the Son is equal to the Father in power; and the same applies to the Holy Ghost in relation to both.

Reply Obj. 1. The words, *the Son cannot of Himself do anything*, do not withdraw from the Son any power possessed by the Father, since it is immediately added, *Whatsoever things the Father doth, the Son doth in like manner* (*Jo.* v. 19); but their meaning is to show that the Son derives His power from the Father, of Whom He receives His nature. Hence, Hilary says: *The unity of the divine nature implies that the Son so acts of Himself* [*per se*], *that He does not act by Himself* [*a se*].[1]

Reply Obj. 2. The Father's *showing* and the Son's *hearing* are to be taken in the sense that the Father communicates knowledge to the Son, as He communicates His essence. The command of the Father can be explained in the same sense, as giving Him from eternity knowledge and will to act, by begetting Him. Or, better still, this may be referred to Christ in His human nature.

Reply Obj. 3. As the same essence is paternity in the Father, and filiation in the Son, so by the same power the Father begets, and the Son is begotten. Hence it is clear that the Son can do whatever the Father can do. But it does not follow that the Son can beget, for to argue thus would imply transition from substance to relation, since generation signifies a divine relation. So the Son has the same power as the Father, but with another relation. For the Father has power as

1. 参见 *De Trin.*, IX (PL 10, 319).

giving, and this is signified when it is said that He *can generate*; but Son has power as *receiving*, and this is signified when it is said that He *can be generated*.

Question XLIII
THE MISSION OF THE DIVINE PERSONS
(*In Eight Articles*)

WE next consider the mission of the divine persons, concerning which there are eight points of inquiry: (1) Whether it is suitable for a divine person to be sent? (2) Whether mission is eternal, or only temporal? (3) In what sense a divine person is invisibly sent? (4) Whether it is fitting that each person be sent? (5) Whether both the Son and the Holy Ghost are invisibly sent? (6) To whom the invisible mission is directed? (7) Visible mission. (8) Whether any person sends Himself visibly or invisibly?

First Article
WHETHER A DIVINE PERSON CAN FITTINGLY BE SENT?

We proceed thus to the First Article: —

Objection 1. It would seem that a divine person cannot fittingly be sent. For one who is sent is less than the sender. But one divine person is not less than another. Therefore one person is not sent by another.

Obj. 2. Further, what is sent is separated from the sender; and so Jerome says, commenting on *Ezechiel* xvi. 53: *What is joined and tied in one body cannot be sent.*[1] But in the divine persons *there is nothing that is separable*, as Hilary says.[2] Therefore one person is not sent by another.

Obj. 3. Further, whoever is sent departs from one place and comes

1. 参见 *In Ezech.*, V, super XVI, 53 (PL 25,164).
2. 参见 *De Trin.*, VII (PL 10, 233).

anew into another. But this does not apply to a divine person, Who is everywhere. Therefore it is not suitable for a divine person to be sent.

On the contrary, It is said (*Jo*. viii. 16): *I am not alone, but I and the Father that sent Me.*

I answer that, the notion of mission includes two things: the relation of the one sent to the sender, and that of the one sent to the end whereto he is sent. That anyone be sent implies a certain kind of procession of the one sent from the sender: either according to command, as the master sends the servant; or according to counsel, as an adviser may be said to send the king to battle; or according to origin, as a tree sends forth its flower. Through the fact that anyone is sent there is also indicated a relation to the term to which one is sent, so that in some way he begins to be present there: either because in no way was he present before in the place whereto he is sent, or because he begins to be there in some way in which he was not there hitherto.

Thus the mission of a divine person is a fitting thing, as meaning in one way the procession of origin from the sender, and as meaning a new way of existing in another. Thus the Son is said to be sent by the Father into the world, inasmuch as He began to exist *visibly* in the world by taking our nature; whereas *He was* previously *in the world* (*Jo*. i. 1).

Reply Obj. 1. Mission implies inferiority in the one sent when it means procession from the principle as sending by command or counsel; for the one commanding is the greater, and the counsellor is the wiser. In God, however, it means only procession of origin, which is according to equality, as was explained above.[1]

Reply Obj. 2. What is so sent as to begin to exist where previously it did not exist, is locally moved by being sent; hence it is necessarily separated locally from the sender. This, however, does not occur in the

---

1. 参见 Q. 42, a. 4 and 6.

mission of a divine person, for the divine person sent neither begins to exist where he did not previously exist, nor ceases to exist where He was. Hence such a mission takes place without a separation, having only distinction of origin.

Reply Obj. 3. This objection rests on the idea of mission according to local motion, which is not in God.

Second Article
WHETHER MISSION IS ETERNAL, OR ONLY TEMPORAL?

We proceed thus to the Second Article: —

Objection 1. It would seem that mission can be eternal. For Gregory says, *The Son is sent even as He is begotten.*[1] But the Son's generation is eternal. Therefore mission is eternal.

Obj. 2. Further, a thing is changed if it becomes something temporally. But a divine person is not changed. Therefore the mission of a divine person is not temporal, but eternal.

Obj. 3. Further, mission implies procession. But the procession of the divine persons is eternal. Therefore mission is also eternal.

On the contrary, It is said (*Gal.* iv. 4): *When the fullness of the time was come, God sent His Son.*

I answer that, A certain difference is to be observed in all the terms that express the origin of the divine persons. For some express only relation to the principle, as *procession* and *going forth.* Others express the term of procession together with the relation to the principle. Of these, some express the eternal term, as *generation* and *spiration*; for generation is the procession of the divine person into the divine nature, and passive spiration is the procession of the subsisting love. Other names express the temporal term with the relation to the principle, as *mission*

1. 参见 *In Evang.*, II, hom. 26 (PL 76, 1198).

and *giving*. For a thing is sent that it may be in something else, and is given that it may be possessed; but that a divine person be possessed by any creature, or exist in it in a new way, is temporal.

Hence *mission* and *giving* have only a temporal signification in God, but *generation* and *spiration* are exclusively eternal; whereas *procession* and *going forth* have, in God, both an eternal and a temporal signification: for the Son has proceeded eternally as God. But He may proceed temporally, to become man as well, according to His visible mission; or He may proceed temporally by dwelling in man according to His invisible mission.

Reply Obj. 1. Gregory speaks of the temporal generation of the Son, not from the Father, but from His mother; or it may be taken to mean that the Son could be sent because He was eternally begotten.

Reply Obj. 2. That a divine person may newly exist in anyone, or be possessed temporally by anyone, does not come from change in the divine person, but from change in the creature; as God Himself is temporally called Lord by a change in the creature.

Reply Obj. 3. Mission not only signifies procession from the principle, but also includes the temporal term of the procession. Hence mission is only temporal. Or we may say that it includes the eternal procession, with the addition of a temporal effect. For the relation of a divine person to His principle must be eternal. Hence the procession may be called a twin procession, eternal and temporal, not that there is a double relation to the principle, but a double term, temporal and eternal.

Third Article
WHETHER THE INVISIBLE MISSION OF A DIVINE PERSON IS ONLY ACCORDING TO THE GIFT OF SANCTIFYING GRACE?

We proceed thus to the Third Article: —

Objection 1. It would seem that the invisible mission of a divine person is not only according to the gift of sanctifying grace. For the sending of a divine person means that He is given. Hence if a divine person is sent only according to the gifts of sanctifying grace, the divine person Himself will not be given, but only His gifts; and this is the error of those who say that the Holy Ghost is not given, but that His gifts are given.

Obj. 2. Further, this preposition, *according to*, denotes the relation of some cause. But a divine person is the cause that the gift of sanctifying grace is possessed, and not conversely, according to *Rom.* v. 5, *the charity of God is poured forth in our hearts by the Holy Ghost, Who is given to us.* Therefore it is improperly said that the divine person is sent according to the gifts of sanctifying grace.

Obj. 3. Further, Augustine says that *the Son, when temporally perceived by the mind, is said to be sent.*[1] But the Son is known not only by sanctifying grace, but also by gratuitous grace, as well as by faith and by knowledge. Therefore a divine person is not sent only according to the gift of sanctifying grace.

Obj. 4. Further, Rabanus says that the Holy Ghost was given to the apostles for the working of miracles.[2] This, however, is not a gift of sanctifying grace, but a gratuitous grace. Therefore a divine person is not given only according to the gift of sanctifying grace.

On the contrary, Augustine says that *the Holy Ghost proceeds temporally for the creature's sanctification.*[3] But mission is a temporal procession. Since, then, the creature's sanctification[4] is by sanctifying grace[5], it follows that the mission of a divine person is only by sanctifying grace.

---

1. 参见 *De Trin.*, IV, 20 (PL 42, 907).
2. 参见 *Enarr. in Epist. Pauli*, XI, super *I Cor.* XII, 11 (PL 112, 109).
3. 参见 *De Trin.*, XV, 27 (PL 42, 1095).
4. sanctification：圣化；神圣化
5. sanctifying grace：圣化的恩宠

I answer that, A divine person is fittingly sent in the sense that He exists newly in anyone, and He is fittingly given as possessed by anyone; but neither of these is otherwise than by sanctifying grace.

For God is in all things in a universal way by His essence, power, and presence, as the cause existing in the effects which participate in His goodness. Above and beyond this universal way, however, there is one special way belonging to the rational nature wherein God is said to be present as the object known is in the knower, and the beloved in the lover. And since the rational creature by its operation of knowledge and love attains to God Himself, according to this special way God is said not only to exist in the rational creature, but also to dwell therein as in His own temple. So no other effect can be put down as the reason why the divine person is in the rational creature in a new way, except sanctifying grace. Hence, the divine person is sent and proceeds temporally only according to sanctifying grace.

Again, we are said to possess only what we can freely use or enjoy. But to have the power of enjoying the divine person can be only according to sanctifying grace. And yet the Holy Ghost is possessed by man, and dwells within him, in the very gift itself of sanctifying grace. Hence the Holy Ghost Himself is given and sent.

Reply Obj. 1. By the gift of sanctifying grace the rational creature is perfected so that it can both freely use the created gift itself, and also enjoy the divine person Himself. And so the invisible mission takes place according to the gift of sanctifying grace; and vet the divine person Himself is given.

Reply Obj. 2. Sanctifying grace disposes the soul to possess the divine person; and this is signified when it is said that the Holy Ghost is given according to the gift of grace. Nevertheless the gift itself of grace is from the Holy Ghost; and this is what is meant by the words, *the charity of God is poured forth in our hearts by the Holy Ghost.*

Reply Obj. 3. Although the Son can be known by us according to other effects, yet He neither dwells in us, nor is He even possessed by us, according to those effects.

Reply Obj. 4. The working of miracles manifests sanctifying grace, as does also the gift of prophecy and any other gratuitous grace. Hence gratuitous grace is called the *manifestation of the Spirit* (*1 Cor.* xii. 7). And so the Holy Ghost is said to be given to the apostles for the working of miracles, because sanctifying grace was given to them along with its outward sign. Were only the sign of sanctifying grace given to them without the grace itself, it would not be said absolutely that the Holy Ghost was given, except with some qualifying term; just as we read of certain ones receiving the gift of the spirit of prophecy, or of miracles, as having from the Holy Ghost the power of prophesying or of working miracles.

Fourth Article
WHETHER THE FATHER CAN BE FITTINGLY SENT?

We proceed thus to the Fourth Article: —

Objection 1. It seems fitting that also the Father should be sent. For being sent means that a divine person is given. But the Father gives Himself since He can be possessed only by His giving Himself. Therefore it can be said that the Father sends Himself.

Obj. 2. Further, a divine person is sent according to the indwelling of grace. But by grace the whole Trinity dwells in us according to *Jo.* xiv. 23: *We will come to him and make Our abode with him.* Therefore each one of the divine persons is sent.

Obj. 3. Further, whatever belongs to one person belongs to them all, except the notions and persons. But mission does not signify any person; nor even a notion, since there are only five notions, as was stated above.[1] Therefore every divine person can be sent.

1. 参见 Q. 32, a. 3.

On the contrary, Augustine says, *The Father alone is never described as having been sent.*[1]

I answer that, The very idea of mission means procession from another, and in God it means procession according to origin, as was above explained. Hence, as the Father is not from another, in no way is it fitting for Him to be sent; but this can belong only to the Son and to the Holy Ghost, to Whom it belongs to be from another.

Reply Obj. 1. In the sense of *giving* as a free bestowal of something, the Father gives Himself, as freely bestowing Himself to be enjoyed by the creature. But as implying the authority of the giver as regards what is given, *to be given* applies in God only to the Person Who is from another; and the same as regards *being sent.*

Reply Obj. 2. Although the effect of grace is also from the Father, Who dwells in us by grace, just as the Son and the Holy Ghost, still He is not described as being sent, for He is not from another. Thus Augustine says that *The Father, when known by anyone temporally, is not said to be sent; for there is no one whence He is, or from whom He proceeds.*[2]

Reply Obj. 3. Mission, meaning procession from the sender, includes the signification of a notion, not of a special notion, but in general; for *to be from another* is common to two of the notions.

Fifth Article
WHETHER IT IS FITTING FOR THE SON TO BE SENT INVISIBLY?

We proceed thus to the Fifth Article: —

Objection. 1. It would seem that it is not fitting for the Son to be

---

1. 参见 *De Trin.*, II , 5 (PL 42, 849); *Contra Serm. Arian.*, IV (PL 42, 686).
2. 参见 *Op. cit.*, IV, 20 (PL 42, 908).

sent invisibly. For the invisible mission of a divine person is according to the gift of grace. But all gifts of grace belong to the Holy Ghost, according to *1 Cor.* xii. 11: *One and the same Spirit worketh all things.* Therefore only the Holy Ghost is sent invisibly.

Obj. 2. Further, the mission of a divine person is according to sanctifying grace. But the gifts belonging to the perfection of the intellect are not gifts of sanctifying grace, since they can be possessed without the gift of charity, according to *1 Cor.* xiii. 2: *If I should have prophecy, and should know all mysteries, and all knowledge, and if I should have all faith so that I could move mountains, and have not charity, I am nothing.* Therefore, since the Son proceeds as the word of the intellect, it seems unfitting for Him to be sent invisibly.

Obj. 3. Further, the mission of a divine person is a procession, as was said above. But the procession of the Son is not the procession of the Holy Ghost. Therefore they are distinct missions, if both are sent; and then one of them would be superfluous, since one would suffice for the creature's sanctification.

On the contrary, It is said of divine Wisdom (*Wis.* ix. 10): *Send her from heaven to Thy Saints, and from the seat of Thy greatness.*

I answer that, Through sanctifying grace, the whole Trinity dwells in the mind, according to *Jo.* xiv. 23: *We will come to him, and will make Our abode with him.* But that a divine person be sent to anyone by invisible grace signifies both that this Person dwells in a new way within someone and that He has His origin from another. Hence, since both to the Son and to the Holy Ghost it belongs to dwell in the soul by grace, and to be from another, it therefore belongs to both of them to be invisibly sent. As to the Father, though He dwells in us by grace, still it does not belong to Him to be from another, and consequently it does not belong to Him to be sent.

Reply Obj. 1. All the gifts, considered as such, are attributed to the Holy Ghost, for He is by His nature the first Gift, since He is Love, as was already stated.[1] Nevertheless, although this is true, some gifts, by reason of their own particular nature, are appropriated in a certain way to the Son; those, namely, which belong to the intellect, and in respect of which we speak of the mission of the Son. Hence Augustine says that *The Son is sent to anyone invisibly, whenever He is known and perceived by anyone* [2].

Reply Obj. 2. The soul is made like to God by grace. Hence for a divine person to be sent to anyone by grace, there must needs be a likening of the soul to the divine person Who is sent, by some gift of grace. Because the Holy Ghost is Love, the soul is assimilated to the Holy Ghost by the gift of charity: hence the mission of the Holy Ghost is according to the gift of charity. But the Son is the Word, not any sort of word, but one Who breathes forth Love. Hence Augustine says: *The Word we speak of is knowledge with love.*[3] Thus the Son is sent not in accordance with every and any kind of intellectual perfection, but according to the intellectual formation or illumination which breaks forth into the affection of love, as is said (*Jo.* vi. 45): *Everyone that hath heard from the Father and hath learned, cometh to Me*; and (*Ps.* xxxviii. 4): *In my meditation a fire shall flame forth.* Thus Augustine plainly says: *The Son is sent, whenever He is known and perceived by anyone.*[4] Now perception implies a certain experimental knowledge; and this is properly called *wisdom* [*sapientia*], as it were, a relishing knowledge[5] [*sapida scientia*], according to *Ecclus.* vi. 23: *The wisdom of doctrine is according to her name.*

Reply Obj. 3. Since mission expresses the origin of the person Who is sent, and His indwelling by grace, as was above explained, if we speak of mission according to origin, in this sense the Son's mission is

---

1. 参见 Q. 38, a. 2.
2. 参见 *De Trin.*, IV, 20 (PL 42, 907).
3. 参见 *Op. cit.*, IX, 10 (PL 42, 969).
4. 参见 *De Trin.*, IV, 20 (PL 42, 907).
5. a relishing knowledge：一种领会的知识；被品尝过的知识

distinguished from the mission of the Holy Ghost, just as generation is distinguished from procession. If we consider mission as regards the effect of grace, in this sense the two missions are united in the root of grace, but are distinguished in the effects of grace, which consist in the illumination of the intellect and the kindling of the affection. Thus it is manifest that one mission cannot be without the other, because neither takes place without sanctifying grace, nor is one person separated from the other.

Sixth Article

WHETHER THE INVISIBLE MISSION IS TO ALL WHO PARTICIPATE GRACE?

We proceed thus to the Sixth Article: —

Objection 1. It would seem that the invisible mission is not to all who participate grace. For the Fathers of the Old Testament had their share of grace. Yet to them was made no invisible mission; for it is said (*Jo.* vii. 39): *The Spirit was not yet given, because Jesus was not yet glorified.* Therefore the invisible mission is not to all partakers in grace.

Obj. 2. Further, progress in virtue is only by grace. But the invisible mission is not according to progress in virtue, because progress in virtue is continuous, since charity always increases or decreases; and thus the mission would be continuous. Therefore the invisible mission is not to all who share in grace.

Obj. 3. Further, Christ and the blessed have fullness of grace. But mission is not to them, for mission implies distance, whereas Christ, as man, and all the blessed are perfectly united to God. Therefore the invisible mission is not to all sharers in grace.

Obj. 4. Further, the Sacraments[1] of the New Law[2] contain grace, and it is not said that the invisible mission is sent to them. Therefore the

1. the Sacraments：圣事；圣礼
2. the New Law：指圣经新约里的法律，相比较于旧约中的梅瑟法律

invisible mission is not to all that have grace.

On the contrary, According to Augustine, the invisible mission is for the creature's sanctification.[1] Now every creature that has grace is sanctified. Therefore the invisible mission is to every such creature.

I answer that, As was above stated, mission in its very meaning implies either that he who is sent begins to exist where he was not before, as occurs to creatures; or that he begins to exist where he was before, but in a new way, in which sense mission is ascribed to the divine persons. Thus mission, as regards the one who receives it, implies two things, the indwelling of grace, and a certain renewal by grace. Thus the invisible mission is to all in whom are to be found these two conditions.

Reply Obj. 1. The invisible mission was directed to the Old Testament Fathers, as appears from what Augustine says, namely, that the invisible mission of the Son *is in man and with men. This was done in former times with the Fathers and Prophets.*[2] Thus the words, *the Spirit was not yet given*, are to be applied to that giving accompanied with a visible sign which took place on the day of Pentecost.

Reply Obj. 2. The invisible mission takes place also as regards progress in virtue or increase of grace. Hence Augustine says that *the Son is sent to each one when He is known and perceived by anyone, so far as He can be known and perceived according to the capacity of the soul, whether journeying towards God, or united perfectly to Him.*[3] Such invisible mission, however, chiefly occurs as regards anyone's proficiency in the performance of a new act, or in the acquisition of a new state of grace; as, for example, the proficiency in reference to the gift of miracles or of prophecy, or in the fervor of charity leading a man to expose himself to the danger of martyrdom[4], or to renounce his possessions, or to undertake any arduous work.

---

1. 参见 *Op. cit.*, XV, 27 (PL 42, 1095)
2. 参见 *Op. cit.*, TV, 20 (PL 42, 907).
3. 同上
4. martyrdom：殉道；殉难

Reply Obj. 3. The invisible mission is directed to the blessed at the very beginning of their beatitude. The invisible mission is made to them subsequently, not by the *intensity* of grace, but by the further revelation of mysteries; which goes on till the day of judgment. Such an increase is by the *extension* of grace, because it extends to a greater number of objects. To Christ the invisible mission was sent at the first moment of His conception; but not afterwards, since from the beginning of His conception He was filled with all wisdom and grace

Reply Obj. 4. Grace resides instrumentally in the sacraments of the New Law, as the form of a thing designed resides in the instruments of the art designing, according to a certain procession from the agent to the subject receiving the operation. But mission is spoken of only as directed to its term. Hence the mission of the divine person is not to the sacraments, but to those who receive grace through the sacraments.

Seventh Article
WHETHER IT IS FITTING FOR THE HOLY GHOST TO BE SENT VISIBLY?

We proceed thus to the Seventh Article: —

Objection 1. It would seem that the Holy Ghost is not fittingly sent in a visible manner. For the Son, as visibly sent to the world, is said to be less than the Father. But the Holy Ghost is never said to be less than the Father. Therefore the Holy Ghost is not fittingly sent in a visible manner.

Obj. 2. Further, the visible mission takes place by way of union to a visible creature, as the Son's mission according to the flesh. But the Holy Ghost did not assume any visible creature; and hence it cannot be said that He exists otherwise in some creatures than in others, unless perhaps as in a sign, as He is also present in the sacraments and in all the figures of the law. Thus the Holy Ghost is either not sent visibly at all, or His visible mission takes place in all these things.

Obj. 3. Further, every visible creature is an effect showing forth the whole Trinity. Therefore the Holy Ghost is not sent by reason of those visible creatures more than any other person.

Obj. 4. Further, the Son was visibly sent according to the noblest of visible creatures, namely, human nature. Therefore if the Holy Ghost is sent visibly, He ought to have been sent according to some kind of rational creatures.

Obj. 5. Further, whatever is done visibly by God is dispensed by the ministry of the angels, as Augustine says.[1] So visible appearances, if there have been any, came by means of the angels. Thus the angels are sent, and not the Holy Ghost.

Obj. 6. Further, if the Holy Ghost is sent in a visible manner, this is only for the purpose of manifesting the invisible mission; for invisible things are made known by the visible. So those to whom there was not an invisible mission ought not to receive the visible mission, and to all who received the invisible mission, whether in the New or in the Old Testament, there ought likewise to be the visible mission; and this is clearly false. Therefore the Holy Ghost is not sent visibly.

On the contrary, It is stated (*Matt.* iii. 16) that, when our Lord was baptized, the Holy Ghost descended upon Him in the shape of a dove.

I answer that, God provides for all things according to the nature of each thing. Now the nature of man requires that he be led to the invisible by visible things, as was explained above.[2] Therefore, the invisible things of God must be made manifest to man by the things that are visible. As God, therefore, in a certain way has demonstrated Himself and His eternal processions to men by visible creatures, according to certain signs, so it was fitting that the invisible missions also of the divine persons should be made manifest by some visible creatures.

---

1. 参见 *De Trin.*, III, 10; 11 (PL 42, 879; 882).
2. 参见 Q. 12, a. 12.

This mode of manifestation applies in different ways to the Son and to the Holy Ghost. For it belongs to the Holy Ghost, Who proceeds as Love, to be the gift of sanctification; but to the Son, as the principle of the Holy Ghost, it belongs to be the author of this sanctification. Thus the Son has been sent visibly as the author of sanctification; the Holy Ghost as the sign of sanctification.

Reply Obj. 1. The Son assumed the visible creature, wherein He appeared, into the unity of His person, so that whatever can be said of that creature can be said of the Son of God; and so, by reason of the nature assumed, the Son is called less than the Father. But the Holy Ghost did not assume the visible creature, in which He appeared, into the unity of His person; so that what is said of it cannot be predicated of Him. Hence He cannot be called less than the Father by reason of any visible creature.

Reply Obj. 2. The visible mission of the Holy Ghost does not apply to the imaginary vision which is that of prophecy, because, as Augustine says: *The prophetic vision is not displayed to corporeal eyes by corporeal shapes, but is shown in the spirit by the spiritual images of bodies. But whoever saw the dove and the fire saw them by their eyes. Nor, again, has the Holy Ghost the same relation to these images that the Son has to the rock, because it is said, 'The rock was Christ'* (*1 Cor. x. 4*). *For that rock was already created, and after the manner of an action was named Christ, Whom it typified; whereas the dove and the fire suddenly appeared to signify only what was happening. They seem, however, to be like to the flame of the burning bush seen by Moses and to the column which the people followed in the desert, and to the lightning and thunder issuing forth when the Law was given on the mountain. For the purpose of the bodily appearances of those things was that they might signify something, and then pass away.*[1] Thus the visible mission is neither displayed by prophetic vision which is imaginary and not corporeal, nor by the sacramental signs of the

1. 参见 *De. Trin.*, II, 6 (PL 42, 852).

Old and New Testament, wherein certain pre-existing things are employed to signify something. But the Holy Ghost is said to be sent visibly, inasmuch as He showed Himself in certain creatures as in signs especially made for that purpose.

Reply Obj. 3. Although the whole Trinity makes those creatures, still they are made in order to show forth in some special way this or that person. For as the Father, Son and Holy Ghost are signified by diverse names, so also can They each one be signified by different things, even though neither separation nor diversity exists among Them.

Reply Obj. 4. It was necessary for the Son to be declared as the author of sanctification, as has been said. Thus the visible mission of the Son was necessarily made according to the rational nature to which it belongs to act, and which is capable of sanctification; whereas any other creature could be the sign of sanctification. Nor was such a visible creature, formed for such a purpose, necessarily assumed by the Holy Ghost into the unity of His person, since it was not assumed or used for the purpose of action, but only for the purpose of a sign; and so likewise it was not required to last beyond what its use required.

Reply Obj. 5. Those visible creatures were formed by the ministry of the angels, not to signify the person of an angel, but to signify the Person of the Holy Ghost. Thus, as the Holy Ghost resided in those visible creatures as the one signified in the sign, on that account the Holy Ghost is said to be sent visibly, and not an angel.

Reply Obj. 6. It is not necessary that the invisible mission should always be made manifest by some visible external sign; but, as is said (*1 Cor.* xii. 7), *the manifestation of the Spirit is given to every man unto profit*, that is, of the Church. This utility consists in the confirmation and propagation of the Faith by such visible signs. This has been done chiefly by Christ and by the apostles, according to *Heb.* ii. 3, *which having begun to be declared by the Lord, was confirmed unto us by them that heard.*

Thus in a special sense, a mission of the Holy Ghost was directed to Christ, to the apostles, and to some of the early saints on whom the Church was in a way founded; in such a manner, however, that the visible mission made to Christ should show forth the invisible mission made to Him, not at that particular time, but at the first moment of His conception. The visible mission was directed to Christ at the time of His baptism by the figure of a dove, a fruitful animal, to show forth in Christ the authority of the giver of grace by spiritual regeneration; hence the Father's voice spoke, *This is My beloved Son* (*Matt.* iii. 17), that others might be regenerated to the likeness of the only Begotten. The Transfiguration showed the mission forth in the appearance of a bright cloud, to show the eminence of His teaching; and hence it was said, *Hear ye Him* (*Matt.* xvii. 5). To the apostles the mission was directed in the form of breathing to show forth the power of their ministry in the dispensation of the sacraments; and hence it was said, *Whose sins you shall forgive, they are forgiven* (*Jo.* xx. 23); and again it was directed to them under the sign of fiery tongues, to show forth the office of teaching; whence it is said that, *they began to speak with divers tongues* (*Acts* ii. 4). The visible mission of the Holy Ghost was fittingly not sent to the Fathers of the Old Testament, because the visible mission of the Son was to be accomplished before that of the Holy Ghost; since the Holy Ghost manifests the Son, as the Son manifests the Father. Visible apparitions of the divine persons were, however, given to the Fathers of the Old Testament; these, however, cannot be called visible missions, because, according to Augustine, they were not made to designate the indwelling of the divine person by grace, but for the manifestation of something else.[1]

1. 参见 Cf. *op. cit.*, II, 17 (PL 42, 866).

Eighth Article

WHETHER A DIVINE PERSON IS SENT ONLY BY THE PERSON WHENCE HE PROCEEDS ETERNALLY?

We proceed thus to the Eighth Article: —

Objection 1. It would seem that a divine person is sent only by the person whence He proceeds eternally. For as Augustine says, *The Father is sent by no one because He is from no one.*[1] Therefore, if a divine person is sent by another, He must be from that other.

Obj. 2. Further, the sender has authority over the one sent. But there can be no authority as regards a divine person except according to origin. Therefore the divine person sent must proceed from the one sending.

Obj. 3. Further, if a divine person can be sent by one whence He does not proceed, then the Holy Ghost may be given by a man, although He proceeds not from him; which is contrary to what Augustine says.[2] Therefore, the divine person is sent only by the one whence He proceeds.

On the contrary, The Son is sent by the Holy Ghost, according to *Isa.* xlviii. 16, *Now the Lord God hath sent Me and His Spirit.* But the Son is not from the Holy Ghost. Therefore a divine person is sent by one from Whom He does not proceed.

I answer that, There are different opinions on this point. Some say that a divine person is sent only by the one whence He proceeds eternally;[3] and so, when it is said that the Son of God is sent by the Holy Ghost, this is to be explained as regards His human nature,

---

1. 参见 *Op. cit.*, IV, 20 (PL 42, 908); *Contra Serm. Arian.*, IV (PL 42, 686).
2. 参见 *De Trin.*, XV, 26; II, 6 (PL 42, 1092; 908).
3. 参见 *Op. cit.*, II, 5 (PL 42, 849); Peter Lombard, *Sent.*, I, xv, 1 (I. 95); St. Bonaventure, *In I Sent.*, d. xv, a. 1, q. 4 (I, 265).

according to which He was sent to preach by the Holy Ghost. Augustine, however, says that the Son is sent by Himself, and by the Holy Ghost,[1] and that the Holy Ghost is sent by Himself, and by the Son;[2] so that to be sent in God does not apply to each person, but only to the person proceeding from another, whereas to send belongs to each person.

There is some truth in both of these opinions. For when a person is described as being sent, the person Himself existing from another is designated, along with the visible or invisible effect which is the purpose of the mission of the divine person. Thus if the sender be designated as the principle of the person sent, in this sense not each person sends; but that person only Who is the principle of the person sent; and thus the Son is sent only by the Father, and the Holy Ghost by the Father and the Son. If, however, the person sending is understood as the principle of the effect which the purpose of the mission, in that sense the whole Trinity sends the person sent. This reason does not prove that a man can send the Holy Ghost, for man cannot cause the effect of grace.

The answers to the objections appear from the above.

1. 参见 *De Trin.*, II, 5 (PL 42, 849); *Contra Maximin.*, II, 20 (PL 42, 789).
2. 参见 *De Trin.*, II, 5; XV, 19 (PL 42, 849; 1084).

TREATISE ON CREATION

Question XLIV
THE PROCESSION OF CREATURES FROM GOD, AND THE FIRST CAUSE OF ALL THINGS
(*In Four Articles*)

AFTER treating of the procession of the divine persons, we must consider the procession of creatures from God. This consideration will be threefold: (1) the production of creatures; (2) the distinction of creatures;[1] (3) their preservation and government.[2] Concerning the first point there are three things to be considered: (1) the first cause of things; (2) the mode of procession of creatures from the first cause;[3] (3) the beginning of the duration of things.[4]

Under the first head there are four points of inquiry: (1) Whether God is the efficient cause of all beings? (2) Whether primary matter is created by God, or is an independent co-ordinate principle with Him? (3) Whether God is the exemplary cause of things, or whether there are other exemplary causes? (4) Whether He is the final cause of things?

First Article
WHETHER IT IS NECESSARY THAT EVERY BEING BE CREATED BY GOD?

We proceed thus to the First Article: —

1. 参见 Q. 47.
2. 参见 Q. 103.
3. 参见 Q. 45.
4. 参见 Q. 46.

Objection 1. It would seem that it is not necessary that every being be created by God. For there is nothing to prevent a thing from being without that which does not belong to its essence, as a man can be found without whiteness. But the relation of the thing caused to its cause does not appear to be essential to beings, for some beings can be understood without it. Therefore they can exist without it; and hence it is possible that some beings should not be created by God.

Obj. 2. Further, a thing requires an efficient cause in order to exist. Therefore whatever cannot not-be does not require an efficient cause. But no necessary thing can not-be, because whatever necessarily exists cannot not-be. Therefore as there are many necessary things in existence, it appears that not all beings are from God.

Obj. 3. Further, among whatever things there is a cause, there can be demonstration by that cause. But in mathematics demonstration is not made *by the efficient cause*, as appears from the Philosopher.[1] Therefore not all beings are from God as from their efficient cause.

On the contrary, It is said (*Rom*. xi. 36): *Of Him, and by Him, and in Him are all things*.

I answer that, It must be said that everything, that in any way is, is from God. For whatever is found in anything by participation must be caused in it by that to which it belongs essentially, as iron becomes heated by fire. Now it has been shown above, when treating of the divine simplicity, that God is self-subsisting being[2] itself,[3] and also that subsisting being can be only one;[4] just as, if whiteness were self-subsisting, it would be one, since whiteness is multiplied by its recipients. Therefore all beings other than God are not their own being, but are beings by participation. Therefore, it must be that all

1. 参见 *Metaph*., II, 2 (996a 29).
2. God is self-subsisting being.：天主是自我存在的存在。
3. 参见 Q. 3, a. 4.
4. 参见 Q. 7, a. 1, ad 3 ; a. 2.

things which are diversified by the diverse participation of being, so as to be more or less perfect, are caused by one First Being[1], Who possesses being most perfectly.

Hence Plato said that unity must come before multitude;[2] and Aristotle said that whatever is greatest in being and greatest in truth is the cause of every being and of every truth, just *as whatever is the greatest in heat is the cause of all heat.*[3]

Reply Obj. 1. Though relation to its cause is not part of the definition of a thing caused, still it follows as a result of what belongs to its nature. For, from the fact that a thing is being by participation, it follows that it is caused. Hence such a being cannot be without being caused, just as man cannot be without having the faculty of laughing. But, since to be caused does not enter into the nature of being taken absolutely, that is why there exists a being that is uncaused.

Reply Obj. 2. This objection has led some to say that what is necessary has no cause.[4] But this is manifestly false in demonstrative sciences, where necessary principles are the causes of necessary conclusions. And therefore Aristotle says that there are some necessary things which have a cause of their necessity.[5] But the reason why an efficient cause is required is not merely because the effect can not-be, but because the effect would not be if the cause were not. For this conditional proposition is true, whether the antecedent and consequent be possible or impossible.

Reply Obj. 3. Although they are not abstract in reality, mathematicals are considered in abstraction by the reason. Now, it belongs to a thing to have an efficient cause according as it has being. And so, although mathematicals do have an efficient cause, it is not according to their

---

1. one First Being：独一的第一存在，指天主
2. 参见 Cf. St. Augustine, *De Civit. Dei*, VIII, 4 (PL 41, 231).
3. 参见 Metaph., Ia, 1 (993b 25).
4. 参见 *Phys.*, VIII, 1 (252a 35).
5. 参见 *Metaph.*, IV, 5 (1015b 9).

relation to their efficient cause that they fall under the consideration of the mathematician. Therefore there is no demonstration by means of an efficient cause in mathematics.

Second Article
WHETHER PRIMARY MATTER IS CREATED BY GOD?

We proceed thus to the Second Article: —

Objection 1. It would seem that primary matter is not created by God. For whatever is made is composed of a subject and of something else.[1] But primary matter has no subject. Therefore primary matter cannot have been made by God.

Obj. 2. Further, action and passion are opposite members of a division. But just as the first active principle is God, so the first passive principle is matter. Therefore God and primary matter are two principles divided against each other, neither of which is from the other.

Obj. 3. Further, every agent produces its like, and thus, since every agent acts in proportion to its actuality, it follows that everything made is in some degree actual. But primary matter, considered in itself, is only in potentiality. Therefore it is against the nature of primary matter to be a thing made.

On the contrary, Augustine says, Two *things hast Thou made, O Lord; one nigh unto Thyself — viz., angels — the other nigh unto nothing* — viz., primary matter.[2]

I answer that, The ancient philosophers gradually, and as it were step by step, advanced in the knowledge of truth.[3] At first, being rather undeveloped, they failed to realize that any beings existed except

1. 参见 Aristotle, *Phys.*, I, 7 (190b 1).
2. 参见 *Confess.*, XII, 7 (PL 32, 828).
3. 参见 Cf. Aristotle, *Metaph.*, I, 3–4 (983b 6–985b 22).

sensible bodies.[1] And those among them who admitted movement did not consider it except according to certain accidents,[2] for instance, according to rarefaction and condensation,[3] through union and separation.[4] And supposing, as they did, that corporeal substance itself was uncreated,[5] they assigned certain causes for these accidental changes, as for instance, friendship, discord,[6] intellect,[7] or something of that kind. An advance was made when they understood that there was a distinction between the substantial form and matter, which latter they held to be uncreated,[8] and when they perceived transmutation to take place in bodies in regard to essential forms. These transmutations they attributed to certain more universal causes, such as the oblique circle, according to Aristotle,[9] or the Ideas, according to Plato.[10]

But we must take into consideration that matter is contracted by its form to a determinate species, just as a substance belonging to a certain species is contracted by a supervening accident[11] to a determinate mode of being, for instance, man by whiteness. Each of these opinions, therefore, considered *being* under some particular aspect, namely, either as *this* being or as *such* a being; and so they assigned particular efficient causes to things.

Then others advanced further and raised themselves to the

---

1. 参见 Cf. Aristotle, *Phys.*, IV, 6 (213a 29); *Metaph.*, II, 5 (1002a 8); St. Augustine, *De Civit. Dei.*, VIII, 2 (PL 41, 225).
2. 参见 Cf. Aristotle, *De Gener.*, II, 9 (335b 24); *Phys.*, I, 4 (187a 30).
3. 参见 Cf. Aristotle, *Phys.*, I, 4 (187a 15).
4. 参见 Cf. Aristotle, *De Gener.*, II, 9 (336a 4).
5. 参见 Cf. Aristotle, *Phys.*, I, 8 (191a 27).
6. 参见 Empedocles, according to Aristotle, *Metaph.*, I, 4 (985a 8); *Phys.*, I, 5 (188b 34).
7. 参见 Anaxagoras, according to Aristotle, *Phys.*, VIII, 1 (250b 24).
8. 参见 Plato, cf. above. q. 15, a. 3, ad 3; below, q. 46, a. 1, obj. 1 and ad 3. — Cf. also St. Thomas, *In Phys.*, I, lect. 15.
9. 参见 *De Gener.*, II, 10 (336a 32).
10. 参见 Cf. *ibid.* — Cf. also *Phaedo* (p. 96A).
11. supervening accident：随后发生的事故

consideration of being as being, and who assigned a cause to things, not only according as they are *these* or *such*, but according as they are *beings*.[1] Therefore, whatever is the cause of things considered as beings, must be the cause of things, not only according as they are *such* by accidental forms, nor according as they are *these* by substantial forms, but also according to all that belongs to their being in any way whatever. And thus it is necessary to say that also primary matter is created by the universal cause of things.

Reply Obj. 1. The Philosopher is speaking of *becoming* in particular — that is, from form to form, either accidental or substantial.[2] But here we are speaking of things according to their coming forth from the universal principle of being. From this coming forth matter itself is not excluded, although it is excluded from the other mode of being made.

Reply Obj. 2. Passion is an effect of action. Hence it is reasonable that the first passive principle should be the effect of the first active principle, since every imperfect thing is caused by one perfect. For the first principle must be most perfect, as Aristotle says.[3]

Reply Obj. 3. The reason adduced does not show that matter is not created, but that it is not created without form; for though everything created is actual, still it is not pure act. Hence it is necessary that even what is potential in it should be created, if all that belongs to its being is created.

Third Article
WHETHER THE EXEMPLARY CAUSE IS ANYTHING OTHER THAN GOD?

We proceed thus to the Third Article: —

1. 参见 Cf. E. Gilson, *L'esprit de la phil. méd.* (Paris: J. Vrin, 1932) I, pp. 240–242.
2. 参见 *Phys.*, I, 7(190b 1).
3. 参见 *Metaph.*, XI, 7 (1072b 29).

Objection 1. It would seem that the exemplary cause[1] is something other than God. For the effect is like its exemplar. But creatures are far from being like God. Therefore God is not their exemplary cause.

Obj. 2. Further, whatever is by participation is reduced to something self-existing, as a thing ignited is reduced to fire, as was stated above. But whatever exists in sensible things exists only by participation of some species. This appears from the fact that in all sensible things is found not only what belongs to the species, but also individuating principles added to the principles of the species. Therefore it is necessary to admit self-existing species, as, for instance, a *per se*[2] man, and a *per se* horse, and the like, which are called the exemplars. Therefore exemplary causes exist outside God.

Obj. 3. Further, sciences and definitions are concerned with species themselves, but not as these are in particular things, because there is no science or definition of particular things. Therefore there are some beings, which are beings or species not existing in singular things, and these are called exemplars. Therefore the same conclusion follows as above.

Obj. 4. Further, this likewise appears from Dionysius, who says that self-subsisting being is before self-subsisting life, and before self-subsisting wisdom.[3]

On the contrary, The exemplar is the same as the idea. But ideas, according to Augustine, *are the master forms which are contained in the divine intelligence.*[4] Therefore the exemplars of things are not outside God.

I answer that, God is the first exemplary cause of all things. In proof whereof we must consider that if for the production of anything an exemplar is necessary, it is in order that the effect may receive a determinate form. For an artificer produces a determinate form

---

1. exemplary cause：模型因
2. per se：自身；本身
3. 参见 *De Div. Nom.*, V, 5 (PG 3, 820).
4. 参见 *Lib. 83 Quaest.*, q. 46 (PL 40, 30).

in matter by reason of the exemplar before him, whether it be the exemplar beheld externally, or the exemplar interiorly conceived in the mind. Now it is manifest that things made by nature receive determinate forms. This determination of forms must be reduced to the divine wisdom as its first principle, for divine wisdom devised the order of the universe residing in the distinction of things. And therefore we must say that in the divine wisdom are the models of all things, which we have called *ideas* — *i.e.*, exemplary forms existing in the divine mind.[1] And although these ideas are multiplied by their relations to things, nevertheless, they are not really distinct from the divine essence, inasmuch as the likeness of that essence can be shared diversely by different things. In this manner, therefore, God Himself is the first exemplar of all things. Moreover, in created things one may be called the exemplar of another by the reason of its likeness to it either in species, or by the analogy of some kind of imitation.

Reply Obj. 1. Although creatures are not so perfect as to be specifically like God in nature, after the manner in which a man begotten is like to the man begetting, still they do attain to likeness to Him, according to the representation in the exemplar known by God; just as a material house is like the house in the architect's mind.

Reply Obj. 2. It is of a man's nature to be in matter, and so a man without matter is impossible. Therefore, although this particular man is a man by participation of the species, he cannot be reduced to anything self-existing in the same species, but to a superior species, such as separate substances. The same applies to other sensible things.

Reply Obj. 3. Although every science and definition is concerned only with beings, still it is not necessary that a thing should have the same way of being as the intellect has of understanding. For through

---

1. 参见 Q. 15, a. 1.

the power of the agent intellect we abstract universals from particular conditions; but it is not necessary that universals should subsist outside the particulars as their exemplars.

Reply Obj. 4. As Dionysius says, by *self-existing*[1] *life and self-existing wisdom* he sometimes denotes God Himself, sometimes the powers given to things themselves;[2] but not any self-subsisting things, as the ancients asserted.

Fourth Article
WHETHER GOD IS THE FINAL CAUSE OF ALL THINGS?

We proceed thus to the Fourth Article: —

Objection 1. It would seem that God is not the final cause[3] of all things. For to act for an end seems to imply need of the end. But God needs nothing. Therefore it does not become Him to act for an end.

Obj. 2. Further, the end of generation, and the form of the thing generated, and the agent cannot be identical, because the end of generation is the form of the thing generated.[4] But God is the first agent producing all things. Therefore He is not the final cause of all things.

Obj. 3. Further, all things desire their end. But all things do not desire God, for all do not even know Him. Therefore God is not the end of all things.

Obj. 4. Further, the final cause is the first of causes. If, therefore, God is the efficient cause and the final cause, it follows that *before* and *after* exist in Him; which is impossible.

On the contrary, It is said (*Prov.* xvi. 4): *The Lord has made all things for*

1. self-existing：自存
2. 参见 *De Div. Nom.*, XI, 6 (PG 3, 953).
3. final cause：终极因
4. 参见 Aristotle, *Phys.*, II, 7 (198a 26).

Himself.

I answer that, Every agent acts for an end, or otherwise one thing would not follow more than another from the action of the agent, unless it were by chance. Now the end of the agent and of the patient considered as such is the same, but in a different way respectively. For the impression which the agent intends to produce, and which the patient intends to receive, are one and the same. Some things, however, are both agent and patient at the same time: these are imperfect agents, and to these it belongs to intend, even in acting, the acquisition of something. But it does not belong to the First Agent, Who is agent only, to act for the acquisition of some end: He intends only to communicate His perfection, which is His goodness; while every creature intends to acquire its own perfection, which is the likeness of the divine perfection and goodness. Therefore the divine goodness is the end of all things.

Reply Obj. 1. To act from need belongs only to an imperfect agent, which by its nature is both agent and patient. But this does not belong to God, and therefore He alone is the most perfectly liberal giver, because He does not act for His own profit, but only out of His own goodness.

Reply Obj. 2. The form of the thing generated is not the end of generation, except inasmuch as it is the likeness of the form of the generator, which intends to communicate its own likeness; otherwise the form of the thing generated would be more noble than the generator, since the end is more noble than the means to the end.

Reply Obj. 3. All things desire God as their end in desiring any particular good, whether this desire be intellectual or sensible, or natural, *i.e.*, without knowledge; for nothing is good and desirable except inasmuch as it participates in the likeness to God.

Reply Obj. 4. Since God is the efficient, the exemplar and the final cause of all things, and since primary matter is from Him, it follows that the first principle of all things is one in reality. But this does not prevent us from thinking that, from the standpoint of our reason, there are many things in God, of which we come to know some before others.

Question XLV
THE MODE OF EMANATION OF THINGS FROM THE FIRST PRINCIPLE
(*In Eight Articles*)

THE next question concerns the mode of the emanation of things from the First Principle which is called creation. On creation there are eight points of inquiry: (1) What is creation? (2) Whether God can create anything? (3) Whether creation is a reality in things? (4) To what things it belongs to be created? (5) Whether it belongs to God alone to create? (6) Whether to create is common to the whole Trinity, or proper to any one Person? (7) Whether any trace of the Trinity is to be found in created things? (8) Whether the work of creation enters into the works of nature and of the will?

First Article
WHETHER TO CREATE IS TO MAKE SOMETHING FROM NOTHING?

We proceed thus to the First Article: —

Objection 1. It would seem that to create is not to make anything from nothing. For Augustine says: *To make concerns what did not exist at all; but to create is to make something by bringing it forth from what was already existing.*[1]

Obj. 2. Further, the nobility of action and of motion is considered

---

1. 参见 *Contra Adv. Legis et Proph.*, I. 23 (PL 42, 633).

from their terms. On this basis, action is nobler if it is from good to good, and from being to being, than if it is from nothing to something. But creation appears to be the most noble action, and first among all actions. Therefore it is not from nothing to something, but rather from being to being.

Obj. 3. Further, the preposition *from* [*ex*] expresses the relation of some cause, and especially of the material cause; as when we say that a statue is made from brass. But *nothing* cannot be the matter of being, nor in any way its cause. Therefore to create is not to make something from nothing.

On the contrary, On the text of *Gen.* i. 1, *In the beginning God created heaven*, etc., the *Gloss* says: *To create is to make something from nothing.*[1]

I answer that, As was said above, we must consider not only the emanation of a particular being from a particular agent, but also the emanation of all being from the universal cause, which is God;[2] and this emanation we designate by the name of *creation*. Now what proceeds by a particular emanation is not presupposed to that emanation. Thus, in the generation of man, we must say that he does not exist before being generated; but man is made from *not-man*, and white from *not-white*. Hence if the emanation of the whole universal being from the first principle be considered, it is impossible that any being should be presupposed to this emanation. Now *nothing* is the same as *no being*. Therefore as the generation of a man presupposes the *non-being* which is *non-man*, so creation, which is the emanation of all being, presupposes the *non-being* which is *nothing*.

Reply Obj. 1. Augustine uses the term *creation* in an equivocal sense, according as to be created signifies improvement in things; as when we say that a bishop is created. This is not the way in which we here use

---

1. 参见 *Glossa ordin.*, super *Gen*, I, 1 (I, 23F).
2. 参见 Q. 44, a. 2.

the term creation, but in the way already stated.

Reply Obj. 2. Changes receive their species and dignity, not from the term *wherefrom*, but from the term *whereto*. Therefore a change is more perfect and excellent when the term *whereto* of the change is more noble and excellent, although the term *wherefrom*, corresponding to the term *whereto*, may be more imperfect: thus generation is absolutely nobler and more excellent than alteration, because the substantial form is nobler than the accidental form; and yet the privation of the substantial form, which is the term *wherefrom* in generation, is more imperfect than the contrary which is the term *wherefrom* in alteration. Similarly, creation is more perfect and more excellent than generation and alteration, because the term *whereto* is the whole substance of the thing; whereas what is understood as the term *wherefrom* is absolutely non-being.

Reply Obj. 3. When anything is said to be made from nothing, the preposition *from* [*ex*] does not signify a material cause, but only an order; as when we say, *from morning comes midday* — *i.e.*, *after* morning comes midday. But we must understand that this preposition *from* [*ex*] can either include the negation expressed when I say the *nothing*, or it can be included in it. If taken in the first sense, then we affirm the order by stating the relation of what now is to its previous non-being. But if the negation includes the preposition, then the order is denied, and the sense is, *It is made from nothing* — *i.e.*, *it is not made from anything*; just as if we were to say, *He speaks of nothing*, because he does not speak of anything. Both uses of *from* are present when we say that something is made from nothing. But in the first way, the preposition *from* [*ex*] expresses order, as has been said. In the second sense, it expresses a relation to a material cause, and denies it.

Second Article
WHETHER GOD CAN CREATE ANYTHING?

We proceed thus to the Second Article: —

Objection 1. It would seem that God cannot create anything, because, according to the Philosopher, the ancient philosophers considered it as a commonly received axiom that *nothing is made from nothing*.[1] But the power of God does not extend to the contraries of first principles; as, for instance, that God could make the whole to be less than its part, or that affirmation and negation be both true at the same time. Therefore God cannot make anything from nothing, or create.

Obj. 2. Further, if to create is to make something from nothing, to be created is to be made. But to be made is to be changed. Therefore creation is change. But every change occurs in some subject, as appears by the definition of motion: for motion is the act of what is in potentiality. Therefore it is impossible for anything to be made out of nothing by God.

Obj. 3. Further, what has been made must have at some time been becoming. But it cannot be said that, at the same time, what is created is becoming and has been made, because in permanent things what is becoming, is not, and what has been made, already is; and so, if we said that it was both, it would follow that something would be, and not be, at the same time. Therefore, when anything is made, its becoming precedes its having been made. But this is impossible, unless there is a subject in which the becoming is sustained. Therefore it is impossible that anything should be made from nothing.

Obj. 4. Further, an infinite distance cannot be crossed. But an infinite distance exists between being and nothing. Therefore it does not happen that something is made from nothing.

On the contrary, It is said (*Gen*. i. 1): *In the beginning God created heaven and earth*; on which the *Gloss* says that *to create is to make something from nothing*.[2]

I answer that, Not only is it not impossible that anything should be

1. 参见 *Phys*., I, 4 (187a 28).
2. 参见 *Glossa ordin*., super *Gen*, I, 1 (I, 23F).

created by God, but it is necessary to say that all things were created by God, as appears from what has been said. For when anyone makes one thing from another, the thing from which he makes it is presupposed to his action, and is not produced by his action; and thus the craftsman produces his works from natural things such as wood or brass, which are caused, not by the action of art, but by the action of nature. So, too, nature itself causes natural things so far as concerns their form, but presupposes matter. If, therefore, God acted only on the condition of a subject presupposed to His action, it would follow that the thing presupposed would not be caused by Him. Now it was shown above that nothing can be unless it is from God, Who is the universal cause of all being.[1] Hence it is necessary to say that God brings things into being from nothing.

Reply Obj. 1. The ancient philosophers, as was said above, considered only the emanation of particular effects from particular causes, which necessarily presuppose something in their action;[2] whence came their common opinion that *nothing is made from nothing*. But this dictum has no place in the first emanation from the universal principle of things.

Reply Obj. 2. Creation is not change, except according to our way of understanding. For change means that the same thing should be different now from what it was previously. Sometimes it is the same actual reality which is different now from what it was before, as happens when the motion is according to quantity, quality and place; but sometimes it is the same being only in potentiality, as in substantial change, the subject of which is matter. But in creation, by which the whole substance of a thing is produced, the same thing can be taken as different now and before only according to our way of understanding, so that a thing is understood as first not existing at all, and afterwards as existing. But *as action and passion coincide as to*

---

1. 参见 Q. 44, a. 1 and 2.
2. 参见 Q. 44, a. 2.

the substance of motion, and differ only according to diverse relations,[1] it must follow that, when motion is withdrawn, there remain only the diverse relations in the Creator and in the creature. But because the mode of signification follows the mode of understanding, as was said above,[2] creation is signified as a change; and on this account it is said that to create is to make something from nothing. And yet *to make* and *to be made* are more suitable expressions here than *to change* and *to be changed*, because *to make* and *to be made* import a relation of cause to the effect, and of effect to the cause, and imply change only as a consequence.

Reply Obj. 3. In things which are made without motion, to become and to be already made are simultaneous, whether such making is the term of motion, as illumination (for a thing is being illuminated and is illuminated at the same time), or whether it is not the term of motion, as the concept is being made in the mind and is made at the same time. In things of this kind, what is being made, is; but when we speak of their being made, we mean that they are from another, and that previously they did not exist. Hence, since creation is without motion, a thing is being created and has been created at the same time.

Reply Obj. 4. This objection proceeds from a false imagination, as if there were an infinite medium between nothing and being; which is plainly false. This false imagination comes from the fact that creation is signified as a change existing between two terms.

Third Article
WHETHER CREATION IS ANYTHING IN THE CREATURE?

We proceed thus to the Third Article: —

Objection 1. It would seem that creation is not anything in the

1. 参见 Aristotle, *Phys.*, III, 3 (202b 20).
2. 参见 Q. 13, a. 1.

creature. For just as creation taken in a passive sense is attributed to the creature, so creation taken in an active sense is attributed to the Creator. But creation taken actively is not anything in the Creator, because otherwise it would follow that in God there would be something temporal. Therefore creation taken passively is not anything in the creature.

Obj. 2. Further, there is no medium between the Creator and the creature. But creation is signified as the medium between them both. For it is not the Creator, as it is not eternal; nor is it a creature, because in that case it would be necessary to suppose another creation to create it, and so on to infinity. Therefore creation is not anything in the creature.

Obj. 3. Further, if creation is anything in addition to created substance, it must be an accident belonging to it. But every accident is in a subject. Therefore a created thing would be the subject of creation, and so the same thing would be the subject and also the term of creation. This is impossible, because the subject is before the accident, and preserves the accident; while the term is after the action and passion whose term it is, and as soon as it exists, action and passion cease. Therefore creation itself is not any thing.

On the contrary, It is greater for a thing to be made according to its entire substance than to be made according to its substantial or accidental form. But generation, taken absolutely or relatively, whereby anything is made according to the substantial or the accidental form, is something in the thing generated. Therefore much more is creation, whereby a thing is made according to its whole substance, something in the thing created.

I answer that, Creation posits something in the created thing only according to relation; for what is created is not made by motion or by change. For what is made by motion or by change is made from something pre-existing. This happens, to be sure, in the particular productions of some beings, but it cannot happen in the production of all being by the universal cause of all beings, which is God. Hence, when God creates, He produces things without motion. Now when motion is removed from action and passion, only relation remains, as was said above. Hence creation in the creature is only a certain relation to the Creator as to the principle of its being; even as in passion, which supposes motion, is implied a relation to the principle of motion.

Reply Obj. 1. Creation signified actively means the divine action, which is God's essence with a relation to the creature. But in God relation to the creature is not a real relation, but only a relation of reason; whereas the relation of the creature to God is a real relation, as was said above in treating of the divine names.[1]

Reply Obj. 2. Because creation is signified as a change, as was said above, and change is a kind of medium between the mover and the moved, therefore creation itself is signified as a medium between the Creator and the creature. Nevertheless passive creation is in the creature, and is a creature. Nor is there need of a further creation in its creation, for since *to be with reference to something else* completely expresses what they are, relations are not referred by any other relations, but by themselves, as was also shown above in treating of the equality of the Persons.[2]

Reply Obj. 3. The creature is the term of creation as signifying a change; but it is the subject of creation taken as a real relation, and is prior to it in being, as the subject is to the accident. Nevertheless, creation has a certain aspect of priority on the part of the object to which it is directed, which is the beginning of the creature. Nor is it necessary to say that a creature is being created during its entire existence; for creation imports a relation of the creature to the Creator *with a certain newness or beginning.*

1. 参见 Q. 13, a. 7.
2. 参见 Q. 42, a. 1, ad 4.

Fourth Article

WHETHER TO BE CREATED BELONGS TO COMPOSITE AND SUBSISTING THINGS?

We proceed thus to the Fourth Article: —

Objection 1. It would seem that to be created does not belong to composite and subsisting things. For in the *Book of Causes* it is said, *The first of creatures is being*[1] But the being of a created thing is not subsistent. Therefore creation properly speaking does not belong to subsisting and composite things.

Obj. 2. Further, whatever is created is from nothing. But composite things are not out of nothing, but out of their component parts. Therefore composite things are not created.

Obj. 3. Further, what is presupposed in the second emanation is properly produced by the first: as natural generation produces the natural thing, which is presupposed in the operation of art. But what is presupposed in natural generation is matter. Therefore matter, and not the composite, is properly speaking that which is created.

On the contrary, It is said (*Gen.* i. 1): *In the beginning God created heaven and earth*. But heaven and earth are subsisting composite things. Therefore creation properly belongs to them.

I answer that, To be created is a kind of coming to be, as was shown above. Now, to be made is directed to the being of a thing. Hence *to be made* and *to be created* properly belong to whatever *being* belongs. Now being belongs properly to subsisting things, whether they be simple, as in the case of separate substances, or composite, as in the case of material substances. For being belongs to that which has being — that is, to what subsists in its own being. But forms and accidents and

1. 参见 *De Causis*, IV (p. 164).

the like are called beings, not as if they themselves were, but because something is by them; as whiteness is called a being because its subject is white by it. Hence, according to the Philosopher, an accident is more properly said to be *of a being* than *a being*.[1] Therefore, just as accidents and forms and other non-subsisting things are to be said to co-exist rather than to exist, so they ought to be called *concreated* rather than *created* things. But properly speaking, it is subsisting beings which are created.

Reply Obj. 1. In the proposition *the first of created things is being*, the word *being* does not refer to that which is created, but to the proper nature of the object of creation. For a created thing is called created because it is a being, not because it is *this* being; since creation is the emanation of all being from the Universal Being, as was said above. We use a similar way of speaking when we say that *the first visible thing is color*, although, strictly speaking, the thing colored is what is seen.

Reply Obj. 2. Creation does not mean the production of a composite thing from pre-existing principles; but the composite is so said to be created that it is brought into being along with all its component principles.

Reply Obj. 3. This reason does not prove that matter alone is created, but that matter does not exist except by creation; for creation is the production of the whole being, and not only of matter.

Fifth Article
WHETHER IT BELONGS TO GOD ALONE TO CREATE?

We proceed thus to the Fifth Article: —

Objection 1. It would seem that it does not belong to God alone to create. For according to the Philosopher, that is perfect which can

---

1. 参见 *Metaph.*, VI, 1 (1028a 18).

make something like itself.[1] But immaterial creatures are more perfect than material creatures, which nevertheless can produce their like; for fire generates fire, and man begets man. Therefore an immaterial substance can make a substance like to itself. But immaterial substance can be made only by creation, since it has no matter from which to be made. Therefore a creature can create.

Obj. 2. Further, the greater the resistance on the part of the thing made, the greater power required in the maker. But a *contrary* resists more than *nothing*. Therefore it requires more power to make something from its contrary (which nevertheless a creature can do) than to make a thing from nothing. All the more therefore can a creature make something out of nothing.

Obj. 3. Further, the power of the maker is considered according to the measure of what is made. But created being is finite, as we proved above when treating of the infinity of God.[2] Therefore only a finite power is needed to produce a creature by creation. But to have a finite power is not contrary to the nature of a creature. Therefore it is not impossible for a creature to create.

On the contrary, Augustine says that neither good nor bad angels can create anything.[3] Much less therefore can any other creatures.

I answer that, It is sufficiently apparent at first glance, according to what has preceded, that to create can be the proper action of God alone.[4] For the more universal effects must be reduced to the more universal and prior causes. Now among all effects the most universal is being itself; and hence it must be the proper effect of the first and most universal cause, God. Hence we find it said that *neither intelligence nor*

1. 参见 *Meteor.*, IV, 3 (380a 14); *De An.*, II, 4 (415a 26).
3. 参见 Q. 7, a. 2, 3 and 4.
3. 参见 *De Trin.*, III, 8 (PL 42, 876).
4. 参见 A. 1; q. 44, a. 1 and 2.

the soul gives being, except inasmuch as it works by divine operation.[1] Now to produce being absolutely, and not merely as this or that being, belongs to the nature of creation. Hence it is manifest that creation is the proper act of God alone.

It is possible, however, for something to participate in the proper action of another, not by its own power, but instrumentally, inasmuch as it acts by the power of another; as air can heat and ignite by the power of fire. And so some have supposed that although creation is the proper act of the universal cause, still some lesser cause, acting by the power of the first cause, can create. And thus Avicenna asserted that the first separate substance created by God created another separate substance after itself, then the substance of the heavens and its soul; and that the substance of the heavens creates the matter of the inferior bodies.[2] And in the same manner the Master of the *Sentences* says that God can communicate to a creature the power of creating, so that the creature can create as God's minister, and not by its own power.[3]

But such a thing cannot be, because the secondary instrumental cause does not share in the action of the superior cause, except inasmuch as by something proper to itself it acts dispositively in relation to the effect of the principal agent. If therefore it produced nothing by means of what is proper to itself, it would be set to work in vain; nor would there be any need for us to use special instruments for special actions. Thus we see that a saw, in cutting wood, which it does by the property of its own form, produces the form of a bench, which is the proper effect of the principal agent. But the proper effect of God creating is what is presupposed to all other effects, and that is

1. 参见 *De Causis*, III (p. 163).
2. 参见 *Metaph.*, IX, 4 (104vb). — Cf. Algazel, *Metaph.*, V (p. 119); Averroes, *Destruct. Destruct.*, III (IX, 23ra; 24rab); *De Causis*, III (p. 163). — Cf. also St. Albert, *Summa de Creatur.*, II, q. 61, a. 2 (XXXV, 524).
3. 参见 Peter Lombard, *Sent.*, IV, v, 3 (II, 575).

being taken absolutely. Hence nothing else can act dispositively and instrumentally towards this effect, since creation does not depend on anything presupposed, which can be disposed by the action of the instrumental agent. So it is impossible for any creature to create, either by its own power, or instrumentally — that is, ministerially.

And above all it is absurd to suppose that a body can create, for no body acts except by touching or moving; and thus it requires in its action some pre-existing thing which can be touched or moved, which is contrary to the very idea of creation.

Reply Obj. 1. A perfect thing participating in any nature makes a likeness to itself, not by absolutely producing that nature, but by applying it to something else. For an individual man cannot be the cause of human nature absolutely, because he would then be the cause of himself; but he is the cause that human nature exists in the man begotten. And thus he presupposes in his action the determinate matter whereby he is an individual man. But just as an individual man participates in human nature, so every created being participates, so to speak, in the nature of being; for God alone is His own being, as we have said above.[1] Therefore no created being can produce a being absolutely, except inasmuch as it causes *being* in some particular subject; and so it is necessary to presuppose that whereby a thing is this particular thing as prior to the action whereby it produces its own like. But in an immaterial substance it is not possible to presuppose anything whereby it is this thing, because it is a *this* by its form, through which it has being. For an immaterial substance is a subsisting form. Therefore an immaterial substance cannot produce another like immaterial substance as regards its being, but only as regards some added perfection; as we may say that a superior angel illumines an inferior, as Dionysius says.[2] In this sense we also speak of paternity

1. 参见 Q. 7, a. 1, ad 3; a. 2.
2. 参见 *De Cael. Hier.*, VIII, 2 (PG 3, 240).

in heaven, as the Apostle says (*Ephes.* iii. 15): *From whom all paternity in heaven and on earth is named.* From which it clearly appears that no created being can cause anything, unless something is presupposed; which is against the nature of creation.

Reply Obj. 2. A thing is made from its contrary accidentally; but properly it is made from the subject which is in potentiality.[1] And so the contrary resists the agent, inasmuch as it keeps the potentiality from the act to which the agent intends to reduce the matter; just as fire intends to reduce the matter of water to an act like to itself, but is impeded by the form and contrary dispositions, by which the potentiality of the water is as it were restrained from being reduced to act. But the more the potentiality is restrained, the more power is required in the agent to reduce the matter to act. Hence a much greater power is required in the agent when no potentiality pre-exists. Thus it appears that it is an act of much greater power to make a thing from nothing than from its contrary.

Reply Obj. 3. The power of the maker is reckoned not only from the substance of the thing made, but also from the mode of its being made; for a greater heat heats not only more, but also more quickly. Therefore, although to create a finite effect does not reveal an infinite power, yet to create it from nothing does reveal an infinite power. This appears from what has been said. For if a greater power is required in the agent in proportion to the distance of the potentiality from act, it follows that the power of that which produces something from no presupposed potentiality (which is how a creating agent produces) is infinite, because there is no proportion between *no potentiality* and the potentiality presupposed by the power of a natural agent, as there is no proportion between *non-being* and *being*. And because no creature has an absolutely infinite power, any more than it has an infinite being, as was proved above,[2] it follows that no creature can create.

---

1. 参见 Aristotle, Phy., I, 7 (190b 27).
2. 参见 Q. 7, a. 2.

Sixth Article
WHETHER TO CREATE IS PROPER TO ANY PERSON?

We proceed thus to the Sixth Article: —

Objection 1. It would seem that to create is proper to some Person. For what is first acts as the cause of what is after; and what is perfect is the cause of what is imperfect. But the procession of a divine Person is prior to the procession of the creature, as well as more perfect, because a divine Person proceeds in perfect likeness to His principle, whereas the creature proceeds according to an imperfect likeness. Therefore the processions of the divine Persons are the cause of the processions of things, and hence to create belongs to a Person.

Obj. 2. Further, the divine Persons are distinguished from each other only by their processions and relations. Therefore whatever difference is attributed to the divine Persons belongs to them according to the processions and relations of the Persons. But the causality on which creatures depend is diversely attributed to the divine Persons; for in the Creed, to the Father is attributed that *He is the Creator of all things visible and invisible*; to the Son is attributed that by Him *all things were made*; and to the Holy Ghost is attributed that He is *Lord and Life-giver.*[1] Therefore the production of creatures belongs to the Persons according to processions and relations.

Obj. 3. Further, if it be said that the causality of God in relation to the creature flows from some essential attribute appropriated to some one Person, this does not appear to be sufficient. For every divine effect is caused by every essential attribute — viz., by power, goodness, and wisdom — and thus does not belong to one more than to another. Therefore no determinate mode of causality ought to be attributed to

---

1. 参见 *Symb. Nicaenum* (Denzinger, no. 54).

one Person more than to another, unless the Persons are distinguished in creating according to relations and processions.

On the contrary, Dionysius says that all caused things are the common work of the whole Godhead.[1]

I answer that, To create is, properly speaking, to cause or produce the being of things. And as every agent produces its like, the principle of action can be considered from the effect of the action; for it is fire that generates fire. To create, therefore, belongs to God according to His being. But God's being is His essence, which is common to the three Persons. Hence to create is not proper to any one Person, but is common to the whole Trinity.

Nevertheless the divine Persons, according to the nature of their procession, have a causality in relation to the creation of things. For as was said above, when treating of the knowledge and will of God, God is the cause of things by His intellect and will, just as the craftsman is cause of the things made by his craft.[2] Now the craftsman works through the word conceived in his intellect, and through the love of his will towards some object. So, too, God the Father made the creature through His Word, which is His Son; and through His Love, which is the Holy Ghost. And so the processions of the Persons are the model of the productions of creatures according as they include the essential attributes, namely, knowledge and will.

Reply Obj. 1. The processions of the divine Persons are the cause of creation, as was above explained.

Reply Obj. 2. As the divine nature, although common to the three Persons, still belongs to them in a kind of order, inasmuch as the Son receives the divine nature from the Father, and the Holy Ghost from both: so likewise the power to create, though common to the three Persons, belongs to them in a kind of order. For the Son receives

1. 参见 *De Div. Nom.*, II, 3 (PG 3, 637).
2. 参见 Q. 14, a. 8; q. 19, a. 4.

it from the Father, and the Holy Ghost from both. Hence to be the Creator is attributed to the Father as to Him Who does not receive the power of creation from another. And of the Son it is said (*Jo.* i. 3), *Through Him all things were made*, inasmuch as He has the same power, but from another; for this preposition *through* usually denotes a mediate cause, or *a principle from a principle*. But to the Holy Ghost, Who has the same power from both, is attributed that by His sway He governs and quickens what is created by the Father through the Son.

Again, the general reason for this attribution may be taken from the appropriation of the essential attributes. For, as was above stated,[1] to the Father is appropriated *power*, which is especially shown in creation; and therefore to be Creator is attributed to the Father. To the Son is appropriated *wisdom*, through which an intellectual agent acts; and therefore it is said: *Through Whom all things were made*. To the Holy Ghost is appropriated *goodness*, to which belong both governance, which brings things to their proper end, and the giving of life. For life consists in a certain interior movement; and the first mover is the end, and goodness.

Reply Obj. 3. Although every effect of God proceeds from each attribute, nevertheless each effect is reduced to that attribute with which it is related according to its proper nature. Thus, the ordering of things is reduced to *wisdom*, and the justification of the sinner to *mercy* and *goodness* poured out superabundantly. But creation, which is the production of the very substance of a thing, is reduced to *power*.

Seventh Article
WHETHER IN CREATURES IS NECESSARILY FOUND A TRACE OF THE TRINITY?

We proceed thus to the Seventh Article: —

---

1. 参见 Q. 39, a. 8.

Objection 1. It would seem that in creatures there is not necessarily found a trace of the Trinity. For anything can be traced through its traces. But the trinity of persons cannot be traced from creatures, as was stated above.[1] Therefore there is no trace of the Trinity in creatures.

Obj. 2. Further, whatever is in creatures is created. Therefore if a trace of the Trinity is found in creatures according to some of their properties, and if everything created has a trace of the Trinity, it follows that we can find a trace of the Trinity in each of these properties; and so on to infinitude.

Obj. 3. Further, the effect represents only its own cause. But the causality on which creatures depend belongs to the common nature, and not to the relations by which the Persons are distinguished and numbered. Therefore in the creature is to be found a trace, not of the Trinity, but of the unity of essence.

On the contrary, Augustine says that *a trace of the Trinity appears in creatures.*[2]

I answer that, Every effect in some degree represents its cause, but diversely. For some effects represent only the causality of the cause, but not its form; as smoke represents fire. Such a representation is called a *trace*; for a trace shows that someone has passed by but not who it is. Other effects represent the cause in terms of a likeness of its form, as fire generated represents fire generating, and as a statue of Mercury represents Mercury; and this is called the representation of *image*. Now the processions of the divine Persons are referred to the acts of intellect and will, as was said above.[3] For the Son proceeds as the Word of the intellect; and the Holy Ghost proceeds as the Love of the will. Therefore in rational creatures, which possess intellect and will, there is found the representation of the Trinity by way of image, inasmuch

---

1. 参见 Q. 32, a. 1.
2. 参见 *De Trin.*, VI, 10 (PL 42, 932).
3. 参见 Q. 27.

as there is found in them a word conceived in the intellect and the love proceeding in the will.

But in all creatures there is found the trace of the Trinity, inasmuch as in every creature are found some things which are necessarily reduced to the divine Persons as to their cause. For every creature subsists in its own being; it has a form by which it is determined to a species; and it has relation to some other thing. Therefore, according as it is a created substance, it represents the cause and principle; and in this manner it reveals the Person of the Father, Who is the *principle from no principle*. According as it has a form and species, it represents the Word, for the form of a thing made by art is from the conception of the craftsman. According as it has relation of order, it represents the Holy Ghost, inasmuch as He is love, because the order of the effect to something else is from the will of the Creator.

And so Augustine says that a trace of the Trinity is found in every creature, according as *it is one individual*, and according *as it is formed by a species*, and according as it *has a certain relation of order.*[1] And to these are also reduced the three characteristics mentioned in the Book of *Wisdom* (xi. 21) namely, *number, weight and measure*. For *measure* refers to the substance of the thing limited by its principles, *number* refers to the species, *weight* refers to the order. To these are likewise reduced the other three mentioned by Augustine, namely, *mode*, *species* and *order*,[2] and also those he mentions in the book of *Eighty-Three Questions: that which exists, that by which it is distinguished, that by which it is like other things.*[3] For a thing exists by its substance, it is distinct by its form, and it agrees by its order. Other similar expressions may be easily reduced to the above.

Reply Obj. 1. The representation of the trace is to be referred to the appropriations: in which manner we are able to arrive at a knowledge

1. 参见 *De Trin.*, VI, 10 (PL 42, 932).
2. 参见 *De Nat. Boni.,* III (PL 42, 553).
3. 参见 *Lib. 83 Quaest.*, q. 18 (PL 40, 15).

of the Trinity of the divine Persons from creatures, as we have said.[1]

Reply Obj. 2. A creature is properly a subsisting thing, in which the above-mentioned three things are to be found. Nor is it necessary that these three things should be found in each thing that exists in the creature; but only to a subsisting being is a trace ascribed in accord with them.

Reply Obj. 3. Even the processions of the Persons are in a way the cause and model of creation, as appears from the above.

Eighth Article
WHETHER CREATION ENTERS INTO THE WORKS OF NATURE AND ART?

We proceed thus to the Eighth Article: —

Objection 1. It would seem that creation enters into the works of nature and art. For in every operation of nature and art some form is produced. But it is not produced from anything, since matter has no part in it. Therefore it is produced from nothing; and thus in every operation of nature and art there is creation.

Obj. 2. Further, the effect is not more powerful than its cause. But in natural things the only agent is the accidental form, which is an active or a passive form. Therefore the substantial form is not produced by the operation of nature; and therefore it must be produced by creation.

Obj. 3. Further, in nature like begets like. But some things are found generated in nature by a thing unlike to them; as is evident in animals generated through putrefaction. Therefore their form is not from nature, but by creation. The same reason applies to other things.

Obj. 4. Further, what is not created is not a creature. If therefore in nature's productions there were not creation, it would follow that

---

1. 参见 Q. 32, a. 1, ad 1.

nature's productions are not creatures; which is heretical.

On the contrary, Augustine distinguishes the work of propagation, which is a work of nature, from the work of creation.[1]

I answer that, This question arises because of forms. Some[2] said that forms do not come into existence by the action of nature, but previously exist in matter; for they asserted that forms are latent. This arose from ignorance concerning matter, and from not knowing how to distinguish between potentiality and act. For since forms pre-exist in matter *potentially*, they asserted that the forms pre-existed absolutely and without qualification. Others,[3] however, said that the forms were given or caused by a separate agent by way of creation, and, accordingly, that to each operation of nature is joined creation. But this opinion arose from ignorance concerning form. For those who held it failed to consider that the form of a natural body is not itself subsisting, but is that by which a thing is. And therefore, since to be made and to be created belong properly to a subsisting thing alone, as was shown above, it does not belong to forms to be made or to be created, but to be *concreated*. What, properly speaking, is made by the natural agent is the *composite*, which is made from matter.

Hence creation does not enter into the works of nature, but for the operation of nature something is presupposed.

Reply Obj. 1. Forms begin to be actual when the composites are made, not as though they are themselves made *directly*, but only *indirectly*.

---

1. 参见 *De Genesi ad Litt.*, V, 11; 20 (PL 34, 330; 335).
2. 参见 Cf. St. Thomas, *De Pot.*, q. 3, a. 8. — The position of Anaxagoras, according to Aristotle, *Phys.*, I, 4 (187a 29).
3. 参见 Cf. *De Pot.*, q. 3, a. 8. — According to Averroes (*In Metaph.*, VII, comm. 31; VIII, 85rv), the doctrine of the "*dator formarum*" was held by Plato. Themistius and Avicenna followed him. — Cf. Avicenna, *Metaph.*, IX, 3 (103vb); St. Thomas, *In II Sent.*, d. xviii, q. 2, a. 3 and *Q. D. de Anima*, a.5.

Reply Obj. 2. The active qualities in nature act by virtue of substantial forms: and therefore the natural agent produces its like not only according to quality, but according to species.

Reply Obj. 3. For the generation of imperfect animals, a universal agent suffices, and this is to be found in the celestial power to which they are assimilated, not in species, but according to a kind of analogy. Nor is it necessary to say that their forms are created by a separate agent. However, for the generation of perfect animals, the universal agent does not suffice, but a proper agent is required, acting as a univocal generator.

Reply Obj. 4. The operation of nature takes place only on the presupposition of created principles; and thus the products of nature are called creatures.

Question XLVI
ON THE BEGINNING OF THE DURATION OF CREATURES
(*In Three Articles*)

NEXT must be considered the beginning of the duration of creatures, about which there are three points for treatment: (1) Whether creatures always existed? (2) Whether that they began to exist is an article of Faith? (3) How God is said to have created heaven and earth in the beginning?

First Article
WHETHER THE UNIVERSE OF CREATURES ALWAYS EXISTED?

We proceed thus to the First Article: —

Objection 1. It would seem that the universe of creatures, which is now called the world, had no beginning, but existed from eternity. For everything which begins to be had, before being, the possibility of being: otherwise its coming to be would have been impossible. If therefore the world began to be, before it began to be it was possible for it to be. But *that which can be* is matter, which is in potentiality to being, which results from a form, and to non-being, which results from privation of form. If therefore the world began to be, matter must have existed before the world. But matter cannot be without form: and if the matter of the world is joined to form, that *is* the world. Therefore the world existed before it began to be: which is impossible.[1]

Obj. 2. Further, nothing which has power to be always, sometimes is and sometimes is not; because as far as the power of a thing lasts, so long does it exist. But every incorruptible thing has the power to be always, for its power does not extend to any determinate time. Therefore no incorruptible thing sometimes is, and sometimes is not. But everything, which has a beginning, at some time is, and at some time is not. Therefore no incorruptible thing begins to be. But there are many incorruptible things in the world, as the celestial bodies and all intellectual substances[2]. Therefore the world did not begin to be.[3]

Obj. 3. Further, what is ungenerated has no beginning. But the Philosopher proves that matter is ungenerated, and also that the heavens are ungenerated.[4] Therefore the universe did not begin to be.[5]

Obj. 4. Further, there is a vacuum where there is not a body, but there could be. But if the world began to be, there was first no body where the body of the world now is; and yet it could be there, otherwise it would not be there now. Therefore before the world there was a vacuum; which is impossible.[6]

Obj. 5. Further, nothing begins anew to be moved except for the fact that either the mover or the thing moved is now otherwise than it was before. But what is now otherwise than it was before is moved. Therefore before every new motion there was a previous motion.

---

1. 参见 Argument of the Peripatetics, according to Maimonides, *Guide*, II 14 (p. 174). — Cf. Averroes, *Destruct. Destruct.*, I (IX, 16ra); *In Phys.*, VIII, comm. 4 (IV, 155r).
2. intellectual substances：理性实体
3. 参见 Aristotle, *De Caelo*, I, 12 (281b 18). — Averroes, *In De Caelo*, I, comm. 119 (V, 38r).
4. 参见 *De Caelo*, I, 3 (270a 13).
5. 参见 An argument of Aristotle, found in Maimonides, *Guide*, II, 13 (p. 173).
6. 参见 Averroes, *In De Caelo*, III,comm. 29 (V, 92v–93r).

Therefore motion always was; and therefore so also was the thing moved, because motion is only in a movable thing.[1]

Obj. 6. Further, every mover is either natural or voluntary. But neither begins to move except by some pre-existing motion. For nature always operates in the same manner: hence unless some change precede either in the nature of the mover, or in the movable thing, there cannot arise from the natural mover a motion which was not there before. As for the will, without itself being changed, it puts off doing what it proposes to do; but this can be only by some imagined change, even if it involves only the passage of time. Thus he who wills to make a house to-morrow, and not to-day, awaits something which will be to-morrow, but is not to-day. At the very least he awaits for to-day to pass, and for to-morrow to come; and this cannot be without change, because time is the number of motion. Therefore it remains that before every new motion, there was a previous motion; and so the same conclusion follows as before.[2]

Obj. 7. Further, whatever is always in its beginning, and always in its end, cannot cease and cannot begin; because what begins is not in its end, and what ceases is not in its beginning. But time is always in its beginning and end, because no part of time exists except *now*, which is the end of the past and the beginning of the future. Therefore time cannot begin or end, and consequently neither can motion, of which time is the number.[3]

Obj. 8. Further, God is before the world either in the order of nature only, or also in duration. If in the order of nature only, therefore, since God is eternal, the world also is eternal. But if God is prior in duration, since what is prior and posterior in duration constitutes time,

---

1. 参见An argument of Aristotle, found in Maimonides, *Guide*, II, 14 (p. 174). — Cf. Averroes, *In Phys.*, VIII, comm. 7 (IV, 156r).
2. 参见 Avicenna, *Metaph.*, IX, 1 (102ra). — Averroes, *In Phys.*, VIII, comm. 8 (IV, 156v); comm. 15 (IV, 158v ff.); *Destruct. Destruct.*, I (IX, 8rb).
3. 参见 Aristotle, *Phys.*, VIII, 1 (251b 19). — Cf. Averroes, *In Phys.*, VIII, comm. 11 (IV, 157v).

it follows that time existed before the world; which is impossible.[1]

Obj. 9. Further, if there is a sufficient cause, there is an effect; for a cause from which there is no effect is an imperfect cause, requiring something else to make the effect follow. But God is the sufficient cause of the world: He is the final cause, by reason of His goodness, the exemplary cause by reason of His wisdom, and the efficient cause by reason of His power, as appears from the above.[2] Since therefore God is eternal, the world also is eternal.[3]

Obj. 10. Further, He who has an eternal action also has an eternal effect. But the action of God is His substance, which is eternal. Therefore the world is eternal.[4]

On the contrary, It is said (*Jo.* xvii. 5), *Glorify Me, O Father, with Thyself with the glory which I had before the world was*; and (*Prov.* viii. 22), *The Lord possessed Me in the beginning of His ways, before He made anything from the beginning.*

I answer that, Nothing except God can be eternal. This statement is far from impossible. For it has been shown above that the will of God is the cause of things.[5] Therefore, things are necessary according as it is necessary for God to will them, since the necessity of the effect depends on the necessity of the cause.[6] Now it was shown above that, absolutely speaking, it is not necessary that God should will anything except Himself.[7] It is not therefore necessary for God to will that the world should always exist; but supposing an eternal world to exist, it exists to the extent that God wills it to exist, since the being of the world depends

---

1. 参见 Avicenna, *Metaph*; IX, 1 (101vab). — Cf. Averroes, *Destruct. Destruct.*, I (IX, 13ra).
2. 参见 Q. 44, a. 1, 3 and 4.
3. 参见 Avicenna, *Metaph.*, IX 1 (101vb). — Cf. Alex. of Hales, *Summa Theol.*, I, no. 64 (I, 93); St. Bonaventure, *In II Sent.*, d. 1, pt. 1, a. 1, q. 2 (II, 20).
4. 参见 Avicenna, *Metaph.*, IX, 1 (101va). — Maimonides, *Guide*, II, 18 (p. 181).
5. 参见 Q. 19, a. 4.
6. 参见 Aristotle, *Metaph.*, IV, 5 (1015b 9).
7. 参见 Q. 19, a, 3.

on the will of God as on its cause. It is not therefore necessary for the world to be always; hence neither can it be proved demonstratively.

Nor are Aristotle's arguments absolutely demonstrative, but only relatively — viz., as against the arguments of some of the ancients who asserted that the world began to be in some actually impossible ways. This appears in three ways.[1] First, because both in *Physics* viii.[2] and in *De Caelo* i.[3] he premises some opinions, such as those of Anaxagoras, Empedocles and Plato, and brings forward arguments to refute them. Secondly, because wherever he speaks of this subject, he quotes the testimony of the ancients, which is not the way of a demonstrator, but of one persuading of what is probable. Thirdly, because he expressly says that there are dialectical problems which we cannot solve demonstratively, as, *whether the world is eternal*.[4]

Reply Obj. 1. Before the world existed, it was possible for the world to be, not, indeed, according to the passive power which is matter, but according to the active power of God. The world was possible also, according as a thing is called absolutely possible, not in relation to any power, but from the sole relation of the terms which are not repugnant[5] to each other; in which sense possible is opposed to impossible, as appears from the Philosopher.[6]

Reply Obj. 2. Whatever has the power always to be, from the fact of having that power cannot sometimes be and sometimes not-be. However, before it received that power, it did not exist. Hence this argument, which is given by Aristotle,[7] does not prove absolutely that incorruptible beings never began to be; it proves that they did

1. 参见 Cf. Maimonides, *Guide*, II, 15 (p. 176).
2. 参见 *Phys.*, VIII, 1 (250b 24; 251b 17).
3. 参见 *De Caelo*, I, 10 (279b 4; 280a 30).
4. 参见 *Top.*, I, 9 (104b 16).
5. repugnant：矛盾的
6. 参见 *Metaph.*, IV, 12 (1019b 19).
7. 参见 *De Caelo*, I, 12 (281b 18).

not begin according to the natural process by which generable and corruptible beings begin to be.

Reply Obj. 3. Aristotle proves that *matter is ungenerated* from the fact that *it has not a subject* from which to derive its existence;[1] and he proves that the heavens are ungenerated, because they have no contrary from which to be generated.[2] Hence it appears that no conclusion follows in either case, except that matter and the heavens did not begin by generation; as some said especially about the heavens.[3] But what we say is that matter and the heavens were produced into being by creation, as appears above.[4]

Reply Obj. 4. The notion of a vacuum is not only that *in which is nothing*, but also implies a space capable of holding a body and in which there is not a body, as appears from Aristotle.[5] But we hold that there was no place or space before the world was.

Reply Obj. 5. The first mover was always in the same state, but the first movable thing was not always so, because it began to be whereas hitherto it was not. This, however, was not through change, but by creation, which is not change, as was said above.[6] Hence it is evident that this argument, which Aristotle gives,[7] is valid against those who admitted the existence of eternal movable things, but not eternal motion, as appears from the opinions of Anaxagoras and Empedocles.[8] But we hold that motion always existed from the moment that movable things began to exist.

Reply Obj. 6. The first agent is a voluntary agent. And although

1. 参见 *Phys.*, I, 9 (192a 28).
2. 参见 *De Caelo*, I, 3 (270a 13).
3. 参见 Cf. *op. cit.*, I, 10 (279a 13).
4. 参见 Q. 45, a. 2.
5. 参见 *Phys.*, IV, 1 (208b 26).
6. 参见 Q. 45, a. 2, ad 2.
7. 参见 *Phys.*, VIII, 1 (251a 25).
8. 参见 Cf. *ibid.* (250b 24).

He had the eternal will to produce some effect, yet He did not produce an eternal effect. Nor is it necessary for some change to be presupposed, not even because of imaginary time. For we must take into consideration the difference between a particular agent, that presupposes something and produces something else, and the universal agent, who produces the whole. The particular agent produces the form, and presupposes the matter; and hence it is necessary that it introduce the form in due proportion into a suitable matter. Hence it is logical to say that the particular agent introduces the form into such matter, and not into another, because of the different kinds of matter. But it is not logical to say so of God Who produces form and matter together; whereas it is logical to say of Him that He produces matter fitting to the form and to the end. Now a particular agent presupposes time just as it presupposes matter. Hence it is logically described as acting in a time *after* and not in a time *before*, according to an imaginary succession of time after time. But the universal agent, who produces both the thing and time, is not correctly described as acting now, and not before, according to an imaginary succession of time succeeding time, as if time were presupposed to His action; but He must be considered as giving time to His effect as much as and when He willed, and according to what was fitting to demonstrate His power. For the world leads more evidently to the knowledge of the divine creating power if it was not always, than if it had always been; since everything which was not always manifestly has a cause; whereas this is not so manifest of what always was.

Reply Obj. 7. As is stated in *Physics* iv., *before and after belong to time*, according as *they are found in motion*.[1] Hence beginning and end in time must be taken in the same way as in motion. Now, granted the eternity of motion, it is necessary that any given moment in motion be

1. 参见 Aristotle, *op. cit.*, IV, 11 (219a 17).

a beginning and an end of motion; which need not be if motion has a beginning. The same applies to the *now* of time. Thus it appears that the view of the instant *now*, as being always the beginning and end of time, presupposes the eternity of time and motion. Hence Aristotle brings forward this argument against those who asserted the eternity of time, but denied the eternity of motion.[1]

Reply Obj. 8. God is prior to the world by priority of duration. But the word *prior* signifies priority, not of time, but of eternity. — Or we may say that it signifies the eternity of imaginary time, and not of time really existing; much as, when we say that above the heavens there is nothing, the word *above* signifies only an imaginary place, according as it is possible to imagine other dimensions beyond those of the body of the heavens.

Reply Obj. 9. Just as the effect of a cause that acts by nature follows from it according to the mode of its form, so likewise it follows from the voluntary agent according to the form preconceived and determined by the agent, as appears from what was said above.[2] Therefore, although God was from eternity the sufficient cause of the world, we may not hold that the world was produced by Him, except as preordained by His will — that is, that it should have being after non-being, in order more manifestly to declare its author.

Reply Obj. 10. Given the action, the effect follows according to the requirement of the form which is the principle of action. But in agents acting by will, what is conceived and preordained is considered as the form which is the principle of action. Therefore, from the eternal action of God an eternal effect does not follow; there follows only such an effect as God has willed, an effect, namely, which has being after non-being.

---

1. 参见 *Op. cit.*, VIII, 1 (251b 29).
2. 参见 Q. 19, a. 4; q. 41, a. 2.

Second Article

WHETHER IT IS AN ARTICLE OF FAITH THAT THE WORLD BEGAN?

We proceed thus to the Second Article: —

Objection 1. It would seem that it is not an article of faith but a demonstrable conclusion that the world began. For everything that is made has a beginning of its duration. But it can be proved demonstratively[1] that God is the producing cause of the world; indeed this is asserted by the more approved philosophers.[2] Therefore it can be demonstratively proved that the world began.[3]

Obj. 2. Further, if it is necessary to say that the world was made by God, it must have been made from nothing, or from something. But it was not made from something, or otherwise the matter of the world would have preceded the world; and against this are the arguments of Aristotle who held that the heavens are ungenerated. Therefore it must be said that the world was made from nothing; and thus it has being after non-being. Therefore it must have begun to be.[4]

Obj. 3. Further, *everything which works by intellect works from some principle*,[5] as is revealed in all works of human art. But God acts by intellect, and therefore His work has a principle, from which to begin. The world, therefore, which is His effect, did not always exist.

Obj. 4. Further, it appears manifestly that certain arts have developed, and certain parts of the world have begun to be inhabited at some fixed time. But this would not be the case if the world had

---

1. demonstratively：推理地
2. 参见 Cf. above, q. 44, a. 2.
3. 参见 Alex. of Hales, *Summa Theol.*, I, no. 64 (I, 95); St. Bonaventure, *In II Sent.*, d. 1, pt. 1, a. 1, q. 3 (II, 22).
4. 参见 Alex, of Hales, *Summa Theol.*, I, no. 64 (I, 93).
5. 参见 Aristotle, *Phys.*, III, 4 (203a 31).

always been in existence. Therefore it is manifest that the world did not always exist.

Obj. 5. Further, it is certain that nothing can be equal to God. But if the world had always been, it would be equal to God in duration. Therefore it is certain that the world did not always exist.[1]

Obj. 6. Further, if the world always was, the consequence is that an infinite number of days preceded this present day. But it is impossible to traverse what is infinite. Therefore we should never have arrived at this present day; which is manifestly false.[2]

Obj. 7. Further, if the world was eternal, generation also was eternal. Therefore one man was begotten of another in an infinite series. But the father is the efficient cause of the son.[3] Therefore in efficient causes there could be an infinite series; which however is disproved in *Metaph.* ii.[4]

Obj. 8. Further, if the world and generation always were, there have been an infinite number of men. But man's soul is immortal. Therefore an infinite number of human souls would now actually exist, which is impossible. Therefore it can be known with certainty that the world began: it is not held by faith alone.[5]

On the contrary, The articles of faith cannot be proved demonstratively, because faith is of things *that appear not*. But that God is the Creator of the world in such a way that the world began to be is an article of faith; for we say, *I believe in one God*, etc.[6] And again, Gregory says that Moses prophesied of the past, saying, *In the beginning God created heaven and earth:* in which words the newness of the

1. 参见 Alex, of Hales, *Summa Theol.*, I, no. 64 (I, 93).
2. 参见 Argument of Algazel in Averroes, *Destruct. Destruct.*, I (IX, 9rb; 10rb); and of the Mutakallimin, found in Maimonides, *Guide*, I, 74 (p. 138).
3. 参见 Aristotle, *Phys.*, II, 3 (194b 30).
4. 参见 Aristotle, *Metaph.*, Ia, 2 (994a 5) — For the use of this argument, cf. the Mutakallimin in Averroes, *Destruct. Destruct.*, I (IX, 12vab).
5. 参 见 Argument of Algazel, found in Averroes, *Destruct. Destrust.*, I (IX, 12vab); and of the Mutakallimin in Maimonides, *Guide*, I, 73 (p. 132).
6. 参见 *Symb. Nicaenum* (Denzinger, no. 54).

world is stated.[1] Therefore the newness of the world is known only by revelation, and hence it cannot be proved demonstratively.

I answer that, That the world did not always exist we hold by faith alone: it cannot be proved demonstratively; which is what was said above of the mystery of the Trinity.[2] The reason for this is that the newness of the world cannot be demonstrated from the world itself. For the principle of demonstration is the essence of a thing. Now everything, considered in its species, abstracts from *here* and *now*; which is why it is said that *universals are everywhere and always*.[3] Hence it cannot be demonstrated that man, or the heavens, or a stone did not always exist.

Likewise, neither can the newness of the world be demonstrated from the efficient cause, which acts by will. For the will of God cannot be investigated by reason, except as regards those things which God must will of necessity; and what He wills about creatures is not among these, as was said above.[4] But the divine will can be manifested by revelation, on which faith rests. Hence that the world began to exist is an object of faith, but not of demonstration or science. And it is useful to consider this, lest anyone, presuming to demonstrate what is of faith, should bring forward arguments that are not cogent; for this would give unbelievers the occasion to ridicule, thinking that on such grounds we believe the things that are of faith.

Reply Obj. 1. As Augustine says, the opinion of philosophers who asserted the eternity of the world was twofold.[5] For some said that the substance of the world was not from God, which is an intolerable error; and therefore it is refuted by proofs that are cogent. Some, however,

---

1. 参见 *In Ezech.*, hom. 1, bk. 1 (PL 76, 786).
2. 参见 Q. 32, a. 1.
3. 参见 Aristotle, *Post. Anal.*, I, 31 (87b 33).
4. 参见 Q. 19, a. 3.
5. 参见 *De Civit. Dei*, XI, 4 (PL 41, 319).

said that the world was eternal, although made by God. *For they hold that the world has a beginning, not of time, but of creation; which means that, in a scarcely intelligible way, it was always made. And they try to explain their meaning thus: for just as, if a foot were always in the dust from eternity, there would always be a footprint which without doubt was caused by him who trod on it, so also the world always was, because its Maker always existed.*[1] To understand this we must consider that an efficient cause which acts by motion of necessity precedes its effect in time; for the effect exists only in the end of the action, and every agent must be the beginning of action. But if the action is instantaneous and not successive, it is not necessary for the maker to be prior in duration to the thing made, as appears in the case of illumination. Hence it is held that it does not follow necessarily that if God is the active cause of the world, He must be prior to the world in duration;[2] because creation, by which He produced the world, is not a successive change, as was said above.[3]

Reply Obj. 2. Those who would hold that the world was eternal, would say that the world was made by God from nothing; not that it was made after nothing, according to what we understand by the term *creation*, but that it was not made from anything. And so some of them even do not reject the term creation, as appears from Avicenna.[4]

Reply Obj. 3. This is the argument of Anaxagoras as reported in *Physics* iii.[5] But it does not lead to a necessary conclusion, except as to that intellect which deliberates in order to find out what should be done; which procedure is like movement. Such is the human intellect, but not the divine intellect.[6]

Reply Obj. 4. Those who hold the eternity of the world hold that

---

1. 参见 *Op. cit.*, X, 31 (PL 41, 311).
2. 参见 Cf. Averroes, *Destruct. Destruct.*, I (IX, 13rb).
3. 参见 Q. 45, a. 2, ad 3.
4. 参见 *Metaph.*, IX, 4 (104va).
5. 参见 Aristotle, *Phys.*, III, 4 (203a 31); VIII, 1 (250b 24).
6. 参见 Q. 14, a. 7.

some region was changed an infinite number of times from being uninhabitable to being inhabitable and *vice versa*.[1] They also hold that the arts, by reason of various corruptions and accidents, were subject to an infinite succession of discovery and decay.[2] Hence Aristotle says that it is absurd to base our opinion of the newness of the whole world on such particular changes.[3]

Reply Obj. 5. Even supposing that the world always was, it would not be equal to God in eternity, as Boethius says;[4] for the divine Being is all being simultaneously without succession, but with the world it is otherwise.

Reply Obj. 6. Passage is always understood as being from term to term. Whatever by-gone day we choose, from it to the present day there is a finite number of days which can be traversed. The objection is founded on the idea that, given two extremes, there is an infinite number of mean terms.

Reply Obj. 7. In efficient causes it is impossible to proceed to infinity *per se*. Thus, there cannot be an infinite number of causes that are *per se* required for a certain effect; for instance, that a stone be moved by a stick, the stick by the hand, and so on to infinity. But it is not impossible to proceed to infinity *accidentally* as regards efficient causes; for instance, if all the causes thus infinitely multiplied should have the order of only one cause, while their multiplication is accidental: *e.g.*, as an artificer acts by means of many hammers accidentally, because one after the other is broken. It is accidental, therefore, that one particular hammer should act after the action of another, and it is likewise accidental to this particular man as generator to be generated by another man; for he generates as a man, and not as the son of another man. For all men generating hold

1. 参见 Cf. St. Augustine, *De Civit. Dei*, XII, 10 (PL 41, 358); Aristotle, *Meteor.*, I, 14 (351a 19).
2. 参见 Cf. St. Augustine, *De Civit. Dei*, XII, 10 (PL 41, 358) ; Averroes, *In Metaph.*, XII, comm. 50 (VIII, 156V).
3. 参见 *Meteor.*, I, 14 (352a 26; 351b 8).
4. 参见 *De Consol.*, V, prose 6 (PL 63, 859).

one grade in the order of efficient causes — viz., the grade of a particular generator. Hence it is not impossible for a man to be generated by man to infinity; but such a thing would be impossible if the generation of this man depended upon this man, and on an elementary body, and on the sun, and so on to infinity.

Reply Obj. 8. Those who hold the eternity of the world evade this argument in many ways. For some do not think it impossible for there to be an actual infinity of souls, as appears from the *Metaphysics* of Algazel, who says that such a thing is an accidental infinity.[1] But this was disproved above.[2] Some say that the soul is corrupted with the body.[3] And some say that of all souls only one remains.[4] But others as Augustine says, asserted on this account a circulation of souls — viz., that souls separated from their bodies again return thither after a course of time.[5] A fuller consideration of this matter will be given later.[6] But be it noted that this argument considers only a particular case. Hence one might say that the world was eternal, or at least some creature as an angel, but not man. But we are considering the question in general, namely, whether any creature can exist from eternity.

Third Article
WHETHER THE CREATION OF THINGS WAS IN THE BEGINNING OF TIME?

We proceed thus to the Third Article: —

---

1. 参见 *Metaph.*, I, tr. 1, div. 6 (p. 40). — Cf. Averroes, *Destruct. Destruct.*, I (IX, 12vab).
2. 参见 Q. 7, a. 4.
3. 参见 Cf. Nemesius, *De Nat. Hom.*, II (PG 40, 537).
4. 参见 Averroes, *Destruct. Destruct.*, I (IX, 10va).
5. 参见 *Serm.* CCXLI, 4 (PG 38, 1135); *De Civit. Dei*, XII, 13 (PL 41, 361). — Cf. Plato *Timaeus* (p. 39a).
6. 参见 Q. 75, a. 6; q. 76, a. 2; q118, a. 3.

Objection 1. It would seem that the creation of things was not in the beginning of time. For whatever is not in time, is not in any part of time. But the creation of things was not in time, for by the creation the substance of things was brought into being; but time does not measure the substance of things, and especially of incorporeal things. Therefore, creation was not in the beginning of time.

Obj. 2. Further, the Philosopher proves that everything which is made, was being made.[1] Hence, to be made implies a *before* and *after*. But in the beginning of time, since it is indivisible, there is no *before* and *after*. Therefore, since to be created is a kind of *being made*, it appears that things were not created in the beginning of time.

Obj. 3. Further, even time itself is created. But time cannot be created in the beginning of time, since time is divisible, and the beginning of time is indivisible. Therefore, the creation of things was not in the beginning of time.

On the contrary, It is said (*Gen.* i. 1): *In the beginning God created heaven and earth.*

I answer that, The words of *Genesis*, *In the beginning God created heaven and earth*, are interpreted in a threefold sense in order to exclude three errors. For some said that the world always was, and that time had no beginning;[2] and to exclude this the words *In the beginning* are interpreted to mean *the beginning of time.*

And some said that there are two principles of creation, one of good things and the other of evil things,[3] against which *In the beginning is* expounded — *in the Son.* For as the efficient principle is appropriated to the Father by reason of power, so the exemplary principle is appropriated to the Son by reason of wisdom; in order that, according

1. 参见 *Phys.*, VI, 6 (237b 10).
2. 参见 Cf. St. Augustine, *De Civit. Dei*, X, 31; XI, 4; XII, 10 (PL 41, 311; 319; 357).
3. 参见 Cf. below, q. 49, a. 3.

to the words (*Ps.* ciii. 24), *Thou hast made all things in wisdom*, it may be understood that God made all things in the beginning — that is, in the Son. As it is said by the Apostle (*Col.* i. 16), *In Him* — viz., the Son — *were created all things.*

But others said that corporeal things were created by God through the medium of spiritual creatures;[1] and to exclude this the words of *Genesis* are interpreted thus: *In the beginning* — *i.e., before* all things — *God created heaven and earth.* For four things are stated to be created together — viz., the empyrean heavens, corporeal matter, by which is meant the earth, time, and the angelic nature.

Reply Obj. 1. Things are said to be created in the beginning of time, not as if the beginning of time were a measure of creation, but because together with time the heavens and earth were created.

Reply Obj. 2. This saying of the Philosopher is understood *of being made* by means of movement, or as the term of movement. For, since in every motion there is *before* and *after*, before any one point in a given motion — that is, while anything is in the process of being moved and made, — there is a *before* and also an *after*, because what is in the beginning of motion or in its term is not in the state of *being moved.* But creation is neither motion nor the term of motion, as was said above.[2] Hence a thing is created in such a way that it was not being created before.

Reply Obj. 3. Nothing is made except as it exists. But nothing of time exists except *now*. Hence time cannot be made except according to some *now*; not because there is time in the first *now*, but because from it time begins.

1. 参见 Cf. above, q. 45, a. 5; below, q. 65, a. 4.
2. 参见 Q. 45, a. 2, ad 3; a. 3.

Question XLVII
ON THE DISTINCTION OF THINGS IN GENERAL
(*In Three Articles*)

AFTER considering the production of creatures, we must turn to the consideration of the distinction among them. This consideration will be threefold — first, the distinction of things in general; secondly, the distinction of good and evil;[1] thirdly, the distinction of spiritual and corporeal creatures.[2]

Under the first head there are three points of inquiry: (1) The multitude or distinction of things. (2) Their inequality. (3) The unity of the world.

First Article
WHETHER THE MULTITUDE AND DISTINCTION OF THINGS IS FROM GOD?

We proceed thus to the First Article: —

Objection 1. It would seem that the multitude and distinction of things does not come from God. For one naturally always makes one. But God is supremely one, as appears from what precedes.[3] Therefore He produces but one effect.

Obj. 2. Further, the representation is assimilated to its exemplar.

---

1. 参见 Q. 48.
2. 参见 Q. 50.
3. 参见 Q. 11, a. 4.

But God is the exemplary cause of His effect, as was said above.[1] Therefore, as God is one, His effect is only one, and not diverse.

Obj. 3. Further, the means are proportioned to the end. But the end of the creature is one — viz., the divine goodness, as was shown above.[2] Therefore the effect of God is but one.

On the contrary, It is said (*Gen.* i. 4, 7) that God *divided the light from the darkness*, and *divided waters from waters*. Therefore the distinction and multitude of things is from God.

I answer that, The distinction of things has been ascribed to many causes. For some attributed the distinction to matter, either by itself or with the agent. Democritus, for instance, and all the ancient natural philosophers, who admitted no cause but matter, attributed it to matter alone;[3] and in their opinion the distinction of things comes from chance according to the motion of matter. Anaxagoras, however, attributed the distinction and multitude of things to matter and to the agent together; and he said that the intellect distinguishes things by separating what is mixed in the matter.[4]

But this cannot stand, for two reasons. First, because, as was shown above, even matter itself was created by God.[5] Hence we must reduce to a higher cause whatever distinction comes from matter. Secondly, because matter is for the sake of the form, and not the form for the matter, and the distinction of things comes from their proper forms. Therefore, the distinction of things is not for the sake of the matter; but rather, on the contrary, created matter is formless, in order that it may be accommodated to different forms.

Others have attributed the distinction of things to secondary agents,

---

1. 参见 Q. 44, a. 3.
2. 参见 Q. 44, a. 4.
3. 参见 Cf. Aristotle, *Phys.*, II, 2 (194a 20); II, 4 (196a 24); III, 4 (203a 34).
4. 参见 Cf. *op. cit.*, III, 4 (203a 23).
5. 参见 Q. 44, a. 2.

as did Avicenna, who said that God by understanding Himself, produced the first intelligence; in which, since it was not its own being, there is necessarily composition of potentiality and act,[1] as will appear later.[2] And so the first intelligence, inasmuch as it understood the first cause, produced the second intelligence; and in so far as it understood itself as in potentiality it produced the body of the heavens, which causes motion, and inasmuch as it understood itself as having actuality it produced the soul of the heavens.

But this opinion cannot stand, for two reasons. First, because it was shown above that to create belongs to God alone;[3] and hence whatever can be caused only by creation is produced by God alone — viz., all those things which are not subject to generation and corruption. Secondly, because, according to this opinion, the universe of things would not proceed from the intention of the first cause, but from the concurrence of many producing causes; and such an effect is an effect produced by chance. Therefore, the perfection of the universe, which consists of the diversity of things, would thus be a thing of chance; which is impossible.

Hence we must say that the distinction and multitude of things is from the intention of the first cause, who is God. For He brought things into being in order that His goodness might be communicated to creatures, and be represented by them. And because His goodness could not be adequately represented by one creature alone, He produced many and diverse creatures, so that what was wanting to one in the representation of the divine goodness might be supplied by another. For goodness, which in God is simple and uniform, in creatures is manifold and divided; and hence the whole universe together participates the divine goodness more perfectly, and represents it better, than any given single creature. And because the

1. 参见 *Metaph.*, IX, 4 (104va); cf. *op. cit.*, I, 7 (73rb).
2. 参见 Q. 50, a. 2, ad 3.
3. 参见 Q. 45, a. 5.

divine wisdom is the cause of the distinction of things, therefore Moses said that things are made distinct by the Word of God, which is the conception of His wisdom; and this is what we read in *Genesis* (i. 3,4): *God said: Be light made. ... And He divided the light from the darkness.*

Reply Obj. 1. The natural agent acts by the form which makes it what it is, and which is only one in one thing; and therefore its effect is one only. But the voluntary agent, such as God is, as was shown above, acts by an intellectual form.[1] Since, therefore, it is not against God's unity and simplicity to understand many things, as was shown above [2] it follows that, although He is one, He can make many things.

Reply Obj. 2. This argument would apply to the representation which perfectly represents the exemplar, and which is multiplied only by reason of matter. Hence the uncreated image, which is perfect, is only one. But no creature perfectly represents the first exemplar, which is the divine essence; and, therefore, it can be represented by many things. Still, according as ideas are called exemplars, the plurality of ideas corresponds in the divine mind to the plurality of things.

Reply Obj. 3. In speculative matters the means of demonstration, which demonstrates the conclusion perfectly, is only one; whereas probable means of proof are many. Likewise when operation is concerned, if the means be equal, so to speak, to the end, only one is necessary. But the creature is not so related to its end, which is God; and hence the multiplication of creatures is necessary.

Second Article
WHETHER THE INEQUALITY OF THINGS IS FROM GOD?

We proceed thus to the Second Article: —

Objection 1. It would seem that the inequality of things is not from

---

1. 参见 Q. 19, a. 4.
2. 参见 Q. 15, a. 2.

God. For it belongs to the best to produce the best. But among things that are best, one is not greater than another. Therefore, it belongs to God, Who is the Best, to make all things equal.

Obj. 2. Further, equality is the effect of unity.[1] But God is one. Therefore, He has made all things equal.

Obj. 3. Further, it is the part of justice to give unequal gifts to unequal things. But God is just in all His works. Since, therefore, no inequality of things is presupposed to the operation whereby He gives being to things, it seems that He has made all things equal.

On the contrary, It is said (*Ecclus*. xxxiii. 7): *Why does one day excel another, and one light another, and one year another year, one sun another sun? By the knowledge of the Lord they were distinguished.*

I answer that, When Origen wished to refute those who said that the distinction of things arose from the contrariety of the principles of good and evil, he said that in the beginning all things were created equal by God.[2] For he asserted that God first created only rational creatures, and all equal; and that inequality arose in them from free choice, since some turned to God more and some less, and others turned more and others less away from God. And so those rational creatures which were turned to God by free choice, were promoted to the various orders of angels according to the diversity of merits. Those however who were turned away from God were bound to bodies according to the diversity of their sin; and this was the cause (he said) of the creation and diversity of bodies.

But according to this opinion, it would follow that the universe of bodily creatures would not be for the sake of the communication of the goodness of God to creatures, but for the sake of the punishment of sin; which is contrary to what is said: *God saw all the things that He had made, and they were very good* (*Gen*. i. 31). And, as Augustine says: *What*

1. 参见 Aristotle, *Metaph*., IV, 15 (1021a 12).
2. 参见 *Peri Archon*, I, 6; 8; II, 9 (PG 11, 166; 178; 229).

can be more stupid than to say that the divine Artist provided this one sun for the one world, not to be an ornament to its beauty, nor for the benefit of corporeal things, but that it happened through the sin of one soul; so that, if a hundred souls had sinned, there would be a hundred suns in the world?[1]

Therefore it must be said that, just as the wisdom of God is the cause of the distinction of things, so the same wisdom is the cause of their inequality. This may be explained as follows. A twofold distinction is found in things: one is a formal distinction among things differing specifically; the other is a material distinction among things differing numerically only. And since matter is for the sake of form, material distinction exists for the sake of formal distinction. Hence we see that in incorruptible things there is only one individual of each species, for the species is sufficiently preserved in the one; whereas in generable and corruptible things there are many individuals of one species for the preservation of the species. Whence it appears that formal distinction is of greater consequence than the material. Now, formal distinction always requires inequality, because, as the Philosopher says,[2] the forms of things are like numbers in which species vary by the addition or subtraction of unity. Hence in natural things species seem to be arranged in a hierarchy: as the mixed things are more perfect than the elements, and plants than minerals, and animals than plants, and men than other animals; and in each of these one species is more perfect than others. Therefore, just as the divine wisdom is the cause of the distinction of things for the sake of the perfection of the universe, so is it the cause of inequality. For the universe would not be perfect if only one grade of goodness were found in things.

Reply Obj. 1. It is the part of the best cause to produce an effect which is best *as a whole*; but this does not mean that He makes every part of the whole the best absolutely, but in proportion to the whole. In

---

1. 参见 *De Civit. Dei*, XI, 23 (PL 41, 337).
2. 参见 Aristotle, *Metaph.*, VII, 3 (1043b 34).

the case of an animal, for instance, its goodness would be taken away if every part of it had the dignity of an eye. In the same way, God made the universe to be best as a whole, according to its requirement as a creature; whereas He did not make each single creature best, but one better than another. And therefore we find it said of each creature, *God saw the light that it was good* (*Gen.* i. 4); and in like manner of each one of the rest. But of all together it is said, *God saw all the things that He had made, and they were very good* (*Gen.* i. 31).

Reply Obj. 2. The first effect of unity is equality, and then comes multiplicity. Therefore from the Father, to Whom, according to Augustine, unity is appropriated,[1] the Son proceeds, to Whom is appropriated equality; and then comes the creature, to which belongs inequality. Nevertheless, creatures share also in a certain equality, namely, that of proportion.

Reply Obj. 3. This is the argument that persuaded Origen;[2] but it holds only as regards the distribution of rewards, the inequality of which is due to unequal merits. But in the constitution of things there is no inequality of parts through any preceding inequality, either of merits or of the disposition of the matter; but inequality comes from the perfection of the whole. This appears also in works done by art; for the roof of a house does not differ from the foundation because it is made of other material. But the builder seeks different materials in order that the house may be perfect in its different parts. Indeed, he would make such materials if he could.

Third Article
WHETHER THERE IS ONLY ONE WORLD?

We proceed thus to the Third Article: —

1. 参见 *De Doct. Christ.*, I, 5 (PL 34, 21).
2. 参见 *Peri Archon*, I, 6; 8; II, 9 (PG 11, 166; 178; 229).

Objection 1. It would seem that there is not only one world, but many. Because, as Augustine says, it is unfitting to say that God has created things without a reason.[1] But for the same reason that He created one, He could create many, since His power is not limited to the creation of one world, but is infinite, as was shown above.[2] Therefore God has produced many worlds.

Obj. 2. Further, nature does what is best, and much more does God. But it is better that there be many worlds than that there be one, because many good things are better than a few. Therefore many worlds have been made by God.

Obj. 3. Further, everything which has a form in matter can be multiplied in number, while the species remains the same, because multiplication in number comes from matter. But the world has form in matter. Thus, when I say *man*, I mean the form, and when I say *this man*, I mean the form in matter; so when we say *world*, the form is signified, and when we say *this world*, the form in matter is signified. Therefore there is nothing to prevent the existence of many worlds.

On the contrary, It is said (*Jo*. i. 10): *The world was made by Him*, where the world is named as one, as if only one existed.

I answer that, The very order of things created by God shows the unity of the world. For this world is called one by the unity of order, whereby some things are ordered to others. But whatever things come from God have relation of order to each other and to God Himself, as was shown above.[3] Hence it is necessary that all things should belong to one world. Therefore only those were able to assert the existence of many worlds who did not acknowledge any ordaining wisdom, but rather believed in chance; as did Democritus, who said that this world, besides an infinite number of other worlds, was made from a coming

1. 参见 *Lib. 83 Quaest.*, c. 46 (PL 40, 30).
2. 参见 Q. 25, a. 2.
3. 参见 Q. 11, a. 3; q. 21, a. 1, ad 3.

together of atoms.[1]

Reply Obj. 1. This argument proves that the world is one because all things must be arranged in one order, and to one end. Therefore from the unity of order in things Aristotle infers the unity of God governing all.[2] In the same way, Plato proves the unity of the world, as a sort of copy, from the unity of the exemplar.[3]

Reply Obj. 2. No agent intends material plurality as the end; for material multitude has no certain limit, but of itself tends to infinity, and the infinite is opposed to the notion of end. Now when it is said that many worlds are better than one, this has reference to material multitude. But the *best*, in this sense, is not the intention of the divine agent; since for the same reason it might be said that if He had made two worlds, it would be better if He had made three; and so on to infinity.

Reply Obj. 3. The world is composed of the whole of its matter. For it is not possible for there to be another earth than this one, since every earth would naturally be carried to this central one, wherever it was. The same applies to the other bodies which are parts of the world.

---

1. 参见 Cf. Aristotle, *De Caelo*, III, 4 (303a 4); Cicero, *De Nat. Deor.*, I, 26 (p. 28) ; St. Ambrose, *In Hexaëm.*, I, 1 (PL 14, 135).
2. 参见 *Metaph.*, XI, 10 (1076a 4).
3. 参见 Cf. St. Thomas, *In De Caelo*, I, lect. 19. — Cf. also Plato, *Timaeus* (p. 31a).

Question XLVIII
THE DISTINCTION OF THINGS IN PARTICULAR
(*In Six Articles*)

WE must now consider the distinction of things in particular. And firstly the distinction of good and evil; then the distinction of spiritual and corporeal creatures.[1]

Concerning the first, we inquire into evil and its cause.[2]

Concerning evil, six points are to be considered: (1) Whether evil is a nature? (2) Whether evil is found in things? (3) Whether good is the subject of evil? (4) Whether evil totally corrupts good? (5) The division of evil into pain [*poena*] and fault [*culpa*]. (6) Which has more the nature of evil, pain or fault?

First Article
WHETHER EVIL IS A NATURE?

We proceed thus to the First Article: —

Objection 1. It would seem that evil is a nature. For every genus is a nature. But evil is a genus, for the Philosopher says that *good and evil are not in a genus, but are genera of other things.*[3] Therefore evil is a nature.

Obj. 2. Further, every difference which constitutes a species is a nature. But evil is a difference constituting a species in the field of

1. 参见 Q. 50.
2. 参见 Q. 49.
3. 参见 Aristotle, *Cat.*, XI (14a 23).

morals; for a bad habit differs in species from a good habit, as does liberality from illiberality. Therefore evil signifies a nature.

Obj. 3. Further, each extreme of two contraries is a nature. But evil and good are not opposed as privation and habit, but as contraries, as the Philosopher shows by the fact that between good and evil there is an intermediate position, and from evil there can be a return to good.[1] Therefore evil signifies a nature.

Obj. 4. Further, what is not, acts not. But evil acts, for it corrupts good. Therefore evil is a being and a nature.

Obj. 5. Further, nothing belongs to the perfection of the universe except what is a being and a nature. But evil belongs to the perfection of the universe of things, for Augustine says that *the admirable beauty oj the universe is made up of all things. In which even what is called evil, well ordered and in its place, makes better known the greatness of the good.*[2] Therefore evil is a nature.

On the contrary, Dionysius says that *Evil is neither a being nor a good.*[3]

I answer that, One opposite is known through the other, as darkness is known through light. Hence, what evil is must be known from the nature of good. Now, we have said above that good is everything that is appetible;[4] and thus, since every nature desires its own being and its own perfection, it must be said also that the being and the perfection of any nature is good. Hence it is impossible that evil signifies any being, or any form or nature. Therefore, by the name *evil* there must be signified some absence of good. And this is what is meant by saying that *evil is neither a being nor a good.* For since being, as such, is good, the absence of being involves the absence of good.

Reply Obj. 1. Aristotle speaks there according to the opinion of

---

1. 参见 *Op. cit.*, X (12a 22; b 26).
2. 参见 *Enchir.*, X (PL 40, 236).
3. 参见 *De Div. Nom.*, IV, 20 (PG 3, 717).
4. 参见 Q. 5, a. 1.

the Pythagoreans, who thought that evil was a kind of nature, and therefore they asserted the existence of good and evil as genera. For Aristotle, especially in his logical works, was in the habit of bringing forward examples that in his time were probable in the opinion of some philosophers. Or, it may be said that, as the Philosopher says, *the first kind of contrariety*[1] *is habit and privation*, being verified in all contraries; for one contrary is always imperfect in relation to another, as black in relation to white, and bitter in relation to sweet. And in this way good and evil are said to be genera, not absolutely, but in regard to contraries; because, just as every form has the nature of good, so every privation, as such, has the nature of evil.

Reply Obj. 2. Good and evil are not constitutive differences except in moral matters, which receive their species from the end, which is the object of the will, the source of all morality[2]. And because good has the nature of an end, for this reason good and evil are specific differences in moral matters — the good in itself, but evil as the absence of the due end. Yet neither does the absence of the due end by itself constitute a species in moral matters, except as the absence is joined to an undue end; just as we do not find the privation of the substantial form in natural things, unless it is joined to another form. Thus, therefore, the evil which is a constitutive difference in morals is a certain good joined to the privation of another good; just as the end proposed by the intemperate man is not the privation of the good of reason, but the delight of sense against the order of reason. Hence evil is not as such a constitutive difference, but by reason of the good that is annexed.

Reply Obj. 3. The answer to this objection appears from the above. For the Philosopher there speaks of good and evil in morality. Now in that respect, between good and evil there is something intermediate, as good is considered something rightly ordered, and evil a thing not only

1. contrariety：相反；矛盾
2. morality：道德；品行

out of right order, but also injurious to another. Hence the Philosopher says that a *prodigal man is foolish, but not evil.*[1] And from this evil in morality, there may be a return to good, but not from any sort of evil; for from blindness there is no return to sight, although blindness is an evil.

Reply Obj. 4. A thing is said to act in a threefold sense. In one way, *formally*, as when we say that whiteness makes white; and in that sense evil considered even as a privation is said to corrupt good, for it is itself a corruption or privation of good. In another sense, a thing is said to *act effectively*, as when a painter makes a wall white. Thirdly, it is said in the sense of the *final cause*, as the end is said to effect by moving the efficient cause. But in these last two ways evil does not effect anything of itself, that is, as a privation, but by virtue of the good annexed to it. For every action comes from some form; and everything which is desired as an end is a perfection. Therefore, as Dionysius says, evil does not act, nor is it desired, except by virtue of some good joined to it: while of itself it is nothing definite, and outside the scope of our will and intention.[2]

Reply Obj. 5. As was said above, the parts of the universe are ordered to each other, according as one acts on the other, and according as one is the end and exemplar of the other.[3] But, as was said above, this can happen to evil only as joined to some good. Hence evil neither belongs to the perfection of the universe, nor comes under the order of the universe, except accidentally, that is, by reason of some good joined to it.

Second Article
WHETHER EVIL IS FOUND IN THINGS?

We proceed thus to the Second Article: —

---

1. 参见 *Eth.*, IV, 1 (1121a 25).
2. 参见 *De Div. Nom.*, IV, 20; 32 (PG 3, 720; 733).
3. 参见 Q. 2, a. 3; q. 19, a. 5, ad 2; q. 21, a. 1, ad 3; q. 44, a. 3.

Objection 1. It would seem that evil is not found in things. For whatever is found in things is either something, or a privation of something, which is a *non-being*. But Dionysius says that evil is distant from the existent, and even more distant from the non-existent.[1] Therefore evil is not at all found in things.

Obj. 2. Further, *being* and *thing* are convertible. If, therefore, evil is a being in things, it follows that evil is a thing; which is contrary to what has been said.

Obj. 3. Further, the whiter white is *the white unmixed with black*, as the Philosopher says.[2] Therefore the good unmixed with evil is the greater good. But God always makes what is better much more than nature does. Therefore in things made by God there is no evil.

On the contrary, On the above assumptions, all prohibitions and penalties would cease, for they are concerned only with evils.

I answer that, As was said above, the perfection of the universe requires that there should be inequality in things, so that every grade of goodness may be realized.[3] Now, one grade of goodness is that of the good which cannot fail. Another grade of goodness is that of the good which can fail in goodness. These grades of goodness are to be found in being itself; for there are some things which cannot lose their being, as incorruptible things, while there are some which can lose it, as corruptible things. As, therefore, the perfection of the universe requires that there should be not only incorruptible beings, but also corruptible beings, so the perfection of the universe requires that there should be some which can fail in goodness and which sometimes do fail. Now it is in this that evil consists, namely, in the fact that a thing fails in goodness. Hence it is clear that evil is found in things in the way that corruption also is found; for corruption itself is an evil.

---

1. 参见 *De Div. Nom.*, IV, 19 (PG 3, 716).
2. 参见 *Top.*, III, 5 (119a 27).
3. 参见 Q. 47, a. 2.

Reply Obj. 1. Evil is distant both from being absolutely and from *non-being* absolutely, because it is neither a habit nor a pure negation, but a privation.

Reply Obj. 2. As the Philosopher says, *being* [*ens*] is said in two ways.[1] In one way, it is considered as signifying the entity of a thing, according as it is divided by the ten categories. In that sense it is convertible with *thing*, and thus no privation is a being, and neither therefore is evil a being. In another sense, *being* is said to be that which signifies the truth of a proposition which consists in composition, revealed by the verb *is*. In this sense, being is what answers to the question, *Does it exist?* It is in this sense that we speak of blindness as being in the eye; or of any other privation. In this way even evil can be called a being. Through ignorance of this distinction, some, considering that things may be evil, or that evil is said to be in things, believed that evil was a positive thing in itself.[2]

Reply Obj. 3. God and nature and any other agent make what is better in the whole, but not what is better in every single part, except in relation to the whole, as was said above.[3] And the whole itself, which is the universe of creatures, is all the better and more perfect if there be some things in it which can fail in goodness, and which do sometimes fail, without God preventing it. This happens, firstly, because *it belongs to Providence, not to destroy, but to save nature*, as Dionysius says.[4] But it belongs to nature that what may fail should sometimes fail. It happens, secondly, because, as Augustine says, *God is so powerful that He can even make good out of evil.*[5] Hence many good things would be taken away if God permitted no evil to exist; for fire would not be generated if air

---

1. 参见 Aristotle, *Metaph.*, IV, 7 (1017a 22).
2. 参见 Cf. a. 1, ad 1; below, q. 49, a. 3.
3. 参见 Q. 47, a. 2, ad 1.
4. 参见 *De Div. Nom.*, IV, 3 (PG 3, 733).
5. 参见 *Enchir.*, XI (PL 40, 236).

was not corrupted, nor would the life of a lion be preserved unless the ass were killed. Neither would avenging justice nor the patience of a sufferer be praised if there were no injustice.

Third Article
WHETHER EVIL IS IN GOOD AS IN ITS SUBJECT?

We proceed thus to the Third Article: —

Objection 1. It would seem that evil is not in good as its subject. For good is something that exists. But Dionysius says that *evil does not exist, nor is it in that which exists.*[1] Therefore, evil is not in good as its subject.

Obj. 2. Further, evil is not a being, whereas good is a being. But *non-being* does not require being as its subject. Therefore, neither does evil require good as its subject.

Obj. 3. Further, one contrary is not the subject of another. But good and evil are contraries. Therefore, evil is not in good as in its subject.

Obj. 4. Further, the subject of whiteness is called white. Therefore, also, the subject of evil is evil. If, therefore, evil is in good as in its subject, it follows that good is evil, against what is said (*Isa.* v. 20): *Woe to you who call evil good, and good evil!*

On the contrary, Augustine says that *evil exists only in good.*[2]

I answer that, As was said above, evil indicates the absence of good. But not every absence of good is evil. For absence of good can be taken in a privative and in a negative sense. Absence of good, taken negatively, is not evil; otherwise, it would follow that what does not exist is evil, and also that every thing would be evil because of not having the good belonging to something else. For instance, a man would be evil because he did not have the swiftness of the roe, or the strength of a lion. But the absence of good, taken in a privative sense,

---

1. 参见 *De Div. Nom.*, IV, 33 (PG 3, 733).
2. 参见 *Enchir.*, XIV (PL 40, 238).

is an evil; as, for instance, the privation of sight is called blindness.

Now, the subject of privation and of form is one and the same — viz., being in potentiality, whether it be being in potentiality absolutely, as primary matter, which is the subject of the substantial form and of the privation of the opposite form; or whether it be being in potentiality relatively, and actuality absolutely, as in the case of a transparent body, which is the subject both of darkness and light. It is, however, manifest that the form which makes a thing actual is a perfection and a good. Hence, every actual being is a good; and likewise every potential being, as such, is a good, as having a relation to good. For as it has being in potentiality, so it has goodness in potentiality. Therefore, the subject of evil is good.

Reply Obj. 1. Dionysius means that evil is not in existing things as a part, or as a natural property of any existing thing.

Reply Obj. 2. *Non-being*, understood negatively, does not require a subject; but privation is negation in a subject, as the Philosopher says, and such a *non-being* is an evil.[1]

Reply Obj. 3. Evil is not in the good opposed to it as in its subject, but in some other good, for the subject of blindness is not *sight*, but *the animal.* Yet it appears, as Augustine says, that the rule of dialectic here fails, the rule, namely, which says that contraries cannot exist together.[2] But this is to be taken according to the universal meaning of good and evil, but not in reference to any particular good and evil. For white and black, sweet and bitter, and like contraries, are considered as contraries only in a special sense, because they exist in some determinate genera; whereas good enters into every genus. Hence one good can coexist with the privation of another good.

Reply Obj. 4. The prophet invokes woe to those who say that good as such is evil. But this does not follow from what is said above, as is clear

1. 参见 *Metaph.*, III, 2 (1004a 15).
2. 参见 *Enchir.*, XIV (PL 40, 238).

from the explanation given.

Fourth Article
WHETHER EVIL CORRUPTS THE WHOLE GOOD?

We proceed thus to the Fourth Article: —

Objection 1. It would seem that evil corrupts the whole good. For one contrary is wholly corrupted by another. But good and evil are contraries. Therefore evil corrupts the whole good.

Obj. 2. Further, Augustine says that *evil injures inasmuch as it takes away good.*[1] But good is all of a piece and uniform. Therefore it is wholly taken away by evil.

Obj. 3. Further, evil, as long as it lasts, causes injury and takes away good. But that from which something is always being removed, is at some time consumed, unless it is infinite, which cannot be said of any created good. Therefore evil wholly consumes good.

On the contrary, Augustine says that *evil cannot wholly consume good.*[2]

I answer that, Evil cannot wholly consume good. To prove this we must consider that there is a threefold good. One kind of good is wholly destroyed by evil, and this is the good opposed to evil ; as light is wholly destroyed by darkness, and sight by blindness. Another kind of good is neither wholly destroyed nor diminished by evil, and that is the good which is the subject of evil; for by darkness the substance of the air is not injured. And there is also a kind of good which is diminished by evil, but is not wholly taken away; and this good is the aptitude of a subject to some actuality.

The diminution, however, of this last kind of good is not to be considered by way of subtraction, as is diminution in quantity, but rather by way of remission, as is diminution in qualities and

1. 参见 *Op. cit.*, XII (PL 40, 237); *De Mor. Eccl.* II, 3 (PL 32, 1347).
2. 参见 *Enchir.*, XII (PL 40, 237).

forms. The remission of this aptitude is to betaken as contrary to its intensity. For this kind of aptitude receives its intensity by the dispositions whereby the matter is prepared for actuality. The more they are multiplied in the subject, the more is it fitted to receive its perfection and form; and, on the contrary, it is decreased by contrary dispositions, whose greater multiplication in the matter, as well as greater intensity, weaken all the more the potentiality in relation to its act.

Therefore, if contrary dispositions cannot be multiplied and intensified to infinity, but only to a certain limit, neither is the aforesaid aptitude diminished or remitted infinitely. This appears in the active and passive qualities of the elements, for coldness and humidity, whereby the aptitude of matter to the form of fire is diminished or remitted, cannot be infinitely multiplied. But if the contrary dispositions can be infinitely multiplied, the aforesaid aptitude is also infinitely diminished or remitted. Nevertheless, it is not wholly taken away, because it always remains in its root, which is the substance of the subject. Thus, if opaque bodies were interposed to infinity between the sun and the air, the aptitude of the air for light would be infinitely diminished; but still it would never be wholly removed while the air remained, which in its very nature is transparent. In the same way, addition in sin can be made to infinitude, whereby the aptitude of the soul for grace is more and more lessened; and these sins are like obstacles interposed between us and God, according to *Isa.* lix. 2: *Our sins have divided between us and God.* Yet the aforesaid aptitude of the soul is not wholly taken away, for it belongs to its very nature.

Reply Obj. 1. The good which is opposed to evil is wholly taken away; but other goods are not wholly removed, as was said above.

Reply Obj. 2. The aforesaid aptitude is intermediate between subject and act. Hence, where it touches act, it is diminished by evil; but where it reaches the subject, it remains as it was. Therefore, although good is like to itself, yet, because of its relation to different things, it is not wholly, but only partially, taken away.

Reply Obj. 3. Some, imagining that the diminution of this kind of good is like the diminution of quantity, said that just as the continuous is infinitely divisible, if the division be made according to the same proportion (for in stance, half of a half, or a third of a third), so is it in the present case.[1] But this explanation does not avail here. For when in a division we keep the same proportion, we continue to subtract less and less; for half of a half is less than half the whole. But a second sin does not necessarily diminish the above mentioned aptitude less than a preceding sin, but perchance either equally or more.

Therefore it must be said that, although this aptitude is a finite thing, still it may be so diminished infinitely, not *per se*, but accidentally, according as the contrary dispositions are also increased infinitely, as was explained.

Fifth Article
WHETHER EVIL IS ADEQUATELY DIVIDED INTO PAIN [POENA] AND FAULT [CULPA]?

We proceed thus to the Fifth Article: —

Objection 1. It would seem that evil is not adequately divided into pain and fault. For every defect is a kind of evil. But in all creatures there is the defect of not being able to preserve themselves in being, which nevertheless is neither a pain nor a fault. Therefore evil is inadequately divided into pain and fault.

Obj. 2. Further, in irrational creatures there is neither fault nor pain; but, nevertheless, they have corruption and defect, which are evils. Therefore not every evil is a pain or a fault.

---

1. 参见 William of Auxerre, *Summa Aurea*, II, tr. 26, q. 5 (fol. 87a).

Obj. 3. Further, temptation is an evil, but it is not a fault, for *temptation which involves no consent is not a sin, but an occasion for the exercise of virtue*, as is said in the *Gloss* on *2 Cor.* xii. 7;[1] nor is it a pain, because temptation precedes the fault, and the pain follows afterwards. Therefore, evil is not sufficiently divided into pain and fault.

Obj. 4. *On the contrary*, It would seem that this division is superfluous; for, as Augustine says, a thing is evil *because it injures*.[2] But whatever injures is penal. Therefore every evil comes under pain.

I answer that, Evil, as was said above, is the privation of good, which chiefly and of itself consists in perfection and act. Act, however, is twofold, first, and second. The first act is the form and integrity of a thing; the second act is its operation. Therefore evil is also twofold. In one way it occurs by the subtraction of the form, or of any part required for the integrity of the thing, as blindness is an evil, just as it is an evil to be wanting in any member of the body. In another way evil exists by the withdrawal of the due operation, either because it does not exist, or because it has not its due mode and order. But because good in itself is the object of the will, evil, which is the privation of good, is found in a special way in rational creatures which have a will. Therefore the evil which comes from the withdrawal of the form and integrity of the thing has the nature of a pain; and especially so on the supposition that all things are subject to divine providence and justice, as was shown above.[3] For it is of the very nature of a pain to be against the will. But the evil which consists in the subtraction of the due operation in voluntary things has the nature of a fault; for it is imputed to anyone as a fault if he should fail as regards perfect action, of which he is master by the will. Therefore every evil in voluntary

---

1. 参见 *Glossa ordin.* (VI, 76E); Peter Lombard, *In II Cor.*, super XII, 7 (PL 192, 84).
2. 参见 *Enchir.*, XII (PL 40, 237); *De Mor. Eccl.*, II, 3 (PL 32, 1347).
3. 参见 Q. 22, a. 2.

things is to be looked upon as a pain or a fault.

Reply Obj. 1. Because evil is the privation of good, and not a pure negation, as was said above, therefore not every defect of good is an evil, but only the defect of the good which is naturally due. For the want of sight is not an evil in a stone, but it is an evil in an animal; since it is against the nature of a stone to see. So, likewise, it is against the nature of a creature to be preserved in being through itself, because being and conservation come from one and the same source. Hence this kind of defect is not an evil for a creature.

Reply Obj. 2. Pain and fault do not divide evil absolutely considered, but evil that is found in voluntary things.

Reply Obj. 3. Temptation, as importing provocation to evil, is always an evil of fault in the tempter; but in the one tempted it is not, properly speaking, a fault, unless through the temptation some change is wrought in the one who is tempted. For thus the action of the agent resides in the patient; and according as the tempted is changed to evil by the tempter he falls into fault.

Reply Obj. 4. In answer to the opposite argument, it must be said that the very nature of pain includes the idea of injury to the agent in himself, whereas the idea of fault includes the idea of injury to the agent in his operation; and thus both are contained in evil, as including the idea of injury.

Sixth Article

WHETHER PAIN HAS THE NATURE OF EVIL MORE THAN FAULT HAS?

We proceed thus to the Sixth Article: —

Objection 1. It would seem that pain has more of evil than fault. For fault is to pain what merit is to reward. But reward has more of good than merit, being its end. Therefore pain has more evil in it than fault has.

Obj. 2. Further, that is the greater evil which is opposed to the greater good. But pain, as was said above, is opposed to the good of the agent, while fault is opposed to the good of the action. Therefore, since the agent is better than the action, it seems that pain is worse than fault.

Obj. 3. Further, the privation of the end is a pain consisting in forfeiting the vision of God; whereas the evil of fault is privation of the order to the end. Therefore pain is a greater evil than fault.

On the contrary, A wise workman chooses a lesser evil in order to prevent a greater, as the surgeon cuts off a member of the body to save the whole body. But divine wisdom inflicts pain to prevent fault. Therefore fault is a greater evil than pain.

I answer that, Fault has more of the nature of evil than pain has — not only more than pain of sense, consisting in the privation of corporeal goods (which is the kind of pain most men comprehend), but also more than any kind of pain, and understanding pain in its most general meaning, so as to include privation of grace or glory.

There is a twofold reason for this. The first is that one becomes evil by the evil of fault, but not by the evil of pain. As Dionysius says, *To be punished is not an evil; but it is an evil to be made worthy of punishment.*[1] The reason for this is that, since good absolutely considered consists in act, and not in potentiality, and the ultimate act is operation, or the use of something possessed, it follows that the absolute good of man consists in good operation, or the good use of something possessed. Now we use all things by the act of the will. Hence from a good will, by which a man uses well what he has, a man is called good, and from a bad will he is called bad. For a man who has a bad will can use ill even the good he has, as when a grammarian[2] of his own will speaks incorrectly. Therefore, because the fault itself consists in the disordered act of the

---

1. 参见 *De Div. Nom.*, IV, 22 (PG 3, 724).
2. grammarian：文法家

will, and the pain consists in the privation of something used by the will, fault has more of evil in it than pain has.

The second reason can be taken from the fact that God is the author of the evil of pain, but not of the evil of fault. And this is because the evil of pain takes away the creature's good, which may be either something created (as sight, destroyed by blindness), or something uncreated (as by being deprived of the vision of God the creature loses its uncreated good). But the evil of fault is properly opposed to uncreated good; for it is opposed to the fulfillment of the divine will, and to divine love whereby the divine good is loved for itself, and not only as it is shared by the creature. Therefore it is plain that fault has more evil in it than pain has.

Reply Obj. 1. Although fault terminates in pain, as merit in reward, yet fault is not intended for the sake of the pain, as merit is for the reward; but rather, on the contrary, pain is brought about so that the fault may be avoided, and thus fault is worse than pain.

Reply Obj. 2. The order of action destroyed by fault is a more perfect good of the agent, since it is the second perfection, than is the good destroyed by pain, which is the first perfection.

Reply Obj. 3. Pain and fault are not to be compared as end and order to the end, because one may be deprived in some way of the end and of the order to the end both by fault and by pain: by pain, according as a man is removed from the end and from the order to the end; by fault, inasmuch as this privation belongs to an action which is not ordered to its due end.

Question XLIX
THE CAUSE OF EVIL
(*In Three Articles*)

WE next inquire into the cause of evil. Concerning this there are three points of inquiry: (1) Whether good can be the cause of evil? (2) Whether the supreme good, God, is the cause of evil? (3) Whether there be any supreme evil, which is the first cause of all evils?

First Article
WHETHER GOOD CAN BE THE CAUSE OF EVIL?

We proceed, thus to the First Article: —

Objection 1. It would seem that good cannot be the cause of evil. For it is said (*Matt.* vii. 18): *A good tree cannot bring forth evil fruit.*

Obj. 2. Further, one contrary cannot be the cause of another. But evil is the contrary to good. Therefore good cannot be the cause of evil.

Obj. 3. Further, a deficient effect can proceed only from a deficient cause. But supposing that evil has a cause, it is a deficient effect; and therefore it has a deficient cause. But everything deficient is an evil. Therefore the cause of evil can be only evil.

Obj. 4. Further, Dionysius says that evil has no cause.[1] Therefore good is not the cause of evil.

On the contrary, Augustine says: *There is no possible source of evil except good.*[2]

---

1. 参见 *Op. cit.*, IV, 30 (PG 3, 732).
2. 参见 *Contra Julian.*, I, 9 (PL 44, 670).

I answer that, It must be said that every evil in some way has a cause. For evil is the absence of the good which is natural and due to a thing. But that anything fall short of its natural and due disposition can come only from some cause drawing it out of its proper disposition. For a heavy thing is not moved upwards except by some impelling force; nor does an agent fail in its action except from some impediment. But only good can be a cause; because nothing can be a cause except inasmuch as it is a being, and every being, as such, is good. And if we consider the special kinds of causes, we see that the agent, the form and the end imply some kind of perfection which belongs to the notion of good. Even matter, as a potentiality to good, has the nature of good.

Now that good is the cause of evil by way of the material cause was shown above.[1] For it was shown that good is the subject of evil. But evil has no formal cause, but is rather a privation of form. So, too, neither has it a final cause, but is rather a privation of order to the proper end; since it is not only the end which has the nature of good, but also the useful, which is ordered to the end. Evil, however, has a cause by way of an agent, not directly, but accidentally.

In proof of this, we must know that evil is caused in action otherwise than in the effect. In action, evil is caused by reason of the defect of some principle of action, either of the principal or the instrumental agent. Thus, the defect in the movement of an animal may happen by reason of the weakness of the motive power, as in the case of children, or by reason only of the ineptitude[2] of the instrument, as in the lame. On the other hand, evil is caused in a thing, but not in the proper effect of the agent, sometimes by the power of the agent, sometimes by reason of a defect, either of the agent or of the matter. It is caused by reason of the power or perfection of the agent when there necessarily follows on the form intended by the agent the privation of

---

1. 参见 Q. 48, a. 3.
2. ineptitude：不合适

another form; as, for instance, when on the form of fire there follows the privation of the form of air or of water. Therefore, as the more perfect the fire is in strength, so much the more perfectly does it impress its own form, so also the more perfectly does it corrupt the contrary. Hence that evil and corruption befall air and water comes from the perfection of the fire, but accidentally; because fire does not aim at the privation of the form of water, but at the introduction of its own form, though by doing this it also accidentally causes the other. But if there is a defect in the proper effect of the fire — as, for instance, that it fails to heat — this comes either by defect of the action, which implies the defect of some principle, as was said above, or by the indisposition of the matter, which does not receive the action of the fire acting on it. But the fact itself that it is a deficient being is accidental to good to which it belongs essentially to act. Hence it is true that evil in no way has any but an accidental cause. Thus good is the cause of evil.

Reply Obj. 1. As Augustine says, *The Lord calls an evil will an evil tree, and a good will a good tree.*[1] Now, a good will does not produce a morally bad act, since it is from the good will itself that a moral act is judged to be good. Nevertheless the movement itself of an evil will is caused by the rational creature, which is good; and thus good is the cause of evil.

Reply Obj. 2. Good does not cause that evil which is contrary to itself, but some other evil. Thus, the goodness of the fire causes evil to the water, and man, good in his nature, causes a morally evil act. Furthermore, as was explained above, this is by accident.[2] Moreover, it does happen sometimes that one contrary causes another by accident: for instance, the exterior surrounding cold heats inasmuch as the heat is confined by it.

Reply Obj. 3. Evil has a deficient cause in voluntary beings otherwise

---

1. 参见 *Contra Julian.*, I, 9 (PL 44, 672).
2. 参见 Q. 19, a. 9.

than in natural things. For the natural agent produces the same kind of effect as it is itself, unless it is impeded by some exterior thing; and this amounts to some defect in it. Hence evil never follows in the effect unless some other evil pre-exists in the agent or in the matter, as was said above. But in voluntary beings the defect of the action comes from an actually deficient will inasmuch as it does not actually subject itself to its proper rule. This defect, however, is not a fault; but fault follows upon it from the fact that the will acts with this defect.

Reply Obj. 4. Evil has no direct cause, but only an accidental cause, as was said above.

Second Article

WHETHER THE HIGHEST GOOD, GOD, IS THE CAUSE OF EVIL?

We proceed thus to the Second Article: —

Objection 1. It would seem that the highest good, God, is the cause of evil. For it is said (*Isa.* xiv. 5, 7): *I am the Lord, and there is no other God, forming the light, and creating darkness, making peace, and creating evil.* It is also said (*Amos* iii. 6), *Shall there be evil in a city, which the Lord hath not done?*

Obj. 2. Further, the effect of the secondary cause is reduced to the first cause. But good is the cause of evil, as was said above. Therefore, since God is the cause of every good, as was shown above,[1] it follows that also every evil is from God.

Obj. 3. Further, as is said by the Philosopher, the cause of both *the safety and danger of the ship* is the same.[2] But God is the cause of the safety of all things. Therefore He is the cause of all perdition and of all evil.

On the contrary, Augustine says that, *God is not the author of evil, because*

---

1. 参见 Q. 2, a. 3; q. 6, a. i and 4.
2. 参见 Aristotle, *Phys.*, II, 3 (195a 3).

He is not the cause of tending to non-being.[1]

I answer that, As appears from what was said, the evil which consists in the defect of action is always caused by the defect of the agent. But in God there is no defect, but the highest perfection, as was shown above.[2] Hence, the evil which consists in defect of action, or which is caused by defect of the agent, is not reduced to God as to its cause.

But the evil which consists in the corruption of some things is reduced to God as the cause. And this appears as regards both natural things and voluntary things. For it was said that some agent, inasmuch as it produces by its power a form which is followed by corruption and defect, causes by its power that corruption and defect. But it is manifest that the form which God chiefly intends in created things is the good of the order of the universe. Now, the order of the universe requires, as was said above, that there should be some things that can, and sometimes do, fail.[3] And thus God, by causing in things the good of the order of the universe, consequently and, as it were by accident, causes the corruptions of things, according to *1 Kings* ii. 6: *The Lord killeth and maketh alive*. But when we read that *God hath not made death* (*Wis*. i. 13), the sense is that God does not will death for its own sake. Nevertheless, the order of justice belongs to the order of the universe; and this requires that penalty should be dealt out to sinners. And so God is the author of the evil which is penalty, but not of the evil which is fault, by reason of what is said above.

Reply Obj. 1. These passages refer to the evil of penalty, and not to the evil of fault.

Reply Obj. 2. The effect of the deficient secondary cause is reduced to the first non-deficient cause as regards what it has of being and perfection, but not as regards what it has of defect; just as whatever

---

1. 参见 *Lib. 83 Quaest.*, q. 21 (PL 40, 16).
2. 参见 Q. 4, a. 1.
3. 参见 Q. 22, a. 2, ad 2; q. 48, a. 2.

there is of motion in the act of limping is caused by the motive power, whereas what is unbalanced in it does not come from the motive power, but from the curvature of the leg. So, too, whatever there is of being and action in a bad action is reduced to God as the cause; whereas whatever defect is in it is not caused by God, but by the deficient secondary cause.

Reply Obj. 3. The sinking of a ship is attributed to the sailor as the cause, from the fact that he does not fulfill what the safety of the ship requires; but God does not fail in doing what is necessary for safety. Hence there is no parity.

Third Article

WHETHER THERE BE ONE HIGHEST EVIL WHICH IS THE CAUSE OF EVERY EVIL?

We proceed thus to the Third Article: —

Objection 1. It would seem that there is one highest evil which is the cause of every evil. For contrary effects have contrary causes. But contrariety is found in things, according to *Ecclus.* xxxiii. 15: *Good is set against evil, and life against death; so also is the sinner against a just man.* Therefore there are contrary principles, one of good, the other of evil.

Obj. 2. Further, if one contrary is in nature, so is the other, as it is said in *De Caelo*, ii.[1] But the highest good is in nature, and is the cause of every good, as was shown above.[2] Therefore, there is also a highest evil opposed to it as the cause of every evil.

Obj. 3. Further, as we find good and better things, so we find evil and worse. But good and better are so considered in relation to what is best. Therefore evil and worse are so considered in relation to some highest evil.

---

1. 参见 Aristotle, *De Caelo*, II, 3 (286a 23).
2. 参见 Q. 2, a. 3; q. 6, a. 2 and 4.

Obj. 4. Further, everything participated is reduced to what is essentially so. But things which are evil among us are evil, not essentially, but by participation. Therefore it is possible to find some highest essential evil, which is the cause of every evil.

Obj. 5. Further, whatever is accidental is reduced to that which is *per se*. But good is the accidental cause of evil. Therefore, we must suppose some highest evil which is the *per se* cause of evils. Nor can it be said that evil has no *per se* cause, but only an accidental cause; for it would then follow that evil would not exist in the majority of cases, but only in a few.

Obj. 6. Further, the evil of the effect is reduced to the evil of the cause; because the deficient effect comes from the deficient cause, as was said above. But we cannot proceed to infinity in this matter. Therefore, we must posit one first evil as the cause of every evil.

On the contrary, The highest good is the cause of every being, as was shown above.[1] Therefore there cannot be any principle opposed to it as the cause of evils.

I answer that, It appears from what precedes that there is no one first principle of evil, as there is one first principle of good.

First, because the first principle of good is essentially good, as was shown above.[2] But nothing can be evil in its very essence. For it was shown above that every being, as such, is good,[3] and that evil can exist only in good as in its subject.[4]

Secondly, because the first principle of good is the highest and perfect good which pre-contains in itself all goodness, as was shown above.[5] But there cannot be a highest evil, for, as was shown above,

1. 参见 Q. 2, a. 3; q. 6, a. 4.
2. 参见 Q. 6, a. 3 and 4.
3. 参见 Q. 5, a. 3.
4. 参见 Q. 48, a. 3.
5. 参见 Q. 6, a. 2.

although evil always lessens good, yet it never wholly consumes it;[1] and thus, since the good always survives, nothing can be wholly and perfectly evil. Therefore, the Philosopher says that *if the wholly evil could be, it would destroy itself.*[2] For if all good were destroyed (which is essential for something to be wholly evil), evil itself would be taken away, since its subject is good.

Thirdly, because the very nature of evil is against the idea of a first principle; both because every evil is caused by good, as was shown above, and because evil can be only an accidental cause, and thus it cannot be the first cause, for the accidental cause is subsequent to an essential cause, as appears in *Physics* ii.[3]

Those, however, who upheld two first principles, one good and the other evil, fell into this error from the same cause, whence also arose other strange notions of the ancients.[4] For they failed to consider the universal cause of all being, and considered only the particular causes of particular effects. Hence on that account, if they found a thing injurious to something by the power of its own nature, they thought that the very nature of that thing was evil; as, for instance, if one were to say that the nature of fire was evil because it burnt the house of some poor man. The judgment, however, of the goodness of anything does not depend upon its reference to any particular thing, but rather upon what it is in itself, and on its reference to the whole universe, wherein every part has its own perfectly ordered place, as was said above.[5] So, too, because they found two contrary particular causes of two contrary particular effects, they did not know how to reduce these contrary particular causes to a universal common cause; and therefore

1. 参见 Q. 48, a. 4.
2. 参见 *Eth.*, IV, 5 (1126a 12).
3. 参见 Aristotle, *Phys.*, II, 6 (198a 8).
4. 参见 Cf. St. Thomas, *C. G.*, II, 41; St. Augustine, *De Haeres.*, 14; 21; 46 (PL 42, 28; 29; 37).
5. 参见 Q. 47, a. 2, ad 1.

they extended the contrariety of causes even to the first principles. But since all contraries agree in something common, it is necessary to search for one common cause for them above their own contrary causes; just as above the contrary qualities of the elements there exists the power of the body of the heavens, and above all things that exist, no matter how, there exists one first principle of being, as was shown above.[1]

Reply Obj. 1. Contraries agree in one genus, and they also agree in the nature of being; and therefore, although they have contrary particular causes, nevertheless we must come at last to one first common cause.

Reply Obj. 2. Privation and habit belong naturally to the same subject. Now the subject of privation is a being in potentiality, as was said above.[2] Hence, since evil is privation of good, as appears from what was said above,[3] it is opposed to that good which has some potentiality, but not to the highest good, who is pure act.

Reply Obj. 3. Increase in intensity is in proportion to the nature of a thing. And just as the form is a perfection, so privation removes a perfection. Hence every form, perfection, and good is intensified by approach to a perfect terminus, while privation and evil are intensified by receding from that term. Hence a thing is not said to be evil and worse by reason of access to the highest evil, in the same way as a thing is said to be good and better by reason of access to the highest good.

Reply Obj. 4. No being is called evil by participation, but by privation of participation. Hence it is not necessary to reduce it to any essential evil.

Reply Obj. 5. Evil can have only an accidental cause, as was shown

1. 参见 Q. 2, a. 3.
2. 参见 Q. 48, a. 3.
3. 同上

above. Hence reduction to any *per se* cause of evil is impossible. Hence, to say that evil is in the majority of cases is absolutely false. For things which are generated and corrupted, in which alone there can be natural evil, are a very small part of the whole universe. Then again, defects in nature are found in every species only in a small number of cases. In man alone does evil manifest itself in the majority of cases. For the good of man as regards the senses of the body is not the good of man as man, but the good according to the reason. More men, however, follow the sense rather than the reason.

Reply Obj. 6. In the causes of evil we do not proceed to infinity, but reduce all evils to some good cause, whence evil follows accidentally.

注 1：该卷本分第一、第二卷两卷本，收录了《神学大全》第一集的所有内容，涉及 119 个问题，共 1688 页。
注 2：托马斯·阿奎那是天主教的一位神父，相关术语均参照天主教的习惯用法。

Thomas Aquinas

BASIC WRITINGS OF SAINT THOMAS AQUINAS II

〔意〕托马斯·阿奎那 著

圣托马斯基本著作

（第二卷）

方补课 导读 注释

上海译文出版社

TREATISE ON THE ANGELS

Question L
THE SUBSTANCE OF THE ANGELS ABSOLUTELY CONSIDERED
(*In Five Articles*)

NEXT we consider the distinction of corporeal and spiritual creatures: first, the purely spiritual creature which in Holy Scripture is called *angel*; secondly, the creature which is wholly corporeal;[1] thirdly, the composite creature, corporeal and spiritual, which is man.[2]

Concerning the angels, we consider first what belongs to their substance; secondly, what belongs to their intellect;[3] thirdly, what belongs to their will;[4] fourthly, what belongs to their creation.[5]

Their substance we consider absolutely, and also in relation to corporeal things.[6]

Concerning their substance, absolutely considered, there are five points of inquiry: (1) Whether there is any creature entirely spiritual and altogether incorporeal? (2) Supposing that an angel is such, we ask whether he is composed of matter and form? (3) We ask concerning their number. (4) Their difference from each other. (5) Their immortality or incorruptibility.

---

1. 参见 Q. 65.
2. 参见 Q. 75.
3. 参见 Q. 54.
4. 参见 Q. 59.
5. 参见 Q. 61.
6. 参见 Q. 51.

First Article
WHETHER AN ANGEL IS ALTOGETHER INCORPOREAL?

We proceed thus to the First Article:—

Objection 1. It would seem that an angel is not entirely incorporeal. For what is incorporeal only in relation to us, and not in relation to God, is not absolutely incorporeal. But Damascene says that *an angel is said to be incorporeal and immaterial as regards us; but compared to God he is corporeal and material.*[1] Therefore he is not absolutely incorporeal.

Obj. 2. Further, nothing is moved except a body, as the Philosopher says.[2] But Damascene says that *an angel is an ever movable intellectual substance.*[3] Therefore an angel is a corporeal substance.

Obj. 3. Further, Ambrose says: *Every creature is limited within its own nature.*[4] But to be limited belongs to bodies. Therefore, every creature is corporeal. Now angels are God's creatures, as appears from *Ps.* cxlviii. 2: *Praise ye* the Lord, *all His angels*; and, farther on (*verse* 4), *For He spoke, and they were made*; *He commanded, and they were created.* Therefore angels are corporeal.

On the contrary, It is said (*Ps.* ciii. 4): *Who makes His angels spirits.*

I answer that, There must be some incorporeal creatures. For what is principally intended by God in creatures is good, and this consists in assimilation to God Himself. Now the perfect assimilation of an effect to a cause is accomplished when the effect imitates the cause according to that whereby the cause produces the effect; as heat makes heat. Now God produces the creature by His intellect and will.[5] Hence, the perfection of the universe requires that there should be intellectual

---

1. 参见 *De Fide Orth.*, II, 3 (PG 94, 866).
2. 参见 Aristotle, *Phys.*, VI, 4 (234b 10).
3. 参见 *De Fide Orth.*, II, 3 (PG 94, 866).
4. 参见 *De Spir. Sancto*, I, 7 (PL 16, 753).
5. 参见 Q. 14, a. 8; q. 19, a. 4.

creatures. Now to understand cannot be the action of a body, nor of any corporeal power; for every body is limited to *here* and *now*. Hence the perfection of the universe requires the existence of an incorporeal creature.

The ancients, however, not properly realizing the meaning of understanding, and failing to make a proper distinction between sense and intellect, thought that nothing existed in the world but what could be apprehended by sense and imagination.[1] And because bodies alone fall under imagination, they supposed that *no being existed except bodies*, as the Philosopher observes.[2] Thence came the error of the Sadducees, who said that there was no spirit (*Acts* xxiii. 8).

But the very fact that intellect is above sense is a reasonable proof that there are some incorporeal realities comprehensible by the intellect alone.

Reply Obj. 1. Incorporeal substances rank between God and corporeal creatures. Now the medium compared to one extreme appears to be the other extreme, as what is tepid compared to heat seems to be cold; and thus it is said that the angels, compared to God, are material and corporeal, not, however, as if anything corporeal existed in them.

Reply Obj. 2. Motion is there taken in the sense in which to understand and to will are called motions. Therefore an angel is called an ever mobile substance, because he is always actually intelligent, and not as if he were sometimes actually and sometimes potentially, as we are. Hence it is clear that the objection rests on an equivocation.

Reply Obj. 3. To be circumscribed by local limits belongs only to bodies; whereas to be circumscribed by essential limits belongs to all creatures, both corporeal and spiritual. Hence Ambrose says that *although some things are not contained in corporeal place, still they are none the*

---

1. 参见 Cf. Aristotle, *De An.*, III, 3 (427a 21).
2. 参见 *Phys.* IV, 6 (213a 29).

less circumscribed by their substance.[1]

Second Article
WHETHER AN ANGEL IS COMPOSED OF MATTER AND FORM?

We proceed thus to the Second Article:—

Objection 1. It would seem that an angel is composed of matter and form[2]. For everything which is contained under any genus is composed of the genus and of the difference which, added to the genus, makes the species. But the genus is taken from the matter, and the difference from the form.[3] Therefore everything which is in a genus is composed of matter and form. But an angel is in the genus of substance. Therefore he is composed of matter and form.[4]

Obj. 2. Further, wherever the properties of matter exist, there matter is.[5] Now the properties of matter are to receive and to substand;[6] whence Boethius says that *a simple form cannot be a subject.* Now the above properties are found in the angel. Therefore an angel is composed of matter and form.[7]

Obj. 3. Further, form is act. So what is only form is pure act. But an angel is not pure act, for this belongs to God alone. Therefore an angel

---

1. 参见 *De Spir. Sancto*, I, 7 (PL 16, 753).
2. matter and form: 质素和形素
3. 参见 Aristotle, *Metaph.*, VII, 2 (1043a 19).—Cf. Boethius, *De Divisione* (PL 64, 879); Avicenna, *Metaph.*, V, 6 (90rb).
4. 参见 Argument of Alex, of Hales, *Summa Theol.*, II, I, no. 106 (II, 135); and of St. Bonaventure, *In II Sent.*, d. iii, a. 1, q. 1 (II, 90).—Cf. Avicebron, *Fons Vitae*, III, 18 (p. 118).
5. 参见 Cf. Avicebron, *Fons Vitae*, IV, 10 (pp. 231–232).
6. 参见 Cf. *op. cit.*, IV, 10 (p. 232); I, 11 (p. 15).—Cf. also St. Albert, *In II Sent.*, d, 1, a. 4 (XXVII, 13).
7. 参见 *De Trin.*, II (PL 64, 1250).—Cf. St. Albert, *In II Sent.*, d. iii, a. 4 (XXVII, 66); St. Bonaventure, *In II Sent.*, d. iii, a. 1, q. 1 (II, 90).

is not only form, but has a form in matter.[1]

Obj. 4. Further, form is properly limited and made finite by matter. So the form which is not in matter is an infinite form. But the form of an angel is not infinite, for every creature is finite. Therefore the form of an angel is in matter.[2]

On the contrary, Dionysius says: *The first creatures are understood to be not only immaterial but also incorporeal.*[3]

I answer that, Some[4] assert that the angels are composed of matter and form, which opinion Avicebron endeavored to establish in his book, the *Fount of Life*. For he supposes that whatever things are distinguished by the intellect are also distinct in reality.[5] Now as regards incorporeal substance, the intellect apprehends something which distinguishes it from corporeal substance, and also something which it has in common with it. Hence Avicebron concludes that what distinguishes incorporeal from corporeal substance is to it as a *form*, and whatever is subject to this distinguishing form, being as it were something common, is its *matter*.[6] Therefore, he asserts, the universal matter of spiritual and corporeal things is the same;[7] from which we are to understand that the form of incorporeal substance is impressed on the matter of spiritual realities, in the same way as the form of quantity is impressed on the matter of corporeal things.[8]

---

1. 参见 Argument of St. Bonaventure, *In II Sent.*, d. iii, a. 1, q. 1 (II, 91).
2. 参见 Cf. *ibid.*—Cf. also St. Albert, *Summa de Creatur.*, II, q. 7, a. 3 (XXXV, 101); Dominic Gundissalinus, *De An.*, VII (p. 56); Avicebron, *Fons Vitae*, IV, 6 (pp. 223–224).
3. 参见 *De Div. Nom.*, IV, 1 (PG 3, 693).
4. 参见 Alex, of Hales and St. Bonaventure especially.—Cf. E. Kleineidam, *Das Problem* (pp. 23–46).
5. 参见 *Fons Vitae*, II, 16 (p. 51); III, 46 (p. 182).
6. 参见 *Op. cit.*, IV, 2–4 (pp. 213–217).—Cf. St. Thomas, *De Subst. Sep.*, TV.
7. 参见 *Fons Vitae*, IV (pp. 211–256).—Cf. Dominic Gundissalinus, *De An.*, VII (p. 53).
8. 参见 Cf. *Fons Vitae*, II, 12 (p. 44).

But one glance is enough to show that there cannot be one matter in spiritual and in corporeal things. For it is not possible that a spiritual and a corporeal form should be received into the same part of matter, or otherwise one and the same thing would be corporeal and spiritual. Hence we are left with the alternative that one part of matter receives the corporeal form, and another receives the spiritual form. Matter, however, is not divisible into parts except as regarded under quantity; for without quantity substance is indivisible, as Aristotle says.[1] It would therefore follow that the matter of spiritual beings is subject to quantity; which cannot be. Therefore, it is impossible that corporeal and spiritual beings should have the same matter.

It is, further, impossible for an intellectual substance to have any kind of matter. For the operation belonging to anything is according to the mode of its substance. Now to understand is an altogether immaterial operation, as appears from its object; for it is from the object that any act receives its specification and nature. For a thing is understood according as it is abstracted from matter; because forms that exist in matter are individual forms which the intellect does not apprehend as such. Hence it must be that every intellectual substance is altogether immaterial.

But things distinguished by the intellect are not necessarily distinguished in reality; for the intellect does not apprehend things according to their mode of being, but according to its own. Hence material things, which are inferior to our intellect, exist in our intellect in a simpler mode than they exist in themselves. Angelic substances[2], on the other hand, are above our intellect. Hence our intellect cannot succeed in apprehending them as they are in themselves, but by its own mode, according as it apprehends composite things. And this is

1. 参见 Cf. Aristotle, *Phys.*, III, 5 (204a 9).
2. Angelic substance: 天使的本体

likewise the way in which it apprehends God.[1]

Reply Obj. 1. It is difference which constitutes the species. Now everything is constituted in a species according as it is determined to some special grade of being, because *the species of things are like numbers*, which differ by the addition and subtraction of unity, as the Philosopher says.[2] But in material things there is one thing which determines to a special grade, and that is the *form*; and another thing which is determined, and this is the *matter*; and hence the *genus* is taken from the latter, and the *difference* from the former. But in immaterial beings, there is no separate determinator and thing determined: each being by its own self holds a determinate grade in being; and therefore in them *genus* and *difference* are not taken from different things, but from one and the same. Nevertheless, there is a difference according to our mode of conception; for, inasmuch as our intellect considers this being as indeterminate, it derives the idea of *genus*, and inasmuch as it considers it determinately, it derives the idea of difference.

Reply Obj. 2. This reason is given in the book the *Fount of Life*, and it would be cogent, supposing that the manner of reception by the intellect and by matter were the same. But this is clearly false. For matter receives form, that thereby it may be constituted in some species, either of air, or of fire, or of something else. But the intellect does not receive form in the same way; otherwise the opinion of Empedocles, that we know earth by earth, and fire by fire, would be true.[3] But the intelligible form is in the intellect according to the very nature of a form; for it is so known by the intellect. Hence such a way of receiving is not that of matter, but of an immaterial substance.

Reply Obj. 3. Although there is no composition of matter and form in an angel, yet there is act and potentiality. And this can be made

---

1. 参见 Q. 3, a. 3, ad 1.
2. 参见 Aristotle, *Metaph.*, VII, 3 (1043b 34).
3. 参见 Cf. Aristotle, *De An.*, I, 2 (404b 13).

evident if we consider the nature of material things, which contain a twofold composition. The first is that of form and matter, from which the nature is constituted. Such a composite nature is not its own being, but being is its act. Hence the nature itself is related to its own being as potentiality to act. Therefore, if there be no matter, and given that the form itself subsists without matter, there nevertheless still remains the relation of the form to its very being, as of potentiality to act. And such a composition must be understood to be in the angels. This is what some say, that an angel is composed of that *whereby he is* and *what is*,[1] or *being* and *what is*, as Boethius says.[2] For *what is* is the form itself subsisting, and the being itself is that whereby the substance is; as the running is whereby the runner runs. But in God *being* and *what is* are not different, as was explained above.[3] Hence God alone is pure act.

Reply Obj. 4. Every creature is absolutely finite, inasmuch as its being is not absolutely subsisting, but is limited to some nature to which it belongs. But there is nothing preventing a creature from being considered relatively infinite. Material creatures are infinite on the part of matter, but finite in their form, which is limited by the matter which receives it. Immaterial created substances, however, are finite in their being, but they are infinite in the sense that their forms are not received in anything else. This would be as if we were to say, for example, that whiteness existing separately is infinite as regards the nature of whiteness, since it is not contracted to any one subject; while its *being* is finite as determined to some one special nature.

That is why it is said that *intelligence is finite from above*, as receiving its being from above itself, and *infinite from below*, as not received in

---

1. 参见 Cf. O. Lottin, in *Revue néo-scolastique de philosophie*, XXXIV, 1932, pp. 25, 28.
2. 参见 *De Hebdom.* (PL 64, 1311).
3. 参见 Q. 3, a. 4.

any matter.[1]

Third Article
WHETHER THE ANGELS EXIST IN ANY GREAT NUMBER?

We proceed thus to the Third Article: —

Objection 1. It would seem that the angels are not in great numbers. For number is a species of quantity, and follows the division of a continuous body. But this cannot be in the angels, since they are incorporeal, as was shown above. Therefore the angels cannot exist in any great number.

Obj. 2. Further, the more a being approaches to unity, so much the less is it multiplied, as is evident in numbers. But among other created natures the angelic nature approaches nearest to God. Therefore, since God is supremely one, it seems that there is the least possible number in the angelic nature.

Obj. 3. Further, the proper effect of separate substances seems to be the movement of the heavenly bodies. But the movements of the heavenly bodies fall within some small determined number, which we can comprehend. Therefore the angels are not in greater number than the movements of the heavenly bodies.

Obj. 4. Dionysius says that *all intelligible and intellectual substances subsist because of the rays of the divine goodness.*[2] But a ray is multiplied only according to the diversity of its recipients. Now it cannot be said that their matter is receptive of an intelligible ray, since intellectual substances are immaterial, as was shown above. Therefore it seems that the multiplication of intellectual substances can be only according to the requirements of the first bodies —that is, the heavenly bodies; namely, so that the descent of these divine rays may somehow reach

---

1. 参见 *De Causis*, XVI (p. 174).
2. 参见 *De Div. Nom.*, IV, 1 (PG 3, 693).

down to them. Hence, the same conclusion is to be drawn as before.

On the contrary, It is said (*Dan.* vii. 10): *Thousands of thousands ministered to Him, and ten thousand times a hundred thousand stood before Him.*

I answer that, There have been various opinions with regard to the number of the separate substances. Plato contended that the separate substances are the species of sensible things.[1] This is as though we were to maintain that human nature is a separate substance of itself. According to this view it would have to be maintained that the number of the separate substances is the number of the species of sensible things.[2] Aristotle, however, refutes this view on the ground that matter is of the nature of the species of sensible things.[3] Consequently, separate substances cannot be the exemplary species of these sensible things; on the contrary, they have their own natures, which are higher than the natures of sensible things. Now Aristotle held that these more perfect natures are related to sensible things in the capacity of movers and ends;[4] and therefore he strove to find out the number of the separate substances on the basis of the number of the primary motions.

But since this appears to be against the teachings of Sacred Scripture, Rabbi Moses the Jew[5], wishing to bring both into harmony, held that the angels, in so far as they are named immaterial substances, are multiplied according to the number of heavenly motions or bodies, as Aristotle held.[6] At the same time he contended that in the Scriptures even men bearing a divine message are called angels, as are even *the powers of natural things*, which manifest God's

---

1. 参见 Cf. Aristotle, *Metaph.*, I, 6 (987b 7).
2. 参见 Cf. *op. cit.*, I, 11 (990b 6).
3. 参见 Cf. *op. cit.*, VII, 1 (1042a 25).
4. 参见 *Op. cit.*, XI, 8 (1073a 33; 1074a 20).
5. Rabbi Moses the Jew: 犹太的梅瑟拉比
6. 参见 *Guide*, II, 4 (p. 157).

almighty power.[1] It is, however, quite foreign to the custom of the Scriptures for the powers of irrational things to be designated as angels.

Hence it must be said that the angels, even inasmuch as they are immaterial substances, exist in exceeding great number, far beyond all material multitude. This is what Dionysius says: *There are many blessed armies of the heavenly intelligences, surpassing the weak and limited reckoning of our material numbers.*[2] The reason for this is that, since it is the perfection of the universe that God chiefly intends in the creation of things, the more perfect some things are, the greater the abundance in which they are created by God. Now, just as in bodies such abundance is determined according to their magnitude, so in incorporeal beings it is determined according to their multitude. We see, in fact, that incorruptible bodies, which are the most perfect of bodies, exceed corruptible bodies almost incomparably in magnitude; for the entire [sublunary] sphere of things active and passive is very small in comparison with the heavenly bodies. Hence it is reasonable to conclude that immaterial substances exceed material substances in multitude as it were incomparably.

Reply Obj. 1. In the angels number is not that of discrete quantity, caused by division of what is continuous, but that which is caused by the distinction of forms, according as multitude is reckoned among the transcendentals[3], as was said above.[4]

Reply Obj. 2. From the fact that the angelic nature is nearest to God, it must needs have least of multitude in its composition, but not so as to be found in few subjects.

---

1. 参见 *Op. cit.*, II, 6 (p. 160, 161).
2. 参见 *De Cael. Hier.*, XIV, 1 (PG 3, 321).
3. the transcendentals: 超验主义者
4. 参见 Q. 30, a. 3.

Reply Obj. 3. This is Aristotle's argument,[1] and it would conclude necessarily if the separate substances existed for the sake of corporeal substances. For thus immaterial substances would exist to no purpose, unless some motion from them were to appear in corporeal things. But it is not true that immaterial substances exist because of the corporeal, because the end is nobler than the means to the end. Hence Aristotle himself says that this is not a necessary argument, but a probable one.[2] He was forced to make use of this argument, since only through sensible things can we come to know the intelligible.

Reply Obj. 4. This argument comes from the opinion of those who held that matter is the cause of the distinction of things. But this was refuted above.[3] Accordingly, the multiplication of the angels is not to be taken according to matter, nor according to bodies, but according to the divine wisdom devising the various orders of immaterial substances.

Fourth Article
WHETHER THE ANGELS DIFFER IN SPECIES?

We proceed thus to the Fourth Article: —

Objection 1. It would seem that the angels do not differ in species. For since the *difference* is nobler than the *genus*, all things which agree in what is noblest in them agree likewise in their ultimate constitutive difference; and so they are the same according to species. But all the angels agree in what is noblest in them — that is to say, in intellectuality. Therefore all the angels are of one species.

Obj. 2. Further, more and less do not change a species. But the

1. 参见 *Metaph.*, XI, 8 (1073a 37).
2. 同上 (1074a 16).
3. 参见 Q. 47, a. 1.

angels seem to differ only from one another according to more and less—namely, as one is simpler than another, and of keener intellect. Therefore the angels do not differ specifically.

Obj. 3. Further, soul and angel are contra-distinguished from each other. But all souls are of one species. So therefore are the angels.

Obj. 4. Further, the more perfect a thing is in nature, the more it ought to be multiplied. But this would not be so if there were but one individual under one species. Therefore there are many angels of one species.

On the contrary, In things of one species there is no gradation of *first* and *second*, as the Philosopher says.[1] But in the angels even of the one order there are first, middle, and last, as Dionysius says.[2] Therefore the angels are not of the same species.

I answer that, Some[3] have said that all spiritual substances, even souls, are of the one species. Others,[4] again, that all the angels are of the one species, but not souls. And others[5] allege that all the angels of one hierarchy, or even of one order, are of the one species.

But this is impossible. For things which agree in species but differ in number, agree in form but are distinguished materially. If, therefore, the angels are not composed of matter and form, as was said above, it follows that it is impossible for two angels to be of one species; just as it would be impossible to say that there are several separate whitenesses, or several humanities, since whitenesses are not several, except in so far as they are in several substances. And even if the angels had matter,

---

1. 参见 Aristotle, *Metaph.*, II, 3 (999a 6).
2. 参见 *De Cael. Hier.*, X, 2 (PG 3, 273).
3. 参见 Cf. *C. G.*, II, 95, where Origen is mentioned (*Peri Archon*, I, 8; II, 9 [PG 11, 176; 229]).
4. 参见 St, Bonaventure, *In II Sent.*, d. iii, pt. 1, a. 2, q. 1 (II, 103); d. ix, a. 1, q. 1 (II, 242).—St. Albert, *In II Sent.*, d. ix, a. 7 (XXVII, 204).—Cf. prop. 81 and 96 of those condemned in 1277: H. Denifle, *Chartularium*, no. 473 (I, 548).
5. 参见 Alex. of Hales, *Summa Theol.*, II, I, no. 113 ; no. 114 (II, 153; 155).

not even then could there be several angels of one species. For it would then be necessary for the principle of the distinction of one from the other to be matter, but not according to the division of quantity, since the angels are incorporeal, but according to the diversity of their powers. Now such diversity of matter causes diversity not merely of species, but of genus.

Reply Obj. 1. *Difference* is nobler than *genus*, as the determined is more noble than the undetermined, and the proper than the common, but not as one nature is nobler than another; otherwise it would be necessary that all irrational animals be of the same species, or that there should be in them some form which is higher than the sensible soul. Therefore irrational animals differ in species according to the various determined degrees of sensitive nature; and in like manner all the angels differ in species according to the diverse degrees of intellectual nature.

Reply Obj. 2. More and less change the species, not according as they are caused by the intensity or weakening of one form, but according as they are caused by forms of diverse degrees; for instance, if we say that fire is more perfect than air. It is in this way that the angels are diversified according to more and less.

Reply Obj. 3. The good of the species preponderates[1] over the good of the individual. Hence it is much better that the species be multiplied in the angels than that individuals be multiplied in one species.

Reply Obj. 4. Numerical multiplication, since it can be drawn out infinitely, is not intended by the agent, but only specific multiplication, as was said above.[2] Hence the perfection of the angelic nature requires the multiplying of species, but not the multiplying of individuals in one species.

---

1. preponderate: 超过；胜过
2. 参见 Q. 47, a. 3, ad 2.

Fifth Article
WHETHER THE ANGELS ARE INCORRUPTIBLE?

We proceed thus to the Fifth Article:—

Objection 1. It would seem that the angels are not incorruptible, for Damascene, speaking of the angel, says that he is *an intellectual substance, partaking of immortality by grace, and not by nature.*[1]

Obj. 2. Further, Plato says in the *Timaeus: O gods of gods, whose maker and father am I: You are indeed my works, dissoluble by nature, yet indissoluble because I so will it.*[2] But by gods such as these Plato can understand only the angels. Therefore the angels are corruptible by their nature.

Obj. 3. Further, according to Gregory, *all things would tend towards nothing, unless the hand of the Almighty preserved them.*[3] But what can be brought to nothing is corruptible. Therefore, since the angels were made by God, it would appear that they are corruptible of their own nature.

On the contrary, Dionysius says that the intellectual substances *have unfailing life, being free from all corruption, death, matter, and generation.*[4]

I answer that, It must necessarily be maintained that the angels are incorruptible of their own nature. The reason for this is that nothing is corrupted except by the separation of its form from matter. Hence, since an angel is a subsisting form, as is clear from what was said above, it is impossible for its substance to be corruptible. For what belongs to anything, considered in itself, can never be separated from it; but what belongs to a thing, considered in relation to something else, can be separated, when that something else, in view of which it belonged to it, is taken away. Roundness can never be taken away

---

1. 参见 *De Fide Orth.*, II, 3 (PG 94, 868).
2. 参见 Plato, *Timaeus*, p. 41a (trans. Chalcidius, XVI, p. 169).
3. 参见 *Moral.*, XVI, 37 (PL 75, 1143).
4. 参见 *De Div. Nom.*, IV, 1 (PG 3, 693).

from the circle, because it belongs to it of itself; but a bronze circle can lose roundness, if the bronze be deprived of its circular shape. Now *to be* belongs to a form considered in itself; for everything is an actual being through its form. Now matter is an actual being by the form. Consequently, a subject composed of matter and form ceases to be actually when the form is separated from the matter. But if the form subsists in its own being, as happens in the angels, as was said above, it cannot lose its being. Therefore, the angel's immateriality is the reason why it is incorruptible by its own nature.

A token of this incorruptibility can be gathered from its intellectual operation; for since everything acts according as it is actual, the operation of a being indicates its mode of being. Now the species and nature of the operation is understood from the object. But an intelligible object, being above time, is everlasting. Hence every intellectual substance is incorruptible of its own nature.

Reply Obj. 1. Damascene is dealing with perfect immortality, which includes complete immutability; since *every change is a kind of death*, as Augustine says.[1] The angels obtain perfect immutability only by grace, as will appear later.[2]

Reply Obj. 2. By the expression *gods* Plato understands the heavenly bodies, which he supposed to be made up of elements, and therefore dissoluble of their own nature; yet they are for ever preserved in existence by the divine will.

Reply Obj. 3. As was observed above,[3] there is a kind of necessary thing which has a cause of its necessity. Hence it is not repugnant to a necessary or incorruptible being to depend for its being on another as its cause. Therefore, when it is said that all things, even the angels, would lapse into nothing, unless preserved by God, this does not

1. 参见 *Contra Maximin.*, II, 12 (PL 42, 768).
2. 参见 Q. 62, a. 2 and 8.
3. 参见 Q. 44, a. 1, ad 2.

mean that there is any principle of corruption in the angels, but that the being of the angels is dependent upon God as its cause. For a thing is not said to be corruptible because God can reduce it to non-being, by withdrawing His act of preservation; but because it has some principle of corruption within itself, or some contrariety, or at least the potentiality of matter.

Question LI
THE ANGELS IN COMPARISON WITH BODIES
(*In Three Articles*)

WE next inquire about the angels in comparison with corporeal things. And in the first place about their comparison with bodies; secondly, of the angels in comparison with corporeal places;[1] and, thirdly, of their comparison with local movement.[2]

Under the first heading there are three points of inquiry: (1) Whether angels have bodies naturally united to them? (2) Whether they assume bodies? (3) Whether they exercise functions of life in the bodies assumed?

First Article
WHETHER THE ANGELS HAVE BODIES NATURALLY UNITED TO THEM?

We proceed thus to the First Article:—

Objection 1. It would seem that angels have bodies naturally united to them. For Origen says: *It is God's attribute alone — that is, it belongs to the Father, the Son, and the Holy Ghost, as a property of nature, that He is understood to exist without any material substance and without any companionship of corporeal addition.*[3] Bernard likewise says: *Let us*

---

1. 参见 Q. 52.
2. 参见 Q. 53.
3. 参见 *Peri Archon*, I, 6 (PG 11, 170).

assign incorporeity to God alone even as we do immortality, whose nature alone, neither for its own sake nor because of anything else, needs the help of any corporeal organ. But it is clear that every created spirit needs corporeal assistance.[1] Augustine also says: *The demons are called aerial animals because their nature is akin to that of aerial bodies.*[2] But the nature of demons and angels is the same. Therefore angels have bodies naturally united to them.

Obj. 2. Further, Gregory calls an angel a rational animal.[3] But every animal is composed of body and soul. Therefore angels have bodies naturally united to them.

Obj. 3. Further, life is more perfect in the angels than in souls. But the soul not only lives, it also gives life to the body. Therefore the angels animate bodies which are naturally united to them.

On the contrary, Dionysius says that *the angels are understood to be incorporeal and immaterial.*[4]

I answer that, The angels have not bodies naturally united to them. For whatever belongs to any nature as an accident is not found universally in that nature. Thus, for instance, to have wings, because it is not of the essence of an animal, does not belong to every animal. But since to understand is not the act of a body, nor of any corporeal power, as will be shown later,[5] it follows that to have a body united to it is not of the nature of an intellectual substance, as such; but it befalls some intellectual substance because of something else. In this way it belongs to the human soul to be united to a body, because it is imperfect and exists potentially in the genus of intellectual substances, not having the fullness of knowledge in its own nature, but acquiring

---

1. 参见 *In Cant.*, Serm. VI (PL 183, 803).
2. 参见 *De Genesi ad Litt.*, III, 10 (PL 34, 284).
3. 参见 *In Evang.*, I, hom. X (PL 76, 1110).
4. 参见 *De Div. Nom.*, IV, 1 (PG 3, 693).
5. 参见 Q. 75, a. 2.

it from sensible things through the bodily senses, as will be explained later on.[1] Now whenever we find something imperfect in any genus we must presuppose something perfect in that genus. Therefore, there are some intellectual substances perfect in intellectual nature, which do not need to acquire knowledge from sensible things. Consequently not all intellectual substances are united to bodies, but some are separated from bodies. These we call angels.

Reply Obj. 1. As was said above, it was the opinion of some that every being is a body,[2] and consequently some seem to have thought that there were no incorporeal substances existing except as united to bodies,[3] so much so that some even held that God was the soul of the world, as Augustine tells us.[4] Now this is contrary to Catholic Faith, which asserts that God is exalted above all things, according to *Psalm* viii. 2: *Thy magnificence is exalted beyond the heavens.* Origen, therefore, through refusing to say such a thing of God, followed the opinion of others regarding the other substances,[5] being deceived here, as also in many other points, by following the opinions of the ancient philosophers. Bernard's expression can be explained to mean that the created spirit needs some bodily instrument, which is not naturally united to it, but assumed for some purpose, as will be explained. Augustine speaks, not as asserting the fact, but merely using the opinion of the Platonists, who maintained that there are some aerial animals, which they termed demons.[6]

Reply Obj. 2. Gregory calls the angel a rational animal metaphorically, because of the likeness to the rational nature.

---

1. 参见 Q. 84, a. 6; q. 89, a. 1.
2. 参见 Q. 50, a. 1.
3. 参见 Cf. Origen, *Peri Archon*, I, 6 (PG 11, 170); Pseudo-Augustine (Alcher of Clairvaux), *De Spir. et An.*, 18 (PL 40, 793).—Cf. below, q. 54, a. 5.
4. 参见 *De Civit. Dei*, VII, 6 (PL 41, 199).
5. 参见 *Peri Archon*, I, 6 (PG 11, 170).
6. 参见 *De Civit. Dei*, VIII, 16; IX, 8 (PL 41, 241; 263).

Reply Obj. 3. To give life effectively is an absolute perfection. Hence it belongs also to God, as is said (*1 Kings* ii. 6): *The Lord killeth, and maketh alive.* But to give life formally belongs to a substance which is part of some nature, and which has not within itself the full nature of the species. Hence an intellectual substance which is not united to a body is more perfect than one which is united to a body.

Second Article
WHETHER ANGELS ASSUME BODIES?

We proceed thus to the Second Article:—

Objection 1. It would seem that angels do not assume bodies. For there is nothing superfluous in the work of an angel, just as there is none in the work of nature. But it would be superfluous for the angels to assume bodies, because an angel has no need for a body, since his own power surpasses every bodily power. Therefore an angel does not assume a body.

Obj. 2. Further, every assumption is terminated in some union, because to assume implies a taking to oneself [*ad se sumere*]. But a body is not united to an angel as to a form, as has been stated; while in so far as it is united to the angel as to a mover, it is not said to be assumed, or otherwise it would follow that all bodies moved by the angels are assumed by them. Therefore the angels do not assume bodies.

Obj. 3. Further, angels do not assume bodies made of earth or water, or they could not suddenly disappear; nor again of fire, otherwise they would burn whatever things they touched; nor again of air, because air is without shape or color. Therefore the angels do not assume bodies.

On the contrary, Augustine says that angels appeared to Abraham under assumed bodies.[1]

---

1. 参见 *Op. cit.*, XVI, 29 (PL 41, 508).

I answer that, Some have maintained that the angels never assume bodies, but that all that we read in Scripture of the apparitions of angels happened in prophetic vision — that is, according to imagination.[1] But this is contrary to the intent of Scripture, for whatever is beheld in imaginary vision is only in the beholder's imagination, and consequently is not seen by everybody. Yet divine Scripture from time to time introduces angels so apparent as to be seen commonly by all: *e.g.*, the angels who appeared to Abraham were seen by him and by his whole family, by Lot, and by the citizens of Sodom; and in like manner the angel who appeared to Tobias was seen by all present. From all this it is clearly shown that such apparitions were beheld by bodily vision, whereby the reality seen exists outside the person beholding it, and can accordingly be seen by all. Now by such vision only a body can be beheld. Consequently, since the angels are not bodies, nor have they bodies naturally united with them, as is clear from what has been said,[2] it follows that they sometimes assume bodies.

Reply Obj. 1. Angels need an assumed body, not for themselves, but on our account, namely, so that by conversing familiarly with men they may give evidence of that intellectual companionship which men expect to have with them in the life to come. Moreover, that angels assumed bodies under the Old Testament was a figurative indication that the Word of God would take a human body; because all the apparitions in the Old Testament were ordained to that whereby the Son of God appeared in the flesh.

Reply Obj. 2. The assumed body is united to the angel not as its form, nor merely as its mover, but as the mover represented by the assumed movable body. For, just as in the Sacred Scripture[3] the

---

1. 参见 Maimonides, *Guide*, II, 6 (p. 162).
2. 参见 A. 1; q. 50, a. 1.
3. the Sacred Scripture: 神圣经典，通常指《圣经》

properties of intelligible things are set forth by the likenesses of sensible things, in the same way by divine power sensible bodies are so fashioned by angels as fittingly to represent the intelligible properties of an angel. And this is what we mean by an angel assuming a body.

Reply Obj. 3. Although air, as long as it is in a state of rarefaction, has neither shape nor color, yet when condensed it can both be shaped and colored, as appears in the clouds. Even so the angels assume bodies of air, condensing it by divine power in so far as is needful for forming the assumed body.

Third Article
WHETHER THE ANGELS EXERCISE FUNCTIONS OF LIFE IN THE BODIES ASSUMED?

We proceed thus to the Third Article:—

Objection 1. It would seem that the angels exercise functions of life in assumed bodies. For a pretense of truth is unbecoming in angels. But it would be pretense if the body assumed by them, which seems to live and to exercise vital functions, did not possess these functions. Therefore the angels exercise functions of life in the assumed body.

Obj. 2. Further, in the works of the angels there is nothing without a purpose. But eyes, nostrils, and the other instruments of the senses, would be fashioned without a purpose in the body assumed by the angel, if he did not perceive by their means. Consequently, the angel perceives by the assumed body; and this is the most special function of life.

Obj. 3. Further, to move hither and thither is one of the functions of life, as the Philosopher says.[1] But the angels are manifestly seen to move in their assumed bodies. For it is said (*Gen.* xviii. 16) that

---

1. 参见 Aristotle, *De An.*, II, 2 (413a 23).

Abraham walked with the angels, who had appeared to him, *bringing them on the way*; and when Tobias said to the angel (*Tob.* v. 7, 8): *Knowest thou the way that leadeth to the city of the Medes?* he answered: *I know it; and I have often walked through all the ways thereof.* Therefore the angels often exercise functions of life in assumed bodies.

Obj. 4. Further, speech is the function of a living subject, for it is produced by the voice, while the voice itself is a sound conveyed from the mouth.[1] But it is evident from many passages of Sacred Scripture that angels spoke in assumed bodies. Therefore in their assumed bodies they exercise functions of life.

Obj. 5. Further, eating is properly an animal function. Hence the Lord after His Resurrection[2] ate with His disciples in proof of having resumed life (*Luke* xxiv. 41). Now when angels appeared in their assumed bodies they ate, and Abraham offered them food, after having previously adored them as God (*Gen.* xviii. 2). Therefore the angels exercise functions of life in assumed bodies.

Obj. 6. Further, to beget offspring is a vital act. But this has befallen the angels in their assumed bodies; for it is related: *After the sons of God went in to the daughters of men, and they brought forth children, these are the mighty men of old, men of renown* (*Gen.* vi. 4). Consequently the angels exercised vital functions in their assumed bodies.

On the contrary, The bodies assumed by angels have no life, as was stated in the previous article. Therefore they cannot exercise functions of life through assumed bodies.

I answer that, Some functions of living subjects have something in common with other operations; just as speech, which is the function of a living creature, agrees with other sounds of inanimate things, in so far as it is sound; and walking agrees with other movements, in so far as it is movement. Consequently vital functions can be performed

---

1. 参见 Aristotle, *De An.*, II, 8 (420b 5).
2. His Resurrection: 指耶稣基督的复活

in assumed bodies by the angels, as to that which is common in such operations, but not as to that which is special to living subjects; because, according to the Philosopher, *that which has the power has the action.*[1] Hence nothing can have a function of life except what has life, which is the potential principle of such action.

Reply Obj. 1. As it is in no wise contrary to truth for intelligible things to be set forth in Scripture under sensible figures, since it is not said for the purpose of maintaining that intelligible things are sensible, but in order that the properties of intelligible things may be understood according to some likeness through sensible figures; so it is not contrary to the truth of the holy angels that their assumed bodies appear to be living men, although they really are not. For the bodies are assumed merely for this purpose, that the spiritual properties and works of the angels may be manifested by the properties of man and of his works. This could not be done so fittingly if they were to assume true men, because the properties of such men would lead us to men, and not to angels.

Reply Obj. 2. Sensation is entirely a vital function. Consequently it can in no way be said that the angels perceive through the organs of their assumed bodies. Yet such bodies are not fashioned in vain, for they are not fashioned for the purpose of sensation through them, but to this end, that by such bodily organs the spiritual powers of the angels may be made manifest; just as by. the eye the power of the angel's knowledge is pointed out, and other powers by the other members, as Dionysius teaches.[2]

Reply Obj. 3. Movement coming from a united mover is a proper function of life, but the bodies assumed by the angels are not thus moved, since the angels are not their forms. Yet the angels are moved accidentally, when such bodies are moved, since they are in them as

---

1. 参见 *De Somno*, I (454a 8).
2. 参见 *De Cael. Hier.*, XV, 3 (PG 3, 328).

movers are in the moved; and thus they are *here* in such a way as not to be *elsewhere*, which cannot be said of God. Accordingly, although God is not moved when the things are moved in which He exists, since He is everywhere, yet the angels are moved accidentally according to the movement of the bodies assumed. But they are not moved according to the movement of the heavenly bodies, even though they be in them as movers in the things moved, because the heavenly bodies do not change place in their entirety; nor for the spirit which moves a sphere is there any fixed locality according to any restricted part of the world's substance, which now is in the east, and now in the west, but according to a fixed quarter, because the *moving power is always in the east*, as is stated in *Physics* viii.[1]

Reply Obj. 4. Properly speaking, the angels do not talk through their assumed bodies; yet there is a semblance of speech, in so far as they fashion sounds in the air like to human voices.

Reply Obj. 5. Properly speaking, the angels cannot be said to eat, because eating involves the taking of food convertible into the substance of the eater.

Although after the Resurrection food was not converted into the substance of Christ's body, but resolved into pre-existing matter, nevertheless Christ had a body of such a nature that food could be changed into it. Hence it was a true eating. But the food taken by angels was neither changed into the assumed body, nor was the body of such a nature that food could be changed into it; consequently, it was not a true eating, but figurative of spiritual eating. This is what the angel said to Tobias: *When I was with you, I seemed indeed to eat and to drink; but I use an invisible meat and drink* (*Tob.* xii. 19).

Abraham offered them food, deeming them to be men. In them, nevertheless, he worshipped God, in the manner in which God is wont

1. 参见 Cf. Aristotle, *De Caelo*, II, 2 (285b 18).

to be in the prophets, as Augustine says.[1]

Reply Obj. 6. As Augustine says, *Many persons affirm that they have had the experience, or have heard from such as have experienced it, that the Satyrs and Fauns, whom the common folk call incubi, have often presented themselves before women, and have sought and procured intercourse with them. Hence it is folly to deny it. But God's holy angels could not fall in such fashion before the deluge. Hence by the sons of God are to be understood the sons of Seth, who were good, while by the daughters of men the Scripture designates those who sprang from the race of Cain. Nor is it to be wondered at that giants should be born of them, for they were not all giants, albeit there were many more before than after the deluge.*[2] Still if some are occasionally begotten from the union of demons, it is not from the seed of such demons, nor from their assumed bodies, but from the seed of men taken for the purpose, as when the demon assumes first the form of a woman, and afterwards of a man; just as they take the seed of other things for other generating purposes, as Augustine says,[3] so that the person born is not the child of a demon, but of a man.

---

1. 参见 *De Civit. Dei*, XVI, 29 (PL 41, 509).
2. 参见 *Op. cit.*, XV, 23 (PL 41, 468).
3. 参见 *De Trin.*, III, 8, 9 (PL 42, 876; 878).

Question LII
THE ANGELS IN RELATION TO PLACE
(*In Three Articles*)

WE now inquire into the place of the angels. Touching this there are three subjects of inquiry: (1) Is the angel in a place? (2) Can he be in several places at once? (3) Can several angels be in the same place?

First Article
WHETHER AN ANGEL IS IN A PLACE?

We proceed thus to the First Article:—

Objection 1. It would seem that an angel is not in a place. For Boethius says: *The common opinion of the learned is that things incorporeal are not in a place.*[1] And again, Aristotle observes that *it is not everything existing which is in a place, but only a movable body.*[2] But an angel is not a body, as was shown above.[3] Therefore an angel is not in a place.

Obj. 2. Further, place is a *quantity having position.* But everything which is in a place has some position. Now to have a position cannot befit an angel, since his substance is devoid of quantity, the proper difference of which is to have position. Therefore an angel is not in a place.

Obj. 3. Further, to be in a place is to be measured and to be contained by such place, as is evident from the Philosopher.[4] But an

---

1. 参见 *De Hebdom.* (PL 64, 1311).
2. 参见 *Phys.*, IV, 5 (212b 28).
3. 参见 Q. 50, a. 1.
4. 参见 *Phys.*, IV, 12 (221a 18).

angel can neither be measured nor contained by a place, because the container is more formal than the contained; as air with regard to water.[1] Therefore an angel is not in a place.

On the contrary, It is said in the Collect: *Let Thy holy angels, who dwell herein, keep us in peace.*

I answer that, It is befitting an angel to be in a place, yet an angel and a body are said to be in a place in quite a different sense. A body is said to be in a place in such a way that it is applied to such place according to the contact of dimensive quantity; but there is no such quantity in the angels, for theirs is a virtual one. Consequently an angel is said to be in a corporeal place by application of the angelic power in any manner whatever to any place.

Accordingly there is no need for saying that an angel can be deemed commensurate with a place, or that he occupies a space in a continuum; for this is proper to a located body which is endowed with dimensive quantity. In similar fashion, it is not necessary on this account for the angel to be contained by a place. For an incorporeal substance virtually contains the thing with which it comes into contact, and is not contained by it: thus, the soul is in the body as containing it, not as contained by it. In the same way, an angel is said to be in a place which is corporeal, not as being contained, but as somehow containing it.

And hereby we have the answers to the objections.

Second Article
WHETHER AN ANGEL CAN BE IN SEVERAL PLACES AT ONCE?

We proceed thus to the Second Article:—

Objection 1. It would seem that an angel can be in several places at

---

1. 参见 *Op. cit.*, IV, 5 (213a 2).

once. For an angel is not less endowed with power than the soul. But the soul is in several places at once, for it is entirely in every part of the body, as Augustine says.[1] Therefore an angel can be in several places at once.

Obj. 2. Further, an angel is in the body which he assumes; and, since the body which he assumes is continuous, it would appear that he is in every part of it. But according to its various parts there are various places. Therefore the angel is at one time in various places.

Obj. 3. Further, Damascene says that *where the angel operates, there he is.*[2] But occasionally he operates in several places at one time, as is evident from the angel destroying Sodom[3] (*Gen.* xix. 25). Therefore an angel can be in several places at the one time.

On the contrary, Damascene says that *while the angels are in heaven, they are not on earth.*[4]

I answer that, An angel's power and nature are finite, whereas the divine power and essence, which is the universal cause of all things, is infinite. Consequently, through His power God touches all things, and is not present merely in some places, but everywhere. Now since the angel's power is finite, it does not extend to all things, but to one determined thing. For whatever is compared with one power must be compared with it as one determined thing. Consequently since all being is compared as one thing to God's universal power, so one particular being is compared as something one to the angelic power. Hence, since the angel is in a place by the application of his power to the place, it follows that he is not everywhere, nor in several places, but in only one place.

Some, however, have been deceived in this matter. For some

---

1. 参见 *De Trin.*, VI, 6 (PL 42, 929); *De Immortal. An.*, XVI (PL 32, 1034); *Contra Epist. Manich.*, XVI (PL 42, 185).
2. 参见 *De Fide Orth.*, I, 13 (PG 94, 853).
3. destroying Sodom: 毁灭的索多玛城。该城因恶行横行而遭毁灭，见圣经创世纪第 19 章。
4. 参见 *Op. cit.*, II, 3 (PG 94, 869).

who were unable to go beyond the reach of their imaginations, supposed the indivisibility of the angel to be like that of a point;[1] and consequently they thought that an angel could be only in a place which is a point. But they were manifestly deceived, because a point is something indivisible, yet having position, whereas the angel is indivisible, and beyond the genus of quantity and position. Consequently there is no occasion for determining in his regard one indivisible place as to position: any place which is either divisible or indivisible, great or small, suffices, according as he deliberately applies his power to a great or to a small body. So the entire body to which he is applied by his power corresponds as one place to him.

Nor, if any angel moves the heavens, is it necessary for him to be everywhere. First of all, because his power is applied only to what is first moved by him. Now there is one part of the heavens in which there is movement first, namely, the part to the east; hence the Philosopher attributes the power of the heavenly mover to the part which is in the east.[2] Secondly, because philosophers do not hold that one separate substance moves all the spheres immediately.[3] Hence it need not be everywhere.

So, then, it is evident that to be in a place pertains quite differently to a body, to an angel, and to God. For a body is in a place in a circumscribed fashion, since it is measured by the place. An angel, however, is not there in a circumscribed fashion, since he is not measured by the place, but definitively, because he is in one place in such a manner that he is not in another. But God is neither circumscriptively nor definitively there, because He is everywhere.

---

1. 参见 Cf. below, q. 52, a. 3.
2. 参见 Cf. Aristotle, *De Caelo*, II, 2 (285b 18).
3. 参见 Cf. Avicenna, *Metaph.*, IX, 2 (103va); Averroes, I*n Metaph.*, XII, comm. 43 (VIII, 153v); comm. 44 (VIII, 153v).—Cf. also Aristotle, *Metaph.*, XII, 8 (1073a 32).

From this we can easily gather an answer to the objections: because the entire subject to which the angelic power is immediately applied is reputed as one place, even though it be continuous.

Third Article
WHETHER SEVERAL ANGELS CAN BE AT THE SAME TIME IN THE SAME PLACE?

We proceed thus to the Third Article:—

Objection 1. It would seem that several angels can be at the same time in the same place. For several bodies cannot be at the same time in the same place, because they fill the place. But angels do not fill a place, because only a body fills a place so that it be not empty, as appears from the Philosopher.[1] Therefore several angels can be in the one place.

Obj. 2. Further, there is a greater difference between an angel and a body than there is between two angels. But an angel and a body are at one time in the same place, because there is no place which is not filled with a sensible body, as is proved in *Physics* iv.[2] Much more, then, can two angels be in the same place.

Obj. 3. Further, the soul is in every part of the body, according to Augustine.[3] But demons, although they do not obsess souls, do occasionally obsess bodies; and thus the soul and the demon are at one time in the same place. For the same reason, consequently, so are all other spiritual substances.

On the contrary, There are not two souls in the same body. Therefore, for a like reason there are not two angels in the same place.

---

1. 参见 *Phys.*, IV, 7 (213b 33).
2. 同上 (214b 12); *op. cit.*, IV, 9 (216b 23).
3. 参见 *De Trin.*, VI, 6 (PL 42, 929); *De Immortal. An.*, XVI (PL 32, 1034); *Contra Epist. Manich.*, XVI (PL 42, 185).

I answer that, There are not two angels in the same place. The reason for this is because it is impossible for two complete causes to be immediately the causes of one and the same thing. This is evident in every class of causes. For there is one proximate form of one thing, and there is one proximate mover, although there may be several remote movers. Nor can it be objected that several individuals may row a boat, since no one of them is a perfect mover, because no one man's strength is sufficient for moving the boat; the fact is rather that all together are as one mover, in so far as their united powers all combine in producing the one movement. Hence, since the angel is said to be in one place by the fact that his power touches the place immediately by way of a perfect container, as was said, there can be but one angel in one place.

Reply Obj. 1. Several angels are not hindered from being in the same place because of their filling the place, but for another reason, as has been said.

Reply Obj. 2. An angel and a body are not in a place in the same way, and hence the conclusion does not follow.

Reply Obj. 3. Not even a demon and a soul are compared to a body according to the same relation of causality, since the soul is its form, while the demon is not. Hence the inference does not follow.

Question LIII
ON THE LOCAL MOVEMENT OF THE ANGELS
(*In Three Articles*)

WE must next consider the local movement of the angels, under which heading there are three points of inquiry: (1) Whether an angel can be moved locally? (2) Whether in passing from place to place he passes through intervening space? (3) Whether the angel's movement is in time or instantaneous?

First Article
WHETHER AN ANGEL CAN BE MOVED LOCALLY?

We proceed thus to the First Article:—

Objection 1. It seems that an angel cannot be moved locally. For, as the Philosopher proves, *nothing which is devoid of parts is moved.*[1] For, while it is in the term *wherefrom*, it is not moved; nor while it is in the term *whereto*, for it is then already moved; and consequently it follows that everything which is moved, while it is being moved, is partly in the term *wherefrom* and partly in the term *whereto*. But an angel is without parts. Therefore an angel cannot be moved locally.

Obj. 2. Further, movement is *the act of an imperfect being*, as the Philosopher says.[2] But a beatified angel is not imperfect. Consequently a beatified angel is not moved locally.

---

1. 参见 *Phys.*, VI, 4 (234b 10); cf. *op. cit.*, VI, 10 (240b 8).
2. 参见 *Op. cit.*, III, 2 (201b 31).

Obj. 3. Further, movement exists simply because of want. But the holy angels have no want. Therefore the holy angels are not moved locally.

On the contrary, It is the same thing for a beatified angel to be moved as for a beatified soul to be moved. But it must necessarily be said that a blessed soul is moved locally, because it is an article of faith that Christ's soul descended into Hell. Therefore a beatified angel is moved locally.

I answer that, A beatified angel can be moved locally. As, however, to be in a place belongs equivocally to a body and to an angel, so likewise does local movement. For a body is in a place in so far as it is contained by the place, and is commensurate with the place. Hence it is necessary for the local movement of a body to be commensurate with the place, and in accord with its requirements. Hence it is that the continuity of movement is according to the continuity of magnitude; and according to priority and posteriority in magnitude is the priority and posteriority of local movement, as the Philosopher says.[1] But an angel is not in a place as commensurate and contained, but rather as containing it. Hence it is not necessary for the local movement of an angel to be commensurate with the place, nor for it to be according to the requirement of the place, so as to have continuity therefrom; but it is a non-continuous movement. For since the angel is in a place only by virtual contact, as was said above,[2] it follows necessarily that the movement of an angel in a place is nothing else than the various contacts of various places successively, and not at once; because an angel cannot be in several places at one time, as was said above.[3] Nor is it necessary for these contacts to be continuous. Nevertheless a certain kind of continuity can be found in such contacts. For, as was

---

1. 参见 Aristotle, *op. cit.*, IV, 11 (219a 12).
2. 参见 Q. 52, a. 1.
3. 参见 Q. 52, a. 2.

said above, there is nothing to hinder us from assigning a divisible place to an angel according to virtual contact;[1] just as a divisible place is assigned to a body through contact with magnitude. Hence as a body successively, and not all at once, quits the place in which it was before (thence arises continuity in its local movement), so likewise an angel can successively quit the divisible place in which he was before, and so his movement will be continuous. And he can all at once quit the whole place, and in the same instant apply himself to the whole of another place, and thus his movement will not be continuous.

Reply Obj. 1. This argument fails of its purpose for a twofold reason. First of all, because Aristotle's demonstration deals with what is indivisible according to quantity, to which corresponds a place necessarily indivisible.[2] And this cannot be said of an angel.

Secondly, because Aristotle's demonstration deals with movement which is continuous. For if the movement were not continuous, it might be said that a thing is moved while it is in the term *wherefrom*, and while it is in the term *whereto*; because the very succession of *wheres*, regarding the same thing, would be called movement, and hence, in whichever of those *wheres* the thing might be, it could be said to be moved. But the continuity of movement prevents this, for nothing which is continuous is in its term, as is clear, because the line is not in the point. Therefore it is necessary for the thing moved to be not totally in either of the terms while it is being moved, but partly in the one, and partly in the other. Therefore, according as the angel's movement is not continuous, Aristotle's demonstration does not hold good in the present case. But according as the angel's movement is held to be continuous, it can be granted that, while an angel is in movement, he is partly in the term *wherefrom*, and partly in the term *whereto* (yet so that such *partness* be not referred to the angel's substance, but to the place);

---

1. 参见 Q. 52, a. 1.
2. 参见 *Phys.*, VI, 4 (234b 10); 10 (240b 8).

because at the outset of his continuous movement the angel is in the whole divisible place from which he begins to be moved, but while he is actually in movement, he is in part of the first place which he quits, and in part of the second place which he occupies. And this very fact that he can occupy the parts of two places pertains to the angel from this, that he can occupy a divisible place by applying his power, just as a body does by application of magnitude. Hence it follows, regarding a body which is movable according to place, that it is divisible according to magnitude; but regarding an angel, that his power can be applied to something which is divisible.

Reply Obj. 2. The movement of that which is in potentiality is the act of that which is imperfect. But the movement which is by application of power is the act of one in act; for a being has power according as it has actuality.

Reply Obj. 3. The movement of that which is in potentiality is because of its own need, but the movement of what is in act is not for any need of its own, but for another's need. In this way, because of our need, the angel is moved locally, according to *Heb.* i. 14: *They are all ministering spirits, sent to minister for them who receive the inheritance of salvation.*

Second Article
WHETHER AN ANGEL PASSES THROUGH INTERMEDIATE SPACE?

We proceed thus to the Second Article:—

Objection 1. It would seem that an angel does not pass through intermediate space. For everything that passes through an intermediate space first travels along a place of its own dimensions, before passing through a greater. But the place corresponding to an angel, who is indivisible, is confined to a point. Therefore if the angel passes through intermediate space, he must traverse an infinite number of points in his movement; which is not possible.

Obj. 2. Further, an angel is of simpler substance than the soul. But our soul, by taking thought, can pass from one extreme to another without going through the middle: for I can think of France and afterwards of Syria, without ever thinking of Italy, which stands between them. Therefore much more can an angel pass from one extreme to another without going through the middle.

On the contrary, If the angel be moved from one place to another, then, when he is in the term *whither*, he is no longer in motion, but is changed. But a process of changing precedes every actual change. Consequently he was being moved while existing in some place. But he was not moved so long as he was in the term *whence*. Therefore, he was moved while he was in mid-space; and so it was necessary for him to pass through intervening space.

I answer that, As was observed above in the preceding article, the local motion of an angel can be continuous, and non-continuous. If it be continuous, the angel cannot pass from one extreme to another without passing through the mid-space; because, as is said by the Philosopher, *The middle is that into which a thing which is continually moved comes, before arriving at the last into which it is moved.*[1] For the order of before and after in continuous movement is according to the order of before and after in magnitude, as he says.[2]

But if an angel's movement be not continuous, it is possible for him to pass from one extreme to another without going through the middle. Which is evident thus. Between the two extreme limits there are infinite intermediate places, whether the places be taken as divisible or as indivisible. This is clearly evident with regard to places which are indivisible, because between every two points that are infinite intermediate points, since no two points follow one another

---

1. 参见 Aristotle, *op. cit.*, V, 3 (226b 23).
2. 参见 *Op. cit.*, IV, 11 (219a 16).

without a middle, as is proved in *Physics* vi.[1] And the same must of necessity be said of divisible places. This is shown from the continuous movement of a body. For a body is not moved from place to place except in time. But in the whole time which measures the movement of a body, there are not two *nows* in which the body moved is not in one place and in another; for if it were in one and the same place in two *nows*, it would follow that it would be at rest there, since to be at rest is nothing else than to be in the same place now and previously. Therefore, since there are infinite *nows* between the first and the last *now* of the time which measures the movement, there must be infinite places between the first from which the movement begins and the last where the movement ceases. This again is made evident from sensible experience. Let there be a body of a palm's length, and let there be a plane measuring two palms, along which it travels. It is evident that the first place from which the movement starts is that of the one palm, and the place wherein the movement ends is that of the other palm. Now it is clear that when it begins to move, it gradually quits the first palm and enters the second. According, then, as the magnitude of the palm is divided, even so are the intermediate places multiplied; because every distinct point in the magnitude of the first palm is the beginning of a place, and a distinct point in the magnitude of the other palm is the limit of the same. Accordingly, since magnitude is infinitely divisible, and the points in every magnitude are likewise infinite in potentiality, it follows that between every two places there are infinite intermediate places.

Now a movable body exhausts the infinity of the intermediate places only by the continuity of its movement; because, as the intermediate places are infinite in potentiality, so likewise must there be reckoned some infinitudes in movement which is continuous.

---

1. 参见 *Op. cit.*, VI, 1 (231b 9).

Consequently, if the movement be not continuous, then all the parts of the movement will be actually numbered. If, therefore, any movable body be moved, but not by continuous movement, it follows either that it does not pass through all the intermediate places, or else that it actually numbers infinite places; which is not possible. Accordingly, then, as the angel's movement is not continuous, he does not pass through all intermediate places.

Now, the actual passing from one extreme to the other, without going through the mid-space, is quite in keeping with an angel's nature; but not with that of a body, because a body is measured by and contained by a place, and hence is bound to follow the laws of place in its movement. But an angel's substance is not subject to place as contained thereby, but is above it as containing it. Hence it is in his power to apply himself to a place just as he wills, either through or without the intervening place.

Reply Obj. 1. The place of an angel is not taken as equal to him according to magnitude, but according to contact of power; and so the angel's place can be divisible, and is not always a mere point. Yet even the intermediate divisible places are infinite, as was said above, but they are consumed by the continuity of the movement, as is evident from the foregoing.

Reply Obj. 2. While an angel is moved locally, his essence is applied to various places, but the soul's essence is not applied to the things thought of, but rather the things thought of are in it. So there is no comparison.

Reply Obj. 3. In continuous movement the actual change is not a part of the movement, but its conclusion: hence to-be-moved must precede having-been-moved. Accordingly, such movement is through the mid-space. But in movement which is not continuous, the change is a part, as a unit is a part of number; and hence the succession of the various places, even without the mid-space, constitutes such movement.

Third Article
WHETHER THE MOVEMENT OF AN ANGEL IS INSTANTANEOUS?

We proceed thus to the Third Article:—

Objection 1. It would seem that an angel's movement is instantaneous. For the greater the power of the mover, and the less the moved resist the mover, the more rapid is the movement. But the power of an angel moving himself exceeds beyond all proportion the power which moves a body. Now the proportion of velocities is reckoned according to the lessening of the time. But between one length of time and any other length of time there is proportion. If therefore a body be moved in time, an angel is moved in an instant.

Obj. 2. Further, the angel's movement is simpler than any bodily change. But some bodily change is effected in an instant, such as illumination; both because the subject is not illuminated successively, in the way that it gets hot successively, and because a ray does not reach sooner what is near than what is remote. Much more therefore is the angel's movement instantaneous.

Obj. 3. Further, if an angel be moved from place to place in time, it is manifest that in the last instant of such time he is in the term *whereto*. Now in the whole of the preceding time, he is either in the place immediately preceding, which is taken as the term *wherefrom*, or else he is partly in the one, and partly in the other. But if he be partly in the one and partly in the other, it follows that he is divisible; which is impossible. Therefore during the whole of the preceding time he is in the term *wherefrom*. Therefore he is at rest there, since to be at rest is to be in the same place now and previously, as was said. Therefore it follows that he is not moved except in the last instant of time.

On the contrary, In every change there is a before and after. Now the before and after of movement is reckoned by time. Consequently every movement is in time. This applies also to the movement of an angel, since there is a before and after in it.

I answer that, Some have maintained that the local movement of an angel is instantaneous.[1] They said that when an angel is moved from place to place, during the whole of the preceding time he is in the term *wherefrom*; but in the last instant of such time he is in the term *whereto*. Nor is there any need for a medium between the terms, just as there is no medium between time and the limit of time. But there is a mid-time between two *nows* of time. Hence they say that a last *now* cannot be assigned in which it was in the term *wherefrom*, just as in illumination, and in the substantial generation of fire, there is no last instant to be assigned in which the air was dark, or in which the matter was under the privation of the form of fire; but a last time can be assigned, so that in the last instant of such time there is light in the air, or the form of fire in the matter. And so illumination and substantial generation are called instantaneous movements[2].[3]

But this does not hold good in the present case, as is shown by the following. It is of the nature of rest that the subject in repose be not otherwise disposed now than it was before; and therefore in every *now* of time which measures rest, the subject reposing is in the same *where* in the first, in the middle and in the last *now*. On the other hand, it is of the very nature of movement for the subject moved to be otherwise now than it was before; and therefore in every *now* of time which measures movement, the movable subject is in various dispositions, and so in the last *now* it must have a different form from what it had before. So it is evident that to rest during the whole time in some [disposition], for instance, in whiteness, is to be in it in every instant of such time. Hence it is not possible for anything to rest in

---

1. 参见 St. Albert, *In I Sent.*, d. xxxvii, a. 23; a. 24 (XXVI, 260; 262); *Summa de Creatur.* I, tr. 4, q. 59 (XXXIV, 627).
2. instantaneous movements: 立刻的行动
3. 参见 Cf. Averroes, *In Phys.*, VI, comm. 59 (IV, 13or).

one term during the whole of the preceding time, and afterwards in the last instant of that time to be in the other term. But this is possible in movement, because to be moved in any whole time is not to be in the same disposition in every instant of that time. Therefore, all such instantaneous changes are terms of a continuous movement: *e.g.*, generation is the term of the alteration of matter, and illumination is the term of the local movement of the illuminating body.

Now the local movement of an angel is not the term of any other continuous movement, but is of itself, depending upon no other movement. Consequently it is impossible to say that during the whole time he is in some place, and that in the last *now* he is in another place; but some *now* must be assigned in which he last was in the preceding place. But where there are many *nows* succeeding one another, there is necessarily time, since time is nothing else than the reckoning of before and after in movement. It remains, then, that the movement of an angel is in time. It is in continuous time if his movement be continuous, and in non-continuous time if his movement be non-continuous; for his movement, as was said, can be of either kind, and the continuity of time comes of the continuity of movement, as the Philosopher says.[1]

But that time, whether it be continuous or not, is not the same as the time which measures the movement of the heavens, and by which are measured all corporeal things, which have their changeableness from the movement of the heavens; for the angel's movement does not depend upon the movement of the heavens.

Reply Obj. 1. If the time of the angel's movement be not continuous, but a kind of succession of *nows*, it will have no proportion to the time which measures the movement of corporeal things, which is continuous, since it is not of the same nature. If, however, it be

1. 参见 Aristotle, *Phys.*, IV, 11 (219a 13).

continuous, it is certainly proportionable, not, indeed, because of the proportion of the mover and the movable, but because of the proportion of the magnitudes in which the movement exists. Besides, the swiftness of the angel's movement is not measured by the quantity of his power, but according to the determination of his will.

Reply Obj. 2. Illumination is the term of a movement, but it is an alteration, not a local movement, as though the light were first moved to what is near, before being moved to what is remote. But the angel's movement is local, and, besides, it is not the term of movement. Hence there is no comparison.

Reply Obj. 3. This objection is based on continuous time. But the time of an angel's movement can be non-continuous. So an angel can be in one place in one instant, and in another place in the next instant, without any time intervening. If the time of the angel's movement be continuous, he is changed through infinite places throughout the whole time which precedes the last *now*, as was already shown. Nevertheless he is partly in one of the continuous places, and partly in another, not because his substance is susceptible of parts, but because his power is applied to a part of the first place and to a part of the second, as was said above.

Question LIV
THE KNOWLEDGE OF THE ANGELS
(*In Five Articles*)

AFTER considering what belongs to the angel's substance, we now proceed to his knowledge. This investigation will be fourfold. In the first place inquiry must be made into his power of knowing; secondly, into his medium of knowing;[1] thirdly, into the things known;[2] and fourthly, into the manner whereby he knows them.[3]

Under the first heading there are five points of inquiry: (1) Is the angel's understanding his substance? (2) Is his being his understanding? (3) Is his substance his power of understanding? (4) Is there in the angels an agent and a possible intellect? (5) Is there in them any other power of knowing besides the intellect?

First Article
WHETHER AN ANGEL'S ACT OF UNDERSTANDING IS HIS SUBSTANCE?

We proceed thus to the First Article:—

Objection 1. It would seem that the angel's act of understanding is his substance. For the angel is both higher and simpler than the active intellect of a soul. But the substance of the agent intellect is its

1. 参见 Q. 55.
2. 参见 Q. 56.
3. 参见 Q. 58.

own action, as is evident from Aristotle[1] and from his Commentator.[2] Therefore much more is the angel's substance his action, that is, his act of understanding.

Obj. 2. Further, the Philosopher says that *the action of the intellect is life.*[3] But *since in living things to live is to be, as he says,*[4] it seems that life is essence. Therefore the action of the intellect is the essence of an angel who understands.

Obj. 3. Further, if the extremes be one, then the middle does not differ from them, because extreme is farther from extreme than the middle is. But in an angel the intellect and the thing understood are the same, at least in so far as he understands his own essence. Therefore the act of understanding, which is between the intellect and the thing understood, is one with the substance of the angel who understands.

On the contrary, The action of anything differs more from its substance than does its being. But no creature's being is its substance, for this belongs to God only, as is evident from what was said above.[5] Therefore neither the action of an angel, nor that of any other creature, is its substance.

I answer that, It is impossible for the action of an angel, or of any other creature, to be its own substance. For an action is properly the actuality of a power, just as being is the actuality of a substance, or of an essence. Now it is impossible for anything which is not a pure act, but which has some admixture of potentiality, to be its own actuality, because actuality is opposed to potentiality. But God alone is pure act. Hence only in God is His substance the same as His being and His

---

1. 参见 *De An.*, III, 5 (430a 18).
2. 参见 Averroes, *In De An.*, III, comm. 19 (VI, 17or).
3. 参见 *Metaph.*, XI, 7 (1072b 27).
4. 参见 Aristotle, *De An.*, II, 4 (415b 13).
5. 参见 Q. 3, a. 4; q. 7, a. 1, ad 3; a. 2; q. 44, a. 1.

action.

Besides, if an angel's act of understanding were his substance, it would be necessary for it to be subsisting. Now a subsisting act of understanding can be but one, just as an abstract subsisting thing can be only one. Consequently an angel's substance would neither be distinguished from God's substance, which is His very act of understanding subsisting in itself, nor from the substance of another angel.

Even more, if the angel were his own act of understanding, there could then be no degrees of understanding more or less perfectly; for this comes about through the diverse participation of the act of understanding.

Reply Obj. 1. When the agent intellect is said to be its own action, such predication is not essential, but concomitant, because, since its very nature consists in act, instantly, so far as lies in itself, action accompanies it; which cannot be said of the possible intellect, for this has no actions until after it has been reduced to act.

Reply Obj. 2. The relation between *life* and *to live* is not the same as that between *essence* and *to be*; it is rather the same as that between *a race* and *to run*, one of which signifies the act in the abstract, and the other in the concrete. Hence it does not follow that, if *to live* is *to be*, *life* is *essence*. Yet life is sometimes used for the essence, for as Augustine says, *Memory and understanding and will are one essence, one life.*[1] But it is not taken in this sense by the Philosopher when he says that *the act of the intellect is life.*[2]

Reply Obj. 3. Action which is transient, passing to some extrinsic thing, is really mediate between the agent and the subject receiving the action. The action which remains within the agent is not really a medium between the agent and its object, but only according to the

1. 参见 *De Trin.*, X, 11 (PL 42, 983).
2. 参见 *Metaph.*, XI, 7 (1072b 27).

manner of signification; for it really follows the union of the object with the agent. For from the union of the object understood with the one who understands results understanding as an effect which differs, as it were, from both.

Second Article
WHETHER IN THE ANGEL TO UNDERSTAND IS TO BE?

We proceed thus to the Second Article:—

Objection 1. It would seem that in the angel to understand is to be. For in living things to live is to be, as the Philosopher says.[1] But *to understand is in a sense to live.*[2] Therefore in the angel to understand is to be.

Obj. 2. Further, cause bears the same relation to cause as effect to effect. But the form whereby the angel exists is the same as the form by which he understands at least himself. Therefore in the angel to understand is to be.

On the contrary, The angel's act of understanding is his movement, as is clear from Dionysius.[3] But to be is not a movement. Therefore in the angel to be is not to understand.

I answer that, The action of the angel, as also the action of any creature, is not his being. For, as it is said, there is a twofold class of action:[4] one, which goes out to something beyond, and causes passion in it, as burning and cutting; the other, which does not go outwards, but remains within the agent, as to feel, to understand, to will; and by such actions nothing outside is changed, but the whole action takes place within the agent. It is quite clear, regarding the

---

1. 参见 Aristotle, *De An.*, II, 4 (415b 13).
2. 参见 *Op. cit.*, II, 2 (413a 23).
3. 参见 *De Div. Nom.*, IV, 8 (PG 3, 704).
4. 参见 Aristotle, *Metaph.*, VIII, 8 (1050a 23).

first kind of action, that it cannot be the agent's very being, because the agent's being is signified as within him, while such an action denotes something as issuing from the agent into the thing done. But the second action of its own nature has infinity, either absolutely or relatively. As an example of infinity absolutely, we have the act *to understand*, of which the object is *the true*, and the act *to will*, of which the object is *the good*. Both of these are convertible with being; and so, to understand and to will, of themselves, bear relation to all things, and each receives its specification from its object. On the other hand, the act of sensation is relatively infinite, for it bears relation to all sensible things; as sight does to all things visible. Now the being of every creature is restricted to one in genus and species, and God's being alone is absolutely infinite, comprehending all things in itself, as Dionysius says.[1] Hence the divine being alone is its own act of understanding and its own act of will.

Reply Obj. 1. *To live* is sometimes taken as the *to be* of living things, sometimes also for a vital operation, that is, for one whereby something is shown to be living. In this way the Philosopher says that to understand is, in a sense, to live, for he there distinguishes the various grades of living things according to the various functions of life.

Reply Obj. 2. The essence of an angel is the formal principle of his entire being, but not the formal principle of his whole act of understanding, since he cannot understand everything by his essence. Consequently the essence of an angel is compared to his being according to its proper nature as such an essence; whereas to his act of understanding it is compared as included in the idea of a more universal object, namely, truth and being. Thus it is evident, that, though it be the same form, yet the essence is not the principle of being and of understanding according to the same formality. On

1. 参见 *De Div. Nom.*, V, 4 (PG 3, 817).

this account it does not follow that in the angel *to be* is the same as *to understand.*

Third Article
WHETHER AN ANGEL'S POWER OF UNDERSTANDING IS HIS ESSENCE?

We proceed thus to the Third Article:—

Objection 1. It would seem that in an angel the power or faculty of understanding is not different from his essence. For, *mind* and *intellect* express the power of understanding. But in many passages of his writings, Dionysius names the angels *intellects* and *minds.*[1] Therefore the angel is his own power of understanding.

Obj. 2. Further, if the angel's power of understanding be anything besides his essence, then it must needs be an accident; for that which is besides the essence of anything, we call its accident. But *a simple form cannot be a subject*, as Boethius states.[2] Thus an angel would not be a simple form, which is contrary to what has been previously said.[3]

Obj. 3. Further, Augustine says that God made the angelic nature *nigh unto Himself*, while He made primary matter *nigh unto nothing.*[4] From this it would seem that the angel is of a simpler nature than primary matter, as being closer to God. But primary matter is its own power. Therefore much more is an angel his own power of understanding.

On the contrary, Dionysius says that *the angels are divided into substance, power and operation.*[5] Therefore substance, power and operation are all

---

1. 参见 *De Cael. Hier.*, II, 1; VI, 1; XII, 2 (PG 3, 137; 200; 292); *De Div. Nom.*, VII, 2 (PG 3, 868).
2. 参见 *De Trin.*, II (PL 64, 1250).
3. 参见 Q. 50, a. 2.
4. 参见 *Confess.*, XII, 7 (PL 32, 828).
5. 参见 *De Cael. Hier.*, XI, 2 (PG 3, 284).

distinct in them.

I answer that, Neither in an angel nor in any creature is the power or operative faculty the same as its essence. The evidence for this is as follows. Since every power is related to an act, the diversity of powers must be according to the diversity of acts; and on this account it is said that each proper act corresponds to its proper power. But in every creature the essence differs from the being, and is compared to it as potentiality is to act, as is evident from what has been already said.[1] Now the act to which the operative power is compared is operation. But in the angel to understand is not the same as to be, nor is any operation in him, nor in any other created thing, the same as his being. Hence the angel's essence is not his power of understanding, nor is the essence of any creature its power of operation.

Reply Obj. 1. An angel is called *intellect* and *mind*, because all his knowledge is intellectual; whereas the soul's knowledge is partly intellectual and partly sensitive.

Reply Obj. 2. A simple form which is pure act cannot be the subject of any accident, because subject is compared to accident as potentiality is to act. God alone is such a form, and it is of such a form that Boethius is there speaking. But a simple form which is not its own being, but is compared to it as potentiality is to act, can be the subject of an accident; and especially of such an accident as follows the species, for such accident belongs to the form, whereas an accident which belongs to the individual, and which does not belong to the whole species, results from the matter, which is the principle of individuation. And such a simple form is an angel.

Reply Obj. 3. The power of matter is a potentiality in regard to substantial being itself, whereas the power of operation regards accidental being. Hence there is no comparison.

---

1. 参见 A. 1; q. 44, a. 1.

Fourth Article

WHETHER THERE IS AN AGENT AND A POSSIBLE INTELLECT IN AN ANGEL?

We proceed thus to the Fourth Article:—

Objection 1. It would seem that there is both an agent and a possible intellect in an angel. The Philosopher says that *in the soul, just as in every nature, there is something whereby it can become all things, and there is something whereby it can make all things.*[1] But an angel is a kind of nature. Therefore there is an agent and a possible intellect in an angel.

Obj. 2. Further, the proper function of the possible intellect is to receive, whereas to illumine is the proper function of the agent intellect, as is made clear in *De Anima* iii.[2] But an angel receives illumination from a higher angel, and illumines a lower one. Therefore there is in him an agent and a possible intellect.

On the contrary, The distinction of agent and possible intellect in us is in relation to the phantasms, which are compared to the possible intellect as colors to sight, but to the agent intellect as colors to light, as is clear from De *Anima* iii.[3] But this is not so in the angel. Therefore there is no agent and possible intellect in the angel.

I answer that, The necessity for admitting a possible intellect in us is derived from the fact that we sometimes understand only in potentiality, and not actually. Hence there must exist some power which, previous to the act of understanding, is in potentiality to intelligibles, but which becomes actualized in their regard when it apprehends them and furthermore when it considers them. This is the power which is named the *possible intellect.* The necessity for admitting

---

1. 参见 *De An.*, III, 5 (430a 14).
2. 参见 *Op. cit.*, III, 4; 5 (429a 15; 430a 14).
3. 参见 *Op. cit.*, III. 5; 7 (430a 15; 431a 14).

an agent intellect is due to this, that the natures of the material things which we know are not immaterial and actually intelligible outside the soul, but are only intelligible in potentiality so long as they are outside the soul. Consequently it is necessary that there should be some power capable of rendering such natures actually intelligible, and this power in us is called the *agent intellect*.

But both of these necessities are absent from the angels. They are not sometimes understanding only in potentiality with regard to such things as they naturally apprehend; nor, again, are their intelligible objects intelligible in potentiality, but they are actually such. For first and principally they understand immaterial things, as will appear later.[1] Therefore there cannot be an agent and a possible intellect in them, except equivocally.

Reply Obj. 1. As the words themselves show, the Philosopher understands those two things to be in every nature in which there can be generation or becoming. Knowledge, however, is not generated in the angels, but is present naturally. Hence there is no need for admitting an agent and a possible intellect in them.

Reply Obj. 2. It is the function of the agent intellect to illumine, not another intellect, but the things which are intelligible in potentiality, in so far as by abstraction it makes them to be actually intelligible. It belongs to the possible intellect to be in potentiality with regard to things which are naturally capable of being known, and sometimes to apprehend them actually. Hence for one angel to illumine another does not belong to the notion of an agent intellect: neither does it belong to the possible intellect for the angel to be illumined with regard to supernatural mysteries[2], to the knowledge of which he is sometimes in potentiality. But if anyone wishes to call these by the names of agent and possible intellect, he will then be speaking equivocally; and it is

---

1. 参见 Q. 84, a. 7; q. 85, a. 1.
2. supernatural mystery: 超自然的奥迹

not about names that we need trouble.

Fifth Article
WHETHER THERE IS ONLY INTELLECTUAL KNOWLEDGE IN THE ANGELS?

We proceed thus to the Fifth Article:—

Objection 1. It would seem that the knowledge of the angels is not exclusively intellectual. For Augustine says that in the angels there is *life which understands and senses.*[1] Therefore there is a sensitive power in them.

Obj. 2. Further, Isidore says that the angels have learned many things by experience.[2] But *experience comes of many remembrances*, as is stated in *Metaph.* i.[3] Consequently they have likewise a power of memory.

Obj. 3. Further, Dionysius says that there is a *perverted phantasy*[4] in the demons.[5] But phantasy belongs to the imaginative power. Therefore the power of the imagination is in the demons, and for the same reason it is in the angels, since they are of the same nature.

On the contrary, Gregory says that *man senses in common with the brutes, and understands with the angels.*[6]

I answer that, In our soul there are certain powers whose operations are exercised through corporeal organs. Such powers are acts of sundry parts of the body, as sight of the eye, and hearing of the ear. There are some other powers of the soul whose operations are not performed through bodily organs, as intellect and will. These are not

---

1. 参见 *De Civit. Dei*, VIII, 6 (PL 41, 231).
2. 参见 *Sent.*, I, 10 (PL 83, 556).
3. 参见 Aristotle, *Metaph.*, I 1 (980b 29).
4. perverted phantasy: 邪恶的想象
5. 参见 *De Div. Nom.*, IV, 23 (PG 3, 725).
6. 参见 *In Evang.*, II, hom. 29 (PL 76, 1214).

acts of any parts of the body. Now the angels have no bodies naturally joined to them, as is manifest from what has already been said.[1] Hence among the soul's powers only intellect and will can belong to them.

The Commentator says the same thing, namely, that the separated substances are divided into intellect and will.[2] And it is in keeping with the order of the universe for the highest intellectual creature to be entirely intelligent, and not in part, as is our soul. For this reason also the angels are called *intellects* and *minds*, as was said above.

A twofold answer can be returned to the contrary objections. First, it may be replied that those authorities are speaking according to the opinion of such men as contended that angels and demons have bodies naturally united to them.[3] Augustine often makes use of this opinion in his books, although he does not mean to assert it. And so he says that *such an inquiry does not call for much labor.*[4] Secondly, it may be said that such authorities and the like are to be understood as by way of likeness. For, since sense has a sure apprehension of its proper sensible object, it is a common usage of speech, when we understand something for certain, to say that we *sense* it. And hence it is that we use the word *sententia* [*sentiment* or *view*]. Experience can be attributed to the angels according to the likeness of the things known, although not by likeness of the power knowing them. For we have experience when we know singulars through the senses. Now the angels likewise know singulars, as we shall show,[5] yet not through the senses. But memory can be allowed in the angels, according as Augustine puts it in the mind;[6] although it cannot belong to them in so far as it is a part

1. 参见 Q. 51, a. 1.
2. 参见 *In Metaph.*, XII, comm. 36 (VIII, 149v).
3. 参见 Cf. above, q. 51, a. 1, ad 1.
4. 参见 Cf. *De Genesi ad Litt.*, II, 17 (PL 34, 278); *De Civit. Dei*, XXI, 10 (PL 41, 724).
5. 参见 Q. 57, a. 2.
6. 参见 *De Trin.*, X, 11 (PL 42, 983).

of the sensitive soul. In like fashion, *a perverted phantasy* is attributed to demons since they have a false practical estimate of what is the true good. In us, deception takes place properly through the phantasy, through which we sometimes hold fast to images of things as if they were the things themselves, as is manifest in sleepers and lunatics.

Question LV
THE MEDIUM OF THE ANGELIC KNOWLEDGE
(*In Three Articles*)

NEXT in order, the question arises as to the medium of the angelic knowledge. Under this heading there are three points of inquiry: (1) Do the angels know everything by their substance, or by some species? (2) If by species, is it by connatural[1] species, or by such as they have derived from things? (3) Do the higher angels know by more universal species than the lower angels?

First Article
WHETHER THE ANGELS KNOW ALL THINGS BY THEIR SUBSTANCE?

We proceed thus to the First Article:—

Objection 1. It would seem that the angels know all things by their substance. For Dionysius says that *the angels, according to the proper nature of a mind, know the things which are happening upon earth.*[2] But the angel's nature is his essence. Therefore the angel knows things by his essence.

Obj. 2. Further, according to the Philosopher, *in things which are without matter, the intellect is the same as the thing understood.*[3] But the thing

---

1. connatural: 先天的；固有的；同性质的
2. 参见 *De Div. Nom.*, VII, 2 (PG 3, 869).
3. 参见 *Metaph.*, XI, 9 (1075a 3).—*De An.*, III, 4 (430a 3).

understood is the same as the one who understands it by reason of the means whereby it is understood. Therefore in beings without matter, such as angels, the medium of understanding is the very substance of the one understanding.

Obj. 3. Further, everything which is contained in another is there according to the mode of the container. But an angel has an intellectual nature. Therefore whatever is in him is there in an intelligible way. But all things are in him, because the lower orders of beings are essentially in the higher, while the higher are in the lower participatively. Hence Dionysius says that God *enfolds the whole in the whole*, *i.e.*, all in all.[1] Therefore the angel knows all things in his substance.

On the contrary, Dionysius says that *the angels are illumined by the forms of things.*[2] Therefore they know by the forms of things, and not by their own substance.

I answer that, The medium through which the intellect understands is compared to the intellect understanding as its form, because it is by the form that an agent acts. Now in order that a power may be perfectly completed by the form, it is necessary for all things to which the power extends to be contained under the form. Hence it is that in things which are corruptible the form does not perfectly complete the potentiality of the matter, because the potentiality of the matter extends to more things than are contained under this or that form. But the intellective power of the angel extends to the understanding all things, since the object of the intellect is universal being or universal truth. The angel's essence, however, does not comprise all things in itself, since it is an essence restricted to a genus and species. But it is proper to the divine essence, which is infinite, to comprise absolutely all things in itself in a perfect way. Therefore God alone knows all

---

1. 参见 *De Div. Nom.*, IV, 7 (PG 3, 701).
2. 参见 *Op. cit.*, IV, 1 (PG 3, 692).

things by His essence. But an angel cannot know all things by his essence, but his intellect must be perfected by some species in order to know things.

Reply Obj. 1. When it is said that the angel knows things according to his own nature, the words *according to* do not determine the medium of such knowledge, which is the likeness of the thing known; but they denote the knowing power, which belongs to the angel of his own nature.

Reply Obj. 2. Just as the sense in act is the sensible in act, as is stated in *De Anima* iii.,[1] not in the sense that the sensitive power itself is the very likeness of the sensible object in the sense, but because one thing is made from both as from act and potentiality, so likewise the intellect in act is said to be the thing understood in act, not because the substance of the intellect is itself the likeness by which it understands, but because that likeness is a form in it. Now, it is precisely the same thing to say *in things which are without matter, the intellect is the same thing as that which is understood*, as to say that *the intellect in act is the thing understood in act*;[2] for a thing is understood actually precisely because it is immaterial.

Reply Obj. 3. The things which are beneath the angel, and those which are above him, are in a measure in his substance, not indeed perfectly, nor according to their own proper natures (because the angel's essence, being finite, is distinguished by its, own nature from other things), but according to some common characteristic of being. Yet all things are perfectly and according to their own natures in God's essence, as in the first and universal operative power, from which proceeds whatever is proper or common to anything. Therefore God has a proper knowledge of all things by His own essence. This the angel has not, but only a common knowledge.

---

1. 参见 Aristotle, *De An.*, III, 8 (431b 23); cf. *op. cit.*, III, 2 (426a 10; a 16).
2. 参见 *Op. cit.*, III, 4 (430a 3).

Second Article

WHETHER THE ANGELS UNDERSTAND BY SPECIES DRAWN FROM THINGS?

We proceed thus to the Second Article:—

Objection 1. It would seem that the angels understand by species drawn from things. For everything understood is apprehended by some likeness within him who understands it. But the likeness of the thing existing in another is there either by way of an exemplar, so that the likeness is the cause of the thing; or else by way of an image, so that it is caused by such thing. Hence all knowledge in the one understanding must either be the cause of the thing understood, or else be caused by it. Now the angel's knowledge is not the cause of existing things; that belongs to the divine knowledge alone. Therefore it is necessary for the species, by which the angelic mind understands, to be derived from things.

Obj. 2. Further, the angelic light is stronger than the light of the agent intellect of the soul. But the light of the agent intellect abstracts intelligible species from phantasms. Therefore the light of the angelic mind can also abstract species from sensible things. So there is nothing to hinder us from saying that the angel understands through species drawn from things.

Obj. 3. Further, the species in the intellect are indifferent to what is present or distant, except in so far as they are taken from sensible things. Therefore, if the angel does not understand by species drawn from things, his knowledge would be indifferent as to things present and distant; and so he would be moved locally to no purpose.

On the contrary, Dionysius says that the *angels do not gather their divine knowledge from things divisible or sensible.*[1]

---

1. 参见 *De Div. Nom.*, VII, 2 (PG 3, 868).

I answer that, The species whereby the angels understand are not drawn from things, but are connatural to them. For we must observe that there is a similarity between the distinction and order of spiritual substances[1] and the distinction and order of corporeal substances. The highest bodies have in their nature a potentiality which is fully perfected by the form; whereas in the lower bodies the potentiality of matter is not entirely perfected by the form, but receives now one form, now another, from some agent. In like fashion also the lower intellectual substances[2]—that is to say, human souls—have a power of understanding which is not naturally complete, but is successively completed in them by their drawing intelligible species from things. But in the higher spiritual substances—that is, the angels—the power of understanding is naturally perfected by intelligible species, in so far as they have such species connatural to them, so as to understand all things which they can know naturally.

The same is evident from the manner of being of such substances. The lower spiritual substances—that is, souls—have a being akin to a body, in so far as they are the forms of bodies; and consequently from their very mode of being it is necessary for them to seek their intelligible perfection from bodies, and through bodies. Otherwise, they would be united to bodies in vain. On the other hand, the higher substances—that is, the angels—are utterly free from bodies, and subsist immaterially and in their own intelligible being; and consequently they attain their intelligible perfection through an intelligible outpouring, whereby they received from God the species of things known, together with their intellectual nature. Hence Augustine says: *The other things which are lower than the angels are so created that they first receive existence in the knowledge of the rational creature, and then in their own nature.*[3]

---

1. spiritual substance: 精神本体
2. intellectual substance: 理性本体
3. 参见 *De Genesi ad Litt.*, II, 8 (PL 34, 269).

Reply Obj. 1. There are likenesses of creatures in the angel's mind, not, indeed, derived from creatures, but from God, Who is the cause of creatures, and in Whom the likenesses of creatures first exist. Hence Augustine says that, *As the model, according to which the creature is fashioned, is in the Word of God before the creature which is fashioned, so the knowledge of the same model exists first in the intellectual creature, and is afterwards the very fashioning of the creature.*[1]

Reply Obj. 2. To go from one extreme to the other it is necessary to pass through the middle. Now the being of a form in the imagination, which is without matter but not without material conditions, stands midway between the being of a form which is in matter, and the being of a form which is in the intellect by abstraction from matter and from material conditions. Consequently, however powerful the angelic mind might be, it could not reduce material forms to an intelligible being, except it were first to reduce them to the being of forms in the imagination; which is impossible, since the angel has no imagination, as was said above.[2] Even granted that he could abstract intelligible species from material things, yet he would not do so; because he would not need them, for he has connatural intelligible species.

Reply Obj. 3. The angel's knowledge is quite indifferent as to what is near or distant. Nevertheless his local movement is not purposeless on that account; for he is not moved to a place for the purpose of acquiring knowledge, but for the purpose of operation.

Third Article
WHETHER THE HIGHER ANGELS UNDERSTAND BY MORE UNIVERSAL SPECIES THAN THE LOWER ANGELS?

We proceed thus to the Third Article:—

1. 参见 *De Genesi ad Litt.*, II, 8 (PL 34, 269).
2. 参见 Q. 54, a. 5.

Objection 1. It would seem that the higher angels do not understand by more universal species than the lower angels. For the universal, seemingly, is what is abstracted from particulars. But angels do not understand by species abstracted from things. Therefore it cannot be said that the species of the angelic intellect are more or less universal.

Obj. 2. Further, whatever is known in particular is more perfectly known than what is known universally, because to know anything universally is, in a fashion, midway between potentiality and act. If, therefore, the higher angels know by more universal forms than the lower, it follows that the higher have a more imperfect knowledge than the lower; which is not befitting.

Obj. 3. Further, the same cannot be the proper likeness of many. But if the higher angel knows various things by one universal form, which the lower angel knows by several special forms, it follows that the higher angel uses one universal form for knowing various things. Therefore he will not be able to have a proper knowledge of each; which seems unbecoming.

On the contrary, Dionysius says that the higher angels have a more universal knowledge than the lower.[1] And in the *Book of Causes* it is said that *the higher angels have more universal forms.*[2]

I answer that, Some things are more exalted than others because they are nearer to and more like the first being, which is God. Now in God the whole plenitude of intellectual knowledge is contained in one thing, that is to say, in the divine essence, by which God knows all things. This plenitude of knowledge is found in created intellects in a lower manner, and less simply. Consequently it is necessary for lower intellects to know by many forms what God knows by one, and by so many the more according as the intellect is lower.

Thus the higher the angel is, by so much the fewer species will he

1. 参见 *De Cael. Hier.*, XII, 2 (PG 3, 292).
2. 参见 *De Causis*, X (p. 170).

be able to apprehend the whole realm of intelligible objects. Therefore his forms must be more universal: each one of them, as it were, must extend to more things. An example of this can in some measure be observed in ourselves. For there are some people who cannot grasp an intelligible truth, unless it be explained to them in every part and detail; and this comes of their weakness of intellect. But there are others of stronger intellect, who can grasp many things from few.

Reply Obj. 1. It is accidental to the universal to be abstracted from particulars, in so far as the intellect knowing it derives its knowledge from things. But if there be an intellect which does not derive its knowledge from things, the universal which it knows will not be abstracted from things, but in a measure will be pre-existing to them: either according to the order of causality, as the universal ideas of things are in the Word of God; or at least in the order of nature, as the universal ideas of things are in the angelic mind.

Reply Obj. 2. To know anything universally can be taken in two senses. In one way, on the part of the thing known, namely, that only the universal nature of the thing is known. To know a thing thus is something less perfect; for he would have an imperfect knowledge of a man who only knew him to be an animal. In another way, on the part of the medium of such universal knowledge. In this way it is more perfect to know a thing in the universal; for the intellect, which by one universal medium can know singulars properly, is more perfect than one which cannot.

Reply Obj. 3. The same cannot be the adequate proper likeness of several things. But if it be a transcending likeness, then it can be taken as the proper form and likeness of many. Just as in man there is a universal prudence[1] with respect to all the acts of the virtues, which can be taken as the proper form and likeness of that prudence

1. universal prudence: 普遍智德

which in the lion leads to acts of magnanimity, and in the fox to acts of wariness; and so on of the rest. The divine essence, because of its eminence, is in like fashion taken as the proper likeness of each thing contained therein. Hence each one is likened to it according to its proper form. The same applies to the universal form which is in the mind of the angel, namely, that because of its excellence many things can be known through it with a proper knowledge.

Question LVI
THE ANGELS' KNOWLEDGE OF IMMATERIAL THINGS
(*In Three Articles*)

WE now inquire into the knowledge of the angels with regard to the things known by them. We shall treat of their knowledge, first, of immaterial things, secondly of things material.[1] Under the first heading there are three points of inquiry: (1) Does an angel know himself? (2) Does one angel know another? (3) Does the angel by his own natural powers know God?

First Article
WHETHER AN ANGEL KNOWS HIMSELF?

We proceed thus to the First Article:—

Objection 1. It would seem that an angel does not know himself. For Dionysius says that *the angels do not know their own powers.*[2] But, when the substance is known, the power is known. Therefore an angel does not know his own essence.

Obj. 2. Further, an angel is a singular substance, otherwise he would not act, since acts belong to subsistent singulars. But nothing singular is intelligible. Therefore, since the angel possesses only knowledge which is intellectual, no angel can know himself.

Obj. 3. Further, the intellect is moved by the intelligible object,

---

1. 参见 Q. 57.
2. 参见 *De Cael. Hier.*, VI, 1 (PG 3, 200).

because, according to *De Anima* iii., *understanding is a kind of passion.*[1] But nothing is moved by, or is passive to, itself; as appears in corporeal things. Therefore the angel cannot understand himself.

On the contrary, Augustine says that *the angel knew himself when he was established, that is, enlightened by truth.*[2]

I answer that, As is evident from what has previously been said, the object is on a different footing in an immanent, and in a transient, action.[3] In a transient action, the object or matter into which the action passes is something separate from the agent, as the thing heated is separate from what gave it heat, and the building from the builder. But in an immanent action, for the action to proceed, the object must be united with the agent; just as the sensible object must be united with sense in order that the sense may actually perceive. And the object which is united to a power bears the same relation to actions of this kind as does the form which is the principle of action in other agents; for as heat is the formal principle of heating in the fire, so the species of the thing seen is the formal principle of sight in the eye.

It must, however, be borne in mind that this likeness of the object exists sometimes only potentially in the knowing power, and then there is only knowledge in potentiality. So, in order that there may be actual knowledge, it is required that the power of knowledge be reduced to an actual possession of the species. But if it always actually possesses the species, it can thereby have actual knowledge without any preceding change or reception. From this it is evident that to be moved by the object is not of the nature of the knower, as knowing, but as only knowing in potentiality. Now, for the form to be the principle of the action, it makes no difference whether it be inherent in something else, or self-subsisting. For heat would give forth heat none the less if it were

1. 参见 Aristotle, *De An.*, III, 4 (429a 14).
2. 参见 *De Genesi ad Litt.*, II, 8 (PL 34, 269).
3. 参见 Q. 14, a. 2; q. 54, a. 2.

self-subsisting, than it does by inhering in something else. Therefore, if in the order of intelligible beings there be any subsisting intelligible form, it will understand itself. And since an angel is immaterial, he is a subsisting form, and consequently actually intelligible. Hence it follows that he understands himself by his form, which is his substance.

Reply Obj. 1. That is the text of the old translation, which is amended in the new one, and runs thus: *furthermore they*, that is to say the angels, *knew their own powers:* instead of which the old translation read —*and furthermore they do not know their own powers.* Although even the reading of the old translation might be kept and made to mean that the angels do not know their own power perfectly; for they do not know that power as it proceeds from the order of the divine wisdom, which is incomprehensible to the angels.

Reply Obj. 2. We have no knowledge of singular corporeal things, not because of their singularity, but because of the matter, which is their principle of individuation[1]. Accordingly, if there be any singular beings subsisting without matter, as are the angels, there is nothing to prevent them from being actually intelligible.

Reply Obj. 3. To be moved and to be passive belongs to the intellect, in so far as it is in potentiality. Hence this does not happen in the angelic intellect, especially as regards the fact that he understands himself. Besides, the action of the intellect is not of the same nature as the action found in corporeal things, which goes out into some other matter.

Second Article
WHETHER ONE ANGEL KNOWS ANOTHER?

We proceed thus to the Second Article:—

---

1. individuation: 赋予个性；个性化

Objection 1. It would seem that one angel does not know another. For the Philosopher says that if the human intellect were to have in itself any one of the natures of sensible things, then such a nature existing within it would prevent it from apprehending external things;[1] as likewise, if the pupil of the eye were colored with some particular color, it could not see every color. But as the human intellect is disposed for understanding corporeal things, so is the angelic mind for understanding immaterial things. Therefore, since the angelic intellect has within itself some one determinate nature from the number of such natures, it would seem that it cannot understand other angelic natures.

Obj. 2. Further, it is stated in the *Book of Causes* that *every intelligence knows what is above it, in so far as it is caused by it; and what is beneath it, in so far as it is its cause.*[2] But one angel is not the cause of another. Therefore one angel does not know another.

Obj. 3. Further, one angel cannot be known to another angel by the essence of the one knowing, because all knowledge is effected according to a likeness. But the essence of the angel knowing is not like the essence of the angel known, except generically, as is clear from what has been said before.[3] Hence, it follows that one angel would not have a particular knowledge of another, but only a general knowledge. In like manner, it cannot be said that one angel knows another by the essence of the angel known, because that whereby the intellect understands is something within the intellect. But the Trinity alone can penetrate the mind. Again, it cannot be said that one angel knows the other by a species, because that species would not differ from the angel understood, since each is immaterial. Therefore in no way does it appear that one angel can understand another.

---

1. 参见 *De An.*, III, 4 (429a 20).
2. 参见 *De Causis*, VIII (p. 168).
3. 参见 Q. 50, a. 4; q. 55, a. 1, ad. 3.

Obj. 4. Further, if one angel did understand another, this would be either by an innate species, in which case it would follow that, if God were now to create another angel, such an angel could not be known by the existing angels; or else he would have to be known by a species drawn from things, and so it would follow that the higher angels could not know the lower, from whom they receive nothing. Therefore in no way does it seem that one angel knows another.

On the contrary, We read in the *Book of Causes* that *every intelligence knows the things which are not corrupted.*[1]

I answer that, As Augustine says, such things as pre-existed from eternity in the Word of God came forth from Him in two ways: first, into the angelic mind; and secondly, so as to subsist in their own natures.[2] They proceeded into the angelic mind in that God impressed upon the angelic mind the likenesses of the things which He produced in their own natural being. Now in the Word of God from eternity there existed not only the likenesses of corporeal things, but likewise the likenesses of all spiritual creatures. So in every one of these spiritual creatures, the likenesses of all things, both corporeal and spiritual, were impressed by the Word of God[3]. This was done in such a way that in every angel there was impressed the likeness of his own species according to both its natural and its intelligible being, so that he should subsist in the nature of his species, and understand himself by it. But the likenesses of other spiritual and corporeal natures were impressed in him only according to their intelligible being, so that by such impressed species he might know corporeal and spiritual creatures.

Reply Obj. 1. The spiritual natures of the angels are distinguished from

---

1. 参见 *De Causis*, XI (p. 171).
2. 参见 *De Genesi ad Litt.*, II. 8 (PL 34, 269).
3. the Word of God: 天主的圣言，指耶稣基督

one another by a certain order, as was already observed.[1] So the nature of an angel does not hinder him from knowing the other angelic natures, since both the higher and lower bear affinity to his nature, and the only difference is according to their diverse degrees of perfection.

Reply Obj. 2. The nature of cause and effect does not lead one angel to know another, except because of likeness, so far as cause and effect are alike. Therefore if likeness without causality be admitted in the angels, this will suffice for one to know another.

Reply Obj. 3. One angel knows another by the species of such an angel existing in his intellect, which differs from the angel whose likeness it is, not according to material and immaterial being, but according to natural and intentional being. The angel is himself a subsisting form in his natural being; but his species in the intellect of another angel is not so, for there it possesses only an intelligible being. In the same way, the form of color on the wall has a natural being; but, in the deferent medium, it has only intentional being.

Reply Obj. 4. God made every creature proportionate to the universe which He determined to make. Therefore had God resolved to make more angels or more natures of things, He would have impressed more intelligible species in the angelic minds; just as a builder would have made larger foundations if he had intended to build a larger house. Hence, for God to add a new creature to the universe means that He would add a new intelligible species to an angel.

Third Article
WHETHER BY HIS OWN NATURAL POWERS AN ANGEL KNOWS GOD?

We proceed thus to the Third Article:—

---

1. 参见 Q. 50, a. 4, ad 1 and 2; q. 10, a. 6; q. 47, a. 2.

Objection 1. It would seem that the angels cannot know God by their natural powers. For Dionysius says that God *by His incomprehensible might is placed above all heavenly minds.*[1] Afterwards he adds that, *since He is above all substances, He is remote from all knowledge.*

Obj. 2. Further, God is infinitely above the intellect of an angel. But what is infinitely beyond cannot be reached. Therefore it appears that an angel cannot know God by his natural powers.

Obj. 3. Further, it is written (*1 Cor.* xiii. 12): *We see now through a glass in a dark manner; but then face to face.* From this it appears that there is a twofold knowledge of God: the one, whereby He is seen in His essence, according to which He is said to be seen face to face; the other whereby He is seen in the mirror of creatures. As was already shown, an angel cannot have the former knowledge by his natural powers.[2] Nor does vision through a mirror belong to the angels, since they do not derive their knowledge of God from sensible things, as Dionysius observes.[3] Therefore the angels cannot know God by their natural powers.

On the contrary, The angels are more powerful in knowledge than men. Yet men can know God through their natural powers, according to *Rom.* i. 19: *what is known of God is manifest in them.* Therefore much more so can the angels.

I answer that, The angels can have some knowledge of God by their own natural powers. In evidence whereof it must be borne in mind that a thing is known in three ways: first, by the presence of its essence in the knower, as light can be seen in the eye, and in this way we have said that an angel knows himself;—secondly, by the presence of its likeness in the power which knows it, as a stone is seen by the eye from the fact that its image is found in the eye;—thirdly, when the likeness

1. 参见 *De Div. Nom.*, I, 4 (PG 3, 593).
2. 参见 Q. 12, a. 4.
3. 参见 *De Div. Nom.*, VII, 2 (PG 3, 868).

of the thing known is not drawn directly from the thing itself, but from something else in which it is made to appear, as when we behold a man in a mirror.

To the first-named kind of knowledge is likened that knowledge of God by which He is seen through His essence; and knowledge such as this is impossible for any creature through its natural powers, as was said above.[1] The third kind comprises the knowledge whereby we know God while we are on earth, by His likeness reflected in creatures, according to *Rom.* i. 20: *The invisible things of God are clearly seen, being understood by the things that are made.* Hence, too, we are said to see God in a mirror. But the knowledge, whereby the angel knows God through his natural powers, stands midway between these two, and is likened to that knowledge whereby a thing is seen through the species abstracted from it. For since God's image is, according to its essence, impressed on the very nature of the angel, the angel knows God in as much as he is the image of God. Yet he does not behold God's essence, because no created likeness is sufficient to represent the divine essence. Such knowledge rather approaches the knowledge of things seen in a mirror, because the angelic nature is itself a kind of mirror representing the divine likeness.

Reply Obj. 1. Dionysius is speaking of the knowledge of comprehension, as his words expressly state. In this way God is not known by any created intellect.

Reply Obj. 2. Since an angel's intellect and essence are infinitely remote from God, it follows that the angel cannot comprehend Him; nor can he see God's essence through his own nature. Yet it does not follow on that account that he can have no knowledge of Him at all; what is rather the case is that, just as God is infinitely remote from the angel, so the knowledge which God has of Himself is infinitely above

1. 参见 Q. 12, a. 4.

the knowledge which an angel has of Him.

Reply Obj. 3. The knowledge which an angel has of God is midway between these two kinds of knowledge; nevertheless it approaches more to one of them, as was said above.

Question LVII
THE ANGELS' KNOWLEDGE OF MATERIAL THINGS
(*In Five Articles*)

WE next investigate the material things which are known by the angels. Under this heading there are five points of inquiry: (1) Whether the angels know the natures of material things? (2) Whether they know singular things? (3) Whether they know the future? (4) Whether they know secret thoughts? (5) Whether they know all the mysteries of grace?

First Article
WHETHER THE ANGELS KNOW MATERIAL THINGS?

We proceed thus to the First Article:—

Objection 1. It would seem that the angels do not know material things. For the thing understood is the perfection of him who understands it. But material things cannot be the perfections of angels, since they are beneath them. Therefore the angels do not know material things.

Obj. 2. Further, intellectual vision is only of such things as exist within the soul by their essence, as is said in the *Gloss.*[1] But material things cannot enter by their essence into man's soul, nor into the

1. 参见 *Glossa ordin.*, super *II Cor.*, XII, 2 (VI, 76A); Peter Lombard, *In II Cor.*, XII, 2 (PL 192, 80).—Cf. St. Augustine, *De Genesi ad Litt.*, XII, 28 (PL 34, 478).

angel's mind. Therefore they cannot be known by intellectual vision, but only by imaginary vision, whereby the images of bodies are apprehended, and by sensible vision, which regards bodies in themselves. Now there is neither imaginary nor sensible vision in the angels, but only intellectual. Therefore the angels cannot know material things.

Obj. 3. Further, material things are not actually intelligible, but are knowable by the apprehension of the sense and the imagination, which are not found in angels. Therefore angels do not know material things.

On the contrary, Whatever the lower power can do, the higher can do likewise. But man's intellect, which in the order of nature is inferior to the angel's, can know material things. Therefore much more can the intellect of an angel.

I answer that, The established order of things requires that higher beings be more perfect than lower, and that whatever is contained deficiently, partially and in manifold manner in the lower beings should be contained in the higher eminently and according to a certain fullness and simplicity. Therefore, in God, as in the highest source of things, all things pre-exist supersubstantially according to the manner of His simple Being itself, as Dionysius says.[1] But among other creatures the angels are nearest to God, and resemble Him most. Hence they share more fully and more perfectly in the divine goodness, as Dionysius says.[2] Consequently, all material things pre-exist in the angels more simply and less materially than in themselves, yet in a more manifold manner and less perfectly than in God.

Now whatever exists in any subject is contained in it after the manner of such subject. But the angels are intellectual beings of their own nature. Therefore, just as God knows material things by His essence, so the angels know them, inasmuch as they are in the angels

1. 参见 *De Div. Nom.*, I, 5; V, 9 (PG 3, 592; 825).
2. 参见 *De Cael. Hier.*, IV, 2 (PG 3, 180).

by their intelligible species.

Reply Obj. 1. The thing understood is the perfection of the one who understands, by reason of the intelligible species which he has in his intellect. And thus the intelligible species which are in the intellect of an angel are the perfections and acts of the angelic intellect.

Reply Obj. 2. Sense does not apprehend the essences of things, but only their outward accidents. In like manner neither does the imagination, for it apprehends only the likenesses of bodies. The intellect alone apprehends the essences of things. Hence it is said that *the object of the intellect is what a thing is,*[1] regarding which it does not err, as neither does sense regarding its proper sensible object. In this way, the essences of material things are in the intellect of a man or an angel as the thing understood is in him who understands, and not according to their real being. But some things are in the intellect or in the soul according to both kinds of being; and in either case there is intellectual vision.

Reply Obj. 3. If an angel were to draw his knowledge of material things from the material things themselves, he would need to make them actually intelligible by abstracting them. But he does not derive his knowledge of them from the material things themselves; he has knowledge of material things by actually intelligible species of things, which species are connatural to him; just as our intellect has, by species which it makes intelligible by abstraction.

Second Article
WHETHER AN ANGEL KNOWS SINGULARS?

We proceed thus to the Second Article:—

Objection 1. It would seem that angels do not know singulars. For

1. 参见 Aristotle, *De An.*, III, 6 (430b 28).

the Philosopher says: *The sense has for its object singulars, but the reason or intellect, universals.*[1] Now, in the angels there is no power of knowing save the intellectual power, as is evident from what was said above.[2] Consequently they do not know singulars.

Obj. 2. Further, all knowledge comes about by some assimilation of the knower to the thing known. But it is not possible for any assimilation to exist between an angel and a singular thing, in so far as it is singular; because, as was observed above, an angel is immaterial,[3] while matter is the principle of singularity. Therefore the angel cannot know singulars.

Obj. 3. Further, if an angel does know singulars, it is either by singular or by universal species. It is not by singular species, because in this way he would need to have an infinite number of species. Nor is it by universal species, since the universal is not a sufficient principle for knowing the singular as such, because singulars are not known in the universal except potentially. Therefore the angel does not know singulars.

On the contrary, No one can guard what he does not know. But angels guard individual men, according to *Ps.* xc. 11: *He hath given His angels charge over Thee.* Consequently the angels know singulars.

I answer that, Some have denied to the angels all knowledge of singulars.[4] In the first place this detracts from the Catholic Faith, which asserts that these lower things are administered by angels, according to *Heb.* i. 14: *They are all ministering spirits.* Now, if they had no knowledge of singulars, they could exercise no provision over what is going on in this world, since acts belong to individuals. This is against

---

1. 参见 *Post. Anal.*, I, 18 (81b 6); 24 (86a 29).
2. 参见 Q. 54, a. 5.
3. 参见 Q. 50, a. 2.
4. 参见 Cf. Maimonides, *Guide*, II, 11 (p. 167); Isaac Israeli, *Lib. de Defin.* (pp. 312, 315).—Cf. also St. Thomas, *De Subst. Sep.*, XI; Maimonides, *Guide*, III, 16 (p. 280).

the text of *Eccles.* v. 5: *Say not before the angel: There is no providence.* Secondly, it is also contrary to the teachings of philosophy, according to which the angels are stated to be the movers of the heavenly spheres, and to move them according to their knowledge and will.[1]

Consequently others have said that the angel possesses knowledge of singulars, but in their universal causes, to which all particular effects are reduced.[2] This would be as if an astronomer were to foretell a coming eclipse from the dispositions of the movements of the heavens. This opinion does not escape the aforesaid difficulties, since to know a singular merely in its universal causes is not to know it as singular, that is, as it exists here and now. The astronomer, knowing from computation of the heavenly movements that an eclipse is about to happen, knows it in the universal; yet he does not know it as taking place now, unless he perceives it by the senses. Now precisely, administration, providence and movement are of singulars in so far as they are here and now existing.

Therefore a different answer must be given. Just as man by his various powers of knowledge knows all classes of things, apprehending universals and immaterial things by his intellect, and things singular and corporeal by the senses, so an angel knows both by one intellectual power. For the order of things runs in this way, that the higher a thing is, the more is its power unified and far-reaching. Thus in man himself it is manifest that the common sense which is higher than the proper sense, although it is but one power, knows everything apprehended by the five outward senses, and some other things which no outer sense knows; for example, the difference between white and sweet. The same is to be observed in other cases. Accordingly, since an angel is above man in the order of nature, it is unbefitting to say that a man knows

---

1. 参见 Cf. Maimonides, *op. cit.*, II, 4 (p. 156), where he refers to Aristotle and the Peripatetics.—Cf. above, q. 52, a. 2.
2. 参见 Avicenna, *Metaph.*, IX, 6 (105vb).—Cf. above, q. 14, a. 11.

by any one of his powers something which an angel by his one power of knowledge, namely, the intellect, does not know. Hence Aristotle pronounces it ridiculous to say that a discord, which is known to us, should be unknown to God.[1]

The manner in which an angel knows singular things can be considered from this, that, just as things proceed from God in order that they may subsist in their own natures, so likewise they proceed in order that they may. exist in the angelic mind. Now it is clear that there goes out to things not only whatever belongs to their universal nature, but likewise the principles of individuation; for God is the cause of the entire substance of a thing, as to both its matter and its form. Moreover, He knows things in the way that He causes them, for His knowledge is the cause of a thing, as was shown above.[2] Therefore, just as by His essence, by which He causes all things, God is the likeness of all things, and knows all things, not only as to their universal natures, but also as to their singularity; so through the species imparted to them do the angels know things, not only as to their universal nature, but likewise in their singularity, in so far as these species are the manifold representations of that one simple essence.

Reply Obj. 1. The Philosopher is speaking of our intellect, which apprehends things only by abstraction.[3] Now, by such abstraction from material conditions the thing abstracted becomes a universal. But this manner of understanding is not in keeping with the nature of the angels, as was said above,[4] and consequently there is no comparison.

Reply Obj. 2. It is not according to their nature that the angels are likened to material things in the manner in which one thing resembles another by agreement in genus, species, or accident; but in the manner

---

1. 参见 Aristotle, *De An.*, I, 5 (410b 4); *Metaph.*, II, 4 (1000b 5).
2. 参见 Q. 14, a. 8.
3. 参见 *Post. Anal.*, I, 18 (81b 8); 24 (86a 29).
4. 参见 Q. 55, a. 2; a. 3, ad 1.

in which the higher bears resemblance to the lower, as the sun does to fire. So, too, in this way there is in God a resemblance of all things, as to both matter and form, in so far as there pre-exists in Him as in its cause whatever is to be found in things. For the same reason, the species in the angel's intellect, which are certain likenesses drawn from the divine essence, are the likenesses of things not only as to their form, but also as to their matter.

Reply Obj. 3. Angels know singulars by universal forms, which nevertheless are the likenesses of things both as to their universal and as to their individuating principles. How it is possible for many things to be known by the same species, has been already stated above.[1]

Third Article
WHETHER ANGELS KNOW THE FUTURE?

We proceed thus to the Third Article:—

Objection 1. It would seem that the angels know future events. For angels are more powerful in knowledge than men. But some men know many future events. Therefore much more do the angels.

Obj. 2. Further, the present and the future are differences of time. But the angel's intellect is above time, because, as is said in the *Book of Causes, an intelligence ranks with eternity,*[2] that is, æviternity. Therefore, to the angel's mind, past and future are not different, but he knows each indifferently.

Obj. 3. Further, the angel does not know by species derived from things, but by innate universal species. But universal species refer equally to present, past and future. Therefore it appears that the angels know indifferently things past, present and future.

Obj. 4. Further, just as a thing is said to be distant in time, so it is

1. 参见 Q. 55, a. 3, ad 3.
2. 参见 *De Causis*, II (p. 162).

said to be distant in place. But angels know things which are distant according to place. Therefore they likewise know things distant according to future time.

On the contrary, That which is the exclusive sign of divinity does not belong to the angels. But to know future events is the exclusive sign of divinity, according to *Isa.* xli. 23: *Show the things that are to come hereafter, and we shall know that ye are gods.* Therefore the angels do not know future events.

I answer that, The future can be known in two ways. First, it can be known in its cause. And thus, future events which proceed necessarily from their causes are known with sure knowledge; as that the sun will rise tomorrow. But events which proceed from their causes in the majority of cases are not known for certain, but conjecturally; and thus the doctor knows beforehand the health of the patient. This manner of knowing future events exists in the angels, and by so much the more than it does in us, as they understand the causes of things both more universally and more perfectly. For example, doctors who penetrate more deeply into the causes of an ailment can pronounce a surer verdict on its future outcome. But events which proceed from their causes in the minority of cases are quite unknown. Such are chance and fortuitous events.

In another way, future events are known in themselves. To know the future in this way belongs to God alone. This refers not merely to those events which happen of necessity, or in the majority of cases, but even to chance and fortuitous events; for God sees all things in His eternity, which, being simple, is present to all time, and embraces all time. And therefore God's single glance is cast over all things which happen in all time as present before Him, and He beholds all things as they are in themselves, as was said before when dealing with God's knowledge.[1]

---

1. 参见 Q. 14, a. 13.

But the intellect of an angel, and every created intellect, falls far short of God's eternity; and hence the future as it is in its own being cannot be known by any created intellect.

Reply Obj. 1. Men cannot know future things except in their causes, or by God's revelation. The angels know the future in the same way, but much more distinctly.

Reply Obj. 2. Although the angel's intellect is above the time according to which corporeal movements are reckoned, yet there is a time in his intellect according to the succession of intelligible conceptions. Of this Augustine says that *God moves the spiritual creature according to time.*[1] And thus, since there is succession in the angel's intellect, not all things that happen through all time are present to it.

Reply Obj. 3. Although the species in the intellect of an angel, in so far as they are species, refer equally to things present, past and future, nevertheless the present, past, and future do not bear the same relations to the species. For present things have a nature according to which they resemble the species in the mind of an angel: and so they can be known by them. But things which are yet to come have not yet a nature whereby they are likened to such species. Consequently, they cannot be known by them.

Reply Obj. 4. Things distant according to place are already existing in nature and share in some species whose likeness is in the angel; whereas this is not true of future things, as has been stated. Consequently there is no comparison.

Fourth Article
WHETHER ANGELS KNOW SECRET THOUGHTS?

We proceed thus to the Fourth Article:—

---

1. 参见 *De Genesi ad Litt.*, VIII, 22 (PL 34, 389).—Cf. *op. cit.*, VIII, 20 (PL 34, 388).

Objection 1. It would seem that the angels know secret thoughts. For Gregory, explaining *Job* xxviii. 17 (*Gold or crystal cannot equal it*), says that *then*, namely in the bliss of those rising from the dead, *one shall be as evident to another as he is to himself, and when once the mind of each is seen, his conscience will at the same time be penetrated.*[1] But those who rise shall be like the angels, as is stated (*Matt.* xxii. 30). Therefore an angel can see what is in another's conscience.

Obj. 2. Further, intelligible species bear the same relation to the intellect as shapes do to bodies. But when a body is seen its shape is seen. Therefore, when an intellectual substance is seen, the intelligible species within it is also seen. Consequently, when one angel beholds another angel or even a soul, it seems that he can see the thoughts of both.

Obj. 3. Further, the ideas in our intellect resemble the angel more than do the images in our imagination, because the former are actually understood, while the latter are understood only potentially. But the images in our imagination can be known by an angel as corporeal things are known, since the imagination is a corporeal power. Therefore it seems that an angel can know the thoughts of the intellect.

On the contrary, What is proper to God does not belong to angels. But it is proper to God to read the secrets of hearts, according to *Jer.* xvii. 9: *The heart is perverse above all things, and unsearchable; who can know it? I am the Lord, Who search the heart.* Therefore angels do not know the secrets of hearts.

I answer that, A secret thought can be known in two ways. First, in its effect. In this way it can be known not only by an angel, but also by man; and with so much the greater subtlety according as the effect is the more hidden. For thought is sometimes discovered not merely by outward act, but also by a change of countenance; and doctors can tell

1. 参见 *Moral.*, XVIII, 48 (PL 76, 84).

some affections of the soul by the pulse. Much more then can angels, or even demons, the more deeply they penetrate these hidden bodily modifications. Hence Augustine says that demons *sometimes with the greatest facility learn man's dispositions, not only when expressed by speech, but even when conceived in thought, when the soul expresses them by certain signs in the body.*[1] Yet he observes in the *Retractations* that *it cannot be asserted how this is done.*[2]

In another way thoughts can be known as they are in the intellect, and affections as they are in the will; and thus God alone can know secret thoughts and the affections of wills. The reason of this is that the will of the rational creature is subject only to God, and He alone can work in it Who is its principal object and last end. This will be developed later.[3] Consequently all that is in the will, and all things that depend only on the will, are known to God alone. Now it is evident that it depends entirely on the will that anyone should actually consider anything; because a man who has a habit of knowledge, or any intelligible species, uses them at will. Hence the Apostle says (*1 Cor.* ii. 11): *For what man knoweth the things of a man, but the spirit of a man that is in him?*

Reply Obj. 1. In the present life one man's thought is not known by another owing to a twofold hindrance, namely, because of the barrier of the body, and because the will shuts up its secrets. The first obstacle will be removed at the Resurrection, and does not exist at all in the angels; while the second will remain, and is in the angels now. Nevertheless the brightness of the body will show forth the quality of the soul in what pertains to its amount of grace and of glory. In this way one will be able to see the mind of another.

Reply Obj. 2. Although one angel sees the intelligible species of

---

1. 参见 *De Divinat. Daemon.*, V (PL 40, 586).
2. 参见 *Retract.*, II, 30 (PL 32, 643).
3. 参见 Q. 105, a. 4; q. 106, a. 2; I–II, q. 9, a. 6.

another because the universality of these species varies in proportion to the nobility of the substance of the angels, yet it does not follow that one angel knows how another makes use of them by actual consideration.

Reply Obj. 3. The appetite of the brute does not control its act, but follows the influence of some other corporeal or spiritual cause. Since, therefore, the angels know corporeal things and their dispositions, they can thereby know what is passing in the appetite or in the imaginative apprehension of brute animals, and even of man, in so far as man's sensitive appetite sometimes acts under the influence of some bodily impression, as always happens in brutes. Yet the angels do not necessarily know the movements of the sensitive appetite and the imaginative apprehension of man, in so far as these are moved by the will and reason; because, *even the lower part of the soul has some share of reason, as obeying its ruler*, as is said in the *Ethics*.[1] Nor does it follow that, if the angel knows what is passing through man's sensitive appetite or imagination, he knows what is in man's thought or will. For the intellect and the will are not subject to the sensitive appetite or the imagination, but can make various uses of them.

Fifth Article
WHETHER THE ANGELS KNOW THE MYSTERIES OF GRACE?

We proceed thus to the Fifth Article:—

Objection 1. It would seem that the angels know the mysteries of grace. For, the mystery of the Incarnation is the most excellent of all mysteries. But the angels knew of it from the beginning, for Augustine says: *This mystery was hidden in God through the ages, yet so that it was*

---

1. 参见 *Eth.*, I, 13 (1102b 31).

known to the princes and powers in heavenly places.[1] And the Apostle says (*1 Tim.* iii. 16): *That great mystery of godliness appeared unto angels.* Therefore the angels know the mysteries of grace.

Obj. 2. Further, the significance of all the mysteries of grace is contained in the divine wisdom. But the angels behold God's wisdom, which is His essence. Therefore they know the mysteries of grace.

Obj. 3. Further, the prophets are enlightened by the angels, as is clear from Dionysius.[2] But the prophets knew the mysteries of grace, for it is said (*Amos* iii. 7): *For the Lord God doth nothing without revealing His secret to His servants the prophets.* Therefore angels know the mysteries of grace.

On the contrary, No one learns what he already knows. Yet even the highest angels seek out and learn the divine mysteries of grace. For it is stated that *Sacred Scripture describes some heavenly essences as questioning Jesus, and learning from Him the knowledge of His divine work for us; and Jesus as teaching them directly.*[3] This is evident in *Isa.* lxiii. 1, where, on the angels asking, *Who is he who cometh up from Edom?* Jesus answered, *It is I, Who speak justice.* Therefore the angels do not know the mysteries of grace.

I answer that, There is a twofold knowledge in the angel. The first is his natural knowledge, according to which he knows things both by his essence and by innate species. By such knowledge the angels cannot know the mysteries of grace. For these mysteries depend upon the pure will of God. Now if an angel cannot learn the thoughts of another angel, which depend upon the will of such angel, much less can he ascertain what depends entirely upon God's will. The Apostle reasons in this fashion (*1 Cor.* ii. 11): *No one knoweth the things of a man, but the spirit of a man that is in him. So, the things also that are of God no*

---

1. 参见 *De Genesi ad Litt.*, V, 19 (PL 34, 334).
2. 参见 *De Cael. Hier.*, IV, 2 (PG 3, 180).
3. 参见 *Op. cit.*, VII, 3 (PG 3, 209).

man knoweth but the Spirit of God.

There is another knowledge in the angels, the knowledge which beatifies them, by which they see the Word, and things in the Word. By such vision they know the mysteries of grace, but not all mysteries, nor do they all know them equally, but just as God wills them to learn by revelation; as the Apostle says (*1 Cor.* ii. 10): *But to us God hath revealed them through His Spirit.* This happens in such a way that the higher angels, beholding the divine wisdom more clearly, learn more and deeper mysteries in the vision of God, which they communicate to the lower angels by illumining them. Some of these mysteries they knew from the very beginning of their creation; others they are taught afterwards, as befits their ministrations.

Reply Obj. 1. One can speak in two ways of the mystery of the Incarnation. First of all, in general, and in this way it was revealed to all from the beginning of their beatitude. The reason for this is, that this mystery is a kind of general principle to which all their duties are ordered. For *all are ministering spirits, sent to minister for them who shall receive the inheritance of salvation* (*Heb.* i. 14); and this is brought about by the mystery of the Incarnation. Hence it was necessary for all of them to be instructed in this mystery from the very beginning.

We can speak of the mystery of the Incarnation[1] in another way, as to its special conditions. Thus not all the angels were instructed on all points from the beginning. Even some of the higher angels learned these afterwards, as appears from the passage of Dionysius already quoted.[2]

Reply Obj. 2. Although the beatified angels behold the divine wisdom, yet they do not comprehend it. So it is not necessary for them to know everything hidden in it.

Reply Obj. 3. Whatever the prophets knew of the mysteries of grace

1. the Incarnation: 道成肉身，指天主子耶稣基督降生成人
2. 同上

by revelation was revealed in a more excellent way to the angels. And although God revealed in general to the prophets what He was one day to do regarding the salvation of the human race, still the apostles knew some particulars of the same, which the prophets did not know. Thus we read (*Ephes* iii. 4,5): *As you, reading, may understand my knowledge in the mystery of Christ, which in other generations was not known to the sons of men, as it is now revealed to His holy apostles.* Among the prophets, indeed, the later ones knew what the former did not know, according to *Ps.* cxviii. 100: *I have had understanding above ancients.* And Gregory says: *The knowledge of divine things increased as time went on.*[1]

---

1. 参见 *In Ezech.*, II, hom. 4 (PL 76, 980).

Question LVIII
THE MODE OF THE ANGELIC KNOWLEDGE
(*In Seven Articles*)

AFTER the foregoing we have now to treat of the mode of the angelic knowledge, concerning which there are seven points of inquiry: (1) Whether the angel's intellect is sometimes in potentiality, and sometimes in act? (2) Whether the angel can understand many things at the same time? (3) Whether the angel's knowledge is discursive? (4) Whether he understands by composing and dividing? (5) Whether there can be falsehood in the angel's intellect? (6) Whether his knowledge can be characterized as *morning* and *evening?* (7) Whether the *morning* and *evening* knowledge are the same, or do they differ?

First Article
WHETHER THE ANGEL'S INTELLECT IS SOMETIMES IN POTENTIALITY, AND SOMETIMES IN ACT?

We proceed thus to the First Article:—

Objection 1. It would seem that the angel's intellect is sometimes in potentiality and sometimes in act. *For movement is the act of what is in potentiality*, as is stated in *Physics* iii.[1] But the angels' minds are moved in understanding, as Dionysius says.[2] Therefore the angelic minds are sometimes in potentiality.

---

1. 参见 Aristotle, *Phys.*, III, 1 (201a 10).
2. 参见 *De Div. Nom.*, IV, 8 (PG 3, 704)

Obj. 2. Further, since desire is of a thing not possessed but possible to have, whoever desires to know anything is in potentiality thereto. But it is said (*1 Pet.* i. 12): *On Whom the angels desire to look.* Therefore the angel's intellect is sometimes in potentiality.

Obj. 3. Further, in the *Book of Causes* it is stated that *an intelligence understands according to the mode of its substance.*[1] But the angel's substance has some admixture of potentiality. Therefore it sometimes understands potentially.

On the contrary, Augustine says: *Since the angels were created, in the eternity of the Word, they enjoy holy and devout contemplation.*[2] Now a contemplating intellect is not in potentiality, but in act. Therefore the intellect of an angel is not in potentiality.

I answer that, As the Philosopher states, the intellect is in potentiality in two ways: first, *as before learning or discovering*, that is, before it has the habit of science; secondly, as *when it possesses the habit of science, but does not actually consider.*[3] In the first way an angel's intellect is never in potentiality with regard to the things to which his natural knowledge extends. For, as the higher, namely, the heavenly, bodies have no potentiality to being that is not fully actualized, in the same way the heavenly intellects, the angels, have no intelligible potentiality which is not fully completed by connatural intelligible species. But with regard to things divinely revealed to them, there is nothing to hinder them from being in potentiality, because thus even the heavenly bodies are at times in potentiality to being enlightened by the sun.

In the second way an angel's intellect can be in potentiality with regard to things known by natural knowledge; for he is not always actually considering everything that he knows by natural knowledge. But as to the knowledge of the Word, and of the things he beholds in

---

1. 参见 *De Causis*, VIII (p. 168).
2. 参见 *De Genesi ad Litt.*, II, 8 (PL 34, 270).
3. 参见 *De An.*, III, 4 (429b 8); *Phys.*, VIII, 4 (255a 33).

the Word, he is never in this way in potentiality; because he is always actually beholding the Word, and the things he sees in the Word. For the beatitude of the angels consists in such vision, and beatitude does not consist in habit, but in act, as the Philosopher says.[1]

Reply Obj. 1. Movement is taken there not as the act of something imperfect, that is, of something existing in potentiality, but as the act of something perfect, that is, of one actually existing. In this way understanding and feeling are termed movements, as stated in *De Anima* iii.[2]

Reply Obj. 2. Such desire on the part of the angels does not exclude the thing desired, but weariness thereof. Or they are said to desire the vision of God with regard to fresh revelations, which they receive from God to fit them for the tasks which they have to perform.

Reply Obj. 3. In the angel's substance there is no potentiality divested of act. In the same way, the angel's intellect is never so in potentiality as to be without act.

Second Article
WHETHER AN ANGEL CAN UNDERSTAND MANY THINGS AT THE SAME TIME?

We proceed thus to the Second Article:—

Objection 1. It would seem that an angel cannot understand many things at the same time. For the Philosopher says that *it may happen that we know many things, but understand only one.*[3]

Obj. 2. Further, nothing is understood unless the intellect be informed by an intelligible species; just as the body is formed by shape. But one body cannot be formed into many shapes. Therefore neither can one

---

1. 参见 *Eth.*, I, 8 (1098b 33).
2. 参见 Aristotle, *De An.*, III, 7 (431a 4).
3. 参见 *Top.*, II, 10 (114b 34).

intellect simultaneously understand various intelligible things.

Obj. 3. Further, to understand is a kind of movement. But no movement terminates in various termini. Therefore many things cannot be understood altogether.

On the contrary, Augustine says: *The spiritual power of the angelic mind most easily comprehends at the same time all things that it wills.*[1]

I answer that, As unity of term is requisite for unity of movement, so unity of object is required for unity of operation. Now it is possible that several things may be taken as several or as one, like the parts of a continuous whole. For if each of the parts be considered by itself, the parts are many and consequently neither by sense nor by intellect are they grasped by one operation, nor all at once. In another way they are taken as forming one in the whole, and thus they are grasped both by sense and intellect all at once and by one operation; and this obtains as long as the entire continuous whole is considered, as is stated in *De anima* iii.[2] In this way our intellect understands together both the subject and the predicate, as being parts of one proposition; and also two things compared together, according as they agree in one point of comparison. From this it is evident that many things, in so far as they are distinct, cannot be understood at once; but in so far as they are comprised under some intelligible unity, they can be understood together. Now everything is actually intelligible according as its likeness is in the intellect. All things, then, which can be known by one intelligible species, are known as one intelligible object, and therefore are understood simultaneously. But things known by various intelligible species are apprehended as different intelligible objects.

Consequently, by such knowledge as the angels have of things through the Word, they know all things under one intelligible species, which is the divine essence. Therefore, as regards such knowledge,

1. 参见 *De Genesi ad Litt.*, IV, 32 (PL 34, 316).
2. 参见 Aristotle, *De An.*, III, 6 (430b 7).

they know all things at once; just as in heaven *our thoughts will not be fleeting, going and returning from one thing to another, but we shall behold all our knowledge at the same time by one glance*, as Augustine says.[1] But by that knowledge wherewith the angels know things by innate species, they can at the one time know all things which can be comprised under one species; but not such as are under various species.

Reply Obj. 1. To understand many things as one is, in a way, to understand one thing.

Reply Obj. 2. The intellect is informed by the intelligible species which it has within it. So it can behold at the same time many intelligible objects under one species, just as one body can by one shape be likened to many bodies.

To the third objection the answer is the same as to the first.

Third Article
WHETHER AN ANGEL'S KNOWLEDGE IS DISCURSIVE?

We proceed thus to the Third Article:—

Objection 1. It would seem that the knowledge of an angel is discursive. For the discursive movement of the intellect comes from the fact that one thing is known through another. But the angels know one thing through another, for they know creatures through the Word. Therefore the intellect of an angel knows discursively.

Obj. 2. Further, whatever a lower power can do, the higher can do. But the human intellect can syllogize, and know causes in effects; all of which pertains to discursiveness. Therefore the intellect of the angel, which is higher in the order of nature, can with greater reason do this.

Obj. 3. Further, Isidore says that *demons learn many things by experience.*[2] But experimental knowledge is discursive for *one experience*

1. 参见 *De Trin.*, XV, 16 (PL 42, 1079).
2. 参见 *Sent.*, I, 10 (PL 83, 556).

comes of many remembrances, and one universal from many experiences, as Aristotle observes.[1] Therefore an angel's knowledge is discursive.

On the contrary, Dionysius says that the *angels do not acquire divine knowledge from separate discourses, nor are they led to something particular from something common.*[2]

I answer that, As has often been stated, the angels hold that grade among spiritual substances which the heavenly bodies hold among corporeal substances;[3] for Dionysius calls them *heavenly minds.*[4] Now, the difference between heavenly and earthly bodies is this, that earthly bodies obtain their last perfection by change and movement, while the heavenly bodies have their last perfection at once from their very nature. So, likewise, the lower, namely, the human, intellects obtain their perfection in the knowledge of truth by a kind of movement and discursive intellectual operation. That is to say, they obtain their perfection by advancing from one thing known to another. But if from the knowledge of a known principle they were straightway to perceive as known all its consequent conclusions, then there would be no place for discursiveness[5] in human intellect. Such is the condition of the angels, because in the truths which they know naturally, they at once behold all things whatsoever that can be known in them.

That is why they are called *intellectual* beings, because even in ourselves the things which are apprehended naturally are said to be understood [*intelligi*]. Hence it is that *intellect* is called the *habit of first principles*. But human souls which acquire the knowledge of truth discursively are called *rational*; and this comes of the feebleness of their intellectual light. For if they possessed the fullness of intellectual light,

---

1. 参见 *Post. Anal.*, II, 15 (100a 4); *Metaph.*, I, 1 (980b 28).
2. 参见 *De Div. Nom.*, VII, 2 (PG 3, 868).
3. 参见 A 1; q. 50, a. 3; q. 55, a. 2.
4. 参见 *De Cael. Hier.*, II, 1 (PG 3, 137); *De Div. Nom.*, I, 4 (PG 3, 593).
5. discursiveness: 推论；散漫

like the angels, then in the first grasping of principles they would at once comprehend all their virtualities, by perceiving whatever could be reasoned out from them.

Reply Obj. 1. Discursion expresses movement of a kind. Now all movement is from something before to something after. Hence discursive knowledge comes about according as from something previously known one attains to the knowledge of what is afterwards known, but which was previously unknown. But if in one thing perceived something else be seen at the same time, just as a thing and its image are seen simultaneously in a mirror, this is not discursive knowledge. And in this way the angels know things in the Word.

Reply Obj. 2. The angels can syllogize, in the sense of knowing a syllogism, and they see effects in causes, and causes in effects; yet they do not in this way acquire knowledge of an unknown truth by syllogizing from causes to effect, or from effects to causes.

Reply Obj. 3. Experience is affirmed of angels and demons simply by way of likeness, namely, inasmuch as they know sensible things present to them, yet without any discursion withal.

Fourth Article
WHETHER THE ANGELS UNDERSTAND BY COMPOSING AND DIVIDING?

We proceed thus to the Fourth Article:—

Objection 1. It would seem that the angels understand by composing and dividing. For, where there is multiplicity of things understood, there is composition of the same, as is said in *De Anima* iii.[1] But there is a multitude of things understood in the angelic intellect, because angels apprehend different things by various species, and not all at one

---

1. 参见 Aristotle, *De An.*, III, 6 (430a 27).

time. Therefore there is composition and division in the angel's mind.

Obj. 2. Further, negation is far more remote from affirmation than are any two opposite natures, because the first of distinctions is that of affirmation and negation. But the angel knows certain distant natures not by one, but by diverse species, as is evident from what was said. Therefore he must know affirmation and negation by diverse species. And so it seems that he understands by composing and dividing.

Obj. 3. Further, speech is a sign of the intellect. But in speaking to men, angels use affirmative and negative enunciations, which are signs of composition and of division in the intellect; as is manifest from many passages of Sacred Scripture. Therefore it seems that the angel understands by composing and dividing.

On the contrary, Dionysius says that *the intellectual power of the angel shines forth with the clear simplicity of divine concepts.*[1] But a simple understanding is without composition and division.[2] Therefore the angel understands without composition or division.

I answer that, As in the intellect, when reasoning, the conclusion is compared with the principle, so in the intellect composing and dividing, the predicate is compared with the subject. For if our intellect were to see at once the truth of the conclusion in the principle, it would never understand by discursion and reasoning. In like manner, if the intellect in apprehending the quiddity of the subject were at once to have knowledge of all that can be attributed to, or removed from, the subject, it would never understand by composing and dividing, but only by understanding the essence. Thus it is evident that for the self-same reason our intellect understands by discursion, and by composing and dividing, namely, that in the first apprehension of anything newly apprehended it cannot at once grasp all that is virtually contained in it. And this comes from the weakness of the intellectual light within us, as has been said. Hence, since

---

1. 参见 *De Div. Nom.*, VII, 2 (PG 3, 868).
2. 参见 Aristotle, *De An.*, III, 6 (430a 27).

the intellectual light is perfect in the angel, for *he is a pure and most clear mirror*, as Dionysius says,[1] it follows that as the angel does not understand by reasoning, so neither does he by composing and dividing.

Nevertheless, he understands the composition and the division of enunciations, just as he apprehends the reasoning of syllogisms; for he understands the composite simply, the movable immovably, and the material immaterially.

Reply Obj. 1. Not every multitude of things understood causes composition, but only that multitude in which one thing understood is attributed to, or denied of, another. But when an angel apprehends the quiddity of anything, he at the same time understands whatever can be either attributed to it or denied of it. Hence, in apprehending the essence, by one simple perception he grasps all that we can learn by composing and dividing.

Reply Obj. 2. The various quiddities of things differ less as to their mode of existing than do affirmation and negation. Yet, as to the way in which they are known, affirmation and negation have something more in common; because directly the truth of an affirmation is known, the falsehood of the opposite negation is known also.

Reply Obj. 3. The fact that angels use affirmative and negative enunciations shows that they know composition and division; it does not show that they know by composing and dividing, but rather by knowing simply the nature of a thing.

Fifth Article
WHETHER THERE CAN BE FALSEHOOD IN THE INTELLECT OF AN ANGEL?

We proceed thus to the Fifth Article:—

---

1. 参见 *De Div. Nom.*, IV, 22 (PG 3, 724).

Objection 1. It would seem that there can be falsehood in the angel's intellect. For perversity pertains to falsehood. But, as Dionysius says, there is a *perverted fancy*[1] in the demons.[2] Therefore it seems that there can be falsehood in the intellect of the angels.

Obj. 2. Further, nescience is the cause of judging falsely. But, as Dionysius says, there can be nescience in the angels.[3] Therefore it seems there can be falsehood in them.

Obj. 3. Further, everything which falls away from the truth of wisdom, and which has a depraved reason, has falsehood or error in its intellect. But Dionysius affirms this of the demons.[4] Therefore it seems that there can be falsehood in the minds of the angels.

On the contrary, The Philosopher says that *the intellect is always true.*[5] Augustine likewise says that *nothing but what is true can be the object of intellect.*[6] Therefore there can be neither deception nor falsehood in the angel's knowledge.

I answer that, The truth of this question depends partly upon what has gone before. For it has been said that an angel understands not by composing and dividing, but by understanding essence. Now *the intellect is always true as regards essence*, just as is the sense regarding its proper object, as is said in *De Anima* iii.[7] But deception and falsehood creep in by accident, when we understand the essence of a thing by some kind of composition, and this happens either when we take the definition of one thing as the definition of another, or when the parts of a definition do not hang together, as if we were to accept as the definition of some creature, *a four-footed flying beast*, for there is no such

---

1. perverted fancy: 颠倒是非的想象
2. 参见 *Op. cit.*, IV, 23 (PG 3, 725).
3. 参见 *De Eccles. Hier.*, VI, 1 (PG 3, 200).
4. 参见 *De Div. Nom.*, VII, 2 (PG 3, 868).
5. 参见 *De An.*, III 10 (433a 26); 6 (430b 27).
6. 参见 *Lib. 83 Quaest.*, q. 32 (PL 40, 22); q. 44 (PL 40, 38).
7. 参见 *De An.*, III, 6 (430b 27).

animal. This happens in composite things, the definition of which is drawn from diverse elements, one of which is as matter to the other. But there is no room for error in understanding simple quiddities, as is stated in *Metaph.* ix,[1] for either they are not grasped at all, and so we know nothing respecting them, or else they are known precisely as they exist.

Thus, therefore, no falsehood, error, or deception can exist of itself in the mind of any angel. Yet it does happen accidentally, but very differently from the way it befalls us. For we sometimes get at the quiddity of a thing by composing and dividing, as when, by division and demonstration, we seek out the truth of a definition. Such is not the method of the angels, but through the essence of a thing they know everything that can be said regarding it. Now it is quite evident that the quiddity of a thing can be a source of knowledge with regard to everything naturally belonging to such a thing, or naturally excluded from it; but not of what is dependent on God's supernatural ordinance. Consequently, owing to their upright will, the good angels, from their knowing the nature of a creature, do not form any judgment as to what pertains to the thing supernaturally, save under the divine ordinance; and hence there can be no error or falsehood in them. But since the demons have turned their intellects away from the divine wisdom through a perversion of will, they at times judge of things absolutely according to their natural conditions. Now they are not deceived as to the natural properties of anything, but they can be misled with regard to supernatural matters; for example, on seeing a dead man, they may suppose that he will not rise again, or, on beholding Christ as man, they may judge Him not to be God.

From all this the answers to the objections on both sides of the question are evident. For the perversity of the demons comes of their

---

1. 参见 Aristotle, *Metaph.*, VIII, 10 (1051b 26).

not being subject to the divine wisdom, while nescience is in the angels as regards things knowable, not naturally, but supernaturally. It is, furthermore, evident that their understanding of essence is always true, save accidentally, according as it is, in an undue manner, referred to some composition or division.

Sixth Article

WHETHER THERE IS A *MORNING* AND AN *EVENING* KNOWLEDGE IN THE ANGELS?

We proceed thus to the Sixth Article:—

Objection 1. It would seem that there is neither an evening nor a morning knowledge in the angels, because evening and morning have an admixture of darkness. But there is no darkness in the knowledge of an angel, since there is no error or falsehood. Therefore the angelic knowledge ought not to be termed morning and evening knowledge.

Obj. 2. Further, between evening and morning the night intervenes, while noonday falls between morning and evening. Consequently, if there be a morning and an evening knowledge in the angels, for the same reason it appears that there ought to be a noonday and a night knowledge.

Obj. 3. Further, knowledge is diversified according to the difference of the objects known. Hence the Philosopher says, *The sciences are divided as things are.*[1] But there is a threefold being of things, namely, *in the Word, in their own natures, and in the angelic knowledge*[2], as Augustine observes.[3] If, therefore, a morning and an evening knowledge be admitted in the angels, because of the being of things in the Word, and in their own nature, then there ought to be admitted a third class of

1. 参见 *De An.*, III, 8 (431b 24).
2. the angelic knowledge: 天使的知识
3. 参见 *De Genesi ad Litt.*, II, 8 (PL 34, 269).

knowledge, because of the being of things in the angelic mind.

On the contrary, Augustine divides the knowledge of the angels into morning and evening knowledge.[1]

I answer that, The expression *morning* and *evening* knowledge was devised by Augustine, who interprets the six days wherein God made all things, not as ordinary days measured by the solar circuit, since the sun was not made until on the fourth day, but as one day, namely, the day of angelic knowledge as directed to six classes of things.[2] Now, just as in the ordinary day, morning is the beginning, and evening the close of day, so, their knowledge of the primordial being of things is called *morning knowledge*[3]; and this is according as things exist in the Word. But their knowledge of the very being of the thing created, as it stands in its own nature, is termed *evening knowledge*[4], because the being of things flows from the Word as from a kind of primordial principle[5], and this flow is *terminated* in the being which they have in themselves.

Reply Obj. 1. Evening and morning in the angelic knowledge are not taken as compared to the admixture of darkness, but as compared to beginning and end. Or else it can be said, as Augustine puts it, that there is nothing to prevent us from calling something light in comparison with one thing, and darkness with respect to another.[6] In the same way the life of the faithful and the just is called light in comparison with the wicked, according to *Ephes* v. 8: *You were heretofore darkness; but now, light in the Lord.* Yet this very life of the faithful, when set in contrast to the life of glory, is termed darkness, according to *2 Pet.* i. 19: *You have the firm prophetic word, whereunto you do well to attend,*

---

1. 参见 *Op. cit.*, IV, 22 (PL 34, 312); *De Civit. Dei*, XI, 7 (PL 41, 322).
2. 参见 *De Genesi ad Litt.*, IV, 22; 26 (PL 34, 312; 314).
3. morning knowledge: 清晨的知识，指万物因存在于天主圣言内而最先存在的知识
4. evening knowledge: 傍晚的知识，指存在于受造物自己本性内的知识
5. primordial principle: 最初的原理；本源
6. 参见 *Op. cit.*, IV, 23 (PL 34, 312).

as to a light that shineth in a dark place. So the angel's knowledge, by which he knows things in their own nature, is day in comparison with ignorance or error; yet it is dark in comparison with the vision of the Word.

Reply Obj. 2. The morning and evening knowledge belong to the day, that is, to the illumined angels, who are quite apart from the darkness, that is, from the evil angels. The good angels, while knowing the creature, do not adhere to it, for that would be to turn to darkness and to night; but they refer this back to the praise of God, in Whom, as in their principle, they know all things. Consequently after *evening* there is no night, but *morning*; so that morning is the end of the preceding day and the beginning of the following, in so far as the angels refer to God's praise their knowledge of the preceding work. Noonday is comprised under the name of day, as the middle between the two extremes. Or else the noon can be referred to their knowledge of God Himself, Who has neither beginning nor end.

Reply Obj. 3. The angels themselves are also creatures. Accordingly the being of things in the angelic knowledge is comprised under evening knowledge, as is the being of things in their own nature.

Seventh Article
WHETHER THE MORNING AND EVENING KNOWLEDGE ARE ONE?

We proceed thus to the Seventh Article:—

Objection 1. It would seem that the morning and the evening knowledge are one. For it is said (*Gen.* i. 5): *There was evening and morning, one day.* But by the expression *day* the knowledge of the angels is to be understood, as Augustine says.[1] Therefore the morning and the

1. 参见 *De Genesi ad Litt.*, IV, 22; 26 (PL 34, 312; 314); *De Civit. Dei*, IX, 7 (PL 41, 322).

evening knowledge of the angels are one and the same.

Obj. 2. Further, it is impossible for one power to have two operations at the same time. But the angels are always using their morning knowledge, because they are always beholding God and things in God, according to *Matt.* xviii. 10. Therefore, if the evening knowledge were different from the morning, the angel could never exercise his evening knowledge.

Obj. 3. Further, the Apostle says (*1 Cor.* xiii. 10): *When that which is perfect is come, then that which is in part shall be done away.* But, if the evening knowledge be different from the morning, it is compared to it as the less perfect to the perfect. Therefore the evening knowledge cannot exist together with the morning knowledge.

On the contrary, Augustine says: *There is a vast difference between knowing anything as it is in the Word of God, and as it is in its own nature; so that the former belongs to the day, and the latter to the evening.*[1]

I answer that, As was observed, the evening knowledge is that by which the angels know things in their proper nature. This cannot be understood to mean that they draw their knowledge from the proper nature of things, in which case the preposition *in* denotes relation to a principle; because, as has been already stated, the angels do not draw their knowledge from things.[2] It follows, then, that when we say *in their proper nature*, we refer to the aspect of the thing known in so far as it is an object of knowledge; that is to say, that the evening knowledge is in the angels in so far as they know the being of things which those things have in their own nature.

Now they know this through a twofold medium, namely, by innate species, and by the likenesses of things existing in the Word. For by beholding the Word, they know not merely that being which things have in the Word, but that being which they have in themselves. In the

1. 参见 *De Genesi ad Litt.*, IV, 23 (PL 34, 312).
2. 参见 Q. 55, a. 2.

same way, God by contemplating Himself sees that being which things have in their own nature. If, therefore, evening knowledge means that when the angels behold the Word, they know the being which things have in their proper nature, then the morning and the evening knowledge are essentially one and the same, and differ only as to the things known. If evening knowledge refers to the fact that through innate ideas the angels know the being which things have in their own natures, then the morning and the evening knowledge differ. Thus Augustine seems to understand the matter when he assigns one as inferior to the other.[1]

Reply Obj. 1. The six days, as Augustine understands them, are taken as the six classes of things known by the angels; so that the day's unit is taken according to the unit of the thing understood, which, nevertheless, can be apprehended by various ways of knowing it.

Reply Obj. 2. There can be two operations of the same power at the one time, if one of them is referred to the other; as is evident when the will at the same time wills the end and the means to the end, and the intellect at the same instant perceives principles and conclusions through the principles, after the acquisition of science. As Augustine says, however, the evening knowledge is referred to the morning knowledge in the angels;[2] hence there is nothing to hinder both from being at the same time in the angels.

Reply Obj. 3. On the coming of what is perfect, the opposite imperfect is done away; just as faith, which is of the things that are not seen, is made void when vision succeeds. But the imperfection of the evening knowledge is not opposed to the perfection of the morning knowledge. For that a thing be known in itself is not opposed to its

---

1. 参见 *De Genesi ad Litt.*, IV, 22; 29 (PL 34, 312; 315); *De Civit. Dei*, XI, 7 (PL 41, 522).
2. 参见 *De Genesi ad Litt.*, TV, 22; 24; 30 (PL 34, 312; 313; 316) ; *De Civit. Dei*, XI, 7 (PL 41, 322).

being known in its cause. Nor, again, is there any inconsistency in knowing a thing through two mediums, one of which is more perfect and the other less perfect; just as we can have a demonstrative and a probable means for reaching the same conclusion. In like manner, a thing can be known by the angel through the uncreated Word, and through an innate species.

Question LIX
THE WILL OF THE ANGELS
(*In Four Articles*)

IN the next place we must treat of things concerning the will of the angels. In the first place we shall treat of the will itself; secondly, of its movement, which is love.[1] Under the first heading there are four points of inquiry: (1) Whether there is will in the angels? (2) Whether the will of the angel is his nature, or his intellect? (3) Is there free choice in the angels? (4) Is there an irascible[2] and a concupiscible appetite[3] in them?

First Article
WHETHER THERE IS WILL IN THE ANGELS?

We proceed thus to the First Article:—

Objection 1. It would seem that there is no will in the angels. For as the Philosopher says, *The will is in the reason.*[4] But there is no reason in the angels, but something higher than reason. Therefore there is no will in the angels, but something higher than the will.

Obj. 2. Further, the will is comprised under the appetite, as is evident from the Philosopher.[5] But appetite argues something imperfect,

---

1. 参见 Q. 60.
2. irascible appetite: 愤怒之情
3. concupiscible appetite: 欲情
4. 参见 *De An.*, III, 9 (432b 5).
5. 参见 *Op. cit.*, 10 (433a 23).

because it is a desire of something not as yet possessed. Therefore, since there is no imperfection in the angels, especially in the blessed ones, it seems that there is no will in them.

Obj. 3. Further, the Philosopher says that the will is a mover which is moved;[1] for it is moved by the understood appetible object. Now the angels are immovable, since they are incorporeal. Therefore there is no will in the angels.

On the contrary, Augustine says that the image of the Trinity is found in the mind according to memory, understanding and will.[2] But God's image is found not only in the mind of man, but also in the angelic mind, since it also is capable of knowing God. Therefore there is will in the angels.

I answer that, We must necessarily say that there is a will in the angels. In evidence thereof, it must be borne in mind that, since all things flow from the divine will, all things in their own way are inclined by appetite towards good, but in different ways. Some are inclined to good by their natural disposition, without knowledge, as plants and inanimate bodies. Such inclination towards good is called *a natural appetite*. Others, again, are inclined towards good, but with some knowledge. Not that they know the very nature of goodness: they rather apprehend some particular good, as is the case with the sense, which knows the sweet, the white, and so on. The inclination which follows this apprehension is called *a sensitive appetite*. Other things, again, have an inclination towards good, but with a knowledge whereby they perceive the nature of goodness. This belongs to the intellect. Things so inclined are most perfectly inclined towards what is good; not, indeed, as if they were guided only by another towards the good, like things devoid of knowledge, nor as if they were guided towards some particular good only, as things which have only sensitive knowledge, but as inclined

1. 参见 *Op. cit.*, 10 (433b 16).
2. 参见 *De Trin.*, X, 12 (PL 42, 984).

towards the universal good itself. Such inclination is termed *will*. Accordingly, since the angels by their intellect know the universal nature of goodness, it is manifest that there is a will in them.

Reply Obj. 1. Reason surpasses sense in a different way from that in which intellect surpasses reason. Reason surpasses sense according to the diversity of the objects known; for sense knows particulars, while reason knows universals. Therefore there must be one appetite tending towards the universal good, which appetite belongs to reason; and another with a tendency towards the particular good, which appetite belongs to sense. But intellect and reason differ as to their manner of knowing, because the intellect knows by simple intuition, while reason knows by discursion from one thing to another. Nevertheless, by such discursion reason comes to know what intellect knows without it, namely, the universal. Consequently, the object presented to the appetitive power on the part of reason and on the part of intellect is the same. Therefore in the angels, who are purely intellectual, there is no appetite higher than the will.

Reply Obj. 2. Although the name of the appetitive part is derived from seeking things not yet possessed, yet the appetitive part reaches out not only to these things, but also to many other things. So, too, the name of a stone [*lapis*] is derived from injuring the foot [*læsio pedis*], though not this alone belongs to a stone. In the same way, the irascible power is so denominated from anger [*ira*], though at the same time there are several other passions in it, as hope, daring, and the rest.

Reply Obj. 3. The will is called a mover which is moved, according as to will and to understand are termed movements of a kind. There is nothing to prevent movement of this kind from existing in the angels, since such movement is the *act of what is perfect*, as is stated in *De Anima* iii.[1]

---

1. 参见 Aristotle, *De An.*, III, 7 (431a 6).

Second Article

WHETHER IN THE ANGELS THE WILL DIFFERS FROM THE INTELLECT?

We proceed thus to the Second Article:—

Objection 1. It would seem that in the angels the will does not differ from the intellect and from the nature. For an angel is more simple than a natural body. But a natural body is inclined through its form towards its end, which is its good. Therefore much more so is the angel. Now the angel's form is either the nature in which he subsists, or else it is some species within his intellect. Therefore the angel is inclined towards the good through his own nature, or through an intelligible species. But such inclination towards the good belongs to the will. Therefore the will of the angel does not differ from his nature or his intellect.

Obj. 2. Further, the object of the intellect is the true, while the object of the will is the good. Now the good and the true differ, not really, but only logically.[1] Therefore will and intellect are not really different.

Obj. 3. Further, the distinction of common and proper does not differentiate the powers, for the same power of sight perceives color and whiteness. But the good and the true seem to be mutually related as common to particular; for the true is a particular good, namely, of the intellect. Therefore the will, whose object is the good, does not differ from the intellect, whose object is the true.

On the contrary, The will in the angels regards good things only, while their intellect regards both good and evil things, for they know both. Therefore the will of the angels is distinct from their intellect.

I answer that, In the angels the will is a faculty or power, which is

---

1. 参见 Cf. above, q. 16, a. 4.

neither their nature nor their intellect. That it is not their nature is manifest from this, that the nature or essence of a thing is completely comprised within it: whatever, then, extends to anything beyond it, is not its essence. Hence we see in natural bodies that the inclination to being does not come from anything superadded to the essence, but from the matter which desires being before possessing it, and from the form which keeps it in such being when once it exists. But the inclination towards something extrinsic comes from something superadded to the essence: *e.g.*, tendency to a place comes from gravity or lightness, while the inclination to make something like itself comes from the active qualities.

Now the will has a natural tendency towards good. Consequently there alone are essence and will identified where the good is wholly contained within the essence of him who wills; that is to say, in God, Who wills nothing beyond Himself except because of His goodness. This cannot be said of any creature, because infinite goodness is outside the essence of any created thing. Accordingly, neither the will of the angel, nor that of any creature, can be the same thing as its essence.

In like manner neither can the will be the same thing as the intellect of angel or man. For knowledge comes about because the thing known is in the knower. Consequently the intellect extends itself to what is outside it, according as what is essentially outside it is naturally capable of being somehow within it. On the other hand, the will goes out to what is beyond it, according as by a kind of inclination it tends somehow to what is outside it. Now it belongs to one power to have within itself something which is outside it, and to another power to tend to what is outside it. Consequently intellect and will must necessarily be different powers in every creature. It is not so with God, for He has within Himself universal being and the universal good. Therefore both intellect and will are His essence.

Reply Obj. 1. A natural body is inclined to its own being by its substantial form; while it is inclined to something outside by something additional, as has been said.

Reply Obj. 2. Powers are not differentiated by any material distinction in their objects, but according to their formal distinction, which is taken from the nature of the object as such. Consequently the diversity derived from the notion of good and true suffices for the diversity intellect from will.

Reply Obj. 3. Because the good and the true are really convertible, it follows that the good is apprehended by the intellect as something true, and that the true is desired by the will as something good. Nevertheless the diversity of their meanings is sufficient for diversifying the powers, as was said above.

Third Article
WHETHER THERE IS FREE CHOICE IN THE ANGELS?

We proceed thus to the Third Article:—

Objection 1. It would seem that there is no free choice in the angels. For the act of free choice is to choose. But there can be no choice with the angels, because choice is *the desire of something after taking counsel*, while counsel is *a kind of inquiry*, according to *Ethics* iii.[1] But the angels' knowledge is not the result of inquiring, for this belongs to the discursiveness of reason. Therefore it appears that there is no free choice in the angels.

Obj. 2. Further, free choice implies indifference to alternatives. But on the part of their intellect there is no such indifference in the angels, because, as was already observed, their intellect is not deceived as to things which are naturally intelligible to them.[2] Therefore neither on the part of their appetitive power can there be free choice.

---

1. 参见 Aristotle, *Eth.*, III, 2 (1112a 15); 3 (1112b 23).
2. 参见 Q. 58, a. 5.

Obj. 3. Further, the natural endowments of the angels belong to them according to degrees of more or less; because in the higher angels the intellectual nature is more perfect than in the lower. But free choice does not admit of degrees. Therefore there is no free choice in them.

On the contrary, Free choice is part of man's dignity. But the angels' dignity surpasses that of men. Therefore, since free choice is in men, with much more reason is it in the angels.

I answer that, Some things there are which act, not from any previous judgment, but, as it were, moved and made to act by others; just as the arrow is directed to the target by the archer. Others act from some kind of judgment, but not from free choice, such as irrational animals; for the sheep flies from the wolf by a kind of judgment whereby it esteems it to be hurtful to itself. Now such a judgment is not a free one, but implanted by nature. Only an agent endowed with an intellect can act with a judgment which is free, in so far as it knows the universal nature of goodness, from which it can judge this or the other thing to be good. Consequently, wherever there is intellect, there is free choice. It is therefore manifest that just as there is intellect, so is there free choice in the angels, and in a higher degree of perfection than in man.

Reply Obj. 1. The Philosopher is speaking of choice as it is in man.[1] Now just as a man's judgment in speculative matters differs from an angel's in that the one needs not to inquire, while the other does, so is it in practical matters. Hence there is choice in the angels, yet not with the inquiring deliberation of counsel, but by the immediate acceptance of truth.

Reply Obj. 2. As was observed already, knowledge is effected by the presence of the known within the knower.[2] Now it is a mark of imperfection in anything not to have within it what it should naturally

1. 参见 *Eth.*, III, 2 (1112a 15) ; 3 (1112b 23).
2. 参见 A. 2; q. 12, a. 4.

have. Consequently an angel would not be perfect in his nature, if his intellect were not determined to every truth which he can know naturally. But the act of the appetitive power comes of this, that the affection is directed to something outside. Yet the perfection of a thing does not come from everything to which it is inclined, but only from something which is higher than it. Therefore it does not argue imperfection in an angel if his will be not determined with regard to things beneath him; but it would argue imperfection in him, were he to be indeterminate to what is above him.

Reply Obj. 3. Free choice exists in a nobler manner in the higher angels than it does in the lower, as also does the judgment of the intellect. Yet it is true that liberty, in so far as the removal of compulsion is considered, is not susceptible[1] of greater and less degree; because privations and negations are not lessened nor increased directly of themselves, but only by their cause, or through the addition of some qualification.

Fourth Article
WHETHER THERE IS AN IRASCIBLE AND A CONCUPISCIBLE APPETITE IN THE ANGELS?

We proceed thus to the Fourth Article:—

Objection 1. It would seem that there is an irascible and a concupiscible[2] appetite in the angels. For Dionysius says that in the demons there is *unreasonable fury and wild concupiscence.*[3] But demons are of the same nature as angels, for sin did not alter their nature. Therefore there is an irascible and a concupiscible appetite in the angels.

---

1. susceptible: 易受影响的；移动感情的
2. concupiscence: 情欲，私欲偏情
3. 参见 *De Div. Nom.*, IV, 23 (PG 3, 725).

Obj. 2. Further, love and joy are in the concupiscible appetite, while anger, hope and fear are in the irascible appetite. But in the Sacred Scriptures these things are attributed both to the good and to the wicked angels. Therefore there is an irascible and a concupiscible appetite in the angels.

Obj. 3. Further, some virtues are said to reside in the irascible appetite and some in the concupiscible. Thus charity and temperance appear to be in the concupiscible, while hope and fortitude are in the irascible. But these virtues are in the angels. Therefore there is both a concupiscible and an irascible appetite in the angels.

On the contrary, The Philosopher says that the irascible and concupiscible are in the sensitive part,[1] which does not exist in angels. Consequently there is no irascible or concupiscible appetite in the angels.

I answer that, The intellective appetite is not divided into irascible and concupiscible; only the sensitive appetite is so divided. The reason for this is because powers are distinguished from one another, not according to a material distinction of their objects, but only according to the formal aspect of object. Hence if to any power there corresponds an object according to some common idea, there will be no distinction of powers according to the diversity of the proper objects contained under that common idea. Just as, if the proper object of the power of sight be color as such, there are not several powers of sight distinguished according to the difference of black and white; whereas if the proper object of a given power were white, as white, then the power of seeing white would be distinguished from the power of seeing black.

Now it is quite evident from what has been said that the object of intellectual appetite, otherwise known as the will, is good according to

1. 参见 *De An.*, III, 9 (432b 6).

the common nature of goodness; nor can there be any appetite except of what is good. Hence, in the intellectual part, the appetite is not divided according to the distinction of some particular good things; but this is rather the way that the sensitive appetite is divided, which is not related to what is good according to its common nature, but to some particular good. Accordingly, since there exists in the angels only an intellectual appetite, their appetite is not distinguished into irascible and concupiscible, but remains undivided, and is called the will.

Reply Obj. 1. Fury and concupiscence are metaphorically said to be in the demons, just as anger is sometimes attributed to God because of the resemblance in the effect.

Reply Obj. 2. Love and joy, in so far as they are passions, are in the concupiscible appetite; but in so far as they name an act of the will, they are in the intellectual part. In this sense, to love is to wish well to anyone; and to be glad is for the will to repose in some good possessed. Universally speaking, therefore, none of these things is said of the angels in the sense of meaning a passion, as Augustine says.[1]

Reply Obj. 3. Charity, as a virtue, is not in the concupiscible appetite, but in the will. For the object of the concupiscible appetite is the good as delectable to the senses, whereas the divine goodness, which is the object of charity, is not such a good. For the same reason it must be said that hope does not reside in the irascible appetite, because the object of the irascible appetite is something arduous belonging to the sensible order. With this the virtue of hope is not concerned, since the object of the virtue of hope is something arduous and divine. Temperance, however, considered as a human virtue, deals with the desires of sensible pleasures, which belong to the concupiscible power. Similarly, fortitude regulates daring and fear, which reside in the irascible part. Consequently, temperance, in so far as it is a human

---

1. 参见 *De Civit.* Dei, IX, 5 (PL 41, 261).

virtue, resides in the concupiscible part, and fortitude in the irascible. But they do not exist in the angels in this manner. For in them there are no passions of concupiscence, nor of fear and daring, to be regulated by temperance and fortitude. But temperance is predicated of them according as they display their will in a controlled way in conformity with the divine will. Fortitude is likewise attributed to them in so far as they firmly carry out the divine will. All of this is done by their will, and not by the irascible or concupiscible appetite.

Question LX
THE LOVE OR DILECTION OF THE ANGELS
(*In Five Articles*)

THE next subject for our consideration is the act of the will, which is *love* or *dilection*; because every act of the appetitive power belongs to love.

Under this heading there are five points of inquiry: (1) Whether there is natural love in the angels? (2) Whether there is in them love of choice? (3) Whether the angel loves himself with natural love or with love of choice? (4) Whether one angel loves another as himself with natural love? (5) Whether the angel loves God more than self with natural love?

First Article
WHETHER THERE IS NATURAL LOVE OR DILECTION IN AN ANGEL?

We proceed thus to the First Article:—

Objection 1. It would seem that there is no natural love or dilection in the angels. For natural love is contradistinguished from intellectual love, as is stated by Dionysius.[1] But an angel's love is intellectual. Therefore it is not natural.

Obj. 2. Further, those who love with natural love are more acted

---

1. 参见 *De Div. Nom.*, IV, 15 (PG 3, 713).

upon than active in themselves; for nothing is master over its own nature. Now the angels are not acted upon, but act of themselves, because they possess free choice, as was shown above.[1] Consequently there is no natural love in them.

Obj. 3. Further, every love is either ordinate or inordinate. Now ordinate love belongs to charity, while inordinate love belongs to wickedness. But neither of these belongs to nature; for charity is above nature, while wickedness is against nature. Therefore there is no natural love in the angels.

On the contrary, Love results from knowledge, for nothing is loved except it be first known, as Augustine says.[2] But there is natural knowledge in the angels. Therefore there is also natural love.

I answer that, We must necessarily say that there is natural love in the angels. In evidence of this we must bear in mind that what comes first is always verified in what comes after it. Now nature comes before intellect, because the nature of every subject is its essence. Consequently whatever belongs to nature must likewise be verified in beings having an intellect. But it is common to every nature to have some inclination; and this is its natural appetite or love. This inclination is found to exist diversely in different natures, in accord with the mode of each nature. Consequently, in the intellectual nature there is to be found a natural inclination according to the mode of will; in the sensitive nature, according to the mode of sensitive appetite; but in a nature devoid of knowledge, only according to the ordination of the nature to something. Therefore, since an angel is an intellectual nature, there must be a natural love in his will.

Reply Obj. 1. Intellectual love is contradistinguished from that natural love which is merely natural, in so far as it belongs to a nature which has not the perfection of either sense or intellect added to its

---

1. 参见 Q. 59, a. 3.
2. 参见 *De Trin.*, VIII, 4; X, 1; 2 (PL 42, 951; 973; 975).

character as a nature.

Reply Obj. 2. All things in the whole world are moved to act by something else, except the First Agent, Who acts in such a manner that He is in no way moved to act by another. In Him, nature and will are the same. So there is nothing unfitting if an angel is moved to act, in so far as a natural inclination is implanted in him by the Author of his nature. Yet he is not so moved to act that he himself does not act, for he has free choice.

Reply Obj. 3. As natural knowledge is always true, so natural love is always well regulated; because natural love is nothing else than the inclination implanted in nature by its Author. To say that a natural inclination is not well regulated, is to derogate from the Author of nature. Yet the rectitude of natural love is different from the rectitude of charity and virtue, for the one rectitude perfects the other. In the same way, the truth of natural knowledge is of one kind, and the truth of infused or acquired knowledge is of another.

Second Article
WHETHER THERE IS LOVE OF CHOICE IN THE ANGELS?

We proceed thus to the Second Article:—

Objection 1. It would seem that there is no love of choice in the angels. For love of choice appears to be rational love, since choice follows counsel, which lies in inquiry, according to *Ethics* iii.[1] Now rational love is contrasted with intellectual love, which is proper to angels, as it is said.[2] Therefore there is no love of choice in the angels.

Obj. 2. Further, the angels have only natural knowledge besides such as is infused, since they do not proceed from principles to acquire the knowledge of conclusions. Hence they are disposed to everything

1. 参见 Aristotle, *Eth.*, III, 2 (1112a 15); 3 (1112b 23).
2. 参见 Pseudo-Dionysius, *De Div. Norm.*, IV, 16 (PG 3, 713).

they can naturally know in the same way that our intellect is disposed towards first principles, which it can know naturally. Now love follows knowledge, as has been already stated. Consequently, besides their infused love, there is only natural love in the angels. Therefore there is no love of choice in them.

On the contrary, We neither merit nor demerit by our natural acts. But by their love the angels merit or demerit. Therefore there is love of choice in them.

I answer that, There exists in the angels a natural love and a love of choice. Their natural love is the principle of their love of choice, because what belongs to that which precedes has always the nature of a principle. Therefore, since nature is first in everything, what belongs to nature must be a principle in everything.

This is clearly evident in man, with respect to both his intellect and his will. For the intellect knows principles naturally, and from such knowledge in man comes the knowledge of conclusions, which are known by him not naturally, but by discovery or by teaching. In like manner, the end acts in the will in the same way as the principle does in the intellect, as is laid down in *Physics* ii.[1] Consequently the will tends naturally to its last end, for every man naturally wills happiness. All other desires are results from this natural desire, since whatever a man wills he wills for the sake of the end. Therefore, that love which is the love of the good that a man naturally wills as an end is his natural love; but the love which comes of this, which is of something loved for the sake of the end, is the love of choice.

There is however a difference on the part of the intellect and on the part of the will. Because, as was stated already, the intellect's knowledge is brought about by the presence of the known within the knower.[2] Now it is the result of the imperfection of man's intellectual

---

1. 参见 Aristotle, *Phys.*, II, 9 (200a 22).
2. 参见 Q. 59, a. 2.

nature that his intellect does not immediately possess all things capable of being understood, but only a few things, from which he is moved in a measure to grasp other things. The act of the appetitive power, on the contrary, follows the inclination of man towards things. Some of these are good in themselves, and consequently are appetible in themselves; others are good only in relation to something else, and are appetible for the sake of something else. Consequently, it does not argue imperfection in the person desiring, for him to seek one thing naturally as his end, and something else from choice as ordained to such end. Therefore, since the intellectual nature of the angels is perfect, only natural and not discursive knowledge is to be found in them; but there is to be found in them both natural love and love of choice.

In saying all this, we are passing over all that pertains to what is above nature, since nature is not the sufficient principle thereof. We shall consider these matters later on.[1]

Reply Obj. 1. Not all love of choice is rational love, according as rational is distinguished from intellectual love. For rational love is the love which follows discursive knowledge. But, as was said above when treating of free choice, not every choice follows a discursive act of the reason, but only human choice.[2] Consequently the conclusion does not follow.

The reply to the second objection follows from what has been said.

Third Article

WHETHER THE ANGEL LOVES HIMSELF WITH BOTH NATURAL LOVE, AND LOVE OF CHOICE?

We proceed thus to the Third Article:—

1. 参见 Q. 62.
2. 参见 Q. 59, a. 3, ad 1.

Objection 1. It would seem that the angel does not love himself both with a natural love and a love of choice. For, as was said, natural love is of the end itself, while love of choice is of the means to the end. But the same thing, under the same relationship, cannot be both the end and a means to the end. Therefore natural love and the love of choice cannot have the same object.

Obj. 2. Further, as Dionysius observes, *Love is a uniting and a binding power.*[1] But uniting and binding imply various things brought together. Therefore the angel cannot love himself.

Obj. 3. Further, love is a kind of movement. But every movement tends towards something else. Therefore it seems that an angel cannot love himself with either natural or elective love.

On the contrary, The Philosopher says: *Love for others comes of love for oneself.*[2]

I answer that, Since the object of love is the good, and the good is to be found both in substance and in accident, as is clear from *Ethics* i.,[3] a thing may be loved in two ways. First, it may be loved as a subsisting good, and secondly, as an accidental or inherent good. That is loved as a subsisting good which is so loved that we wish well to it. But that which we love for something else is loved as an accidental or inherent good. Thus, knowledge is loved, not that any good may come to it, but that it may be possessed. This kind of love has been called by the name of *concupiscence*, while the first is called *friendship*.

Now among things devoid of knowledge it is manifest that everything naturally seeks to procure what is good for itself; as fire seeks to mount upwards. Consequently, both the angel and man naturally seek their own good and perfection. This is to love the self. Hence the angel and man naturally love the self, in so far as by natural

1. 参见 *De Div. Nom.*, IV, 15 (PG 3, 713).
2. 参见 *Eth.*, IX, 4 (1166a 1).
3. 参见 *Op. cit.*, I, 6 (1096a 19).

appetite each desires what is good for himself. On the other hand, each loves himself with the love of choice, in so far as from choice he wishes for something which will benefit himself.

Reply Obj. 1. It is not under the same, but under quite different aspects, that an angel or a man loves himself with natural and with elective love, as was observed above.

Reply Obj. 2. As to be one means more than to be united, so there is more oneness in love which is directed to the self than in love which is directed to other things united to the self. The reason why Dionysius used the terms *uniting* and *binding* was to show the derivation of love from self to things outside self, on the analogy of the derivation of *uniting* from *unity*.

Reply Obj. 3. As love is an action which remains within the agent, so it is also a movement which abides within the lover, without tending of necessity towards something else. Rather, it can be reflected back upon the lover so that he loves himself; just as knowledge is reflected back upon the knower in such a way that he knows himself.

Fourth Article
WHETHER AN ANGEL LOVES ANOTHER AS HIMSELF WITH NATURAL LOVE?

We proceed thus to the Fourth Article:—

Objection 1. It would seem that an angel does not love another as himself with natural love. For love follows knowledge. But one angel does not know another as he knows himself, because he knows himself by his essence, while he knows another by his likeness, as was said above.[1] Therefore it seems that one angel does not love another as himself with natural love.

---

1. 参见 Q. 56, a. 1 and 2.

Obj. 2. Further, the cause is more powerful than the effect, and the principle than what is derived from it. But love for another comes from love for self, as the Philosopher says.[1] Therefore one angel does not love another as himself, but loves himself more.

Obj. 3. Further, natural love is of something as an end, and is unremovable. But no angel is the end of another; and again, such love can be severed from him, as is the case with the demons, who have no love for the good angels. Therefore an angel does not love another as himself with natural love.

On the contrary, That seems to be natural which is found in all, even in such as are devoid of reason. But, *every beast loves its like*, as is said, *Ecclus.* xiii. 19. Therefore an angel naturally loves another as he loves himself.

I answer that, As was observed, both angel and man naturally love themselves. Now what is one with a thing is that thing itself, and consequently every thing loves what is one with itself. So, if this be one with it by natural union, it loves it with natural love; but if it be one with it by non-natural union, then it loves it with non-natural love. Thus a man loves his fellow citizen with a love of political virtue, while he loves a blood relation with natural love, in so far as he is one with him in the principle of natural generation.

Now it is evident that what is generically or specifically one with another is one according to nature. And so it is with a natural love that everything loves another which is one with it in species, in so far as it loves its own species. This is manifest even in things devoid of knowledge. For fire has a natural inclination to communicate its form to another thing, wherein consists this other thing's good, just as it is naturally inclined to seek its own good, namely, to be borne upwards.

Hence, it must be said that one angel loves another with natural

1. 参见 *Eth.*, IX, 4 (1166a 1).

love, in so far as he is one with him in nature. But so far as an angel has something else besides nature in common with another angel, or differs from him in other respects, he does not love him with natural love.

Reply Obj. 1. The expression *as himself* in one way can qualify knowledge and love on the part of the one known and loved. And thus one angel knows another as himself, because he knows the other to be, just as he knows himself to be. In another way the expression can qualify knowledge and love on the part of the knower and the lover. And thus one angel does not know another as himself, because he knows himself by his essence, and the other not by the other's essence. In like manner, he does not love another as he loves himself, because he loves himself by his own will; but he does not love another by the other's will.

Reply Obj. 2. The expression *as* does not denote equality, but likeness. For since natural love rests upon natural unity, the angel naturally loves less what is less one with him. Consequently he loves more what is numerically one with himself, than what is one only generically or specifically. But it is natural for him to have a like love for another as for himself in this respect, that as he loves himself in wishing well to himself, so he loves another in wishing well to him.

Reply Obj. 3. Natural love is said to be of the end, not as of that end to which the good is willed, but rather as of that good which one wills for oneself, and in consequence for another, as united to oneself. Nor can such natural love be stripped even from the wicked angels, without their still retaining a natural love towards the good angels, in so far as they share the same nature with them. But they hate them, in so far as they are unlike them according to righteousness and unrighteousness.

Fifth Article
WHETHER AN ANGEL BY NATURAL LOVE LOVES GOD MORE THAN HE LOVES HIMSELF?

We proceed thus to the Fifth Article:—

Objection 1. It would seem that the angel does not love God by natural love more than he loves himself. For, as was stated, natural love rests upon natural union. Now the divine nature is far above the angelic nature. Therefore, according to natural love, the angel loves God less than self, or even than another angel.

Obj. 2. Further, *That because of which a thing is such, is yet more so.* But every one loves another with natural love for his own sake, because one thing loves another as good for itself. Therefore the angel does not love God more than himself with natural love.

Obj. 3. Further, nature is self-centred in its operation, for we behold every agent acting naturally for its own preservation. But nature's operation would not be self-centred were it to tend towards anything else more than to nature itself. Therefore the angel does not love God more than himself from natural love.

Obj. 4. Further, it is proper to charity to love God more than self. But to love from charity is not natural to the angels; for *it is poured out upon their hearts by the Holy Spirit Who is given to them*, as Augustine says.[1] Therefore the angels do not love God more than themselves by natural love.

Obj. 5. Further, natural love always lasts while nature endures. But the love of God more than of self does not remain in the angel or man who sins; for, as Augustine says, *Two loves have made two cities, namely, love of self unto the contempt of God has made the earthly city, while love of God unto the contempt of self has made the heavenly city.*[2] Therefore it is not natural to love God more than self.

On the contrary, All the moral precepts of law come from the law of nature. But the precept of loving God more than self is a moral precept of law. Therefore, it is of the law of nature. Consequently the angel loves God more than himself with a natural love.

---

1. 参见 *De Civit. Dei*, XII, 9 (PL 41, 357).
2. 参见 *Op. cit.*, XIV, 28 (PL 41, 436).

I answer that, Some[1] have maintained that an angel loves God more than himself with natural love. This refers to the love of concupiscence, since the angel seeks for himself the divine good rather than his own good. In a fashion this refers to the love of friendship, in so far as he naturally desires a greater good to God than to himself; because he naturally wishes God to be God, while as for himself, he wills to have his own nature. But absolutely speaking, out of natural love the angel loves himself more than he does God, because he naturally loves himself before God, and with greater intensity.

The falsity of such an opinion stands in evidence, if one but consider whither natural movement tends in the natural order of things. For the natural inclination of things devoid of reason shows the nature of the natural inclination residing in the will of an intellectual nature. Now, in natural things, everything which, as such, naturally belongs to another, is principally and more strongly inclined towards that other to which it belongs than towards itself. Such a natural inclination is evidenced from things which are moved according to nature; because *according as a thing is moved naturally, it has an inborn aptitude to be thus moved*, as is stated in *Physics* ii.[2] For we observe that the part naturally exposes itself in order to safeguard the whole; as, for instance, the hand is without deliberation exposed to the blow for the whole body's safety. And since reason imitates nature, we find the same imitation among the political virtues; for it belongs to the virtuous citizen to expose himself to the danger of death for the conservation of the whole body politic; and if man were a natural part of the state, then such an inclination would be natural to him.

Consequently, since God is the universal good, and under this good both man and angel and all creatures are comprised, for every creature

---

1. 参见 William of Auxerre, *Summa Aurea*, II, tr. 1, ch. 4 (fol, 36rb).—Cf. St. Albert, *In II Sent.*, d. iii, a. 18 (XXVII, 98).
2. 参见 Aristotle, *Phys.*, II, 8 (199a 9).

in regard to its entire being naturally belongs to God, it follows that angel and man alike love God with a natural love before themselves and with a greater love. Otherwise, if either of them loved himself more than God, it would follow that natural love would be perverse, and that it would not be perfected, but destroyed, by charity.

Reply Obj. 1. Such reasoning holds good of things adequately divided, of which one is not the cause of the existence and goodness of the other; for in such natures each loves itself naturally more than it does the other, inasmuch as it is more one with itself than it is with the other. But where one is the whole cause of the existence and goodness of the other, that one is naturally more loved than the self; because, as we said above, each part naturally loves the whole more than itself, and each individual naturally loves the good of its species more than its own individual good. Now God is not only the good of one species, but the absolutely universal good. Hence everything in its own way naturally loves God more than itself.

Reply Obj. 2. When it is said that God is loved by an angel *in so far* as He is good to the angel, if the expression *in so far* denotes an end, then it is false; for he does not naturally love God for his own good, but for God's sake. If it denotes the nature of the love in the lover, then it is true; for it would not be in the nature of anyone to love God, except from this, that everything is dependent on that good which is God.

Reply Obj. 3. Nature's operation is self-centred not merely as to what is singular in it, but much more as to what is common; for everything is inclined to preserve not merely its individuality, but likewise its species. And much more has everything a natural inclination towards what is the absolutely universal good.

Reply Obj. 4. God, in so far as He is the universal good, from Whom every natural good depends, is loved by everything with natural love. So far as He is the good which of its very nature beatifies all with supernatural beatitude. He is loved with the love of charity.

Reply Obj. 5. Since in God the divine substance and the universal good are one and the same, all who behold God's essence are by the same movement of love moved towards the divine essence according as it is distinct from other things, and according as it is the universal good. And because He is naturally loved by all so far as He is the universal good, it is impossible that whoever sees Him in His essence should not love Him. But such as do not behold His essence know Him by some particular effects, which are sometimes opposed to their will. So in this way they are said to hate God; although, so far as He is the universal good of all, every thing naturally loves God more than itself.

Question LXI
THE PRODUCTION OF THE ANGELS IN THE ORDER OF NATURAL BEING
(*In Four Articles*)

AFTER dealing with the nature of the angels, their knowledge and will, it now remains for us to treat of their creation, or, speaking in a general way, of their origin. Such consideration is threefold. In the first place we must see how they were brought into natural being; secondly, how they were made perfect in grace or glory;[1] and thirdly, how some of them became wicked.[2]

Under the first heading there are four points of inquiry: (1) Whether the angel has a cause of his being? (2) Whether he has existed from eternity? (3) Whether he was created before corporeal creatures? (4) Whether the angels were created in the empyrean heaven?

First Article
WHETHER THE ANGELS HAVE A CAUSE OF THEIR BEING?

We proceed thus to the First Article:—

Objection 1. It would seem that the angels have no cause of their being. For the first chapter of *Genesis* treats of things created by God. But there is no mention of angels. Therefore the angels were not created by God.

Obj. 2. Further, the Philosopher says that if any substance be a

1. 参见 Q. 62.
2. 参见 Q. 63.

form without matter, *straightway it has being and unity of itself, and has no cause of its being and unity.*[1] But the angels are immaterial forms, as was shown above.[2] Therefore they have no cause of their being.

Obj. 3. Further, whatever is produced by any agent, from the very fact of its being produced, receives form from it. But since the angels are forms, they do not derive their form from any agent. Therefore the angels have no producing cause.

On the contrary, It is said (*Ps.* cxlviii. 2): *Praise ye Him all His angels*; and further on (*verse* 5): *For He spoke and they were made.*

I answer that, It must be affirmed that angels and all things other than God were made by God. For God alone is His own being; while in everything else the essence differs from the being of the thing, as was shown above.[3] From this it is clear that God alone is being of His own essence, while all other things are beings by participation. Now whatever is by participation is caused by what is essentially; as everything ignited is caused by fire. Consequently the angels, of necessity, were created by God.

Reply Obj. 1. Augustine says that the angels were not passed over in that account of the first creation of things, but are designated by the name of *heavens*, or *of light*.[4] And they were either passed over, or else designated by the names of corporeal things, because Moses was addressing an uncultured people, as yet incapable of understanding an incorporeal nature. And if it had been divulged that there were creatures existing beyond corporeal nature, it would have proved to them an occasion of idolatry, to which they were inclined, and from which Moses especially meant to remove them.

Reply Obj. 2. Substances that are subsisting forms have no *formal*

---

1. 参见 *Metaph.*, VII. 6 (1045a 36).
2. 参见 Q. 50, a. 2.
3. 参见 Q. 3, a. 4; q. 7, a. 1, ad 3; a. 2; q. 44, a. 1.
4. 参见 *De Civit. Dei*, XI, 9; 33 (PL 41, 323; 347).

cause of their being and unity, nor such an active cause as produces its effect by changing the matter from a state of potentiality to actuality; but they have a cause productive of their entire substance.

From this the solution of the third difficulty is manifest.

Second Article
WHETHER THE ANGEL WAS PRODUCED BY GOD FROM ETERNITY?

We proceed thus to the Second Article:—

Objection 1. It would seem that the angel was produced by God from eternity. For God is the cause of the angel by His being, for He does not act through something added to His essence. But His being is eternal. Therefore He produced the angels from eternity.

Obj. 2. Further, everything which exists at one period and not at another, is subject to time. But the angel is above time, as is laid down in the *Book of Causes*.[1] Therefore the angel is not at one time existing and at another non-existing, but exists always.

Obj. 3. Further, Augustine proves the soul's incorruptibility by the fact that through the intellect it is capable of truth.[2] But as truth is incorruptible, so is it eternal. Therefore the intellectual nature of the soul and of the angel is not only incorruptible, but likewise eternal.

On the contrary, It is said (*Prov.* viii. 22) in the person of begotten Wisdom: *The Lord possessed me in the beginning of His ways, before He made anything from the beginning.* But, as was shown above, the angels were made by God. Therefore at one time the angels were not.

I answer that, God alone, Father, Son, and Holy Ghost, is from eternity. The Catholic Faith holds this without doubt; and everything to the contrary must be rejected as heretical. For God so produced

---

1. 参见 *De Causis*, II (p. 163).—Cf. above, q. 57, a. 3.
2. 参见 *Solil.*, II, 19 (PL 32, 901).

creatures that He made them *from nothing*; that is, after nothing had been.

Reply Obj. 1. God's being is His will. So the fact that God produced the angels and other creatures by His being does not exclude that He made them also by His will. But, as was shown above, God's will does not act by necessity in producing creatures.[1] Therefore He produced such as He willed, and when He willed.

Reply Obj. 2. An angel is above that time which is the measure of the movement of the heavens, because he is above every movement of a corporeal nature. Nevertheless, he is not above the time which is the measure of the succession of his being after his non-being, and which is also the measure of the succession which is in his operations. Hence Augustine says that *God moves the spiritual creature according to time.*[2]

Reply Obj. 3. Angels and intellectual souls are incorruptible by the very fact of their having a nature by which they are capable of truth. But they did not possess this nature from eternity; it was bestowed upon them when God Himself willed it. Consequently it does not follow that the angels existed from eternity.

Third Article
WHETHER THE ANGELS WERE CREATED BEFORE THE CORPOREAL WORLD?

We proceed thus to the Third Article:—

Objection 1. It would seem that the angels were created before the corporeal world. For Jerome says: *Six thousand years of our time have not yet elapsed; yet how shall we measure the time, how shall we count the ages, in which the Angels, Thrones, Dominations, and the other orders served God?*[3]

---

1. 参见 Q. 19, a. 3; q. 46, a. 1.
2. 参见 *De Genesi ad Litt.*, VIII, 20; 22 (PL 34, 388; 389).
3. 参见 *In Epist. ad Tit.*, I, 2 (PL 26, 594).

Damascene also says: *Some say that the angels were begotten before all creation;*[1] as Gregory the Theologian declares, *He first of all devised the angelic and heavenly powers, and the devising was the making thereof.*[2]

Obj. 2. Further, the angelic nature stands midway between the divine and the corporeal natures. But the divine nature is from eternity, while corporeal nature is from time. Therefore the angelic nature was produced before time was made, and after eternity.

Obj. 3. Further, the angelic nature is more remote from the corporeal nature than one corporeal nature is from another. But one corporeal nature was made before another; hence it is that there are the six days of the production of things set forth in the beginning of *Genesis*. Much more, therefore, was the angelic nature made before every corporeal nature.

On the contrary, It is said (*Gen.* i. 1): *In the beginning God created heaven and earth.* Now, this would not be true if anything had been created previously. Consequently the angels were not created before corporeal nature.

I answer that, There is a twofold opinion on this point to be found in the writings of the Fathers. The more probable one holds that the angels were created at the same time as corporeal creatures. For the angels are part of the universe, for they do not constitute a universe of themselves; but both they and corporeal creatures unite in constituting one universe. This stands in evidence from the relationship of creature to creature, because the mutual relationship of creatures makes up the good of the universe. But no part is perfect if separate from the whole. Consequently it is improbable that God, Whose *works are perfect*, as it is said in *Deut.* xxxii. 4, should have created angelic creatures before other creatures. At the same time the contrary is not to be deemed

---

1. 参见 *De Fide Orth.*, II, 3 (PG 94, 873).
2. 参见 *Orat.* XXXVIII, *In Theoph.* (PG 36, 320).

erroneous; especially because of the opinion of Gregory Nazianzen,[1] whose authority in Christian doctrine is of such weight that no one has ever presumed to attack his teaching, as is also the case with the doctrine of Athanasius, as Jerome says.[2]

Reply Obj. 1. Jerome is speaking according to the teaching of the Greek Fathers, all of whom hold the creation of the angels to have taken place previously to that of the corporeal world.

Reply Obj. 2. God is not a part of, but far above, the whole universe, possessing within Himself the entire perfection of the universe in a more eminent way. But an angel is a part of the universe. Hence the comparison does not hold.

Reply Obj. 3. All corporeal creatures are one in matter; but the angels do not agree with them in matter. Consequently, the creation of the matter of the corporeal creature involves in a manner the creation of all things; but the creation of the angels does not involve the creation of the universe.

If the contrary view be held, then in the text of *Genesis* i. (*In the beginning God created heaven and earth*), the words, *In the beginning*, must be interpreted, "In the Son," or "In the beginning of time" ; but not, "In the beginning, before which there was nothing," unless we say, "Before which there was nothing of the nature of corporeal creatures."

Fourth Article
WHETHER THE ANGELS WERE CREATED IN THE EMPYREAN HEAVEN?

We proceed thus to the Fourth Article:—

Objection 1. It would seem that the angels were not created in the empyrean heaven. For the angels are incorporeal substances. Now a

1. 参见 *Orat.* XXXVIII, *In Theoph.* (PG 36, 320).
2. 参见 Cf. Rufinus, in PG 35, 305.

substance which is incorporeal is not dependent upon a body for its being, and, as a consequence, neither is it for its production. Therefore the angels were not created in any corporeal place.

Obj. 2. Further, Augustine remarks that the angels were created in the upper part of the air;[1] therefore not in the empyrean heaven.

Obj. 3. Further, the empyrean heaven is said to be the highest heaven. If therefore the angels were created in the empyrean heaven, it would not beseem them to mount up to a still higher heaven. And this is contrary to what is said in *Isaias* in the person of the sinning angel: *I will ascend into heaven* (*Isa.* xiv. 13).

On the contrary, Strabo, commenting on the text *In the beginning God created heaven and earth*, says: *By heaven he does not mean the visible firmament, but the empyrean, that is, the fiery or intellectual firmament, which is not so named from its heat, but from its splendor; and which was filled with angels directly it was made.*[2]

I answer that, As was observed, one universe is made up of corporeal and spiritual creatures. Consequently spiritual creatures were so created as to bear some relationship to the corporeal creature, and to rule over every corporeal creature. Hence it was fitting for the angels to be created in the highest corporeal place, as presiding over all corporeal nature; whether it be called the empyrean heaven[3], or whatever else it be called. So Isidore says that the highest heaven is the heaven of the angels, in explaining the passage of *Deuteronomy* x. 14: *Behold heaven is the Lord's thy God, and the heaven of heaven.*[4]

Reply Obj. 1. The angels were not created in a corporeal place as if depending upon a body either as to their being or as to their production; because God could have created them before all corporeal

---

1. 参见 *De Genesi ad Litt.*, III, 10; VIII, 20 (PL 34, 284; 388).
2. 参见 Cf. *Glossa ordin.*, super *Gen.* I, 1 (I, 23F).
3. the empyrean heaven: 苍天
4. 参见 *De Ord. Creatur.*, VI (PL 83, 927).

creation, as many holy Doctors hold. They were made in a corporeal place, on the contrary, in order to show their relationship to corporeal nature, and that they are by their power in touch with bodies.

Reply Obj. 2. By *the upper part of the air* Augustine possibly means the highest part of the heavens, to which air has a kind of affinity owing to its thinness and transparency. Or else he is not speaking of all the angels, but only of such as sinned, who, in the opinion of some, belonged to the lower angelic orders. But there is nothing to hinder us from saying that the higher angels, as having an exalted and universal power over all corporeal things, were created in the highest place of the corporeal creature; while the other angels, as having more restricted powers, were created among the inferior bodies.

Reply Obj. 3. Isaias is not speaking there of any corporeal heavens, but of the heaven of the Blessed Trinity, unto which the sinning angel wished to ascend, when he desired to be equal in some manner to God, as will appear later on.[1]

---

1. 参见 Q. 63, a. 3.

Question LXII
THE PERFECTION OF THE ANGELS IN THE ORDER OF GRACE AND OF GLORY
(*In Nine Articles*)

WE have now to inquire how the angels were made in the order of grace and of glory; under which heading there are nine points of inquiry: (1) Were the angels created in beatitude? (2) Did they need grace in order to turn to God? (3) Were they created in grace? (4) Did they merit their beatitude? (5) Did they at once enter into beatitude after merit? (6) Did they receive grace and glory according to their natural capacities? (7) After entering into glory, did their natural love and knowledge remain? (8) Could they have sinned afterwards? (9) After entering into glory, could they advance farther?

First Article
WHETHER THE ANGELS WERE CREATED IN BEATITUDE?

We proceed thus to the First Article:—

Objection 1. It would seem that the angels were created in beatitude. For it is stated that *the angels who continue in the beatitude wherein they were created do not of their nature possess the excellence they have.*[1] Therefore the angels were created in beatitude.

Obj. 2. Further, the angelic nature is nobler than the corporeal. But the corporeal creature straightway from its creation was perfectly

1. 参见 Gennadius, *De Eccles. Dogm.*, LIX (PL 58, 995).

formed and complete; nor did its informity come before its formation temporally, but only naturally, as Augustine says.[1] Therefore neither did God create the angelic nature unformed and imperfect. But the formation and perfection of the angelic nature are derived from its beatitude, whereby it enjoys God. Therefore it was created in beatitude.

Obj. 3. Further, according to Augustine,[2] the things which we read as being made in the works of the six days, were all made together at one time; and so all the six days must have existed instantly from the beginning of creation. But, according to Augustine's exposition, in those six days, *the morning* was the angelic knowledge, according to which they knew the Word and things in the Word.[3] Therefore, straightway from their creation they knew the Word, and things in the Word. But the beatitude of the angels comes of seeing the Word. Consequently the angels were in beatitude straightway from the very beginning of their creation.

On the contrary, To be established or confirmed in the good is of the nature of beatitude. But the angels were not confirmed in the good as soon as they were created. The fall of some of them shows this. Therefore the angels were not in beatitude from their creation.

I answer that, By the name of beatitude is understood the ultimate perfection of the rational or of the intellectual nature; and hence it is that it is naturally desired, since everything naturally desires its ultimate perfection. Now there is a twofold ultimate perfection of the rational or intellectual nature. The first is one which it can procure of its own natural power; and this is in a measure called beatitude or happiness. Hence Aristotle says that man's ultimate happiness consists in the most perfect contemplation, by which the highest intelligible,

---

1. 参见 *De Genesi ad Litt.*, I, 15; V, 5 (PL 34, 257; 326).
2. 参见 *Op. cit.*, IV, 34; V, 5 (PL 34, 319; 326).
3. 参见 *Op. cit.*, IV, 22 (PL 34, 312).

God, can be contemplated in this life.[1] Above this happiness there is still another, to which we look forward in the future, whereby *we shall see God as He is* (*1 John* iii. 2). This is beyond the nature of every created intellect, as was shown above.[2]

So we must say that, as regards the first beatitude, which the angel could procure by his natural power, he was created blessed. For the angel does not acquire such beatitude by any discursive motion, as man does, but, as was observed above, is straightway in possession of it, owing to his natural dignity.[3] But the angels did not have from the beginning of their creation that ultimate beatitude which is beyond the power of nature. For such beatitude is no part of their nature, but its end; and consequently they ought not to have it immediately from the beginning.

Reply Obj. 1. Beatitude is there taken for that natural perfection which the angel had in the state of innocence.

Reply Obj. 2. The corporeal creature instantly in the beginning of its creation could not have the perfection to which it is brought by its operation; and so, according to Augustine, the growing of plants from the earth did not take place at once among the first works, in which only the germinating power of the plants was placed in the earth.[4] In the same way, the angelic creature had the perfection of its nature in the beginning of its creation; but it did not have the perfection to which it had to come by its operation.

Reply Obj. 3. The angel has a twofold knowledge of the Word, one which is natural, the other from glory. By his natural knowledge he knows the Word through His likeness shining in his nature; and by his knowledge of glory he knows the Word through His essence. By both

---

1. 参见 *Eth.*, X, 7 (1177a 12); 8 (1178b 23).
2. 参见 Q. 12, a. 4.
3. 参见 Q. 58, a. 3.
4. 参见 *De Genesi ad Litt.*, V, 4; 5 (PL 34, 324; 328).

kinds of knowledge the angel knows things in the Word; imperfectly by his natural knowledge, and perfectly by his knowledge of glory. Therefore the first knowledge of things in the Word was present to the angel from the outset of his creation; while the second was not, but only when the angels became blessed by turning to the good. And this is properly termed their *morning* knowledge.

Second Article
WHETHER AN ANGEL NEEDED GRACE IN ORDER TO TURN TO GOD?

We proceed thus to the Second Article:—

Objection 1. It would seem that the angel had no need of grace in order to turn to God. For we have no need of grace for what we can accomplish naturally. But the angel naturally turns to God, because he loves God naturally, as is clear from what has been said.[1] Therefore the angel did not need grace in order to turn to God.

Obj. 2. Further, We seem to need help only for difficult tasks. Now it was not a difficult task for the angel to turn to God, because there was no obstacle in him to such turning. Therefore the angel had no need of grace in order to turn to God.

Obj. 3. Further, to turn oneself to God is to dispose oneself for grace. Hence it is said (*Zach.* i. 3): *Turn ye to Me, and I will turn to you.* But we do not stand in need of grace in order to prepare ourselves for grace, for thus we should go on to infinity. Therefore the angel did not need grace to turn to God.

On the contrary, It was by turning to God that the angel reached to beatitude. If, then, he had needed no grace in order to turn to God, it would follow that he did not require grace in order to possess

---

1. 参见 Q. 60, a. 5.

everlasting life. But this is contrary to the saying of the Apostle (*Rom.* vi. 23): *The grace of God is life everlasting.*

I answer that, The angels stood in need of grace in order to turn to God as the object of beatitude. For, as was observed above, the natural movement of the will is the principle of all that we will.[1] But the will's natural inclination is directed towards what is in keeping with its nature. Therefore, if there is anything which is above nature, the will cannot be inclined towards it, unless helped by some other and supernatural principle. Thus it is clear that fire has a natural tendency to give forth heat and to generate fire, whereas to generate flesh is beyond the natural power of fire, and so fire has no tendency to it, except in so far as it is moved instrumentally by the nutritive soul.

Now it was shown above, when we were treating of God's knowledge, that to see God in His essence, wherein the ultimate beatitude of the rational creature consists, is beyond the nature of every created intellect.[2] Consequently no rational creature can have the movement of the will directed towards such a beatitude, except it be moved thereto by a supernatural agent. This is what we call the help of grace. Therefore it must be said that an angel could not of his own will be turned to such beatitude, except by the help of grace.

Reply Obj. 1. The angel loves God naturally, so far as God is the author of his natural being. But here we are speaking of turning to God in so far as God bestows beatitude by the vision of His essence.

Reply Obj. 2. A thing is *difficult* which is beyond a power; and this happens in two ways. First of all, because it is beyond the natural order of the power. In this case, if it can be attained by some help, it is said to be *difficult*; but if it can in no way be attained, then it is *impossible*. Thus, it is impossible for a man to fly. In another way a thing may be beyond a power, not according to its natural order, but owing to

---

1. 参见 Q. 60, a. 2.
2. 参见 Q. 12, a. 4.

some intervening hindrance. Thus, to mount upwards is not contrary to the natural order of the motive power of the soul, because the soul, considered in itself, can be moved in any direction; but the soul is hindered from so doing by the weight of the body. Consequently, it is difficult for a man to mount upwards. To be turned to his ultimate beatitude, however, is difficult for man both because it is beyond his nature, and because he has a hindrance from the corruption of the body and the infection of sin. But it is difficult for an angel only because it is supernatural.

Reply Obj. 3. Every movement of the will towards God can be termed a conversion to God. And so there is a threefold conversion to God. The first is by the perfect love of God, and belongs to a creature already enjoying the possession of God. For such conversion consummate grace[1] is required. The second conversion to God is that which merits beatitude; and for this there is required habitual grace[2], which is the principle of merit. The third conversion is that whereby a man disposes himself so that he may have grace. For this no habitual grace is required, but the operation of God, Who draws the soul towards Himself, according to *Lament.* v. 21: *Convert us, O Lord, to Thee, and we shall be converted.* Hence it is clear that there is no need to go on to infinity.

Third Article
WHETHER THE ANGELS WERE CREATED IN GRACE?

We proceed thus to the Third Article:—

Objection 1. It would seem that the angels were not created in grace. For Augustine says that the angelic nature was first made without form, and was called *heaven*, but afterwards received its form, and was

1. consummate grace: 完成的恩宠
2. habitual grace: 常备恩宠；宠爱

then called *light*.[1] But such formation comes from grace. Therefore they were not created in grace.

Obj. 2. Further, grace turns the rational creature towards God. If, therefore, the angel had been created in grace, no angel would ever have turned away from God.

Obj. 3. Further, grace comes midway between nature and glory. But the angels were not beatified in their creation. Therefore it seems that they were not created even in grace; but that they were first created in nature only, then received grace, and finally they were beatified.

On the contrary, Augustine says, *Who wrought the good will of the angels? Who, but He Who created them with His will, that is, with the pure love wherewith they cling to Him; at the same time producing their nature and bestowing grace on them?*[2]

I answer that, There are conflicting opinions on this point. Some[3] hold that the angels were created only in a natural state, while others[4] maintain that they were created in grace. However, it seems more probable, and more in keeping with the sayings of holy men, that they were created in sanctifying grace. For we see that all things which were produced by the work of the divine government as creatures to come forth in the course of time under God's activity, were created in the first fashioning of things according to seedlike forms, as Augustine says.[5] Such were trees, animals, and the rest. Now it is evident that sanctifying grace bears the same relation to beatitude as the seedlike form in nature does to the natural effect; and hence grace is called the *seed of God* (*1 John* iii. 9). Just as, therefore, in Augustine's opinion, it is

---

1. 参见 *De Genesi ad Litt.*, II, 8; I, 3; 9; III, 20 (PL 34, 269; 247; 248; 292).
2. 参见 *De Civit. Dei*, XII, 9 (PL 41, 357).
3. 参见 William of Auxerre, *Summa Aurea*, II, tr. 1, ch. 1 (fol. 35rb); Alex. of Hales, *Summa Theol.*, II, I, no. 100 (II, 126); St. Bonaventure, *In II Sent.*, d. iv, a. 1, q. 2 (II, 134).
4. 参见 St. Albert, *In II Sent.*, d. iii, a. 12 (XXVII, 85).
5. 参见 *De Genesi ad Litt.*, VIII, 3; V, 4; 23 (PL 34, 374; 324; 338).

contended that the seedlike forms of all natural effects were implanted in the first creation of corporeal creatures, so, straightway from the beginning, the angels were created in grace.

Reply Obj. 1. Such informity in the angels can be understood either by comparison with their formation in glory, and thus the absence of formation preceded formation by priority of time; or else it can be understood of formation according to grace, and thus it did not precede in the order of time, but in the order of nature. This priority of nature Augustine also holds with regard to the formation of corporeal things.[1]

Reply Obj. 2. Every form inclines the subject after the mode of the subject's nature. Now it is the mode of an intellectual nature to be inclined freely towards the objects it desires. Consequently the movement of grace does not impose necessity; but he who has grace can fail to make use of it, and can sin.

Reply Obj. 3. Although in the order of nature grace comes midway between nature and glory, nevertheless, in the order of time, glory is not simultaneous with nature within the created nature; because glory is the end of the operation of nature helped by grace. But grace stands, not as the end of operation, because it is not from works, but as the principle of right operation. Therefore it was fitting for grace to be given straightway with nature.

Fourth Article
WHETHER A BEATIFIED ANGEL MERITS HIS BEATITUDE?

We proceed thus to the Fourth Article:—

Objection 1. It would seem that the beatified angel did not merit his beatitude. For merit arises from the difficulty of the meritorious act[2].

---

1. 参见 *Op. cit.*, I, 15; V, 5 (PL 34, 257; 326).
2. the meritorious act: 功行，有功行为

But the angel experienced no difficulty in acting rightly. Therefore righteous action was not meritorious for him.

Obj. 2. Further, we do not merit by merely natural operations. But it was quite natural for the angel to turn to God. Therefore he did not thereby merit beatitude.

Obj. 3. Further, if a beatified angel merited his beatitude, he did so either before he had it, or else afterwards. But it was not before, because, in the opinion of many, he had no grace before whereby to merit it. Nor did he merit it afterwards, because thus he would be meriting it now; which is clearly false, because in that case a lower angel could by meriting rise to the rank of a higher, and the distinct degrees of grace would not be permanent; which is not admissible. Consequently the angel did not merit his beatitude.

On the contrary, It is stated (*Apoc.* xxi. 17) that the *measure of the angel* in that heavenly Jerusalem is *the measure of a man*. But man can reach beatitude only by merit. Therefore the same is the case with the angel.

I answer that, Perfect beatitude is natural only to God, because *to be* and *to be blessed* are one and the same thing in Him. To be blessed, however, is not the nature of the creature, but is its ultimate end. Now everything attains its ultimate end by its operation. But this operation leading to the end is either productive of the end. when the end is not beyond the power of the agent working for the end, as the healing art is productive of health; or else it is deserving of the end, when the end is beyond the capacity of the agent striving to attain it, and is, therefore, expected from another's bestowing. Now it is evident from what has gone before that ultimate beatitude exceeds both angelic and human nature.[1] It remains, then, that both man and angel merited their beatitude.

And if the angel was created in grace, without which there is no

---

1. 参见 A. 1; q. 12, a. 4.

merit, there would be no difficulty in saying that he merited beatitude. So, too, if one were to say that the angel in any way had grace before he had glory. But if he had no grace before entering upon beatitude, it would then have to be said that he had beatitude without merit, even as we have grace. This, however, is quite foreign to the idea of beatitude, which has the notion of an end, and is the reward of virtue, as also the Philosopher says.[1] Or else it will have to be said, as some others have maintained,[2] that the angels merit beatitude by their present ministrations, while in beatitude. This is quite contrary, again, to the notion of merit, since merit conveys the idea of a means to an end. But what is already in its end cannot, properly speaking, be moved towards such end; and so no one merits what he already enjoys. Or else it will have to be said that one and the same act of turning to God, so far as it comes of free choice, is meritorious; and so far as it attains the end, is the fruition of beatitude. Even this view will not stand, because free choice is not the sufficient cause of merit; and, consequently, an act cannot be meritorious as coming from free choice, except in so far as it is informed by grace. But it cannot at the same time be informed by imperfect grace, which is the principle of meriting, and by perfect grace, which is the principle of fruition. Hence it does not appear to be possible for anyone to enjoy beatitude, and at the same time to merit it.

Consequently it is better to say that the angel had grace before he was admitted to beatitude, and that by such grace he merited beatitude.

Reply Obj. 1. The angel's difficulty of working righteously does not come from any contrariety or hindrance of natural powers; but from the fact that the good work is beyond his natural capacity.

---

1. 参见 *Eth.*, I, 7 (1097a 34); 9 (1099b 16).
2. 参见 Cf. Peter Lombard, *Sent.*, II, v, 6 (I, 329).—Cf. also St. Albert, *In II Sent.*, d. v, a. 7 (XXVII, 124).

Reply Obj. 2. An angel did not merit beatitude by a natural conversion towards God; but by the conversion of charity, which comes through grace.

The answer to the third objection is evident from what we have said.

Fifth Article

WHETHER THE ANGEL OBTAINED BEATITUDE IMMEDIATELY AFTER ONE ACT OF MERIT?

We proceed thus to the Fifth Article:—

Objection 1. It would seem that the angel did not possess beatitude instantly after one act of merit. For it is more difficult for a man to do well than for an angel. But man is not rewarded at once after one act of merit. Therefore neither was the angel.

Obj. 2. Further, an angel could act at once, and in an instant, from the very outset of his creation, for even natural bodies begin to be moved in the very instant of their creation; and if the movement of a body could be instantaneous, like the operations of intellect and will, it would have movement in the first instant of its generation. Consequently, if the angel merited beatitude by one act of his will, he merited it in the first instant of his creation; and so, if their beatitude was not retarded, then the angels were in beatitude in the first instant.

Obj. 3. Further, there must be many intervals between things which are far apart. But the beatific state of the angels is very far remote from the state of their nature. Merit comes between. Therefore the angel would have to pass through many stages of merit in order to reach beatitude.

On the contrary, Man's soul and an angel are ordained alike for beatitude. Hence it is that equality with the angels is promised to the saints (*Luke* xx. 36). Now the soul separated from the body, if it has merit deserving beatitude, enters at once into beatitude, unless there be some obstacle. Therefore so does an angel. Now an angel instantly, in his first act of charity, had the merit of beatitude. Therefore, since there was no obstacle within him, he passed at once into beatitude by only one meritorious act.

I answer that, The angel was beatified instantly after the first act of charity, whereby he merited beatitude. The reason for this is that grace perfects nature according to the mode of nature; just as every perfection is received in the subject capable of perfection, according to its mode. Now it is proper to the angelic nature to receive its natural perfection not discursively, but to have it at once naturally, as was shown above.[1] But just as the angel is of his nature inclined to natural perfection, so he is by merit inclined to glory. Hence instantly after merit the angel secured beatitude. Now the merit of beatitude in angel and man alike can be from one act alone, because man merits beatitude by every act informed by charity. Hence it remains that an angel was beatified straightway after one act informed by charity.

Reply Obj. 1. Man, according to his nature, was not intended to secure his ultimate perfection at once, like the angel. Hence a longer way was given to man than to the angel for securing beatitude.

Reply Obj. 2. The angel is above the time of corporeal things, and hence the various instants pertaining to the angels are not to be taken except as reckoning the succession of their acts. Now the act which merited beatitude could not be in them simultaneously with the act of beatitude which is fruition; since the one belongs to imperfect grace and the other to consummate grace. Consequently, it is necessary to suppose a diversity of instants, in one of which the angel merited beatitude, and in another was beatified.

Reply Obj. 3. It is of the nature of an angel instantly to attain the perfection to which he is ordained. Consequently, only one meritorious

---

1. 参见 A. 1; q. 58, a. 3.

act is required, which can be called an *interval* in so far as through it the angel is directed to beatitude.

Sixth Article
WHETHER THE ANGELS RECEIVED GRACE AND GLORY ACCORDING TO THE DEGREE OF THEIR NATURAL GIFTS?

We proceed thus to the Sixth Article:—

Objection 1. It would seem that the angels did not receive grace and glory according to the degree of their natural gifts. For grace is bestowed of God's absolute will. Therefore the degree of grace depends on God's will, and not on the degree of their natural gifts.

Obj. 2. Further, a human act seems to be more closely allied with grace than nature is, because a human act is preparatory to grace. But grace does not come *of works*, as is said *Rom.* xi. 6. Therefore much less does the degree of grace depend upon the degree of the natural gifts.

Obj. 3. Further, man and angel are alike ordained for beatitude or grace. But man does not receive more grace according to the degree of his natural gifts. Therefore neither does the angel.

On the contrary, There is the saying of the Master of the *Sentences* that *those angels who were created with more subtle natures and of keener intelligence in wisdom, were likewise endowed with greater gifts of grace.*[1]

I answer that, It is reasonable to suppose that gifts of graces and perfection of beatitude were bestowed on the angels according to the degree of their natural gifts. The reason for this can be drawn from two sources. First of all, on the part of God, Who, according to the order of His wisdom, established various degrees in the angelic nature. Now just as the angelic nature was made by God for attaining grace and beatitude, so likewise the grades of the angelic nature seem to be

---

1. 参见 *Sent.*, II, iii, 2 (I, 318).

ordained to the various degrees of grace and glory. For example, when a builder is engaged in preparing stones for building a house, from the fact that he prepares some more artistically and more fittingly than others, it is clear that he is setting them apart for a more ornate part of the house. So it seems that God destined those angels for greater gifts of grace and fuller beatitude whom He made of a higher nature.

Secondly, the same is evident on the part of the angel. The angel is not composed of diverse natures, so that the inclination of the one might thwart or retard the tendency of the other; as happens in man, in whom the movement of his intellectual part is either retarded or thwarted by the inclination of his sensitive part. But when there is nothing to retard or thwart it, nature is moved with its whole power. So it is reasonable to suppose that the angels who had a higher nature were turned to God more strongly and efficaciously. The same thing happens in men, since greater grace and glory are bestowed according to the greater earnestness of their turning to God. Hence it appears that the angels who had the greater natural powers had the more grace and glory.

Reply Obj. 1. As grace comes of God's will alone, so likewise does the nature of the angel; and just as God's will ordained nature for grace, so did it ordain the various degrees of nature to the various degrees of grace.

Reply Obj. 2. The acts of the rational creature are from the creature itself, whereas nature is immediately from God. Accordingly, it seems rather that grace is bestowed according to the degree of nature than according to works.

Reply Obj. 3. Diversity of natural gifts is in one way in the angels, who are themselves different specifically, and in quite another way in men, who differ only numerically. For specific difference is because of the end, while numerical difference is because of the matter. Furthermore, there is something in man which can thwart or impede the movement of his intellectual nature; but not in the angels.

Consequently the argument is not the same for both.

Seventh Article
WHETHER NATURAL KNOWLEDGE AND LOVE REMAIN IN THE BEATIFIED ANGELS?

We proceed thus to the Seventh Article:—

Objection 1. It would seem that natural knowledge and love do not remain in the beatified angels. For it is said (*1 Cor.* xiii. 10): *When that which is perfect is come, then that which is in part shall be done away.* But natural love and knowledge are imperfect in comparison with beatified knowledge and love. Therefore with the coming of beatitude, natural knowledge and love cease.

Obj. 2. Further, where one suffices, another is superfluous. But the knowledge and love of glory suffice for the beatified angels. Therefore it would be superfluous for their natural knowledge and love to remain.

Obj. 3. Further, the same power has not two simultaneous acts, as the same line cannot, at the same end, be terminated in two points. But the beatified angels are always exercising their beatified knowledge and love; for, as is said *Ethics* i., happiness consists not in habit, but in act.[1] Therefore there can never be natural knowledge and love in the angels.

On the contrary, So long as a nature endures, its operation remains. But beatitude does not destroy nature, since it is its perfection. Therefore it does not take away natural knowledge and love.

I answer that, Natural knowledge and love remain in the angels. For in the way that principles of operations are mutually related, so are the operations themselves. Now it is manifest that nature is to beatitude as

---

1. 参见 Aristotle, *Eth.*, I, 8 (1098b 33).

first to second, because beatitude is superadded to nature. But the first must always be preserved in the second. Consequently nature must be preserved in beatitude; and in like manner the act of nature must be preserved in the act of beatitude.

Reply Obj. 1. The advent of a perfection removes the opposite imperfection. Now the imperfection of nature is not opposed to the perfection of beatitude, but underlies it; just as the imperfection of the power underlies the perfection of the form, and the power is not taken away by the form, but the privation which is opposed to the form. In the same way, the imperfection of natural knowledge is not opposed to the perfection of the knowledge of glory; for nothing hinders us from knowing a thing through various means, as a thing may be known at the one time through a probable means and through a demonstrative one. In like manner, an angel can know God by His essence, and this pertains to his knowledge of glory; and at the same time he can know God by his own essence, which belongs to his natural knowledge.

Reply Obj. 2. All things which make up beatitude are sufficient of themselves. But in order to be, they presuppose the natural gifts; because no beatitude is self-subsisting, except the uncreated beatitude.

Reply Obj. 3. There cannot be two operations in the one power at one time, except the one be ordained to the other. But natural knowledge and love are ordained to the knowledge and love of glory. Accordingly, there is nothing to hinder natural knowledge and love from existing in the angel conjointly with those of glory.

Eighth Article
WHETHER A BEATIFIED ANGEL CAN SIN?

We proceed thus to the Eighth Article:—

Objection 1. It would seem that a beatified angel can sin. For, as was said above, beatitude does not do away with nature. But it is of the very notion of a created nature that it can fail. Therefore a beatified angel can sin.

Obj. 2. Further, rational powers are related to opposites, as the Philosopher observes.[1] But the will of the angel in beatitude does not cease to be rational. Therefore it is inclined towards good and evil.

Obj. 3. Further, it belongs to the liberty of choice that man be able to choose good or evil. But the liberty of choice is not lessened in the beatified angels. Therefore they can sin.

On the contrary, Augustine says that *there is in the holy angels that nature which cannot sin.*[2] Therefore the holy angels cannot sin.

I answer that, The beatified angels cannot sin. The reason for this is that their beatitude consists in seeing God through His essence. Now, God's essence is the very essence of goodness. Consequently the angel beholding God is disposed towards God in the same way as anyone else not seeing God is to the common nature of goodness; But it is impossible for any man either to will or to do anything except aiming at what is good; or for him to wish to turn away from good precisely as such. Therefore the beatified angel can neither will nor act, except as aiming towards God. Now whoever wills or acts in this manner cannot sin. Consequently the beatified angel cannot sin.

Reply Obj. 1. Created good, considered in itself, can fail. But from its perfect union with the uncreated good, such as is the union of beatitude, it is rendered unable to sin, for the reason already alleged.

Reply Obj. 2. The rational powers are related to opposites in the things to which they are not inclined naturally; but as to the things to which they have a natural ordination, they are not related to opposites. For the intellect cannot but assent to naturally known principles, and in the same way the will cannot help clinging to the good as good; because the will is naturally ordained to the good as to its proper object. Consequently the will of the angels is related to opposites, as

---

1. 参见 *Metaph.*, VIII, 2 (1046b 5); 5 (1048a 8).
2. 参见 *De Genesi ad Litt.*, XI, 7 (PL 34, 433).

to doing many things, or not doing them. But they have no tendency to opposites with regard to God Himself, Whom they see to be the very nature of goodness; but in all things their aim is towards God, whichever alternative they choose. And this without sin.

Reply Obj. 3. Free choice in its election of means to an end is disposed in the same way as the intellect is to conclusions. Now it is evident that it belongs to the power of the intellect to be able to proceed to different conclusions, according to given principles; but for it to proceed to some conclusion in violation of the order of the principles comes of its own defect. Hence it belongs to the perfection of its liberty that free choice is able to elect various means while maintaining the order of the end. But it comes of the defect of liberty for it to choose anything by turning away from the order of the end; and this is to sin. Hence there is greater liberty of will in the angels who cannot sin than there is in ourselves who can.

Ninth Article
WHETHER THE BEATIFIED ANGELS ADVANCE IN BEATITUDE?

We proceed thus to the Ninth Article:—

Objection 1. It would seem that the beatified angels can advance in beatitude. For charity is the principle of merit. But there is perfect charity in the angels. Therefore the beatified angels can merit. Now, as merit increases, the reward of beatitude increases. Therefore the beatified angels can progress in beatitude.

Obj. 2. Further, Augustine says that *God makes use of us for our own gain, and for His own goodness.*[1] *The same thing happens to the angels, whom He uses for spiritual ministrations*; since *they are all ministering spirits, sent*

1. 参见 *De Doc. Christ.*, I, 32 (PL 34, 32).

to minister for them who shall receive the inheritance of salvation (*Heb.* i. 14). This would not be for their profit were they not to merit thereby, nor to advance in beatitude. It remains, then, that the beatified angels can merit, and can advance in beatitude.

Obj. 3. Further, it argues imperfection for anyone not occupying the foremost place not to be able to advance. But the angels are not in the highest degree of beatitude. Therefore, if unable to ascend higher, it would appear that there is imperfection and defect in them; which is not admissible.

On the contrary, Merit and progress belong to this present state of life. But angels are not wayfarers, but possessors of beatitude. Consequently the beatified angels can neither merit nor advance in beatitude.

I answer that, In every movement, the mover's intention is centred upon one determined end, to which he intends to lead the movable subject; because intention looks to the end, to which endlessness is repugnant. Now since the rational creature cannot of its own power attain to its beatitude, which consists in the vision of God, as is clear from what has gone before,[1] it is evident that it needs to be moved by God towards its beatitude. Therefore there must be some one determined thing to which every rational creature is directed as to its last end.

Now this one determinate object cannot, in the vision of God, consist precisely in that which is seen; for the Supreme Truth is seen by all the blessed in various degrees. But it is on the part of the mode of vision that diverse terms are fixed beforehand by the intention of Him Who directs towards the end. For it is impossible that because the rational creature is led on the vision of the Supreme Essence, it should also be led to the supreme mode of vision, which is comprehension; for this belongs only to God, as is evident from what was said above.[2]

1. 参见 A. 1; q. 12, a. 4.
2. 参见 Q. 12, a. 7; q. 14, a. 3.

But since infinite efficacy is required for comprehending God, while the creature's efficacy in beholding is only finite; and since every finite thing is in infinite degrees removed from the infinite: —it is possible for the rational creature to understand God more or less clearly according to infinite degrees. And as beatitude consists in vision, so the degree of vision lies in a determinate mode of the vision.

Therefore every rational creature is so led by God to the end of its beatitude, that from God's predestination it is brought even to a determinate degree of beatitude. Consequently, when that degree is once secured, it cannot pass to a higher degree.

Reply Obj. 1. Merit belongs to a being which is moving towards its end. Now the rational creature is moved towards its end, not merely passively, but also by working actively. Now if the end is within the power of the rational creature, then its action is said to procure the end, as man acquires knowledge by reflection; but if the end be beyond its power, and is looked for from another, then its action will be meritorious of such an end. But what is already in the ultimate term is not said to be moved, but to have been moved. Consequently, to merit belongs to the imperfect charity of this life; whereas perfect charity does not merit but rather enjoys the reward. In the same way, in the case of acquired habits, the operation preceding the habit is productive of the habit, but the operation from an acquired habit is already perfect and enjoyable. So, too, the act of perfect charity has not the nature of merit, but rather belongs to the perfection of the reward.

Reply Obj. 2. A thing can be termed useful in two ways. First of all, as being on the way to an end; and in this way the merit of beatitude is useful. Secondly, as the part is useful for the whole; as the wall for a house. In this way the angelic ministerings are useful for the beatified angels, inasmuch as they are a part of their beatitude; for to pour out acquired perfection upon others is of the nature of what is perfect, considered as perfect.

Reply Obj. 3. Although a beatified angel is not absolutely in the highest degree of beatitude, yet he is in the highest degree relatively to himself, according to divine predestination. Nevertheless the joy of the angels can be increased with regard to the salvation of such as are saved by their ministrations, according to *Luke* xv. 10: *There is joy before the angels of God upon one sinner doing penance.* Such joy belongs to their accidental reward, which can be increased unto the judgment day. Hence some writers say that they can merit as to their accidental reward.[1] But it is better to say that he who is beatified cannot merit unless he be both wayfarer and comprehensor; which is true only of Christ. For the blessed acquire such joy by virtue of their beatitude, rather than merit it.

---

1. 参见 William of Auvergne, *De Univ.*, IIa IIae, 156 (I, pt. II, 1007).

Question LXIII
THE MALICE OF THE ANGELS WITH REGARD TO SIN
(*In Nine Articles*)

IN the next place we must consider how angels became evil. The first consideration concerns the evil of fault; the second, the evil of punishment.[1] Under the first heading there are nine points of inquiry: (1) Can there be evil of fault in the angels? (2) What kind of sins can be in them? (3) What did the angel seek in sinning? (4) Supposing that some became evil by a sin of their own choosing, are any of them naturally evil? (5) Supposing that it is not so, could any one of them become evil in the first instant of his creation by an act of his own will? (6) Supposing that he did not, was there any interval between his creation and fall? (7) Was the highest of them who fell absolutely the highest among the angels? (8) Was the sin of the foremost angel the cause of the others sinning? (9) Did as many sin as remained steadfast?

First Article
WHETHER THE EVIL OF FAULT CAN BE IN THE ANGELS?

We proceed thus to the First Article:—

Objection 1. It would seem that there can be no evil of fault in the angels. For there can be no evil except in things which are in potentiality, as is said by the Philosopher,[2] because the subject of

---

1. 参见 Q. 64.
2. 参见 Aristotle, *Metaph.*, VIII, 9 (1051a 18).

privation is a being in potentiality. But the angels have not being in potentiality, since they are subsisting forms. Therefore there can be no evil of fault in them.

Obj. 2. Further, the angels are higher than the heavenly bodies. But philosophers say that there cannot be evil in the heavenly bodies.[1] Therefore neither can there be in the angels.

Obj. 3. Further, what is natural to a thing is always in it. But it is natural for the angels to be moved by the movement of love towards God. Therefore such love cannot be withdrawn from them. But in loving God they do not sin. Consequently the angels cannot sin.

Obj. 4. Further, desire is only of what is good or apparently good. Now for the angels there can be no apparent good which is not a true good; because in them either there can be no error at all, or at least not before guilt. Therefore the angels can desire only what is truly good. But no one sins by desiring what is truly good. Consequently the angel does not sin by desire.

On the contrary, It is said (*Job.* iv. 18): *In His angels He found wickedness.*

I answer that, An angel or any other rational creature, considered in his own nature, can sin; and whatever creature can not-sin, possesses this as a gift of grace, and not from the condition of nature. The reason of this is that to sin is nothing else than to deviate from that rectitude which an act ought to have, whether we speak of sin in nature, art, or morals. That act alone, the rule of which is the very power of the agent, can never fall short of rectitude. Were the craftsman's hand the rule itself of carving, he could not carve the wood otherwise than rightly; but if the rightness of carving depends upon another rule, then the carving may be right or faulty. Now the divine will is the sole rule of God's act, because it is not referred to any higher end. But every created will has rectitude of act so far only as it is regulated

---

1. 参见 Aristotle, *Metaph.*, VIII, 9 (1051a 19); Avicenna, *Metaph.*, IX, 6 (106ra); Averroes, *In Metaph.*, IX, comm. 19 (VIII, 115r).

according to the divine will, to which the last end is to be referred; just as every desire of a subordinate ought to be regulated by the will of his superior, for instance, the soldier's will, according to the will of his commanding officer. Thus only in the divine will can there be no sin, whereas in the will of every creature, considered according to its nature, there can be sin.

Reply Obj. 1. In the angels there is no potentiality to natural being. Yet there is potentiality in their intellectual part, as regards their being inclined to this or the other object. In this respect there can be evil in them.

Reply Obj. 2. The heavenly bodies have none but a natural operation. Therefore, just as there can be no evil of corruption in their nature, so neither can there be evil of disorder in their natural action. But besides their natural action, there is the action of free choice in the angels, by reason of which evil may be in them.

Reply Obj. 3. It is natural for the angel to turn to God by the movement of love, according as God is the source of his natural being. But for him to turn to God as the object of supernatural beatitude comes of infused love, from which he could be turned away by sinning.

Reply Obj. 4. Mortal sin occurs in two ways in the act of free choice. First, when something evil is chosen, as man sins by choosing adultery, which is of itself evil. Such sin always comes of ignorance or error, or otherwise what is evil would never be chosen as good. The adulterer errs in the particular, choosing this delight of an inordinate act as something good to be performed now, from the inclination of passion or of habit; even though he does not err in his universal judgment, but retains a right opinion in this respect. There can be no sin of this sort in the angel; for there are no passions in the angels to fetter the reason or the intellect, as is manifest from what has been said above,[1] nor,

---

1. 参见 Q. 59, a. 4.

again, could any habit inclining to sin precede their first sin.

In another way, sin comes of free choice by electing something good in itself, but not according to the proper measure or rule. In this way, the defect which induces sin is only on the part of the choice, which is not properly regulated except as concerns the thing chosen; just as if one were to pray, without heeding the order established by the Church. Such a sin does not presuppose ignorance, but merely absence of consideration of the things which ought to be considered. In this way the angel sinned, by turning himself freely to his own good, without regard for the rule of the divine will.

Second Article
WHETHER ONLY THE SIN OF PRIDE AND ENVY CAN EXIST IN AN ANGEL?

We proceed thus to the Second Article:—

Objection 1. It would seem that there can be other sins in the angels besides those of pride and envy. Because whosoever can delight in any kind of sin, can fall into that sin itself. But the demons delight even in the obscenities of carnal sins, as Augustine says.[1] Therefore there can be also carnal sins in the demons.

Obj. 2. Further, as pride and envy are spiritual sins, so are sloth, avarice and anger. But spiritual sins belong to the spirit, just as carnal sins belong to the flesh. Therefore not only can there be pride and envy in the angels, but likewise sloth and avarice.

Obj. 3. Further, according to Gregory *many vices spring from pride, and in like manner from envy.*[2] But, if the cause is granted, the effect follows. If, therefore, there can be pride and envy in the angels, for the same reason there can likewise be other vices in them.

---

1. 参见 *De Civit. Dei*, II, 4; 26 (PL 41, 50; 74).
2. 参见 *Moral.*, XXXI, 45 (PL 76, 620).

On the contrary, Augustine says that the devil *is not a fornicator nor a drunkard, nor anything of the like sort; but he is proud and envious.*[1]

I answer that, Sin can exist in a subject in two ways: first, by actual guilt, and secondly, by affection. As to guilt, all sins are in the demons, since by leading men to all sins they incur the guilt of all sins. But as to affection, only those sins can be in the demons which can affect a spiritual nature. Now a spiritual nature cannot be affected by such pleasures as pertain to bodies, but only by such as can be found in spiritual beings; because nothing is affected except with regard to something which is in some way suited to its nature. But there can be no sin when anyone is incited to a good of the spiritual order, unless in such affection the rule of the superior be not kept. Such is precisely the sin of pride,—not to be subject to a superior where subjection is due. Consequently the first sin of the angel can be none other than pride.

Yet, as a consequence, it was possible also for envy to be in them, since for the appetite to tend to the desire of something involves on its part resistance to anything contrary. Now the envious man grieves over the good possessed by another, inasmuch as he deems his neighbor's good to be a hindrance to his own. But another's good could not be deemed a hindrance to the good coveted by the wicked angel, except inasmuch as he coveted a singular excellence, which would cease to be singular because of the excellence of some other. So, after the sin of pride, there followed the evil of envy in the sinning angel, whereby he grieved over man's good, and also over the divine excellence, according as against the devil's will God makes use of man for the divine glory.

Reply Obj. 1. The demons do not delight in the obscenities of the sins of the flesh, as if they themselves were disposed to carnal pleasures. It is wholly through envy that they take pleasure in all sorts of human

---

1. 参见 *De Civit. Dei*, XIV, 3 (PL 41, 406).

sins, so far as these are hindrances to man's good.

Reply Obj. 2. Avarice, considered as a special kind of sin, is the immoderate greed of temporal possessions which serve the use of human life, and which can be estimated in value by money; and to these possessions the demons are not at all inclined, any more than they are to carnal pleasures[1]. Consequently avarice properly so called cannot be in them. But if every immoderate greed of possessing any created good be termed avarice, in this way avarice is contained under the pride which is in the demons. Anger, on the other hand, implies passion, and so does concupiscence; and consequently they can exist only metaphorically in the demons. Sloth is a kind of sadness, whereby a man becomes sluggish in spiritual exercises because they weary the body; and this does not apply to the demons. So it is evident that pride and envy are the only spiritual sins which can be found in demons; but with the condition that envy is not to be taken for a passion, but for a will resisting the good of another.

Reply Obj. 3. Under envy and pride, as found in the demons, are comprised all other sins derived from them.

Third Article
WHETHER THE DEVIL DESIRED TO BE AS GOD?

We proceed thus to the Third Article:—

Objection 1. It would seem that the devil did not desire to be as God. For what does not fall under apprehension does not fall under desire, because only the apprehended good moves the appetite, whether sensible, rational, or intellectual. Now sin is possible only in such desire. But for any creature to be God's equal does not fall under apprehension, because it implies a contradiction; for if the finite equals

---

1. carnal pleasure: 肉身的快乐

the infinite, then it would itself be infinite. Therefore an angel could not desire to be as God.

Obj. 2. Further, the natural end can always be desired without sin. But to become like God is the end to which every creature naturally tends. If, therefore, the angel desired to be as God, not by equality, but by likeness, it would seem that he did not thereby sin.

Obj. 3. Further, the angel was created with greater fulness of wisdom than man. But no man, save he be mad, ever chooses to be the equal of an angel, still less of God; because choice aims at only things which are possible, regarding which one takes deliberation. Therefore much less did the angel sin by desiring to be as God.

On the contrary, It is said, in the person of the devil (*Isa.* xiv. 13, 14), *I will ascend into heaven .... I will be like the Most High.* And Augustine says of the devil that being *inflated with pride, he wished to be called God.*[1]

I answer that, Without doubt the angel sinned by seeking to be as God. But *to be as God* can be understood in two ways: first, by equality; secondly, by likeness. He could not seek to be as God in the first way, because by natural knowledge he knew that this was impossible; nor was there any habit preceding his first sinful act, or any passion fettering his mind, so as to lead him to choose what was impossible by causing him to fail in the order of the particular, as sometimes happens in ourselves. And even supposing it were possible, it would be against the natural desire, because there exists in everything the natural desire to preserve its own nature, which would not be preserved were it to be changed into another nature. Consequently, no creature of a lower order can ever covet the grade of a higher nature, just as an ass does not desire to be a horse; for were it to be so upraised, it would cease to be itself. But herein the imagination plays us false; for one is liable to think that, because

1. 参见 Cf. Ambrosiaster, *De Quaest. Vet. et Nov. Test.*, I, q. 113 (PL 35, 2341).

a man seeks to occupy a higher grade as to accidentals, which can increase without the destruction of the subject, he can also seek a higher grade of nature, to which he could not attain without ceasing to be. Now it is quite evident that God surpasses the angels, not merely in accidentals, but also in degree of nature; and one angel surpasses another. Consequently it is impossible for one angel of lower degree to desire equality with a higher: and still more to covet equality with God.

On the other hand, to desire to be as God according to likeness can happen in two ways. In one way, as to that likeness whereby everything is made to be likened unto God. And so, if anyone desire in this way to be Godlike, he commits no sin; provided that he desires such likeness in proper order, that is to say, that he may obtain it of God. But he would sin were he to desire to be like God even in the right way, but of his own power, and not of God's. In another way, one may desire to be like God in some respect which is not natural to one: *e.g.*, if one were to desire to create heaven and earth, which is proper to God; in which desire there would be sin. It was in this way that the devil desired to be as God. Not that he desired to resemble God by being subject to no one else absolutely, for thus he would be desiring his own *non-being*, since no creature can exist except by participating being under God. But he desired resemblance with God in this, that he desired as the last end of his beatitude something which he could attain by the virtue of his own nature, turning his appetite away from the supernatural beatitude which is attained by God's grace. Or, if he desired as his last end that likeness to God which is bestowed by grace, he sought to have it by the power of his own nature, and not from divine assistance according to God's ordering. This harmonizes with Anselm's opinion, who says *that he sought that to which he would have come had he stood fast.*[1]

1. 参见 *De Casu Diab.*, VI (PL 158, 337).

These two views in a manner coincide, because, according to both, the devil sought to have final beatitude of his own power, whereas this is proper to God alone.

Since, furthermore, what exists of itself is the cause of what exists through another, it follows from this that the devil sought to have dominion over others. In this also he perversely wished to be like unto God.

From this we have the answer to all the objections.

Fourth Article
WHETHER ANY OF THE DEMONS ARE NATURALLY WICKED?

We proceed thus to the Fourth Article:—

Objection 1. It would seem that some demons are naturally wicked. For Porphyry says, as quoted by Augustine, *There is a class of demons of crafty nature, pretending that they are gods and the souls of the dead.*[1] But to be deceitful is to be evil. Therefore some demons are naturally wicked.

Obj. 2. Further, as the angels are created by God, so are men. But some men are naturally wicked, of whom it is said (*Wis.* xii. 10): *Their malice was natural.* Therefore some angels can be naturally wicked.

Obj. 3. Further, some irrational animals have wicked dispositions by nature: thus the fox is naturally sly, and the wolf naturally rapacious; and yet they are God's creatures. Therefore, although the demons are God's creatures, they can be naturally wicked.

On the contrary, Dionysius says that *the demons are not naturally wicked.*[2]

I answer that, Everything which is, so far as it is and has a particular nature, tends naturally towards some good, since it comes from a

---

1. 参见 *De Civit. Dei*, X, 11 (PL 41, 289).
2. 参见 *De Div. Nom.*, IV, 23 (PG 3, 724).

good principle; for the effect always reverts to its principle. Now a particular good may happen to have some evil connected with it; and thus fire has this evil connected with it that it consumes other things. But no evil can be connected with the universal good. If, then, there be anything whose nature is ordered towards some particular good, it can tend naturally to some evil, not as evil, but accidentally, as connected with some good. But if anything of its nature be ordered to the good in general, then of its own nature it cannot be inclined to evil. Now it is manifest that every intellectual nature is ordered to the good in general, which it can apprehend and which is the object of the will. Hence, since the demons are intellectual substances, they can in no wise have a natural inclination towards any evil whatsoever; and consequently they cannot be naturally evil.

Reply Obj. 1. Augustine in the same text rebukes Porphyry for saying that the demons are naturally deceitful. He himself maintained that they are not naturally so, but of their own will. Now the reason why Porphyry held that they are naturally deceitful was that, as he contended, demons are animals with a sensitive nature. Now the sensitive nature is inclined towards some particular good, with which evil may be connected. In this way, then, it can have a natural inclination to evil; yet only accidentally, inasmuch as evil is connected with good.

Reply Obj. 2. The malice of some men can be called natural, either because of custom which is a second nature, or because of the natural proclivity on the part of the sensitive nature to some inordinate passion, as some people are said to be naturally wrathful or lustful; but not on the part of the intellectual nature.

Reply Obj. 3. Brute animals have a natural inclination in their sensitive nature towards certain particular goods, with which certain evils are connected; and thus the fox in seeking its food has a natural inclination to do so with a certain skill coupled with deceit. Therefore it is not evil in the fox to be sly, since it is natural to him; just as it is not evil in the dog to be fierce, as Dionysius observes.[1]

Fifth Article
WHETHER THE DEVIL WAS WICKED BY THE FAULT OF HIS OWN WILL IN THE FIRST INSTANT OF HIS CREATION?

We proceed thus to the Fifth Article:—

Objection 1. It would seem that the devil was wicked by the fault of his own will in the first instant of his creation. For it is said of the devil (*Jo.* viii. 44): *He was a murderer from the beginning.*

Obj. 2. Further, according to Augustine, the informity in the creature did not precede its formation in the order of time, but merely in the order of nature.[2] Now according to him the *heaven*, which is said to have been created in the beginning, signifies the as yet unformed angelic nature;[3]and when it is said that God said: *Be light made: and light was made*, we are to understand the formation of the angel by turning to the Word. Consequently, the nature of the angel was created, and light was made, in the one instant. But at the same moment that light was made, it was made distinct from *darkness*, whereby the angels who sinned are denoted. Therefore in the first instant of their creation some of the angels were made blessed, and some sinned.

Obj. 3. Further, sin is opposed to merit. But some intellectual nature can merit in the first instant of its creation: *e.g.*, the soul of Christ, or also the good angels. Therefore the demons likewise could sin in the first instant of their creation.

Obj. 4. Further, the angelic nature is more powerful than corporeal nature. But a corporeal thing begins to have its operation in the

---

1. 参见 *Op. cit.*, IV, 25 (PG 3, 728).
2. 参见 *De Gen. ad Litt.*, I, 15; V, 5 (PL 34, 257; 269).
3. 参见 *Op. cit.*, II, 8 (PL 34, 269) ; cf. *op. cit.*, I, 3; 4; 9; III, 20 (PL 34, 218; 219; 259; 292).

first instant of its creation; as fire begins to move upwards in the first instant it is produced. Therefore the angel could also have his operation in the first instant of his creation. Now this operation was either ordinate or inordinate. If ordinate, then, since he had grace, he thereby merited beatitude. But with the angels reward follows immediately upon merit, as was said above.[1] Consequently they would have become blessed at once; and so they would never have sinned, which is false. It remains, then, that they sinned by inordinate action in their first instant.

On the contrary, It is written (*Gen.* i. 31): *God saw all the things that He had made, and they were very good.* But among them were also the demons. Therefore the demons were at some time good.

I answer that, Some[2] have maintained that the demons were wicked straightway in the first instant of their creation; not indeed by their nature, but by the sin of their own will, *for as soon as he was made, the devil refused righteousness.* As Augustine says, *if anyone subscribes to this opinion, he does not agree with those Manichean heretics who say that the devil's nature is evil of itself.*[3] Since this opinion, however, is in contradiction with the authority of Scripture, —for it is said of the devil under the figure of the prince of Babylon (*Isa.* xiv. 12): *How art thou fallen ... O Lucifer, who didst rise in the morning!* and it is said to the devil in the person of the King of Tyre (*Ezech.* xxviii. 13): *Thou wast in the pleasures of the paradise of God,*—consequently, this opinion was quite reasonably rejected by the masters as erroneous.[4]

Hence others[5] have said that the angels, in the first instant of their creation, could have sinned, but did not. Yet this view also is

---

1. 参见 Q. 62, a. 5.
2. 参见 Cf. Peter Lombard, *Sent.*, II, iii, 4 (I, 319).
3. 参见 *De Civit. Dei*, XI, 13 (PL 41, 329).
4. 参见 Cf. H. Denifie, *Chartularium*, no. 128 (I, 171).
5. 参见 Cf. St. Bonaventure, *In II Sent.*, d. iii, pt. 2, a. 1, q. 2 (II, 117).

repudiated by some,[1] because, when two operations follow one upon the other, it seems impossible for each operation to terminate in the one instant. Now it is clear that the angel's sin was an act subsequent to his creation. But the term of the creative act is the angel's very being, while the term of the sinful act is the being wicked. It seems, then, an impossibility for the angel to have been wicked in the first instant of his being.

This argument, however, does not seem adequate. For it holds good only in such movements as are measured by time, and take place successively. And thus, if local movement follows an alteration, then the alteration and the local movement cannot be terminated in the same instant. But if the changes are instantaneous, then all at once and in the same instant there can be a term to the first and the second change; and thus in the same instant in which the moon is lit up by the sun, the air is lit up by the moon. Now, it is manifest that creation is instantaneous, as is also the movement of free choice in the angels; for, as has already been stated, they have no occasion for comparison or discursive reasoning.[2] Consequently, there is nothing to hinder the term of creation and of free choice from being in the same instant.

We must therefore reply that, on the contrary, it was impossible for the angel to sin in the first instant by an inordinate act of free choice. For although a thing can begin to act in the first instant of its being, nevertheless, that operation which begins with the being comes from the agent from which it has its being; just as upward movement in fire comes from its productive cause. Therefore, if there be anything which derives its being from a defective cause, which can be the cause of a defective action, it can in the first instant of its being have a defective operation; just as a leg, which is defective from birth, through a defect in the principle of generation, begins at once to limp. But the cause

---

1. 参见 St. Albert, *In II Sent.*, d. iii, a. 14 (XXVII, 87).
2. 参见 Q. 58, a. 3.

which brought the angels into existence, namely, God, cannot be the cause of sin. Consequently it cannot be said that the devil was wicked in the first instant of his creation.

Reply Obj. 1. As Augustine says, *when it is stated that* "the devil sins from the beginning" (*1 John* iii. 2), *he is not to be thought of as sinning from the beginning wherein he was created, but from the beginning of sin.*[1] That is to say, he never went back from his sin.

Reply Obj. 2. That distinction of light and darkness, whereby the sins of the demons are understood by the term darkness, must be taken as according to God's foreknowledge. Hence Augustine says that *He alone could discern light and darkness, Who also could foreknow, before they fell, those who would fall.*[2]

Reply Obj. 3. All that is in merit is from God, and consequently an angel could merit in the first instant of his creation. The same reason does not hold good of sin, as has been said.

Reply Obj. 4. God did not distinguish between the angels before the turning away of some of them, and the turning of others to Himself, as Augustine says.[3] Therefore, as all were created in grace, all merited in their first instant. But some of them at once placed an impediment to their beatitude, thereby destroying their preceding merit; and consequently they were deprived of the beatitude which they had merited.

Sixth Article
WHETHER THERE WAS ANY INTERVAL BETWEEN THE CREATION AND THE FALL OF THE ANGEL?

We proceed thus to the Sixth Article:—

---

1. 参见 *De Civit. Dei*, XI, 15 (PL 41, 330).
2. 参见 *Op. cit.*, XI, 19 (PL 41, 333).
3. 参见 *Op. cit.*, XI, 11 (PL 41, 327).

Objection 1. It would seem that there was some interval between the angel's creation and his fall. For, it is said (*Ezech.* xxviii. 15): *Thou didst walk perfect in thy ways from the day of thy creation, until iniquity was found in thee.* But since walking is continuous movement, it requires an interval. Therefore there was some interval between the devil's creation and his fall.

Obj. 2. Further, Origen says that *the serpent of old did not, from the first, walk upon his breast and belly.*[1] This refers to his sin. Therefore the devil did not sin at once after the first instant of his creation.

Obj. 3. Further, capability of sinning is common alike to man and angel. But there was some delay between man's formation and his sin. Therefore, for the like reason there was some interval between the devil's formation and his sin.

Obj. 4. Further, the instant wherein the devil sinned was distinct from the instant wherein he was created. But there is a middle time between every two instants. Therefore there was an interval between his creation and his fall.

On the contrary, It is said of the devil (*Jo.* viii. 44): *He stood not in the truth*; and, as Augustine says, *we must understand this in the sense that he was in the truth, but did not remain in it.*[2]

I answer that, There is a twofold opinion on this point. But the more probable one, which is also more in harmony with the teachings of the Saints, is that the devil sinned at once after the first instant of his creation. This must be maintained if it be held that he elicited an act of free choice in the first instant of his creation, and that he was created in grace, as we have said.[3] For since the angels attain beatitude by one meritorious act, as was said above,[4] if the devil, created in

---

1. 参见 *In Ezech.*, hom. I (PG 13, 671).
2. 参见 *De Civit. Dei*, XI, 15 (PL 41, 330).
3. 参见 A. 5; q. 62, a. 3.
4. 参见 Q. 62, a. 5.

grace, merited in the first instant, he would at once have received beatitude after that first instant, had he not immediately placed an impediment by sinning.

If, however, it be contended that the angel was not created in grace, or that he could not elicit an act of free choice in the first instant, then there is nothing to prevent some interval being interposed between his creation and fall.

Reply Obj. 1. Sometimes in Holy Scripture instantaneous spiritual movements are represented by corporeal movements which are measured by time. In this way by *walking* we are to understand the movement of free choice tending towards good.

Reply Obj. 2. Origen says, *The serpent of old did not, from the first, walk upon his breast and belly,*[1] because of the first instant in which he was not wicked.

Reply Obj. 3. An angel has an inflexible free choice after once choosing; and consequently, if after the first instant, in which he had a natural movement to good, he had not at once placed a barrier to beatitude, he would have been confirmed in good. It is not so with man, and therefore the argument does not hold good.

Reply Obj. 4. It is true to say that there is a middle time between every two instants, in so far as time is continuous, as it is proved *Physics* vi.[2] But in the angels, who are not subject to the movement of the heavens which is first to be measured by continuous time, time is taken to mean the succession of their mental acts, or of their affections. So the first instant in the angels is understood to correspond to the operation of the angelic mind, whereby it turns itself into itself by its evening knowledge; because on the first day evening is mentioned, but not morning. This operation was good in them all. From such an operation, however, some of them were converted to the praise

1. 参见 *In Ezech.*, hom. I (PG 13, 671).
2. 参见 Aristotle, *Phys.*, VI, 1 (231b 9); cf. *op. cit.*, IV, 11 (219a 13).

of the Word by their morning knowledge; while others, absorbed in themselves, became night, *swelling up with pride*, as Augustine says.[1] Hence the first act was common to them all, but in their second they were separated. Consequently they were all of them good in the first instant, but in the second the good were set apart from the wicked.

Seventh Article

WHETHER THE HIGHEST ANGEL AMONG THOSE WHO SINNED WAS THE HIGHEST OF ALL?

We proceed thus to the Seventh Article:—

Objection 1. It would seem that the highest among the angels who sinned was not the highest of all. For it is stated (*Ezech.* xxviii. 14): *Thou wast a cherub stretched out, and protecting, and I set thee in the holy mountain of God.* Now the order of the Cherubim[2] is under the order of the Seraphim[3], as Dionysius says.[4] Therefore, the highest angel among those who sinned was not the highest of all.

Obj. 2. Further, God made the intellectual nature in order that it might attain to beatitude. If therefore the highest of the angels sinned, it follows that the divine ordinance was frustrated in the noblest creature; which is unfitting.

Obj. 3. Further, the more a being is inclined towards anything, so much the less can it fall away from it. But the higher an angel is, so much the more is he inclined towards God. Therefore so much the less can he turn away from God by sinning. And so it seems that the angel who sinned was not the highest of all, but one of the lower angels.

---

1. 参见 *De Genesi ad Litt.*, IV, 24 (PL 34, 313).
2. the Cherubim: 革鲁宾天使，智天使
3. the Seraphim: 色辣芬天使，六翼天使，炽天使
4. 参见 *De Cael. Hier.*, VII, 1 (PG 3, 205).

On the contrary, Gregory says that the chief angel who sinned, *being set over all the hosts of angels*, surpassed them in brightness, *and was by comparison the most illustrious among them.*[1]

I answer that, Two things have to be considered in sin, namely, the proneness to sin, and the motive for sinning. If, then, in the angels we consider the proneness to sin, it seems that the higher angels were less likely to sin than the lower. On this account Damascene says that the highest of those who sinned was set over the terrestrial order[2].[3] This opinion seems to agree with the view of the Platonists, which Augustine quotes.[4] For they said that all the gods were good, whereas some of the demons were good, and some bad; and they named as *gods* the intellectual substances which are above the lunar sphere, and called by the name of *demons* the intellectual substances which are beneath it, yet higher than men in the order of nature. Nor is this opinion to be rejected as contrary to faith, because the whole corporeal creation is governed by God through the angels, as Augustine says.[5] Consequently there is nothing to prevent us from saying that the lower angels were divinely set aside for presiding over the lower bodies, the higher over the higher bodies, and the highest to stand before God. And in this sense Damascene says that they who fell were of the lower grade of angels; although in that order some of them remained good.

But if the motive for sinning be considered, we find that it existed in the higher angels more than in the lower. For, as has been said, the demons' sin was pride, and the motive of pride is excellence, which was greater in the higher spirits. Hence Gregory says that he who

---

1. 参见 *In Evang.*, II, hom. 34 (PL 76, 1250).
2. the terrestrial order: 地上的阶级；人间的阶级
3. 参见 *De Fide Orth.*, II, 4 (PG 94, 873).
4. 参见 *De Civit. Dei*, VIII, 13; 14; X, 11 (PL 41, 237; 238; 289).
5. 参见 *De Trin.*, III, 4 (PL 42, 873).

sinned was the very highest of all.[1] This seems to be the more probable view, because the angels' sin did not come of any proneness, but of free choice alone. Consequently the argument which is drawn from the motive in sinning seems to have the more weight. Yet this must not be prejudicial to the other view; because there might be some motive for sinning in him also who was the chief of the lower angels.

Reply Obj. 1. *Cherubim* is interpreted as *fullness of knowledge*, while *Seraphim* means *those who are on fire*, or *who set on fire*. Consequently Cherubim is derived from knowledge, which is compatible with mortal sin; but Seraphim is derived from the heat of charity, which is incompatible with mortal sin. Therefore the first angel who sinned is called, not a Seraph, but a Cherub.

Reply Obj. 2. The divine intention is not frustrated either in those who sin, or in those who are saved; for God knows beforehand the end of both, and He procures glory from both, saving these because of His goodness, and punishing those because of His justice. But the intellectual creature, when it sins, falls away from its due end. Nor is this unfitting in any exalted creature; because the intellectual creature has so been made by God, that it lies within its own choice to act for its end.

Reply Obj. 3. However great was the inclination towards good in the highest angel, there was no necessity imposed upon him; and consequently it was in his power to choose not to follow it.

Eighth Article
WHETHER THE SIN OF THE HIGHEST ANGEL WAS THE CAUSE OF THE OTHERS SINNING?

We proceed thus to the Eighth Article:—

Objection 1. It would seem that the sin of the highest angel was not

---

1. 参见 *In Evang.*, II, hom. 34 (PL 76, 1250).—Cf. *Moral.*, XXXII, 23 (PL 76, 664).

the cause of the others sinning. For the cause precedes the effect. But, as Damascene observes, they all sinned at the one time.[1] Therefore the sin of one was not the cause of the others sinning.

Obj. 2. Further, an angel's first sin can be only pride, as was shown above. But pride seeks excellence. Now it is more contrary to excellence for anyone to be subject to an inferior than to a superior; and so it does not appear that the demons sinned by desiring to be subject to a higher angel rather than to God. Yet the sin of one angel would have been the cause of the others sinning, if he had induced them to be his subjects. Therefore it does not appear that the sin of the highest angel was the cause of the others sinning.

Obj. 3. Further, it is a greater sin to wish to be subject to another against God, than to wish to be over another against God; because there is present a lesser motive for sinning. If, therefore, the sin of the foremost angel was the cause of the others sinning, in that he induced them to subject themselves to him, then the lower angels would have sinned more deeply than the highest one; which is contrary to the *Gloss* on *Ps.* ciii. 26 (*This dragon which Thou hast formed*): *He who was the more excellent in nature than the rest became the greater in malice.*[2] Therefore the sin of the highest angel was not the cause of the others sinning.

On the contrary, It is said (*Apoc.* xii. 4) that the dragon *drew* with him *the third part of the stars of heaven.*

I answer that, The sin of the highest angel was the cause of the others sinning; not indeed as compelling them, but as inducing them by a kind of exhortation. A token thereof appears in this, that all the demons are subjects of that highest one, as is evident from our Lord's words: *Go, you cursed, into everlasting fire, which was prepared for the devil*

---

1. 参见 *De Fide Orth.*, II, 4 (PG 94, 876).
2. 参见 *Glossa ordin.*, (III, 241A); Peter Lombard, *In Psalm.*, super CIII, 26 (PL 191, 941).—Cf. St. Augustine, *Enarr. in Psalm.*, *Ps.* CIII, serm. 4, v. 26 (PL 37, 1381).

and his angels (*Matt.* xxv. 41). For the order of divine justice exacts that whosoever consents to another's evil suggestion shall be subjected to him in his punishment; according to (*2 Pet.* ii. 19): *By whom a man is overcome, of the same also he is the slave.*

Reply Obj. 1. Although the demons all sinned in the one instant, yet the sin of one could be the cause of sin for the rest. For the angel needs no delay of time for choice, exhortation, or consent, as does man, who requires deliberation in order to choose and consent, and vocal speech in order to exhort; both of which are the work of time. And it is evident that even man begins to speak in the very instant when he takes thought; and in the last instant of speech, another who catches his meaning can assent to what is said, as is especially evident with regard to primary concepts, which everyone accepts directly they are heard. If, then, we take away the time for speech and deliberation which is required in us, in the same instant in which the highest angel expressed his affection by intelligible speech, it was possible for the others to consent thereto.

Reply Obj. 2. Other things being equal, he who is proud would rather be subject to a superior than to an inferior. Yet he chooses rather to be subject to an inferior than to a superior, if he can procure an advantage under an inferior which he cannot under a superior. Consequently it was not against the demons' pride for them to wish to serve an inferior by yielding to his rule; for they wanted to have him as their prince and leader, so that they might attain their ultimate beatitude of their own natural powers; and particularly so as in the order of nature they were even then subject to the highest angel.

Reply Obj. 3. As was observed above, an angel has nothing in him to retard his action,[1] but with his whole might he is moved to whatsoever he is moved, be it good or bad. Consequently, since the highest angel had greater natural power than the lower angels, he fell into sin with

1. 参见 Q. 62. a. 6.

intenser movement, and therefore he became the greater in malice.

Ninth Article
WHETHER THOSE WHO SINNED WERE AS MANY AS THOSE WHO REMAINED FIRM?

We proceed thus to the Ninth Article:—

Objection 1. It would seem that more angels sinned than stood firm. For, as the Philosopher says, *Evil is in many, but good is in few.*[1]

Obj. 2. Further, justice and sin are to be found in the same way in men and in angels. But there are more wicked men to be found than good, according to *Eccles.* i. 15: *The number of fools is infinite.* Therefore for the same reason it is so with the angels.

Obj. 3. Further, the angels are distinguished according to persons and orders. Therefore if more angelic persons stood firm, it would appear that those who sinned were not from all the orders.

On the contrary, It is said (*4 Kings* vi. 16): *There are more with us than with them*; which is explained as referring to the good angels who are with us to aid us, and the wicked spirits who are our foes.

I answer that, More angels stood firm than sinned. For sin is contrary to the natural inclination, while that which is against the natural order happens in a smaller number; for nature procures its effect either always or more often than not.

Reply Obj. 1. The Philosopher is speaking with regard to men, in whom evil comes to pass from seeking after sensible pleasures, which are known to most men, and from forsaking the good dictated by reason, which good is known to few. In the angels there is only an intellectual nature, and hence the argument does not hold.

And from this we have the answer to the second difficulty.

---

1. 参见 *Eth.*, II, 6 (1106b 28); cf. *Top.*, II, 6 (112b 11).

Reply Obj. 3. According to those who hold that the chief devil belonged to the lower order of the angels, who are set over earthly affairs,[1] it is evident that some of every order did not fall, but only those of the lowest order. According to those who maintain that the chief devil was of the highest order,[2] it is probable that some fell of every order; just as men are taken up into every order to compensate for the angelic ruin. In this view, the liberty of free choice is the more confirmed, which in every degree of creature can be turned to evil. In the Sacred Scripture, however, the names of some orders, as of Seraphim and Thrones, are not attributed to demons; since they are derived from the ardor of love and from God's indwelling, which are not consistent with mortal sin. Yet the names of Cherubim, Powers, and Principalities are attributed to them, because these names are derived from knowledge and from power, which can be common to both good and bad.

---

1. 参见 St. John Damascene, *De Fide Orth.*, II, 4 (PG 94, 873).
2. 参见 St. Gregory, *In Evang.*, II, hom. 34 (PL 76, 1250).—Cf. William of Auvergne, *De Univ.*, IIa IIae, 11 (I, pt. II, 854).

Question LXIV
THE PUNISHMENT OF THE DEMONS
(*In Four Articles*)

IT now remains as a sequel to deal with the punishment of the demons, under which heading there are four points of inquiry: (1) The darkening of their intellect. (2) The obstinacy of their will. (3) Their grief. (4) Their place of punishment.

First Article
WHETHER THE DEMONS' INTELLECT IS DARKENED BY PRIVATION OF THE KNOWLEDGE OF ALL TRUTH?

We proceed thus to the First Article:—

Objection 1. It would seem that the demons' intellect is darkened by being deprived of the knowledge of all truth. For if they knew any truth at all, they would most of all know themselves; which is to know separated substances. But this is not in keeping with their unhappiness, for it seems to belong to great happiness, so much so that some writers have assigned as man's last happiness the knowledge of the separated substances.[1] Therefore the demons are deprived of all knowledge of truth.

Obj. 2. Further, what is most manifest in its nature seems to be specially manifest to the angels, whether good or bad. That the same is not most manifest with regard to ourselves, comes from the weakness

---

1. 参见 Cf. below, q. 88, a. 1.

of our intellect which draws its knowledge from phantasms; just as it comes from the weakness of its eye that the owl cannot behold the light of the sun. But the demons cannot know God, Who is most manifest in Himself, because He is the sovereign truth; and this is because they are not clean of heart, by which alone can God be seen. Therefore neither can they know other things.

Obj. 3. Further, according to Augustine the proper knowledge of the angels is twofold; namely, morning and evening.[1] But the demons have no morning knowledge, because they do not see things in the Word; nor have they the evening knowledge, because this evening knowledge refers the things known to the Creator's praise. And so, after *evening* comes *morning* (*Gen.* i.). Therefore the demons can have no knowledge of things.

Obj. 4. Further, the angels at their creation knew the mystery of the kingdom of God, as Augustine says.[2] But the demons are deprived of such knowledge: *for if they had known it, they would never have crucified the Lord of glory*, as is said *1 Cor.* ii. 8. Therefore, for the same reason, they are deprived of all other knowledge of truth.

Obj. 5. Further, whatever truth anyone knows is known either naturally, as we know first principles, or by deriving it from someone else, as we know by learning, or by long experience, as the things we learn by discovery. Now the demons cannot know the truth by their own nature, because, as Augustine says, the good angels are separated from them as light is from darkness.[3] Now every manifestation is made through light, as is said *Ephes.* v . 13. In like manner, they cannot learn by revelation, nor by learning from the good angels, because *there is no fellowship of light with darkness* (*2 Cor.* vi. 14). Nor can they learn by long experience, because experience comes from the senses. Consequently

1. 参见 *De Genesi ad Litt.*, IV, 22 (PL 34, 317); *De Civit. Dei*, XI, 7 (PL 41, 322).
2. 参见 *De Genesi ad Litt.*, V, 19 (PL 34, 334).
3. 参见 *De Civit. Dei*, XI, 19 ; 33 (PL 41, 333; 346).

there is no knowledge of truth in them.

On the contrary, Dionysius says that *certain gifts were bestowed upon the demons which, we say, have not been changed at all, but remain entire and most brilliant.*[1] Now, the knowledge of truth stands among those natural gifts. Consequently there is some knowledge of truth in them.

I answer that, The knowledge of truth is twofold: one which comes from nature, and one which comes from grace. The knowledge which comes from grace is likewise twofold: the first is purely speculative, as when divine secrets are imparted to an individual; the other is affective, and produces love for God. This knowledge properly belongs to the gift of wisdom.

Of these three kinds of knowledge the first was neither taken away nor lessened in the demons. This follows from the very nature of the angel, who, according to his nature, is an intellect or mind. For, because of the simplicity of his substance, nothing can be removed from his nature, so as to punish him by subtracting from his natural powers, as a man is punished by being deprived of a hand or foot or of something else. Therefore Dionysius says that the natural gifts remain entire in them.[2] Consequently, their natural knowledge is not diminished. The second kind of knowledge, however, which comes through grace, and consists in speculation, has not been utterly taken away from them, but lessened; because of such divine secrets only so much is revealed to them as is necessary. That is done either by means of the angels, or *through some temporal workings of divine power*, as Augustine says;[3] but it is not done in the same degree as to the holy angels, to whom many more things are revealed, and more fully, in the Word Himself. But of the third knowledge, as likewise of charity, they are utterly deprived.

---

1. 参见 *De Div. Nom.*, IV, 23 (PG 3, 725).
2. 同上
3. 参见 *De Civit. Dei*, IX, 21 (PL 41, 274).

Reply Obj. 1. Happiness consists in self-application to something higher. The separated substances are above us in the order of nature, and hence man can have happiness of a kind by knowing the separated substances, although his perfect happiness consists in knowing the first substance, namely, God. But it is quite connatural for one separate substance to know another, just as it is connatural for us to know sensible natures. Hence, just as man's happiness does not consist in knowing sensible natures, so neither does the angel's happiness consist in knowing separated substances.

Reply Obj. 2. What is most manifest in its nature is hidden from us because it surpasses the bounds of our intellect, and not merely because our intellect draws knowledge from phantasms. Now the divine substance surpasses the proportion not only of the human intellect, but even of the angelic. Consequently, not even an angel can of his own nature know God's substance. Yet because of the perfection of his intellect he can of his nature have a higher knowledge of God than man can have. Such a knowledge of God remains also in the demons. For although they do not possess the purity which comes with grace, nevertheless they have purity of nature; and this suffices for the knowledge of God which belongs to them from their nature.

Reply Obj. 3. The creature is darkness in comparison with the excellence of the divine light; and therefore the creature's knowledge in its own nature is called *evening* knowledge. For the evening is akin to darkness, yet it possesses some light; but when the light fails utterly, then it is night. So, then, the knowledge of things in their own nature, when referred to the praise of the Creator, as it is in the good angels, has something of the divine light, and can be called evening knowledge; but if it be not referred to God, as is the case with the demons, it is not called evening, but *nocturnal* knowledge. Accordingly we read in *Genesis* (i. 5) that the darkness, which God separated from the light, *He called night.*

Reply Obj. 4. All the angels had some knowledge from the very beginning respecting the mystery of God's kingdom, which found its completion in Christ; and most of all from the moment when they were beatified by the vision of the Word, which the demons never had. Yet all the angels did not fully nor equally apprehend it; and hence the demons much less fully understood the mystery of the Incarnation, when Christ was in the world. For, as Augustine observes, *It was not manifested to them as it was to the holy angels, who enjoy a participated eternity of the Word; but it was made known by some temporal effects, so as to strike terror into them.*[1] For had they fully and with certitude known that he was the Son of God, and the effect of His passion, they would never have procured the crucifixion of the Lord of glory.

Reply Obj. 5. The demons know a truth in three ways. First, by the subtlety of their nature. For although they are darkened by the privation of the light of grace, yet they are enlightened by the light of their intellectual nature. Secondly, by revelation from the holy angels. For while not agreeing with them in conformity of will, they do agree, nevertheless, by their likeness of intellectual nature, according to which they can accept what is manifested by others. Thirdly, they know by long experience, but not as deriving it from the senses. However, when the likeness of their innate intelligible species finds realization in individual things, they know some things as present, which previously they did not know as future, as we said when dealing with the knowledge of the angels.[2]

Second Article
WHETHER THE WILL OF THE DEMONS IS OBSTINATE IN EVIL?

We proceed thus to the Second Article:—

---

1. 参见 *De Civit. Dei*, IX, 21 (PL 41, 274).
2. 参见 Q. 57, a. 3, ad 3.

Objection 1. It would seem that the will of the demons is not obstinate in evil. For liberty of choice belongs to the nature of an intellectual being, which nature remains in the demons. But liberty of choice is directly and firstly ordained to good rather than to evil. Therefore the demons' will is not so obstinate in evil as not to be able to return to what is good.

Obj. 2. Further, since God's mercy is infinite, it is greater than the demons' malice, which is finite. But no one returns from the malice of sin to the goodness of justice save through God's mercy. Therefore even the demons can return from their state of malice to the state of justice.

Obj. 3. Further, if the demons have a will obstinate in evil, then their will would be especially obstinate in the sin whereby they fell. But that sin, namely, pride, is no longer in them, because the motive for the sin, namely, the demon's excellence, no longer remains. Therefore the demon is not obstinate in malice.

Obj. 4. Further, Gregory says that man can be reinstated by another, since he fell through another.[1] But, as was already observed, the lower demons fell through the highest one.[2] Therefore their fall can be repaired by another. Consequently they are not obstinate in malice.

Obj. 5. Further, whoever is obstinate in malice never performs any good work. But the demon performs some good works, for he confesses the truth, saying to Christ: *I know Who Thou art, the holy one of God* (*Mark* i. 24). *The demons also believe and tremble* (*Jas.* ii. 19). And Dionysius observes that *they desire what is good and best, which is, to be, to live, to understand.*[3] Therefore they are not obstinate in malice.

On the contrary, It is said (*Ps.* lxxiii. 23): *The pride of them that hate Thee ascendeth continually*; and this is understood of the demons. Therefore

1. 参见 *Moral.*, IV, 3 (PL 75, 642).
2. 参见 Q. 63, a. 8.
3. 参见 *De Div. Nom.*, IV, 23 (PG 3, 725).

they remain ever obstinate in their malice.

I answer that, It was Origen's opinion that every creaturely will can by reason of free choice be inclined to good and evil; with the exception of the soul of Christ because of the union of the Word.[1] Such a view, however, deprives angels and saints of true beatitude, because everlasting stability is of the very nature of true beatitude. That is why it is termed *life everlasting*. It is also contrary to the authority of Sacred Scripture, which declares that demons and wicked men shall be sent *into everlasting punishment*, and the good brought *into everlasting life*. Consequently, such an opinion must be considered erroneous, and in accord with Catholic Faith it must be held firmly both that the will of the good angels is confirmed in good, and that the will of the demons is obstinate in evil.

We must seek for the cause of this obstinacy, not in the gravity of the sin, but in the condition of their nature or state. For as Damascene says, *death is to men, what the fall is to the angels*.[2] Now it is clear that all the mortal sins of men, grave or less grave, are pardonable before death; whereas after death they are without remission, and endure for ever.

To find, then, the cause of this obstinacy, it must be borne in mind that the appetitive power is in all things proportioned to the apprehensive power, whereby it is moved as the movable by its mover. For the sensitive appetite seeks a particular good, while the will seeks the universal good, as was said above;[3] just as the sense apprehends particulars, while the intellect apprehends universals. Now the angel's apprehension differs from man's in this respect, that by his intellect the angel apprehends immovably (just as we apprehend immovably first principles, the object of the habit of intellect, with immobility);

1. 参见 *Peri Archon*, I, 6; 8 (PG 11, 168; 178).
2. 参见 *De Fide Orth.*, II, 4 (PG 94, 877).
3. 参见 Q. 59, a. 1.

whereas man by his reason apprehends movably, proceeding discursively from one thing to another, and having the way open by which he may proceed to either of two opposites. Consequently man's will adheres to a thing movably, and with the power of forsaking it and of clinging to the opposite; whereas the angel's will adheres fixedly and immovably. Therefore, if the angel's will be considered before its adhesion, it can freely adhere either to this or to its opposite (namely, in such things as he does not will naturally); but after he has once adhered, he clings immovably. So it is customary to say that man's free choice is flexible to the opposite both before and after choice; but the angel's free choice is flexible to either opposite before the choice, but not after. Therefore the good angels, who always adhered to justice, were confirmed therein, whereas the wicked ones, sinning, are obstinate in sin. Later on we shall treat of the obstinacy of men who are damned.[1]

Reply Obj. 1. The good and wicked angels have free choice, but according to the manner and condition of their state, as has been said.

Reply Obj. 2. God's mercy delivers from sin those who repent. But such as are not capable of repenting, cling immovably to sin, and are not delivered by the divine mercy.

Reply Obj. 3. The devil's first sin still remains in him according to desire, although not in the sense that he believes that he can obtain what he desired. Even so, if a man were to believe that he can commit murder, and wills to commit it, and afterwards the power is taken from him, nevertheless, the will to murder can stay with him, so that he would he had done it, or still would do it if he could.

Reply Obj. 4. The fact that man sinned from another's suggestion is not the whole cause why man's sin is pardonable. Consequently the argument does not hold good.

---

1. 参见 *S. T.*, Suppl., q. 98, a. 1 and 3.

Reply Obj. 5. A demon's act is twofold. One comes of deliberate will, and this is properly called his own act. Such an act on the demon's part is always wicked, because, although at times he does something good, yet he does not do it well; as when he tells the truth in order to deceive, and when he believes and confesses, yet not willingly, but compelled by the evidence of things. Another kind of act is natural to the demon, and this can be good, and bears witness to the goodness of nature. Yet he abuses even such good acts to evil purpose.

Third Article
WHETHER THERE IS SORROW IN THE DEMONS?

We proceed thus to the Third Article:—

Objection 1. It would seem that there is no sorrow in the demons. For since sorrow and joy are opposites, they cannot be together in the same subject. But there is joy in the demons. For Augustine says: *The devil has power over them who despise God's commandments*[1], *and he rejoices over this sinister power.*[2] Therefore there is no sorrow in the demons.

Obj. 2. Further, sorrow is the cause of fear; for those things cause fear, while they are future, which cause sorrow when they are present. But there is no fear in the demons, according to *Job.* xli. 24, *Who was made to fear no one.* Therefore there is no grief in the demons.

Obj. 3. Further, it is a good thing to be sorry for evil. But the demons can do no good action. Therefore they cannot be sorry, at least for the evil of sin; which applies to the worm of conscience.

On the contrary, The demon's sin is greater than man's sin. But man is punished with sorrow because of the pleasure taken in sin, according to *Apoc.* xviii. 7, *As much as she hath glorified herself, and lived in delicacies, so much torment and sorrow give ye to her.* Consequently much more is the

1. God's commandments: 天主的诫命，通常指十诫
2. 参见 *De Genesi contra Manich.*, II, 17 (PL 34, 209).

devil punished with the grief of sorrow, because he especially glorified himself.

I answer that, Fear, sorrow, joy, and the like, so far as they are passions, cannot exist in the demons; for thus they are proper to the sensitive appetite, which is a power in a corporeal organ. According, however, as they denote simple acts of the will, they can be in the demons. And it must be said that there is sorrow in them; because sorrow, as denoting a simple act of the will, is nothing else than the resistance of the will to what is, or to what is not. Now it is evident that the demons would wish many things not to be, which are, and others to be, which are not; for, out of envy, they would wish others to be damned, who are saved. Consequently, sorrow must be said to exist in them, and especially because it is of the very notion of punishment that it be repugnant to the will. Moreover, they are deprived of happiness, which they desire naturally. In the same way, their wicked will is curbed in many respects.

Reply Obj. 1. Joy and sorrow are opposites about the same thing, but not about different things. Hence there is nothing to hinder a man from being sorry for one thing, and joyful for another, especially so far as sorrow and joy imply simple acts of the will. For, not merely in different things, but even in one and the same thing, there can be something that we will, and something that we will not.

Reply Obj. 2. As there is sorrow in the demons over present evil, so also there is fear of future evil. Now when it is said, *He was made to fear no one,* this is to be understood of the fear of God which restrains from sin. For it is written elsewhere that *the devils believe and tremble* (*Jas.* ii. 19).

Reply Obj. 3. To be sorry for the evil of sin because of the sin bears witness to the goodness of the will, to which the evil of sin is opposed. But to be sorry for the evil of punishment, or for the evil of sin because of the punishment, bears witness to the goodness of nature, to which the evil of punishment is opposed. Hence Augustine says that *sorrow for good lost by punishment is the witness to a good nature.*[1] Consequently, since the demon has a perverse and obstinate will, he is not sorry for the evil of sin.

Fourth Article
WHETHER OUR ATMOSPHERE IS THE DEMONS' PLACE OF PUNISHMENT?

We proceed thus to the Fourth Article:—

Objection 1. It would seem that this atmosphere is not the demons' place of punishment. For a demon is a spiritual nature. But a spiritual nature is not affected by place. Therefore there is no place of punishment for demons.

Obj. 2. Further, man's sin is not graver than the demons'. But man's place of punishment is hell. Much more, therefore, is it the demons' place of punishment; and consequently not the cloudy atmosphere.

Obj. 3. Further, the demons are punished with the pain of fire. But there is no fire in the cloudy atmosphere. Therefore the cloudy atmosphere is not the place of punishment for the demons.

On the contrary, Augustine says, that *the cloudy atmosphere is as a prison to the demons until the judgment day.*[2]

I answer that, The angels in their own nature stand midway between God and men. Now the order of divine providence so disposes, that it procures the welfare of the inferior orders through the superior. But man's welfare is disposed by divine providence in two ways. First of all, directly, when a man is brought to good and withheld from evil; and this is fittingly done through the good angels. In another way, indirectly, as when anyone assailed is exercised by fighting against opposition. It was fitting for this procuring of man's welfare to be

---

1. 参见 *De Civit. Dei*, XIX, 13 (PL 41, 641).
2. 参见 *De Genesi ad Litt.*, III, 10 (PL 34, 285).

brought about through the wicked angels, lest they should cease to be of service in the natural order after their fall. Consequently, a twofold place of punishment is due to the demons: one, by reason of their sin, and this is hell; another, in order that they may tempt men, and thus the cloudy atmosphere is their due place of punishment.

Now the procuring of men's salvation is prolonged even to the judgment day. Consequently, the ministry of the angels and wrestling with demons endure until then. Hence until then the good angels are sent to us here, and the demons are in this dark atmosphere for our trial; although some of them are even now in hell, to torment those whom they have led astray, just as some of the good angels are with the holy souls in heaven. But after the judgment day all the wicked, both men and angels, will be in hell, and the good in heaven.

Reply Obj. 1. A place is not penal to angel or soul as if affecting the nature by changing it, but as affecting the will by saddening it: because the angel or the soul apprehends that it is in a place not agreeable to its will.

Reply Obj. 2. One soul is not set over another in the order of nature, as the demons are over men in the order of nature; consequently there is no parallel.

Reply Obj. 3. Some[1] have maintained that the pain of sense for demons and souls is postponed until the judgment day, and that the beatitude of the saints is likewise postponed until the judgment day. But this is erroneous, and contrary to the teaching of the Apostle (*2 Cor.* v. 1): *If our earthly house of this habitation be dissolved, we have a house in heaven.* Others,[2] again, while not admitting the same of souls, admit it as to demons. But it is better to say that the same judgment is passed upon wicked souls and wicked angels, even as on good souls and good angels.

---

1. 参见 On these, cf. St. Thomas, *C. G.*, IV, 91.
2. 参见 William of Auvergne, *De Univ.*, IIa IIae, 70 (I, pt. II, 970).

Consequently, it must be said that a heavenly place belongs to the glory of the angels, and yet their glory is not lessened by their coming to us, for they consider that place to be their own; just as in the same way we say that the bishop's honor is not lessened while he is not actually sitting on his throne. In like manner, it must be said that although the demons are not actually bound within the fire of hell while they are in this dark atmosphere, nevertheless, their punishment is not lessened, because they know that such confinement is their due. Hence it is said in a *Gloss* upon *Jas*. iii. 6: *They carry the fire of hell with them wherever they go.*[1] Nor is this contrary to what is said (*Luke* viii. 31), *They besought the Lord not to cast them into the abyss*; for they asked for this, deeming it to be a punishment for them to be cast out of a place where they could injure men. Hence it is stated, *They besought Him that He would not expel them out of the country* (*Mark* v. 10).

---

1. 参见 *Glossa ordin.*, super *James*, III, 6 (VI, 213F).

TREATISE ON THE WORK OF THE SIX DAYS

Question LXV
THE WORK OF CREATION OF CORPOREAL CREATURES
(*In Four Articles*)

FROM the consideration of spiritual creatures we proceed to that of corporeal creatures, in the production of which, as Holy Scripture makes mention, three works are found, namely, the work of creation, as given in the words, *In the beginning God created heaven and earth* (*Gen.* i. 1); the work of distinction, as given in the words, *He divided the light from the darkness, and the waters that are above the firmament from the waters that are under the firmament* (*Gen.* i. 4, 7); and the work of adornment, expressed thus, *Let there be lights in the firmament* (*Gen.* i. 14).

First, then, we must consider the work of creation; secondly, the work of distinction;[1] and thirdly, the work of adornment.[2] Under the first head there are four points of inquiry: (1) Whether corporeal creatures are from God? (2) Whether they were created because of God's goodness? (3) Whether they were created by God through the medium of the angels? (4) Whether the forms of bodies are from the angels or immediately from God?

First Article
WHETHER CORPOREAL CREATURES ARE FROM GOD?

We proceed thus to the First Article:—

1. 参见 Q. 66.
2. 参见 Q. 70.

Objection 1. It would seem that corporeal creatures are not from God. For it is said (*Eccles.* iii. 14): *I have learned that all the works which God hath made, continue for ever.* But visible bodies do not continue for ever, for it is said (*2 Cor.* iv. 18): *The things which are seen are temporal, but the things which are not seen are eternal.* Therefore God did not make visible bodies.

Obj. 2. Further, it is said (*Gen.* i. 31): *God saw all the things that He had made, and they were very good.* But corporeal creatures are evil, since we find them harmful in many ways; as may be seen in serpents, in the sun's heat, and other like things. Now a thing is called evil, in so far as it is harmful. Corporeal creatures, therefore, are not from God.

Obj. 3. Further, what is from God does not withdraw us from God, but leads us to Him. But corporeal creatures withdraw us from God. Hence the Apostle says (*2 Cor.* iv. 18): *While we look not at the things which are seen.* Corporeal creatures, therefore, are not from God.

On the contrary, It is said (*Ps.* cxlv. 6): *Who made heaven and earth, the sea, and all things that are in them.*

I answer that, Certain heretics maintain that visible things are not created by the God Who is good, but by an evil principle, and allege in proof of their error the words of the Apostle (*2 Cor.* iv. 4), *The god of this world hath blinded the minds of unbelievers.*[1] But this position is altogether untenable. For, if things that differ agree in some point, there must be some cause for that agreement, since things diverse in nature cannot be united of themselves. Hence, whenever in different things some one thing common to all is found, it must be that these different things receive that one thing from some one cause, as different bodies that are hot receive their heat from fire. But *being* is found to be common to all things, however otherwise different. There must, therefore, be one principle of being from which all things in whatever way existing have

1. 参见 The opinion of the Manicheans: cf. above, q. 49, a. 3.

their being, whether they are invisible and spiritual, or visible and corporeal. But the devil is called the god of this world, not as having created it, but because worldlings serve him, of whom also the Apostle says, speaking in the same sense, *Whose god is their belly* (*Phil.* iii. 19).

Reply Obj. 1. All the creatures of God in some respects continue for ever, at least as to matter, since what is created will never be annihilated, even though it be corruptible. But the nearer a creature approaches God, Who is immovable, the more it also is immovable. For corruptible creatures endure for ever as regards their matter, though they change as regards their substantial form. But incorruptible creatures endure with respect to their substance, though they are mutable in other respects, such as place, as are the heavenly bodies; or the affections, as are spiritual creatures. But the Apostle's words, *The things which are seen are temporal*, though true even as regards such things considered in themselves (in so far as every visible creature is subject to time, either as to being or as to movement), are intended to apply to visible things in so far as they are offered to man as rewards. For such rewards, as consist in these visible things, are temporal; while those that are invisible endure forever. Hence he had said before (*2 Cor.* iv. 17): It *worketh for us ... an eternal weight of glory*.

Reply Obj. 2. Corporeal creatures according to their nature are good, though this good is not universal, but partial and limited. The consequence of this particularity and limitedness is a certain opposition of contrary qualities, though each quality is good in itself. To those, however, who estimate things, not by the nature thereof, but by the good they themselves can derive therefrom, everything which is harmful to themselves seems absolutely evil. For they do not reflect that what is in some way injurious to one person, to another is beneficial, and that even to themselves the same thing may be evil in some respects, but good in others. And this could not be, if bodies were essentially evil and harmful.

Reply Obj. 3. Creatures of themselves do not withdraw us from God, but lead us to Him; for *the invisible things of God are clearly seen, being understood by the things that are made* (*Rom.* i. 20). If, then, they withdraw men from God, it is the fault of those who use them foolishly. Thus it is said (*Wis.* xiv. 11): *Creatures are turned into a snare to the feet of the unwise.* And the very fact that they can thus withdraw us from God proves that they came from Him, for they cannot lead the foolish away from God except by the allurements of some good that they have from Him.

Second Article

WHETHER CORPOREAL THINGS WERE MADE FOR THE SAKE OF GOD'S GOODNESS?

We proceed thus to the Second Article:—

Objection 1. It would seem that corporeal creatures were not made because of God's goodness. For it is said (*Wis.* i. 14) that God *created all things that they might be.* Therefore all things were created for their own being's sake, and not for the sake of God's goodness.

Obj. 2. Further, good has the nature of an end, and therefore the greater good in things is the end of the lesser good. But spiritual creatures are related to corporeal creatures as the greater good to the lesser. Corporeal creatures, therefore, are created for the sake of spiritual creatures, and not for the sake of God's goodness.

Obj. 3. Further, justice does not give unequal things except to the unequal. Now God is just. Therefore inequality not created by God must precede all inequality created by Him. But an inequality not created by God can arise only from free choice, and consequently all inequality results from the different movements of free choice. Now, corporeal creatures are unequal to spiritual creatures. Therefore the former were made for the sake of some movements of free choice, and not for the sake of God's goodness.

On the contrary, It is said (*Prov.* xvi. 4): *The Lord hath made all things for Himself.*

I answer that, Origen held that corporeal creatures were not made according to God's original purpose, but in punishment of the sin of spiritual creatures.[1] For he maintained that in the beginning God made spiritual creatures only, and all of equal nature. Now, some of these, by the use of free choice, turned to God, and, according to the measure of their conversion, were given a higher or a lower rank, retaining their simplicity; while others turned from God, and became bound to different kinds of bodies according to the degree of their turning away.[2] But this position is erroneous. In the first place, because it is contrary to Scripture, which, after narrating the production of each kind of corporeal creatures, subjoins, *God saw that it was good* (*Gen.* i.), as if to say that everything was brought into being for the reason that it was good for it to be. But according to Origen's opinion, the corporeal creature was made, not because it was good that it should be, but that the evil in another might be punished. Secondly, because it would follow that the present arrangement of the corporeal world would arise from mere chance. For if the sun's body was made what it is that it might serve for a punishment suitable to some sin of a spiritual creature, it would follow, if other spiritual creatures had sinned in the same way as the one to punish whom the sun had been created, that many suns would exist in the world; and so of other things. But such a consequence is altogether inadmissible.

Hence we must set aside this theory as false, and consider that the entire universe is constituted by all creatures, as a whole consists of its parts. Now if we wish to assign an end to any whole, and to the parts of that whole, we shall find, first, that each and every part exists for the sake of its proper act, as the eye for the act of seeing; secondly, that less honorable parts exist for the more honorable, as the senses for the intellect, the lungs for the heart; and, thirdly, that all parts are for the

1. 参见 Cf. *Peri Archon*, II, 5 (PG 11, 329).—Cf. above, q. 47, a. z.
2. 参见 *Op. cit.*, I, 6; 8; II, 9; III, 5 (PG 11, 166; 178; 229; 329).

perfection of the whole, just as matter is for form, since the parts are, as it were, the matter of the whole; Furthermore, the whole man is for the sake of an extrinsic end, namely, the fruition of God. So, even in the parts of the universe every creature exists for its own proper act and perfection, and the less noble for the nobler, as those creatures that are less noble than man exist for the sake of man. Furthermore, each and every creature exists for the perfection of the entire universe. Further still, the entire universe, with all its parts, is ordained towards God as its end, inasmuch as it imitates, as it were, and shows forth the divine goodness to the glory of God. Reasonable creatures, however, have in some special and higher manner God as their end, since they can attain to Him by their own operations, by knowing and loving Him. Thus it is plain that the divine goodness is the end of all corporeal things.

Reply Obj. 1. In that any creature possesses being, it represents the divine Being and Its goodness. And, therefore, the fact that God created all things that they might have being does not exclude that He created them for His own goodness.

Reply Obj. 2. The proximate end does not exclude the ultimate end. Therefore that corporeal creatures were, in a manner, made for the sake of the spiritual does not prevent their being made for the sake of God's goodness.

Reply Obj. 3. Equality of justice has its place in retribution, since equal rewards or punishments are due to equal merit or demerit. But this does not apply to things in their first establishment. For just as an architect, without injustice, places stones of the same kind in different parts of a building, not because of any antecedent difference in the stones, but with a view to securing that perfection of the entire building which could not be obtained except by the different positions of the stones; even so, God from the beginning, to secure perfection in the universe, has set therein creatures of various and unequal natures, according to His wisdom, and without injustice, since no diversity of merit is presupposed.

Third Article
WHETHER CORPOREAL CREATURES WERE PRODUCED BY GOD THROUGH THE MEDIUM OF THE ANGELS?

We proceed thus to the Third Article:—

Objection 1. It would seem that corporeal creatures were produced by God through the medium of the angels. For, as all things are governed by the divine wisdom, so by it all things were made, according to *Ps.* ciii. 24: *Thou hast made all things in wisdom*. But *it belongs to wisdom to ordain*, as stated in the beginning of the *Metaphysics*.[1] Hence in the government of things the lower is ruled by the higher in a certain fitting order, as Augustine says.[2] Therefore in the production of things it was ordained that the corporeal should be produced by the spiritual, as the lower by the higher.

Obj. 2. Further, diversity of effects shows diversity of causes, since like always produces like. If then all creatures, both spiritual and corporeal, were produced immediately by God, there would be no diversity in creatures, for one would not be further removed from God than another. But this is clearly false, for the Philosopher says that some things are corruptible because they are far removed from God.[3]

Obj. 3. Further, infinite power is not required to produce a finite effect. But every body is finite. Therefore, it could be, and was, produced by the finite power of spiritual creatures; for in such beings there is no distinction between *to be* and *to be able*, especially as no dignity befitting a being according to its nature is denied to them, unless it be in punishment of a fault.

---

1. 参见 Aristotle, *Metaph.*, I, 2 (982a 18).
2. 参见 *De Trin.*, III, 4 (PL 42, 873).
3. 参见 *De Gener.*, II, 10 (336b 30).

On the contrary, It is said (*Gen.* i. 1): *In the beginning God created heaven and earth*; by which are understood corporeal creatures. These therefore, were produced immediately by God.

I answer that, Some have maintained that creatures proceeded from God by degrees, in such a way that a first creature proceeded from Him immediately, and in its turn produced another, and so on until the production of corporeal creatures.[1] But this position is untenable, since the first production of corporeal creatures is by creation, by which matter itself is produced; for in the act of coming into being the imperfect must be made before the perfect. Now it is impossible that anything should be created, save by God alone.

In proof of this we must consider that the higher the cause, the more numerous the things to which its causality extends. Now the underlying principle in things is always more universal than that which informs and restricts it; and thus, being is more universal than living, living than understanding, and matter than form. The more widely, then, one thing underlies others, the more directly does that thing proceed from a higher cause. Thus the thing that primarily underlies all things belongs properly to the causality of the supreme cause. Therefore no secondary cause can produce anything, unless there is presupposed in the produced thing something that is caused by a higher cause. But creation is the production of a thing in its entire substance, without presupposing anything, either uncreated or created. Hence it remains that nothing can create except God alone, Who is the first cause. Therefore, in order to show that all bodies were created immediately by God, Moses said: *In the beginning God created heaven and earth.*

Reply Obj. 1. In the production of things an order exists, but not such that one creature is created by another, for that is impossible; but

---

1. 参见 Avicenna: cf. above, q. 45, a. 5. —Cf. also Avicebron, *Fons Vitae*, II, 24 (p. 71); III, 2 (p. 76); III, 6 (p. 90).—Cf. below, q. 74, a. 3, ad 5.

rather such that by the divine wisdom diverse grades are constituted in creatures.

Reply Obj. 2. God Himself, though one, has knowledge of many and different things without detriment to the simplicity of His nature, as has been shown above.[1] Hence, by His wisdom He is the cause of diverse things, produced according to the diversity of what is known by Him, even as an artificer, by apprehending diverse forms, produces diverse works of art.

Reply Obj. 3. The amount of power in an agent is measured not only by the thing made, but also by the manner of making it; for one and the same thing is made in one way by a greater power, in another by a lesser. But the production of finite things, where nothing is presupposed as existing, is the work of infinite power, and, as such, can belong to no creature.

Fourth Article
WHETHER THE FORMS OF BODIES ARE FROM THE ANGELS?

We proceed thus to the Fourth Article:—

Objection 1. It would seem that the forms of bodies are from the angels. For Boethius says: *From forms that are without matter come the forms that are in matter.*[2] But forms that are without matter are spiritual substances, and forms that are in matter are the forms of bodies. Therefore, the forms of bodies are from spiritual substances.

Obj. 2. Further, all that is such by participation is reduced to that which is such by its essence. But spiritual substances are forms essentially, whereas corporeal creatures have forms by participation. Therefore the forms of corporeal things are derived from spiritual

---

1. 参见 Q. 15, a. 2.
2. 参见 *De Trin.*, I (PL 64, 1250).

substances.

Obj. 3. Further, spiritual substances have more power as causes than the heavenly bodies. But the heavenly bodies give form to things here below, for which reason they are said to cause generation and corruption. Much more, therefore, are material forms derived from spiritual substances.

On the contrary, Augustine says: *We must not suppose that this corporeal matter serves the angels at their nod, but rather that it obeys God thus.*[1] But corporeal matter may be said to serve at the nod of that being from which it receives its form. Corporeal forms, then, are not from the angels, but from God.

I answer that, It was the opinion of some that all corporeal forms are derived from the spiritual substances which we call the angels. And there are two ways in which this has been held.

Plato held that the forms of corporeal matter are derived from, and formed by, Forms immaterially subsisting,[2] by a kind of participation.[3] Thus he held that there exists an immaterial man, and an immaterial horse,[4] and so forth, and that from such the individual sensible things that we see are constituted, in so far as in corporeal matter there abides the impression received from these separate forms, by a kind of assimilation, or, as he calls it, *participation*. And, according to the Platonists, the order of forms corresponds to the order of those separate substances.[5] For example, there is a separate substance, which is a horse and the cause of all horses, above this is separate life, or *per se* life, as they term it, which is the cause of all life, and above this again is that which they call being itself, which is the cause of all being.

---

1. 参见 *De Trin.*, III, 8 (PL 42, 875).
2. 参见 Cf. Aristotle, *Metaph.*, I, 9 (991b 3).
3. 参见 Cf. *op. cit.*, I, 6 (987b 9).
4. 参见 Cf. *op. cit.*, II, 2 (997b 8).
5. 参见 *De Causis*, I (p. 161).—Cf. Proclus, *Elem. of Theol.*, prop. 101 (p. 90).—Cf. also Pseudo-Dionysius, *De Div. Nom.*, V, 1 (PG 3, 816).

Avicenna,[1] however, and certain others,[2] have maintained that the forms of corporeal things do not subsist *per se* in matter, but in the intellect only. Thus they say that from forms existing in the intellect of spiritual creatures (called *intelligences* by them, but *angels* by us) proceed all the forms of corporeal matter, as the form of his handiwork proceeds from the forms in the mind of the craftsman.[3] This theory seems to be the same as that of certain heretics of modern times, who say that God indeed created all things, but that the devil formed corporeal matter, and differentiated it into species.[4]

But all these opinions seem to have a common origin. They all, in fact, sought for a cause of forms as though the form were of itself brought into being. But, as Aristotle proves, what is made, properly speaking, is the *composite*.[5] Now, such are the forms of corruptible things that at one time they exist and at another time they do not exist, without being themselves generated or corrupted; but they become generated or corrupted by reason of the generation or corruption of the *composites*. For forms themselves do not have being, but composites have being through forms; for according to a thing's mode of being is the mode in which it is brought into being. Since, then, like is produced from like, we must not look for the cause of corporeal forms in any immaterial form, but in something that is composite, as this fire is generated by that fire. Corporeal forms, therefore, are caused, not as emanations from some immaterial form, but by the reduction of matter from potentiality to act by some composite agent. But since the composite agent, which is a body, is moved by a created spiritual substance, as Augustine says,[6] it follows further that even corporeal

1. 参见 *Metaph.*, VII, 2 (96rb).
2. 参见 Avicebron, *Fons Vitae*, III, 23 (p. 132).
3. 参见 Avicenna, *Metaph.*, IX, 3 (103vb); *De An.*, IV, 4 (20vb).
4. 参见 The Albigensians: cf. Denzinger, no. 428.
5. 参见 *Metaph.*, VII, 8 (1033b 17); 9 (1034b 10).
6. 参见 *De Trin.*, III, 4 (PL 42, 873).

forms are derived from spiritual substances, not as emanating from them, but as the term of their movement. And, further still, the species of the angelic intellect, which are, as it were, certain seminal principles of corporeal forms, must be referred to God as the first cause.

But in the first production of corporeal creatures no transmutation from potentiality to act can have taken place. Accordingly, the corporeal forms that bodies had when first produced came immediately from God, Whose bidding alone matter obeys, as its own proper cause. To signify this, Moses prefaces each divine work with the words, *God said, Let this thing be*, or *that*, to denote the formation of all things by the Word of God, from Whom, according to Augustine, is *all form and fitness and concord of parts.*[1]

Reply Obj. 1. By immaterial forms Boethius understands the exemplars of things in the mind of God. In the same way, the Apostle says (*Heb.* xi. 3): *By faith we understand that the world was framed by the Word of God; that from invisible things visible things might be made.* But if by immaterial forms he understands the angels, we must say that from them come material forms, not by emanation, but by motion.

Reply Obj. 2. Forms received into matter are to be referred, not to self-subsisting forms of the same nature, as the Platonists held, but either to intelligible forms of the angelic intellect, from which they proceed by movement, or, still higher, to the exemplars in the divine intellect, by which even the seeds of forms are implanted in created things, that they may be able to be brought by movement into act.

Reply Obj. 3. The heavenly bodies inform earthly ones by movement, not by emanation.

---

1. 参见 *Tract.* I, super *Ioann.*, I, 3 (PL 35, 1386).

Question LXVI
THE ORDER OF CREATION TOWARDS DISTINCTION
(*In Four Articles*)

WE must next consider the work of distinction. And first, the ordering of creation towards distinction; secondly, the distinction itself. Under the first head there are four points of inquiry: (1) Whether the informity of created matter preceded in time its formation? (2) Whether the matter of all corporeal things is the same? (3) Whether the empyrean heaven was created contemporaneously with formless matter? (4) Whether time was created simultaneously with it?

First Article
WHETHER INFORMITY OF CREATED MATTER PRECEDED IN TIME ITS FORMATION?

We proceed thus to the First Article:—

Objection 1. It would seem that the informity of matter preceded in time its formation. For it is said (*Gen.* i. 2): *The earth was void and empty*, or *invisible and shapeless*, according to another version; by which is understood *the informity of matter*, as Augustine says.[1] Therefore matter was formless until it received its form.

Obj. 2. Further, nature in its working imitates the working of God, as a secondary cause imitates a first cause. But in the working of

---

1. 参见 *Confess.*, XII, 12 (PL 32, 831); *De Genesi ad Litt.*, II, 11 (PL 34, 272).

nature, informity precedes form in time. It does so, therefore, in the divine working.

Obj. 3. Further, matter is higher than accident, for matter is part of substance. But God can make an accident exist without a subject, as in the Sacrament of the Altar. He could, therefore, cause matter to exist without form.

On the contrary, An imperfect effect proves imperfection in the agent. But God is an absolutely perfect agent; wherefore it is said of Him (*Deut.* xxxii. 4): *The works of God are perfect.* Therefore the work of His creation was at no time formless. Further, the formation of corporeal creatures was effected by the work of distinction. But confusion is opposed to distinction, as informity to formation. If, therefore, informity preceded in time the formation of matter, it follows that at the beginning confusion, called by the ancients chaos,[1] existed in the corporeal creation.

I answer that, On this point holy men differ in opinion. Augustine, for instance, believes that the informity of matter was not prior in time to its formation, but only in origin or the order of nature.[2] But others, as Basil,[3] Ambrose,[4] and Chrysostom,[5] hold that the informity of matter preceded in time its formation. And although these opinions seem mutually contradictory, in reality they differ but little; for Augustine takes the informity of matter in a different sense from the others. In his sense, it means the absence of all form, and if we thus understand it, we cannot say that the informity of matter was prior in time either to its formation or to its distinction. As to formation, the argument is clear. For if formless matter preceded in

---

1. 参见 Cf. Aristotle, *Phys.*, I, 4 (187a 23); *Metaph.*, XI, 2 (1069b 22).
2. 参见 *Confess.*, XII, 12 (PL 32, 843); *De Genesi ad Litt.*, I, 15 (PL 34, 257).
3. 参见 *In Hexaëm.*, hom. II (PG 29, 29).
4. 参见 *In Hexaëm.*, VII (PL 14, 148).
5. 参见 *In Genesim*, hom. II (PG 53, 30).

duration, it already existed; for this is implied by duration, since the end of creation is being in act, and act itself is a form. To say, then, that matter preceded, but without form, is to say that being existed actually, yet without act, which is a contradiction in terms. Nor can it be said that it possessed some common form, on which afterwards supervened different forms, to distinguish it. For this would be to hold the opinion of the ancient natural philosophers, who maintained that primary matter was some corporeal reality in act, as fire, air, water, or some intermediate substance. Hence, followed the dictum that to be made means merely to be altered.[1] For since the preceding form bestowed actual substantial being, and made some particular thing to be, it would follow that the supervening form would not, absolutely speaking, make an actual being, but *this* actual being; which is the proper effect of an accidental form. Thus the forms after the first would be merely accidents, implying not generation, but alteration. Hence we must assert that primary matter was not created altogether formless nor under any one common form, but under distinct forms. And so, if the informity of matter be taken as referring to the condition of primary matter, which in itself is formless, this informity did not precede in time its formation or distinction, but only in origin and nature, as Augustine says; in the same way as potentiality is prior to act, and the part to the whole. But the other holy writers understand by informity, not the exclusion of all form, but the absence of that beauty and comeliness which are now apparent in the corporeal creation. Accordingly they say that the informity of corporeal matter preceded its form in duration. And so, when this is considered, it appears that Augustine agrees with them in some respects, and in others disagrees, as will be shown later.[2]

As far as may be gathered from the text of *Genesis*, a threefold

1. 参见 Aristotle, *Phys.*, I, 4 (187a 12).
2. 参见 Q. 69, a. 1; q. 74, a. 2.

beauty was wanting to corporeal creatures, for which reason they were said to be without form. For the beauty of light was wanting to all that transparent body, which we call the heavens, whence it is said that *darkness was upon the face of the deep*. And the earth lacked beauty in two ways: first, that beauty which it acquired when its watery veil was withdrawn, and so we read that *the earth was void*, or *invisible*, inasmuch as the waters covered and concealed it from view; secondly, that which it derives from being adorned by herbs and plants, for which reason it is called *empty*, or, according to another reading, *shapeless* —that is, unadorned. Thus after the mention of two created natures, the heaven and the earth, the informity of the heaven is indicated by the words, *darkness was upon the face of the deep*, since the air is included under heaven; and the informity of the earth, by the words, *the earth was void and empty*.

Reply Obj. 1. The word *earth* is taken differently in this passage by Augustine, and by other writers. Augustine holds that by the words *earth* and *water*, in this passage, primarily matter itself is signified.[1] For it was impossible for Moses to make the idea of such matter intelligible to an ignorant people, except under the similitude of well-known things. Hence he uses a variety of figures in speaking of it, calling it not water only, nor earth only, lest they should think it to be in very truth water or earth. At the same time, it has so far a likeness to earth in that it is susceptible of form, and to water in its adaptability[2] to a variety of forms. In this respect, then, the earth is said to be *void and empty*, or *invisible and shapeless*, because matter is known by means of form. Hence, considered in itself, it is called *invisible* or *void*, and its potentiality is filled by form; and that is why Plato says that matter is *place*.[3] But other holy writers understand by earth the element *earth*,

---

1. 参见 *Confess*., XII, 12 (PL 32, 831); *De Genesi ad Litt*., II, 11 (PL 34, 272).
2. adaptability: 适应性
3. 参见 Cf. Aristotle, *Phys*., IV, 2 (209b 11; b 15).

and we have said how, in this sense, the earth was, according to them, without form.

Reply Obj. 2. Nature produces an actual effect from being in potentiality; and consequently in the operations of nature potentiality must precede act in time, and informity must precede formation. But God produces being in act out of nothing, and can, therefore, produce a perfect thing in an instant, according to the greatness of His power.

Reply Obj. 3. Accident, inasmuch as it is a form, is a kind of act; whereas matter, as such, is essentially being in potentiality. Hence it is more repugnant that matter should be in act without form, than for an accident to be without a subject.

In reply to the first argument in the contrary sense, we say that if, according to some holy writers, informity was prior in time to the informing of matter, this arose, not from want of power on God's part, but from His wisdom, and from the design of preserving due order in the disposition of creatures by developing the perfect from the imperfect.

In reply to the second argument, we say that certain of the ancient natural philosophers maintained confusion devoid of all distinction;[1] except Anaxagoras, who taught that the intellect alone was distinct and without admixture.[2]

But previous to the work of distinction, Holy Scripture enumerates several kinds of differentiation, the first being that of the heaven from the earth, in which even a material distinction is expressed, as will be shown later.[3] This is signified by the words, *In the beginning God created heaven and earth.*

The second distinction mentioned is that of the elements according to their forms, since both *earth* and *water* are named. *Air* and *fire* are

1. 参见 Cf. Aristotle, *Phys.*, I, 4 (187a 29).
2. 参见 Cf. *op. cit.*, VIII, 5 (256b 26); *Metaph.*, I, 8 (989b 15).
3. 参见 A. 3; q. 68, a. 1, ad 1.

not mentioned by name because the corporeal nature of these would not be so evident as that of earth and water to the ignorant people to whom Moses spoke. Plato, nevertheless, understood air to be signified by the words, *Spirit of God*, since spirit is another name for air, and considered that by the word heaven is meant fire, for he held heaven to be composed of fire, as Augustine relates.[1] But Rabbi Moses, though otherwise agreeing with Plato, says that fire is signified by the word darkness, since, said he, fire does not shine in its own sphere.[2] However, it seems more reasonable to hold to what we stated above; because by the words *Spirit of God* Scripture usually means the Holy Ghost, Who is said to *move over the waters*, not, indeed, in bodily shape, but as the craftsman's will may be said to move over the material to which he intends to give a form.

The third distinction is that of place. For the earth is said to be under the waters that rendered it invisible, while the air, the subject of darkness, is described as being above the waters: *Darkness was upon the face of the deep.* The remaining distinctions will appear from what follows.[3]

Second Article
WHETHER THE FORMLESS MATTER OF ALL CORPOREAL THINGS IS THE SAME?

We proceed thus to the Second Article:—

Objection 1. It would seem that the formless matter of all corporeal things is the same. For Augustine says: *I find two things Thou hast made, one formed, the other formless;*[4] and he says that the latter was the invisible

---

1. 参见 *De Civit. Dei*, VIII, 11 (PL 41, 236).
2. 参见 *Guide*, II, 30 (p. 213).
3. 参见 Q. 71.
4. 参见 *Confess.*, XII, 12 (PL 34, 831).

and shapeless earth, whereby, he adds, the matter of all corporeal things is designated. Therefore the matter of all corporeal things is the same.

Obj. 2. Further, the Philosopher says: *Things that are one in genus are one in matter.*[1] But all corporeal things are in the same genus of body. Therefore the matter of all bodies is the same.

Obj. 3. Further, different acts befit different potentialities, and one act befits one potentiality. But all bodies have the same form, corporeity. Therefore all bodies have the same matter.

Obj. 4. Further, matter, considered in itself, is only in potentiality. But distinction is due to forms. Therefore matter considered in itself is the same in all corporeal things.

On the contrary, Things of which the matter is the same are mutually interchangeable, and mutually active or passive, as it is said.[2] But heavenly and earthly bodies do not act upon each other mutually. Therefore their matter is not the same.

I answer that, On this question the opinions of philosophers have differed. Plato and all who preceded Aristotle held that all bodies are of the nature of the four elements.[3] Hence, since the four elements have one common matter, as their mutual generation and corruption prove, it followed that the matter of all bodies is the same. But the fact of the incorruptibility of some bodies was ascribed by Plato, not to the condition of matter, but to the will of the artificer, God, Whom he represents as saying to the heavenly bodies: *By your own nature you are subject to dissolution, but by My will you are indissoluble, for My will is more powerful than the link that binds you together.*[4] But this theory Aristotle

---

1. 参见 *Metaph.*, IV, 6 (1016a 24).
2. 参见 Aristotle, *De Gener.*, I, 6 (322b 18).
3. 参见 Cf. Aristotle, *Phys.*, I, 4 (187a 12).
4. 参见 Plato, *Timaeus*, p. 41a, trans. Chalcidius, XVI (p. 169).

disproves by the natural movements of bodies.[1] For since, he says, the heavenly bodies have a natural movement, different from that of the elements, it follows that they have a different nature from them. For movement in a circle, which is proper to the heavenly bodies, is not by contraries, whereas the movements of the elements are mutually opposite, one tending upwards, another downwards; and so, for this reason, a heavenly body is without contrariety, whereas the elemental bodies have contrariety in their nature. And as generation and corruption are from contraries, it follows that, whereas the elements are corruptible, the heavenly bodies are incorruptible.

But in spite of this difference of natural corruptibility[2] and incorruptibility[3], Avicebron taught the unity of matter in all bodies, arguing from the unity of the corporeal form.[4] And, indeed, if corporeity were one form in itself, on which the other forms that distinguish bodies from each other supervene, this argument would necessarily be true; for the form of corporeity would inhere in matter immutably, and all bodies would thus be incorruptible so far as concerns the form of corporeity. But corruption would then be merely accidental through the disappearance of the later forms—that is to say, it would be corruption, not pure and simple, but relatively so, since a being in act would subsist as the subject of the privation. In this same way, too, the ancient natural philosophers taught that the substratum of bodies was some actual being, such as air or fire.

But supposing that no form in corruptible bodies remains subsisting beneath generation and corruption, it follows necessarily that the matter of corruptible and incorruptible bodies is not the same. For matter, as it is in itself, is in potentiality to form. Considered in

---

1. 参见 *De Caelo*, I, 2 (269a 30); 3 (270a 12).
2. corruptibility: 腐败性；堕落性
3. incorruptibility: 清廉，高尚
4. 参见 *Fons Vitae*, I, 17 (pp. 21, 22).

itself, then, matter is in potentiality to the forms of all those things to which it is common. But in receiving any one form it is in act only as regards that form. Hence it remains in potentiality to all the other forms. And this is the case even where some forms are more perfect than others, and contain these others virtually in themselves. For potentiality in itself is indifferent with respect to perfection and imperfection, so that under an imperfect form it is in potentiality to a perfect form, and *vice versa*. Matter, therefore, while existing under the form of an incorruptible body, would be in potentiality to the form of a corruptible body; and as it does not actually possess the latter, it has both form and the privation of form, for the lack of a form in that which is in potentiality thereto is privation. But this condition belongs to a corruptible body. It is therefore impossible that bodies by nature corruptible, and those by nature incorruptible, should possess the same matter.

Neither can we say, as Averroes imagines,[1] that a heavenly body itself is the matter of the heaven, being in potentiality with regard to place, though not to being, and that its form is a separate substance united to it as its mover. For it is impossible to suppose any being in act, unless in its totality it be act and form, or be something which has act or form. If, then, we were to think of this separate substance, which is held to be a mover, as removed, then, if the heavenly body is not something having form—that is, something composed of a form and the subject of that form—it follows that in its totality it is form and act. But every such thing is something actually intelligible, which the heavenly bodies are not, being sensible. It follows, then, that the matter of the heavenly bodies, considered in itself, is in potentiality to that form alone which it actually possesses. Nor does it concern the point at issue to inquire whether this is a soul or any other thing.[2] Hence this form perfects this

1. 参见 *De Subst. Orbis*, III (IX, 5va).
2. 参见 Cf. below, q. 70, a. 3.

matter in such a way that there remains in it no potentiality with respect to being, but only to place, as Aristotle says.[1] So, then, the matter of the heavenly bodies and of the elements is not the same, except by analogy, in so far as they agree in the motion of potentiality.

Reply Obj. 1. Augustine follows in this the opinion of Plato, who does not admit a fifth essence.[2] Or we may say that formless matter is one with the unity of order, just as all bodies are one in the order of corporeal creatures.

Reply Obj. 2. If genus is taken physically, *corruptible and incorruptible beings are not in the same genus*, because of their diverse modes of potentiality, as is said *Metaph.* x.[3] Logically considered, however, there is but one genus of all bodies, since they are all included in the one notion of corporeity.

Reply Obj. 3. The form of corporeity is not one and the same in all bodies, not being other than the various forms by which bodies are distinguished, as was stated above.

Reply Obj. 4. Since potentiality is said in relation to act, a being in potentiality is diverse according to its relation to a diverse act; as sight is in relation to color, and hearing to sound. Therefore, the reason why the matter of celestial bodies is different from that of the elemental bodies is that it is not in potentiality to an elemental form.

Third Article
WHETHER THE EMPYREAN HEAVEN WAS CREATED AT THE SAME TIME AS FORMLESS MATTER?

We proceed thus to the Third Article:—

---

1. 参见 *Metaph.*, XI, 2 (1069a 26).
2. 参见 Cf. Nemesius, *De Nat. Hom.*, V (PG 40, 625).—Cf. St. Thomas, *In De Caelo*, I, lect. 4.
3. 参见 Aristotle, *Metaph.*, IX, 10 (1058b 28).

Objection 1. It would seem that the empyrean heaven was not created at the same time as formless matter. For the empyrean, if it is anything at all, must be a sensible body. But all sensible bodies are movable, and the empyrean heaven is not movable. For if it were so, its movement would be ascertained by the movement of some visible body, which is not the case. The empyrean heaven, then, was not created contemporaneously with formless matter.

Obj. 2. Further, Augustine says that *the lower bodies are governed by the higher in a certain order.*[1] If, therefore, the empyrean heaven is the highest of bodies, it must necessarily exercise some influence on bodies below it. But this does not seem to be the case, especially as it is presumed to be without movement; for one body cannot move another unless itself also be moved. Therefore the empyrean heaven was not created together with formless matter.

Obj. 3. Further, if it be held that the empyrean heaven is the place of contemplation, and not ordained to natural effects,[2] on the contrary, Augustine says: *In so far as we apprehend eternal things by the mind, so far are we not of this world;*[3] from which it is clear that contemplation lifts the mind above the things of this world. Corporeal place, therefore, cannot be the seat of contemplation.

Obj. 4. Further, among the heavenly bodies exists a body, partly transparent and partly luminous, which we call the sidereal heaven. There exists also a heaven wholly transparent, called by some the aqueous or crystalline heaven.[4] If, then, there exists a still higher heaven, it must be wholly luminous. But this cannot be, for then the air would be constantly illumined, and there would be no night. Therefore the empyrean heaven was not created together with formless matter.

---

1. 参见 *De Trin.*, III, 4 (PL 42, 873).
2. 参见 Cf. St. Albert, *In II Sent.*, d. 2, a. 5 (XXVII, 54).
3. 参见 *De Trin.*, IV, 20 (PL 42, 907).
4. 参见 Cf. below, q. 68, a. 2 and 4.

On the contrary, Strabo says that in the passage, *In the beginning God created heaven and earth, heaven denotes not the visible firmament, but the empyrean or fiery heaven.*[1]

I answer that, The empyrean heaven rests only on the authority of Strabo and Bede, and also of Basil; all of whom agree in one respect, namely, in holding it to be the place of the blessed. Strabo[2] and Bede[3] say that *as soon as created it was filled with the angels*; and Basil says: *Just as the lost are driven into the lowest darkness, so the reward for worthy deeds is laid up in the light beyond this world, where the just shall obtain the abode of rest.*[4] But they differ in the reasons on which they base their statement. Strabo[5] and Bede[6] teach that there is an empyrean heaven, because the firmament, which they take to mean the sidereal heaven, is said to have been made, not in the beginning, but on the second day; whereas the reason given by Basil is that otherwise God would seem to have made darkness His first work,[7] as the Manicheans falsely assert, when they call the God of the Old Testament the God of darkness.

These arguments, however, are not very cogent. For the question of the firmament, said to have been made on the second day, is solved in one way by Augustine,[8] and in another by other holy writers.[9] But the question of the darkness is explained, according to Augustine, by supposing that informity, signified by darkness, preceded form not by duration, but by origin.[10] According to others, however, since darkness is not a creature, but a privation of light, it is a proof of divine wisdom,

---

1. 参见 Cf. *Glossa ordin.*, super *Gen.*, I, 1 (I, 23F).
2. 同上
3. 参见 *Hexaëm.*, I, super *Gen.* I, 6 (PL 91, 18).
4. 参见 *In Hexaëm.*, hom. II (PG 29, 41).
5. 参见 Cf. *Glossa ordin.*, super *Gen.*, I, 6 (I, 24G).
6. 参见 *Hexaëm.*, I, super *Gen.*, I, 2 (PL 91, 14).
7. 参见 *In Hexaëm.*, hom. II (PG 29, 37).
8. 参见 *De Genesi ad Litt.*, I, 9 (PL 34, 252).
9. 参见 St. Bede, *Hexaëm.*, I, super *Gen.*, I, 2; 6 (PL 91, 13; 18).
10. 参见 *Contra Adv. Legis et Proph.*, I, 8; 9 (PL 42, 609; 610).

that the things it created from nothing it produced first in an imperfect state, and afterwards brought them to perfection.[1]

But a better reason can be drawn from the state of glory itself. For in the reward to come a twofold glory is looked for, a spiritual one and a corporeal one consisting not only in the glorification of human bodies, but also in the renovation of the whole world. Now the spiritual glory began with the beginning of the world, in the blessedness of the angels, equality with whom is promised to the saints. It was fitting, then, that even from the beginning there should be made some inauguration of bodily glory in something corporeal, free at the very outset from the servitude of corruption and change, and wholly luminous, even as the whole bodily creation, after the Resurrection, is expected to be. So, then, that heaven is called the empyrean, *i.e.*, fiery, not from its heat, but from its brightness.[2]

It is to be noticed, however, that according to Augustine Porphyry *sets the demons apart from the angels by supposing that the former inhabit the air, the latter the ether, or empyrean.*[3] But Porphyry, as a Platonist, held the heaven, known as sidereal, to be fiery, and therefore called it empyrean or ethereal, taking ethereal to denote the burning of flame,[4] and not as Aristotle understands it, swiftness of movement.[5] This much has been said to prevent anyone from supposing that Augustine maintained an empyrean heaven in the sense understood by modern writers.[6]

Reply Obj. 1. Sensible bodies are movable in the present state of the world, for by the movement of corporeal creatures the multiplication of the elect is advanced. But when glory is finally consummated, the movement of bodies will cease. And such must have been from the

1. 参见 St. Bede, *Hexaëm.*, I, super *Gen.*, I. 2 (PL 91, 15).
2. 参见 Cf. *Glossa ordin.*, super *Gen.*, I, 1 (I, 23F).
3. 参见 *De Civit. Dei*, X, 9 (PL 41, 287).
4. 参见 Cf. below, q. 68, a. 1.
5. 参见 *De Caelo*, I, 3 (270b 20); *Meteor.*, I, 3 (339b 21).
6. 参见 Cf. below, q. 68, a. 4.

beginning the condition of the empyrean.

Reply Obj. 2. It is not improbable, as some assert,[1] that the empyrean heaven, having the state of glory for its ordained end, does not influence inferior bodies of another order—those, namely, that are directed only to natural ends. Yet it seems more probable to say that it does influence bodies that are moved, even though it remains motionless, just as angels of the highest rank, who are turned to God alone, influence those of lower degree who act as messengers, though they themselves are not sent, as Dionysius teaches.[2] For this reason it may be said that the influence of the empyrean upon that which is called the first heaven, and is moved, produces therein not something that comes and goes as a result of movement, but something of a fixed and stable, nature, *e.g.*, the power of conserving and causing, or some other eminent thing of this sort.

Reply Obj. 3. Corporeal place is assigned to contemplation, not as necessary, but as congruous, so that the external splendor may correspond to that which is within. Hence Basil says: *The ministering spirit could not live in darkness, but made his habitual dwelling in light and joy.*[3]

Reply Obj. 4. As Basil says: *It is certain that the heavens were created spherical in shape, of dense body, and sufficiently strong to separate what is outside it from what it encloses. On this account they darken the region external to them, for the light by which they themselves are lit up is shut out from that region.*[4] But since the body of the firmament, though solid, is transparent, because it does not exclude light (as is clear from the fact that we can see the stars through the intervening heavens), we may also say that the empyrean has light, not condensed so as to emit

---

1. 参见 St. Albert, *In II Sent.*, d. 2, a. 5 (XXVII, 54).
2. 参见 *De Cael. Hier.*, XIII, 3 (PG 3, 301).
3. 参见 *In Hexaëm.*, hom. II (PG 29, 41).
4. 同上

rays, as the sun does, but of a more subtle nature. Or it may have the brightness of glory which differs from mere natural brightness.

Fourth Article
WHETHER TIME WAS CREATED SIMULTANEOUSLY WITH FORMLESS MATTER?

We proceed thus to the Fourth Article:—

Objection 1. It would seem that time was not created simultaneously with formless matter. For Augustine says: *I find two things that Thou didst create before time was*, namely, the primary corporeal matter, and the angelic nature.[1] Therefore time was not created with formless matter.

Obj. 2. Further, time is divided by day and night. But in the beginning there was neither day nor night, for these began when *God divided the light from the darkness.* Therefore in the beginning time was not.

Obj. 3. Further, time is the measure of the firmament's[2] movement; and the firmament is said to have been made on the second day. Therefore in the beginning time was not.

Obj. 4. Further, movement precedes time, and therefore should be reckoned among the first things created, rather than time.

Obj. 5. Further, as time is the extrinsic measure of created things, so is place. Place, then, as truly as time, must be reckoned among the things first created.

On the contrary, Augustine says: *Both spiritual and corporeal creatures were created at the beginning of time.*[3]

I answer that, It is commonly said that the first things created

---

1. 参见 *Confess.*, XII, 12 (PL 32, 831).
2. firmament: 穹苍，苍天
3. 参见 *De Genesi ad Litt.*, I, 1 (PL 34, 247).

were these four—the angelic nature, the empyrean heaven, formless corporeal matter, and time.[1] It must be observed, however, that this is not the opinion of Augustine. For he specifies only two things as first created—the angelic nature and corporeal matter—making no mention of the empyrean heaven.[2] But these two, namely, the angelic nature and formless matter, precede formation, by nature only, and not by duration; and therefore, as they precede formation, so do they precede movement and time. Time, therefore, cannot be included among them. But the enumeration above given is that of other holy writers, who hold that the informity of matter preceded its form in duration; in which case it is necessary to posit the existence of time as the measure of that duration, for otherwise there would be no such measure.

Reply Obj. 1. The teaching of Augustine rests on the opinion that the angelic nature and formless matter precede time by origin or nature.

Reply Obj. 2. Just as in the opinion of some holy writers matter was in some measure formless before it received its form, so time was in a manner formless before it was formed and distinguished into day and night.

Reply Obj. 3. If the movement of the firmament did not begin immediately from the beginning, then the time that preceded was the measure, not of the firmament's movement, but of the first movement of whatsoever kind. For it is accidental to time to be the measure of the firmament's movement, in so far as this is the first movement. But if the first movement were another than this, time would have been its measure, for everything is measured by the first of its kind. And it must be granted that forthwith from the beginning there was movement of some kind, at least in the succession of conceptions and affections in the angelic mind. Now movement without time cannot be

1. 参见 St. Albert, *Summa de Creatur.*, I (XXXIX, 307).
2. 参见 *Confess.*, XII, 12 (PL 32, 831).

conceived, since time is nothing else than the measure of priority and succession in movement.

Reply Obj. 4. Among the first created things are to be reckoned those which have a general relationship to things. And, therefore, among these time must be included, as having the nature of a common measure; but not movement, which is related only to the movable subject.

Reply Obj. 5. Place is said to be in the empyrean heaven considered as the boundary of the universe. And since place has reference to things permanent, it was created at once in its totality. But since time is not permanent, it was created only in its beginning; just as even at the present moment we cannot lay hold of any part of time save the *now*.

Question LXVII
THE WORK OF DISTINCTION IN ITSELF
(*In Four Articles*)

WE must consider next the work of distinction in itself. First, the work of the first day; secondly, the work of the second day;[1] thirdly, the work of the third day.[2]

Under the first head there are four points of inquiry: (1) Whether *light* is used in its proper sense in speaking of spiritual things? (2) Whether corporeal light is a body? (3) Whether light is a quality? (4) Whether light was fittingly made on the first day?

First Article
WHETHER *LIGHT* IS USED IN ITS PROPER SENSE IN SPEAKING OF SPIRITUAL THINGS?

We proceed thus to the First Article:—

Objection 1. It would seem that light is used in its proper sense in spiritual things. For Augustine says that *in spiritual things light is better and surer, and that Christ is not called Light in the same sense as He is called the Stone; the former is to be taken properly, and the latter metaphorically.*[3]

Obj. 2. Further, Dionysius includes *Light* among the intelligible names of God.[4] But such names are used in their proper sense in spiritual

---

1. 参见 Q. 68.
2. 参见 Q. 69.
3. 参见 *De Genesi ad Litt.*, IV, 28 (PL 34, 315).
4. 参见 *De Div. Nom.*, IV, 5 (PG 3, 700).

things. Therefore light is used in its proper sense in spiritual matters.

Obj. 3. Further, the Apostle says (*Ephes.* v. 13): *All that is made manifest is light.* But to be made manifest belongs more properly to spiritual things than to corporeal. Therefore so does light.

On the contrary, Ambrose says that *Splendor* is among the names which are said of God metaphorically.[1]

I answer that, Any name may be considered in two ways—that is to say, either in its primary imposition, or according to usage. This is clearly shown in the word *sight*, which was originally applied to the act of the sense of sight, and then, as this sense is the noblest and most trustworthy of the senses, was extended in common speech to all knowledge obtained through the other senses. Thus we say, *See how it tastes*, or *smells*, or *burns*. Further, sight is applied to knowledge obtained through the intellect, as in those words: *Blessed are the clean of heart, for they shall see God* (*Matt.* v. 8). And thus it is with the word light. In its primary meaning, it was intended to signify that which produces clarity in the sense of sight; afterwards it was extended to that which produces clarity in any sort of knowledge. If, then, the word *light* is taken in its primary meaning, it is to be understood metaphorically when applied to spiritual things, as Ambrose says.[2] But if it is taken in its common usage, as applied to clarity of every kind, it may properly be applied to spiritual things.

The answer to the objections will sufficiently appear from what has been said.

Second Article
WHETHER LIGHT IS A BODY?

We proceed thus to the Second Article:—

---

1. 参见 *De Fide*, II, Prol. (PL 16, 584).
2. 同上

Objection 1. It would seem that light is a body. For Augustine says that *light takes the first place among bodies.*[1] Therefore light is a body.

Obj. 2. Further, the Philosopher says that *light is a species of fire.*[2] But fire is a body, and therefore so is light.

Obj. 3. Further, the powers of movement, intersection and reflection belong properly to bodies. But all these are attributes of light and its rays. Moreover, different rays of light, as Dionysius says,[3] are united and separated, which seems impossible unless they are bodies. Therefore light is a body.

On the contrary, Two bodies cannot occupy the same place simultaneously. But this is the case with light and air. Therefore light is not a body.

I answer that, Light cannot be a body, for three reasons. First, on the part of place. For the place of any one body is different from that of any other, nor is it possible, naturally speaking, for any two bodies, of whatever nature, to exist simultaneously in the same place, since contiguity requires distinction of place.

The second reason is from the nature of movement. For if light were a body, its diffusion would be the local movement of a body. Now no local movement of a body can be instantaneous, since everything that moves from one place to another must pass through the intervening space before reaching the end. But the diffusion of light is instantaneous. Nor can it be argued that the time required is too short to be perceived; for though this may be the case in short distances, it cannot be so in distances so great as that which separates the East from the West. Yet as soon as the sun is at the horizon, the whole hemisphere is illuminated from end to end. It must also be borne in

---

1. 参见 *De Lib. Arb.*, III, 5 (PL 32, 1279).
2. 参见 *Top.*, V, 5 (134b 29).
3. 参见 *De Div. Nom.*, II, 4 (PG 3, 641).

mind, on the part of movement, that whereas all bodies have their natural determinate movement, the movement of light is indifferent as regards direction, proceeding equally in a circle as in a straight line. Hence it appears that the diffusion of light is not the local movement of a body.

The third reason is from generation and corruption. For if light were a body, it would follow that whenever the air is darkened by the absence of a luminary, the body of light would be corrupted, and its matter would receive a new form. But unless we are to say that darkness also is a body, this does not appear to be the case. Neither does it appear from what matter a body can be daily generated large enough to fill the intervening hemisphere. Also it would be absurd to say that a body of so great bulk is corrupted by the mere absence of a luminary. And should anyone reply that it is not corrupted, but approaches and moves round with the sun, we may ask why it is that when a lighted candle is obscured by the intervening object the whole room is darkened? It is not that the light is condensed round the candle when this is done, since it burns no more brightly then than it burned before.

Since, therefore, these things are repugnant, not only to reason, but to the sense as well, we must conclude that light cannot be a body.

Reply Obj. 1. Augustine takes light to be a luminous body in act—in other words, to be fire, the noblest of the four elements.

Reply Obj. 2. By *light*, Aristotle refers to fire existing in its own proper matter; just as fire in aerial matter is called *flame*, and in earthly matter *coal*. Nor must too much attention be paid to the instances adduced by Aristotle in his works on logic, as he merely mentions them as probable opinions according to the judgment of others.

Reply Obj. 3. All these properties are assigned to light metaphorically, and might in the same way be attributed to heat. For since movement from place to place is naturally the first movement, as is proved in *Physics* viii.,[1] we use terms belonging to local movement in speaking of alteration and movement of all kinds. For even the word *distance* is extended from the idea of remoteness of place to that of all contraries, as is said *Metaph.* x.[2]

Third Article
WHETHER LIGHT IS A QUALITY?

We proceed thus to the Third Article:—

Objection 1. It would seem that light is not a quality. For every quality remains in its subject even after the active cause of the quality be removed, just as heat remains in water removed from the fire. But light does not remain in the air when the source of light is withdrawn. Therefore light is not a quality.

Obj. 2. Further, every sensible quality has its opposite, as cold is opposed to hot, and black to white. But this is not the case with light, since darkness is merely a privation of light. Light therefore is not a sensible quality.

Obj. 3. Further, a cause is more potent than its effect. But the light of the heavenly bodies is a cause of substantial forms among these sublunary bodies.[3] It also gives to colors their spiritual being, by making them actually visible. Light, then, is not a sensible quality, but rather a substantial or spiritual form.

On the contrary, Damascene says that light is a species of quality.[4]

I answer that, Some writers[5] have said that the light in the air has not a natural being such as the color on a wall has, but only an intentional

---

1. 参见 Aristotle, *Phys.*, VIII, 7 (260a 28).
2. 参见 Aristotle, *Metaph.*, IX, 4 (1055a 9).
3. 参见 Avicenna, *Metaph.*, IX, 2 (102rb).
4. 参见 *De Fide Orth.*, I, 8 (PG 94, 816).
5. 参见 St. Bonaventure, *In II Sent.*, d. 13, a. 3, q. 2 (II, 328).—Cf. Averroes, *In De An.*, II, comm. 70 (VI, 140v).

being, as the likeness of color in the air. But this cannot be the case for two reasons. First, because light gives a name to the air, since by it the air becomes actually luminous. But color does not do this, for we do not speak of the air as colored. Secondly, because light produces natural effects, for by the rays of the sun bodies are warmed, and natural changes cannot be brought about by intentions.

Others[1] have said that light is the substantial form of the sun; but this also seems impossible for two reasons. First, because substantial forms are not of themselves objects of the senses, for the essence is the object of the intellect, as it is said in the *De Anima* iii.;[2] whereas light is visible of itself. In the second place, because it is impossible that what is the substantial form of one thing should be the accidental form of another; since substantial forms of their very nature constitute species, and therefore always and everywhere accompany the species. But light is not the substantial form of air, for if it were, the air would be destroyed when light is withdrawn. Hence it cannot be the substantial form of the sun.

We must say, then, that as heat is an active quality consequent on the substantial form of fire, so light is an active quality consequent on the substantial form of the sun, or of any other body that is of itself luminous, if there is any such body. An indication of this is that the rays of different stars produce different effects according to the diverse natures of bodies.

Reply Obj. 1. Since quality is consequent upon substantial form, the mode in which the subject receives a quality differs as the mode differs in which a subject receives a substantial form. For when matter receives its form perfectly, the qualities consequent upon the form are firm and enduring; as when, for instance, water is converted into fire.

---

1. 参见 St. Bonaventure, *In II Sent.*, d. 13, a. 2, q. 2. (II, 320).—On this and the preceding opinion, cf. St. Thomas, *In De An.*, II, lect. 14.
2. 参见 Aristotle, *De An.*, III, 6 (430b 28).

When, however, the substantial form is received imperfectly, so as to be, as it were, in process of being received, rather than fully impressed, the consequent quality lasts for a time but is not permanent; as may be seen when water which has been heated returns in time to its natural state. But light is not produced by the transmutation[1] of matter, as though matter were in receipt of a substantial form, and light were a certain inception of substantial form. For this reason light disappears on the disappearance of its active cause.

Reply Obj. 2. It is accidental to light not to have a contrary, inasmuch as it is the natural quality of the first corporeal cause of change, which is itself removed from contrariety.

Reply Obj. 3. Just as heat acts towards inducing the form of fire, as an instrumental cause in the power of the substantial form, so light acts instrumentally in the power of the heavenly bodies, towards producing substantial forms; and also towards rendering colors actually visible, inasmuch as it is a quality of the first sensible body.

Fourth Article

WHETHER THE PRODUCTION OF LIGHT IS FITTINGLY ASSIGNED TO THE FIRST DAY?

We proceed thus to the Fourth Article:—

Objection 1. It would seem that the production of light is not fittingly assigned to the first day. For light, as was stated above, is a quality. But qualities are accidents, and as such should have, not the first, but a subordinate place. The production of light, then, ought not to be assigned to the first day.

Obj. 2. Further, it is light that distinguishes night from day, and this is effected by the sun, which is recorded as having been made on the

---

1. transmutation: 变化；变形；演变

fourth day. Therefore the production of light could not have been on the first day.

Obj. 3. Further, night and day are brought about by the circular movement of a luminous body. But movement of this kind belongs to the firmament, and we read that the firmament was made on the second day. Therefore the production of light, dividing night from day, ought not to be assigned to the first day.

Obj. 4. Further, if it be said that spiritual light is here spoken of, it may be replied that the light made on the first day dispels the darkness. But in the beginning spiritual darkness did not exist, for even the demons were in the beginning good, as has been shown.[1] Therefore the production of light ought not to be assigned to the first day.

On the contrary, That without which there could not be day must have been made on the first day. But there can be no day without light. Therefore light must have been made on the first day.

I answer that, There are two opinions as to the production of light. Augustine seems to say that Moses could not have fittingly passed over the production of the spiritual creature, and therefore when we read, *In the beginning God created heaven and earth*, a spiritual nature as yet formless is to be understood by the word *heaven*, and the formless matter of the corporeal creature by the word *earth*.[2] And spiritual nature was formed first, as being of higher dignity than corporeal. The forming, therefore, of this spiritual nature is signified by the production of light. That is to say, the light in question is a spiritual light. For a spiritual nature receives its formation by the illumination whereby it is led to adhere to the Word of God.

Other writers think that the production of spiritual creatures was purposely omitted by Moses, and give various reasons. Basil says that

---

1. 参见 Q. 63, a. 5.
2. 参见 *De Genesi ad Litt.*, I, 1; 3; 4; 9 (PL 34, 247; 248; 249; 252).

Moses begins his narrative from the beginning of the time which belongs to sensible things; but that the spiritual or angelic creation is passed over, as having been created beforehand.[1]

Chrysostom gives as a reason for the omission that Moses was addressing an ignorant people, to whom material things alone appealed, and whom he was endeavoring to draw away from the worship of idols.[2] It would have been to them a pretext for idolatry if he had spoken to them of natures spiritual in substance and nobler than all corporeal creatures; for they would have paid them divine worship, since they were prone to worship as gods even the sun, moon and stars, which was forbidden them (*Deut.* iv. 19).

But Scripture also mentioned several kinds of formlessness, in regard to the corporeal creature (*Gen.* i. 2). One is where we read that *the earth was void and empty*, and another where it is said that *darkness was upon the face of the deep.* Now it was necessary, for two reasons, that the informity of darkness should be removed first of all by the production of light. In the first place because light is a quality of the first body, as was stated, and thus it was fitting that the world should be first formed according to light. The second reason is because light is a common quality. For light is common to terrestrial and celestial bodies. But just as in knowledge we proceed from general principles, so do we in work of every kind. For the living thing is generated before the animal, and the animal before man, as is shown in *De Gener. Anim.*[3] It was fitting, then, as an evidence of the divine wisdom, that among the works of distinction the production of light should take first place, since light is a form of the primary body, and because it is a more common quality.

Basil, furthermore, adds a third reason: that all other things are

1. 参见 *In Hexaëm.*, hom. I (PG 29, 4).
2. 参见 *In Genesim*, hom. V (PG 53, 52).
3. 参见 Aristotle, *De Gener. Anim.*, II, 3 (736b 2).

made manifest by light.[1] And there is yet a fourth, already touched upon in the objections, namely, that day cannot be unless light exists. It had to be made, therefore, on the first day.

Reply Obj. 1. According to the opinion of those who hold that the informity of matter preceded its formation in duration,[2] matter must be held to have been created in the beginning with substantial forms, afterwards receiving those that are accidental, among which light holds the first place.

Reply Obj. 2. In the opinion of some the light here spoken of was a kind of luminous cloud, and that on the making of the sun this returned to the matter of which it had been formed.[3] But this cannot well be maintained, since in the beginning of *Genesis* Holy Scripture records the establishment of that order of nature which henceforth is to endure. We cannot, then, say that what was made at that time afterwards ceased to exist.

Others, therefore, hold that this luminous cloud continues in existence, but so closely attached to the sun as to be indistinguishable.[4] But this is as much as to say that it is superfluous, whereas none of God's works has been made in vain. On this account it is held by some that the sun's body was made out of this cloud. This, too, is impossible—to those at least who believe that the sun is different in its nature from the four elements, and by nature incorruptible. For in that case its matter cannot take on another form.

I answer, then, with Dionysius,[5] that the light was the sun's light, formless as yet, being already the solar substance, and possessing

---

1. 参见 *In Hexaëm.*, hom. II (PG 29, 44).
2. 参见 Cf. above, q. 66, a. 1.
3. 参见 Reported anonymously by Alex. of Hales, *Summa Theol.*, II, I, no. 263 (II, 323).
4. 参见 For this and the following opinion, cf. Peter Lombard, *Sent.*, II, xiii, 5 (I, 366).
5. 参见 *De Div. Nom.*, IV, 4 (PG 3, 700).

illuminative power in a general way, to which was afterwards added the special and determinative power required to produce determinate effects. Thus, then, in the production of this light a triple distinction was made between light and darkness. First, as to cause, inasmuch as in the substance of the sun we have the cause of light, and in the opaque nature of the earth the cause of darkness. Secondly, as to place, for in one hemisphere there was light, in the other darkness. Thirdly, as to time, because there was light for one part of time and darkness for another in the same hemisphere; and this is signified by the words *He called the light day, and the darkness night.*

Reply Obj. 3. Basil says that day and night were then caused by expansion and contraction of light, rather than by movement.[1] But Augustine objects to this, that there was no reason for this process of expansion and contraction, since there were neither men nor animals on the earth at that time, for whose service this was required.[2] Nor does the nature of a luminous body seem to admit of the withdrawal of light, so long as the body is actually present; though this might be effected by miracle. As to this, however, Augustine remarks that in the first founding of the order of nature we must not look for miracles, but for what is in accordance with the nature of things.[3] We hold, then, that the movement of the heavens is twofold. Of these movements, one is common to the entire heaven, and is the cause of day and night. This, as it seems, had its beginning on the first day. The other varies in proportion as it affects various bodies, and by its variations is the cause of the succession of days, months, and years. Thus it is that in the account of the first day the distinction between day and night alone is mentioned; for this distinction was brought about by the common movement of the heavens. The further distinction into successive

---

1. 参见 *In Hexaëm.*, hom. II (PG 29, 48).
2. 参见 *De Genesi ad Litt.*, I, 16 (PL 34, 258).
3. 参见 *Op. cit.*, II, 1 (PL 34, 263).

days, seasons and years recorded as begun on the fourth day, in the words *let them be for seasons, and for days, and years,* is due to particular movements.

Reply Obj. 4. As Augustine teaches, informity did not precede formation in duration;[1] and so we must understand the production of light to signify the formation of spiritual creatures, not, indeed, with the perfection of glory, in which they were not created, but with the perfection of grace, which they possessed from their creation, as was said above.[2] Thus the division of light from darkness will denote the distinction of the spiritual creature from other created things as yet without form. On the other hand, if all created things received their formation at the same time, the darkness must be held to mean the spiritual darkness of the wicked, not as existing from the beginning, for the devil was not created wicked, but such as God foresaw would exist.

---

1. 参见 *Confess.*, XII, 29 (PL 32, 843); *De Genesi ad Litt.*, I, 15 (PL 34, 257).
2. 参见 Q. 62, a. 3.

Question LXVIII
THE WORK OF THE SECOND DAY
(*In Four Articles*)

WE must next consider the work of the second day. Under this head there are four points of inquiry: (1) Whether the firmament was made on the second day? (2) Whether there are waters above the firmament? (3) Whether the firmament divides waters from waters? (4) Whether there is more than one heaven?

First Article
WHETHER THE FIRMAMENT WAS MADE ON THE SECOND DAY?

We proceed thus to the First Article:—

Objection 1. It would seem that the firmament was not made on the second day. For it is said (*Gen.* i. 8): *God called the firmament heaven.* But the heaven was made before the days, as is clear from the words, *In the beginning God created heaven and earth.* Therefore the firmament was not made on the second day.

Obj. 2. Further, the work of the six days is ordered conformably to the order of divine wisdom. Now it would ill become the divine wisdom to make afterwards that which is naturally first. But though the firmament naturally precedes the earth and the waters, these are mentioned before the formation of light, which was on the first day. Therefore the firmament was not made on the second day.

Obj. 3. Further, all that was made in the six days was formed out of matter created before the days began. But the firmament cannot have been formed out of pre-existing matter, for, if so, it would be liable to generation and corruption. Therefore the firmament was not made on the second day.

On the contrary, It is written (*Gen.* i. 6): *God said: let there be a firmament*, and further on (*verse* 8): *And the evening and morning were the second day.*

I answer that, In discussing questions of this kind two rules are to be observed, as Augustine teaches.[1] The first is, to hold the truth of Scripture without wavering. The second is that, since Holy Scripture can be explained in a multiplicity of senses, one should adhere to a particular explanation only in such measure as to be ready to abandon it, if it be proved with certainty to be false; lest Holy Scripture be exposed to the ridicule of unbelievers, and obstacles be placed to their believing.

We say, therefore, that the words which speak of the firmament as made on the second day can be understood in two senses. They may be understood, first, of the starry firmament. In that case, our explanations will vary according to the diversity of opinions on the firmament.[2] Some believed it to be composed of the elements; and this was the opinion of Empedocles, who, however, held further that the body of the firmament was not susceptible of dissolution, because its parts are, so to say, not in conflict, but in harmony.[3] Others held the firmament to be of the nature of the four elements, not, indeed, compounded of them, but being as it were a simple element. Such was the opinion of Plato, who held that it was made of fire.[4] Others, again, have held that the heaven is hot of the nature of the four elements, but is itself a fifth body, existing over and above these. This is the opinion

---

1. 参见 *De Genesi ad Litt.*, I, 18; 19; 21 (PL 34, 260; 261; 262).
2. 参见 Besides the authors cited, cf. St. Basil, *In Hexaëm.*, hom. I (PG 29, 26); St. John Damascene, *De Fide Orth.*, II, 6 (PG 94, 879).
3. 参见 Cf. Aristotle, *De Gener.*, I, 2 (315a 3).
4. 参见 *Timaeus*, p. 40a, trans. Chalcidius, XV (p. 168). Cf. St. Augustine, *De Genesi ad Litt.*, II, 3 (PL 34, 265).

of Aristotle.[1]

According to the first opinion, it may, strictly speaking, be granted that the firmament was made, even as to its substance, on the second day. For it is part of the work of creation to produce the substance of the elements, while it belongs to the work of distinction and adornment to form things out of pre-existing elements.

But the belief that the firmament was made in its substance on the second day is incompatible with the opinion of Plato, according to whom the making of the firmament implies the production of the element of fire. This production, however, belongs to the work of creation—at least, according to those who hold that informity of matter preceded in time its formation, since the first form received by matter is the elemental.

Still less compatible with the belief that the substance of the firmament was produced on the second day is the opinion of Aristotle,[2] seeing that the mention of days denotes succession of time, whereas the firmament, being naturally incorruptible, is of a matter not susceptible of change of form, and therefore could not be made out of matter existing antecedently in time.

Hence to produce the substance of the firmament belongs to the work of creation. But its formation, in some degree, belongs to the second day, according to both of these opinions; for as Dionysius says, the light of the sun was without form during the first three days, and afterwards, on the fourth day, received its form.[3]

If, however, we take these days to denote an order of nature, as Augustine holds,[4] and not succession in time, there is then nothing to prevent our saying, while holding any one of the opinions given above,

---

1. 参见 *De Caelo*, I, 2 (269b 13).
2. 参见 *Op. cit.*, I, 3 (270a 12).
3. 参见 *De Div. Nom.*, IV, 4 (PG 3, 700).
4. 参见 *De Genesi ad Litt.*, IV, 34; V, 5 (PL 34, 319; 325).

that the substantial formation of the firmament belongs to the second day.

Another possible explanation is to understand by the firmament that was made on the second day, not that in which the stars are set, but the part of the atmosphere where the clouds are collected, and which has received the name of firmament from the firmness and density of the air. *For a body is called firm* that is dense and solid, as distinguished *from a mathematical body*, as is remarked by Basil.[1] If, then, this explanation is adopted, none of these opinions will be found repugnant to reason. Augustine, in fact, recommends it thus: *I consider this view of the question worthy of all commendation, as neither contrary to faith nor difficult to be proved and believed.*[2]

Reply Obj. 1. According to Chrysostom, Moses prefaces his record by speaking of the works of God collectively, in the words, *In the beginning God created heaven and earth*, and then proceeds to explain them part by part. In somewhat the same way, one might say: *This house was constructed by that builder*, and then add: *First he laid the foundations, then built the walls, and thirdly, put on the roof.*[3] In accepting this explanation we are, therefore, not bound to hold that a different heaven is spoken of in the words, *In the beginning God created heaven and earth*, and when we read that the firmament was made on the second day.

We may also say that the heaven recorded as created in the beginning is not the same as that made on the second day; and there are several senses in which this may be understood. Augustine says that the heaven recorded as made on the first day is the formless spiritual nature, and that the heaven of the second day is the corporeal

1. 参见 *In Hexaëm.*, hom. III (PG 29, 64).
2. 参见 *De Genesi ad Litt.*, II, 4 (PL 34, 266).
3. 参见 *In Genesim*, hom. II (PG 53, 30).

heaven.[1] According to Bede[2] and Strabo,[3] the heaven made on the first day is the empyrean, and the firmament made on the second day, the starry heaven. According to Damascene, that of the first day was *spherical in form and without stars*,[4] the same, in fact, that the philosophers speak of, calling it the ninth sphere, and the primary movable body that moves with a diurnal movement;[5] while by the firmament made on the second day he understands the starry heaven. According to another theory, touched upon by Augustine,[6] the heaven made on the first day was the starry heaven itself, and the firmament made on the second day was that region of the air where the clouds are collected, which is also called heaven, but equivocally. And to show that the word is here used in an equivocal sense, it is expressly said that *God called the firmament heaven*; just as in a preceding verse it is said that *God called the light day* (since the word *day* is also used to denote a space of twenty-four hours). Other instances of a similar use occur, as pointed out by Rabbi Moses.[7]

The second and third objections are sufficiently answered by what has been already said.

Second Article
WHETHER THERE ARE WATERS ABOVE THE FIRMAMENT?

We proceed thus to the Second Article:—

Objection 1. It would seem that there are not waters above the firmament. For water is by nature heavy, and heavy things tend

---

1. 参见 *De Genesi ad Litt.*, I, 9 (PL 34, 252).
2. 参见 *Hexaëm.*, I, super *Gen.* I, 2 (PL 91, 13).
3. 参见 Cf. *Glossa ordin.*, super *Gen.* I, 1 (I, 23F).—Cf. above, q. 66, a. 3.
4. 参见 *De Fide Orth.*, II, 6 (PG 94, 880).
5. 参见 *E.g.*, Michael Scot: cf. below, a. 2, ad 3; a. 3.
6. 参见 *De Genesi ad Litt.*, II, 1; 4 (PL 34, 363; 365).
7. 参见 *Guide*, II, 30 (p. 213); cf. below, q. 69, a. 1, ad 5.

naturally downwards, not upwards. Therefore there are not waters above the firmament.

Obj. 2. Further, water is fluid by nature, and fluids cannot rest on a sphere, as experience shows. Therefore, since the firmament is a sphere, there cannot be water above it.

Obj. 3. Further, water is an element, and ordered to the generation of composite bodies, according to the relation in which imperfect things stand towards perfect. But bodies of composite nature have their place upon the earth, and not above the firmament, so that water would be useless there. But none of God's works are useless. Therefore there are not waters above the firmament.

On the contrary, It is written (*Gen.* i. 7): [*God*] *divided the waters that were under the firmament from those that were above the firmament.*

I answer with Augustine that, *These words of Scripture have more authority than the most exalted human intellect. Hence, whatever these waters are, and whatever their mode of existence, we cannot for a moment doubt that they are there.*[1] As to the nature of these waters, all are not agreed. Origen says that the waters that are above the firmament are *spiritual substances.*[2] Therefore it is written (*Ps.* cxlviii. 4): *Let the waters that are above the heavens praise the name of the Lord*; and (*Dan.* iii. 60): *Ye waters that are above the heavens, bless the Lord.* To this Basil answers that these words do not mean that these waters are rational creatures, but that *the thoughtful contemplation of them by those who understand fulfills the glory of the Creator.*[3] Hence in the same context, fire, hail, and other like creatures, are invoked in the same way, though no one would attribute reason to these.

We must hold, then, these waters to be material, but their exact nature will be differently defined according as opinions on the

---

1. 参见 *De Genesi ad Litt.*, II, 5 (PL 34, 267).
2. 参见 Cf. Epiphanius, in the trans. of St. Jerome, *Epist.* LI (PL 22, 523).
3. 参见 *In Hexaëm.*, hom. III (PG 29, 76).

firmament differ. For if by *firmament* we understand the starry heaven, and if we understand it as being of the nature of the four elements, for the same reason it may be believed that the waters above the heaven are of the same nature as the elemental waters. But if by firmament we understand the starry heaven, not, however, as being of the nature of the four elements, then the waters above the firmament will not be of the same nature as the elemental waters. Rather just as, according to Strabo, one heaven is called empyrean, that is, fiery, solely because of its splendor,[1] so this other heaven, which is above the starry heaven, will be called aqueous solely because of its transparence.[2] Again, if the firmament is held to be of a nature other than the elements, it may still be said[3] to divide the waters, if we understand by water not the element but formless matter. Augustine, in fact, says that whatever divides bodies from bodies can be said to divide waters from waters.[4]

If, however, we understand by the firmament that part of the air in which the clouds are collected, then the waters above the firmament must rather be the vapors resolved from the waters which are raised above a part of the atmosphere, and from which the rain falls. But to say, as do some writers alluded to by Augustine,[5] that waters resolved into vapor may be lifted above the starry heaven, is a mere absurdity. The solid nature of the firmament, the intervening region of fire, wherein all vapor must be consumed, the tendency in light and rarefied bodies to drift to one spot beneath the vault of the moon, as well as the fact that vapors are perceived not to rise even to the tops of the higher mountains,—all go to show the impossibility of this. Nor is it less absurd to say, in support of this opinion, that bodies may be

---

1. 参见 Cf. *Glossa ordin.*, super *Gen.*, I, 1 (I, 23F).
2. 参见 Cf. St. Albert, *In II Sent.*, d. xiv, a. 2 (XXVII, 260).
3. 参见 Cf. *op. cit.* d. xiv, a. 1 (XXVII, 258).
4. 参见 *De Genesi Contra Manich.*, I, 7 (PL 34, 179).
5. 参见 *Op. cit.*, II, 4 (PL 34, 265).

rarefied infinitely,[1] since natural bodies cannot be infinitely rarefied or divided, but up to a certain point only.

Reply Obj. 1. Some have attempted to solve this difficulty by supposing that in spite of the natural weight of water, it is kept in its place above the firmament by the divine power. Augustine, however, will not admit this solution, but says, *It is our business here to inquire how God has constituted the natures of His creatures, not how far it may have pleased Him to work on them by way of miracle.*[2] We leave this view, then, and answer that according to the last two opinions on the firmament and the waters, the solution appears from what has been said. According to the first opinion, an order of the elements must be supposed different from that given by Aristotle,[3] that is to say, that the waters surrounding the earth are of a dense consistency, and those around the firmament of a rarer consistency, in proportion to the respective density of the earth and of the heaven.

Or by the water, as stated, we may understand the matter of bodies to be signified.

Reply Obj. 2. The solution is clear from what has been said, according to the last two opinions. But according to the first opinion, Basil gives two replies.[4] He answers, first, that a body seen as concave from beneath need not necessarily be rounded, or convex, above; secondly, that the waters above the firmament are not fluid, but exist outside it in a solid state, as a mass of ice. This is the crystalline heaven[5] of some writers.[6]

Reply Obj. 3. According to the third opinion given, the waters above the firmament have been raised in the form of vapors, and

---

1. 参见 Cf. *ibid.*
2. 参见 *De Genesi ad Litt.*, II, 1 (PL 34, 263).
3. 参见 *De Caelo*, II, 4 (287a 32).
4. 参见 *In Hexaëm.*, hom. III (PG 29, 60).
5. the crystalline heaven: 水晶体的天空
6. 参见 Cf. *ibid.* (PG 29, 62).

serve to give rain to the earth. But according to the second opinion, they are above the heaven that is wholly transparent and starless. This, according to some, is the *primum mobile*, the cause of the daily revolution of the entire heaven, whereby the continuance of generation is secured.[1] In the same way, the starry heaven, by the zodiacal movement, is the cause whereby different bodies are generated or corrupted,[2] through the rising and setting of the stars,[3] and their various influences. But according to the first opinion, these waters are set there to temper the heat of the celestial bodies, as Basil supposes.[4] And Augustine says that some have considered this to be proved by *the extreme cold of Saturn owing to its nearness to the waters that are above the firmament.*[5]

Third Article

WHETHER THE FIRMAMENT DIVIDES WATERS FROM WATERS?

We proceed thus to the Third Article:—

Objection 1. It would seem that the firmament does not divide waters from waters. For bodies that are of one and the same species have naturally one and the same place. But the Philosopher says: *All water is the same in species.*[6] Water therefore cannot be distinct from water by place.

Obj. 2. Further, should it be said that the waters above the firmament differ in species from those under the firmament, it may be

---

1. 参见 Cf. St. Albert, *In II Sent.*, d. xiv, a. 2; d. xv, a. 3 (XXVII, 260; 275).—Cf. P. Duhem, *Le Système du Monde* (III, 336; 352).
2. 参见 Cf. P. Duhem, *op. cit.* (II, 149).
3. 参见 *Op. cit.* (II, 242).
4. 参见 *In Hexaëm.*, hom. III (PG 29, 69).
5. 参见 *De Genesi ad Litt.*, II, 5 (PL 34, 266).
6. 参见 *Top.*, I, 5 (103a 29).

argued, on the contrary, that things distinct in species need nothing else to distinguish them. If, then, these waters differ in species, it is not the firmament that distinguishes them.

Obj. 3. Further, it would appear that what distinguishes waters from waters must be something which is in contact with them on either side, as a wall standing in the midst of a river. But it is evident that the waters below do not reach up to the firmament. Therefore the firmament does not divide the waters from the waters.

On the contrary, It is written (*Gen.* i. 6): *Let there be a firmament made amidst the waters; and let it divide the waters from the waters.*

I answer that, The text of *Genesis*, considered superficially, might lead to the adoption of a theory similar to that held by certain philosophers of antiquity, who taught that water was a body infinite in dimension, and the primary element of all bodies.[1] Thus in the words, *Darkness was upon the face of the deep*, the word *deep* might be taken to mean the infinite mass of water, understood as the principle of all other bodies. These philosophers also taught that not all corporeal things are confined beneath the heaven perceived by our senses, but that a body of water, infinite in extent, exists above that heaven.[2] On this view the firmament of heaven might be said to divide the waters without from those within—that is to say, from all bodies under the heaven, since they took water to be the principle of them all.

As, however, this theory can be shown to be false by solid reasons, it cannot be held to be the sense of Holy Scripture. It should rather be considered that Moses was speaking to ignorant people, and that out of consideration for their weakness he put before them only such things as are apparent to sense. Now even the most uneducated can perceive by their senses that earth and water are corporeal, whereas it

---

1. 参见 The opinion of Thales according to Aristotle, *Metaph.*, I, 3 (983b 20).
2. 参见 Cf. Avicenna, *Metaph.*, IX, 2 (103va); St. John Damascene, *De Fide Orth.*, II, 6 (PG 94, 879).

is not evident to all that air also is corporeal, for there have even been philosophers who said that air is nothing, and called a space filled with air a vacuum.[1]

Moses, then, while he expressly mentions water and earth, makes no express mention of air by name, to avoid setting before ignorant persons something beyond their knowledge. In order, however, to express the truth to those capable of understanding it, he implies in the words, *Darkness was upon the face of the deep*, the existence of air as attendant, so to say, upon the water. For it may be understood from these words that over the face of the water a transparent body was extended, the subject of light and darkness, which, in fact, is the air.

Whether, then, we understand by the firmament the starry heaven, or the cloudy region of the air, it is true to say that it divides the waters from the waters, according as we take water to denote formless matter, or any kind of transparent body as fittingly designated under the name of waters. For the starry heaven divides the lower transparent bodies from the higher, and the cloudy region divides the higher part of the air, where the rain and similar things are generated, from the lower part, which is connected with the water and included under that name.

Reply Obj. 1. If by the firmament is understood the starry heaven, the waters above are not of the same species as those beneath. But if by the firmament is understood the cloudy region of the air, both these waters are of the same species, and two places are assigned to them, though not for the same purpose, the higher being the place of their begetting, the lower, the place of their repose.

Reply Obj. 2. If the waters are held to differ in species, the firmament cannot be said to divide the waters, as the cause of their distinction,

---

1. 参见 Cf. Aristotle, *Phys.*, IV, 6 (213a 27).

but only as the boundary of each.

Reply Obj. 3. Because the air and other similar bodies are invisible, Moses includes all such bodies under the name of water, and thus it is evident that waters are found on each side of the firmament, whatever be the sense in which the word is used.

Fourth Article

WHETHER THERE IS ONLY ONE HEAVEN?

We proceed thus to the Fourth Article:—

Objection 1. It would seem that there is only one heaven. For the heaven is contrasted with the earth, in the words, *In the beginning God created heaven and earth*. But there is only one earth. Therefore there is only one heaven.

Obj. 2. Further, that which consists of the entire sum of its own matter, must be one; and such is the heaven, as the Philosopher proves.[1] Therefore there is but one heaven.

Obj. 3. Further, whatever is predicated of many things univocally is predicated of them according to one common notion. But if there are more heavens than one, they are so called univocally, for if equivocally only, they could not properly be called many. If, then, they are many, there must be some common notion by reason of which each is called heaven. But this common notion cannot be assigned. Therefore there cannot be more than one heaven.

On the contrary, It is said (*Ps.* cxlviii. 4): *Praise Him ye heavens of heavens.*

I answer that, On this point there seems to be a diversity of opinion between Basil and Chrysostom. The latter says that there is only one heaven and that the words *heavens of heavens* are merely the translation of the Hebrew idiom according to which the word is always used in the

---

1. 参见 *De Caelo*, I, 9 (279a 7).

plural, just as in Latin there are many nouns that are wanting in the singular.[1] On the other hand, Basil, whom Damascene follows,[2] says that there are many heavens.[3] The difference, however, is more verbal than real. For Chrysostom means by the one heaven the whole body that is above the earth and the water, for which reason the birds that fly in the air are called *birds of heaven* (*Ps.* viii. 9). But since in this body there are many distinct parts, Basil said that there are more heavens than one.

In order, then, to understand the distinction of heavens, it must be borne in mind that Scripture speaks of heaven in a threefold sense. Sometimes it uses the word in its proper and natural meaning, when it denotes that body on high which is luminous actually or potentially, and incorruptible by nature. In this body there are three heavens: the first is the empyrean, which is wholly luminous;[4] the second is the aqueous or crystalline, wholly transparent; and the third is called the starry heaven, in part transparent, and in part actually luminous, and divided into eight spheres. One of these is the sphere of the fixed stars, the other seven are the spheres of the planets. These may be called the eight heavens.

In the second place, the name heaven is applied to a body that participates in any property of the heavenly body, as sublimity and luminosity, actual or potential. Thus Damascene holds as one heaven all the space between the waters and the moon's orb, calling it the aerial. According to him, then, there are three heavens, the aerial, the starry, and one higher than both these, of which the Apostle is understood to speak when he says of himself that he was *rapt to the third*

1. 参见 *In Genesim*, hom. IV (PG 53, 41).
2. 参见 *De Fide Orth.*, II, 6 (PG 94, 880; 884).
3. 参见 *In Hexaëm.*, hom. III (PG 29, 56).
4. 参见 This name and those following can be found in *Glossa ordin.*, super *Gen.*, I, 1 (I 23F).

heaven (*2 Cor.* xii. 2).

But since this space contains two elements, namely, fire and air, and in each of these there is what is called a higher and a lower region, Rabanus subdivides this space into four distinct heavens.[1] The higher region of fire he calls the fiery heaven, the lower, the Olympian heaven from a lofty mountain of that name; the higher region of air he calls, from its fiery brightness, the ethereal heaven, the lower, the aerial heaven. When, therefore, these four heavens are added to the three enumerated above, there are seven corporeal heavens in all, in the opinion of Rabanus.

Thirdly, there are metaphorical uses of the word heaven, as when this name is applied to the Blessed Trinity, Who is the Light and the Most High Spirit. It is explained by some, as thus applied, in the words, *I will ascend into heaven* (*Isa.* xiv. 13), whereby the devil is represented as seeking to make himself equal with God. Sometimes also spiritual blessings, the recompense of the Saints, are signified by the word heaven and, in fact, they are so signified, according to Augustine,[2] in the words, *Your reward is very great in heaven* (*Matt.* v. 12).

Again, three kinds of supernatural visions, bodily, imaginative, and intellectual, are sometimes called heavens, in reference to which Augustine expounds Paul's rapture *to the third heaven.*[3]

Reply Obj. 1. The earth stands in relation to the heavens as the center of a circle to its circumference. But as one center may have many circumferences, so, though there is but one earth, there may be many heavens.

Reply Obj. 2. The argument holds good as to the heavens in so far as it denotes the entire sum of corporeal creation, for in that sense there

1. 参见 Cf. St. Bede, *In Pentat.*, super *Gen.*, I,1 (PL 91, 192).
2. 参见 *De Serm. Dom.*, I, 5 (PL 34, 1237).
3. 参见 *De Genesi ad Litt.*, XII, 28; 29; 34 (PL 34, 478; 479; 482).

is only one heaven.

Reply Obj. 3. All the heavens have in common sublimity and some degree of luminosity, as appears from what has been said.

Question LXIX
THE WORK OF THE THIRD DAY
(*In Two Articles*)

WE next consider the work of the third day. Under this head there are two points of inquiry: (1) The gathering together of the waters. (2) The production of plants.

First Article
WHETHER IT WAS FITTING THAT THE GATHERING TOGETHER OF THE WATERS SHOULD TAKE PLACE, AS RECORDED, ON THE THIRD DAY?

We proceed thus to the First Article:—

Objection 1. It would seem that it was not fitting that the gathering together of the waters should take place on the third day. For what was made on the first and second days is expressly said to have been *made* in the words, *God said: Be light made* (*Gen.* i. 3), and *Let there be a firmament made* (*Gen.* i. 6). But the third day is contradistinguished from the first and second days. Therefore the work of the third day should have been described as a making, not as a gathering together.

Obj. 2. Further, the earth hitherto had been completely covered by the waters, and that is why it was described as *invisible*. There was then no place on the earth in which the waters could be gathered together.

Obj. 3. Further, things which are not in continuous contact cannot occupy one place. But not all the waters are in continuous contact, and therefore all were not gathered together into one place.

Obj. 4. Further, a gathering together is a mode of local movement.

But the waters flow naturally, and take their course towards the sea. In their case, therefore, a divine precept of this kind was unnecessary.

Obj. 5. Further, the earth is given its name at its first creation by the words, *In the beginning God created heaven and earth* (*Gen.* i. 1). Therefore the imposition of its name on the third day seems to be recorded without necessity.

On the contrary, The authority of Scripture suffices (*Gen.* i. 9).

I answer that, It is necessary to reply differently to this question according to the different interpretations given by Augustine and other holy writers.[1] For according to Augustine, in all his commentaries on *Genesis*, there is no order of duration, but only of origin and nature. He says[2] that the spiritual and corporeal natures were first created formless (the latter are first indicated by the words *earth* and *water*[3]) in the sense that this formlessness preceded formation, not in time, but only in origin.[4] Nor did one formation precede another in duration, but merely in the order of nature.[5] Agreeably, then, to this order, the formation of the highest or spiritual nature is recorded in the first place, where it is said that light was made on the first day. For as the spiritual nature is higher than the corporeal, so the higher bodies are nobler than the lower. Hence the formation of the higher bodies is indicated in the second place, by the words, *Let there be made a firmament*; by which is to be understood the impression of celestial forms on formless matter, that preceded with priority, not of time, but of origin only. In the third place, the impression of elemental forms on formless matter is recorded, also with a priority of origin only. Therefore the words, *Let the waters be gathered together, and the dry land*

---

1. 参见 Cf. above, q. 66, a. 1.
2. 参见 *De Genesi ad Litt.*, I, 1; 3; 4; 9; V, 5 (PL 34, 247; 248; 249; 252; 325).
3. 参见 *Op. cit.*, I, 15 (PL 34, 257).
4. 同上
5. 参见 *Op. cit.*, IV, 34; V, 5 (PL 34, 319; 325).

appear (*Gen.* i. 9), mean that corporeal matter was impressed with the substantial form of water, so as to have such movement, and with the substantial form of earth, so as to have such an appearance.[1]

According, however, to other holy writers an order of duration in the works is to be understood, by which is meant that the formlessness of matter precedes its formation, and one form another, in the order of time.[2] Nevertheless, they do not hold that the formlessness of matter implies the total absence of form, for heaven, earth and water already existed, since these three are named as already clearly perceptible to the senses; rather they understand by formlessness the want of due distinction and of perfect beauty, and in respect of these three Scripture mentions three kinds of formlessness. Heaven, the highest of them, was without form so long as *darkness* filled it, because it was the source of light. The formlessness of water, which holds the middle place, is called the *deep*, because, as Augustine says, this word signifies the mass of waters without order.[3] Thirdly, the formless state of the earth is touched upon when the earth is said to be *void* or *invisible*, because it was covered by the waters.

Thus, then, the formation of the highest body took place on the first day. And since time results from the movement of the heavens, and is the numerical measure of the movement of the highest body, from this formation resulted the distinction of time, namely, that of night and day. On the second day the intermediate body, water, was formed, receiving from the firmament a sort of distinction and order (so that *water* is to be understood as including other things, as explained above[4]). On the third day the earth, the lowest body, received its form by the withdrawal of the waters, and there resulted the distinction in

---

1. 参见 *Op. cit.*, II, 11 (PL 34, 272).
2. 参见 Cf. above, q. 66, a. 1.
3. 参见 *Contra Faust.*, XXII, 11 (PL 42,405).
4. 参见 Q. 68, a. 3.

the lowest body, namely, of land and sea. Hence Scripture, having expressed the formless state of the earth appropriately by saying that it was *invisible* or *void*, expresses the manner in which it received its form by the equally suitable words, *Let the dry land appear.*

Reply Obj. 1. According to Augustine, Scripture does not say of the work of the third day, that it was made, as it says of those that precede, in order to show that higher and spiritual forms, such as the angels and the heavenly bodies, are perfect and stable in being, whereas inferior forms are imperfect and mutable.[1] Hence the impression of such forms is signified by the gathering of the waters, and the appearing of the land. For *water*, to use Augustine's words, *glides and flows away, the earth abides.*[2] Others, again, hold that the work of the third day was perfected on that day only as regards movement from place to place, and that for this reason Scripture could not speak of it as made.[3]

Reply Obj. 2. This argument is easily solved, according to Augustine's opinion, because we need not suppose that the earth was first covered by the waters, and that these were afterwards gathered together, but that they were produced in this very gathering together.[4] But according to the other writers, there are three solutions, which Augustine gives.[5] The first supposes that the waters were heaped up to a greater height at the place where they were gathered together, for it has been proved in regard to the Red Sea that the sea is higher than the land, as Basil remarks.[6] The second explains the water that

1. 参见 *De Genesi ad Litt.*, II, 11 (PL 34, 273).
2. 同上
3. 参见 Cf. Peter Lombard, *Sent.*, II, xiv, 8 (I, 372); St. Bede, *Hexaëm.*, I, super *Gen.*, I, 8 (PL 91, 20).
4. 参见 *De Genesi contra Manich.*, I, 12 (PL 34, 181); *De Genesi ad Litt.*, II, 11 (PL 34, 272).
5. 参见 *Op. cit.*, I, 12 (PL 34, 255).
6. 参见 *In Hexaëm.*, hom. IV (PG 29, 84).

covered the earth as being rarefied or nebulous, which was afterwards condensed when the waters were gathered together. The third suggests the existence of hollows in the earth, to receive the confluence of waters. Of the above the first seems the most probable.

Reply Obj. 3. All the waters have the sea as their goal, into which they flow by channels hidden or apparent; and this may be the reason why they are said to be gathered together into one place. Or, *one place* is to be understood not simply, but as contrasted with the place of the dry land, so that the sense would be, *Let the waters be gathered together in one place*, that is, apart from the dry land. That the waters occupied more places than one seems to be implied by the words that follow, *The gathering together of the waters He called seas.*

Reply Obj. 4. The divine command gives bodies their natural movement; and by these natural movements they are said to *fulfill His word.* Or we may say that it was according to the nature of water completely to cover the earth, just as the air completely surrounds both water and earth. But as a necessary means towards an end, namely, that plants and animals might be on the earth, it was necessary for the waters to be withdrawn from a portion of the earth. Some philosophers attribute this uncovering of the earth's surface to the action of the sun lifting up the vapors and thus drying the land.[1] Scripture, however, attributes it to the divine power, not only in *Genesis*, but also in *Job* (xxxviii. 10), where in the person of the Lord it is said, *I set My bounds around the sea*; and in *Jer.* (v. 22), where it is written: *Will you not then fear Me, saith the Lord, who have set the sand a bound for the sea?*

Reply Obj. 5. According to Augustine, primary matter is meant by the word *earth*, where it is first mentioned; but in the present passage it is to be taken for the element itself.[2] Or it may be said with Basil that the earth is mentioned in the first passage in respect of its nature, but

---

1. 参见 Aristotle, *Meteor.*, II, 1 (353b 5).
2. 参见 *De Genesi contra Manich.*, I, 7; 12 (PL 34, 178; 182).

here in respect of its principal property, namely, dryness.[1] Therefore it is written: *He called the dry land, Earth.* It may also be said with Rabbi Moses, that the expression, *He called*, denotes throughout an equivocal use of the name imposed.[2] Thus we find it said at first that *He called the light day*, for the reason that, later on, a period of twenty-four hours is also called day, where it is said that *there was evening and morning, one day.* In like manner, it is said that *the firmament*, that is, the air, *He called heaven*, for that which was first created was also called *heaven.* And here, again, it is said that *the dry land*, that is, the part from which the waters had withdrawn, *He called, Earth*, as distinct from the sea; although the name earth is equally applied to that which is covered with waters or not. So by the expression *He called* we are to understand throughout that *the nature or property He bestowed corresponded to the name He gave.*

Second Article
WHETHER IT WAS FITTING THAT THE PRODUCTION OF PLANTS SHOULD TAKE PLACE ON THE THIRD DAY?

We proceed thus to the Second Article:—

Objection 1. It would seem that it was not fitting that the production of plants should take place on the third day. For plants have life, as animals have. But the production of animals belongs to the work, not of distinction, but of adornment. Therefore the production of plants, as also belonging to the work of adornment, ought not to be recorded as taking place on the third day, which is devoted to the work of distinction.

Obj. 2. Further, a work by which the earth is accursed should have been recorded apart from the work by which it receives its form. But

1. 参见 *In Hexaëm.*, hom. IV (PG 29, 89).
2. 参见 *Guide*, II, 30 (p. 213).

the words of *Gen.* iii. 17, *Cursed is the earth in thy work, thorns and thistles shall it bring forth to thee*, show that by the production of certain plants the earth was accursed. Therefore the production of plants in general should not have been recorded on the third day, which is concerned with the work of formation.

Obj. 3. Further, as plants are firmly fixed to the earth, so are stones and metals, which nevertheless are not mentioned in the work of formation. Plants, therefore, ought not to have been made on the third day.

On the contrary, It is said (*Gen.* i. 12): *The earth brought forth the green herb*; after which there follows, *The evening and the morning were the third day.*

I answer that, On the third day, as was said above, the formless state of the earth comes to an end. But this state is described as twofold. On the one hand, the earth was *invisible* or *void*, being covered by the waters; on the other hand, it was *shapeless* or *empty*, that is, without that comeliness which it owes to the plants that clothe it, as it were, with a garment. Thus, therefore, in either respect this formless state ends on the third day: the first, when *the waters were gathered together into one place and the dry land appeared*; the second, when the *earth brought forth the green herb.*

But concerning the production of plants, Augustine's opinion differs from that of others. For other commentators, in accordance with the surface meaning of the text, consider that the plants were produced in act in their various species on this third day;[1] whereas Augustine says that the earth is said to have then produced plants and trees *in their causes, that is, it received then the power to produce them.*[2] He supports this view by the authority of Scripture, for it is said (*Gen.* ii. 4, 5): *These*

---

1. 参见 *Glossa ordin.*, super *Gen.*, I, 11 (I, 25F); St. Bede, *Hexaëm.*, I, super *Gen.* I, 11 (PL 91, 21).
2. 参见 *De Genesi ad Litt.*, V, 4; VIII, 3 (PL 34, 325; 374).

are the generations of the heaven and the earth, when they were created, in the day that ... God made the heaven and the earth, and every plant of the field before it sprung up in the earth, and every herb of the ground before it grew. Therefore, the production of plants in their causes, within the earth, took place before they sprang up from the earth's surface. And this is confirmed by reason, as follows. In these first days, God created all things in their origin or causes, and from this work He subsequently rested. Yet afterwards, by governing His creatures, in the work of propagation, *He worketh until now.* Now the production of plants from out the earth is a work of propagation, and therefore they were not produced in act on the third day, but in their causes only. However, in accordance with other writers, it may be said that the first constitution of species belongs to the work of the six days, but the reproduction among them of like from like, to the government of the universe. And Scripture indicates this in the words, *before it sprung up in the earth,* and *before it grew,* that is, before like was produced from like; just as now happens in the order of nature through seeds. Therefore Scripture says pointedly (*Gen.* i. 11): *Let the earth bring forth the green herb, and such as may seed,* as indicating the production of perfect species, from which the seeds of others should arise. Nor does the question where the seminal power may reside, whether in root, stem, or fruit, affect the argument.

Reply Obj. 1. Life in plants is hidden, since they lack sense and local movement, by which the animate and the inanimate are chiefly discernible. And therefore, since they are immovably fixed in the earth, their production is treated as a part of the earth's formation.

Reply Obj. 2. Even before the earth was accursed, thorns and thistles had been produced, either virtually or actually. But they were not produced in punishment of man; as though the earth, which he tilled to gain his food, produced unfruitful and noxious plants. Hence it was said: "Shall it bring forth to *thee.*"

Reply Obj. 3. Moses put before the people such things only as were manifest to their senses, as we have said.[1] But minerals are generated in hidden ways within the bowels of the earth. Moreover, they seem hardly specifically distinct from earth, and would seem to be species thereof. For this reason he makes no mention of them.

---

1. 参见 Q. 68, a. 3.

Question LXX
THE WORK OF ADORNMENT, AS REGARDS THE FOURTH DAY
(*In Three Articles*)

WE must next consider the work of adornment, first as to each day by itself, secondly as to all seven days in general.[1]

In the first place, then, we consider the work of the fourth day; secondly that of the fifth day;[2] thirdly that of the sixth day;[3] and fourthly, such matters as belong to the seventh day.[4]

Under the first head there are three points of inquiry: (1) The production of the luminaries. (2) The end of their production. (3) Whether they are living beings?

First Article
WHETHER THE LUMINARIES OUGHT TO HAVE BEEN PRODUCED ON THE FOURTH DAY?

We proceed thus to the First Article:—

Objection 1. It would seem that the luminaries ought not to have been produced on the fourth day. For the heavenly luminaries are by nature incorruptible bodies, and so their matter cannot exist without their form. But their matter was produced in the work of creation,

---

1. 参见 Q. 74.
2. 参见 Q. 71.
3. 参见 Q. 72.
4. 参见 Q. 73.

before there was any day; so therefore were their forms. It follows, then, that the luminaries were not produced on the fourth day.

Obj. 2. Further, the luminaries are, as it were, vessels of light. But light was made on the first day. The luminaries, therefore, should have been made on the first day, not on the fourth.

Obj. 3. Further, the luminaries are fixed in the firmament, as plants are fixed in the earth. For, the Scripture says, *He set them in the firmament.* But plants are described as produced when the earth, to which they are attached, received its form. The luminaries, therefore, should have been produced at the same time as the firmament, that is to say, on the second day.

Obj. 4. Further, plants are an effect of the sun, moon, and the other luminaries. Now, cause precedes effect in the order of nature. The luminaries, therefore, ought not to have been produced on the fourth day, but on the third or before.

Obj. 5. Further, as astronomers say, there are many stars larger than the moon. Therefore the sun and the moon alone are not correctly described as the *two great lights.*

On the contrary, Suffices the authority of Scripture (*Gen.* i. 14).

I answer that, In recapitulating the divine works, Scripture says (*Gen.* fi. 1): *So the heavens and the earth were finished and all the furniture of them*, thereby indicating that the work was threefold. In the first work, that of *creation*, the heaven and the earth were produced, but as yet without form. In the second, or work of *distinction*, the heaven and the earth were perfected, either by adding substantial form to formless matter, as Augustine holds,[1] or by giving them the order and beauty due to them, as other holy writers suppose.[2] To these two works is added the work of *adornment*, which differs from perfection. For the perfection of the heaven and the earth appears to be concerned with those things

1. 参见 *De Genesi ad Litt.*, II, 11 (PL 34, 272).
2. 参见 Cf. above, q. 66, a. 1; q. 69, a. 1.

that belong to them intrinsically, but the adornment, those that are extrinsic, just as the perfection of a man lies in his proper parts and forms, and his adornment, in clothing or the like. The distinction of certain things is made most evident by their local movement, as separating one from another. Hence, to the work of adornment belongs the production of things having movement in the heavens and upon the earth. But it has been stated above that three things are recorded as created, namely, the heaven, the water, and the earth.[1] These three furthermore received their formation through the three days' work of distinction. Heaven was formed on the first day; on the second day the waters were separated; and on the third, the earth was divided into sea and dry land. So also is it in the work of adornment. On the first day of this work, which is the fourth of creation, are produced the luminaries, to adorn the heaven by their movements; on the second day, which is the fifth, birds and fishes are called into being, to make beautiful the intermediate element, for they move in air and water, which are here taken as one; while on the third day, which is the sixth, animals are brought forth, to move upon the earth and adorn it. It must also be noted here that Augustine's opinion on the production of the luminaries is not at variance with that of other holy writers.[2] For he says that they were made actually and not merely virtually, since the firmament has not the power of producing luminaries, as the earth has of producing plants.[3] Therefore Scripture does not say: *Let the firmament produce lights*, though it says: *Let the earth bring forth the green herb*.

Reply Obj. 1. In Augustine's opinion there is no difficulty here.[4] For

---

1. 参见 Q. 69, a. 1.
2. 参见 Cf. *Glossa ordin.*, super *Gen.*, I, 14 (I, 26B); St. Bede, *Hexaëm.*, I, super *Gen.*, I, 14 (PL 91, 21).
3. 参见 *De Genesi ad Litt.*, V, 5 (PL 34, 326).
4. 参见 *Op. cit.*, IV, 34; V, 5 (PL 34, 319; 325).

he does not hold a succession of time in these works, and so there was no need for the matter of the luminaries to exist under another form. Nor is there any difficulty in the opinion of those who hold the heavenly bodies to be of the nature of the four elements,[1] since it may be said that they were formed out of matter already existing, as animals and plants were formed. For those, however, who hold the heavenly bodies to be of another nature from the elements, and naturally incorruptible,[2] the answer must be that the luminaries were substantially created in the beginning, but that their substance, at first formless, is formed on this day, by receiving not its substantial form, but a determination of power. As to the fact that the luminaries are not mentioned as existing from the beginning, but only as made on the fourth day, Chrysostom explains this by the need of guarding the people from the danger of idolatry;[3] since the luminaries are proved not to be gods, by the fact that they were not from the beginning.

Reply Obj. 2. No difficulty exists if we follow Augustine in holding the light made on the first day to be spiritual, and that made on this day to be corporeal.[4] If, however, the light made on the first day is understood to be itself corporeal,[5] then it must be held to have been produced on that day merely as light in general; and that on the fourth day the luminaries received a definite power to produce determinate effects. Thus we observe that the rays of the sun have one effect, those of the moon another, and so forth. Hence, speaking of such a determination of power, Dionysius says that the sun's light, which previously was without form, was formed on the fourth day.[6]

---

1. 参见 Cf. above, q. 68, a. 1.
2. 参见 Cf. *ibid.*
3. 参见 *In Genesim*, hom. VI (PG 53, 58).
4. 参见 *De Genesi ad Litt.*, I, 12 (PL 34, 255).
5. 参见 Cf. Peter Lombard, *Sent.*, II, xiii, 2 (I, 364).—Cf. above, q. 67, a. 4, ad 2.
6. 参见 *De Div. Nom.*, IV, 4 (PG 3, 700).

Reply Obj. 3. According to Ptolemy, the luminaries are not fixed in the spheres, but have their own movement distinct from the movement of the spheres.[1] Hence Chrysostom says that God is said to have set them in the firmament, not because He fixed them there immovably, but because He bade them be there, even as He placed man in paradise, to be there.[2] In the opinion of Aristotle, however, the stars are fixed in their spheres, and in reality have no other movement but that of the spheres; and yet our senses perceive the movement of the luminaries and not that of the spheres.[3] But Moses describes what is obvious to sense, out of condescension to popular ignorance, as we have already said.[4] The objection, however, falls to the ground if we regard the firmament made on the second day as being in nature distinct from that in which the stars are placed, even though the distinction is not apparent to the senses (whose testimony Moses follows, as was stated above). For although to the senses there appears but one firmament, yet if we admit a higher and a lower firmament, the lower will be that which was made on the second day, and on the fourth the stars were fixed in the higher firmament.

Reply Obj. 4. In the words of Basil, plants were recorded as produced before the sun and moon to prevent idolatry, since those who believe the heavenly bodies to be gods hold that plants originate primarily from these bodies.[5] Although as Chrysostom remarks,[6] the sun, moon and stars co-operate in the work of production by their movements, just as the farmer co-operates by his labor.

Reply Obj. 5. As Chrysostom says, the two luminaries are called great, not so much with regard to their dimensions as to their

---

1. 参见 *Syntaxis Matkematica*, I, 7 (I, 27^{14-20}).
2. 参见 *In Genesim*, hom. VI (PG 53, 59).
3. 参见 *De Caelo*, II, 8 (289b 32).
4. 参见 Q. 68, a. 3.
5. 参见 *In Hexaëm.*, hom. V (PG 29, 96).
6. 参见 *In Genesim*, hom. VI (PG 53, 58).

influence and power.[1] For though the stars be of greater bulk than the moon, yet the influence of the moon is more perceptible to the senses in this lower world. Moreover, as far as the senses are concerned, its apparent size is greater.

Second Article
WHETHER THE CAUSE ASSIGNED FOR THE PRODUCTION OF THE LUMINARIES IS REASONABLE?

We proceed thus to the Second Article:—

Objection 1. It would seem that the cause assigned for the production of the luminaries is not reasonable. For it is said (*Jer.* x. 2): *Be not afraid of the signs of heaven, which the heathens fear.* Therefore the luminaries were not made to be signs.

Obj. 2. Further, sign is contradistinguished from cause. But the luminaries are the cause of what takes place upon the earth. Therefore they are not signs.

Obj. 3. Further, the distinction of seasons and days began from the first day. Therefore the luminaries were not made *for seasons, and days, and years*, that is, in order to distinguish them.

Obj. 4. Further, nothing is made for the sake of that which is inferior to itself, since the end is better than the means. But the luminaries are nobler than the earth. Therefore they were not made *to enlighten it.*

Obj. 5. Further, the new moon cannot be said *to rule the night.* But such it probably did when first made; for men begin to count from the new moon. The moon, therefore, was not made to *rule the night.*

On the contrary, Suffices the authority of Scripture (*Gen.* i. 14).

I answer that, As we have said above, a corporeal creature can be considered as made either for the sake of its own actuality, or for other

---

1. 参见 *In Genesim*, hom. VI (PG 53, 58).

creatures, or for the whole universe, or for the glory of God.[1] Of these reasons only that which points out the usefulness of these things to man is touched upon by Moses, in order to withdraw his people from idolatry. Hence it is written (*Deut.* iv. 19): *Lest perhaps lifting up thy eyes to heaven, thou see the sun and the moon and all the stars of heaven, and being deceived by error thou adore and serve them, which the Lord thy God created for the service of all nations.* Now, he explains this service at the beginning of *Genesis* as threefold. First, the luminaries are of service to man, in regard to sight, which directs him in his works, and is most useful for perceiving things. In reference to this he says: *Let them shine in the firmament and give life to the earth.* Secondly, as regards the changes of the seasons, which prevent weariness, preserve health, and provide for the necessities of food; all of which could not be secured if it were always summer or winter. In reference to this he says: *Let them be for seasons, and for days, and years.* Thirdly, as regards the convenience of business and work, in so far as from the luminaries in the heavens is indicated fair or rainy weather, favorable to various occupations. And in this respect he says: *Let them be for signs.*

Reply Obj. 1. The luminaries in the heavens are set for signs of changes effected in corporeal creatures, but not of those changes which depend upon free choice.

Reply Obj. 2. We are sometimes brought to the knowledge of hidden effects through their sensible causes, and conversely. Hence nothing prevents a sensible cause from being a sign. But he says *signs*, rather than *causes*, to guard against idolatry.

Reply Obj. 3. The general division of time into day and night took place on the first day, as regards the diurnal movement, which is common to the whole heavens and may be understood to have begun on that first day. But the particular distinctions of days and seasons

---

1. 参见 Q. 65, a. 2.

and years, according as one day is hotter than another, one season than another, and one year than another, are due to certain particular movements of the stars; and these movements may have had their beginning on the fourth day.

Reply Obj. 4. Light was given to the earth for the service of man, who, by reason of his soul, is nobler than the heavenly bodies. Nor is it untrue to say that a higher creature may be made for the sake of a lower, considered not in itself, but as ordained to the good of the universe.

Reply Obj. 5. When the moon is at its perfection, it rises in the evening and sets in the morning, and thus it rules the night; and it was quite probably made in its full perfection, as were plants yielding seed, as also were animals and man himself. For although the perfect is developed from the imperfect by natural processes, yet, absolutely speaking, the perfect must exist before the imperfect. Augustine, however, does not say this, for he says that it is not unfitting that God made things imperfect, which He afterwards perfected.[1]

Third Article
WHETHER THE LUMINARIES OF HEAVEN ARE LIVING BEINGS?

We proceed thus to the Third Article:—

Objection 1. It would seem that the luminaries of heaven are living beings. For the nobler a body is, the more nobly it should be adorned. But a body less noble than the heaven is adorned with living beings, with fish, birds, and the beasts of the field. Therefore the luminaries of heaven, as pertaining to its adornment, should be living beings also.

Obj. 2. Further, the nobler a body is, the nobler must be its form.

---

1. 参见 *De Genesi ad Litt.*, II, 15 (PL 34, 276).

But the sun, moon and stars are nobler bodies than plants or animals, and must therefore have nobler forms. Now the noblest of all forms is the soul, as being the first principle of life. Hence Augustine says: *Every living substance stands higher in the order of nature than one that has not life.*[1] The luminaries of heaven, therefore, are living beings.

Obj. 3. Further, a cause is nobler than its effect. But the sun, moon and stars are a cause of life, as is especially evidenced in the case of animals generated from putrefaction, which receive life through the power of the sun and stars. Much more, therefore, have the heavenly bodies a living soul.

Obj. 4. Further, the movements of the heavens and the heavenly bodies are natural.[2] Now natural movement is from an intrinsic principle. But the principle of movement in the heavenly bodies is a substance capable of apprehension, which is moved as he who desires is moved by the object desired.[3] Therefore, the apprehending principle is intrinsic to the heavenly bodies, and consequently they are living beings.

Obj. 5. Further, the first of movables is the heavens. Now, of all things that are endowed with movement the first moves itself, as is proved in *Physics* viii.,[4] because what is of itself precedes that which is by another. But only beings that are living move themselves, as is shown in the same book.[5] Therefore the heavenly bodies are living beings.

On the contrary, Damascene says, *Let no one esteem the heavens or the heavenly bodies to be living beings, for they have neither life nor sense.*[6]

I answer that, Philosophers have differed on this question.

---

1. 参见 *De Vera Relig.*, XXIX (PL 34, 145).
2. 参见 Aristotle, *De Caelo*, I, 2 (269a 30).
3. 参见 Aristotle, *Metaph.*, XI, 7 (1072a 26).
4. 参见 Aristotle, *Phys.*, VIII, 5 (256a 21).
5. 参见 *Op. cit.*, VIII, 4 (255a 6).
6. 参见 *De Fide Orth.*, II, 6 (PG 94, 885).

Anaxagoras, for instance, as Augustine mentions, *was condemned by the Athenians for teaching that the sun was a fiery mass of stone, and neither a god nor even a living being.*[1] On the other hand, the Platonists held that the heavenly bodies have life.[2] Nor was there less diversity of opinion among the Doctors of the Church. It was the belief of Origen[3] and Jerome[4] that these bodies were alive, and the latter seems to explain in that sense the words (*Eccles.* i. 6), *The spirit goeth forward, surveying all places round about.* But Basil[5] and Damascene[6] maintain that the heavenly bodies are inanimate. Augustine leaves the matter in doubt, without committing himself to either theory, though he goes so far as to say that if the heavenly bodies are really living beings, their souls must be akin to the angelic nature.[7]

In examining the truth of this question, where such diversity of opinion exists, we shall do well to bear in mind that the union of soul and body exists for the sake of the soul and not of the body; for the form does not exist for the matter, but the matter for the form. Now the nature and power of the soul are apprehended through its operation, which to a certain extent is also its end. Yet for some of these operations, as sensation and nutrition, our body is a necessary instrument. Hence it is clear that the sensitive and nutritive souls must be united to a body in order to exercise their functions. There are, however, operations of the soul which are not exercised through the medium of the body, though the body ministers, as it were, to their production. The intellect, for example, makes use of the phantasms

---

1. 参见 *De Civit. Dei*, XVIII, 41 (PL 41, 601).
2. 参见 Cf. Macrobius, *In Somn. Scipion.*, I, 14 (pp. 540–541); Avicenna, *Metaph.*, IX, 2 (102vb).
3. 参见 *Peri Archon*, I, 7 (PG 11, 173).
4. 参见 *In Eccles.*, super I, 6 (PL 23, 1068).
5. 参见 *In Hexaëm.*, hom. III (PG 29, 76).
6. 参见 *De Fide Orth.*, II, 6 (PG 94, 885).
7. 参见 *De Genesi ad Litt.*, II, 18 (PL 34, 279); *Enchir.*, LVIII (PL 40, 260).

derived from the bodily senses, and thus far is dependent on the body, although capable of existing apart from it. It is not, however, possible that the functions of nutrition, growth and generation, through which the nutritive soul operates, can be exercised by the heavenly bodies, for such operations are incompatible with a body naturally incorruptible. Equally impossible is it that the functions of the sensitive soul can pertain to a heavenly body, since all the senses depend on the sense of touch, which perceives elemental qualities, and all the organs of the senses require a certain proportion in the admixture of elements; whereas the nature of the heavenly bodies is not elemental.

It follows, then, that of the operations of the soul the only ones left to be attributed to the heavenly bodies are those of understanding and moving; for appetite follows both sensitive and intellectual perception, and is in proportion thereto. But since the operation of the intellect is not exercised through the body, it needs a body as its instrument only to supply phantasms through the senses. Moreover, the operations of the sensitive soul, as we have seen, cannot be attributed to the heavenly bodies. Accordingly, the union of a soul to a heavenly body cannot be for the purpose of the operations of the intellect. So the only reason for which a soul is joined to a heavenly body is motion. Now, in order to move the heavenly body, the soul need not be united to the latter as its form; but by contact of power, as a mover is united to that which he moves And so Aristotle, after showing that the first mover is made up of two parts, the moving and the moved, goes on to show the nature of the union between these two parts.[1] This, he says, is effected by contact which is mutual if both are bodies, but on the part of one only, if one is a body and the other not.[2] The Platonists themselves explain the union of soul and body in the same way, as a contact of

1. 参见 *Phys.*, VIII, 5 (257a 33).
2. 同上 (258a 20).

a moving power with the thing moved;[1] and since Plato holds the heavenly bodies to be living beings, this means nothing else but that spiritual substances are united to them as movers to the things moved. A proof that the heavenly bodies are moved by the direct influence and contact of some spiritual substance, and not by nature, like heavy and light bodies, lies in the fact that whereas nature moves to one fixed end, in which having attained it, it rests; this does not appear in the movement of heavenly bodies. Hence it follows that they are moved by some intellectual substances. Augustine appears to be of the same opinion when he expresses his belief that all *bodies* are ruled *through the spirit of life.*[2]

From what has been said, then, it is clear that the heavenly bodies are not living beings in the same sense as plants and animals, but only equivocally. It will also be seen that the difference of opinion between those who affirm, and those who deny, that these bodies have life, is not a difference in reality but in words.

Reply Obj. 1. Certain things belong to the adornment of the universe by reason of their proper movement; and in this way the heavenly luminaries agree with others that conduce to that adornment, for they are moved by a living substance.

Reply Obj. 2. One being may be nobler than another absolutely, but not in a particular respect. While, then, it is not conceded that the heavenly bodies are nobler forms than the souls of animals absolutely, it must be conceded that they are superior to them with regard to their role as forms, since they perfect their matter entirely, so that it is not in potentiality to other forms; whereas a soul does not do this. So, too, as regards movement, the power that moves the heavenly bodies is of a nobler kind.

Reply Obj. 3. Since the heavenly body is a moved mover, it has

1. 参见 Cf. below, q. 76, a. 1.
2. 参见 *De Trin.*, III, 4 (PL 42, 873).

the nature of an instrument, which acts in the power of the agent. Therefore, since this agent is a living substance, the heavenly body can impart life in virtue of that agent.

Reply Obj. 4. The movements of the heavenly bodies are natural, not because of their active principle, but because of their passive principle; that is to say, from a certain natural aptitude for being so moved by an intelligent power.

Reply Obj. 5. The heaven is said to move itself in as far as it is composed of mover and moved, not by the union of the mover, as the form, with the moved, as the matter, but by contact with the motive power, as we have said. So far, then, the principle that moves it may be called intrinsic, and consequently so can its movement be called natural with respect to that active principle; just as we say that voluntary movement is natural to the animal as animal.[1]

1. 参见 Aristotle, *Phys.*, VIII, 4 (254b 14).

Question LXXI
THE WORK OF THE FIFTH DAY
(*In One Article*)

WE must next consider the work of the fifth day.

Objection 1. It would seem that this work is not fittingly described. For the waters produce that which the power of water suffices to produce. But the power of water does not suffice for the production of every kind of fishes and birds, since we find that many of them are generated from seed. Therefore the words, *Let the waters bring forth the creeping creature having life, and the fowl that may fly over the earth*, do not fittingly describe this work.

Obj. 2. Further, fishes and birds are not produced from water only, but earth seems to predominate over water in their composition, as is shown by the fact that their bodies tend naturally to the earth and rest upon it. It is not, then, fittingly said that fishes and birds are produced from water.

Obj. 3. Further, fishes move in the waters, and birds in the air. If, then, fishes are produced from the waters, birds ought to be produced from the air, and not from the waters.

Obj. 4. Further, not all fishes creep through the waters, for some, as a sea-calf, have feet and walk on land. Therefore the production of fishes is not sufficiently described by the words, *Let the waters bring forth the creeping creature having life.*

Obj. 5. Further, land animals are more perfect than birds and fishes, which appears from the fact that they have more distinct members, and generation of a higher order. For they bring forth living beings, whereas birds and fishes bring forth eggs. But the more perfect has precedence in the order of nature. Therefore fishes and birds ought not to have been produced on the fifth day, before land animals.

On the contrary, Suffices the authority of Scripture (*Gen.* i. 20).

I answer that, As was said above, the order of the work of adornment corresponds to the order of the work of distinction.[1] Hence, just as among the three days assigned to the work of distinction, the middle, or second, day is devoted to the work of the distinction of water, which is the intermediate body, so in the three days of the work of adornment, the middle day, which is the fifth, is assigned to the adornment of the intermediate body by the production of birds and fishes. Hence, just as Moses makes mention of the luminaries and of light on the fourth day, to show that the fourth day corresponds to the first day on which he had said that the light was made, so on this fifth day he mentions the waters and the firmament of heaven to show that the fifth day corresponds to the second. It must, however, be observed that Augustine differs from other writers in his opinion about the production of fishes and birds, just as he differs about the production of plants. For while others say that fishes and birds were produced actually on the fifth day,[2] he holds that the nature of the waters produced them on that day potentially.[3]

Reply Obj. 1. It was laid down by Avicenna that animals of all kinds can be generated by various minglings of the elements, and, even naturally, without any kind of seed.[4] This, however, seems repugnant to the fact that nature produces its effects by determinate means; and, consequently, those things that are naturally generated from seed cannot be generated naturally in any other way. It ought, then,

---

1. 参见 Q. 70, a. 1.
2. 参见 Cf. St. Basil, *In Hexaëm.*, hom. VII (PG 29, 148); St. Ambrose, *In Hexaëm.*, V, 1 (PL 14, 219); St. Bede, *In Hexaëm.*, I, super *Gen.*, I, 20 (PL 91, 25).
3. 参见 *De Genesi ad Litt.*, V, 5 (PL 34, 326).
4. 参见 *De Anim.*, XV, 1 (59va).

rather to be said that in the natural generation of all animals that are generated from seed, the active principle lies in the formative power of the seed, but that in the case of animals generated from putrefaction, the formative power is the influence of the heavenly bodies. The material principle, however, in the generation of either kind of animals, is either some element, or something compounded of the elements. But at the first beginning of the world, the active principle was the Word of God, Who produced animals from material elements, either in act, as some holy writers say,[1] or virtually, as Augustine teaches.[2] Not as though water or earth has in itself the power of producing all animals, as Avicenna held;[3] rather, it is from the power originally placed in the elements that they are able to produce animals either from elemental matter by the power of seed or the influence of the stars.

Reply Obj. 2. The bodies of birds and fishes may be considered from two points of view. If considered in themselves, it will be evident that the earthly element must predominate, since the element that is least active, namely, the earth, must be the most abundant in quantity in order that the mingling may be duly tempered in the body of the animal. But if considered as by nature constituted to move with certain specific motions, thus they have some special affinity with the bodies in which they move. Hence the words in which their generation is here described.

Reply Obj. 3. The air, as not being so apparent to the senses, is not enumerated by itself, but with other things: partly with the water, because the lower region of the air is thickened by watery exhalations; partly with the heaven as to the higher region. But birds move in the

1. 参见 Cf. St. Basil, *In Hexaëm.*, hom. VIII (PG 29, 163); St. Ambrose, *In Hexaëm.*, VI, 2 (PL 14, 258); St. Bede, *In Hexaëm.*, I, super *Gen.*, I, 24 (PL 94, 27).
2. 参见 *De Genesi ad Litt.*, V, 5 (PL 34, 326).
3. 参见 *De Anim.*, XV, 1 (59va).

lower part of the air, and so are said to fly *beneath the firmament*, even if the firmament be taken to mean the region of clouds. Hence the production of birds is ascribed to the water.

Reply Obj. 4. Nature passes from one extreme to another through the medium. Therefore there are creatures of intermediate type between the animals of the air and those of the water, having something in common with both; and they are reckoned as belonging to that class to which they are most allied, through the characters possessed in common with that class, rather than with the other. But in order to include among fishes all such intermediate forms as have special characters like to theirs, the words, *Let the waters bring forth the creeping creature having life*, are followed by these: *God created great whales*, etc.

Reply Obj. 5. The order in which the production of these animals is given has reference to the order of those bodies which they are set to adorn, rather than to the superiority of the animals themselves. Moreover, in generation also the more perfect is reached through the less perfect.

Question LXXII
THE WORK OF THE SIXTH DAY
(*In One Article*)

WE must now consider the work of the sixth day.

Objection 1. It would seem that this work is not fittingly described. For as birds and fishes have a living soul, so also have land animals. But these animals are not themselves living souls. Therefore the words, *Let the earth bring forth the living creature*, should rather have been, *Let the earth bring forth the living fourfooted creatures.*

Obj. 2. Further, a genus ought not be divided against its species. But beasts and cattle are quadrupeds. Therefore quadrupeds ought not to be enumerated as a class with beasts and cattle.

Obj. 3. Further, just as other animals belong to a determinate genus and species, so also does man. But in the making of man nothing is said of his genus and species, and therefore nothing ought to have been said about them in the production of other animals; whereas it is said *according to its genus* and *in its species.*

Obj. 4. Further, land animals are more like man, whom God is recorded to have blessed, than are birds and fishes. But as birds and fishes are said to be blessed, this should have been said, with much more reason, of the other animals as well.

Obj. 5. Further, certain animals are generated from putrefaction, which is a kind of corruption. But corruption is repugnant to the first founding of the world. Therefore such animals should not have been produced at that time.

Obj. 6. Further, certain animals are poisonous, and injurious to man. But there ought to have been nothing injurious to man before man sinned. Therefore, either such animals ought not to have been made by God at all, since He is the Author of good, or at least not until man had sinned.

On the contrary, Suffices the authority of Scripture (*Gen.* i. 24).

I answer that, As on the fifth day, the intermediate body, namely the water, is adorned, and thus that day corresponds to the second day; so the sixth day, on which the lowest body, or the earth, is adorned by the production of land animals, corresponds to the third day. Hence the earth is mentioned in both places. And here again Augustine says that the production was potential,[1] and other holy writers that it was actual.[2]

Reply Obj. 1. The different grades of life which are found in different living creatures can be discovered from the various ways in which the Scripture speaks of them, as Basil says.[3] The life of plants, for instance, is very imperfect and difficult to discern, and hence, in speaking of their production, nothing is said of their life, but only their generation is mentioned, since only in generation is a vital act observed in them. For the powers of nutrition and growth are subordinate to the generative life, as will be shown later on.[4] But among animals, those that live on land are, generally speaking, more perfect than birds and fishes, not because the fish is devoid of memory, as Basil upholds[5] and Augustine rejects,[6] but because their members are more distinct and their generation of a higher order (although some imperfect animals, such as bees and ants, are more intelligent in certain ways). Scripture,

---

1. 参见 *De Genesi ad Litt.*, V, 5 (PL 34, 326).
2. 参见 Cf. St. Basil, *In Hexaëm.*, hom. VIII (PG 29, 163) ; St. Ambrose, *In Hexaëm.*, VI, 2 (PL 14, 258): St. Bede, *In Hexaëm.*, I, super *Gen.*, I, 24 (PL 91, 27).
3. 参见 *In Hexaëm.*, hom. VIII (PG 29, 165).
4. 参见 Q. 78, a. 2.
5. 参见 *In Hexaëm.*, hom. VIII (PG 29, 165).
6. 参见 *De Genesi ad Litt.*, III, 8 (PL 34, 283).

therefore, does not call fishes *living creatures*, but *creeping creatures having life*; whereas it does call land animals *living creatures* because of their more perfect life, and seems to imply that fishes are merely bodies having in them something of a soul, while land animals, from the higher perfection of their life, are, as it were, living souls with bodies subject to them. But the life of man, as being the most perfect grade, is not said to be produced, like the life of other animals, by the earth or water, but immediately by God.

Reply Obj. 2. By *cattle*, domestic animals are signified, which in any way are of service to man; but by *beasts*, wild animals such as bears and lions are designated. By *creeping things* those animals are meant which either have no feet and cannot rise from the earth, as serpents, or those whose feet are too short to lift them far from the ground, as the lizard and tortoise. But since certain animals, as deer and goats, seem to fall under none of these classes, the word *quadrupeds* is added. Or perhaps the word *quadruped* is used first as being the genus, to which the others are added as species, for even some reptiles, such as lizards and tortoises, are four-footed.

Reply Obj. 3. In other animals, and in plants, mention is made of genus and species, to denote the generation of like from like. But it was unnecessary to do so in the case of man, as what had already been said of other creatures might be understood of him. Again, animals and plants may be said to be produced according to their kinds, to signify their remoteness from the divine image and likeness, whereas man is said to be made *to the image and likeness of God.*

Reply Obj. 4. The blessing of God gives power to multiply by generation, and, having been mentioned in the preceding account of the making of birds and fishes, could be understood of the beasts of the earth, without requiring to be repeated. The blessing, however, is repeated in the case of man, since in him generation of children has a special relation to the fulfillment of the number of the elect, and to prevent *anyone from saying that there was any sin whatever in the act of begetting children.* As to plants, *since they experience neither desire of propagation, nor sensation in generating, they are deemed unworthy of a formal blessing.*[1]

Reply Obj. 5. Since the generation of one thing is the corruption of another, it was not incompatible with the first formation of things that from the corruption of the less perfect the more perfect should be generated. Hence animals generated from the corruption of inanimate things, or of plants, may have been generated then. But those generated from the corruption of animals could not have been produced then otherwise than potentially.

Reply Obj. 6. In the words of Augustine: *If an unskilled person enters the workshop of an artificer, he sees in it many appliances of which he does not understand the use, and which, if he is a foolish fellow, he considers unnecessary. Moreover, should he carelessly fall into the fire, or wound himself with a sharp-edged tool, he is under the impression that many of the things there are hurtful; whereas the craftsman, knowing their use, laughs at his folly. And thus some people presume to find fault with many things in this world, through not seeing the reasons for their existence. For though not required for the furnishing of our house, these things are necessary for the perfection of the universe.*[2] And since before he sinned man would have used the things of this world conformably to the order designed, poisonous animals would not have injured him.

---

1. 参见 St. Augustine, *De Genesi ad Litt.*, III, 13 (PL 34, 288).
2. 参见 *De Genesi contra Manich.*, I, 16 (PL 34, 185).

Question LXXIII
THE THINGS THAT BELONG TO THE SEVENTH DAY
(*In Three Articles*)

WE must next consider the things that belong to the seventh day. Under this head there are three points of inquiry: (1) About the completion of the works. (2) About the resting of God. (3) About the blessing and sanctifying of this day.

First Article
WHETHER THE COMPLETION OF THE DIVINE WORKS OUGHT TO BE ASCRIBED TO THE SEVENTH DAY?

We proceed thus to the First Article:—

Objection 1. It would seem that the completion of the divine works ought not to be ascribed to the seventh day. For all things that are done in this world belong to the divine works. But the consummation of the world will be at the end of the world (*Matt.* xiii. 39, 40). Moreover, the time of Christ's Incarnation[1] is a time of completion; wherefore it is called *the time of fullness* (*Gal.* iv. 4). And Christ Himself, at the moment of His death, cried out, *It is consummated* (*Jo.* xix. 30). Hence the completion of the divine works does not belong to the seventh day.

Obj. 2. Further, the completion of a work is an act in itself. But we do

1. Christ's Incarnation: 基督降生成人

not read that God acted at all on the seventh day, but rather that He rested from all His work. Therefore the completion of the works does not belong to the seventh day.

Obj. 3. Further, nothing is said to be complete to which many things are added, unless they are merely superfluous; for a thing is called perfect to which nothing is wanting that it ought to possess. But many things were made after the seventh day, as the production of many individual beings, and even of certain new species that are frequently appearing, especially in the case of animals generated from putrefaction. Also, God creates daily new souls. Again, the work of the Incarnation was a new work, of which it is said (*Jer.* xxxi. 22): *The Lord hath created a new thing upon the earth.* Miracles also are new works, of which it is said (*Ecclus.* xxxvi. 6): *Renew thy signs, and work new miracles.* Moreover, all things will be made new when the saints are glorified, according to *Apoc.* xxi. 5: *And He that sat on the throne said: Behold I make all things new.* Therefore the completion of the divine works ought not to be attributed to the seventh day.

On the contrary, It is said (*Gen.* ii. 2): *On the seventh day God ended His work which he had made.*

I answer that, The perfection of a thing is twofold, first and second. The *first* perfection is that according to which a thing is substantially perfect; and this perfection is the form of the whole, which results from the fact that the whole has its parts complete. But the *second* perfection is the end, which is either an operation (as the end of the harpist is to play the harp), or something that is attained by an operation (as the end of the builder is the house that he makes by building). But the first perfection is the cause of the second, because the form is the principle of operation. Now the final perfection, which is the end of the whole universe, is the perfect beatitude of the saints at the consummation of the world. But the first perfection is the completeness of the universe at its first founding, and this is what is ascribed to the seventh day.

Reply Obj. 1. The first perfection is the cause of the second, as we said above. Now, for the attaining of beatitude two things are required, nature and grace. Therefore, as said above, the perfection of beatitude will be at the end of the world. But this consummation[1] existed previously in its causes, as to nature, at the first founding of the world, and as to grace, in the Incarnation of Christ. For, *Grace and truth came by Jesus Christ* (*Jo.* i. 17). So, then, on the seventh day there was the consummation of nature, in Christ's Incarnation there was the consummation of grace, and at the end of the world there will be the consummation of glory.

Reply Obj. 2. God did act on the seventh day, not by creating new creatures, but by directing and moving His creatures to the work proper to them; and thus He made some beginning of the *second* perfection. So, according to our version of the Scripture, the completion of the works is attributed to the seventh day, though according to the other it is assigned to the sixth.[2] Either version, however, may stand, since the completion of the universe as to the completeness of its parts belongs to the sixth day, but its completion as regards their operation, to the seventh. It may also be added that in continuous movement, so long as any further movement is possible, movement cannot be called completed till it comes to rest, for rest denotes consummation of movement. Now God might have made many other creatures besides those which He made in the six days; and hence, by the fact that He ceased making them on the seventh day, He is said on that day to have consummated His work.

Reply Obj. 3. Nothing entirely new was afterwards made by God, but all things subsequently made had in a sense been made before in the work of the six days. Some things, indeed, had a previous existence materially, as the rib from the side of Adam out of which God formed Eve; while others existed not only in matter but also in their causes, as

---

1. consummation: 完成；圆满；极致
2. 参见 The Septuagint.

those individual creatures that are now generated existed in the first of their kind. Species, also, that are new, if any such appear, existed beforehand in various active powers; so that animals, and perhaps even new species of animals, are produced by putrefaction by the power which the stars and elements received at the beginning. Again, animals of new kinds arise occasionally from the union of individuals belonging to different species, as the mule is the offspring of an ass and a mare; but even these existed previously in their causes, in the works of the six days. Some also existed beforehand by way of likeness, as the souls now created. And the work of the Incarnation itself was thus foreshadowed, for, as we read (*Phil.* ii. 7), The Son of God *was made in the likeness of men.* And again, the glory that is spiritual was anticipated in the angels by way of likeness; and that of the body, in the heavens, especially the empyrean. Hence it is written (*Eccles.* i. 10), *Nothing under the sun is new, for it hath already gone before, in the ages that were before us.*

Second Article

WHETHER GOD RESTED ON THE SEVENTH DAY FROM ALL HIS WORK?

We proceed thus to the Second Article:—

Objection 1. It would seem that God did not rest on the seventh day from all His work. For it is said (*Jo.* v. 17), *My Father worketh until now, and I work.* God, then, did not rest on the seventh day from all His works.

Obj. 2. Further, rest is opposed to movement, or to labor, which movement causes. But, as God produced His work without movement and without labor, He cannot be said to have rested on the seventh day from His work.

Obj. 3. Further, should it be said that God rested on the seventh day by causing man to rest, against this it may be argued that rest is set down in contradistinction to His work. Now the words *God created* or *made* this thing or the other cannot be explained to mean that He made man create or make these things. Therefore the resting of God cannot be explained as His making man to rest.

On the contrary, It is said (*Gen.* ii. 2): *God rested on the seventh day from all the work which He had done.*

I answer that, Rest is, properly speaking, opposed to movement, and consequently to the labor that arises from movement. But although *movement*, strictly speaking, belongs to bodies, yet the term is applied also to spiritual things, and in a twofold sense. On the one hand, every operation may be called a movement, and thus the divine goodness is said to move and go forth to things, in communicating itself to them, as Dionysius says.[1] On the other hand, the desire that tends to a thing outside itself is said to move towards it. Hence rest is taken in two senses, in one sense meaning a cessation from work, in the other, the satisfying of desire. Now, in either sense God is said to have rested on the seventh day. First, because He ceased from creating new creatures on that day, for, as was said above, He made nothing afterwards that had not existed previously, in some degree, in the first works; secondly, because He Himself had no need of the things that He had made, but was happy in the fruition of Himself. Hence, when all things were made He is not said to have rested *in* His works, as though needing them for His own happiness, but to have rested *from* them, as in fact resting in Himself, since He suffices for Himself and fulfills His own desire. And even though from all eternity He rested in Himself, yet the rest in Himself, which He took after He had finished His works, is that rest which belongs to the seventh day. And this, says Augustine, is the meaning of God's resting from His works on that day.[2]

Reply Obj. 1. God indeed *worketh until now* by preserving and providing for the creatures He has made, but not by the making of new

---

1. 参见 *De Div. Nom.*, II, 4 (PG 3, 640).
2. 参见 *De Genesi ad Litt.*, IV, 15 (PL 34, 306).

ones.

Reply Obj. 2. Rest is here not opposed to labor or to movement, but to the production of new creatures and to the desire tending to an external object.

Reply Obj. 3. Even as God rests in Himself alone and is happy in the enjoyment of Himself, so our own sole happiness lies in the enjoyment of God. Thus, too, does He make us find rest in Himself both from His works and our own. It is not, then, unreasonable to say that God rested in giving rest to us. Still, this explanation must not be set down as the only one; but the other is rather the first and principal explanation.

Third Article
WHETHER BLESSING AND SANCTIFYING ARE DUE TO THE SEVENTH DAY?

We proceed thus to the Third Article:—

Objection 1. It would seem that blessing and sanctifying are not due to the seventh day. For it is usual to call a time blessed or holy because some good thing has happened in it, or some evil has been avoided. But whether God works or ceases from work, nothing accrues to Him or is lost to Him. Therefore no special blessing and sanctifying are due to the seventh day.

Obj. 2. Further, the Latin *benedictio* [*blessing*] is derived from *bonitas* [*goodness*]. But it is the nature of good to spread and communicate itself, as Dionysius says.[1] The days, therefore, in which God produced creatures deserved a blessing rather than the day on which He ceased producing them.

Obj. 3. Further, over each creature a blessing was pronounced, as

---

1. 参见 *De Div. Nom.*, IV, 20 (PG 3, 720); cf. *op. cit.*, IV, 4; 1 (PG 3, 697; 693).

upon each work it was said, *God saw that it was good.* Therefore it was not necessary that after all had been produced, the seventh day should be blessed.

On the contrary, It is written (*Gen.* ii. 3), *God blessed the seventh day and sanctified it, because in it He had rested from all His work.*

I answer that, as was said above, God's rest on the seventh day is understood in two ways. First, in that He ceased from producing new works, though He still preserves and provides for the creatures He has made. Secondly, in that after all His works He rested in Himself. According to the first meaning, a blessing befits the seventh day, since, as we explained, the blessing referred to the increase by multiplication;[1] for which reason God said to the creatures which He blessed: *Increase and multiply.* Now, this increase is effected through God's providence over His creatures, securing the generation of like from like. And according to the second meaning, it is right that the seventh day should have been sanctified, since the special sanctification of every creature consists in resting in God. For this reason things dedicated to God are said to be sanctified.

Reply Obj. 1. The seventh day is said to be sanctified, not because anything can accrue to God, or be taken from Him, but because something is added to creatures by their multiplying, and by their resting in God.

Reply Obj. 2. In the first six days, creatures were produced in their first causes; but after being thus produced, they are multiplied and preserved, and this work also belongs to the divine goodness. And the perfection of this goodness is also made most clear by the knowledge that in it alone God finds His own rest, and we may find ours in its fruition.

---

1. 参见 Q. 72, a. 4.

Reply Obj. 3. The good mentioned in the works of each day belongs to the first establishment of nature; but the blessing attached to the seventh day, to its propagation.

Question LXXIV
ON ALL THE SEVEN DAYS IN COMMON
(*In Three Articles*)

WE next consider all the seven days in common: and there are three points of inquiry: (1) As to the sufficiency of these days. (2) Whether they are all one day, or more than one? (3) As to certain modes of speaking which Scripture uses in narrating the works of the six days.

First Article
WHETHER THESE DAYS ARE SUFFICIENTLY ENUMERATED?

We proceed thus to the First Article:—

Objection 1. It would seem that these days are not sufficiently enumerated. For the work of creation is no less distinct from the works of distinction and adornment than these two works are from one another. But separate days are assigned to distinction and to adornment, and therefore separate days should be assigned to creation.

Obj. 2. Further, air and fire are nobler elements than earth and water. But one day is assigned to the distinction of water, and another to the distinction of the land. Therefore, other days ought to be devoted to the distinction of fire and air.

Obj. 3. Further, fish differ from birds as much as birds differ from the beasts of the earth, whereas man differs more from other animals than all animals whatsoever differ from each other. But one day is devoted to the production of fishes, and another to that of the beasts of the earth. Another day, then, ought to be assigned to the production of birds, and another to that of man.

Obj. 4. Further, it would seem that some of the days are superfluous. Light, for instance, stands to the luminaries in the relation of accident to subject. But the subject is produced at the same time as the accident proper to it. The light and the luminaries, therefore, ought not to have been produced on different days.

Obj. 5. Further, these days are devoted to the first establishment of the world. But as on the seventh day nothing was newly established, that day ought not to be enumerated with the others.

I answer that, The plan of the distinction of these days is made clear by what has been said above, namely, that the parts of the world had first to be distinguished, and then each part adorned and filled, as it were, by the beings that inhabit it.[1] Now the parts into which the corporeal creation is divided are three, according to some holy writers, namely, the *heaven*, or highest part, the *water*, or middle part, and the *earth*, or lowest part.[2] (Thus the Pythagoreans teach that perfection consists in three things, the beginning, the middle, and the end.[3]) The first part, then, is distinguished on the first day, and adorned on the fourth, the middle part distinguished on the second day, and adorned on the fifth, and the third part distinguished on the third day, and adorned on the sixth. But Augustine, while agreeing with the above writers as to the last three days, differs as to the first three,[4] for, according to him, spiritual creatures are formed on the first day, and corporeal on the two others: the higher bodies are formed on the first of these two days, and the lower on the second. Thus, then, the perfection of the divine works corresponds to the perfection of the number six, which is the sum of its aliquot parts, one, two, three; since one day is assigned to the forming of spiritual creatures, two to that of

1. 参见 Q. 70, a. 1.
2. 参见 Cf. St. Basil, *In Hexaëm.*, hom. I (PG 29, 19).
3. 参见 Aristotle, *De Caelo*, I, 1 (268a 10).
4. 参见 Cf. above, q. 70, a. 1; q. 72; q. 73.

corporeal creatures, and three to the work of adornment.

Reply Obj. 1. According to Augustine,[1] the work of creation belongs to the production of formless matter, and of the formless spiritual nature, both of which are outside of time, as he himself says.[2] Thus, then, the creation of either is set down before there was any day. But it may also be said, following other holy writers,[3] that the works of distinction and adornment imply certain changes in the creature which are measurable by time; whereas the work of creation lies only in the divine act producing the substance of beings instantaneously. For this reason, therefore, every work of distinction and adornment is said to take place *in a day*, but creation *in the beginning*, which denotes something indivisible.

Reply Obj. 2. Fire and air, as not distinctly known by the unlettered, are not expressly named by Moses among the parts of the world, but reckoned with the intermediate part, or water, especially as regards the lowest part of the air; or with the heaven, to which the higher region of air approaches, as Augustine says.[4]

Reply Obj. 3. The production of animals is recorded with reference to their adornment of the various parts of the world. Therefore the days of their production are separated or united according as the animals adorn the same parts of the world, or different parts.

Reply Obj. 4. The nature of light, as existing in a subject, was made on the first day; and the making of the luminaries on the fourth day does not mean that their substance was produced anew, but that they then received a formation that they had not before, as was said above.[5]

Reply Obj. 5. According to Augustine,[6] after all that has been

---

1. 参见 Cf. above, q. 70, a. 1.
2. 参见 *Confess.*, XII, 12; 13 (PL 32, 831; 832).
3. 参见 Cf. above, q. 66, a. 1.
4. 参见 *De Genesi ad Litt.*, II, 3; 13; III, 7 (PL 34, 265; 274; 283).
5. 参见 Q. 70, a. 1, ad 2.
6. 参见 *De Genesi ad Litt.*, IV, 15 (PL 34, 306).

recorded as assigned to the six days, something distinct is attributed to the seventh,—namely, that on it God rested in Himself from His works. And for this reason it was right that the seventh day should be mentioned after the six. It may also be said, with other writers,[1] that the world entered on the seventh day upon a new state, in that nothing new was to be added to it, and that therefore the seventh day is mentioned after the six, from its being devoted to cessation from work.

Second Article
WHETHER ALL THESE DAYS ARE ONE DAY?

We proceed thus to the Second Article:—

Objection 1. It would seem that all these days are one day. For it is written (*Gen*, ii. 4, 5): *These are the generations of the heaven and the earth, when they were created, in the day that the Lord ... made the heaven and the earth, and every plant of the field, before it sprung up in the earth.* Therefore the day in which God made *the heaven and the earth, and every plant of the field*, is one and the same day. But He made the heaven and the earth on the first day, or rather before there was any day; but the plant of the field He made on the third day. Therefore the first and third days are but one day, and for a like reason all the rest.

Obj. 2. Further, it is said (*Ecclus.* xviii. 1): *He that liveth for ever, created all things together.* But this would not be the case if the days of these works were more than one. Therefore they are not many but one only.

Obj. 3. Further, on the seventh day God ceased from all new works. If, then, the seventh day is distinct from the other days, it follows that He did not make that day; which is not admissible.

Obj. 4. Further, the entire work ascribed to one day God perfected in an instant, for with each work are the words [*God*] *said, ... and it*

---

1. 参见 Cf. above, q. 66, a. 1; q. 69, a. 2.

was ... done. If, then, He had reserved His next work for another day, it would follow that for the remainder of a day He would have ceased from working and left it vacant, which would be superfluous. The day, therefore, of the preceding work is one with the day of the work that follows.

On the contrary, It is written (*Gen.* i. 8), *The evening and the morning were the second day ... the third day*, and so on. But where there is second and third there are more than one. There was not, therefore, only one day.

I answer that, On this question Augustine differs from other expositors. His opinion is that all the days that are called seven are one day represented in a sevenfold aspect;[1] while others consider there were seven distinct days, and not one only.[2] Now, these two opinions, taken as explaining the literal text of *Genesis*, are certainly widely different. For Augustine understands by the word *day* the knowledge in the mind of the angels, and hence, according to him, the first day denotes their knowledge of the first of the divine work, the second day their knowledge of the second work, and similarly with the rest. Thus, then, each work is said to have been wrought in some one of these days, inasmuch as God wrought nothing in the universe without impressing the knowledge of it on the angelic mind, which can know many things at the same time, especially in the Word, in Whom all angelic knowledge is perfected and terminated. So the distinction of days denotes the natural order of the things known, and not a succession in the knowledge acquired, or in the things produced. Moreover, angelic knowledge is appropriately called *day*, since light, the cause of day, is to be found in the spiritual order, as Augustine observes.[3] In the

---

1. 参见 *De Genesi ad Litt.*, IV, 26; 33; V, 3; 23 (PL 34, 314; 318; 323; 338); *De Civit. Dei*, XI, 9 (PL 41, 324).—Cf. Pseudo-Augustine, *Dial. 65 Quaest.*, q. 26 (PL 40, 741).
2. 参见 St. Basil, *In Hexaëm.*, hom. II (PG 29, 49); St. Ambrose, *In Hexaëm.*, I, 10 (PL 14, 155).—Cf. St. Gregory, *Moral.*, XXXII, 12 (PL 76, 644).
3. 参见 *De Genesi ad Litt.*, IV, 28 (PL 34, 315).

opinion of the others, however, the days signify a succession both in time, and in the things produced.

If, however, these two explanations are looked at as referring to the mode of production, they will be found not greatly to differ, if the diversity of opinion existing on two points, as already shown,[1] between Augustine and other writers is taken into account. First, because Augustine takes the earth and the water, as first created, to signify matter totally without form: but the making of the firmament, the gathering of the waters, and the appearing of dry land, to denote the impression of forms upon corporeal matter. But other holy writers take the earth and the water, as first created, to signify the elements of the universe themselves existing under their proper forms, and the works that follow to mean some sort of distinction in bodies previously existing, as also has been shown.[2] Secondly, some writers hold that plants and animals were produced actually in the work of the six days;[3] Augustine, that they were produced potentially.[4] Now the opinion of Augustine, that the works of the six days were simultaneous, is consistent with either view of the mode of the production of things. For the other writers agree with him that in the first production of things matter existed under the substantial form of the elements, and they agree with him also that in the first establishment of the world animals and plants did not exist actually. There remains, however, a difference as to four points; since, according to the latter, there was a time, after the first production of creatures, in which light did not exist, the firmament had not been formed, and the earth was still covered by the waters, nor, fourthly, had the heavenly bodies been formed.[5]

---

1. 参见 Q. 69, a. 1; q. 67, a. 1.
2. 参见 Q. 69, a. 1.
3. 参见 Cf. above, q. 69, a. 2; q. 71, a. 1.
4. 参见 Cf. above, q. 69, a. 2; q. 71; q. 72.
5. 参见 Cf. above, q. 69, a. 1.

These views are not consistent with Augustine's explanation. In order, therefore, to be impartial, we must meet the arguments of either side.

Reply Obj. 1. On the day on which God created the heaven and the earth, He created also every plant of the field, not, indeed, actually, but *before it sprung up in the earth*, that is, potentially. And this work Augustine ascribes to the third day,[1] but other writers to the first establishment of the world.[2]

Reply Obj. 2. God created all things together so far as regards their substance considered as somehow formless. But He did not create all things together, so far as regards that formation of things which lies in distinction and adornment. Hence the word *creation* is significant.

Reply Obj. 3. On the seventh day God ceased from making new beings, but not from providing for their increase, and to this latter work it belongs that the first day is succeeded by other days.

Reply Obj. 4. All things were not distinguished and adorned together, not from a want of power on God's part, as requiring time in which to work, but that due order might be observed in the establishment of the world. Hence it was fitting that different days should be assigned to the different states of the world, as each succeeding work added to the world a fresh state of perfection.

Reply Obj. 5. According to Augustine, the order of days refers to the natural order of the works attributed to the days.[3]

Third Article
WHETHER SCRIPTURE USES SUITABLE WORDS TO EXPRESS THE WORK OF THE SIX DAYS?

We proceed thus to the Third Article:—

---

1. 参见 *De Genesi ad Litt.*, V, 5; VIII. 3 (PL 34, 326; 374).
2. 参见 Cf. above, q. 69, a. 2.
3. 参见 *De Genesi ad Litt.*, IV, 34; 35; V, 5 (PL 34, 319; 320; 326).

Objection 1. It would seem that Scripture does not use suitable words to express the works of the six days. For as light, the firmament, and other similar works were made by the Word of God, so were the heaven and the earth. For *all things were made by Him* (*Jo.* i. 3). Therefore in the creation of heaven and earth, as in the other works, mention should have been made of the Word of God.

Obj. 2. Further, the water was created by God, yet its creation is not mentioned. Therefore the creation of the world is not sufficiently described.

Obj. 3. Further, it is said (*Gen.* i. 31): *God saw all the things that He had made, and they were very good.* It ought, then, to have been said of each work, *God saw that it was good.* The omission, therefore, of these words in the work of creation and in that of the second day is not fitting.

Obj. 4. Further, the Spirit of God is God Himself. But it does not befit God to move and to occupy place. Therefore the words, *The Spirit of God moved over the waters*, are unbecoming.

Obj. 5. Further, what is already made is not made over again. Therefore to the words, *God said: Let the firmament be made ... and it was so*, it is superfluous to add, *God made the firmament.* And the like is to be said of other works.

Obj. 6. Further, evening and morning do not sufficiently divide the day, since the day has many parts. Therefore the words, *The evening and morning were the second day* or, *the third day*, are not suitable.

Obj. 7. Further, *first*, not *one*, corresponds to *second* and *third*. It should therefore have been said that, *The evening and the morning were the first day*, rather than *one day*.

Reply Obj. 1. According to Augustine, the person of the Son is mentioned both in the first creation of the world, and in its distinction and adornment, but differently in either place.[1] For distinction

1. 参见 *Op. cit.*, I, 4 (PL 34, 249).

and adornment belong to the work by which the world receives its formation. But just as the formation of a work of art is by means of the form of the art in the mind of the artist, which may be called his intelligible word, so the formation of every creature is by the Word of God; and for this reason in the works of distinction and adornment the Word is mentioned. But in creation the Son is mentioned as the beginning, by the words, *In the beginning God created*, since by creation is understood the production of formless matter. But according to those who hold that the elements were created from the first under their proper forms, another explanation must be given. Thus, Basil says that the words, *God said*, signify a divine command.[1] Such a command, however, could not have been given before creatures had been produced that could obey it.

Reply Obj. 2. According to Augustine,[2] by the heaven is understood the formless spiritual nature, and by the earth, the formless matter of all corporeal things. And thus no creature is omitted. But, according to Basil,[3] the heaven and the earth, as the two extremes, are alone mentioned, while the intervening things are left to be understood, since all these move heavenwards, if light, or earthwards, if heavy. And others[4] say that under the word, *earth*, Scripture is accustomed to include all the four elements, just as after the words, *Praise the Lord from the earth*, is added, *fire*, *hail*, *snow*, *and ice* (*Ps.* cxlviii. 7, 8).

Reply Obj. 3. In the account of the creation there is found something to correspond to the words, *God saw that it was good*, used in the work of distinction and adornment, and this appears from the consideration that the Holy Spirit is Love. Now there are two things, says Augustine,

---

1. 参见 *In Hexaëm.*, hom. II; III (PG 29, 45 ; 53).
2. 参见 *De Genesi ad Litt.*, I, 1; 4; 9 (PL 34, 247; 249; 252).
3. 参见 *In Hexaëm.*, hom. I (PG 29, 17).
4. 参见 Peter Lombard, *Sent.*, II, xii, 1 (I, 358); Maimonides, *Guide*, II, 30 (p. 213).

for which God loves His creatures, their being and their permanence. That they might exist, and exist permanently, therefore, *the Spirit of God*[1], it is said, *moved over the waters*[2]—that is to say, over that formless matter, signified by water, even as the love of the artist moves over the materials of his art, that out of them he may form his work. And the words, *God saw that it was good*, signify that the things that He had made were to endure, since they express a certain satisfaction taken by God in His works, as of an artist in his art. This does not mean, of course, that He knew the creature otherwise, or that the creature was pleasing to Him otherwise, than before He made it. Thus in either work, of creation and of formation, the Trinity of Persons[3] is implied. In creation the Person of the Father is indicated by God the Creator, the Person of the Son by the beginning, in which He created, and the Person of the Holy Ghost by the Spirit that moved over the waters. But in the formation of creatures, the Person of the Father is indicated by God that speaks, the Person of the Son by the Word in Which He speaks, and the Person of the Holy Spirit by the satisfaction with which God saw that what was made was good.

And if the words, *God saw that it was good*, are not said of the work of the second day, this is because the work of distinguishing the waters was only begun on that day, but perfected on the third. Hence these words, which are said of the third day, refer also to the second. Or it may be that Scripture does not use these words of approval of the second day's work, because this is concerned with the distinction of things not evident to the senses of mankind. Or, again, because by the firmament is simply understood the cloudy region of the air, which is not one of the permanent parts of the universe, nor of the principal divisions of the world. The above three reasons are given by Rabbi

---

1. the Spirit of God: 天主的神，指三位一体的天主的第三位，即圣神
2. 参见 *De Genesi ad Litt.*, I, 8 (PL 34, 251).
3. the Trinity of Persons: 三位一体的三位

Moses,[1] and to these may be added a mystical one derived from numbers and assigned by some writers, according to whom the work of the second day is not marked with approval because the second number is an imperfect number, as receding from the perfection of unity.[2]

Reply Obj. 4. Rabbi Moses understands by the *Spirit of the Lord*, the air or the wind, as Plato also did,[3] and says that it is so called according to the custom of Scripture, in which these things are throughout attributed to God. But according to the holy writers, the Spirit of the Lord signifies the Holy Ghost, Who is said to *move over the water*—that is to say, over what Augustine holds to mean formless matter,[4] lest it should be supposed that God loved of necessity the works He was to produce, as though He stood in need of them. For a love that is born of need is subject to the things that it loves. Moreover, it is fittingly implied that the Spirit moved over that which was incomplete and unfinished, since that movement is not one of place, but of pre-eminent power, as Augustine says.[5] It is the opinion, however, of Basil that the Spirit moved over the element of water, *fostering and quickening its nature and impressing vital power, as the hen broods over her chickens.*[6] For water has especially a life-giving power, since many animals are generated in water, and the seed of all animals is liquid. Also the life of the soul is given by the water of baptism, according to *Jo.* iii. 5: *Unless a man be born again of water and the Holy Ghost, he cannot enter into the kingdom of God.*

Reply Obj. 5. According to Augustine, these three phrases denote the

---

1. 参见 *Guide*, II, 30 (p. 215).
2. 参见 *Glossa ordin.*, super *Gen.*, I, 6 (I, 25B).
3. 参见 Cf. above, q. 66, a. 1, ad 5.
4. 参见 *De Genesi contra Manich.*, I, 7 (PL 34, 179).
5. 参见 *De Genesi ad Litt.*, I, 7 (PL 34, 251).
6. 参见 *In Hexaëm.*, hom. II (PG 29, 44).

threefold being of creatures.[1] First, their being in the Word is denoted by the command *Let ... be made*; secondly, their being in the angelic mind, signified by the words, *It was ... done*; thirdly, their being in their proper nature, by the words *He made*. And because the formation of the angels is recorded on the first day, it was not necessary there to add, *He made*. It may also be said, following other writers,[2] that the words, *He said*, and, *Let ... be made*, denote God's command, and the words, *It was done*, the fulfilment of that command. But as it was necessary, for the sake of those especially who have asserted that all visible things were made by the angels,[3] to mention how things were made, it is added, in order to remove that error, that God Himself made them. Hence, in each work, after the words, *It was done*, some act of God is expressed by some such words as, *He made*, or, *He divided*, or, *He called*.

Reply Obj. 6. According to Augustine,[4] by the *evening* and the *morning* are understood the evening and the morning knowledge of the angels, which has been explained.[5] But, according to Basil,[6] the entire period takes its name, as is customary, from its more important part, the day. An instance of this is found in the words of Jacob, *The days of my pilgrimage* (*Gen*. xlvii. 9), where night is not mentioned at all. But the evening and the morning are mentioned as being the ends of the day, since day begins with morning and ends with evening, or because evening denotes the beginning of night, and morning the beginning of day. It seems fitting, also, that where the first distinction of creatures is described, divisions of time should be denoted only by what marks their beginning. And the reason for mentioning the evening first is

---

1. 参见 *De Genesi ad Litt*., II, 8 (PL 34, 269).
2. 参见 St. Basil, St. John Chrysostom, St. Ambrose and St. Bede.
3. 参见 Cf. St. Thomas, *Expositio in I Decretalem* (P. Mandonnet, *Opuscula*, IV, p. 333).
4. 参见 *De Genesi ad Litt*., IV, 22 (PL 34, 312).
5. 参见 Q. 58, a. 6 and 7.
6. 参见 *In Hexaëm*., hom. II (PG 29, 49).

that as the evening ends the day, which begins with the light, the termination of the light at evening precedes the termination of the darkness, which ends with the morning. But Chrysostom's explanation is that thereby it is intended to show that the natural day does not end with the evening, but with the morning.[1]

Reply Obj. 7. The words *one day* are used when day is first established, to denote that one day is made up of twenty-four hours. Hence, by mentioning *one*, the measure of a natural day is fixed. Another reason may be to signify that a day is completed by the return of the sun to the point from which it commenced its course. And yet another, because at the completion of a week of seven days, the first day returns, which is one with the eighth day. The three reasons assigned above are those given by Basil.[2]

---

1. 参见 *In Genesim*, hom. V (PG 53, 52).
2. 参见 *In Hexaëm.*, hom. II (PG 29, 49).

TREATISE ON MAN

Question LXXV
ON MAN WHO IS COMPOSED OF A SPIRITUAL AND A CORPOREAL SUBSTANCE: AND FIRST, CONCERNING WHAT BELONGS TO THE ESSENCE OF THE SOUL.
(*In Seven Articles*)

HAVING treated of the spiritual and of the corporeal creature, we now proceed to treat of man, who is composed of a spiritual and of a corporeal substance. We shall treat first of the nature of man, and secondly of his origin.[1] Now the theologian considers the nature of man in relation to the soul, but not in relation to the body, except in so far as the body has relation to the soul. Hence the first object of our consideration will be the soul. And since Dionysius says that three things are to be found in spiritual substances—essence, power and operation[2] —we shall treat first of what belongs to the essence of the soul; secondly, of what belongs to its power;[3] thirdly, of what belongs to its operation.[4]

Concerning the first, two points have to be considered; the first is the nature of the soul considered in itself; the second is the union of the soul with the body.[5] Under the first head there are seven points of

1. 参见 Q. 90.
2. 参见 *De Cael. Hier.*, XI, 2 (PG 3, 284).
3. 参见 Q. 77.
4. 参见 Q. 84.
5. 参见 Q. 76.

inquiry.

(1) Whether the soul is a body? (2) Whether the human soul is something subsistent? (3) Whether the souls of brute animals are subsistent? (4) Whether the soul is man, or is man composed of soul and body? (5) Whether the soul is composed of matter and form? (6) Whether the soul is incorruptible? (7) Whether the soul is of the same species as an angel?

First Article
WHETHER THE SOUL IS A BODY?

We proceed thus to the First Article:—

Objection 1. It would seem that the soul is a body. For the soul is the mover of the body. Nor does it move unless moved. First, because apparently nothing can move unless it is itself moved, since nothing gives what it has not. For instance, what is not hot does not give heat. Secondly, because if there be anything that moves and is itself not moved, it must be the cause of eternal and uniform movement, as we find proved *Physics* viii.[1] Now this does not appear to be the case in the movement of an animal, which is caused by the soul. Therefore the soul is a moved mover. But every moved mover is a body. Therefore the soul is a body.

Obj. 2. Further, all knowledge is caused by means of a likeness. But there can be no likeness of a body to an incorporeal thing. If, therefore, the soul were not a body, it could not have knowledge of corporeal things.

Obj. 3. Further, between the mover and the moved there must be contact. But contact is only between bodies. Since, therefore, the soul moves the body, it seems that the soul must be a body.

---

1. 参见 Aristotle, *Phys.*, VIII, 10 (267b 3).

On the contrary, Augustine says that the soul *is simple in comparison with the body, inasmuch as it does not occupy space by any bulk.*[1]

I answer that, To seek the nature of the soul, we must premise that the soul is defined as the first principle of life in those things in our world which live; for we call living things *animate*, and those things which have no life, *inanimate*. Now life is shown principally by two activities, knowledge and movement. The philosophers of old, not being able to rise above their imagination, supposed that the principle of these actions was something corporeal;[2] for they asserted that only bodies were real things, and that what is not corporeal is nothing.[3] Hence they maintained that the soul is some sort of body.[4] This opinion can be proved in many ways to be false; but we shall make use of only one proof, which shows quite universally and certainly that the soul is not a body.

It is manifest that not every principle of vital action is a soul, for then the eye would be a soul, as it is a principle of vision; and the same might be applied to the other instruments of the soul. But it is the *first* principle of life which we call the soul. Now, though a body may be a principle of life, as the heart is a principle of life in an animal, yet no body can be the first principle of life. For it is clear that to be a principle of life, or to be a living thing, does not belong to a body as a body, since, if that were the case, every body would be a living thing, or a principle of life. Therefore a body is competent to be a living thing, or even a principle of life, as *such* a body. Now that it is actually such a body it owes to some principle which is called its act. Therefore the soul, which is the first principle of life, is not a body, but the act

---

1. 参见 *De Trin.*, VI, 6 (PL 42, 929).
2. 参见 Democritus and Empedocles, according to Aristotle, *De An.*, I, 2 (404a 1; b 11).
3. 参见 Cf. above, q. 50, a. 1.
4. 参见 Cf. Macrobius, *In Somn. Scipion.*, I, 14 (p. 543); Nemesius, *De Nat. Hom.*, II (PG 40, 536); St. Augustine, *De Civit. Dei*, VIII, 5 (PL 41, 230).

of a body; just as heat, which is the principle of calefaction[1], is not a body, but an act of a body.

Reply Obj. 1. Since everything which is moved must be moved by something else, a process which cannot be prolonged indefinitely, we must allow that not every mover is moved. For, since to be moved is to pass from potentiality to actuality, the mover gives what it has to the thing moved, inasmuch as it causes it to be in act. But, as is shown in *Physics* viii., there is a mover which is altogether immovable, and which is not moved either essentially or accidentally; and such a mover can cause an eternally uniform movement.[2] There is, however, another kind of mover, which, though not moved essentially, is moved accidentally; and for this reason it does not cause a uniform movement. Such a mover is the soul. There is, again, another mover, which is moved essentially—namely, the body. And because the philosophers of old believed that nothing existed but bodies, they maintained that every mover is moved, and that the soul is moved essentially, and is a body.[3]

Reply Obj. 2. It is not necessary that the likeness of the thing known be actually in the nature of the knower. But given a being which knows potentially, and afterwards knows actually, the likeness of the thing known must be in the nature of the knower, not actually, but only potentially; and thus color is not actually in the pupil of the eye, but only potentially. Hence it is necessary, not that the likeness of corporeal things be actually in the nature of the soul, but that there be a potentiality in the soul for such a likeness. But the ancient naturalists did not know how to distinguish between actuality and potentiality;[4] and so they held that the soul must be a body in order to have

1. calefaction: 热化效应；发热作用；温暖
2. 参见 Aristotle, *Phys.*, VIII, 5 (258b 4); 6 (258b 15); 10 (267b 3).
3. 参见 Cf. Aristotle, *De An.*, I, 2 (403b 29).
4. 参见 Cf. Aristotle, *De Gener.*, I, 10 (327b 23).

knowledge of a body, and that it must be composed of the principles of which all bodies are formed.

Reply Obj. 3. There are two kinds of contact, that of *quantity*, and that of *power*. By the former a body can be touched only by a body; by the latter a body can be touched by an incorporeal reality, which moves that body.

Second Article
WHETHER THE HUMAN SOUL IS SOMETHING SUBSISTENT?

We proceed thus to the Second Article:—

Objection 1. It would seem that the human soul is not something subsistent. For that which subsists is said to be *this particular thing*. Now *this particular thing* is said not of the soul, but of that which is composed of soul and body. Therefore the soul is not something subsistent.

Obj. 2. Further, everything subsistent operates. But the soul does not operate, for, as the Philosopher says, *to say that the soul feels or understands is like saying that the soul weaves or builds.*[1] Therefore the soul is not subsistent.

Obj. 3. Further, if the soul were something subsistent, it would have some operation apart from the body. But it has no operation apart from the body, not even that of understanding; for the act of understanding does not take place without a phantasm, which cannot exist apart from the body. Therefore the human soul is not something subsistent.

On the contrary, Augustine says: *Whoever understands that the nature of the mind is that of a substance and not that of a body, will see that those who maintain the corporeal nature of the mind are led astray because they associate with the mind those things without which they are unable to think*

---

1. 参见 *De An.*, I, 4 (408b 11).

of any nature—i.e., imaginary pictures of corporeal things.[1] Therefore the nature of the human mind is not only incorporeal, but it is also a substance, that is, something subsistent.

I answer that, It must necessarily be allowed that the principle of intellectual operation, which we call the soul of man, is a principle both incorporeal and subsistent. For it is clear that by means of the intellect man can know all corporeal things. Now whatever knows certain things cannot have any of them in its own nature, because that which is in it naturally would impede the knowledge of anything else. Thus we observe that a sick man's tongue, being unbalanced by a feverish and bitter humor, is insensible to anything sweet, and everything seems bitter to it. Therefore, if the intellectual principle contained within itself the nature of any body, it would be unable to know all bodies. Now every body has its own determinate nature. Therefore it is impossible for the intellectual principle to be a body. It is also impossible for it to understand by means of a bodily organ, since the determinate nature of that organ would likewise impede knowledge of all bodies; as when a certain determinate color is not only in the pupil of the eye, but also in a glass vase, the liquid in the vase seems to be of that same color.

Therefore the intellectual principle, which we call the mind or the intellect, has essentially an operation in which the body does not share. Now only that which subsists in itself can have an operation in itself. For nothing can operate but what is actual, and so a thing operates according as it is; for which reason we do not say that heat imparts heat, but that what is hot gives heat. We must conclude, therefore, that the human soul, which is called intellect or mind, is something incorporeal and subsistent.

Reply Obj. 1. *This particular thing* can be taken in two senses. Firstly,

---

1. 参见 *De Trin.*, X, 7 (PL 42, 979).

for anything subsistent; secondly, for that which subsists and is complete in a specific nature. The former sense excludes the inherence of an accident or of a material form; the latter excludes also the imperfection of the part, so that a hand can be called *this particular thing* in the first sense, but not in the second. Therefore, since the human soul is a part of human nature, it can be called *this particular thing* in the first sense, as being something subsistent; but not in the second, for in this sense the composite of body and soul is said to be *this particular thing*.

Reply Obj. 2. Aristotle wrote those words as expressing, not his own opinion, but the opinion of those who said that to understand is to be moved, as is clear from the context.[1] Or we may reply that to operate through itself belongs to what exists through itself. But for a thing to exist through itself, it suffices sometimes that it be not inherent, as an accident or a material form; even though it be part of something. Nevertheless, that is rightly said to subsist through itself which is neither inherent in the above sense, nor part of anything else. In this sense, the eye or the hand cannot be said to subsist through itself; nor can it for that reason be said to operate through itself. Hence the operation of the parts is through each part attributed to the whole. For we say that man sees with the eye, and feels with the hand, and not in the same sense as when we say that what is hot gives heat by its heat; for heat, strictly speaking, does not give heat. We may therefore say that the soul understands just as the eye sees; but it is more correct to say that man understands through the soul.

Reply Obj. 3. The body is necessary for the action of the intellect, not as its organ of action, but on the part of the object; for the phantasm[2] is to the intellect what color is to the sight. Neither does such a dependence on the body prove the intellect to be non-subsistent, or

1. 参见 *De An.*, I, 4 (408a 34).
2. phantasm: 幻想；幽灵；错觉

otherwise it would follow that an animal is non-subsistent simply because it requires external sensibles for sensation.

Third Article
WHETHER THE SOULS OF BRUTE ANIMALS ARE SUBSISTENT?

We proceed thus to the Third Article:—

Objection 1. It would seem that the souls of brute animals are subsistent. For man is of the same genus as other animals, and, as we have shown, the soul of man is subsistent. Therefore the souls of other animals are subsistent.

Obj. 2. Further, the relation of the sensitive power to sensible objects is like the relation of the intellectual power to intelligible objects. But the intellect, without the body, apprehends intelligible objects. Therefore the sensitive power, without the body, perceives sensible objects. Therefore, since the souls of brute animals are sensitive, they are subsistent, for the same reason that the human soul, which is intellectual, is subsistent.

Obj. 3. Further, the soul of brute animals moves the body. But the body is not a mover, but is moved. Therefore the soul of brute animals has an operation apart from the body.

On the contrary, Is what is written in the book *De Ecclesiasticis Dogmatibus: Man alone we believe to have a subsistent soul; whereas the souls of animals are not subsistent.*[1]

I answer that, The early philosophers[2] made no distinction between sense and intellect, and referred both to a corporeal principle, as has been said. Plato, however, drew a distinction between intellect and sense, but he referred both to an incorporeal principle, maintaining

---

1. 参见 Gennadius, *De Eccles. Dogm.*, XVI (PL 58, 984).
2. 参见 Empedocles, according to Aristotle, *De An.*, III, 3 (427a 21).

that sensing, like understanding, belongs to the soul as such.[1] From this it follows that even the souls of brute animals are subsistent.[2] But Aristotle held that, of the operations of the soul, understanding alone is performed without a corporeal organ.[3] On the other hand, sensation and the attendant operations of the sensitive soul are evidently accompanied with change in the body; and thus, in the act of vision, the pupil of the eye is affected by the likeness of color. So with the other senses. Hence it is clear that the sensitive soul has no *per se* operation of its own, and that every operation of the sensitive soul belongs to the composite. Therefore we conclude that as the souls of brute animals have no *per se* operations they are not subsistent. For the operation of anything follows the mode of its being.

Reply Obj. 1. Although man is of the same *genus* as other animals, he is of a different *species*. Now, specific difference is derived from the difference of form; nor does every difference of form necessarily imply a diversity of *genus*.

Reply Obj. 2. The relation of the sensitive power to the sensible object is in one way the same as that of the intellectual power to the intelligible object, in so far as each is in potentiality to its object. But in another way their relations differ, inasmuch as the impression of the sensible on the sense is accompanied with change in the body; so that when the intensity of the sensible is excessive, the sense is corrupted. This is a thing that never occurs in the case of the intellect. For an intellect that understands the highest of intelligible objects is more able afterwards to understand those that are lower.—If, however, in the process of intellectual operation the body is weary, this result is accidental, inasmuch as the intellect requires the operation of the

---

1. 参见 Cf. Nemesius, *De Nat. Hom.*, VI (PG 40, 637); Plato, *Theaetet.* (p. 184c). — Cf. also St. Augustine, *De Musica*, VI, 5 (PL 32, 1168).
2. 参见 Cf. Nemesius, *De Nat. Hom.*, II (PL 40, 582).
3. 参见 *De An.*, III, 4 (429a 24).

sensitive powers in the production of the phantasms.

Reply Obj. 3. A motive power is of two kinds. One, the appetitive power, which commands motion. The operation of this power in the sensitive soul is not without the body; for anger, joy and passions of a like nature are accompanied by some change in the body. The other motive power is that which executes motion in adapting the members for obeying the appetite; and the act of this power does not consist in moving, but in being moved. Whence it is clear that to move is not an act of the sensitive soul without the body.

Fourth Article
WHETHER THE SOUL IS MAN?

We proceed thus to the Fourth Article:—

Objection 1. It would seem that the soul is man. For it is written (*2 Cor.* iv. 16): *Though our outward man is corrupted, yet the inward man is renewed day by day.* But that which is within man is the soul. Therefore the soul is the inward man.

Obj. 2. Further, the human soul is a substance. But it is not a universal substance. Therefore it is a particular substance. Therefore it is a *hypostasis* or a person; and it can be only a human person. Therefore the soul is a man, for a human person is a man.

On the contrary, Augustine commends Varro as holding *that man is not the soul alone, nor the body alone, but both soul and body.*[1]

I answer that, The assertion, *the soul is a man*, can be taken in two senses. First, that man is a soul, though this particular man (Socrates, for instance) is not a soul, but composed of soul and body. I say this, because some held that the form alone belongs to the species,[2] while

---

1. 参见 *De Civit. Dei*, XIX, 3 (PL 41, 626).
2. 参见 Averroes, *In Metaph.*, VII, comm. 21; comm. 24 (VIII, 80v; 82v).—Cf. St. Thomas, *In Metaph.*, VII, lect. 9.

matter is part of the individual, and not of the species. This cannot be true, for to the nature of the species belongs what the definition signifies, and in natural things the definition does not signify the form only, but the form and the matter. Hence, in natural things the matter is part of the species; not, indeed, signate matter, which is the principle of individuation, but common matter. For just as it belongs to the nature of this particular man to be composed of this soul, of this flesh, and of these bones, so it belongs to the nature of man to be composed of soul, flesh, and bones; for whatever belongs in common to the substance of all the individuals contained under a given species must belong also to the substance of the species.

That *the soul is a man* may also be understood in this sense, namely, that this soul is this man. Now this could be held if it were supposed that the operation of the sensitive soul were proper to it without the body; because in that case all the operations which are attributed to man would belong only to the soul. But each thing is that which performs its own operations, and consequently that is man which performs the operations of a man. But it has been shown above that sensation is not the operation of the soul alone. Since, then, sensation is an operation of man, but not proper to the soul, it is clear that man is not only a soul, but something composed of soul and body.—Plato, through supposing that sensation was proper to the soul, could maintain man to be *a soul making use of a body*.[1]

Reply Obj. 1. According to the Philosopher, each thing seems to be chiefly what is most important in it.[2] Thus, what the governor of a state does, the state is said to do. In this way sometimes what is most important in man is said to be man: sometimes it is the intellectual part which, in accordance with truth, is called the *inward* man; and sometimes the sensitive part with the body is called man in the opinion

1. 参见 Cf. Nemesius, *De Nat. Hom.*, I (PG 40, 505).—Plato, *Alcib.* (p. 130c).
2. 参见 *Eth.*, IX, 8 (1168b 31).

of those who remain the slaves of sensible things. And this is called the *outward* man.

Reply Obj. 2. Not every particular substance is a hypostasis or a person, but that which has the complete nature of its species. Hence a hand, or a foot, is not called a hypostasis, or a person; nor, likewise, is the soul alone so called, since it is a part of the human species.

Fifth Article

WHETHER THE SOUL IS COMPOSED OF MATTER AND FORM?

We proceed thus to the Fifth Article:—

Objection 1. It would seem that the soul is composed of matter and form. For potentiality is opposed to actuality. Now, whatsoever things are in actuality participate in the First Act, which is God. It is by participation in God that all things are good, beings, and living things, as is clear from the teachings of Dionysius.[1] Therefore, whatsoever things are in potentiality participate in the first potentiality. But the first potentiality is primary matter. Therefore, since the human soul is, after a manner, in potentiality (which appears from the fact that sometimes a man is potentially understanding), it seems that the human soul must participate in primary matter, as a part of itself.

Obj. 2. Further, wherever the properties of matter are found, there matter is. But the properties of matter are found in the soul—namely, to be a subject, and to be changed. For the soul is subject to science, and virtue; and it changes from ignorance to knowledge and from vice to virtue. Therefore there is matter in the soul.[2]

Obj. 3. Further, things which have no matter have no cause of their

---

1. 参见 *De Div. Nom.*, V, 5 (PG 3, 820).
2. 参见 Cf. St. Bonaventure, *In II Sent.*, d. iii, pt. 1, a. 1, q, 1 (II, 89).

being, as the Philosopher says in *Metaph.* viii.[1] But the soul has a cause of its being, since it is created by God. Therefore the soul has matter.

Obj. 4. Further, what has no matter, and is only a form, is a pure act, and is infinite. But this belongs to God alone. Therefore the soul has matter.[2]

On the contrary, Augustine proves that the soul was made neither of corporeal matter, nor of spiritual matter.[3]

I answer that, The soul has no matter. We may consider this question in two ways. First, from the notion of a soul in general, for it belongs to the notion of a soul to be the form of a body. Now, either it is a form in its entirety, or by virtue of some part of itself. If in its entirety, then it is impossible that any part of it should be matter, if by matter we understand something purely potential; for a form, as such, is an act, and that which is purely potential cannot be part of an act, since potentiality is repugnant to actuality as being its opposite. If, however, it be a form by virtue of a part of itself, then we shall call that part the soul, and that matter, which it actualizes first, we shall call the *primary animate*.

Secondly, we may proceed from the specific notion of the human soul, inasmuch as it is intellectual. For it is clear that whatever is received into something is received according to the condition of the recipient. Now a thing is known in as far as its form is in the knower. But the intellectual soul knows a thing in its nature absolutely: for instance, it knows a stone absolutely as a stone; and therefore the form of a stone absolutely, as to its proper formal notion, is in the intellectual soul. Therefore the intellectual soul itself is an absolute form, and not something composed of matter and form. For if the

---

1. 参见 Aristotle, *Metaph.*, VII, 6 (1045b 4).
2. 参见 Cf. above, q. 50, a. 2; St. Bonaventure, *In I Sent.*, d. viii, pt. 2, a. 1. q. 2 (I, 167).
3. 参见 *De Genesi ad Litt.*, VII, 7; 8; 9 (PL 34, 359, 360).

intellectual soul were composed of matter and form, the forms of things would be received into it as individuals, and so it would only know the individual; just as it happens with the sensitive powers which receive forms in a corporeal organ. For matter is the principle by which forms are individuated. It follows, therefore, that the intellectual soul, and every intellectual substance which has knowledge of forms absolutely, is exempt from composition of matter and form.

Reply Obj. 1. The First Act is the universal principle of all acts, because It is infinite, *precontaining all things* in its power, as Dionysius says.[1] Therefore It is participated in by things, not as a part of themselves, but by diffusion of Its processions. Now as potentiality is receptive of act, it must be proportionate to act. But the acts received which proceed from the First Infinite Act, and are participations thereof, are diverse, so that there cannot be one potentiality which receives all acts, in the same way that there is one act from which all participated acts are derived; for then the receptive potentiality would equal the active potentiality of the First Act. Now the receptive potentiality in the intellectual soul is other than the receptive potentiality of primary matter, as appears from the diversity of the things received by each. For primary matter receives individual forms; whereas the intellect receives absolute forms. Hence the existence of such a potentiality in the intellectual soul does not prove that the soul is composed of matter and form.

Reply Obj. 2. To be a subject and to be changed belong to matter by reason of its being in potentiality. Just as, therefore, the potentiality of the intellect is one thing and the potentiality of primary matter another, so in each is there a different manner of subjection and change. For the intellect is subject to knowledge, and is changed from ignorance to knowledge, by reason of its being in potentiality with

---

1. 参见 *De Div. Nom.*, V, 9 (PG 3, 825).

regard to the intelligible species.

Reply Obj. 3. The form causes matter to be, and so does the agent; and so, the agent causes matter to be in so far as it changes it to the actuality of the form. A subsistent form, however, does not owe its being to some formal principle, nor has it a cause changing it from potentiality to act. So after the words quoted above, the Philosopher concludes that in things composed of matter and form *there is no other cause but that which moves from potentiality to act; while whatsoever things have no matter are truly beings in themselves.*[1]

Reply Obj. 4. Everything participated is compared to the participator as its act. But whatever created form be supposed to subsist *per se*, must have being by participation, for *even life*, or anything of that sort, is a *participator of being*, as Dionysius says.[2] Now participated being is limited by the capacity of the participator; so that God alone, Who is His own being, is pure act and infinite. But in intellectual substances, there is composition of actuality and potentiality, not, indeed, of matter and form, but of form and participated being. Therefore some say that they are composed of that *whereby they are* and that *which they are*;[3] for being itself is that by which a thing is.

Sixth Article
WHETHER THE HUMAN SOUL IS CORRUPTIBLE?

We proceed thus to the Sixth Article:—

Objection 1. It would seem that the human soul is corruptible. For those things that have a like beginning and process seemingly have a like end. But the beginning, by generation, of men is like that of animals, for they are made from the earth. And the process of life is

---

1. 参见 *Metaph.*, VII, 6 (1045b 21).
2. 参见 *De Div. Nom.*, V, 5 (PG 3, 820).
3. 参见 Cf. above, q. 50, a. 2, ad 3.

alike in both; because *all things breathe alike, and man hath nothing more than the beast*, as it is written (*Eccles.* iii. 19). Therefore, as the same text concludes, *the death of man and beast is one, and the condition of both is equal.* But the souls of brute animals are corruptible. Therefore the human soul too is corruptible.

Obj. 2. Further, whatever is out of nothing can return to nothingness, because the end should correspond to the beginning. But as it is written (*Wis.* ii. 2), *We are born of nothing*; and this is true, not only of the body, but also of the soul. Therefore, as is concluded in the same passage, *After this we shall be as if we had not been*, even as to our soul.

Obj. 3. Further, nothing is without its own proper operation. But the operation proper to the soul, which is to understand through a phantasm, cannot be without the body. For the soul understands nothing without a phantasm, and *there is no phantasm without the body*, as the Philosopher says.[1] Therefore the soul cannot survive the dissolution of the body.

On the contrary, Dionysius says that human souls owe to divine goodness that they are *intellectual*, and that they have *an incorruptible substantial life.*[2]

I answer that, We must assert that the intellectual principle which we call the human soul is incorruptible. For a thing may be corrupted in two ways—in itself and accidentally. Now it is impossible for any subsistent being to be generated or corrupted accidentally, that is, by the generation or corruption of something else. For generation and corruption belong to a thing in the same way that being belongs to it, which is acquired by generation and lost by corruption. Therefore, whatever has being in itself cannot be generated or corrupted except in itself; while things which do not subsist, such as accidents and material forms, acquire being or lose it through the generation or

---

1. 参见 Aristotle, *De An.*, I, 1 (403a 9).
2. 参见 *De Div. Nom.*, IV, 2 (PG 3, 696).

corruption of composites. Now it was shown above that the souls of brutes are not self-subsistent, whereas the human soul is, so that the souls of brutes are corrupted, when their bodies are corrupted, while the human soul could not be corrupted unless it were corrupted in itself. This is impossible, not only as regards the human soul, but also as regards anything subsistent that is a form alone. For it is clear that what belongs to a thing by virtue of the thing itself is inseparable from it. But being belongs to a form, which is an act, by virtue of itself. And thus, matter acquires actual being according as it acquires form; while it is corrupted so far as the form is separated from it. But it is impossible for a form to be separated from itself; and therefore it is impossible for a subsistent form to cease to exist.

Granted even that the soul were composed of matter and form, as some pretend,[1] we should nevertheless have to maintain that it is incorruptible. For corruption is found only where there is contrariety, since generation and corruption are from contraries and into contraries. Therefore the heavenly bodies, since they have no matter subject to contrariety, are incorruptible. Now there can be no contrariety in the intellectual soul; for it is a receiving subject according to the manner of its being, and those things which it receives are without contrariety. Thus, the notions even of contraries are not themselves contrary, since contraries belong to the same science. Therefore it is impossible for the intellectual soul to be corruptible.

Moreover we may take a sign of this from the fact that everything naturally aspires to being after its own manner. Now, in things that have knowledge, desire ensues upon knowledge. The senses indeed do not know being, except under the conditions of *here* and *now*, whereas the intellect apprehends being absolutely, and for all time; so that everything that has an intellect naturally desires always to exist. But a

1. 参见 Cf. above, a. 5 and q. 50, a. 2.

natural desire cannot be in vain. Therefore every intellectual substance is incorruptible.

Reply Obj. 1. Solomon reasons thus in the person of the foolish, as expressed in the words of *Wis.* ii. Therefore the saying that man and animals have a like beginning in generation is true of the body; for all animals alike are made of earth. But it is not true of the soul. For while the souls of brutes are produced by some power of the body, the human soul is produced by God. To signify this, it is written of other animals: *Let the earth bring forth the living soul* (*Gen.* i. 24); while of man it is written (*Gen.* ii. 7) that *He breathed into his face the breath of life.* And so in the last chapter of *Ecclesiastes* (xii. 7) it is concluded: *The dust returns into its earth from whence it was; and the spirit returns to God Who gave it.* Again, the process of life is alike as to the body, concerning which it is written (*Eccles.* iii. 19): *All things breathe alike*, and (*Wis.* ii. 2), *The breath in our nostrils is smoke.* But the process is not alike in the case of the soul, for man has understanding whereas animals do not. Hence it is false to say: *Man has nothing more than beasts.* Thus death comes to both alike as to the body, but not as to the soul.

Reply Obj. 2. As a thing can be created, not by reason of a passive potentiality, but only by reason of the active potentiality of the Creator, Who can produce something out of nothing, so when we say that a thing can be reduced to nothing, we do not imply in the creature a potentiality to non-being, but in the Creator the power of ceasing to sustain being. But a thing is said to be corruptible because there is in it a potentiality to non-being.

Reply Obj. 3. To understand through a phantasm is the proper operation of the soul by virtue of its union with the body. After separation from the body, it will have another mode of understanding, similar to other substances separated from bodies, as will appear later on.[1]

---

1. 参见 Q. 89, a. 1.

Seventh Article

WHETHER THE SOUL IS OF THE SAME SPECIES AS AN ANGEL?

We proceed thus to the Seventh Article:—

Objection 1. It would seem that the soul is of the same species as an angel. For each thing is ordained to its proper end by the nature of its species, whence is derived its inclination for that end. But the end of the soul is the same as that of an angel—namely, eternal happiness. Therefore they are of the same species.

Obj. 2. Further, the ultimate specific difference is the noblest, because it completes the nature of the species. But there is nothing nobler either in an angel or in the soul than their intellectual being. Therefore the soul and the angel agree in the ultimate specific difference. Therefore they belong to the same species.

Obj. 3. Further, it seems that the soul does not differ from an angel except in its union with the body. But as the body is outside the essence of the soul, it does not seem to belong to its species. Therefore the soul and an angel are of the same species.

On the contrary, Things which have different natural operations are of different species. But the natural operations of the soul and of an angel are different, since, as Dionysius says, *Angelic minds have simple and blessed intellects, not gathering their knowledge of divine things from visible things.*[1] Subsequently he says the contrary of this about the soul. Therefore the soul and an angel are not of the same species.

I answer that, Origen held that human souls and angels are all of the same species,[2] and this because he supposed that in these substances the difference of degree was accidental, resulting from their free

---

1. 参见 *De Div. Nom.*, VII, 2 (PG 3, 868).
2. 参见 *Peri Archon*, III, 5 (PG 11, 329).

choice,[1] as we have seen above.[2] But this cannot be, for in incorporeal substances there cannot be diversity of number without diversity of species and inequality of nature; because, as they are not composed of matter and form, but are subsistent forms, it is clear that there is necessarily among them a diversity in species. For a separate form cannot be understood otherwise than as one of a single species. Thus, supposing a separate whiteness to exist, it could only be one, for one whiteness does not differ from another except as in this or that subject. But diversity of species is always accompanied by diversity of nature. Thus, in the species of colors, one is more perfect than another; and the same applies to other species, because differences which divide a *genus* are contrary to one another. Contraries, however, are compared to one another as the perfect to the imperfect, since the *principle of contrariety is habit and privation*, as is written, *Metaph.* x.[3]

The same would follow if the aforesaid substances were composed of matter and form. For if the matter of one be distinct from the matter of another, it is required either that the form be the principle of the distinction of matter—that is to say, that the matter is distinct because of its relation to diverse forms, in which case there would still result a difference of species and an inequality of nature; or else that the matter is the principle of the distinction of forms. But one matter cannot be distinct from another, except by a distinction of quantity, which has no place in these incorporeal substances, such as an angel and the soul. Hence, it is not possible for the angel and the soul to be of the same species. How it is that there can be many souls of one species will be explained later.[4]

Reply Obj. 1. This argument is concerned with the proximate

1. 参见 *Op. cit.*, I, 6; 8; II, 9; III, 5 (PG 11, 166; 178; 229; 329).
2. 参见 Q. 47, a. 2.
3. 参见 Aristotle, *Metaph.*, IX, 4 (1055a 33).
4. 参见 Q. 76, a. 2, ad 1.

and natural end. Eternal happiness, however, is the ultimate and supernatural end.

Reply Obj. 2. The ultimate specific difference is the noblest because it is the most determinate, in the same way as actuality is nobler than potentiality. Thus, however, that which is intellectual is not the noblest, because it is indeterminate and common to many degrees of intellectuality; just as the sensible is common to many degrees of sensible being. Hence, just as all sensible things are not of one species, so neither are all intellectual beings of one species.

Reply Obj. 3. The body is not of the essence of the soul, but the soul, by nature of its essence, can be united to the body; so that, properly speaking, it is not even the soul, but rather the *composite*, which is in the species. And the very fact that the soul in a certain way requires the body for its operation proves that the soul is endowed with a grade of intellectuality inferior to that of an angel, who is not united to a body.

Question LXXVI
THE UNION OF BODY AND SOUL
(*In Eight Articles*)

WE now consider the union of the soul with the body, on which there are eight points for inquiry: (1) Whether the intellectual principle is united to the body as its form? (2) Whether the intellectual principle is multiplied numerically according to the number of bodies, or is there one intellect for all men? (3) Whether in a body, the form of which is an intellectual principle, there is some other soul? (4) Whether in that body there is any other substantial form? (5) Of the qualities required in the body of which the intellectual principle is the form? (6) Whether the intellectual soul is joined to the body by means of accidental dispositions? (7) Whether the intellectual soul is united to such a body by means of another body? (8) Whether the soul is wholly in each part of the body?

First Article
WHETHER THE INTELLECTUAL PRINCIPLE IS UNITED TO THE BODY AS ITS FORM?

We proceed thus to the First Article:—

Objection 1. It seems that the intellectual principle is not united to the body as its form. For the Philosopher says that *the intellect is separate*, and that it is not the act of any body.[1] Therefore it is not united to the

1. 参见 *De An.*, III, 4 (429b 5).

body as its form.

Obj. 2. Further, every form is determined according to the nature of the matter of which it is the form; otherwise no proportion would be required between matter and form. Therefore if the intellect were united to the body as its form, since every body has a determinate nature, it would follow that the intellect has a determinate nature; and thus, it would not be capable of knowing all things, as is clear from what has been said.[1] This is contrary to the nature of the intellect. Therefore the intellect is not united to the body as its form.

Obj. 3. Further, whatever receptive power is an act of a body, receives a form materially and individually; for what is received must be received according to the condition of the receiver. But the form of the thing understood is not received into the intellect materially and individually, but rather immaterially and universally. Otherwise, the intellect would not be capable of knowing immaterial and universal objects, but only individuals, like the senses. Therefore the intellect is not united to the body as its form.

Obj. 4. Further, power and action have the same subject, for the same subject is what can, and does, act. But intellectual action is not the action of a body, as appears from the above.[2] Therefore neither is the intellectual power a power of the body. But a virtue or a power cannot be more abstract or more simple than the essence from which the virtue or power is derived. Therefore, neither is the substance of the intellect the form of a body.

Obj. 5. Further, whatever has being in itself is not united to the body as its form, because a form is that *by which* a thing exists; which means that the very being of a form does not belong to the form by itself. But the intellectual principle has being in itself and is subsistent, as was

---

1. 参见 Q. 75, a. 2.
2. 同上

said above.[1] Therefore it is not united to the body as its form.

Obj. 6. Further, whatever exists in a thing by reason of its nature exists in it always. But to be united to matter belongs to the form by reason of its nature, because form is the act of matter, not by any accidental quality, but by its own essence; or otherwise matter and form would not make a thing substantially one, but only accidentally one. Therefore, a form cannot be without its own proper matter. But the intellectual principle, since it is incorruptible, as was shown above,[2] remains separate from the body, after the dissolution of the body. Therefore the intellectual principle is not united to the body as its form.

On the contrary, According to the Philosopher in *Metaph*. viii., difference is derived from the form.[3] But the difference which constitutes man is *rational*, which is said of man because of his intellectual principle. Therefore the intellectual principle is the form of man.

I answer that, We must assert that the intellect which is the principle of intellectual operation is the form of the human body. For that whereby primarily anything acts is a form of the thing to which the act is attributed. For instance, that whereby a body is primarily healed is health, and that whereby the soul knows primarily is knowledge; hence health is a form of the body, and knowledge is a form of the soul. The reason for this is that nothing acts except so far as it is in act; and so, a thing acts by that whereby it is in act. Now it is clear that the first thing by which the body lives is the soul. And as life appears through various operations in different degrees of living things, that whereby we primarily perform each of all these vital actions is the soul. For the soul is the primary principle of our nourishment, sensation, and local

1. 参见 Q. 75, a. 2.
2. 参见 Q. 75, a. 6.
3. 参见 *Metaph.*, VII, 2 (1043a 19).

movement; and likewise of our understanding. Therefore this principle by which primarily we understand, whether it be called the intellect or the intellectual soul, is the form of the body. This is the demonstration used by Aristotle.[1]

But if anyone say that the intellectual soul is not the form of the body,[2] he must explain how it is that this action of understanding is the action of this particular man; for each one is conscious that it is he himself who understands. Now an action may be attributed to anyone in three ways, as is clear from the Philosopher.[3] For a thing is said to move or act, either by virtue of its whole self, for instance, as a physician heals; or by virtue of a part, as a man sees by his eye; or through an accidental quality, as when we say that something that is white builds, because it is accidental to the builder to be white. So when we say that Socrates or Plato understands, it is clear that this is not attributed to him accidentally, since it is ascribed to him as man, which is predicated of him essentially. We must therefore say either that Socrates understands by virtue of his whole self, as Plato maintained, holding that man is an intellectual soul;[4] or that the intellect is a part of Socrates. The first cannot stand, as was shown above, because it is one and the same man who is conscious both that he understands and that he senses.[5] But one cannot sense without a body, and therefore the body must be some part of man. It follows therefore that the intellect by which Socrates understands is a part of Socrates, so that it is in some way united to the body of Socrates.

As to this union, the Commentator held that it is through the

---

1. 参见 *De An.*, II, 2 (414a 12).
2. 参见 Cf. St. Albert, *Summa de Creatur.*, II, q. 4, a. 1 (XXXV, 34).—Cf. also Avicenna, *De An.*, I, 1 (11b); V, 4 (24va).
3. 参见 *Phys.*, V, 1 (224a 31).
4. 参见 Cf. above, q. 75, a. 4.
5. 同上

intelligible species,[1] as having a double subject, namely, the possible intellect and the phantasms which are in the corporeal organs. Thus, through the intelligible species, the possible intellect *is linked* to the body of this or that particular man. But this link or union does not sufficiently explain the fact that the act of the intellect is the act of Socrates. This can be clearly seen from comparison with the sensitive power, from which Aristotle proceeds to consider things relating to the intellect. For the relation of phantasms to the intellect is like the relation of colors to the sense of sight, as he says *De Anima* iii.[2] Therefore, just as the species of colors are in the sight, so the species of phantasms are in the possible intellect. Now it is clear that because the colors, the likenesses of which are in the sight, are on a wall, the action of seeing is not attributed to the wall; for we do not say that the wall sees, but rather that it is seen. Therefore, from the fact that the species of phantasms are in the possible intellect, it does not follow that Socrates, in whom are the phantasms, understands, but that he or his phantasms are understood.

Some,[3] however, have tried to maintain that the intellect is united to the body as its mover, and hence that the intellect and body form one thing in such a way that the act of the intellect could be attributed to the whole. This is, however, absurd for many reasons. First, because the intellect does not move the body except through the appetite, whose movement presupposes the operation of the intellect. The reason therefore why Socrates understands is not because he is moved by his intellect, but rather, contrariwise, he is moved by his intellect because he understands.—Secondly, because, since Socrates is an individual in a nature of one essence composed of matter and form,

---

1. 参见 *In De An.*, III, comm. 5 (VI, 164v).
2. 参见 Aristotle, *De An.*, III, 7 (431a 14).
3. 参见 Cf. William of Auvergne, *De An.*, I, 7 (II. Suppl., 72); VI. 35 (II, Suppl., 194).

if the intellect be not the form, it follows that it must be outside the essence, and then the intellect is to the whole Socrates as a motor to the thing moved. But to understand is an action that remains in the agent, and does not pass into something else, as does the action of heating. Therefore the action of understanding cannot be attributed to Socrates for the reason that he is moved by his intellect.—Thirdly, because the action of a mover is never attributed to the thing moved, except as to an instrument, just as the action of a carpenter is attributed to a saw. Therefore, if understanding is attributed to Socrates as the action of his mover, it follows that it is attributed to him as to an instrument. This is contrary to the teaching of the Philosopher, who holds that understanding is not possible through a corporeal instrument.[1]—Fourthly, because, although the action of a part be attributed to the whole, as the action of the eye is attributed to a man, yet it is never attributed to another part, except perhaps accidentally; for we do not say that the hand sees because the eye sees. Therefore, if the intellect and Socrates are united in the above manner, the action of the intellect cannot be attributed to Socrates. If, however, Socrates be a whole composed of a union of the intellect with whatever else belongs to Socrates, but with the supposition that the intellect is united to the other parts of Socrates only as a mover, it follows that Socrates is not one absolutely, and consequently neither a being absolutely, for a thing is a being according as it is one.

There remains, therefore, no other explanation than that given by Aristotle—namely, that this particular man understands because the intellectual principle is his form.[2] Thus from the very operation of the intellect it is made clear that the intellectual principle is united to the body as its form.

The same can be clearly shown from the nature of the human

---

1. 参见 *De An.*, III, 4 (429a 26).
2. 参见 *Op. cit.*, II, 2 (414a 12).—Cf. *C. G.*, II, 59.

species. For the nature of each thing is shown by its operation. Now the proper operation of man as man is to understand, for it is in this that he surpasses all animals. Whence Aristotle concludes that the ultimate happiness of man must consist in this operation as properly belonging to him.[1] Man must therefore derive his species from that which is the principle of this operation. But the species of each thing is derived from its form. It follows therefore that the intellectual principle is the proper form of man.

But we must observe that the nobler a form is, the more it rises above corporeal matter, the less it is subject to matter, and the more it excels matter by its power and its operation. Hence we find that the form of a mixed body has an operation not caused by its elemental qualities. And the higher we advance in the nobility of forms, the more we find that the power of the form excels the elementary matter; as the vegetative soul excels the form of the metal, and the sensitive soul excels the vegetative soul. Now the human soul is the highest and noblest of forms. Therefore, in its power it excels corporeal matter by the fact that it has an operation and a power in which corporeal matter has no share whatever. This power is called the intellect.

It is well to remark, furthermore, that if anyone held that the soul is composed of matter and form,[2] it would follow that in no way could the soul be the form of the body. For since form is an act, and matter is being only in potentiality, that which is composed of matter and form cannot in its entirety be the form of another. But if it is a form by virtue of some part of itself, then that part which is the form we call the soul, and that of which it is the form we call the *primary animate*, as was said above.[3]

---

1. 参见 *Eth.*, X, 7 (1177a 17).
2. 参见 Cf. above, q. 75, a. 5; q. 50, a. 2.
3. 参见 Q. 75, a. 5.

Reply Obj. 1. As the Philosopher says,[1] the highest natural form (namely, the human soul) to which the consideration of the natural philosopher is directed is indeed separate, but it exists in matter. He proves this from the fact that *man and the sun generate man from matter.* It is separate according to its intellectual power, because an intellectual power is not the power of a corporeal organ, as the power of seeing is the act of the eye; for understanding is an act which cannot be performed by a corporeal organ, as can the act of seeing. But it exists in matter in so far as the soul itself, to which this power belongs, is the form of the body, and the term of human generation. And so the Philosopher says that *the intellect is separate,*[2] because it is not the power of a corporeal organ.

From this it is clear how to answer the Second and Third objections. For in order that man may be able to understand all things by means of his intellect, and that his intellect may understand all things immaterial and universal, it is sufficient that the intellectual power be not the act of the body.

Reply Obj. 4. The human soul, by reason of its perfection, is not a form immersed in matter, or entirely embraced by matter. Therefore there is nothing to prevent some power of the soul from not being the act of the body, although the soul is essentially the form of the body.

Reply Obj. 5. The soul communicates that being in which it subsists to the corporeal matter, out of which and the intellectual soul there results one being; so that the being of the whole composite is also the being of the soul. This is not the case with other non-subsistent forms. For this reason the human soul retains its own being after the dissolution of the body; whereas it is not so with other forms.

Reply Obj. 6. To be united to the body belongs to the soul by reason of itself, just as it belongs to a light body by reason of itself to be

1. 参见 *Phys.*, II, 2 (194b 12).
2. 参见 *De An.*, III, 4 (429b 5).

raised up. And just as a light body remains light, when removed from its proper place, retaining meanwhile an aptitude and an inclination for its proper place, so the human soul retains its proper being when separated from the body, having an aptitude and a natural inclination to be united to the body.

Second Article
WHETHER THE INTELLECTUAL PRINCIPLE IS MULTIPLIED ACCORDING TO THE NUMBER OF BODIES?

We proceed thus to the Second Article:—

Objection 1. It would seem that the intellectual principle is not multiplied according to the number of bodies, but that there is one intellect in all men. For an immaterial substance is not multiplied numerically within one species. But the human soul is an immaterial substance, since it is not composed of matter and form, as was shown above.[1] Therefore there are not many human souls in one species. But all men are of one species. Therefore there is but one intellect in all men.

Obj. 2. Further, when the cause is removed, the effect is also removed. Therefore, if human souls were multiplied according to the number of bodies, it would follow that if the bodies were removed, the number of souls would not remain, but from all the souls there would be but a single remainder. This is heretical, for it would do away with the distinction of rewards and punishments.

Obj. 3. Further, if my intellect is distinct from your intellect, my intellect is an individual, and so is yours; for individuals are things which differ in number but agree in one species.[2] Now whatever is received into anything must be received according to the condition

---

1. 参见 Q. 75, a. 5.
2. 参见 Cf. Averroes, *In De An.*, III, comm. 5 (VI, 166r).

of the receiver. Therefore the species of things would be received individually into my intellect, and also into yours; which is contrary to the nature of the intellect, which knows universals.

Obj. 4. Further, the thing understood is in the intellect which understands. If, therefore, my intellect is distinct from yours, what is understood by me must be distinct from what is understood by you; and consequently it will be reckoned *as something individual*, and be only *potentially something understood.*[1] Hence, the common intention will have to be abstracted from both, since from things which are diverse something intelligible and common to them may be abstracted. But this is contrary to the nature of the intellect, for then the intellect would not seem to be distinct from the imagination. It seems to follow, therefore, that there is one intellect in all men.

Obj. 5. Further, when the disciple receives knowledge from the teacher, it cannot be said that the teacher's knowledge begets knowledge in the disciple, because then knowledge too would be an active form, such as heat is; which is clearly false. It seems, therefore, that the same individual knowledge which is in the teacher is communicated to the disciple.[2] This cannot be, unless there is one intellect in both. Seemingly, therefore, the intellect of the disciple and teacher is but one; and, consequently, the same applies to all men.

Obj. 6. Further, Augustine says: *If I were to say that there are many human souls, I should laugh at my self.*[3] But the soul seems to be one chiefly because of the intellect. Therefore there is one intellect of all men.

On the contrary, The Philosopher says that the relation of universal causes to what is universal is like the relation of particular causes to

---

1. 参见 Cf. Averroes, *In De An.*, III, comm. 5 (VI, 163v–164r).
2. 同上 (VI. 166rv).
3. 参见 *De Quant. An.*, XXXII (PL 32, 1073).

individuals.[1] But it is impossible that a soul, one in species, should belong to animals of different species. Therefore it is impossible that one individual intellectual soul should belong to several individuals.

I answer that, It is absolutely impossible for one intellect to belong to all men. This is clear if, as Plato maintained, man is the intellect itself.[2] For if Socrates and Plato have one intellect, it would follow that Socrates and Plato are one man, and that they are not distinct from each other, except by something outside the essence of each. The distinction between Socrates and Plato would then not be other than that of one man with a tunic and another with a cloak; which is quite absurd.

It is likewise clear that this is impossible if, according to the opinion of Aristotle, it is supposed that the intellect is a part or a power of the soul which is the form of man.[3] For it is impossible for many distinct individuals to have one form, just as it is impossible for them to have one being. For the form is the principle of being.

Again, this is clearly impossible, whatever one may hold as to the manner of the union of the intellect to this or that man. For it is manifest that, if there is one principal agent, and two instruments, we can say without qualification that there is one agent but several actions; as when one man touches several things with his two hands, there will be one who touches, but two contacts. If, on the contrary, we suppose one instrument and several principal agents, we can say that there are several agents, but one act; for example, if there be many pulling a ship by means of a rope, those who pull will be many, but the pulling will be one. If, however, there is one principal agent, and one instrument, we say that there is one agent and one action; as when the smith strikes with one hammer, there is one striker and

---

1. 参见 *Phys.*, II, 3 (195b 26).
2. 参见 Cf. above, q. 75, a. 4.
3. 参见 *De An.*, II, 2 (414a 13) ; 3 (414a 32).

one stroke. Now it is clear that no matter how the intellect is united or joined to this or that man, the intellect has the primacy among all the other things which pertain to man, for the sensitive powers obey the intellect, and are at its service. So if we suppose two men to have two intellects and one sense,—for instance, if two men had one eye,—there would be two seers, but one seeing. But if the intellect is held to be one, no matter how diverse may be all those things which the intellect uses as instruments, it is in no way possible to say that Socrates and Plato are more than one understanding man. And if to this we add that to understand, which is the act of the intellect, is not produced by any organ other than the intellect itself, it will further follow that there is but one agent and one action; in other words, all men are but one "understander," and have but one act of understanding,—I mean, of course, in relation to one and the same intelligible object.

Now, it would be possible to distinguish my intellectual action from yours by the distinction of the phantasms—because there is one phantasm of a stone in me, and another in you—if the phantasm itself, according as it is one thing in me and another in you, were a form of the possible intellect. For the same agent produces diverse actions through diverse forms. Thus, through the diverse forms in things in relation to the same eye, there are diverse "seeings." But the phantasm itself is not the form of the possible intellect; the intelligible species abstracted from phantasms is such a form. Now in one intellect, from different phantasms of the same species, only one intelligible species is abstracted; as appears in one man, in whom there may be different phantasms of a stone, and yet from all of them only one intelligible species of a stone is abstracted, by which the intellect of that one man, by one operation, understands the nature of a stone, notwithstanding the diversity of phantasms. Therefore, if there were one intellect for all men, the diversity of phantasms in this man and in that would not cause a diversity of intellectual operation in this man and that man, as the Commentator imagines.[1] It follows, therefore, that it is altogether impossible and inappropriate to posit one intellect for all men.

Reply Obj. 1. Although the intellectual soul, like the angel, has no matter from which it is produced, yet it is the form of a certain matter; in which it is unlike an angel. Therefore, according to the division of matter, there are many souls of one species; while it is quite impossible for many angels to be of one species.

Reply Obj. 2. Everything has unity in the same way that it has being, and consequently we must judge of the multiplicity of a thing as we judge of its being. Now it is clear that the intellectual soul is according to its very being united to the body as its form. And yet, after the dissolution of the body, the intellectual soul retains its own being. In like manner, the multiplicity of souls is in proportion to the multiplicity of bodies; and yet, after the dissolution of the bodies, the souls remain multiplied in their being.

Reply Obj. 3. The individuality of the understanding being, or of the species whereby it understands, does not exclude the understanding of universals; or otherwise, since separate intellects are subsistent substances, and consequently individual, they could not understand universals. But it is the materiality of the knower, and of the species whereby he knows, that impedes the knowledge of the universal. For as every action is according to the mode of the form by which the agent acts, as heating is according to the mode of the heat, so knowledge is according to the mode of the species by which the knower knows. Now it is clear that the common nature becomes distinct and multiplied by reason of the individuating principles which come from the matter. Therefore if the form, which is the means of knowledge, is material —that is, not abstracted from material conditions—its likeness to the nature of a species or genus will be according to the

1. 参见 *In De An.*, III, comm. 5 (VI, 166v).

distinction and multiplication of that nature by means of individuating principles; so that the knowledge of the nature in its community will be impossible. But if the species be abstracted from the conditions of individual matter, there will be a likeness of the nature without those things which make it distinct and multiplied. And thus there will be knowledge of the universal. Nor does it matter, as to this particular point, whether there be one intellect or many; because, even if there were but one, it would necessarily be an individual intellect, and the species whereby it understands, an individual species.

Reply Obj. 4. Whether the intellect be one or many, what is understood is one. For what is understood is in the intellect, not in itself, but according to its likeness; for *the stone is not in the soul, but its likeness is*, as is said *De Anima* iii.[1] Yet it is the stone which is understood, not the likeness of the stone, except by a reflection of the intellect on itself. Otherwise, the objects of sciences would not be things, but only intelligible species. Now it is possible for different things, according to different forms, to be likened to the same thing. And since knowledge is begotten according to the assimilation of the knower to the thing known, it follows that the same thing can be known by several knowers; as is apparent in regard to the senses, for several see the same color by means of diverse likenesses. In the same way several intellects understand one thing. But there is this difference, according to the opinion of Aristotle,[2] between the sense and the intellect—that a thing is perceived by the sense according to that disposition which it has outside the soul—that is, in its individuality; whereas, though the nature of the thing understood is outside the soul, yet its mode of being outside the soul is not the mode of being according to which it is known. For the common nature is understood as apart from the individuating principles; whereas such is not its

1. 参见 Aristotle, *De An.*, III, 8 (431b 29).
2. 同上 (432a 2).

mode of being outside the soul. (But according to the opinion of Plato, the thing understood exists outside the soul in the same way as it is understood.[1] For Plato supposed that the natures of things exist separate from matter.)

Reply Obj. 5. One knowledge exists in the disciple and another in the teacher. How it is caused will be shown later on.[2]

Reply Obj. 6. Augustine denies such a plurality of souls as would involve a denial of their communication in the one nature of the species.

Third Article

WHETHER BESIDES THE INTELLECTUAL SOUL THERE ARE IN MAN OTHER SOULS ESSENTIALLY DIFFERENT FROM ONE ANOTHER?

We proceed thus to the Third Article:—

Objection 1. It would seem that besides the intellectual soul there are in man other souls essentially different from one another, namely, the sensitive soul and the nutritive soul. For corruptible and incorruptible are not of the same substance. But the intellectual soul is incorruptible, whereas the other souls, namely, the sensitive and the nutritive, are corruptible, as was shown above.[3] Therefore in man the essence of the intellectual soul[4], the sensitive soul and the nutritive soul[5], cannot be the same.

Obj. 2. Further, if it be said that the sensitive soul in man is incorruptible, against this is the dictum that the *corruptible and the*

---

1. 参见 Cf. above, q. 6, a. 4.
2. 参见 Q. 117, a. 1.
3. 参见 Q. 75, a. 6.
4. the intellectual soul: 灵魂
5. the nutritive soul: 生魂

incorruptible differ generically, according to the Philosopher in *Metaph*. x.[1] But the sensitive soul in the horse, the lion, and other brute animals, is corruptible. If, therefore, in man it be incorruptible, the sensitive soul[2] in man and brute animals will not be of the same *genus*. Now, an animal is so called because it has a sensitive soul; and, therefore, *animal* will not be one genus common to man and other animals, which is absurd.

Obj. 3. Further, the Philosopher says that the embryo is an animal before it is a man.[3] But this would be impossible if the essence of the sensitive soul were the same as that of the intellectual soul; for an animal is such by its sensitive soul, while a man is a man by the intellectual soul. Therefore in man the essence of the sensitive soul is not the same as the essence of the intellectual soul.

Obj. 4. Further, the Philosopher says in *Metaph*. viii., that the genus is taken from the matter, and difference from the form.[4] But *rational*, which is the difference constituting man, is taken from the intellectual soul; while he is called *animal* by reason of his having a body animated by a sensitive soul. Therefore the intellectual soul is compared to the body animated by a sensitive soul as form to matter. Therefore in man the intellectual soul is not essentially the same as the sensitive soul, but presupposes it as a material subject.

On the contrary, It is said in the book *De Ecclesiasticis Dogmatibus*: *Nor do we say that there are two souls in one man, as James and other Syrians write,—one, animal, by which the body is animated, and which is mingled with the blood; the other, spiritual, which obeys the reason; but we say that it is one and the same soul in man which both gives life to the body by being united to it*,

1. 参见 Aristotle, *Metaph*., IX, 10 (1059a 10).
2. the sensitive soul: 觉魂
3. 参见 *De Gener. Anim*., II, 3 (736a 35).
4. 参见 *Metaph*., VII, 2 (1043a 5; a 19); cf. *op. cit*., VI, 12 (1038a 6).

and orders itself by its own reason.[1]

I answer that, Plato held that there were several souls in one body, distinct even according to organs. To these souls he referred the different vital actions, saying that the nutritive power is in the liver, the concupiscible in the heart, and the knowing power in the brain.[2] Which opinion is rejected by Aristotle with reference to those parts of the soul which use corporeal organs.[3] His reason is that in those animals which continue to live when they have been divided, in each part are observed the operations of the soul, such as those of sense and appetite. Now this would not be the case if the various principles of the soul's operations were essentially diverse in their distribution through the various parts of the body. But with regard to the intellectual part, Aristotle seems to leave it in doubt whether it be *only logically* distinct from the other parts of the soul, *or also locally.*

The opinion of Plato could be maintained if, as he held, the soul were united to the body, not as its form, but as its mover. For nothing incongruous is involved if the same movable thing be moved by several movers; and still less if it be moved according to its various parts. If we suppose, however, that the soul is united to the body as its form, it is quite impossible for several essentially different souls to be in one body. This can be made clear by three reasons.

In the first place, an animal in which there were several souls would not be absolutely one. For nothing is absolutely one except by one form, by which a thing has being; because a thing has both being and unity from the same source, and therefore things which are denominated by various forms are not absolutely one; as, for

---

1. 参见 Gennadius, *De Eccles. Dogm.*, XV (PL 58, 984).—Cf. Pseudo-Augustine (Alcher of Clairvaux), *De Spir. et An.*, 48 (PL 40, 814).
2. 参见 Cf. Averroes, *In De An.*, I, comm. 90 (VI, 125v).—Cf. also Plato, *Timaeus* (p. 69e).
3. 参见 *De An.*, II, 2 (413b 13).

instance, *a white man*. If, therefore, man were *living* by one form, the vegetative soul, and *animal* by another form, the sensitive soul, and *man* by another form, the intellectual soul, it would follow that man is not absolutely one. Thus Aristotle argues in *Metaph*. viii., against Plato, that if the Idea of an animal is distinct from the Idea of a biped, then a biped animal is not absolutely one.[1] For this reason, against those who hold that there are several souls in the body, he asks, *what contains them?*—that is, what makes them one?[2] It cannot be said that they are united by the unity of the body; because it is rather the soul that contains the body and makes it one, than the reverse.

Secondly, this is proved to be impossible by the mode in which one thing is predicated of another. Those things which are derived from various forms are predicated of one another either accidentally (if the forms are not ordered one to another, as when we say that something white is sweet), or essentially, in the second mode of essential predication (if the forms are ordered one to another, as when the subject enters into the definition of the predicate; and thus a surface is presupposed for color, so that if we say that a body with a surface is colored, we have the second mode of essential predication). Therefore, if we have one form by which a thing is an animal, and another form by which it is a man, it follows either that one of these two things could not be predicated of the other, except accidentally (supposing these two forms not to be ordered to one another), or that one would be predicated of the other according to the second mode of essential predication, if one soul be presupposed to the other. But both of these consequences are clearly false. For *animal* is predicated of man essentially and not accidentally, and man is not part of the definition of an animal, but the other way about. Therefore it is of necessity by the same form that a thing is animal and man. Otherwise man would

1. 参见 *Metaph*., VII, 6 (1045a 14).
2. 参见 *De An*., I, 5 (411b 6).

not really be the being which is an animal, so that animal could be essentially predicated of man.

Thirdly, this is shown to be impossible by the fact that when one operation of the soul is intense it impedes another; which could never be the case unless the principle of such actions were essentially one.

We must therefore conclude that the sensitive soul, the intellectual soul and the nutritive soul are in man numerically one and the same soul. This can easily be explained, if we consider the differences of species and forms. For we observe that the species and forms of things differ from one another as the perfect and the less perfect; just as in the order of things, the animate are more perfect than the inanimate, animals more perfect than plants, and man more perfect than brute animals. Furthermore, in each of these genera there are various degrees. For this reason Aristotle compares the species of things to numbers, which differ in species by the addition or subtraction of unity.[1] He also compares the various souls to the species of figures, one of which contains another, as a pentagon contains and exceeds a tetragon.[2] Thus the intellectual soul contains virtually whatever belongs to the sensitive soul of brute animals, and to the nutritive soul of plants. Therefore, just as a surface which is of a pentagonal shape is not tetragonal by one shape, and pentagonal by another — since a tetragonal shape would be superfluous, as being contained in the pentagonal — so neither is Socrates a man by one soul, and an animal by another; but by one and the same soul he is both animal and man.

Reply Obj. 1. The sensitive soul is incorruptible, not by reason of its being sensitive, but by reason of its being intellectual. When, therefore, a soul is sensitive only, it is corruptible; but when the intellectual is joined to the sensitive, then the sensitive soul is incorruptible. For

1. 参见 *Metaph.*, VII, 3 (1043b 34).
2. 参见 *De An.*, II, 3 (414b 28).

although the sensitive does not give incorruptibility, yet it cannot deprive the intellectual of its incorruptibility.

Reply Obj. 2. Not forms, but composites, are classified either generically or specifically. Now man is corruptible like other animals. And so the difference of corruptible and incorruptible which is on the part of the forms does not involve a generic difference between man and the other animals.

Reply Obj. 3. The embryo has first of all a soul which is merely sensitive, and when this is removed, it is supplanted by a more perfect soul, which is both sensitive and intellectual, as will be shown farther on.[1]

Reply Obj. 4. We must not base the diversity of natural things on the various logical notions or intentions which follow from our manner of understanding; for reason can apprehend one and the same thing in various ways. Therefore since, as we have said, the intellectual soul contains virtually what belongs to the sensitive soul, and something more, reason can consider separately what belongs to the power of the sensitive soul, as something imperfect and material. And because it observes that this is something common to man and to other animals, it forms thence the notion of the *genus*. On the other hand, that wherein the intellectual soul exceeds the sensitive soul, the reason takes as formal and perfecting; and thence it gathers the *difference* of man.

Fourth Article
WHETHER IN MAN THERE IS ANOTHER FORM BESIDES THE INTELLECTUAL SOUL?

We proceed thus to the Fourth Article:—

Objection 1. It would seem that in man there is another form besides

---

1. 参见 Q. 118, a. 2, ad 2.

the intellectual soul. For the Philosopher says that *the soul is the act of a physical body which has life potentially.*[1] Therefore the soul is to the body as a form to matter. But the body has a substantial form by which it is a body. Therefore some other substantial form in the body precedes the soul.

Obj. 2. Further, man moves himself as every animal does. *Now everything that moves itself is divided into two parts, of which one moves, and the other is moved*, as the Philosopher proves.[2] But the part which moves is the soul. Therefore the other part must be such that it can be moved. But primary matter cannot be moved since it is a being only potentially,[3] while everything that is moved is a body. Therefore in man and in every animal there must be another substantial form, by which the body is constituted.

Obj. 3. Further, the order of forms depends on their relation to primary matter; for *before* and *after* apply by comparison to some beginning. Therefore, if there were not in man some other substantial form besides the rational soul, and if the rational soul[4] inhered immediately to primary matter, it would follow that it ranks among the most imperfect forms which inhere to matter immediately.

Obj. 4. Further, the human body is a mixed body. Now mixture does not result from matter alone; for then we should have mere corruption. Therefore the forms of the elements must remain in a mixed body; and these are substantial forms. Therefore in the human body there are other substantial forms besides the intellectual soul.

On the contrary, Of one thing there is but one substantial being. But the substantial form gives substantial being. Therefore of one thing there is but one substantial form. But the soul is the substantial

---

1. 参见 *De An.*, II, 1 (412a 28).
2. 参见 Aristotle, *Phys.*, VIII, 5 (257b 12).
3. 参见 *Op. cit.*, V, 1 (225a 25).
4. the rational soul: 智魂；灵魂

form of man. Therefore it is impossible that there be in man another substantial form besides the intellectual soul.

I answer that, If we supposed that the intellectual soul is not united to the body as its form, but only as its mover, as the Platonists maintain, it would necessarily follow that in man there is another substantial form by which the body is established in its being as movable by the soul.[1] If, however, the intellectual soul is united to the body as its substantial form, as we have said above, it is impossible for another substantial form besides the intellectual soul to be found in man.

In order to make this evident, we must consider that the substantial form differs from the accidental form in this, that the accidental form does not make a thing *to be absolutely*, but *to be such*, as heat does not make a thing to be absolutely, but only to be hot. Therefore by the coming of the accidental form a thing is not said to be made or generated absolutely, but to be made such, or to be in some particular disposition; and in like manner, when an accidental form is removed, a thing is said to be corrupted, not absolutely, but relatively. But the substantial form gives being absolutely, and hence by its coming a thing is said to be generated absolutely, and by its removal to be corrupted absolutely. For this reason, the old natural philosophers, who held that primary matter was some actual being—for instance, fire or air, or something of that sort—maintained that nothing is generated absolutely, or corrupted absolutely, but that *every becoming is nothing but an alteration*, as we read *Physics* i.[2] Therefore, if besides the intellectual soul there pre-existed in matter another substantial form by which the subject of the soul were made an actual being, it would follow that the soul does not give being absolutely, and consequently that it is not the substantial form; and so at the advent of the soul

---

1. 参见 Cf. Alex. of Hales, *Summa Theol.*, II, I, no. 344 (II, 419).
2. 参见 Aristotle, *Phys.*, I, 4 (187a 30).

there would not be absolute generation, nor at its removal absolute corruption. All of which is clearly false.

Whence we must conclude that there is no other substantial form in man besides the intellectual soul; and that just as the soul contains virtually the sensitive and nutritive souls, so does it contain virtually all inferior forms, and does alone whatever the imperfect forms do in other things. The same is to be said of the sensitive soul in brute animals, and of the nutritive soul in plants, and universally of all more perfect forms in relation to the imperfect.

Reply Obj. 1. Aristotle does not say that the soul is the act of a body only, but *the act of a physical organic body which has life potentially*; and that this potentiality *does not exclude the soul.*[1] Whence it is clear that in the being of which the soul is called the act, the soul itself is included; as when we say that heat is the act of what is hot, and light of what is lucid. And this means, not that the lucid is lucid in separation from light, but that it is lucid through light. In like manner, the soul is said to be the *act of a body*, etc., because it is by the soul that the body is a body, and is organic, and has life potentially. When the first act is said to be *in potentiality*, this is to be understood in relation to the second act, which is operation. Now such a potentiality *does not remove*—that is, does not exclude—the soul.

Reply Obj. 2. The soul does not move the body by its essence, as the form of the body, but by the motive power, whose act presupposes that the body is already actualized by the soul: so that the soul by its motive power is the part which moves; and the animate body is the part moved.

Reply Obj. 3. There are in matter various degrees of perfection, as *to be*, *to live*, *to sense*, *to understand.* Now what is added is always more perfect. Therefore that form which gives matter only the first degree of

---

1. 参见 *De An.*, II, 2 (412a 27; b 25).

perfection is the most imperfect, while that form which gives the first, second, and third degree, and so on, is the most perfect: and yet it is present to matter immediately.

Reply Obj. 4. Avicenna held that the substantial forms of the elements remain entire in the mixed body, and that the mixture is made by the contrary qualities of the elements being reduced to an equilibrium.[1] But this is impossible. For the various forms of the elements must necessarily be in various parts of matter, and for the distinction of the parts we must suppose dimensions, without which matter cannot be divisible. Now matter subject to dimension is not to be found except in a body. But several distinct bodies cannot be in the same place. Whence it follows that the elements in the mixed body would be distinct as to position. Hence, there would not be a real mixture which affects the whole, but only a mixture that seems so to the sense because of the juxtaposition of very small particles.

Averroes[2] maintained that the forms of elements, by reason of their imperfection, are between accidental and substantial forms, and so can be *more* or *less*; and therefore in the mixture they are modified and reduced to an equilibrium, so that one form emerges among them. But this is even more impossible. For the substantial being of each thing consists in something indivisible, and every addition and subtraction varies the species, as in numbers, according to *Metaph.* viii.[3] Consequently, it is impossible for any substantial form to receive *more* or *less*. Nor is it less impossible for anything to be between substance and accident.

Therefore we must say, in accordance with the Philosopher,[4] that

---

1. 参见 Cf. Averroes, *In De Gener.*, I, comm. 90 (V, 167r).
2. 参见 *In De Caelo*, III, comm. 67 (V, 105r).
3. 参见 Aristotle, *Metaph.*, VII, 3 (1044a 9).
4. 参见 *De Gener.*, I, 10 (327b 22).

the forms of the elements remain in the mixed body, not actually, but virtually. For the proper qualities of the elements remain, though modified; and in these qualities is the power of the elementary forms. This quality of the mixture is the proper disposition for the substantial form of the mixed body; for instance, the form of a stone, or of any sort of soul.

Fifth Article
WHETHER THE INTELLECTUAL SOUL IS FITTINGLY UNITED TO SUCH A BODY?

We proceed thus to the Fifth Article:—

Objection 1. It would seem that the intellectual soul is not fittingly united to such a body. For matter must be proportionate to the form. But the intellectual soul is an incorruptible form. Therefore it is not fittingly united to a corruptible body.

Obj. 2. Further, the intellectual soul is a perfectly immaterial form. A proof of this is its operation in which corporeal matter does not share. But the more subtle is the body, the less has it of matter. Therefore the soul should be united to a most subtle body, to fire, for instance, and not to a mixed body, still less to a terrestrial body[1].

Obj. 3. Further, since the form is the principle of the species, one form cannot produce a variety of species. But the intellectual soul is one form. Therefore, it should not be united to a body which is composed of parts belonging to various species.

Obj. 4. Further, a more perfect form should have a more perfect subject. But the intellectual soul is the most perfect of souls. Therefore since the bodies of other animals are naturally provided with a covering, for instance, with hair instead of clothes, and hoofs instead

1. terrestrial body: 地上的身体

of shoes, and are, moreover, naturally provided with arms, as claws, teeth, and horns:—it seems that the intellectual soul should not have been united to a body which is imperfect, in being deprived of the above means of protection.

On the contrary, The Philosopher says that *the soul is the act of a physical organic body having life potentially.*[1]

I answer that, Since the form is not for the matter, but rather the matter for the form, we must gather from the form the reason why the matter is such as it is; and not conversely. Now the intellectual soul, as we have seen above,[2] holds in the order of nature the lowest place among intellectual substances. So much so, that it is not naturally endowed with the knowledge of truth, as the angels are, but has to gather knowledge from individual things by way of the senses, as Dionysius says.[3] But nature never fails anyone in what is necessary, and therefore the intellectual soul had to be endowed not only with the power of understanding, but also with the power of sensing. Now the action of the senses is not performed without a corporeal instrument. Therefore the intellectual soul had to be united to a body which could be the fitting organ of sense.

Now all the other senses are based on the sense of touch. But the organ of touch requires to be a medium between contraries, such as hot and cold, wet and dry, and the like, of which the sense of touch has the perception; and in this way it is in potentiality with regard to contraries, and is able to perceive them. Therefore the more the organ of touch is reduced to an equable complexion, the more sensitive will be the touch. But the intellectual soul has the power of sense in all its completeness, because what belongs to the inferior nature pre-

---

1. 参见 *De An.*, II, 1 (412a 27; b 5).
2. 参见 Q. 55, a. 2.
3. 参见 *De Div. Nom.*, VII, 2 (PG 3, 868).

exists more perfectly in the superior, as Dionysius says.[1] Therefore the body to which the intellectual soul is united had to be a mixed body, above others reduced to the most equable complexion. For this reason, among animals man has the better sense of touch. And among men, those who have the better sense of touch have the better intellect. A sign of which is that we observe *those who are refined in body are well endowed in mind*, as is stated in *De Anima* ii.[2]

Reply Obj. 1. Perhaps someone might try to avoid this objection by saying that before sin the human body was incorruptible. But such an answer does not seem sufficient, because before sin the human body was immortal, not by nature, but by a gift of divine grace; or otherwise its immortality[3] would not be forfeited through sin, as neither was the immortality of the devil.

Therefore we answer in another way. Now in matter two conditions are to be found: one which is chosen in order that the matter be suitable to the form; the other which follows necessarily as a result of a previous disposition. The artisan, for instance, chooses iron for the making of a saw, because it is suitable for cutting through hard material; but that the teeth of the saw may become blunt and rusted, follows from a necessity imposed by the matter itself. So the intellectual soul requires a body of equable complexion, which, however, is corruptible by necessity of its matter. If, however, it be said that God could avoid this necessity, we answer that in the establishment of natural things, the question is not what God can do, but what befits the natures of things, as Augustine says.[4] God, however, provided in this case by applying a remedy against death in the gift of grace.

1. 参见 *Op. cit.*, V, 3 (PG 3, 817).
2. 参见 Aristotle, *De An.*, II, 9 (421a 26).
3. immortality: 不朽；长生不老；永生
4. 参见 *De Genesi ad Litt.*, II, 1 (PL 34, 263).

Reply Obj. 2. A body is not necessary to the intellectual soul by reason of its intellectual operation considered as such, but because of the sensitive power, which requires an organ of equable temperament[1]. Therefore the intellectual soul had to be united to such a body, and not to a simple element, or to a mixed body, in which fire was in excess; because otherwise there could not be an equability of temperament. And this body of an equable temperament has a dignity of its own in being remote from contraries. In this it resembles in a way a heavenly body[2].

Reply Obj. 3. The parts of an animal, for instance, the eye, hand, flesh, and bones, and so forth, do not make the species, but the whole does; and therefore, properly speaking, we cannot say that these have diverse species, but diverse dispositions. This is suitable to the intellectual soul, which, although it be one in its essence, yet because of its perfection, is manifold in its power. And so, for its various operations the soul requires various dispositions in the parts of the body to which it is united. For this reason we observe that there is a greater variety of parts in perfect than in imperfect animals; and in these a greater variety than in plants.

Reply Obj. 4. The intellectual soul, as comprehending universals, has a power that is open to infinite things. Therefore it cannot be limited by nature to certain fixed natural judgments or even to certain fixed means whether of defense or of clothing, as is the case with other animals, whose souls are endowed with a knowledge and a power for fixed particular things. Instead of all these, man has by nature his reason and his hands, which are *the organs of organs*,[3] since by their means man can make for himself instruments of an infinite variety, and for any number of purposes.

---

1. equable temperament: 温和的性情
2. heavenly body: 天体
3. 参见 Aristotle, *De An.*, III, 8 (432a 1–2).

Sixth Article

WHETHER THE INTELLECTUAL SOUL IS UNITED TO THE BODY THROUGH THE MEDIUM OF ACCIDENTAL DISPOSITIONS?

We proceed thus to the Sixth Article:—

Objection 1. It would seem that the intellectual soul is united to the body through the medium of accidental dispositions. For every form resides in its own disposed matter. But dispositions to a form are accidents. Therefore we must presuppose accidents to be in matter before the substantial form; and therefore before the soul, since the soul is a substantial form.

Obj. 2. Further, diverse forms of one species require diverse parts of matter. But diverse parts of matter are unintelligible without division in measurable quantity. Therefore we must suppose dimensions in matter before the substantial forms, which are many belonging to one species.

Obj. 3. Further, what is spiritual is connected with what is corporeal by virtual contact. But the virtue of the soul is its power. Therefore it seems that the soul is united to the body by means of a power, which is an accident.

On the contrary, Accident is posterior to substance, both in the order of time and in the order of reason, as the Philosopher says in *Metaph.* vii.[1] Therefore it is unintelligible that any accidental form exist in matter before the soul, which is the substantial form.

I answer that, If the soul were united to the body merely as a mover, there would be nothing to prevent the existence of certain dispositions mediating between the soul and the body; on the contrary, they would

---

1. 参见 Aristotle, *Metaph.*, VI, 1 (1028a 32).

be necessary, for on the part of the soul there would be required the power to move the body, and on the part of the body, a certain aptitude to be moved by the soul.

If, however, the intellectual soul is united to the body as the substantial form, as we have already said above, it is impossible for any accidental disposition to come between the body and the soul, or between any substantial form whatever and its matter. The reason is this. Since matter is in potentiality to all acts in a certain order, what is absolutely first among the acts must be understood as being first in matter. Now the first among all acts is being. Therefore, it is impossible for matter to be apprehended as being hot, or quantified, before actually being. But matter has actual being by the substantial form, which makes it to be absolutely, as we have said above. Therefore it is impossible for any accidental dispositions to pre-exist in matter before the substantial form, and consequently before the soul.

Reply Obj. 1. As appears from what has been already said, the more perfect form virtually contains whatever belongs to the inferior forms; and therefore while remaining one and the same, it perfects matter according to the various degrees of perfection. For the same essential form makes man an *actual being*, a *body*, a *living being*, an *animal*, and a *man*. Now it is clear that to every *genus* follow its own proper accidents. Therefore as matter is apprehended as perfected in its being, before it is understood as corporeal, and so on, so those accidents which belong to being are understood to exist before corporeity. And thus, dispositions are understood in matter before the form, not as regards all its effects, but as regards the subsequent effect.

Reply Obj. 2. Dimensions of quantity are accidents consequent upon the corporeity which belongs to the whole matter. Hence, once matter is understood as corporeal and measurable, it can be understood as distinct in its various parts, and as receptive of different forms according to further degrees of perfection. For although it is essentially the same form which gives to matter the various degrees of perfection, as we have said, yet it is considered as different according to the way that the reason thinks of it.

Reply Obj. 3. A spiritual substance, which is united to a body as its mover only, is united to it by power or virtue. But the intellectual soul is united to the body as a form by its very being; but it guides and moves the body by its power and virtue.

Seventh Article

WHETHER THE SOUL IS UNITED TO THE ANIMAL BODY BY MEANS OF A BODY?

We proceed thus to the Seventh Article:—

Objection 1. It seems that the soul is united to the animal body by means of a body. For Augustine says that *the soul administers the body by light* (that is, by fire) *and by air, which are most akin to a spirit.*[1] But fire and air are bodies. Therefore the soul is united to the human body by means of a body.

Obj. 2. Further, a link between two things seems to be that thing the removal of which involves the cessation of their union. But when breathing ceases, the soul is separated from the body. Therefore the breath, which is a subtle body, is the means of union between soul and body.

Obj. 3. Further, things which are very distant from one another are not united except by something between them. But the intellectual soul is very distant from the body, both because it is incorporeal and because it is incorruptible. Therefore it seems to be united to the body by means of an incorruptible body; and such would be some heavenly light, which would harmonize the elements, and unite them together.

---

1. 参见 *De Genesi ad Litt.*, VII, 19; (PL 34, 364).

On the contrary, The Philosopher says: *We need not ask if the soul and body are one, just as neither do we ask if wax and its shape are one.*[1] But the shape is united to the wax without a body intervening. Therefore also the soul is thus united to the body.

I answer that, If the soul, following the opinion of the Platonists, were united to the body merely as a mover, it would be right to say that some other bodies must intervene between the soul and body of man, or of any animal whatever; for a mover naturally moves what is distant from it by means of something nearer.

If, however, the soul is united to the body as its form, as we have said above, it is impossible for it to be united by means of another body. The reason for this is that a thing is one according as it is a being. Now the form; through itself, makes a thing to be actual, since it is itself essentially an act; nor does it give being by means of something else. Hence, the unity of a thing composed of matter and form is by virtue of the form itself, which by reason of its very nature is united to matter as its act. Nor is there any other cause of union except the agent, which causes matter to be in act, as the Philosopher says in *Metaph.* viii.[2]

From this it is clear how false are the opinions of those who maintained the existence of some mediate bodies between the soul and body of man. Of these, certain Platonists[3] said that the intellectual soul has an incorruptible body naturally united to it, from which it is never separated, and by means of which it is united to the corruptible body of man. Others[4] said that the soul is united to the body by means

---

1. 参见 *De An.*, II, 1 (412b 6).
2. 参见 Aristotle, *Metaph.*, VII, 6 (1045b 21).
3. 参见 Cf. above, q. 51, a. 1, ad 1.
4. 参见 Pseudo-Augustine (Alcher of Clairvaux), *De Spir. et An.*, XIV (PL 40, 789); Costa-Ben-Luca, *De Differ. An. et Spir.*, IV (p. 138).—Cf. Avicebron, *Fons Vitae*, III, 2; V, 15 (pp. 75, 284).

of a corporeal spirit. Others,[1] again, said it is united to the body by means of light, which, they say, is a body and of the nature of the fifth essence; so that the vegetative soul would be united to the body by means of the light of the sidereal heaven, the sensible soul, by means of the light of the crystal heaven, and the intellectual soul by means of the light of the empyrean heaven. Now all this is fictitious and ridiculous. For light is not a body, and the fifth essence does not enter materially into the composition of a mixed body (since it is unchangeable), but only virtually; and lastly, because the soul is immediately united to the body as the form to matter.

Reply Obj. 1. Augustine speaks there of the soul as it moves the body; whence he uses the word *administration*. It is true that it moves the grosser parts of the body by the more subtle parts. And the first instrument of the motive power is a kind of spirit, as the Philosopher says in *De causa motus animalium*.[2]

Reply Obj. 2. The union of soul and body ceases at the cessation of breath, not because this is the means of union, but because of the removal of that disposition by which the body is disposed for such a union. Nevertheless the breath is a means of moving, as the first instrument of motion.

Reply Obj. 3. The soul is indeed very distant from the body, if we consider the condition of each separately; so that if each had a separate being, many means of connection would have to intervene. But inasmuch as the soul is the form of the body, it does not have being apart from the being of the body, but by its own being it is united to the body immediately. This is the case with every form

---

1. 参见 St. Bonaventure, *In II Sent.*, d. xiii, a. 2, q. 2, ad 5 (II, 321); d. xvii, a. 2, q. 2 (II, 421). —Cf. also, St. Augustine, *De Genesi ad Litt.*, VII, 19 (PL 34, 364); Avicenna, *De An.*, IV, 5 (21ra); Gundissalinus, *De An.*, X (p, 102).
2. 参见 *De Causa Mot. Anim.*, X (703a 9).

which, if considered as an act, is very distant from matter, which is a being only in potentiality.

Eighth Article
WHETHER THE WHOLE SOUL IS IN EACH PART OF THE BODY?

We proceed thus to the Eighth Article:—

Objection 1. It would seem that the whole soul is not in each part of the body. For the Philosopher says: *It is not necessary for the soul to be in each part of the body; it suffices that it be in some principle of the body causing the other parts to live, for each part has a natural movement of its own.*[1]

Obj. 2. Further, the soul is in the body of which it is the act. But it is the act of an organic body. Therefore it exists only in an organic body. But each part of the human body is not an organic body. Therefore the whole soul is not in each part.

Obj. 3. Further, the Philosopher says that the relation of a part of the soul to a part of the body, such as the sight to the pupil of the eye, is the same as the relation of the whole soul to the whole body of an animal.[2] If, therefore, the whole soul is in each part of the body, it follows that each part of the body is an animal.

Obj. 4. Further, all the powers of the soul are rooted in the essence of the soul. If, therefore, the whole soul be in each part of the body, it follows that all the powers of the soul are in each part of the body; and thus, the sight will be in the ear, and hearing in the eye, and this is absurd.

Obj. 5. Further, if the whole soul is in each part of the body, each part of the body is immediately dependent on the soul. Thus one part would not depend on another, nor would one part be nobler than

---

1. 参见 *Op. cit.*, X (703a 34).
2. 参见 Aristotle, *De An.*, II, 1 (412b 17; b 27).

another; which is clearly untrue. Therefore the soul is not in each part of the body.

On the contrary, Augustine says that *in each body the whole soul is in the whole body and wholly in each part.*[1]

I answer that, As we have said, if the soul were united to the body merely as its mover, we might say that it is not in each part of the body, but only in one part, through which it would move the others. But since the soul is united to the body as its form, it must necessarily be in the whole body, and in each part thereof. For it is not an accidental form, but the substantial form of the body. Now the substantial form perfects not only the whole, but each part of the whole. For since a whole consists of parts, a form of the whole which does not give being to each of the parts of the body is a form consisting in composition and order, such as the form of a house; and such a form is accidental. But the soul is a substantial form, and therefore it must be the form and the act, not only of the whole, but also of each part. Therefore, on the withdrawal of the soul, just as we do not speak of an animal or a man unless equivocally (as we speak of a painted animal or a stone animal), so it is with the hand, the eye, the flesh and bones, as the Philosopher says.[2] A proof of which is that, on the withdrawal of the soul, no part of the body retains its proper work; although that which retains its species or form retains the action of the species. But act is in that of which it is the act, and therefore the soul must be in the whole body, and in each part thereof.

That it is entire in each part of the body may be concluded from this, that since a whole is that which is divided into parts, there are three kinds of totality, corresponding to three kinds of division. There is a whole which is divided into parts of quantity, as a whole line, or a whole body. There is also a whole which is divided into logical

1. 参见 *De Trin.*, VI, 6 (PL 42, 929).
2. 参见 *De An.*, II, 1 (412b 10; b 17); *Meteor.*, IV, 12 (389b 31).

and essential parts: as a thing defined is divided into the parts of a definition, and a composite into matter and form. There is, further, a third kind of whole which is potential, divided into virtual parts.

The first kind of totality does not apply to forms, except perhaps accidentally; and then only to those forms which have an indifferent relationship to a quantitative whole and its parts. Thus, whiteness, as far as its essence is concerned, is equally disposed to be in the whole surface, and in each part of the surface; and, therefore, when the surface is divided, the whiteness is accidentally divided. But a form which requires variety in the parts, such as a soul, and especially the soul of perfect animals, is not equally related to the whole and the parts. Hence it is not divided accidentally, namely, through the division of quantity. Quantitative totality[1], therefore, cannot be attributed to the soul, either essentially or accidentally. But the second kind of totality, which depends on logical and essential perfection, properly and essentially belongs to forms; and likewise virtual totality, because a form is the principle of operation. Therefore if it be asked whether the whole whiteness is in the whole surface and in each part thereof, it is necessary to distinguish. If we mean the quantitative totality which whiteness has accidentally, then the whole whiteness is not in each part of the surface. The same is to be said of totality of power, since the whiteness which is in the whole surface moves the sight more than the whiteness which is in a small part thereof. But if we mean totality of species and essence, then the whole whiteness is in each part of a surface.

Since, however, the soul has no quantitative totality, neither essentially, nor accidentally, as we have seen, it is enough to say that the whole soul is in each part of the body by totality of perfection and of essence, but not by totality of power. For it is not in each part of the

1. quantitative totality: 数量上的整体性

body with regard to each of its powers; but with regard to sight, it is in the eye, and with regard to hearing, it is in the ear, and so forth. We must observe, however, that since the soul requires a variety of parts, its relation to the whole is not the same as its relation to the parts; for to the whole it is compared primarily and essentially as to its proper and proportionate perfectible[1]: but to the parts, secondarily, inasmuch as they are ordained to the whole.

Reply Obj. 1. The Philosopher is speaking there of the motive power of the soul.

Reply Obj. 2. The soul is the act of an organic body, as of its primary and proportionate perfectible.

Reply Obj. 3. An animal is that which is composed of a soul and a whole body, which is the soul's primary and proportionate perfectible. *Thus* the soul is not in a part. Whence it does not follow that a part of an animal is an animal.

Reply Obj. 4. Some of the powers of the soul are in it according as it exceeds the entire capacity of the body, namely, the intellect and the will; and hence these powers are not said to be in any part of the body. Other powers are common to the soul and body; wherefore each of these powers need not be wherever the soul is, but only in that part of the body which is adapted to the operation of such a power.

Reply Obj. 5. One part of the body is said to be nobler than another because of the various powers, of which the parts of the body are the organs. For that part which is the organ of a nobler power is a nobler part of the body; as is also that part which serves the same power in a nobler manner.

---

1. proportionate perfectible: 相称可完成的

Question LXXVII
WHAT BELONGS TO THE POWERS OF THE SOUL IN GENERAL
(*In Eight Articles*)

WE proceed to consider those things which belong to the powers of the soul, first, in general, and secondly, in particular.[1] Under the first head there are eight points of inquiry: (1) Whether the essence of the soul is its power? (2) Whether there is one power of the soul, or several? (3) How the powers of the soul are distinguished from one another? (4) Of the order of the powers, one to another. (5) Whether the powers of the soul are in it as in their subject? (6) Whether the powers flow from the essence of the soul? (7) Whether one power rises from another? (8) Whether all the powers of the soul remain in the soul after death?

First Article
WHETHER THE ESSENCE OF THE SOUL IS ITS POWER?

We proceed thus to the First Article:—

Objection 1. It would seem that the essence of the soul is its power. For Augustine says that *mind, knowledge and love are in the soul substantially, or, what is the same thing, essentially;*[2] and that *memory, understanding and will are one life, one mind, one essence.*[3]

Obj. 2. Further, the soul is nobler than primary matter. But primary

1. 参见 Q. 78.
2. 参见 *De Trin.*, IX, 4 (PL 42, 963).
3. 参见 *Op. cit.*, X, 11 (PL 42, 984).

matter is its own potentiality. Much more therefore is the soul its own power.

Obj. 3. Further, the substantial form is simpler than the accidental form; a sign of which is that the substantial form is not intensified or relaxed, but is indivisible. But the accidental form is its own power. Much more therefore is that substantial form which is the soul.

Obj. 4. Further, we sense by the sensitive power and we understand by the intellectual power. But *that by which we first sense and understand* is the soul, according to the Philosopher.[1] Therefore the soul is its power.

Obj. 5. Further, whatever does not belong to the essence is an accident. Therefore, if the power of the soul is something else beside the essence thereof, it is an accident; which is contrary to Augustine, who says that the foregoing [i.e., the trinities mentioned in objection 1] *are not in the soul as in a subject, as color or shape, or any other quality, or quantity, is in a body; for such a thing does not exceed the subject in which it is, whereas the mind can love and know other things.*[2]

Obj. 6. Further, *a simple form cannot be a subject.*[3] But the soul is a simple form, since it is not composed of matter and form, as we have said above.[4] Therefore the power of the soul cannot be in it as in a subject.

Obj. 7. Further, an accident is not the principle of a substantial difference. But *sensitive* and *rational* are substantial differences; and they are taken from sense and reason, which are powers of the soul. Therefore the powers of the soul are not accidents; and so it would seem that the power of the soul is its own essence.

On the contrary, Dionysius says that *heavenly spirits are divided into essence, power, and operation.*[5] Much more, then, in the soul is the essence

---

1. 参见 *De An.*, II, 2 (414a 12).
2. 参见 *De Trin.*, IX, 4 (PL 42, 963).
3. 参见 Boethius, *De Trin.*, II (PL 64, 1250).
4. 参见 Q. 75, a. 5.
5. 参见 *De Cael. Hier.*, XI, 2 (PG 3, 284).

distinct from the virtue or power.

I answer that, It is impossible to admit that the power of the soul is its essence, although some have maintained it.[1] For the present purpose this may be proved in two ways. First, because, since potency and act divide being and every kind of being, we must refer a potency and its act to the same genus. Therefore, if the act be not in the genus of substance, the potency which is said in relation to that act cannot be in the genus of substance. Now the operation of the soul is not in the genus of substance, for this belongs to God alone, whose operation is His own substance. Therefore the divine potency or power which is the principle of His operation is the divine essence itself. This cannot be true either of the soul or of any creature, as we have said above when speaking of the angels.[2] Secondly, this may be also shown to be impossible in the soul. For the soul by its very essence is an act. Therefore, if the very essence of the soul were the immediate principle of operation, whatever has a soul would always have actual vital actions, as that which has a soul is always an actually living thing. For, as a form, the soul is not an act ordained to a further act; it is rather the ultimate term of generation. Therefore, for it to be in potentiality to another act does not belong to it according to its essence as a form, but according to its power. So the soul itself, as the subject of its power, is called the first act, with a further relation to the second act.[3] Now we observe that what has a soul is not always actual with respect to its vital operations. Hence it is also said in the definition of the soul that it is *the act of a body having life potentially*; which potentiality, however, *does not exclude the soul.*[4] Therefore it follows that the essence of the soul is

---

1. 参见 William of Auvergne, *De An.*, III, 4 (II, Suppl., 89).—Cf. Peter Lombard, *Sent.*, I, iii, 2 (I, 35).
2. 参见 Q. 54, a. 3.
3. 参见 Aristotle, *De An.*, II, 1 (412a 27).
4. 同上 (412a 25).

not its power. For nothing is in potentiality by reason of an act, as act.

Reply Obj. 1. Augustine is speaking of the mind as it knows and loves itself. Thus knowledge and love, as referred to the soul as known and loved, are substantially or essentially in the soul, for the very substance or essence of the soul is known and loved. In the same way are we to understand what he says in the other passage, that those things are *one life, one mind, one essence.* Or, as some say,[1] this passage is true in the sense in which the potential whole is predicated of its parts, being midway between the universal whole and the integral whole. For the universal whole is in each part according to its entire essence and power, as animal in a man and in a horse; and therefore it is properly predicated of each part. But the integral whole is not in each part, either according to its whole essence, or according to its whole power. Therefore in no way can it be predicated of each part. Yet in a way it is predicated, though improperly, of all the parts together; as if we were to say that the wall, roof and foundations are a house. But the potential whole is in each part according to its whole essence, not, however, according to its whole power. Therefore it can in a way be predicated of each part, but not so properly as the universal whole. In this sense, Augustine says that the memory, understanding and will are the one essence of the soul.

Reply Obj. 2. The act to which primary matter is in potentiality is the substantial form. Therefore the potentiality of matter is nothing else but its essence.

Reply Obj. 3. Action belongs to the composite, as does being; for to act belongs to what exists. Now the composite has being substantially through the substantial form; and it operates by the power which results from the substantial form. Hence an active accidental form is to the substantial form of the agent (for instance, heat compared to the form of fire) as the power of the soul is to the soul.

---

1. 参见 St. Albert, *In I Sent.*, d iii, a. 34 (XXV, 140).

Reply Obj. 4. That the accidental form is a principle of action is due to the substantial form. Therefore the substantial form is the first principle of action, but not the proximate principle. In this sense the Philosopher says that *the soul is that whereby we understand and sense.*

Reply Obj. 5. If we take accident as meaning what is divided against substance, then there can be no medium between substance and accident; for they are divided by affirmation and negation, that is, according to being in a subject, and not being in a subject. In this sense, since the power of the soul is not its essence, it must be an accident. It belongs to the second species of accident, that of quality. But if we take accident as one of the five predicables, in this sense there is a medium between substance and accident. For the substance is all that belongs to the essence of a thing. But whatever is beyond the essence of a thing cannot be called accident in this sense; but only what is not caused by the essential principle of the species. For *property* does not belong to the essense of a thing, but is caused by the essential principles of the species; and hence it is a medium between the essence and accident thus understood. In this sense the powers of the soul may be said to be a medium between substance and accident, as being natural properties of the soul. When Augustine says that knowledge and love are not in the soul as accidents in a subject, this must be understood in the sense given above, inasmuch as they are compared to the soul, not as loving and knowing, but as loved and known. His argument holds good in this sense; for if love were in the soul loved as in a subject, it would follow that an accident transcends its subject, since even other things are loved through the soul.

Reply Obj. 6. Although the soul is not composed of matter and form, yet it has an admixture of potentiality, as we have said above,[1] and for this reason it can be the subject of an accident. The statement quoted

---

1. 参见 Q. 75，a. 5, ad 4.

is verified in God, Who is Pure Act; and it is in treating of this subject that Boethius employs the phrase.

Reply. Obj. 7. Rational and sensitive, as differences, are not taken from the powers of sense and reason, but from the sensitive and rational soul itself. But because substantial forms, which in themselves are unknown to us, are known by their accidents, nothing prevents us from sometimes substituting accidents for substantial differences.

Second Article
WHETHER THERE ARE SEVERAL POWERS OF THE SOUL?

We proceed thus to the Second Article:—

Objection 1. It would seem that there are not several powers of the soul. For the intellectual soul approaches nearest to the likeness of God. But in God there is one simple power. So, too, therefore, in the intellectual soul.

Obj. 2. Further, the higher a power is, the more unified it is. But the intellectual soul excels all other forms in power. Therefore above all others it has one virtue or power.

Obj. 3. Further, to operate belongs to what is in act. But by the one essence of the soul, man has actual being in the different degrees of perfection, as we have seen above.[1] Therefore by the one power of the soul he performs operations of various degrees.

On the contrary, The Philosopher places several powers in the soul.[2]

I answer that, Of necessity we must place several powers in the soul. To make this evident, we observe that, as the Philosopher says,[3] the lowest order of things cannot acquire perfect goodness, but they acquire a certain imperfect goodness, by few movements. Those which belong to a higher order acquire perfect goodness by

1. 参见 Q. 76, a. 3 and 4.
2. 参见 *De An.*, II, 3 (414a 31).
3. 参见 *De Caelo*, II, 12 (292a 22).

many movements. Those yet higher acquire perfect goodness by few movements, and the highest perfection is found in those things which acquire perfect goodness without any movement whatever. Thus he is least of all disposed to health, who can only acquire imperfect health by means of a few remedies. Better disposed is he who can acquire perfect health by means of many remedies, and better still, he who can by few remedies; but best of all is he who has perfect health without any remedies. We conclude, therefore, that things which are below man acquire a certain limited goodness, and so have a few determinate operations and powers. But man can acquire universal and perfect goodness, because he can acquire beatitude. Yet he is in the lowest degree, according to his nature, of those to whom beatitude is possible; and therefore the human soul requires many and various operations and powers. But to angels a smaller variety of powers is sufficient. In God, however, there is no power or action beyond His own Essence.

There is yet another reason why the human soul abounds in a variety of powers:—it is on the confines of spiritual and corporeal creatures, and therefore the powers of both meet together in the soul.

Reply Obj. 1. The intellectual soul approaches to the divine likeness, more than inferior creatures, in being able to acquire perfect goodness, although by many and various means; and in this it falls short of more perfect creatures.

Reply Obj. 2. A unified power is superior if it extends to equal things. But a multiform power is superior to it, if it is over many things.

Reply Obj. 3. One thing has one substantial being, but may have several operations. So there is one essence in the soul, but several powers.

Third Article
WHETHER THE POWERS ARE DISTINGUISHED BY THEIR ACTS AND OBJECTS?

We proceed thus to the Third Article:—

Objection 1. It would seem that the powers of the soul are not distinguished by acts and objects. For nothing is determined to its species by what is subsequent and extrinsic to it. But the act is subsequent to the power, and the object is extrinsic to it. Therefore the soul's powers are not specifically distinct by acts and objects.

Obj. 2. Further, contraries are what differ most from each other. Therefore if the powers are distinguished by their objects, it follows that the same power could not have contrary objects. This is clearly false in almost all the powers, for the power of vision extends to white and black, and the power of taste to sweet and bitter.

Obj. 3. Further, if the cause be removed, the effect is removed. Hence if the difference of powers came from the difference of objects, the same object would not come under different powers. This is clearly false, for the same thing is known by the cognitive power, and desired by the appetitive.

Obj. 4. Further, that which of itself is the cause of anything, is the cause thereof, wherever it is. But various objects which belong to various powers belong also to some one power; as sound and color belong to sight and hearing, which are different powers, yet come under the one power of common sense. Therefore the powers are not distinguished according to the difference of their objects.

On the contrary, Things that are subsequent are distinguished by what precedes. But the Philosopher says that *acts and operations precede the powers according to the reason; and these again are preceded by their opposites*,[1] that is, their objects. Therefore the powers are distinguished according to their acts and objects.

I answer that, A power as such is directed to an act. Therefore we must derive the nature of a power from the act to which it is directed; and consequently the nature of a power is diversified according as the

---

1. 参见 *De An.*, II, 4 (415a 18).

nature of the act is diversified. Now the nature of an act is diversified according to the various natures of the objects. For every act is either of an active power or of a passive power. Now, the object is to the act of a passive power as the principle and moving cause; for color is the principle of vision, inasmuch as it moves the sight. On the other hand, to the act of an active power the object is a term and an end; just as the object of the power of growth is perfect quantity, which is the end of growth. Now, from these two things an act receives its species, namely, from its principle, or from its end or term. For the act of heating differs from the act of cooling in this, that the former proceeds from something hot, which is the active principle, to heat; while the latter proceeds from something cold, which is the active principle, to cold. Therefore the powers are of necessity distinguished by their acts and objects.

Nevertheless, we must observe that things which are accidental do not change the species. For since to be colored is accidental to an animal, its species is not changed by a difference of color, but by a difference in that which belongs to the nature of an animal, that is to say, by a difference in the sensitive soul, which is sometimes found accompanied by reason, and sometimes not. Hence *rational* and *irrational* are differences dividing animal, constituting its various species. In like manner, therefore, not any variety of objects diversifies the powers of the soul, but a difference in that to which the power of its very nature is directed. Thus the senses of their very nature are directed to the passive quality which of itself is divided into color, sound, and the like, and therefore there is one sensitive power with regard to color, namely, sight, and another with regard to sound, namely, hearing. But it is accidental to a passive quality, for instance, to something colored, to be a musician or a grammarian, great or small, a man or a stone. Therefore by reason of such differences the powers of the soul are not distinguished.

Reply Obj. 1. Act, though subsequent in being to power, is, nevertheless, prior to it in intention and logically; as the end is with regard to the agent. And the object, although extrinsic, is, nevertheless, the principle or end of the action; and the conditions which are intrinsic to a thing are proportionate to its principle and end.

Reply Obj. 2. If any power were to have one of two contraries as such for its object, the other contrary would belong to another power. But the power of the soul does not regard the nature of the contrary as such, but rather the common aspect of both contraries; as sight does not regard white as such, but as color. This is because, of two contraries, one, in a manner, includes the nature of the other, since they are to one another as perfect and imperfect.

Reply Obj. 3. Nothing prevents things which coincide in subject from being considered under different aspects; and therefore they can belong to various powers of the soul.

Reply Obj. 4. The higher power of itself regards a more universal formality in its object than the lower power; because the higher a power is, to a greater number of things does it extend. Therefore many things are combined in the one formality of the object, which the higher power considers of itself; while they differ in the formalities regarded by the lower powers of themselves. Thus it is that various objects belong to various lower powers; which objects, however, are subject to one higher power.

Fourth Article

WHETHER AMONG THE POWERS OF THE SOUL THERE IS ORDER?

We proceed thus to the Fourth Article:—

Objection 1. It would seem that there is no order among the powers of the soul. For in those things which come under one division, there is no before and after, but all are naturally simultaneous. But the powers of the soul are contradistinguished from one another. Therefore there is no order among them.

Obj. 2. Further, the powers of the soul are related to their objects, and to the soul itself. On the part of the soul, there is no order among the powers, because the soul is one. In like manner, there is no order among them in relation to the objects, which are various and dissimilar, as color and sound. Therefore there is no order among the powers of the soul.

Obj. 3. Further, where there is order among powers, we find that the operation of one depends on the operation of another. But the action of one power of the soul does not depend on that of another; for sight can act independently of hearing, and conversely. Therefore there is no order among the powers of the soul.

On the contrary, The Philosopher compares the parts or powers of the soul to figures.[1] But figures have an order among themselves. Therefore the powers of the soul also have order.

I answer that, Since the soul is one, and the powers are many, and since a number of things that proceed from one must proceed in a certain order, there must be some order among the powers of the soul. Accordingly we may observe a triple order among them, two of which correspond to the dependence of one power on another, while the third is taken from the order of the objects. Now the dependence of one power on another can be taken in two ways: according to the order of nature, inasmuch as perfect things are by their nature prior to imperfect things; and according to the order of generation and time, inasmuch as from being imperfect, a thing comes to be perfect. Thus, according to the first kind of order among the powers, the intellectual powers are prior to the sensitive powers; wherefore they direct them and command them. Likewise the sensitive powers are prior according to this order to the powers of the nutritive soul.

---

1. 参见 *Op. cit.*, II, 3 (414b 20).

In the second kind of order, it is the other way about. For the powers of the nutritive soul are prior in generation to the powers of the sensitive soul; and therefore they prepare the body for the actions of the sensitive powers. The same is to be said of the sensitive powers with regard to the intellectual. But in the third kind of order, certain sensitive powers are ordered among themselves, namely, sight, hearing, and smelling. For the visible comes naturally first, since it is common to higher and lower bodies. On the other hand, sound is audible in the air, which is naturally prior to the mingling of elements, of which odor is the result.

Reply Obj. 1. The species of a given genus are to one another as before and after, like numbers and figures, if considered in their being; although they may be said to be simultaneous, according as they receive the predication of the genus common to them.

Reply Obj. 2. This order among the powers of the soul is both on the part of the soul (which, though it be one according to its essence, is disposed to various acts in a certain order), and on the part of the objects, and furthermore on the part of the acts, as we have said above.

Reply Obj. 3. This argument holds good as regards those powers among which order of the third kind exists. Those powers, however, among which the two other kinds of order exist, are such that the action of one depends on another.

Fifth Article
WHETHER ALL THE POWERS OF THE SOUL ARE IN THE SOUL AS THEIR SUBJECT?

We proceed thus to the Fifth Article:—

Objection 1. It would seem that all the powers of the soul are in the soul as their subject. For as the powers of the body are to the body, so the powers of the soul are to the soul. But the body is the subject of the corporeal powers. Therefore the soul is the subject of the powers of the soul.

Obj. 2. Further, the operations of the powers of the soul are attributed to the body by reason of the soul; because, as the Philosopher says, *the soul is that by which we sense and understand primarily.*[1] But the first principles of the operations of the soul are the powers. Therefore the powers are primarily in the soul.

Obj. 3. Further, Augustine says that the soul senses certain things, not through the body, but in fact, without the body, as fear and the like; and some things it senses through the body.[2] But if the sensitive powers were not in the soul alone as their subject, the soul could not sense anything without the body. Therefore the soul is the subject of the sensitive powers; and for a similar reason, of all the other powers.

On the contrary, The Philosopher says that *sensation belongs neither to the soul, nor to the body, but to the composite.*[3] Therefore the sensitive power is in the composite as its subject. Therefore the soul alone is not the subject of all the powers.

I answer that, The subject of operative power is that which is able to operate; for every accident denominates its proper subject. Now it is the same being which is able to operate, and which does operate. Therefore the *subject of power* is of necessity *the subject of operation*, as again the Philosopher says in the beginning of *De Somno et Vigilia.*[4] Now, it is clear from what we have said above that some operations of the soul are performed without a corporeal organ, as to understand and to will.[5] Hence the powers of these operations are in the soul as their subject. But some operations of the soul are performed by means of corporeal organs, as seeing by the eye, and hearing by the ear. And so it is with all the other operations of the nutritive and sensitive parts.

---

1. 参见 Aristotle, *Op. cit.*, II, 2 (414a 12).
2. 参见 *De Genesi ad Litt.*, XII, 7; 24 (PL 34, 459; 474).
3. 参见 *De Somno*, I (454a 7).
4. 同上 (454a 8).
5. 参见 Q. 75, a. 2 and 3; q. 76, a. 1, ad 1.

Therefore, the powers which are the principles of these operations have their subject in the composite, and not in the soul alone.

Reply Obj. 1. All the powers are said to belong to the soul, not as their subject, but as their principle; because it is by the soul that the composite has the power to perform such operations.

Reply Obj. 2. All such powers are in the soul before they are in the composite; not, however, as in their subject, but as in their principle.

Reply Obj. 3. Plato's opinion was that sensation is an operation proper to the soul, just as understanding is.[1] Now in many things relating to philosophy, Augustine makes use of the opinions of Plato, not asserting them as true, but reporting them. However, as far as the present question is concerned, when it is said that the soul senses some things with the body, and some without the body, this can be taken in two ways. Firstly, the words *with the body or without the body* may determine the act of sense in its mode of proceeding from the one who senses. *Thus* the soul senses nothing without the body, because the action of sensation cannot proceed from the soul except by a corporeal organ. Secondly, they may be understood as determining the act of sense on the part of the object sensed. *Thus* the soul senses some things with the body, that is, things existing in the body, as when it feels a wound or something of that sort; while it senses some things without the body, that is, which do not exist in the body, but only in the apprehension of the soul, as when it feels sad or joyful on hearing something.

Sixth Article
WHETHER THE POWERS OF THE SOUL FLOW FROM ITS ESSENCE?

We proceed thus to the Sixth Article:—

---

1. 参见 Cf. above, q. 75, a. 3.

Objection 1. It would seem that the powers of the soul do not flow from its essence. For different things do not proceed from one simple thing. But the essence of the soul is one and simple. Since, therefore, the powers of the soul are many and diverse, they cannot proceed from its essence.

Obj. 2. Further, that from which a thing proceeds is its cause. But the essence of the soul cannot be said to be the cause of the powers, as is clear if one considers the different kinds of causes. Therefore the powers of the soul do not flow from its essence.

Obj. 3. Further, emanation signifies some sort of movement. But nothing is moved by itself, as the Philosopher proves,[1] except, perhaps, by reason of a part of itself; as an animal is said to be moved by itself, because one part of it moves and another is moved. But the soul is not moved, as the Philosopher proves.[2] Therefore the soul does not produce its powers within itself.

On the contrary, The powers of the soul are its natural properties. But the subject is the cause of its proper accidents; whence it is also included in the definition of accident, as is clear from *Metaph.* vii.[3] Therefore the powers of the soul proceed from its essence as from their cause.

I answer that, The substantial and the accidental forms partly agree and partly differ. They agree in this, that each is an act, and that by each of them something is in some way actual. They differ, however, in two respects. First, because the substantial form makes a thing to be absolutely, and its subject is only potentially a being. But the accidental form does not make a thing to be absolutely, but to be such, or so great, or in some particular condition; for its subject is an actual being. Hence it is clear that actuality is found in the substantial form prior to

---

1. 参见 Aristotle, *Phys.*, VII, 1 (241b 24).
2. 参见 Aristotle, *De An.*, I, 4 (408a 34).
3. 参见 Aristotle, *Metaph.*, VI, 4 (1029b 30).

its being found in its subject; and since that which is first in a genus is the cause in that genus, the substantial form causes actual being in its subject. On the other hand, actuality is found in the subject of the accidental form prior to its being found in the accidental form; and therefore the actuality of the accidental form is caused by the actuality of the subject. So the subject, inasmuch as it is in potentiality, is receptive of the accidental form; but inasmuch as it is in act, it produces it. This I say of the proper and *per se* accident; for with regard to the extraneous accident, the subject is receptive only, and such an accident is caused by an extrinsic agent. Secondly, substantial and accidental forms differ, because, since that which is the less principal exists for the sake of that which is the more principal, matter exists for the sake of the substantial form; while, on the contrary, the accidental form exists for the sake of the completeness of the subject.

Now it is clear, from what has been said, that either the subject of the soul's powers is the soul itself alone, which can be the subject of an accident according as it has something of potentiality, as we have said above, or else this subject is the composite. But the composite is actual by the soul. Whence it is clear that all the powers of the soul, whether their subject be the soul alone or the composite, flow from the essence of the soul as from their principle; for it has already been said that an accident is caused by the subject according as the subject is actual, and is received into it according as it is in potentiality.

Reply Obj. 1. From one simple thing many things may proceed naturally in a certain order; or, again, if there be diversity of recipients. Thus, from the one essence of the soul many and diverse powers proceed, both because order exists among these powers and also by reason of the diversity of the corporeal organs.

Reply Obj. 2. The subject is both the final cause, and in a way the active cause, of its proper accident. It is also as it were the material cause, inasmuch as it is receptive of the accident. From this we may gather that the essence of the soul is the cause of all its powers, as their end, and as their active principle; and of some, as receptive of them.

Reply Obj. 3. The emanation of proper accidents from their subject is not by way of transmutation, but by a certain natural resultance; just as one thing results naturally from another, as color from light.

Seventh Article
WHETHER ONE POWER OF THE SOUL ARISES FROM ANOTHER?

We proceed thus to the Seventh Article:—

Objection 1. It would seem that one power of the soul does not arise from another. For if several things arise together, one of them does not arise from another. But all the powers of the soul are created at the same time with the soul. Therefore one of them does not arise from another.

Obj. 2. Further, the power of the soul arises from the soul as an accident from its subject. But one power of the soul cannot be the subject of another, because nothing is the accident of an accident. Therefore one power does not arise from another.

Obj. 3. Further, one opposite does not arise from the other opposite, but everything arises from that which is like it in species. Now the powers of the soul are oppositely divided, as diverse species. Therefore one of them does not proceed from another.

On the contrary, Powers are known by their actions. But the action of one power is caused by the action of another power, as the action of the imagination by the action of the senses. Therefore one power of the soul is caused by another.

I answer that, In things which proceed from one according to a natural order, just as the first is the cause of all, so that which is nearer to the first is, in a way, cause of those which are more remote. Now it has been shown above that among the powers of the soul there are several kinds of order. Therefore one power of the soul proceeds from the essence of the soul by the medium of another. But since the essence of the soul is compared to the powers both as an active and final principle, and as a receptive principle, either separately by itself, or together with the body; and since the agent and the end are more perfect, while the receptive principle, as such, is less perfect:—it follows that those powers of the soul which precede the others in the order of perfection and nature are the principles of the others after the manner of an end and an active principle. For we see that sense is for the sake of the intellect, and not the other way about. Sense, moreover, is a certain imperfect participation of the intellect, and therefore, according to its natural origin, it proceeds from the intellect as the imperfect from the perfect. But considered as receptive principles, the more imperfect powers are principles with regard to the others; and thus the soul, according as it has the sensitive power, is considered as the subject, and as something material in relation to the intellect. On this account, the more imperfect powers precede the others in the order of generation, for the animal is generated before the man.

Reply Obj. 1. As the power of the soul flows from the essence, not by a transmutation, but by a certain natural resultance, and is simultaneous with the soul, so is it the case with one power as regards another.

Reply Obj. 2. An accident cannot of itself be the subject of an accident; but one accident is received in a substance prior to another, as quantity prior to quality. In this sense, one accident is said to be the subject of another (as surface is of color) inasmuch as a substance receives one accident through the means of another. The same thing may be said of the powers of the soul.

Reply Obj. 3. The powers of the soul are opposed to one another as perfect and imperfect; as also are the species of numbers and figures. But this opposition does not prevent the origin of one from another, because imperfect things naturally proceed from perfect things.

Eighth Article

WHETHER ALL THE POWERS REMAIN IN THE SOUL WHEN SEPARATED FROM THE BODY?

We proceed thus to the Eighth Article:—

Objection 1. It would seem that all the powers of the soul remain in the soul separated from the body. For we read in the *De Spiritu et Anima* that *the soul withdraws from the body, taking with itself sense and imagination, reason and intellect and intelligence, concupiscibility and irascibility.*[1]

Obj. 2. Further, the powers of the soul are its natural properties. But properties are always in that to which they belong, and are never separated from it. Therefore the powers of the soul are in it even after death.

Obj. 3. Further, the powers even of the sensitive soul are not weakened when the body becomes weak; because, as the Philosopher says, *If an old man were given the eye of a young man, he would see just as well as a young man.*[2] But weakness is the road to corruption. Therefore the powers of the soul are not corrupted when the body is corrupted, but remain in the separated soul.

Obj. 4. Further, memory is a power of the sensitive soul, as the Philosopher proves.[3] But memory remains in the separated soul, for it was said to the rich glutton whose soul was in hell: *Remember that thou didst receive good things during thy lifetime* (*Luke* xvi. 25). Therefore memory remains in the separated soul; and consequently the other powers of the sensitive part.

Obj. 5. Further, joy and sorrow are in the concupiscible part, which

---

1. 参见 Pseudo-Augustine (Alcher of Clairvaux), *De Spir. et An.*, XV (PL 40, 791).
2. 参见 Aristotle, *De An.*, I, 4 (408b 21).
3. 参见 *De Mem. et Rem.*, I (450a 12).

is a power of the sensitive soul. But it is clear that separate souls grieve or rejoice at the pains or rewards which they receive. Therefore the concupiscible power remains in the separate soul.

Obj. 6. Further, Augustine says that, just as the soul, when the body lies senseless, yet not quite dead, sees some things by imaginary vision,[1] so also when by death the soul is quite separate from the body. But the imagination is a power of the sensitive part. Therefore, a power of the sensitive part remains in the separate soul; and consequently all the other powers.

On the contrary, It is said that *of two substances only does man consist: the soul with its reason, and the body with its senses.*[2] Therefore when the body is dead, the sensitive powers do not remain.

I answer that, As we have already said, all the powers of the soul belong to the soul alone as their principle. But some powers belong to the soul alone as their subject: such are intellect and will. These powers must remain in the soul, after the destruction of the body. But other powers are in the composite as in their subject; as all the powers of the sensitive and nutritive parts. Now accidents cannot remain after the destruction of the subject. Therefore, when the composite is destroyed, such powers do not remain actually; but they remain virtually in the soul, as in their principle or root.

So it is false that, as some say, these powers remain in the soul even after the corruption of the body.[3] It is much more false that, as they also say, the acts of these powers remain in the separate soul;[4] because these powers have no act apart from a corporeal organ.

Reply Obj. 1. That book has no authority, and so what is there

---

1. 参见 *De Genesi ad Litt.*, XII, 32 (PL 34, 480).
2. 参见 Gennadius, *De Eccles. Dogm.*, XXIX (PL 58,985).
3. 参见 Pseudo-Augustine (Alcher of Clairvaux), *De Spir. et An.*, XV (PL 40, 791).
4. 参见 *Op. cit.*, XXX (PL 40, 800).

written can be ignored with the same facility as it was said; although we may say that the soul takes with itself these powers, not actually, but virtually.

Reply Obj. 2. These powers, which we say do not actually remain in the separate soul, are not the properties of the soul alone, but of the composite.

Reply Obj. 3. These powers are said not to be weakened when the body becomes weak, because the soul remains unchangeable, and is the virtual principle of these powers.

Reply Obj. 4. The recollection spoken of there is to be taken in the same way as Augustine places memory in the mind;[1] which is not in the way that memory is a part of the sensitive soul.

Reply Obj. 5. In the separate soul, sorrow and joy are not in the sensitive, but in the intellectual appetite, as in the angels.

Reply Obj. 6. Augustine in that passage is speaking as inquiring, not as asserting. Therefore he retracted some things which he had said there.[2]

---

1. 参见 *De Trin.*, X, 11; XIV, 7 (PL 42, 983; 1043).
2. 参见 *Retract.*, II, 24 (PL 32, 640).

Question LXXVIII
THE POWERS OF THE SOUL IN PARTICULAR
(*In Four Articles*)

WE next treat of the powers of the soul in particular. The theologian, however, has only to inquire specifically concerning the intellectual and appetitive powers, in which the virtues reside. And since the knowledge of these powers depends to a certain extent on the other powers, our consideration of the powers of the soul in particular will be divided into three parts: first, we shall consider those powers which are a preamble to the intellect; secondly, the intellectual powers;[1] thirdly, the appetitive powers.[2]

Under the first head there are four points of inquiry: (1) The powers of the soul considered generally. (2) The species of powers in the vegetative part of the soul. (3) The exterior senses. (4) The interior senses.

First Article
WHETHER THERE ARE TO BE DISTINGUISHED FIVE GENERA OF POWERS IN THE SOUL?

We proceed thus to the First Article:—

Objection 1. It would seem that there are not to be distinguished five genera of powers in the soul —namely, vegetative, sensitive, appetitive,

---

1. 参见 Q. 79.
2. 参见 Q. 80.

locomotive, and intellectual. For the powers of the soul are called its parts. But only three parts of the soul are commonly assigned—namely, the vegetative soul, the sensitive soul, and the rational soul. Therefore there are only three genera of powers in the soul, and not five.

Obj. 2. Further, the powers of the soul are the principles of its vital operations. Now, in four ways is a thing said to live. For the Philosopher says: *In several ways a thing is said to live, and even if only one of these is present, the thing is said to live; as intellect and sense, local movement and rest, and lastly, movement of decrease and increase due to nourishment.*[1] Therefore there are only four genera of powers cf the soul, as the appetitive is excluded.

Obj. 3. Further, a special kind of soul ought not to be assigned as regards what is common to all the powers. Now desire is common to each power of the soul. For sight desires its appropriate visible object: whence we read (*Ecclus.* xl. 22): *The eye desireth favor and beauty, but more than these green sown fields.* In the same way, every other power desires its appropriate object. Therefore the appetitive power should not be made a special genus of the powers of the soul.

Obj. 4. Further, the moving principle in animals is sense, or intellect, or appetite, as the Philosopher says.[2] Therefore the motive power should not be added to the above as a special genus of soul.

On the contrary, The Philosopher says: *The powers are the vegetative, the sensitive, the appetitive, the locomotive, and the intellectual.*[3]

I answer that, There are five genera among the powers of the soul, as above numbered. Of these, three are called souls, and four are called modes of living. The reason of this diversity is that the various souls are distinguished according as the operation of the soul transcends the operation of the corporeal nature in various ways; for the whole

---

1. 参见 *De An.*, II, 2 (413a 22).
2. 参见 *Op. cit.*, III, 10 (433a 9).
3. 参见 *Op. cit.*, II, 3 (414a 31).

corporeal nature is subject to the soul, and is related to it as its matter and instrument. There exists, therefore, an operation of the soul which so far exceeds the corporeal nature that it is not even performed by any corporeal organ; and such is the operation of the *rational soul*. Below this, there is another operation of the soul, which is indeed performed through a corporeal organ, but not through a corporeal quality, and this is the operation of the *sensitive soul*. For though hot and cold, wet and dry, and other such corporeal qualities are required for the work of the senses, yet they are not required in such a way that the operation of the senses takes place by the power of such qualities; but only for the proper disposition of the organ. The lowest of the operations of the soul is that which is performed by a corporeal organ and by the power of a corporeal quality. Yet this transcends the operation of the corporeal nature; because the movements of bodies are caused by an extrinsic principle, while these operations are from an intrinsic principle. For this is common to all the operations of the soul, since every animate thing, in some way, moves itself. Such is the operation of the *vegetative soul*; for digestion, and what follows, is caused instrumentally by the action of heat, as the Philosopher says.[1]

Now the powers of the soul are distinguished generically by their objects. For the higher a power is, the more universal is the object to which it extends, as we have said above.[2] But the object of the soul's operation may be considered in a triple order. For in the soul there is a power whose object is only the body that is united to that soul; and the powers of this genus are called *vegetative*, for the vegetative power acts only on the body to which the soul is united. There is another genus in the powers of the soul which regards a more universal object—namely, every sensible body, and not only the body to which the soul is united. And there is yet another genus in the powers of the

1. 参见 Aristotle, *Op. cit.*, II, 4 (416b 25).
2. 参见 Q. 77, a. 3, ad 4.

soul which regards a still more universal object—namely, not only the sensible body, but universally all being. Therefore it is evident that the latter two genera of the soul's powers have an operation in regard not merely to that which is united to them, but also to something extrinsic. Now, since whatever operates must in some way be united to the object in relation to which it operates, it follows of necessity that this something extrinsic, which is the object of the soul's operation, must be related to the soul in a twofold manner. First, inasmuch as this something extrinsic has a natural aptitude to be united to the soul, and to be by its likeness in the soul. In this way there are two kinds of powers—namely, the *sensitive*, in regard to the less common object, the sensible body; and the *intellectual*, in regard to the most common object, universal being. Secondly, inasmuch as the soul itself has an inclination and tendency to the external thing. And in this way there are again two kinds of powers in the soul: one —*the appetitive* —according to which the soul is referred to something extrinsic as to an end, which is first in the intention; the other—the *locomotive* power[1]—according to which the soul is referred to something extrinsic as to the term of its operation and movement; for every animal is moved for the purpose of realizing its desires and intentions.

The modes of living, on the other hand, are distinguished according to the degrees of living things. There are some living things in which there exists only vegetative power, as plants. There are others in which along with the vegetative there exists also the sensitive, but not the locomotive, power; and such are immovable animals, as shellfish. There are others which, besides this, have locomotive powers, as do the perfect animals, which require many things for their life, and consequently need movement to seek necessaries of life from a

1. the locomotive power: 运动机能

distance. And there are some living things which along with these have intellectual power—namely, men. But the appetitive power does not constitute a degree of living things; because *wherever there is sense there is also appetite.*[1]

Thus the first two objections are hereby solved.

Reply Obj. 3. *Natural appetite* is that inclination which each thing has, of its own nature, for something; wherefore by its natural appetite each power desires what is suitable to itself. But *animal appetite* follows from the apprehended form. This sort of appetite requires a special power in the soul—apprehension alone does not suffice. For a thing is desired according as it exists in its own nature, whereas in the apprehensive power it exists, not according to its own nature, but according to its likeness. Whence it is clear that sight desires naturally a visible object for the purpose of its act only—namely, for the purpose of seeing; but the animal by its appetitive power desires the thing seen, not merely for the purpose of seeing it, but also for other purposes. But if the soul did not require the things perceived by the senses, except for the sake of the actions of the senses (that is, for the purpose of sensing them), there would be no need for a special genus of appetitive powers, since the natural appetite of the powers would suffice.

Reply Obj. 4. Although sense and appetite are principles of movement in perfect animals, yet sense and appetite, as such, are not sufficient to cause movement, unless another power be added to them; for immovable animals have sense and appetite, and yet they have not the power of motion. Now this motive power is not only in the appetite and sense as commanding the movement, but also in the parts of the body, to make them obey the appetite of the soul which moves them. Of this we have a sign in the fact that when the members are deprived of their natural disposition, they do not move in obedience to the

1. 参见 Aristotle, *De An.*, II, 3 (414b 1).

appetite.

Second Article

WHETHER THE PARTS OF THE VEGETATIVE SOUL ARE FITTINGLY ENUMERATED AS THE NUTRITIVE, AUGMENTATIVE, AND GENERATIVE?

We proceed thus to the Second Article:—

Objection 1. It would seem that the parts of the vegetative soul are not fittingly enumerated as the nutritive, augmentative, and generative. For these are called *natural* powers. But the powers of the soul are above the natural powers. Therefore we should not class the above powers as powers of the soul.

Obj. 2. Further, we should not assign a particular power of the soul to that which is common to living and non-living things. But generation is common to all things that can be generated and corrupted, whether living or not living. Therefore the generative power should not be classed as a power of the soul.

Obj. 3. Further, the soul is more powerful than the body. But the body by the same active power gives species and due quantity; much more, therefore, does the soul. Therefore the augmentative power of the soul is not distinct from the generative power.

Obj. 4. Further, everything is preserved in being by that whereby it has being. But the generative power is that whereby a living thing acquires being. Therefore by the same power the living thing is preserved. Now the nutritive power is directed to the preservation of the living thing, being *a power which is capable of preserving whatever receives it.*[1] Therefore we should not distinguish the nutritive power from the generative.

---

1. 参见 Aristotle, *op. cit.*, II, 4 (416b 14).

On the contrary, The Philosopher says that the operations of this soul are *generation, the use of food, and growth.*[1]

I answer that, The vegetative part has three powers. For the vegetative part, as we have said, has for its object the body itself, living by the soul; and for this body a triple operation of the soul is required. One is whereby it acquires being, and to this is directed the *generative* power. Another is whereby the living body acquires its due quantity, and to this is directed the *augmentative* power. Another is whereby the body of a living thing is preserved in its being and in its due quantity, and to this is directed the *nutritive* power.

We must, however, observe a difference among these powers. The nutritive and the augmentative have their effect where they exist, since the body itself united to the soul grows and is preserved by the augmentative and nutritive powers which exist in one and the same soul. But the generative power has its effect, not in one and the same body, but in another; for a thing cannot generate itself. Therefore the generative power in a way approaches to the dignity of the sensitive soul, which has an operation extending to extrinsic things, although in a more excellent and more universal manner; for that which is highest in an inferior nature approaches to that which is lowest in the higher nature, as is made clear by Dionysius.[2] Therefore, of these three powers, the generative has the greater finality, nobility and perfection, as the Philosopher says, for it belongs to a thing which is already perfect *to produce another like unto itself*.[3] Furthermore, the generative power is served by the augmentative and nutritive powers; and the augmentative power by the nutritive.

Reply Obj. 1. Such powers are called natural, both because they produce an effect like that of nature, which also gives being, quantity

---

1. 参见 Aristotle, *op. cit.*, II, 4 (415a 25; b 23).
2. 参见 *De Div. Nom.*, VII, 3 (PG 3, 872).
3. 参见 Aristotle, *De An.*, II, 4 (416b 24).

and preservation (although the above powers accomplish these things in a more perfect way); and because these powers perform their actions instrumentally, through the active and passive qualities, which are the principles of natural actions.

Reply Obj. 2. Generation in inanimate things is entirely from an extrinsic source; whereas the generation of living things is in a higher way, through something in the living thing itself, which is the semen containing the formative principle of the body. Therefore, there must be in the living thing a power that prepares this semen; and this is the generative power.

Reply Obj. 3. Since the generation of living things is from a semen, it is necessary that in the beginning an animal of small size be generated. For this reason it must have a power in the soul, whereby it is brought to its appropriate size. But the inanimate body is generated from determinate matter by an extrinsic agent; and therefore it receives at once its nature and its quantity, according to the condition of the matter.

Reply Obj. 4. As we have said above, the operation of the vegetative principle is performed by means of heat, the property of which is to consume humidity. Therefore, in order to restore the humidity thus lost, the nutritive power is required, whereby the food is changed into the substance of the body. This is also necessary for the action of the augmentative and generative powers.

Third Article
WHETHER THE FIVE EXTERIOR SENSES ARE PROPERLY DISTINGUISHED?

We proceed thus to the Third Article:—

Objection 1. It would seem inaccurate to distinguish five exterior senses. For sense can know accidents. But there are many kinds of accidents. Therefore, since powers are distinguished by their objects, it seems that the senses are multiplied according to the number of the kinds of accidents.

Obj. 2. Further, magnitude and shape, and other so-called *common sensibles*, are *not sensibles by accident*, but are contradistinguished from them by the Philosopher.[1] Now the diversity of the proper objects diversifies the powers. Since, therefore, magnitude and shape are further from color than sound is, it seems that there is much more need for another sensitive power that can grasp magnitude or shape than for that which grasps color or sound.

Obj. 3. Further, one sense regards one contrariety; as sight regards white and black. But the sense of touch grasps several contrarieties, such as hot or cold, moist or dry, and the like. Therefore, it is not a single sense but several. Therefore there are more than five senses.

Obj. 4. Further, a species is not divided against its genus. But taste is a kind of touch. Therefore it should not be classed as a distinct sense from touch.

On the contrary, The Philosopher says: *There is none other besides the five senses.*[2]

I answer that, The reason of the distinction and number of the senses has been assigned by some on the basis of the organs, in which one or other of the elements preponderates, as water, air, or the like.[3] By others it has been assigned to the medium, which is either in conjunction or extrinsic, and is either water or air, or the like. Others[4] have ascribed it to the diverse natures of the sensible qualities, according as such quality belongs to a simple body or results from complexity.

---

1. 参见 Aristotle, *op. cit.*, II, 6 (418a 8).
2. 参见 *Op. cit.*, III, 1 (424b 22).
3. 参见 Cf. St. Albert, *Summa de Creatur.*, II, q. 34, a. 4 (XXXV, 304); Alex. of Hales, *Summa Theol.*, II, I, no. 356 (II, 432).
4. 参见 Cf. St. Bonaventure, *Itin. Mentis In Deum.*, II (V, 300).

But none of these explanations is apt. For the powers are not for the organs, but the organs for the powers, and therefore there are not various powers for the reason that there are various organs, but, on the contrary, for this has nature provided a variety of organs, that they might be suitable to the diversity of powers. In the same way, nature provided various mediums for the various senses, according to what suited the acts of the powers. Now to be cognizant of the natures of sensible qualities does not pertain to the senses, but to the intellect. The reason of the number and distinction of the exterior senses must therefore be ascribed to that which belongs to the senses properly and *per se*. Sense is a passive power, and is naturally immuted by the exterior sensible. Hence, the exterior cause of such immutation is what is *per se* perceived by the sense, and according to the diversity of that exterior cause are the sensitive powers diversified.

Now, immutation is of two kinds, one natural, the other spiritual. Natural immutation takes place when the form of that which causes the immutation is received, according to its natural being, into the thing immuted, as heat is received into the thing heated. But spiritual immutation takes place when the form of what causes the immutation is received, according to a spiritual mode of being, into the thing immuted, as the form of color is received into the pupil which does not thereby become colored. Now, for the operation of the senses, a spiritual immutation is required, whereby an intention of the sensible form is effected in the sensile organ. Otherwise, if a natural immutation alone sufficed for the sense's action, all natural bodies would have sensation when they undergo alteration.

But in some senses we find spiritual immutation only, as in *sight*, while in others we find not only a spiritual but also a natural immutation, and this either on the part of the object only, or likewise on the part of the organ. On the part of the object, we find local natural immutation in sound, which is the object of *hearing*; for sound is caused by percussion and commotion of the air. We find natural immutation by alteration in odor, which is the object of *smelling*; for in order to give off an odor, a body must be in a measure affected by heat. On the part of the organ, natural immutation takes place in *touch* and *taste*; for the hand that touches something hot becomes hot, while the tongue is moistened by the humidity of flavors. But the organs of smelling and hearing are not affected in their respective operations by any natural immutation, except accidentally.

Now, the sight, which is without natural immutation either in its organ or in its object, is the most spiritual, the most perfect, and the most universal of all the senses. After this comes the hearing and then the smell, which require a natural immutation on the part of the object; while local motion is more perfect than, and naturally prior to, the motion of alteration, as the Philosopher proves.[1] Touch and taste are the most material of all (of their distinction we shall speak later on). Hence it is that the three other senses are not exercised through a medium united to them, to obviate any natural immutation in their organ; as happens as regards these two senses.

Reply Obj. 1. Not every accident has in itself a power of immutation, but only qualities of the third species, according to which there can be alteration. Therefore only such qualities are the objects of the senses, because *the senses are affected by the same things whereby inanimate bodies are affected*, as is stated in *Physics* vii.[2]

Reply Obj. 2. Size, shape, and the like, which are called *common sensibles*, are midway between *accidental sensibles* and *proper sensibles*, which are the objects of the senses. For the proper sensibles first, and of their very nature, affect the senses, since they are qualities that cause alteration. But the common sensibles are all reducible to quantity. As to size and number, it is clear that they are species of

---

1. 参见 Aristotle, *Phys.*, VIII, 7 (260a 28).
2. 参见 *Op. cit.*, VII, 2 (244b 12).

quantity. Shape is a quality about quantity, since the nature of shape consists in fixing the bounds of magnitude. Movement and rest are sensed according as the subject is affected in one or more ways in the magnitude of the subject or of its local distance, as in the movement of growth or of locomotion, or again, according as it is affected in some sensible qualities, as in the movement of alteration; and thus to sense movement and rest is, in a way, to sense one thing and many. Now quantity is the proximate subject of the qualities that cause alteration, as surface is of color. Therefore the common sensibles do not move the senses first and of their own nature, but by reason of sensible quality; as the surface by reason of color. Yet they are not accidental sensibles, for they produce a certain diversity in the immutation of the senses. For sense is immuted differently by a large and by a small surface; since whiteness itself is said to be great or small, and therefore is divided according to its proper subject.

Reply Obj. 3. As the Philosopher seems to say, the sense of touch is generically one, but is divided into several specific senses, and for this reason it extends to various contrarieties.[1] These senses, however, are not separate from one another in their organ, but are spread together throughout the whole body, so that their distinction is not evident. But taste, which perceives the sweet and the bitter, accompanies touch in the tongue, but not in the whole body; so it is easily distinguished from touch. We might also say that all those contrarieties agree, each in some proximate genus, and all in a common genus, which is the common and formal object of touch. Such a common genus is, however, unnamed, just as the proximate genus of hot and cold is unnamed.

Reply Obj. 4. The sense of taste, according to a saying of the Philosopher, is a kind of touch existing only in the tongue.[2] It is not

---

1. 参见 *De An.*, II, 11 (422b 17).
2. 参见 *Op. cit.*, II, 9 (421a 18); 11 (423a 17).

distinct from touch in general, but only from the species of touch distributed in the body. But if touch is only one sense, because of the common formality of its object, we must say that taste is distinguished from touch by reason of a different kind of immutation. For touch involves a natural, and not only a spiritual, immutation in its organ, by reason of the quality which is its proper object. But the organ of taste is not necessarily immuted by a natural immutation according to the quality which is its proper object, so that the tongue itself becomes sweet or bitter, but according to the quality which is a preamble to, and on which is based, the flavor; which quality is moisture, the object of touch.

Fourth Article

WHETHER THE INTERIOR SENSES ARE SUITABLY DISTINGUISHED?

We proceed thus to the Fourth Article:—

Objection 1. It would seem that the interior senses are not suitably distinguished. For the common is not divided against the proper. Therefore the common sense should not be numbered among the interior sensitive powers, in addition to the proper exterior senses.

Obj. 2. Further, there is no need to assign an interior power of apprehension when the proper and exterior sense suffices. But the proper and exterior senses suffice for us to judge of sensible things; for each sense judges of its proper object. In like manner, they seem to suffice for the perception of their own actions; for since the action of the sense is, in a way, between the power and its object, it seems that sight must be much more able to perceive its own vision, as being nearer to it, than the color; and in like manner with the other senses. Therefore for this purpose there is no need to assign an interior power, called the common sense.

Obj. 3. Further, according to the Philosopher, the imagination and the memory are passions of the *first sensitive*.[1] But passion is not divided against its subject. Therefore memory and imagination should not be assigned as powers distinct from sense.

Obj. 4. Further, the intellect depends on the senses less than any power of the sensitive part. But the intellect knows nothing but what it receives from the senses; whence we read that *those who lack one sense lack one kind of knowledge*.[2] Therefore much less should we assign to the sensitive part a power, which they call the *estimative* power[3], for the perception of representations which the sense does not perceive.

Obj. 5. Further, the action of the *cogitative* power[4], which consists in comparing, uniting and dividing, and the action of the *reminiscence*, which consists in the use of a kind of syllogism for the sake of inquiry, are not less distant from the actions of the *estimative* and *memorative* powers[5], than the action of the estimative is from the action of the imagination. Therefore either we must add the cogitative and reminiscitive powers[6] to the estimative and memorative powers, or the estimative and memorative powers should not be made distinct from the imagination.

Obj. 6. Further, Augustine describes three kinds of vision, namely, corporeal, which is an action of the sense; spiritual, which is an action of the imagination or phantasy; and intellectual, which is an action of the intellect.[7] Therefore there is no interior power between the sense and intellect, besides the imagination.

On the contrary, Avicenna assigns five interior sensitive powers, namely, *common sense*, *phantasy*, *imagination*, *the estimative and the*

---

1. 参见 *De Mem. et Rem.*, I (450a 10).
2. 参见 Aristotle, *Post. Anal.*, I, 18 (81a 38).
3. the estimative power: 估量的技能
4. the cogitative power: 思考力
5. the memorative power: 记忆力
6. the reminiscitive power: 回忆能力
7. 参见 *De Genesi ad Litt.*, XII, 6; 7; 24 (PL 34, 458; 459; 474).

memorative.[1]

I answer that, As nature does not fail in necessary things, there must needs be as many actions of the sensitive soul as may suffice for the life of a perfect animal. If any of these actions cannot be reduced to one and the same principle, they must be assigned to diverse powers; since a power of the soul is nothing else than the proximate principle of the soul's operation.

Now we must observe that for the life of a perfect animal, the animal should apprehend a thing not only at the actual time of sensation, but also when it is absent. Otherwise, since animal motion and action follow apprehension, an animal would not be moved to seek something absent; the contrary of which we may observe especially in perfect animals, which are moved by progression, for they are moved towards something apprehended and absent. Therefore, through the sensitive soul an animal must not only receive the species of sensible things, when it is actually affected by them, but it must also retain and preserve them. Now to receive and retain are, in corporeal things, reduced to diverse principles; for moist things are apt to receive, but retain with difficulty, while it is the reverse with dry things. Therefore, since the sensitive power is the act of a corporeal organ, it follows that the power which receives the species of sensible things must be distinct from the power which preserves them.

Again, we must observe that if an animal were moved by pleasing and disagreeable things only as affecting the sense, there would be no need to suppose that an animal has a power besides the apprehension of those forms which the senses perceive, and in which the animal takes pleasure, or from which it shrinks with horror. But the animal needs to seek or to avoid certain things, not only because they are pleasing or otherwise to the senses, but also because of other

---

1. 参见 *De An.*, I, 5 (51b); IV, 1 (17va).

advantages and uses, or disadvantages; just as the sheep runs away when it sees a wolf, not because of its color or shape, but as a natural enemy. So, too, a bird gathers together straws, not because they are pleasant to the sense, but because they are useful for building its nest. Animals, therefore, need to perceive such intentions, which the exterior sense does not perceive. Now some distinct principle is necessary for this, since the perception of sensible forms comes by an immutation caused by the sensible, which is not the case with the perception of the above intentions.

Thus, therefore, for the reception of sensible forms, the *proper sense* and the *common sense* are appointed. Of their distinction we shall speak later. But for the retention and preservation of these forms, the *phantasy* or *imagination* is appointed, being as it were a storehouse of forms received through the senses. Furthermore, for the apprehension of intentions which are not received through the senses, the *estimative* power is appointed: and for their preservation, the *memorative* power, which is a storehouse of such intentions. A sign of which we have in the fact that the principle of memory in animals is found in some such intention, for instance, that something is harmful or otherwise. And the very character of something as past, which memory observes, is to be reckoned among these intentions.

Now, we must observe that as to sensible forms there is no difference between man and other animals; for they are similarly immuted by external sensibles. But there is a difference as to the above intentions: for other animals perceive these intentions only by some sort of natural instinct, while man perceives them also by means of a certain comparison. Therefore the power which in other animals is called the *natural estimative* in man is called the *cogitative*, which by some sort of comparison discovers these intentions.[1] Therefore

1. 参见 Cf. Alex. of Hales, *Summa Theol.*, II, I, no. 357 (II, 434).—Cf. also Averroes, *Colliget*, II, 20 (X, 17va).

it is also called the *particular reason*, to which medical men assign a particular organ, namely, the middle part of the head;[1] for it compares individual intentions, just as the intellectual reason compares universal intentions. As to the memorative power, man has not only memory, as other animals have, in the sudden recollection of the past, but also *reminiscence*[2], by seeking syllogistically, as it were, for a recollection of the past by the application of individual intentions. Avicenna,[3] however, assigns between the estimative and the imaginative a fifth power, which combines and divides imaginary forms; as when from the imaginary form of gold, and the imaginary form of a mountain, we compose the one form of a golden mountain, which we have never seen. But this operation is not to be found in animals other than man, in whom the imaginative power suffices for this purpose. Averroes also attributes this action to the imagination, in his book *De sensu et sensibilibus*.[4] So there is no need to assign more than four interior powers of the sensitive part—namely, the common sense, the imagination, and the estimative and memorative powers.

Reply Obj. 1. The interior sense is called *common* not by predication, as if it were a genus, but as the common root and principle of the exterior senses.

Reply Obj. 2. The proper sense judges of the proper sensible by discerning it from other things which come under the same sense; for instance, by discerning white from black or green. But neither sight nor taste can discern white from sweet, because what discerns between two things must know both. Hence, the discerning judgment must be assigned to the common sense. To it, as to a common term, all apprehensions of the senses must be referred, and by it, again, all the

1. 参见 Avicenna, *De An.*, I, 5 (5rb); Averroes, *Colliget*, II, 20 (X, 17va).
2. reminiscence: 旧事；回忆
3. 参见 *De An.*, IV, 1 (17va).
4. 参见 *De Sensu et Sensibili* (VI, 193v).

intentions of the senses are perceived; as when someone sees that he sees. For this cannot be done by the proper sense, which knows only the form of the sensible by which it is immuted. In this immutation the action of sight is completed, and from it follows another immutation in the common sense which perceives the act of seeing.

Reply Obj. 3. Just as one power arises from the soul by means of another, as we have seen above,[1] so likewise the soul is the subject of one power through another. In this way the imagination and the memory are called passions of the *first sensitive*.

Reply Obj. 4. Although the operation of the intellect has its origin in the senses, yet, in the thing apprehended through the senses, the intellect knows many things which the senses cannot perceive. In like manner does the estimative power, though in a less perfect way.

Reply Obj. 5. The cogitative and memorative powers in man owe their excellence not to that which is proper to the sensitive part, but to a certain affinity and proximity to the universal reason, which, so to speak, overflows into them. Therefore they are not distinct powers, but the same, yet more perfect than in other animals.

Reply Obj. 6. Augustine calls that vision spiritual which is effected by the images of bodies in the absence of bodies. Whence it is clear that it is common to all interior apprehensions.

1. 参见 Q. 77, a. 7.

Question LXXIX
THE INTELLECTUAL POWERS
(*In Thirteen Articles*)

THE next question concerns the intellectual powers, under which head there are thirteen points of inquiry: (1) Whether the intellect is a power of the soul, or its essence? (2) If it is a power, whether it is a passive power? (3) If it is a passive power, whether there must be an agent intellect? (4) Whether it is something in the soul? (5) Whether the agent intellect is one in all? (6) Whether memory is in the intellect? (7) Whether the memory is distinct from the intellect? (8) Whether the reason is a distinct power from the intellect? (9) Whether the superior and inferior reason are distinct powers? (10) Whether intelligence is a power distinct from the intellect? (11) Whether the speculative and practical intellect are distinct powers? (12) Whether *synderesis* is some power of the intellectual part? (13) Whether the conscience is a power of the intellectual part?

First Article
WHETHER THE INTELLECT IS A POWER OF THE SOUL?

We proceed thus to the First Article:—

Objection 1. It would seem that the intellect is not a power of the soul, but the essence of the soul. For the intellect seems to be the same as the mind. Now the mind is not a power of the soul, but the essence; for Augustine says: *Mind and spirit are not names of relations, but denominate the essence.*[1]

---

1. 参见 *De Trin.*, IX, 2 (PL 42, 962).

Therefore the intellect is the essence of the soul.

Obj. 2. Further, different genera of the soul's powers are not united in some one power, but only in the essence of the soul. Now the appetitive and the intellectual are different genera of the soul's powers, as the Philosopher says;[1] but they are united in the mind, for Augustine places the intelligence and will in the mind.[2] Therefore the mind and intellect of man is the very essence of the soul, and not a power.

Obj. 3. Further, according to Gregory, in a homily for the Ascension, *man understands with the angels.*[3] But angels are called *minds* and *intellects.* Therefore the mind and intellect of man is not a power of the soul, but the soul itself.

Obj. 4. Further, a substance is intellectual by the fact that it is immaterial. But the soul is immaterial through its essence. Therefore it seems that the soul must be intellectual through its essence.

On the contrary, The Philosopher assigns the intellect as a power of the soul.[4]

I answer that, In accordance with what has been already shown, it is necessary to say that the intellect is a power of the soul, and not the very essence of the soul.[5] For the essence of that which operates is then alone the immediate principle of operation, when operation itself is its being; for as power is related to operation as to its act, so is essence related to being. But in God alone is His act of understanding the same as His very Being. Hence, in God alone is His intellect His essence; while in other intellectual creatures, the intellect is a power.

Reply Obj. 1. Sense is sometimes taken for the power, and sometimes

---

1. 参见 Aristotle, *De An.*, II, 3 (414a 31).
2. 参见 *De Trin.*, X, 11 (PL 42, 983).
3. 参见 *In Evang.*, II, hom. 29 (PL 76, 1214).
4. 参见 *De An.*, II, 3 (414a 32).
5. 参见 Q. 54, a. 3; q. 77, a. 1.

for the sensitive soul; for the sensitive soul takes its name from its chief power, which is sense. And in like manner the intellectual soul is sometimes called intellect, as from its chief power; and thus we read that the *intellect is a substance.*[1] And in this sense also Augustine says that the mind is spirit or essence.[2]

Reply Obj. 2. The appetitive and intellectual powers are different genera of powers in the soul, by reason of the different natures of their objects. But the appetitive power agrees partly with the intellectual power, and partly with the sensitive, in its mode of operation either through a corporeal organ or without it; for appetite follows apprehension. It is in this way that Augustine puts the will in the mind; and the Philosopher, in the reason.[3]

Reply Obj. 3. In the angels there is no other power besides the intellect and the will, which follows the intellect. This is the reason why an angel is called a *mind* or an *intellect*, because his whole power consists in this. But the soul has many other powers, such as the sensitive and nutritive powers, and therefore the comparison fails.

Reply Obj. 4. The immateriality of a created intelligent substance is not its intellect; but rather through its immateriality it has the power of understanding. Therefore it follows, not that the intellect is the substance of the soul, but that it is its virtue and power.

Second Article
WHETHER THE INTELLECT IS A PASSIVE POWER?

We proceed thus to the Second Article:—

Objection 1. It would seem that the intellect is not a passive power. For everything is passive by its matter, and acts by its form. But the

---

1. 参见 Aristotle, *De An.*, I, 4 (408b 18).
2. 参见 *De Trin.*, IX, 2; XIV, 16 (PL 42, 962; 1053).
3. 参见 *De An.*, III, 9 (432b 5).

intellectual power results from the immateriality of the intelligent substance. Therefore it seems that the intellect is not a passive power.

Obj. 2. Further, the intellectual power is incorruptible, as we have said above.[1] But *if the intellect is passive, it is corruptible.*[2] Therefore the intellectual power is not passive.

Obj. 3. Further, the *agent is nobler than the patient*, as Augustine[3] and Aristotle[4] say. But all the powers of the vegetative part are active, and yet they are the lowest among the powers of the soul. Much more, therefore, are all the intellectual powers, which are the highest, active.

On the contrary, The Philosopher says that *to understand is in a way to be passive.*[5]

I answer that, To be passive may be taken in three ways. Firstly, in its most strict sense, when from a thing is taken something which belongs to it by virtue either of its nature, or of its proper inclination; as when water loses coolness by heating, and as when a man becomes ill or sad. Secondly, less strictly, a thing is said to be passive when something, whether suitable or unsuitable, is taken away from it. And in this way not only he who is ill is said to be passive, but also he who is healed; not only he that is sad, but also he that is joyful; or whatever way he be altered or moved. Thirdly, in a wide sense a thing is said to be passive, from the very fact that what is in potentiality to something receives that to which it was in potentiality, without being deprived of anything. And accordingly, whatever passes from potentiality to act may be said to be passive, even when it is perfected. It is *thus* that to understand is to be passive. This is clear from the following reason. For the intellect, as we have seen above, has an operation extending

---

1. 参见 Q. 75, a. 6.
2. 参见 Aristotle, *De An.*, III, 5 (430a 24).
3. 参见 *De Genesi ad Litt.*, XII, 16 (PL 34, 467).
4. 参见 *De An.*, III, 5 (430a 18).
5. 参见 *Op. cit.*, III, 4 (429b 24).

to universal being.[1] We may therefore see whether an intellect is in act or potentiality by observing first of all the nature of the relation of the intellect to universal being. For we find an intellect whose relation to universal being is that of the act of all being; and such is the divine intellect, which is the essence of God, in which, originally and virtually, all being pre-exists as in its first cause. Therefore the divine intellect is not in potentiality, but is pure act. But no created intellect can be an act in relation to the whole universal being; for then it would needs be an infinite being. Therefore no created intellect, by reason of its very being, is the act of all things intelligible; but it is compared to these intelligible things as a potentiality to act.

Now, potentiality has a double relation to act. There is a potentiality which is always perfected by its act. Such is the case with the matter of the heavenly bodies.[2] And there is another potentiality which is not always in act, but proceeds from potentiality to act; as we observe in things that are corrupted and generated. Hence the angelic intellect is always in act as regards those things which it can understand, by reason of its proximity to the first intellect, which is pure act, as we have said above. But the human intellect, which is the lowest in the order of intellects and most remote from the perfection of the divine intellect, is in potentiality with regard to things intelligible, and is at first *like a clean tablet on which nothing is written*, as the Philosopher says.[3] This is made clear from the fact that at first we are only in potentiality towards understanding, and afterwards we are made to understand actually. And so it is evident that with us to understand is *in a way to be passive*, taking passion in the third sense. And consequently the intellect is a passive power.

Reply Obj. 1. This objection is verified of passion in the first and

---

1. 参见 Q. 78, a. 1.
2. 参见 Q. 58, a. 1.
3. 参见 *De An.*, III, 4 (430a 1).

second senses, which belong to primary matter. But in the third sense, passion is in anything which is reduced from potentiality to act.

Reply Obj. 2. *Passive intellect* is the name given by some to the sensitive appetite, in which are the passions of the soul;[1] which appetite is also called *rational by participation*, because it *obeys the reason*.[2] Others give the name of passive intellect to the cogitative power, which is called the *particular reason*.[3] And in each case *passive* may be taken in the two first senses, since this so-called intellect is the act of a corporeal organ. But the intellect which is in potentiality to things intelligible, and which for this reason Aristotle calls the *possible intellect*,[4] is not passive except in the third sense; for it is not an act of a corporeal organ. Hence it is incorruptible.

Reply Obj. 3. The agent is nobler than the patient, if the action and the passion are referred to the same thing; but not always, if they refer to different things. Now the intellect is a passive power in regard to the whole universal being, while the vegetative power is active in regard to some particular thing, namely, the body as united to the soul. Therefore nothing prevents such a passive power being nobler than such an active one.

Third Article
WHETHER THERE IS AN AGENT INTELLECT?

We proceed thus to the Third Article:—

Objection 1. It would seem that there is no agent intellect. For as the senses are to things sensible, so is our intellect to things intelligible.

---

1. 参见 Themistius, *In De An.*, III, 5 (II, 186). —Cf. Averroes, *In De An.*, III, 20 (VI, 170v).
2. 参见 Aristotle, *Eth.*, I, 13 (1102b 25).
3. 参见 Cf. Averroes, *In De An.*, III, 20 (VI, 171r).
4. 参见 *De An.*, III, 4 (429a 22).

But because sense is in potentiality to things sensible, there is not said to be an *agent sense*, but only a passive one. Therefore, since our intellect is in potentiality to things intelligible, it seems that we cannot say that there is an agent intellect, but only a passive one.[1]

Obj. 2. Further, if we say that also in the senses there is something active, such as light,[2] on the contrary, light is required for sight, inasmuch as it makes the medium to be actually luminous; for color of its own nature moves the luminous medium. But in the operation of the intellect there is no appointed medium that has to be brought into act. Therefore there is no necessity for an agent intellect.

Obj. 3. Further, the likeness of the agent is received into the patient according to the nature of the patient. But the possible intellect is an immaterial power. Therefore its immaterial nature suffices for forms to be received into it immaterially. Now a form is intelligible in act from the very fact that it is immaterial. Therefore there is no need for an agent intellect to make the species actually intelligible.[3]

On the contrary, The Philosopher says: *As in every nature, so in the soul, there is something by which it becomes all things, and something by which it makes all things.*[4] Therefore we must admit an agent intellect.

I answer that, According to the opinion of Plato, there is no need for an agent intellect in order to make things actually intelligible, but perhaps in order to provide intellectual light to the intellect, as will be explained farther on.[5] For Plato supposed that the forms of natural things subsisted apart from matter, and consequently that they are intelligible;[6] for a thing is actually intelligible from the very fact that it is immaterial. And he called such forms *species or ideas*. From a

---

1. 参见 An argument of William of Auvergne, *De An.*, VII, 4 (II, Suppl., 207).
2. 参见 Cf. *ibid.*
3. 参见 Cf. *op. cit.*, VII, 5 (II, Suppl., 210).
4. 参见 *De An.*, III, 5 (430a 10).
5. 参见 A. 4; q. 84, a. 6.
6. 参见 Cf. above, q. 6, a. 4.

participation in these, he said that even corporeal matter was formed, in order that individuals might be naturally established in their proper genera and species,[1] and also that our intellect was formed by such participation in order to have knowledge of the genera and species of things.[2] But since Aristotle did not allow that the forms of natural things exist apart from matter, and since forms existing in matter are not actually intelligible,[3] it follows that the natures or forms of the sensible things which we understand are not actually intelligible. Now nothing is reduced from potentiality to act except by something in act; as the senses are made actual by what is actually sensible. We must therefore assign on the part of the intellect some power to make things actually intelligible, by the abstraction of the species from material conditions. And such is the necessity for positing an agent intellect.

Reply Obj. 1. Sensible things are found in act outside the soul; and hence there is no need for an agent sense. Therefore it is clear that, in the nutritive part, all the powers are active, whereas in the sensitive part all are passive; but in the intellectual part, there is something active and something passive.

Reply Obj. 2. There are two opinions as to the effect of light. For some say that light is required for sight, in order to make colors actually visible.[4] And according to this, the agent intellect is required for understanding in like manner and for the same reason as light is required for seeing. But in the opinion of others, light is required for sight, not for the colors to become actually visible, but in order that the medium may become actually luminous, as the Commentator says on *De Anima* ii.[5] And according to this, Aristotle's comparison

---

1. 参见 Cf. Aristotle, *Metaph.*, I, 9 (991b 3); Plato, *Phaedo* (p. 100d).—Cf. above, q. 15, a. 3.
2. 参见 Cf. below, q. 84, a. 1; a. 4.
3. 参见 Cf. *Metaph.*, II, 4 (999b 18); VII, 3 (1043b 19).
4. 参见 Avempace: cf. Averroes, *In De An.*, II, comm. 67 (VI, 140r).
5. 同上

of the agent intellect to light[1] is verified in this, that as it is required for understanding, so is light required for seeing; but not for the same reason.

Reply Obj. 3. If the agent pre-exist, it may well happen that its likeness is received variously into various things, because of their dispositions. But if the agent does not pre-exist, the disposition of the recipient has nothing to do with the matter. Now the intelligible in act is not something existing in nature, provided, of course, that we are thinking of the nature of sensible things, which do not subsist without matter. And therefore in order to understand them, the immaterial nature of the possible intellect would not suffice but for the presence of the agent intellect, which makes things actually intelligible by way of abstraction.

Fourth Article

WHETHER THE AGENT INTELLECT IS SOMETHING IN THE SOUL?

We proceed thus to the Fourth Article:—

Objection 1. It would seem that the agent intellect is not something in the soul. For the effect of the agent intellect is to give light for the purpose of understanding. But this is done by something higher than the soul, according to *Jo.* i. 9, *He was the true light that enlighteneth every man coming into this world.* Therefore the agent intellect is not something in the soul.[2]

Obj. 2. Further, the Philosopher says of the agent intellect, *that it does not sometimes understand and sometimes not understand.*[3] But our soul does

1. 参见 *De An.*, III, 5 (430a 15).—Cf. Averroes, *In De An.*, II, comm. 67 (VI, 140r); III, comm. 18 (VI, 169v).
2. 参见 Cf. William of Auvergne, *De An.*, VII, 6 (II, Suppl., 211).
3. 参见 *De An.*, III, 5 (430a 22).

not always understand, but sometimes it understands, and sometimes it does not understand. Therefore the agent intellect is not something in our soul.[1]

Obj. 3. Further, agent and patient suffice for action. If, therefore, the possible intellect, which is a passive power, is something belonging to the soul; and also the agent intellect, which is an active power:—it follows that man would always be able to understand when he wished, which is clearly false. Therefore the agent intellect is not something in our soul.[2]

Obj. 4. Further, the Philosopher says that the agent intellect is *a substance in actual being.*[3] But nothing can be in potentiality and in act with regard to the same thing. If, therefore, the possible intellect, which is in potentiality to all things intelligible, is something in the soul, it seems impossible for the agent intellect to be also something in our soul.

Obj. 5. Further, if the agent intellect is something in the soul, it must be a power. For it is neither a passion nor a habit, since habits and passions do not have the nature of agents in regard to what the soul receives; but passion is rather the very action of the passive power, while habit is something which results from acts. Now every power flows from the essence of the soul. It would therefore follow that the agent intellect flows from the essence of the soul. And thus it would not be in the soul by way of participation from some higher intellect; which is unfitting. Therefore the agent intellect is not something in our soul.

On the contrary, The Philosopher says that *it is necessary for these differences*, namely, the possible and agent intellect, *to be in the soul.*[4]

---

1. 参见 Cf. William of Auvergne, *De An.*, VII, 3 (II, Suppl., 206).
2. 参见 Cf. *op. cit.*, VII, 4 (II, Suppl., 208).
3. 参见 *De An.*, III, 5 (430a 18).
4. 参见 *Op. cit.*, III, 5 (430a 13).

I answer that, The agent intellect, of which the Philosopher speaks, is something in the soul. In order to make this evident, we must observe that above the intellectual soul of man we must needs suppose a superior intellect, from which the soul acquires the power of understanding. For what is such by participation, and what is movable, and what is imperfect, always requires the pre-existence of something essentially such, immovable and perfect. Now the human soul is called intellectual by reason of a participation in intellectual power, a sign of which is that it is not wholly intellectual but only in part. Moreover it reaches to the understanding of truth by reasoning, with a certain discursiveness and movement. Even more, it has an imperfect understanding, both because it does not understand everything, and because, in those things which it does understand, it passes from potentiality to act. Therefore there must needs be some higher intellect, by which the soul is helped to understand.

Therefore some held that this intellect, substantially separate, is the agent intellect,[1] which by lighting up the phantasms, as it were, makes them to be actually intelligible. But, even supposing the existence of such a separate agent intellect, it would still be necessary to assign to the human soul some power participating in that superior intellect, by which power the human soul makes things to be actually intelligible. Such is also the case in other perfect natural things, among which, besides the universal active causes, each one is endowed with its proper powers derived from those universal causes: for the sun alone does not generate man, but in man himself there is the power of begetting man; and in like manner with other perfect animals. Now among these sublunary things nothing is more perfect than the human soul. Therefore we must say that in the soul is some power derived

---

1. 参见 Alexander of Aphrodisias, *De Intellectu et Intellecto* (p. 76); Averroes, *In De An.*, III, comm. 18 (VI, 169v); comm. 19 (VI, 170r); Avicenna, *De An.*, V, 5 (25rb); *Metaph.*, IX, 3 (104rb).

from a higher intellect, whereby it is able to illumine the phantasms.

And we know this by experience, since we perceive that we abstract universal forms from their particular conditions; which is to make them actually intelligible. Now no action belongs to anything except through some principle formally inherent therein, as we have said above of the possible intellect.[1] Therefore the power which is the principle of this action must be something in the soul. For this reason Aristotle compared the agent intellect to light, which is something received into the air,[2] while Plato compared the separate intellect, whose light touches the soul, to the sun, as Themistius says in his commentary on *De Anima* iii.[3]

But the separate intellect, according to the teaching of our Faith, is God Himself, Who is the soul's Creator, and only beatitude; as will be shown later on.[4] Therefore the human soul derives its intellectual light from Him, according to *Ps.* iv. 7, *The light of Thy countenance, O Lord, is signed upon us.*

Reply Obj. 1. That true light illumines as a universal cause, from which the human soul derives a particular power, as we have explained.

Reply Obj. 2. The Philosopher says those words not of the agent intellect, but of the intellect in act; of which he had already said: *Knowledge in act is the same as the thing.*[5] Or, if we refer those words to the agent intellect, then they are said because it is not owing to the agent intellect that sometimes we do, and sometimes we do not understand, but to the intellect which is in potentiality.

Reply Obj. 3. If the relation of the agent intellect to the possible

---

1. 参见 Q. 76, a. 1.
2. 参见 *De An.*, III, 5 (430a 15).
3. 参见 *In De An.*, III 5 (II, 191); cf. Plato, *Republic*, VI (p. 508).
4. 参见 Q. 90, a. 3; I–II, q. 3, a. 7.
5. 参见 *De An.*, III, 5 (430a 19).

intellect were that of an active object to a power (as, for instance, of the visible in act to the sight), it would follow that we could understand all things instantly, since the agent intellect is that which makes all things in act. But the agent intellect is not an object, rather is it that whereby the objects are made to be in act; and for this, besides the presence of the agent intellect, we require the presence of phantasms, the good disposition of the sensitive powers, and practice in this sort of operation. For from one thing understood, other things come to be understood, as from terms propositions are made, and from first principles, conclusions. From this point of view, it matters not whether the agent intellect is something belonging to the soul, or something separate from the soul.

Reply Obj. 4. The intellectual soul is indeed actually immaterial, but it is in potentiality to the determinate species of things. On the contrary, phantasms are actual likenesses of certain species, but they are immaterial in potentiality. Therefore nothing prevents one and the same soul, inasmuch as it is actually immaterial, from having a power by which it makes things actually immaterial, by abstraction from the conditions of individual matter (this power is called the *agent intellect*), and another power, receptive of such species, which is called the *possible intellect* by reason of its being in potentiality to such species.

Reply Obj. 5. Since the essence of the soul is immaterial, created by the supreme intellect, nothing prevents the power which it derives from the supreme intellect, and whereby it abstracts from matter, from proceeding from the essence of the soul, in the same way as its other powers.

Fifth Article
WHETHER THE AGENT INTELLECT IS ONE IN ALL?

We proceed thus to the Fifth Article:—

Objection 1. It would seem that there is one agent intellect in all.

For what is separate from the body is not multiplied according to the number of bodies. But the agent intellect is *separate*, as the Philosopher says.[1] Therefore it is not multiplied in the multitude of human bodies, but is one for all men.

Obj. 2. Further, the agent intellect is the cause of the universal, which is one in many. But that which is the cause of unity is still more itself one. Therefore the intellect is the same in all.

Obj. 3. Further, all men agree in the first intellectual concepts. But to these they assent by the agent intellect. Therefore all are united in one agent intellect.

On the contrary, The Philosopher says that the agent intellect is as a light.[2] But light is not the same in the various illuminated things. Therefore the same agent intellect is not in various men.

I answer that, The truth about this question depends on what we have already said. For if the agent intellect were not something belonging to the soul, but were some separate substance, there would be one agent intellect for all men. And this is what they mean who hold that there is one agent intellect for all. But if the agent intellect is something belonging to the soul, as one of its powers, we are bound to say that there are as many agent intellects as there are souls, which are multiplied according to the number of men, as we have said above.[3] For it is impossible that one and the same power belong to various substances.

Reply Obj. 1. The Philosopher proves that the agent intellect is separate by the fact that the possible intellect is separate; because, as he says, *the agent is more noble than the patient.*[4] Now the possible intellect is said to be separate because it is not the act of any corporeal organ.

---

1. 参见 *De An.*, III, 5 (430a 17).
2. 同上 (430a 15).
3. 参见 Q. 76, a. 2.
4. 参见 *De An.*, III, 5 (430a 18).

And in this sense the agent intellect is also called *separate*; but not as a separate substance.

Reply Obj. 2. The agent intellect is the cause of the universal, by abstracting it from matter. But for this purpose it need not be one in all intelligent beings; but it must be one in relation to all those things from which it abstracts the universal, with respect to which things the universal is one. And this befits the agent intellect inasmuch as it is immaterial.

Reply Obj. 3. All things which are of one species enjoy in common the action which accompanies the nature of the species, and consequently the power which is the principle of such action; but not in such a way that the power be identical in all. Now to know the first intelligible principles is an action belonging to the human species. Therefore all men enjoy in common the power which is the principle of this action; and this power is the agent intellect. But there is no need for it to be identical in all; although it must be derived by all from one principle. And thus the possession by all men in common of first principles proves the unity of the separate intellect, which Plato compares to the sun, but not the unity of the agent intellect, which Aristotle compares to light.[1]

Sixth Article
WHETHER MEMORY IS IN THE INTELLECTUAL PART OF THE SOUL?

We proceed thus to the Sixth Article:—

Objection 1. It would seem that memory is not in the intellectual part of the soul. For Augustine says that to the higher part of the soul belong those things which are not *common to man and beast.*[2] But

1. 参见 *De An.*, III, 5 (430a 15).
2. 参见 *De Trin.*, XII, 2; 8 (PL 42, 999; 1005).

memory is common to man and beast, for he says that *beasts can sense corporeal things through the senses of the body, and commit them to memory.*[1] Therefore memory does not belong to the intellectual part of the soul.

Obj. 2. Further, memory is of the past. But the past is said of something according to a fixed time. Memory, therefore, knows a thing under the condition of a fixed time; which involves knowledge under the conditions of *here* and *now*. But this is not the province of the intellect, but of the sense. Therefore memory is not in the intellectual part, but only in the sensitive part.

Obj. 3. Further, in the memory are preserved the species of those things of which we are not actually thinking. But this cannot happen in the intellect, because the intellect is reduced to act by the fact that the intelligible species are received into it. Now for the intellect to be in act is for it to be understanding in act; and therefore the intellect actually understands all things of which it has the species. Therefore the memory is not in the intellectual part.

On the contrary, Augustine says that *memory, understanding and will are one mind.*[2]

I answer that, Since it is of the nature of the memory to preserve the species of those things which are not apprehended actually, we must first of all consider whether the intelligible species can thus be preserved in the intellect. For Avicenna held that this was impossible.[3] He admitted that this could happen in the sensitive part, as to some powers, inasmuch as they are acts of corporeal organs, in which certain species may be preserved without actual apprehension; but in the intellect, which has no corporeal organ, nothing but what is intelligible exists. Hence, every thing of which the likeness exists in the intellect must be actually understood. Thus, therefore, according to

1. 参见 *Op. cit.*, XII, 2 (PL 42, 999).
2. 参见 *Op. cit.*, X, 11 (PL 42, 983).
3. 参见 *De An.*, V, 6 (26rb).

him, as soon as we cease to understand something actually, the species of that thing ceases to be in our intellect, and if we wish to understand that thing anew, we must turn to the agent intellect, which he held to be a separate substance, in order that the intelligible species may thence flow again into our possible intellect. And from the practice and repetition of turning to the agent intellect there is formed, according to him, a certain aptitude in the possible intellect for turning itself to the agent intellect; which aptitude he calls *the habit of science*. According, therefore, to this supposition, nothing is preserved in the intellectual part that is not actually understood; and hence it would not be possible to admit memory in the intellectual part.

But this opinion is clearly opposed to the teaching of Aristotle. For he says that, when the possible intellect *is identified with each thing as knowing it, it is said to be in act*, and that *this happens when it can operate through itself. And, even then, it is in potentiality, but not in the same way as before learning and discovering.*[1] Now, the possible intellect is said to become each thing, inasmuch as it receives the intelligible species of each thing. To the fact, therefore, that it receives the species of intelligible things it owes its being able to operate when it wills, but not so that it be always operating; for even then it is in potentiality in a certain sense, though otherwise than before the act of understanding—namely, in the sense that whoever has habitual knowledge is in potentiality to actual consideration.

The foregoing opinion is also opposed to reason. For what is received into something is received according to the condition of the recipient. But the intellect is of a more stable nature, and is more immovable, than corporeal matter. If, therefore, corporeal matter holds the forms which it receives, not only while it actually does something through them, but also after ceasing to act through them, much more

1. 参见 *De An.*, III, 4 (429b 5).

does the intellect receive the species unchangeably and lastingly, whether it receive them from things sensible, or from some superior intellect.

Thus, therefore, if we take memory only for the power of retaining species, we must say that it is in the intellectual part. But if in the notion of memory we include its object as something past, then the memory is not in the intellectual, but only in the sensitive part, which apprehends individual things. For past, as past, since it signifies being under a condition of fixed time, is something individual.

Reply Obj. 1. Memory, if considered as retentive of species, is not common to us and other animals. For species are not retained in the sensitive part of the soul only, but rather in the body and soul united, since the memorative power is the act of some organ. But the intellect in itself is retentive of species, without the association of any corporeal organ. Therefore the Philosopher says that *the soul is the seat of the species, not the whole soul, but the intellect.*[1]

Reply Obj. 2. The condition of *pastness* may be referred to two things—namely, to the object known, and to the act of knowledge. These two are found together in the sensitive part, which apprehends something from the fact of its being immuted by a present sensible. Therefore, at one and the same time an animal remembers that he sensed before in the past, and that he sensed some past sensible thing. But as concerns the intellectual part, the past is accidental, and is not in itself a part of the object of the intellect, for the intellect understands man as man; and to man, as man, it is accidental that he exist in the present, past, or future. But on the part of the act, the condition of being past, even as such, may be understood to be in the intellect, as well as in the senses. For our soul's act of understanding is an individual act, existing in this or that time, inasmuch as a

1. 参见 *De An.*, III, 4 (429a 27).

man is said to understand now, or yesterday, or tomorrow. And this is not incompatible with what is intellectual, for such an act of understanding, though something individual, is yet an immaterial act, as we have said above of the intellect.[1] And therefore, just as the intellect understands itself, though it be itself an individual intellect, so also it understands its act of understanding, which is an individual act, in the past, present, or future. In this way, then, the notion of memory, in as far as it regards past events, is preserved in the intellect, according as it understands that it previously understood; but not in the sense that it understands the past as something *here* and *now*.

Reply Obj. 3. The intelligible species is sometimes in the intellect only in potentiality, and then the intellect is said to be in potentiality. Sometimes the intelligible species is in the intellect according to the ultimate completion of the act, and then the intellect understands in act. And sometimes the intelligible species is in a middle state, between potentiality and act; and then we have habitual knowledge. In this last way the intellect retains the species, even when it does not understand in act.

Seventh Article
WHETHER THE INTELLECTUAL MEMORY IS A POWER DISTINCT FROM THE INTELLECT?

We proceed thus to the Seventh Article:—

Objection 1. It would seem that the intellectual memory is distinct from the intellect. For Augustine assigns to the mind memory, understanding and will.[2] But it is clear that the memory is a distinct power from the will. Therefore it is also distinct from the intellect.

Obj. 2. Further, the principle of distinction among the powers in

---

1. 参见 Q. 76, a. 1.
2. 参见 *De Trin.*, X, 11 (PL 42, 983) ; cf. *op. cit.*, XIV, 7 (PL 42, 1043).

the sensitive part is the same as in the intellectual part. But memory in the sensitive part is distinct from sense, as we have said.[1] Therefore memory in the intellectual part is distinct from the intellect.

Obj. 3. Further, according to Augustine, memory, understanding and will are equal to one another, and one flows from the other.[2] But this could not be if memory and intellect were the same power. Therefore they are not the same power.

On the contrary, From its nature the memory is the treasury or storehouse of species. But the Philosopher attributes this to the intellect, as we have said.[3] Therefore the memory is not another power from the intellect.

I answer that, As has been said above, the powers of the soul are distinguished according to the different character of their objects,[4] for each power is defined in reference to that thing to which it is directed and which is its object. It has also been said above that if any power is directed by its nature to an object according to the common nature of the object, that power will not be differentiated according to the individual differences under that object;[5] just as the power of sight, in relation to its object under the common nature of color, is not differentiated by differences of black and white. Now, the intellect is related to its object under the common nature of being, since the possible intellect is that *by which we become all things*. Therefore the possible intellect is not differentiated by any difference of being. Nevertheless there is a distinction between the power of the agent intellect and of that of the possible intellect; because as regards the same object, the active power, which makes the object to be in act,

---

1. 参见 Q. 78, a. 4.
2. 参见 *De Trin.*, X, 11; XI, 7 (PL 42, 983; 993).
3. 参见 *De An.*, III, 4 (429a 27).—Cf. a. 6, ad 1.
4. 参见 Q. 77, a. 3.
5. 参见 Q. 59, a. 4.

must be distinct from the passive power, which is moved by the object existing in act. Thus the active power is compared to its object as a being in act is to a being in potentiality; whereas the passive power, on the contrary, is compared to its object as a being in potentiality is to a being in act.

Therefore there can be no other difference of powers in the intellect but that of possible and agent. Hence, it is clear that memory is not a distinct power from the intellect, for it belongs to the nature of a passive power to retain as well as to receive.

Reply Obj. 1. Although it is said that memory, intellect and will are three powers,[1] this is not in accordance with the intention of Augustine, who says expressly that *if we take memory, intelligence and will as always present in the soul, whether we actually attend to them or not, they seem to pertain to the memory only. And by intelligence I mean that by which we understand when actually thinking; and by will I mean that love or affection which unites the child and its parents.*[2] Therefore it is clear that Augustine does not take the above three for three powers; but by memory he understands the soul's habit of retention, by intelligence, the act of the intellect, and by will, the act of the will.

Reply Obj. 2. Past and present may differentiate the sensitive powers, but not the intellectual powers, for the reason given above.

Reply Obj. 3. Intelligence arises from memory, as act from habit; and in this way it is equal to it, but not as a power to a power.

Eighth Article
WHETHER THE REASON IS DISTINCT FROM THE INTELLECT?

We proceed thus to the Eighth Article:—

---

1. 参见 Peter Lombard, *Sent.* I, iii, 2 (I, 35).
2. 参见 *De Trin.*, XIV, 7 (PL 42, 1043).

Objection 1. It would seem that the reason is a distinct power from the intellect. For it is stated in the *De Spiritu et Anima* that *when we wish to rise from lower things to higher, first the sense comes to our aid, then imagination, then reason, then the intellect.*[1] Therefore the reason is distinct from the intellect, just as imagination is from sense.

Obj. 2. Further, Boethius says that intellect is compared to reason, as eternity to time.[2] But it does not belong to the same power to be in eternity and to be in time. Therefore reason and intellect are not the same power.

Obj. 3. Further, man has intellect in common with the angels, and sense in common with the brutes. But reason, which is proper to man, and by which he is called a rational animal, is a power distinct from sense. Therefore it is equally true to say that it is distinct from the intellect, which properly belongs to the angels and which enables them to be called intellectual.

On the contrary, Augustine says that *that in which man excels irrational animals is reason, or mind, or intelligence, or whatever appropriate name we like to give it.*[3] Therefore reason, intellect and mind are one power.

I answer that, Reason and intellect in man cannot be distinct powers. We shall understand this clearly if we consider their respective acts. For to understand is to apprehend intelligible truth absolutely, and to reason is to advance from one thing understood to another, so as to know an intelligible truth. And therefore the angels, who possess a perfect knowledge of intelligible truth according to the mode of their nature, have no need to advance from one thing to another; they rather apprehend the truth of things absolutely and without discursiveness, as Dionysius says.[4] But man arrives at

---

1. 参见 Pseudo-Augustine (Alcher of Clairvaux), *De Spir. et An.*, XI (PL 40, 780).
2. 参见 *De Consol.*, TV, prose 6 (PL 63, 818).
3. 参见 *De Genesi ad Litt.*, III, 20 (PL 34, 292).
4. 参见 *De Div. Nom.*, VII, 2 (PG 3, 868).

the knowledge of intelligible truth by advancing from one thing to another; and therefore he is called *rational*.[1] Reasoning, therefore, is compared to understanding as movement is to rest, or acquisition to possession; of which one belongs to the perfect, the other to the imperfect. And since movement always proceeds from something immovable, and ends in something at rest, hence it is that human reasoning, in the order of inquiry and discovery, proceeds from certain things absolutely understood— namely, the first principles; and, again, in the order of judgment returns by analysis to first principles, in the light of which it examines what it has found. Now it is clear that rest and movement are not to be referred to different powers, but to one and the same, even in natural things, since by the very same nature a thing is moved towards a certain place, and rests in that place. Much more, therefore, by the same power do we understand and reason. And so it is clear that in man reason and intellect are the same power.

Reply Obj. 1. That enumeration[2] is made according to the order of actions, not according to the distinction of powers. Moreover, that book is not of great authority.

Reply Obj. 2. The answer is clear from what we have said. For eternity is compared to time as the immovable to movable. And that is why Boethius compared the intellect to eternity, and reason to time.

Reply Obj. 3. Other animals are so much lower than man that they cannot attain to the knowledge of truth, which reason seeks. But man attains, although imperfectly, to the knowledge of intelligible truth, which the angels know. Therefore the knowing power in the angels is not of a different genus from the knowing power in the human reason, but is compared to it as the perfect to the imperfect.

---

1. 参见 *De Div. Nom.*, VII, 2 (PG 3, 868).
2. enumeration: 列举；计数；细目

Ninth Article

WHETHER THE HIGHER AND LOWER REASON ARE DISTINCT POWERS?

We proceed thus to the Ninth Article:—

Objection 1. It would seem that the higher and lower reason are distinct powers. For Augustine says that the image of the Trinity is in the higher part of the reason, and not in the lower.[1] But the parts of the soul are its powers. Therefore the higher and lower reason are two powers.

Obj. 2. Further, nothing flows from itself. Now, the lower reason flows from the higher, and is ruled and directed by it. Therefore the higher reason is another power from the lower.

Obj. 3. Further, the Philosopher says that *the scientific part* of the soul, by which the soul knows necessary things, is another principle and another part from the *opinionative* and *reasoning* part by which it knows contingent things.[2] And he proves this from the principle that for those things which are *generically different, generically different parts of the soul are ordained.*[3] Now contingent and necessary are generically different, as corruptible and incorruptible. Since, therefore, necessary is the same as eternal, and temporal the same as contingent, it seems that what the Philosopher calls the *scientific* part must be the same as the higher reason, which, according to Augustine, *is intent on the consideration and consultation of things eternal;*[4] and that what the Philosopher calls the *reasoning* or *opinionative* part is the same as the lower reason, which, according to Augustine, *is intent on the ordering of temporal things.*

1. 参见 *De Trin.*, XII, 4 (PL 42, 1000).
2. 参见 *Eth.*, VI, 1 (1139a 6).
3. 同上 (1139a 8).
4. 参见 *De Trin.*, XII, 7 (PL 42, 1005).

Therefore the higher reason is another power than the lower.

Obj. 4. Further, Damascene says that *opinion rises from imagination; and then the mind, by judging of the truth or error of the opinion, discovers the truth. Hence* mens [mind] *is derived from* metiendo [measuring]. *And therefore the intellect regards those things which are already subject to judgment and true decision.*[1] Therefore the opinionative power[2], which is the lower reason, is distinct from mind and intellect, by which we may understand the higher reason.

On the contrary, Augustine says that *the higher and lower reason are distinct only by their functions.*[3] Therefore they are not two powers.

I answer that, The higher and lower reason, as they are understood by Augustine, can in no way be two powers of the soul. For he says that *the higher reason is that which is intent on the contemplation and consultation of things eternal.*[4] In other words, in contemplation it sees them in themselves, and in consultation it takes its rules of action from them. But he calls the lower reason that which *is intent on the ordering of temporal things.*[5] Now these two—namely, eternal and temporal—are related to our knowledge in this way, that one of them is the means of knowing the other. For in the order of discovery, we come through temporal things to the knowledge of things eternal, according to the words of the Apostle (*Rom.* i. 20): *The invisible things of God are clearly seen, being understood by the things that are made.* But in the order of judgment, from eternal things already known, we judge of temporal things, and according to the laws of eternal things we order temporal things.

But it may happen that the medium and what is attained thereby

---

1. 参见 *De Fide Orth.*, II, 22 (PG 94, 941).
2. the opinionative power: 武断能力；臆度能力
3. 参见 *De Trin.* XII, 4 (PL 42, 1000).
4. 同上 (PL 42, 1004).
5. 同上

belong to different habits; as the first indemonstrable principles belong to the *habit of intellect*, whereas the conclusions which we draw from them belong to the *habit of science*. And so it happens that from the principles of geometry we may draw conclusions in another science—for example, optics. But it is to one and the same power of the reason that both medium and term belong. For the act of the reason is, as it were, a movement from one thing to another. But the same movable thing passes through the medium and reaches the end. Therefore the higher and lower reasons are one and the same power. But according to Augustine they are distinguished by the functions of their actions, and according to their various habits, for wisdom is attributed to the higher reason, science to the lower.

Reply Obj. 1. We can speak of parts, in whatever way a thing is divided. Hence, so far as reason is divided according to its various acts, the higher and lower reason are called parts; but not because they are different powers.

Reply Obj. 2. The lower reason is said to flow from the higher, or to be ruled by it, in so far as the principles used by the lower reason are drawn from and directed by the principles of the higher reason.

Reply Obj. 3. The *scientific* part, of which the Philosopher speaks,[1] is not the same as the higher reason; for necessary truths are found even among temporal things, of which natural philosophy and mathematics treat. And the *opinionative* and *ratiocinative* part is more limited than the lower reason, for it regards only things contingent. Neither must we say, without any qualification, that the power by which the intellect knows necessary things is distinct from the power by which it knows contingent things, for it knows both under the same objective aspect—namely, under the aspect of being and truth. Hence, necessary things, which have perfect being in truth, it knows perfectly, since it penetrates

1. 参见 *Eth.*, VI, 1 (1139a 12); 5 (1140b 26).

to their very essence, from which it demonstrates their proper accidents. On the other hand, it knows contingent things imperfectly, since they have only imperfect being and truth. Now perfect and imperfect in action do not vary the power, but they vary the actions as to the mode of acting; and consequently they vary the principles of the actions and the habits themselves. That is why the Philosopher posits two parts of the soul, namely, the *scientific* and the *ratiocinative*,[1] not because they are two powers, but because they are distinct according to diverse aptitudes for receiving diverse habits (concerning whose diversity he there intends to inquire). For contingent and necessary, though differing according to their proper genera, nevertheless agree in the common nature of being, which is the object of the intellect, and to which they are diversely related as perfect and imperfect.

Reply Obj. 4. That distinction given by Damascene is according to the diversity of the acts, not according to the diversity of the powers.[2] For *opinion* signifies an act of the intellect which leans to one side of a contradiction, though in fear of the other. While to *judge* or *measure* [mensurare] is an act of the intellect applying fixed principles to the examination of propositions. From this is taken the word *mens* [mind]. Lastly, to *understand* is to adhere to the formed judgment with approval.

Tenth Article
WHETHER INTELLIGENCE IS A POWER DISTINCT FROM INTELLECT?

We proceed thus to the Tenth Article:—

Objection 1. It would seem that the intelligence is another power than the intellect. For we read in the *De Spiritu et Anima* that *when we*

---

1. 参见 *Op. cit.*, VI, 1 (1139a 12).
2. 参见 *De Fide Orth.*, II, 22 (PG 94, 941).

wish to rise from lower to higher things, first the sense comes to our aid, then imagination, then reason, then intellect, and afterwards intelligence.[1] But imagination and sense are distinct powers. Therefore intellect and intelligence are also distinct.

Obj. 2. Further, Boethius says that *sense considers man in one way, imagination in another, reason in another, intelligence in another.*[2] But intellect is the same power as reason. Therefore intelligence seems to be a distinct power from intellect, just as reason is a distinct power from imagination and sense.

Obj. 3. Further, *actions come before powers*, as the Philosopher says.[3] But intelligence is an act separate from the others which are attributed to the intellect. For Damascene says that *the first movement is called intelligence. But that intelligence which is about a certain thing is called intention; that which remains and conforms the soul to that which is understood is called invention, and invention when it remains where it is, examining and judging of itself, is called phronesis* (that is, wisdom), *and phronesis, if dilated, makes thought, that is, orderly internal speech; from which, they say, comes speech expressed by the tongue.*[4] Therefore it seems that intelligence is some special power.

On the contrary, The Philosopher says that *intelligence is of indivisible things in which there is nothing false.*[5] But the knowledge of these things belongs to the intellect. Therefore intelligence is not another power than the intellect.

I answer that, This term *intelligence* properly signifies the very act of the intellect, which is to understand. However, in some works translated from the Arabic, the separate substances, which we call

---

1. 参见 Pseudo-Augustine (Alcher of Clairvaux), *De Spir. et An.*, XI (PL 40, 780).
2. 参见 *De Consol.*, V, prose 4 (PL 63, 849).
3. 参见 Aristotle, *De An.*, II, 4 (415a 18).
4. 参见 *De Fide Orth.*, II, 22 (PG 94, 941).
5. 参见 *De An.*, III, 6 (430a 26).

angels, are called *intelligences*,[1] and perhaps for this reason, that such substances are always actually understanding. But in works translated from the Greek, they are called *intellects* or *minds*.[2] Thus intelligence is distinct from intellect, not as power is from power, but as act is from power. And such a division is recognized even by the philosophers.[3] For sometimes they posit four intellects—namely, the *agent intellect*, the *possible intellect*, the *habitual intellect*, and the *acquired intellect*. Of which four, the agent and possible intellects are different powers; just as in all things the active power is distinct from the passive. But the three which are not the agent intellect are distinguished as three states of the possible intellect, which is sometimes in potentiality only, and thus it is called *possible*; sometimes it is in the first act, which is knowledge, and thus it is called the *habitual intellect*[4]; and sometimes it is in the second act, which is the actual use of knowledge, and thus it is called the *intellect in act*[5], or the *acquired intellect*.

Reply Obj. 1. If this authority is accepted, intelligence there means the act of the intellect. And thus it is divided against intellect as act against power.

Reply Obj. 2. Boethius takes intelligence as meaning that act of the intellect which transcends the act of the reason. Therefore he there says that *reason belongs only to the human race, as intelligence alone belongs to God*.[6] For it belongs to God to understand all things without any investigation.

Reply Obj. 3. All those acts which Damascene enumerates[7] belong

1. 参见 Cf. Avicenna, *Metaph.*, X, 1 (107va).
2. 参见 Cf. above, q. 54, a. 3, ad 1.
3. 参见 Cf. Alexander of Aphrodisias, *De Intellectu et Intellecto* (p. 74); Avicenna, *De An.*, I, 5 (5vb).
4. the habitual intellect: 习性理智
5. the acquired intellect: 习得理智
6. 参见 *De Consol.*, V, prose 5 (PL 63, 854).
7. 参见 *De Fide Orth.*, II, 22 (PG 94, 941).

to one power—namely, the intellectual power. For this power first apprehends something absolutely, and this act is called *intelligence*. Secondly, it directs what it apprehends to the knowledge of something else, or to some operation, and this is called *intention*. And when it goes on in search of what it *intends*, it is called *invention*. When, in the light of something known as certain, it examines what it has found, it is said to know or to be wise, which belongs to *phronesis* or *wisdom*; for *it belongs to the wise man to judge*, as the Philosopher says.[1] And when once it has obtained something as certain, as being fully examined, it thinks about the means of making it known to others; and this is the ordering of *interior speech*[2], from which proceeds *external speech*[3]. And so, not every difference of acts diversifies the powers, but only that which cannot be reduced to one and the same principle, as we have said above.[4]

Eleventh Article
WHETHER THE SPECULATIVE AND PRACTICAL INTELLECTS ARE DISTINCT POWERS?

We proceed thus to the Eleventh Article:—

Objection 1. It would seem that the speculative and practical intellects are distinct powers. For the *apprehensive* and the *motive* are different kinds of powers, as is clear from *De Anima* ii.[5] But the speculative intellect[6] is merely an apprehensive power; while the practical intellect[7] is a motive power. Therefore they are distinct powers.

Obj. 2. Further, the different nature of the object differentiates the

---

1. 参见 Aristotle, *Metaph.*, I, 2 (982a 18).
2. interior speech: 内在的言语
3. external speech: 外在的言语
4. 参见 Q. 78, a. 4.
5. 参见 Aristotle, *De An.*, II, 3 (414a 31).
6. the speculative intellect: 思辨理智
7. the practical intellect: 实践理智

power. But the object of the speculative intellect is *truth*, and of the practical, *good*; which differ in nature. Therefore the speculative and practical intellects are distinct powers.

Obj. 3. Further, in the intellectual part, the practical intellect is compared to the speculative, as the estimative is compared to the imaginative power in the sensitive part. But the estimative differs from the imaginative as power from power, as we have said above.[1] Therefore so does the speculative intellect differ from the practical.

On the contrary, The speculative intellect by extension becomes practical.[2] But one power is not changed into another. Therefore the speculative and practical intellects are not distinct powers.

I answer that, The speculative and practical intellects are not distinct powers. The reason for this is, as we have said above, that what is accidental to the nature of the object of a power does not differentiate that power;[3] for it is accidental to a colored thing to be a man, or to be great or small. Hence all such things are apprehended by the same power of sight. Now, to a thing apprehended by the intellect, it is accidental whether it be directed to operation or not; but it is according to this that the speculative and practical intellects differ. For it is the speculative intellect which directs what it apprehends, not to operation, but to the sole consideration of truth; while the practical intellect is that which directs what it apprehends to operation. And this is what the Philosopher says, namely, that *the speculative differs from the practical in its end.*[4] Whence each is named from its end: the one speculative, the other practical—*i.e.*, operative.

Reply Obj. 1. The practical intellect is a motive power, not as executing movement, but as directing towards it; and this belongs to it

---

1. 参见 Q. 78, a. 4.
2. 参见 Aristotle, *De An.*, III, 10 (433a 14).
3. 参见 Q. 77, a. 3.
4. 参见 *De An.*, III, 10 (433a 14).

according to its mode of apprehension.

Reply Obj. 2. Truth and good include one another; for truth is something good, or otherwise it would not be desirable, and good is something true, or otherwise it would not be intelligible. Therefore, just as the object of the appetite may be something true, as having the aspect of good (for example, when some one desires to know the truth), so the object of the practical intellect is the good directed to operation, under the aspect of truth. For the practical intellect knows truth, just as the speculative, but it directs the known truth to operation.

Reply Obj. 3. Many differences differentiate the sensitive powers, which do not differentiate the intellectual powers, as we have said above.[1]

Twelfth Article
WHETHER SYNDERESIS IS A SPECIAL POWER OF THE SOUL DISTINCT FROM THE OTHERS?

We proceed thus to the Twelfth Article:—

Objection 1. It would seem that *synderesis* is a special power, distinct from the others. For those things which fall under one division seem to be of the same genus. But in the *Gloss* of Jerome on *Ezech.* i. 6, *synderesis*[2] is divided against the irascible[3], the concupiscible[4], and the rational, which are powers.[5] Therefore *synderesis* is a power.

Obj. 2. Further, opposites are of the same genus. But *synderesis* and sensuality seem to be opposed to one another, because *synderesis* always

1. 参见 A. 7, ad 2; q. 77, a. 3, ad 4.
2. synderesis: 良知；对道德行为原则的先天知识
3. the irascible: 愤情
4. the concupiscible: 欲情
5. 参见 *Glossa ordin.* (IV, 210 E).—St. Jerome, *In Ezech.*, I, super I, 6 (PL 25, 22).

inclines to good, while sensuality[1] always inclines to evil (whence it is signified by the serpent, as is clear from Augustine[2]). It seems, therefore, that *synderesis* is a power just as sensuality is.

Obj. 3. Further, Augustine says that in the natural power of judgment there are certain *rules and seeds of virtue, both true and unchangeable.*[3] But this is what we call *synderesis*. Since, therefore, the unchangeable rules which guide our judgment belong to the reason as to its higher part, as Augustine says,[4] it seems that *synderesis* is the same as reason, and thus is a power.

On the contrary, According to the Philosopher, *rational powers* are related to *opposites*.[5] But *synderesis* does not regard opposites, but inclines to good only. Therefore *synderesis* is not a power. For if it were a power, it would be a rational power, since it is not found in brute animals.

I answer that, *Synderesis* is not a power, but a habit. However, some[6] have held that it is *a power higher than reason*, while others[7] said that it is *reason itself, not as reason, but as a nature*. In order to make this question clear, we must observe, as we have said above, that man's act of reasoning, since it is a kind of movement, proceeds from the understanding of certain things (namely, those which are naturally known without any investigation on the part of reason) as from an immovable principle; it also terminates in the understanding, inasmuch as, by means of those naturally known principles, we judge of those things which we have discovered by reasoning. Now it is clear that, as the speculative reason reasons about speculative matters, so

---

1. sensuality: 肉欲
2. 参见 *De Trin.*, XII, 12; 13 (PL 42, 1007; 1009).
3. 参见 *De Lib. Arb.*, II, 10 (PL 32, 1256).
4. 参见 *De Trin.*, XII, 2 (PL 42, 999).
5. 参见 *Metaph.*, VIII, 2 (1046b 5).
6. 参见 William of Auxerre, *Summa Aurea*, II, tr. 2, ch. 1 (fol. 65vb).
7. 参见 Alex. of Hales, *Summa Theol.*, II, I, no. 418 (II, 493).

the practical reason reasons about practical matters. Therefore we must be naturally endowed with not only speculative principles, but also practical principles. Now the first speculative principles bestowed on us by nature do not belong to a special power, but to a special habit, which is called *the understanding of principles*, as the Philosopher explains.[1] Hence, the first practical principles, bestowed on us by nature, do not belong to a special power, but to a special natural habit, which we call *synderesis*. Whence *synderesis* is said to incline to good, and to murmur at evil, inasmuch as through first principles we proceed to discover, and judge of what we have discovered. It is therefore clear that *synderesis* is not a power, but a natural habit.

Reply Obj. 1. The division given by Jerome is taken from the diversity of acts, and not from the diversity of powers. Now diverse acts can belong to one power.

Reply Obj. 2. In like manner, the opposition of sensuality to *synderesis* is an opposition of acts, and not of the different species of one genus.

Reply Obj. 3. Such unchangeable notions are the first practical principles, concerning which no one errs; and they are attributed to reason as to a power, and to *synderesis* as to a habit. Therefore we judge naturally both by our reason and by *synderesis*.

Thirteenth Article
WHETHER CONSCIENCE IS A POWER?

We proceed thus to the Thirteenth Article:—

Objection 1. It would seem that conscience is a power; for Origen says that *conscience is a correcting and guiding spirit accompanying the soul, by which it is led away from evil and made to cling to good.*[2] But in the soul, spirit designates a power—either the mind itself, according to

1. 参见 *Eth.*, VI, 6 (1141a 7).
2. 参见 *In Rom.*, II, super II, 15 (PG 14, 892).

the text (*Ephes.* iv. 13), *Be ye renewed in the spirit of your mind*—or the imagination, whence imaginary vision is called *spiritual*, as Augustine says.[1] Therefore conscience is a power.

Obj. 2. Further, nothing is a subject of sin, except a power of the soul. But conscience is a subject of sin; for it is said of some that *their mind and conscience are defiled* (*Titus* i. 15). Therefore it seems that conscience is a power.

Obj. 3. Further, conscience must of necessity be either an act, a habit or a power. But it is not an act, for thus it would not always exist in man. Nor is it a habit, for it would not be one thing but many, since we are directed in our actions by many habits of knowledge. Therefore conscience is a power.

On the contrary, Conscience can be laid aside. But a power cannot be laid aside. Therefore conscience is not a power.

I answer that, Properly speaking conscience is not a power, but an act. This is evident both from the very name and from those things which in the common way of speaking are attributed to conscience. For conscience, according to the very nature of the word, implies the relation of knowledge to something; for *conscientia* may be resolved into *cum alio scientia* [knowledge applied to an individual case]. But the application of knowledge to something is done by some act. Therefore from this explanation of the name it is clear that conscience is an act.

The same is manifest from the things which are attributed to conscience. For conscience is said to witness, to bind, or incite, and also to accuse, torment, or rebuke. And all these follow the application of knowledge or science to what we do. This application is made in three ways. In one way, in so far as we recognize that we have done or not done something: *Thy conscience knoweth that thou hast often spoken evil of others* (*Eccles.* vii. 23); and according to this, conscience is said

---

1. 参见 *De Genesi ad Litt.*, XII, 7; 24 (PL 34, 459; 474).

to witness. In another way, in so far as through the conscience we judge that something should be done or not done; and in this sense, conscience is said to incite or to bind. In the third way, in so far as by conscience we judge that something done is well done or ill done, and in this sense conscience is said to excuse, accuse, or torment. Now, it is clear that all these things follow the actual application of knowledge to what we do. Therefore, properly speaking, conscience denominates an act. But since habit is a principle of act, sometimes the name conscience is given to the first natural habit, namely, *synderesis*. Thus Jerome calls *synderesis* conscience;[1] Basil calls the *natural power of judgment*[2] conscience; and Damascene says that conscience is the *law of our intellect*.[3] For it is customary for causes and effects to be called after one another.

Reply Obj. 1. Conscience is called a spirit, so far as spirit is the same as mind, because conscience is a certain pronouncement of the mind.

Reply Obj. 2. Defilement is said to be in the conscience, not as in a subject, but as the thing known is in knowledge, namely, in so far as someone knows that he is defiled.

Reply Obj. 3. Although an act does not always remain in itself, yet it always remains in its cause, which is a power and a habit. Now all the habits by which conscience is formed, although many, nevertheless have their efficacy from one first habit, the habit of first principles, which is called *synderesis*. Hence, there is a special reason why this habit is sometimes called conscience, as we have said above.

---

1. 参见 *In Ezech.*, I, super I, 6 (PL 25, 22). Cf. *Glossa ordin.* (IV, 210 F).
2. 参见 *Hom.* XII. *In Princ. Prov.* (PG 31, 404).
3. 参见 *De Fide Orth.*, IV, 22 (PG 94, 1089).

Question LXXX
THE APPETITIVE POWERS IN GENERAL
(*In Two Articles*)

NEXT we consider the appetitive powers, concerning which there are four heads of consideration: first, the appetitive powers in general; second, sensuality;[1] third, the will;[2] fourth, free choice.[3] Under the first there are two points of inquiry. (1) Whether the appetite should be considered a special power of the soul? (2) Whether the appetite is divided into intellectual and sensitive as distinct powers?

First Article
WHETHER THE APPETITE IS A SPECIAL POWER OF THE SOUL?

We proceed thus to the First Article:—

Objection 1. It would seem that the appetite is not a special power of the soul. For no power of the soul is to be assigned for those things which are common to animate and to inanimate beings. But appetite is common to animate and inanimate beings, since *all desire good*, as the Philosopher says.[4] Therefore the appetite is not a special power of the soul.

---

1. 参见 Q. 81.
2. 参见 Q. 82.
3. 参见 Q. 83.
4. 参见 Aristotle, *Eth.*, I, 1 (1094a 3).

Obj. 2. Further, powers are differentiated by their objects. But what we desire is the same as what we know. Therefore the appetitive power is not distinct from the apprehensive power.

Obj. 3. Further, the common is not divided from the proper. But each power of the soul desires some particular desirable thing—namely, its own suitable object. Therefore, with regard to the object which is the desirable in general, we should not assign some particular power distinct from the others, called the appetitive power.

On the contrary, The Philosopher distinguishes the appetitive from the other powers.[1] Damascene also distinguishes the appetitive from the cognitive powers.[2]

I answer that, It is necessary to assign an appetitive power to the soul. To make this evident, we must observe that some inclination follows every form: for example, fire, by its form, is inclined to rise, and to generate its like. Now, the form is found to have a more perfect existence in those things which participate in knowledge than in those which lack knowledge. For in those which lack knowledge, the form is found to determine each thing only to its own being—that is, to the being which is natural to each. Now this natural form is followed by a natural inclination, which is called the natural appetite. But in those things which have knowledge, each one is determined to its own natural being by its natural form, but in such a manner that it is nevertheless receptive of the species of other things. For example, sense receives the species of all sensible things, and the intellect, of all intelligible things; so that the soul of man is, in a way, all things by sense and intellect. In this way, those beings that have knowledge approach, in a way, to a likeness to God, *in Whom all things pre-exist*, as Dionysius says.[3]

---

1. 参见 *De An.*, II, 3 (414a 31); cf. *op. cit.*, III, 10 (433a 9).
2. 参见 *De Fide Orth.*, II, 22 (PG 94, 941).
3. 参见 *De Div. Nom.*, V, 5 (PG 3, 820).

Therefore, just as in those beings that have knowledge forms exist in a higher manner and above the manner of natural forms, so there must be in them an inclination surpassing the natural inclination, which is called the natural appetite. And this superior inclination belongs to the appetitive power of the soul, through which the animal is able to desire what it apprehends, and not only that to which it is inclined by its natural form. And so it is necessary to assign an appetitive power to the soul.

Reply Obj. 1. Appetite is found in things which have knowledge, above the common manner in which it is found in all things, as we have said above. Therefore it is necessary to assign to the soul a particular power.

Reply Obj. 2. What is apprehended and what is desired are the same in reality, but differ in aspect; for a thing is apprehended as something sensible or intelligible, whereas it is desired as suitable or good. Now, it is diversity of aspect in the objects, and not material diversity, which demands a diversity of powers.

Reply Obj. 3. Each power of the soul is a form or nature, and has a natural inclination to something. Hence each power desires, by natural appetite, that object which is suitable to itself. Above this natural appetite is the animal appetite, which follows the apprehension, and by which something is desired, not as suitable to this or that power (such as sight for seeing, or sound for hearing), but as suitable absolutely to the animal.

Second Article
WHETHER THE SENSITIVE AND INTELLECTUAL APPETITES ARE DISTINCT POWERS?

We proceed thus to the Second Article:—

Objection 1. It would seem that the sensitive and intellectual appetites are not distinct powers. For powers are not differentiated by accidental differences, as we have seen above.[1] But it is accidental to the appetible object whether it be apprehended by the sense or by the intellect. Therefore the sensitive and intellectual appetites are not distinct powers.

Obj. 2. Further, intellectual knowledge is of universals, and is thereby distinguished from sensitive knowledge, which is of individuals. But there is no place for this distinction in the appetitive part. For since the appetite is a movement of the soul to individual things, every act of the appetite seems to be towards individual things. Therefore the intellectual appetite is not distinguished from the sensitive.

Obj. 3. Further, just as under the apprehensive power the appetitive is subordinate as a lower power, so also is the motive power. But the motive power which in man follows the intellect is not distinct from the motive power which in animals follows sense. Therefore, for a like reason, neither is there distinction in the appetitive part.

On the contrary, The Philosopher distinguishes a double appetite, and says that the higher appetite moves the lower.[2]

I answer that, We must needs say that the intellectual appetite is a distinct power from the sensitive appetite. For the appetitive power is a passive power, which is naturally moved by the thing apprehended. Therefore *the apprehended appetible is a mover which is not moved, while the appetite is a moved mover*, as the Philosopher says in *De Anima* iii. and in *Metaph.* xii.[3] Now things passive and movable are differentiated according to the distinction of the corresponding active and motive principles, for the motive must be proportionate to the movable, and the active to the passive. Indeed, the passive power itself has its very nature from its relation to its active principle. Therefore, since what

1. 参见 Q. 77, a. 3.
2. 参见 *De An.*, III, 9 (432b 5); 10 (433a 23); 11 (434a 12).
3. 参见 *Op. cit.*, III, 10 (433b 16); *Metaph.*, XI, 7 (1072a 26).

is apprehended by the intellect and what is apprehended by sense are generically different, consequently, the intellectual appetite is distinct from the sensitive.

Reply Obj. 1. It is not accidental to the thing desired to be apprehended by the sense or the intellect. On the contrary, this belongs to it by its nature, for the appetible does not move the appetite except as it is apprehended. Hence differences in the thing apprehended are of themselves differences in the appetible. And so the appetitive powers are distinguished according to the distinction of the things apprehended as according to their proper objects.

Reply Obj. 2. The intellectual appetite, though it tends to individual things which exist outside the soul, yet it tends to them as standing under the universal; as when it desires something because it is good. Therefore the Philosopher says that hatred can be of a universal, as when *we hate every kind of thief.*[1] In the same way, by the intellectual appetite we may desire the immaterial good, which is not apprehended by sense, such as knowledge, virtue and the like.

Reply Obj. 3. As the Philosopher says, a universal opinion does not move except by means of a particular opinion;[2] and in like manner the higher appetite moves by means of the lower. Therefore, there are not two distinct motive powers following the intellect and the sense.

---

1. 参见 *Rhetor.*, II, 4 (1382a 5).
2. 参见 Aristotle, *De An.*, III, 11 (434a 16).

Question LXXXI
THE POWER OF SENSUALITY
(*In Three Articles*)

NEXT we have to consider the power of sensuality, concerning which there are three points of inquiry: (1) Whether sensuality is only an appetitive power? (2) Whether it is divided into *irascible* and *concupiscible* as distinct powers? (3) Whether the irascible and concupiscible powers obey reason?

First Article
WHETHER SENSUALITY IS ONLY APPETITIVE?

We proceed thus to the First Article:—

Objection 1. It would seem that sensuality is not only appetitive, but also cognitive. For Augustine says that *the sensual movement of the soul which is directed to the bodily senses is common to us and beasts.*[1] But the bodily senses belong to the apprehensive powers. Therefore sensuality is a cognitive power.

Obj. 2. Further, things which come under one division seem to be of one genus. But Augustine divides sensuality against the higher and lower reason, which belong to knowledge.[2] Therefore sensuality also is apprehensive.

Obj. 3. Further, in man's temptations sensuality stands in the place of the serpent. But in the temptation of our first parents, the serpent

---

1. 参见 *De Trin.* XII, 12 (PL 42, 1007).
2. 同上

presented himself as one giving information and proposing sin, which belong to the cognitive power. Therefore sensuality is a cognitive power.

On the contrary, Sensuality is defined as *the appetite of things belonging to the body.*[1]

I answer that, The name *sensuality* seems to be taken from the sensual movement, of which Augustine speaks,[2] just as the name of a power is taken from its act, for instance, sight from seeing. Now the sensual movement is an appetite following sensible apprehension. For the act of the apprehensive power is not so properly called a movement as the act of the appetite; since the operation of the apprehensive power is completed in the very fact that the thing apprehended is in the one that apprehends, while the operation of the appetitive power is completed in the fact that he who desires is borne towards the desirable thing. Hence it is that the operation of the apprehensive power is likened to rest; whereas the operation of the appetitive power is rather likened to movement. Therefore by sensual movement we understand the operation of the appetitive power. Thus, sensuality is the name of the sensitive appetite.

Reply Obj. 1. By saying that the sensual movement of the soul is directed to the bodily senses, Augustine does not give us to understand that the bodily senses are included in sensuality, but rather that the movement of sensuality is a certain inclination to the bodily senses, since we desire things which are apprehended through the bodily senses. And thus the bodily senses pertain to sensuality as a sort of gateway.

Reply Obj. 2. Sensuality is divided against higher and lower reason, as having in common with them the act of movement; for the apprehensive power, to which belong the higher and lower reason, is a

---

1. 参见 Cf. Peter Lombard, *Sent.*, II, xxiv, 4 (I, 421).
2. 参见 *De Trin.*, XII, 12; 13 (PL 42, 1007; 1009).

motive power; as is appetite, to which sensuality pertains.

Reply Obj. 3. The serpent not only showed and proposed sin, but also incited to the commission of sin. And in this, sensuality is signified by the serpent.

Second Article

WHETHER THE SENSITIVE APPETITE IS DIVIDED INTO THE IRASCIBLE AND CONCUPISCIBLE AS DISTINCT POWERS?

We proceed thus to the Second Article:—

Objection 1. It would seem that the sensitive appetite is not divided into the irascible and concupiscible as distinct powers. For the same power of the soul regards both sides of a contrariety, as sight regards both black and white, according to the Philosopher.[1] But suitable and harmful are contraries. Since, then, the concupiscible power regards what is suitable, while the irascible is concerned with what is harmful, it seems that irascible and concupiscible are the same power in the soul.

Obj. 2. Further, the sensitive appetite regards only what is suitable according to the senses. But such is the object of the concupiscible power. Therefore there is no sensitive appetite differing from the concupiscible.

Obj. 3. Further, hatred is in the irascible part, for Jerome says on *Matt.* xiii. 33: *We ought to have the hatred of vice in the irascible power.*[2] But hatred is contrary to love, and is in the concupiscible part. Therefore the concupiscible and irascible are the same powers.

On the contrary, Gregory of Nyssa and Damascene assign two parts to

---

1. 参见 Aristotle, *De An.*, II, 11 (422b 23).
2. 参见 *In Matt.*, I, super XIII, 33 (PL 26, 94).

the sensitive appetite, the irascible and the concupiscible.[1]

I answer that, The sensitive appetite is one generic power, and is called sensuality; but it is divided into two powers, which are species of the sensitive appetite—the irascible and the concupiscible. In order to make this clear, we must observe that in natural corruptible things there is needed an inclination not only to the acquisition of what is suitable and to the avoiding of what is harmful, but also to resistance against corruptive and contrary forces which are a hindrance to the acquisition of what is suitable, and are productive of harm. For example, fire has a natural inclination, not only to rise from a lower place, which is unsuitable to it, towards a higher place, which is suitable, but also to resist whatever destroys or hinders its action. Therefore, since the sensitive appetite is an inclination following sensitive apprehension (just as natural appetite is an inclination following the natural form), there must needs be in the sensitive part two appetitive powers:—one, through which the soul is inclined absolutely to seek what is suitable, according to the senses, and to fly from what is hurtful, and this is called the *concupiscible*; and another, whereby an animal resists the attacks that hinder what is suitable, and inflict harm, and this is called the *irascible*. Whence we say that its object is something arduous, because its tendency is to overcome and rise above obstacles.

Now these two inclinations are not to be reduced to one principle. For sometimes the soul busies itself with unpleasant things, against the inclination of the concupiscible appetite, in order that, following the impulse of the irascible appetite, it may fight against obstacles. And so even the passions of the irascible appetite counteract the passions of the concupiscible appetite; since concupiscence, on being roused, diminishes anger, and anger, being roused, very often diminishes

1. 参见 Cf. Nemesius, *De Nat. Hom.*, XVI; XVII (PL 40, 672; 676); Damascene, *De Fide Orth.*, II, 12 (PG 94, 928).

concupiscence. This is clear also from the fact that the irascible is, as it were, the champion and defender of the concupiscible, when it rises up against what hinders the acquisition of the suitable things which the concupiscible desires, or against what inflicts harm, from which the concupiscible flies. And for this reason all the passions of the irascible appetite rise from the passions of the concupiscible appetite and terminate in them. For instance, anger rises from sadness, and, having wrought vengeance, terminates in joy. For this reason also the quarrels of animals are about things concupiscible—namely, food and sex, as the Philosopher says.[1]

Reply Obj. 1. The concupiscible power regards both what is suitable and what is unsuitable. But the object of the irascible power is to resist the onslaught of the unsuitable.

Reply Obj. 2. Just as in the apprehensive powers of the sensitive part there is an estimative power, which perceives those things which do not impress the senses, as we have said above,[2] so also in the sensitive appetite there is an appetitive power which regards something as suitable, not because it pleases the senses, but because it is useful to the animal for self-defence. And this is the irascible power.

Reply Obj. 3. Hatred belongs absolutely to the concupiscible appetite, but by reason of the strife which arises from hatred it may belong to the irascible appetite.

Third Article
WHETHER THE IRASCIBLE AND CONCUPISCIBLE APPETITES OBEY REASON?

We proceed thus to the Third Article:—

Objection 1. It would seem that the irascible and concupiscible

---

1. 参见 Aristotle, *Hist. Anim.*, VIII, 1 (589a 2).
2. 参见 Q. 78. a. 2.

appetites do not obey reason. For irascible and concupiscible are parts of sensuality. But sensuality does not obey reason; which is why it is signified by the serpent, as Augustine says.[1] Therefore the irascible and concupiscible appetites do not obey reason.

Obj. 2. Further, what obeys a certain thing does not resist it. But the irascible and concupiscible appetites resist reason, according to the Apostle (*Rom.* vii. 23): *I see another law in my members fighting against the law of my mind.* Therefore the irascible and concupiscible appetites do not obey reason.

Obj. 3. Further, as the appetitive power is inferior to the rational part of the soul, so also is the sensitive power. But the sensitive part of the soul does not obey reason, for we neither hear nor see just when we wish. Therefore, in like manner, neither do the powers of the sensitive appetite, the irascible and concupiscible, obey reason.

On the contrary, Damascene says that *the part of the soul which is obedient and amenable to reason is divided into concupiscence and anger.*[2]

I answer that, In two ways do the irascible and concupiscible powers obey the higher part, in which are the intellect or reason, and the will: first, as to the reason, and secondly, as to the will. They obey the reason in their own acts, because in other animals the sensitive appetite is naturally moved by the estimative power; for instance, a sheep, esteeming the wolf as an enemy, is afraid. In man the estimative power, as we have said above, is replaced by the cogitative power, which is called by some *the particular reason*, because it compares individual intentions.[3] Hence, in man the sensitive appetite is naturally moved by this particular reason. But this same particular reason is naturally guided and moved according to the universal reason; and that is why in syllogisms particular conclusions are drawn from

1. 参见 *De Trin.*, XII, 12; 13 (PL 42, 1007; 1009).
2. 参见 *De Fide Orth.*, II, 12 (PG 94, 928).
3. 参见 Q. 78, a. 4.

universal propositions. Therefore it is clear that the universal reason directs the sensitive appetite, which is divided into concupiscible and irascible, and that this appetite obeys it. But because to draw particular conclusions from universal principles is not the work of the intellect, as such, but of the reason, hence it is that the irascible and concupiscible are said to obey the reason rather than to obey the intellect. Anyone can experience this in himself; for by applying certain universal considerations, anger or fear or the like may be lessened or increased.

To the will also is the sensitive appetite subject in execution, which is accomplished by the motive power. For in other animals movement follows at once the concupiscible and irascible appetites. For instance, the sheep, fearing the wolf, flies at once, because it has no superior counteracting appetite. On the contrary, man is not moved at once according to the irascible and concupiscible appetites; but he awaits the command of the will, which is the superior appetite. For wherever there is order among a number of motive powers, the second moves only by virtue of the first; and so the lower appetite is not sufficient to cause movement, unless the higher appetite consents. And this is what the Philosopher says, namely, that *the higher appetite moves the lower appetite, as the higher sphere moves the lower.*[1] In this way, therefore, the irascible and concupiscible are subject to reason.

Reply Obj. 1. Sensuality is signified by the serpent in what is proper to it as a sensitive power. But the irascible and concupiscible powers denominate the sensitive appetite rather on the part of the act, to which they are led by the reason, as we have said.

Reply Obj. 2. As the Philosopher says: *We observe in an animal a despotic and a politic principle; for the soul dominates the body by a despotic rule, but the intellect dominates the appetite by a politic and royal rule.*[2] For that rule is called despotic whereby a man rules his slaves, who have not the

1. 参见 *De An.*, III, 11 (434a 12).
2. 参见 *Polit.*, I, 2 (1254b 2).

means to resist in any way the orders of the one that commands them, since they have nothing of their own. But that rule is called politic and royal by which a man rules over free subjects, who, though subject to the government of the ruler, have nevertheless something of their own, by reason of which they can resist the orders of him who commands. And so, the soul is said to rule the body by a despotic rule, because the members of the body cannot in any way resist the sway of the soul, but at the soul's command both hand and foot, and whatever member is naturally moved by voluntary movement, are at once moved. But the intellect or reason is said to govern the irascible and concupiscible by a politic rule because the sensitive appetite has something of its own, by virtue whereof it can resist the commands of reason. For the sensitive appetite is naturally moved, not only by the estimative power in other animals, and in man by the cogitative power which the universal reason guides, but also by the imagination and the sense. Whence it is that we experience that the irascible and concupiscible powers do resist reason, inasmuch as we sense or imagine something pleasant, which reason forbids, or unpleasant, which reason commands. And so from the fact that the irascible and concupiscible resist reason in something, we must not conclude that they do not obey it.

Reply Obj. 3. The exterior senses require for their acts exterior sensible things by which to be immuted, whose presence does not lie in the power of the reason. But the interior powers, both appetitive and apprehensive, do not require exterior things. Therefore they are subject to the command of reason, which can not only incite or modify the affections of the appetitive power, but can also form the phantasms of the imagination.

Question LXXXII
THE WILL
(*In Five Articles*)

WE next consider the will. Under this head there are five points of inquiry: (1) Whether the will desires something of necessity? (2) Whether it desires everything of necessity? (3) Whether it is a higher power than the intellect? (4) Whether the will moves the intellect? (5) Whether the will is divided into irascible and concupiscible?

First Article
WHETHER THE WILL DESIRES SOMETHING OF NECESSITY?

We proceed thus to the First Article:—

Objection 1. It would seem that the will desires nothing of necessity. For Augustine says that if anything is necessary, it is not voluntary.[1] But whatever the will desires is voluntary. Therefore nothing that the will desires is desired of necessity.

Obj. 2. Further, *the rational powers*, according to the Philosopher, *extend to opposite things.*[2] But the will is a rational power, because, as he says, *the will is in the reason.*[3] Therefore the will extends to opposite things, and hence is determined to nothing of necessity.

Obj. 3. Further, by the will we are masters of our own actions. But we are not masters of that which is of necessity. Therefore the act of

---

1. 参见 *De Civit. Dei*, V, 10 (PL 41, 152).
2. 参见 *Metaph.*, VIII, 2 (1046b 5).
3. 参见 Aristotle, *De An.*, III, 9 (432b 5).

the will cannot be necessitated.

On the contrary, Augustine says that *all desire happiness with one will.*[1] Now if this were not necessary, but contingent, there would at least be a few exceptions. Therefore the will desires something of necessity.

I answer that, The word *necessity* is employed in many ways. For that which must be is necessary. Now that a thing must be may belong to it by an intrinsic principle:—either material, as when we say that everything composed of contraries is of necessity corruptible;—or formal, as when we say that it is necessary for the three angles of a triangle to be equal to two right angles. And this is *natural* and *absolute necessity*. In another way, that a thing must be belongs to it by reason of something extrinsic, which is either the end or the agent. The necessity is imposed on something by the end when without it the end is not to be attained or so well attained: for instance, food is said to be necessary for life, and a horse is necessary for a journey. This is called the *necessity of the end*, and sometimes also *utility*. The necessity is imposed by the agent when someone is forced by some agent, so that he is not able to do the contrary. This is called the *necessity of coercion*.

Now this necessity of coercion is altogether repugnant to the will. For we call *violent* that which is against the inclination of a thing. But the very movement of the will is an inclination to something. Therefore, just as a thing is called *natural* because it is according to the inclination of nature, so a thing is called *voluntary* because it is according to the inclination of the will. Therefore, just as it is impossible for a thing to be at the same time violent and natural, so it is impossible for a thing to be absolutely coerced, or violent, and voluntary.

But the necessity of the end is not repugnant to the will, when the end cannot be attained except in one way; and thus from the will to

1. 参见 *De Trin.*, XIII, 4 (PL 42, 1018).

cross the sea arises in the will the necessity to desire a ship.

In like manner, neither is natural necessity repugnant to the will. Indeed, just as the intellect of necessity adheres to first principles, so the will must of necessity adhere to the last end, which is happiness; for the end is in practical matters what the principle is in speculative matters, as is said in *Physics* ii.[1] For what befits a thing naturally and immovably must be the root and principle of all else pertaining thereto, since the nature of a thing is the first in everything, and every movement arises from something immovable.

Reply Obj. 1. The words of Augustine are to be understood of the necessity of coercion. But natural necessity *does not take away the liberty of the will*, as he himself says in the same work.[2]

Reply Obj. 2. The will, so far as it desires a thing naturally, corresponds rather to the intellect of natural principles than to the reason, which extends to contraries. Hence, in this respect, it is rather an intellectual than a rational power.

Reply Obj. 3. We are masters of our own actions by reason of our being able to choose this or that. But choice regards, not the end, but *the means to the end*, as the Philosopher says.[3] Consequently, the desire of the ultimate end is not among those actions of which we are masters.

Second Article
WHETHER THE WILL DESIRES OF NECESSITY WHATEVER IT DESIRES?

We proceed thus to the Second Article:—

Objection 1. It would seem that the will desires of necessity all that

---

1. 参见 Aristotle, *Phys.*, II, 9 (200a 21).
2. 参见 *De Civit. Dei*, V, 10 (PL 41, 152).
3. 参见 Aristotle, *Eth.*, III, 2 (111b 27).

it desires. For Dionysius says that *evil is outside the scope of the will.*[1] Therefore the will tends of necessity to the good which is proposed to it.

Obj. 2. Further, the object of the will is compared to the will as the mover to the movable thing. But the movement of the movable necessarily follows the mover. Therefore it seems that the will's object moves it of necessity.

Obj. 3. Further, just as the thing apprehended by sense is the object of the sensitive appetite, so the thing apprehended by the intellect is the object of the intellectual appetite, which is called the will. But what is apprehended by the sense moves the sensitive appetite of necessity, for Augustine says that *animals are moved by things seen.*[2] Therefore it seems that whatever is apprehended by the intellect moves the will of necessity.

On the contrary, Augustine says that *it is the will by which we sin and live well.*[3] Thus, the will extends to opposites. Therefore it does not desire of necessity all things whatsoever it desires.

I answer that, The will does not desire of necessity whatsoever it desires. In order to make this evident we must observe that, just as the intellect naturally and of necessity adheres to first principles, so the will adheres to the last end, as we have said already. Now there are some intelligible things which have no necessary connection with first principles: *e.g.*, contingent propositions, the denial of which does not involve a denial of first principles. And to such the intellect does not assent of necessity. But there are some propositions which have a necessary connection with first principles, namely, demonstrable conclusions, a denial of which involves a denial of first principles. And to these the intellect

---

1. 参见 *De Div. Nom.*, IV, 32 (PG 3, 732).
2. 参见 *De Genesi ad Litt.*, IX, 14 (PL 34, 402).
3. 参见 *Retract.*, I, 9 (PL 32, 596); *De Civit. Dei*, V, 10 (PL 41, 152).

assents of necessity, when once it is aware (by demonstration) of the necessary connection of these conclusions with the principles; but it does not assent of necessity until through the demonstration it recognizes the necessity of such a connection.

It is the same with the will. For there are certain particular goods which have not a necessary connection with happiness, because without them a man can be happy; and to such the will does not adhere of necessity. But there are some things which have a necessary connection with happiness, namely, those by means of which man adheres to God, in Whom alone true happiness consists. Nevertheless, until through the certitude produced by seeing God the necessity of such a connection be shown, the will does not adhere to God of necessity, nor to those things which are of God. But the will of the man who sees God in His essence of necessity adheres to God, just as now we desire of necessity to be happy. It is therefore clear that the will does not desire of necessity whatever it desires.

Reply Obj. 1. The will can tend to nothing except under the aspect of good. But because good is of many kinds, for this reason the will is not of necessity determined to one.

Reply Obj. 2. The mover of necessity causes movement in the movable thing only when the power of the mover exceeds the movable thing in such a way that its entire capacity is subject to the mover. But as the capacity of the will is for the universal and perfect good, it is not subjected to any particular good. And therefore it is not of necessity moved by it.

Reply Obj. 3. The sensitive power does not compare different things with each other, as reason does; but it apprehends simply some one thing. Therefore, according to that one thing, it moves the sensitive appetite in a determinate way. But the reason is a power that compares several things together. Therefore the intellectual appetite—that is, the will—may be moved by several things, but not of necessity by one thing.

Third Article

WHETHER THE WILL IS A HIGHER POWER THAN THE INTELLECT?

We proceed thus to the Third Article:—

Objection 1. It would seem that the will is a higher power than the intellect. For the object of the will is the good and the end. But the end is the first and highest cause. Therefore the will is the first and highest power.

Obj. 2. Further, in the order of natural things we observe a progress from imperfect things to perfect. And this also appears in the powers of the soul, for sense precedes the intellect, which is more noble. Now the act of the will, according to a natural order, follows the act of the intellect. Therefore the will is a more noble and perfect power than the intellect.

Obj. 3. Further, habits are proportioned to their powers, as perfections to what they make perfect. But the habit which perfects the will —namely, charity —is more noble than the habits which perfect the intellect; for it is written (*1 Cor.* xiii. 2): *If I should know all mysteries, and if I should have all faith, and have not charity, I am nothing.* Therefore the will is a higher power than the intellect.

On the contrary, The Philosopher holds the intellect to be the highest power of the soul.[1]

I answer that, The superiority of one thing over another can be considered in two ways: *absolutely* and *relatively*. Now a thing is considered to be such absolutely when it is considered such in itself; but relatively, when it is such in relation to something else. If therefore the intellect and will be considered with regard to themselves, then

1. 参见 *Eth.*, X 7 (1177a 20).

the intellect is the higher power. And this is clear if we compare their respective objects to one another. For the object of the intellect is more simple and more absolute than the object of the will. For the object of the intellect is the very notion of the appetible good; and the appetible good, the notion of which is in the intellect, is the object of the will. Now the more simple and the more abstract a thing is, the nobler and higher it is in itself; and therefore the object of the intellect is higher than the object of the will. Therefore, since the proper nature of a power is according to its order to its object, it follows that the intellect, in itself and absolutely, is higher and nobler than the will.

But relatively, and by comparison with something else, we find that the will is sometimes higher than the intellect; and this happens when the object of the will occurs in something higher than that in which occurs the object of the intellect. Thus, for instance, I might say that hearing is relatively nobler than sight, inasmuch as something in which there is sound is nobler than something in which there is color, though color is nobler and simpler than sound. For, as we have said above, the act of the intellect consists in this—that the likeness of the thing understood is in the one who understands;[1] while the act of the will consists in this—that the will is inclined to the thing itself as existing in itself. And therefore the Philosopher says in *Metaph.* vi. that *good and evil*, which are objects of the will, *are in things*, but *truth and error*, which are objects of the intellect, *are in the mind.*[2] When, therefore, the thing in which there is good is nobler than the soul itself, in which is the understood likeness, then, by comparison with such a thing, the will is higher than the intellect. But when the thing which is good is less noble than the soul, then, even in comparison with that thing, the intellect is higher than the will. Hence, the love of God is better than the knowledge of God; but, on the contrary, the knowledge of corporeal

1. 参见 Q. 16, a. 1; q. 27, a. 4.
2. 参见 *Metaph.*, V, 4 (1027b 25).

things is better than the love of them. Absolutely, however, the intellect is nobler than the will.

Reply Obj. 1. The notion of cause is perceived by comparing one thing to another, and in such a comparison the notion of good is found to be nobler; but truth signifies something more absolutely, and extends to the notion of good itself. Thus, the good is something true. But, again, the true is something good. For the intellect is a given reality, and truth is its end. And among other ends this is the most excellent: just as is the intellect among the other powers.

Reply Obj. 2. What precedes in the order of generation and time is less perfect, for in one and the same thing potentiality precedes act, and imperfection precedes perfection. But what precedes absolutely and in the order of nature is more perfect; for thus act precedes potentiality. And in this way the intellect precedes the will, as the motive power precedes the movable thing, and as the active precedes the passive; for it is the *apprehended* good that moves the will.

Reply Obj. 3. This argument is verified of the will as compared with what is above the soul. For charity is the virtue by which we love God.

Fourth Article
WHETHER THE WILL MOVES THE INTELLECT?

We proceed thus to the Fourth Article:—

Objection 1. It would seem that the will does not move the intellect. For what moves excels and precedes what is moved, because what moves is an agent, and *the agent is nobler than the patient*, as Augustine says,[1] and the Philosopher.[2] But the intellect excels and precedes the will, as we have said above. Therefore the will does not move the intellect.

---

1. 参见 *De Genesi ad Litt.*, XII, 16 (PL 34, 467).
2. 参见 *De An.*, III, 5 (430a 18).

Obj. 2. Further, what moves is not moved by what is moved, except perhaps accidentally. But the intellect moves the will, because the good apprehended by the intellect moves without being moved; whereas the appetite is a moved mover. Therefore the intellect is not moved by the will.

Obj. 3. Further, we can will nothing but what we understand. If, therefore, in order to understand, the will moves by willing to understand, that act of the will must be preceded by another act of the intellect, and this act of the intellect by another act of the will, and so on indefinitely, which is impossible. Therefore the will does not move the intellect.

On the contrary, Damascene says: *It is in our power to learn an art or not, as we will.*[1] But a thing is in our power by the will, and we learn an art by the intellect. Therefore the will moves the intellect.

I answer that, A thing is said to move in two ways: First, as an end, as when we say that the end moves the agent. In this way the intellect moves the will, because the understood good is the object of the will, and moves it as an end. Secondly, a thing is said to move as an agent, as what alters moves what is altered, and what impels moves what is impelled. In this way the will moves the intellect, and all the powers of the soul, as Anselm says.[2] The reason is, because wherever we have order among a number of active powers, that power which is related to the universal end moves the powers which refer to particular ends. And we may observe this both in nature and in political things. For the heavens, which aims at the universal preservation of things subject to generation and corruption, moves all inferior bodies, each of which aims at the preservation of its own species or of the individual. So too, a king, who aims at the common good of the whole kingdom, by his rule moves all the governors of cities, each of whom rules over his own

---

1. 参见 *De Fide Orth.*, II, 26 (PG 94, 960).
2. 参见 Eadmer, *De Similit.*, II (PL 159, 605).

particular city. Now the object of the will is the good and the end in general, whereas each power is directed to some suitable good proper to it, as sight is directed to the perception of color, and the intellect to the knowledge of truth. Therefore the will as an agent moves all the powers of the soul to their respective acts, except the natural powers of the vegetative part, which are not subject to our choice.

Reply Obj. 1. The intellect may be considered in two ways: as apprehensive of universal being and truth, and as a reality and a particular power having a determinate act. In like manner also the will may be considered in two ways: according to the common nature of its object—that is to say, as appetitive of universal good—and as a determinate power of the soul having a determinate act. If, therefore, the intellect and will be compared with one another according to the universality of their respective objects, then, as we have said above, the intellect is absolutely higher and nobler than the will. If, however, we take the intellect in relation to the common nature of its object and the will as a determinate power, then again the intellect is higher and nobler than the will, because under the notion of being and truth is contained both the will itself, its act, and its object. Therefore the intellect understands the will, its act, and its object, just as it understands other species of things, as stone or wood, which are contained in the common notion of being and truth. But if we consider the will in relation to the common nature of its object, which is good, and the intellect as a reality and a special power, then the intellect itself, its act, and its object, which is the true, each of which is some species of good, are contained under the common notion of good. And in this way the will is higher than the intellect, and can move it. From this we can easily understand why these powers include one another in their acts, because the intellect understands that the will wills, and the will wills the intellect to understand. In the same way, the good is contained under the true, inasmuch as it is an understood truth, and the true under the good, inasmuch as it is a desired good.

Reply Obj. 2. The intellect moves the will in one sense, and the will moves the intellect in another, as we have said above.

Reply Obj. 3. There is no need to go on indefinitely, but we must stop at the intellect as preceding all the rest. For every movement of the will must be preceded by apprehension, whereas every apprehension is not preceded by an act of the will; but the principle of counselling and understanding is an intellectual principle higher than our intellect — namely, God; as Aristotle also says, explaining in this way that there is no need to proceed indefinitely.[1]

Fifth Article
WHETHER WE SHOULD DISTINGUISH IRASCIBLE AND CONCUPISCIBLE PARTS IN THE SUPERIOR APPETITE?

We proceed thus to the Fifth Article:—

Objection 1. It would seem that we ought to distinguish irascible and concupiscible parts in the superior appetite, which is the will. For the concupiscible power is so called from *concupiscere* [*to desire*], and the irascible part from *irasci* [*to be angry*]. But there is a concupiscence[2] which cannot belong to the sensitive appetite, but only to the intellectual, which is the will: *e.g.*, the concupiscence of wisdom, of which it is said (*Wis.* vi. 21): *The concupiscence of wisdom bringeth to the eternal kingdom.* There is also a certain anger which cannot belong to the sensitive appetite, but only to the intellectual; as when our anger is directed against vice. And so, Jerome commenting on *Matt.* xiii. 33, warns us *to have the hatred of vice in the irascible part.*[3] Therefore we should distinguish irascible and concupiscible parts in the intellectual soul as well as in the sensitive.

---

1. 参见 *Eth. Eudem.*, VII, 14 (1248a 26).
2. concupiscence: 强烈的邪欲
3. 参见 *In Matt.*, I, super XIII, 33 (PL 26, 94).

Obj. 2. Further, as is commonly said, charity is in the concupiscible, and hope in the irascible part. But they cannot be in the sensitive appetite, because their objects are not sensible, but intellectual. Therefore we must assign an irascible and a concupiscible power to the intellectual part.

Obj. 3. Further, it is said that *the soul has these powers* —namely, the irascible, concupiscible and rational—*before it is united to the body.*[1] But no power of the sensitive part belongs to the soul alone, but to the soul and body united, as we have said above.[2] Therefore the irascible and concupiscible powers are in the will, which is the intellectual appetite.

On the contrary, Gregory of Nyssa says that the irrational part of the soul is divided into the desiderative and irascible,[3] and Damascene says the same.[4] And the Philosopher says *that the will is in the reason, while in the irrational part of the soul are concupiscence and anger*, or *desire and spirit.*[5]

I answer that, The irascible and concupiscible are not parts of the intellectual appetite, which is called the will. For, as was said above, a power which is directed to an object according to some common notion is not differentiated by special differences which are contained under that common notion.[6] For instance, because sight is related to what is visible under the common notion of something colored, the visual power is not multiplied according to the different kinds of color; but if there were a power concerned with white as white, and not as something colored, it would be distinct from a power concerned with black as black.

---

1. 参见 Pseudo-Augustine (Alcher of Clairvaux), *De Spir. et An.*, XVI (PL 40, 791).
2. 参见 Q. 77, a. 5 and 8.
3. 参见 Cf. Nemesius, *De Nat. Hom.*, XVI; XVII (PG 40, 672; 676).
4. 参见 *De Fide Orth.*, XII (PG 94, 928).
5. 参见 *De An.*, III, 11 (432b 5).
6. 参见 Q. 59, a. 4; q. 79, a. 7.

Now the sensitive appetite is not related to the common notion of good, because neither do the senses apprehend the universal. Therefore the parts of the sensitive appetite are differentiated by the different notions of particular good; for the concupiscible is related to its proper sort of good, which is something pleasant to the senses and suitable to nature; whereas the irascible is related to that sort of good which is something that wards off and repels what is hurtful. But the will is related to the good according to the common notion of good, and therefore in the will, which is the intellectual appetite, there is no differentiation of appetitive powers, so that there be in the intellectual appetite an irascible power distinct from a concupiscible power; just as neither on the part of the intellect are the apprehensive powers multiplied, although they are on the part of the senses.

Reply Obj. 1. Love, concupiscence and the like can be understood in two ways. Sometimes they are taken as passions—arising, that is, with a certain commotion of spirit. And thus they are commonly understood, and in this sense they are only in the sensitive appetite. They may, however, be taken in another way, in so far as they are simple affections without passion or commotion of spirit, and thus they are acts of the will. And in this sense, too, they are attributed to the angels and to God. But if taken in this sense, they do not belong to different powers, but only to one power, which is called the will.

Reply Obj. 2. The will itself may be said to be irascible, insofar as it wills to repel evil, not from any sudden movement of passion, but from a judgment of the reason. And in the same way the will may be said to be concupiscible because of its desire for good. And thus in the irascible and concupiscible are charity and hope—that is, in the will as ordered to such acts.

And in this way, too, we may understand the words quoted from the *De Spiritu et Anima*, namely, that the irascible and concupiscible powers are in the soul before it is united to the body (as long as we understand priority of nature, and not of time): although there is no need to have faith in what that book says.

Whence the answer to the third objection is clear.

Question LXXXIII
FREE CHOICE
(*In Four Articles*)

WE now inquire concerning free choice. Under this head there are four points of inquiry: (1) Whether man has free choice? (2) What is free choice—a power, an act, or a habit? (3) If it is a power, is it appetitive or cognitive? (4) If it is appetitive, is it the same power as the will, or distinct?

First Article
WHETHER MAN HAS FREE CHOICE?

We proceed thus to the First Article:—

Objection 1. It would seem that man has not free choice. For whoever has free choice does what he wills. But man does not what he wills, for it is written (*Rom.* vii. 19): *For the good which I will I do not, but the evil which I will not, that I do.* Therefore man has not free choice.

Obj. 2. Further, whoever has free choice has in his power to will or not to will, to do or not to do. But this is not in man's power, for it is written (*Rom.* ix. 16): *It is not of him that willeth*—namely, to will—*nor of him that runneth*—namely, to run. Therefore man has not free choice.

Obj. 3. Further, he is free who is his own master, as the Philosopher says.[1] Therefore what is moved by another is not free. But God moves the will, for it is written (*Prov.* xxi. 1): *The heart of the king is in the hand*

---

1. 参见 Aristotle, *Metaph.*, I, 2 (982b 26).

of the Lord; *whithersoever He will He shall turn it*; and (*Phil.* ii 13): *It is God Who worketh in you both to will and to accomplish.* Therefore man has not free choice.

Obj. 4. Further, whoever has free choice is master of his own actions. But man is not master of his own actions, for it is written (*Jer.* x. 23): *The way of a man is not his*, *neither is it in a man to walk.* Therefore man has not free choice.

Obj. 5. Further, the Philosopher says: *According as each one is*, *such does the end seem to him.*[1] But it is not in our power to be such as we are, for this comes to us from nature. Therefore it is natural to us to follow some particular end, and therefore we are not free in so doing.

On the contrary, It is written (*Ecclus.* xv. 14): *God made man from the beginning*, *and left him in the hand of his own counsel*; and the *Gloss* adds: *That is*, *in the liberty of choice.*[2]

I answer that, Man has free choice, or otherwise counsels, exhortations, commands, prohibitions, rewards and punishments would be in vain. In order to make this evident, we must observe that some things act without judgment, as a stone moves downwards; and in like manner all things which lack knowledge. And some act from judgment, but not a free judgment; as brute animals. For the sheep, seeing the wolf, judges it a thing to be shunned, from a natural and not a free judgment; because it judges, not from deliberation, but from natural instinct. And the same thing is to be said of any judgment in brute animals. But man acts from judgment, because by his apprehensive power he judges that something should be avoided or sought. But because this judgment, in the case of some particular act, is not from a natural instinct, but from some act of comparison in the reason, therefore he acts from free judgment and retains the power of being inclined to various things. For reason in contingent matters

1. 参见 *Eth.*, III, 5 (1114a 32).
2. 参见 *Glossa interl*, (III, 401v); cf. *Glossa ordin.* (III, 401E).

may follow opposite courses, as we see in dialectical syllogisms[1] and rhetorical arguments[2]. Now particular operations are contingent, and therefore in such matters the judgment of reason may follow opposite courses, and is not determinate to one. And in that man is rational, it is necessary that he have free choice.

Reply Obj. 1. As we have said above, the sensitive appetite, though it obeys the reason, yet in a given case can resist by desiring what the reason forbids.[3] This is therefore the good which man does not when he wishes—namely, *not to desire against reason*, as Augustine says.[4]

Reply Obj. 2. Those words of the Apostle are not to be taken as though man does not wish or does not run of his free choice, but because free choice is not sufficient thereto unless it be moved and helped by God.

Reply Obj. 3. Free choice is the cause of its own movement, because by his free choice man moves himself to act. But it does not of necessity belong to liberty that what is free should be the first cause of itself, as neither for one thing to be cause of another need it be the first cause. God, therefore, is the first cause, Who moves causes both natural and voluntary. And just as by moving natural causes He does not prevent their actions from being natural, so by moving voluntary causes He does not deprive their actions of being voluntary; but rather is He the cause of this very thing in them, for He operates in each thing according to its own nature.

Reply Obj. 4. *Man's way* is said *not to be his* in the execution of his choice, wherein he may be impeded, whether he will or not. The choice itself, however, is in us, but presupposes the help of God.

---

1. dialectical syllogism: 辩证性推论
2. rhetorical argument: 修辞性论证
3. 参见 Q. 81, a. 3, ad 2.
4. 参见 *Glossa interl.*, super *Rom.*, VII, 19 (VI, 17r).—Cf. St. Augustine, *Serm. ad Popul.*, serm. CLIV, 3 (PL 38, 834).

Reply Obj. 5. Quality in man is of two kinds: natural and adventitious. Now the natural quality may be in the intellectual part, or in the body and its powers. From the very fact, therefore, that man is such by virtue of a natural quality which is in the intellectual part, he naturally desires his last end, which is happiness. This desire is, indeed, a natural desire, and is not subject to free choice, as is clear from what we have said above.[1] But on the part of the body and its powers, man may be such by virtue of a natural quality, inasmuch as he is of such a temperament or disposition due to any impression whatever produced by corporeal causes, which cannot affect the intellectual part, since it is not the act of a corporeal organ. And such as a man is by virtue of a corporeal quality, such also does his end seem to him, because from such a disposition a man is inclined to choose or reject something. But these inclinations are subject to the judgment of reason, which the lower appetite obeys, as we have said.[2] Therefore this is in no way prejudicial to free choice.

The adventitious qualities are habits and passions, by virtue of which a man is inclined to one thing rather than to another. And yet even these inclinations are subject to the judgment of reason. Such qualities, too, are subject to reason, as it is in our power either to acquire them, whether by causing them or disposing ourselves to them, or to reject them. And so there is nothing in this that is repugnant to free choice.

Second Article
WHETHER FREE CHOICE IS A POWER?

We proceed thus to the Second Article:—

Objection 1. It would seem that free choice is not a power. For free

---

1. 参见 Q. 82, a. 1 and 2.
2. 参见 Q. 81, a. 3.

choice is nothing but a free judgment. But judgment denominates an act, not a power. Therefore free choice is not a power.

Obj. 2. Further, free choice is defined as *the faculty of the will and reason.*[1] But faculty denominates the facility of power, which is due to a habit. Therefore free choice is a habit. Moreover Bernard says that free choice is *the soul's habit of disposing of itself.*[2] Therefore it is not a power.

Obj. 3. Further, no natural power is forfeited through sin. But free choice is forfeited through sin, for Augustine says that *man, by abusing free choice, loses both it and himself.*[3] Therefore free choice is not a power.

On the contrary, Nothing but a power, seemingly, is the subject of a habit. But free choice is the subject of grace, by the help of which it chooses what is good. Therefore free choice is a power.

I answer that, Although *free choice*, in its strict sense, denotes an act, in the common manner of speaking we call free choice that which is the principle of the act by which man judges freely. Now in us the principle of an act is both power and habit; for we say that we know something both by science and by the intellectual power. Therefore free choice must be either a power,[4] or a habit,[5] or a power with a habit.[6] That it is neither a habit nor a power together with a habit can be clearly proved in two ways. First of all, because, if it is a habit, it must be a natural habit; for it is natural to man to have free choice. But there is no natural habit in us with respect to those things which come under free choice, for we are naturally inclined to those things of which we have natural habits, for instance, to assent to first principles. Now those things to which we are naturally inclined are not subject

1. 参见 Peter Lombard, *Sent.*, II, xxiv, 3 (I, 421).
2. 参见 St. Bernard, *De Gratia et Libero Arbitrio*, I (PL 182, 1002).
3. 参见 *Enchir.*, XXX (PL 40, 246).
4. 参见 St. Albert, *Summa de Creatur.*, II, q. 70, a. 2 (XXXV, 575).
5. 参见 St. Bonaventure, *In II Sent.*, d. xxv, pt. 1, a. 1, q. 4 (II, 601).
6. 参见 Alex, of Hales, *Summa Theol.*, II, I, no. 390 (II, 486).

to free choice, as we have said in the case of the desire of happiness.[1] Therefore it is against the very notion of free choice that it should be a natural habit; and that it should be a non-natural habit is against its nature. Therefore in no sense is it a habit.

Secondly, this is clear because habits are defined as that *by reason of which we are well or ill disposed with regard to actions and passions.*[2] For by temperance we are well-disposed as regards concupiscences, and by intemperance ill-disposed; and by science we are well-disposed to the act of the intellect when we know the truth, and by the contrary habit ill-disposed. But free choice is indifferent to choosing well or ill, and therefore it is impossible that it be a habit. Therefore it is a power.

Reply Obj. 1. It is not unusual for a power to be named from its act. And so from this act, which is a free judgment, is named the power which is the principle of this act. Otherwise, if free choice denominated an act, it would not always remain in man.

Reply Obj. 2. *Faculty* sometimes denominates a power ready for operation, and in this sense faculty is used in the definition of free choice. But Bernard takes habit, not as divided against power, but as signifying any aptitude by which a man is somehow disposed to an act.[3] This may be both by a power and by a habit, for by a power man is, as it were, empowered to do the action, and by the habit he is apt to act well or ill.

Reply Obj. 3. Man is said to have lost free choice by falling into sin, not as to natural liberty, which is freedom from coercion, but as regards freedom from fault and unhappiness. Of this we shall treat later in the treatise on Morals in the second part of this work.[4]

---

1. 参见 Q. 82, a. 1 and 2.
2. 参见 Aristotle, *Eth.*, II, 5 (1105b 25).
3. 参见 *De Grat. et Lib. Arb.*, I (PL 182,1002).
4. 参见 *S. T.*, I–II, q. 85; q. 109.

Third Article
WHETHER FREE CHOICE IS AN APPETITIVE POWER?

We proceed thus to the Third Article:—

Objection 1. It would seem that free choice is not an appetitive, but a cognitive power. For Damascene says that *free choice straightway accompanies the rational power.*[1] But reason is a cognitive power. Therefore free choice is a cognitive power.

Obj. 2. Further, free choice is so called as though it were a free judgment. But to judge is an act of a cognitive power. Therefore free choice is a cognitive power.

Obj. 3. Further, the principal function of free choice is election. But election seems to belong to knowledge, because it implies a certain comparison of one thing to another; which belongs to the cognitive power. Therefore free choice is a cognitive power.

On the contrary, The Philosopher says that election is *the desire of those things which are in our power.*[2] But desire is an act of the appetitive power. Therefore election is also. But free choice is that by which we elect. Therefore free choice is an appetitive power.

I answer that, The proper act of free choice is election, for we say that we have a free choice because we can take one thing while refusing another; and this is to elect. Therefore we must consider the nature of free choice by considering the nature of election. Now two things concur in election: one on the part of the cognitive power, the other on the part of the appetitive power. On the part of the cognitive power, counsel is required, by which we judge one thing to be preferred to another; on the part of the appetitive power, it is required that the appetite should accept the judgment of counsel. Therefore Aristotle leaves it in doubt whether election belongs principally to the

---

1. 参见 *De Fide Orth.*, II, 27 (PG 94, 949).
2. 参见 *Eth.*, III, 3 (1113a 11).

appetitive or the cognitive power: since he says that election is either *an appetitive intellect or an intellectual appetite.*[1] But he inclines to its being an intellectual appetite when he describes election as *a desire proceeding from counsel.*[2] And the reason of this is because the proper object of election is the means to the end. Now the means, as such, has the nature of that good which is called *useful*; and since the good, as such, is the object of the appetite, it follows that election is principally an act of an appetitive power. And thus free choice is an appetitive power.

Reply Obj. 1. The appetitive powers accompany the apprehensive, and in this sense Damascene says that free choice straightway accompanies the rational power.

Reply Obj. 2. Judgment, as it were, concludes and terminates counsel. Now counsel is terminated, first, by the judgment of reason; secondly, by the acceptation of the appetite. Hence the Philosopher says that, *having formed a judgment by counsel, we desire in accordance with that counsel.*[3] And in this sense election itself is a judgment from which free choice takes its name.

Reply Obj. 3. This comparison which is implied in the term election belongs to the preceding counsel, which is an act of reason. For though the appetite does not make comparisons, yet inasmuch as it is moved by the apprehensive power which does compare, it has some likeness of comparison, by choosing one in preference to another.

Fourth Article
WHETHER FREE CHOICE IS A POWER DISTINCT FROM THE WILL?

We proceed thus to the Fourth Article:—

---

1. 参见 *Op. cit.*, VI, 2 (1139b 4).
2. 参见 *Op. cit.*, III, 3 (1113a 11).
3. 同上

Objection 1. It would seem that free choice is a power distinct from the will.[1] For Damascene says that θέλησις is one thing and βούλησις another.[2] But θέλησις is will, while βούλησις seems to be free choice, because βούλησις, according to him, is the will as concerning an object by way of comparison between two things. Therefore it seems that free choice is a power distinct from the will.

Obj. 2. Further, powers are known by their acts. But election, which is the act of free choice, is distinct from the will, because *the will regards the end, whereas choice regards the means to the end.*[3] Therefore free choice is a power distinct from the will.

Obj. 3. Further, the will is the intellectual appetite. But on the part of the intellect there are two powers —agent and possible. Therefore, also on the part of the intellectual appetite there must be another power besides the will. And this, seemingly, can be only free choice. Therefore free choice is a power distinct from the will.

On the contrary, Damascene says free choice is nothing else than the will.[4]

I answer that, The appetitive powers must be proportionate to the apprehensive powers, as we have said above.[5] Now, as on the part of intellectual apprehension we have intellect and reason, so on the part of the intellectual appetite we have will and free choice, which is nothing else but the power of election. And this is clear from their relations to their respective objects and acts. For the act of *understanding* implies the simple acceptation of something, and hence we say that we understand first principles, which are known of themselves without any comparison. But to *reason*, properly speaking, is

---

1. 参见 Cf. St. Albert, *Summa de Creatur.*, II, q. 70, a. 2 (XXXV, 577).
2. 参见 *De Fide Orth.*, XXII (PG 94, 944).
3. 参见 Aristotle, *Eth.*, III, 2 (1111b 26).
4. 参见 *De Fide Orth.*, XIV (PG 94, 1037).
5. 参见 Q. 64, a. 2; q. 80, a. 2.

to come from one thing to the knowledge of another, and so, properly speaking, we reason about conclusions, which are known from the principles. In like manner, on the part of the appetite, to *will* implies the simple appetite for something, and so the will is said to regard the end, which is desired for itself. But to *elect* is to desire something for the sake of obtaining something else, and so, properly speaking, it regards the means to the end. Now in appetitive matters, the end is related to the means, which is desired for the end, in the same way as, in knowledge, principles are related to the conclusion to which we assent because of the principles. Therefore it is evident that as *intellect* is to *reason*, so *will* is to the *elective power*, which is free choice. But it has been shown above that it belongs to the same power both to understand and to reason,[1] even as it belongs to the same power to be at rest and to be in movement. Hence it belongs also to the same power to will and to elect. And on this account will and the free choice are not two powers, but one.

Reply Obj. 1. βουλησις is distinct from θέλησις because of a distinction, not of powers, but of acts.

Reply Obj. 2. Election and will—that is, the act of willing—are different acts, yet they belong to the same power, as do *to understand* and *to reason*, as we have said.

Reply Obj. 3. The intellect is compared to the will as moving the will. And therefore there is no need to distinguish in the will an *agent* and a *possible* will.

---

1. 参见 Q. 79, a. 8.

Question LXXXIV
HOW THE SOUL WHILE UNITED TO THE BODY UNDERSTANDS CORPOREAL THINGS BENEATH IT
(*In Eight Articles*)

WE now have to consider the acts of the soul in regard to the intellectual and the appetitive powers, for the other powers of the soul do not come directly under the consideration of the theologian. Now the acts of the appetitive part of the soul come under the consideration of the science of morals, and so we shall treat of them in the second part of this work, to which the consideration of moral matters belongs. But of the acts of the intellectual part we shall treat now. In treating of these acts, we shall proceed in the following order. First, we shall inquire how the soul understands when united to the body; secondly, how it understands when separated from the body.[1]

The former of these inquiries will be threefold: (1) How the soul understands bodies, which are beneath it. (2) How it understands itself and things contained in itself.[2] (3) How it understands immaterial substances, which are above it.[3]

In treating of the knowledge of corporeal things, there are three points to be considered: (1) Through what does the soul know them? (2) How and in what order does it know them?[4] (3) What does it know

---

1. 参见 Q. 89.
2. 参见 Q. 87.
3. 参见 Q. 88.
4. 参见 Q. 85.

in them?[1]

Under the first head there are eight points of inquiry: (1) Whether the soul knows bodies through the intellect? (2) Whether it understands them through its essence, or through any species? (3) If through some species, whether the species of all things intelligible are naturally innate in the soul? (4) Whether these species are derived by the soul from certain separate immaterial forms? (5) Whether our soul sees in the eternal exemplars all that it understands? (6) Whether it acquires intellectual knowledge from the senses? (7) Whether the intellect can, through the species of which it is possessed, actually understand, without turning to the phantasms? (8) Whether the judgment of the intellect is hindered by an obstacle in the sensitive powers?

First Article
WHETHER THE SOUL KNOWS BODIES THROUGH THE INTELLECT?

We proceed thus to the First Article:—

Objection 1. It would seem that the soul does not know bodies through the intellect. For Augustine says that *bodies cannot be understood by the intellect: nor indeed anything corporeal unless it can be perceived by the senses.*[2] He says also that intellectual vision is of those things that are in the soul by their essence.[3] But such are not bodies. Therefore the soul cannot know bodies through the intellect.

Obj. 2. Further, as sense is to the intelligible, so is the intellect to the sensible. But the soul can by no means, through the senses, understand spiritual things, which are intelligible. Therefore by no means can it, through the intellect, know bodies, which are sensible.

---

1. 参见 Q. 86.
2. 参见 *Solil.*, II, 4 (PL 32, 888).
3. 参见 *De Genesi ad Litt.*, XII, 24 (PL 34, 474).

Obj. 3. Further, the intellect is concerned with things that are necessary and unchangeable. But all bodies are movable and changeable. Therefore the soul cannot know bodies through the intellect.

On the contrary, Science is in the intellect. If, therefore, the intellect does not know bodies, it follows that there is no science of bodies; and thus perishes the science of nature, which treats of movable bodies.

I answer, In order to elucidate this question, that the early philosophers, who inquired into the natures of things, thought there was nothing in the world save bodies.[1] And because they observed that all bodies are subject to motion, and considered them to be ever in a state of flux, they were of the opinion that we can have no certain knowledge of the reality of things. For what is in a continual state of flux cannot be grasped with any degree of certitude, for it passes away before the mind can form a judgment on it. As Heraclitus said, *it is not possible to touch the water in a passing stream twice* (as the Philosopher relates[2]).

After these came Plato, who, wishing to save the certitude of our knowledge of truth through the intellect, maintained that, besides these corporeal things, there is another genus of beings, separate from matter and movement, which he called *species* or *ideas*, by participation in which each one of these singular and sensible things is said to be either a man, or a horse, or the like.[3] And so, he said that sciences and definitions, and whatever pertains to the act of the intellect, is not referred to these sensible bodies, but to those immaterial and separate beings;[4] so that, according to this, the soul does not understand these

---

1. 参见 Cf. above, q. 44, a. 2.
2. 参见 *Metaph.*, III, 5 (1010a 14).
3. 参见 Cf. Aristotle, *op. cit.*, I, 6 (987b 6; b 7); I, 9 (992b 7).—Cf. also Plato, *Theaetet.* (p. 156a).
4. 参见 Cf. Avicenna, *Metaph.*, VII, 2 (96ra).

corporeal things, but their separated species.

Now this is clearly false for two reasons. First, because, since those species are immaterial and immovable, knowledge of movement and matter (which is proper to natural philosophy) would be excluded from among the sciences, and likewise all demonstration through moving and material causes. Secondly, because it seems ridiculous, when we seek for knowledge of things which are to us manifest, to introduce other beings, which cannot be the substances of the things with which we began, since they differ from them in being. Hence, granted that we have a knowledge of those separate substances, we cannot for that reason claim to form judgments concerning these sensible things.

Now it seems that Plato strayed from the truth because, having observed that all knowledge takes place through some kind of similitude,[1] he thought that the form of the thing known must of necessity be in the knower in the same manner as in the thing known itself. But it was his opinion that the form of the thing understood is in the intellect under conditions of universality, immateriality[2], and immobility; which is apparent from the very operation of the intellect, whose act of understanding is universal, and characterized by a certain necessity; for the mode of action corresponds to the mode of the agent's form. Therefore he concluded that the things which we understand must subsist in themselves under the same conditions of immateriality and immobility[3].

But there is no necessity for this. For even in sensible things it is to be observed that the form is otherwise in one sensible than in another. For instance, whiteness may be of great intensity in one, and of a less intensity in another; in one we find whiteness with sweetness, in another without sweetness. In the same way, the sensible form is

---

1. 参见 Cf. *ibid.* (96rb).—Cf. also, Aristotle, *De An.*, I, 2 (404b 17).
2. immateriality: 无形；非物质
3. immobility: 固定性；静止

in one way in the thing which is external to the soul, and in another way in the senses, which receive the forms of sensible things without receiving matter, such as the color of gold without receiving gold. So, too, the intellect, according to its own mode, receives under conditions of immateriality and immobility the species of material and movable bodies; for the received is in the receiver according to the mode of the receiver. We must conclude, therefore, that the soul knows bodies through the intellect by a knowledge which is immaterial, universal and necessary.

Reply Obj. 1. These words of Augustine are to be understood as referring to the medium of intellectual knowledge, and not to its object. For the intellect knows bodies by understanding them, not indeed through bodies, nor through material and corporeal likenesses, but through immaterial and intelligible species, which can be in the soul by their own essence.

Reply Obj. 2. As Augustine says, it is not correct to say that as the sense knows only bodies so the intellect knows only spiritual things;[1] for it would follow that God and the angels would not know bodies. The reason for this diversity is that the lower power does not extend to those things that belong to the higher power; whereas the higher power accomplishes in a more excellent manner what belongs to the lower power.

Reply Obj. 3. Every movement presupposes something immovable. For when a change of quality occurs, the substance remains unmoved; and when there is a change of substantial form, matter remains unmoved. Moreover, mutable things have immovable dispositions; for instance, though Socrates be not always sitting, yet it is an immovable truth that whenever he does sit he remains in one place. For this reason there is nothing to hinder our having an immovable science of

---

1. 参见 *De Civit. Dei*, XXII, 29 (PL 41, 800).

movable things.

Second Article
WHETHER THE SOUL UNDERSTANDS CORPOREAL THINGS THROUGH ITS ESSENCE?

We proceed thus to the Second Article:—

Objection 1. It would seem that the soul understands corporeal things through its essence. For Augustine says that the soul *collects and lays hold of the images of bodies which are formed in the soul and of the soul; for in forming them it gives them something of its own substance.*[1] But the soul understands bodies by the likenesses of bodies. Therefore the soul knows bodies through its essence, which it employs for the formation of such likenesses, and from which it forms them.

Obj. 2. Further, the Philosopher says that *the soul, after a fashion, is everything.*[2] Since, therefore, like is known by like, it seems that the soul knows corporeal things through itself.

Obj. 3. Further, the soul is superior to corporeal creatures. Now lower things are in higher things in a more eminent way than in themselves, as Dionysius says.[3] Therefore all corporeal creatures exist in a more excellent way in the essence of the soul than in themselves. Therefore the soul can know corporeal creatures through its essence.

On the contrary, Augustine says that *the mind gathers the knowledge of corporeal things through the bodily senses.*[4] But the soul itself cannot be known through the bodily senses. Therefore it does not know corporeal things through itself.

I answer that, The ancient philosophers held that the soul knows

---

1. 参见 *De Trin.* X, 5 (PL 42, 977) .
2. 参见 *De An.*, III, 8 (431b 21).
3. 参见 *De Cael. Hier.*, XII, 2 (PG 3, 293).
4. 参见 *De Trin.*, IX, 3 (PL 42, 963).

bodies through its essence. For it was universally admitted that *like is known by like.*[1] But they thought that the form of the thing known is in the knower in the same way as in the thing known. The Platonists however were of a contrary opinion. For Plato, having observed that the intellectual soul has an immaterial nature,[2] and an immaterial mode of knowing,[3] held that the forms of the things known subsist immaterially. But the earlier natural philosophers, observing that the things known are corporeal and material, held that they must exist materially even in the soul that knows them. And therefore, in order to ascribe to the soul a knowledge of all things, they held that it has the same nature in common with all.[4] And because the nature of an effect is determined by its principles, they ascribed to the soul the nature of a principle.[5] Hence it is that those who thought fire to be the principle of all, held that the soul had the nature of fire,[6] and in like manner as to air[7] and water.[8] Lastly, Empedocles, who held the existence of four material elements and two principles of movement,[9] said that the soul was composed of these.[10] Consequently, since they held that things existed in. the soul materially, they maintained that all the soul's knowledge is material, thus failing to distinguish intellect from sense.[11]

But this opinion will not hold. First, because in the material principle of which they were speaking, effects do not exist save in

---

1. 参见 Cf. Aristotle, *De An.*, I, 5 (409b 24).
2. 参见 Cf. Nemesius, *De Nat. Hom.*, II (PG 40, 572); St. Augustine, *De Civit. Dei*, VIII, 5 (PL 41, 230).
3. 参见 Cf. Aristotle, *Metaph.*, I, 6 (987b 6).
4. 参见 Cf. Aristotle, *De An.*, I, 5 (409b 24).
5. 参见 Cf. *op. cit.*, I, 2 (404b 110).
6. 参见 A theory of Democritus, according to Aristotle, *De An.*, I, 2 (405a 5).
7. 参见 A theory of Diogenes, according to Aristotle, *ibid.*, (405a 21); and of Anaximenes, according to Macrobius, *In Somn. Scipion.*, I, 14 (p. 543).
8. 参见 A theory of Hippo, according to Aristotle, *De An.*, I, 2 (405b 1).
9. 参见 Cf. Aristotle, *De Gener.*, I, 1 (314a 16).
10. 参见 Cf. Aristotle, *De An.*, I, 5 (410a 3); I, 4 (408a 19).
11. 参见 Cf. *op. cit.*, III, 3 (427a 21).

potentiality. But a thing is not known according as it is in potentiality, but only according as it is in act, as is shown in *Metaph.* ix.;[1] therefore neither is a power known except through its act. It was therefore insufficient to ascribe to the soul the nature of the principles of things in order to guarantee to the soul a knowledge of all things; it was further necessary to admit in the soul the natures and forms of each individual effect, for instance, of bone, flesh, and the like. Thus does Aristotle argue against Empedocles.[2] Secondly, because if it were necessary for the thing known to exist materially in the knower, there would be no reason why things which have a material existence outside the soul should be devoid of knowledge; why, for instance, if by fire the soul knows fire, that fire also which is outside the soul should not have knowledge of fire.

We must conclude, therefore, that the material things known must needs exist in the knower, not materially, but rather immaterially. The reason for this is that the act of knowledge extends to things outside the knower; for we know even the things that are outside us. Now by matter the form of a thing is determined to some one thing. Therefore it is clear that knowledge is in inverse ratio to materiality. Consequently, things that are not receptive of forms, save materially, have no power of knowledge whatever— such as plants, as the Philosopher says.[3] But the more immaterially a being receives the form of the thing known, the more perfect is its knowledge. Therefore the intellect, which abstracts the species not only from matter, but also from the individuating conditions of matter, knows more perfectly than the senses, which receive the form of the thing known, without matter indeed, but subject to material conditions. Moreover, among the senses themselves, sight has the most perfect knowledge, because

1. 参见 Aristotle, *Metaph.*, VIII, 9 (1051a 29).
2. 参见 *De An.*, I, 5 (409b 23).
3. 参见 *Op. cit.*, II, 12 (424a 32).

it is the least material, as we have remarked above.[1] So, too, among intellects, the more perfect is the more immaterial.

It is therefore clear from the foregoing, that if there be an intellect which knows all things by its essence, then its essence must needs have all things in itself immaterially; much as the early philosophers held that the essence of the soul must be composed actually of the principles of all material things in order to know all things. Now it is proper to God that His essence comprise all things immaterially, as effects pre-exist virtually in their cause. God alone, therefore, understands all things through His essence; but neither the human soul nor the angels can do so.

Reply Obj. 1. Augustine in that passage is speaking of an imaginary vision, which takes place through the images of bodies. To the formation of such images the soul gives part of its substance, just as a subject is given in order to be informed by some form. In this way the soul makes such images from itself; not that the soul or some part of the soul be turned into this or that image, but just as we say that a body is made into something colored because of its being informed with color. That this is the sense is clear from the sequel. For he says that the soul *keeps something*—namely, not informed with such an image—*which is able freely to judge of the species of these images*, and that this is the *mind* or *intellect*.[2] And he says that the part which is informed with these images—namely, the imagination—is *common to us and beasts*.

Reply Obj. 2. Aristotle did not hold that the soul was actually composed of all things, as did the earlier naturalists; he said that the soul is all things, *after a fashion*, inasmuch as it is in potentiality to all—through the senses, to all sensible things; through the intellect, to all intelligible things.

---

1. 参见 Q. 78, a. 3.
2. 参见 *De Trin.*, X, 5 (PL 42, 977).

Reply Obj. 3. Every creature has a finite and determinate being. Therefore, although the essence of a higher creature has a certain likeness to a lower creature, inasmuch as they share in a common genus, yet it has not a complete likeness thereof, because it is determined to a certain species other than the species of the lower creature. But the divine essence is a perfect likeness of all that may be found to exist in things created, being the universal principle of all.

Third Article
WHETHER THE SOUL UNDERSTANDS ALL THINGS THROUGH INNATE SPECIES?

We proceed thus to the Third Article:—

Objection 1. It would seem that the soul understands all things through innate species. For Gregory says, in a homily for the Ascension[1], that *man has understanding in common with the angels.*[2] But angels understand all things through innate species: wherefore in the *Book of Causes* it is said that *every intelligence is full of forms.*[3] Therefore the soul also has innate species of things, by means of which it understands corporeal things.

Obj. 2. Further, the intellectual soul is more excellent than corporeal primary matter. But primary matter was created by God under the forms to which it has potentiality. Therefore much more is the intellectual soul created by God with intelligible species. And so the soul understands corporeal things through innate species.

Obj. 3. Further, no one can answer the truth except concerning what he knows. But even a person untaught, and devoid of acquired knowledge, answers the truth to every question if put to him in

---

1. the Ascension: 耶稣升天
2. 参见 *In Evang.*, II, hom. 29 (PL 76, 1214).
3. 参见 *De Causis*, X (p. 170).

orderly fashion, as we find related in the *Meno* of Plato concerning a certain individual.[1] Therefore we have some knowledge of things even before we acquire knowledge; which would not be the case unless we had innate species. Therefore the soul understands corporeal things through innate species.

On the contrary, The Philosopher, speaking of the intellect, says that it is like *a tablet on which nothing is written.*[2]

I answer that, Since form is the principle of action, a thing must be related to the form which is the principle of an action in the same way as it is to that action. For instance, if upward motion is from lightness, then that which moves upwards only potentially must needs be only potentially light, but that which actually moves upwards must needs be actually light. Now we observe that man sometimes is only a potential knower, both as to sense and as to intellect. And he is reduced from such potentiality to act:—through the action of sensible objects on his senses, to the act of sensation; by instruction or discovery, to the act of understanding. Therefore we must say that the cognitive soul is in potentiality both to the likenesses which are the principles of sensing, and to the likenesses which are the principles of understanding. For this reason Aristotle held that the intellect by which the soul understands has no innate species, but is at first in potentiality to all such species.[3]

But since that which actually has a form is sometimes unable to act according to that form because of some hindrance (as a light thing may be hindered from moving upwards), for this reason Plato held that man's intellect is naturally filled with all intelligible species, but that, by being united to the body, it is hindered from the realization

1. 参见 *Meno* (p. 82b).—Cf. St. Augustine, *De Trin.*, II, 15 (PL 42, 1011).
2. 参见 *De An.*, III, 4 (430a 1).
3. 同上 (429b 30).

of its act.[1] But this seems to be unreasonable. First, because, if the soul has a natural knowledge of all things, it seems impossible for the soul so far to forget the existence of such knowledge as not to know itself to be possessed of it. For no man forgets what he knows naturally, *e.g.*, that every whole is larger than its part, and the like. And especially unreasonable does this seem if we suppose that it is natural to the soul to be united to the body, as we have established above;[2] for it is unreasonable that the natural operation of a thing be totally hindered by that which belongs to it naturally. Secondly, the falseness of this opinion is clearly proved from the fact that if a sense be wanting, the knowledge of what is apprehended through that sense is also wanting. For instance, a man who is born blind can have no knowledge of colors. This would not be the case if the soul had innate likenesses of all intelligible things. We must therefore conclude that the soul does not know corporeal things through innate species.

Reply Obj. 1. Man indeed has understanding in common with the angels, but not in the same degree of perfection; just as the lower grades of bodies, which merely exist, according to Gregory, have not the same degree of perfection as the higher bodies. For the matter of the lower bodies is not totally completed by its form, but is in potentiality to forms which it has not; whereas the matter of the heavenly bodies is totally completed by its form, so that it is not in potentiality to any other form, as we have said above.[3] In the same way the angelic intellect is perfected by intelligible species, in accordance with its nature; whereas the human intellect is in potentiality to such species.

Reply Obj. 2. Primary matter has substantial being through its form, and consequently it had need to be created under some form; for

---

1. 参见 Cf. Aristotle, *Metaph.*, I, 9 (993a 1).
2. 参见 Q. 76, a. 1.
3. 参见 Q. 66, a. 2.

otherwise it would not be in act. But when once it exists under one form it is in potentiality to others. On the other hand, the intellect does not receive substantial being through the intelligible species; and therefore there is no comparison.

Reply Obj. 3. If questions be put in an orderly fashion, they proceed from universal self-evident principles to what is particular. Now by such a process knowledge is produced in the soul of the learner. Therefore, when he answers the truth to a subsequent question, this is not because he had knowledge previously, but because he then acquires such knowledge for the first time. For it matters not whether the teacher proceed from universal principles to conclusions by questioning or by asserting; for in either case the intellect of the listener is assured of what follows by that which preceded.

Fourth Article
WHETHER THE INTELLIGIBLE SPECIES ARE DERIVED BY THE SOUL FROM CERTAIN SEPARATE FORMS?

We proceed thus to the Fourth Article:—

Objection 1. It would seem that the intelligible species are derived by the soul from some separate forms. For whatever is such by participation is caused by what is such essentially; for instance, that which is on fire is reduced to fire as its cause. But the intellectual soul, in so far as it is actually understanding, participates in the intelligibles themselves; for, in a manner, the intellect in act is the thing understood in act. Therefore that which in itself and in its essence is understood in act, is the cause that the intellectual soul actually understands. Now that which in its essence is actually understood is a form existing without matter. Therefore the intelligible species, by which the soul understands, are caused by some separate forms.

Obj. 2. Further, the intelligible is to the intellect as the sensible is to the sense. But the sensible species which are in the senses, and by which we sense, are caused by the sensible things which exist actually outside the soul. Therefore the intelligible species, by which our intellect understands, are caused by some things actually intelligible, existing outside the soul. But these can be nothing else than forms separate from matter. Therefore the intelligible forms of our intellect are derived from some separate substances.

Obj. 3. Further, whatever is in potentiality is reduced to act by something actual. If, therefore, our intellect, previously in potentiality, afterwards actually understands, this must needs be caused by some intellect which is always in act. But this is a separate intellect. Therefore the intelligible species, by which we actually understand, are caused by some separate substances.

On the contrary, If this were true, we should not need the senses in order to understand. And this is proved to be false especially from the fact that if a man be wanting in a sense, he cannot have any knowledge of the sensibles corresponding to that sense.

I answer that, Some have held that the intelligible species of our intellect are derived from certain separate Forms or substances. And this in two ways. For Plato, as we have said, held that the forms of sensible things subsist by themselves without matter: *e.g.*, the Form of a man which he called man-in-himself, and the Form or Idea of a horse which he called horse-in-itself, and so forth. He said therefore that these Forms are partici pated both by our soul and by corporeal matter: by our soul, for knowledge,[1] and by corporeal matter for being;[2] so that, just as corporeal matter, by participating the Idea of a stone, becomes an individual stone, so our intellect, by participating the Idea of a stone, is made to understand a stone. Now the participation of an Idea takes place by some likeness of the Idea in

1. 参见 Cf. St. Augustine, *Lib. 83 Quaest.*, q. 46 (PL 40, 30).
2. 参见 Cf. Aristotle, *Metaph.*, I, 9 (991b 3).—Plato, *Phaedo* (p. 100d).

the participator, in the way that a model is participated by a copy.[1] So just as he held that the sensible forms, which are in corporeal matter, are derived from the Ideas as certain likenesses of them, so he held that the intelligible species of our intellect are likenesses of the Ideas, derived therefrom.[2] And for this reason, as we have said above, he referred sciences and definitions to those Ideas.

But since it is contrary to the nature of sensible things that their forms should subsist without matter, as Aristotle proves in many ways,[3] Avicenna, setting this opinion aside, held that the intelligible species of all sensible things, instead of subsisting in themselves without matter, pre-exist immaterially in some separate intellects.[4] From the first of these intellects, said he, such species are derived by a second, and so on to the last separate intellect, which he called the *agent intellect*. From the agent intellect, according to him, intelligible species flow into our souls, and sensible species into corporeal matter.[5] And so Avicenna agrees with Plato in this, that the intelligible species of our intellect are derived from certain separate Forms; but these Plato held to subsist of themselves, while Avicenna placed them in the agent intellect. They differ, too, in this respect, that Avicenna held that the intelligible species do not remain in our intellect after it has ceased actually to understand, and that it needs to turn [to the agent intellect] in order to receive them anew.[6] Consequently, he does not hold that the soul has innate knowledge, as Plato, who held that the participations of the Ideas remain immovably in the soul.[7]

But in this opinion no sufficient reason can be assigned for the soul

---

1. 参见 Cf. Aristotle, *Metaph.*, I, 9 (991a 21).—Plato, *Timaeus* (pp. 28a, 30c).
2. 参见 Cf. Avicenna, *De An.*, V, 5 (25rb) ; *Metaph.*, IX, 4 (105ra).
3. 参见 *Metaph.*, VI, 14 (1039a 24).
4. 参见 *De An.*, V, 5 (25rb); *Metaph.*, IX, 4 (105ra).
5. 参见 *De An.*, V, 6 (26rb); *Metaph.*, IX, 5 (105rb).—Cf. above, q. 65, a. 4.
6. 参见 *De An.*, V, 6 (26rb).—Cf. *C. G.*, II, 74.
7. 参见 Cf. Aristotle, *Metaph.*, I, 7 (988b 3); *Top.*, II, 7 (113a 27).

being united to the body. For it cannot be said that the intellectual soul is united to the body for the sake of the body, since neither is form for the sake of matter, nor is the mover for the sake of the thing moved, but rather the reverse. Especially does the body seem necessary to the intellectual soul for the latter's proper operation, which is to understand; since as to its being, the soul does not depend on the body. But if the soul by its very nature had an inborn aptitude for receiving intelligible species only through the influence of certain separate principles, and were not to receive them from the senses, it would not need the body in order to understand. Hence, it would be united to the body to no purpose.

But if it be said that our soul needs the senses in order to understand, in that it is in some way awakened by them to the consideration of those things whose intelligible species it receives from the separate principles,[1] even this seems an insufficient explanation. For this awakening does not seem necessary to the soul, except in as far as it is overcome by sleep, as the Platonists expressed it, and by forgetfulness, through its union with the body;[2] and thus the senses would be of no use to the intellectual soul except for the purpose of removing the obstacle which the soul encounters through its union with the body.[3] Consequently, the reason for the union of the soul with the body still remains unexplained.

And if it be said, with Avicenna, that the senses are necessary to the soul because by them it is roused to turn to the agent intellect from which it receives the species,[4] neither is this a sufficient explanation. Because if it is natural for the soul to understand through species

1. 参见 Cf. William of Auvergne, *De Univ.*, IIa IIae, 76 (I, pt. II, 929); IIIa IIae, 3 (I, pt. II, 1018).
2. 参见 Pseudo-Augustine (Alcher of Clairvaux, *De Spir. et An.*, I (PL 40, 781).
3. 参见 Cf. below, q. 89, a. 1.
4. 参见 *De An.*, V, 5 (25rb).

derived from the agent intellect, it would follow that the soul can turn to the agent intellect from the inclination of its very nature, or through being roused by another sense to turn to the agent intellect, and receive the species of those sensible things for which we are missing a sense. And thus a man born blind could have knowledge of colors; which is clearly untrue. We must therefore conclude that the intelligible species, by which our soul understands, are not derived from separate forms.

Reply Obj. 1. The intelligible species which are participated by our intellect are reduced, as to their first cause, to a first principle which is by its essence intelligible—namely, God. But they proceed from that principle by way of the forms of sensible and material things, from which we gather knowledge, as Dionysius says.[1]

Reply Obj. 2. Material things, as to the being which they have outside the soul, may be actually sensible, but not actually intelligible. Therefore there is no comparison between sense and intellect.

Reply Obj. 3. Our possible intellect is reduced from potentiality to act by some being in act, that is, by the agent intellect, which is a power of the soul, as we have said;[2] and not by any separate intellect, as a proximate cause, although perchance as a remote cause.

Fifth Article
WHETHER THE INTELLECTUAL SOUL KNOWS MATERIAL THINGS IN THE ETERNAL EXEMPLARS?

We proceed thus to the Fifth Article:—

Objection 1. It would seem that the intellectual soul does not know material things in the eternal exemplars. For that in which anything is known must itself be known more and antecedently. But the

---

1. 参见 *De Div. Nom.*, VII, 2 (PG 3, 886).
2. 参见 Q. 79, a. 4.

intellectual soul of man, in the present state of life, does not know the eternal exemplars, for it does not know God in Whom the eternal exemplars exist, but is *united to God as to the unknown*, as Dionysius says.[1] Therefore the soul does not know all in the eternal exemplars.

Obj. 2. Further, it is written (*Rom.* i. 20) that *the invisible things of God are clearly seen ... by the things that are made.* But among the invisible things of God are the eternal exemplars. Therefore the eternal exemplars are known through creatures, and not the converse.

Obj. 3. Further, the eternal exemplars are nothing else but ideas, for Augustine says that *ideas are permanent exemplars existing in the divine mind.*[2] If therefore we say that the intellectual soul knows all things in the eternal exemplars, we come back to the opinion of Plato who said that all knowledge is derived from them.

On the contrary, Augustine says: *If we both see that what you say is true, and if we both see that what I say is true, where do we see this, I pray? Neither do I see it in you, nor do you see it in me; but we both see it in the unchangeable truth which is above our minds.*[3] Now the unchangeable truth is contained in the eternal exemplars. Therefore the intellectual soul knows all truths in the eternal exemplars.

I answer that, As Augustine says: *If those who are called philosophers said by chance anything that was true and consistent with our faith, we must claim it from them as from unjust possessors. For some of the doctrines of the pagans are spurious imitations or superstitious inventions, which we must be careful to avoid when we renounce the society of the pagans.*[4] Consequently whenever Augustine, who was imbued with the doctrines of the Platonists, found in their teaching anything consistent with faith, he adopted it; and those things which he found contrary to faith he amended. Now

---

1. 参见 *De Myst. Theol.*, I, 3 (PG 3, 1001); cf. *De Div. Nom.*, I, 1 (PG 3, 585).
2. 参见 *Lib. 83 Quaest.*, q. 46 (PL 40, 30).
3. 参见 *Confess.*, XII, 25 (PL 32, 840).
4. 参见 *De. Doc. Christ.*, II, 40 (PL 34, 63).

Plato held, as we have said above, that the forms of things subsist of themselves apart from matter. These he called Ideas, and he said that our intellect knows all things by participation in them; so that just as corporeal matter, by participating in the Idea of a stone, becomes a stone, so our intellect, by participating in the same Idea, has knowledge of a stone. But it seems contrary to faith that the forms of things should subsist of themselves without matter outside the things themselves, as the Platonists held, asserting that *life-in-itself* and *wisdom-in-itself* are certain creative substances, as Dionysius relates.[1] Therefore, in the place of the Ideas defended by Plato, Augustine said that the exemplars of all creatures existed in the divine mind. It is according to these that all things are formed, as well as that the human soul knows all things.[2]

When, therefore, the question is asked: Does the human soul know all things in the eternal exemplars? we must reply that one thing is said to be known in another in two ways. First, as in an object itself known; as one may see in a mirror the images of the things reflected therein. In this way the soul, in the present state of life, cannot see all things in the eternal exemplars; but thus the blessed, who see God and all things in Him, know all things in the eternal exemplars. Secondly, one thing is said to be known in another as in a principle of knowledge; and thus we might say that we see in the sun what we see by the sun. And thus we must needs say that the human soul knows all things in the eternal exemplars, since by participation in these exemplars we know all things. For the intellectual light itself, which is in us, is nothing else than a participated likeness of the uncreated light, in which are contained the eternal exemplars. Whence it is written (*Ps.* iv. 6, 7), *Many say: who showeth us good things?* which question the Psalmist[3]

1. 参见 *De Div. Nom.*, XI, 6 (PG 3, 956).
2. 参见 *Lib. 83 Quaest.*, q. 46 (PL 40, 30).
3. the Psalmist:《圣经》中圣咏的作者

answers, *The light of Thy countenance, O Lord, is signed upon us*; as though to say: By the seal of the divine light in us, all things are made known to us.

But since besides the intellectual light which is in us, intelligible species, which are derived from things, are required in order that we may have knowledge of material things, therefore this knowledge is not due merely to a participation of the eternal exemplars, as the Platonists held, maintaining that the mere participation in the Ideas sufficed for knowledge.[1] Therefore Augustine says: *Although the philosophers prove by convincing arguments that all things occur in time according to the eternal exemplars, were they able to see in the eternal exemplars, or to find out from them, how many kinds of animals there are and the origin of each? Did they not seek for this information from the story of times and places?*[2]

Now that Augustine did not understand all things to be known in their *eternal exemplars* or in *the unchangeable truth*, as though the eternal exemplars themselves were seen, is clear from what he says, viz., that *not each and every rational soul can be said to be worthy of that vision*, namely, of the eternal exemplars, *but only those that are holy and pure*,[3] such as the souls of the blessed.

From what has been said the objections are easily solved.

Sixth Article
WHETHER INTELLECTUAL KNOWLEDGE IS DERIVED FROM SENSIBLE THINGS?

We proceed thus to the Sixth Article:—

Objection 1. It would seem that intellectual knowledge is not derived

1. 参见 Cf. below, q. 87, a. 1.—Cf. also, St. Bonaventure, *Quaest. Disp. de Scientia Dei*, q. 4 (V, 17).
2. 参见 *De Trin.*, IV, 16 (PL 42, 902).
3. 参见 *Lib. 83 Quaest.*, q. 46 (PL 40, 30).

from sensible things. For Augustine says that *we cannot expect to acquire the pure truth from the senses of the body.*[1] This he proves in two ways. First, because, *whatever the bodily senses reach is continually being changed; and what is never the same cannot be perceived.* Secondly, because, *whatever we perceive by the body, even when not present to the senses, may be present in their images, as when we are asleep or angry; yet we cannot discern by the senses whether what we perceive be the sensible things themselves, or their deceptive images. Now nothing can be perceived which cannot be distinguished from its counterfeit.* And so he concludes that we cannot expect to learn the truth from the senses. But intellectual knowledge apprehends the truth. Therefore intellectual knowledge cannot be conveyed by the senses.

Obj. 2. Further, Augustine says: *We must not think that the body can make any impression on the spirit, as though the spirit were to subject itself like matter to the body's action; for that which acts is in every way more excellent than that which it acts on.*[2] Whence he concludes that *the body does not cause its image in the spirit, but the spirit itself causes it in itself.* Therefore intellectual knowledge is not derived from sensible things.

Obj. 3. Further, an effect does not surpass the power of its cause. But intellectual knowledge extends beyond sensible things, for we understand some things which cannot be perceived by the senses. Therefore intellectual knowledge is not derived from sensible things.

On the contrary, The Philosopher proves that the origin of knowledge is from the senses.[3]

I answer that, On this point the philosophers held three opinions. For Democritus held that *all knowledge is caused by images issuing from the bodies we think of and entering into our souls,* as Augustine says in his letter to Dioscorus.[4] And Aristotle says that Democritus held that

---

1. 参见 *Op. cit.*, q. 9 (PL 40, 13).
2. 参见 *De Genesi ad Litt.*, XII, 16 (PL 34, 467).
3. 参见 *Metaph.*, I, 1 (981a 2); *Post. Anal.*, II, 15 (100a 3).
4. 参见 *Epist.* CXVIII, 4 (PL 33, 446).

knowledge is caused by a *discharge of images.*[1] And the reason for this opinion was that both Democritus and the other early philosophers did not distinguish between intellect and sense, as Aristotle relates.[2] Consequently, since the sense is immuted by the sensible, they thought that all our knowledge is caused merely by an immutation from sensible things. This immutation Democritus held to be caused by a discharge of images.

Plato, on the other hand, held that the intellect differs from sense, and that it is an immaterial power not making use of a corporeal organ for its action.[3] And since the incorporeal cannot be affected by the corporeal, he held that intellectual knowledge is not brought about by sensible things immuting the intellect, but by the participation in separate intelligible forms by the intellect, as we have said above. Moreover he held that sense is a power operating through itself. Consequently not even the sense itself, since it is a spiritual power, is affected by sensible things; but the sensible organs are affected by the sensible, with the result that the soul is in a way roused to form within itself the species of the sensible. Augustine seems to touch on this opinion where he says that the *body feels not, but the soul through the body, which it makes use of as a kind of messenger, for reproducing within itself what is announced from without.*[4] Thus according to Plato, neither does intellectual knowledge proceed from sensible knowledge, nor does sensible knowledge itself come entirely from sensible things; but these rouse the sensible soul to sensation, and the senses likewise rouse the intellect to the act of understanding.

Aristotle chose a middle course. For with Plato he agreed that

---

1. 参见 *De Divinat.*, II (464a 5).
2. 参见 *De An.*, III, 3 (427a 17).
3. 参见 Cf. above, q. 75, a. 3.
4. 参见 *De Genesi ad Litt.*, XII, 24 (PL 34, 475).

inteliect and sense are different.[1] But he held that the sense has not its proper operation without the cooperation of the body; so that *to sense is not an act of the soul alone*, but of the *composite*.[2] And he held the same in regard to all the operations of the sensitive part. Since, therefore, it is not incongruous that the sensible things which are outside the soul should produce some effect in the *composite*, Aristotle agreed with Democritus in this, that the operations of the sensitive part are caused by the impression of the sensible on the sense; not indeed by a discharge, as Democritus said, but by some kind of operation. Democritus, it must be remembered, maintained that every action is by way of a discharge of atoms, as we gather from *De Gener.* i.[3] But Aristotle held that the intellect has an operation in which the body does not share.[4] Now nothing corporeal can make an impression on the incorporeal. And therefore, in order to cause the intellectual operation, according to Aristotle, the impression caused by sensible bodies does not suffice, but something more noble is required, *for the agent is more noble than the patient*, as he says.[5] Not, be it observed, in the sense that the intellectual operation is effected in us by the mere impression of some superior beings, as Plato held; but that the higher and more noble agent which he calls the agent intellect, of which we have spoken above,[6] causes the phantasms received from the senses to be actually intelligible, by a process of abstraction.

According to this opinion, then, on the part of the phantasms, intellectual knowledge is caused by the senses. But since the phantasms cannot of themselves immute the possible intellect, but require to be made actually intelligible by the agent intellect, it cannot be said

---

1. 参见 *De An.*, III, 3 (427b 6).
2. 参见 *De Somno*, I (454a 7).
3. 参见 Aristotle, *De Gener.*, I, 8 (324b 25).
4. 参见 *De An.*, III, 4 (429a 24).
5. 参见 *Op. cit.*, III, 5 (430a 18).
6. 参见 Q. 79, a. 3 and 4.

that sensible knowledge is the total and perfect cause of intellectual knowledge, but rather is in a way the matter of the cause.

Reply Obj. 1. These words of Augustine mean that truth is not entirely from the senses. For the light of the agent intellect is needed, through which we know the truth of changeable things unchangeably, and discern things themselves from their likenesses.

Reply Obj. 2. In this passage Augustine speaks not of intellectual but of imaginary knowledge. And since, according to the opinion of Plato, the imagination has an operation which belongs to the soul only, Augustine, in order to show that corporeal images are impressed on the imagination, not by bodies but by the soul, uses the same argument as Aristotle does in proving that the agent intellect must be separate, namely, because *the agent is more noble than the patient.*[1] And without doubt, according to the above opinion, in the imagination there must needs be not only a passive but also an active power. But if we hold, according to the opinion of Aristotle,[2] that the action of the imaginative power is an action of the *composite*, there is no difficulty; because the sensible body is more noble than the organ of the animal, in so far as it is compared to it as a being in act to a being in potentiality; even as the object actually colored is compared to the pupil which is potentially colored. Now, although the first immutation of the imagination is through the agency of the sensible, since *the phantasm is a movement produced in accordance with sensation,*[3] nevertheless, it may be said that there is in man an operation which by division and composition forms images of various things, even of things not perceived by the senses. And Augustine's words may be taken in this sense.

Reply Obj. 3. Sensitive knowledge is not the entire cause of

---

1. 参见 *De An.*, III, 5 (430a 18).
2. 参见 *Op. cit.*, I, 1 (403a 5).
3. 参见 *Op. cit.*, III, 3 (429a 1).

intellectual knowledge. And therefore it is not strange that intellectual knowledge should extend beyond sensitive knowledge.

Seventh Article

WHETHER THE INTELLECT CAN UNDERSTAND ACTUALLY THROUGH THE INTELLIGIBLE SPECIES OF WHICH IT IS POSSESSED, WITHOUT TURNING TO THE PHANTASMS?

We proceed thus to the Seventh Article:—

Objection 1. It would seem that the intellect can understand actually through the intelligible species of which it is possessed, without turning to the phantasms. For the intellect is made actual by the intelligible species by which it is informed. But if the intellect is in act, it understands. Therefore the intelligible species suffices for the intellect to understand actually, without turning to the phantasms.

Obj. 2. Further, the imagination is more dependent on the senses than the intellect on the imagination. But the imagination can actually imagine in the absence of the sensible. Therefore much more can the intellect understand without turning to the phantasms.

Obj. 3. There are no phantasms of incorporeal things, for the imagination does not transcend time and space. If, therefore, our intellect cannot under stand anything actually without turning to the phantasms, it follows that it cannot understand anything incorporeal. Which is clearly false, for we understand truth, and God, and the angels.

On the contrary, The Philosopher says that *the soul understands nothing without a phantasm.*[1]

I answer that, In the state of the present life, in which the soul is united to a corruptible body, it is impossible for our intellect to

---

1. 参见 *Op. cit.*, III, 7 (431a 16).

understand anything actually, except by turning to phantasms. And of this there are two indications. First of all because the intellect, being a power that does not make use of a corporeal organ, would in no way be hindered in its act through the lesion of a corporeal organ, if there were not required for its act the act of some power that does make use of a corporeal organ. Now sense, imagination and the other powers belonging to the sensitive part make use of a corporeal organ. Therefore it is clear that for the intellect to understand actually, not only when it acquires new knowledge, but also when it uses knowledge already acquired, there is need for the act of the imagination and of the other powers. For when the act of the imagination is hindered by a lesion of the corporeal organ, for instance, in a case of frenzy, or when the act of the memory is hindered, as in the case of lethargy, we see that a man is hindered from understanding actually even those things of which he had a previous knowledge. Secondly, anyone can experience this of himself, that when he tries to understand something, he forms certain phantasms to serve him by way of examples, in which as it were he examines what he is desirous of understanding. For this reason it is that when we wish to help someone to understand something, we lay examples before him, from which he can form phantasms for the purpose of understanding.

Now the reason for this is that the power of knowledge is proportioned to the thing known. Therefore the proper object of the angelic intellect, which is entirely separate from a body, is an intelligible substance separate from a body. Whereas the proper object of the human intellect, which is united to a body, is the quiddity or nature existing in corporeal matter; and it is through these natures of visible things that it rises to a certain knowledge of things invisible. Now it belongs to such a nature to exist in some individual, and this cannot be apart from corporeal matter; for instance, it belongs to the nature of a stone to be in an individual stone, and to the nature of a horse to be in an individual horse, and so forth. Therefore the nature of a stone or any material thing cannot be known completely and truly, except in as much as it is known as existing in the individual. Now we apprehend the individual through the sense and the imagination. And, therefore, for the intellect to understand actually its proper object, it must of necessity turn to the phantasms in order to perceive the universal nature existing in the individual. But if the proper object of our intellect were a separate form, or if, as the Platonists say, the natures of sensible things subsisted apart from the individual, there would be no need for the intellect to turn to the phantasms whenever it understands.

Reply Obj. 1. The species preserved in the possible intellect exist there habitually when it does not understand them actually, as we have said above.[1] Therefore for us to understand actually, the fact that the species are preserved does not suffice; we need further to make use of them in a manner befitting the things of which they are the species, which things are natures existing in individuals.

Reply Obj. 2. Even the phantasm is the likeness of an individual thing; and so the imagination does not need any further likeness of the individual, whereas the intellect does.

Reply Obj. 3. Incorporeal beings, of which there are no phantasms, are known to us by comparison with sensible bodies of which there are phantasms. Thus we understand truth by considering a thing in which we see the truth; and God, as Dionysius says,[2] we know as cause, by way of excess and by way of remotion. Other incorporeal substances we know, in the state of the present life, only by way of remotion or by some comparison to corporeal things. Hence, when we understand something about these beings, we need to turn to the phantasms of bodies, although there are no phantasms of these beings themselves.

---

1. 参见 Q. 79, a. 6.
2. 参见 *De Div. Nom.*, I, 5 (PG 3, 593).

Eighth Article

WHETHER THE JUDGMENT OF THE INTELLECT IS HINDERED THROUGH SUSPENSION OF THE SENSITIVE POWERS?

We proceed thus to the Eighth Article:—

Objection 1. It would seem that the judgment of the intellect is not hindered by suspension of the sensitive powers. For the superior does not depend on the inferior. But the judgment of the intellect is higher than the senses. Therefore the judgment of the intellect is not hindered through suspension of the senses.

Obj. 2. Further, to syllogize is an act of the intellect. But during sleep the senses are suspended, as is said in *De Somno et Vigilia*,[1] and yet it sometimes happens to us to syllogize while asleep. Therefore the judgment of the intellect is not hindered through suspension of the senses.

On the contrary, What a man does while asleep, against the moral law, is not imputed to him as a sin, as Augustine says.[2] But this would not be the case if man, while asleep, had free use of his reason and intellect. Therefore the judgment of the intellect is hindered by suspension of the senses.

I answer that, As we have said above, our intellect's proper and proportionate object is the nature of a sensible thing. Now a perfect judgment concerning anything cannot be formed, unless all that pertains to that thing be known; especially if that be ignored which is the term and end of judgment. For the Philosopher says that *as the end of practical science is a work, so the end of the science of nature is that*

1. 参见 Aristotle, *De Somno*, I (454b 13).
2. 参见 *De Genesi ad Litt.*, XII, 15 (PL 34, 466).

which is perceived principally through the senses.[1] For the smith does not seek the knowledge of a knife except for the purpose of producing this individual knife; and in like manner the natural philosopher does not seek to know the nature of a stone and of a horse, save for the purpose of knowing the essential properties of those things which he perceives with his senses. Now it is clear that a smith cannot judge perfectly of a knife unless he knows what making this particular knife means; and in like manner the natural philosopher cannot judge perfectly of natural things, unless he knows sensible things. But in the present state of life, whatever we understand we know by comparison with natural sensible things. Consequently it is not possible for our intellect to form a perfect judgment while the senses are suspended, through which sensible things are known to us.

Reply Obj. 1. Although the intellect is superior to the senses, nevertheless in a manner it receives from the senses, and its first and principal objects are founded in sensible things. Hence, suspension of the senses necessarily involves a hindrance to the judgment of the intellect.

Reply Obj. 2. The senses are suspended in the sleeper through certain evaporations and the escape of certain exhalations, as we read in *De Somno et Vigilia.*[2] And, therefore, according to the disposition of such evaporation, the senses are more or less suspended. For when the movement of the vapors is very agitated, not only are the senses suspended, but also the imagination, so that there are no phantasms; as happens especially when a man falls asleep after much eating and drinking. If, however, the movement of the vapors be somewhat less violent, phantasms appear, but distorted and without sequence; as happens in a case of fever. And if the movement be still more attenuated, the phantasms will have a certain sequence; as happens

1. 参见 *De Caelo*, III, 7 (306a 16).
2. 参见 Aristotle, *De Somno*, III (456b 17).

especially towards the end of sleep, and in sober men and those who are gifted with a strong imagination. If the movement be very slight, not only does the imagination retain its freedom, but even the common sense is partly freed; so that sometimes while asleep a man may judge that what he sees is a dream, discerning, as it were, between things and their images. Nevertheless, the common sense remains partly suspended, and therefore, although it discriminates some images from reality, yet it is always deceived in some particular. Therefore, while a man is asleep, according as sense and imagination are free, so is the judgment of his intellect unfettered, though not entirely. Consequently, if a man syllogizes while asleep, when he wakes up he invariably recognizes a flaw in some respect.

Question LXXXV
THE MODE AND ORDER OF UNDERSTANDING
(*In Eight Articles*)

WE come now to consider the mode and order of understanding. Under this head there are eight points of inquiry: (1) Whether our intellect understands by abstracting species from the phantasms? (2) Whether the intelligible species abstracted from the phantasms are what our intellect understands, or that whereby it understands? (3) Whether our intellect naturally first understands the more universal? (4) Whether our intellect can know many things at the same time? (5) Whether our intellect understands by composition and division? (6) Whether the intellect can err? (7) Whether one intellect can understand the same thing better than another? (8) Whether our intellect understands the indivisible before the divisible?

First Article
WHETHER OUR INTELLECT UNDERSTANDS CORPOREAL AND MATERIAL THINGS BY ABSTRACTION FROM PHANTASMS?

We proceed thus to the First Article:—

Objection 1. It would seem that our intellect does not understand corporeal and material things by abstraction from the phantasms. For the intellect is false if it understands a thing otherwise than as it is. Now the forms of material things do not exist in abstraction from the particular things represented by the phantasms. Therefore, if we understand material things by the abstraction of species from phantasms, there will be error in the intellect.

Obj. 2. Further, material things are those natural things which include matter in their definition. But nothing can be understood apart from that which enters into its definition. Therefore material things cannot be understood apart from matter. Now matter is the principle of individuation. Therefore material things cannot be understood by the abstraction of the universal from the particular; and this is to abstract intelligible species from the phantasm.

Obj. 3. Further, the Philosopher says that the phantasm is to the intellectual soul what color is to the sight.[1] But seeing is not caused by abstraction of species from color, but by color impressing itself on the sight. Therefore neither does the act of understanding take place by the abstraction of something from the phantasms, but by the phantasms impressing themselves on the intellect.

Obj. 4. Further, the Philosopher says that there are two things in the intellectual soul—the possible intellect and the agent intellect.[2] But it does not belong to the possible intellect to abstract the intelligible species from the phantasm, but to receive them already abstracted. Neither does it seem to be the function of the agent intellect, which is related to phantasms as light is to colors; since light does not abstract anything from colors, but rather acts on them. Therefore in no way do we understand by abstraction from phantasms.

Obj. 5. Further, the Philosopher says that *the intellect understands the species in the phantasms;*[3] and not, therefore, by abstraction.

On the contrary, The Philosopher says that *things are intelligible in proportion as they are separable from matter.*[4] Therefore material things

---

1. 参见 Aristotle, *De An.*, III, 7 (431a 14).
2. 参见 *Op. cit.*, III, 5 (430a 14).
3. 参见 *Op. cit.*, III, 7 (431b 2).
4. 参见 *Op. cit.*, III, 4 (429b 21).

must needs be understood according as they are abstracted from matter and from material images, namely, phantasms.

I answer that, As stated above, the object of knowledge is proportionate to the power of knowledge.[1] Now there are three grades of the cognitive powers. For one cognitive power, namely, the sense, is the act of a corporeal organ. And therefore the object of every sensitive power is a form as existing in corporeal matter; and since such matter is the principle of individuation, therefore every power of the sensitive part can have knowledge only of particulars. There is another grade of cognitive power which is neither the act of a corporeal organ, nor in any way connected with corporeal matter. Such is the angelic intellect, the object of whose cognitive power is therefore a form existing apart from matter; for though angels know material things, yet they do not know them save in something immaterial, namely, either in themselves or in God. But the human intellect holds a middle place; for it is not the act of an organ, and yet it is a power of the soul, which is the form of the body, as is clear from what we have said above.[2] And therefore it is proper to it to know a form existing individually in corporeal matter, but not as existing in this individual matter. But to know what is in individual matter, yet not as existing in such matter, is to abstract the form from individual matter which is represented by the phantasms. Therefore we must needs say that our intellect understands material things by abstracting from phantasms; and that through material things thus considered we acquire some knowledge of immaterial things, just as, on the contrary, angels know material things through the immaterial.

But Plato, considering only the immateriality of the human intellect, and not that it is somehow united to the body, held that the objects of the intellect are separate Ideas, and that we understand,

---

1. 参见 Q. 84, a. 7.
2. 参见 Q. 76, a. 1.

not by abstraction, but rather by participating in abstractions, as was stated above.[1]

Reply Obj. 1. Abstraction may occur in two ways. First, by way of composition and division, and thus we may understand that one thing does not exist in some other, or that it is separate from it. Secondly, by way of a simple and absolute consideration; and thus we understand one thing without considering another. Thus, for the intellect to abstract one from another things which are not really abstract from one another, does, in the first mode of abstraction, imply falsehood. But, in the second mode of abstraction, for the intellect to abstract things which are not really abstract from one another, does not involve falsehood, as clearly appears in the case of the senses. For if we said that color is not in a colored body, or that it is separate from it, there would be error in what we thought or said. But if we consider color and its properties, without reference to the apple which is colored, or if we express in word what we thus understand, there is no error in such an opinion or assertion; for an apple is not essential to color, and therefore color can be understood independently of the apple. In the same way, the things which belong to the species of a material thing, such as a stone, or a man, or a horse, can be thought without the individual principles which do not belong to the notion of the species. This is what we mean by abstracting the universal from the particular, or the intelligible species from the phantasm; in other words, this is to consider the nature of the species apart from its individual principles represented by the phantasms. If, therefore, the intellect is said to be false when it understands a thing otherwise than as it is, that is so, if the word *otherwise* refers to the thing understood; for the intellect is false when it understands a thing to be otherwise than as it is. Hence, the intellect would be false if it abstracted the species of a stone from

---

1. 参见 Q. 84, a. 1.

its matter in such a way as to think that the species did not exist in matter, as Plato held.[1] But it is not so, if the word *otherwise* be taken as referring to the one who understands. For it is quite true that the mode of understanding, in one who understands, is not the same as the mode of a thing in being; since the thing understood is immaterially in the one who understands, according to the mode of the intellect, and not materially, according to the mode of a material thing.

Reply Obj. 2. Some have thought that the species of a natural thing is a form only, and that matter is not part of the species.[2] If that were so, matter would not enter into the definition of natural things. Therefore we must disagree and say that matter is twofold, common and *signate*, or individual: common, such as flesh and bone; individual, such as this flesh and these bones. The intellect therefore abstracts the species of a natural thing from the individual sensible matter, but not from the common sensible matter. For example, it abstracts the species of *man* from *this flesh and these bones*, which do not belong to the species as such, but to the individual,[3] and need not be considered in the species. But the species of man cannot be abstracted by the intellect from *flesh and bones.*

Mathematical species, however, can be abstracted by the intellect not only from individual sensible matter, but also from common sensible matter. But they cannot be abstracted from common intelligible matter, but only from individual intelligible matter. For sensible matter is corporeal matter as subject to sensible qualities, such as being cold or hot, hard or soft, and the like; while intelligible matter is substance as subject to quantity. Now it is manifest that quantity is in substance before sensible qualities are. Hence quantities,

---

1. 参见 Cf. above, q. 84, a. 4.
2. 参见 Averroes, *In Metaph.*, VII, comm. 21 (VIII, 80v; 81r); comm. 34 (VIII, 87r).—Cf. St. Thomas, *In Metaph.*, VII, lect. 9.
3. 参见 Aristotle, *Metaph.*, VI, 10 (1035b 28).

such as number, dimension, and figures, which are the terminations of quantity, can be considered apart from sensible qualities, and this is to abstract them from sensible matter. But they cannot be considered without understanding the substance which is subject to the quantity, for that would be to abstract them from common intelligible matter. Yet they can be considered apart from this or that substance, and this is to abstract them from individual intelligible matter.

But some things can be abstracted even from common intelligible matter, such as *being*, *unity*, *potency*, *act*, and the like, all of which can exist without matter, as can be verified in the case of immaterial substances. And because Plato failed to consider the twofold kind of abstraction, as above explained, he held that all those things which we have stated to be abstracted by the intellect, are abstract in reality.[1]

Reply Obj. 3. Colors, as being in individual corporeal matter, have the same mode of being as the power of sight; and therefore they can impress their own image on the eye. But phantasms, since they are images of individuals, and exist in corporeal organs, have not the same mode of being as the human intellect, as is clear from what we have said, and therefore they have not the power of themselves to make an impression on the possible intellect. But through the power of the agent intellect, there results in the possible intellect a certain likeness produced by the turning of the agent intellect toward the phantasms. This likeness represents what is in the phantasms, but includes only the nature of the species. It is thus that the intelligible species is said to be abstracted from the phantasm; not that the identical form which previously was in the phantasm is subsequently in the possible intellect, as a body transferred from one place to another.

Reply Obj. 4. Not only does the agent intellect illumine phantasms, it does more; by its power intelligible species are abstracted from

---

1. 参见 Cf. above, q. 84, a. 1; cf. also q. 50, a. 2.

phantasms. It illumines phantasms because, just as the sensitive part acquires a greater power by its conjunction with the intellectual part, so through the power of the agent intellect phantasms are made more fit for the abstraction of intelligible intentions from them. Now the agent intellect abstracts intelligible species from phantasms inasmuch as by its power we are able to take into our consideration the natures of species without individual conditions. It is in accord with their likenesses that the possible intellect is informed.

Reply Obj. 5. Our intellect both abstracts the intelligible species *from* phantasms, inasmuch as it considers the natures of things universally, and yet understands these natures *in* the phantasms, since it cannot understand the things, of which it abstracts the species, without turning to phantasms, as we have said above.[1]

Second Article

WHETHER THE INTELLIGIBLE SPECIES ABSTRACTED FROM PHANTASMS ARE RELATED TO OUR INTELLECT AS THAT WHICH IS UNDERSTOOD?

We proceed thus to the Second Article:—

Objection 1. It would seem that the intelligible species abstracted from phantasms are related to our intellect as that which is understood. For the understood in act is in the one who understands: since the understood in act is the intellect itself in act. But nothing of what is understood is in the actually understanding intellect save the abstracted intelligible species. Therefore this species is what is actually understood.

Obj. 2. Further, what is actually understood must be in something; or else it would be nothing. But it is not in something outside the soul;

---

1. 参见 Q. 84, a. 7.

for, since what is outside the soul is material, nothing therein can be actually understood. Therefore what is actually understood is in the intellect. Consequently it can be nothing else than the aforesaid intelligible species.

Obj. 3. Further, the Philosopher says that *words are signs of the passions in the soul.*[1] But words signify the things understood, for we express by word what we understand. Therefore these passions of the soul, viz., the intelligible species, are what is actually understood.

On the contrary, The intelligible species is to the intellect what the sensible species is to the sense. But the sensible species is not *what* is perceived, but rather that *by which* the sense perceives. Therefore the intelligible species is not what is actually understood, but that by which the intellect understands.

I answer that, Some[2] have asserted that our intellectual powers know only the impressions made on them; as, for example, that sense is cognizant only of the impression made on its own organ. According to this theory, the intellect understands only its own impressions, namely, the intelligible species which it has received.

This is, however, manifestly false for two reasons. First, because the things we understand are also the objects of science. Therefore, if what we understand is merely the intelligible species in the soul, it would follow that every science would be concerned, not with things outside the soul, but only with the intelligible species within the soul; just as, according to the teaching of the Platonists, all the sciences are about Ideas, which they held to be that which is actually understood.[3] Secondly, it is untrue, because it would lead to the

---

1. 参见 *Perih.*, I, 1 (16a 3).
2. 参见 The reference seems to be to Protagoras and to Heraclitus: cf. Aristotle, *Metaph.*, VIII, 3 (1047a 6); III, 3 (1005b 25).
3. 参见 Q. 84, a. 1 and 4.

opinion of the ancients who maintained that *whatever seems, is true,*[1] and that consequently contradictories are true simultaneously. For if a power knows only its own impressions, it can judge only of them. Now a thing *seems* according to the impression made on the cognitive power. Consequently the cognitive power will always judge of its own impression as such; and so every judgment will be true. For instance, if taste perceived only its own impression, when anyone with a healthy taste perceives that honey is sweet, he would judge truly, and if anyone with a corrupt taste perceives that honey is bitter, this would be equally true; for each would judge according to the impression on his taste. Thus every opinion, in fact, every sort of apprehension, would be equally true.

Therefore it must be said that the intelligible species is related to the intellect as that by which it understands. Which is proved thus. Now action is twofold, as it is said in *Metaph.* ix:[2] one which remains in the agent (for instance, to see and to understand), and another which passes into an external object (for instance, to heat and to cut). Each of these actions proceeds in virtue of some form. And just as the form from which proceeds an act tending to something external is the likeness of the object of the action, as heat in the heater is a likeness of the thing heated, so the form from which proceeds an action remaining in the agent is a likeness of the object. Hence that by which the sight sees is the likeness of the visible thing; and the likeness of the thing understood, that is, the intelligible species, is the form by which the intellect understands. But since the intellect reflects upon itself, by such reflection it understands both its own act of understanding, and the species by which it understands. Thus the intelligible species is secondarily that which is understood; but that which is primarily understood is the thing, of which the species is the likeness.

---

1. 参见 Cf. Aristotle, *Metaph.*, III, 5 (1009a 8).
2. 参见 *Op. cit.*, VIII, 8 (1050a 23).

This also appears from the opinion of the ancient philosophers, who said that *like is known by like.*[1] For they said that the soul knows the earth outside itself by the earth within itself; and so of the rest. If, therefore, we take the species of the earth instead of the earth, in accord with Aristotle who says *that a stone is not in the soul, but only the likeness of the stone,*[2] it follows that by means of its intelligible species the soul knows the things which are outside it.

Reply Obj. 1. The thing understood is in the knower by its own likeness. It is in this sense that we say that the thing actually understood is the intellect in act, because the likeness of the thing understood is the form of the intellect, just as the likeness of a sensible thing is the form of the sense in act. Hence it does not follow that the abstracted intelligible species is what is actually understood; but rather that it is the likeness thereof.

Reply Obj. 2. In these words *the thing actually understood* there is a double meaning:—the thing which is understood, and the fact that it is understood. In like manner, the words *abstract universal* mean two things, the nature of a thing and its abstraction or universality. Therefore the nature itself which suffers the act of being understood, or the act of being abstracted, or the intention of universality, exists only in individuals; but that it is understood, abstracted or considered as universal is in the intellect. We see something similar to this in the senses. For the sight sees the color of the apple apart from its smell. If therefore it be asked where is the color which is seen apart from the smell, it is quite clear that the color which is seen is only in the apple; but that it be perceived apart from the smell, this is owing to the sight, inasmuch as sight receives the likeness of color and not of smell. In like manner, the humanity which is understood exists only in this or

1. 参见 The opinion of Empedocles, according to Aristotle, *De An.*, I, 5 (409b 26); and of Plato: cf. *op. cit.*, I. 2 (404b 17).
2. 参见 *Op. cit.*, III, 8 (431b 29).

that man; but that humanity be apprehended without the conditions of individuality, that is, that it be abstracted and consequently considered as universal, befalls humanity inasmuch as it is perceived by the intellect, in which there is a likeness of the specific nature, but not of the individual principles.

Reply Obj. 3. There are two operations in the sensitive part. One is limited to immutation, and thus the operation of the senses takes place when the senses are impressed by the sensible. The other is formation, inasmuch as the imagination forms for itself an image of an absent thing, or even of something never seen. Both of these operations are found in the intellect. For in the first place there is the passion of the possible intellect as informed by the intelligible species; and then the possible intellect, as thus informed, then forms a definition, or a division, or a composition, which is expressed by language. And so, the notion signified by a *term* is a definition; and a *proposition* signifies the intellect's division or composition. Words do not therefore signify the intelligible species themselves; but that which the intellect forms for itself for the purpose of judging of external things.

Third Article
WHETHER THE MORE UNIVERSAL IS FIRST IN OUR INTELLECTUAL COGNITION?

We proceed thus to the Third Article:—

Objection 1. It would seem that the more universal is not first in our intellectual cognition. For what is first and more known in its own nature is secondarily and less known in relation to ourselves. But universals come first as regards their nature, because *that is first which does not involve the existence of its correlative.* Therefore universals are secondarily known by our intellect.

Obj. 2. Further, the composite precedes the simple in relation to us. But universals are the more simple. Therefore they are known secondarily by us.

Obj. 3. Further, the Philosopher says that the object defined comes in our knowledge before the parts of its definition.[1] But the more universal is part of the definition of the less universal, as *animal* is part of the definition of *man*. Therefore universals are secondarily known by us.

Obj. 4. Further, we know causes and principles by their effects. But universals are principles. Therefore universals are secondarily known by us.

On the contrary, *We must proceed from the universal to the singular.*[2]

I answer that, In our knowledge there are two things to be considered. First, that intellectual knowledge in some degree arises from sensible knowledge. Now because sense has singular and individual things for its object, and intellect has the universal for its object, it follows that our knowledge of the former comes before our knowledge of the latter. Secondly, we must consider that our intellect proceeds from a state of potentiality to a state of actuality; and that every power thus proceeding from potentiality to actuality comes first to an incomplete act, which is intermediate between potentiality and actuality, before accomplishing the perfect act. The perfect act of the intellect is complete knowledge, when the object is distinctly and determinately known; whereas the incomplete act is imperfect knowledge, when the object is known indistinctly, and as it were confusedly. A thing thus imperfectly known is known partly in act and partly in potentiality. Hence the Philosopher says that *what is manifest and certain is known to us at first confusedly; afterwards we know it by distinguishing its principles and elements.*[3] Now it is evident that to know something that comprises many things, without a proper knowledge of

1. 参见 *Phys.*, I, 1 (184b 11).
2. 同上 (184a 23).
3. 同上 (184a 21).

each thing contained in it, is to know that thing confusedly. In this way we can have knowledge not only of the universal whole, which contains parts potentially, but also of the integral whole; for each whole can be known confusedly, without its parts being known distinctly. But to know distinctly what is contained in the universal whole is to know the less common; and thus to know *animal* indistinctly is to know it as *animal*, whereas to know *animal* distinctly is to know it as *rational* or *irrational animal*, that is, to know a man or a lion. And so our intellect knows *animal* before it knows man; and the same reason holds in comparing any more universal concept with the less universal.

Moreover, as sense, like the intellect, proceeds from potentiality to act, the same order of knowledge appears in the senses. For by sense we judge of the more common before the less common, in reference both to place and time. In reference to place, when a thing is seen afar off it is seen to be a body before it is seen to be an animal, and to be an animal before it is seen to be a man, and to be a man before it is seen to be Socrates or Plato. The same is true as regards time, for a child can distinguish man from not-man before he distinguishes this man from that, and therefore *children at first call all men fathers, and later on distinguish each one from the others.*[1] The reason of this is clear: he who knows a thing indistinctly is in a state of potentiality as regards its principle of distinction; just as he who knows *genus* is in a state of potentiality as regards *difference*. Thus it is evident that indistinct knowledge is midway between potentiality and act.

We must therefore conclude that knowledge of the singular and individual is prior, as regards us, to the knowledge of the universal, just as sensible knowledge is prior to intellectual knowledge. But in both sense and intellect the knowledge of the more common precedes the knowledge of the less common.

---

1. 参见 *Phys.*, I, 1 (184b 12).

Reply Obj. 1. The universal can be considered in two ways. First, the universal nature may be considered together with the intention of universality. And since the intention of universality—viz., the relation of one and the same to many—is due to intellectual abstraction, the universal thus considered is subsequent in our knowledge. Hence it is said that the *universal animal is either nothing or something subsequent.*[1] But according to Plato, who held that universals are subsistent, the universal considered thus would be prior to the particular, for the latter, according to him, are mere participations in the subsistent universals which he called Ideas.[2]

Secondly, the universal can be considered according to the nature itself (for instance, *animality* or *humanity*) as existing in the individual. And thus we must distinguish two orders of nature: one, by way of generation and time; and thus the imperfect and the potential come first. In this way the more common comes first in the order of nature. This appears clearly in the generation of man and animal; for *the animal is generated before man*, as the Philosopher says.[3] The other order is the order of perfection or of the intention of nature. For instance, act considered absolutely is naturally prior to potentiality, and the perfect to the imperfect; and thus the less common comes naturally before the more common, as man comes before animal. For the intention of nature does not stop at the generation of animal, but aims at the generation of man.

Reply Obj. 2. The more common universal may be compared to the less common as a whole, and as a part. As a whole, inasmuch as in the more universal there is potentially contained not only the less universal, but also other things; as in *animal* is contained not only *man* but also *horse*. As a part, inasmuch as the less common universal contains in its notion not only the more common, but also more;

---

1. 参见 Aristotle, *De An.*, I, 1 (402b 7).
2. 参见 Cf. above, q. 84, a. 1.
3. 参见 Aristotle, *De Gener. Anim.*, II, 3 (736b 2).

as *man* contains not only *animal* but also *rational*. Therefore *animal* considered in itself is in our knowledge before *man*; but *man* comes before *animal* considered as a part of the notion of man.

Reply Obj. 3. A part can be known in two ways. First, absolutely considered in itself; and thus nothing prevents the parts from being known before the whole, as stones are known before a house is known. Secondly, as belonging to a certain whole; and thus we must needs know the whole before its parts. For we know a house confusedly before we know its different parts. So, likewise, that which defines is known before the thing defined is known; otherwise the thing defined would not be made known by the definition. But as parts of the definition they are known after. For we know man confusedly as man before we know how to distinguish all that belongs to human nature.

Reply Obj. 4. The universal, as understood with the intention of universality, is, in a certain manner, a principle of knowledge, in so far as the intention of universality results from the mode of understanding, which is by way of abstraction. But that which is a principle of knowledge is not of necessity a principle of being, as Plato thought, since at times we know a cause through its effect, and substance through accidents. Therefore the universal thus considered, according to the opinion of Aristotle, is neither a principle of being, nor a substance, as he makes clear.[1] But if we consider the generic or specific nature itself as existing in the singular, thus in a way it has the character of a formal principle in regard to singulars; for the singular is the result of matter, while the nature of the species is from the form. But the generic nature is compared to the specific nature rather after the fashion of a material principle, because the generic nature is taken from that which is material in a thing, while the nature of the species is taken from that which is formal. Thus the notion of

---

1. 参见 Aristotle, *Metaph.*, VI, 13 (1038b 8).

animal is taken from the sensitive part, whereas the notion of man is taken from the intellectual part. Thus it is that the ultimate intention of nature is towards the species and not the individual, or the genus; because the form is the end of generation, while matter is for the sake of the form. Neither is it necessary that the knowledge of any cause or principle should be subsequent in relation to us, since through sensible causes we sometimes become acquainted with unknown effects, and sometimes conversely.

Fourth Article
WHETHER WE CAN UNDERSTAND MANY THINGS AT THE SAME TIME?

We proceed thus to the Fourth Article:—

Objection 1. It would seem that we can understand many things at the same time. For intellect is above time, whereas the succession of before and after belongs to time. Therefore the intellect does not understand different things in succession, but at the same time.

Obj. 2. Further, there is nothing to prevent different forms not opposed to each other from actually being in the same subject, as, for instance, color and smell are in the apple. But intelligible species are not opposed to each other. Therefore there is nothing to prevent the same intellect from being in act as regards different intelligible species. Thus it can understand many things at the same time.

Obj. 3. Further, the intellect understands a whole at the same time, such as a man or a house. But a whole contains many parts. Therefore the intellect understands many things at the same time.

Obj. 4. Further, we cannot know the difference between two things unless we know both at the same time;[1] and the same is to be said of

---

1. 参见 Aristotle, *De An.*, III, 2 (426b 22).

any other comparison. But our intellect knows the difference between one thing and another. Therefore it knows many things at the same time.

On the contrary, It is said that *understanding is of one thing only, science is of many.*[1]

I answer that, The intellect can, indeed, understand many things as one, but not as many, that is to say, by *one* but not by *many* intelligible species. For the mode of every action follows the form which is the principle of that action. Therefore whatever things the intellect can understand under one species, it can understand together. Hence it is that God sees all things at the same time, because He sees all in one, that is, in His essence. But whatever things the intellect understands under different species, it does not understand at the same time. The reason for this is that it is impossible for one and the same subject to be perfected at the same time by many forms of one genus and diverse species, just as it is impossible for one and the same body at the same time to have different colors or different shapes. Now all intelligible species belong to one genus, because they are the perfections of one intellectual power even though the things which the species represent belong to different genera. Therefore it is impossible for one and the same intellect to be perfected at the same time by different intelligible species so as actually to understand different things.

Reply Obj. 1. The intellect is above that time which is the measure of the movement of corporeal things. But the multitude itself of intelligible species causes a certain succession of intelligible operations, according as one operation is prior to another. And this succession is called time by Augustine, who says that *God moves the spiritual creature through time.*[2]

Reply Obj. 2. Not only is it impossible for opposite forms to exist

---

1. 参见 Aristotle, *Top.*, II, 10 (114b 34).
2. 参见 *De Genesi ad Litt.*, VIII, 20; 22 (PL 34, 388; 389).

at the same time in the same subject, but neither can any forms belonging to the same genus, although they be not opposed to one another, as is clear from the examples of colors and shapes.

Reply Obj. 3. Parts can be understood in two ways. First, in a confused way, as existing in the whole; and thus they are known through the one form of the whole, and so are known together. In another way, they are known distinctly; and thus each is known by its species, and hence they are not understood at the same time.

Reply Obj. 4. If the intellect sees the difference or comparison between one thing and another, it knows both in relation to their difference or comparison; just as it knows the parts in the whole, as we said above.

Fifth Article
WHETHER OUR INTELLECT UNDERSTANDS BY COMPOSITION AND DIVISION?

We proceed thus to the Fifth Article:—

Objection 1. It would seem that our intellect does not understand by composition and division. For composition and division are only of many, whereas the intellect cannot understand many things at the same time. Therefore it cannot understand by composition and division.

Obj. 2. Further, every composition and division implies past, present, or future time. But the intellect abstracts from time, as also from other particular conditions. Therefore the intellect does not understand by composition and division.

Obj. 3. Further, the intellect understands things by an assimilation to them. But composition and division are not in things; for nothing is in things but the thing which is signified by the predicate and the subject, and which is one and the same thing, provided that the composition be true; for *man* is truly what *animal* is. Therefore the intellect does not act by composition and division.

On the contrary, Words signify the conceptions of the intellect, as the Philosopher says.[1] But in words we find composition and division, as appears in affirmative and negative propositions. Therefore the intellect acts by composition and division.

I answer that, The human intellect must of necessity understand by composition and division. For since the intellect passes from potentiality to act, it has a likeness to generable things, which do not attain to perfection all at once but acquire it by degrees. In the same way, the human intellect does not acquire perfect knowledge of a thing by the first apprehension; but it first apprehends something of the thing, such as its quiddity, which is the first and proper object of the intellect; and then it understands the properties, accidents, and various dispositions affecting the essence. Thus it necessarily relates one thing with another by composition or division; and from one composition and division it necessarily proceeds to another, and this is *reasoning*.

But the angelic and the divine intellects, like all incorruptible beings, have their perfection at once from the beginning. Hence the angelic and the divine intellect have the entire knowledge of a thing at once and perfectly; and hence, in knowing the quiddity of a thing, they know at once whatever we can know by composition, division and reasoning. Therefore the human intellect knows by composition, division and reasoning. But the divine and the angelic intellects have a knowledge of composition, division, and reasoning, not by the process itself, but by understanding the simple essence.

Reply Obj. 1. Composition and division of the intellect are made by differentiating and comparing. Hence the intellect knows many things by composition and division, by knowing the difference and comparison of things.

---

1. 参见 *Perih.*, I, 1 (16a 3).

Reply Obj. 2. Although the intellect abstracts from phantasms, it does not understand actually without turning to the phantasms, as we have said.[1] And in so far as the intellect turns to phantasms, composition and division involve time.

Reply Obj. 3. The likeness of a thing is received into the intellect according to the mode of the intellect, not according to the mode of the thing. Hence, although something on the part of the thing corresponds to the composition and division of the intellect, still, it does not exist in the same way in the intellect and in the thing. For the proper object of the human intellect is the quiddity of a material thing, which is apprehended by the senses and the imagination. Now in a material thing there is a twofold composition. First, there is the composition of form with matter. To this corresponds that composition of the intellect whereby the universal whole is predicated of its part: for the genus is derived from common matter, while the difference that completes the species is derived from the form, and the particular from individual matter. The second composition is of accident with subject; and to this composition corresponds that composition of the intellect whereby accident is predicated of subject, as when we say *the man is white*. Nevertheless, the composition of the intellect differs from the composition of things; for the components in the thing are diverse, whereas the composition of the intellect is a sign of the identity of the components. For the above composition of the intellect was not such as to assert that *man is whiteness*; but the assertion, *the man is white*, means that *the man is something having whiteness*. In other words, *man* is identical in subject with the *being having whiteness*. It is the same with the composition of form and matter. For *animal* signifies that which has a sensitive nature; *rational*, that which has an intellectual nature; *man*, that which has both; and *Socrates*, that which has all these things

---

1. 参见 A. 1; q. 84, a. 7.

together with individual matter. And so, according to this kind of identity our intellect composes one thing with another by means of predication.

Sixth Article
WHETHER THE INTELLECT CAN BE FALSE?

We proceed thus to the Sixth Article:—

Objection 1. It would seem that the intellect can be false, for the Philosopher says that *truth and falsehood are in the mind.*[1] But the *mind* and *intellect* are the same, as is shown above.[2] Therefore falsehood may be in the intellect.

Obj. 2. Further, opinion and reasoning belong to the intellect. But falsehood exists in both. Therefore falsehood can be in the intellect.

Obj. 3. Further, sin is in the intellectual part. But sin involves falsehood, for *those err that work evil* (*Prov.* xiv. 22). Therefore falsehood can be in the intellect.

On the contrary, Augustine says that *everyone who is deceived, does not rightly understand that wherein he is deceived.*[3] And the Philosopher says that *the intellect is always true.*[4]

I answer that, The Philosopher compares the intellect with the sense on this point.[5] For the sense is not deceived in its proper object (as sight in regard to color), save accidentally, through some hindrance to the sensible organ. For example, the taste of a fever-stricken person judges a sweet thing to be bitter, because his tongue is vitiated by ill humors. The sense, however, may be deceived as regards common

---

1. 参见 *Metaph.*, V, 4 (1027b 27).
2. 参见 Q. 72.
3. 参见 *Lib. 83 Quaest.*, q. 32 (PL 40, 22).
4. 参见 *De An.*, III, 10 (433a 26).
5. 参见 *Op. cit.*, III, 6 (430b 29).

sensible objects, as size or figure; as when, for example, it judges the sun to be only a foot in diameter, whereas in reality it exceeds the earth in size. Much more is the sense deceived concerning accidental sensible objects; as when it judges that vinegar is honey because the color is similar. The reason of this is evident. Every power, as such, is essentially directed to its proper object; and things of this kind are always uniform. Hence, so long as the power exists, its judgment concerning its own proper object does not fail. Now the proper object of the intellect is the *quiddity* in a thing. Hence, properly speaking, the intellect is not in error concerning this quiddity; whereas it may go astray as regards the accompaniments of the essence or quiddity in the thing, either in referring one thing to another, in what concerns composition or division, or also in the process of reasoning. That is why it is also true that the intellect cannot err in regard to those propositions which are understood as soon as their terms are understood. Such is the case with first principles, from which there also arises infallible truth in the certitude of science with respect to its conclusions.

The intellect, however, may be accidentally deceived in the quiddity of composite things, not by the defect of its organ, for the intellect is a power that is independent of an organ, but on the part of the composition affecting the definition. This may happen, for instance, when the definition of a thing is false in relation to something else, as the definition of a circle predicated of a triangle; or when a definition is false in itself as involving the composition of things incompatible, as, for instance, to describe anything as *a rational winged animal*. Hence as regards simple things, in whose definitions there is no composition, we cannot be deceived; but if we fail, we fail completely in understanding them, as is said in *Metaph*. ix.[1]

---

1. 参见 Aristotle, *Metaph*., VIII, 10 (1052a 1).

Reply Obj. 1. The Philosopher says that falsehood is in the intellect in regard to composition and division. The same answer applies to the *second objection* concerning opinion and reasoning; as well as to the *third objection*, concerning the error of the sinner, who errs in the practical judgment of the appetible object. But in the absolute consideration of the quiddity of a thing, and of those things which are known thereby, the intellect is never deceived. In this sense are to be understood the authorities quoted in proof of the opposite conclusion.

Seventh Article
WHETHER ONE PERSON CAN UNDERSTAND ONE AND THE SAME THING BETTER THAN ANOTHER CAN?

We proceed thus to the Seventh Article:—

Objection 1. It would seem that one person cannot understand one and the same thing better than another can. For Augustine says: *Whoever understands a thing otherwise than as it is, does not understand it at all. Hence it is clear that there is a perfect understanding, than which none other is more perfect; and therefore there are not infinite degrees of understanding a thing, nor can one person understand a thing better than another can.*[1]

Obj. 2. Further, the intellect is true in its act of understanding. But truth, being a certain equality between thought and thing, is not subject to more or less; for a thing cannot be said to be more or less equal. Therefore a thing cannot be more or less understood.

Obj. 3. Further, the intellect is that which most pertains to the form in man. But different forms cause different species. Therefore if one man understands better than another, it would seem that they do not belong to the same species.

On the contrary, Experience shows that some understand more

---

1. 参见 *Lib. 83 Quaest.*, q. 32 (PL 40, 22).

profoundly than do others; as one who carries a conclusion to its first principles and ultimate causes understands it better than the one who reduces it only to its proximate causes.

I answer that, To say that a thing is understood more by one than by another may be taken in two senses. First, so that the word *more* be taken as determining the act of understanding as regards the thing understood; and thus, one cannot understand the same thing more than another, because to understand it otherwise than as it is, either better or worse, would be to be deceived rather than to understand, as Augustine argues. In another sense, the word *more* can be taken as determining the act of understanding on the part of the one who understands. In this way, one may understand the same thing better than someone else, through having a greater power of understanding; just as a man may see a thing better with his bodily sight, whose power is greater, and whose sight is more perfect. The same applies to the intellect in two ways. First, as regards the intellect itself, which is more perfect. For it is plain that the better the disposition of a body, the better the soul allotted to it; which clearly appears in things of different species. The reason for this is that act and form are received into matter according to the capacity of matter; and thus because some men have bodies of better disposition, their souls have a greater power of understanding. Hence, it is said that *those who have soft flesh are of apt mind.*[1] Secondly, this occurs in regard to the lower powers of which the intellect needs its operation; for those in whom the imaginative, cogitative and memorative powers are of better disposition, are better disposed to understand.

The reply to the first objection is clear from the above; and likewise the reply to the second, for the truth of the intellect consists in this, that the intellect understands a thing as it is.

---

1. 参见 Aristotle, *De An.*, II, 9 (421a 25).

Reply Obj. 3. The difference of form which is due only to the different disposition of matter causes, not a specific, but only a numerical, difference: for different individuals have different forms, diversified according to the diversity of matter.

Eighth Article
WHETHER THE INTELLECT UNDERSTANDS THE INDIVISIBLE BEFORE THE DIVISIBLE?

We proceed thus to the Eighth Article:—

Objection 1. It would seem that the intellect understands the indivisible before the divisible. For the Philosopher says that we *understand and know from the knowledge of principles and elements.*[1] But indivisibles are the principles and elements of divisible things. Therefore the indivisible is known to us before the divisible.

Obj. 2. Further, the definition of a thing contains what is known antecedently, for a definition *proceeds from the first and more known*, as is said *Topic.* vi.[2] But the indivisible is included in the definition of the divisible, as a point comes into the definition of a line; for, as Euclid says, *a line is length without breadth, the extremities of which are two points.*[3] So, too, unity comes into the definition of number, for *number is multitude measured by one*, as is said in *Metaph.* x.[4] Therefore our intellect understands the indivisible before the divisible.

Obj. 3. Further, *Like is known by like.* But the indivisible is more like to the intellect than is the divisible, because *the intellect is simple.*[5] Therefore our intellect first knows the indivisible.

---

1. 参见 *Phys.*, I, 1 (184a 12).
2. 参见 Aristotle, *Top.*, VI, 4 (141a 32).
3. 参见 *Geometria*, trans. Boethius, I (PL 63, 1307).
4. 参见 Aristotle, *Metaph.*, IX, 6 (1057a 3).
5. 参见 Aristotle, *De An.*, III, 4 (429a 18; b 23).

On the contrary, It is said that *the indivisible is made known as a privation*.[1] But privation is known secondarily. Therefore so is the indivisible.

I answer that, The object of our intellect in its present state is the quiddity of a material thing, which it abstracts from phantasms, as was stated above.[2] And since that which is known first and of itself by our cognitive power is its proper object, we must consider its relationship to that quiddity in order to discover in what order the indivisible is known. Now the indivisible is threefold, as is said in *De Anima* iii.[3] First, the continuous is indivisible, since it is actually undivided, although potentially divisible. This indivisible is known to us before its division, which is a division into parts, because confused knowledge is prior to distinct knowledge, as we have said above. Secondly, there is the indivisible in species, as man's nature is something indivisible. This way, also, the indivisible is understood before its division into the parts of the nature, as we have said above; and also before the intellect composes and divides by affirmation and negation. The reason of this priority is that both these kinds of indivisible are understood by the intellect of itself as its proper object. The third kind of indivisible is what is altogether indivisible, as a point and unity, which cannot be divided either actually or potentially. And this indivisible is known secondarily, through the privation of divisibility. Therefore a point is defined by way of privation *as that which has no parts*;[4] and in like manner the notion of *one* is that it is *indivisible*, as is stated in *Metaph.* x.[5] And the reason for this posteriority is that this indivisible has a certain opposition to a corporeal being, the quiddity of which is the

---

1. 参见 *Op. cit.*, III, 6 (430b 21).
2. 参见 A. 1; q. 84, a. 7.
3. 参见 Aristotle, *De An.*, III, 6 (430b 6).
4. 参见 Euclid, *Geometria*, I (PL 63, 1307).
5. 参见 Aristotle, *Metaph.*, IX, 1 (1052b 16).

primary and proper object of the intellect.

But if our intellect understood by participation in certain separate indivisibles, as the Platonists maintained,[1] it would follow that such an indivisible is prior in the understanding, for, according to the Platonists, it is first in being participated by things.[2]

Reply Obj. 1. In the acquisition of knowledge, principles and elements are not always first; for sometimes from sensible effects we arrive at the knowledge of principles and intelligible causes. But in perfect knowledge, the knowledge of effects always depends on the knowledge of principles and elements; for, as the Philosopher says in the same passage, *Then do we consider that we know, when we can resolve principles into their causes.*[3]

Reply Obj. 2. A point is not included in the definition of a line in general; for it is manifest that in a line of indefinite length, and also in a circular line, there is no point, save potentially. Euclid defines a straight line of definite length, and therefore he includes a point in the definition as the limit in the definition of that which is limited.[4]—Unity, however, is the measure of number: wherefore it is included in the definition of a measured number. But it is not included in the definition of the divisible, but rather conversely.

Reply Obj. 3. The likeness through which we understand is the species of the thing known in the knower. Hence, a thing is prior in being known, not according to the likeness of its nature to the knowing power, but according to its agreement with the proper object of that power. Otherwise, sight would perceive hearing rather than color.

---

1. 参见 Cf. above, q. 84, a. 1 and 4.
2. 参见 Cf. *De Causis*, I (p. 161).
3. 参见 *Phys.*, I, 1 (184a 12).
4. 参见 *Geometria*, I (PL 63, 1307).

Question LXXXVI
WHAT OUR INTELLECT KNOWS IN MATERIAL THINGS
(*In Four Articles*)

WE now have to consider what our intellect knows in material things. Under this head there are four points of inquiry: (1) Whether it knows singulars? (2) Whether it knows infinite things? (3) Whether it knows contingent things? (4) Whether it knows future things?

First Article
WHETHER OUR INTELLECT KNOWS SINGULARS?

We proceed thus to the First Article:—

Objection 1. It would seem that our intellect knows singulars. For whoever knows a composition, knows the terms of composition. But our intellect knows this composition: *Socrates is a man*, for the intellect can form a proposition to this effect. Therefore our intellect knows this singular, *Socrates.*

Obj. 2. Further, the practical intellect directs to action. But action has relation to singular things. Therefore the intellect knows the singular.

Obj. 3. Further, our intellect understands itself. But in itself it is a singular, or otherwise it would have no action of its own; for actions belong to singulars. Therefore our intellect knows singulars.

Obj. 4. Further, a superior power can do whatever is done by an inferior power. But sense knows the singular. Much more, therefore, can the intellect know it.

On the contrary, The Philosopher says that *the universal is known by reason, and the singular is known by sense.*[1]

I answer that, Our intellect cannot know the singular in material things directly and primarily. The reason for this is that the principle of singularity in material things is individual matter; whereas our intellect, as we have said above,[2] understands by abstracting the intelligible species from such matter. Now what is abstracted from individual matter is universal. Hence our intellect knows directly only universals. But indirectly, however, and as it were by a kind of reflexion, it can know the singular, because, as we have said above,[3] even after abstracting the intelligible species, the intellect, in order to understand actually, needs to turn to the phantasms in which it understands the species, as is said in *De Anima* iii.[4] Therefore it understands the universal directly through the intelligible species, and indirectly the singular represented by the phantasm. And thus it forms the proposition, *Socrates is a man.*

Therefore the reply to the first objection is clear.

Reply Obj. 2. The choice of a particular thing to be done is as the conclusion of a syllogism formed by the practical intellect, as is said in *Ethics* vii.[5] But a singular proposition cannot be directly concluded from a universal proposition, except through the medium of a singular proposition. Therefore the universal principle of the practical intellect does not move save through the medium of the particular apprehension of the sensitive part, as is said in *De Anima* iii.[6]

Reply Obj. 3. Intelligibility is incompatible with the singular not as such, but as material; for nothing can be understood otherwise than

---

1. 参见 *Phys.*, I, 5 (189a 5).
2. 参见 Q. 85, a. 1.
3. 参见 Q. 84, a. 7.
4. 参见 Aristotle, *De An.*, III, 7 (431b 2).
5. 参见 Aristotle, *Eth.*, VII, 3 (1147a 28).
6. 参见 Aristotle, *De An.*, III, 11 (434a 16).

immaterially. Therefore if there be an immaterial singular such as the intellect, there is no reason why it should not be intelligible.

Reply Obj. 4. The higher power can do what the lower power can, but in a more eminent way. And so, what the sense knows materially and concretely, which is to know the singular directly, the intellect knows immaterially and in the abstract, which is to know the universal.

Second Article
WHETHER OUR INTELLECT CAN KNOW INFINITE THINGS?

We proceed thus to the Second Article:—

Objection 1. It would seem that our intellect can know the infinite. For God excels all infinite things. But our intellect can know God, as we have said above.[1] Much more, therefore, can our intellect know all other infinite things.

Obj. 2. Further, our intellect can naturally know *genera* and *species*. But there is an infinity of species in some genera, as in number, proportion and figure. Therefore our intellect can know the infinite.

Obj. 3. Further, if one body can coexist with another in the same place, there is nothing to prevent an infinite number of bodies being in one place. But one intelligible species can exist with another in the same intellect, for many things can be habitually known at the same time. Therefore our intellect can have a habitual knowledge of an infinite number of things.

Obj. 4. Further, since the intellect is not a corporeal power, as we have said,[2] it appears to be an infinite power. But an infinite power has a capacity for an infinite number of things. Therefore our intellect can know the infinite.

On the contrary, It is said that the *infinite, considered as such, is*

1. 参见 Q. 12, a. 1.
2. 参见 Q. 76, a. 1.

unknown.[1]

I answer that, Since a power is proportioned to its object, the intellect must be related to the infinite in the same way as is its object, which is the quiddity of a material thing. Now in material things the infinite does not exist actually, but only potentially, which is to say, successively, as is said in *Physics* iii.[2] Therefore infinity is potentially in our intellect through its considering successively one thing after another; because never does our intellect understand so many things, that it cannot understand more.

On the other hand, our intellect cannot understand the infinite either actually or habitually. Not actually, for our intellect can know actually at the same time only what it knows through one species. But the infinite is not represented by one species, for if it were it would be something whole and complete. Consequently it cannot be understood except by a successive consideration of one part after another, as is clear from its definition; for the infinite is that *from which, however much we may take, there always remains something to be taken.*[3] Thus the infinite could not be known actually, unless all its parts were counted; which is impossible.

For the same reason we cannot have habitual knowledge of the infinite: because our habitual knowledge results from actual consideration; since by understanding we acquire knowledge, as is said in *Ethics* ii.[4] Hence, it would not be possible for us to have a habit of an infinity of things distinctly known, unless we had already considered the entire infinity, counting them according to the succession of our knowledge; which is impossible. And so, neither actually or habitually can our intellect know the infinite, but only potentially, as was

---

1. 参见 Aristotle, *Phys.*, I, 4 (187b 7).
2. 参见 *Op. cit.*, III, 6 (204a 20).
3. 同上 (207a 7).
4. 参见 Aristotle, *Eth.*, I, 1 (1103a 33).

explained above.

Reply Obj. 1. As we have said above,[1] God is called infinite because He is a form unlimited by matter; whereas in material things, the term *infinite* is applied to that which is deprived of any formal termination. And since form is known in itself, whereas matter cannot be known without form, hence it is that the material infinite is in itself unknown. But the formal infinite, God, is of Himself known; but He is unknown to us by reason of our feeble intellect, which in its present state has a natural aptitude[2] only for material things. Therefore we cannot know God in our present life except through material effects. In the future life this defect of our intellect will be removed by the state of glory, when we shall be able to see the essence of God Himself, but without being able to comprehend Him.

Reply Obj. 2. The nature of our intellect is to know species abstracted from phantasms; and therefore it cannot know actually or habitually species of numbers or figures that have not been imagined, except in a general way and in universal principles; and this is to know them potentially and confusedly.

Reply Obj. 3. If two or more bodies were in the same place, there would be no need for them to occupy the place successively, in order for the things placed to be counted according to this succession of occupation. On the other hand, the intelligible species enter our intellect successively because many things cannot be actually understood at the same time; and therefore there must be a definite and not an infinite number of species in our intellect.

Reply Obj. 4. In the way in which our intellect is infinite in power, so does it know the infinite. For its power is indeed infinite inasmuch as it is not terminated by corporeal matter. Moreover it can know the universal, which is abstracted from individual matter, and which

---

1. 参见 Q. 7, a. 1.
2. natural aptitude: 天赋

consequently is not limited to one individual, but, considered in itself, extends to an infinite number of individuals.

Third Article
WHETHER OUR INTELLECT CAN KNOW CONTINGENT THINGS?

We proceed thus to the Third Article:—

Objection 1. It would seem that the intellect cannot know contingent things: because, as the Philosopher says, the objects of *understanding*, *wisdom* and *science* are not contingent, but necessary things.[1]

Obj. 2. Further, as is stated in *Physics* iv., *what sometimes is and sometimes is not, is measured by time.*[2] Now the intellect abstracts from time, and from other material conditions. Therefore, as it is proper to a contingent thing sometime to be and sometime not to be, it seems that contingent things are not known by the intellect.

On the contrary, Every science is in the intellect. But some sciences are of contingent things, as the moral sciences, which consider human actions subject to free choice; and, again, the sciences of nature in as far as they consider things generable and corruptible. Therefore the intellect knows contingent things.

I answer that, Contingent things can be considered in two ways: either as contingent, or as containing some element of necessity. For every contingent thing has in it something necessary. For example, that Socrates runs, is in itself contingent; but the relation of running to motion is necessary, for it is necessary that Socrates move if he runs. Now contingency[3] arises from matter, for contingency is a potentiality to be or not to be, and potentiality belongs to matter; whereas

---

1. 参见 Aristotle, *Eth.*, VI, 6 (1040b 31).
2. 参见 Aristotle, *Phys.*, IV, 12 (221b 29).
3. contingency: 意外事故

necessity results from form, because whatever is consequent on form is of necessity in the subject. But matter is the principle of individuation, whereas the universal comes from the abstraction of the form from particular matter. Moreover it was laid down above that the intellect of itself and directly has the universal for its object; while the object of sense is the singular, which in a certain way is the indirect object of the intellect, as we have said above. Therefore the contingent, considered as such, is known directly by sense and indirectly by the intellect; while the universal and necessary principles of contingent things are known by the intellect. Hence if we consider knowable things in their universal principles, then all science is of necessary things. But if we consider the things themselves, thus some sciences are of necessary things, some of contingent things.

From which the replies to the objections are clear.

Fourth Article
WHETHER OUR INTELLECT KNOWS THE FUTURE?

We proceed thus to the Fourth Article:—

Objection 1. It would seem that our intellect knows the future. For our intellect knows by means of intelligible species which abstract from the *here* and *now*, and are thus related indifferently to all time. But it can know the present. Therefore it can know the future.

Obj. 2. Further, man, while his senses are in suspension, can know some future things, as in sleep, and in frenzy. But the intellect is freer and more vigorous when removed from sense. Therefore the intellect of its own nature can know the future.

Obj. 3. The intellectual knowledge of man is superior to any knowledge in brutes. But some animals know the future; and thus crows by their frequent cawing foretell rain. Therefore much more can the intellect know the future.

On the contrary, It is written (*Eccles.* viii. 6, 7), *There is great affliction for man, because he is ignorant of things past; and things to come he cannot know by any messenger.*

I answer that, We must apply the same distinction to future things as we applied above to contingent things. For future things considered as subject to time are singular, and the human intellect knows them by reflexion only, as stated above. But the principles of future things may be universal; and thus they may enter the domain of the intellect and become the objects of science.

Speaking, however, of the knowledge of the future in a general way, we must observe that the future may be known in two ways: either in itself, or in its cause. The future cannot be known in itself save by God alone, to Whom even that is present which in the course of events is future, inasmuch as from eternity His glance embraces the whole course of time, as we have said above when treating of God's knowledge.[1] But in so far as it exists in its cause, the future can be known also by us. Now if the cause be such as to have a necessary connection with its future result, then the future is known with scientific certitude, just as the astronomer foresees the future eclipse. If, however, the cause be such as to produce a certain result more frequently than not, then the future can be known more or less conjecturally, according as its cause is more or less inclined to produce the effect.

Reply Obj. 1. This argument holds of that knowledge which is drawn from universal causal principles; from these the future may be known, according to the order of the effects to the cause.

Reply Obj. 2. As Augustine says, the soul has a certain power of forecasting, so that by its nature it can know the future;[2] and so, when withdrawn from corporeal sense, and, as it were, concentrated on itself, it shares in the knowledge of the future. —Such an opinion as

---

1. 参见 Q. 14, a. 13.
2. 参见 Cf. *De Genesi ad Litt.*, XII, 13 (PL 34, 464).

this would be reasonable if we were to admit that the soul receives knowledge by participating in the Ideas, as the Platonists maintained,[1] because in that case the soul by its nature would know the universal causes of all effects, and would only be impeded in its knowledge by the body; and hence when withdrawn from the corporeal senses it would know the future.

But since it is connatural to our intellect to know things, not thus, but by receiving its knowledge from the senses, it is not natural for the soul to know the future when withdrawn from the senses. Rather does it know the future by the impression of superior spiritual and corporeal causes: of spiritual causes, when by divine power the human intellect is enlightened through the ministry of angels, and the phantasms are directed to the knowledge of future events; or, by the influence of demons, when the imagination is moved regarding the future known to the demons, as was explained above.[2] The soul is naturally more inclined to receive these impressions of spiritual causes when it is withdrawn from the senses, as it is then nearer to the spiritual world, and freer from external distractions.—The same may also come from superior corporeal causes. For it is clear that superior bodies influence inferior bodies. Hence, since sensitive powers are the acts of corporeal organs, the influence of the heavenly bodies causes the imagination to be affected, and so, as the heavenly bodies cause many future events, the imagination receives certain signs of some such events. These signs are perceived more at night and while we sleep than in the daytime and while we are awake, because, as is stated in *De Somno et Vigilia* ii., *impressions made by day are evanescent. The night air is calmer, when silence reigns; and hence bodily impressions are made in sleep, when slight internal movements are felt more than in wakefulness, and such movements produce in*

---

1. 参见 Cf. q. 84, a. 1 and 4; q. 87, a. 1.
2. 参见 Q. 57, a. 3.

the imagination images from which the future may be foreseen.[1]

Reply Obj. 3. Brute animals have no power above the imagination to regulate their images, as man has his reason, and therefore their imagination follows entirely the influence of the heavenly bodies. Thus from such animals' movements some future things, such as rain and the like, may be known rather than from human movements directed by reason. Hence the Philosopher says that *some who are most imprudent are most far-seeing; for their intelligence is not burdened with cares, but is as it were barren and bare of all anxiety, moving at the caprice of whatever is brought to bear on it.*[2]

1. 参见 Aristotle, *De Divinat.*, II (464a 12).
2. 同上 (464a 18).

Question LXXXVII
HOW THE INTELLECTUAL SOUL KNOWS ITSELF AND ALL THAT IS WITHIN ITSELF
(*In Four Articles*)

WE have now to consider how the intellectual soul knows itself and all that is within itself. Under this head there are four points of inquiry: (1) Whether the soul knows itself by its own essence? (2) Whether it knows its own habits? (3) How does the intellect know its own act? (4) How does it know the act of the will?

First Article
WHETHER THE INTELLECTUAL SOUL KNOWS ITSELF BY ITS ESSENCE?

We proceed thus to the First Article:—

Objection 1. It would seem that the intellectual soul knows itself by its own essence. For Augustine says that *the mind knows itself by itself, because it is incorporeal.*[1]

Obj. 2. Further, both angels and human souls belong to the genus of intellectual substance. But an angel understands himself by his own essence. Therefore so does the human soul.

Obj. 3. Further, *in things without matter, the intellect and that which is understood are the samer.*[2] But the human mind is without matter, not

---

1. 参见 *De Trin.*, IX, 3 (PL 42, 963).
2. 参见 Aristotle, *De An.*, III, 4 (430a 3).

being the act of a body, as was stated above.[1] Therefore the intellect and its object are the same in the human mind; and therefore the human mind understands itself by its own essence.

On the contrary, It is said that the *intellect understands itself in the same way as it understands other things.*[2] But it understands other things, not by their essence, but by their likenesses. Therefore it does not understand itself by its own essence.

I answer that, Everything is knowable so far as it is in act, and not so far as it is in potentiality;[3] for a thing is a being, and is true, and therefore knowable, according as it is actual. This is quite clear as regards sensible things, for the eye does not see what is potentially, but what is actually, colored. In like manner, it is clear that the intellect, so far as it knows material things, does not know save what is in act; and hence it does not know primary matter except as proportionate to form, as is stated *Physics* i.[4] Consequently immaterial substances are intelligible by their own essence, according as each one is actual by its own essence.

Therefore it is that the essence of God, the pure and perfect act, is absolutely and perfectly in itself intelligible; and hence God by His own essence knows Himself, and all other things also. The angelic essence belongs, indeed, to the genus of intelligible things as *act*, but not as a *pure act*, nor as a *complete act*; and hence the angel's act of intelligence is not completed by his essence. For, although an angel understands himself by his own essence, still he cannot understand all other things by his own essence; he rather knows things other than himself by their likenesses. Now the human intellect is only potential in the genus of intelligible beings, just as primary matter is potential in

1. 参见 Q. 76, a. 1.
2. 参见 Aristotle, *De An.*, III, 4 (430a. 2).
3. 参见 Aristotle, *Metaph.*, VIII, 9 (1051a 29).
4. 参见 Aristotle, *Phys.*, I, 7 (191a 8).

the genus of sensible beings; and hence it is called *possible*.[1] Therefore in its essence the human intellect is potentially understanding. Hence it has in itself the power to understand, but not to be understood, except as it is made actual. For even the Platonists asserted that an order of intelligible beings existed above the order of intellects, since the intellect understands only by participation in the intelligible;[2] for that which participates is below what it participates.

If, therefore, the human intellect, as the Platonists held, became actual by participating in separate intelligible Forms, it would understand itself by such a participation in incorporeal beings. But as in this life our intellect has material and sensible things for its proper object, as was stated above,[3] it understands itself according as it is made actual by the species abstracted from sensible things, through the light of the agent intellect, which not only actualizes the intelligibles themselves, but also, by their instrumentality[4], actualizes the possible intellect. Therefore the intellect knows itself, not by its essence, but by its act. This happens in two ways: In the first place, singularly, as when Socrates or Plato perceives that he has an intellectual soul because he perceives that he understands. In the second place, universally, as when we consider the nature of the human mind from a knowledge of the intellectual act. It is true, however, that the judgment and power of this knowledge, by which we know the nature of the soul, comes to us according to the derivation of our intellectual light from the divine truth which contains the exemplars of all things, as was stated above.[5] Hence Augustine says: *We gaze on the inviolable truth whence we can as perfectly as possible define,*

---

1. 参见 Aristotle, *De An.*, III, 4 (428a 22).
2. 参 见 Cf. Dionysius, *De Div. Nom.*, IV, 1 (PG 3, 693); *De Causis*, IX (p. 169). Cf. also Proclus, *Elem. of Theol.*, prop. 163 and 164 (p. 142).
3. 参见 Q. 84, a. 7.
4. instrumentality: 手段；工具；媒介
5. 参见 Q. 84, a. 5.

not what each man's mind is, but what it ought to be in the light of the eternal exemplars.[1] There is, however, a difference between these two kinds of knowledge, and it consists in this that the mere presence of the mind suffices for the first; since the mind itself is the principle of action whereby it perceives itself, and hence it is said to know itself by its own presence. But as regards the second kind of knowledge, the mere presence of the mind does not suffice, but there is further required a careful and subtle inquiry. Hence many are ignorant of the soul's nature, and many have erred about it. So Augustine says concerning such mental inquiry: *Let the mind strive not to see itself as if it were absent, but to discern itself as present*[2]—*i.e.*, to know how it differs from other things; which is to know its essence and nature.

Reply Obj. 1. The mind knows itself by means of itself, because at length it arrives at a knowledge of itself, though led thereto by its own act:—because it is itself that it knows, since it loves itself, as Augustine says in the same passage. Now a thing can be called self-evident in two ways, either because we can know it by nothing else except itself, as first principles are called self-evident; or because it is not accidentally knowable, as color is visible of itself, whereas substance is visible accidentally.

Reply Obj. 2. The essence of an angel is as an act in the genus of intelligible beings, and therefore it is both intellect and the thing understood. Hence an angel apprehends his own essence through himself; not so the human intellect, which is either altogether in potentiality to intelligible things,—as is the possible intellect,—or is the act of the intelligible abstracted from the phantasms,—as is the agent intellect.

Reply Obj. 3. This saying of the Philosopher is universally true in every kind of intellect. For as the sense in act is the sensible in act,

---

1. 参见 *De Trin.*, IX, 6 (PL 42, 966).
2. 参见 *Op. cit.*, X, 9 (PL 42, 980).

by reason of the sensible likeness which is the form of sense in act, so likewise the intellect in act is the object understood in act, by reason of the likeness of the thing understood, which is the form of the intellect in act. So the human intellect, which becomes actual by the species of the thing understood, is itself understood by the same species as by its own form. Now to say that in *things without matter the intellect and what is understood are the same*, is equal to saying that *as regards things actually understood the intellect and what is understood are the same.* For a thing is actually understood in that it is immaterial. But a distinction must be drawn, since the essences of some things are immaterial, as the separate substances called angels, each of which is understood and understands; whereas there are other things whose essences are not without matter but only their abstract likenesses. Hence the Commentator says that the proposition quoted is true only of separate substances;[1] because in a sense it is verified in their regard, and not in regard to other substances, as was already stated.

Second Article
WHETHER OUR INTELLECT KNOWS THE HABITS OF THE SOUL BY THEIR ESSENCE?

We proceed thus to the Second Article:—

Objection 1. It would seem that our intellect knows the habits of the soul by their essence. For Augustine says: *Faith is not seen in the heart wherein it abides in the same way as the soul of a man may be seen by another from the movement of the body; but we know most certainly that it is there, and conscience proclaims its existence.*[2] The same applies to the other habits of the soul. Therefore the habits of the soul are not known by their acts, but by themselves.

---

1. 参见 *In De An.*, III, comm. 15 (VI 169r).
2. 参见 *De Trin.*, XIII, 1 (PL 42, 1014).

Obj. 2. Further, material things outside the soul are known because their likenesses are present in the soul, and are said therefore to be known by their likenesses. But the soul's habits are present by their essence in the soul. Therefore the habits of the soul are known by their essence.

Obj. 3. Further, *whatever is the cause that a thing is such, is still more so.* But habits and intelligible species cause things to be known by the soul. Therefore they are still more known by the soul in themselves.

On the contrary, Habits, like powers, are the principles of acts. But, as it is said, *acts and operations are logically prior to powers.*[1] Therefore in the same way they are prior to habits; and thus habits, like the powers, are known by their acts.

I answer that, A habit is intermediate between mere power and mere act. Now, it has been said that nothing is known but as it is actual; and therefore so far as a habit fails in being a perfect act, it falls short in being of itself knowable, and can be known only by its act. Thus, for example, anyone knows he has a habit from the fact that he can produce the act proper to that habit; or he may inquire into the nature and character of the habit by considering the act. The first kind of knowledge of the habit arises from its being present, for the very fact of its presence causes the act whereby it is known. The second kind of knowledge of the habit arises from a careful inquiry, as was explained above concerning the mind.

Reply Obj. 1. Although faith is not known by external movements of the body, it is perceived by the subject wherein it resides by the interior act of the heart. For no one knows that he has faith except because he knows that he believes.

Reply Obj. 2. Habits are present in our intellect, not as its object,—since, in the present state of life, our intellect's object is the nature

---

1. 参见 Aristotle, *De An.*, II, 4 (415a 18).

of a material thing, as was stated above[1]—but as that by which it understands.

Reply Obj. 3. The axiom, *whatever is the cause that a thing is such, is still more so*, is true of things that are of the same order, for instance, of the same kind of cause. For example, we may say that health is desirable because of life, and therefore that life is more desirable still. But if we take things of different orders, the axiom is not true; for we may say that health is caused by medicine, but it does not follow that medicine is more desirable than health, for health belongs to the order of final causes, whereas medicine belongs to the order of efficient causes. So of two things belonging essentially to the order of the objects of knowledge, the one which causes the other to be known will be the more known, as principles are more known than conclusions. But a habit as such does not belong to the order of objects of knowledge; nor are things known because of the habit as because of an object known, but rather as because of a disposition or form whereby the subject knows. Therefore the argument does not hold.

Third Article
WHETHER OUR INTELLECT KNOWS ITS OWN ACT?

We proceed thus to the Third Article:—

Objection 1. It would seem that our intellect does not know its own act. For what is known is the object of the knowing power. But the act differs from the object. Therefore the intellect does not know its own act.

Obj. 2. Further, whatever is known is known by some act. If, then, the intellect knows its own act, it knows it by some act, and again it knows that act by some other act. This is to proceed indefinitely,

---

1. 参见 Q. 84, a. 7; q. 85, a. 8; q. 86, a. 2.

which seems impossible.

Obj. 3. Further, the intellect has the same relation to its act as sense has to its act. But the proper sense does not perceive its own act, for this belongs to the common sense, as is stated in *De Anima* iii.[1] Therefore neither does the intellect understand its own act.

On the contrary, Augustine says: *I understand that I understand.*[2]

I answer that, As was stated above, a thing is known according as it is in act. Now the ultimate perfection of the intellect consists in its own operation. For this is not an act tending to something else in which lies the perfection of the work accomplished, as building is the perfection of the thing built; but it remains in the agent as its perfection and act, as is said in *Metaph.* ix.[3] Therefore the first thing of the intellect that is understood is its own act of understanding. This occurs in different ways with different intellects. For there is an intellect, namely, the divine, which is its own act of understanding, so that in God the understanding of His understanding and the understanding of His essence are one and the same act, because His essence is His act of understanding. But there is another intellect, the angelic, which is not its own act of understanding, as we have said above;[4] and yet the first object of that act is the angelic essence[5]. Therefore, although there is a logical distinction between the act whereby he understands that he understands, and that whereby he understands his essence, yet he understands both by one and the same act; because to understand his own essence is the proper perfection of his essence, and by one and the same act is a thing, together with its perfection, understood. And there is yet another, namely, the human intellect, which is not its own

---

1. 参见 Aristotle, *De An.*, III, 2 (425b 12).
2. 参见 *De Trin.*, X, 11 (PL 42, 983).
3. 参见 Aristotle, *Metaph.*, VIII, 8 (1050a 36).
4. 参见 Q. 79, a. 1.
5. the angelic essence: 天使的本质

act of understanding, nor is its own essence the first object of its act of understanding, for this object is the nature of a material thing. And therefore that which is first known by the human intellect is an object of this kind, and that which is known secondarily is the act by which that object is known; and through the act the intellect itself is known, whose perfection is the act itself of understanding. For this reason did the Philosopher assert that objects are known before acts, and acts before powers.[1]

Reply Obj. 1. The object of the intellect is something universal, namely, *being* and *the true*, in which the act of understanding is itself comprised. Therefore the intellect can understand its own act; but not primarily, since the first object of our intellect, in this state of life, is not every being and everything true, but *being* and *true* as found in material things, as we have said above,[2] from which it acquires knowledge of all other things.

Reply Obj. 2. The act of the human intellect is not the act and perfection of the nature understood, as if the nature of the material thing and the act of the intellect could be understood by one act; just as a thing and its perfection are understood by one act. Hence the act whereby the intellect understands a stone is distinct from the act whereby it understands that it understands a stone; and so on. Nor is it incongruous for the intellect to be infinite potentially, as was explained above.[3]

Reply Obj. 3. The proper sense perceives by reason of the immutation in the material organ caused by the external sensible. A material thing, however, cannot immute itself, but one is immuted by another; and therefore the act of the proper sense is perceived by the common sense. The intellect, on the contrary, does not have understanding by

---

1. 参见 *De An.*, II, 4 (415a 16).
2. 参见 Q. 84, a. 7.
3. 参见 Q. 86, a. 2.

the material immutation[1] of an organ; and so there is no comparison.

Fourth Article
WHETHER THE INTELLECT UNDERSTANDS THE ACT OF THE WILL?

We proceed thus to the Fourth Article:—

Objection 1. It would seem that the intellect does not understand the act of the will. For nothing is known by the intellect, unless it be in some way present in the intellect. But the act of the will is not in the intellect, since the will and the intellect are distinct powers. Therefore the act of the will is not known by the intellect.

Obj. 2. Further, the act is specified by the object. But the object of the will is not the same as the object of the intellect. Therefore the act of the will also is specifically distinct from the object of the intellect. Therefore the act of the will is not known by the intellect.

Obj. 3. Augustine says of the soul's affections that *they are known neither by images, as bodies are known; nor by their presence, like the arts; but by certain notions.*[2] Now it does not seem that there can be in the soul any other notions of things except either the essences of the things known or their likenesses. Therefore it seems impossible for the intellect to know the affections of the soul, which are the acts of the will.

On the contrary, Augustine says: *I understand that I will.*[3]

I answer that, As was stated above, the act of the will is nothing but an inclination consequent on the form understood; just as natural appetite is an inclination consequent on the natural form.[4] Now the inclination of a thing resides in it according to its mode of being; and

---

1. the material immutation: 物质变化
2. 参见 *Confess.*, X, 17 (PL 32, 790).
3. 参见 *De Trin.*, X, 11 (PL 42, 983).
4. 参见 Q. 59, a. 1.

hence natural inclination resides in a natural thing naturally, and the inclination called the sensible appetite is in the sensible thing sensibly; and likewise the intelligible inclination, which is the act of the will, is in the intelligent being intelligibly, as in its principle and proper subject. Hence the Philosopher expresses himself thus, that *the will is in the reason.*[1] Now whatever is intelligibly in an intelligent subject is understood by that subject. Therefore the act of the will is understood by the intellect, both inasmuch as one perceives that one wills, and inasmuch as one knows the nature of this act, and consequently, the nature of the principle which is the habit or power.

Reply Obj. 1. This argument would hold good if the will and the intellect were in different subjects, in addition to being distinct powers; for then whatever was in the will would not be in the intellect. But as both are rooted in the same substance of the soul, and since one is in a way the principle of the other, consequently what is in the will is, in a way, also in the intellect.

Reply Obj. 2. The *good* and the *true*, which are the objects of the will and of the intellect, differ logically, but one is contained in the other, as we have said above;[2] for the true is a particular good, and the good is a particular true. Therefore the objects of the will fall under the intellect, and those of the intellect can fall under the will.

Reply Obj. 3. The affections of the soul are in the intellect, not by likeness only, as are bodies, nor as being present in their subject, as are the arts; but as the thing caused is in its principle, which contains some notion of the thing caused. And so Augustine says that the soul's affections are in the memory by certain notions.

---

1. 参见 *De An.*, III, 9 (432b 5).
2. 参见 Q. 16, a. 4, ad 1; q. 82, a. 4, ad 1.

Question LXXXVIII
HOW THE HUMAN SOUL KNOWS WHAT IS ABOVE ITSELF
(*In Three Articles*)

WE must now consider how the human soul knows what is above itself, viz, immaterial substances. Under this head there are three points of inquiry: (1) Whether the human soul in the present state of life can understand the immaterial substances, called angels, in themselves? (2) Whether it can arrive at the knowledge thereof by the knowledge of material things? (3) Whether God is the first object of our knowledge?

First Article
WHETHER THE HUMAN SOUL IN THE PRESENT STATE OF LIFE CAN UNDERSTAND IMMATERIAL SUBSTANCES IN THEMSELVES?

We proceed thus to the First Article:—

Objection 1. It would seem that the human soul in the present state of life can understand immaterial substances in themselves. For Augustine says: *As the mind itself acquires the knowledge of corporeal things by means of the corporeal senses, so it gains through itself the knowledge of incorporeal things.*[1] But these are the immaterial substances. Therefore the human mind understands immaterial substances[2].

---

1. 参见 *De Trin.*, IX, 3 (PL 42, 963).
2. immaterial substance: 非物质本体

Obj. 2. Further, like is known by like. But the human mind is more akin to immaterial than to material things; since its own nature is immaterial, as is clear from what we have said above.[1] Since then our mind understands material things, much more is it able to understand immaterial things.

Obj. 3. Further, the fact that objects which are in themselves most eminently sensible are not most perceived by us, comes from the fact that sense is corrupted by their very excellence. But the intellect is not subject to such a corrupting influence from the excellence of its object, as is stated in *De Anima* iii.[2] Therefore things which are in themselves in the highest degree of intelligibility are likewise to us most intelligible. Since material things, however, are intelligible only so far as we make them actually so, by abstracting them from material conditions, it is clear that those substances are more intelligible in themselves whose nature is immaterial. Therefore they are much more known to us than are material things.

Obj. 4. Further, the Commentator says that, *nature would be frustrated in its end* were we unable to understand abstract substances, *because it would have made what in itself is naturally intelligible not to be understood at all.*[3] But in nature nothing is idle or purposeless. Therefore immaterial substances can be understood by us.

Obj. 5. Further, as the sense is to the sensible, so is the intellect to the intelligible. But our sight can see all things corporeal, whether superior and incorruptible, or sublunary and corruptible. Therefore our intellect can understand all intelligible substances, including the superior and immaterial.

On the contrary, It is written (*Wis.* ix. 16): *The things that are in heaven who shall search out?* But these substances are said to be in heaven,

---

1. 参见 Q. 76, a. 1.
2. 参见 Aristotle, *De An.*, III, 4 (429b 2).
3. 参见 *In Metaph.*, *II*, comm. 1 (VIII, 14v).

according to *Matthew* xviii. 10, *Their angels in heaven*, etc. Therefore immaterial substances cannot be known by human investigation.

I answer that, In the opinion of Plato, immaterial substances are not only understood by us, but are also the objects we understand first of all. For Plato taught that immaterial subsisting Forms, which he called *Ideas*, are the proper objects of our intellect, and are thus first and essentially understood by us.[1] Furthermore, material things are known by the soul inasmuch as imagination and sense are joined to the intellect.[2] Hence the purer the intellect is, so much the more clearly does it perceive the intelligible reality of immaterial things.[3]

But in Aristotle's opinion, which experience corroborates, our intellect in its present state of life has a natural relation to the natures of material things;[4] and therefore it can understand only by turning to the phantasms, as we have said above.[5] Thus it clearly appears that immaterial substances, which do not fall under sense and imagination, cannot be known by us first and essentially, according to the mode of knowledge of which we have experience.

Nevertheless Averroes teaches that in this present life man can in the end arrive at the knowledge of separate substances by being joined or united to some separate substance, which he calls the *agent intellect*, and which, being a separate substance itself, can naturally understand separate substances.[6] Hence, when it is perfectly united to us, so that through it we are able to understand perfectly, we too shall be able to understand separate substances; just as in the present life, through the possible intellect united to us, we can understand material things.

---

1. 参见 Cf. q. 84, a. 4.
2. 参见 Cf. Macrobius, *In Somn. Scipion.*, I, 12 (pp. 531–532).
3. 参见 Cf. Cicero, *Tusc. Disp.*, I, 30 (p. 254).—Cf. also Plato, *Phaedo* (p. 80).
4. 参见 *De An.*, III, 7 (431a 16).
5. 参见 Q. 84, a. 7.
6. 参见 *In De An.*, III, comm. 36, pt. 5 (VI, 178v).

Now he said that the agent intellect is united to us as follows.[1] For since we understand by means of both the agent intellect and intelligible objects (as, for instance, we understand conclusions by principles understood), the agent intellect must be compared to the objects understood, either as the principle agent is to the instrument, or as form to matter. For an action is ascribed to two principles in one of these two ways: to a principal agent and to an instrument, as cutting to the workman and the saw; to a form and its subject, as heating to heat and fire. In both these ways the agent intellect can be compared to the intelligible object as perfection is to the perfectible, and as act is to potentiality. Now a subject is made perfect and receives its perfection at one and the same time, as the reception of what is actually visible synchronizes with the reception of light in the eye. Therefore the possible intellect receives the intelligible object and the agent intellect together. And the more numerous the intelligible objects received, so much the nearer do we come to the point of perfect union between ourselves and the agent intellect; so much so, that when we shall have understood all the intelligible objects, the agent intellect will become perfectly united to us, and through it we shall understand all things material and immaterial. In this he makes the ultimate happiness of man to consist.[2] Nor, as regards the present inquiry, does it matter whether the possible intellect in that state of happiness understands separate substances through the agent intellect, as he himself maintains, or whether (as he imputes to Alexander) the possible intellect can never understand separate substances (because according to him it is corruptible), but man understands separate substances through the agent intellect.[3]

All this, however, is untrue. First, because, supposing the agent

1. 参见 *In De An.*, III, comm. 36, pt. 5 (VI, 179rv).
2. 参见 *De An. Beatitud.*, I (IX, 64ra).—Cf. Avicenna, *De An.*, V, 6 (26va).
3. 参见 Averroes, *In De An.*, III, comm. 36, pt. 2 (VI, 176r).

intellect to be a separate substance, we could not formally understand through it; for the formal medium of an agent's action is its form and act, since every agent acts according to its actuality, as was said of the possible intellect.[1] Secondly, this opinion is untrue because the agent intellect, supposing it to be a separate substance, would not be joined to us in its substance, but only in its light, as participated in what we understood. But this would not extend to the other acts of the agent intellect so as to enable us to understand immaterial substances; just as when we see colors set off by the sun, we are not united to the substance of the sun so as to act like the sun, but only its light is united to us, that we may see the colors.

Thirdly, this opinion is untrue because, granted that, as was above explained, the agent intellect were united to us in substance, still it is not said that it is wholly united to us on the basis of one intelligible object, or two; but rather on the basis of all intelligible objects. But all such objects together do not equal the power of the agent intellect, as it is a much greater thing to understand separate substances than to understand all material things. Hence it clearly follows that the knowledge of all material things would not make the agent intellect to be so united to us as to enable us to understand separate substances through it.

Fourthly, this opinion is untrue because it is hardly possible for anyone in this world to understand all material things; and thus no one, or very few, would reach perfect felicity. This is against what the Philosopher says, that happiness is a *kind of common good, communicable to all capable of virtue.*[2] Further, it is against reason that only the few of any species attain to the end of the species.

Fifthly, the Philosopher expressly says that happiness is *an operation*

---

1. 参见 Q. 76, a. 1.
2. 参见 *Eth.*, I, 9 (1099b 18).

according to perfect virtue;[1] and after enumerating many virtues in the tenth book of the *Ethics*, he concludes that ultimate happiness, consisting in the knowledge of the highest things intelligible, is attained through the virtue of *wisdom*,[2] which in the sixth book he had named as *the chief of the speculative sciences.*[3] Hence Aristotle clearly placed the ultimate felicity of man[4] in that knowledge of separate substances which is obtainable by speculative science; and not in any union with the agent intellect, as some have imagined.

Sixthly, as was shown above,[5] the agent intellect is not a separate substance, but a power of the soul, extending itself actively to the same objects to which the possible intellect extends receptively; because, as Aristotle states, the possible intellect is *all things potentially*, and the agent intellect is *all things in act.*[6] Therefore both intellects, according to the present state of life, extend only to material things, which are made actually intelligible by the agent intellect, and are received in the possible intellect. Hence, in the present state of life, we cannot understand separate immaterial substances in themselves, either by the possible or by the agent intellect.

Reply Obj. 1. Augustine may be taken to mean that the knowledge of incorporeal things in the mind can be gained through the mind itself. This is so true that philosophers also say that the knowledge concerning the soul is a principle for the knowledge of separate substances.[7] For by knowing itself, the soul attains to some knowledge of incorporeal substances, such as is within its compass; not that the knowledge of itself gives it a perfect and absolute knowledge of them.

---

1. 参见 *Op. cit.*, I, 10 (1101a 14).
2. 参见 *Op. cit.*, X, 7 (1177a 21); 8 (1179a 30).
3. 参见 *Op. cit.*, VI, 7 (1141a 20).
4. the ultimate felicity: 终极幸福
5. 参见 Q. 79, a. 4.
6. 参见 Aristotle, *De An.*, III, 5 (430a 14).
7. 参见 Averroes, *In De An.*, I, comm. 2 (VI, 108v) ; III, comm. 5 (VI, 166r).

Reply Obj. 2. The likeness of nature is not a sufficient principle of knowledge. Otherwise, what Empedocles said would be true—that the soul needs to have the nature of all in order to know all.[1] But knowledge requires that the likeness of the thing known be in the knower, as a kind of form in the knower. Now our possible intellect, in the present state of life, is such that it can be informed with the likenesses abstracted from phantasms: and therefore it knows material things rather than immaterial substances.

Reply Obj. 3. There must needs be some proportion between the object and the power of knowledge; such as of the active to the passive, and of perfection to the perfectible. Hence that sensible objects of great excellence are not grasped by the senses is due not merely to the fact that they corrupt the organ, but also to their not being proportionate to the sensitive powers. And it is thus that immaterial substances are not proportionate to our intellect, in our present state of life, so that it cannot understand them.

Reply Obj. 4. This argument of the Commentator fails in several ways. First, because if separate substances are not understood by us, it does not follow that they are not understood by any intellect; for they are understood by themselves, and by one another.

Secondly, to be understood by us is not the end of separate substances and only that is vain and purposeless which fails to attain its end. It does not follow, therefore, that immaterial substances are purposeless, even if they are not at all understood by us.

Reply Obj. 5. Sense knows bodies, whether superior or inferior, in the same way, that is, by the sensible thing acting on the organ. But we do not understand material and immaterial substances in the same way. The former we understand by abstraction, which is impossible in the case of the latter, for there are no phantasms of what is immaterial.

---

1. 参见 Cf. Aristotle, *De An.*, I, 2 (404b 11).

Second Article

WHETHER OUR INTELLECT CAN COME TO UNDERSTAND IMMATERIAL SUBSTANCES THROUGH ITS KNOWLEDGE OF MATERIAL THINGS?

We proceed thus to the Second Article:—

Objection 1. It would seem that our intellect can come to know immaterial substances through the knowledge of material things. For Dionysius says that *the human mind cannot be raised up to immaterial contemplation of the heavenly hierarchies, unless it uses thereto material guidance according to its own nature.*[1] Therefore we can be led by material things to know immaterial substances.

Obj. 2. Further, science resides in the intellect. But there are sciences and definitions of immaterial substances; for Damascene defines an angel,[2] and we find angels discussed both in theology and in philosophy. Therefore immaterial substances can be understood by us.

Obj. 3. Further, the human soul belongs to the genus of immaterial substances. But it can be understood by us through its act, by which it understands material things. Therefore other immaterial substances also can be understood by us, through their effects in material things.

Obj. 4. Further, the only cause which cannot be comprehended through its effects is that which infinitely transcends them, and this belongs to God alone. Therefore other created immaterial substances can be understood by us through material things.

On the contrary, Dionysius says that *intelligible things cannot be understood through sensible things, nor composite things through simple, nor incorporeal things through corporeal.*[3]

---

1. 参见 *De Cael. Hier.*, I, 3 (PG 3, 124).
2. 参见 *De Fide Orth.*, II, 3 (PG 94, 865).
3. 参见 *De Div. Nom.*, I, 1 (PG 3, 588).

I answer that, Averroes says that a philosopher named Avempace taught that by the understanding of material substances we can be led, according to true philosophical principles, to the knowledge of immaterial substances.[1] For since the nature of our intellect is to abstract the quiddity of material things from matter, anything material residing in that abstracted quiddity can again be made subject to abstraction; and as the process of abstraction cannot go on forever, it must arrive at length at the understanding of a quiddity that is absolutely without matter; and this would be the understanding of immaterial substance.

Now this opinion would be true, were immaterial substances the forms and species of these material things, as the Platonists supposed.[2] But supposing, on the contrary, that immaterial substances differ altogether from the quiddity of material things, it follows that, however much our intellect may abstract the quiddity of a material thing from matter, it could never arrive at anything like an immaterial substance. Therefore we are not able to understand immaterial substances perfectly through material substances.

Reply Obj. 1. From material things we can rise to some sort of knowledge of immaterial things, but not to a perfect knowledge; for there is no proper and adequate proportion between material and immaterial things, and the likenesses drawn from material things for the understanding of immaterial things are very unlike them, as Dionysius says.[3]

Reply Obj. 2. Science treats of higher things principally by way of remotion. Thus Aristotle explains the heavenly bodies by denying to them the properties of sublunary bodies.[4] Hence it follows that much

1. 参见 *In De An.*, III, comm. 36, pt. 3 (VI, 177v–178v).
2. 参见 Cf. above, q. 84, a. 1.
3. 参见 *De Cael. Hier.*, II, 2 (PG 3, 137).
4. 参见 *De Caelo*, I, 3 (269b 18).

less can immaterial substances be known by us in such a way as to make us know their quiddity; but we may have a knowledge of them from the sciences by way of negation and by their relation to material things.

Reply Obj. 3. The human soul understands itself through its own act of understanding, which is proper to it, showing perfectly its power and nature. But the power and nature of immaterial substances cannot be perfectly known through such an act, nor through any other and material thing, because there is no proportion between the latter and the power of the former.

Reply Obj. 4. Created immaterial substances are not in the same natural genus as material substances, for they do not agree in power or in matter; but they belong to the same logical genus, because even immaterial substances are in the predicament of substance, since their essence is distinct from their being. But God has no community with material things either in a natural genus or in a logical genus; because God is not in a genus at all, as was stated above.[1] Hence through the likenesses derived from material things we can know something positive concerning the angels, according to some common notion, though not according to their specific nature; whereas we cannot acquire any such knowledge at all about God.

Third Article
WHETHER GOD IS THE FIRST OBJECT KNOWN BY THE HUMAN MIND?

We proceed thus to the Third Article:—

Objection 1. It would seem that God is the first object known by the human mind. For that object in which all others are known, and by

---

1. 参见 Q. 3, a. 5.

which we judge others, is the first thing known to us; as light is to the eye, and first principles to the intellect. But we know all things in the light of the first truth, and thereby judge of all things, as Augustine says.[1] Therefore God is the first object known to us.

Obj. 2. Further, whatever causes a thing to be such is more so. But God is the cause of all our knowledge; for He is *the true light which enlighteneth every man that cometh into this world* (*Jo.* i. 9). Therefore God is our first and most known object.

Obj. 3. Further, what is first known in an image is the exemplar to which the image is formed. But in our mind is *the image of God*, as Augustine says.[2] Therefore God is the first object known to our mind.

On the contrary, No man hath seen God at any time (*Jo.* i. 18).

I answer that, Since the human intellect in the present state of life cannot understand immaterial created substances, much less can it understand the essence of the uncreated substance. Hence it must be said absolutely that God is not the first object of our knowledge. Rather do we know God through creatures, according to the Apostle (*Rom.* i. 20): *the invisible things of God are clearly seen, being understood by the things that are made.* Now the first object of our knowledge in this life is the *quiddity of a material thing*, which is the proper object of our intellect, as appears above in many passages.[3]

Reply Obj. 1. We see and judge of all things in the light of the first truth, insofar as the light itself of our intellect, whether natural or gratuitous, is nothing else than an impression of the first truth upon it, as was stated above.[4] Hence, since the light itself of our intellect is not that which the intellect understands, but the medium whereby it

---

1. 参见 *De Trin.*, XII, 2 (PL 42, 999); *De Vera Relig.*, XXXI (PL 34, 147); *Confess.*, XII, 25 (PL 32, 840).
2. 参见 *De Trin.*, XII, 4 (PL 42; 1000).
3. 参见 Q. 84, a. 7; q. 85, a. 8; q. 87, a. 2, ad 2.
4. 参见 Q. 12, a. 11, ad 3; q. 84, a. 5.

understands, much less can it be said that God is the first thing known by our intellect.

Reply Obj. 2. The axiom, *Whatever causes a thing to be such is more so*, must be understood of things belonging to one and the same order, as was explained above.[1] Other things than God are known because of God, not as if He were the first known object, but because He is the first cause of our power of knowledge.

Reply Obj. 3. If there existed in our souls a perfect image of God, as the Son is the perfect image of the Father, our mind would know God at once. But the image in our mind is imperfect; and hence the argument does not hold.

---

1. 参见 Q. 87, a. 2, ad 3.

Question LXXXIX
THE KNOWLEDGE OF THE SEPARATED SOUL
(*In Eight Articles*)

WE must now consider the knowledge of the separated soul. Under this head there are eight points of inquiry: (1) Whether the soul separated from the body can understand? (2) Whether it understands separate substances? (3) Whether it understands all natural things? (4) Whether it understands singulars? (5) Whether the habits of science acquired in this life remain? (6) Whether the soul can use the habit of science here acquired? (7) Whether local distance impedes the separated soul's knowledge? (8) Whether souls separated from the body know what happens here?

First Article
WHETHER THE SEPARATED SOUL CAN UNDERSTAND ANYTHING?

We proceed thus to the First Article:—

Objection 1. It would seem that the soul separated from the body can understand nothing at all. For the Philosopher says that *the understanding is corrupted together with its interior principle.*[1] But by death all human interior principles are corrupted. Therefore understanding itself is corrupted.

---

1. 参见 *De An.*, I, 4 (408b 24).

Obj. 2. Further, the human soul is hindered from understanding when the senses are impeded, and by a distracted imagination[1], as was explained above.[2] But death destroys the senses and imagination, as we have shown above.[3] Therefore after death the soul understands nothing.

Obj. 3. Further, if the separated soul understands, this must be by means of some species. But it does not understand by means of innate species, because it has none such, being at first *like a tablet on which nothing is written.* Nor does it understand by species abstracted from things, for it does not then possess the organs of sense and imagination which are necessary for the abstraction of species; nor yet does it understand by means of species formerly abstracted and retained in the soul, for if that were so, a child's soul would have no means of understanding at all; nor finally does it understand by means of intelligible species divinely infused, for such knowledge would not be natural, such as we treat of now, but the effect of grace. Therefore the soul apart from the body understands nothing.

On the contrary, The Philosopher says: *If the soul had no proper operation, it could not be separated from the body.*[4] But the soul is separated from the body, and therefore it has a proper operation, and especially that which consists in understanding. Therefore the soul can understand when it is apart from the body.

I answer that, The difficulty in solving this question arises from the fact that the soul united to the body can understand only by turning to the phantasms, as experience shows. Did this not proceed from the soul's very nature, but accidentally, through its being bound up with

---

1. distracted imagination: 错乱的想象
2. 参见 Q. 84, a. 7 and 8.
3. 参见 Q. 77, a. 8.
4. 参见 *De An.*, I, 1 (403a 11).

the body, as the Platonists said,[1] the difficulty would vanish; for in that case, when the burden of the body was once removed,[2] the soul would at once return to its own nature, and would understand intelligible things simply, without turning to phantasms, as is exemplified in the case of other separate substances. In that case, however, the union of soul and body would not be for the soul's good, for evidently it would understand worse in the body than out of it; but the union would be for the good of the body, which would be absurd, since matter exists for the sake of the form, and not the form for the sake of the matter. But if we hold that the nature of the soul requires it to understand by turning to the phantasms, it will seem, since death does not change its nature, that it can then naturally understand nothing, since the phantasms are wanting to which it may turn.

To solve this difficulty, we must consider that nothing acts except so far as it is actual, and therefore the mode of action in every agent follows from the mode of its being. Now the soul has one mode of being when in the body, and another when apart from it, though its nature remains the same. But this does not mean that its union with the body is accidental, for, on the contrary, such a union belongs to it according to the very character of its nature, just as the nature of a light body is not changed when it is in its proper place, which is natural to it, and outside its proper place, which is beside its nature. The soul, therefore, when united to the body, consistently with that mode of being, has a mode of understanding by turning to corporeal phantasms, which are in corporeal organs; but when it is separated from the body, it has a mode of understanding by turning to pure intelligibles, as is proper to other separate substances. Hence it is as natural for the soul to understand by turning to the phantasms,

---

1. 参见 Cf. Cicero, *Tusc. Disp.*, I, 31 (pp. 255–256).—Cf. also Plato, *Phaedo* (p. 67d).
2. 参见 Cf. Avicenna, *De An.*, V, 5 (25va).

as it is for it to be joined to the body. But to be separated from the body is not in accordance with its nature, and likewise to understand without turning to the phantasms is not natural to it. That is why it is united to the body in order that it may have a mode of being and operation suitable to its nature. But here again a difficulty arises. For since a being is always ordered to what is best, and since it is better to understand by turning to pure intelligibles than by turning to the phantasms, God should have established the soul's nature in such a way that the nobler way of understanding would have been natural to it, and it would not have needed the body for that purpose.

In order to resolve this difficulty, we must consider that while it is true that in itself it is nobler to understand by turning to something higher than to understand by turning to phantasms, nevertheless such a mode of understanding was less perfect if we consider to what extent it lay within the power of the soul. This will appear if we consider that every intellectual substance possesses intellective power by the influence of the divine light. This light is one and simple in its first principle, and the farther off intellectual creatures are from the first principle so much the more is the light divided and diversified, as is the case with lines radiating from the center of a circle. Hence it is that God by His essence understands all things, while the superior intellectual substances understand by means of a number of species, which nevertheless are fewer and more universal and bestow a deeper comprehension of things, because of the efficaciousness of the intellectual power of such natures; but inferior intellectual natures possess a greater number of species, which are also less universal, and bestow a lower degree of comprehension, in proportion as they recede from the intellectual power of the higher intellectual substances. If, therefore, inferior substances received species in the same degree of universality as the superior substances, since they are not so strong in understanding, the knowledge which they would derive through these species would be imperfect, and of a general and confused nature. We can see this to a certain extent in men, for those who are of weaker intellect fail to acquire perfect knowledge through the universal conceptions of those who have a better understanding, unless things are explained to them singly and in detail. Now it is clear that in the order of nature human souls hold the lowest place among intellectual substances; for the perfection of the universe required various grades of being. If, therefore, God had willed human souls to understand in the same way as separate substances, it would follow that human knowledge, so far from being perfect, would be confused and general. Therefore, to make it possible for human souls to possess a perfect and proper knowledge of things, they were so made that their nature required them to be joined to bodies, and thus to receive a proper knowledge of sensible things from the sensible things themselves. So, too, we see in the case of uneducated men that they have to be taught by sensible examples.

It is clear then that it was for the soul's good that it was united to a body, and that it understands by turning to the phantasms. Nevertheless it is possible for it to exist apart from the body, and also to understand in another way.

Reply Obj. 1. The Philosopher's words, if carefully examined, will show that he said this on the basis of a previous supposition, namely, that understanding is a movement of body and soul as united, just as is sensation, for he had not as yet explained the difference between intellect and sense.[1] We may also say that he is referring to the way of understanding by turning to phantasms.

This is also the meaning of the second objection.

Reply Obj. 3. The separated soul does not understand by innate species, nor by species then abstracted, nor only by retained species, as the objection proves; but the soul in that state understands by means

1. 参见 *De An.*, I, 4 (408b 6).

of participated species resulting from the influence of the divine light, shared by the soul as by other separate substances, though in a lesser degree. Hence, as soon as it ceases to act by turning to the body, the soul turns at once to what is above it; nor is this way of knowledge unnatural, for God is the author of the influx both of the light of grace and of the light of nature.

Second Article
WHETHER THE SEPARATED SOUL UNDERSTANDS SEPARATE SUBSTANCES?

We proceed thus to the Second Article:—

Objection 1. It would seem that the separated soul does not understand separate substances. For the soul is more perfect when joined to the body than when existing apart from it; for it is an essential part of human nature, and every part of a whole is more perfect when it exists in that whole. But the soul in the body does not understand separate substances, as was shown above.[1] Therefore much less is it able to do so when apart from the body.

Obj. 2. Further, whatever is known is known either by its presence or by its species. But separate substances cannot be known to the soul by their presence, for God alone can enter into the soul; nor by means of species abstracted by the soul from an angel, for an angel is more simple than a soul. Therefore the separated soul cannot at all understand separate substances.

Obj. 3. Further, some philosophers said that the ultimate happiness of man consists in the knowledge of separate substances. If, therefore, the separated soul can understand separate substances, its happiness would be secured by its separation alone; which cannot reasonably be said.

---

1. 参见 Q. 88, a. 1.

On the contrary, Souls apart from the body know other separated souls; as we see in the case of the rich man in hell, who saw Lazarus and Abraham (*Luke* xvi. 23). Therefore separated souls see the devils and the angels.

I answer that, as Augustine says, *our mind acquires the knowledge of incorporeal things by itself* —*i.e.*, by knowing itself.[1] Therefore, from the knowledge which the separated soul has of itself, we can judge how it knows other separate beings. Now it was said above that as long as it is united to the body, the soul understands by turning to phantasms.[2] Hence, it does not understand itself save through becoming actually understanding by means of species abstracted from phantasms; for thus it understands itself through its own act, as was shown above.[3] When, however, it is separated from the body, it understands no longer by turning to phantasms, but by turning to what is intelligible through itself; and so in that state it understands itself through itself. Now, every separate substance *understands what is above itself and what is below itself, according to the mode of its substance*;[4] for a thing is understood according as it is in the one who understands, and one thing is in another according to the nature of that in which it is. Now the mode of being of a separated soul is inferior to that of an angel, but is the same as that of other separated souls. Therefore the soul apart from the body has perfect knowledge of other separated souls, but it has an imperfect and defective knowledge of the angels so far as its natural knowledge is concerned. But the knowledge of glory is otherwise.

Reply Obj. 1. The separated soul is, to be sure, less perfect, if we consider the nature in which it communicates with the nature of the body; but it has a greater freedom for understanding, since the burden and care of the

---

1. 参见 *De Trin.*, IX, 3 (PL 42, 963).—Cf. q. 88, a. 1, ad 1.
2. 参见 A. 1; q. 84, a. 7.
3. 参见 Q. 87, a. 1.
4. 参见 *De Causis*, VIII (p. 168).

body are a clog upon the clearness of intelligence in the present life.

Reply Obj. 2. The separated soul understands the angels by means of divinely impressed likenesses; which, however, fail to give a perfect knowledge of them, for the nature of the soul is inferior to that of an angel.

Reply Obj. 3. Man's ultimate happiness consists, not in the knowledge of any separate substances, but in the knowledge of God, Who is seen only through grace. The knowledge of other separate substances, if perfectly understood, gives great happiness—not final and ultimate happiness. But the separated soul does not understand them perfectly, as was shown above.

Third Article
WHETHER THE SEPARATED SOUL KNOWS ALL NATURAL THINGS?

We proceed thus to the Third Article:—

Objection 1. It would seem that the separated soul knows all natural things. For the likenesses of all natural things exist in separate substances. Therefore, as separated souls know separate substances, they also know all natural things.

Obj. 2. Further, whoever understands the greater intelligible will be all the more able to understand the lesser intelligible. But the separated soul understands immaterial substances, which are most intelligible. Therefore much more can it understand all natural things, which are in a lower degree of intelligibility.

On the contrary, The devils have a greater natural knowledge than the separated soul, yet they do not know all natural things, but have to learn many things by long experience, as Isidore says.[1] Therefore neither can the separated soul know all natural things.

---

1. 参见 *Sent.*, I, 10 (PL 83, 556).

Further, if the soul, as soon as it was separated, gained knowledge of all natural things, the efforts of men to know would be vain and profitless. But this is incongruous. Therefore the separated soul does not know all natural things.

I answer that, As was stated above, the separated soul, like the angels, understands by means of species received from the influence of the divine light. Nevertheless, as the soul by nature is inferior to an angel, to whom this kind of knowledge is natural, the soul apart from the body does not receive perfect knowledge through such species, but only a general and confused kind of knowledge. Separated souls, therefore, have the same relation to an imperfect and confused knowledge of natural things by means of such species as the angels have to the perfect knowledge of them. Now through such species angels know all natural things perfectly, because all that God has produced in the respective natures of things has been produced by Him in the angelic intelligence, as Augustine says.[1] Hence it follows that separated souls know all natural things, not with a certain and proper knowledge, but in a general and confused manner.

Reply Obj. 1. Even an angel does not understand all natural things through his substance, but through certain species, as was stated above.[2] So it does not follow that the soul knows all natural things because it knows separate substances.

Reply Obj. 2. As the separated soul does not understand separate substances perfectly, so neither does it know all natural things perfectly; but it knows them confusedly, as was explained above.

Reply Obj. 3. Isidore speaks of the knowledge of the future which neither angels, nor demons, nor separated souls, know except so far as future things pre-exist in their causes or are known by divine revelation. But we are here treating of the knowledge of natural things.

---

1. 参见 *De Genesi ad Litt.*, II, 8 (PL 34, 269).
2. 参见 Q. 55, a. 1; q. 87, a. 1.

Reply Obj. 4. Knowledge acquired here by inquiry is proper and perfect, but the knowledge of which we speak is confused. Hence it does not follow that the search to learn is in vain.

Fourth Article
WHETHER THE SEPARATED SOUL KNOWS SINGULARS?

We proceed thus to the Fourth Article:—

Objection 1. It would seem that the separated soul does not know singulars. For no cognitive power besides the intellect remains in the separated soul, as is clear from what has been said above.[1] But the intellect does not know singulars, as we have shown.[2] Therefore the separated soul does not know singulars.

Obj. 2. Further, the knowledge of the singular is more determinate than knowledge of the universal. But the separated soul has no determinate knowledge of the species of natural things; and therefore much less does it know singulars.

Obj. 3. Further, if it knows singulars, yet not by sense, for the same reason it would know all singulars. But it does not know all singulars. Therefore it knows none.

On the contrary, The rich man in hell said: *I have five brethren* (*Luke* xvi. 28).

I answer that, Separated souls know some singulars, but not all, and not even all present singulars. To understand this, we must consider that there is a twofold way of knowing things, one by means of abstraction from phantasms, and in this way singulars cannot be directly known by the intellect, but only indirectly, as was stated above.[3] The other way of understanding is by the infusion of species by God, and in that

---

1. 参见 Q. 77, a. 8.
2. 参见 Q. 86, a. 1.
3. 同上

way it is possible for the intellect to know singulars. For just as God knows all things, universal and singular, by His essence, as the cause of universal and individual principles,[1] so likewise separate substances can know singulars by species which are a kind of participated likeness of the divine essence. There is this difference, however, between angels and separated souls, namely, that through these species the angels have a perfect and proper knowledge of things, whereas separated souls have only a confused knowledge. Hence the angels, by reason of their perfect intellect, know through these species not only the specific natures of things, but also the singulars contained in those species; whereas separated souls know by these species only those singulars to which they are determined by former knowledge in this life, or by some affection, or by natural relation, or by the divine plan; because whatever is received into anything is determined according to the mode of the recipient.

Reply Obj. 1. The intellect does not know the singular by way of abstraction; neither does the separated soul know it thus, but in the way explained above.

Reply Obj. 2. The knowledge of the separated soul is confined to those species or individuals to which the soul has some kind of determinate relation, as we have said.

Reply Obj. 3. The separated soul has not the same relation to all singulars, but one relation to some, and another to others. Therefore there is not the same reason why it should know all singulars.

Fifth Article
WHETHER THE HABIT OF SCIENCE HERE ACQUIRED REMAINS IN THE SEPARATED SOUL?

We proceed thus to the Fifth Article:—

---

1. 参见 Q. 14, a. 11; q. 57, a. 2.

Objection 1. It would seem that the habit of science acquired in this life does not remain in the soul separated from the body; for the Apostle says: *Knowledge shall be destroyed* (*1 Cor.* xiii. 8).

Obj. 2. Further, some in this world who are less good enjoy knowledge denied to others who are better. If, therefore, the habit of science remained in the soul after death, it would follow that some who are less good would, even in the future life, excel some who are better; which seems unreasonable.

Obj. 3. Further, separated souls will possess science by influence of the divine light. Supposing, therefore, that science here acquired remained in the separated soul, it would follow that two forms of the same species would coexist in the same subject, which cannot be.

Obj. 4. Further, the Philosopher says that *a habit is a quality hard to remove: yet sometimes science is destroyed by sickness or the like.*[1] But in this life there is no change so thorough as death. Therefore it seems that the habit of science is destroyed by death.

On the contrary, Jerome says: *Let us learn on earth that kind of science which will remain with us in heaven.*[2]

I answer that, Some say that the habit of science resides, not in the intellect itself, but in the sensitive powers, namely, the imaginative, cogitative, and memorative, and that the intelligible species are not preserved in the possible intellect.[3] If this were true, it would follow that when the body is destroyed by death, the habit of science acquired here would be entirely destroyed.[4]

But, since knowledge resides in the intellect, which is *the abode of species*, as the Philosopher says, the habit of science here acquired must be partly in the aforesaid sensitive powers, and partly in the

---

1. 参见 *Cat.*, VIII (8b 28).
2. 参见 *Epist.*, LIII (PL 22, 549).
3. 参见 Avicenna, *De An.*, V, 6 (26va).
4. 参见 Cf. Dominic Gundissalinus, *De An.*, X (p. 97).

intellect.[1] This can be seen by considering the very actions from which the habit of science arises. For *habits are like the actions whereby they are acquired.*[2] Now the actions of the intellect, by which science is acquired in the present life, are performed through the turning of the intellect to the phantasms in the aforesaid sensitive powers. Hence through such acts the possible intellect acquires a certain facility in acting through the species received; and the aforesaid sensitive powers acquire a certain aptitude in seconding the action of the intellect when it turns to them to consider the intelligible object. But just as the intellectual act resides chiefly and formally in the intellect itself, while it resides materially and dispositively[3] in the inferior powers, so the same distinction is to be applied to habit.

Science, therefore, acquired in the present life does not remain in the separated soul, as regards what belongs to the sensitive powers; but as regards what belongs to the intellect itself, it must remain. For, as the Philosopher says, a form may be corrupted in two ways: first, directly, when corrupted by its contrary, as heat by cold; secondly, indirectly, when its subject is corrupted.[4] Now it is evident that the science which is in the human intellect is not corrupted through the corruption of the subject, for the intellect is incorruptible, as was stated above.[5] Neither can the intelligible species in the possible intellect be corrupted by their contrary; for there is no contrary to intelligible intentions, above all as regards the simple comprehension of what a thing is. But contrariety may exist in the intellect as regards composition and division, or also reasoning, according as what is false in a proposition or an argument is contrary to truth. And thus

1. 参见 Aristotle, *De An.*, III, 4 (429a 27).
2. 参见 Aristotle, *Eth.*, II, 1 (1103b 21).
3. dispositively: 决定性地
4. 参见 *De Long. et Brev. Vitae*, II (465a 23).
5. 参见 Q. 75, a. 1, ad 2 ; q. 75, a. 6.

science is at times corrupted by its contrary when a false argument leads anyone away from the knowledge of truth. For this reason the Philosopher in the above work mentions two ways in which science is corrupted directly:[1] namely, *forgetfulness* on the part of the memorative power, and *deception* on the part of a false argument. But these have no place in the separated soul. Therefore we must conclude that the habit of science, so far as it is in the intellect, remains in the separated soul.

Reply Obj. 1. The Apostle is not speaking of knowledge as a habit, but as to the act of knowing; and hence he says, in proof of the assertion quoted, *Now, I know in part* (*1 Cor.* xiii. 12).

Reply Obj. 2. As a less good man may exceed a better man in bodily stature, so the same kind of man may have a habit of science in the future life which a better man may not have. This, however, cannot be compared with the other prerogatives enjoyed by the better man.

Reply Obj. 3. These two kinds of science are not of the same species, so there is no impossibility.

Reply Obj. 4. This objection considers the corruption of science on the part of the sensitive powers.

Sixth Article
WHETHER THE ACT OF SCIENCE ACQUIRED HERE REMAINS IN THE SEPARATED SOUL?

We proceed thus to the Sixth Article:—

Objection 1. It would seem that the act of science here acquired does not remain in the separated soul. For the Philosopher says that when the body is corrupted, *the soul neither remembers nor loves.*[2] But to consider what is previously known is an act of memory. Therefore the separated soul cannot retain an act of science here acquired.

---

1. 参见 *De Long. et Brev. Vitae*, II (465a 23).
2. 参见 *De An.*, I, 4 (408b 27).

Obj. 2. Further, intelligible species cannot have greater power in the separated soul than they have in the soul united to the body. But in this life we cannot understand by intelligible species without turning to phantasms, as was shown above.[1] Therefore the separated soul cannot do so, and thus it cannot understand at all by intelligible species acquired in this life.

Obj. 3. Further, the Philosopher says that *habits produce acts similar to those whereby they are acquired.*[2] But a habit of science is acquired here by acts of the intellect turning to phantasms. Therefore it cannot produce any other acts. These acts, however, are not adapted to the separated soul. Therefore the soul in the state of separation cannot produce any act of science acquired in this life.

On the contrary, It was said to Dives in hell (*Luke* xvi. 25): *Remember thou didst receive good things in thy lifetime.*

I answer that, An act offers two things for our consideration, its species and its mode. Its species comes from the object, to which the knowing power is directed by the species, which is the likeness of the object; whereas the mode is gathered from the power of the agent. Thus, that a person sees a stone is due to the species of the stone in his eye; but that he see it clearly, is due to the eye's visual power. Therefore, since the intelligible species remain in the separated soul, as was stated above, and since the state of the separated soul is not the same as it is in this life, it follows that through the intelligible species acquired in this life the soul apart from the body can understand what it understood formerly, but in a different way; that is, not by turning to phantasms, but by a mode suited to a soul existing apart from the body. Thus the act of knowledge here acquired remains in the separated soul, but in a different mode.

Reply Obj. 1. The Philosopher speaks of remembrance, according as

---

1. 参见 Q. 84, a. 7.
2. 参见 *Eth.*, II, 1 (1103b 21).

memory belongs to the sensitive part, but not as belonging in a way to the intellect, as was explained above.[1]

Reply Obj. 2. The different mode of understanding is produced by the different state of the intelligent soul, not by diversity in the power of the species.

Reply Obj. 3. The acts which produce a habit are like the acts caused by that habit in species, but not in mode. For example, to do just things, but not justly, that is, with enjoyment, causes the habit of political justice, whereby we act with enjoyment.

Seventh Article
WHETHER LOCAL DISTANCE IMPEDES THE KNOWLEDGE IN THE SEPARATED SOUL?

We proceed thus to the Seventh Article:—

Objection 1. It would seem that local distance impedes the separated soul's knowledge. For Augustine says that *the souls of the dead are where they cannot know what is done here.*[2] But they know what is done among themselves. Therefore local distance impedes the knowledge in the separated soul.

Obj. 2. Further, Augustine says that *the demons' rapidity of movement enables them to tell things unknown to us.*[3] But agility of movement would be useless in that respect unless their knowledge was impeded by local distance; which, therefore, is a much greater hindrance to the knowledge of the separated soul, whose nature is inferior to the demon's.

Obj. 3. Further, as there is distance of place, so is there distance of time. But distance of time impedes knowledge in the separated soul,

---

1. 参见 Q. 79, a. 6.
2. 参见 *De Cura pro Mort.*, XIII (PL 40, 605).
3. 参见 *De Divinat. Daemon.*, III (PL 40, 584).

for the soul is ignorant of the future. Therefore it seems that distance of place also impedes its knowledge.

On the contrary, It is written (*Luke* xvi. 23), that Dives, *lifting up his eyes, when he was in torment, saw Abraham afar off.* Therefore local distance does not impede knowledge in the separated soul.

I answer that, Some have held that the separated soul knows the singular by abstraction from the sensible.[1] If that were so, it might be said that local distance would impede its knowledge; for either the sensible would need to act upon the separated soul, or the separated soul upon the sensible, and in either case a determinate distance would be necessary. This is, however, impossible, because abstraction of the species from the sensible is done through the senses and the other sensible powers, which do not remain actually in the soul apart from the body. But the soul when separated understands singulars by species derived from the divine light, which is indifferent to what is near or distant. Hence knowledge in the separated soul is not hindered by local distance.

Reply Obj. 1. Augustine says that the souls of the departed cannot see what is done here, not because they are *there*, as if impeded by local distance, but for some other cause, as we shall explain.

Reply Obj. 2. Augustine speaks there in accordance with the opinion that demons have bodies naturally united to them, and so have sensitive powers, which require local distance.[2] In the same book he expressly sets down this opinion,[3] though apparently rather by way of narration than of assertion, as we may gather from *De Civitate Dei* xxi.[4]

Reply Obj. 3. The future, which is distant in time, does not actually

---

1. 参见 Cf. Cassiodorus, *De An.*, II (PL 70, 1286); Pseudo-Augustine (Alcher of Clairvaux), *De Spir. et An.*, XXX (PL 40, 800).
2. 参见 Cf. above, q. 51, a. 1, ad 1.
3. 参见 *De Divinat. Daemon.*, III (PL 40, 584).
4. 参见 *De Civit. Dei*, XXI, 10 (PL 41, 724).

exist, and therefore is not knowable in itself; for so far as a thing falls short of being, so far does it fall short of being knowable. But what is locally distant exists actually, and is in itself knowable. Hence we cannot argue from distance of time to distance of place.

Eighth Article
WHETHER SEPARATED SOULS KNOW WHAT TAKES PLACE ON EARTH?

We proceed thus to the Eighth Article:—

Objection 1. It would seem that separated souls know what takes place on earth; for otherwise they would have no care for it, as they have, according to what Dives said (*Luke* xvi. 27, 28), *I have five brethren ... he may testify unto them, lest they also come into the place of torments.* Therefore separated souls know what passes on earth.

Obj. 2. Further, the dead often appear to the living, asleep or awake, and tell them of what takes place here; as Samuel appeared to Saul (*1 Kings*, xxviii. 11). But this could not be unless they knew what takes place here. Therefore they know what takes place on earth.

Obj. 3. Further, separated souls know what happens among themselves. If, therefore, they do not know what takes place among us, it must be by reason of local distance; which has been shown to be false.

On the contrary, It is written (*Job* xiv. 21): *He will not understand whether his children come to honor or dishonor.*

I answer that, By natural knowledge, of which we are treating now, the souls of the dead do not know what passes on earth. This follows from what has been laid down, since the separated soul has knowledge of singulars by being in a way determined to them, either by some vestige of previous knowledge or affection, or by the divine order. Now the departed souls are in a state of separation from the company of the living, both by divine order and by their mode of being, and they are joined to the world of incorporeal spiritual substances. Hence they are ignorant of what goes on among us. Of this Gregory gives the reason thus: *The dead do not know how the living act, for the life of the spirit is far from the life of the flesh; and so, as corporeal things differ from incorporeal in genus, so they are distinct in knowledge.*[1] Augustine seems to say the same when he asserts that *the souls of the dead have no concern in the affairs of the living.*[2]

Gregory and Augustine, however, seem to be divided in opinion as regards the souls of the blessed in heaven, for Gregory continues the passage above quoted: *The case of the holy souls is different, for since they see the light of Almighty God, we cannot believe that external things are unknown to them.*[3] But Augustine expressly says: *The dead, even the saints, do not know what is done by the living or by their own children,*[4] according to the quotation of the *Gloss* on the text, *Abraham hath not known us* (*Isa.* lxiii. 16).[5] He confirms this opinion by saying that he was not visited, nor consoled in sorrow by his mother, as when she was alive, and he could not think it possible that she was less kind when in a happier state; and again by the fact that the Lord promised to king Josias that he should die, lest he should see his people's afflictions (*4 Kings*, xxii. 20). Yet Augustine says this in doubt; and premises, *Let every one take what I say as he pleases.* Gregory, on the other hand, is positive, since he says, *We cannot believe.* His opinion, indeed, seems to be the more probable one,—that the souls of the blessed who see God do know all that passes here. For they are equal to the angels, of whom Augustine himself says that they know what happens among those living on earth.[6] But as the souls of the blessed are most perfectly united to

1. 参见 *Moral.*, XII, 21 (PL 75, 999).
2. 参见 *De Cura pro Mort.*, XIII; XVI (PL 40, 604; 607).
3. 参见 *Moral.*, XII, 21 (PL 75, 999).
4. 参见 *De Cura pro Mort.*, XIII (PL 40, 604).
5. 参见 *Glossa interl.* (IV, 102v).
6. 参见 *De Cura pro Mort.*, XV (PL 40, 605).

divine justice, they do not suffer from sorrow, nor do they interfere in mundane affairs, except in accordance with divine justice.

Reply Obj. 1. The souls of the departed may care for the living, even if ignorant of their state; just as we care for the dead by pouring forth prayer on their behalf, though we are ignorant of their state. Moreover, the affairs of the living can be made known to them, not immediately, but souls who pass hence thither, or by angels and demons, or even by *the revelation of the Holy Ghost*, as Augustine says in the same book.[1]

Reply Obj. 2. That the dead appear to the living in any way whatever is either by the special dispensation[2] of God, in order that the souls of the dead may enter into the affairs of the living (this is to be accounted as miraculous) ; or else such apparitions occur through the instrumentality of bad or good angels, without the knowledge of the departed, as may likewise happen when the living appear in dreams, without their own knowledge, to others living, as Augustine says in the same book.[3] And so it may be said of Samuel that he appeared through a divine revelation, according to *Ecclus.* xlvi. 23: *He slept, and told the king the end of his life.* Or, again, this apparition was procured by the demons; unless, indeed, the authority of *Ecclesiasticus* be set aside because it is not received by the Jews as part of the canonical Scriptures.

Reply Obj. 3. This kind of ignorance does not proceed from the obstacle of local distance, but from the cause mentioned above.

---

1. 参见 *De Cura pro Mort.*, XV (PL 40, 606).
2. the special dispensation: 特许
3. 参见 *Op. cit.*, XII (PL 40, 600).

Question XC
THE FIRST PRODUCTION OF MAN'S SOUL
(*In Four Articles*)

AFTER the foregoing, we must consider the first production of man, concerning which there are four subjects of treatment: (1) the production of man himself; (2) the end of this production;[1] (3) the state and condition of the first man;[2] (4) the place of his abode;[3] concerning the production of man, there are three things to be considered: (1) the production of man's soul; (2) the production of man's body;[4] (3) the production of woman.[5]

Under the first head there are four points of inquiry: (1) Whether man's soul was something made, or a part of the divine substance? (2) Whether, if made, it was created? (3) Whether it was made by angelic instrumentality? (4) Whether it was made before the body?

First Article
WHETHER THE SOUL WAS MADE, OR WAS OF GOD'S SUBSTANCE?

We proceed thus to the First Article:—

Objection 1. It would seem that the soul was not made, but was

---

1. 参见 Q. 93.
2. 参见 Q. 94.
3. 参见 Q. 102.
4. 参见 Q. 91.
5. 参见 Q. 92.

of God's substance. For it is written (*Gen.* ii. 7): *God formed man of the slime of the earth, and breathed into his face the breath of life, and man was made a living soul.* But he who breathes sends forth something of himself. Therefore the soul, whereby man lives, is a part of the divine substance.

Obj. 2. Further, as was explained above, the soul is a simple form.[1] But a form is an act. Therefore the soul is a part of God's substance.

Obj. 3. Further, things that exist and do not differ are the same. But God and the mind exist, and in no way differ, for they could be differentiated only by certain differences, and thus would be composite. Therefore God and the human mind are the same.

On the contrary, Augustine mentions certain opinions which he calls *exceedingly and evidently perverse, and contrary to the Catholic Faith*, among which the first is the opinion that *God made the soul, not out of nothing, but from Himself.*[2]

I answer that, To say that the soul is of the divine substance involves a manifest improbability. For, as is clear from what has been said,[3] the human soul is sometimes in a state of potentiality to the act of understanding, —acquires knowledge somehow from things, —and has various powers: all of which are incompatible with the divine nature, which is a pure act,—receives nothing from any other,—and admits of no diversity in itself, as we have proved.[4]

This error seems to have originated from two views of the ancients. For those who first began to observe the nature of things, being unable to rise above their imagination, supposed that nothing but bodies existed.[5] Therefore they said that God was a body, which

---

1. 参见 Q. 75, a. 5.
2. 参见 *De Orig An.*, III, 15 (PL 44, 522).
3. 参见 Q. 77, a. 2; q. 79, a. 2; q. 84, a. 6.
4. 参见 Q. 3, a. 1 and 7; q. 9, a. 1.
5. 参见 Cf. above, q. 44, a. 2.

they considered to be the principle of other bodies.[1] And since they held that the soul was of the same nature as that body which they regarded as the first principle, as is stated in *De Anima* i.,[2] it followed that the soul was of the substance of God Himself. According to this supposition, the Manichæans also, thinking that God was a corporeal light, held that the soul was a part of that light bound to the body.[3]

Then a further step in advance was made, and some surmised the existence of something incorporeal, not apart from the body, but the form of a body.[4] In this spirit Varro said, *God is a soul governing the world by movement and reason*, as Augustine relates.[5] So some supposed man's soul to be part of that one soul,[6] just as man is a part of the whole world; for they were unable to go so far as to understand the different degrees of spiritual substance, except according to the distinction of bodies.

But, all these theories are impossible, as was proved above.[7] Hence, it is evidently false that the soul is of the substance of God.

Reply Obj. 1. The term *breathe* is not to be taken in the material sense; but as regards the act of God, to breathe [*spirare*] is the same as to *make a spirit*. Moreover, in the material sense, man by breathing does not send forth anything of his own substance, but an extraneous thing.

Reply Obj. 2. Although the soul is a simple form in its essence, yet it is not its own being, but is a being by participation, as was explained above.[8] Therefore it is not a pure act like God.

Reply Obj. 3. That which differs, properly speaking, differs by

1. 参见 Cf. *C. G.*, I, 20; St. Augustine, *De Civit. Dei*, VIII, 2; 5 (PL 41, 226; 239).
2. 参见 Aristotle, *De An.*, I, 2 (405a 3).
3. 参见 Cf. St. Augustine, *De Haeres.*, 46 (PL 42, 35); *De Genesi ad Litt.*, VII, 11 (PL 34, 361).
4. 参见 Cf. above, q. 44, a. 2.
5. 参见 *De Civit. Dei*, VII, 6; IV, 31 (PL 41, 199; 138).
6. 参见 Macrobius, *In Somn. Scipion.*, I, 14 (p. 540).
7. 参见 Q. 3, a. 1 and 8; q. 50, a. 2, ad 4; q. 75, a. 1.
8. 参见 Q. 75, a. 5, ad 4.

something; wherefore we seek for difference where we also find resemblance. For this reason, things which differ must in some way be composite, since they differ in something, and in something resemble each other. In this sense, although all that differ are diverse, yet all things that are diverse do not differ, as is said in *Metaph.* x.[1] For simple beings are diverse through themselves, and do not differ from one another by differences as their components. For instance, a man and an ass differ by the difference of rational and irrational; but we cannot say that these again differ by some further difference.

Second Article
WHETHER THE SOUL WAS PRODUCED BY CREATION?

We proceed thus to the Second Article:—

Objection 1. It would seem that the soul was not produced by creation. For that which has in itself something material is produced from matter. But the soul is in part material, since it is not a pure act. Therefore the soul was made of matter; and hence it was not created.

Obj. 2. Further, every actuality of matter is educed from the potentiality of that matter; for since matter is in potentiality to act, any act pre-exists in matter potentially. But the soul is the act of corporeal matter, as is clear from its definition.[2] Therefore the soul is educed from the potentiality of matter.

Obj. 3. Further, the soul is a form. Therefore, if the soul is created, all other forms also are created. Thus no forms would come into existence by generation; which is not true.

On the contrary, It is written (*Gen.* i. 27): *God created man to His own image.* But man is in the image of God according to his soul. Therefore the soul was created.

---

1. 参见 Aristotle, *Metaph.*, IV, 9 (1018a 11).
2. 参见 Aristotle, *De An.*, II, 1 (412a 27).

I answer that, The rational soul can be made only by creation, which, however, is not true of other forms. The reason is that, since to be made is the way to being, a thing must be made in such a way as is suitable to its mode of being. Now that properly exists which itself has being, as it were, subsisting in its own being. Therefore, only substances are properly and truly called beings, whereas an accident has not being, but something is by it, and so far is it called a being: for instance, whiteness is called a being because by it something is white. Hence it is said in *Metaph.* vii. that an accident should be described as *of something rather than as something.*[1] The same is to be said of all non-subsistent forms. Therefore, properly speaking, it does not belong to any non-subsisting form to be made; but such are said to be made by the fact that the composite substances are made. On the other hand, the rational soul is a subsistent form, as was explained above,[2] and so it is competent to be and to be made. And since it cannot be made of pre-existing matter, —whether corporeal, which would render it a corporeal being,—or spiritual, which would involve the transmutation of one spiritual substance into another, we must conclude that it cannot come to be except by creation.

Reply Obj. 1. The soul's simple essence is as the material element, while its participated being is its formal element; which participated being necessarily accompanies the soul's essence, because being naturally follows the form. The same reason holds if the soul is supposed to be composed of some spiritual matter, as some maintain,[3] because that sort of matter is not in potentiality to another form, as neither is the matter of a celestial body; or otherwise the soul would be corruptible. Hence, the soul cannot in any way be made of pre-existent matter.

---

1. 参见 Aristotle, *Metaph.*, VI, 1 (1028a 25).
2. 参见 Q. 75, a. 2.
3. 参见 Cf. above, q. 50, a. 2; q. 75, a. 6.

Reply Obj. 2. The education of an act from the potentiality of matter is nothing else than that something becomes actual that previously was in potentiality. But since the rational soul does not depend in its being on corporeal matter, but is subsistent, and exceeds the capacity of corporeal matter, as we have seen,[1] it is not educed from the potentiality of matter.

Reply Obj. 3. As we have said, there is no comparison between the rational soul and other forms.

Third Article
WHETHER THE RATIONAL SOUL IS PRODUCED BY GOD IMMEDIATELY?

We proceed thus to the Third Article:—

Objection 1. It would seem that the rational soul is not immediately made by God, but by the instrumentality of the angels. For spiritual things have more order than corporeal things. But inferior bodies are produced by means of the superior, as Dionysius says.[2] Therefore the inferior spirits, that is, the rational souls, also are produced by means of the superior spirits, the angels.

Obj. 2. Further, the end corresponds to the beginning of things; for God is the beginning and end of all things. Therefore the coming of things from their beginning corresponds to their return to their end. But *inferior things return through the higher*, as Dionysius says.[3] Therefore the inferior are likewise brought into being by the higher, that is, souls by angels.

Obj. 3. Further, *that is perfect which can produce its like*, as is stated in

---

1. 参见 Q. 75, a. 2.
2. 参见 *De Div. Nom.*, IV, 4 (PG 3, 697).
3. 参见 *De Eccles. Hier.*, V, 4 (PG 3, 504).

Meteor. iv.[1] But spiritual substances are much more perfect than the corporeal. Therefore, since bodies produce their like in their own species, much more are angels able to produce something specifically inferior to themselves; and such is the rational soul.

On the contrary, It is written (*Gen.* ii. 7) that God Himself *breathed into the face of man the breath of life.*

I answer that, Some have held that angels, acting by the power of God, produce rational souls.[2] But this is quite impossible, and against faith. For it has been proved that the rational soul cannot be produced except by creation. Now, God alone can create, for the first agent alone can act without presupposing the existence of anything; while a second cause always presupposes something derived from the first cause, as was above explained.[3] Now every agent that presupposes something to its act acts by producing a change. Therefore everything else acts by producing a change, whereas God alone acts by creation. Since, therefore, the rational soul cannot be produced by a change in matter, it cannot be produced save immediately by God.

Thus the replies to the objections are clear. For that bodies produce their like or something inferior to themselves, and that the higher things direct the inferior,—all these things are effected through some change.

Fourth Article
WHETHER THE HUMAN SOUL WAS PRODUCED BEFORE THE BODY?

We proceed thus to the Fourth Article:—

Objection 1. It would seem that the human soul was made before the

---

1. 参见 Aristotle, *Meteor.*, IV, 3 (380a 14).
2. 参见 Avicenna, *Metaph.*, IX, 4 (104vb).—Cf. also *De Causis*, III (p. 163).
3. 参见 Q. 65, a. 3.

body. For the work of creation preceded the work of distinction and adornment, as was shown above.[1] But the soul was made by creation, whereas the body was made at the end of the work of adornment, as we have said.[2] Therefore the soul of man was made before the body.

Obj. 2. Further, the rational soul has more in common with the angels than with brute animals. But angels were created before bodies, or at least, in the beginning with corporeal matter; whereas the body of man was formed on the sixth day, when brute animals also were made. Therefore the soul of man was created before the body.

Obj. 3. Further, the end is proportioned to the beginning. But in the end the soul outlasts the body. Therefore in the beginning it was created before the body.

On the contrary, The proper act is produced in its proper potentiality. Therefore, since the soul is the proper act of the body, the soul was produced in the body.

I answer that, Origen held that not only the soul of the first man, but also the souls of all men were created at the same time as the angels, before their bodies.[3] For he thought that all spiritual substances, whether souls or angels, are equal in their natural condition, and differ only by merit; so that some of them—namely, the souls of men or of heavenly bodies —are united to bodies, while others remain in their different orders entirely free from matter. Of this opinion we have already spoken,[4] and so we need say nothing about it here.

Augustine,[5] however, says that the soul of the first man was created at the same time as the angels, before the body, for another reason. For he supposes that the body of man, during the work of the six days,

---

1. 参见 Q. 66, a. 1; q. 70, a. 1.
2. 参见 Q. 72.
3. 参见 *Peri Archon*, I, 6; 8; II, 9 (PG 11, 166; 178; 229).
4. 参见 Q. 47, a. 2.
5. 参见 *De Genesi ad Litt.*, VII, 24; 28 (PL 34, 368; 370).

was produced, not actually, but only according to some *causal principles*; which cannot be said of the soul, because neither was it made of any pre-existing corporeal or spiritual matter, nor could it be produced from any created seminal principle. Therefore it seems that the soul itself was created together with the angels during the work of the six days when all things were made; and that afterwards the soul was inclined by its own will to the care of the body. But he does not say this by way of assertion, as his words prove. For he says: *We may believe, if neither Scripture nor reason forbids, that man was made on the sixth day, in the sense that the causal principle of his body was created in the elements of the world, but that the soul itself was already created.*[1]

Now this could be upheld by those who hold that the soul has of itself a complete species and nature,[2] and that it is not united to the body as its form, but as its administrator. But if the soul is united to the body as its form, and is naturally a part of human nature, the above supposition is quite impossible. For it is clear that God made the first things in their perfect natural state, as their species required. Now the soul, as a part of human nature, has its natural perfection only as united to the body. Therefore it would have been unfitting for the soul to be created without the body.

Therefore, if we admit the opinion of Augustine about the work of the six days,[3] we may say that the human soul preceded in the work of the six days according to a certain generic likeness, so far as it has intellectual nature in common with the angels; but it was itself created at the same time as the body. According to other saints, however, both the body and soul of the first man were produced in the work of the six days.[4]

---

1. 参见 *Op. cit.*, VII, 24 (PL 34, 368).
2. 参见 Cf. above, q. 76, a. 1.
3. 参见 *De Genesi ad Litt.*, IV, 26; 33; V, 3; 23 (PL 34, 314; 318; 323; 338).
4. 参见 Cf. above, q. 74, a. 2.

Reply Obj. 1. If the soul by its nature were a complete species, so that it might be created by itself, this reason would prove that the soul was created by itself in the beginning. But as the soul is naturally the form of the body, it was necessarily created, not separately, but in the body.

Reply Obj. 2. The same observation applies to the second objection. For if the soul had of itself a complete species, it would have something still more in common with the angels. But, as the form of the body, it belongs to the genus animal as a formal principle.

Reply Obj. 3. That the soul remains after the body is due to a defect of the body, namely, death. This defect was not due when the soul was first created.

Question XCI
THE PRODUCTION OF THE BODY OF THE FIRST MAN
(*In Four Articles*)

WE have now to consider the production of the body of the first man. Under this head there are four points of inquiry: (1) The matter from which it was produced. (2) The author by whom it was produced. (3) The disposition it received in its production. (4) The mode and order of its production.

First Article
WHETHER THE BODY OF THE FIRST MAN WAS MADE OF THE SLIME OF THE EARTH?

We proceed thus to the First Article:—

Objection 1. It would seem that the body of the first man was not made of the slime of the earth. For it is an act of greater power to make something out of nothing than out of something; because *not being* is farther from actuality than *being in potentiality*. But since man is the most noble of God's lower creatures, it was fitting that in the production of man's body the power of God should be most clearly shown. Therefore it should not have been made of the slime of the earth, but out of nothing.

Obj. 2. Further, the heavenly bodies are nobler than earthly bodies. But the human body has the greatest nobility, since it is perfected by the noblest form, which is the rational soul. Therefore it should not be made of an earthly body, but of a heavenly body.

Obj. 3. Further, fire and air are nobler bodies than earth and water, as is clear from their fineness. Therefore, since the human body is most noble, it should rather have been made of fire and air than of the slime of the earth.

Obj. 4. Further, the human body is composed of the four elements. Therefore it was not made of the slime of the earth, but of the four elements.

On the contrary, It is written (*Gen.* ii. 7): *God made man of the slime of the earth.*

I answer that, As God is perfect, in His works He bestowed perfection on all according to their capacity: *God's works are perfect* (*Deut.* xxxii. 4). Now He Himself is absolutely perfect by the fact that *all things are precontained* in Him, not as component parts, but as *united in one simple whole*, as Dionysius says;[1] just as various effects pre-exist in their cause, according to its one power. This perfection is bestowed on the angels, according as all things which are produced by God in nature through diverse forms come under their knowledge. But on man this perfection is bestowed in an inferior way. For he does not possess a natural knowledge of all natural things, but is in a manner composed of all things, since he has in himself a rational soul of the genus of spiritual substances, and in likeness to the heavenly bodies he is removed from contraries by an equable temperament. As to the elements, he has them in their very substance, yet in such a way that the higher elements, fire and air, predominate in him by their power; for life is mostly found where there is heat, which is from fire, and where there is moisture, which is of the air. But the inferior elements abound in man by their substance, for otherwise the mingling of elements would not be evenly balanced, unless the inferior elements, which have the less power, predominated in quantity. Therefore the

1. 参见 *De Div. Nom.*, V, 9 (PG 3, 825).

body of man is said to have been formed from the slime of the earth, because earth and water mingled are called slime. So, too, man is called *a miniature world*[1],[2] because all creatures of the world are in a way to be found in him.

Reply Obj. 1. The power of the divine creator was manifested in man's body in that its matter was produced by creation. But it was fitting that the human body should be made of the four elements, that man might have something in common with inferior bodies, as being on the boundary between spiritual and corporeal substances.

Reply Obj. 2. Although a heavenly body is in itself nobler than an earthly body, yet for the operations of the rational soul the heavenly body is less adapted. For the rational soul receives the knowledge of reality in a way through the senses, whose organs cannot be formed of a heavenly body which is impassible. Nor is it true that something of the fifth essence enters materially into the composition of the human body, as some say, who suppose that the soul is united to the body by means of some sort of light.[3] For, first of all, what they say is false —that light is a body. Secondly, it is impossible for something to be taken from the fifth essence, or from a heavenly body, and to be mingled with the elements, since a heavenly body is impassible; and so it does not enter into the composition of mixed bodies, except as its power produces some effect.

Reply Obj. 3. If fire and air, whose action is of greater power, predominated also in quantity in the human body, they would entirely draw the rest into themselves, and there would be no equality in the mixture, such as is required in the composition of man for the sense of touch, which is the foundation of the other senses. For the organ of

---

1. miniature world: 小宇宙；微型世界
2. 参见 Cf. Aristotle, *Phys.*, VIII, 2 (252b 26); Nemesius, *De Nat. Hom.*, I (PG 40, 533).
3. 参见 Cf. above, q. 76, a. 7.

any particular sense must not have actually the contraries of which that sense has the perception, but only potentially. This can take place either in such a way that it is entirely without the whole *genus* of such contraries, —thus, for instance, the pupil of the eye is without color, so as to be in potentiality to all colors (this is not possible in the organ of touch, since it is composed of the elements whose qualities are perceived by touch); or so that the organ is a mean between two contraries, as must needs be the case with touch, for the mean is in potentiality to the extremes.

Reply Obj. 4. In the slime of the earth are earth, and water joining the parts of the earth together. Of the other elements Scripture makes no mention, both because they are less in quantity in the human body, as we have said, and because in the account of the creation no mention is made of fire and air, which are not perceived by senses of backward people such as those to whom the Scripture was immediately addressed.

Second Article

WHETHER THE HUMAN BODY WAS IMMEDIATELY PRODUCED BY GOD?

We proceed thus to the Second Article:—

Objection 1. It would seem that the human body was not produced by God immediately. For Augustine says that *corporeal things are disposed by God through the angels.*[1] But the human body was formed from corporeal matter, as was stated above. Therefore it should have been produced by the instrumentality of the angels, and not immediately by God.

Obj. 2. Further, whatever can be made by a created power, is not necessarily produced immediately by God. But the human body can

1. 参见 *De Trin.*, III, 4 (PL 42, 873).

be produced by the created power of a heavenly body, for even certain animals are produced from putrefaction by the active power of a heavenly body; and Albumazar says that man is not generated where heat and cold are extreme, but only in temperate regions.[1] Therefore, the human body was not necessarily produced immediately by God.

Obj. 3. Further, nothing is made out of corporeal matter except by some material change. But all corporeal change is caused by a movement of a heavenly body, which is the first of movements. Therefore, since the human body was produced from corporeal matter, it seems that a heavenly body had part in its production.

Obj. 4. Further, Augustine says[2] that man's body was made, during the work of the six days, according to the causal principles which God inserted in the corporeal creation; and that afterwards it was actually formed. But what pre-exists in the corporeal creature according to causal principles can be produced through some corporeal power. Therefore the human body was produced by some created power, and not immediately by God.

On the contrary, It is written (*Ecclus.* xvii. 1): *God created man out of the earth.*

I answer that, The first formation of the human body could not be by the instrumentality of any created power, but was immediately from God. Some, indeed, supposed that the forms which are in corporeal matter are derived from some immaterial forms;[3] but the Philosopher refutes this opinion for the reason that *forms cannot be made in themselves, but only composites can*,[4] as we have explained.[5] And because the agent must be like its effect, it is not fitting that a pure form, not existing in

1. 参见 Cf. P. Duhem, *Système du Monde* (II, 369).
2. 参见 *De Genesi ad Litt.*, VII, 24 (PL 34, 368).
3. 参见 Cf. above, q. 45, a. 8; q. 65, a. 4.
4. 参见 *Metaph.*, VI, 8 (1033b 16).
5. 参见 Q. 45, a. 8; q. 65, a. 4; q. 90, a. 2.

matter, should produce a form which is in matter, and which is made only by the fact that the composite is made. So it is a form which is in matter that can be the cause of another form that is in matter, according as composite is made by composite. Now God, though He is absolutely immaterial, can alone by His own power produce matter by creation; and so He alone can produce a form in matter, without the aid of any preceding material form. For this reason the angels cannot transform a body except by making use of certain seminal principles, as Augustine says.[1] Therefore, as no pre-existing body had been formed, through whose power another body of the same species could be generated, the first human body was of necessity made immediately by God.

Reply Obj. 1. Although the angels are to some extent the ministers of God, as regards what He does in bodies, yet God does something in bodies beyond the angels' power, as, for instance, raising the dead, or giving sight to the blind; and by this power He formed the body of the first man from the slime of the earth. Nevertheless, the angels could act as ministers in the formation of the body of the first man, in the same way as they will do at the last resurrection, by gathering the dust.

Reply Obj. 2. Perfect animals, produced from seed, cannot be made by the sole power of a heavenly body, as Avicenna imagined;[2] although the power of a heavenly body may assist by co-operation in the work of natural generation, for as the Philosopher says, *man and the sun beget man from matter.*[3] For this reason, a place of moderate temperature is required for the production of man and other perfect animals. But the power of the heavenly bodies suffices for the production of some imperfect animals from properly disposed matter; for it is clear that more conditions are required to produce a perfect than an imperfect

1. 参见 *De Trin.*, III, 8; 9 (PL 42, 876; 878).
2. 参见 Cf. above, q. 71, a. 1, ad 1.
3. 参见 *Phys.*, II, 2 (194b 13).

thing.

Reply Obj. 3. The movement of the heavens causes natural changes, but not changes that surpass the order of nature and are caused by the divine power alone, as for the dead to be raised to life, or the blind to see; and the making of man from the slime of the earth is a work of this sort.

Reply Obj. 4. An effect may be said to pre-exist according to causal principles in creatures, in two ways. First, both in active and in passive potentiality, so that not only can it be produced out of pre-existing matter, but also that some pre-existing creature can produce it. Secondly, in passive potentiality only, that is, that it can be produced out of pre-existing matter by God. In this sense, according to Augustine, the human body pre-existed in the works produced in their causal principles.

Third Article
WHETHER THE BODY OF MAN WAS GIVEN AN APT DISPOSITION?

We proceed thus to the Third Article:—

Objection 1. It would seem that the body of man was not given an apt disposition. For since man is the noblest of animals, his body ought to be the best disposed in what is proper to an animal, that is, in sense and movement. But some animals have sharper senses and quicker movement than man; and thus dogs have a keener smell, and birds a swifter flight. Therefore man's body was not aptly disposed.

Obj. 2. Further, that is perfect which lacks nothing. But the human body lacks more than the bodies of other animals, for these are provided with covering and natural arms of defense, in which man is lacking. Therefore the human body is very imperfectly disposed.

Obj. 3. Further, man is more distant from plants than he is from the brutes. But plants are erect in stature, while brutes are prone in stature.

Therefore man should not be of erect stature.

On the contrary, It is written (*Eccles.* vii. 30): *God made man right.*

I answer that, All natural things were produced by the divine art, and so may be called God's works of art. Now every artist intends to give to his work the best disposition; not absolutely the best, but the best as regards the proposed end. And even if this entails some defect, the artist cares not. Thus, for instance, when a man makes himself a saw for the purpose of cutting, he makes it of iron, which is suitable for the object in view; and he does not prefer to make it of glass, though this be a more beautiful material, because this very beauty would be an obstacle to the end he has in view. Therefore God gave to each natural being the best disposition; not absolutely so, but in view of its proper end. This is what the Philosopher says: *And because it is better so, not absolutely, but for each one's substance.*[1]

Now the proximate end of the human body is the rational soul and its operations; for matter is for the sake of the form, and instruments are for the actions of the agent. I say, therefore, that God fashioned the human body in that disposition which was best according as it was most suited to such a form and to such operations. If defect exists in the disposition of the human body, it is well to observe that such defect arises, as a necessary result of the matter, from the conditions required in the body in order to make it suitably proportioned to the soul and its operations.

Reply Obj. 1. The sense of touch, which is the foundation of the other senses, is more perfect in man than in any other animal; and for this reason man must have the most equable temperament of all animals. Moreover, man also excels all other animals in the interior sensitive powers, as is clear from what we have said above.[2] But by a kind of necessity, man falls short of the other animals in some of

---

1. 参见 *Op. cit.*, II, 7 (198b 8).
2. 参见 Q. 78, a. 4.

the exterior senses; and thus of all animals he has the weakest sense of smell. For of all animals man needs the largest brain as compared to the body; and this both for his greater freedom of action in the interior powers required for the intellectual operations, as we have seen above,[1] and in order that the low temperature of the brain may modify the heat of the heart, which has to be considerable in man for him to be able to stand up erect. So it happens that the size of the brain, by reason of its humidity, is an impediment to the smell, which requires dryness. In the same way, we may suggest a reason why some animals have a keener sight, and a more acute hearing than man, namely, because of a hindrance to his senses arising necessarily from the perfect equability of his temperament. The same reason suffices to explain why some animals are more rapid in movement than man, since this excellence of speed is inconsistent with the equability of the human temperament.

Reply Obj. 2. Horns and claws, which are the weapons of some animals, and toughness of hide and quantity of hair or feathers, which are the clothing of animals, are signs of an abundance of the earthly element; which does not agree with the equability and softness of the human temperament. Therefore such things do not suit the nature of man. Instead of these, he has reason and hands whereby he can make himself arms and clothes, and other necessaries of life, of infinite variety. And so the hand is called by Aristotle *the organ of organs.*[2] Moreover it was more becoming to a rational nature, which is capable of conceiving an infinite number of things, to have the power of devising for itself an infinite number of instruments.

Reply Obj. 3. An upright stature was becoming to man for four reasons. First, because the senses are given to man, not only for the purpose of procuring the necessaries of life, for which they are

---

1. 参见 Q. 84, a. 7.
2. 参见 Aristotle, *De An.*, III, 8 (432a 1).

bestowed on other animals, but also for the purpose of knowledge. Hence, whereas the other animals take delight in the things of sense only as ordered to food and sex, man alone takes pleasure in the beauty of sensible things for its own sake. Therefore, as the senses are situated chiefly in the face, other animals have the face turned to the ground, as it were for the purpose of seeking food and procuring a livelihood; whereas man has his face erect, in order that by the senses, and chiefly by sight, which is more subtle and reveals many differences in things, he may freely survey the sensible things around him, both heavenly and earthly, so as to gather intelligible truth from all things. Secondly, for the greater freedom of the acts of the interior powers, which requires that the brain, wherein these actions are, in a way, performed, be not low down, but lifted up above other parts of the body. Thirdly, because if man's figure were prone to the ground, he would need to use his hands as fore-feet, and thus their utility for other purposes would cease. Fourthly, because if man's figure were prone to the ground, and he used his hands as fore-feet, he would be obliged to take hold of his food with his mouth. Thus he would have a protruding mouth, with thick and hard lips, and also a hard tongue, so as to keep it from being hurt by exterior things; as we see in other animals. Now such a disposition would completely hinder speech, which is the proper work of the reason.

Nevertheless, though of erect stature, man is far above plants. For man's superior part, his head, is turned towards the superior part of the world, and his inferior part is turned towards the inferior world; and therefore he is perfectly disposed as to the general situation of his body. Plants have the superior part turned towards the lower world, since their roots correspond to the mouth; and their inferior part towards the upper world. But brute animals have a middle disposition, for the superior part of the animal is that by which it takes food, and the inferior part that by which it rids itself of the surplus.

Fourth Article

WHETHER THE PRODUCTION OF THE HUMAN BODY IS FITTINGLY DESCRIBED IN SCRIPTURE?

We proceed thus to the Fourth Article:—

Objection 1. It would seem that the production of the human body is not fittingly described in Scripture (*Gen.* i. 26; ii. 7). For, as the human body was made by God, so also were the other works of the six days. But in the other works it is written, *God said: Let it be made, and it was made.* Therefore the same should have been said of man.

Obj. 2. Further, the human body was made by God immediately, as was explained above. Therefore it was not fittingly said, *Let us make man.*

Obj. 3. Further, the form of the human body is the soul itself which is the breath of life. Therefore, having said, *God made man of the slime of the earth*, it should not have added: *And He breathed into him the breath of life.*

Obj. 4. Further, the soul, which is the breath of life, is in the whole body, and chiefly in the heart. Therefore it was not fittingly said: *He breathed into his face the breath of life.*

Obj. 5. Further, the male and female sex belong to the body, while the image of God belongs to the soul. But the soul, according to Augustine, was made before the body.[1] Therefore, having said: *To His image He made them*, it should not have added, *male and female He created them.*

On the contrary, Is the authority of Scripture.

Reply Obj. 1. As Augustine observes,[2] man does not surpass other things in the fact that God Himself made man, as though He did not

---

1. 参见 *De Genesi ad Litt.*, VII, 24; 28 (PL 34, 368; 370).
2. 参见 *Op. cit.*, VI, 12 (PL 34, 362).

make other things; since it is written (*Ps.* ci. 26), *The work of Thy hands is the heaven*, and elsewhere (*Ps.* xciv. 5), *His hands laid down the dry land.* But man surpasses other things in this, that he is made in God's image. Yet in describing man's production, Scripture uses a special way of speaking in order to show that other things were made for man's sake. For we are accustomed to perform with more deliberation and care what we principally intend.

Reply Obj. 2. We must not imagine that when God said *Let us make man*, He spoke to the angels, as some perversely thought.[1] But by these words is signified the plurality of the divine Person, Whose image is more clearly expressed in man.

Reply Obj. 3. Some have thought that man's body was formed first in priority of time, and that afterwards the soul was infused into the already formed body.[2] But it is inconsistent with the perfection of the first production of things that God should have made either the body without the soul, or the soul without the body, since each is a part of human nature. This is especially unfitting as regards the body, for the body depends on the soul, and not the soul on the body.

To remove the difficulty some[3] have said that the words, *God made man*, must be understood of the production of the body with the soul; and that the subsequent words, *and He breathed into his face the breath of life*, should be understood of the Holy Ghost, just as the Lord breathed on His Apostles, saying, *Receive ye the Holy Ghost* (*Jo.* xx. 22). But this explanation, as Augustine says, is excluded by the very words of Scripture.[4] For we read farther on, *And man was made a living soul*;

1. 参见 Anonymously reported in Peter Lombard, *Sent.*, II, xvi, 2 (I, 379).
2. 参见 Cf. *op. cit.*, II, xvii, 2 (I, 383); St. Augustine, *De Genesi ad Litt.*, VII, 24 (PL 34, 368).—Cf. also Hugh of St. Victor, *De Sacram.*, I, pt. 6, ch. 3 (PL 176, 265).
3. 参见 Anonymously reported by St. Augustine, *De Civit. Dei*, XIII, 24 (PL 41, 398).
4. 同上 (PL 41, 401).

which words the Apostle (*1 Cor.* xv. 45) refers not to spiritual life, but to animal life. Therefore, by the *breath of life* we must understand the soul, so that the words, *He breathed into his face the breath of life*, are a sort of exposition of what had gone before; for the soul is the form of the body.

Reply Obj. 4. Since vital operations are more clearly seen in man's face, because of the senses which are there found, therefore Scripture says that the breath of life was breathed into man's face.

Reply Obj. 5. According to Augustine, the works of the six days were done all at one time.[1] Therefore, according to him, man's soul, which he holds to have been made with the angels, was not made before the sixth day; but on the sixth day itself both the soul of the first man was made actually, and his body was made in its causal principles. But other doctors hold that on the sixth day both the body and soul of man were made actually.[2]

---

1. 参见 *De Genesi ad Litt.*, IV, 33; 34 (PL 34, 318; 319).
2. 参见 Cf. above, q. 90, a. 4.

Question XCII
THE PRODUCTION OF WOMAN
(*In Four Articles*)

WE must next consider the production of the woman. Under this head there are four points of inquiry: (1) Whether woman should have been made in that first production of things? (2) Whether woman should have been made from man? (3) Whether of man's rib? (4) Whether woman was made immediately by God?

First Article
WHETHER WOMAN SHOULD HAVE BEEN MADE IN THE FIRST PRODUCTION OF THINGS?

We proceed thus to the First Article:—

Objection 1. It would seem that woman should not have been made in the first production of things. For the Philosopher says that the *female is a misbegotten male.*[1] But nothing misbegotten or defective should have been in the first production of things. Therefore woman should not have been made at that first production.

Obj. 2. Further, subjection and limitation were a result of sin, for to the woman was it said after sin (*Gen.* iii. 16): *Thou shalt be under the man's power*; and Gregory says that, *Where there is no sin, there is no inequality.*[2] But woman is naturally of less strength and dignity than man, *for*

---

1. 参见 *De Gener. Anim.*, II, 3 (737a 27).
2. 参见 *Moral.*, XXI, 15 (PL 76, 203).

the agent is always more honorable than the patient, as Augustine says.[1] Therefore woman should not have been made in the first production of things before sin.

Obj. 3. Further, occasions of sin should be cut off. But God foresaw that woman would be an occasion of sin to man. Therefore He should not have made woman.

On the contrary, It is written (*Gen.* ii. 18): *It is not good for man to be alone; let us make him a helper like to himself.*

I answer that, It was necessary for woman to be made, as the Scripture says, as *a helper* to man; not, indeed, as a helpmate in other works, as some say,[2] since man can be more efficiently helped by another man in other works; but as a helper in the work of generation. This can be made clear if we observe the mode of generation carried out in various living things. Some living things do not possess in themselves the power of generation, but are generated by an agent of another species; and such are those plants and animals which are generated, without seed, from suitable matter through the active power of the heavenly bodies. Others possess the active and passive generative power together, as we see in plants which are generated from seed. For the noblest vital function in plants is generation, and so we observe that in these the active power of generation invariably accompanies the passive power. Among perfect animals, the active power of generation belongs to the male sex, and the passive power to the female. And as among animals there is a vital operation nobler than generation, to which their life is principally directed, so it happens that the male sex is not found in continual union with the female in perfect animals, but only at the time of coition; so that we may consider that by coition the male and female are one, as in

1. 参见 *De Genesi ad Litt.*, XII, 16 (PL 34, 467).
2. 参见 Anonymously reported by St. Augustine, *De Genesi ad Litt.*, IX, 3 (PL 34, 395).

plants they are always united, even though in some cases one of them preponderates, and in some the other. But man is further ordered to a still nobler work of life, and that is intellectual operation. Therefore there was greater reason for the distinction of these two powers in man; so that the female should be produced separately from the male, and yet that they should be carnally united for generation. Therefore directly after the formation of woman, it was said: *And they shall be two in one flesh* (*Gen.* ii. 24).

Reply Obj. 1. As regards the individual nature, woman is defective and misbegotten, for the active power in the male seed tends to the production of a perfect likeness according to the masculine sex; while the production of woman comes from defect in the active power, or from some material indisposition, or even from some external influence, such as that of a south wind, which is moist, as the Philosopher observes.[1] On the other hand, as regards universal human nature, woman is not misbegotten, but is included in nature's intention as directed to the work of generation. Now the universal intention of nature depends on God, Who is the universal Author of nature. Therefore, in producing nature, God formed not only the male but also the female.

Reply Obj. 2. Subjection is twofold. One is servile, by virtue of which a superior makes use of a subject for his own benefit; and this kind of subjection began after sin. There is another kind of subjection, which is called economic or civil, whereby the superior makes use of his subjects for their own benefit and good; and this kind of subjection existed even before sin. For the good of order would have been wanting in the human family if some were not governed by others wiser than themselves. So by such a kind of subjection woman is naturally subject to man, because in man the discernment of reason predominates. Nor

---

1. 参见 Aristotle, *De Gener. Anim.*, IV, 2 (766b 33).

is inequality among men excluded by the state of innocence, as we shall prove.[1]

Reply Obj. 3. If God had deprived the world of all those things which proved an occasion of sin, the universe would have been imperfect. Nor was it fitting for the common good to be destroyed in order that individual evil might be avoided; especially as God is so powerful that He can direct any evil to a good end.

Second Article

WHETHER WOMAN SHOULD HAVE BEEN MADE FROM MAN?

We proceed thus to the Second Article:—

Objection 1. It would seem that woman should not have been made from man. For sex belongs both to man and animals. But in the other animals the female was not made from the male. Therefore neither should it have been so with man.

Obj. 2. Further, things of the same species are of the same matter. But male and female are of the same species. Therefore, as man was made of the slime of the earth, so woman should have been made of the same, and not from man.

Obj. 3. Further, woman was made to be a helpmate to man in the work of generation. But close relationship makes a person unfit for that office; and hence near relations are debarred from intermarriage, as is written (*Lev.* xviii. 6). Therefore woman should not have been made from man.

On the contrary, It is written (*Ecclus.* xvii. 5): *He created of him*, that is, out of man, *a helpmate like to himself*, that is, woman.

I answer that, When all things were first made, it was more suitable

---

1. 参见 Q. 96, a. 3.

for woman to be formed from man than for this to happen in other animals. First, in order thus to give the first man a certain dignity consisting in this, that as God is the principle of the whole universe, so the first man, in likeness to God, was the principle of the whole human race. Hence Paul says that *God made the whole human race from one* (*Acts* xvii. 26). Secondly, that man might love woman all the more, and cleave to her more closely, knowing her to be fashioned from himself. Hence it is written (*Gen.* ii. 23, 24): *She was taken out of man, wherefore a man shall leave father and mother, and shall cleave to his wife.* This was most necessary in the human species, in which the male and female live together for life; which is not the case with other animals. Thirdly, because, as the Philosopher says, the human male and female are united, not only for generation, as with other animals, but also for the purpose of domestic life, in which each has his or her particular duty, and in which the man is the head of the woman.[1] Therefore it was suitable for the woman to be made out of man, as out of her principle. Fourthly, there is a sacramental reason for this. For by this is signified that the Church takes her origin from Christ. Therefore the Apostle says (*Ephes.* v. 32): *This is a great sacrament; but I speak in Christ and in the Church.*

Reply Obj. 1 is clear from the foregoing.

Reply Obj. 2. Matter is that from which something is made. Now created nature has a determinate principle, and since it is determined to one thing, it has also a determinate mode of proceeding. Therefore from determinate matter it produces something in a determinate species. On the other hand, the divine power, being infinite, can produce things of the same species out of any matter, such as a man from the slime of the earth, and a woman from a man.

Reply Obj. 3. A certain affinity arises from natural generation,

---

1. 参见 *Eth.*, VIII, 12 (1162a 19).

and this is an impediment to matrimony. Woman, however, was not produced from man by natural generation, but by the divine power alone. Hence Eve is not called the daughter of Adam. And so this argument does not prove.

Third Article
WHETHER THE WOMAN WAS FITTINGLY MADE FROM THE RIB OF MAN?

We proceed thus to the Third Article:—

Objection 1. It would seem that woman should not have been formed from the rib of man. For the rib was much smaller than the woman's body. Now from a smaller thing a larger thing can be made only—either by addition (and then the woman ought to have been described as made out of that which was added, rather than out of the rib itself); —or by rarefaction, because, as Augustine says: *A body cannot increase in bulk except by rarefaction.*[1] But woman's body is not more rarefied than man's —at least, not in the proportion of a rib to Eve's body. Therefore Eve was not formed from a rib of Adam.

Obj. 2. Further, in those things which were first created there was nothing superfluous. Therefore a rib of Adam belonged to the integrity of his body. So, if a rib was removed, his body remained imperfect; which is unreasonable to suppose.

Obj. 3. Further, a rib cannot be removed from man without pain. But there was no pain before sin. Therefore it was not right for a rib to be taken from the man, that Eve might be made from it.

On the contrary, It is written (*Gen.* ii. 22): *God built the rib, which He took from Adam, into a woman.*

I answer that, It was right for woman to be made from a rib of man.

---

1. 参见 *De Genesi ad Litt.*, X, 26 (PL 34, 428).

First, to signify the social union of man and woman, for the woman should neither use authority over man, and so she was not made from his head; nor was it right for her to be subject to man's contempt as his slave, and so she was not made from his feet. Secondly, for the sacramental signification; for from the side of Christ sleeping on the Cross the Sacraments flowed —namely, blood and water —on which the Church was established.

Reply Obj. 1. Some[1] say that woman's body was formed by a material increase, without anything being added, in the same way as our Lord multiplied the five loaves. But this is quite impossible. For such an increase of matter would either be by a change of the very substance of the matter itself, or by a change of its dimensions. It was not by a change of the substance of the matter, both because matter, considered in itself, is quite unchangeable, since it has a potential existence, and has nothing but the nature of a subject; and because multiplication and size are extraneous to the essence of matter itself. And so, the multiplication of matter is quite unintelligible, as long as the matter itself remains the same without anything added to it, unless it receives greater dimensions. This implies rarefaction[2], which is for the same matter to receive greater dimensions, as the Philosopher says.[3] To say, therefore, that the same matter is enlarged, without being rarefied, is to combine contradictories —viz., the definition with the absence of the thing defined.

Therefore, as no rarefaction is apparent in such multiplications[4] of matter, we must admit an addition of matter, either by creation or, what is more probable, by conversion. Hence Augustine says that

---

1. 参见 Hugh of St. Victor, *De Sacram.*, I, pt. 6, ch. 36 (PL 176, 284); Peter Lombard, *Sent.*, II, xviii, 4 (I, 389).
2. rarefaction: 变稀薄；稀薄
3. 参见 *Phys.*, IV, 9 (217a 25).
4. multiplication: 繁殖；乘法

Christ filled five thousand men with five loaves, in the same way as from a few seeds He produces the harvest of corn[1] —that is, by transformation of the nourishment. Nevertheless, we say that the crowds were fed with five loaves, or that woman was made from the rib, because an addition was made to the already existing matter of the loaves and of the rib.

Reply Obj. 2. The rib belonged to the integral perfection of Adam, not as an individual, but as the principle of the human race; just as the semen belongs to the perfection of the begetter, and is released by a natural and pleasurable operation. Much more, therefore, was it possible that by the divine power the body of woman should be produced from the man's rib.

From this it is clear how to answer the third objection.

Fourth Article
WHETHER WOMAN WAS FORMED IMMEDIATELY BY GOD?

We proceed thus to the Fourth Article:—

Objection 1. It would seem that woman was not formed immediately by God. For no individual is produced immediately by God from another individual alike in species. But woman was made from man, who is of the same species. Therefore she was not made immediately by God.

Obj. 2. Further, Augustine says that corporeal things are governed by God through the angels.[2] But woman's body was formed from corporeal matter. Therefore it was made through the ministry of the angels, and not immediately by God.

Obj. 3. Further, those things which pre-exist in creatures in their causal principles are produced by the power of some creature, and not immediately by God, But woman's body was produced in its causal

1. 参见 *Tract.* XXIV, super *Ioann.*, VI, 2 (PL 35, 1593).
2. 参见 *De Trin.*, III, 4 (PL 42, 873).

principles among the first created works, as Augustine says.[1] Therefore it was not produced immediately by God.

On the contrary, Augustine says, in the same work: *God alone, to Whom all nature owes its existence, could form or fashion woman from man's rib.*[2]

I answer that, As was said above, the natural generation of every species is from some determinate matter. Now the matter whence man is naturally begotten is the human semen of man or woman. Therefore an individual of the human species cannot be generated naturally from any other matter. Now God alone, the author of nature, can bring an effect into being outside the ordinary course of nature. Therefore God alone could produce either man from the slime of the earth, or woman from the rib of man.

Reply Obj. 1. This argument is good when an individual is begotten, by natural generation, from that which is like it in species.

Reply Obj. 2. As Augustine says,[3] we do not know whether the angels were employed by God in the formation of woman; but it is certain that, as the body of man was not formed by the angels from the slime of the earth, so neither was the body of woman formed by them from the man's rib.

Reply Obj. 3. As Augustine says: *The first creation of things did not demand that woman should be made thus; it made it possible for her to be thus made.*[4] Therefore the body of woman pre-existed according to these causal principles in the first works of God, not according to an active potentiality, but according to a passive potentiality ordered to the active power of God.

---

1. 参见 *De Genesi ad Litt.*, IX, 15 (PL 34, 404).
2. 同上 (PL 34, 403).
3. 同上 (PL 34, 404).
4. 参见 *Op. cit.*, IX, 18 (PL 34, 407).

Question XCIII
THE END OR TERM OF THE PRODUCTION OF MAN
(*In Nine Articles*)

WE now treat of the end or term of man's production, inasmuch as he is said to be made *to the image and likeness of God.* There are under this head nine points of inquiry: (1) Whether the image of God is in man? (2) Whether the image of God is in irrational creatures? (3) Whether the image of God is in the angels more than in man? (4) Whether the image of God is in every man? (5) Whether the image of God is in man by comparison with the essence, or with all the divine Persons, or with one of them? (6) Whether the image of God is in man, as to his mind only? (7) Whether the image of God is in man's powers, or in his habits and acts? (8) Whether the image of God is in man by comparison with every object? (9) On the difference between *image* and *likeness.*

First Article
WHETHER THE IMAGE OF GOD IS IN MAN?

We proceed thus to the First Article:—

Objection 1. It would seem that the image of God is not in man. For it is written (*Isa.* xl. 18): *To whom have you likened God? or what image will you make for Him?*

Obj. 2. Further, to be the image of God is the property of the First-Begotten, of Whom the Apostle says (*Col.* i. 15): *Who is the image of the invisible God, the First-Born of every creature.* Therefore the image of God is not to be found in man.

Obj. 3. Further, Hilary says that *an image is of the same species as that which it represents*; and he also says that *an image is the undivided and united likeness of one thing adequately representing another.*[1] But there is no species common to both God and man, nor can there be a comparison of equality between God and man. Therefore there can be no image of God in man.

On the contrary, It is written (*Gen.* i. 26): *Let Us make man to Our own image and likeness.*

I answer that, As Augustine says, *where an image exists, there forthwith is likeness*; *but where there is likeness, there is not necessarily an image.*[2] Hence it is clear that *likeness* is essential to *image*; and that an image adds something to likeness—namely, that it is copied from something else. For an *image* is so called because it is produced as an imitation of something else; and so an egg, however much like and equal to another egg, is not called an image of the other egg, because it is not copied from it.

But equality does not belong to the essence of an image, for, as Augustine says in the same place, *where there is an image there is not necessarily equality*, as we see in a person's image reflected in a glass. Yet equality is of the essence of a perfect image, for in a perfect image nothing is wanting that is to be found in that of which it is a copy. Now it is manifest that in man there is some likeness to God, copied from God as from an exemplar; yet this likeness is not one of equality, for such an exemplar infinitely excels its copy. Therefore there is in man a likeness to God, not, indeed, a perfect likeness, but imperfect. And Scripture signifies the same thing when it says that man was made *to* God's likeness; for the preposition *to* signifies a certain approach, as of something at a distance.

---

1. 参见 *De Synod.* (PL 10, 490).
2. 参见 *Lib. 83 Quaest.*, q. 74 (PL 40, 85).

Reply Obj. 1. The Prophet speaks of bodily images made by man. Therefore he says pointedly: *What image will you make for Him?* But God made a spiritual image to Himself in man.

Reply Obj. 2. *The First-Born of creatures* is the perfect Image of God, reflecting perfectly that of which He is the Image; and so He is said to be the *Image*, and never *to the image*. But man is said to be both *image* by reason of the likeness, and *to the image* by reason of the imperfect likeness. And since the perfect likeness to God cannot be except in an identical nature, the Image of God exists in His first-born Son as the image of the king is in his son, who is of the same nature as himself; whereas it exists in man as in an alien nature, as the image of the king is in a silver coin, as Augustine explains in *De decem Chordis*.[1]

Reply Obj. 3. As unity means absence of division, a species is said to be the *same* in so far as it is *one*. Now a thing is said to be one not only numerically, specifically, or generically, but also according to a certain analogy or proportion. In this sense a creature is one with God, or like to Him; but when Hilary speaks *of a thing which adequately represents another*, this is to be understood of a perfect image.

Second Article

WHETHER THE IMAGE OF GOD IS TO BE FOUND IN IRRATIONAL CREATURES?

We proceed thus to the Second Article:—

Objection 1. It would seem that the image of God is to be found in irrational creatures. For Dionysius says: *Effects are contingent images of their causes*.[2] But God is the cause not only of rational, but also of irrational, creatures. Therefore the image of God is to be found in irrational creatures.

---

1. 参见 *Serm.* IX, 8 (PL 38, 82).
2. 参见 *De Div. Nom.*, II, 8 (PG 3, 645).

Obj. 2. Further, the more distinct a likeness is, the nearer it approaches to the nature of an image. But Dionysius says that *the solar ray has a very great likeness to the divine goodness.*[1] Therefore it is made to the image of God.

Obj. 3. Further, the more perfect anything is in goodness, the more it is like God. But the whole universe is more perfect in goodness than man; for though each individual thing is good, all things together are called *very good* (*Gen.* i. 31). Therefore the whole universe is to the image of God, and not only man.

Obj. 4. Further, Boethius says of God: *Holding the world in His mind, and forming it to His image.*[2] Therefore the whole world is to the image of God, and not only the rational creature.

On the contrary, Augustine says: *Man's excellence consists in the fact that God made him to His own image by giving him an intellectual soul, which raises him above the beasts of the field.*[3] Therefore things without intellect are not made to God's image.

I answer that, Not every likeness, not even what is copied from something else, is sufficient to make an image. For if the likeness be only generic, or existing by virtue of some common accident, this does not suffice for one thing to be the image of another. For instance, a worm, though it may originate from man, cannot be called man's image, merely because of the generic likeness; nor, if anything is made white like something else, can we say that it is the image of that thing, for whiteness is an accident belonging to many species. Consequently, the nature of an image requires likeness in species (as the image of the king exists in his son), or, at least, in some specific accident, and chiefly in the shape (as we speak of a man's image in copper). Whence

---

1. 参见 *Op. cit.*, IV, 4 (PG 3, 697).
2. 参见 *De Consol.*, III, verse 9 (PL 63, 759).
3. 参见 *De Genesi ad Litt.*, VI, 12 (PL 34, 348).

Hilary says pointedly that *an image is of the same species.*[1]

Now it is manifest that specific likeness follows the ultimate difference. Hence, some things are like God first and most commonly because they exist; secondly, because they live; and thirdly because they know or understand. These last, as Augustine says, *approach so near to God in likeness, that among all creatures nothing comes nearer to Him.*[2] It is therefore clear that, properly speaking, intellectual creatures alone are made to God's image.

Reply Obj. 1. Everything imperfect is a participation of what is perfect. Therefore even what falls short of the nature of an image, so far as it possesses any sort of likeness to God participates in some degree in the nature of an image. So Dionysius says that effects are *contingent images of their causes*, that is, as much as they happen [*contingit*] to be so, but not absolutely.

Reply Obj. 2. Dionysius compares the solar ray to divine goodness, as regards its causality, not as regards its natural dignity, which is required for the nature of an image.

Reply Obj. 3. The universe is more perfect in goodness than the intellectual creature as regards extension and diffusion; but intensively and collectively the likeness to the divine goodness is found rather in the intellectual creature, which has a capacity for the highest good. Or we may say that a part is not rightly divided against the whole, but only against another part. Therefore, when we say that the intellectual nature alone is to the image of God, we do not mean that the universe is not to God's image in any of its parts, but that other parts are excluded.

Reply Obj. 4. Boethius here uses the word *image* to express the likeness which the product of art bears to the artistic exemplar in the mind of the artist. Thus every creature is an image of the exemplary

---

1. 参见 *De Synod.* (PL 10, 490).
2. 参见 *Lib. 83 Quaest.*, q. 51 (PL 40, 32).

likeness it has in the divine mind. We are not, however, using the word *image* in this sense, but as it implies a likeness in nature, that is, inasmuch as all things, as beings, are like to the First Being: as living beings, like to the First Life; and as intelligent beings, like to the Supreme Wisdom.

Third Article

WHETHER THE ANGELS ARE MORE TO THE IMAGE OF GOD THAN MAN IS?

We proceed thus to the Third Article:—

Objection 1. It would seem that the angels are not more to the image of God than man is. For Augustine says in a sermon that God granted to no other creature besides man to be to His image.[1] Therefore it is not true to say that the angels are more than man to the image of God.

Obj. 2. Further, according to Augustine, *man is so much to God's image that he is formed by God without the interposition of any creature; and therefore nothing is more joined to Him.*[2] But a creature is called God's image so far as it is joined to God. Therefore the angels are not more to the image of God than man.

Obj. 3. Further, a creature is said to be to God's image so far as it is of an intellectual nature. But intellectual nature does not admit of intensity or remission; for it is not an accidental thing, since it is a substance. Therefore the angels are not more to the image of God than man.

On the contrary, Gregory says: *The angel is called a "seal of resemblance"* (*Ezech.* xxviii. 12) *because in him the resemblance of the divine image is wrought with greater expression.*[3]

---

1. 参见 *Serm.* XLIII, 2 (PL 38, 255).
2. 参见 *Lib. 83 Quaest.*, q. 51 (PL 40, 33).
3. 参见 *In Evang.*, II, hom. 34 (PL 76, 1250).

I answer that, We may speak of God's image in two ways. First, we may consider in it that in which the notion of image chiefly consists, that is, the intellectual nature. From this point of view, the image of God is more perfect in the angels than in man, because their intellectual nature is more perfect, as is clear from what has been said.[1] Secondly, we may consider the image of God in man as regards its accidental qualities, and from this point of view, we may observe in man a certain imitation of God, consisting in the fact that man proceeds from man, as God from God; and also in the fact that the whole human soul is in the whole body, and again, in every part, as God is in regard to the whole world. In these and like things, the image of God is more perfect in man than it is in the angels. But these do not of themselves pertain to the nature of the divine image in man, unless we presuppose the first likeness, which is in the intellectual nature; or otherwise even brute animals would be to God's image. Therefore, as in their intellectual nature the angels are more to the image of God than man is, we must grant that, absolutely speaking, the angels are more to the image of God than man is, but that man is relatively more like to God.

Reply Obj. 1. Augustine excludes inferior creatures lacking reason from the image of God; but not the angels.

Reply Obj. 2. Just as fire is said to be specifically the most subtle of bodies, while, nevertheless, one kind of fire is more subtle than another, so we say that nothing is more like to God than the human soul in the genus of intellectual nature; because, as Augustine had said previously, *things which have knowledge are so near to Him in likeness that of all creatures none are nearer.* Therefore this does not mean that the angels are not more to God's image.

Reply Obj. 3. When we say that *substance does not admit of more or less,*[2]

---

1. 参见 Q. 58, a. 3; q. 75, a. 7, ad 3; q. 79, a. 8.
2. 参见 Aristotle, *Cat.*, V (3b 33).

we do not mean that one species of substance is not more perfect than another, but that one and the same individual does not participate in its specific nature at one time more than at another; and we mean that the nature of substance is not shared among different individuals in a greater or lesser degree.

Fourth Article
WHETHER THE IMAGE OF GOD IS FOUND IN EVERY MAN?

We proceed thus to the Fourth Article:—

Objection 1. It would seem that the image of God is not found in every man. For the Apostle says that *man is the image of God, but woman is the image of man* (*1 Cor.* xi. 7). Therefore, as woman is an individual of the human species, it is clear that every individual is not an image of God.

Obj. 2. Further, the Apostle says (*Rom.* viii. 29): *Whom God foreknew, He also predestinated to be made conformable to the image of His Son.* But all men are not predestined. Therefore all men have not the conformity of the image.

Obj. 3. Further, likeness belongs to the nature of the image, as was above explained. But by sin man becomes unlike God. Therefore he loses the image of God.

On the contrary, it is written (*Ps.* xxxviii. 7): *Surely man passeth as an image.*

I answer that, Since man is said to be to the image of God by reason of his intellectual nature, he is the most perfectly like God according as his intellectual nature can most imitate God. Now the intellectual nature imitates God chiefly in this, that God understands and loves Himself. Therefore the image of God may be considered in man in three ways. First, inasmuch as man possesses a natural aptitude for understanding and loving God; and this aptitude consists in the very nature of the mind, which is common to all men. Secondly, inasmuch as man actually or habitually knows and loves God, though imperfectly; and this image consists in the conformity of grace. Thirdly, inasmuch as man knows God actually and loves Him perfectly; and this image consists in the likeness of glory. Therefore on the words, *The light of Thy countenance, O Lord, is signed upon us* (*Ps.* iv. 7), the *Gloss* distinguishes a threefold image, of *creation*, of *re-creation*, and of *likeness*.[1] The first is found in all men, the second only in the just, the third only in the blessed.

Reply Obj. 1. The image of God, in its principal signification, namely the intellectual nature, is found both in man and in woman. Hence after the words, *To the image of God He created him*, it is added, *Male and female He created them* (*Gen.* i. 27). Moreover it is said *them* in the plural, as Augustine remarks, lest it should be thought that both sexes were united in one individual.[2] But in a secondary sense the image of God is found in man, and not in woman, for man is the beginning and end of woman, just as God is the beginning and end of every creature. So when the Apostle had said that *man is the image and glory of God, but woman is the glory of man*, he adds his reason for saying this: *For man is not of woman, but woman of man; and man was not created for woman, but woman for man.*

Reply Objs. 2 and 3. These reasons refer to the image consisting in the conformity of grace and glory.

Fifth Article
WHETHER THE IMAGE OF GOD IS IN MAN ACCOR DING TO THE TRINITY OF PERSONS?

We proceed thus to the Fifth Article:—

Objection 1. It would seem that the image of God does not exist in

---

1. 参见 *Glossa ordin.* (III, 92A).
2. 参见 *De Genesi ad Litt.*, III, 22 (PL 34, 294).

man as to the Trinity of Persons. For Augustine says: *One in essence is the Godhead of the Holy Trinity, and one is the image to which man was made.*[1] And Hilary says: *Man is made to the image of that which is common in the Trinity.*[2] Therefore the image of God in man is of the divine essence, and not of the Trinity of Persons.

Obj. 2. Further, it is said that the image of God in man is to be referred to eternity.[3] Damascene also says that the image of God in man belongs to him as *an intelligent being endowed with free choice and self-movement.*[4] Gregory of Nyssa also asserts that, when Scripture says that *man was made to the image of God, it means that, human nature was made a participator of all good; for the Godhead is the fullness of goodness.*[5] Now all these things belong more to the unity of the essence than to the distinction of the Persons. Therefore the image of God in man regards, not the Trinity of Persons, but the unity of the essence.

Obj. 3. Further, an image leads to the knowledge of that of which it is the image. Therefore, if there is in man the image of God as to the Trinity of Persons, since man can know himself by his natural reason, it follows that by his natural knowledge man could know the Trinity of the divine Persons; which is untrue, as was shown above.[6]

Obj. 4. Further, the name *image* is not applicable to any of the Three Persons, but only to the Son; for Augustine says that *the Son alone is the image of the Father.*[7] Therefore, if in man there were an image of God as regards the Person, this would not be an image of the Trinity, but only of the Son.

On the contrary, Hilary says: *The plurality of the divine Persons is proved*

---

1. 参见 Cf. Fulgentius, *De Fide ad Petrum*, I (PL 65, 674).
2. 参见 *De Trin.*, V (PL 10, 134).
3. 参见 Gennadius, *De Eccles. Dogm.*, 88 (PL 58, 1000).
4. 参见 *De Fide Orth.*, II, 12 (PG 94, 920).
5. 参见 *De Hom. Opif.*, XVI (PG 44, 184).
6. 参见 Q. 32, a. 1.
7. 参见 *De Trin.*, VI, 2 (PL 42, 925).

from the fact that man is said to have been made to the image of God.[1]

I answer that, as we have seen, the distinction of the divine Persons is only according to origin, or, rather, relations of origin.[2] Now the mode of origin is not the same in all things, but in each thing is adapted to its nature. For animate things are produced in one way, and inanimate in another; animals in one way, and plants in another. Hence it is manifest that the distinction of the divine Persons is suitable to the divine nature. Therefore, to be to the image of God by imitation of the divine nature does not exclude being to the image of God by the representation of the divine Persons; but rather one follows from the other. We must, therefore, say that in man there exists the image of God, both as regards the divine nature and as regards the Trinity of Persons; for in God Himself there is one nature in Three Persons.

Thus it is clear how to solve the first two objections.

Reply Obj. 3. This argument would hold if the image of God in man represented God in a perfect manner. But, as Augustine says, there is a great difference between the trinity within ourselves and the divine Trinity.[3] Therefore, as he there says: *We see, rather than believe, the trinity which is in ourselves; whereas we believe rather than see that God is a Trinity.*[4]

Reply Obj. 4. Some have said that in man there is an image only of the Son. Augustine rejects this opinion.[5] First, because as the Son is like to the Father by an equality of essence, it would follow of necessity that if man is made to the likeness of the Son, he is made to the likeness of the Father. Secondly, because if man were made only to the image of the Son, the Father would not have said, *Let Us make man to* Our *own image and likeness*; but *to* Thy *image*. When, therefore, it is

1. 参见 *De Trin.*, IV (PL 10, 111).
2. 参见 Q. 40, a. 2.
3. 参见 *De Trin.*, XV, 20; 23 (PL 42, 1088; 1090).
4. 参见 *Op. cit.*, XV, 6 (PL 42, 1064).
5. 参见 *Op. cit.*, XII, 6 (PL 42, 1001).

written, *He made him to the image of God* (*Gen.* i. 27), the sense is not that the Father made man to the image of the Son only, Who is God, as some have explained it, but that the divine Trinity made man to Its image, that is, of the whole Trinity.

When it is said that God *made man to His image*, this can be understood in two ways. First, so that this preposition *to* points to the term of the making, and then the sense is, *Let Us make man in such a way that Our image may be in him.* Secondly, this preposition *to* may point to the exemplary cause, as when we say, *This book is made [like] to that one.* Thus the image of God is the very essence of God, which is incorrectly called an image, according as image signifies the *exemplar*. Or, as some say, the divine essence is called an image because thereby one Person imitates another.[1]

Sixth Article

WHETHER THE IMAGE OF GOD IS IN MAN AS REGARDS THE MIND ONLY?

We proceed thus to the Sixth Article:—

Objection 1. It would seem that the image of God is not only in man's mind. For the Apostle says (*1 Cor.* xi. 7) that *man is the image ... of God.* But man is not only mind. Therefore the image of God is not to be observed only in his mind.

Obj. 2. Further, it is written (*Gen.* i. 27): *God created man to His own image; to the image of God He created him; male and female He created them.* But the distinction of male and female is in the body. Therefore the image of God is also in the body, and not only in the mind.

Obj. 3. Further, an image seems to apply principally to the shape of a thing. But shape belongs to the body. Therefore the image of God is

---

1. 参见 Cf. St. Hilary, *De Trin.*, IV (PL 10, 111).

to be seen also in man's body, and not only in his mind.

Obj. 4. Further, according to Augustine, there is a threefold vision in us, *corporeal*, *spiritual*, or imaginary, and *intellectual*.[1] Therefore, if in the intellectual vision that belongs to the mind there exists in us a trinity by reason of which we are made to the image of God, for the like reason there must be another trinity in the others.

On the contrary, The Apostle says (*Ephes.* iv. 23, 24): *Be renewed in the spirit of your mind, and put on the new man.* Whence we are given to understand that our renewal, which consists in putting on the new man, belongs to the mind. Now he says (*Col.* iii. 10): *Putting on the new* man, *him who is renewed unto knowledge* of God, *according to the image of Him that created him*; where the renewal which consists in putting on the new man is ascribed to the image of God. Therefore to be to the image of God belongs only to the mind.

I answer that, Although in all creatures there is some kind of likeness to God, in the rational creature alone do we find a likeness of *image*, as we have explained above; whereas in other creatures we find a likeness by way of a *trace*. Now the intellect or mind is that whereby the rational creature excels other creatures. Hence, this image of God is not found even in the rational creature except in the mind. In the other parts, however, which the rational creature may happen to possess, we find the likeness of a *trace*, as is the case in the other creatures to which, in reference to such parts, the rational creature can be likened. We may easily understand the reason for this if we consider the ways in which a *trace* and an *image* represent anything. An *image* represents something according to a likeness in species, as we have said; while a *trace* represents something in the manner of an effect, which represents the cause in such a way as not to attain to the likeness of species. For the imprints which are left by the movements of animals are called *traces*;

---

1. 参见 *De Genesi ad Litt.*, XII, 7; 24 (PL 34, 459; 474).

so also ashes are a trace of fire, and the desolation of the land a trace of a hostile army.

We may therefore observe such a difference between rational creatures and others, both as to the representation of the likeness of the divine nature in creatures, and as to the representation in them of the uncreated Trinity. For as to the likeness of the divine nature, rational creatures seem to attain, after a fashion, to the representation of the species, inasmuch as they imitate God not only in being and life, but also in understanding, as was above explained; whereas other creatures do not understand, although we observe in them a certain trace of the intellect that created them, if we consider their disposition. Likewise, just as the uncreated Trinity is distinguished by the procession of the Word from the Speaker, and of Love from both of these, as we have seen,[1] so we may say that in rational creatures, wherein we find a procession of the word in the intellect, and a procession of love in the will, there exists an image of the uncreated Trinity according to a certain representation of the species. In other creatures, however, we do not find the principle of the word, the word, and love; but we do see in them a certain trace of the existence of these in the cause that produced them. For the fact that a creature has a limited and finite substance proves that it proceeds from a principle; its species points to the interior word of the maker, just as the structure of a house points to the idea of the architect, and order points to the maker's love, by reason of which he directs the effect to some good, just as the use of the house points to the will of the architect. So we find in man a likeness to God by way of an *image* in his mind; but in the other parts of his being by way of a *trace*.

Reply Obj. 1. Man is called the image of God, not because he is essentially an image, but because the image of God is impressed on

---

1. 参见 Q. 28, a. 3.

his mind; as a coin is an image of the king, as having the image of the king. Therefore there is no need to consider the image of God as existing in every part of man.

Reply Obj. 2. As Augustine says, some have thought that the image of God was not in man individually, but severally.[1] They held that *the man represents the Person of the Father; that those born of man denote the person of the Son; and that woman is a third person in likeness to the Holy Ghost, since she so proceeded from man as not to be his son or daughter.* All of this is manifestly absurd. First, because it would follow that the Holy Ghost is the principle of the Son, just as woman is the principle of man's offspring; secondly, because one man would be to the image of only one Person; thirdly, because in that case Scripture should not have mentioned the image of God in man until after the birth of offspring. Therefore we must observe that when Scripture had said, *to the image of God He created him*, it added, *male and female He created them*, not to imply that the image of God came through the distinction of sex, but that the image of God belongs to both sexes, since it is in the mind, wherein there is no distinction of sexes. Therefore the Apostle (*Col.* iii. 10), after saying, *According to the image of Him that created him*, added, *Where there is neither male nor female* [Vulg., *neither Gentile nor Jew*; cf. *Gal.* iii. 28].

Reply Obj. 3. Although the image of God in man is not to be found in his bodily shape, yet because *the body of man alone among terrestrial animals is not inclined prone on its stomach, but is adapted to look upward to the heavens, for this reason we may rightly say that it is made to God's image and likeness, rather than the bodies of other animals*, as Augustine remarks.[2] But this is not to be understood as though the image of God were in man's body; but in the sense that the very shape of the human body represents the image of God in the soul by way of a trace.

Reply Obj. 4. Both in corporeal and in imaginary vision we may find

1. 参见 *De Trin.*, XII, 5 (PL 42, 1000).
2. 参见 *Lib. 83 Quaest.*, q. 51 (PL 40, 33).

a trinity, as Augustine says.[1] For in corporeal vision, there is first the species of the exterior body; secondly, the act of vision, which occurs by the impression on the sight of a certain likeness of the said species; thirdly, the intention of the will applying the sight to see, and to rest fixed on what is seen.

Likewise, in imaginary vision we find first the species kept in the memory; secondly, the vision itself, which is caused by the sight of the soul, that is, the power of imagination, when it is informed by the species; and thirdly, we find the intention of the will joining both together.

But each of these trinities falls short of the divine image. For the species of the external body is extrinsic to the essence of the soul, while the species in the memory, though not extrinsic to the soul, is adventitious to it; and thus in both cases the species falls short of representing the connaturality and co-eternity of the divine Persons. The corporeal vision, too, does not proceed only from the species of the external body, but from this and, at the same time, from the sense of the seer; and in like manner, imaginary vision is not from the species only which is preserved in the memory, but also from the imagination. For these reasons the procession of the Son from the Father alone is not suitably represented. Lastly, the intention of the will, joining the two together, does not proceed from them either in corporeal or spiritual vision; and so the procession of the Holy Ghost from the Father and the Son is not properly represented.

Seventh Article
WHETHER THE IMAGE OF GOD IS TO BE FOUND IN THE ACTS OF THE SOUL?

We proceed thus to the Seventh Article:—

---

1. 参见 *De Trin.*, XI, 2 (PL 42, 985).

Objection 1. It would seem that the image of God is not found in the acts of the soul. For Augustine says that *man was made to God's image, inasmuch as we are and know that we are, and love this being and knowing.*[1] But to be does not signify an act. Therefore the image of God is not to be found in the soul's acts.

Obj. 2. Further, Augustine assigns God's image in the soul to these three things — mind, knowledge and love.[2] But mind does not signify an act, but rather the power or even the essence of the intellectual soul. Therefore the image of God does not extend to the acts of the soul.

Obj. 3. Further, Augustine assigns the image of the Trinity in the soul to *memory, understanding and will.*[3] But these three are *natural powers of the soul*, as the Master of the *Sentences* says.[4] Therefore the image of God is in the powers, and does not extend to the acts of the soul.

Obj. 4. Further, the image of the Trinity always remains in the soul. But an act does not always remain. Therefore the image of God does not extend to the acts.

On the contrary, Augustine assigns a trinity in the lower parts of the soul according to actual vision, sensible and imaginative.[5] Therefore, the trinity in the mind, by reason of which man is like to God's image, must likewise be referred to actual vision.

I answer that, As was above explained, a certain representation of the species belongs to the nature of an image. Hence, if the image of the divine Trinity is to be found in the soul, we must look for it where the soul approaches the nearest to a representation of the species of the divine Persons. Now the divine Persons are distinct from each other by reason of the procession of the Word from the Speaker, and the

---

1. 参见 *De Civit. Dei*, XI, 26 (PL 41, 339).
2. 参见 *De Trin.*, IX, 12 (PL 42, 972).
3. 参见 *Op. cit.*, X, 12 (PL 42, 984).
4. 参见 *Sent.*, I, iii, 2 (I, 35).
5. 参见 *De Trin.*, XI, 2 (PL 42, 985).

procession of Love connecting both. But in our soul, the inner word *cannot exist without actual thought*, as Augustine says.[1] Therefore, first and chiefly, the image of the Trinity is to be found in the acts of the soul, that is, inasmuch as, from the knowledge which we possess, by actual thought we form an inner word, and thence break forth into love. But, since the principles of acts are the habits and powers, and since everything exists virtually in its principle, therefore, secondarily and consequently, the image of the Trinity may be considered as existing in the powers, and still more in the habits, inasmuch as the acts exist virtually in the habits.

Reply Obj. 1. Our being bears the image of God so far as it is proper to us, and excels that of the other animals; and such being belongs to us in so far as we are endowed with a mind. Therefore, this trinity is the same as that which Augustine mentions, and which consists in mind, knowledge and love.[2]

Reply Obj. 2. Augustine observed this trinity first in the mind. But though the mind knows itself entirely in a certain way, yet in a way it does not know itself —namely, as being distinct from other things (and thus it also seeks itself, as Augustine subsequently proves[3]). For this reason, because knowledge does not fully comprehend the mind, Augustine takes three things in the soul, namely, memory, understanding and will, as belonging properly to the mind, since everyone is conscious of possessing them; and he assigns the image of the Trinity preeminently to these three, as though the first assignation were in a way deficient.

Reply Obj. 3. As Augustine proves, we may be said to understand and will, or love, certain things, both when we actually consider them, and

---

1. 参见 *Op. cit.*, XIV, 7 (PL 42, 1043).
2. 参见 *Op. cit.*, IX, 12 (PL 42, 972).
3. 参见 *Op. cit.*, X, 4; 8 (PL 42, 976; 979).

when we do not think of them.[1] When they are not under our actual consideration, they are objects of our memory only, which, in his opinion, is nothing else than habitual retention of knowledge and love. *But since*, as he says, *a word cannot be there without actual thought* (*for we think everything that we say, even if we speak with that interior word belonging to no nation's tongue*), *this image consists chiefly in these three things, memory, understanding and will. And by understanding I mean here that whereby we understand with actual thought; and by will, love, or dilection I mean that which unites this child with its parent.*[2] From which it is clear that he places the image of the divine Trinity more in actual understanding and will, than in these as existing in the habitual retention of the memory; although even thus the image of the Trinity exists in the soul in a certain degree, as he says in the same place. Thus it is clear that memory, understanding and will are not three *powers*, as it is stated in the *Sentences*.

Reply Obj. 4. Someone could answer by referring to Augustine's statement that *the mind always remembers itself, always understands itself, always loves itself.*[3] Some take this to mean that the soul always actually understands and loves itself.[4] But he excludes this interpretation by adding that *it does not always think of itself as actually distinct from other things.*[5] Thus it is clear that the soul always understands and loves itself, not actually, but habitually; though we might say that by perceiving its own act, it understands itself whenever it understands anything. But since it is not always actually understanding, as in sleep, we must say that these acts, although not always actually existing, yet exist always in their principles, the habits and powers. Therefore, Augustine says: *If*

1. 参见 *Op. cit.*, XIV, 7 (PL 42, 1042).
2. 同上 (PL 42, 1043).
3. 参见 *Op. cit.*, XIV, 6; X, 12 (PL 42, 1042; 984).
4. 参见 Cf. St. Bonaventure, *In I Sent.*, d. iii, pt. 2, a. 2, q. 1 (I, 88).
5. 参见 St. Augustine, *De Trin.*, XIV, 6 (PL 42, 1042).

the rational soul is made to the image of God in the sense that it can make use of reason and intellect to understand and consider God, then the image of God was in the soul from the beginning of its existence.[1]

Eighth Article
WHETHER THE IMAGE OF THE DIVINE TRINITY IS IN THE SOUL ONLY BY COMPARISON WITH GOD AS ITS OBJECT?

We proceed thus to the Eighth Article:—

Objection 1. It would seem that the image of the divine Trinity is not in the soul only by comparison with God as its object. For the image of the divine Trinity is to be found in the soul, as was shown above, according as the word in us proceeds from the speaker, and love from both. But this is to be found in us as regards any object. Therefore the image of the divine Trinity is in our mind as regards any object.

Obj. 2. Further, Augustine says that *when we seek a trinity in the soul, we seek it in the whole of the soul, without separating the engagement of the reason in temporal activities from the contemplation of eternal things.*[2] Therefore the image of the Trinity is to be found in the soul, even as regards temporal objects.

Obj. 3. Further, it is by grace that we can know and love God. If, therefore, the image of the Trinity is found in the soul by reason of the memory, understanding and will or love of God, this image is not in man by nature but by grace, and thus is not common to all.

Obj. 4. Further, the saints in heaven are most perfectly conformed to the image of God by the beatific vision[3]. And so it is written (*2 Cor.* iii. 18): *We ... are transformed into the same image from glory to glory.* But temporal things are known by the beatific vision. Therefore the image

---

1. 参见 *Op. cit.*, XIV, 4 (PL 42, 1040).
2. 参见 *Op. cit.*, XII, 4 (PL 42, 1000).
3. the beatific vision: 荣福直观；享见天主

of God exists in us even according to temporal things.

On the contrary, Augustine says: *The image of God exists in the mind, not because it has a remembrance of itself, loves itself and understands itself; but because it can also remember, understand and love God by Whom it was made.*[1] Much less, therefore, is the image of God in the soul in respect of other objects.

I answer that, As was above explained, image means a likeness which in some degree, however small, attains to a representation of the species. Therefore we must seek the image of the divine Trinity[2] in the soul according as it represents the divine Persons by a representation of species, so far as this is possible to a creature. Now the divine Persons, as was stated above, are distinguished from each other according to the procession of the word from the speaker, and the procession of love from both. Moreover the Word of God is born of God by the knowledge of Himself, and Love proceeds from God according as He loves Himself. But it is clear that diversity of objects diversifies the species of word and love; for in the human mind the species of a stone is specifically different from that of a horse, and the love regarding each of them is also specifically different. Hence we refer the divine image in man to the verbal concept born of the knowledge of God, and to the love derived therefrom. Thus the image of God is found in the soul according as the soul turns to God, or possesses a nature that enables it to turn to God. Now the mind may turn towards a thing in two ways: directly and immediately, or indirectly and mediately; as, for instance, when anyone sees a man reflected in a looking-glass he may be said to be turned towards that man. And so Augustine says that *the mind remembers itself, understands itself and loves itself. If we perceive this, we perceive a trinity, not, indeed, God, but, nevertheless, what is already the image*

1. 参见 *Op. cit.*, XIV, 12 (PL 42, 1048).
2. the divine Trinity: 天主圣三

of God.[1] But this is true, not because the mind turns to itself absolutely, but because thereby it can further turn to God, as appears from the authority quoted above.[2]

Reply Obj. 1. For the notion of an image it is not enough that something proceed from another; it is also necessary to observe what it is that proceeds from another, namely, that it is the Word of God that proceeds from the knowledge of God.

Reply Obj. 2. In all the soul we may see a kind of trinity, not, however, as though besides engagement in temporal things and the contemplation of eternal things, *any third thing should be required to make up the trinity*, as he adds in the same passage.[3] Rather, in that part of the reason which is concerned with temporal things, *although a trinity may be found, yet the image of God is not to be seen there*, as he says farther on; for this knowledge of temporal things is adventitious to the soul. Moreover, even the habits whereby temporal things are known are not always present; but sometimes they are actually present, and sometimes present only in memory even after they begin to exist in the soul. Such is clearly the case with faith, which comes to us temporally for this present life; while in the future life faith will no longer exist, but only the remembrance of faith.

Reply Obj. 3. The meritorious knowledge and love of God can be in us only by grace. Yet there is a certain natural knowledge and love, as we have seen above.[4] So, too, it is natural that the mind can make use of reason in order to understand God. In this sense we have already said that the image of God always abides in the mind, *whether this image of God be so obsolete*, as it were clouded, *as almost to amount to nothing* (as in those who have not the use of reason), *or obscured and disfigured* (as in

---

1. 参见 *Op. cit.*, XIV, 8 (PL 42, 1044).
2. 参见 *Op. cit.*, XIV, 12 (PL 42, 1048).
3. 参见 *Op. cit.*, XII, 4 (PL 42, 1000).
4. 参见 Q. 12, a. 12; q. 56, a. 3; q. 60, a. 5.

sinners), or *clear and beautiful* (as in the just), as Augustine says.[1]

Reply Obj. 4. By the vision of glory temporal things will be seen in God Himself; and so such a vision of temporal things will belong to the image of God. This is what Augustine means when he says that *in that nature to which the mind will blissfully adhere, whatever it sees it will see as unchangeable.*[2] For in the uncreated Word are the likenesses of all creatures.

Ninth Article

WHETHER LIKENESS IS PROPERLY DISTINGUISHED FROM IMAGE?

We proceed thus to the Ninth Article:—

Objection 1. It would seem that *likeness* is not properly distinguished from *image*. For *genus* is not properly distinguished from *species*. Now *likeness* is to *image* as genus to species, because, *where there is image, forthwith there is likeness, but not conversely*, as Augustine says.[3] Therefore *likeness* is not properly distinguished from *image*.

Obj. 2. Further, the nature of the image consists not only in the representation of the divine Persons, but also in the representation of the divine essence, to which representation belong immortality and indivisibility. So it is not true to say that the *likeness is in the essence because it is immortal and indivisible; whereas the image is in other things.*[4]

Obj. 3. Further, the image of God in man is threefold,—the image of nature, of grace and of glory, as was above explained. But innocence and justice belong to grace. Therefore it is incorrectly said *that the image is taken from memory, understanding and will, while the likeness is from*

---

1. 参见 *De Trin.*, XIV, 4 (PL 42, 1040).
2. 参见 *Op. cit.*, XIV, 14 (PL 42, 1051).
3. 参见 *Lib. 83 Quaest.*, q. 74 (PL 40, 85).
4. 参见 Cf. Peter Lombard, *Sent.*, II, xvi, 3 (I, 381).

innocence and justice.[1]

Obj. 4. Further, knowledge of truth belongs to the intellect, and love of virtue to the will; which two things are parts of the image. Therefore it is incorrect to say that *the image consists in the knowledge of truth, and the likeness in the love of virtue.*[2]

On the contrary, Augustine says *Some consider that these two were mentioned not without reason, namely 'image' and 'likeness,' since, if they meant the same, one would have sufficed.*[3]

I answer that, Likeness is a kind of unity, for oneness in quality causes likeness, as the Philosopher says.[4] Now, since *one* is a transcendental, it is both common to all, and adapted to each single thing, just as the good and the true. Hence, just as the good can be compared to some individual thing both as prior and as subsequent to it, as signifying some perfection in it, so also in the same way there exists a kind of comparison between *likeness* and *image*. For the good is prior to man, inasmuch as man is some particular good; and, again, the good is subsequent to man, inasmuch as we may say of a certain man that he is good by reason of his perfect virtue. In like manner, likeness may be considered as prior to image, inasmuch as it is something more common than image, as we have said above; and, again, it may be considered as subsequent to image, inasmuch as it signifies a certain perfection of the image. For we say that an image is like or unlike what it represents, according as the representation is perfect or imperfect.

Thus likeness may be distinguished from image in two ways. First, as prior to it, and as existing in more things; and in this sense likeness regards things which are more common than the properties of an

---

1. 参见 Cf. Peter Lombard, *Sent.*, II, xvi, 3 (I, 381).
2. 同上
3. 参见 *Lib. 83 Quaest.*, q. 51 (PL 40, 33).
4. 参见 Aristotle, *Metaph.*, IV, 15 (1021a 11).

intellectual nature, wherein the image is properly to be seen. In this sense it is said that *the spirit* (namely, the mind) *without doubt was made to the image of God. But the other parts of man*, belonging to the soul's inferior parts, or even to the body, *are in the opinion of some made to God's likeness.*[1] In this sense Augustine also says that the likeness of God is found in the soul's incorruptibility;[2] for corruptible and incorruptible are differences of being in general. But likeness may be considered in another way, as signifying the expression and perfection of the image. In this sense Damascene says that the image signifies *an intelligent being, endowed with free choice and self-movement, whereas likeness signifies a likeness of power, as far as this may be possible in man.*[3] In the same sense, *likeness* is said to belong to *the love of virtue*; for there is no virtue without love of virtue.

Reply Obj. 1. Likeness is not distinct from *image* according to the common nature of *likeness* (for thus it is included in the nature of *image*); but so far as any *likeness* falls short of *image*, or again, as it perfects the *image*.

Reply Obj. 2. The soul's essence belongs to the *image*, as representing the divine essence in those things which belong to the intellectual nature; but not in those conditions consequent upon being in general, such as simplicity and indissolubility[4].

Reply Obj. 3. Even certain virtues are natural to the soul, at least, in their seeds, by reason of which we may say that a natural *likeness* exists in the soul. Nor is it unfitting to use the term *image* from one point of view, and from another the term *likeness*.

Reply Obj. 4. Love of the word, which is knowledge loved, belongs to the nature of *image*; but love of virtue belongs to *likeness*, as does virtue.

---

1. 参见 *Lib. 83 Quaest.*, q. 51 (PL 40, 33).
2. 参见 St. Augustine, *De Quant. An.*, II (PL 32, 1037).
3. 参见 *De Fide Orth.*, II, 12 (PG 94, 920).
4. indissolubility: 不溶性；不稳定性

Question XCIV
THE STATE AND CONDITION OF THE FIRST MAN AS REGARDS HIS INTELLECT
(*In Four Articles*)

WE next consider the state or condition of the first man: first, as regards his soul; secondly as regards his body.[1] Concerning the first there are two things to be considered: (1) The condition of man as to his intellect; (2) the condition of man as to his will.[2]

Under the first head there are four points of inquiry: (1) Whether the first man saw the essence of God? (2) Whether he could see separate substances, that is, the angels? (3) Whether he possessed all knowledge? (4) Whether he could err or be deceived?

First Article
WHETHER THE FIRST MAN SAW GOD THROUGH HIS ESSENCE?

We proceed thus to the First Article:—

Objection 1. It would seem that the first man saw God through His essence. For man's happiness consists in the vision of the divine essence. But the first man, *while established in Paradise, led a life of happiness in the enjoyment of all things*, as Damascene says.[3] And Augustine says: *If man was gifted with the same affections as now, how*

---

1. 参见 Q. 97.
2. 参见 Q. 95.
3. 参见 *De Fide Orth.*, II, 11 (PG 94, 912).

happy must he have been in Paradise, that place of ineffable[1] *happiness!*[2] Therefore the first man in Paradise saw God through His essence.

Obj. 2. Further, Augustine says that *the first man lacked nothing which his good will might obtain.*[3] But a good will can obtain nothing better than the vision of the divine essence. Therefore man saw God through His essence.

Obj. 3. Further, the vision of God in His essence is that whereby God is seen without a medium or enigma. But man in the state of innocence *saw God immediately*, as the Master of the *Sentences* asserts.[4] He also saw without an enigma[5], for an enigma implies obscurity, as Augustine says.[6] Now, obscurity resulted from sin. Therefore man in the first state saw God through His essence.

On the contrary, The Apostle says (*1 Cor.* xv. 46): *That was not first which is spiritual, but that which is natural.* But to see God through His essence is most spiritual. Therefore the first man, in the first state of his natural life, did not see God through His essence.

I answer that, The first man did not see God through His essence if we consider the ordinary state of that life; unless, perhaps, it be said that he saw God in rapture when *God cast a deep sleep upon Adam* (*Gen.* ii. 21). The reason for this is that, since in the divine essence is beatitude itself, the intellect of a man who sees the divine essence has the same relation to God as a man has to beatitude. Now it is clear that man cannot willingly be turned away from beatitude, since he desires it naturally and necessarily, and shuns unhappiness. Therefore no one who sees the essence of God can willingly turn away from God, which means to sin. Hence all who see God through His essence are so firmly established in

1. ineffable: 不可言喻的；不可说出的
2. 参见 *De Civit. Dei*, XIV, 10 (PL 41, 417).
3. 同上
4. 参见 *Sent.*, IV, i, 5 (II, 747).
5. enigma: 难以理解的问题；奥秘
6. 参见 *De Trin.*, XV, 9 (PL 42, 1069).

the love of God, that for eternity they can never sin. Therefore, as Adam did sin, it is clear that he did not see God through His essence.

Nevertheless, he knew God with a more perfect knowledge than we do now. Thus his knowledge was in a way midway between our knowledge in the present state, and the knowledge we shall have in heaven, when we see God through His essence. To make this clear, we must consider that the vision of God through His essence is contradistinguished from the vision of God through His creatures. Now the higher a creature is, and the more like God, the more clearly is God seen in it; just as a man is seen more clearly through a mirror in which his image is more clearly expressed. Thus God is seen in a much more perfect manner through His intelligible effects than through those which are sensible or corporeal. But in his present state, man is impeded as regards the full and clear consideration of God's intelligible effects, because he is distracted by and occupied with sensible things. Now, it is written (*Eccles.* vii. 30): *God made man right.* And man was made right by God in this sense, that in him the lower powers were subjected to the higher, and the higher nature was made so as not to be impeded by the lower. Hence, the first man was not impeded by exterior things from a clear and steady contemplation of the intelligible effects which he perceived by the radiation of the first truth, whether by a natural or by a gratuitous knowledge. Hence Augustine says that *perhaps God used to speak to the first human beings as He speaks to the angels, by shedding on their mind a ray of the unchangeable truth, yet without bestowing on them the experience of which the angels are capable in the participation of the divine essence.*[1] Therefore, through these intelligible effects of God, man knew God then more clearly than we now know Him.

Reply Obj. 1. Man was happy in Paradise, but not with that perfect happiness to which he was destined, which consists in the vision of

---

1. 参见 *De Genesi ad Litt.*, XI, 33 (PL 34, 447).

the divine essence. He was, however, endowed with *a life of happiness in a certain measure*, as Augustine says,[1] in so far as he was gifted with a certain natural integrity and perfection.

Reply Obj. 2. A good will is a well-ordered will. But the will of the first man would have been ill-ordered had he wished to have, while in the state of merit, what had been promised to him as a reward.

Reply Obj. 3. A medium is twofold: one through which, and, at the same time, in which, something is seen, as, for example, a man is seen through a mirror, and is seen with the mirror; another kind of medium is that whereby we attain to the knowledge of something unknown, such as the medium in a demonstration. God was seen without this second kind of medium, but not without the first kind. For there was no need for the first man to attain to the knowledge of God by demonstration drawn from some effect, such as we need; since he knew God simultaneously in His effects, especially in the intelligible effects, according to his capacity. Again, we must remark that the obscurity which is implied in the word enigma may be of two kinds. First, so far as every creature is something obscure when compared with the immensity of the divine splendor; and thus Adam saw God in an enigma, because he saw Him in a created effect. Secondly, we may take obscurity as an effect of sin, so far as man is impeded in the consideration of intelligible things by being preoccupied with sensible things; in which sense Adam did not see God in an enigma.

Second Article
WHETHER ADAM IN THE STATE OF INNOCENCE SAW THE ANGELS THROUGH THEIR ESSENCE?

We proceed thus to the Second Article:—

1. 参见 *Op. cit.*, XI, 18 (PL 34, 438).

Objection 1. It would seem that Adam, in the state of innocence, saw the angels through their essence. For Gregory says: *In Paradise man was accustomed to enjoy the words of God, and by purity of heart and loftiness of vision to have the company of the good angels.*[1]

Obj. 2. Further, the soul in the present state is impeded from the knowledge of separate substances by union with a corruptible body which *is a load upon the soul*, as is written in *Wisdom* ix. 15. Therefore the separated soul can see separate substances, as was above explained.[2] But the body of the first man was not a load upon his soul, for it was not corruptible. Therefore he was able to see separate substances.

Obj. 3. Further, one separate substance knows another separate substance by knowing itself.[3] But the soul of the first man knew itself. Therefore it knew separate substances.

On the contrary, The soul of Adam was of the same nature as ours. But our souls cannot now understand separate substances. Therefore neither could Adam's soul.

I answer that, The *state* of the human soul may be distinguished in two ways. First, according to a diversity of the mode of its natural being, and in this way the state of the separate soul is distinguished from the state of the soul joined to the body. Secondly, the state of the soul is distinguished according to integrity and corruption, while the state of natural being remains the same; and thus the state of innocence is distinguished from the state of man after sin. For in the state of innocence, man's soul was adapted to the work of perfecting and governing the body, even as now. Hence, the first man is said to have been made into a *living soul* (*Gen.* ii. 7), that is, a soul giving life to the body,—namely, animal life. But he was endowed with integrity as to this life, in that the body was entirely subject to the soul, hindering

1. 参见 *Dial.*, IV, 1 (PL 77, 317).
2. 参见 Q. 89, a. 2.
3. 参见 *De Causis*, XIII (p. 172).

it in no way, as we have said above. Now it is clear from what has been already said that, since the soul is adapted to perfecting and governing the body, as regards animal life, it is fitting that it should have that mode of understanding which is by turning to phantasms.[1] Therefore this mode of understanding was becoming also to the soul of the first man.

Now, in virtue of this mode of understanding, there are three degrees of movement in the soul, as Dionysius says.[2] The first is by the soul passing from exterior things to concentrate its powers on itself; the second is by the soul ascending so as to be associated with the united superior powers, namely, the angels; the third is when the soul is led on yet further to the supreme good, that is, to God.

In virtue of the first movement of the soul from exterior things to itself, the soul's knowledge reaches its perfection. This is because the intellectual operation of the soul has a natural ordination to external things, as we have said above,[3] and so by the knowledge of these things our intellectual operation can be known perfectly, as an act through its object. And through the intellectual operation itself, the human intellect can be known perfectly, as a power through its proper act. But in the second movement we do not find perfect knowledge. Because, since the angel does not understand by turning to phantasms, but in a far more excellent way, as we have said above,[4] the above-mentioned mode of knowledge, by which the soul knows itself, is not sufficient to lead it to the knowledge of an angel. Much less does the third movement lead to perfect knowledge, for even the angels themselves, by the fact that they know themselves, are not able to arrive at the knowledge of the divine substance, by reason of its surpassing

---

1. 参见 Q. 84, a. 7; q. 85. a. 1; q. 89, a. 1.
2. 参见 *De Div. Nom.*, IV, 9 (PG 3, 705).
3. 参见 Q. 87, a. 3.
4. 参见 Q. 55, a. 2.

excellence.

Therefore the soul of the first man could not see the angels in their essence. Nevertheless he had a more excellent mode of knowledge regarding the angels than we possess, because his knowledge of interior intelligible things within him was more certain and fixed than our knowledge. And it is because of this excellence of knowledge that Gregory says that *he enjoyed the company of the angelic spirits.*[1]

This makes clear the reply to the first objection.

Reply Obj. 2. That the soul of the first man fell short of the knowledge of separate substances was not owing to the fact that the body was a load upon it; but to the fact that its connatural object fell short of the excellence of separate substances. We, in our present state, fall short because of both these reasons.

Reply Obj. 3. The soul of the first man was not able to arrive at the knowledge of separate substances by means of its self-knowledge, as we have shown above; for even each separate substance knows others in its own measure.

Third Article
WHETHER THE FIRST MAN KNEW ALL THINGS?

We proceed thus to the Third Article:—

Objection 1. It would seem that the first man did not know all things. For if he had such knowledge, it would be either by acquired species, or by connatural species, or by infused species. Not, however, by acquired species, for this kind of knowledge is acquired by experience, as is stated in *Metaph.* i.;[2] and the first man had not then gained experience of all things. Nor through connatural species, because

1. 参见 *Dial.*, IV, 1 (PL 77, 317).
2. 参见 Aristotle, *Metaph.*, I, 1 (980b 28).

he was of the same nature as we are; and our soul, as Aristotle says, is *like a tablet on which nothing is written.*[1] And if his knowledge came by infused species, it would have been of a different kind from ours, which we acquire from things themselves.

Obj. 2. Further, individuals of the same species have the same way of arriving at perfection. Now other men have not, from the beginning, knowledge of all things, but they acquire it in the course of time according to their capacity. Therefore neither did Adam know all things when he was first created.

Obj. 3. Further, the present state of life is given to man in order that his soul may advance in knowledge and merit; for the soul seems to be united to the body for that purpose. Now man would have advanced in merit in that state of life; therefore also in knowledge. Therefore he was not endowed with the knowledge of all things.

On the contrary, Man named the animals (*Gen.* ii. 20). But names should be adapted to the nature of things. Therefore Adam knew the natures of all the animals; and in like manner he was possessed of the knowledge of all other things.

I answer that, It is natural for the perfect to come before the imperfect, as act comes before potentiality; for whatever is in potentiality is made actual only by something actual. And since God first created things not only for their own existence, but also that they might be principles of other things, so creatures were produced in their perfect state to be the principles as regards others. Now man can be the principle of another man, not only by corporeal generation, but also by instruction and government. Hence, just as the first man was produced in his perfect bodily state for the work of generation, so also was his soul established in a perfect state to instruct and govern others.

Now no one can instruct others unless he has knowledge; and so

---

1. 参见 Aristotle, *De An.*, III, 4 (430a 1).

the first man was established by God in such a manner as to have the knowledge of all those things for which man has a natural aptitude. And such are whatever are virtually contained in the first self-evident principles, that is, whatever truths man is naturally able to know. Moreover, in order to direct his own life and that of others, man needs to know not only those things which can be naturally known, but also things surpassing natural knowledge, because the life of man is directed to a supernatural end; just as it is necessary for us to know the truths of faith in order to direct our own lives. Therefore the first man was endowed with such a knowledge of these supernatural truths as was necessary for the direction of human life in that state. But those things which cannot be known by merely human effort, and which are not necessary for the direction of human life, were not known by the first man: *e.g.*, the thoughts of men, future contingent events, and some individual facts, as for instance the number of pebbles in a stream, and the like.

Reply Obj. 1. The first man had knowledge of all things by divinely infused species. Yet his knowledge was not different from ours; just as the eyes which Christ gave to the man born blind were not different from those given by nature.

Reply Obj. 2. To Adam, as being the first man, was due a degree of perfection which was not due to other men, as is clear from what was said above.

Reply Obj. 3. Adam would have advanced in natural knowledge, not in the number of things known, but in the manner of knowing; because what he knew speculatively he would subsequently have known by experience. But as regards supernatural knowledge, he would also have advanced in the number of things known, by further revelation; just as the angels advance by further illuminations. Moreover there is no comparison between advance in knowledge and advance in merit; since one man cannot be a principle of merit to another, although he can be to another a principle of knowledge.

Fourth Article

WHETHER MAN IN HIS FIRST STATE COULD HAVE BEEN DECEIVED?

We proceed thus to the Fourth Article:—

Objection 1. It would seem that man in his first state could have been deceived. For the Apostle says (*1 Tim.* ii. 14) that *the woman being seduced was in the transgression*[1].

Obj. 2. Further, the Master of the *Sentences* says that *woman was not frightened at the serpent speaking, because she thought that he had received the faculty of speech from God.*[2] But this was untrue. Therefore before sin woman was deceived.

Obj. 3. Further, it is natural that the farther off anything is from us, the smaller it seems to be. Now, the nature of the eyes is not changed by sin. Therefore this would have been the case in the state of innocence. Therefore man would have been deceived in the size of what he saw, just as he is deceived now.

Obj. 4. Further, Augustine says that in sleep the soul adheres to the images of things as if they were the things themselves.[3] But in the state of innocence man would have eaten and consequently have slept and dreamed. Therefore he would have been deceived, adhering to images as to realities.

Obj. 5. Further, the first man would have been ignorant of other men's thoughts, and of future contingent events, as was stated above. So if anyone had told him what was false about these things, he would have been deceived.

On the contrary, Augustine says: *To regard what is true as false, is not*

---

1. transgression: 犯罪；违反
2. 参见 Peter Lombard, *Sent.*, II, xxi, 4 (I, 405).
3. 参见 *De Genesi ad Litt.*, XII, 2 (PL 44, 455).

natural to man as created, but is a punishment of man condemned.[1]

I answer that, In the opinion of some, deception may mean two things.[2] It may mean any slight surmise[3], in which one adheres to what is false, as though it were true, but without the assent of belief; or it may mean a firm belief. Thus, before sin, Adam could not be deceived in either of these ways as regards those things to which his knowledge extended; but as regards things to which his knowledge did not extend, he might have been deceived, if we take deception in the wide sense of the term for any surmise without assent of belief. This opinion was held with the idea that it is not harmful to man to entertain a false opinion in such matters, and that provided he does not assent rashly, he is not to be blamed.

Such an opinion, however, is not in harmony with the integrity of the first state of life; because, as Augustine says, in that state of life *sin was avoided without struggle, and while it remained so, no evil could exist.*[4] Now it is clear that as truth is the good of the intellect, so falsehood is its evil, as the Philosopher says.[5] Hence, as long as the state of innocence continued, it was impossible for the human intellect to assent to falsehood as if it were truth. For as some perfections, such as clarity, were lacking in the bodily members of the first man, though no evil could be therein, so there could be in his intellect the absence of some knowledge, but no false opinion.

This is clear also from the very rectitude of the first state, by virtue of which, while the soul remained subject to God, the lower powers in man were subject to the higher, and were no impediment to their action. And from what has preceded it is clear that as regards its

---

1. 参见 *De Lib. Arb.*, III, 18 (PL 32, 1296).
2. 参见 Cp. also St. Bonaventure, *In II Sent.*, d. xxiii, a. 2, q. 2 (II, 540).
3. surmise: 推测；猜测
4. 参见 *De Civit. Dei*, XIV, 10 (PL 41, 417).
5. 参见 Aristotle, *Eth.*, VI, 2 (1139a 28).

proper object the intellect is always true.[1] Hence, it is never deceived of itself, but whatever deception occurs is due to some lower power, such as the imagination or the like. Hence we see that when the natural power of judgment is free we are not deceived by such images, but only when it is not free, as is the case in sleep. Therefore, it is clear that the rectitude of the first state was incompatible with any deception of the intellect.

Reply Obj. 1. Though woman was deceived before she sinned in deed, still it was not till she had already sinned by interior pride. For Augustine says that *woman would not have believed the words of the serpent, had she not already acquiesced in the love of her own power, and in a presumption of self-conceit.*[2]

Reply Obj. 2. Woman thought that the serpent had received this faculty, not as acting in accordance with nature, but by virtue of some supernatural operation. We need not, however, follow the Master of the *Sentences* in this point.

Reply Obj. 3. Were anything presented to the imagination or sense of the first man, not in accordance with the nature of things, he would not have been deceived, for his reason would have enabled him to judge the truth.

Reply Obj. 4. A man is not accountable for what occurs during sleep, as he has not then the use of his reason, wherein consists man's proper action.

Reply Obj. 5. If anyone had said something untrue as regards future contingencies, or as regards secret thoughts, man in the first state would not have believed that it was so, but that such a thing was possible; which would not have been to entertain a false opinion.

It might also be said that he would have been divinely guided from above, so as not to be deceived in a matter to which his knowledge did

1. 参见 Q. 17, a. 3; q. 85, a. 6.
2. 参见 *De Genesi ad Litt.*, XI, 30 (PL 34, 445).

not extend.

If any object, as some do,[1] that he was not guided when tempted, though he was then most in need of guidance, we reply that man had already sinned in his heart, and that he failed to have recourse to the divine aid.

1. 参见 Cf. Peter Lombard, *Sent.*, II, xxiii, 1 (I, 417).

Question XCV
OF THINGS PERTAINING TO THE FIRST MAN'S WILL, NAMELY, GRACE AND JUSTICE
(*In Four Articles*)

WE next consider what belongs to the will of the first man, concerning which there are two points for treatment: (1) The grace and justice of the first man; (2) the use of justice as regards his dominion over other things.[1]

Under the first head there are four points of inquiry: (1) Whether the first man was created in grace? (2) Whether in the state of innocence he had passions of the soul? (3) Whether he had all the virtues? (4) Whether what he did would have been as meritorious as now?

First Article
WHETHER THE FIRST MAN WAS CREATED IN GRACE?

We proceed thus to the First Article:—

Objection 1. It would seem that the first man was not created in grace. For the Apostle, distinguishing between Adam and Christ, says (*1 Cor.* xv. 45): *The first Adam was made into a living soul; the last Adam into a quickening spirit.* But the spirit is quickened by grace. Therefore Christ alone was made in grace.

Obj. 2. Further, Augustine says that *Adam did not possess the Holy*

1. 参见 Q. 96.

Ghost.[1] But whoever possesses grace has the Holy Ghost. Therefore Adam was not created in grace.

Obj. 3. Further, Augustine says that *God so ordered the life of angels and men, as to show first what they could do by free choice, then what they could do by His grace, and by the discernment of justice.*[2] God thus first created men and angels in the natural liberty of choice only, and afterwards bestowed grace on them.

Obj. 4. Further, the Master of the *Sentences* says: *When man was created, he was given sufficient help to stand, but not sufficient to advance.*[3] But whoever has grace can advance by merit. Therefore the first man was not created in grace.

Obj. 5. Further, the reception of grace requires the consent of the recipient, since thereby a kind of spiritual marriage takes place between God and the soul. But consent to grace presupposes the prior existence of the one consenting. Therefore man did not receive grace in the first moment of his creation.

Obj. 6. Further, nature is more distant from grace than grace is from glory, which is but grace consummated. But in man grace precedes glory. Therefore much more did nature precede grace.

On the contrary, Man and angel are alike ordained to grace. But the angels were created in grace, for Augustine says: *God at the same time fashioned their nature and endowed them with grace.*[4] Therefore man also was created in grace.

I answer that, Some[5] say that man was not created in grace, but that grace was bestowed on him subsequently before sin. Now many

---

1. 参见 Ambrosiaster, *De Quaest. Vet. et Nov. Test.*, I, q. 123 (PL 35, 2371).
2. 参见 *De Corrept. et Grat.*, X (PL 44, 932).
3. 参见 Peter Lombard, *Sent.*, II, xxiv, 1 (I, 419).
4. 参见 *De Civit. Dei*, XII, 9 (PL 41, 357).
5. 参见 William of Auxerre, *Summa Aurea*, II, tr. 1, ch. 1 (fol. 35rb); Alex. of Hales, *Summa Theol.*, II, I, no. 505 (II, 729); St. Bonaventure, *In II Sent.*, d. xxix, a. 2, q. 2 (II, 703).

authorities of the saints declare that man possessed grace in the state of innocence.[1]

But the very rectitude of the first state, with which man was endowed by God, seems to require that, as others say,[2] he was created in grace, according to *Eccles.* vii. 30, *God made man right.* For this rectitude consisted in his reason being subject to God, the lower powers to reason, and the body to the soul. Now the first subjection was the cause of both the second and the third, since while reason was subject to God, the lower powers remained subject to reason, as Augustine says.[3] Now it is clear that such a subjection of the body to the soul and of the lower powers to reason was not from nature, or otherwise it would have remained after sin; for even in the demons the natural gifts remained after sin, as Dionysius declares.[4] Hence it is clear that also the first subjection, by virtue of which reason was subject to God, was not a merely natural gift, but a supernatural endowment of grace; for it is not possible that the effect should be of greater efficacy than the cause. Hence Augustine says that *as soon as they disobeyed the divine command, and forfeited divine grace, they were ashamed of their nakedness; for they felt the impulse of disobedience in the flesh, as though it were a punishment corresponding to their own disobedience.*[5] Hence if the loss of grace dissolved the obedience of the flesh to the soul, we may gather that the inferior powers were subjected to the soul through grace existing in the soul.

Reply Obj. 1. The Apostle in these words means to show that there is a spiritual body, if there is an animal body, inasmuch as the life of the spiritual body began in Christ, who is *the firstborn of the dead* (*Col.* i. 18),

1. 参见 Cf. St. Jerome, *In Ephes.*, III, super IV, 30 (PL 26, 546); St. Augustine, *De Civit. Dei*, XIII, 13 (PL 41, 386).
2. 参见 St. Albert, *In II Sent.*, d. iii, a. 12 (XXVII, 85).
3. 参见 *De Civit. Dei*, XIII, 13 (PL 41, 386).
4. 参见 *De Div. Nom.*, IV, 23 (PG 3, 725).
5. 参见 *De Civit. Dei*, XIII, 13 (PL 41, 386).

as the body's animal life began in Adam. From the Apostle's words, therefore, we cannot gather that Adam had no spiritual life in his soul, but that he had not spiritual life as regards the body.

Reply Obj. 2. As Augustine says in the same passage, it is not disputed that Adam, like other just men, was in some degree gifted with the Holy Ghost; but *he did not possess the Holy Ghost as the faithful possess Him now*,[1] who are admitted to eternal happiness directly after death.

Reply Obj. 3. This passage from Augustine does not assert that angels or men were created with the natural liberty of choice before they possessed grace, but that God shows first what their free choice could do before being confirmed in grace, and what they acquired afterwards by being so confirmed.

Reply Obj. 4. The Master here speaks according to the opinion of those who held that man was not created in grace, but only in a state of nature. We may also say that, though man was created in grace, yet it was not by virtue of the nature wherein he was created that he could advance by merit, but by virtue of the grace which was added.

Reply Obj. 5. As the motion of the will is not continuous, there is nothing against the first man having consented to grace even in the first moment of his creation.

Reply Obj. 6. We merit glory by an act of grace, but we do not merit grace by an act of nature. Hence the comparison fails.

Second Article
WHETHER PASSIONS EXISTED IN THE SOUL OF THE FIRST MAN?

We proceed thus to the Second Article:—

---

1. 参见 Ambrosiaster, *De Quaest. Vet. et Nov. Test.*, I, q. 123 (PL 35, 2371).

Objection 1. It would seem that the first man's soul had no passions. For by the passions of the soul *the flesh lusteth against the spirit* (*Gal.* v. 17). But this did not happen in the state of innocence. Therefore in the state of innocence there were no passions of the soul.

Obj. 2. Further, Adam's soul was nobler than his body. But his body was impassible. Therefore no passions were in his soul.

Obj. 3. Further, the passions of the soul are restrained by the moral virtues. But in Adam the moral virtues were perfect. Therefore the passions were entirely excluded from him.

On the contrary, Augustine says that *in our first parents there was undisturbed love of God*,[1] and other passions of the soul.

I answer that, The passions of the soul are in the sensual appetite, the object of which is good and evil. Therefore some passions of the soul are directed to what is good, as love and joy, others to what is evil, as fear and sorrow. And since, in the first state, evil was neither present nor imminent, nor was any good wanting which a good will could desire to have then, as Augustine says,[2] therefore Adam had no passion with evil as its object, such as fear, sorrow, and the like; neither had he passions in respect of good not possessed, but to be possessed then, as burning concupiscence. But those passions which regard present good, as joy and love, or which regard future good to be had at the proper time, as desire and hope that casteth not down, existed in the state of innocence; otherwise, however, than as they exist in ourselves. For our sensual appetite, wherein the passions reside, is not entirely subject to reason, and hence at times our passions forestall and hinder reason's judgment, and at other times they follow after reason's judgment, according as the sensual appetite obeys reason to some extent. But in the state of innocence, the inferior appetite was wholly subject to reason, so that in that state the passions of the soul existed only as

1. 参见 *De Civit. Dei*, XIV, 10 (PL 41, 417).
2. 同上

consequent upon the judgment of reason.

Reply Obj. 1. The *flesh lusts against the spirit* by the rebellion of the passions against reason; which could not occur in the state of innocence.

Reply Obj. 2. The human body was impassible in the state of innocence as regards the passions which alter the disposition of nature, as will be explained later on.[1] So, too, the soul was impassible as regards the passions which impede the free use of reason.

Reply Obj. 3. The perfection of moral virtue does not wholly take away the passions, but regulates them; *for the temperate man desires as he ought to desire, and what he ought to desire*, as is stated in *Ethics* iii.[2]

Third Article
WHETHER ADAM HAD ALL THE VIRTUES?

We proceed thus to the Third Article:—

Objection 1. It would seem that Adam had not all the virtues. For some virtues are directed to curb the excesses of the passions; and thus immoderate concupiscence is restrained by temperance, and immoderate fear by fortitude. But in the state of innocence no immoderation existed in the passions. Therefore neither did these virtues then exist.

Obj. 2. Further, some virtues are concerned with the passions which have evil as their object, as meekness with anger, and fortitude with fear. But these passions did not exist in the state of innocence, as was stated above. Therefore neither did those virtues exist then.

Obj. 3. Further, penance is a virtue that regards sin already committed. Mercy, too, is a virtue concerned with unhappiness. But in the state of innocence neither sin nor unhappiness existed. Therefore

---

1. 参见 Q. 97, a. 2.
2. 参见 Aristotle, *Eth.*, III, 12 (1119b 16).

neither did those virtues exist.

Obj. 4. Further, perseverance is a virtue. But Adam possessed it not, as is proved by his subsequent sin. Therefore he did not possess every virtue.

Obj. 5. Further, faith is a virtue. But it did not exist in the state of innocence, for it implies an obscurity of knowledge which seems to be incompatible with the perfection of the first state.

On the contrary, Augustine says in a homily: *The prince of sin overcame Adam who was made from the slime of the earth to the image of God, adorned with modesty, restrained by temperance, refulgent with brightness.*[1]

I answer that, In the state of innocence man in a certain sense possessed all the virtues. This can be proved from what precedes. For it was shown above that such was the rectitude of the first state, that reason was subject to God, and the lower powers to reason. Now the virtues are nothing but those perfections whereby reason is directed to God, and the inferior powers regulated according to the dictate of reason, as will be explained in the Treatise on the Virtues.[2] Therefore the rectitude of the first state required that man should in a measure possess every virtue.

It must, however, be noted that some virtues of their very nature do not involve imperfection, such as charity and justice; and these virtues did exist in the first state absolutely, both in habit and in act. But other virtues are of such a nature as to imply imperfection either in their act or on the part of the matter. Now if this imperfection be consistent with the perfection of the first state, then such virtues could exist in that state; as faith, which is of things not seen, and hope, which is of things not yet possessed. For the perfection of that state did not extend to the vision of the divine essence and the possession of God with the enjoyment of final beatitude. Hence faith and hope could exist

---

1. 参见 Pseudo-Augustine, *Serm. contra Iudaeos*, II (PL 42, 1117).
2. 参见 *S. T.*, I–II, q. 56, a. 4 and 6; q. 63, a. 2.

in the first state, both as to habit and as to act. But any virtue, which implies imperfection incompatible with the perfection of the first state, could exist in that state as a habit, but not as to the act: for instance, penance, which is sorrow for sin committed, and mercy, which is sorrow for others' unhappiness, because sorrow, guilt and unhappiness are incompatible with the perfection of the first state. Therefore such virtues existed as habits in the first man, but not as to their acts; for he was so disposed that he would repent, if there had been a sin for which to repent, and had he seen unhappiness in his neighbor, he would have done his best to remedy it. This is in accordance with what the Philosopher says: *Shame, which regards what is ill done may be found in a virtuous man, but only conditionally; for he is so disposed that he would be ashamed if he did wrong.*[1]

Reply Obj. 1. It is accidental to temperance and fortitude to subdue superabundant passion, in so far as they are in a subject which happens to have superabundant passions; but those virtues are *per se* competent to moderate the passions.

Reply Obj. 2. Passions which have evil for their object are incompatible with the perfection of the first state, if that evil be in the one affected by the passion. Such is the case with fear and sorrow. But passions which relate to evil in another are not incompatible with the perfection of the first state, for in that state man could hate the demons' malice, as he could love God's goodness. Thus the virtues which relate to such passions could exist in the first state, both in habit and in act. Virtues, however, relating to passions which regard evil in the same subject, if relating to such passions only, could not exist actually in the first state, but only in habit, as we have said above of penance and of mercy. But there are other virtues which have relation not to such passions only, but to others. Such are temperance,

---

1. 参见 *Eth.*, IV, 9 (1128b 29).

which relates not only to sorrow, but also to joy, and fortitude, which relates not only to fear, but also to daring and hope. Thus the act of temperance could exist in the first state, so far as it moderates pleasure; and in like manner fortitude, as moderating daring and hope, but not as moderating sorrow and fear.

Reply Obj. 3 appears from what has been said above.

Reply Obj. 4. Perseverance may be taken in two ways: in one sense as a particular virtue, signifying a habit whereby a man makes a choice of persevering in good. In this sense Adam possessed perseverance. In another sense, it is taken as a circumstance of virtue, signifying a certain uninterrupted continuation of virtue; in which sense Adam did not possess perseverance.

Reply Obj. 5 appears from what has been said above.

Fourth Article
WHETHER THE WORKS OF THE FIRST MAN WERE LESS MERITORIOUS THAN OURS ARE?

We proceed thus to the Fourth Article:—

Objection 1. It would seem that the works of the first man were less meritorious than ours are. For grace is given to us through the mercy of God, Who succors most those who are most in need. Now we are more in need of grace than was man in the state of innocence. Therefore grace is more copiously poured out upon us, and since grace is the source of merit, our works are more meritorious.

Obj. 2. Further, struggle and difficulty are required for merit. For it is written (*2 Tim.* ii. 5): *He ... is not crowned except he strive lawfully*; and the Philosopher says: *The object of virtue is the difficult and the good.*[1] But there is more strife and difficulty now. Therefore there is greater

1. 参见 *Op. cit.*, II, 3 (1105a 9).

efficacy for merit.

Obj. 3. Further, the Master says that *man would not have merited in resisting temptation, whereas he does merit now, when he resists.*[1] Therefore our works are more meritorious than in the first state.

On the contrary, if such were the case, man would be better off after sinning.

I answer that, Merit, as regards degree, may be gauged in two ways. First, in its root, which is grace and charity. Merit thus measured corresponds in degree to the essential reward, which consists in the enjoyment of God; for the greater the charity whence our actions proceed, the more perfectly shall we enjoy God. Secondly, the degree of merit is measured by the degree of the action itself. This degree is of two kinds, absolute and proportional. The widow who put two mites into the treasury performed a deed of absolutely less degree than others who put great sums therein. But in proportionate degree the widow gave more, as Our Lord[2] said, because she gave more in proportion to her means. In each of these cases the degree of merit corresponds to the accidental reward, which consists in rejoicing in a created good.

We conclude therefore that in the state of innocence man's works were more meritorious than after sin was committed, if we consider the degree of merit on the part of grace, which would have been more copious as meeting with no obstacle in human nature. And in like manner, it would have been more meritorious, if we consider the absolute degree of the work done; because, as man would have had greater virtue, he would have performed greater works. But if we consider the proportional degree, a greater reason for merit exists after sin, because of man's weakness; because a small deed is more beyond the capacity of one who works with difficulty than a great deed is

---

1. 参见 Peter Lombard, *Sent.*, II, xxiv, 1 (I, 420).
2. Our Lord: 我们的主，指耶稣基督

beyond one who performs it easily.

Reply Obj. 1. After sin man requires grace for more things than before sin, but he does not need grace more. For even before sin man required grace to obtain eternal life, which is the chief reason for the need of grace. But after sin man required grace also for the remission of sin, and for the support of his weakness.

Reply Obj. 2. Difficulty and struggle belong to the degree of merit according to the proportional degree of the work done, as was explained above. It is also a sign of the will's promptitude that it strives after what is difficult to itself; for the promptitude[1] of the will is caused by the intensity of charity. Yet it may happen that a person performs an easy deed with as prompt a will as another, who is ready to do even what may be difficult to him, performs an arduous deed. But the actual difficulty, by its penal character, enables the deed to satisfy for sin.

Reply Obj. 3. The first man would not have gained merit in resisting temptation, according to the opinion of those who say that he did not possess grace; even as now there is no merit to those who have not grace. But in this point there is a difference, inasmuch as in the first state there was no interior impulse to evil, as in our present state. Hence man was more able then than now to resist temptation without grace.

---

1. promptitude: 敏捷；迅速

Question XCVI
THE MASTERSHIP BELONGING TO MAN IN THE STATE OF INNOCENCE
(*In Four Articles*)

WE next consider the mastership which belonged to man in the state of innocence. Under this head there are four points of inquiry: (1) Whether man in the state of innocence was master over the animals? (2) Whether he was master over all creatures? (3) Whether in the state of innocence all men were equal? (4) Whether in that state man would have been master over men?

First Article
WHETHER IN THE STATE OF INNOCENCE ADAM HAD MASTERSHIP OVER THE ANIMALS?

We proceed thus to the First Article:—

Objection 1. It would seem that in the state of innocence Adam had no mastership over the animals. For Augustine says that the animals were brought to Adam, under the direction of the angels, to receive their names from him.[1] But the angels need not have intervened thus, if man himself were master over the animals. Therefore in the state of innocence man had no mastership of the animals.

Obj. 2. Further, it is unfitting that beings hostile to one another should be brought under the mastership of one. But many animals are

---

1. 参见 *De Genesi ad Litt.*, IX, 14 (PL 34, 402).

hostile to one another, as the sheep and the wolf. Therefore all animals were not brought under the mastership of man.

Obj. 3. Further, Jerome says: *God gave man mastership over the animals, although before sin he had no need of them; for God foresaw that after sin animals would become useful to man.*[1] Therefore, before sin, it was at least unfitting for man to make use of his mastership.

Obj. 4. Further, it is proper to a master to command. But a command is not given rightly save to a rational being. Therefore man had no mastership over the irrational animals.

On the contrary, It is written (*Gen.* i. 26): *Let him have dominion over the fishes of the sea, and the birds of the air, and the beasts of the earth.*

I answer that, As was above stated, for his disobedience to God, man was punished by the disobedience of those creatures which should be subject to him.[2] Therefore in the state of innocence, before man had disobeyed, nothing disobeyed him that was naturally subject to him. Now all animals are naturally subject to man. This can be proved in three ways. First, from the order observed by nature. For just as in the generation of things we perceive a certain order of procession of the perfect from the imperfect (thus matter is for the sake of form, and the imperfect form, for the sake of the perfect), so also is there order in the use of natural things. For the imperfect are for the use of the perfect: plants make use of the earth for their nourishment, animals make use of plants, and man makes use of both plants and animals. Therefore it is in keeping with the order of nature that man should be master over animals. Hence the Philosopher says that the hunting of wild animals is just and natural, because man thereby exercises a natural right.[3] Secondly, this is proved from the order of divine providence which always governs inferior things by the superior. Therefore, since

1. 参见 St. Bede, *Hexaëm.*, I, super *Gen.*, I, 26 (PL 91, 200).
2. 参见 Q. 95, a. 1.
3. 参见 *Polit.*, I, 3 (1256b 24).

man, being made to the image of God, is above other animals, these are rightly subject to his government. Thirdly, this is proved from a property of man and of other animals. For we see in the latter a certain participation of prudence by means of a natural judgment, in regard to certain particular acts; whereas man possesses a universal prudence as regards all practical matters. Now whatever is participated is subject to what is essentially and universally so. Therefore the subjection of other animals to man is natural.

Reply Obj. 1. A higher power can do many things that an inferior power cannot do to those which are subject to them. Now an angel is naturally higher than man. Therefore certain things in regard to animals could be done by angels, which could not be done by man: for instance, the rapid gathering together of all the animals.

Reply Obj. 2. In the opinion of some, those animals which now are fierce and kill others would, in that state, have been tame, not only in regard to man, but also in regard to other animals.[1] But this is quite unreasonable. For the nature of animals was not changed by man's sin, as if those whose nature now it is to devour the flesh of others, as the lion and falcon, would then have lived on herbs. Nor does Bede's *Gloss* on *Gen.* i. 30 say that trees and herbs were given as food to all animals and birds, but to some.[2] Thus there would have been a natural antipathy[3] between some animals. They would not, however, on this account have been excepted from the mastership of man; as neither at present are they for that reason excepted from the mastership of God, Whose providence has ordained all this. Of this providence man would have been the executor, as appears even now

1. 参见 Alex. of Hales, *Summa Theol.*, II, I, no. 522 (II, 781); St. Bonaventure, *In II Sent.*, d. xv, a. 2, q. 1 (II, 383).
2. 参见 *Glossa ordin.*, super *Gen.*, I, 30 (I, 28 F); St. Bede, *In Pentat.*, super *Gen.*, I, 30 (PL 91, 202).
3. antipathy: 反感；厌恶

in regard to domestic animals, since fowls are given by men as food to trained falcons.

Reply Obj. 3. In the state of innocence man would not have had any bodily need of animals:—neither for clothing, since then they were naked and not ashamed, for there were no inordinate motions of concupiscence,—nor for food, since they fed on the trees of paradise,—nor to carry him about, for his body was strong enough for that purpose. But man needed animals in order to have experimental knowledge of their natures. This is signified by the fact that God led the animals to man, that he might give them names expressive of their respective natures.

Reply Obj. 4. All animals have by natural judgment a certain participation in prudence and reason, which accounts for the fact that cranes follow their leader, and bees obey their queen. So all animals would have obeyed man of their own accord, as in the present state some domestic animals obey him.

Second Article
WHETHER MAN WOULD HAVE HAD MASTERSHIP OVER ALL OTHER CREATURES?

We proceed thus to the Second Article:—

Objection 1. It would seem that in the state of innocence man would not have had mastership over all other creatures. For an angel naturally has a greater power than man. But, as Augustine says, *corporeal matter would not have obeyed even the holy angels.*[1] Much less therefore would it have obeyed man in the state of innocence.

Obj. 2. Further, the only powers of the soul existing in plants are nutritive, augmentative and generative. Now these do not naturally

---

1. 参见 *De Trin.*, III, 8 (PL 42, 875).

obey reason, as we can see in the case of any one man. Therefore, since it is by his reason that man is competent to have mastership, it seems that in the state of innocence man had no dominion over plants.

Obj. 3. Further, whosoever is master of a thing, can change it. But man could not have changed the course of the heavenly bodies, for this belongs to God alone, as Dionysius says.[1] Therefore man had no dominion over them.

On the contrary, It is written (*Gen.* i. 26): *That he may have dominion over ... every creature.*

I answer that, Man in a certain sense contains all things, and so according as he is master of what is within himself, in the same way he can have mastership over other things. Now we may consider four things in man: his *reason*, which makes him like to the angels; his *sensitive powers*, whereby he is like the animals; his *natural powers*, which liken him to the plants; and *the body* itself, wherein he is like to inanimate things. Now in man reason has the position of a master and not of a subject. Therefore man had no mastership over the angels in the first state. So when we read *all creatures*, we must understand the creatures which are not made to God's image. Over the sensitive powers, as the irascible and concupiscible, which obey reason in some degree, the soul has mastership by commanding. So in the state of innocence man had mastership over the animals by commanding them. But of the natural powers and the body itself man is master, not by commanding, but by using them. Thus also in the state of innocence man's mastership over plants and inanimate things consisted, not in commanding or in changing them, but in making use of them without hindrance.

The answers to the objections appear from the above.

---

1. 参见 *Epist.* VII, 2 (PG 3, 1080).

Third Article

WHETHER IN THE STATE OF INNOCENCE MEN WOULD HAVE BEEN EQUAL?

We proceed thus to the Third Article:—

Objection 1. It would seem that in the state of innocence all would have been equal. For Gregory says: *Where there is no sin, there is no inequality.*[1] But in the state of innocence there was no sin. Therefore all were equal.

Obj. 2. Further, likeness and equality are the basis of mutual love, according to *Ecclus.* xiii. 19, *Every beast loveth its like; so also every man him that is nearest to himself.* Now in that state there was among men an abundance of love, which is the bond of peace. Therefore all would have been equal in the state of innocence.

Obj. 3. Further, when the cause ceases, the effect also ceases. But the cause of present inequality among men seems to arise, on the part of God, from the fact that He rewards some and punishes others; and on the part of nature, from the fact that some, through a defect of nature, are born weak and deficient, and others strong and perfect, which would not have been the case in the first state.

On the contrary, It is written (*Rom.* xiii. 1): *The things which are of God, are well ordered.* But order consists chiefly in inequality, for Augustine says: *Order disposes things equal and unequal in their proper place.*[2] Therefore in the first state, which would have been most proper and orderly, inequality would exist.

I answer that, We must needs admit that in the first state there would have been some inequality, at least as regards sex, because generation depends upon diversity of sex; and likewise as regards age, for some

---

1. 参见 *Moral.*, XXI, 15 (PL 76, 203).
2. 参见 *De Civit. Dei*, XIX, 13 (PL 41, 640).

would have been born of others, nor would sexual union have been sterile.

Moreover, as regards the soul, there would have been inequality as to justice and knowledge. For man worked, not of necessity, but of his own free choice, by virtue of which man can apply himself, more or less, to action, desire or knowledge. Hence some would have made a greater advance in justice and knowledge than others.

There could also have been bodily disparity[1]. For the human body was not entirely exempt from the laws of nature, so as not to receive from exterior sources more or less advantage and help; since it was likewise dependent on food wherewith to sustain life.

So we may say that, according to the climate, or the movement of the stars, some would have been born more robust in body than others, and also greater, and more beautiful, and in all ways better disposed; so that, however, in those who were thus surpassed, there would have been no defect or fault either in soul or body.

Reply Obj. 1. By those words Gregory means to exclude such inequality as exists between virtue and vice, the result of which is that some are placed in subjection to others as a penalty.

Reply Obj. 2. Equality is the cause of equality in mutual love. Yet between those who are unequal there can be a greater love than between equals, although there be not an equal response; for a father naturally loves his son more than a brother loves his brother, although the son does not love his father as much as he is loved by him.

Reply Obj. 3. The cause of inequality could be on the part of God; not indeed that He would punish some and reward others, but that He would exalt some above others, so that the beauty of order would the more shine forth among men. Inequality might also arise on the part of nature, as was above described, without any defect of nature.

---

1. bodily disparity: 身体差异

Fourth Article

WHETHER IN THE STATE OF INNOCENCE MAN WOULD HAVE BEEN MASTER OVER MAN?

We proceed thus to the Fourth Article:—

Objection 1. It would seem that in the state of innocence man would not have been master over man. For Augustine says: *God willed that man, who was endowed with reason and made to His image, should rule over none but irrational creatures; not over men, but over cattle.*[1]

Obj. 2. Further, what came into the world as a penalty for sin would not have existed in the state of innocence. But man was made subject to man as a penalty; for after sin it was said to woman (*Gen.* iii. 16): *Thou shalt be under thy husband's power.* Therefore in the state of innocence man would not have been subject to man.

Obj. 3. Further, subjection is opposed to liberty. But liberty is one of the chief blessings, and would not have been lacking in the state of innocence, *where nothing was wanting that man's good will could desire*, as Augustine says.[2] Therefore man would not have been master over man in the state of innocence.

On the contrary, The condition of man in the state of innocence was not more exalted than the condition of the angels. But among the angels some rule over others, and so one order is called that of *Dominations*. Therefore it was not beneath the dignity of the state of innocence that one man should be subject to another.

I answer that, Mastership has a twofold meaning. First, it is opposed to slavery, in which sense a master means one to whom another is subject as a slave. In another sense, mastership is referred in a general way to any kind of subject; and in this sense even he who has the

1. 参见 *Op. cit.*, XIX, 15 (PL 41, 643).
2. 参见 *Op. cit.*, XIV, 10 (PL 41, 417).

office of governing and directing free men can be called a master. In the state of innocence man could have been a master of men, not in the former, but in the latter sense. This distinction is founded on the reason that a slave differs from a free man in that the latter *has the disposal of himself*, as is stated in the beginning of the *Metaphysics*,[1] whereas a slave is ordered to another. And so, that man is master of another as his slave when he assigns the one, whose master he is, to his own—namely, the master's use. And since every man's proper good is desirable to himself, and consequently it is a grievous matter to anyone to yield to another what ought to be one's own, therefore such dominion implies of necessity a pain inflicted on the subject; and consequently in the state of innocence such a mastership would not have existed between man and man.

But a man is the master of a free subject by directing him either towards his proper welfare, or to the common good. Such a mastership would have existed in the state of innocence between man and man, for two reasons. First, because man is naturally a social being, and so in the state of innocence he would have led a social life. Now a social life cannot exist among a number of people unless under the governance of one to look after the common good; for many, as such, seek many things, whereas one attends only to one. Hence the Philosopher says, in the beginning of the *Politics*, that wherever many things are directed to one, we shall always find one at the head directing them.[2] Secondly, if one man surpassed another in knowledge and justice, this would not have been fitting unless these gifts conduced to the benefit of others, according to *1 Pet.* iv. 10, *As every man hath received grace, ministering the same one to another.* Therefore Augustine says: *Just men command not by the love of domineering, but by the service of counsel*; and: *The natural order of things requires this*; *and thus did God make*

1. 参见 Aristotle, *Metaph.*, I, 2 (982b 26).
2. 参见 *Polit.*, I, 2 (1254a 28).

man.[1]

From this appear the replies to the objections which are founded on the first-mentioned mode of mastership.

1. 参见 *De Civit. Dei*, XIX, 14 (PL 41, 643).

Question XCVII
THE PRESERVATION OF THE INDIVIDUAL IN THE FIRST STATE
(*In Four Articles*)

WE next consider what belongs to the bodily state of the first man: first, as regards the preservation of the individual; secondly, as regards the preservation of the species.[1]

Under the first head there are four points of inquiry: (1) Whether man in the state of innocence was immortal? (2) Whether he was impassible? (3) Whether he stood in need of food? (4) Whether he would have obtained immortality by the tree of life?

First Article
WHETHER IN THE STATE OF INNOCENCE MAN WOULD HAVE BEEN IMMORTAL?

We proceed thus to the First Article:—

Objection 1. It would seem that in the state of innocence man was not immortal. For the term *mortal* belongs to the definition of man. But if you take away the definition, you take away the thing defined. Therefore, as long as man was man, he could not be immortal.

Obj. 2. Further, *corruptible and incorruptible are generically distinct*, as the Philosopher says.[2] But there can be no change from one genus to another. Therefore if the first man was incorruptible, man could not be

1. 参见 Q. 98.
2. 参见 Aristotle, *Metaph.*, IX, 10 (1058b 28).

corruptible in the present state.

Obj. 3. Further, if man was immortal in the state of innocence, this would have been due either to nature or to grace. But not to nature, for since nature does not change within the same species, he would have been immortal also now. Likewise, neither would this be owing to grace, for the first man recovered grace by repentance, according to *Wisdom* x. 2: *He brought him out of his sins.* Hence he would have regained his immortality; which is clearly not the case. Therefore man was not immortal in the state of innocence.

Obj. 4. Further, immortality is promised to man as a reward, according to *Apoc.* xxi. 4: *Death shall be no more.* But man was not created in the state of reward, but that he might deserve the reward. Therefore man was not immortal in the state of innocence.

On the contrary, It is written (*Rom.* v. 12): *By sin death came into the world.* Therefore man was immortal before sin.

I answer that, A thing may be incorruptible in three ways. First, on the part of matter—that is to say, either because it possesses no matter, like an angel, or because it possesses matter that is in potentiality to one form only, like the heavenly bodies. Such things as these are incorruptible by their very nature. Secondly, a thing is incorruptible in its form, inasmuch as, being by nature corruptible, it yet has an inherent disposition which preserves it wholly from corruption. And this is called the incorruptibility of glory, because, as Augustine says, *God made man's soul of such a powerful nature, that from its fullness of beatitude there redounds to the body a fullness of health and the vigor of incorruption.*[1] Thirdly, a thing may be incorruptible on the part of its efficient cause, and it is in this sense that man would have been incorruptible and immortal in the state of innocence. For, as Augustine says, *God made man immortal as long as he did not sin; so that he*

1. 参见 *Epist.* CXVIII, 3 (PL 33, 439).

might achieve for himself life or death.[1] For man's body was indissoluble, not by reason of any intrinsic vigor of immortality, but by reason of a supernatural force given by God to the soul, whereby it was enabled to preserve the body from all corruption so long as it itself remained subject to God. This entirely agrees with reason, for since the rational soul surpasses the capacity of corporeal matter, as was above explained,[2] it was most properly endowed in the beginning with the power of preserving the body in a manner surpassing the capacity of corporeal matter.

Reply Obj. 1 and 2. These objections are founded on natural incorruptibility and immortality.

Reply Obj. 3. This power of preserving the body from corruption was not natural to the soul, but the gift of grace. And though man recovered grace for the remission of guilt and the merit of glory, yet he did not recover grace for the immortality which was lost; for this was reserved for Christ to accomplish, by Whom the defect of nature was to be restored into something better, as we shall explain further on.[3]

Reply Obj. 4. The promised reward of the immortality of glory differs from the immortality which was bestowed on man in the state of innocence.

Second Article
WHETHER IN THE STATE OF INNOCENCE MAN WOULD HAVE BEEN PASSIBLE?

We proceed thus to the Second Article:—

Objection 1. It seems that in the state of innocence man would have been passible. For *sensation is a kind of passion.* But in the state of

---

1. 参见 Cf. Ambrosiaster, *De Quaest. Vet. et Nov. Test.*, q. 19 (PL 35, 2227).
2. 参见 Q. 76, a. 1.
3. 参见 *S. T.*, III, q. 14, a. 4, ad 1.

innocence man would have been sensitive. Therefore he would have been passible.

Obj. 2. Further, sleep is a kind of passion. Now, man slept in the state of innocence, according to *Gen.* ii. 21, *God cast a deep sleep upon Adam.* Therefore he would have been passible.

Obj. 3. Further, the same passage goes on to say that He *took a rib out of Adam.* Therefore he was passible even to the degree of the cutting out of part of his body.

Obj. 4. Further, man's body was soft. But a soft body is naturally passible as regards a hard body; therefore if a hard body had come in contact with the soft body of the first man, the latter would have suffered from the impact. Therefore the first man was passible.

On the contrary, Had man been passible, he would have been also corruptible, because excessive suffering wastes the substance itself.

I answer that, *Passion* may be taken in two senses. First, in its proper sense, and thus a thing is said to suffer when changed from its natural disposition. For passion is the effect of action, and in nature contraries are mutually active or passive, according as one thing changes another from its natural disposition. Secondly, *passion* can be taken in a general sense for any kind of change, even if belonging to the perfection of nature. Thus *understanding and sensation are said to be passions.*[1] In this second sense, man was passible in the state of innocence, and was passive both in soul and body. In the first sense, man was impassible, both in soul and body, as he was likewise immortal; for he could curb his passion, as he could avoid death, so long as he refrained from sin.

Thus it is clear how to reply to the first two objections, since sensation and sleep do not remove from man his natural disposition, but are ordered to his natural welfare.

Reply Obj. 3. As was already explained, the rib was in Adam as

---

1. 参见 Aristotle, *De An.*, III, 4 (429a 13).

the principle of the human race, as the semen in man, who is a principle through generation.[1] Hence as man does not suffer any natural deterioration by seminal issue, so neither did he through the separation of the rib.

Reply Obj. 4. In the state of innocence, man's body could be preserved from suffering injury from a hard body, partly by the use of his reason, whereby he could avoid what was harmful; and partly also by divine providence, which so preserved him, that nothing of a harmful nature could come upon him unawares.

Third Article
WHETHER IN THE STATE OF INNOCENCE MAN HAD NEED OF FOOD?

We proceed thus to the Third Article:—

Objection 1. It would seem that in the state of innocence man did not require food. For food is necessary for man to restore what he has lost. But Adam's body suffered no loss, as being incorruptible. Therefore he had no need of food.

Obj. 2. Further, food is needed for nourishment. But nourishment involves passibility. Since, then, man's body was impassible, it does not appear how food could be needful to him.

Obj. 3. Further, we need food for the preservation of life. But Adam could preserve his life otherwise, for had he not sinned, he would not have died. Therefore he did not require food.

Obj. 4. Further, the consumption of food involves voiding of the surplus, which seems unsuitable to the state of innocence. Therefore it seems that in the first state man did not take food.

On the contrary, It is written (*Gen.* ii. 16): *Of every tree in Paradise ye shall*

---

1. 参见 Q. 92, a. 3, ad 2.

eat.

I answer that, In the state of innocence man had an animal life requiring food, but after the resurrection he will have a spiritual life needing no food. In order to make this clear, we must observe that the rational soul is both a soul and a spirit. It is called a soul by reason of what it possesses in common with other souls —that is, as giving life to the body. Hence it is written (*Gen.* ii. 7): *Man was made into a living soul*, that is, a soul giving life to the body. But the soul is called a spirit according to what properly belongs to itself, and not to other souls, namely, an immaterial intellectual power.

Thus in the first state, the rational soul communicated to the body what belonged to itself as a soul; and so the body was called *animal* (*1 Cor.* xv. 44) through having its life from the soul. Now the first principle of life in these sublunary creatures, as the Philosopher says, is the vegetative soul,[1] whose operations are the use of food, generation and growth. Therefore such operations befitted man in the state of innocence. But in the final state, after the resurrection, the soul will in a way communicate to the body what properly belongs to itself as a spirit: immortality, for everyone; impassibility, glory and power, for the good, whose bodies will be called *spiritual* (*1 Cor.* xv. 44). So, after the resurrection, man will not require food; whereas he required it in the state of innocence.

Reply Obj. 1. As Augustine says, *How could man have an immortal body, which was sustained by food? Since an immortal being needs neither food nor drink.*[2] For we have explained that the immortality of the first state was based on a supernatural force in the soul, and not on any intrinsic disposition of the body. Hence, by the action of heat, the body might lose part of its moisture; and to prevent the entire consumption of the moisture, man was obliged to take food.

---

1. 参见 Aristotle, *De An.*, II, 4 (415a 23); III, 9 (432b 8).
2. 参见 Cf. Ambrosiaster, *De Quaest. Vet. et Nov. Test.*, I, q. 19 (PL 35, 2227).

Reply Obj. 2. A certain passion and alteration attends nutriment, on the part of the food changed into the substance of the being nourished. So we cannot thence conclude that man's body was passible, but that the food taken was passible; although even this kind of passion conduced to the perfection of the nature.

Reply Obj. 3. If man had not taken food he would have sinned, as he also sinned by taking the forbidden fruit. For he was told, at the same time, to abstain from the tree of the knowledge of good and evil, and to eat of every other tree of Paradise.

Reply Obj. 4. Some say that in the state of innocence man would not have taken more than necessary food, so that there would have been nothing superfluous.[1] This, however, is unreasonable to suppose, as implying that there would have been no fæcal matter. Therefore there was need for voiding the surplus, yet so disposed by God as not to be unbefitting.

Fourth Article
WHETHER IN THE STATE OF INNOCENCE MAN WOULD HAVE ACQUIRED IMMORTALITY BY THE TREE OF LIFE?

We proceed thus to the Fourth Article:—

Objection 1. It would seem that the tree of life could not be the cause of immortality. For nothing can act beyond its own species, since an effect does not exceed its cause. But the tree of life was corruptible, or otherwise it could not be taken as food; since food is changed into the substance of the being nourished. Therefore the tree of life could not give incorruptibility or immortality.

Obj. 2. Further, effects caused by the powers of plants and other natural agencies are natural. If therefore the tree of life caused

---

1. 参见 Cf. Alex. of Hales, *Summa Theol.*, II, I, no. 457 (II, 592).

immortality, this would have been natural immortality.

Obj. 3. Further, this would seem to return to the ancient fable that the gods, by eating a certain food, became immortal; which the Philosopher ridicules.[1]

On the contrary, It is written (*Gen.* iii. 22): *Lest perhaps he put forth his hand, and take of the tree of life, and eat, and live for ever.* Further, Augustine says: *A taste of the tree of life warded off corruption of the body ; and even after sin man would have remained immortal, had he been allowed to eat of the tree of life.*[2]

I answer that, The tree of life in a certain way was the cause of immortality, but not absolutely. To understand this, we must observe that in the first state man possessed, for the preservation of life, two remedies, against two defects. One of these defects was the loss of moisture by the action of natural heat, which acts as the soul's instrument. As a remedy against such loss man was provided with food, taken from the other trees of paradise, as now we are provided with the food, which we take for the same purpose. The second defect, as the Philosopher says, arises from the fact that the moisture which is caused from extraneous sources lessens the specific active power when it is added to what was already moist;[3] just as water added to wine takes at first the taste of wine, but then, as more water is added, the strength of the wine is diminished, till the wine becomes watery. In like manner, we may observe that at first the active power of the species is so strong that it is able to transform so much of the food as is required to replace the lost tissue, and also what suffices for growth. Later on, however, the assimilated food does not suffice for growth, but only replaces what is lost. Last of all, in old age, it does not suffice even for this purpose; whereupon the body declines, and finally dies from

1. 参见 *Metaph.*, II, 4 (1000a 12).
2. 参见 Cf. Ambrosiaster, *De Quaest. Vet. et Nov. Test.*, I, q. 19 (PL 35, 2227).
3. 参见 *De Gener.*, I, 5 (322a 28).

natural causes. Against this defect man was provided with a remedy in the tree of life; for its effect was to strengthen the power of the species against the weakness resulting from the admixture of extraneous nutriment. Therefore Augustine says: *Man had food to appease his hunger, drink to slake his thirst, and the tree of life to banish the dissolution of old age*;[1] and: *The tree of life, like a drug, warded off all bodily corruption.*[2]

Yet it did not absolutely cause immortality, for neither was the soul's intrinsic power of preserving the body due to the tree of life, nor was it of such efficacy as to give the body a disposition to immortality, whereby it might become indissoluble; which is clear from the fact that every bodily power is finite. So the power of the tree of life could not go so far as to give the body the prerogative of living for an infinite time, but only for a definite time. For it is manifest that the greater a power is, the more durable is its effect. Therefore, since the power of the tree of life was finite, man's life was to be preserved for a definite time by partaking of it once; and when that time had elapsed, man was to be either transferred to a spiritual life, or had need to eat once more of the tree of life.

From this the replies to the objections clearly appear. For the first proves that the tree of life did not absolutely cause immortality; while the others show that it caused incorruption by warding off corruption, according to the explanation above given.

---

1. 参见 *De Civit. Dei*, XIV, 26 (PL 41, 434).
2. 参见 Cf. Ambrosiaster, *De Quaest. Vet. et Nov. Test.*, I, q. 19 (PL 35, 2228).

Question XCVIII
THE PRESERVATION OF THE SPECIES
(*In Two Articles*)

WE next consider what belongs to the preservation of the species; and, first, of generation; secondly, of the state of the offspring.[1] Under the first head there are two points of inquiry: (1) Whether in the state of innocence there would have been generation? (2) Whether generation would have been through coition?

First Article
WHETHER IN THE STATE OF INNOCENCE GENERATION WOULD HAVE EXISTED?

We proceed thus to the First Article:—

Objection 1. It would seem that there would have been no generation in the state of innocence. For, as is stated in *Physics* v., *corruption is contrary to generation.*[2] But contraries affect the same subject. Now there would have been no corruption in the state of innocence. Therefore neither would there have been generation.

Obj. 2. Further, the object of generation is the preservation in the species of that which is corruptible in the individual. Therefore there is no generation in those individuals which last forever. But in the state of innocence man would have lived forever. Therefore in the state of innocence there would have been no generation.

---

1. 参见 Q. 99.
2. 参见 Aristotle, *Phys.*, V, 5 (229b 12).

Obj. 3. Further, by generation man is multiplied. But the multiplication of masters requires the division of property, to avoid confusion of mastership. Therefore, since man was made master of the animals, it would have been necessary to make a division of rights when the human race increased by generation. This is against the natural law, according to which all things are in common, as Isidore says.[1] Therefore there would have been no generation in the state of innocence.

On the contrary, It is written (*Gen.* i. 28): *Increase and multiply, and fill the earth.* But this increase could not come about save by generation, since the original number of mankind was only two. Therefore there would have been generation in the state of innocence.

I answer that, In the state of innocence there would have been generation of offspring for the multiplication of the human race. Otherwise, man's sin would have been very necessary, for such a great blessing to be its result. We must, therefore, observe that by his nature man is established, as it were, midway between corruptible and incorruptible creatures, since his soul is naturally incorruptible, while his body is naturally corruptible. We must also observe that nature's purpose appears to be different as regards corruptible and incorruptible things. For that seems to be the direct purpose of nature, which is invariable and perpetual; while what is only for a time is seemingly not the chief purpose of nature, but, as it were, subordinate to something else. Otherwise, when it ceased to exist, nature's purpose would become void.

Therefore, since in corruptible things none is everlasting and permanent except the species, it follows that the chief purpose of nature is the good of the species, for the preservation of which natural generation is ordained. On the other hand, incorruptible substances survive, not only in the species, but also in the individual; and

---

1. 参见 *Etymol.*, V, 4 (PL 82, 199).

therefore even the individuals are included in the chief purpose of nature.

Hence it belongs to man to beget offspring, because of his naturally corruptible body. But on the part of the soul, which is incorruptible, it is fitting that the multitude of individuals should be the direct purpose of nature, or rather of the Author of nature, Who alone is the creator of the human soul. Hence, to provide for the multiplication of the human race, He established the begetting of offspring even in the state of innocence.

Reply Obj. 1. In the state of innocence, the human body was in itself corruptible, but it could be preserved from corruption by the soul. Therefore, since generation belongs to corruptible things, man was not to be deprived of it.

Reply Obj. 2. Although generation in the state of innocence might not have been required for the preservation of the species, yet it would have been required for the multiplication of individuals.

Reply Obj. 3. In our present state, a division of possessions is necessary because of the multiplicity of masters, inasmuch as community of possession is a source of strife, as the Philosopher says.[1] In the state of innocence, however, the wills of men would have been so ordered that without any danger of strife they would have used in common, according to each one's need, those things of which they were masters—a state of things to be observed even now among many good men.

Second Article
WHETHER IN THE STATE OF INNOCENCE THERE WOULD HAVE BEEN GENERATION BY COITION?

We proceed thus to the Second Article:—

1. 参见 *Polit.*, II, 2 (1263a 21).

Objection 1. It would seem that generation by coition would not have existed in the state of innocence. For, as Damascene says, the first man in the terrestrial Paradise was *like an angel.*[1] But in the future state of the resurrection, when men will be like to the angels, *they shall neither marry nor be married*, as it is written *Matt.* xxii. 30. Therefore neither in Paradise would there have been generation by coition.

Obj. 2. Further, our first parents were created at the age of perfect development. Therefore, if generation by coition had existed before sin, they would have had intercourse even in Paradise; which was not the case, according to Scripture (*Gen.* iv. 1).

Obj. 3. Further, in carnal intercourse, more than at any other time, man becomes like the beasts, because of the vehement[2] delight which he takes therein. Hence it is that continence is praiseworthy, whereby man refrains from such pleasures. But man is compared to beasts by reason of sin, according to *Psalm* xlviii. 13: *Man, when he was in honor, did not understand; he is compared to senseless beasts, and is become like to them.* Therefore, before sin, there would have been no such intercourse of man and woman.

Obj. 4. Further, in the state of innocence there would have been no corruption. But virginal integrity is corrupted by intercourse. Therefore there would have been no such thing in the state of innocence.

On the contrary, God made man and woman before sin (*Gen.* i. 27 and ii. 22). But nothing is vain in God's works. Therefore, even if man had not sinned, there would have been such intercourse, to which the distinction of sex is ordained. Moreover, we are told that woman was made to be a help to man (*Gen.* ii. 18, 20). But she was not fitted to help man except in generation, because another man would have proved a more effective help in anything else. Therefore there would

1. 参见 *De Fide Orth.*, II, 11 (PG 94, 916).
2. vehement: 热烈的；激烈的

have been such generation also in the state of innocence.

I answer that, Some of the earlier doctors, considering the nature of concupiscence as regards generation in our present state, concluded that in the state of innocence generation would not have been effected in the same way.[1] Thus Gregory of Nyssa says that in Paradise the human race would have been multiplied by some other means, as the angels were multiplied without coition by the operation of the divine power.[2] He adds that God made man male and female before sin, because He foreknew the mode of generation which would take place after sin, which He foresaw. But this is unreasonable. For what is natural to man was neither acquired nor forfeited by sin. Now it is clear that generation by coition is natural to man by reason of his animal life, which he possessed even before sin, as was above explained,[3] just as it is natural to other perfect animals. This is made clear by the corporeal members deputed to this work. So we cannot allow that these members would not have had a natural use, as other members had, before sin.

Thus, as regards generation by coition, there are, in the present state of life, two things to be considered. One, which comes from nature, is the union of man and woman; for in every act of generation there is an active and a passive principle. Therefore, since wherever there is distinction of sex, the active principle is male and the passive is female, the order of nature demands that for the purpose of generation there should be concurrence of male and female. The second thing to be observed is a certain deformity of excessive concupiscence, which in the state of innocence would not have existed, when the lower powers were entirely subject to reason. Hence Augustine says: *We must be far*

---

1. 参见 St. John Chrysostom, *In Genesim*, hom. XVI; XVIII (PG 53, 126; 153); St. John Damascene, *De Fide Orth.*, II, 30; IV, 24 (PG 94, 976; 1208).
2. 参见 *De Hom. Opif.*, XVII (PG 44, 189).
3. 参见 Q. 97, a. 3.

from supposing that offspring could not be begotten without concupiscence. All the bodily members would have been equally moved by the will, without ardent or wanton incentive, with calmness of soul and body.[1]

Reply Obj. 1. In Paradise man would have been like an angel in his spirituality of mind, yet with an animal life in his body. After the resurrection, man will be like an angel, spiritualized in soul and body. Therefore there is no parallel.

Reply Obj. 2. As Augustine says, our first parents did not come together in Paradise, for they were ejected from Paradise because of sin shortly after the creation of woman; or for the reason that, having received the general divine command relative to generation, they awaited the special command relative to the time.[2]

Reply Obj. 3. Beasts are without reason. In this way man becomes, as it were, like them in coition, because he cannot moderate concupiscence. In the state of innocence nothing of this kind would have happened that was not regulated by reason, not because delight of sense would be less, as some say[3] (rather indeed would sensible delight have been the greater in proportion to the greater purity of nature and the greater sensibility of the body), but because the force of concupiscence would not have so inordinately thrown itself into such pleasure, being curbed by reason, whose place it is not to lessen sensual pleasure, but to prevent the force of concupiscence from cleaving to it immoderately. By *immoderately* I mean going beyond the bounds of reason, as a sober person does not take less pleasure in food taken in moderation than the glutton, but his concupiscence lingers less in such pleasures. This is what Augustine means by the

---

1. 参见 *De Civit. Dei*, XIV, 26 (PL 41, 434).
2. 参见 *De Genesi ad Litt.*, IX, 4 (PL 34, 395).
3. 参见 St. Bonaventure, *In II Sent.*, d. xx, a. 1, q. 3 (II, 481) ; Alex. of Hales, *Summa Theol.*, II, I, no. 496 (II, 703).

words quoted,[1] which do not exclude intensity of pleasure from the state of innocence, but the ardor of lust and restlessness of the soul. Therefore continence would not have been praiseworthy in the state of innocence, whereas it is praiseworthy in our present state, not because it removes fecundity, but because it excludes inordinate desire. In that state fecundity[2] would have been without lust.

Reply Obj. 4. As Augustine says: In that state *intercourse would have been without prejudice to virginal integrity. For the semen could enter without the impairment of the genital organs, just as now the menstrual flow in a virgin does not impair her integrity. And just as in giving birth the mother was then relieved, not by groans of pain, but by the instigations of maturity, so in conceiving, the union was one, not of lustful desire, but of deliberate action.*[3]

1. 参见 *De Civit. Dei*, XIV, 26 (PL 41, 434).
2. fecundity: 多产；富饶
3. 同上

Question XCIX
THE CONDITION OF THE OFFSPRING AS TO THE BODY
(*In Two Articles*)

We must now consider the condition of the offspring—first, as regards the body; secondly, as regards virtue;[1] thirdly, in knowledge.[2] Under the first head there are two points of inquiry: (1) Whether in the state of innocence children would have had full powers of the body immediately after birth? (2) Whether all infants would have been of the male sex?

First Article
WHETHER IN THE STATE OF INNOCENCE CHILDREN WOULD HAVE HAD PERFECT STRENGTH OF BODY AS TO THE USE OF ITS MEMBERS IMMEDIATELY AFTER BIRTH?

We proceed thus to the First Article:—

Objection 1. It would seem that in the state of innocence children would have had perfect strength of the body, as to the use of its members, immediately after birth. For Augustine says of children: *This weakness of the body befits their weakness of mind.*[3] But in the state of innocence there would have been no weakness of mind. Therefore neither would there have been weakness of body in infants.

---

1. 参见 Q. 101.
2. 参见 Q. 100.
3. 参见 *De Pecc. Remiss. et Bapt. Parv.*, I, 38 (PL 44, 150).

Obj. 2. Further, some animals at birth have sufficient strength to use their members. But man is nobler than other animals. Therefore much more is it natural to man to have strength to use his members at birth; and thus it appears to be a punishment of sin that he has not that strength.

Obj. 3. Further, inability to secure a proffered pleasure causes affliction. But if children had not full strength in the use of their members, they would often have been unable to procure something pleasurable offered to them; and so they would have been afflicted, which was not possible before sin. Therefore, in the state of innocence, children would not have been deprived of the use of their members.

Obj. 4. Further, the weakness of old age seems to correspond to that of infancy. But in the state of innocence there would have been no weakness of old age. Therefore neither would there have been such weakness in infancy.

On the contrary, Everything generated is first imperfect. But in the state of innocence children would have been begotten by generation. Therefore from the first they would have been imperfect in bodily size and power.

I answer that, By faith alone do we hold truths which are above nature, and what we believe rests on authority. Therefore, in making any assertion, we must be guided by the nature of things, except in those things which are above nature, and are made known to us by divine authority. Now it is clear that it is as natural as it is befitting to the principles of human nature that children do not have sufficient strength for the use of their members immediately after birth. Because in proportion to other animals man has naturally a larger brain. Hence, it is natural, because of the considerable humidity of the brain in children, that the nerves which are instruments of movement should not be equal to the task of moving the members. On the other hand, no Catholic doubts it possible for a child to have, by divine power, the use of its members immediately after birth.

Now we have it on the authority of Scripture that *God made man right* (*Eccles.* vii. 30); which rightness, as Augustine says, consists in the perfect subjection of the body to the soul.[1] As, therefore, in the first state it was impossible to find in the human members anything repugnant to man's well-ordered will, so it was impossible for those members to fail in executing the will's commands. Now the human will is well ordered when it tends to acts which are befitting to man. But the same acts are not befitting to man at every season of life. We must, therefore, conclude that children would not have had sufficient strength for the use of their members for the purpose of performing every kind of act; but only for the acts befitting the state of infancy, such as suckling, and the like.

Reply Obj. 1. Augustine is speaking of the weakness which we observe in children even as regards those acts which befit the state of infancy; as is clear from his preceding remark that *even when close to the breast, and longing for it, they are more apt to cry than to suckle.*[2]

Reply Obj. 2. The fact that some animals have the use of their members immediately after birth is due, not to their superiority, since more perfect animals are not so endowed, but to the dryness of the brain, and to the fact that the operations proper to such animals are imperfect, so that a small amount of strength suffices them.

Reply Obj. 3 is clear from what we have said above. We may add that they would have desired nothing except with an ordinate will, and only what was befitting to their state of life.

Reply Obj. 4. In the state of innocence man would have been born, yet not subject to corruption. Therefore in that state there could have been certain infantile defects which result from birth; but not senile defects leading to corruption.

---

1. 参见 *De Civit. Dei*, XIII, 13 (PL 41, 386); *De Pecc. Remiss. et Bapt. Parv.*, I, 16 (PL 44, 120).
2. 参见 *Op. cit.*, I, 38 (PL 44, 150).

Second Article

WHETHER, IN THE FIRST STATE, WOMEN WOULD HAVE BEEN BORN?

We proceed thus to the Second Article:—

Objection 1. It would seem that in the first state women would not have been born. For the Philosopher says that woman is a *misbegotten male*,[1] as though she were a product outside the purpose of nature. But in that state nothing would have been unnatural in human generation. Therefore in that state women would not have been born.

Obj. 2. Further, every agent produces its like, unless prevented by insufficient power or ineptness of matter: *e.g.*, a small fire cannot burn green wood. But in generation, the active power is in the male. Since, therefore, in the state of innocence man's active power would not have been subject to defect, nor would there have been any inept matter on the part of woman, it seems that males would always have been born.

Obj. 3. Further, in the state of innocence generation is ordered to the multiplication of the human race. But the race could have been sufficiently multiplied by the first man and woman, from the fact that they would have lived forever. Therefore, in the state of innocence, there would have been no need for women to be born.

On the contrary, nature's process in generation would have been in harmony with the manner in which it was established by God. But God established male and female in human nature, as it is written (*Gen.* i. 27 and ii. 22). Therefore also in the state of innocence male and female would have been born.

I answer that, Nothing belonging to the completeness of human nature would have been lacking in the state of innocence. And as

---

1. 参见 *De Gener. Anim.*, II, 3 (737a 27).

different grades belong to the perfection of the universe, so also diversity of sex belongs to the perfection of human nature. Therefore in the state of innocence both sexes would have been begotten.

Reply Obj. 1. Woman is said to be a *misbegotten male*, as being a product outside the purpose of nature considered in the individual case, but not against the purpose of universal nature, as was above explained.[1]

Reply Obj. 2. The generation of woman is not occasioned either by a defect of the active force or by inept matter, as the objection supposes; but sometimes by an extrinsic accidental cause. Thus the Philosopher says: *The northern wind favors the generation of males, and the southern wind that of females.*[2] Sometimes the generation of woman is occasioned also by some impression in the soul, which may easily have some effect on the body. Especially could this be the case in the state of innocence, when the body was more subject to the soul; so that by the mere will of the parent the sex of the offspring might be diversified.

Reply Obj. 3 The offspring would have been begotten in possession of an animal life, to which belong both the use of food and generation. Hence it was fitting that all should generate, and not only the first parents. From this it seems to follow that males and females would have been equal in number.

---

1. 参见 Q. 92, a. 1, ad 1.
2. 参见 *Hist. Anim.*, VI, 19 (547a 1).

Question C
THE CONDITION OF THE OFFSPRING AS REGARDS JUSTICE
(*In Two Articles*)

WE now have to consider the condition of the offspring as to justice. Under this head there are two points of inquiry: (1) Whether men would have been born in a state of justice? (2) Whether they would have been born confirmed in justice?

First Article
WHETHER MEN WOULD HAVE BEEN BORN IN A STATE OF JUSTICE?

We proceed thus to the First Article:—

Objection 1. It would seem that in the state of innocence men would not have been born in a state of justice. For Hugh of St. Victor says: *Before sin, the first man would have begotten children sinless, but not heirs to their father's justice.*[1]

Obj. 2. Further, justice is effected by grace, as the Apostle says (*Rom.* v. 16, 21). Now grace is not transfused from one to another, for thus it would be natural, but is infused by God alone. Therefore children would not have been born just.

Obj. 3. Further, justice is in the soul. But the soul is not transmitted from the parent. Therefore neither would justice have been transmitted

1. 参见 *De Sacram.*, I, pt. 6, ch. 24 (PL 176, 278).

from parents to the children.

On the contrary, Anselm says: *As long as man did not sin, he would have begotten children endowed with justice together with the rational soul.*[1]

I answer that, Man naturally begets what is specifically like to himself. Hence whatever accidental qualities result from the nature of the species must be alike in parent and child, unless nature fails in its operation, which would not have occurred in the state of innocence. But individual accidents do not necessarily exist alike in parent and child. Now original justice, in which the first man was created, was an accident pertaining to the nature of the species, not as caused by the principles of the species, but only as a gift conferred by God on the entire human nature. This is clear from the fact that opposites are of the same genus. For original sin, which is opposed to original justice, is called the sin of nature, and hence is transmitted from the parent to the offspring; and for this reason, the children would have been assimilated to their parents also as regards original justice.

Reply Obj. 1. These words of Hugh are to be understood as referring, not to the habit of justice, but to the execution of the act thereof.

Reply Obj. 2. Some say that children would have been born, not with the *justice of grace*, which is the principle of merit, but with *original justice*.[2] But the root of original justice, which conferred rectitude on the first man when he was made, consists in the supernatural subjection of the reason to God, which subjection results from sanctifying grace, as was above explained.[3] For this reason we must conclude that if children were born in original justice, they would also have been born in grace; just as we have said above that the first man was created in grace.[4] This grace, however, would not have been natural, for it would

1. 参见 *De Concep. Virg.*, X (PL 158, 144).
2. 参见 Alex. of Hales, *Summa Theol.*, II, I, no. 499 (II, 712); no. 500 (II. 714).
3. 参见 Q. 95, a. 1.
4. 同上

not have been transfused by virtue of the semen; but it would have been conferred on man immediately on his receiving a rational soul. In the same way, the rational soul, which is not transmitted by the parent, is infused by God as soon as the human body is ready to receive it.

From this the reply to the third objection is clear.

Second Article

WHETHER IN THE STATE OF INNOCENCE CHILDREN WOULD HAVE BEEN BORN CONFIRMED IN JUSTICE?

We proceed thus to the Second Article:—

Objection 1. It would seem that in the state of innocence children would have been born confirmed in justice. For Gregory says on the words of *Job* iii. 13 *(For now I should have been asleep*, etc.*): If no sinful corruption had infected our first parent, he would not have begotten 'children of hell'* ; *no children would have been born of him but such as were destined to be saved by the Redeemer.*[1] Therefore all would have been born confirmed in justice.

Obj. 2. Further, Anselm says: *If our first parents had so lived as not to yield to temptation, they would have been confirmed in grace, so that with their offspring they would have been henceforth unable to sin.*[2] Therefore the children would have been born confirmed in justice.

Obj. 3. Further, good is stronger than evil. But by the sin of the first man there resulted, in those born of him, the necessity of sin. Therefore, if the first man had persevered in justice, his descendants would have derived from him the necessity of preserving justice.

Obj. 4. Further, the angels who remained faithful to God, while the others sinned, were at once confirmed in grace, so as to be henceforth unable to sin. In like manner, therefore, man would have been

1. 参见 *Moral.*, IV, 31 (PL 75, 671).
2. 参见 *Cur Deus Homo*, I, 18 (PL 158, 387).

confirmed in grace if he had persevered. But he would have begotten children like himself. Therefore they also would have been born confirmed in justice.

On the contrary, Augustine says: *Happy would have been the whole human race if neither they*—that is, our first parents—*had committed any evil to be transmitted to their descendants, nor any of their race had committed any sin for which they would have been condemned.*[1] From which words we gather that even if our first parents had not sinned, any of their descendants might have done evil; and therefore they would not have been born confirmed in justice.

I answer that, It does not seem possible that in the state of innocence children would have been born confirmed in justice. For it is clear that at their birth they would not have had greater perfection than their parents at the time of begetting. Now the parents, as long as they begot children, would not have been confirmed in justice. For the rational creature is confirmed in justice through the beatitude given by the clear vision of God; and when once it has seen God, it cannot but cleave to Him Who is the essence of goodness, wherefrom no one can turn away, since nothing is desired or loved but under the aspect of good. I say this according to the general law; for it may be otherwise in the case of special privilege, such as we believe was granted to the Virgin Mother of God[2]. And as soon as Adam would have attained to that happy state of seeing God in His essence, he would have become spiritual in soul and body; and his animal life would have ceased, wherein alone there is generation. Hence it is clear that children would not have been born confirmed in justice.

Reply Obj. 1. If Adam had not sinned, he would not have begotten *children of hell* in the sense that they would contract from him sin which is the cause of hell; but by sinning of their own free choice they could

1. 参见 *De Civit. Dei*, XIV, 10 (PL 41, 417).
2. the Virgin Mother of God: 天主之母童贞玛利亚

have become *children of hell*. If, however, they did not become *children of hell* by falling into sin, this would not have been owing to their being confirmed in justice, but to divine providence preserving them free from sin.

Reply Obj. 2. Anselm does not say this by way of assertion, but only as an opinion, which is clear from his mode of expression as follows: *It seems that if they had lived, etc.*

Reply Obj. 3. This argument is not conclusive, though Anselm seems to have been influenced by it, as appears from his words above quoted.[1] For the necessity of sin incurred by the descendants through the sin of the first parent would not have been such that they could not return to justice. For this is the case only with the damned. Therefore neither would the parents have transmitted to their descendants the necessity of not sinning, which is only in the blessed.

Reply Obj. 4. There is no comparison between man and the angels, for man's free choice is changeable, both before and after choice, whereas the angel's is not changeable, as we have said above in treating of the angels.[2]

---

1. 参见 *Cur Deus Homo*, I, 18 (PL 158, 387).
2. 参见 Q. 64, a. 2.

Question CI
THE CONDITION OF THE OFFSPRING AS REGARDS KNOWLEDGE
(*In Two Articles*)

WE next consider the condition of the offspring as to knowledge. Under this head there are two points of inquiry: (1) Whether in the state of innocence children would have been born with perfect knowledge? (2) Whether they would have had perfect use of reason at the moment of birth?

First Article
WHETHER IN THE STATE OF INNOCENCE CHILDREN WOULD HAVE BEEN BORN WITH PERFECT KNOWLEDGE?

We proceed thus to the First Article:—

Objection 1. It would seem that in the state of innocence children would have been born with perfect knowledge. For Adam would have begotten children like himself. But Adam was gifted with perfect knowledge.[1] Therefore children would have been born of him with perfect knowledge.

Obj. 2. Further, ignorance is a result of sin, as Bede says.[2] But ignorance is a privation of knowledge. Therefore before sin children would have had perfect knowledge as soon as they were born.

Obj. 3. Further, children would have been gifted with justice from

---

1. 参见 Q. 94, a. 3.
2. 参见 *In Luc.*, III, super X, 30 (PL 92, 469).

birth. But knowledge is required for justice, since it directs our actions. Therefore they would also have been gifted with knowledge.

On the contrary, The human soul is naturally *like a blank tablet on which nothing is written*, as the Philosopher says.[1] But the nature of the soul is the same now as it would have been in the state of innocence. Therefore, the souls of children would have been without knowledge at birth.

I answer that, As was above stated, concerning matters which are above nature, we rely on authority alone;[2] and so, when authority is wanting, we must be guided by the ordinary course of nature. Now it is natural for man to acquire knowledge through the senses, as was above explained.[3] And so, the reason why the soul is united to the body is that it needs it for its proper operation; and this would not be so if the soul were endowed at birth with knowledge not acquired through the sensitive powers. We must therefore conclude that, in the state of innocence, children would not have been born with perfect knowledge; but in course of time they would have acquired knowledge without difficulty, by discovery or learning.

Reply Obj. 1. The perfection of knowledge was an individual accident of our first parent, so far as he was established as the father and teacher of the whole human race. Therefore he begot children like himself, not in that respect, but only in those accidents which were natural or conferred gratuitously on the whole nature.

Reply Obj. 2. Ignorance is a privation of knowledge due at some particular time. This would not have been in children from their birth, for they would have possessed the knowledge due to them at that time. Hence, no ignorance would have been in them, but only nescience in regard to certain matters. Such nescience was even in the holy angels,

---

1. 参见 Aristotle, *De An.*, III, 4 (430a 1).
2. 参见 Q. 99, a. 1.
3. 参见 Q. 55, a. 2; q. 84, a. 7.

according to Dionysius.[1]

Reply Obj. 3. Children would have had sufficient knowledge to direct them to works of justice, in which men are guided by universal principles of right; and this knowledge of theirs would have been much more complete than what we have now by nature, as is true also of their knowledge of other universal principles.

Second Article
WHETHER CHILDREN WOULD HAVE HAD PERFECT USE OF REASON AT BIRTH?

We proceed thus to the Second Article:—

Objection 1. It would seem that children would have had perfect use of reason at birth. For that children have not perfect use of reason in our present state arises because the soul is weighed down by the body; which was not the case in paradise, because, as it is written, *The corruptible body is a load upon the soul* (*Wis.* ix. 15). Therefore, before sin and the corruption which resulted therefrom, children would have had the perfect use of reason at birth.

Obj. 2. Further, some animals at birth have the use of their natural powers, as the lamb at once flies from the wolf. Much more, therefore, would men in the state of innocence have had perfect use of reason at birth.

On the contrary, In all things produced by generation, nature proceeds from the imperfect to the perfect. Therefore children would not have had the perfect use of reason from the very outset.

I answer that, As was stated above, the use of reason depends in a certain manner on the use of the sensitive powers.[2] So it is that when the senses are impeded and the interior sensitive powers hampered,

---

1. 参见 *De Cael. Hier.*, VII, 3 (PG 3, 209).
2. 参见 Q. 84, a. 7.

man has not the perfect use of reason, as we see in those who are asleep or delirious. Now the sensitive powers belong to corporeal organs, and therefore, so long as their organs are hindered, their own action is of necessity hindered also; and likewise, consequently, the use of reason. Now children are hindered in the use of these powers because of the moisture of the brain; and so they have perfect use neither of these powers nor of reason. Therefore, in the state of innocence, children would not have had the perfect use of reason, which they would have enjoyed later on in life. Yet they would have had a more perfect use than they have now, as to matters pertaining to that particular state, as was explained above regarding the use of their members.[1]

Reply Obj. 1. The corruptible body is a load upon the soul because it hinders the use of reason even in those matters which belong to man at all ages.

Reply Obj. 2. Even other animals have not at birth such a perfect use of their natural powers as they have later on. This is clear from the fact that birds teach their young to fly; and the like may be observed in other animals. Moreover a special impediment exists in man from the humidity of the brain, as we have said above.[2]

---

1. 参见 Q. 99, a. 1.
2. 同上

Question CII
ON MAN'S ABODE, WHICH IS PARADISE
(*In Four Articles*)

WE next consider man's abode, which is paradise. Under this head there are four points of inquiry: (1) Whether paradise is a corporeal place? (2) Whether it is a place apt for human habitation? (3) For what purpose was man placed in paradise? (4) Whether he should have been created in paradise?

First Article
WHETHER PARADISE IS A CORPOREAL PLACE.

We proceed thus to the First Article:—

Objection 1. It would seem that paradise is not a corporeal place. For Bede says that *paradise reaches to the lunar circle.*[1] But no earthly place answers that description, both because it is contrary to the nature of the earth to be raised up so high, and because beneath the moon is the region of fire, which would consume the earth. Therefore paradise is not a corporeal place.

Obj. 2. Further, Scripture mentions four rivers as rising in paradise (*Gen.* ii. 10). But the rivers there mentioned have visible sources elsewhere, as is clear from the Philosopher.[2] Therefore paradise is not a corporeal place.

Obj. 3. Further, although men have explored the entire habitable

---

1. 参见 Cf. *Glossa ordin.*, super *Gen.*, II, 8 (I, 36 F).
2. 参见 *Meteor.*, I, 13 (350b 18).

world, yet none have made mention of the place of paradise.[1] Therefore it is not a corporeal place.

Obj. 4. Further, the tree of life is described as growing in paradise (*Gen.* ii. 9). But the tree of life is a spiritual thing, for it is written of Wisdom that *She is a tree of life to them that lay hold on her* (*Prov.* iii. 18). Therefore paradise also is not a corporeal, but a spiritual, place.

Obj. 5. Further, if paradise be a corporeal place, the trees of paradise must also be corporeal. But it seems they were not, for corporeal trees were produced on the third day, while the planting of the trees of paradise is recorded after the work of the six days (*Gen.* ii. 8, 9). Therefore paradise was not a corporeal place.

On the contrary, Augustine says: *Three general opinions prevail about paradise. Some understand a place merely corporeal, others a place entirely spiritual, while others, whose opinion, I confess, pleases me, hold that paradise was both corporeal and spiritual.*[2]

I answer that, As Augustine says: *Nothing prevents us from holding, within proper limits, a spiritual paradise; so long as we believe in the truth of the events narrated as having there occurred.*[3] For whatever Scripture tells us about paradise is set down as a matter of history; and wherever Scripture makes use of this method, we must hold to the historical truth of the narrative as a foundation of whatever spiritual explanation we may offer. And so paradise, as Isidore says, *is a place situated in the east, its name being the Greek for garden.*[4] It was fitting that it should be in the east, for it is to be believed that it was situated in the most excellent part of the earth. Now the east is the right hand of the heavens, as the Philosopher explains,[5] and the right hand is nobler

---

1. 参见 Cf. St. Albert, *De Nat. Locorum*, I, 6 (IX, 527); III, 1 (IX, 566).
2. 参见 *De Genesi ad Litt.*, VIII, 1 (PL 34, 371).
3. 参见 *De Civit. Dei*, XIII, 21 (PL 41, 395).
4. 参见 *Etymol.*, XIV, 3 (PL 82, 496).
5. 参见 *De Caelo*, II, 2 (285b 16).

than the left. Hence it was fitting that God should place the earthly paradise in the east.

Reply Obj. 1. Bede's assertion is untrue, if taken in its obvious sense. It may, however, be explained to mean that paradise reaches to the moon, not literally, but figuratively; because, as Isidore says, the atmosphere there is of *a continually even temperature.*[1] In this respect it is like the heavenly bodies, which are devoid of opposing elements. Yet mention is made of the lunar sphere rather than of the other spheres, because, of all the heavenly bodies, it is nearest to us. Moreover, of all heavenly bodies the moon is the most akin to the earth; hence it is observed to be overshadowed by clouds and thus to approach the state of opaqueness[2]. Others say that paradise reached to the lunar sphere (*i.e.*, to the middle space of the air, where rain, and wind, and the like arise), because the moon is said to have influence on such changes.[3] But in this sense it would not be a fit place for human dwelling, since it is uneven in temperature, and not attuned to the human temperament, as is the lower atmosphere in the neighborhood of the earth.

Reply Obj. 2. Augustine says: *It is probable that man has no idea where paradise was, and that the rivers, whose sources are said to be known, flowed for some distance underground, and then sprang up elsewhere. For who is not aware that such is the case with some other streams?*[4]

Reply Obj. 3. The situation of paradise is shut off from the habitable world by mountains, or seas, or some torrid region, which cannot be crossed; and so people who have written about topography[5] make no mention of it.

Reply Obj. 4. The tree of life is a material tree, so called because its

---

1. 参见 *Etymol.*, XIV, 3 (PL 82, 496).
2. opaqueness: 不透明的；难以理解的
3. 参见 Peter Lombard, *Sent.*, II, xvii, 5 (I, 386).
4. 参见 *De Genesi ad Litt.*, VIII, 7 (PL 34, 378).
5. topography: 地形学

fruit was endowed with a life-preserving power, as was above stated.[1] Yet it had a spiritual signification; as the rock in the desert was of a material nature, and yet signified Christ (*1 Cor.* x. 4). In like manner, the tree of the knowledge of good and evil was a material tree, so called in view of future events; because, after eating of it, man was to learn, by experience of the consequent punishment, the difference between the good of obedience and the evil of rebellion. However, as some say, it could spiritually signify free choice.[2]

Reply Obj. 5. According to Augustine,[3] the plants were not produced actually on the third day, but in their seminal principles; whereas, after the work of the six days, the plants, both of paradise and others, were actually produced. According to other holy writers, we ought to say that all the plants were actually produced on the third day, including the trees of paradise; and what is said of the trees of paradise being planted after the work of the six days is to be understood, they say, by way of recapitulation[4].[5] Whence our text reads: *The Lord God had planted a paradise of pleasure from the beginning* (*Gen.* ii. 8).

Second Article
WHETHER PARADISE WAS A PLACE ADAPTED TO BE THE ABODE OF MAN?

We proceed thus to the Second Article:—

Objection 1. It would seem that paradise was not a place adapted to be the abode of man. For man and angels are similarly ordered to beatitude. But the angels from the very beginning of their existence

---

1. 参见 Q. 97, a. 4.
2. 参见 St. Augustine, *De Civit. Dei*, XIII, 21 (PL 41, 395).
3. 参见 *De Genesi ad Litt.*, V, 4; VIII, 3 (PL 34, 324; 371).
4. recapitulation: 概括；重述要点
5. 参见 Cf. above, q. 69, a. 2.

were made to dwell in the abode of the blessed—that is, the empyrean heaven. Therefore the place of man's habitation should have been there also.

Obj. 2. Further, if some definite place were required for man's abode, this would be required on the part either of the soul or of the body. If on the part of the soul, the place would be in heaven, which is adapted to the nature of the soul; since the desire of heaven is implanted in all. On the part of the body, however, there was no need for any other place than the one provided for other animals. Therefore paradise was not at all adapted to be the abode of man.

Obj. 3. Further, a place which contains nothing is purposeless. But after sin, paradise was not occupied by man. Therefore if it were adapted as a dwelling-place for man, it seems that God made paradise to no purpose.

Obj. 4. Further, since man is of an even temperament, a fitting place for him should be of even temperature. But paradise was not of an even temperature; for it is said to have been on the equator[1] —a location of extreme heat, since twice in the year the sun passes vertically over the heads of its inhabitants.[2] Therefore paradise was not a fit dwelling-place for man.

On the contrary, Damascene says: *Paradise was a divinely ordered region, and a worthy dwelling of him who was made to God's image.*[3]

I answer that, As was stated above, man was incorruptible and immortal, not because his body had a disposition to incorruptibility, but because in his soul there was a power preserving the body from corruption.[4] Now the human body may be corrupted from within or

---

1. 参见 St. Albert, *Summa de Creatur.*, II, q. 79, a. 1 (XXXV, 640); *In II Sent.*, d. xvii, a. 4 (XXVII, 304); St. Bonaventure, *In II Sent.*, d. xvii, dub. 3 (II, 427).
2. 参见 Cf. St. Albert, *De Nat. Locorum*, I, 6 (IX, 539).
3. 参见 *De Fide Orth.*, II, 11 (PG 94, 913).
4. 参见 Q. 97, a. 1.

from without. From within, the body is corrupted by the consumption of moisture and by old age, as was explained above;[1] and such corruption man was able to ward off by means of food. Among those things which corrupt the body from without, the chief seems to be an atmosphere of unequal temperature; and to such corruption a remedy is found in an atmosphere of equable nature. In paradise both conditions were found, because, as Damascene says: *Paradise was permeated with the all-pervading brightness of a temperate, pure and exquisite atmosphere, and decked with ever-flowering plants.*[2] Whence it is clear that paradise was most fit to be a dwelling-place for man, and in keeping with his original state of immortality.

Reply Obj. 1. The empyrean heaven is the highest of corporeal places, and is outside the region of change. By the first of these two conditions, it is a fitting abode for the angelic nature. For, as Augustine says, *God rules corporeal creatures through spiritual creatures.*[3] Hence it is fitting that the spiritual nature should be established above the entire corporeal nature, as presiding over it. By the second condition, it is a fitting abode for the state of beatitude, which is endowed with the highest degree of stability. Thus the abode of beatitude was suited to the very nature of the angel; and therefore he was created there. But it is not suited to man's nature, since man is not set as a ruler over the entire corporeal creation; but it is a fitting abode for man in regard only to his beatitude. Therefore he was not placed from the beginning in the empyrean heaven, but was destined to be transferred thither in the state of his final beatitude.

Reply Obj. 2. It is ridiculous to assert that any particular place is natural to the soul or to any spiritual substance, though some particular place may have a certain fitness in regard to spiritual

---

1. 参见 Q. 97, a. 4.
2. 参见 *De Fide Orth.*, II, 11 (PG 94, 913).
3. 参见 *De Trin.*, III, 4 (PL 42, 873).

substances. For the earthly paradise was a place adapted to man, as regards both his body and his soul—that is, inasmuch as in his soul was the power which preserved the human body from corruption. This could not be said of the other animals. Therefore, as Damascene says: *No irrational animal inhabits paradise*;[1] although, by a certain dispensation, the animals were brought thither by God to Adam, and the serpent was able to trespass therein by the complicity[2] of the devil.

Reply Obj. 3. Paradise did not become useless through being unoccupied by man after sin, just as a certain immortality was not conferred on man in vain, though he was to lose it. For thereby we learn God's benevolence towards man, and what man lost by sin. On the other hand, some say that Enoch and Elias still dwell in that paradise.[3]

Reply Obj. 4. Those who say that paradise was on the equinoctial line are of the opinion that such a location is most temperate because of the unvarying equality of day and night; that it is never too cold there, because the sun is never too far off; and never too hot, because, although the sun passes over the heads of the inhabitants, it does not remain long in that position. However, Aristotle distinctly says that such a region is uninhabitable because of the heat.[4] This seems to be more probable, for even those regions where the sun does not pass vertically overhead, are extremely hot because of the mere proximity[5] of the sun. But whatever be the truth of the matter, we must hold that paradise was situated in a most temperate situation, whether on the equator or elsewhere.

---

1. 参见 *De Fide Orth.*, II, 11 (PG 94, 913).
2. complicity: 合谋；串通
3. 参见 St. Augustine, *De Genesi ad Litt.*, IX, 6 (PL 34, 396).
4. 参见 *Meteor.*, II, 5 (362b 25).
5. proximity: 接近；附近

Third Article

WHETHER MAN WAS PLACED IN PARADISE TO WORK AND GUARD IT?

We proceed thus to the Third Article:—

Objection 1. It would seem that man was not placed in paradise to work and guard it. For what was brought on him as a punishment of sin would not have existed in paradise in the state of innocence. But the cultivation of the soil was a punishment of sin (*Gen.* iii. 17). Therefore man was not placed in paradise to work and guard it.

Obj. 2. Further, there is no need of a guardian when there is no fear of trespass with violence. But in paradise there was no fear of trespass with violence. Therefore there was no need for man to guard paradise.

Obj. 3. Further, if man was placed in paradise to work and guard it, man would apparently have been made for the sake of paradise, and not contrariwise; which seems to be false. Therefore man was not placed in paradise to work and guard it.

On the contrary, It is written (*Gen.* ii. 15): *The Lord God took man and placed him in the paradise of pleasure, to dress and keep it.*

I answer that, As Augustine says, these words of *Genesis* may be understood in two ways.[1] First, in the sense that God placed man in paradise that He might Himself work in man and guard him, by sanctifying him (for if this work cease, man at once relapses into darkness, as the air grows dark when the light ceases to shine), and by guarding man from all corruption and evil. Secondly, it might mean that man might work and guard paradise, which working would not have involved labor, as it did after sin; but it would have been joyous because man would have experienced the power of nature. Nor would

1. 参见 *De Genesi ad Litt.*, VIII, 10 (PL 34, 380).

man have guarded paradise against a trespasser; but he would have striven to guard paradise for himself lest he should lose it by sin. All of which was for man's good; and so, paradise was ordered to man's benefit, and not conversely.

Whence the Replies to the Objections are made clear.

Fourth Article
WHETHER MAN WAS CREATED IN PARADISE?

We proceed thus to the Fourth Article:—

Objection 1. It would seem that man was created in paradise. For the angel was created in his dwelling-place —namely, the empyrean heaven. But before sin paradise was a fitting abode for man. Therefore it seems that man was created in paradise.

Obj. 2. Further, other animals remain in the place where they are produced, as the fish in water, and walking animals on the earth from which they were made. Now man would have remained in paradise after he was created.[1] Therefore he was created in paradise.

Obj. 3. Further, woman was made in paradise. But man is greater than woman. Therefore much more should man have been made in paradise.

On the contrary, It is written (*Gen.* ii. 15): *God took man and placed him in paradise.*

I answer that, Paradise was a fitting abode for man as regards the incorruptibility of the first state. Now this incorruptibility was man's, not by nature, but by a supernatural gift of God. Therefore that this might be attributed to the grace of God, and not to human nature, God made man outside of paradise, and afterwards placed him in paradise to live during the whole of his animal life; and, having

1. 参见 Q. 97, a. 4.

attained to the spiritual life, to be transferred thence to heaven.

Reply Obj. 1. The empyrean heaven was a fitting abode for the angels as regards their nature, and therefore they were created there.

In the same way I reply to the second objection, for those places befit those animals in their nature.

Reply Obj. 3. Woman was made in paradise, not by reason of her own dignity, but because of the dignity of the principle from which her body was formed. For the same reason the children would have been born in paradise, where their parents were already.

TREATISE ON THE DIVINE GOVERNMENT

Question CIII
THE GOVERNMENT OF THINGS IN GENERAL
(*In Eight Articles*)

HAVING considered the creation of things and their distinction, we now consider in the third place the government thereof, and (1) the government of things in general; (2) in particular, the effects of this government.[1] Under the first head there are eight points of inquiry: (1) Whether the world is governed by someone? (2) What is the end of this government? (3) Whether the world is governed by one? (4) On the effects of this government. (5) Whether all things are subject to the divine government? (6) Whether all things are immediately governed by God? (7) Whether the divine government is frustrated in anything? (8) Whether anything is contrary to the divine providence?

First Article
WHETHER THE WORLD IS GOVERNED BY ANYONE?

We proceed thus to the First Article:—

Objection 1. It would seem that the world is not governed by anyone. For it belongs to those things to be governed which move or work for an end. But natural things which make up the greater part of the world do not move, or work for an end, for they have no knowledge of their end. Therefore the world is not governed.

---

1. 参见 Q. 104.

Obj. 2. Further, those things are governed which are moved towards some object. But the world does not appear to be so directed, but has stability in itself. Therefore it is not governed.

Obj. 3. Further, what is necessarily determined by its own nature to one particular course does not require any external principle of government. But the principal parts of the world are by a certain necessity determined to something particular in their actions and movements. Therefore the world does not require to be governed.

On the contrary, It is written (*Wis.* xiv. 3): *But Thou, O Father, governest all things by Thy Providence.* And Boethius says: *Thou Who governest this universe by mandate eternal.*[1]

I answer that, Certain ancient philosophers denied the government of the world, saying that all things happened by chance.[2] But such an opinion can be refuted as impossible in two ways. First, by the observation of things themselves. For we observe that in nature things happen always or nearly always for the best; which would not be the case unless some sort of providence directed nature towards good as an end. And this is to govern. Therefore the unfailing order we observe in things is a sign of their being governed. For instance, if we were to enter a well-ordered house, we would gather from the order manifested in the house the notion of a governor, as Cicero says, quoting Aristotle.[3] Secondly, this is clear from a consideration of the divine goodness, which, as we have said above, is the cause of the production of things in being.[4] For as *it belongs to the best to produce the best*, it is not fitting that the supreme goodness of God should produce things without giving them their perfection. Now a thing's ultimate perfection consists in the attainment of its end. Therefore it belongs to the divine

---

1. 参见 *De Consol.*, III, verse 9 (PL 63, 758).
2. 参见 Democritus and Epicurus: cf. above, q. 22, a. 2.
3. 参见 *De Nat. Deor.*, II, 5 (IV, 111).
4. 参见 Q. 44, a. 4; q. 65, a. 2.

goodness, as it brought things into being, so to lead them to their end. And this is to govern.

Reply Obj. 1. A thing moves or operates for an end in two ways. First, in moving itself to the end, as do man and other rational creatures; and such beings have a knowledge of their end, and of the means to the end. Secondly, a thing is said to move or operate for an end, as though moved or directed thereto by another, as an arrow is directed to the target by the archer, who knows the end unknown to the arrow. Hence, as the movement of the arrow towards a definite end shows clearly that it is directed by someone with knowledge, so the unvarying course of natural things which are without knowledge shows clearly that the world is governed by some reason.

Reply Obj. 2. In all created things there is a stable element, even if this be only primary matter, and something belonging to movement, if under movement we include operation. Now things need governing as to both, because even that which is stable, since it is created from nothing, would return to nothingness were it not sustained by a governing hand, as will be explained later.[1]

Reply Obj. 3. The natural necessity inherent in those beings which are determined to a particular course is a kind of impression from God, directing them to their end; just as the necessity whereby the arrow is moved so as to fly towards a certain point is an impression from the archer, and not from the arrow. But there is a difference, inasmuch as that which creatures receive from God is their nature, while that which natural things receive from man in addition to their nature is something violent. Therefore, just as the violent necessity in the movement of the arrow shows the action of the archer, so the natural necessity of things shows the government of divine providence.

---

1. 参见 Q. 104, a. 1.

Second Article

WHETHER THE END OF THE GOVERNMENT OF THE WORLD IS SOMETHING OUTSIDE THE WORLD?

We proceed thus to the Second Article:—

Objection 1. It would seem that the end of the government of the world is not something existing outside the world. For the end of the government of a thing is that to which the thing governed is brought. But that to which a thing is brought is some good in the thing itself; and thus a sick man is brought back to health, which is something good in him. Therefore the end of the government of things is some good, not outside, but existing within the things themselves.

Obj. 2. Further, the Philosopher says: *Some ends are operations*; *some are works*[1] —*i.e.*, products of operations. But nothing can be produced by the whole universe outside itself, and operation exists in the agent. Therefore nothing extrinsic can be the end of the government of things.

Obj. 3. Further, the good of a multitude seems to consist in order and peace, which is the *tranquillity of order*, as Augustine says.[2] But the world is composed of a multitude of things. Therefore the end of the government of the world is a peaceful order in things themselves. Therefore the end of the government of the world is not an extrinsic good.

On the contrary, It is written (*Prov*. xvi. 4): *The Lord hath made all things for Himself*. But God is outside the entire order of the universe. Therefore the end of all things is something extrinsic to them.

I answer that, As the end of a thing corresponds to its beginning, it is not possible to be ignorant of the end of things if we know their

---

1. 参见 *Eth.*, I, 1 (1094a 4).
2. 参见 *De Civit. Dei*, XIX, 13 (PL 41, 640).

beginning. Therefore, since the beginning of all things is something outside the universe, namely, God, as is clear from what has been said above,[1] we must conclude that the end of all things is some extrinsic good. This can be proved by reason. For it is clear that good has the nature of an end. And so the particular end of anything consists in some particular good, while the universal end of all things is a universal good. A universal good is good of itself by virtue of its essence, which is the very essence of goodness; whereas a particular good is good by participation. Now it is manifest that in the whole created universe there is not a good which is not such by participation. Therefore that good which is the end of the whole universe must be a good outside the universe.

Reply Obj. 1. We may acquire some good in many ways: first, as a form existing in us, such as health or knowledge; secondly, as something done by us, as a builder attains his end by building a house; thirdly, as something good possessed or acquired by us, as the buyer of a field attains his end when he enters into possession. Therefore nothing prevents something outside the universe from being the good to which it is directed.

Reply Obj. 2. The Philosopher is speaking of the ends of various arts.[2] For the end of some arts consists in the operation itself, as the end of a harpist is to play the harp; whereas the end of other arts consists in something produced, as the end of a builder is not the act of building, but the house he builds. Now it may happen that something extrinsic is the end not only as made, but also as possessed or acquired, or even as represented, as if we were to say that Hercules is the end of the statue made to represent him. Therefore we may say that some good outside the whole universe is the end of the government of the universe, as something possessed and represented; for each thing tends

1. 参见 Q. 44, a. 1.
2. 参见 *Eth.*, I, 1 (1094a 1).

to participate in it, and to assimilate itself to it, as far as is possible.

Reply Obj. 3. The end of the universe, namely, the order of the universe itself, is a good existing in it. This good, however, is not its ultimate end, but is ordered to an extrinsic good as to an ultimate end; just as the order in an army is ordered to the general, as is stated in *Metaph.* xii.[1]

Third Article
WHETHER THE WORLD IS GOVERNED BY ONE?

We proceed thus to the Third Article:—

Objection 1. It would seem that the world is not governed by one. For we judge the cause by the effect. Now, we see in the government of the universe that things are not moved and do not operate uniformly, but some contingently and some of necessity, and according to other and various differences. Therefore the world is not governed by one.

Obj. 2. Further, things which are governed by one do not act against each other, except by the inexperience, the incapacity or the unskilfulness of the ruler; which cannot apply to God. But created things do not harmonize, and act against each other; as is evident in the case of contraries. Therefore the world is not governed by one.

Obj. 3. Further, in nature we always find what is the better. But it *is better that two should be together than one* (*Eccles.* iv. 9). Therefore the world is not governed by one, but by many.

On the contrary, We confess one God and one Lord, according to the words of the *Apostle* (*1 Cor.* viii. 6): *To us there is but one God, the Father ... and one Lord*; and both of these pertain to government. For to the Lord belongs dominion over subjects; and the name *God* is taken from providence, as was stated above.[2] Therefore the world is governed by

---

1. 参见 Aristotle, *Metaph.*, XI, 10 (1075a 15).
2. 参见 Q. 13, a. 8.

one.

I answer that, We must of necessity say that the world is governed by one. For since the end of the government of the world is that which is essentially good, which is the greatest good, the government of the world must be the best kind of government. Now the best government is government by one. The reason for this is that government is nothing but the directing of the things governed to the end; which consists in some good. But unity belongs to the notion of goodness, as Boethius proves from this, that, as all things desire good, so do they desire unity, without which they would cease to exist.[1] For a thing so far exists as it is one. Whence we observe that things resist division, as far as they can, and that the dissolution of a thing arises from some defect in the thing. Therefore the intention of a ruler over a multitude is unity, or peace. Now the proper cause of unity is that which is one. For it is clear that several cannot be the cause of unity or concord, except so far as they are united. Furthermore, what is one in itself is a more apt and a better cause of unity than several things united. Therefore a multitude is better governed by one than by several. From this it follows that the government of the world, being the best form of government, must be by one. This is expressed by the Philosopher: *Things refuse to be ill governed; and multiplicity of authorities is a bad thing. Therefore there should be one ruler.*[2]

Reply Obj. 1. Movement is *the act of a thing moved, caused by the mover.* Therefore dissimilarity of movements is caused by the diversity of things moved, which is essential to the perfection of the universe,[3] and not by a diversity of governors.

Reply Obj. 2. Although contraries do not agree with each other in their proximate ends, nevertheless they agree in the ultimate end, so

---

1. 参见 *De Consol.*, III, prose 11 (PL 63, 771).
2. 参见 *Metaph.*, XI, 10 (1076a 3).
3. 参见 Q. 47, a. 1 and 2; q. 48, a. 2.

far as they are included in the one order of the universe.

Reply Obj. 3. If we consider individual goods, then two are better than one. But if we consider the essential good, then no addition of good is possible.

Fourth Article
WHETHER THE EFFECT OF GOVERNMENT IS ONE OR MANY?

We proceed thus to the Fourth Article:—

Objection 1. It would seem that there is but one effect of the government of the world, and not many. For the effect of government is that which is caused in the things governed. This is one, namely, the good which consists in order, as may be seen in the example of an army. Therefore the government of the world has but one effect.

Obj. 2. Further, from one there naturally proceeds but one. But the world is governed by one, as we have proved. Therefore the effect of this government is but one.

Obj. 3. Further, if the effect of government is not one by reason of the unity of the governor, it must be many by reason of the many things governed. But these are too numerous to be counted. Therefore we cannot assign any definite number to the effects of government.

On the contrary, Dionysius says: *God contains all and fills all by His providence and perfect goodness.*[1] But government belongs to providence. Therefore there are certain definite effects of the divine government.

I answer that, The effect of any action may be judged from its end, because it is by action that the attainment of the end is effected. Now the end of the government of the world is the essential good, to the participation and similarity of which all things tend. Consequently the

---

1. 参见 *De Div. Nom.*, XII, 2 (PG 3, 969).

effect of the government of the world may be taken in three ways. First, on the part of the end itself, and in this way there is but one effect, that is, assimilation to the highest good. Secondly, the effect of the government of the world may be considered on the part of those things by means of which the creature is made like to God. Thus there are, in general, two effects of government. For the creature is assimilated to God in two respects. First, with regard to this, that God is good, and thus the creature becomes like Him by being good; and secondly, with regard to this, that God is the cause of goodness in others, and thus the creature becomes like God by moving others to be good. Therefore there are two effects of government, the preservation of things in their goodness, and the moving of things to good. Thirdly, we may consider the effects of the government of the world in particular instances, and in this way they are without number.

Reply Obj. 1. The order of the universe includes both the preservation of the things created by God and their movement. For it is in reference to these two things that we find order among things, namely, inasmuch as one is better than another, and one is moved by another.

From what has been said above, we can gather the replies to the other two objections.

Fifth Article
WHETHER ALL THINGS ARE SUBJECT TO THE DIVINE GOVERNMENT?

We proceed thus to the Fifth Article:—

Objection 1. It would seem that not all things are subject to the divine government. For it is written (*Eccles.* ix. 11): *I saw that under the sun the race is not to the swift, nor the battle to the strong, nor bread to the wise, nor riches to the learned, nor favor to the skilful, but time and chance in all.* But things subject to the divine government are not ruled by chance.

Therefore those things which are under the sun are not subject to the divine government.

Obj. 2. Further, the Apostle says (*1 Cor.* ix. 9): *God hath no care for oxen.* But he that governs has care for the things he governs. Therefore all things are not subject to the divine government.

Obj. 3. Further, what can govern itself needs not to be governed by another. But the rational creature can govern itself. For it is master of its own act, and acts of itself; nor is it made to act by another, which seems proper to things which are governed. Therefore all things are not subject to the divine government.

On the contrary, Augustine says: *Not only heaven and earth, not only man and angel, but even the bowels of the lowest animal, even the wing of the bird, the flower of the plant, the leaf of the tree, hath God endowed with every fitting detail of their nature.*[1] Therefore all things are subject to His government.

I answer that, For the same reason is God the ruler of things as He is their cause, because the same cause gives being that gives perfection; and this belongs to government. Now God is the cause, not of some particular kind of being, but of the whole universal being, as was proved above.[2] Therefore, as there can be nothing which is not created by God, so there can be nothing which is not subject to His government. This can also be proved from the nature of the end of government. For a man's government extends over all those things which come under the end of his government. Now the end of the divine government is the divine goodness, as we have shown. Therefore, as there can be nothing that is not ordered to the divine goodness as its end, as is clear from what we have said above,[3] it is impossible for anything to escape from the divine government.

Foolish therefore was the opinion of those who said that the

---

1. 参见 *De Civit. Dei*, V, 11 (PL 41, 154).
2. 参见 Q. 44, a. 1 and 2.
3. 参见 Q. 44, a. 4; q. 65, a. 2.

corruptible lower world,[1] or individual things,[2] or that even human affairs,[3] were not subject to the divine government. These are represented as saying, *God hath abandoned the earth* (*Ezech.* ix. 9).

Reply Obj. 1. Those things are said to be under the sun which are generated and corrupted according to the sun's movement. In all such things we find chance; not that everything is by chance which occurs in such things, but that in each one there is an element of chance. And the very fact that an element of chance is found in these things proves that they are subject to government of some kind. For unless corruptible things were governed by a higher being, they would tend to nothing definite, especially those which possess no kind of knowledge. So nothing in them would happen unintentionally; which constitutes the nature of chance. Therefore to show how things happen by chance and yet according to the ordering of a higher cause, he does not say absolutely that he observes chance in all things, but *time and chance*, that is to say, that defects may be found in these things according to some order of time.

Reply Obj. 2. Government implies a certain change effected by the governor in the things governed. Now every movement is the act of a movable thing, caused by the moving principle, as is laid down in *Physics* iii.[4] Now every act is proportioned to that of which it is an act. Consequently, diverse movable things must be moved diversely, even as regards movement by one and the same mover. Thus, by the one art of the divine governor things are diversely governed according to their diversity. Some, according to their nature, act of themselves, having dominion over their actions; and these are governed by God, not only in this, that they are moved by God Himself, Who works in

---

1. 参见 Cf. above, q. 22, a. 2.
2. 参见 Q. 57, a. 2.
3. 参见 Cf. St. Augustine, *De Civit. Dei*, V, 9 (PL 41, 148).
4. 参见 Aristotle, *Phys.*, III, 3 (202a 14).

them interiorly, but also in this, that they are induced by Him to do good and to fly from evil, by precepts and prohibitions, rewards and punishments. But irrational creatures, which do not act but are only acted upon, are not thus governed by God. Hence, when the Apostle says that *God hath no care for oxen*, he does not wholly withdraw them from the divine government, but only as regards the way in which rational creatures are governed.

Reply Obj. 3. The rational creature governs itself by its intellect and will, both of which require to be governed and perfected by the divine intellect and will. Therefore, above the government whereby the rational creature governs itself as master of its own act, it requires to be governed by God.

Sixth Article
WHETHER ALL THINGS ARE IMMEDIATELY GOVERNED BY GOD?

We proceed thus to the Sixth Article:—

Objection 1. It would seem that all things are governed by God immediately. For Gregory of Nyssa reproves the opinion of Plato who divides providence into three parts.[1] The first he ascribes to the supreme god, who watches over heavenly things and all universal realities; the second providence he attributes to the secondary deities, who go the round of the heavens to watch over generation and corruption; while he ascribes a third providence to certain demons who are guardians on earth of human actions. Therefore it seems that all things are immediately governed by God.

Obj. 2. Further, it is better that a thing be done by one, if possible, than by many, as the Philosopher says.[2] But God can by Himself

1. 参见 Cf. Nemesius, *De Nat. Hom.* XLIV (PG 40, 794).
2. 参见 Aristotle, *Phys.*, VIII, 6 (259a 8).

govern all things without any intermediary cause. Therefore it seems that He governs all things immediately.

Obj. 3. Further, in God nothing is defective or imperfect. But it seems to be imperfect in a ruler to govern by means of others; and thus an earthly king, by reason of not being able to do everything himself, and because he cannot be everywhere at the same time, requires to govern by means of ministers. Therefore God governs all things immediately.

On the contrary, Augustine says: *As the lower and grosser bodies are ruled in a certain orderly way by bodies of greater subtlety and power, so all bodies are ruled by the rational spirit of life; and the sinful and unfaithful spirit is ruled by the good and just spirit of life, and this spirit by God Himself.*[1]

I answer that, In government there are two things to be considered: the nature of government, which is providence itself; and the execution of government. As to the nature of government, God governs all things immediately; whereas in its execution, He governs some things by means of others.

The reason for this is that, since God is the very essence of goodness, everything must be attributed to God in its highest degree of goodness. Now the highest degree of goodness in any practical order, function or knowledge (and such is the nature of government) consists in knowing the individuals within whose domain the action takes place. Thus, the best physician is not the one who gives his attention only to general principles, but who can consider the least details; and so on in other things. Therefore we must say that God possesses, in its very essence, the government of all things, even of the very least.

But since things which are governed should be brought to perfection by government, this government will be so much the better in the degree that the things governed are brought to perfection. Now it is

1. 参见 *De Trin.*, III, 4 (PL 42, 873).

a greater perfection for a thing to be good in itself and also the cause of goodness in others, than only to be good in itself. Therefore God so governs things that He makes some of them to be causes of others in government; as in the case of a teacher, who not only imparts knowledge to his pupils, but also makes some of them to be the teachers of others.

Reply Obj. 1. Plato's opinion is to be rejected, because he held that God did not govern all things immediately, even as concerns the nature of government; and this is clear from the fact that he divided providence, which is the nature of government, into three parts.

Reply Obj. 2. If God governed alone, things would be deprived of the perfection of causality. Therefore all that is effected by many would not be accomplished by one.

Reply Obj. 3. That an earthly king should have ministers to execute his laws is a sign not only of his imperfection, but also of his dignity; because from the array of ministers the kingly power is brought into greater evidence.

Seventh Article
WHETHER ANYTHING CAN HAPPEN OUTSIDE THE ORDER OF THE DIVINE GOVERNMENT?

We proceed thus to the Seventh Article:—

Objection 1. It would seem possible that something may occur outside the order of the divine government. For Boethius says that *God disposes all by good.*[1] Therefore, if nothing happens outside the order of the divine government, it would follow that no evil exists.

Obj. 2. Further, nothing that is in accordance with the pre-ordination of a ruler occurs by chance. Therefore, if nothing occurs outside

1. 参见 *De Consol.*, III, prose 12 (PL 63, 779).

the order of the divine government, it follows that there is nothing fortuitous and by chance.

Obj. 3. Further, the order of divine providence is certain and unchangeable, because it is in accord with an eternal design. Therefore, if nothing happens outside the order of the divine government, it follows that all things happen by necessity, and nothing is contingent; which is false. Therefore it is possible for something to occur outside the order of the divine government.

On the contrary, It is written (*Esth.* xiii. 9): *O Lord, Lord, almighty King, all things are in Thy power, and there is none that can resist Thy will.*

I answer that, It is possible for an effect to happen outside the order of some particular cause, but not outside the order of the universal cause. The reason for this is that no effect happens outside the order of a particular cause, except through some other and impeding cause; which other cause must itself be reduced to the first universal cause. Thus, indigestion may occur outside the order of the nutritive power by some such impediment as the coarseness of the food, which again is to be ascribed to some other cause, and so on till we come to the first universal cause. Therefore, as God is the first universal cause, not of one genus only, but of all being, it is impossible for anything to occur outside the order of the divine government; but from the very fact that from one point of view something seems to evade the order of divine providence considered in regard to one particular cause, it must necessarily come back to that order as regards some other cause.

Reply Obj. 1. There is nothing wholly evil in the world, for evil is always founded on good, as was shown above.[1] Therefore something is said to be evil because it escapes from the order of some particular good. If it escaped wholly from the order of the divine government, it would wholly cease to exist.

---

1. 参见 Q. 48, a. 3.

Reply Obj. 2. Things are said to be by chance as regards some particular cause from whose order they escape. But as to the order of divine providence, *nothing in the world happens by chance*, as Augustine declares.[1]

Reply Obj. 3. Certain effects are said to be contingent as compared to their proximate causes, which may fail in their effects; and not as though anything could happen entirely outside the order of divine government. The very fact that something occurs outside the order of some proximate cause is owing to some other cause, itself subject to the divine government.

Eighth Article

WHETHER ANYTHING CAN RESIST THE ORDER OF THE DIVINE GOVERNMENT?

We proceed thus to the Eighth Article:—

Objection 1. It would seem possible that some resistance can be made to the order of the divine government. For it is written (*Isa.* iii. 8): *Their tongue and their devices are against the Lord.*

Obj. 2. Further, a king does not justly punish those who do not rebel against his commands. Therefore if no one rebelled against God's commands, no one would be justly punished by God.

Obj. 3. Further, everything is subject to the order of the divine government. But some things oppose others. Therefore some things rebel against the order of the divine government.

On the contrary, Boethius says:[2] *There is nothing that can desire or is able to resist this sovereign good. It is this sovereign good therefore that ruleth all mightily and ordereth all sweetly*, as is said (*Wis.* viii. 1) of divine wisdom.

I answer that, We may consider the order of divine providence in two

---

1. 参见 *Lib. 83 Quaest.*, q. 24 (PL 40, 17).
2. 参见 *De Consol.*, III, prose 12 (PL 63, 779).

ways: in general, inasmuch as it proceeds from the governing cause of all; and in particular, inasmuch as it proceeds from some particular cause which executes the order of the divine government.

Considered in the first way, nothing can resist the order of the divine government. This can be proved in two ways: First, from the fact that the order of the divine government is wholly directed to good, and everything by its own operation and effort tends to good only; *for no one acts intending evil*, as Dionysius says.[1] Secondly, from the fact that, as we have said above, every inclination of anything, whether natural or voluntary, is nothing but a kind of impression from the first mover; just as the inclination of the arrow towards a fixed point is nothing but an impulse received from the archer. Hence, every agent, whether natural or voluntary, attains to its divinely appointed end, as though of its own accord. For this reason God is said *to order all things sweetly* (*Wis.* viii. 1).

Reply Obj. 1. Some are said to think, speak or act against God, not because they entirely resist the order of the divine government (for even the sinner intends the attainment of a certain good), but because they resist some particular good, which belongs to their nature or state. Therefore they are justly punished by God.

Reply Obj. 2 is clear from the above.

Reply Obj. 3. From the fact that one thing opposes another, it follows that some one thing can resist the order of a particular cause, but not that order which depends on the universal cause of all things.

---

1. 参见 *De Div. Nom.*, IV, 31 (PG 3, 732).

Question CIV
THE SPECIAL EFFECTS OF THE DIVINE GOVERNMENT
(*In Four Articles*)

WE next consider the effects of the divine government in particular, concerning which four points of inquiry arise: (1) Whether creatures need to be kept in being by God? (2) Whether they are immediately conserved by God? (3) Whether God can reduce anything to nothingness? (4) Whether anything is reduced to nothingness?

First Article
WHETHER CREATURES NEED TO BE KEPT IN BEING BY GOD?

We proceed thus to the First Article:—

Objection 1. It would seem that creatures do not need to be kept in being by God. For what cannot not-be does not need to be kept in being, just as that which cannot depart does not need to be kept from departing. But some creatures by their very nature cannot not-be. Therefore not all creatures need to be kept in being by God. The middle proposition is proved thus. That which of itself is included in the nature of a thing is necessarily in that thing, and its contrary cannot be in it; and thus a multiple of two must necessarily be even, and cannot possibly be an odd number. Now being follows necessarily upon a form, because everything is a being actually in so far as it has a form. But some creatures are subsistent forms, as we have said of the angels.[1] Hence, to be belongs to them of themselves. The same reasoning applies to those creatures whose matter is in potentiality to one form only, as was explained above of the heavenly bodies.[2] Hence such creatures as these have in their nature to be necessarily, and cannot not-be. For there can be no potentiality to not-being, either in the form which has being of itself, or in matter existing under a form which it cannot lose, since it is not in potentiality to any other form.

Obj. 2. Further, God is more powerful than any created agent. But a created agent, even after ceasing to act, can cause its effect to be preserved in being. Thus, the house continues to stand after the builder has ceased to build; and water remains hot for some time after the fire has ceased to heat. Much more, therefore, can God cause His creature to be kept in being, after He has ceased to create it.

Obj. 3. Further, nothing violent can occur, except it have some active cause. But tendency to not-being is unnatural and violent to any creature, since all creatures naturally desire to be. Therefore no creature can tend to not-being, except through some active cause of corruption. Now there are creatures of such a nature that nothing can cause them to be corrupted. Such are spiritual substances and heavenly bodies. Therefore such creatures cannot tend to not-being, even if God were to withdraw His action.

Obj. 4. Further, if God keeps creatures in being, this is done by some action. Now every action of an agent, if that action be efficacious, produces something in the effect. Therefore the conserving power of God must produce something in the creature. But this is not so, because this action does not give being to the creature, since being is not given to that which already is; nor does it add anything new to the creature, because either God would not keep the creature in being continually, or He would be continually adding something new to the

1. 参见 Q. 50, a. 2 and 5.
2. 参见 Q. 66, a. 2.

creature,—either of which is unreasonable. Therefore creatures are not kept in being by God.

On the contrary, It is written (*Heb.* i. 3): *Upholding all things by the word of His power.*

I answer that, Both reason and faith require us to say that creatures are kept in being by God. To make this clear, we must consider that a thing is conserved by another in two ways. First, indirectly and accidentally, and thus a person is said to conserve anything by removing the cause of its corruption; as a man may be said to conserve a child, whom he guards from falling into the fire. In this way God conserves some things, but not all, for there are some things of such a nature that nothing can corrupt them, so that it is not necessary to keep them from corruption. Secondly, a thing is said to conserve another essentially and directly, namely, in so far as what is conserved depends on the conserver in such a way that it cannot exist without it. In this manner all creatures need to be conserved by God. For the being of every creature depends on God, so that not for a moment could it subsist, but would fall into nothingness, were it not kept in being by the operation of the divine power, as Gregory says.[1]

This is made clear as follows. Every effect depends on its cause, so far as it is its cause. But we must observe that an agent may be the cause of the *becoming* of its effect, but not directly of its *being*. This may be seen both in artificial and in natural things. For the builder causes the house in its *becoming*, but he is not the direct cause of its *being*. For it is clear that the *being* of the house is a result of its form, which consists in the putting together and arrangement of the materials, and which results from the natural qualities of certain things. Thus a cook prepares the food by applying the natural activity of fire; and in the same way a builder constructs a house, by making use of cement,

1. 参见 *Moral.*, XVI, 37 (PL 75, 1143).

stones and wood, which are able to be put together in a certain order and to conserve it. Therefore the *being* of the house depends on the nature of these materials, just as its *becoming* depends on the action of the builder. The same principle applies to natural things. For if an agent is not the cause of a form as such, neither will it be directly the cause of the *being* which results from that form; but it will be the cause of the effect only in its *becoming*.

Now it is clear that of two things in the same species one cannot be essentially the cause of the other's form as such, since it would then be the cause of its own form, since both forms have the same nature; but it can be the cause of this form inasmuch as it is in matter—in other words, it may be the cause that *this matter* receives *this form*. And this is to be the cause of *becoming*, as when man begets man, and fire causes fire. Thus, whenever a natural effect is such that it has an aptitude to receive from its active cause an impression specifically the same as in that active cause, then the *becoming* of the effect depends on the agent, but not its *being*. Sometimes, however, the effect has not this aptitude to receive the impression of its cause in the same way as it exists in the agent; as may be seen clearly in all agents which do not produce an effect of the same species as themselves. Thus, the heavenly bodies cause the generation of inferior bodies which differ from them in species. Such an agent can be the cause of a form as such, and not merely as being joined to this matter; and consequently it is not merely the cause of *becoming* but also the cause of *being*.

Therefore, as the becoming of a thing cannot continue when the action of the agent, which causes the *becoming* of the effect, ceases, so neither can the *being* of a thing continue after the action of the agent, which is the cause of the effect not only in *becoming* but also in *being*, has ceased. This is why hot water retains heat after the cessation of the fire's action; while, on the contrary, the air does not continue to be lit up, even for a moment, when the sun ceases to act upon it. For water is a matter susceptive of the fire's heat in the same way as it exists in the fire. Therefore, if it were to be reduced to the perfect form of fire, it would retain that form always; whereas if it has the form of fire imperfectly and inchoately, the heat will remain for a time only, by reason of the imperfect participation in the principle of heat. On the other hand, air is not of such a nature as to receive light in the same way as it exists in the sun, namely, to receive the form of the sun, which is the principle of light. Therefore, since it has no root in the air, the light ceases with the action of the sun.

Now every creature may be compared to God as the air is to the sun which illumines it. For as the sun possesses light by its nature, and as the air is illumined by participating light from the sun, though not participating in the sun's nature, so God alone is Being by virtue of His own essence (since His essence is His being), whereas every creature has being by participation, so that its essence is not its being. Therefore, as Augustine says: *If the ruling power of God were withdrawn from His creatures, their nature would at once cease, and all nature would collapse.*[1] In the same work he says: *As the air becomes light by the presence of the sun, so is man illumined by the presence of God, and in His absence returns at once to darkness.*[2]

Reply Obj. 1. *Being* necessarily results from the form of a creature, given the influence of the divine action; just as light results from the diaphanous nature of the air, given the action of the sun. Hence, the potentiality to not-being in spiritual creatures and heavenly bodies is rather something in God, Who can withdraw His influence, than in the form or matter of those creatures.

Reply Obj. 2. God cannot communicate to a creature that it be conserved in being after the cessation of the divine influence; as neither can He make it not to have received its being from Himself. For the creature needs to be conserved by God in so far as the being of an effect depends on the cause of its being. Hence, there is no

---

1. 参见 *De Genesi ad Litt.*, IV, 12 (PL 34, 304).
2. 参见 *Op. cit.*, VIII, 12 (PL 34, 383).

comparison with an agent that is not the cause of *being*, but only of *becoming*.

Reply Obj. 3. This argument holds in regard to that conservation which consists in the removal of corruption; but all creatures do not need to be conserved thus, as was stated above.

Reply Obj. 4. The conservation of things by God is not by a new action, but by a continuation of that action whereby He gives being, which action is without either motion or time; so also the conservation of light in the air is by the continual influence of the sun.

Second Article
WHETHER GOD CONSERVES EVERY CREATURE IMMEDIATELY?

We proceed thus to the Second Article:—

Objection 1. It would seem that God conserves every creature immediately. For God creates and conserves things by the same action, as was stated above. But God created all things immediately. Therefore He conserves all things immediately.

Obj. 2. Further, a thing is nearer to itself than to another. But it cannot be given to a creature to conserve itself. Much less therefore can it be given to a creature to conserve another. Therefore God conserves all things without any intermediate conserving cause.

Obj. 3. Further, an effect is kept in being by the cause, not only of its *becoming*, but also of its *being*. But all created causes do not seem to cause their effects except in their becoming, for they cause only by moving, as was stated above.[1] Therefore they are not causes that keep their effects in being.

On the contrary, A thing is kept in being by that which gives it being. But God gives being to things by means of certain intermediate causes.

---

1. 参见 Q. 45, a. 3.

Therefore He also keeps things in being by means of certain causes.

I answer that, As was stated above, a thing keeps another in being in two ways: first, indirectly and accidentally, by removing or hindering the action of a corrupting cause; secondly, directly and essentially, by the fact that on it depends the other's being, as the being of the effect depends on the cause. And in both ways a created thing keeps another in being. For it is clear that even in corporeal things there are many causes which hinder the action of corrupting agents, and for that reason are called *conserving*; just as salt preserves meat from putrefaction, and in like manner with many other things. It happens also that an effect depends on a creature as to its being. For when we have many ordered causes, it necessarily follows that, while the effect depends first and principally on the first cause, it also depends in a secondary way on all the intermediate causes. Therefore the first cause is the principal cause of the conservation of the effect, which is to be referred to all the intermediate causes in a secondary way; and all the more so, as the intermediate cause is higher and nearer to the first cause.

For this reason, even in corporeal things, the conservation and endurance of things is ascribed to higher causes. Thus, the Philosopher says that the first, namely the diurnal, movement is the cause of the continuation of things generated; whereas the second movement, which is according to the zodiac, is the cause of diversity owing to generation and corruption.[1] In like manner, astronomers ascribe to Saturn, the highest of the planets, those things which are permanent and fixed.[2] So we conclude that God keeps certain things in being, by means of certain causes.

Reply Obj. 1. God created all things immediately, but in the creation itself He established an order among things, so that some depend on

---

1. 参见 *Metaph.*, XI, 6 (1072a 9).
2. 参见 Cf. Averroes, *In Metaph.*, XII, comm. 44 (VIII, 153v).

others, by which they are conserved in being; though He remains the principal cause of their conservation.

Reply Obj. 2. An effect is conserved by its proper cause, on which it depends. Hence, just as no effect can be its own cause, but can produce another effect, so no effect can be endowed with the power of self-conservation, but only with the power of conserving another.

Reply Obj. 3. No created being can cause another to acquire a new form or disposition, except by virtue of some change; for the created being acts always on something presupposed. But after causing the form or disposition in the effect, without any fresh change in the effect, the cause conserves that form or disposition; as in the air, when it is lit up anew, we must allow some change to have taken place, while the conservation of the light is without any further change in the air due to the presence of the source of light.

Third Article
WHETHER GOD CAN ANNIHILATE ANYTHING?

We proceed thus to the Third Article:—

Objection 1. It would seem that God cannot annihilate anything. For Augustine says that *God is not the cause of anything tending to not-being.*[1] But He would be such a cause if He were to annihilate anything. Therefore He cannot annihilate anything.

Obj. 2. Further, by His goodness God is the cause why things exist, since, as Augustine says, *because God is good, we exist.*[2] But God cannot cease to be good. Therefore He cannot cause things to cease to exist; which would be the case were He to annihilate anything.

Obj. 3. Further, if God were to annihilate anything, it would be by His action. But this cannot be, because the term of every action

1. 参见 *Lib. 83 Quaest.*, q. 21 (PL 40, 16).
2. 参见 *De Doct. Christ.*, I, 32 (PL 34, 32).

is some being. Thus, the action of a corrupting cause has its term in something generated; for when one thing is generated another undergoes corruption. Therefore God cannot annihilate anything.

On the contrary, It is written (*Jer.* x. 24): *Correct me, O Lord, but yet with judgment; and not in Thy jury, lest Thou bring me to nothing.*

I answer that, Some have held that God, in giving being to creatures, acted from natural necessity.[1] Were this true, God could not annihilate anything, since His nature cannot change. But, as we have said above,[2] such an opinion is entirely false, and absolutely contrary to the Catholic Faith, which confesses that God created things freely, according to *Ps.* cxxxiv. 6: *Whatsoever the Lord pleased, He hath done.* Therefore that God gives being to a creature depends on His will; nor does He conserve things in being otherwise than by continually giving being to them, as we have said. Therefore, just as before things existed, God was free not to give them being, and so not to make them, so, after they have been made, He is free not to give them being, and thus they would cease to exist. This would be to annihilate them.

Reply Obj. 1. Not-being has no essential cause; for nothing is a cause except inasmuch as it is a being, and a being essentially as such is a cause of being. Therefore, God cannot cause a thing to tend to not-being, but a creature has this tendency of itself, since it is produced from nothing. But indirectly God can cause things to be reduced to not-being by withdrawing His action from them.

Reply Obj. 2. God's goodness is the cause of things, not as though by natural necessity, because the divine goodness does not depend on creatures; but by a free will. Therefore, just as without prejudice to His goodness He might not have brought things into being, so, without prejudice to His goodness, He might not conserve things in being.

Reply Obj. 3. If God were to annihilate anything, this would not

---

1. 参见 Cf. above, q. 25, a. 5.
2. 参见 Q. 19, a. 4.

imply an action on God's part, but a mere cessation of His action.

Fourth Article
WHETHER ANYTHING IS ANNIHILATED?

We proceed thus to the Fourth Article:—

Objection 1. It would seem that something is annihilated. For the end corresponds to the beginning. But in the beginning there was nothing but God. Therefore all things must tend to this end, that there shall be nothing but God. Therefore creatures will be reduced to nothing.

Obj. 2. Further, every creature has a finite power. But no finite power extends to the infinite. Therefore the Philosopher proves that *a finite power cannot move in infinite time.*[1] Therefore a creature cannot last for an infinite duration; and so at some time it will be reduced to nothing.

Obj. 3. Further, forms and accidents have no matter as part of themselves. But at some time they cease to exist. Therefore they are reduced to nothing.

On the contrary, It is written (*Eccles.* iii. 14): *I have learned that all the works that God hath made continue forever.*

I answer that, Some of the things which God does in creatures occur in accordance with the natural course of things; others happen miraculously, and not in accordance with the natural order, as will be explained.[2] Now whatever God wills to do according to the natural order of things may be observed from the natures themselves of things; but those things which occur miraculously are ordered to the manifestation of grace, according to the Apostle, *To each one is given the manifestation of the Spirit, unto profit* (*1 Cor.* xii. 7). He goes on to mention, among other things, the working of miracles.

Now the nature of creatures shows that none of them is annihilated.

---

1. 参见 Aristotle, *Phys.*, VIII, 10 (266a 12).
2. 参见 Q. 105, a. 6.

For, either they are immaterial, and therefore have no potentiality to not-being, or they are material, and then they continue to exist, at least in matter, which is incorruptible, since it is the subject of generation and corruption. Moreover, the annihilation of things does not pertain to the manifestation of grace, since the power and goodness of God are rather manifested by the conservation of things in being. Therefore we must conclude by denying absolutely that anything at all will be annihilated.

Reply Obj. 1. That things were brought into being from not-being clearly shows the power of Him Who made them; but that they should be reduced to nothing would hinder that manifestation, since the power of God is conspicuously shown in His preserving all things in being, according to the Apostle: *Upholding all things by the word of His power* (*Heb.* i. 3).

Reply Obj. 2. A creature's potentiality to being is merely receptive; the active power belongs to God Himself, from Whom being is derived. Therefore, the infinite duration of things is a consequence of the infinity of the divine power. To some things, however, is given a determinate power of duration for a certain time, in that they may be hindered from receiving the influx of being, which comes from Him, by some contrary agent to which a finite power cannot offer resistance for an infinite time, but only for a limited time. So things which have no contrary, though they have a finite power, continue to exist forever.

Reply Obj. 3. *Forms* and *accidents* are not complete beings, since they do not subsist, but each one of them is something *of a being*; for each is called a being, because something is by it. Yet according to their mode of being, they are not entirely reduced to nothingness; not that any part of them survives, but that they remain in the potentiality of the matter, or of the subject.

Question CV
THE MOVEMENT OF GOD IN CREATURES
(*In Eight Articles*)

WE now consider the second effect of the divine government, *i.e.*, the moving of creatures by God: and first whether God moves creatures; secondly, the movement of one creature by another.[1]

Under the first head there are eight points of inquiry: (1) Whether God can move immediately the matter to the form? (2) Whether He can immediately move a body? (3) Whether He can move the intellects? (4) Whether He can move the will? (5) Whether God works in every agent? (6) Whether He can do anything outside the order imposed on things? (7) Whether all that God thus does is miraculous? (8) On the diversity of miracles.

First Article
WHETHER GOD CAN MOVE THE MATTER IMMEDIATELY TO THE FORM?

We proceed thus to the First Article:—

Objection 1. It would seem that God cannot move the matter immediately to receive the form. For, as the Philosopher proves, nothing can bring a form into any particular matter, except that form which is in matter; because like begets like.[2] But God is not a form in matter. Therefore He cannot cause a form in matter.

---

1. 参见 Q. 106.
2. 参见 *Metaph.*, VI, 8 (1033b 23).

Obj. 2. Further, any agent inclined to several effects will produce none of them, unless it is determined to a particular one by some other cause. As the Philosopher says, a universal judgment does not move except by means of some particular apprehension.[1] But the divine power is the universal cause of all things. Therefore it cannot produce any particular form, except by means of a particular agent.

Obj. 3. As universal being depends on the first universal cause, so determinate being depends on determinate particular causes, as we have seen above.[2] But the determinate being of a particular thing is from its own form. Therefore the forms of things are produced by God only by means of particular causes.

On the contrary, It is written (*Gen.* ii. 7): *God formed man of the slime of the earth.*

I answer that, God can move matter immediately to a form. For whatever is in passive potentiality can be reduced to act by the active power which extends over that potentiality. Therefore, since the divine power extends over matter, as having been produced by God, matter can be reduced to act by the divine power; and this is what is meant by matter being moved to a form, for a form is nothing else but the act of matter.

Reply Obj. 1. An effect is assimilated to the active cause in two ways. First, according to the same species, as man is generated by man, and fire by fire. Secondly, by being virtually contained in the cause, as the form of the effect is virtually contained in its cause. Thus animals, produced by putrefaction, and plants and minerals are like the sun and stars, by whose power they are produced. In this way the effect is like its active cause as regards all that over which the power of that cause extends. Now the power of God extends to both matter and form, as

---

1. 参见 Aristotle, *De An.*, III, 11 (434a 16).
2. 参见 Q. 104, a. 2.

we have said above.[1] Therefore, if a composite thing be produced, it is likened to God by way of a virtual inclusion; and it is likened to the composite generator by a likeness of species. Therefore, just as the composite generator can move matter to a form by generating a composite thing like itself, so also can God. But no other form not existing in matter can do this, because the power of no other separate substance extends over matter. Hence angels and demons act on visible matter, not by imprinting forms in matter, but by making use of corporeal seminal principles.

Reply Obj. 2. This argument would hold if God acted from natural necessity. But since He acts by His will and intellect, which knows the particular and not only the universal natures of all forms, it follows that He can determinately imprint this or that form on matter.

Reply Obj. 3. The fact that secondary causes are ordered to determinate effects is due to God; and so, since God ordains other causes to determinate effects, He can also produce determinate effects by Himself without any other cause.

Second Article
WHETHER GOD CAN MOVE A BODY IMMEDIATELY?

We proceed thus to the Second Article:—

Objection 1. It would seem that God cannot move a body immediately. For *as the mover and the moved must exist simultaneously*, as the Philosopher says,[2] it follows that there must be some contact between the mover and the moved. But there can be no contact between God and a body, for Dionysius says: *There is no contact with God.*[3] Therefore God cannot move a body immediately.

---

1. 参见 Q. 14, a. 11; q. 44, a. 2.
2. 参见 Aristotle, *Phys.*, VII, 2 (243a 4).
3. 参见 *De Div. Nom.*, I, 5 (PG 3, 593).

Obj. 2. Further, God is an unmoved mover. But such also is the desirable object when apprehended. Therefore God moves as the object of desire and apprehension. But He cannot be apprehended except by the intellect, which is neither a body nor a corporeal power. Therefore God cannot move a body immediately.

Obj. 3. Further, the Philosopher proves that an infinite power moves instantaneously.[1] But it is impossible for a body to be moved in one instant, for since every movement is between opposites, it would follow that two opposites would exist at once in the same subject; which is impossible. Therefore a body cannot be moved immediately by an infinite power. But God's power is infinite, as we have explained above.[2] Therefore God cannot move a body immediately.

On the contrary, God produced the works of the six days immediately, among which is included the movement of bodies, as is clear from *Gen.* i. 9: *Let the waters be gathered together into one place.* Therefore God can move a body immediately.

I answer that, It is erroneous to say that God cannot Himself produce all the determinate effects which are produced by any created cause. Therefore, since bodies are moved immediately by created causes, we cannot possibly doubt that God can move immediately any bodies whatever. This follows from what is stated above. For every movement of any body whatever either results from a form, as the movements of things heavy and light result from the form which they have from their generating cause, for which reason the generator is called the mover; or else it tends to a form, as heating tends to the form of heat. Now it belongs to the same cause to imprint a form, to dispose to that form, and to give the movement which results from that form; for fire not only generates fire, but it also heats and moves things upwards. Therefore, since God can imprint a form immediately

---

1. 参见 *Phys.*, VIII, 10 (266a 31).
2. 参见 Q. 25, a. 2.

in matter, it follows that He can move any body whatever in respect of any movement whatever.

Reply Obj. 1. There are two kinds of contact: corporeal contact (when two bodies touch each other) and virtual contact (as the cause of sadness is said to touch the one made sad). According to the first kind of contact, God, as being incorporeal, neither touches, nor is touched. But according to virtual contact, He touches creatures by moving them, but He is not touched, because the natural power of no creature can reach up to Him. Thus did Dionysius understand the words. *There is no contact with God*; that is, so that God Himself be touched.

Reply Obj. 2. God moves as the object of desire and apprehension, but it does not follow that He always moves as being desired and apprehended by that which is moved; but rather as being desired and known by Himself, for He does all things because of His own goodness.

Reply Obj. 3. The Philosopher intends to prove that the power of the first mover is not a power in a magnitude. This is his argument.[1] The power of the first mover is infinite (which he proves from the fact that the first mover can move in infinite time[2]). Now an infinite power, if it were a power in any magnitude, would move without time, which is impossible. Therefore the infinite power of the first mover must be in something which is without magnitude. Whence it is clear that for a body to be moved without time can be the result only of an infinite power. The reason is that every power in a magnitude moves in its entirety, since it moves by a necessity of nature. But an infinite power surpasses out of all proportion any finite power. Now the greater the power of the mover, the greater is the velocity of the movement. Therefore, since a finite power moves in a determinate time, it follows that an infinite power does not move in any time; for between one time

1. 参见 *Phys.*, VIII, 10 (266a 10).
2. 同上 (267b 25).

and any other time there is some proportion. On the other hand, a power which is not in a magnitude is the power of an intelligent being, which operates in its effects according to what is fitting to them; and therefore, since it cannot be fitting for a body to be moved without time, it does not follow that it moves without time.

Third Article
WHETHER GOD MOVES THE CREATED INTELLECT IMMEDIATELY?

We proceed thus to the Third Article:—

Objection 1. It would seem that God does not immediately move the created intellect. For the action of the intellect is from the being in which it resides, since it does not pass into external matter, as is stated in *Metaph.* ix.[1] But the action of what is moved by another does not proceed from that wherein it is, but from the mover. Therefore the intellect is not moved by another; and so apparently God cannot move the created intellect.

Obj. 2. Further, anything which in itself has a sufficient principle of movement is not moved by another. But the movement of the intellect is its act of understanding. Thus, we say that to understand or to sense is a kind of movement, as the Philosopher says.[2] But the intelligible light with which the intellect is endowed is a sufficient principle of understanding. Therefore it is not moved by another.

Obj. 3. Further, as the senses are moved by the sensible, so the intellect is moved by the intelligible. But God is not intelligible to us, but exceeds the capacity of our intellect. Therefore God cannot move our intellect.

On the contrary, The teacher moves the intellect of the one taught.

---

1. 参见 Aristotle, *Metaph.*, VIII, 8 (1050a 36).
2. 参见 *De An.*, III, 7 (431a 6).

But it is written (*Ps.* xciii. 10) that God *teaches man knowledge*. Therefore God moves the human intellect.

I answer that, As in corporeal movement that is called the mover which gives the form that is the principle of movement, so that is said to move the intellect which is the cause of the form that is the principle of the intellectual operation called the movement of the intellect. Now there is a twofold principle of intellectual operation in the intelligent being: one is the intellectual power itself, which principle exists also in the one who understands in potentiality; while the other is the principle of actual understanding, namely, the likeness of the thing understood. So a thing is said to move the intellect, whether it gives to him who understands the power of understanding, or impresses on him the likeness of the thing understood.

Now God moves the created intellect in both ways. For He is the first and immaterial being; and as intellectuality[1] is a result of immateriality, it follows that He is the first intelligent being. Therefore, since in each order the first is the cause of all that follows, we must conclude that from Him proceeds all intellectual power. In like manner, since He is the first being, and all other beings pre-exist in Him as in their first cause, it follows that they exist intelligibly in Him, after the mode of His own nature. For as the intelligible exemplars of everything exist first of all in God, and are derived from Him by other intellects in order that these may actually understand, so also are they derived by creatures that they may subsist. Therefore God so moves the created intellect that He gives it the power of understanding, whether natural, or superadded; and He impresses on the created intellect the intelligible species, and maintains and preserves both power and species in being.

Reply Obj. 1. The intellectual operation is performed by the intellect

1. intellectuality: 智力；知性

in which it exists as by a secondary cause; but it proceeds from God as from its first cause. For by Him the power to understand is given to the one who understands.

Reply Obj. 2. The intellectual light together with the likeness of the thing understood is a sufficient principle of understanding; but it is a secondary principle, and depends upon the first principle.

Reply Obj. 3. The intelligible object moves our human intellect in so far as it somehow impresses on it its own likeness, by means of which the intellect is able to understand it. But the likenesses which God impresses on the created intellect are not sufficient to enable the created intellect to understand God through His Essence, as we have seen above.[1] Hence He moves the created intellect, and yet He cannot be intelligible to it, as we have explained.[2]

Fourth Article
WHETHER GOD CAN MOVE THE CREATED WILL?

We proceed thus to the Fourth Article:—

Objection 1. It would seem that God cannot move the created will. For whatever is moved from without, is forced. But the will cannot be forced. Therefore it is not moved from without. Therefore it cannot be moved by God.

Obj. 2. Further, God cannot make two contradictories to be true at the same time. But this would follow if He moved the will; for to be voluntarily moved means to be moved from within, and not by another. Therefore God cannot move the will.

Obj. 3. Further, movement is attributed to the mover rather than to the one moved; and so homicide is not ascribed to the stone, but to the thrower. Therefore, if God moves the will, it follows that voluntary

---

1. 参见 Q. 12, a. 2; q. 56, a. 3.
2. 参见 Q. 12, a. 4.

actions are not imputed to man for reward or blame. But this is false. Therefore God does not move the will.

On the contrary, It is written (*Phil.* ii. 13): *It is God who worketh in us both to will and to accomplish.*

I answer that, Just as the intellect is moved by the object and by the giver of the power of understanding, as was stated above, so the will is moved by its object, which is the good, and by Him who creates the power of willing. Now the will can be moved by any good as its object, but by God alone is it moved sufficiently and efficaciously. For nothing can move a movable thing sufficiently unless the active power of the mover surpasses or at least equals the potentiality of the movable thing. Now the potentiality of the will extends to the universal good, for its object is the universal good, just as the object of the intellect is universal being. But every created good is some particular good, and God alone is the universal good. Therefore He alone fills the capacity of the will, and moves it sufficiently as its object. In like manner, the power of willing is caused by God alone. For to will is nothing but to be inclined towards the object of the will, which is the universal good. But to incline towards the universal good belongs to the first mover, to whom the ultimate end is proportioned; just as in human affairs to him that presides over the community belongs the directing of his subjects to the common weal. Therefore in both ways it belongs to God to move the will; but especially in the second way by an interior inclination of the will.

Reply Obj. 1. A thing moved by another is forced if it is moved against its natural inclination. But if it is moved by another which gives to it its natural inclination, it is not forced. Thus, a heavy body, made to move downward by that which produced it, is not forced. In like manner God, while moving the will, does not force it, because He gives the will its own natural inclination.

Reply Obj. 2. To be moved voluntarily is to be moved from within, that is, by an interior principle. But this interior principle may be caused by an exterior principle; and so to be moved from within is not repugnant to being moved by another.

Reply Obj. 3. If the will were so moved by another as in no way to be moved from within itself, the act of the will would not be imputed for reward or blame. But since its being moved by another does not prevent its being moved from within itself, as we have stated, it does not thereby forfeit the motive for merit or demerit.

Fifth Article
WHETHER GOD WORKS IN EVERY AGENT?

We proceed thus to the Fifth Article:—

Objection 1. It would seem that God does not work in every agent. For we must not attribute any insufficiency to God. If therefore God works in every agent, He works sufficiently in each one. Hence it would be superfluous for the created agent to work at all.

Obj. 2. Further, the same work cannot proceed at the same time from two sources, just as neither can one and the same movement belong to two movable things. Therefore if the creature's operation is from God operating in the creature, it cannot at the same time proceed from the creature; and so no creature works at all.

Obj. 3. Further, the maker is the cause of the operation of the thing made, as giving it the form whereby it operates. Therefore, if God is the cause of the operation of the things made by Him, this would be inasmuch as He gives them the power of operating. But this is in the beginning, when He makes them. Thus it seems that God does not operate any further in the operating creature.

On the contrary, It is written (*Isa.* xxvi. 12): *Lord, Thou hast wrought all our works in us.*

I answer that, Some have understood God to work in every agent in such a way that no created power has any effect in things, but that God alone is the immediate cause of everything wrought; for instance, that it is not fire that gives heat, but God in the fire, and so forth.[1] But this is impossible. First, because the order of cause and effect would be taken away from created things, and this would imply a lack of power in the Creator; for it is due to the power of the cause, that it bestows active power on its effect. Secondly, because the operative powers which are seen to exist in things would be bestowed on things to no purpose, if things produced nothing through them. Indeed, all things created would seem, in a way, to be purposeless, if they lacked an operation proper to them; since the purpose of everything is its operation. For the less perfect is always for the sake of the more perfect. Consequently, just as the matter is for the sake of the form, so the form which is the first act is for the sake of its operation, which is the second act; and thus operation is the end of the creature. We must therefore understand that God works in things in such a manner that things have also their proper operation.

In order to make this clear, we must observe that of the four causes matter is not a principle of action, but the subject that receives the effect of action. On the other hand, the end, the agent and the form are principles of action, but in a certain order. For the first principle of action is the end which moves the agent, the second is the agent, and the third is the form of that which the agent applies to action (although the agent also acts through its own form). This may be clearly seen in things made by art. For the craftsman is moved to action by the end, which is the thing wrought, for instance a chest or a bed, and he applies to action the axe which cuts because it is sharp.

Thus then does God work in every agent, according to these three things. First, as an end. For since every operation is for the sake of some good, real or apparent, and since nothing is good, either really or apparently, except in so far as it participates in a likeness to the

1. 参见 Cf. above, q. 45, a. 8.—Cf. also Averroes, *In Metaph.*, IX, comm. 7 (VIII, 109r).

highest good, which is God, it follows that God Himself is the cause of every operation as its end. Again, it is to be observed that where there are several agents in order, the second always acts in virtue of the first; for the first agent moves the second to act. And thus all agents act in virtue of God Himself; and so, He is the cause of action in every agent. Thirdly, we must observe that God not only moves things to operate, as it were applying their forms and powers to operation, just as the workman applies the axe to cutting (who nevertheless did not himself give the axe its form), but He also gives created agents their forms and preserves them in being. Therefore He is the cause of action not only by giving the form which is the principle of action, as the generator is said to be the cause of movement in things heavy and light, but also as conserving the forms and powers of things; just as the sun is said to be the cause of the manifestation of colors, inasmuch as it gives and conserves the light by which colors are made manifest. And since the form of a thing is within the thing, and all the more so, as it approaches nearer to the first and universal cause; and because in all things God Himself is properly the cause of universal being which is innermost in all things: —it follows that God works intimately in all things. For this reason in Holy Scripture the operations of nature are attributed to God as operating in nature, according to *Job* x. 11: *Thou hast clothed me with skin and flesh: Thou hast put me together with bones and sinews.*

Reply Obj. 1. God works sufficiently in things as a first cause, but it does not follow from this that the operation of secondary agents is superfluous.

Reply Obj. 2. One action does not proceed from two agents of the same order. But nothing hinders the same action from proceeding from a primary and a secondary agent.

Reply Obj. 3. God not only gives things their forms, but He also conserves them in being, and applies them to act, and is moreover the end of every action, as was explained above.

Sixth Article

WHETHER GOD CAN DO ANYTHING OUTSIDE THE ESTABLISHED ORDER OF NATURE?

We proceed thus to the Sixth Article:—

Objection 1. It would seem that God cannot do anything outside the established order of nature. For Augustine says: *God, the Maker and Creator of each nature, does nothing against nature.*[1] But that which is outside the natural order seems to be against nature. Therefore God can do nothing outside the natural order.

Obj. 2. Further, as the order of justice is from God, so is the order of nature. But God cannot do anything outside the order of justice, for then He would be doing something unjust. Therefore He cannot do anything outside the order of nature.

Obj. 3. Further, God established the order of nature. Therefore, if God does anything outside the order of nature, it would seem that He is changeable; which cannot be said.

On the contrary, Augustine says: *God sometimes does things which are contrary to the wonted course of nature.*[2]

I answer that, From each cause there results a certain order to its effects, since every cause is a principle; and so, according to the multiplicity of causes, there results a multiplicity of orders, subject one to the other, just as cause is subject to cause. Hence, a higher cause is not subject to a cause of a lower order, but conversely. An example of this may be seen in human affairs. On the father of a family depends the order of the household; which order is contained in the order of the city; which order again depends on the ruler of the city; while this last order depends on that of the king, by whom the whole kingdom is

---

1. 参见 *Contra Faust.*, XXVI, 3 (PL 42, 480).
2. 同上 (PL 42, 481).

ordered.

If, therefore, we consider the order of things according as it depends on the first cause, God cannot do anything against this order; for, if He did so, He would act against His foreknowledge[1], or His will, or His goodness. But if we consider the order of things according as it depends on any secondary cause, thus God can do something outside such order. For He is not subject to the order of secondary causes, but, on the contrary, this order is subject to Him, as proceeding from Him, not by a natural necessity, but by the choice of His own will; for He could have created another order of things. Therefore God can do something outside this order created by Him, when He chooses,—for instance, by producing the effects of secondary causes without them, or by producing certain effects to which secondary causes do not extend. So Augustine says: *God acts against the wonted course of nature, but by no means does He act against the supreme law; because He does not act against Himself.*[2]

Reply Obj. 1. In natural things something may happen outside this natural order, in two ways. It may happen by the action of an agent which did not give them their natural inclination, as, for example, when a man moves a heavy body upwards, which does not owe to him its natural inclination to move downwards. Now this would be against nature. It may also happen by the action of the agent on whom the natural inclination depends, and this is not against nature, as is clear in the ebb and flow of the tide, which is not against nature, although it is against the natural movement of water, which is moved downward; for it is owing to the influence of a heavenly body, on which the natural inclination of lower bodies depends. Therefore since the order of nature is given to things by God, if He does anything outside this order, it is not against nature. Hence Augustine says: *That is natural to*

---

1. foreknowledge: 预知；先见之明
2. 参见 *Contra Faust.*, XXVI, 3 (PL 42, 481).

each thing which is caused by Him from Whom is all limit, number and order in nature.[1]

Reply Obj. 2. The order of justice arises by relation to the first cause, which is the rule of all justice; and that is why God can do nothing against such an order.

Reply Obj. 3. God fixed a certain order in things in such a way that at the same time He reserved to Himself whatever He intended to do otherwise than by a particular cause. So when He acts outside this order, He does not change.

Seventh Article
WHETHER WHATEVER GOD DOES OUTSIDE THE NATURAL ORDER IS MIRACULOUS?

We proceed thus to the Seventh Article:—

Objection 1. It would seem that not everything which God does outside the natural order of things is miraculous. For the creation of the world and of souls, and the justification of the unrighteous, are done by God outside the natural order; for these effects are not accomplished by the action of any natural cause. Yet these things are not called miracles. Therefore not everything that God does outside the natural order is a miracle.

Obj. 2. Further, a miracle is *something difficult, which seldom occurs, surpassing the faculty of nature, and going so far beyond our hopes as to compel our astonishment.*[2] But some things outside the order of nature are not arduous, for they occur in small things, such as the recovery of some precious stone or the healing of the sick. Nor are they of rare occurrence, since they happen frequently; as when the sick were placed in the streets, to be healed by the shadow of Peter (*Acts* v. 15). Nor do

---

1. 参见 *Contra Faust.*, XXVI, 3 (PL 42, 480).
2. 参见 St. Augustine, *De Util. Cred.*, XVI (PL 42, 90).

they surpass the ability of nature; as when people are cured of a fever. Nor are they beyond our hopes, since we all hope for the resurrection of the dead, which nevertheless will be outside the course of nature. Therefore not all things that are outside the course of nature are miraculous.

Obj. 3. Further, the term *miracle* is derived from admiration. Now admiration concerns things manifest to the senses. But sometimes things happen outside the order of nature which are not manifest to the senses; as when the Apostles were endowed with knowledge without studying or being taught. Therefore not everything that occurs outside the order of nature is miraculous.

On the contrary, Augustine says: *Where God does anything against that order of nature which we know and are accustomed to observe, we call it a miracle.*[1]

I answer that, The term *miracle* is derived from admiration, which arises when an effect is manifest, whereas its cause is hidden; as when a man sees an eclipse without knowing its cause, as the Philosopher says in the beginning of his *Metaphysics*.[2] Now the cause of a manifest effect may be known to one, but unknown to others. Hence a thing is wonderful to one man, and not at all to others; as an eclipse is to a rustic, but not to an astronomer. Now a miracle is so called as being full of wonder, in other words, as having a cause absolutely hidden from all. This cause is God. Therefore those things which God does outside the causes which we know are called miracles.

Reply Obj. 1. Creation, and the justification of the unrighteous, though done by God alone, are not, properly speaking, miracles, because they are not of a nature to proceed from any other cause; so they do not occur outside the order of nature, since they do not belong to the capacity of nature.

---

1. 参见 *Contra Faust.*, XXVI, 3 (PL 42, 481).
2. 参见 Aristotle, *Metaph.*, I, 2 (982b 16).

Reply Obj. 2. An arduous thing is called a miracle, not because of the excellence of the thing wherein it is done, but because it surpasses the ability of nature. So, too, a thing is called unusual, not because it does not often happen, but because it is outside the usual natural course of things. Furthermore, a thing is said to be above the ability of nature, not only by reason of the substance of the thing done, but also because of the manner and order in which it is done. Again, a miracle is said to go beyond the hope *of nature*, not above the hope *of grace*, which hope comes from faith, whereby we believe in the future resurrection.

Reply Obj. 3. The knowledge of the Apostles, although not manifest in itself, yet was made manifest in its effect, from which it was shown to be wonderful.

Eighth Article
WHETHER ONE MIRACLE IS GREATER THAN ANOTHER?

We proceed thus to the Eighth Article:—

Objection 1. It would seem that one miracle is not greater than another. For Augustine says: *In miraculous deeds, the whole measure of the deed is the power of the doer.*[1] But by the same power of God all miracles are done. Therefore one miracle is not greater than another.

Obj. 2. Further, the power of God is infinite. But the infinite exceeds the finite beyond all proportion; and therefore no more reason exists to wonder at one effect thereof than at another. Therefore one miracle is not greater than another.

On the contrary, The Lord says, speaking of miraculous works (*Jo.* xiv. 12): *The works that I do, he also shall do, and greater than these shall he do.*

I answer that, Nothing is called a miracle by comparison with the

---

1. 参见 *Epist.* CXXXVII, 2 (PL 33, 519).

divine power, because no action is of any account compared with the power of God, according to *Isa.* xl. 15: *Behold the Gentiles are as a drop from a bucket, and are counted as the smallest grain of a balance.* But a thing is called a miracle by comparison with the power of nature, which it surpasses. So the more the power of nature is surpassed, the greater is the miracle. Now the power of nature is surpassed in three ways: first, in the substance of the deed, for instance, if two bodies occupy the same place, or if the sun goes backwards, or if a human body is glorified. Such things nature is absolutely unable to do; and these hold the highest rank among miracles. Secondly, a thing surpasses the power of nature, not in the deed, but in that wherein it is done; as the raising of the dead, and giving sight to the blind, and the like. For nature can give life, but not to the dead, and it can give sight, but not to the blind. Such hold the second rank in miracles. Thirdly, a thing surpasses nature's power in the measure and order in which it is done; as when a man is cured of a fever suddenly by God, without treatment or the usual process of nature, or as when by divine power the air is suddenly condensed into rain, without a natural cause, as occurred at the prayers of Samuel[1] and Elias.[2] These hold the lowest place in miracles. Moreover, each of these kinds has various degrees, according to the different ways in which the power of nature is surpassed.

From this it is clear how to reply to the objections, arguing as they do from the power of God.

---

1. 参见 *I Kings*, XII, 18.
2. 参见 *III Kings*, XVIII, 44.

Question CVI
HOW ONE CREATURE MOVES ANOTHER
(*In Four Articles*)

WE next consider how one creature moves another. This consideration will be threefold: (1) How the angels move, who are purely spiritual creatures; (2) how bodies move;[1] (3) how man moves, who is composed of a spiritual and a corporeal nature.[2]

Concerning the first point, there are three things to be considered: (1) how an angel acts on an angel; (2) how an angel acts on a corporeal creature;[3] (3) how an angel acts on man.[4]

The first of these raises the question of the illumination and speech of the angels;[5] and of their mutual co-ordination, both of the good[6] and of the bad angels.[7]

Concerning their illumination, there are four points of inquiry: (1) Whether one angel moves the intellect of another by illumination? (2) Whether one angel moves the will of another? (3) Whether an inferior angel can illumine a superior angel? (4) Whether a superior angel illumines an inferior angel in all that he himself knows?

---

1. 参见 Q. 115.
2. 参见 Q. 117.
3. 参见 Q. 110.
4. 参见 Q. 111.
5. 参见 Q. 107.
6. 参见 Q. 108.
7. 参见 Q. 109.

First Article
WHETHER ONE ANGEL ILLUMINES ANOTHER?

We proceed thus to the First Article:—

Objection 1. It would seem that one angel does not illumine another. For the angels possess now the same beatitude which we hope to obtain. But one man will not then illumine another, according to *Jer.* xxxi. 34: *They shall teach no more every man his neighbor, and every man his brother.* Therefore neither does an angel illumine another now.

Obj. 2. Further, light in the angels is threefold: of nature, of grace, and of glory. But an angel is illumined with the light of nature by the Creator, with the light of grace by the Justifier, with the light of glory by the Beatifier; all of which comes from God. Therefore one angel does not illumine another.

Obj. 3. Further, light is a form in the mind. But the rational mind is *informed by God alone, without created intervention*, as Augustine says.[1] Therefore one angel does not illumine the mind of another.

On the contrary, Dionysius says that *the angels of the second hierarchy are cleansed, illumined and perfected by the angels of the first hierarchy.*[2]

I answer that, One angel illumines another. To make this clear, we must observe that intellectual light is nothing else than a manifestation of truth, according to *Ephes.* v. 13: *All that is made manifest is light.* Hence to illumine means nothing else than to communicate to others the manifestation of known truth. As the Apostle says (*Ephes.* iii. 8): *To me the least of all the saints is given this grace ... to enlighten all men, that they may see what is the dispensation of the mystery which hath been hidden from eternity in God.* Therefore one angel is said to illumine another by manifesting the truth which he knows himself. Hence Dionysius says: *Theologians plainly show that the orders of the heavenly beings are taught divine science by*

---

1. 参见 *Lib. 83 Quaest.*, q. 51 (PL 40, 33).
2. 参见 *De Cael. Hier.*, VIII, 1 (PG 3, 240).

the highest minds.[1]

Now since two things concur in understanding, as we have said,[2] namely, the intellectual power, and the likeness of the thing understood, in both of these one angel can manifest a known truth to another. First, by strengthening his intellectual power. For just as the power of an imperfect body is strengthened by the proximity of a more perfect body,—for instance, the less hot is made hotter by the presence of what is hotter, so the intellectual power of an inferior angel is strengthened by the turning of a superior angel to him. For in spiritual beings, for one to turn to another corresponds to proximity in corporeal things. Secondly, one angel manifests the truth to another as regards the likeness of the thing understood. For the superior angel receives the knowledge of truth by a kind of universal conception, to receive which the inferior angel's intellect is not sufficiently powerful; for it is natural to him to receive truth in a more particular manner. Therefore the superior angel particularizes, in a way, the truth which he conceives universally, so that it can be grasped by the inferior angel; and thus he proposes it to his knowledge. Thus it is among men that the teacher, in order to adapt himself to others, divides into many points the knowledge which he possesses in the universal. This is thus expressed by Dionysius: *Every intellectual substance with provident power divides and multiplies the uniform knowledge bestowed on it by one nearer to God, so as to lead its inferiors upwards by analogy.*[3]

Reply Obj. 1. All the angels, both inferior and superior, see the essence of God immediately, and in this respect one does not teach another. It is of this truth that the prophet speaks; wherefore he adds: *They shall teach no more every man his brother, saying: Know the Lord, for all shall know Me, from the least of them even to the greatest.* But all the

1. 参见 *Op. cit.*, VII, 3 (PG 3, 209).
2. 参见 Q. 105, a. 3.
3. 参见 *De Cael. Hier.*, XV, 3 (PG 3, 332).

exemplars of the divine works, which are known in God as in their cause, God knows in Himself, because He comprehends Himself; but of others who see God, each one knows the more exemplars, the more perfectly he sees God. Hence a superior angel knows more about the exemplars of the divine works than an inferior angel, and concerning these the former illumines the latter; and as to this Dionysius says that the angels *are illumined by the exemplars of existing things.*[1]

Reply Obj. 2. An angel does not illumine another by giving him the light of nature, grace, or glory, but by strengthening his natural light, and by manifesting to him truths concerning the state of nature, of grace, and of glory, as was explained above.

Reply Obj. 3. The rational mind is formed immediately by God, either as the image from the exemplar, inasmuch as it is made to the image of God alone, or as a subject by the ultimate perfecting form. For the created mind is always considered to be unformed, except it adhere to the first truth; while other kinds of illumination that proceed from man or angel are, as it were, dispositions to this ultimate form.

Second Article
WHETHER ONE ANGEL MOVES ANOTHER ANGEL'S WILL?

We proceed thus to the Second Article:—

Objection 1. It would seem that one angel can move another angel's will. Because, according to Dionysius quoted above, just as one angel illumines another, so does he cleanse and perfect another.[2] But cleansing and perfecting seem to belong to the will; for the former seems to point to the stain of sin which pertains to the will, while to be perfected is to obtain an end, which is the object of the will. Therefore an angel can move another angel's will.

---

1. 参见 *De Div. Nom.*, IV, 1 (PG 3, 693).
2. 参见 *De Cael. Hier.*, VIII, 1 (PG 3, 240).

Obj. 2. Further, as Dionysius says: *The names of the angels designate their properties.*[1] Now the Seraphim are so called because they are *aflame* or *ablaze*; and this is by love, which belongs to the will. Therefore one angel moves another angel's will.

Obj. 3. Further, the Philosopher says that the higher appetite moves the lower.[2] But as the intellect of the superior angel is higher, so also is his will. It seems, therefore, that the superior angel can change the will of another angel.

On the contrary, To him it belongs to change the will, to whom it belongs to justify it, for justice is the rectitude of the will. But God alone justifies. Therefore one angel cannot change another angel's will.

I answer that, As was said above, the will is changed in two ways: on the part of the object, and on the part of the power.[3] On the part of the object, both the good itself, which is the object of the will, moves the will, as the appetible moves the appetite; and he who points out the object, as, for instance, one who proves something to be good. But as we have said above, other goods in a measure incline the will, yet nothing sufficiently moves the will save the universal good, and that is God.[4] And this good He alone shows, that it may be seen by the blessed, Who, when Moses asked: *Show me Thy glory*, answered: *I will show thee all good* (*Exod.* xxxiii. 18, 19). Therefore an angel does not move the will sufficiently, either as the object or as showing the object. But he inclines the will as something lovable, and as manifesting some created good ordered to God's goodness. And thus he can incline the will to the love of the creature or of God, by way of persuasion.

---

1. 参见 *Op. cit.*, VII, 1 (PG 3, 205).
2. 参见 *De An.*, III, 11 (434a 13).
3. 参见 Q. 105, a. 4.
4. 同上

But on the part of the power, the will cannot be moved at all save by God. For the operation of the will is a certain inclination of the one who wills to the thing willed. And He alone can change this inclination, Who bestowed on the creature the power to will; just as that agent alone can change the natural inclination, that can give the power which the natural inclination follows. Now God alone gave to the creature the power to will, because He alone is the author of the intellectual nature. Therefore an angel cannot move another angel's will.

Reply Obj. 1. Cleansing and perfecting are to be understood as illuminations. And since God illumines by changing the intellect and will, He cleanses by removing defects of intellect and will, and perfects unto the end of the intellect and will. But the illumination caused by an angel concerns the intellect, as was explained above; and therefore an angel is to be understood as cleansing from the defect of nescience in the intellect, and as perfecting unto the consummate end of the intellect, which is the known truth. Thus Dionysius says that *in the heavenly hierarchy the chastening of the inferior essence is an illumination of things unknown, that leads them to more perfect knowledge.*[1] For instance, we might say that corporeal sight is cleansed by the removal of darkness, illumined by the diffusion of light, and perfected by being brought to the perception of the colored thing.

Reply Obj. 2. One angel can induce another by persuasion to love God, as was explained above.

Reply Obj. 3. The Philosopher is speaking of the lower sensitive appetite, which can be moved by the superior intellectual appetite, because it belongs to the same nature of the soul, and because the inferior appetite is a power in a corporeal organ. But this does not apply to the angels.

---

1. 参见 *De Eccles. Hier.*, VI, pt. 3, § 6 (PG 3, 537).

Third Article

WHETHER AN INFERIOR ANGEL CAN ILLUMINE A SUPERIOR ANGEL?

We proceed thus to the Third Article:—

Objection 1. It would seem that an inferior angel can illumine a superior angel. For the ecclesiastical hierarchy is derived from, and represents, the heavenly hierarchy ; and hence the heavenly Jerusalem is called *our mother* (*Gal.* iv. 26). But in the Church even superiors are illumined and taught by their inferiors, as the Apostle says (*1 Cor.* xiv. 31): *You may all prophesy one by one, that all may learn and all may be exhorted.* Therefore, likewise in the heavenly hierarchy, the superiors can be illumined by inferiors.

Obj. 2. Further, as the order of corporeal substances depends on the will of God, so also does the order of spiritual substances. But, as was said above, God sometimes acts outside the order of corporeal substances.[1] Therefore he also sometimes acts outside the order of spiritual substances, by illumining inferiors otherwise than through their superiors. Therefore in that way the inferiors illumined by God can illumine superiors.

Obj. 3. Further, one angel illumines the other to whom he turns, as was above explained. But since this turning to another is voluntary, the highest angel can turn to the lowest passing over the others. Therefore he can illumine him immediately; and thus the latter can illumine his superiors.

On the contrary, Dionysius says that *this is the divine unalterable law, that inferior things are led to God by the superior.*[2]

I answer that, The inferior angels never illumine the superior, but

---

1. 参见 Q. 105, a. 6.
2. 参见 *De Cael. Hier.*, IV, 3 (PG 3, 181); *De Eccles. Hier.*, V, pt. 1, § 4 (PG 3, 504).

are always illumined by them. The reason is, because, as was above explained,[1] one order is under another, as cause is under cause; and hence as cause is ordered to cause, so is order to order. Therefore there is no incongruity if sometimes anything is done outside the order of the inferior cause, that it be ordered to a superior cause, as in human affairs the command of the governor is passed over from obedience to the prince. So it happens that God works miraculously outside the order of corporeal nature, in order that men may be ordered to the knowledge of Him. But the passing over of the order that belongs to spiritual substances in no way belongs to the ordering of men to God, since the angelic operations are not made known to us, as are the operations of sensible bodies. Thus the order which belongs to spiritual substances is never passed over by God; so that the inferiors are always moved by the superior, and not conversely.

Reply Obj. 1. The ecclesiastical hierarchy imitates the heavenly in some degree, but not by a perfect likeness. For in the heavenly hierarchy the perfection of the order is in proportion to its nearness to God. Hence, those who are the nearer to God are the more sublime in grade, and more clear in knowledge; and on that account the superiors are never illumined by the inferiors. But in the ecclesiastical hierarchy, sometimes those who are the nearer to God in sanctity are in the lowest grade, and are not conspicuous for science; and some also are eminent in one kind of science, and fail in another. On this account superiors may be taught by inferiors.

Reply Obj. 2. As was above explained, there is no similarity between what God does outside the order of corporeal nature, and that of spiritual nature. Hence the argument does not hold.

Reply Obj. 3. An angel turns voluntarily to illumine another angel, but the angel's will is always regulated by the divine law which

---

1. 参见 Q. 105, a. 6.

established the order in the angels.

Fourth Article
WHETHER THE SUPERIOR ANGEL ILLUMINES THE INFERIOR AS REGARDS ALL HE HIMSELF KNOWS?

We proceed thus to the Fourth Article:—

Objection 1. It would seem that the superior angel does not illumine the inferior concerning all he himself knows. For Dionysius says that the superior angels have a more universal knowledge, and the inferior a more particular and individual knowledge.[1] But more is contained under a universal knowledge than under a particular knowledge. Therefore not all that the superior angels know is known by the inferior, through the illuminations of the superior.

Obj. 2. Further, the Master of the *Sentences* says that the superior angels had long known the mystery of the Incarnation, whereas the inferior angels did not know it until it was accomplished.[2] Thus we find that on some of the angels inquiring, as it were, in ignorance: *Who is this King of glory?* other angels, who knew, answered: *The Lord of Hosts, He is the King of glory*, as Dionysius expounds.[3] But this would not apply if the superior angels illumined the inferior concerning all they know themselves. Therefore they do not do so.

Obj. 3. Further, if the superior angels illumine the inferior about all they know, nothing that the superior angels know would be unknown to the inferior angels. Therefore the superior angels could communicate nothing more to the inferior; which appears open to objection. Therefore the superior angels illumine the inferior in all things.

---

1. 参见 *De Cael. Hier.*, XII, 2 (PG 3, 293).
2. 参见 *Sent.*, II, xi, 2 (I, 356).
3. 参见 *De Cael. Hier.*, XV, 3 (PG 3, 209).

On the contrary, Gregory says: *In that heavenly country, though there are some excellent gifts, yet nothing is held individually.*[1] And Dionysius says: *Each heavenly essence communicates to the inferior the gift derived from the superior*, as was quoted above.[2]

I answer that, Every creature participates in the divine goodness, so as to diffuse the good it possesses to others; for it is of the nature of good to communicate itself to others. Hence corporeal agents also give their likeness to others so far as they can. Hence, the more an agent is established in the share of the divine goodness, so much the more does it strive to transmit its perfections to others as far as possible. Hence the Blessed Peter admonishes those who by grace share in the divine goodness, saying: *As every man hath received grace, ministering the same one to another, as good stewards of the manifold grace of God* (*1 Pet.* iv. 10). Much more therefore do the holy angels, who enjoy the plenitude of participation of the divine goodness, impart the same to those below them.

Nevertheless this gift is not received so excellently by the inferior as by the superior angels. Therefore the superior always remain in a higher order, and have a more perfect knowledge; just as the teacher understands the same thing better than the pupil who learns from him.

Reply Obj. 1. The knowledge of the superior angels is said to be more universal with reference to the more eminent mode of understanding.

Reply Obj. 2. The Master's words are not to be so understood as if the inferior angels were entirely ignorant of the mystery of the Incarnation; but that they did not know it as fully as the superior angels, and that they progressed in the knowledge of it afterwards when the mystery was accomplished.

Reply Obj. 3. Till the Judgment Day some new things are always

---

1. 参见 Peter Lombard, *Sent.* II, ix, 3 (I, 346); cf. St. Gregory. *In Evang.*, II, hom. 34 (PL 76, 1255).
2. 参见 *De Cael. Hier.*, XV, 3 (PG 3, 332).

being revealed by God to the highest angels, concerning the course of the world, and especially the salvation of the elect. Hence there is always something for the superior angels to make known to the inferior.

Question CVII
THE SPEECH OF THE ANGELS
(*In Five Articles*)

WE now consider the speech of the angels. Here there are five points of inquiry: (1) Whether one angel speaks to another? (2) Whether the inferior speaks to the superior? (3) Whether an angel speaks to God? (4) Whether the angelic speech is subject to local distance? (5) Whether all the speech of one angel to another is known to all?

First Article
WHETHER ONE ANGEL SPEAKS TO ANOTHER?

We proceed thus to the First Article:—

Objection 1. It would seem that one angel does not speak to another. For Gregory says that, in the state of the resurrection, *each one's body will not hide his mind from his fellows.*[1] Much less, therefore, is one angel's mind hidden from another. But speech manifests to another what lies hidden in the mind. Therefore it is not necessary that one angel should speak to another.

Obj. 2. Further, speech is twofold: interior, whereby one speaks to oneself, and exterior, whereby one speaks to another. But exterior speech takes place by some sensible sign, as by voice, or gesture, or some bodily member, as the tongue, or the fingers; and this cannot apply to the angels. Therefore one angel does not speak to another.

---

1. 参见 *Moral.*, XVIII, 48 (PL 76, 84).

Obj. 3. Further, the speaker incites the hearer to listen to what he says. But it does not appear that one angel incites another to listen, for this happens among us by some sensible sign. Therefore one angel does not speak to another.

On the contrary, The Apostle says (*1 Cor.* xiii. 1): *If I speak with the tongues of men and of angels.*

I answer that, The angels speak in a certain way. But, as Gregory says: *It is fitting that our mind, rising above the properties of bodily speech, should be lifted to the sublime and unknown methods of interior speech.*[1]

To understand how one angel speaks to another, we must consider that, as we explained above when treating of the actions and powers of the soul, the will moves the intellect to its operation.[2] Now an intelligible object is present to the intellect in three ways: first, habitually, or in the memory, as Augustine says;[3] secondly, as actually considered or conceived; thirdly, as related to something else. Now it is clear that the intelligible object passes from the first to the second stage by the command of the will; and hence in the definition of habit these words occur, *which anyone uses when he wills.*[4] So, too, the intelligible object passes from the second to the third stage by the will. For by the will the concept of the mind is ordered to something else, as, for instance, either to the performing of an action, or to being made known to another. Now when the mind turns to the actual consideration of what it knows habitually, then a person speaks to himself; for the concept of the mind is called *the interior word.* And by the fact that the concept of the angelic mind is ordered to be made known to another by the will of the angel himself, the concept of one angel is made known to another; and in this way one angel speaks to

---

1. 参见 *Op. cit.*, II, 7 (PL 75, 559).
2. 参见 Q. 82, a. 4.
3. 参见 *De Trin.*, XIV, 6; 7 (PL 42, 1042; 1043).
4. 参见 Averroes, *In De An.*, III, comm. 18 (VI, 169v).

another. For to speak to another means nothing other than to make known the mental concept to another.

Reply Obj. 1. Our mental concept is hidden by a twofold obstacle. The first is in the will, which can retain the concept of the intellect within, or can direct it externally. In this way God alone can see the mind of another, according to *1 Cor.* ii. 11: *What man knoweth the things of a man, but the spirit of a man that is in him?* The other obstacle whereby the mental concept is excluded from another one's knowledge comes from the body; and so it happens that even when the will directs the concept of the mind to be made known, it is not at once made known to another, but some sensible sign must be used. Gregory alludes to this fact when he says: *To other eyes we seem to stand aloof as though behind the wall of the body; and when we wish to make ourselves known, we go out as it were by the door of the tongue to show what we really are.*[1] But an angel is under no such obstacle, and so he can make his concept known to another at once.

Reply Obj. 2. External speech, made by the voice, is a necessity for us because of the obstacle of the body. Hence it does not befit an angel, but only interior speech does, which includes not only the interior speech by mental concept, but also its being ordered to another's knowledge by the will. So the tongue of an angel expresses metaphorically the angel's power by which he manifests his mental concept.

Reply Obj. 3. There is no need to draw the attention of the good angels, inasmuch as they always see each other in the Word; for as one always sees the other, so he always sees what is directed to himself. But because even in the state of nature they could speak to each other, and because even now the bad angels speak to each other, we must say that the intellect is moved by the intelligible object just as sense is affected

---

1. 参见 *Moral.*, II, 7 (PL 75, 559).

by the sensible object. Therefore, as sense is aroused by the sensible object, so the mind of an angel can be aroused to attention by some intelligible power.

Second Article
WHETHER THE INFERIOR ANGEL SPEAKS TO THE SUPERIOR?

We proceed thus to the Second Article:—

Objection 1. It would seem that the inferior angel does not speak to the superior. For on the text (*1 Cor.* xiii. 1), *If I speak with the tongues of men and of angels*, the *Gloss* remarks that the speech of the angels is an illumination by which the superior illumines the inferior.[1] But the inferior never illumines the superior, as was above explained.[2] Therefore neither do the inferior speak to the superior.

Obj. 2. Further, as was said above,[3] to illumine means merely to acquaint one man with what is known to another; and this is to speak. Therefore to speak and to illumine are the same; so the same conclusion follows.

Obj. 3. Further, Gregory says: *God speaks to the angels by the very fact that He shows to their hearts His hidden and invisible things.*[4] But this is to illumine them. Therefore, whenever God speaks, He illumines. In the same way every angelic speech is an illumination. Therefore an inferior angel can in no way speak to a superior angel.

On the contrary, According to the exposition of Dionysius,[5] the inferior angels said to the superior: *Who is this King of Glory* (*Ps.* xxiii.

---

1. 参见 *Glossa ordin.* (VI, 53 E).
2. 参见 Q. 106, a. 3.
3. 参见 Q. 106, a. 1.
4. 参见 *Moral.*, II, 7 (PL 75, 559).
5. 参见 *De Cael. Hier.*, VII, 3 (PG 3, 209).

10)?

I answer that, The inferior angels can speak to the superior. To make this clear, we must consider that all angelic illumination is angelic speech. On the other hand, not all speech is an illumination, because, as we have said, for one angel to speak to another angel means nothing else but that by his own will he directs his mental concept in such a way that it becomes known to the other. Now what the mind conceives may be reduced to a twofold principle: to God Himself, Who is the primal truth, and to the will of the one who understands, whereby we actually consider anything. But because truth is the light of the intellect, and God Himself is the rule of all truth, hence it is that the manifestation of what is conceived by the mind, as depending on the primary truth, is both speech and illumination; as when one man says to another: *Heaven was created by God*; or, *Man is an animal.* The manifestation, however, of what depends on the will of the one who understands cannot be called an illumination, but is only a speech; as when one says to another: *I wish to learn this*; *I wish to do this or that.* The reason is that the created will is not a light, nor a rule of truth, but participates in light. Hence to communicate what comes from the created will is not, as such, an illumination. For to know what you may will, or what you may understand, does not belong to the perfection of my intellect; but only to know the truth in reality.

Now it is clear that the angels are called superior or inferior by comparison with this principle, God; and therefore illumination, which depends on the principle which is God, is conveyed only by the superior angels to the inferior. But as regards the will as the principle, he who wills is first and supreme; and therefore the manifestation of what belongs to the will is conveyed to others by the one who wills. In *this* manner both the superior angels speak to the inferior, and the inferior speak to the superior.

From this clearly appear the replies to the first and second objections.

Reply Obj. 3. Every speech of God to the angels is an illumination. For, since the will of God is the rule of truth, it belongs to the perfection and illumination of the created mind to know even what God wills. But the same does not apply to the will of the angels, as was explained above.

Third Article
WHETHER AN ANGEL SPEAKS TO GOD?

We proceed thus to the Third Article:—

Objection 1. It would seem that an angel does not speak to God. For speech makes known something to another. But an angel cannot make known anything to God, Who knows all things. Therefore an angel does not speak to God.

Obj. 2. Further, to speak is to direct the mental concept to another, as was shown above. But an angel always orders his mental concept to God. So if an angel speaks to God, he always speaks to God; which in some ways appears to be unreasonable, since an angel sometimes speaks to another angel. Therefore it seems that an angel never speaks to God.

On the contrary, It is written (*Zach.* i. 12): *The angel of the Lord answered and said: O Lord of hosts, how long wilt Thou not have mercy on Jerusalem?* Therefore an angel speaks to God.

I answer that, As was said above, the angel speaks by ordering his mental concept to some other being. Now one thing is ordered to another in a twofold manner. In one way, for the purpose of giving one thing to another, as in natural things the agent is ordered to the patient, and in human speech the teacher is ordered to the disciple; and in this sense an angel in no way speaks to God either of what concerns the truth, or of whatever depends on the created will; because God is the principle and source of all truth and of every will. In another way, one thing is ordered to another to receive something, as in natural things that which is receptive is ordered to the agent, and in human speech the disciple to the teacher; and in this way an angel speaks to God, either by consulting the divine will about what ought to be done, or by admiring the divine excellence which he can never comprehend. Thus Gregory says that *the angels speak to God when, by contemplating what is above themselves, they rise to a movement of admiration.*[1]

Reply Obj. 1. Speech is not always for the purpose of making something known to another, but is sometimes ultimately ordered to the purpose of having something manifested to the speaker himself; as when the disciples ask instruction from the teacher.

Reply Obj. 2. The angels are always speaking to God in the sense of praising and admiring Him and His works; but they speak to Him by consulting Him about what ought to be done whenever they have to perform any new work, concerning which they desire illumination.

Fourth Article
WHETHER LOCAL DISTANCE INFLUENCES THE ANGELIC SPEECH?

We proceed thus to the Fourth Article:—

Objection 1. It would seem that local distance affects the angelic speech. For as Damascene says: *An angel works where he is.*[2] But speech is an angelic operation. Therefore, as an angel is in a determinate place, it seems that an angel's speech is limited by the bounds of that place.

Obj. 2. Further, a speaker cries out because of the distance of the hearer. But it is said of the Seraphim that *they cried one to another* (*Isa.* vi. 3). Therefore in the angelic speech local distance has some effect.

On the contrary, It is said that the rich man in hell spoke to Abraham, notwithstanding the local distance (*Luke* xvi. 24). Much less therefore

---

1. 参见 *Moral.*, II, 7 (PL 75, 560).
2. 参见 *De Fide Orth.*, I, 13 (PG 94, 853).

does local distance impede the speech of one angel to another.

I answer that, The angelic speech consists in an intellectual operation, as was explained above. Now intellectual operation in an angel abstracts from the *here and now*. For even our own intellectual operation takes place by abstraction from the *here and now*, except accidentally on the part of the phantasms, which do not exist at all in an angel. But in that which is abstracted from *here and now*, neither difference of time nor local distance has any influence whatever. Hence in the angelic speech local distance is no impediment.

Reply Obj. 1. The angelic speech, as was above explained, is interior, but it is perceived by another; and therefore it exists in the angel who speaks, and consequently where the angel is who speaks. But just as local distance does not prevent one angel from seeing another, so neither does it prevent an angel from perceiving what is directed to him on the part of another; and this is to perceive his speech.

Reply Obj. 2. The cry mentioned is not a bodily voice raised by reason of the local distance, but is taken to signify the magnitude of what is said, or the intensity of the affection, according to what Gregory says: *The less one desires, the less one cries out.*[1]

Fifth Article
WHETHER ALL THE ANGELS KNOW WHAT ONE SPEAKS TO ANOTHER?

We proceed thus to the Fifth Article:—

Objection 1. It would seem that all the angels know what one speaks to another. For unequal local distance is the reason why all men do not know what one man says to another. But in the angelic speech local distance has no effect, as was explained above. Therefore all the angels

---

1. 参见 *Moral.*, II, 7 (PL 75, 560).

know what one speaks to another.

Obj. 2. Further, all the angels have intellectual power in common. So if the mental concept of one ordered to another is known by one, it is for the same reason known by all.

Obj. 3. Further, illumination is a kind of speech. But the illumination of one angel by another extends to all the angels, because, as Dionysius says: *Each one of the heavenly beings communicates what he learns to the others.*[1] Therefore the speech of one angel to another extends to all.

On the contrary, One man can speak to another alone. Much more can this be the case among the angels.

I answer that, As was explained above, the mental concept of one angel can be perceived by another when the angel who possesses the concept refers it by his will to another. Now a thing can be ordered through some cause to one thing and not to another. Consequently, the concept of one angel may be known by one and not by another; and therefore an angel can perceive the speech of one angel to another, while others do not, not through the obstacle of local distance, but because of such an ordination on the part of the will, as was explained above.

From this appear the replies to the first and second objections.

Reply Obj. 3. Illumination is of those truths that emanate from the first rule of truth, which is the principle common to all the angels; and in that way all illumination is common to all. But speech may be of something ordered to the principle of the created will, and this is proper to each angel; and in this way it is not necessary that these speeches should be common to all.

---

1. 参见 *De Cael. Hier.*, XV, 3 (PG 3, 332).

Question CVIII
THE ANGELIC DEGREES OF HIERARCHIES AND ORDERS
(*In Eight Articles*)

WE next consider the degrees of the angels in their hierarchies and orders, for it was said above that the superior angels illumine the inferior angels, and not conversely.[1]

Under this head there are eight points of inquiry: (1) Whether all the angels belong to one hierarchy? (2) Whether in one hierarchy there is only one order? (3) Whether in one order there are many angels? (4) Whether the distinction of hierarchies and orders is natural? (5) The names and properties of each order. (6) The comparison of the orders to one another. (7) Whether the orders will outlast the Day of Judgment? (8) Whether men are taken up into the angelic orders?

First Article
WHETHER ALL THE ANGELS ARE OF ONE HIERARCHY?

We proceed thus to the First Article:—

Objection 1. It would seem that all the angels belong to one hierarchy. For since the angels are supreme among creatures, it is evident that they are ordered for the best. But the best ordering of a multitude is for it to be governed by one authority, as the Philosopher shows.[2]

1. 参见 Q. 106, a. 3.
2. 参见 *Metaph.* XI, 10 (1076a 4); *Polit.*, IV, 2 (1289a 40); cf. *Eth.*, VIII, 10 (1160a 35).

Therefore as a hierarchy is nothing but a sacred principality, it seems that all the angels belong to one hierarchy.

Obj. 2. Further, Dionysius says that *hierarchy is order, knowledge and action.*[1] But all the angels agree in being all ordered to God, Whom they know, and by Whom in their actions they are ruled. Therefore all the angels belong to one hierarchy.

Obj. 3. Further, the sacred principality called hierarchy is to be found among men and angels. But all men are of one hierarchy. Therefore likewise all the angels are of one hierarchy.

On the contrary, Dionysius distinguishes three hierarchies of angels.[2]

I answer that, Hierarchy means a sacred principality, as was above explained. Now principality includes two things: the ruler himself and the multitude ordered under the ruler. Therefore because there is one God, ruler not only of all the angels but also of men and all creatures, so there is one hierarchy, not only of all the angels, but also of all rational creatures, who can be participators of sacred things. For as Augustine says: *There are two cities, that is, two societies, one of the good angels and men, the other of the wicked.*[3]

But if we consider the principality on the part of the multitude ordered under the ruler, then principality is said to be *one* according as the multitude can be subject in *one* way to the government of the prince. And those that cannot be governed in the same way by a ruler belong to different principalities. And thus, under one king there are different cities, which are governed by different laws and administrators. Now it is evident that men do not receive the divine illuminations in the same way as do the angels; for the angels receive them in their intelligible purity, whereas men receive them under

---

1. 参见 *De Cael. Hier.*, III, 1 (PG 3, 164).
2. 参见 *Op. cit.*, VI, 2 (PG 3, 200).
3. 参见 *De Civit. Dei*, XII, 1 (PL 41, 349).

sensible signs, as Dionysius says.[1] Therefore there must needs be a distinction between the human and the angelic hierarchy.

In the same manner we distinguish three angelic hierarchies. For it was shown above, in treating of angelic knowledge, that the superior angels have a more universal knowledge of the truth than the inferior angels.[2] This universal knowledge has three grades among the angels. For the exemplars of things, concerning which the angels are illumined, can be considered in a threefold manner. First, as proceeding from God as the first universal principle. This mode of knowledge belongs to the first hierarchy, connected immediately with God, and, *as it were, placed in the vestibule of God*, as Dionysius says.[3] Secondly, according as these exemplars depend on universal created causes which in some way are already multiplied; and this mode belongs to the second hierarchy. Thirdly, according as these exemplars are applied to particular things as depending on their causes; and this mode belongs to the lowest hierarchy. All this will appear more clearly when we treat of each of the orders. In this way are the hierarchies distinguished on the part of the multitude of subjects.

Hence it is clear that those err and speak against the opinion of Dionysius who place a hierarchy in the divine Persons, and call it the *supercelestial* hierarchy.[4] For in the divine Persons there exists, indeed, a natural order, but there is no hierarchical order; for as Dionysius says: *The hierarchical order is so directed that some be cleansed, illumined and perfected; and that others cleanse, illumine and perfect.*[5] And far be it from us to apply to this the divine Persons!

Reply Obj. 1. This objection considers principality on the part of

---

1. 参见 *De Cael. Hier.*, I, 2 (PG 3, 140).
2. 参见 Q. 55, a. 3.
3. 参见 *De Cael. Hier.*, VII, 2 (PG 3, 208).
4. 参见 William of Auvergne, *De Univ.*, IIa–IIae, ch. 140 (I, pt. II, 990).—Cf. St. Bonaventure, *In II Sent.*, d. ix, praenot. (II, 240).
5. 参见 *De Cael. Hier.*, III, 2 (PG 3, 165).

the ruler, inasmuch as a multitude is best ruled by one ruler, as the Philosopher asserts in those passages.[1]

Reply Obj. 2. As regards knowing God Himself, Whom all see in one way—that is, in His Essence—there is no hierarchical distinction among the angels; but there is such a distinction as regards the exemplars of created things, as was explained above.

Reply Obj. 3. All men are of one species, and have one connatural mode of understanding. But this is not the case in the angels, and hence the same argument does not apply to both.

Second Article
WHETHER THERE ARE SEVERAL ORDERS IN ONE HIERARCHY?

We proceed thus to the Second Article:—

Objection 1. It would seem that in the one hierarchy there are not several orders. For when a definition is multiplied, the thing defined is also multiplied. But a hierarchy is an order, as Dionysius says.[2] Therefore, if there are many orders, there is not one hierarchy only, but many.

Obj. 2. Further, different orders are different grades, and grades among spirits are constituted by different spiritual gifts. But among the angels all the spiritual gifts are common to all, for nothing is possessed individually. Therefore there are not different orders of angels.

Obj. 3. Further, in the ecclesiastical hierarchy the orders are distinguished according to the actions of *cleansing*, *illumining* and *perfecting*. For the order of deacons is *cleansing*, the order of priests

---

1. 参见 *Metaph.*, XI, 10 (1076a 4); *Eth.*, VIII, to (1160a 35); *Polit.*, IV, 2 (1289a 40).
2. 参见 *De Cael. Hier.*, III, 1 (PG 3, 164).

is *illumining*, and of bishops *perfecting*, as Dionysius says.[1] But each of the angels cleanses, illumines and perfects. Therefore there is no distinction of orders among the angels.

On the contrary, The Apostle says (*Ephes.* i. 20, 21) that *God has set the Man Christ above all principality and power, and virtue, and dominion.* Now these are the various orders of the angels, and some of them belong to one hierarchy, as will be explained.

I answer that, As was explained above, one hierarchy is one principality—that is, one multitude ordered in one way under the government of one ruler. Now such a multitude would not be ordered, but confused, if there were not in it different orders. So the nature of a hierarchy requires diversity of orders. This diversity of orders arises from the diversity of offices and actions. We see this in one city where there are different orders according to the different actions; for there is one order of those who judge, and another of those who fight, and another of those who labor in the fields, and so forth.

But although one city thus comprises several orders, all may be reduced to three, when we consider that every multitude has a beginning, a middle and an end. So in every city, a threefold order of men is to be seen. Some of them are supreme, as the nobles, others are the last, as the common people, while others hold a place between these, as the middle-class [*populus honorabilis*]. In the same way, we find in each angelic hierarchy the orders distinguished according to their actions and offices, and all this diversity is reduced to three—namely, to the summit, the middle and the base; and so in every hierarchy Dionysius places three orders.[2]

Reply Obj. 1. Order is twofold. In one way it is taken as the order comprehending in itself different grades, and in that way a hierarchy is called an order. In another way one grade is called an order, and in

1. 参见 *De Eccles. Hier.*, V, pt. 1, § 6 (PG 3, 505).
2. 参见 *De Cael. Hier.*, VI (PG 3, 200).

that sense the several orders of one hierarchy are so called.

Reply Obj. 2. All things are possessed in common by the angelic society; some things, however, are held more excellently by some than by others. Now each gift is more perfectly possessed by the one who can communicate it than by the one who cannot communicate it; as the hot thing which can communicate heat is more perfect than what is unable to give heat. And the more perfectly anyone can communicate a gift, the higher grade he occupies; as he is in the more perfect grade of teaching who can teach a higher science. By this similitude we can reckon the diversity of grades or orders among the angels, according to their different offices and actions.

Reply Obj. 3. The inferior angel is superior to the highest man of our hierarchy, according to the words, *He that is the lesser in the kingdom of heaven is greater than he*—namely, John the Baptist, than whom *there hath not risen a greater among them that are born of women* (*Matt.* xi. 11). Hence the lesser angel of the heavenly hierarchy can not only cleanse, but also illumine and perfect, and in a higher way than can the orders of our hierarchy. Thus the heavenly orders are not distinguished by reason of these, but by reason of other differences in their acts.

Third Article
WHETHER THERE ARE MANY ANGELS IN ONE ORDER?

We proceed thus to the Third Article:—

Objection 1. It seems that there are not many angels in one order. For it was shown above that all the angels are unequal.[1] But equals belong to one order. Therefore there are not many angels in one order.

Obj. 2. Further, it is superfluous for a thing to be done by many which can be done sufficiently by one. But that which belongs to one

1. 参见 Q. 50, a. 4.

angelic office can be done sufficiently by one angel; and so much more sufficiently than the one sun does what belongs to the office of the sun, according as the angel is more perfect than a heavenly body. If, therefore, the orders are distinguished by their offices, as was stated above, several angels in one order would be superfluous.

Obj. 3. Further, it was said above that all the angels are unequal. Therefore, if several angels (for instance, three or four) are of one order, the lowest one of the superior order will be more akin to the highest of the inferior order than with the highest of his own order; and thus he does not seem to be more of one order with the latter than with the former. Therefore there are not many angels of one order.

On the contrary, It is written: *The Seraphim cried to one another* (*Isa.* vi. 3). Therefore there are many angels in the one order of the Seraphim.

I answer that, Whoever knows anything perfectly is able to distinguish its acts, powers, and nature, down to the minutest details; whereas he who knows a thing in an imperfect manner can distinguish it only in a general way, and only as regards a few points. Thus, one who knows natural things imperfectly can distinguish their orders in a general way, placing the heavenly bodies in one order, inanimate inferior bodies in another, plants in another, and animals in another; while he who knows natural things perfectly is able to distinguish different orders in the heavenly bodies themselves, and in each of the other orders.

Now our knowledge of the angels is imperfect, as Dionysius says.[1] Hence we can distinguish the angelic offices and orders only in a general way; and so we place many angels in one order. But if we knew the offices and distinctions of the angels perfectly, we should know perfectly that each angel has his own office and his own order among things, and much more so than any star, though this be hidden from

1. 参见 *De Cael. Hier.*, VI, 1 (PG 3, 200).

us.

Reply Obj. 1. All the angels of one order are in some way equal, namely, according to the common likeness according to which they are placed in that order; but absolutely speaking they are not equal. Hence Dionysius says that in one and the same order of angels there are those who are first, middle and last.[1]

Reply Obj. 2. That special distinction of orders and offices, wherein each angel has his own office and order, is hidden from us.

Reply Obj. 3. As in a surface which is partly white and partly black, the two parts on the borders of white and black are more akin as regards their position than any other two white parts, but are less akin in quality; so two angels who are on the boundary of two orders are more akin in propinquity of nature than one of them is akin to the others of its own order, but less akin in their fitness for similar offices, which fitness, indeed, extends to a definite limit.

Fourth Article
WHETHER THE DISTINCTION OF HIERARCHIES AND ORDERS COMES FROM THE ANGELIC NATURE?

We proceed thus to the Fourth Article:—

Objection 1. It would seem that the distinction of hierarchies and of orders is not from the nature of the angels. For hierarchy is a *sacred principality*, and Dionysius places in its definition that *it approaches a resemblance to God, as far as may be.*[2] But sanctity and resemblance to God is in the angels by grace, and not by nature. Therefore the distinction of hierarchies and orders in the angels is by grace, and not by nature.

Obj. 2. Further, the Seraphim are called *ardent* or *ablaze*, as Dionysius

---

1. 参见 *Op. cit.*, X, 2 (PG 3, 273).
2. 参见 *Op. cit.*, III, 1 (PG 3, 164).

says.[1] This belongs to charity which comes not from nature but from grace; for *it is poured forth in our hearts by the Holy Ghost Who is given to us* (*Rom.* v. 5). *This is said not only of holy men, but also of the holy angels*, as Augustine says.[2] Therefore the angelic orders are not from nature, but from grace.

Obj. 3. Further, the ecclesiastical hierarchy is copied from the heavenly. But the orders among men are not from nature, but by the gift of grace; for it is not a natural gift for one to be a bishop, and another a priest, and another a deacon. Therefore neither in the angels are the orders from nature, but from grace only.

On the contrary, The Master says that *an angelic order is a multitude of heavenly spirits, who are likened to each other by some gift of grace, just as they agree also in the participation of natural gifts*.[3] Therefore the distinction of orders among the angels is not only by gifts of grace, but also by gifts of nature.

I answer that, The order of government, which is the order of a multitude under authority, is derived from its end. Now the end of the angels may be considered in two ways. First, according to the ability of their nature to know and love God by natural knowledge and love; and according to their relation to this end the orders of the angels are distinguished by natural gifts. Secondly, the end of the angelic multitude can be taken from what is above their natural powers, which consists in the vision of the divine essence, and in the changeless fruition of His goodness. To this end they can reach only by grace. Hence, as regards this end, the orders in the angels are adequately distinguished by the gifts of grace, but dispositively by natural gifts; for to the angels are given gratuitous gifts according to the capacity of their natural gifts, which is not the case with men, as was above

1. 参见 *Op. cit.*, VII, 1 (PG 3, 205).
2. 参见 *De Civit. Dei*, XII, 9 (PL 41, 357).
3. 参见 Peter Lombard, *Sent.*, II, ix, 2 (I, 345).

explained.[1] Hence among men the orders are distinguished according to gratuitous gifts only, and not according to natural gifts.

From the above the replies to the objections are evident.

Fifth Article
WHETHER THE ORDERS OF THE ANGELS ARE PROPERLY NAMED?

We proceed thus to the Fifth Article:—

Objection 1. It would seem that the orders of the angels are not properly named. For all the heavenly spirits are called *Angels* and *Virtues* and *heavenly Powers*;[2] but common names should not be appropriated to individuals. Therefore the orders of the *Angels* and the *Virtues* are ineptly named.

Obj. 2. Further, it belongs to God alone to be Lord, according to the words, *Know ye that the Lord He is God* (*Ps.* xcix. 3). Therefore one order of the heavenly spirits is not properly called *Dominations*.

Obj. 3. Further, the name *Domination* seems to imply government, and likewise the names *Principalities* and *Powers*. Therefore these three names do not seem to be properly applied to three orders.

Obj. 4. Further, archangels[3] are as it were angel princes. Therefore this name ought not to be given to any other order than to the *Principalities*.

Obj. 5. Further, the name *Seraphim* is derived from ardor, which pertains to charity; and the name *Cherubim* from science. But charity and science are gifts common to all the angels. Therefore they ought not to be names of any particular orders.

Obj. 6. Further, Thrones are seats. But from the fact that God is

---

1. 参见 Q. 62, a. 6.
2. 参见 Pseudo-Dionysius, *De Cael. Hier.*, V (PG 3, 196).
3. archangel: 总领天使

known and loved by the rational creature He is said to sit within it. Therefore there ought not to be any order of *Thrones* besides the *Cherubim* and *Seraphim*. Therefore it appears that the orders of angels are not properly named.

On the contrary is the authority of Holy Scripture wherein they are so named. For the name *Seraphim* is found in *Isaias* vi. 2; the name *Cherubim* in *Ezechiel* i. [*cf.* x. 15, 20]; *Thrones* in *Colossians* i. 16; *Dominations*, *Virtues*, *Powers* and *Principalities* are mentioned in *Ephesians* i. 21; the name *Archangels* in the canonical epistle of St. Jude (9), and the name Angels is found in many places of Scripture.

I answer that, As Dionysius says, in the names of the angelic orders it is necessary to observe that the proper name of each order expresses its property.[1] Now to see what is the property of each order, we must consider that in ordered things, something may be found in a threefold manner: by way of property, by way of excess, and by way of participation. A thing is said to be in another by way of property, if it is adequate and proportionate to its nature; by excess, when an attribute is less than that to which it is attributed, but is possessed thereby in an eminent manner, as we have stated concerning all the names which are attributed to God;[2] by participation, when an attribute is possessed by something not fully but partially, as holy men are called gods by participation. Therefore, if anything is to be called by a name designating its property, it ought not to be named from what it participates imperfectly, nor from that which it possesses in excess, but from that which is equal to it. For instance, when we wish properly to name a man, we should call him a *rational substance*, but not an *intellectual substance*, which is the proper name of an angel; for simple intelligence belongs to an angel as a property, and to a man by participation. Nor again do we call him a *sensible substance*, which is the

1. 参见 *Op. cit.*, VII, 1 (PG 3, 205).
2. 参见 Q. 13, a. 2.

proper name of a brute; for sense is less than the property of a man, and belongs to man in a more excellent way than to other animals.

So we must consider that in the angelic orders all spiritual perfections are common to all the angels, and that they are all more excellently in the superior than in the inferior angels. But, as in these perfections there are grades, the superior perfection belongs to the superior order as its property, whereas it belongs to the inferior by participation; and conversely, the inferior perfection belongs to the inferior order as its property, and to the superior by way of excess. Hence, the superior order is denominated from the superior perfection.

So in this way Dionysius explains the names of the orders according as they befit the spiritual perfections they signify.[1] Gregory, on the other hand, in expounding these names seems to regard more the exterior ministrations; for he says that *Angels are so called as announcing the least things; and the Archangels, the greatest; by the Virtues miracles are wrought; by the Powers hostile powers are repulsed; and the Principalities preside over the good spirits themselves.*[2]

Reply Obj. 1. Angel means *messenger*. So all the heavenly spirits, so far as they make known divine things, are called *angels*. But the superior angels enjoy a certain excellence, as regards this manifestation, from which the superior orders are denominated. The lowest order of angels possess no excellence above the common manifestation, and therefore it is denominated from manifestation alone; and thus the common name remains as it were proper to the lowest order, as Dionysius says.[3] Or we may say that the lowest order can be specially called the order of *angels*, inasmuch as they announce things to us immediately.

Virtue can be taken in two ways. First, commonly, considered as the medium between the essence and the operation; and in that sense all

1. 参见 *De Cael. Hier.*, VII, 1; VIII, 1; IX, 1 (PG 3, 205; 237; 257).
2. 参见 *In Evang.*, II, hom. 34 (PL 76, 12 50).
3. 参见 *De Cael. Hier.*, V (PG 3, 196).

the heavenly spirits are called heavenly virtues, as also *heavenly essences.*[1] Secondly, as meaning a certain excellence of strength, and thus it is the proper name of an angelic order. Hence Dionysius says[2] that the *name 'virtues' signifies a certain virile and immovable strength*, first, in regard to those divine operations which befit them; secondly, in regard to receiving divine gifts. Thus it signifies that they undertake fearlessly the divine behests appointed to them; and this seems to imply strength of mind.

Reply Obj. 2. As Dionysius says: *Domination is attributed to God in a special manner, by way of excess: but the divine Scripture gives the more illustrious heavenly princes the name of Lord by participation, through whom the inferior angels receive the divine gifts.*[3] Hence Dionysius also states that the name *Domination* means first *a certain liberty, free from servile condition and common subjection, such as that of plebeians*[4], *and from tyrannical oppression*, endured sometimes even by the great. Secondly, it signifies *a certain rigid and inflexible supremacy which does not bend to any servile act, or to the act of those who are subject to or oppressed by tyrants.* Thirdly, it signifies *the desire and participation of the true dominion which belongs to God.*[5] In the same way, the name of each order signifies the participation of what belongs to God; as the name *Virtues* signifies the participation of the divine virtue; and the same principle applies to the rest.

Reply Obj. 3. The names *Domination*, *Power* and *Principality* belong to government in different ways. The place of a lord is only to prescribe what is to be done. So Gregory says that *some companies of the angels, because others are subject in obedience to them, are called Dominations.*[6] The name *Power* points out a kind of order, according to what the Apostle

1. 参见 *De Cael. Hier.*, V (PG 3, 196).
2. 参见 *Op. cit.*, VIII, 1 (PG 3, 237).
3. 参见 *De Div. Nom.*, XII, 2; 4 (PG 3, 969; 972).
4. plebeians: 平民
5. 参见 *De Cael. Hier.*, VIII, 1 (PG 3, 237).
6. 参见 *In Evang.*, II, hom. 34 (PL 76, 1251).

says, *He that resisteth the power, resisteth the ordination of God* (*Rom.* xiii. 2). And so Dionysius says that the name *Power* signifies a kind of ordination both as regards the reception of divine things, and as regards the divine actions performed by superiors towards inferiors, by leading them upward.[1] Therefore, to the order of *Powers* it belongs to regulate what is to be done by those who are subject to them. To preside [*principari*], as Gregory says, is to *be first among others*,[2] as being first in carrying out what is ordered to be done. And so Dionysius says that the name of *Principalities* signifies *one who leads in a sacred order*.[3] For those who lead others, being first among them, are properly called *princes*, according to the words, *Princes went before joined with singers* (*Ps.* lxvii. 26).

Reply Obj. 4. The *Archangels*, according to Dionysius, are between the *Principalities* and the *Angels*.[4] A mean compared to one extreme seems like the other, as participating in the nature of both extremes; and thus tepid seems cold compared to hot, and hot compared to cold. So the *Archangels* are called the *angel princes*, since they are princes as regards the *Angels*, and angels as regards the *Principalities*. But according to Gregory, they are called *Archangels*, because they preside over the one order of the *Angels*, as announcing great things; and the *Principalities* are so called as presiding over all the heavenly *Virtues* who fulfill the divine commands.[5]

Reply Obj. 5. The name *Seraphim* does not come from charity only, but from the excess of charity, expressed by the term ardor or fire. Hence Dionysius expounds the name *Seraphim* according to the properties of fire containing an excess of heat.[6] Now in fire we may

---

1. 参见 *De Cael. Hier.*, VIII, 1 (PG 3, 240).
2. 参见 *In Evang.*, II, hom. 34 (PL 76, 1251).
3. 参见 *De. Cael Hier.*, IX, 1 (PG 3, 257).
4. 参见 *Op. cit.*, IX, 2 (PG 3, 257).
5. 参见 *In Evang.*, II, hom. 34 (PL 76, 1250).
6. 参见 *De Cael. Hier.*, VII, 1 (PG 3, 205).

consider three things. First, the movement which is upwards and continuous. This signifies that they are borne inflexibly towards God. Secondly, the active force which is *heat*, which is not found in fire by itself, but exists with a certain sharpness, as being of most penetrating action, and reaching even to the smallest things, and as it were, with superabundant fervor. Thus is signified the action of the Seraphim exercised powerfully upon those who are subject to them, rousing them to a like fervor, and cleansing them wholly by their heat. Thirdly, we consider in fire its brightness, which signifies that these angels have in themselves an inextinguishable light, and that they also perfectly illumine others.

In the same way, the name *Cherubim* comes from a certain excess of science, and hence it is interpreted *fullness of science*. This Dionysius expounds in regard to four things: the perfect vision of God, the full reception of the divine light, their contemplation in God of the beauty of the divine order, and in regard to the fact that, possessing this science fully, they pour it forth copiously upon others.[1]

Reply Obj. 6. The order of the *Thrones* excels the inferior orders as having an immediate knowledge of the exemplars of the divine works; whereas the *Cherubim* have the excellence of science and the *Seraphim* the excellence of ardor. And although these two excellent attributes include the third, yet the gift belonging to the *Thrones* does not include the other two; and so the order of the *Thrones* is distinguished from the orders of the *Cherubim* and the *Seraphim*. For it is a common rule in all things that the excellence of the inferior is contained in the superior, but not conversely. However, Dionysius explains the name *Thrones* by its likeness to material seats,[2] in which we may consider four things. First, the site, because seats are raised above the earth; and so the angels who are called *Thrones* are raised up to the immediate

1. 参见 *De Cael. Hier.*, VII, 1 (PG 3, 205).
2. 同上

knowledge of the exemplars of things in God. Secondly, because in material seats is displayed strength, since a person sits firmly on them. But here the reverse is the case: for the angels themselves are made firm by God. Thirdly, because the seat receives him who sits thereon, and he can be carried thereupon; and so the angels receive God in themselves, and in a certain way bear Him to the inferior creatures. Fourthly, because in its shape a seat is open on one side to receive the one sitting; and thus the angels are promptly open to receive God and to serve Him.

Sixth Article
WHETHER THE GRADES OF THE ORDERS ARE PROPERLY ASSIGNED?

We proceed thus to the Sixth Article:—

Objection 1. It would seem that the grades of the orders are not properly assigned. For the order of prelates is the highest. But the names of *Dominations*, *Principalities* and *Powers* of themselves imply prelacy. Therefore these orders ought to be supreme.

Obj. 2. Further, the nearer an order is to God, the higher it is. But the order of *Thrones* is the nearest to God, for nothing is nearer to the one sitting than the seat. Therefore the order of the *Thrones* is the highest.

Obj. 3. Further, knowledge comes before love, and intellect is higher than will. Therefore the order of *Cherubim* seems to be higher than the *Seraphim*.

Obj. 4. Further, Gregory places the *Principalities* above the *Powers*.[1] These therefore are not placed immediately above the archangels, as Dionysius says.[2]

---

1. 参见 *In Evang.*, II, hom. 34 (PL 76, 1249).
2. 参见 *De Cael. Hier.*, VI, 2; IX, 1 (PG 3, 200; 257).

On the contrary, Dionysius places in the highest hierarchy the *Seraphim* as the first, the *Cherubim* as the middle, the *Thrones* as the last; in the middle hierarchy he places the *Dominations*, as the first, the *Virtues* in the middle, the *Powers* last; in the lowest hierarchy the *Principalities* first, then the *Archangels*, and lastly the *Angels*.[1]

I answer that, The grades of the angelic orders are assigned by Gregory and Dionysius, who agree as regards all except the *Principalities* and *Virtues*. For Dionysius places the *Virtues* beneath the *Dominations*, and above the *Powers*; and the *Principalities* beneath the *Powers* and above the *Archangels*.[2] Gregory, however, places the *Principalities* between the *Dominations* and the *Powers*; and the *Virtues* between the *Powers* and the *Archangels*.[3] Both of these distributions may claim authority from the words of the Apostle, who enumerates (*Ephes*. i. 20, 21) the middle orders, beginning from the lowest, saying that *God set him, i.e.*, Christ, *on His right hand in the heavenly places above all Principality and Power, and Virtue, and Dominion*. Here he places *Virtues* between *Powers* and *Dominations*, according to the placing of Dionysius. Writing however to the Colossians (i. 16), numbering the same orders from the highest, he says: *Whether Thrones, or Dominations, or Principalities, or Powers, all things were created by Him and in Him*. Here he places the *Principalities* between *Dominations* and *Powers*, as does also Gregory.

Let us then first examine the reason for the ordering of Dionysius. Here we must observe that, as we said above, the highest hierarchy contemplates the exemplars of things in God Himself, the second in the universal causes, and the third in their application to particular effects. And because God is the end not only of the angelic ministrations, but also of the whole creation, it belongs to

---

1. 参见 *Op. cit.*, VI, 2 (PG 3, 200).
2. 同上
3. 参见 *In Evang.*, II, hom. 34 (PL 76, 1249).

the first hierarchy to consider the end; to the middle one belongs the universal disposition of what is to be done; and to the last belongs the application of this disposition to the effect, which is the carrying out of the work. For it is clear that these three tnings exist in every kind of operation. So Dionysius, considering the properties of the orders as derived from their names, placed in the first hierarchy those orders whose names are taken from their relation to God, namely, the *Seraphim*, *Cherubim* and *Thrones*; he placed in the middle hierarchy those orders whose names denote a certain kind of common government or disposition, the *Dominations*, *Virtues*, and *Powers*; and he placed in the third hierarchy the orders whose names denote the execution of the work, namely, the *Principalities*, *Angels* and *Archangels*.[1]

As regards the end, three things may be considered. For firstly we consider the end, then we acquire perfect knowledge of the end, and thirdly we fix our intention on the end; of which the second is by addition to the first, and the third by addition to both. And because God is the end of creatures, as the leader is the end of an army, as the Philosopher says,[2] so a somewhat similar order may be seen in human affairs. For there are some who enjoy the dignity of being able with familiarity to approach the king or leader; others in addition are privileged to know his secrets; and others above these always abide with him, in a close union. According to this similitude, we can understand the disposition in the orders of the first hierarchy. For the *Thrones* are raised up so as to be the familiar recipients of God in themselves, in the sense of knowing immediately the exemplars of things in Himself; and this is proper to the whole of the first hierarchy. The *Cherubim* know the divine secrets supereminently. But the *Seraphim* excel in what is the supreme excellence of all, in being united to God Himself; so that they may be called *Thrones*, from the common

1. 参见 *De Cael. Hier.*, VI, 2 ; VIII, 1; IX, 1 (PG 3, 200; 237; 257).
2. 参见 Aristotle, *Metaph.*, XI, 10 (1075a 15).

attribute of the whole hierarchy, just as, from what is common to all the heavenly spirits together, they are all called *Angels*.

As regards government, three things are comprised therein, of which the first is to appoint those things which are to be done, and this belongs to the *Dominations*; the second is to give the power of carrying out what is to be done, which belongs to the *Virtues*; the third is to order how what has been commanded or decided can be carried out by others, which belongs to the *Powers*.

The execution of the angelic ministrations consists in announcing divine things. Now in the execution of any action there are beginners and leaders; as in singing, the precentors, and in war, generals and officers. This office belongs to the *Principalities*. There are others who simply execute what is to be done, and these are the *Angels*. Others hold a middle place, and these are the *Archangels*, as was above explained.

This explanation of the orders is quite a reasonable one. For the highest in an inferior order always has affinity to the lowest in the higher order; as the lowest animals are near to the plants. Now the first order is that of the divine Persons, which terminates in the Holy Ghost, Who is Love proceeding, with Whom the highest order of the first hierarchy has affinity, denominated as it is from the fire of love. The lowest order of the first hierarchy is that of the *Thrones*, who, according to their name, are akin to the *Dominations*; for the *Thrones*, according to Gregory, are so called *because through them God accomplishes His judgments*,[1] since they are illumined by Him in a manner adapted to the immediate illumination of the second hierarchy, to which belongs the disposition of the divine ministrations. The order of the *Powers* is akin to the order of the *Principalities*; for as it belongs to the *Powers* to impose order on those subject to them, this ordering

---

1. 参见 *In Evang.*, II, hom. 34 (PL 76, 1252).

is plainly shown at once in the name *Principalities*, who, as presiding over the government of peoples and kingdoms (which occupies the first and principal place in the divine ministrations), are the first in the execution thereof. For the good of a nation is more divine than the good of one man; and hence it is written, *The prince of the kingdom of the Persians resisted me* (*Dan.* x. 13).

The disposition of the orders which is mentioned by Gregory is also reasonable. For since the *Dominations* appoint and order what belongs to the divine ministrations, the orders subject to them are arranged according to the disposition of those things in which the divine ministrations are effected. Now, as Augustine says, *bodies are ruled in a certain order: the inferior by the superior, and all of them by the spiritual creature; and the bad spirit by the good spirit.*[1] So the first order after the *Dominations* is called that of *Principalities*, who rule even over good spirits. Then come the *Powers*, who coerce the evil spirits, even as evil-doers are coerced by earthly powers, as it is written (*Rom.* xiii. 3, 4). After these come the *Virtues*, who have power over corporeal nature in the working of miracles. After these are the *Angels* and the *Archangels*, who announce to men either great things above reason, or small things within the purview of reason.

Reply Obj. 1. The angels' subjection to God is greater than their presiding over inferior things; and the latter is derived from the former. Thus the orders which derive their name from *presiding* are not the first and highest; but rather the orders deriving their name from their nearness and relation to God.

Reply Obj. 2. The nearness to God, designated by the name of the *Thrones*, belongs also to the *Cherubim* and *Seraphim*, and in a more excellent way, as was above explained.

Reply Obj. 3. As was above explained, knowledge takes place

---

1. 参见 *De Trin.*, III, 4 (PL 42, 873).

according as the thing known is in the knower; but love, as the lover is united to the thing loved.[1] Now higher things are in a nobler way in themselves than in lower things; whereas lower things are in higher things in a nobler way than they are in themselves. Therefore to know lower things is better than to love them; and to love the higher things, God above all, is better than to know them.

Reply Obj. 4. A careful comparison will show that little or no difference exists in reality between the dispositions of the orders according to Dionysius and Gregory. For Gregory expounds the name *Principalities* from their *presiding over good spirits*,[2] which befits the *Virtues* according as this name expresses a certain strength, giving efficacy to the inferior spirits in the execution of the divine ministrations. Again, according to Gregory, the *Virtues* seem to be the same as the *Principalities* of Dionysius. For to work miracles holds the first place in the divine ministrations, since thereby the way is prepared for the announcements of the archangels and the angels.

Seventh Article
WHETHER THE ORDERS WILL OUTLAST THE DAY OF JUDGMENT?

We proceed thus to the Seventh Article:—

Objection 1. It would seem that the orders of angels will not outlast the Day of Judgment. For the Apostle says (*1 Cor.* xv. 24) that Christ will *bring to naught all principality and power, when He shall have delivered up the kingdom to God and the Father.* This will be in the final consummation. Therefore, for the same reason, all other orders will be abolished in that state.

Obj. 2. Further, to the office of the angelic orders it belongs to

---

1. 参见 Q. 16, a. 1; q. 27, a. 3.
2. 参见 *In Evang.*, II, hom. 34 (PL 76, 1251).

cleanse, illumine and perfect. But after the Day of Judgment one angel will not cleanse, illumine, or perfect another, because they will not advance any more in knowledge. Therefore the angelic orders would remain for no purpose.

Obj. 3. Further, the Apostle says of the angels (*Heb.* i. 14), that *they are all ministering spirits, sent to minister to them who shall receive the inheritance of salvation.* Whence it appears that the angelic offices are directed to the purpose of leading men to salvation. But all the elect are in pursuit of salvation until the Day of Judgment. Therefore the angelic offices and orders will not outlast the Day of Judgment.

On the contrary, It is written (*Judg.* v. 20): *Stars remaining in their order and courses*, which is applied to the angels.[1] Therefore the angels will always remain in their orders.

I answer that, In the angelic orders we may consider two things, the distinction of grades, and the execution of their offices. The distinction of grades among the angels takes place according to the difference of grace and nature, as was above explained. These differences will always remain in the angels, for the differences of natures could not be taken from them unless they themselves were to be corrupted; and the difference of glory will also always remain in them according to the difference of preceding merit. As to the execution of the angelic offices, it will to a certain degree remain after the Day of Judgment, and to a certain degree will cease. It will cease according as their offices are directed towards leading others to their end; but it will remain according as it agrees with the attainment of the end. Thus also the various ranks of soldiers have different duties to perform in battle and in triumph.

Reply Obj. 1. The principalities and powers will come to an end in that final consummation as regards their office of leading others to

---

1. 参见 *Glossa interl.*, super *Judg.*, V, 20 (II, 38r).

their end; because, when the end is attained, it is no longer necessary to tend towards the end. This is clear from the words of the Apostle, *When He shall have delivered up the kingdom of God and the Father, i.e.*, when He shall have led the faithful to the enjoyment of God Himself.

Reply Obj. 2. The actions of angels over the other angels are to be considered according to a likeness to our own intellectual actions. In ourselves we find many intellectual actions which are ordered according to the order of cause and effect; as when we gradually arrive at one conclusion by many middle terms. Now it is manifest that the knowledge of this conclusion depends on all the preceding middle terms not only in the new acquisition of science, but also as regards the preserving of the science acquired. A proof of this is that when anyone forgets any of the preceding middle terms, he can have opinion or belief about the conclusion, but not science, since he is ignorant of the order of causes. So, too, since the inferior angels know the nature of the divine works by the light of the superior angels, their knowledge depends on the light of the superior angels not only as regards the acquisition of science, but also as regards the preserving of the knowledge possessed. Hence, although after the Judgment the inferior angels will not progress in the knowledge of some things, still this will not prevent their being illumined by the superior angels.

Reply Obj. 3. Although after the Day of Judgment men will not be led any more to salvation by the ministry of the angels, still those who are already saved will be illumined through the angelic ministry.

Eighth Article
WHETHER MEN ARE TAKEN UP INTO THE ANGELIC ORDERS?

We proceed thus to the Eighth Article:—

Objection 1. It would seem that men are not taken up into the orders of the angels. For the human hierarchy is stationed beneath the lowest heavenly hierarchy, as the lowest under the middle hierarchy, and the middle beneath the first. But the angels of the lowest hierarchy are never transferred into the middle, or the first. Therefore neither are men transferred to the angelic orders.

Obj. 2. Further, certain offices belong to the orders of the angels, as to guard, to work miracles, to coerce the demons, and the like; which do not appear to belong to the souls of the saints. Therefore they are not transferred to the angelic orders.

Obj. 3. Further, as the good angels lead to good, so do the demons to what is evil. But it is erroneous to say that the souls of bad men are changed into demons; for Chrysostom rejects this.[1] Therefore it does not seem that the souls of the saints will be transferred to the orders of angels.

On the contrary, The Lord says of the saints that *they will be as the angels of God* (*Matt.* xxii. 30).

I answer that, As was above explained, the orders of the angels are distinguished according to the conditions of nature and according to the gifts of grace. Considered only as regards the grade of nature, men can in no way be assumed into the angelic orders; for the distinction of natures will always remain. In view of this distinction, some have asserted that men can in no way be transferred to an equality with the angels.[2] But this is erroneous, contradicting as it does the promise of Christ saying that the children of the resurrection will be equal to the angels in heaven (*Luke* xx. 36). For whatever belongs to nature is as matter in the notion of an order; while that which perfects is from grace, which depends on the liberality of God, and not on the order

1. 参见 *Hom.* XXVIII (PG 57, 354).
2. 参见 Eustratius, *In Eth. Nicom.*, VI, 6 [1141a 3–8], ed. G. Heylbut (in *Comm. in Arist. Graeca*, XX, Berlin: G. Reiner, 1892), p. 318^{1-6}.—Cf. St. Albert, *In Eth.*, VI, tr. 6, ch. 18 (VII, 433).

of nature. Therefore by the gift of grace men can merit glory in such a degree as to be equal to the angels, in each of the angelic grades; and this implies that men are taken up into the orders of the angels. Some, however, say that not all who are saved are assumed into the angelic orders, but only virgins or the perfect; and that the others will constitute their own order, as it were corresponding to the whole society of the angels.[1] But this is against Augustine, who says that *there will not be two societies of men and of angels, but only one; because the beatitude of all is to cleave to God alone.*[2]

Reply Obj. 1. Grace is given to the angels in proportion to their natural gifts. This, however, does not apply to men, as was above explained.[3] So, as the inferior angels cannot be transferred to the natural grade of the superior, neither can they be transferred to the superior grade of grace; whereas men can ascend to the grade of grace, but not of nature.

Reply Obj. 2. The angels, according to the order of nature, are between us and God; and therefore according to universal law not only human affairs are administered by them, but also all corporeal matters. But holy men even after this life are of the same nature with ourselves; and hence according to universal law they do not administer human affairs, *nor do they interfere in the things of the living*, as Augustine says.[4]

Still, by a certain special dispensation it is sometimes granted to some of the saints, whether living or dead, to exercise these offices, by working miracles, by coercing the demons, or by doing something of that kind, as Augustine says in the same work.

Reply Obj. 3. It is not erroneous to say that men are transferred to

---

1. 参见 Cf. St. Bonaventure, *In II Sent.*, d. ix, a. 1, q. 7 (II, 254).
2. 参见 *De Civit. Dei*, XII, 9 (PL 41, 357).
3. 参见 A. 4; q. 62, a. 6.
4. 参见 *De Cura pro Mort.*, XIII; XVI (PL 40, 604; 607).

the penalty of demons; but some erroneously stated that the demons are nothing but the souls of the dead; and it is this that Chrysostom rejects.[1]

1. 参见 Cf. *In Matt.*, hom. 28 (PG 57, 353).

Question CIX
THE ORDERING OF THE BAD ANGELS
(*In Four Articles*)

WE now consider the ordering of the bad angels, concerning which there are four points of inquiry: (1) Whether there are orders among the demons? (2) Whether among them there is precedence? (3) Whether one illumines another? (4) Whether they are subject to the precedence of the good angels?

First Article
WHETHER THERE ARE ORDERS AMONG THE DEMONS?

We proceed thus to the First Article:—

Objection 1. It would seem that there are no orders among the demons. For order belongs to good, as also mode and species, as Augustine says;[1] and on the contrary, disorder belongs to evil. But there is nothing disorderly in the good angels. Therefore in the bad angels there are no orders.

Obj. 2. Further, the angelic orders are contained under a hierarchy. But the demons are not in a hierarchy, which is defined as a holy principality; for they are void of all holiness. Therefore among the demons there are no orders.

Obj. 3. Further, the demons fell from every one of the angelic orders, as is commonly supposed. Therefore, if some demons are said to

---

1. 参见 *De Nat. Boni*, III, (PL 42, 553).

belong to an order, because they fell from that order, it would seem necessary to give them the names of each of those orders. But we never find that they are called *Seraphim*, or *Thrones*, or *Dominations*. Therefore on the same ground they are not to be placed in any other order.

On the contrary, The Apostle says (*Ephes*. vi. 12): *Our wrestling ... is against principalities and powers, against the rulers of the world of this darkness*.

I answer that, As was explained above,[1] order in the angels is considered both according to the grade of nature, and according to that of grace. Now grace has a twofold state, the imperfect, which is that of merit, and the perfect, which is that of consummate glory.

If therefore we consider the angelic orders in the light of the perfection of glory, then the demons are not in the angelic orders, and never were. But if we consider them in relation to imperfect grace, then the demons were once in the orders of angels, but fell away from them; for we said above that all the angels were created in grace.[2] But if we consider them in the light of nature, in that view they are still in those orders, because they have not lost their natural gifts, as Dionysius says.[3]

Reply Obj. 1. Good can exist without evil, whereas evil cannot exist without good;[4] so there is order in the demons, in so far as they possess a good nature.

Reply Obj. 2. If we consider the ordering of the demons on the part of God Who orders them, it is sacred; for He uses the demons for Himself. But on the part of the demons' will, it is not a sacred thing, because they abuse their nature for evil.

Reply Obj. 3. The name *Seraphim* is given from the ardor of charity,

---

1. 参见 Q. 108, a. 4, 7 and 8.
2. 参见 Q. 62, a. 3.
3. 参见 *De Div. Nom*., IV, 23 (PG 3, 725).
4. 参见 Q. 49, a. 3.

the name *Thrones* from the divine indwelling, and the name *Dominations* imports a certain liberty; all of which are opposed to sin. Therefore these names are not given to the angels who sinned.

Second Article
WHETHER AMONG THE DEMONS THERE IS PRECEDENCE?

We proceed thus to the Second Article:—

Objection 1. It would seem that there is no precedence among the demons. For every precedence is according to some order of justice. But the demons are wholly fallen from justice. Therefore there is no precedence among them.

Obj. 2. Further, there is no precedence where obedience and subjection do not exist. But these cannot be without concord, which is not to be found among the demons, according to the text, *Among the proud there are always contentions* (*Prov.* xiii. 10). Therefore there is no precedence among the demons.

Obj. 3. If there be precedence among them, it is either according to nature, or according to their sin or punishment. But it is not according to their nature, for subjection and service do not come from nature, but from subsequent sin; neither is it according to sin or punishment, because in that case the superior demons, who have sinned the most grievously, would be subject to the inferior. Therefore there is no precedence among the demons.

On the contrary, On *1 Cor.* xv. 24, the *Gloss* says: *While the world lasts, angels will preside over angels, men over men, and demons over demons.*[1]

I answer that, Since action follows the nature of a thing, where natures are subordinate, actions also must be subordinate to each other. Thus it is in corporeal things, for since the inferior bodies

---

1. 参见 *Glossa ordin.* (VI, 58 B).

by natural order are below the heavenly bodies, their actions and movements are subject to the actions and movements of the heavenly bodies. Now it is plain from what we have said that the demons are by natural order subject to others; and hence their actions are subject to the action of those above them. This is what we mean by precedence, namely, that the action of the subject should be under the action of the superior. So the very natural disposition of the demons requires that there should be authority among them. This agrees, too, with divine wisdom, which leaves nothing inordinate, and which *reacheth from end to end mightily, and ordereth all things sweetly* (*Wis.* viii. 1).

Reply Obj. 1. The authority of the demons is not founded on their justice, but on the justice of God ordering all things.

Reply Obj. 2. The concord of the demons, whereby some obey others, does not arise from mutual friendships, but from their common wickedness, whereby they hate men, and fight against God's justice. For it belongs to wicked men to be joined and subject to those whom they see to be stronger, in order to carry out their own wickedness.

Reply Obj. 3. The demons are not equal in nature, and so among them there exists a natural precedence; which is not the case with men, who are naturally equal. That the inferior are subject to the superior is not for the benefit of the superior, but rather to their detriment; because since to do evil belongs in a pre-eminent degree to unhappiness, it follows that to preside in evil is to be more unhappy.

Third Article
WHETHER THERE IS ILLUMINATION IN THE DEMONS?

We proceed thus to the Third Article:—

Objection 1. It would seem that illumination is in the demons. For illumination means the manifestation of the truth. But one demon can manifest truth to another, because the superior excel in natural knowledge. Therefore the superior demons can illumine the inferior.

Obj. 2. Further, a body abounding in light can illumine a body deficient in light, as the sun illumines the moon. But the superior demons abound in the participation of natural light. Therefore it seems that the superior demons can illumine the inferior.

On the contrary, Illumination is not without cleansing and perfecting, as was stated above.[1] But to cleanse does not befit the demons, according to the words: *What can be made clean by the unclean?* (*Ecclus.* xxxiv. 4). Therefore neither can they illumine.

I answer that, There can be no illumination properly speaking among the demons. For, as was explained above, illumination properly speaking is the manifestation of truth in reference to God, Who illumines every intellect.[2] Another kind of manifestation of truth is speech, as when one angel manifests his concept to another. Now the demon's perversity does not lead one to order another to God, but rather to lead away from the divine order; and so one demon does not illumine another, but one can make known his mental concept to another by way of speech.

Reply Obj. 1. Not every kind of manifestation of the truth is illumination, but only that which was above described.

Reply Obj. 2. According to what belongs to natural knowledge, there is no necessity for the manifestation of truth either in the angels, or in the demons; for, as was above expounded, they know from the first all that belongs to their natural knowledge.[3] So the greater fullness of natural light in the superior demons does not prove that they illumine others.

Fourth Article
WHETHER THE GOOD ANGELS HAVE PRECEDENCE OVER

---

1. 参见 Q. 106, a. 1; a. 2, ad 1.
2. 参见 Q. 107, a. 2.
3. 参见 Q. 55, a. 2; q. 58, a. 2; q. 79, a. 2.

THE BAD ANGELS?

We proceed thus to the Fourth Article:—

Objection 1. It would seem that the good angels have no precedence over the bad angels. For the angels' precedence is especially connected with illumination. But the bad angels, being darkness, are not illumined by the good angels. Therefore the good angels do not rule over the bad.

Obj. 2. Further, superiors are guilty of negligence for the evil deeds of their subjects. But the demons do much evil. Therefore, if they are subject to the good angels, it seems that negligence is to be charged to the good angels; which cannot be admitted.

Obj. 3. Further, the angels' precedence follows upon the order of nature, as was explained above. But if demons fell from every order, as is commonly said, many of the demons are superior to many good angels according to nature. Therefore the good angels have no precedence over all the bad angels.

On the contrary, Augustine says that *the treacherous and sinful spirit of life is ruled by the rational, pious and just spirit of life*;[1] and Gregory says that *the Powers are the angels to whose charge are subjected the hostile powers.*[2]

I answer that, The whole order of precedence is first and originally in God, and is shared by creatures according as they are the nearer to God. For those creatures which are more perfect and nearer to God have the power to act on others. Now the greatest perfection, and that which brings them nearest to God, belongs to the creatures who enjoy God, as the holy angels. Of this perfection the demons are deprived. Therefore the good angels have precedence over the bad, who are ruled by them.

Reply Obj. 1. Many things concerning the divine mysteries are made

1. 参见 *De Trin.*, III, 4 (PL 42, 873).
2. 参见 *In Evang.*, II, hom. 34 (PL 76, 1251).

known by the holy angels to the bad angels, whenever the divine justice requires the demons to do anything for the punishment of the evil, or for the trial of the good; as in human affairs the judge's assessors make known his sentence to the executioners. This revelation, if compared to the angelic revealers, can be called an illumination, inasmuch as they direct it to God; but it is not an illumination on the part of the demons, for these do not direct it to God, but to the fulfillment of their own wickedness.

Reply Obj. 2. The holy angels are the ministers of the divine wisdom. Hence, as the divine wisdom permits some evil to be done by bad angels or men, for the sake of the good that follows, so also the good angels do not entirely restrain the bad from inflicting harm.

Reply Obj. 3. An angel who is inferior in the order of nature presides over demons, although these may be naturally superior, because the power of divine justice to which the good angels cleave is stronger than the natural power of the angels. Hence likewise among men, *the spiritual man judgeth all things* (*1 Cor.* ii. 15); and the Philosopher says that *the virtuous man is the rule and measure of all human acts.*[1]

1. 参见 *Eth.*, X, 5 (1176a 17).

Question CX
HOW ANGELS ACT ON BODIES
(*In Four Articles*)

WE now consider how the angels preside over the corporeal creatures. Under this head there are four points of inquiry: (1) Whether the corporeal creature is governed by the angels? (2) Whether the corporeal creature obeys the mere will of the angels? (3) Whether the angels by their own power can immediately move bodies locally? (4) Whether the good or bad angels can work miracles?

First Article
WHETHER THE CORPOREAL CREATURE IS GOVERNED BY THE ANGELS?

We proceed thus to the First Article:—

Objection 1. It would seem that the corporeal creature is not governed by the angels. For whatever possesses a determinate mode of action needs not to be governed by any superior power; for we require to be governed lest we do what we ought not. But corporeal things have their actions determined by the nature divinely bestowed upon them. Therefore they do not need the government of angels.

Obj. 2. Further, inferior things are ruled by the superior. But some corporeal things are inferior, and others are superior. Therefore they need not be governed by the angels.

Obj. 3. Further, the different orders of the angels are distinguished by different offices. But if corporeal creatures were ruled by the angels, there would be as many angelic offices as there are species of things.

So also there would be as many orders of angels as there are species of things; which is against what is laid down above.[1] Therefore the corporeal creature is not governed by angels.

On the contrary, Augustine says that *all bodies are ruled by the rational spirit of life*;[2] and Gregory says that *in this visible world nothing takes place without the agency of the invisible creature.*[3]

I answer that, It is generally found both in human affairs and in natural things that every particular power is governed and ruled by a universal power; as, for example, the bailiff's power is governed by the power of the king. Among the angels also, as was explained above, the superior angels who preside over the inferior possess a more universal knowledge.[4] Now it is manifest that the power of any individual body is more particular than the power of any spiritual substance; for every corporeal form is a form individuated by matter, and determined to the *here and now*, whereas immaterial forms are absolute and intelligible. Therefore, just as the inferior angels, who have the less universal forms, are ruled by the superior, so are all corporeal things ruled by the angels. This is laid down not only by the holy doctors, but also by all philosophers who admit the existence of incorporeal substances.

Reply Obj. 1. Corporeal things have determinate actions, but they exercise such actions only according as they are moved, because it belongs to a body not to act unless moved. Hence a corporeal creature must be moved by a spiritual creature.

Reply Obj. 2. The reason alleged is according to the opinion of Aristotle who laid down that the heavenly bodies are moved by spiritual substances.[5] The number of these substances he endeavored

---

1. 参见 Q. 108, a. 2.
2. 参见 *De Trin.*, III, 4 (PL 42, 873).
3. 参见 *Dial.*, IV, 6 (PL 77, 329).
4. 参见 Q. 55, a. 3; q. 106, a. 1; q. 108, a. 1.
5. 参见 *Metaph.*, XI, 8 (1073a 32).

to assign according to the number of motions apparent in the heavenly bodies. But he did not say that there were any spiritual substances with immediate rule over the inferior bodies, except perhaps human souls; and this was because he did not consider that any operations were exercised in the inferior bodies except the natural ones, for which the movement of the heavenly bodies sufficed. But because we assert that many things are performed in the inferior bodies besides the natural corporeal actions, for which the movements of the heavenly bodies are not sufficient, therefore in our opinion we must assert that the angels possess an immediate governance not only over the heavenly bodies, but also over the inferior bodies.

Reply Obj. 3. Philosophers have held different opinions about immaterial substances. For Plato laid down that immaterial substances were the natures and species of sensible bodies,[1] and that some were more universal than others;[2] and so he held that immaterial substances preside immediately over all sensible bodies, and different ones over different bodies.[3] But Aristotle held that immaterial substances are not the species of sensible bodies, but something higher and more universal;[4] and so he did not attribute to them any immediate governance over single bodies, but only over the universal agents, the heavenly bodies.[5] Avicenna followed a middle course.[6] For he agreed with Plato in supposing some spiritual substance to govern immediately in the sphere of active and passive elements; because, as Plato also said, he held that the forms of these sensible things are derived from immaterial substances. But he differed from Plato because he supposed only one immaterial substance to govern over all

1. 参见 Cf. above, q. 84, a. 1 and 4.
2. 参见 Cf. above, q. 65, a. 4.
3. 参见 Cf. above, q. 22, a. 3.
4. 参见 *Metaph.*, VI, 8 (1033b 27).
5. 参见 *Op. cit.*, XI, 8 (1073a 32).—Cf. Maimonides, *Guide*, III, 17 (p. 282).
6. 参见 *Metaph.*, IX, 3 (104rb) ; 4 (104vb).—Cf. above, q. 65, a. 4; q. 84, a. 4.

inferior bodies, which he called the *agent intelligence*.

The holy doctors held with the Platonists that different spiritual substances were placed over corporeal things. For Augustine says: *Every visible thing in this world has an angelic power placed over it.*[1] So, too, Damascene says: *The devil was one of the angelic powers who presided over the terrestrial order.*[2] And on the text, *When the ass saw the angel* (*Num.* xxii. 23), Origen says that *the world has need of angels who preside over beasts, and over the birth of animals, and trees, and plants, and over the increase of all other things.*[3] The reason for this, however, is not that an angel is more fitted by his nature to preside over animals than over plants. For each angel, even the least, has a higher and more universal power than any kind of corporeal thing. The reason is to be sought in the order of divine wisdom, which places different rulers over different things. Nor does it follow that there are more than nine orders of angels, because, as was explained above, the orders are distinguished by their general offices.[4] Hence, just as (according to Gregory) all the angels whose proper office it is to preside over the demons are of the order of the *powers*, so to the order of the *virtues* do those angels seem to belong who preside over purely corporeal creatures; for by their ministration miracles are sometimes performed.[5]

Second Article
WHETHER CORPOREAL MATTER OBEYS THE MERE WILL OF AN ANGEL?

We proceed thus to the Second Article:—

---

1. 参见 *Lib. 83 Quaest.*, q. 79 (PL 40, 90).
2. 参见 *De Fide Orth.*, II, 4 (PG 94, 873).
3. 参见 *In Num.*, hom. XIV (PG 12, 680).
4. 参见 Q. 108, a. 2.
5. 参见 *In Evang.*, II, hom. 34 (PL 76,1251).

Objection 1. It would seem that corporeal matter obeys the mere will of an angel. For the power of an angel excels the power of the soul. But corporeal matter obeys a conception of the soul; for the body of man is changed by a conception of the soul as regards heat and cold, and sometimes even as regards health and sickness. Therefore much more is corporeal matter changed by a conception of an angel.

Obj. 2. Further, whatever can be done by an inferior power can be done by a superior power. Now the power of an angel is superior to corporeal power. But a body by its power is able to transform corporeal matter, as appears when fire begets fire. Therefore much more efficaciously can an angel by his power transform corporeal matter.

Obj. 3. Further, all corporeal nature is under angelic administration, as appears above; and thus it appears that bodies are as instruments to the angels, for an instrument is essentially a moved mover. Now in effects there is something that is due to the power of their principal agents, and which cannot be due to the power of the instrument; and this it is that takes the principal place in the effect. For example, digestion is due to the power of natural heat, which is the instrument of the nutritive soul; but that living flesh is thus generated is due to the power of the soul. Again, the cutting of the wood is from the saw; but that it assumes at length the form of a bed is from the power of the craftsman. Therefore the substantial form, which takes the principal place in the corporeal effects, is due to the angelic power. Therefore matter obeys the angels in receiving its form.

On the contrary, Augustine says, *It is not to be thought that this visible matter obeys the rebel angels; for it obeys God alone.*[1]

I answer that, The Platonists asserted that the forms which are in matter are caused by immaterial forms, because they said that the material forms are participations of immaterial forms.[2] Avicenna

---

1. 参见 *De Trin.*, III, 8.(PL 42, 875).
2. 参见 Cf. above, q. 65, a. 4.

followed them in this opinion to some extent, for he said that all forms which are in matter proceed from the conception of the *agent intelligence*;[1] and that corporeal agents act only dispositively towards forms.[2] They seem to have been deceived, on this point, through supposing a form to be something made in itself, and thus to be the effect of a formal principle. But, as the Philosopher proves, what is made, properly speaking, is the composite;[3] for this, properly speaking, is what subsists. But the form is called a being, not as *that which* is, but as *that by which* something is. Consequently neither is a form, properly speaking, made, for that can be made which can be, since to be made is nothing but the way to being.

Now it is manifest that what is made is like to the maker, for every agent makes its like. So whatever makes natural things has a likeness to composites, and this either because it is itself composite, as when fire begets fire, or because the whole *composite* as to both matter and form is within its power; and this belongs to God alone. Therefore every informing of matter is either immediately from God, or from some corporeal agent; but not immediately from an angel.

Reply Obj. 1. Our soul is united to the body as its form, and so it is not surprising for the body to be formally changed by the soul's conception; especially as the movement of the sensitive appetite, which is accompanied by a certain bodily change, is subject to the command of reason. An angel, however, has not the same relation with natural bodies; and hence the argument does not hold.

Reply Obj. 2. Whatever an inferior power can do, that a superior power can do, not in the same way, but in a more excellent way. For example, the intellect knows sensible things in a more excellent way than sense knows them. So an angel can change corporeal matter in a

---

1. 参见 Cf. above, q. 84, a. 4.
2. 参见 *Metaph.*, IX, 3 (103vb).
3. 参见 *Metaph.*, VI, 8 (1033b 17).

more excellent way than can corporeal agents, that is, by moving the corporeal agents themselves, as a superior cause.

Reply Obj. 3. There is nothing to prevent some natural effect from taking place by angelic power, for which the power of corporeal agents would not suffice. This, however, is not to obey an angel's will (as neither does matter obey the mere will of a cook, when by regulating the fire according to the prescription of his art he produces a dish that the fire could not have produced by itself); since to reduce matter to the act of the substantial form does not exceed the power of a corporeal agent, for it is natural for like to make like.

Third Article
WHETHER BODIES OBEY THE ANGELS AS REGARDS LOCAL MOTION?

We proceed thus to the Third Article:—

Objection 1. It would seem that bodies do not obey the angels in local motion. For the local motion of natural bodies follows on their forms. But the angels do not cause the forms of natural bodies, as was stated above.[1] Therefore neither can they cause in them local motion.

Obj. 2. Further, the Philosopher proves that local motion is the first of all movements.[2] But the angels cannot cause other movements by a formal change of the matter. Therefore neither can they cause local motion.

Obj. 3. Further, the corporeal members obey the conception of the soul as regards local movement, as having in themselves some principle of life. In natural bodies, however, there is no vital principle. Therefore they do not obey the angels in local motion.

On the contrary, Augustine says that the angels use corporeal seminal

1. 参见 A. 2; q. 65, a. 4; q. 91, a. 2.
2. 参见 Aristotle, *Phys.*, VIII, 7 (260a 28).

principles to produce certain effects.[1] But they cannot do this without causing local movement. Therefore bodies obey them in local motion.

I answer that, As Dionysius says, *divine wisdom has joined the ends of the first to the principles of the second.*[2] Hence it is clear that the inferior nature at its highest point is in conjunction with superior nature. Now corporeal nature is below the spiritual nature. But among all corporeal movements the most perfect is local motion, as the Philosopher proves.[3] The reason for this is that what is moved locally is not as such in potentiality to anything intrinsic, but only to something extrinsic—that is, to place. Therefore corporeal nature has a natural aptitude to be moved immediately by the spiritual nature as regards place. Hence also the philosophers asserted that the highest bodies are moved locally by the spiritual substances.[4] Hence we see that the soul moves the body first and chiefly by a local motion.

Reply Obj. 1. There are in bodies other local movements besides those which result from the forms. For instance, the ebb and flow of the sea does not follow from the substantial form of the water, but from the influence of the moon. Much more, therefore, can local movements result from the power of spiritual substances.

Reply Obj. 2. The angels, by causing local motion, as the first motion, can thereby cause other movements; that is, by employing corporeal agents to produce these effects, as a smith employs fire to soften iron.

Reply Obj. 3. The power of an angel is not as limited as is the power of the soul. Hence the motive power of the soul is limited to the body united to it, which is vivified by it, and by which it can move other things. But an angel's power is not limited to any body, and hence it can move locally bodies not joined to it.

---

1. 参见 *De Trin.*, III, 8; 9 (PL 42, 875; 878).
2. 参见 *De Div. Nom.*, VII, 3 (PG 3, 872).
3. 参见 Aristotle, *Phys.*, VIII, 7 (261a 14).
4. 参见 Cf. above, q. 57, a. 2.

Fourth Article
WHETHER ANGELS CAN WORK MIRACLES?

We proceed thus to the Fourth Article:—

Objection 1. It would seem that the angels can work miracles. For Gregory says: *Those spirits are called virtues by whom signs and miracles are quite often done.*[1]

Obj. 2. Further, Augustine says that *magicians work miracles by private contract, good Christians by public justice, and bad Christians by the signs of public justice.*[2] But magicians work miracles because they are *heard by the demons*, as he says elsewhere in the same work.[3] Therefore the demons can work miracles. Therefore much more can the good angels.

Obj. 3. Further, Augustine says in the same work that *it is not absurd to believe that all the things we see happen may be brought about by the lower powers that dwell in our atmosphere.*[4] But when an effect of natural causes is produced outside the order of natural cause, we call it a miracle, as, for instance, when anyone is cured of a fever without the operation of nature. Therefore the angels and demons can work miracles.

Obj. 4. Further, a superior power is not subject to the order of an inferior cause. But corporeal nature is inferior to an angel. Therefore an angel can work outside the order of corporeal agents; which is to work miracles.

On the contrary, It is written of God (*Ps.* cxxxv. 4): *Who alone doth great wonders.*

I answer that, A miracle properly so called takes place when something is done outside the order of nature. But it is not enough

---

1. 参见 *In Evang.*, II, hom. 34 (PL 76, 1251).
2. 参见 *Lib. 83 Quaest.*, q. 79 (PL 40, 92).
3. 参见 Pseudo-Augustine, *Viginti unius Sent.*, IV (PL 40, 726).
4. 同上

for a miracle if something is done outside the order of any particular nature; for otherwise anyone would perform a miracle by throwing a stone upwards, as such a thing is outside the order of the stone's nature. So for a miracle is required that it be beyond the order of the whole created nature. But God alone can do this, because whatever an angel or any other creature does by its own power is according to the order of created nature; and thus it is not a miracle. Hence God alone can work miracles.

Reply Obj. 1. Some angels are said to work miracles either because God works miracles at their request, in the same way as holy men are said to work miracles, or because they exercise a kind of ministry in the miracles which take place, as in gathering the dust in the general resurrection, or by doing something of that kind.

Reply Obj. 2. Properly speaking, as was said above, miracles are things done outside the order of the whole of created nature. But as we do not know all the power of created nature, it follows that when anything is done outside the order of created nature by a power unknown to us, it is called a miracle as regards ourselves. So when the demons do anything of their own natural power, these things are called *miracles* not in an absolute sense, but in reference to ourselves. In this way the magicians work miracles through the demons; and these miracles are said to be done by *private contract*, because every power of the creature, in the universe, may be compared to the power of a private person in a city. Hence when a magician does anything by compact with the devil, this is done as it were by private contract. On the other hand, the divine justice is in the whole universe as the public law is in the city. Therefore good Christians, so far as they work miracles by divine justice, are said to work miracles by *public justice*; but bad Christians by *the signs of public justice*, for example, by invoking the name of Christ, or by making use of other sacred signs.

Reply Obj. 3. Spiritual powers are able to effect whatever happens in this visible world, by employing corporeal seminal principles by local movement.

Reply Obj. 4. Although the angels can do something outside the order of corporeal nature, yet they cannot do anything outside the whole created order; and it is this which is essential to a miracle, as was above explained.

Question CXI
THE ACTION OF THE ANGELS ON MAN
(*In Four Articles*)

WE now consider the action of the angels on man, and inquire: (1) How far they can change them by their own natural power; (2) how they are sent by God to the ministry of men;[1] (3) how they guard and protect men.[2] Under the first head there are four points of inquiry: (1) Whether an angel can illumine the human intellect? (2) Whether he can change man's will? (3) Whether he can change man's imagination? (4) Whether he can affect man's senses?

First Article
WHETHER AN ANGEL CAN ILLUMINE MAN?

We proceed thus to the First Article:—

Objection 1. It would seem that an angel cannot illumine man. For man is illumined by faith, and hence Dionysius attributes illumination to baptism, *as the sacrament of faith.*[3] But faith is immediately from God, according to *Ephes.* ii. 8: *By grace you are saved through faith, and that not of yourselves, for it is the gift of God.* Therefore man is not illumined by an angel, but immediately by God.

Obj. 2. Further, on the words, *God hath manifested it to them* (*Rom.* i. 19), the *Gloss* observes that *not only natural reason availed for the*

---

1. 参见 Q. 112.
2. 参见 Q. 113.
3. 参见 *De Eccles. Hier.*, II, pt. 1; pt. 3, § 3 (PG 3, 392; 397).

manifestation of divine truths to men, but God also revealed them by His work,[1] that is, by His creature. But both are immediately from God —that is, natural reason and the creature. Therefore God illumines man immediately.

Obj. 3. Further, whoever is illumined is conscious of being illumined. But man is not conscious of being illumined by angels. Therefore he is not illumined by them.

On the contrary, Dionysius says that the revelation of divine things reaches men through the ministry of the angels.[2] But such revelation is an illumination, as we have stated.[3] Therefore men are illumined by the angels.

I answer that, Since the order of divine providence disposes that lower things be subject to the actions of the higher, as was explained above,[4] just as the inferior angels are illumined by the superior, so men, who are inferior to the angels, are illumined by them.

The modes of each of this illumination are in one way alike and in another way unlike. For, as was shown above, the illumination which consists in making known divine truth has two functions,[5] namely, according as the inferior intellect is strengthened by the action of the superior intellect, and according as the intelligible species which are in the superior intellect are proposed to the inferior so as to be grasped by them. This takes place in the angels when the superior angel divides his universal concept of the truth according to the capacity of the inferior angel, as was explained above.[6]

The human intellect, however, cannot grasp the universal truth itself

---

1. 参见 *Glossa ordin.* (VI, 5 B); Peter Lombard, *In Rom.*, super I, 19 (PL 191, 1326).
2. 参见 *De Cael. Hier.*, IV, 2 (PG 3, 180).
3. 参见 Q. 106, a. 1; q. 107, a. 2.
4. 参见 Q. 109, a. 2; q. 110, a. 1.
5. 参见 Q. 106, a. 1.
6. 同上

unveiled, because its nature requires it to understand by turning to the phantasms, as was above explained.[1] So the angels propose intelligible truth to men under the likenesses of sensible things, according to what Dionysius says, namely, that *it is impossible for the divine ray to shine on us, otherwise than shrouded by the variety of the sacred veils.*[2] On the other hand, the human intellect, as the inferior, is strengthened by the action of the angelic intellect. And in these two ways man is illumined by an angel.

Reply Obj. 1. Two things concur in the virtue of faith: first, the habit of the intellect whereby it is disposed to obey the will tending to divine truth. For the intellect assents to the truth of faith, not as convinced by the reason, but as commanded by the will ; and so, as Augustine says, *No one believes except willingly.*[3] In this respect faith comes from God alone. Secondly, faith requires that what is to be believed be proposed to the believer; and this is accomplished by man, according to *Rom.* x. 17, *Faith cometh by hearing*, but principally by the angels, by whom divine things are revealed to men. Hence the angels have some part in the illumination of faith. However, men are illumined by the angels not only concerning what is to be believed, but also as regards what is to be done.

Reply Obj. 2. Natural reason, which is immediately from God, can be strengthened by an angel, as we have said above. Again, the more the human intellect is strengthened, so much higher an intelligible truth can be elicited from the species derived from creatures. Thus man is assisted by an angel so that he may obtain from creatures a more perfect knowledge of God.

Reply Obj. 3. Intellectual operation and illumination can be understood in two ways. First, on the part of the thing understood, and thus whoever understands, or is illumined, knows that he understands

---

1. 参见 Q. 84, a. 7.
2. 参见 *De Cael. Hier.*, I, 2 (PG 3, 121).
3. 参见 *Tract.* XXVI, super *Ioann.*, VI, 44 (PL 35, 1607).

or is illumined because he knows that the thing is made known to him. Secondly, on the part of the principle, and thus it does not follow that whoever understands a truth, knows what the intellect is, which is the principle of the intellectual operation. In like manner, not everyone who is illumined by an angel knows that he is illumined by him.

Second Article
WHETHER THE ANGELS CAN CHANGE THE WILL OF MAN?

We proceed thus to the Second Article:—

Objection 1. It would seem that the angels can change the will of man. For, upon the text, *Who maketh His angels spirits and His ministers a flame of fire* (*Heb.* i. 7), the *Gloss* notes that *they are fire, as being spiritually fervent, and as burning away our vices.*[1] This could not be, however, unless they changed the will. Therefore the angels can change the will.

Obj. 2. Further, Bede says that *the devil does not send wicked thoughts, but kindles them.*[2] Damascene, however, says that he also sends them, for he remarks that *every malicious act and unclean passion is contrived by the demons and put into men.*[3] In like manner, the good angels likewise introduce and kindle good thoughts. But this could be only if they changed the will. Therefore the will is changed by them.

Obj. 3. Further, the angel, as was above explained, illumines the human intellect by way of the phantasms. But just as the imagination which serves the intellect can be changed by an angel, so can the sensitive appetite which serves the will, because it also is a power using a corporeal organ. Therefore just as the angel illumines the intellect, so can he change the will.

On the contrary, To change the will belongs to God alone, according

---

1. 参见 Peter Lombard, *In Hebr.*, super I, 7 (PL 192, 410).
2. 参见 *In Matt.*, III, super XV, 11 (PL 92, 75).
3. 参见 *De Fide Orth.*, II, 4 (PG 94, 877).

to *Prov.* xxi. 1: *The heart of the king is in the hand of the Lord, whithersoever He will He shall turn it.*

I answer that, The will can be changed in two ways. First, from within, in which way, since the movement of the will is nothing but the inclination of the will to the thing willed, God alone can thus change the will, because He gives the power of such an inclination to the intellectual nature. For just as the natural inclination is from God alone Who gives the nature, so the inclination of the will is from God alone, Who causes the will.

Secondly, the will is moved from without. As regards an angel, this can happen only in one way, —by the good apprehended by the intellect. Hence in as far as anyone may be the reason why anything is apprehended as an appetible good, so far does he move the will. In this way also God alone can move the will efficaciously; but an angel and man move the will by way of persuasion, as was above explained.[1]

In addition to this mode, the human will can be moved from without in another way, namely, by the passion residing in the sensitive appetite; and thus by concupiscence or anger the will is inclined to will something. In this manner the angels, as being able to rouse such passions, can move the will; not, however, by necessity, for the will always remain free to consent to, or to resist, passion.

Reply Obj. 1. Those who act as God's ministers, either men or angels, are said to burn away vices and to incite to virtue by way of persuasion.

Reply Obj. 2. The demon cannot put thoughts in our minds by causing them from within, since the use of the cogitative power is subject to the will. Nevertheless, the devil is called the kindler of thoughts, inasmuch as he incites to thought, or to the desire of the things thought, by way of persuasion or by rousing the passions.

---

1. 参见 Q. 106, a. 2.

Damascene calls this kindling *a putting in*, because such a work is accomplished within. But good thoughts are attributed to a higher principle, namely, God, though they may be procured by the ministry of the angels.

Reply Obj. 3. The human intellect in its present state can understand only by turning to the phantasms; but the human will can will something following the judgment of reason rather than the passion of the sensitive appetite. Hence the comparison does not hold.

Third Article
WHETHER AN ANGEL CAN CHANGE MAN'S IMAGINATION?

We proceed thus to the Third Article:—

Objection 1. It would seem that an angel cannot change man's imagination. For the phantasy, as is said in *De Anima* iii., is *a motion caused by the sense in act.*[1] But if this motion were caused by an angel, it would not be caused by the sense in act. Therefore it is contrary to the nature of the phantasy, which is the act of the imaginative power, to be changed by an angel.

Obj. 2. Further, since the forms in the imagination are spiritual, they are nobler than the forms existing in sensible matter. But an angel cannot impress forms upon sensible matter.[2] Therefore he cannot impress forms on the imagination, and hence cannot change it.

Obj. 3. Further, Augustine says: *One spirit by intermingling with another can communicate his knowledge to the other spirit by these images, so that the latter either understands it himself, or accepts it as understood by the other.*[3] But it does not seem that an angel can be mingled with the human imagination, nor that the imagination can receive the knowledge of an

1. 参见 Aristotle, *De An.*, III, 3 (429a 1).
2. 参见 Q. 110, a. 2.
3. 参见 *De Genesi ad Litt.*, XII, 12 (PL 34, 464).

angel. Therefore it seems that an angel cannot change the imagination.

Obj. 4. Further, in imaginative vision man cleaves to the likenesses of things as to the things themselves. But in this there is deception. Hence, as a good angel cannot be the cause of deception, it seems that he cannot cause imaginative vision, by changing the imagination.

On the contrary, Those things which are seen in dreams are seen by imaginative vision. But the angels reveal things in dreams, as appears from *Matt.* i. 20; ii. 13, 19, in regard to the angel who appeared to Joseph in dreams. Therefore an angel can move the imagination.

I answer that, Both good and bad angels by their own natural power can move the human imagination. This may be explained as follows. For it was said above that corporeal nature obeys the angel as regards local movement, so that whatever can be caused by the local movement of bodies is subject to the natural power of the angels.[1] Now it is manifest that imaginative apparitions are sometimes caused in us by the local movement of animal spirits and humors. Hence Aristotle says, when assigning the cause of visions in dreams, that *when an animal sleeps, the blood descends in abundance to the sensitive principle, and movements descend with it.*[2] These movements are the impressions left from the movements of sensible things, which movements are preserved in the animal spirits, *and move the sensitive principle*; so that a certain appearance ensues, as if the sensitive principle were being then changed by the external things themselves. Indeed, the commotion of the spirits and humors may be so great that such appearances may even occur to those who are awake, as is seen in mad people, and the like. Hence, just as this happens by a natural disturbance of the humors, and sometimes also by the will of man who voluntarily imagines what he previously experienced, so also the same may be done by the power of a good or a bad angel, sometimes with alienation

1. 参见 Q. 110, a. 3.
2. 参见 *De Somno*, III (461b 11).

from the bodily senses, sometimes without such alienation.

Reply Obj. 1. The first principle of the imagination is from the sense in act. For we cannot imagine what we have never perceived by the senses, either wholly or partly; as a man born blind cannot imagine color. Sometimes, however, the imagination is informed in such a way that the act of the imaginative movement arises from the impressions preserved within.

Reply Obj. 2. An angel changes the imagination, not by the impression of an imaginative form in no way previously received from the senses (for he cannot make a man born blind to imagine color), but by the local movement of the spirits and humors, as was explained above.

Reply Obj. 3. The commingling of the angelic spirit with the human imagination is not a mingling of essences, but by reason of an effect which he produces in the imagination in the way stated above; so that he shows man what he [the angel] knows, but not in the way he knows.

Reply Obj. 4. An angel causing an imaginative vision sometimes illumines the intellect at the same time, so that it knows what these images signify; and then there is no deception. But sometimes by the angelic operation only the likenesses of things appear in the imagination; but neither then is deception caused by the angel, but by the defect in the intellect of him to whom such things appear. Thus neither was Christ a cause of deception when He spoke many things to the people in parables, which He did not explain to them.

Fourth Article
WHETHER AN ANGEL CAN AFFECT THE HUMAN SENSES?

We proceed thus to the Fourth Article:—

Objection 1. It seems that an angel cannot affect the human senses. For the sensitive operation is a vital operation. But such an operation does not come from an extrinsic principle. Therefore the sensitive operation cannot be caused by an angel.

Obj. 2. Further, the sensitive operation is nobler than the nutritive. But the angel cannot affect the nutritive power, nor other natural forms. Therefore neither can he affect the sensitive power.

Obj. 3. Further, the senses are naturally moved by the sensible objects. But an angel cannot change the order of nature.[1] Therefore an angel cannot affect the senses, but these are affected always by the sensible object.

On the contrary, The angels who overturned Sodom *struck the people of Sodom with blindness* or ἀορασία, *so that they could not find the door* (*Gen.* xix. 11). The same is recorded of the Syrians whom Eliseus led into Samaria (*4 Kings* vi. 18).

I answer that, The senses may be affected in a twofold manner: from without, as when they are affected by the sensible thing; and from within, for we see that the senses are affected when the spirits and humors are disturbed. For example, a sick man's tongue, charged with choleric humor, tastes everything as bitter, and the like with the other senses. Now an angel, by his natural power, can work a change in the senses in both ways. For an angel can offer the senses a sensible thing from without, formed either by nature or by the angel himself, as when he assumes a body, as we have said above.[2] Likewise he can move the spirits and humors from within, as we said above, whereby the senses are affected in various ways.

Reply Obj. 1. The principle of the sensitive operation cannot be without the interior principle which is the sensitive power; but this interior principle can be moved in many ways by the exterior principle, as was above explained.

Reply Obj. 2. By the interior movement of the spirits and humors an angel can do something towards changing the act of the nutritive

---

1. 参见 Q. 110, a. 4.
2. 参见 Q. 51, a. 2.

power; and also of the appetitive and sensitive powers, and of any other power using a corporeal organ.

Reply Obj. 3. An angel can do nothing outside the entire order of creatures, but he can outside some particular order of nature, since he is not subject to that order; and thus in some special way an angel can work a change in the senses outside the common mode of nature.

Question CXII
THE MISSION OF THE ANGELS
(*In Four Articles*)

WE next consider the mission of the angels. Under this head arise four points of inquiry: (1) Whether any angels are sent on works of ministry? (2) Whether all are sent? (3) Whether those who are sent, assist? (4) From what orders they are sent.

First Article
WHETHER THE ANGELS ARE SENT ON WORKS OF MINISTRY?

We proceed thus to the First Article:—

Objection 1. It would seem that the angels are not sent on works of ministry. For every mission is to some determinate place. But intellectual actions do not determine a place, for intellect abstracts from the *here* and *now*. Since therefore the angelic actions are intellectual, it appears that the angels are not sent to perform their own actions.

Obj. 2. Further, the empyrean heaven is the place that beseems the angelic dignity. Therefore, if they are sent to us in ministry, it seems that something of their dignity would be lost; which is unseemly.

Obj. 3. Further, external occupation hinders the contemplation of wisdom. Hence it is said: *He that is less in action, shall receive wisdom* (*Ecclus.* xxxviii. 25). So if some angels are sent on external ministrations, they would seem to be hindered from contemplation. But the whole of their beatitude consists in the contemplation of

God. So if they were sent, their beatitude would be lessened; which is unfitting.

Obj. 4. Further, to minister is the part of an inferior; and hence it is written (*Luke* xxii. 27): *Which is the greater, he that sitteth at table, or he that serveth? is not he that sitteth at table?* But the angels are naturally greater than we are. Therefore they are not sent to administer to us.

On the contrary, It is written (*Exod.* xxiii. 20): *Behold I will send My angels who shall go before thee.*

I answer that, From what has been said above,[1] it may be shown that some angels are sent in ministry by God. For, as we have already stated, in treating of the mission of the divine Persons, he is said to be sent who in any way proceeds from another so as to begin to be where he was not, or to be in another way, where he already was.[2] Thus the Son or the Holy Ghost is said to be sent as proceeding from the Father by origin; and He begins to be in a new way, by grace or by the nature assumed, where He was before by the presence of His Godhead. For it belongs to God to be present everywhere, because, since He is the universal cause, His power reaches to all being; and hence He exists in all things.[3]

An angel's power, however, as a particular agent, does not reach to the whole universe, but reaches to one thing in such a way as not to reach another; and so he is *here* in such a manner as not to be *there*. But it is clear from what was above stated that the corporeal creature is governed by the angels.[4] Hence, whenever an angel has to perform any work concerning a corporeal creature, the angel applies himself anew to that body by his power; and in that way begins to be there anew. Now all this takes place by divine command. Hence it follows that an

---

1. 参见 Q. 108, a. 6.
2. 参见 Q. 43, a. 1.
3. 参见 Q. 8, a. 1.
4. 参见 Q. 110, a. 1.

angel is sent by God.

Yet the action performed by the angel who is sent proceeds from God as from its first principle, at Whose nod and by Whose authority the angels work; and it is reduced to God as to its last end. Now this is what is meant by a minister; for a minister is an intelligent instrument; and an instrument is moved by another, and its action is ordered to another. Hence actions of the angels are called *ministries*; and for this reason they are said to be sent in ministry.

Reply Obj. 1. An operation can be intellectual in two ways. In one way, as dwelling in the intellect itself, as contemplation. Such an operation does not demand to occupy a place; indeed, as Augustine says: *Even we ourselves, as mentally tasting something eternal, are not in this world.*[1] In another sense an action is said to be intellectual because it is regulated and commanded by some intellect; and in that sense intellectual operations evidently have sometimes a determinate place.

Reply Obj. 2. The empyrean heaven belongs to the angelic dignity by way of some congruity; for it is congruous that the higher body should be set aside for that nature which occupies a rank above all bodies. Yet an angel does not derive any dignity from the empyrean heaven. Hence, when he is not actually in the empyrean heaven, nothing of his dignity is lost; just as neither does a king lessen his dignity when not actually sitting on the regal throne which suits his dignity.

Reply Obj. 3. Among men, the purity of contemplation is obscured by exterior occupation, because we give ourselves to action through the sensitive powers, whose action when intense impedes the action of the intellectual powers. An angel, on the contrary, regulates his exterior actions by intellectual operation alone. Hence it follows that his external occupations in no respect impede his contemplation: because, given two actions, one of which is the rule and the reason of

---

1. 参见 *De Trin.*, IV, 20 (PL 42, 907).

the other, one does not hinder but helps the other. Therefore Gregory says that *the angels do not go abroad in such a manner as to lose the delights of inward contemplation.*[1]

Reply Obj. 4. In their external actions, the angels chiefly minister to God, and secondarily to us. This is not because we are superior to them, absolutely speaking, but because, since every man or angel by cleaving to God is made one spirit with God, he is thereby superior to every creature. Hence the Apostle says (*Phil.* ii. 3): *Esteeming others better than themselves.*

Second Article
WHETHER ALL THE ANGELS ARE SENT IN MINISTRY?

We proceed thus to the Second Article:—

Objection 1. It would seem that all the angels are sent in ministry. For the Apostle says (*Heb.* i. 14): *All are ministering spirits, sent to minister.*

Obj. 2. Further, among the orders, the highest is that of the Seraphim, as was stated above.[2] But a Seraph was sent to purify the lips of the prophet (*Isa.* vi. 6, 7). Therefore much more are the inferior orders sent.

Obj. 3. Further, the divine Persons infinitely excel all the angelic orders. But the divine Persons are sent. Therefore much more are even the highest angels sent.

Obj. 4. Further, if the superior angels are not sent to external ministries, this can be only because the superior angels execute the divine ministries by means of the inferior angels. But since all the angels are unequal, as was stated above,[3] each angel has an angel inferior to himself except the last one. Therefore only the last angel

---

1. 参见 *Moral.*, II, 3 (PL 75, 556).
2. 参见 Q. 108, a. 6.
3. 参见 Q. 50, a. 4; q. 108, a. 3, ad 1.

would be sent in ministry; which contradicts the words, *Thousands of thousands ministered to Him* (*Dan.* vii. 10).

On the contrary, Gregory, quoting Dionysius,[1] says that *the higher ranks fulfill no exterior service.*[2]

I answer that, As appears from what has been said above,[3] the order of divine providence has so disposed not only among the angels, but also in the whole universe, that inferior things are administered by the superior. By the divine dispensation, however, this order is sometimes not observed as regards corporeal things, for the sake of a higher order, that is, according as it is suitable for the manifestation of grace. And so, that a man born blind was given to see,[4] that Lazarus was raised from the dead,[5] was accomplished immediately by God without the action of the heavenly bodies. So, too, both good and bad angels can work some effect in these bodies independently of the heavenly bodies, by the condensation of the clouds into rain, and by producing some such effects. Nor can anyone doubt that God can immediately reveal things to men without the help of the angels, and the superior angels without the inferior. From this standpoint, some have said that ordinarily the superior angels are not sent, but only the inferior; and yet that sometimes, by divine dispensation, the superior angels also are sent.[6]

This, however, does not seem to be reasonable, because order among the angels is according to the gifts of grace. Now the order of grace has no order above itself for the sake of which it should be passed over; as the order of nature is passed over for the sake of grace. It must likewise be observed that the order of nature in the working

1. 参见 *In Evang.*, II, hom. 34 (PL 76, 1254).
2. 参见 *De Cael. Hier.*, XIII, 2 (PG 3, 300).
3. 参见 Q. 106, a. 3; q. 110, a. 1.
4. 参见 *Jo.* IX, 1.
5. 参见 *Jo.* XI, 43.
6. 参见 Pseudo-Dionysius, *De Cael. Hier.*, XIII, 2 (PG 3, 300).

of miracles is passed over for the confirmation of faith; which purpose would receive no additional support if the angelic order were passed over, since this could not be perceived by us. Furthermore, there is nothing in the divine ministries above the capacity of the inferior orders. Hence Gregory says that *those who announce the highest things are called archangels*. For this reason *the archangel Gabriel was sent to the Virgin Mary*;[1] and yet, as he says further on, this was the greatest of all the divine ministries. Thus with Dionysius we must say, without any qualification, that the superior angels are never sent to the external ministry.[2]

Reply Obj. 1. As in the missions of the divine Persons there is a visible mission, in regard to the corporeal creature, and an invisible mission, in regard to a spiritual effect, so likewise in the angelic missions, there is an external mission, in respect of some administration of corporeal things (and on such a mission not all the angels are sent), and an interior mission, in respect of some intellectual effect, according as one angel illumines another (and in this way all the angels are sent).

It may also be said that the Apostle wishes to prove that Christ is greater than the angels who were chosen as the messengers of the law, in order that He might show the excellence of the new over the old law. Hence there is no need to apply this to any other angels besides those who were sent to give the law.

Reply Obj. 2. According to Dionysius, the angel who was sent to purify the prophet's lips was one of the inferior order;[3] but he was called a *Seraph*, that is, *burning* in an equivocal sense, because he came to *burn* the lips of the prophet. It may also be said that the superior angels communicate their own proper gifts, whereby they are denominated, through the ministry of the inferior angels. Thus one

---

1. 参见 *In Evang.*, II, hom. 34 (PL 76, 1250).
2. 参见 *De Cael. Hier.*, XIII, 2 (PG 3, 300).
3. 同上

of the Seraphim is described as purifying by fire the prophet's lips, not as if he did so immediately, but because an inferior angel did so by his power; as the Pope is said to absolve a man even when he gives absolution by means of someone else.

Reply Obj. 3. The divine Persons are not sent in ministry, but are said to be sent in an equivocal sense, as appears from what has been said.[1]

Reply Obj. 4. A manifold grade exists in the divine ministries. Hence there is nothing to prevent angels, though unequal, from being sent immediately in ministry; in such a manner, however, that the superior are sent to the higher ministries, and the lower to the inferior ministries.

Third Article
WHETHER ALL THE ANGELS WHO ARE SENT, ASSIST?

We proceed thus to the Third Article:—

Objection 1. It would seem that the angels who are sent also assist. For Gregory says: *So the angels are sent, and assist; for, though the angelic spirit is limited, yet the supreme Spirit, God, is not limited.*[2]

Obj. 2. Further, the angel was sent to administer to Tobias. Yet he said, *I am the angel Raphael, one of the seven who stand before the Lord* (*Tob.* xii. 15). Therefore the angels who are sent, assist.

Obj. 3. Further, every holy angel is nearer to God than Satan is. Yet Satan was present to God, according to *Job.* i. 6: *When the sons of God came to stand before the Lord, Satan also was present among them.* Therefore much more do the angels, who are sent to minister, assist.

Obj. 4. Further, if the inferior angels do not assist, the reason is because they receive the divine illumination, not immediately, but

---

1. 参见 Q. 43. a. 1.
2. 参见 *In Evang.*, II, hom. 34 (PL 76, 1255).

through the superior angels. But every angel receives the divine illumination from a superior, except the one who is highest of all. Therefore only the highest angel would assist; which is contrary to the text of *Dan.* vii. 10: *Ten thousand times a hundred thousand stood before Him.* Therefore the angels who are sent also assist.

On the contrary, Gregory says, on *Job* xxv. 3 (*Is there any numbering of His soldiers?*): *Those powers assist, who do not go forth as messengers to men.*[1] Therefore those who are sent in ministry do not assist.

I answer that, The angels are spoken of as *assisting* and *administering*, after the likeness of those who attend upon a king. Some of them always wait upon him, and hear his commands immediately; while there are others to whom the royal commands are conveyed by those who are in attendance— for instance, those who are placed at the head of the administration of various cities. These are said to administer, not to assist.

We must therefore observe that all the angels gaze upon the divine essence immediately; and in regard to this, all, even those who minister, are said to assist. Hence Gregory says that *those who are sent on the external ministry of our salvation can always assist and see the face of the Father.*[2] Yet not all the angels can perceive the secrets of the divine mysteries in the splendor itself of the divine essence, but only the superior angels who announce them to the inferior. And in this respect only the superior angels belonging to the highest hierarchy are said to assist, whose special prerogative it is to be immediately illumined by God, as Dionysius says.[3]

From this may be deduced the reply to the first and second objections, which are based on the first mode of assisting.

Reply Obj. 3. Satan is not described as having assisted, but as present

---

1. 参见 *Moral.*, XVII, 13 (PL 76, 20).
2. 参见 *Op. cit.*, II, 3 (PL 75, 556).
3. 参见 *De Cael. Hier.*, VII, 3 (PG 3, 209).

among the assistants; for, as Gregory says, *though he has lost beatitude, still he has retained a nature like to the angels.*[1]

Reply Obj. 4. All the assistants see some things immediately in the splendor of the divine essence. Hence it may be said that it is the prerogative of the whole of the highest hierarchy to be immediately illumined by God. But the higher ones among them see more than is seen by the inferior, and illumine the other on what they see; just as among those who are present to the king, one knows more of the king's secrets than another.

Fourth Article
WHETHER ALL THE ANGELS OF THE SECOND HIERARCHY ARE SENT?

We proceed thus to the Fourth Article:—

Objection 1. It would seem that all the angels of the second hierarchy are sent. For all the angels either assist or minister, according to *Daniel* vii. 10. But the angels of the second hierarchy do not assist, for they are illumined by the angels of the first hierarchy, as Dionysius says.[2] Therefore all the angels of the second hierarchy are sent in ministry.

Obj. 2. Further, Gregory says that *there are more who minister than who assist.*[3] This would not be the case if the angels of the second hierarchy were not sent in ministry. Therefore all the angels of the second hierarchy are sent to minister.

On the contrary, Dionysius says that the *Dominations are above all subjection.*[4] But to be sent implies subjection. Therefore the *Dominations* are not sent to minister.

---

1. 参见 *Moral.*, II, 4 (PL 75, 557).
2. 参见 *De Cael. Hier.*, VIII, 1 (PG 3, 240).
3. 参见 *Moral.*, XVII, 13 (PL 76, 20).
4. 参见 *De Cael. Hier.*, VIII, 1 (PG 3, 237).

I answer that, As was above stated, to be sent to external ministry properly belongs to an angel according as by divine command he acts in relation to any corporeal creature; which is a part of the execution of the divine ministry. Now the angelic properties are manifested by their names, as Dionysius says,[1] and therefore the angels of those orders are sent to external ministry whose names signify some kind of administration. But the name *Dominations* does not signify any such administration, but only disposition and command in administering. On the other hand, the names of the inferior orders imply administration, for the *Angels* and *Archangels* are so called from *announcing*, the *Virtues* and *Powers* are so called in respect of some act; and it is right that the *Prince*, according to what Gregory says, *be first among the workers.*[2] Hence it belongs to these five orders to be sent to external ministry, but not to the four superior orders.

Reply Obj. 1. The *Dominations* are reckoned among the ministering angels, not as exercising, but as disposing and commanding what is to be done by others; just as an architect does not put his hands to the production of his art, but only disposes and orders what others are to do.

Reply Obj. 2. A twofold reason may be given in assigning the number of the assisting and ministering angels. For Gregory says that those who minister are more numerous than those who assist, because he takes the words (*Dan.* vii. 10) *thousands of thousands ministered to Him*, not in a multiple but in a partitive sense, to mean *thousands out of thousands*; and thus the number of those who minister is indefinite, to signify how large it is, while the number of assistants is finite as in the words added, *and ten thousand times a hundred thousand assisted Him.* This explanation rests on the opinion of the Platonists, who said that the nearer things are to the one first principle, the smaller they are in

1. 参见 *Op. cit.*, VII, 1; VIII, 1 (PG 3, 205; 237).
2. 参见 *In Evang.*, II, hom. 34 (PL 76, 1251).

number;[1] just as the nearer a number is to unity, the lesser it is than multitude. This opinion holds as regards the number of orders, as six administer and three assist.

Dionysius, however, declares that the multitude of angels surpasses all material multitude;[2] so that, just as the superior bodies exceed the inferior in magnitude to an immeasurable degree, so the superior incorporeal natures surpass all corporeal natures in multitude, because whatever is better is more intended and more multiplied by God. Hence, as the assistants are superior to the ministers, there will be more assistants than ministers. In this way, the words *thousands of thousands* are taken by way of multiplication, to signify *a thousand times a thousand.* And because ten times a hundred is a thousand, if it were said *ten times a hundred thousand* it would mean that there are as many assistants as ministers: but since it is written *ten thousand times a hundred thousand*, we are given to understand that the assistants are much more numerous than the ministers. Nor is this said to signify that this is the precise number of angels, but rather that it is much greater, in that it exceeds all material multitude. This is signified by the multiplication together of the greatest numbers, namely ten, a hundred, and a thousand, as Dionysius remarks in the same passage.

---

1. 参见 *De Causis*, IV (p. 164); Proclus, *Elem. of Theol.*, prop. 62 (p. 58); Pseudo-Dionysius, *De Div. Nom.*, XIII, 2 (PG 3, 280); Avicenna, *Metaph.*, IX, 4 (104vb).
2. 参见 *De Cael. Hier.*, XIV (PG 3, 321).

Question CXIII
THE GUARDIANSHIP OF THE GOOD ANGELS
(*In Eight Articles*)

WE next consider the guardianship exercised by the good angels; and their warfare against the bad angels.[1] Under the first head eight points of inquiry arise: (1) Whether men are guarded by angels? (2) Whether to each man is assigned a single guardian angel? (3) Whether guardianship belongs only to the lowest order of angels? (4) Whether it is fitting for each man to have an angel guardian? (5) When does an angel's guardianship of a man begin? (6) Whether the angel guardians always watch over men? (7) Whether the angel grieves over the loss of the one guarded? (8) Whether rivalry exists among the angels as regards their guardianship?

First Article
WHETHER MEN ARE GUARDED BY THE ANGELS?

We proceed thus to the First Article:—

Objection 1. It would seem that men are not guarded by the angels. For guardians are deputed to some because they either know not how, or are not able, to guard themselves, as children and the sick. But man is able to guard himself by his free choice, and knows how by his natural knowledge of the natural law. Therefore man is not guarded by

---

1. 参见 Q. 114.

an angel.

Obj. 2. Further, a strong guard makes a weaker one superfluous. But men are guarded by God, according to *Ps.* cxx. 4: *He shall neither slumber nor sleep, that keepeth Israel.* Therefore man does not need to be guarded by an angel.

Obj. 3. Further, the loss of the guarded redounds to the negligence of the guardian; and hence it was said to a certain one: *Keep this man; and if he shall slip away, thy life shall be for his life* (*3 Kings* xx. 39). Now many perish daily, through falling into sin, whom the angels could help by visible appearance, or by miracles, or in some such way. The angels would therefore be negligent if men are given to their guardianship. But that is clearly false. Therefore the angels are not the guardians of men.

On the contrary, It is written (*Ps.* xc. 11): *He hath given His angels charge over thee, to keep in all thy ways.*

I answer that, According to the plan of the divine providence, we find that in all things the movable and variable are moved and regulated by the immovable and invariable: *e.g.*, all corporeal things by immovable spiritual substances, and the inferior bodies by the superior which are invariable in substance. We ourselves also are regulated as regards conclusions, about which we may have various opinions, by the principles which we hold in an invariable manner. It is moreover manifest that as regards things to be done human knowledge and affection can vary and fail from good in many ways; and so it was necessary that angels should be deputed to the guardianship of men, in order to regulate them and move them to good.

Reply Obj. 1. By free choice man can avoid evil to a certain degree, but not in any sufficient degree; for he is weak in affection towards good because of the manifold passions of the soul. So, too, universal knowledge of the natural law, which by nature belongs to man, to a certain degree directs man to good, but not in a sufficient degree; because in the application of the universal principles of law to particular actions man can fail in many ways. Hence it is written (*Wis.* ix. 14): *The thoughts of mortal men are fearful, and our counsels uncertain.* Thus man needs to be guarded by the angels.

Reply Obj. 2. Two things are required for good action. First, that the affection be inclined to good, which is effected in us by the habit of moral virtue. Secondly, that reason should discover fitting ways to accomplish the good of virtue; and this the Philosopher attributes to prudence.[1] As regards the first, God guards man immediately by infusing into him grace and the virtues; as regards the second, God guards man as his universal teacher, Whose precepts reach man by way of the angels, as was stated above.[2]

Reply Obj. 3. Just as men depart from the natural instigation of good by reason of a sinful passion, so also do they depart from the instigation of the good angels, which takes place invisibly when they illumine man that he may do what is right. Hence that men perish is not to be imputed to the negligence of the angels, but to the malice of men. That they sometimes appear to men visibly outside the ordinary course of nature comes from a special grace of God, as likewise that miracles occur outside the order of nature.

Second Article
WHETHER EACH MAN IS GUARDED BY AN ANGEL?

We proceed thus to the Second Article:—

Objection 1. It would seem that each man is not guarded by an angel. For an angel is stronger than a man. But one man suffices to guard many men. Therefore much more can one angel guard many men.

Obj. 2. Further, the lower things are brought to God through the

---

1. 参见 *Eth.*, VI, 12 (1144a 8).
2. 参见 Q. III, a. 1.

medium of the higher, as Dionysius says.[1] But as all the angels are unequal,[2] there is only one angel between whom and men there is no intermediate. Therefore there is only one angel who immediately guards men.

Obj. 3. Further, the greater angels are deputed to the greater offices. But it is not a greater office to keep one man more than another, since all men are naturally equal. Since, therefore, of all the angels one is greater than another, as Dionysius says,[3] it seems that different men are not guarded by different angels.

On the contrary, On the text, *Their angels in heaven*, etc. (*Matt.* viii. 10), Jerome says: *Great is the dignity of souls, for each one to have an angel deputed to guard it from its birth.*[4]

I answer that, Each man has an angel guardian appointed to him. This rests upon the fact that the guardianship of angels belongs to the execution of divine providence concerning men. But God's providence acts differently as regards men and as regards other corruptible creatures, for the are related differently to incorruptibility. For men are incorruptible not only in the common species, but also in the proper forms of each individual, which are the rational souls; and this cannot be said of other and corruptible things. Now it is manifest that the providence of God is chiefly exercised towards what remains forever; whereas as regards things which pass away, the providence of God acts so as to order their existence to the things which are perpetual. Hence, the providence of God is related to each man as it is to every genus or species of things corruptible. But, according to Gregory,[5] the different orders are deputed to the different *genera of things*, for

1. 参见 *De Cael. Hier.*, IV, 3 (PG 3, 181).
2. 参见 Q. 50, a. 4.
3. 参见 *De Cael. Hier.*, X, 2; 3 (PG 3, 273).
4. 参见 *In Matt.*, III, super XVIII, 10 (PL 26, 135).
5. 参见 *In Evang.*, II, hom. 34 (PL 76, 1251).

instance, the *Powers* to coerce the demons, the *Virtues* to work miracles in corporeal things; and it is also probable that the different species are presided over by different angels of the same order. Hence it is likewise reasonable to suppose that different angels are appointed to the guardianship of different men.

Reply Obj. 1. A guardian may be assigned to a man for two reasons: first, inasmuch as a man is an individual, and thus to one man one guardian is due; and sometimes several are appointed to guard one. Secondly, inasmuch as a man is part of a community, and thus one man is appointed as guardian of a whole community, to whom it belongs to oversee what concerns the individual man in his relation to the whole community, namely, external works, which are sources of strength or weakness to others. But angel guardians are given to men also as regards invisible and hidden things, pertaining to the salvation of each one in himself. Hence individual angels are appointed to guard individual men.

Reply Obj. 2. As was stated above, all the angels of the first hierarchy are, as to some things, illumined by God directly;[1] but, as to other things, only the superior are directlv illumined by God, and these reveal them to the inferior. And the same also applies to the inferior orders. For a lower angel is illumined in some respects by one of the highest, and in other respects by the one immediately above him. Thus it is possible that some one angel illumines a man immediately, and yet has other angels beneath him whom he illumines.

Reply Obj. 3. Although men are equal in nature, still inequality exists among them according as divine providence orders some to the greater, and others to the lesser things, according to *Ecclus.* xxxiii. 11, 12: *With much knowledge the Lord hath divided them, and diversified their ways: some of them hath He blessed and exalted, and some of them hath He*

1. 参见 Q. 112, a. 3, ad 4.

cursed and brought low. Thus it is a greater office to guard one man than another.

Third Article
WHETHER TO GUARD MEN BELONGS ONLY TO THE LOWEST ORDER OF ANGELS?

We proceed thus to the Third Article:—

Objection 1. It would seem that the guardianship of men does not belong only to the lowest order of the angels. For Chrysostom says that the text (*Matt.* xviii. 10) *Their angels in heaven*, etc., is understood, not of any angels, but of the highest.[1] Therefore the highest angels guard men.

Obj. 2. Further, the Apostle says that angels *are sent to minister for them who shall receive the inheritance of salvation* (*Heb.* i. 14); and thus it seems that the mission of the angels is directed to the guardianship of men. But five orders are sent in external ministry.[2] Therefore all the angels of the five orders are deputed to the guardianship of men.

Obj. 3. Further, for the guardianship of men it seems especially necessary to coerce the demons, which belongs most of all to the *Powers*, according to Gregory;[3] and to work miracles, which belongs to the *Virtues*. Therefore these orders are also deputed to the work of guardianship, and not only the lowest order.

On the contrary, In a *Psalm* (xc. 11), the guardianship of men is attributed to the *Angels*, who belong to the lowest order, according to Dionysius.[4]

I answer that, As was stated above, man is guarded in two ways.

---

1. 参见 *In Matt.*, hom. LIX, super XVIII, 10 (PG 58, 579).
2. 参见 Q. 112, a. 4.
3. 参见 *In Evang.*, II, hom. 34 (PL 76, 1251).
4. 参见 *De Cael. Hier.*, IX, 2 (PG 3, 260).

In one way by particular guardianship, according as to each man an angel is appointed to guard him; and such guardianship belongs to the lowest order of the angels, whose place it is, according to Gregory, to announce the *lesser things*.[1] For it seems to be the least of the angelic offices to procure what concerns the salvation of only one man. The other kind of guardianship is universal, multiplied according to the different orders. For the more universal an agent is, the higher it is. Thus, the guardianship of the human race belongs to the order of *Principalities*, or perhaps to the *Archangels*, whom we call the *angel princes*. Hence, Michael, whom we call an archangel, is also called *one of the princes* (*Dan*. x. 13). Moreover, all corporeal natures are guarded by the *Virtues*; and likewise the demons by the *Powers*, and the good spirits by the *Principalities* or *Dominationsy*, according to Gregory's opinion.[2]

Reply Obj. 1. Chrysostom can be taken to mean the highest within the lowest order of angels; for, as Dionysius says, in each order there are first, middle, and last.[3] It is, however, probable that the greater angels are deputed to keep those chosen by God for the higher degree of glory.

Reply Obj. 2. Not all the angels who are sent have guardianship of individual men; but some orders have a universal guardianship, greater or less, as was explained above.

Reply Obj. 3. Even inferior angels exercise the offices of the superior, inasmuch as they share in their gifts, and are executors of the superiors' power; and in this way all the angels of the lowest order can coerce the demons, and work miracles.

Fourth Article
WHETHER ANGELS ARE APPOINTED TO THE GUARDIANSHIP

1. 参见 *In Evang.*, II, hom. 34 (PL 76, 1250).
2. 同上 (PL 76, 1251).
3. 参见 *De Cael. Hier.*, X, 2 (PG 3, 273).

OF ALL MEN?

We proceed thus to the Fourth Article:—

Objection 1. It would seem that angels are not appointed to the guardianship of all men. For it is written of Christ (*Phil.* ii. 7) that He was *made in the likeness of men, and in habit found as a man*. If therefore angels are appointed to the guardianship of all men, Christ also would have had an angel guardian. But this is unseemly, for Christ is greater than all the angels. Therefore angels are not appointed to the guardianship of all men.

Obj. 2. Further, Adam was the first of all men. But it was not fitting that he should have an angel guardian, at least in the state of innocence; for then he was not beset by any dangers. Therefore angels are not appointed to the guardianship of all men.

Obj. 3. Further, angels are appointed to the guardianship of men, that they may take them by the hand and guide them to eternal life, encourage them to good works, and protect them against the assaults of the demons. But men who are foreknown to damnation never attain to eternal life. Unbelievers also, though at times they perform good works, do not perform them well, for they have not a right intention; for *faith directs the intention*, as Augustine says.[1] Moreover, the coming of Antichrist will be *according to the working of Satan*, as it is written (*2 Thess.* ii. 9). Therefore angels are not deputed to the guardianship of all men.

On the contrary is the authority of Jerome quoted above, who says that *each soul has an angel appointed to guard it*.[2]

I answer that, Man while in this state of life, is, as it were, on a road by which he should journey towards heaven. On this road man is threatened by many dangers both from within and from without,

---

1. 参见 *Enarr. in Psalm.*, ps. XXXI, Enarr. ii (PL 36, 259).
2. 参见 *In Matt.*, III, super XVIII, 10 (PL 26, 135).

according to *Ps.* clxi. 4: *In this way wherein I walked, they have hidden a snare for me.* And therefore as guardians are appointed for men who have to pass by an unsafe road, so an angel guardian is assigned to each man as long as he is a wayfarer. When, however, he arrives at the end of life, he no longer has a guardian angel; but in the kingdom he will have an angel to reign with him, in hell a demon to punish him.

Reply Obj. 1. Christ as man was guided immediately by the Word of God, and therefore needed not to be guarded by an angel. Again, as regards His soul, He was a comprehensor, although in regard to His passible body, he was a wayfarer. In this latter respect it was right that He should have, not a guardian angel as superior to Him, but a ministering angel as inferior to Him. Whence it is written (*Matt.* iv. 11) that *angels came and ministered to Him.*

Reply Obj. 2. In the state of innocence, man was not threatened by any peril from within, because within him all was well ordered, as we have said above.[1] But peril threatened from without because of the snares of the demons, as was proved by the event. For this reason he needed a guardian angel.

Reply Obj. 3. Just as the foreknown, the unbelievers, and even Antichrist, are not deprived of the interior help of natural reason, so neither are they deprived of that exterior help granted by God to the whole human race,—namely, the guardianship of the angels. And although the help which they receive therefrom does not result in their deserving eternal life by good works, it does nevertheless conduce to their being protected from certain evils which would hurt both themselves and others. For even the demons are held off by the good angels, lest they hurt as much as they would. In like manner Antichrist will not do as much harm as he would wish.

---

1. 参见 Q. 95, a. 1 and 3.

Fifth Article

WHETHER AN ANGEL IS APPOINTED TO GUARD A MAN FROM HIS BIRTH?

We proceed thus to the Fifth Article:—

Objection 1. It would seem that an angel is not appointed to guard a man from his birth. For angels are *sent to minister for them who shall receive the inheritance of salvation*, as the Apostle says (*Heb.* i. 14). But men begin to receive the inheritance of salvation when they are baptized. Therefore an angel is appointed to guard a man from the time of his baptism, not of his birth.

Obj. 2. Further, men are guarded by angels in as far as angels illumine them by teaching. But children are not capable of instruction as soon as they are born, for they have not the use of reason. Therefore angels are not appointed to guard children as soon as they are born.

Obj. 3. Further, a child has a rational soul for some time before birth, just as well as after. But it does not appear that an angel is appointed to guard a child before its birth, for they are not then admitted to the sacraments of the Church. Therefore angels are not appointed to guard men from the moment of their birth.

On the contrary, Jerome says that *each soul has an angel appointed to guard it from its birth.*[1]

I answer that, As Origen observes, there are two opinions on this matter.[2] For some have held that the angel guardian is appointed at the time of baptism, others, that he is appointed at the time of birth. The latter opinion Jerome approves, and with reason. For those benefits which are conferred by God on man as a Christian begin with his baptism; such as receiving the Eucharist, and the like. But those

1. 参见 *In Matt.*, III, super XVIII, 10 (PL 26, 135).
2. 参见 *In Matt.*, tr. XIII (PG 13, 1165).

benefits which are conferred by God on man as a rational being are bestowed on him at his birth, for then it is that he receives that nature. Among the latter benefits we must count the guardianship of angels, as we have said above. Therefore, from the very moment of his birth man has an angel guardian appointed to him.

Reply Obj. 1. Angels are sent to minister, and that efficaciously, only for those who shall receive the inheritance of salvation, if we consider the ultimate effect of their guardianship, which is the realizing of that inheritance. But for all that, the angelic ministrations are not withdrawn from others, even though they are not so efficacious as to bring them to salvation. Efficacious, nevertheless, they are, inasmuch as they ward off many evils.

Reply Obj. 2. Guardianship is ordained to illumination by instruction, as to its ultimate and principal effect. Nevertheless, it has many other effects consistent with childhood, for instance, to ward off the demons, and to prevent both bodily and spiritual harm.

Reply Obj. 3. As long as the child is in the mother's womb, it is not entirely separate, but by reason of a certain intimate tie is still part of her; just as the fruit while hanging on the tree is part of the tree. And therefore it can be said, with some degree of probability, that the angel who guards the mother guards the child while in the womb. But when the child becomes separate from the mother at birth, an angel guardian is appointed to it, as Jerome says.[1]

Sixth Article
WHETHER THE ANGEL GUARDIAN EVER FORSAKES A MAN?

We proceed thus to the Sixth Article:—

---

1. 参见 *In Matt.*, III, super XVIII, 10 (PL 26, 135).

Objection 1. It would seem that the angel guardian sometimes forsakes the man whom he is appointed to guard. For it is said (*Jer.* li. 9) in the person of the angels: *We would have cured Babylon, but she is not healed: let us forsake her.* And (*Isa.* v. 5) it is written: *I will take away the hedge* —that is, *the guardianship of the angels*, according to the *Gloss*[1] —*and it shall be wasted.*

Obj. 2. Further, God's guardianship excels that of the angels. But God forsakes man at times, according to *Ps.* xxi. 2: *O God, my God, look upon me: why hast Thou forsaken me?* Much more therefore does an angel guardian forsake man.

Obj. 3. Further, according to Damascene, *When the angels are here with us, they are not in heaven.*[2] But sometimes they are in heaven. Therefore sometimes they forsake us.

On the contrary, The demons are ever assailing us, according to *1 Pet.* v. 8: *Your adversary the devil, as a roaring lion, goeth about, seeking whom he may devour.* All the more therefore do the good angels ever guard us.

I answer that, As appears above, the guardianship of the angels is an effect of divine providence in regard to man. Now it is evident that neither man, nor anything at all, is entirely withdrawn from the providence of God; for in as far as a thing participates being, so far is it subject to the providence that extends over all being. So God is said to forsake man, according to the ordering of His providence, only in so far as He allows man to suffer some defect of punishment or of fault. In like manner, it must be said that the angel guardian never forsakes a man entirely; but sometimes he leaves him in some particular, for instance, by not preventing him from being subject to some trouble, or even from falling into sin, according to the ordering of the divine judgments. In this sense Babylon and the House of Israel are said to have been forsaken by the angels, because their angel guardians did

1. 参见 *Glossa interl.*, super *Isaias*, V, 5 (IV, 14r).
2. 参见 *De Fide Orth.*, II, 3 (PG 94, 869).

not prevent them from being subject to tribulation.

From this the answers are clear to the first and second objections.

Reply Obj. 3. Although an angel may forsake a man sometimes locally, he does not for that reason forsake him as to the effect of his guardianship, for even when he is in heaven he knows what is happening to man; nor does he need time for his local motion, for he can be with man in an instant.

Seventh Article

WHETHER ANGELS GRIEVE FOR THE ILLS OF THOSE WHOM THEY GUARD?

We proceed thus to the Seventh Article:—

Objection 1. It would seem that angels grieve for the ills of those whom they guard. For it is written (*Isa.* xxxiii. 7): *The angels of peace shall weep bitterly.* But weeping is a sign of grief and sorrow. Therefore angels grieve for the ills of those whom they guard.

Obj. 2. Further, according to Augustine, *sorrow is for those things that happen against our will.*[1] But the loss of the man whom he has guarded is against the guardian angel's will. Therefore angels grieve for the loss of men.

Obj. 3. Further, as sorrow is contrary to joy, so penance is contrary to sin. But angels rejoice about one sinner doing penance, as we are told in *Luke* xv. 7. Therefore they grieve for the just man who falls into sin.

Obj. 4. Further, on *Numbers* xviii. 12 (*Whatsoever first-fruits they offer,* etc.) the *Gloss* of Origen says: *The angels are brought to judgment as to whether men have fallen through their negligence or through their own fault.*[2] But it is reasonable for anyone to grieve for the ills which have brought

1. 参见 *De Civit. Dei*, XIV, 15 (PL 41, 424).
2. 参见 Cf. *In Num.*, hom. XI (PG 12, 647).

him to judgment. Therefore angels grieve for men's sins.

On the contrary, Where there is grief and sorrow, there is not perfect happiness. And so it is written: *Death shall be no more, nor mourning, nor crying, nor sorrow* (*Apoc.* xxi. 4). But the angels are perfectly happy. Therefore they have no cause for grief.

I answer that, Angels do not grieve, either for the sins or for the pains of men. For grief and sorrow, according to Augustine, are for those things which occur against our will.[1] But nothing happens in the world contrary to the will of the angels and the other blessed, because their will cleaves entirely to the ordering of divine justice; and nothing happens in the world save what is effected or permitted by divine justice. Therefore, absolutely speaking, nothing occurs in the world against the will of the blessed. For as the Philosopher says,[2] that is called unreservedly voluntary which a man wills in a particular case, and at a particular time, having considered all the circumstances. And yet, universally speaking, such a thing might not have been voluntary; and thus the sailor does not will the casting of his cargo into the sea, considered universally and absolutely, but because of the threatened danger to his life he wills it. Therefore this is voluntary rather than involuntary, as is stated in the same passage. Therefore, universally and absolutely speaking, the angels do not will the sins and the pains of men; but they do will the fulfillment of the ordering of divine justice in this matter, in respect of which some are subjected to pains and are allowed to fall into sin.

Reply Obj. 1. These words of Isaias may be understood of the angels, *i.e.*, the messengers, of Ezechias, who wept because of the words of Rabsaces, as related *Isa.* xxxvii. 2 *seqq.* This would be the literal sense. According to the allegorical sense, the *angels of peace* are the apostles and preachers who weep for men's sins. If according to the anagogical

1. 参见 *De Civit. Dei*, XIV, 15 (PL 41, 424).
2. 参见 *Eth.*, III, 1 (1110a 9).

sense this passage be expounded of the blessed angels, then the expression is metaphorical, and signifies that universally speaking the angels will the salvation of mankind; for it is only metaphorically that we attribute passions to God and the angels.

The reply to the second objection appears from what has been said.

Reply Obj. 3. Both in man's repentance and in man's sin there remains one reason for the angel's joy, namely, the fulfillment of the ordering of the divine providence.

Reply Obj. 4. The angels are brought into judgment for the sins of men, not as guilty, but as witnesses to convict man of weakness.

Eighth Article

WHETHER THERE CAN BE STRIFE OR DISCORD AMONG THE ANGELS?

We proceed thus to the Eighth Article:—

Objection 1. It would seem that there can be strife or discord among the angels. For it is written (*Job* xxv. 2): *Who maketh peace in His high places.* But strife is opposed to peace. Therefore among the high angels there is no strife.

Obj. 2. Further, where there is perfect charity and just authority there can be no strife. But all this exists among the angels. Therefore there is no strife among the angels.

Obj. 3. Further, if we say that angels strive for those whom they guard, one angel must needs take one side, and another angel the opposite side. But if one side is in the right the other side is in the wrong. It will follow, therefore, that a good angel is a compounder of wrong; which is unseemly. Therefore there is no strife among good angels.

On the contrary, It is written in the person of Gabriel (*Dan.* x. 13): *The prince of the kingdom of the Persians resisted me one and twenty days.* But this prince of the Persians was the angel deputed to the guardianship of the kingdom of the Persians. Therefore one good angel resists the others; and thus there is strife among them.

I answer that, This question is occasioned by the above words of Daniel.[1] Jerome explains it by saying that the prince of the kingdom of the Persians is the angel who opposed the setting free of the people of Israel, for whom Daniel was praying, whose prayers were being offered to God by Gabriel.[2] And this resistance of his may have been caused by some prince of the demons having led the Jewish captives in Persia into sin; which sin was an impediment to the efficacy of the prayer which Daniel put up for that same people.

But according to Gregory, the prince of the kingdom of Persia was a good angel appointed to the guardianship of that kingdom.[3] To see therefore how one angel can be said to resist another, we must note that the divine judgments in regard to various kingdoms and various men are executed by the angels. Now in their actions the angels are ruled by the divine judgment. But it happens at times in various kingdoms or various men that there are contrary merits or demerits, so that one of them is subject to or placed over another. As to what is the ordering of divine wisdom on such matters, the angels cannot know it unless God reveal it to them; and so they need to consult divine wisdom thereupon. Hence, inasmuch as they consult the divine will concerning various contrary and opposing merits, they are said to resist one another. This does not mean that their wills are in opposition, since they are all of one mind as to the fulfillment of the divine judgment; but that the things about which they seek knowledge are in opposition.

From this the answers to the objections are clear.

---

1. 参见 Cf. Alex, of Hales, *Summa Theol.*, II, I, no. 223 (II, 277).
2. 参见 *In Dan.*, super X, 13 (PL 25, 581).
3. 参见 *Moral.*, XVII, 12 (PL 76, 19).

Question CXIV
THE ASSAULTS OF THE DEMONS
(*In Five Articles*)

WE now consider the assaults of the demons. Under this head there are five points of inquiry: (1) Whether men are assailed by the demons? (2) Whether to tempt is proper to the devil? (3) Whether all the sins of men are to be set down to the assaults or temptations of the demons? (4) Whether they can work real miracles for the purpose of leading men astray? (5) Whether the demons who are overcome by men are hindered from making further assaults?

First Article
WHETHER MEN ARE ASSAILED BY THE DEMONS?

We proceed thus to the First Article:—

Objection 1. It would seem that men are not assailed by the demons. For angels are sent by God to guard man. But demons are not sent by God, for the demons' intention is the loss of souls, whereas God's is the salvation of souls. Therefore demons are not deputed to assail man.

Obj. 2. Further, it is not a fair fight for the weak to be set against the strong, and the ignorant against the astute. But men are weak and ignorant, whereas the demons are strong and astute. It is not therefore to be permitted by God, the author of all justice, that men should be assailed by demons.

Obj. 3. Further, the assaults of the flesh and the world are enough for man's exercise. But God permits His elect to be assailed that they may be exercised. Therefore there is no need for them to be assailed by the demons.

On the contrary, The Apostle says (*Ephes.* vi. 12): *Our wrestling is not against flesh and blood, but against Principalities and Powers, against the rulers of the world of this darkness, against the spirits of wickedness in the high places.*

I answer that, Two things may be considered in the assault of the demons—the assault itself, and its ordering. The assault itself is due to the malice of the demons, who through envy endeavor to hinder man's progress, and through pride usurp a semblance of divine power, by deputing certain ministers to assail man, even as the angels of God in their various offices minister to man's salvation. But the ordering of the assault is from God, Who knows how to make orderly use of evil by ordering it to good. On the other hand, in regard to the angels, both their guardianship and its ordering are to be referred to God as their first author.

Reply Obj. 1. The wicked angels assail men in two ways. First, by instigating them to sin; and thus they are not sent by God to assail us, but are sometimes permitted to do so according to God's just judgments. But sometimes their assault is a punishment to man; and thus they are sent by God, as the lying spirit was sent to punish Achab, King of Israel, as is related in *3 Kings* (xxii. 20). For punishment is referred to God as its first author. Nevertheless the demons, who are sent to punish, do so with an intention other than that for which they are sent; for they punish from hatred or envy, whereas they are sent by God because of His justice.

Reply Obj. 2. In order that the conditions of the fight be not unequal, there is for man the promised recompense, to be gained principally through the grace of God, secondarily through the guardianship of the angels. Therefore, Eliseus said to his servant (*4 Kings* vi. 16): *Fear not, for there are more with us than with them.*

Reply Obj. 3. The assault of the flesh and the world would suffice for the exercise of human weakness; but it does not suffice for the demon's malice, which makes use of both the above in assailing men. But by the divine ordinance this tends to the glory of the elect.

Second Article
WHETHER TO TEMPT IS PROPER TO THE DEVIL?

We proceed thus to the Second Article:—

Objection 1. It would seem that to tempt is not proper to the devil. For God is said to tempt, according to *Genesis* xxii. 1, *God tempted Abraham.* Moreover, man is tempted by the flesh and the world. Again, man is said to tempt God, and to tempt man. Therefore it is not proper to the devil to tempt.

Obj. 2. Further, to tempt is a sign of ignorance. But the demons know what happens among men. Therefore the demons do not tempt.

Obj. 3. Further, temptation is the road to sin. Now sin dwells in the will. Since therefore the demons cannot change man's will, as appears from what has been said above,[1] it seems that it is not in their province to tempt.

On the contrary, It is written (*1 Thess.* iii. 5): *Lest perhaps he that tempteth should have tempted you*; to which the *Gloss* adds, *that is, the devil, whose office it is to tempt.*[2]

I answer that, To tempt is, properly speaking, to make trial of something. Now we make trial of something in order to know something about it, and hence the immediate end of every tempter is knowledge. But sometimes another end, either good or bad, is sought to be acquired through that knowledge: a good end, when, for instance, one desires to know of someone, what sort of a man he is as to knowledge, or virtue, with a view to his promotion; a bad

1. 参见 Q. 111, a. 2.
2. 参见 *Glossa interl.* (VI, 110v).

end, when that knowledge is sought with the purpose of deceiving or ruining him.

From this we can gather how various beings are said to tempt in various ways. For man is said to tempt, sometimes, merely for the sake of knowing something; and for this reason it is a sin to tempt God, since man, being as it were uncertain, presumes to make an experiment of God's power. Sometimes, too, he tempts in order to help; sometimes in order to hurt. The devil, however, always tempts in order to hurt by urging man into sin. In this sense it is said to be his proper office to tempt; for though at times man tempts thus, he does this as minister of the devil. God is said to tempt that He may know, in the same sense as that is said to know which makes others to know. Hence it is written (*Deut.* xiii. 3): *The Lord your God trieth you, that it may appear whether you love Him.*

The flesh and the world are said to tempt as the instruments or matter of temptations, inasmuch as one can know what sort of a man someone is according as he follows or resists the desires of the flesh, and according as he despises worldly advantages and adversity; of which things the devil also makes use in tempting.

Thus the reply to the first objection is clear.

Reply Obj. 2. The demons know what happens outwardly among men; but the inward disposition of man God alone knows, Who is the *weigher of spirits* (*Prov.* xvi. 2). It is this disposition that makes man more prone to one vice than to another. Hence the devil tempts in order to explore this inward disposition of man, so that he may tempt him to that vice to which he is most prone.

Reply Obj. 3. Although a demon cannot change the will, yet, as was stated above,[1] he can change the inferior powers of man, in a certain degree; and by these powers, though the will cannot be forced, it can

---

1. 参见 Q. 111, a. 3 and 4.

nevertheless be inclined.

Third Article
WHETHER ALL SINS ARE DUE TO THE TEMPTATION OF THE DEVIL?

We proceed thus to the Third Article:—

Objection 1. It would seem that all sins are due to the temptation of the devil. For Dionysius says that *the multitude of demons is the cause of all evils, both to themselves and to others.*[1] And Damascene says that *all malice and all uncleanness have been devised by the devil.*[2]

Obj. 2. Further, of every sinner can be said what the Lord said of the Jews (*Jo.* viii. 44): *You are of your father the devil.* But this was in as far as they sinned through the devil's instigation. Therefore every sin is due to the devil's instigation.

Obj. 3. Further, as angels are deputed to guard men, so demons are deputed to assail men. But every good thing we do is due to the suggestion of the good angels, because the divine gifts are borne to us by the angels. Therefore all the evil we do is due to the instigation of the devil.

On the contrary, It is written: *Not all our evil thoughts are stirred up by the devil, but sometimes they arise from the movement of our free choice.*[3]

I answer that, One thing can be the cause of another in two ways, directly and indirectly. Indirectly, as, when an agent is the cause of a disposition to a certain effect, it is said to be the occasional and indirect cause of that effect. For instance, we might say that he who dries the wood is the cause of the wood burning. In this way we must admit that the devil is the cause of all our sins, because it was he

1. 参见 *De Div. Nom.*, IV, 18 (PG 3, 716).
2. 参见 *De Fide Orth.*, II, 4 (PG 94, 877).
3. 参见 Gennadius, *De Eccles. Dogm.*, LXXXII (PL 58, 999).

who instigated the first man to sin, from whose sin there resulted a proneness to sin in the whole human race. And in this sense we must take the words of Damascene[1] and Dionysius.[2]

But a thing is said to be the direct cause of something when its action tends directly to it. And in this way the devil is not the cause of every sin, for not all sins are committed at the devil's instigation, but some are due to free choice and the corruption of the flesh. For, as Origen says,[3] even if there were no devil, men would have the desire for food and sex and such pleasures, with regard to which many disorders may arise unless those desires be curbed by reason, especially if we presuppose the corruption of our natures. Now it is in the power of free choice to curb this appetite and keep it in order. Consequently there is no need for all sins to be due to the instigation of the devil. But those sins which are due to the devil's instigation man perpetrates *through being deceived by the same blandishments*[4] *as were our first parents*, as Isidore says.[5]

Thus the answer to the first objection is clear.

Reply Obj. 2. When man commits sin without being thereto instigated by the devil, he nevertheless becomes a child of the devil by it, in so far as he imitates him who was the first to sin.

Reply Obj. 3. Man can of his own accord fall into sin, but he cannot advance towards merit without the divine assistance, which is borne to man by the ministry of the angels. For this reason the angels take part in all our good works, whereas all our sins are not due to the demons' instigation. Nevertheless there is no kind of sin which is not sometimes due to the demons' suggestion.

---

1. 参见 *De Fide Orth.*, II, 4 (PG 94, 877).
2. 参见 *De Div. Nom.*, IV, 18 (PG 3, 716).
3. 参见 *Peri Archon*, III, 2 (PG 11, 305).
4. blandishments: 奉承；讨好
5. 参见 *Sent.*, III, 5 (PL 83, 664).

Fourth Article
WHETHER DEMONS CAN LEAD MEN ASTRAY BY MEANS OF REAL MIRACLES?

We proceed thus to the Fourth Article:—

Objection 1. It would seem that the demons cannot lead men astray by means of real miracles. For the activity of the demons will show itself especially in the works of Antichrist. But as the Apostle says (*2 Thess.* ii. 9), his *coming is according to the working of Satan, in all power, and signs, and lying wonders.* Much more therefore at other times do the demons perform lying wonders.

Obj. 2. Further, true miracles are wrought by some corporeal change. But demons are unable to change the nature of a body, for Augustine says: *I cannot believe that the human body can receive the members of a beast by means of a demon's art or power.*[1] Therefore the demons cannot work real miracles.

Obj. 3. Further, an argument is useless which may prove both ways. If therefore real miracles can be wrought by demons to persuade one of what is false, they will be useless to confirm the teaching of faith. This is unfitting, for it is written (*Mark* xvi. 20): *The Lord working withal, and confirming the word with signs that followed.*

On the contrary, Augustine says: *Often by means of the magic art miracles are wrought like those which are wrought by the servants of God.*[2]

I answer that, As is clear from what has been said above, if we take a miracle in the strict sense, the demons cannot work miracles, nor can any creature, but God alone;[3] for in the strict sense, a miracle is something done outside the order of the entire created nature, under

1. 参见 *De Civit. Dei*, XVIII, 18 (PL, 41, 575).
2. 参见 Pseudo-Augustine, *Viginti unius Sent.*, IV (PL 40, 726).
3. 参见 Q. 110, a. 4.

which order every power of a creature is contained. But sometimes miracle may be taken, in a wide sense, for whatever exceeds human power and experience. And thus demons can work miracles, that is, things which rouse man's astonishment, by reason of their being beyond his power and outside his sphere of knowledge. For even a man, by doing what is beyond the power and knowledge of another, leads him to marvel at what he has done, so that in a way he seems to that man to have worked a miracle.

It is to be noted, however, that although these works of demons which appear marvellous to us are not real miracles, they are sometimes nevertheless something real. Thus the magicians of Pharaoh by the demons' power produced real serpents and frogs (*Exod.* vii. 12; viii. 7). And *when fire came down from heaven and at one blow consumed Job's servants and sheep, when the storm struck down his house and with it his children — these were the work of Satan, not phantoms*, as Augustine says.[1]

Reply Obj. 1. As Augustine says, in the same place, the works of Antichrist may be called lying wonders *either because he will deceive men's senses by means of phantoms, so that he will not really do what he will seem to do; or because, if he work real prodigies, they will lead those into falsehood who believe in him.*[2]

Reply Obj. 2. As we have said above,[3] corporeal matter does not obey either good or bad angels at their will, so that demons could by their power transmute matter from one form to another; but they can employ certain seminal principles that exist in the elements of the world in order to produce these effects, as Augustine says.[4] Therefore it must be admitted that all the transformations of corporeal things which can be produced by certain natural powers, to which we must

1. 参见 *De Civit. Dei*, XX, 19 (PL 41, 687).
2. 同上
3. 参见 Q. 110, a. 2.
4. 参见 *De Trin.*, III, 8; 9 (PL 42, 875; 877).

assign the seminal principles above mentioned, can be produced by the operation of the demons, by the employment of these principles; such as the transformation of certain things into serpents or frogs, which can be produced by putrefaction. On the contrary, those transformations of bodies which cannot be produced by the power of nature, cannot in reality be effected by the operation of the demons; for instance, that the human body be changed into the body of a beast, or that the body of a dead man return to life. And if at times something of this sort seems to be effected by the operation of demons, it is not real but a mere semblance of reality.

Now this may happen in two ways. First, from within. In this way a demon can work on man's imagination and even on his corporeal senses, so that something seems otherwise than it is, as was explained above.[1] It is said indeed that this can be done sometimes by the power of certain bodies. Secondly, from without. For just as from air he can form a body of any form and shape, and assume it so as to appear in it visibly, so, in the same way he can clothe any corporeal thing with any corporeal form, so as to appear therein. This is what Augustine says: *Man's imagination, which, whether thinking or dreaming, takes the forms of an innumerable number of things, appears to other men's senses as it were embodied in the semblance of some animal.*[2] This is not to be understood as though the imagination itself or the images formed therein were identified with that which appears embodied to the senses of another man; but that the demon, who forms an image in a man's imagination, can offer the same picture to another man's senses.

Reply Obj. 3. As Augustine says: *When magicians do what holy men do, they do it for a different end and by a different law. The former do it for their own glory, the latter, for the glory of God; the former, by certain private compacts, the latter by the evident assistance and command of God, to Whom*

---

1. 参见 Q. 111, a. 3 and 4.
2. 参见 *De Civit. Dei*, XVIII, 18 (PL 41, 575).

every creature is subject.[1]

Fifth Article

WHETHER A DEMON, WHO IS OVERCOME BY MAN, IS FOR THIS REASON HINDERED FROM MAKING FURTHER ASSAULTS?

We proceed thus to the Fifth Article:—

Objection 1. It would seem that a demon, who is overcome by a man, is not for that reason hindered from any further assault. For Christ overcame the tempter most effectively. Yet afterwards the demon assailed Him by instigating the Jews to kill Him. Therefore it is not true that the devil when conquered ceases his assaults.

Obj. 2. Further, to inflict punishment on one who has been worsted in a fight is to incite him to a sharper attack. But this is not befitting God's mercy. Therefore the conquered demons are not prevented from further assaults.

On the contrary, It is written (*Matt.* iv. 11): *Then the devil left Him*, *i.e.*, Christ Who overcame him.

I answer that, Some say that when once a demon has been overcome he can no more tempt any man at all, neither to the same nor to any other sin.[2] And others say that he can tempt others, but not the same man.[3] This seems more probable as long as we understand it to be so for a certain definite time; and so it is written (*Luke* iv. 13): *All temptation being ended, the devil departed from Him for a time.* There are two reasons for this. One is on the part of God's clemency. For as Chrysostom says, *the devil does not tempt man for just as long as he likes, but for as long as God allows; for although He allows him to tempt for a short time,*

---

1. 参见 *Lib. 83 Quaest.*, q. 79 (PL 40, 92).
2. 参见 Origen, *In Lib. Iesu Nave*, hom. XV (PG 12, 903).
3. 参见 Cited anonymously by St. Albert, *In II Sent.*, d. vi, a. 9 (XXVII, 138).

He orders him off because of our weakness.[1] The other reason is taken from the astuteness of the devil. As to this, Ambrose says on *Luke* iv. 13: *The devil is afraid of persisting, because he shrinks from frequent defeat.*[2] That the devil does nevertheless sometimes return to the assault is apparent from *Matthew* xii. 44: *I will return into my house from whence I came out.*

From what has been said, the objections can easily be solved.

1. 参见 *In Matt.*, hom. XIII (PG 57, 214).
2. 参见 *In Lucam*, IV, super IV, 13 (PL 15, 1707).

Question CXV
THE ACTION OF THE CORPOREAL CREATURE
(*In Six Articles*)

WE have now to consider the action of the corporeal creature, and fate, which is ascribed to certain bodies.[1] Concerning corporeal actions there are six points of inquiry: (1) Whether a body can be active? (2) Whether there exist in bodies certain seminal principles? (3) Whether the heavenly bodies are the causes of what is done here by the inferior bodies? (4) Whether they are the cause of human acts? (5) Whether demons are subject to their influence? (6) Whether the heavenly bodies impose necessity on those things which are subject to their influence?

First Article
WHETHER A BODY CAN BE ACTIVE?

We proceed thus to the First Article:—

Objection 1. It would seem that no bodies are active. For Augustine says: *There are things that are acted upon, but do not act, such are bodies; there is one Who acts but is not acted upon, and this is God; there are things that both act and are acted upon, and these are the spiritual substances.*[2]

Obj. 2. Further, every agent except the first agent requires in its work a subject susceptible of its action. But *there is no substance below the corporeal substance which can be susceptible of the latter's action, since it*

1. 参见 Q. 116.
2. 参见 *De Civit. Dei*, V, 9 (PL 41, 151).

belongs to the lowest degree in beings.[1] Therefore corporeal substance is not active.

Obj. 3. Further, every corporeal substance is limited by quantity. But *quantity hinders substance from movement and action, because it surrounds it and penetrates it*; just as a cloud hinders the air from receiving light. *A sign of this is that the more a body increases in quantity, the heavier it is and the more difficult to move.*[2] Therefore no corporeal substance is active.

Obj. 4. Further, the power of action in every agent is according to its propinquity to the first active cause. But *bodies, being most composite, are most remote from the first active cause, which is most simple.*[3] Therefore no bodies are active.

Obj. 5. Further, if a body is an agent, the term of its action is either a substantial, or an accidental, form. But it is not a substantial form, for it is not possible to find in a body any principle of action, save an active quality, which is an accident; and an accident cannot be the cause of a substantial form, since the cause is always more excellent than the effect. Likewise, neither is it an accidental form, for *an accident does not extend beyond its subject*, as Augustine says.[4] Therefore no bodies are active.

On the contrary, Dionysius says that among other qualities of corporeal fire, *it shows its greatness in its action and power on that of which it lays hold.*[5]

I answer that, It is apparent to the senses that some bodies are active. But concerning the action of bodies there have been three errors. For some denied all action to bodies. This is the opinion of Avicebron in his book *The Fount of Life*, where, by the arguments mentioned above,

---

1. 参见 Avicebron, *Fons Vitae*, II, 9 (p. 40).
2. 参见 *Op. cit.*, II, 9 and 10 (p. 41).
3. 同上，10 (p. 41).
4. 参见 *De Trin.*, IX, 4 (PL 42, 963).—Cf. Maimonides, *Guide*, I, 73 (p. 124).
5. 参见 *De Cael. Hier.*, XV, 2 (PG 3, 329).

he endeavors to prove that no bodies act, but that all the actions which seem to be the actions of bodies are the actions *of some spiritual power that penetrates all bodies*;[1] so that, according to him, it is not fire that heats, but a spiritual power which penetrates, by means of the fire. This opinion seems to be derived from that of Plato. For Plato held that all forms existing in corporeal matter are participated and determined and limited to it, while the separate Forms are absolute and as it were universal.[2] Therefore he said that these separate Forms are the causes of the forms that exist in matter.[3] Therefore inasmuch as the form which is in corporeal matter is determined to this matter individuated by quantity, Avicebron held that the corporeal form is determined and limited by quantity, as the principle of individuation, so as to be unable by action to extend to any other matter; and that the spiritual and immaterial form alone, which is not limited by quantity, can proceed to act upon something else.[4]

But this does not prove that the corporeal form is not an agent, but that it is not a universal agent. For in proportion as a thing is participated, so, of necessity, must that be participated which is proper to it; and thus in proportion to the participation of light is the participation of visibility. But to act, which is nothing else than to make something to be in act, is essentially proper to an act as such; and so it is that every agent produces its like. So to the fact that it is a form not determined by matter subject to quantity, a thing owes its being an indeterminate and universal agent; but to the fact that it is determined to this matter, it owes its being a limited and particular agent. Therefore, if the form of fire were separate, as the Platonists supposed, it would be, in a fashion, the cause of every ignition. But

1. 参见 Avicebron, *Fons Vitae*, II, 10 (p. 42).
2. 参见 Cf. above, q, 84, a. 1.
3. 参见 Cf. St. Thomas, *De Pot.*, q. 3, a. 8.
4. 参见 *Fons Vitae*, II, 9 and 10 (p. 41).

this form of fire, which is in this corporeal matter, is the cause of this ignition which passes from this body to that. Hence such an action is effected by the contact of two bodies.

But this opinion of Avicebron goes further than that of Plato. For Plato held only substantial Forms to be separate,[1] while he reduced accidents to the material principles which are *the great* and *the small*, which he considered to be the first contraries,[2] even as others made these contraries to be *the rare* and *the dense*.[3] Consequently both Plato and Avicenna, who follow him to a certain extent, held that corporeal agents act through their accidental forms, by disposing matter for the substantial form; but that the ultimate perfection attained by the introduction of the substantial form is due to an immaterial principle. And this is the second opinion concerning the action of bodies (of which we have spoken above when treating of creation[4]).

The third opinion is that of Democritus, who held that action takes place through the issue of atoms from the corporeal agent, while passion consists in the reception of the atoms in the pores of the passive body. This opinion is disproved by Aristotle.[5] For it would follow that a body would not be passive as a whole, and that the quantity of the active body would be diminished through its action; which things are manifestly untrue.

We must therefore say that a body acts, according as it is in act, on another body, according as it is in potentiality.

Reply Obj. 1. This passage of Augustine is to be understood of the whole corporeal nature considered as a whole, which thus has no nature inferior to it on which it can act; as the spiritual nature acts on

---

1. 参见 Cf. Aristotle, *Metaph.*, I, 9 (990b 29).
2. 参见 Cf. Aristotle, *Phys.*, I, 4 (187a 17).
3. 参见 The opinion of the ancient physicists, according to Aristotle, *Phys.*, I, 4 (187a 15).
4. 参见 Q. 45, a. 8.—Cf. q. 65, a. 4.
5. 参见 *De Gener.*, I, 8 (325a 23).

the corporeal, and the uncreated nature on the created. Nevertheless one body is inferior to another inasmuch as it is in potentiality to that which the other has in act.

From this follows the solution of the second objection.—But it must be observed that when Avicebron argues thus, *There is a mover who is not moved, namely, the first maker of all; therefore, on the other hand, there exists something moved which is purely passive*,[1] this is to be conceded. But this latter is primary matter, which is a pure potentiality, just as God is pure act. Now a body is composed of potentiality and act; and therefore it is both active and passive.

Reply Obj. 3. Quantity does not entirely hinder the corporeal form from action, as was stated above; but quantity hinders it from being a universal agent, inasmuch as a form is individuated by being in matter subject to quantity. The proof taken from the weight of bodies is not to the point. First, because addition of quantity does not cause weight, as is proved in the *De Caelo*.[2] Secondly, because it is false that weight retards movement. On the contrary, the heavier a thing, the more it moves with its own movement. Thirdly, because action is not effected by local movement, as Democritus held, but by the fact that something is reduced from potentiality to act.

Reply Obj. 4. A body is not that which is most distant from God, for it participates something of a likeness to the divine being, inasmuch as it has a form. That which is most distant from God is primary matter, which is in no way active, since it is a pure potentiality.

Reply Obj. 5. The term of a body's action is both an accidental form and a substantial form. For the active quality, such as heat, although itself an accident, acts nevertheless by virtue of the substantial form, as its instrument; and so its action can terminate in a substantial form, just as natural heat, as the instrument of the soul, has an action

1. 参见 *Fons Vitae*, II, 10 (p. 12).
2. 参见 Aristotle, *De Caelo*, IV, 2 (308b 5).

terminating in the generation of flesh. But by its own virtue it produces an accident. Nor is it against the nature of an accident to surpass its subject in acting, but to surpass it in being; unless indeed one were to imagine that an accident transfers its identical self from the agent to the patient. In this way Democritus explained action by an issue of atoms.

Second Article
WHETHER THERE ARE ANY SEMINAL PRINCIPLES IN CORPOREAL MATTER?

We proceed thus to the Second Article:—

Objection 1. It would seem that there are no seminal principles in corporeal matter. For principle implies something of a spiritual order. But in corporeal matter nothing exists spiritually, but only materially, that is, according to the mode of that in which it is. Therefore there are no seminal principles in corporeal matter.

Obj. 2. Further, Augustine says that demons produce certain results by employing with a hidden movement certain seeds, which they know to exist in matter.[1] But bodies, not principles, can be employed with local movement. Therefore it is unreasonable to say that there are seminal principles in corporeal matter.

Obj. 3. Further, seeds are active principles. But there are no active principles in corporeal matter, since, as we have said above, matter is not competent to act. Therefore there are no seminal principles in corporeal matter.

Obj. 4. Further, there are said to be certain *causal principles* which seem to suffice for the production of things.[2] But seminal principles

1. 参见 *De Trin.*, III, 8; 9 (PL 42, 876; 878).
2. 参见 St. Bonaventure, *In II Sent.*, d. xviii, a. 1, q. 2 (II, 438).—Cf. St. Augustine, *De Genesi ad Litt.*, VI, 14 (PL 34, 349).

are not causal principles, for miracles are outside the scope of seminal principles, but not of causal principles. Therefore it is unreasonable to say that there are seminal principles in corporeal matter.

On the contrary, Augustine says: *Of all the things which are generated in a corporeal and visible fashion, certain seeds lie hidden in the corporeal things of this world.*[1]

I answer that, It is customary to name things after what is more perfect, as the Philosopher says.[2] Now in the whole corporeal nature, living bodies are the most perfect, and so even the term *nature* has been transferred from living things to all natural things. For the term itself, *nature*, as the Philosopher says, was first applied to signify the generation of living things, which is called *nativity*.[3] And because living things are generated from a principle united to them, as fruit from a tree, and the offspring from the mother, to whom it is united, consequently the term *nature* has been applied to every principle of movement existing in that which is moved. Now it is manifest that the active and passive principles of the generation of living things are the seeds from which living things are generated. Therefore Augustine fittingly gave the name *seminal principles* [*seminales rationes*] to all those active and passive virtues which are the causes of natural generation and movement.[4]

These active and passive principles may be considered in several orders. For in the first place, as Augustine says, they are principally and originally in the Word of God, as in *exemplary principles*.[5] Secondly, they are in the elements of the world, where they were produced altogether at the beginning, as in *universal causes*. Thirdly, they are

---

1. 参见 *De Trin.*, III, 8 (PL 42, 875).
2. 参见 Aristotle, *De An.*, II, 4 (416b 23).
3. 参见 *Metaph.*, IV, 4 (1014b 16).
4. 参见 *De Trin.*, III, 8 (PL 42, 875).
5. 参见 *De Genesi ad Litt.*, VI, 10 (PL 34, 346).

in those things which, in the succession of time, are produced by universal causes, for instance in this plant, and in that animal, as in *particular causes*. Fourthly, they are in the *seeds* produced from animals and plants. And these again are compared to further particular effects, as the primordial universal causes to the first effects produced.

Reply Obj. 1. These active and passive virtues of natural things, though not called principles by reason of their being in corporeal matter, can nevertheless be so called in respect of their origin, for they are derived from the divine exemplary principles.

Reply Obj. 2. These active and passive virtues are in certain parts of corporeal things; and when they are employed with local movement for the production of certain results, we speak of the demons as employing seeds.

Reply Obj. 3. The seed of the male is the active principle in the generation of an animal. But that can be called seed also which the female contributes as the passive principle. And thus the word *seed* covers both active and passive principles.

Reply Obj. 4. From the words of Augustine, when speaking of these seminal principles, it is easy to gather that they are also causal principles, just as a seed is a kind of cause; for he says that *as a mother is pregnant with the unborn offspring, so is the world itself pregnant with the causes of unborn beings.*[1] Nevertheless, the *exemplary principles* can be called *causal*, but not, strictly speaking, *seminal*, because a seed is not a separate principle, and because miracles are not wrought outside the scope of causal principles. Likewise neither are miracles wrought outside the scope of the passive virtues so implanted in the creature, that the latter can be used to any purpose that God commands. But miracles are said to be wrought outside the scope of the natural active virtues, and the passive potentialities which are ordered to such active

1. 参见 *De Trin.*, III, 9 (PL 42, 878).

virtues, and this is what is meant when we say that they are wrought outside the scope of seminal principles.

Third Article
WHETHER THE HEAVENLY BODIES ARE THE CAUSE OF WHAT IS PRODUCED IN BODIES HERE BELOW?

We proceed thus to the Third Article:—

Objection 1. It would seem that the heavenly bodies are not the cause of what is produced in bodies here below. For Damascene says: *We say that they*—namely, the heavenly bodies—*are not the cause of generation or corruption; they are rather signs of storms and atmospheric changes.*[1]

Obj. 2. Further, for the production of anything, an agent and matter suffice. But in things here below there is passive matter; and there are contrary agents—heat and cold, and the like. Therefore for the production of things here below, there is no need to ascribe causality to the heavenly bodies.

Obj. 3. Further, an agent produces its like. Now it is to be observed that everything which is produced here below is produced through the action of heat and cold, moisture and dryness, and other such qualities, which do not exist in the heavenly bodies. Therefore the heavenly bodies are not the cause of what is produced here below.

Obj. 4. Further, Augustine says: *Nothing is more corporeal than sex.*[2] But sex is not caused by the heavenly bodies. A sign of this is that of twins born under the same constellation[3], one may be male, the other female. Therefore the heavenly bodies are not the cause of things produced in bodies here below.

On the contrary, Augustine says: *Bodies of a grosser and inferior nature*

---

1. 参见 *De Fide Orth.*, II, 7 (PG 94,893).
2. 参见 *De Civit. Dei*, V, 6 (PL 41, 146).
3. constellation: 星座；星群；一群杰出的人

are ruled in a certain order by those of a more subtle and powerful nature.[1] And Dionysius says that *the light of the sun conduces to the generation of sensible bodies, moves them to life, and gives them nourishment, growth and perfection.*[2]

I answer that, Every multitude proceeds from unity, and what is immovable is always uniform, whereas what is moved has many ways of being. For this reason, it must be observed that throughout the whole of nature, all movement proceeds from the immovable. Therefore, the more immovable certain things are, the more are they the cause of those things which are more movable. Now the heavenly bodies are of all bodies the most immovable, for they are not moved save locally. Hence, the movements of bodies here below, which are various and multiform movements, must be referred to the movement of the heavenly bodies as to their cause.

Reply Obj. 1. These words of Damascene are to be understood as denying that the heavenly bodies are the first cause of generation and corruption here below; for this was affirmed by those who held that the heavenly bodies are gods.

Reply Obj. 2. The active principles of bodies here below are only the active qualities of the elements, such as hot and cold and the like. If, therefore, the substantial forms of inferior bodies were not diversified save according to such accidents (the principles of which the early natural philosophers held to be the *rare and the dense*[3]), there would be no need to suppose some principle above these inferior bodies, for they would be of themselves sufficient to act. But to anyone who considers the matter rightly, it is clear that those accidents are merely material dispositions in regard to the substantial forms of natural bodies. Now matter is not of itself sufficient to act, and therefore it is necessary to suppose some active principle above these material dispositions.

---

1. 参见 *De Trin.*, III, 4 (PL 42, 873).
2. 参见 *De Div. Nom.*, IV, 4 (PG 3, 700).
3. 参见 Cf. Aristotle, *Phys.*, I, 4 (187a 15).

This is why the Platonists maintained the existence of separate species, by participation of which the inferior bodies receive their substantial forms. But this does not seem enough. For the separate species, since they are supposed to be immovable, would always have the same mode of being; and consequently there would be no variety in the generation and corruption of inferior bodies, which is clearly false.

Therefore, as the Philosopher says, it is necessary to suppose a movable principle, which by reason of its presence or absence causes variety in the generation and corruption of inferior bodies.[1] Such are the heavenly bodies. Consequently, whatever generates here below, moves to the production of the species as the instrument of a heavenly body. Thus the Philosopher says that *man and the sun generate man.*[2]

Reply Obj. 3. The heavenly bodies have not a specific likeness to the bodies here below. Their likeness consists in this, that by reason of their universal power, whatever is generated in inferior bodies is contained in them. In this way also we say that all things are like God.

Reply Obj. 4. The actions of heavenly bodies are variously received in inferior bodies, according to the various dispositions of matter. Now it happens at times that the matter in human conception is not wholly disposed to the male sex; and so it is formed sometimes into a male, sometimes into a female. Augustine quotes this as an argument against divination by stars; because the effects of the stars are varied even in corporeal things, according to the various dispositions of matter.

Fourth Article
WHETHER THE HEAVENLY BODIES ARE THE CAUSE OF HUMAN ACTIONS?

We proceed thus to the Fourth Article:—

1. 参见 *De Gener.*, II, 10 (336a 15).
2. 参见 *Phys.*, II, 2 (194b 13).

Objection 1. It would seem that the heavenly bodies are the cause of human actions. For since the heavenly bodies are moved by spiritual substances, as was stated above,[1] they act as instruments in the power of these substances. But such spiritual substances are superior to our souls. Therefore it seems that they can cause impressions on our souls, and thereby cause human actions.

Obj. 2. Further, everything multiform is reducible to a uniform principle. But human actions are various and multiform. Therefore it seems that they are reducible to the uniform movements of heavenly bodies, as to their principles.

Obj. 3. Further, astrologers often foretell the truth concerning the outcome of wars, and other human actions, of which the intellect and will are the principles. But they could not do this by means of the heavenly bodies unless these were the cause of human actions. Therefore the heavenly bodies are the cause of human actions.

On the contrary, Damascene says that *the heavenly bodies are by no means the cause of human actions.*[2]

I answer that, The heavenly bodies can directly and of themselves act on bodies, as was stated above. They can act directly indeed on those powers of the soul which are the acts of corporeal organs, but accidentally; because the acts of such powers must needs be hindered by obstacles in the organs. Thus an eye when disturbed cannot see well. Therefore if the intellect and will were powers affixed to corporeal organs, as some maintained, holding that intellect does not differ from sense,[3] it would follow of necessity that the heavenly bodies are the cause of human choice and action. It would also follow that man is led by natural instinct to his actions, just as other animals, in which there are no powers other than those which

1. 参见 Q. 110, a. 3.
2. 参见 *De Fide Orth.*, II, 7 (PG 94, 893).
3. 参见 Cf. Aristotle, *De An.*, III, 3 (427a 21).

are affixed to corporeal organs: for whatever is done here below in virtue of the action of heavenly bodies is done naturally. It would therefore follow that man has no free choice, and that he would have determinate actions, like other natural things. All of which is manifestly false, and contrary to how men live.

It must be observed, however, that indirectly and accidentally, the impressions of heavenly bodies can reach the intellect and will, inasmuch, namely, as both intellect and will receive something from the inferior powers which are affixed to corporeal organs. But in this the intellect and will are differently situated. For the intellect receives of necessity from the inferior apprehensive powers, and so, if the imaginative, cogitative or memorative powers be disturbed, the action of the intellect is, of necessity, also disturbed. The will, on the contrary, does not of necessity follow the inclination of the inferior appetite; for although the passions in the irascible and concupiscible part have a certain force in inclining the will, nevertheless, the will retains the power of following the passions or repressing them. Therefore the impressions of the heavenly bodies, by virtue of which the inferior powers can be changed, have less influence on the will, which is the proximate cause of human actions, than on the intellect.

To maintain therefore that heavenly bodies are the cause of human actions is proper to those who hold that intellect does not differ from sense. And so, some of these said that *such is the will of men, as is the day which the father of men and of gods brings on.*[1] Since, therefore, it is manifest that intellect and will are not acts of corporeal organs, it is impossible that the heavenly bodies should be the cause of human actions.

Reply Obj. 1. The spiritual substances that move the heavenly bodies do indeed act on corporeal things by means of the heavenly bodies;

1. 参见 Homer, *Odyssey*, XVIII, 136.

but they act immediately on the human intellect by illumining it. On the other hand, they cannot compel the will, as was stated above.[1]

Reply Obj. 2. Just as the multiformity of corporeal movements is reducible to the uniformity of the heavenly movement as to its cause, so the multiformity of actions proceeding from the intellect and the will is reduced to a uniform principle which is the divine intellect and will.

Reply Obj. 3. The majority of men follow their passions, which are movements of the sensitive appetite, in which movements heavenly bodies can co-operate; but few are wise enough to resist these passions. Consequently astrologers are able to foretell the truth in the majority of cases, especially in a general way. But not in particular cases, for nothing prevents a man from resisting his passions by his free choice. Hence, the astrologers themselves are wont to say that *the wise man is stronger than the stars*,[2] inasmuch as, namely, he conquers his passions.

Fifth Article
WHETHER HEAVENLY BODIES CAN ACT ON THE DEMONS?

We proceed thus to the Fifth Article:

Objection 1. It would seem that heavenly bodies can act on the demons. For the demons, according to certain phases of the moon, can harass men, who on that account are called lunatics[3], as appears from *Matthew* iv. 24 and xvii. 14. But this would not be if they were not subject to the heavenly bodies. Therefore the demons are subject to them.

Obj. 2. Further, necromancers observe certain constellations in order to invoke the demons. But these would not be invoked through the

---

1. 参见 Q. 111, a. 2.
2. 参见 Cf. *C.G.*, III, 85; St. Albert, *In II Sent.*, d. xv, a. 4 (XXVII, 276).
3. lunatics: 疯子

heavenly bodies unless they were subject to them. Therefore they are subject to them.

Obj. 3. Further, heavenly bodies are more powerful than inferior bodies. But the demons are confined to certain inferior bodies, namely, *herbs, stones, animals, and to certain sounds and words, forms and figures,* as Porphyry says, quoted by Augustine.[1] Much more therefore are the demons subject to the action of heavenly bodies.

On the contrary, The demons are superior, in the order of nature, to the heavenly bodies. But the *agent is superior to the patient,* as Augustine says.[2] Therefore the demons are not subject to the action of heavenly bodies.

I answer that, There have been three opinions about the demons. In the first place the Peripatetics denied the existence of demons, and held that what is ascribed to the demons, according to the necromantic art, is effected by the power of the heavenly bodies. This is what Augustine relates as having been held by Porphyry, namely, that *on earth men fabricate certain powers useful in producing certain effects of the stars.*[3] But this opinion is manifestly false. For we know by experience that many things are done by demons, for which the power of heavenly bodies would in no way suffice: for instance, that a man in a state of delirium should speak an unknown tongue, recite poetry and authors of whom he has no previous knowledge; and that necromancers make statues to speak and move, and other like things.

For this reason the Platonists were led to hold that demons are *animals with an aerial body and a passive soul,* as Apuleius says, quoted by Augustine.[4] And this is the second of the opinions mentioned above, according to which it could be said that demons are subject to

1. 参见 *De Civit. Dei*, X, 11 (PL 41, 290).
2. 参见 *De Genesi ad Litt.*, XII, 16 (PL 34, 467).
3. 参见 *De Civit. Dei*, X, 11 (PL 41, 290).
4. 参见 *Op. cit.*, VIII, 16 (PL 41, 241).

heavenly bodies in the same way as we have said that man is subject thereto. But this opinion is proved to be false from what we have said above. For we hold that demons are spiritual substances not united to bodies.[1] Hence it is clear that they are subject to the action of heavenly bodies neither essentially nor accidentally, neither directly nor indirectly.

Reply Obj. 1. That demons harass men, according to certain phases of. the moon, happens in two ways. First, they do so in order to *defame God's creature*, namely, the moon, as Jerome[2] and Chrysostom[3] say. Secondly, because as they are unable to effect anything save by means of natural forces, as was stated above,[4] they take into account the aptitude of bodies for the intended result. Now it is manifest that *the brain is the most moist of all the parts of the body*, as Aristotle says.[5] Therefore it is the most subject to the action of the moon, the property of which is to move what is moist. And it is precisely in the brain that animal powers culminate. Hence the demons, according to certain phases of the moon, disturb man's imagination, when they observe that the brain is thereto disposed.

Reply Obj. 2. Demons, when summoned through certain constellations, come for two reasons. First, in order to lead man into the error of believing that there is some divine power in the stars. Secondly, because they consider that under certain constellations corporeal matter is better disposed for the result for which they are summoned.

Reply Obj. 3. As Augustine says,[6] *the demons are enticed through various kinds of stones, herbs, trees, animals, songs, rites, not as an animal is enticed by*

---

1. 参见 Q. 51, a. 1.
2. 参见 *In Matt.*, I, super IV, 24 (PL 26, 34).
3. 参见 *In Matt.*, hom. LVII (PG 58, 562).
4. 参见 Q. 114, a. 4, ad 2.
5. 参见 *De Part. Anim.*, II, 7 (652a 27); *De Somno*, III (457b 29).
6. 参见 *De Civit. Dei*, XXI, 6 (PL 41, 717).

food, but as a spirit by signs; that is to say, inasmuch as these things are offered to them in token of the honor due to God, of which they are covetous.

Sixth Article
WHETHER HEAVENLY BODIES IMPOSE NECESSITY ON THINGS SUBJECT TO THEIR ACTION?

We proceed thus to the Sixth Article:—

Objection 1. It would seem that heavenly bodies impose necessity on things subject to their action. For given a sufficient cause, the effect follows of necessity. But heavenly bodies are a sufficient cause of their effects. Since, therefore, heavenly bodies, with their movements and dispositions, are necessary beings, it seems that their effects follow of necessity.

Obj. 2. Further, an agent's effect results of necessity in matter, when the power of the agent is such that it can subject the matter to itself entirely. But the entire matter of inferior bodies is subject to the power of heavenly bodies, since this is a higher power than theirs. Therefore the effect of the heavenly bodies is of necessity received in corporeal matter.

Obj. 3. Further, if the effect of the heavenly body does not follow of necessity, this is due to some hindering cause. But any corporeal cause, that might possibly hinder the effect of a heavenly body, must of necessity be reducible to some heavenly principle, since the heavenly bodies are the causes of all that takes place here below. Therefore, since that heavenly principle also is necessary, it follows that the effect of the other heavenly body is necessarily hindered. Consequently it would follow that all that takes place here below happens of necessity.

On the contrary, The Philosopher says : *It is not incongruous that many of the signs observed in bodies of occurrences in the heavens, such as rain and wind, should not be fulfilled.*[1] Therefore not all the effects of heavenly bodies take place of necessity.

I answer that, This question is partly solved by what was said above, and in part presents some difficulty. For it was shown that although the action of heavenly bodies produces certain inclinations in corporeal nature, the will nevertheless does not of necessity follow these inclinations. Therefore there is nothing to prevent the effect of heavienly bodies from being hindered by the action of the will, not only in man himself, but also in other things to which human action extends.

But in natural things there is no such principle, endowed with freedom to follow or not to follow the impressions produced by heavenly agents. Therefore it seems that in such things, at least, everything happens of necessity. This is in line with the reasoning of some of the ancients who, supposing that everything that is has a cause, and that, given the cause, the effect follows of necessity, concluded that all things happen of necessity.[2] This opinion is refuted by Aristotle as to this double supposition.[3]

For, in the first place, it is not true that, given any cause whatever, the effect must follow of necessity. For some causes are so ordered to their effects as to produce them, not of necessity, but in the majority of cases, and in the minority to fail in producing them. But that such causes do fail in the minority of cases is due to some hindering cause, and consequently the above-mentioned difficulty seems not to be avoided, since the cause in question is hindered of necessity.

Therefore we must say, in the second place, that everything that is a being through itself, has a cause; but what is accidentally, has not a cause, because it is not truly a being, since it is not truly one. For

1. 参见 *De Divinat.*, II (463b 22).
2. 参见 Avicenna, *Sufficientia*, I, 13 (21ra); *Metaph.*, I, 7 (73ra).
3. 参见 *Metaph.*, V, 3 (1027a 31).

that which is *white* has a cause, and likewise that which is *musical* has a cause; but that which is *white-musical* has not a cause, because it is not truly a being, nor truly one. Now it is manifest that a cause which hinders the action of a cause so ordered to its effect as to produce it in the majority of cases, clashes sometimes with this cause by accident; and therefore the clashing of these two causes, inasmuch as it is accidental, has no cause. Consequently, what results from this clashing of causes is not to be reduced to a further preexisting cause, from which it follows of necessity. For instance, that a terrestrial body should take fire in the higher regions of the air and fall to the earth is caused by some heavenly power; and again, that there be on the surface of the earth some combustible matter, is reducible to some heavenly principle. But that the burning body should alight on this matter and set it on fire is not caused by a heavenly body, but is accidental. Consequently not all the effects of heavenly bodies happen of necessity.

Reply Obj. 1. The heavenly bodies are causes of effects that take place here below through the means of particular inferior causes, which can fail in their effects in the minority of cases.

Reply Obj. 2. The power of a heavenly body is not infinite. Therefore it requires a determinate disposition in matter, both as to local distance and as to other conditions, in order to produce its effect. Hence, as local distance hinders the effect of a heavenly body (for the sun has not the same effect in heat in Dacia as in Ethiopia), so the grossness of matter, its low or high temperature or other such disposition, can hinder the effect of a heavenly body.

Reply Obj. 3. Although the cause that hinders the effect of another cause can be reduced to a heavenly body as its cause, nevertheless the clashing of two causes, being accidental, is not reduced to the causality of a heavenly body, as was stated above.

Question CXVI
ON FATE
(*In Four Articles*)

WE come now to the consideration of fate. Under this head there are four points of inquiry: (1) Is there such a thing as fate? (2) Where is it? (3) Is it unchangeable? (4) Are all things subject to fate?

First Article
WHETHER THERE BE SUCH A THING AS FATE?

We proceed thus to the First Article:—

Objection 1. It would seem that fate is nothing. For Gregory says in a homily for the Epiphany: *Far be it from the hearts of the faithful to think that fate is anything real.*[1]

Obj. 2. Further, what happens by fate is not unforeseen, for as Augustine says, *fate is understood to be derived from the verb 'fari' which means to speak*,[2] as though things were said to happen by fate, which are 'fore-spoken' by one who decrees them to happen. Now what is foreseen is neither fortuitous nor by chance. If therefore things happen by fate, there will be neither fortune nor chance in the world.

On the contrary, What does not exist cannot be defined. But Boethius defines fate thus: *Fate is a disposition inherent in changeable things, by which providence connects each one with its proper order.*[3]

---

1. 参见 *In Evang.*, I, hom. 11 (PL 76, 1112).
2. 参见 *De Civit. Dei*, V, 9 (PL 41, 150).
3. 参见 *De Consol.*, IV, prose 6 (PL 63, 815).

I answer that, In this world some things seem to happen by fortune or chance. Now it happens sometimes that something is fortuitous or by chance, as compared to inferior causes, which, if compared to some higher cause, is directly intended. For instance, if two servants, who do not know that they will meet, are sent by their master to the same place, the meeting of the two servants if referred to themselves is by chance: but as compared to the master who had ordered it, it is directly intended.

Now there were some who refused to refer to a higher cause such events which by fortune or chance take place here below. These denied the existence of fate and providence, as Augustine relates of Tully.[1] And this is contrary to what we have said above about providence.[2]

On the other hand, some have considered that everything that takes place here below by fortune or by chance, whether in natural things or in human affairs, is to be reduced to a superior cause, namely, the heavenly bodies.[3] According to these, fate is nothing else than *a disposition of the stars under which each one is begotten or born.*[4] But this will not hold. First, as to human affairs : because we have proved above that human actions are not subject to the action of heavenly bodies, save accidentally and indirectly.[5] Now the cause of fate, since it has the ordering of things that happen by fate, must of necessity be directly and of itself the cause of what takes place. Secondly, as to all things that happen accidentally: for it has been said that what is accidental is, properly speaking, neither a being nor a unity.[6] But every action

1. 参见 *De Civit. Dei*, V, 9 (PL 41, 148).—Cf. Cicero, *De Divinat.*, II, 5 (pp. 68–69); 10 (p. 74).
2. 参见 Q. 22, a. 2.
3. 参见 The opinion of Posidonius, according to St. Augustine, *De Civit. Dei*, V, 7 (PL 41, 454).
4. 参见 *Op. cit.*, V, 1 (PL 41, 141).
5. 参见 Q. 115, a. 4.
6. 参见 Q. 115, a. 6.

of nature terminates in some one thing. Therefore it is impossible for that which is accidental to be the proper effect of an active natural principle. No natural cause can therefore have for its proper effect that a man intending to dig a grave should find a treasure. Now it is manifest that a heavenly body acts after the manner of a natural principle, and so its effects in this world are natural. It is therefore impossible that any active power of a heavenly body be the cause of what happens by accident here below, whether by fortune or by chance.

We must therefore say that what happens here by accident, both in natural things and in human affairs, is reduced to a pre-ordaining cause, which is the divine providence. For nothing hinders that which happens by accident from being considered as one by an intellect, or otherwise the intellect could not form this proposition: *The digger of a grave found a treasure.* And just as an intellect can apprehend this, so can it effect it. For instance, someone who knows of a place where a treasure is hidden might instigate a rustic, ignorant of this, to dig a grave there. Consequently, nothing hinders what happens here by accident, whether by fortune or by chance, from being reduced to some ordering cause which acts by the intellect, especially the divine intellect. For God alone can change the will, as was shown above.[1] Consequently the ordering of human actions, the principle of which is the will, must be ascribed to God alone.

Thus, therefore, inasmuch as all that happens here below is subject to the divine providence, as being pre-ordained and as it were *fore-spoken*, we can admit the existence of *fate*; although the holy doctors have avoided the use of this term because of those who twisted its application to a certain force resulting from the position of the stars. Hence Augustine says: *If anyone ascribes human affairs to fate, meaning*

1. 参见 Q. 105, a. 4; q. 106, a. 2; q. 111, a. 2.

thereby the will or power of God, let him keep to his opinion, but hold his tongue.[1] For this reason Gregory denies the existence of fate.[2] Therefore the first objection's solution is manifest.

Reply Obj. 2. Nothing hinders certain things from happening by fortune or by chance, if compared to their proximate causes, but not if compared to the divine providence, whereby *nothing happens at random in the world*, as Augustine says.[3]

Second Article

WHETHER FATE IS IN CREATED THINGS?

We proceed thus to the Second Article:—

Objection 1. It would seem that fate is not in created things. For Augustine says that the *divine will or power itself is called fate.*[4] But the divine will or power is not in creatures, but in God. Therefore fate is not in creatures but in God.

Obj. 2. Further, fate is compared to things that happen by fate, as their cause; as the very use of the word proves. But the universal cause that of itself effects what takes place by accident here below is God alone, as was stated above. Therefore fate is in God, and not in creatures.

Obj. 3. Further, if fate is in creatures, it is either a substance or an accident; and whichever it is, it must be multiplied according to the number of creatures. Since, therefore, fate seems to be only one thing, it seems that fate is not in creatures, but in God.

On the contrary, Boethius says: *Fate is a disposition inherent in changeable*

---

1. 参见 *De Civit. Dei*, V, 1 (PL 41, 141).
2. 参见 *In Evang.*, I, hom. 11 (PL 76, 1112).
3. 参见 *Lib. 83 Quaest.*, q. 24 (PL 40, 17).
4. 参见 *De Civit. Dei*, V, 1 (PL 41, 141).

things.[1]

I answer that, As is clear from what has been stated above, divine providence produces effects through intermediate causes.[2] We can therefore consider the ordering of effects in two ways. First, as being in God Himself, and thus the ordering of the effects is called *providence.* But if we consider this ordering as being in the intermediate causes assigned by God to the production of certain effects, thus it has the nature of *fate.* This is what Boethius says: *Fate is worked out when divine providence is served by certain spirits, whether it is by the soul, or by all nature itself which obeys Him, whether by the heavenly movements of the stars, whether by the angelic power, or by the ingenuity of the demons, whether by some of these, or by all, that the chain of fate is forged.*[3] Of each of these things we have spoken above.[4] It is therefore manifest that fate is in the created causes themselves, as assigned by God to the production of their effects.

Reply Obj. 1. The ordering itself of second causes, which Augustine calls the *series of causes,*[5] has not the nature of fate, except as dependent on God. Therefore the divine power or will can be called fate, as being the cause of fate. But essentially fate is the very disposition or *series, i.e.,* order, of second causes.

Reply Obj. 2. Fate has the nature of a cause, just as much as the second causes themselves, the ordering of which is called fate.

Reply Obj. 3. Fate is called a disposition, not that disposition which is a species of quality, but in the sense in which it signifies order, which is not a substance, but a relation. And if this order be considered in relation to its principle, it is one; and thus fate is one. But if it be considered in relation to its effects, or to the intermediate causes, this

---

1. 参见 *De Consol.*, IV, prose 6 (PL 63, 815).
2. 参见 Q. 22, a. 3; q. 103, a. 6.
3. 参见 *De Consol.*, IV, prose 6 (PL 63, 815).
4. 参见 A. 1; q. 104, a. 2; q. 110, a. 1; q. 113 and 114.
5. 参见 *De Civit. Dei*, V, 8 (PL 41, 148).

fate is multiple. In this sense the poet wrote: *Thy fates draw thee.*[1]

Third Article
WHETHER FATE IS UNCHANGEABLE?

We proceed thus to the Third Article:—

Objection 1. It seems that fate is not unchangeable. For Boethius says: *As reasoning is to the intellect, as the begotten is to that which is, as time to eternity, as the circle to its center, so is the fickle chain of fate to the unwavering simplicity of providence.*[2]

Obj. 2. Further, the Philosopher says: *If we be moved, what is in us is moved.*[3] But fate is a *disposition inherent in changeable things*, as Boethius says.[4] Therefore fate is changeable.

Obj. 3. Further, if fate is unchangeable, what is subject to fate happens unchangeably and of necessity. But things ascribed to fate seem principally to be contingencies. Therefore there would be no contingencies in the world, but all things would happen of necessity.

On the contrary, Boethius says that fate is an unchangeable disposition.[5]

I answer that, The disposition of second causes, which we call fate, can be considered in two ways: first, in regard to the second causes, which are thus disposed or ordered; secondly, in relation to the first principle, namely, God, by Whom they are ordered. Some, therefore, have held that the series itself or disposition of causes was necessary in itself, so that all things would happen of necessity,[6] since each effect has a cause, and given a cause the effect must follow of necessity. But

1. 参见 Hildebert of Lavardin, *Versus de Excidio Troiae* (PL 171, 1449 D).
2. 参见 *De Consol.*, IV, prose 6 (PL 63, 817).
3. 参见 *Top.*, II, 7 (113a 29).
4. 参见 *De Consol.*, IV, prose 6 (PL 63, 815).
5. 同上 (PL 63, 816).
6. 参见 Cf. above, q. 115, a. 6.

this is false, as was proved above.[1]

Others, on the other hand, held that fate is changeable, even as dependent on the divine providence. Hence the Egyptians said that fate could be changed by certain sacrifices, as Gregory of Nyssa says.[2] This too has been disproved above for the reason that it is repugnant to the unchangeableness of the divine providence.[3]

We must therefore say that fate, considered in regard to second causes, is changeable; but as subject to divine providence, it derives a certain unchangeableness, not of absolute but of conditional necessity. In this sense we say that this conditional proposition is true and necessary : *If God foreknew that this would happen, it will happen.* Hence, Boethius, having said that the chain of fate is fickle, shortly afterwards adds,—*which, since it is derived from an unchangeable providence, must also itself be unchangeable.*[4]

From this the answers to the objections are clear.

Fourth Article
WHETHER ALL THINGS ARE SUBJECT TO FATE?

We proceed thus to the Fourth Article:—

Objection 1. It seems that all things are subject to fate. For Boethius says: *The chain of fate moves the heaven and the stars, tempers the elements to one another, and models them by a reciprocal transformation. By fate all things that are born into the world and perish are renewed in a uniform progression of offspring and seed. By fate the actions and fortunes of men are joined in an indissoluble web of causes.*[5] Nothing therefore seems to be excluded from

---

1. 参见 Cf. above, q. 115, a. 6.
2. 参见 Cf. Nemesius, *De Nat. Hom.*, XXXVI (PG 40, 745).
3. 参见 Q. 23, a. 8.
4. 参见 *De Consol.*, IV, prose 6 (PL 63, 817).
5. 同上

the domain of fate.

Obj. 2. Further, Augustine says that fate is something real, as referred to the divine will and power.[1] But the divine will is the cause of all things that happen, as Augustine says.[2] Therefore all things are subject to fate.

Obj. 3. Further, Boethius says that fate *is a disposition inherent in changeable things.*[3] But all creatures are changeable, and God alone is truly unchangeable, as was stated above.[4] Therefore fate is in all things.

On the contrary, Boethius says that *some things subject to providence are above the ordering of fate.*[5]

I answer that, As was stated above, fate is the ordering of second causes to effects foreseen by God. Whatever, therefore, is subject to second causes, is subject also to fate. But whatever is done immediately by God, since it is not subject to second causes, neither is it subject to fate: *e.g.*, creation, the glorification of spiritual substances, and the like. And this is what Boethius says, viz., that *those things which are near God have a state of immobility, and exceed the changeable order of fate.*[6] Hence it is clear that *the farther a thing is from the First Mind, the more it is involved in the chain of fate,*[7] since so much the more it is bound up with second causes.

Reply Obj. 1. All the things mentioned in this passage are done by God by means of second causes, and for this reason they are contained in the order of fate. But it is not the same with everything else, as was stated above.

---

1. 参见 *De Civit. Dei*, V, 1; 8 (PL 41,141; 148).
2. 参见 *De Trin.*, III, 1 (PL 42, 871); *Enchir.*, XCV (PL 40, 276).
3. 参见 *De Consol.*, IV, prose 6 (PL 63, 815).
4. 参见 Q. 9, a. 2.
5. 参见 *De Consol.*, IV, prose 6 (PL 63, 816).
6. 同上
7. 同上

Reply Obj. 2. Fate is to be referred to the divine will and power as to its first principle. Consequently, it does not follow that whatever is subject to the divine will or power is subject also to fate, as has already been stated.

Reply Obj. 3. Although all creatures are in some way changeable, yet some of them do not proceed from changeable created causes. And these, therefore, are not subject to fate, as was stated above.

Question CXVII
OF THINGS PERTAINING TO THE ACTION OF MAN
(*In Four Articles*)

WE have next to consider those things which pertain to the action of man, who is composed of a created corporeal and spiritual nature. In the first place we shall consider the action of man, and secondly the propagation of man from man.[1] As to the first, there are four points of inquiry: (1) Whether one man can teach another, as being the cause of his knowledge? (2) Whether man can teach an angel? (3) Whether by the power of his soul man can change corporeal matter? (4) Whether the separated soul of man can move bodies by local movement?

First Article
WHETHER ONE MAN CAN TEACH ANOTHER?

We proceed thus to the First Article:—

Objection 1. It would seem that one man cannot teach another. For the Lord says (*Matt.* xxiii. 8): *Be not you called Rabbi:* on which the *Gloss* of Jerome says, *Lest you give to men the honor due to God.*[2] Therefore to be a teacher is properly an honor due to God. But it belongs to a teacher to teach. Therefore man cannot teach, but this is proper to God.

Obj. 2. Further, if one man teaches another, this is only inasmuch as he acts through his own knowledge, so as to cause knowledge in

---

1. 参见 Q. 118.
2. 参见 *Glossa interl.*, super *Matt.*, XXIII, 8 (V, 71r).

the other. But the quality through which anyone acts so as to produce his like, is an active quality. Therefore it follows that knowledge is an active quality just as heat is.

Obj. 3. Further, for knowledge we require intellectual light, and the species of the thing understood. But a man cannot cause either of these in another man. Therefore a man cannot by teaching cause knowledge in another man.

Obj. 4. Further, the teacher does nothing in regard to a disciple save to propose to him certain signs, so as to signify something by words or gestures. But it is not possible to teach anyone so as to cause knowledge in him, by putting signs before him. For these are signs either of things that he knows, or of things he does not know. If of things that he knows, he to whom these signs are proposed is already in the possession of knowledge, and does not acquire it from the teacher. If they are signs of things that he does not know, he can learn nothing from them. For instance, if one were to speak Greek to a man who knows only Latin, he would learn nothing thereby. Therefore in no way can a man cause knowledge in another by teaching him.

On the contrary, The Apostle says (*1 Tim.* ii. 7): *Whereunto I am appointed a preacher and an apostle ... a doctor of the Gentiles in faith and truth.*

I answer that, On this question there have been various opinions. For Averroes, commenting on *De anima* iii., maintains that all men have one possible intellect in common,[1] as was stated above.[2] From this it followed that the same intelligible species belong to all men. Consequently, he held that one man does not cause another to have a knowledge distinct from that which he has himself; but that he communicates the identical knowledge which he has himself, by moving him to order rightly the phantasms in his soul, so that they

---

1. 参见 *In De An.*, III, comm. 5 (VI, 163v–166v).
2. 参见 Q. 76, a. 2.

be rightly disposed for intelligible apprehension. This opinion is true so far as knowledge is the same in the disciple and the teacher, if we consider the identity of the thing known; for the same objective truth is known by both of them. But so far as he maintains that all men have but one possible intellect, and the same intelligible species, differing only according to the diversity of phantasms, his opinion is false, as was stated above.[1]

Besides this, there is the opinion of the Platonists, who held that our souls are possessed of knowledge from the very beginning, through the participation of separate Forms, as was stated above;[2] but that the soul is hindered, through its union with the body, from the free consideration of those things which it knows. According to this, the disciple does not acquire fresh knowledge from his teacher, but is roused by him to consider what he knows; so that to learn would be nothing else than to remember.[3] In the same way they held that natural agents act only dispositively towards the reception of forms, which matter acquires by a participation in separate species.[4] But against this we have proved above that the possible intellect of the human soul is in pure potentiality to intelligibles,[5] as Aristotle says.[6]

We must therefore decide the question differently, by saying that the teacher causes knowledge in the learner by reducing him from potentiality to act, as the Philosopher says.[7] In order to make this clear, we must observe that of effects proceeding from an exterior principle, some proceed from the exterior principle alone, as the form of a house is caused to be in matter by art alone. But other effects

---

1. 参见 Q. 76, a. 2.
2. 参见 Q. 84, a. 3.
3. 同上
4. 参见 Cf. above q. 115, a. 1.
5. 参见 Q. 79, a. 2; q. 84, a. 3.
6. 参见 *De An.*, III, 4 (429b 30).
7. 参见 Aristotle, *Phys.*, VIII, 4 (225b 1).

proceed sometimes from an exterior principle, sometimes from an interior principle; and thus health is caused in a sick man sometimes by an exterior principle (namely, by the medical art), sometimes by an interior principle (as when a man is healed by the power of nature). In these latter effects two things must be noticed. First, that art in its work imitates nature, for just as nature heals a man by alteration, digestion and rejection of the matter that caused the sickness, so does art. Secondly, we must remark that the exterior principle, art, acts, not as principal agent, but as helping the principal agent, which is the interior principle, by strengthening it, and by furnishing it with instruments and assistance, of which the interior principle makes use in producing the effect. Thus the physician strengthens nature, and administers food and medicine which nature is to use for the intended end.

Now knowledge is acquired in man, both from an interior principle, as is clear in one who procures knowledge by discovery; and from an exterior principle, as is clear in one who learns by instruction. For in every man there is a certain principle of knowledge, namely the light of the agent intellect, through which certain universal principles of all the sciences are naturally understood as soon as proposed to the intellect. Now when anyone applies these universal principles to certain particular things, the memory or experience of which he acquires through the senses, then, advancing by discovery from the known to the unknown, he obtains knowledge of what he knew not before. Therefore anyone who teaches leads the disciple from things known by the disciple to the knowledge of things previously unknown to him; for, as the Philosopher says: *All teaching and all learning proceed from previous knowledge.*[1]

Now the teacher leads the disciple in two ways from the preknown

---

1. 参见 Aristotle, *Post. Anal.*, I, 1 (71a 1).

to knowledge of the unknown. First, by proposing to him certain helps or means of instruction, which his intellect can use for the acquisition of science. For instance, he may put before him certain less universal propositions, of which nevertheless the disciple is able to judge from previous knowledge; or he may propose to him some sensible examples, either by way of likeness or of opposition, or something of the sort, from which the intellect of the learner is led to the knowledge of a truth previously unknown. Secondly, by strengthening the intellect of the learner; not, indeed, by some active power as though of a higher nature (as was explained above of the angelic illuminations[1]), because all human intellects are of one grade in the natural order; but inasmuch as he proposes to the disciple the order from principles to conclusions, for the disciple may not have sufficient power of reasoning to be able to draw the conclusions from the principles. Hence the Philosopher says that *a demonstration is a syllogism that causes science.*[2] In this way a demonstrator causes his hearers to know.

Reply Obj. 1. As was stated above, the teacher only brings exterior help, as the physician who heals; but just as the interior nature is the principal cause of the healing, so the interior light of the intellect is the principal cause of knowledge. But both of these are from God. Therefore as of God is it written: *Who healeth all thy diseases* (*Ps.* cii. 3), so of Him is it written: *He that teacheth man knowledge* (*Ps.* xciii. 10), inasmuch as *the light of His countenance is signed upon us* (*Ps.* iv. 7), through which light all things are shown to us.

Reply Obj. 2. The teacher does not, as Averroes argues, cause knowledge in the disciple after the manner of a natural active cause.[3] Hence, knowledge need not be an active quality; it is rather the principle by which one is directed in teaching, just as art is the principle by which

1. 参见 Q. 106, a. 1; q. 111, a. 1.
2. 参见 Aristotle, *Post. Anal.*, I, 2 (71b 17).
3. 参见 *In De An.*, III, comm.5 (VI, 166rv).

one is directed in working.

Reply Obj. 3. The teacher does not cause the intellectual light in the disciple, nor does he cause the intelligible species directly; but he moves the disciple by teaching, so that the latter, by the power of his own intellect, forms intelligible concepts, the signs of which are proposed to him from the outside.

Reply Obj. 4. The signs proposed by the teacher to the disciple are of things known in a general and confused manner; but not known in the particular and distinctly. Therefore when anyone acquires knowledge by himself, he cannot be called self-taught, or be said to have been his own teacher; for perfect knowledge did not precede in him, such as is required in a teacher.

Second Article
WHETHER MAN CAN TEACH THE ANGELS?

We proceed thus to the Second Article:—

Objection 1. It would seem that men can teach angels. For the Apostle says (*Ephes.* iii. 10): *That the manifold wisdom of God may be made known to the principalities and powers in the heavenly places through the Church.* But the Church is the congregation of all the faithful. Therefore some things are made known to angels through men.

Obj. 2. Further, the superior angels, who are illumined immediately concerning divine things by God, can instruct the inferior angels, as was stated above.[1] But some men are instructed immediately concerning divine things by the Word of God, as appears principally of the apostles from *Heb.* i. 1, 2: *Last of all, in these days* [*God*] *hath spoken to us by His Son.* Therefore some men have been able to teach the angels.

Obj. 3. Further, the inferior angels are instructed by the superior. But

1. 参见 Q. 106, a. 1; q. 112, a. 3.

some men are higher than some angels, since some men are taken up to the highest angelic orders, as Gregory says in a homily.[1] Therefore some of the inferior angels can be instructed by men concerning divine things.

On the contrary, Dionysius says that every divine illumination is borne to men by the ministry of the angels.[2] Therefore angels are not instructed by men concerning divine things.

I answer that, As was stated above, the inferior angels can indeed speak to the superior angels, by making their thoughts known to them; but concerning divine things superior angels are never illumined by inferior angels.[3] Now it is manifest that in the same way as inferior angels are subject to the superior, the highest men are subject even to the lowest angels. This is clear from Our Lord's words (*Matt.* xi. 11): *There hath not risen among them that are born of women a greater than John the Baptist; yet he that is lesser in the kingdom of heaven is greater than he.* Therefore angels are never illumined by men concerning divine things. But men can by means of speech make known to angels the thoughts of their hearts; because it belongs to God alone to know the heart's secrets.

Reply Obj. 1. Augustine thus explains this passage of the Apostle, who in the preceding verses says: *To me, the least of all the saints, is given this grace ... to enlighten all men, that they may see what is the dispensation of the mystery which hath been hidden from eternity in God* (*Ephes.* iii. 8).—*Hidden, yet so that the multiform wisdom of God was made known to the principalities and powers in the heavenly places — that is, through the Church.*[4] As though to say: This mystery was hidden from men, but not from the Church in heaven, which is contained in the Principalities and Powers

1. 参见 *In Evang.*, II, hom. 34 (PL 76, 1252).
2. 参见 Cf. *De Cael. Hier.*, IV, 2 (PG 3, 180).
3. 参见 Q. 107, a. 2.
4. 参见 *De Genesi ad Litt.*, V, 19 (PL 34, 335).

who knew it *from all ages, but not before all ages: because the Church was at first there, where after the resurrection this Church composed of men will be gathered together.*

It can also be explained otherwise that *what is hidden, is known by the angels, not only in God, but also here when it takes place and is made public,* as Augustine says further on. Thus when the mysteries of Christ and the Church were fulfilled by the apostles, some things concerning these mysteries became apparent to the angels, which were hidden from them before. In this way we can understand what Jerome says—that from the preaching of the apostles the angels learned certain mysteries;[1] that is to say, through the preaching of the apostles, the mysteries were realized in the things themselves. Thus, by the preaching of Paul, the Gentiles were converted, of which mystery the Apostle is speaking in the passage quoted.

Reply Obj. 2. The apostles were instructed immediately by the Word of God, not according to His divinity, but according as He spoke in His human nature. Hence the argument does not hold.

Reply Obj. 3. Certain men, even in this state of life, are greater than certain angels, not actually, but virtually. That is, they are greater inasmuch as they have such great charity, that they can merit a higher degree of beatitude than that possessed by certain angels. In the same way we might say that the seed of a great tree is virtually greater than a small tree, though actually it is much smaller.

Third Article
WHETHER MAN BY THE POWER OF HIS SOUL CAN CHANGE CORPOREAL MATTER?

We proceed thus to the Third Article:—

---

1. 参见 *In Ephes.*, II, super III, 10 (PL 26, 515).

Objection 1. It would seem that man by the power of his soul can change corporeal matter. For Gregory says: *Saints work miracles, sometimes by prayer, sometimes by their power; and thus Peter, by prayer, raised the dead Tabitha to life, and by his reproof delivered to death the lying Ananias and Saphira.*[1] But in the working of miracles a change is wrought in corporeal matter. Therefore men, by the power of the soul, can change corporeal matter.

Obj. 2. Further, on these words (*Gal.* iii. 1): *Who hath bewitched you, that you should not obey the truth?* the Gloss says that *some have blazing eyes, who by a single look bewitch others, especially children.*[2] But this would not be unless the power of the soul could change corporeal matter. Therefore man can change corporeal matter by the power of his soul.

Obj. 3. Further, the human body is nobler than other inferior bodies. But by the apprehension of the human soul the human body is changed to heat and cold, as appears when a man is angry or afraid; indeed this change sometimes goes so far as to bring on sickness and death. Much more, then, can the human soul by its power change corporeal matter.

On the contrary, Augustine says: *Corporeal matter obeys God alone at will.*[3]

I answer that, As was stated above, corporeal matter is not changed save either by some agent composed of matter and form, or by God Himself, in Whom both matter and form pre-exist virtually, as in the primordial cause of both.[4] Hence, of the angels also we have stated that they cannot change corporeal matter by their natural power, except by employing corporeal agents for the production of certain effects. Much less therefore can the soul, by its natural power, change corporeal

---

1. 参见 *Dial.*, II, 30 (PL 66, 188).
2. 参见 *Glossa ordin.* (VI, 82 A).
3. 参见 *De Trin.*, III, 8 (PL 42, 875).
4. 参见 Q. 110, a. 2.

matter, except by means of bodies.

Reply Obj. 1. The saints are said to work miracles by the power of grace, not of nature. This is clear from what Gregory says in the same place: *Those who are sons of God, in power, as John says, —what wonder is there that they should work miracles by that power?*[1]

Reply Obj. 2. Avicenna assigns the cause of bewitchment to the fact that corporeal matter has a natural tendency to obey spiritual substance rather than natural contrary agents.[2] Therefore when the soul is of strong imagination, it can change corporeal matter. This he says is the cause of the 'evil eye.'

But it has been shown above that corporeal matter does not obey spiritual substances at will, but the Creator alone.[3] Therefore it is better to say that by a strong imagination the spirits of the body united to that soul are changed. This change in the spirits takes place especially in the eyes, to which the more subtle spirits can reach. And the eyes infect the air which is in contact with them to a certain distance; in the same way as a new and clear mirror contracts a tarnish from the look of a menstruating woman, as Aristotle says.[4] Hence, when a soul is vehemently moved to wickedness, as occurs mostly in little old women, according to the above explanation, the countenance becomes venomous and hurtful, especially to children, who have a tender and most impressionable body. It is also possible that by God's permission, or from some hidden deed, the spiteful demons co-operate in this, as the witches may have some compact with them.

Reply Obj. 3. The soul is united to the body as its form; and the sensitive appetite, which in a way obeys the reason as was stated

1. 参见 *Dial.*, II, 30 (PL 66, 188).
2. 参见 *De An.*, IV, 4 (20vb).
3. 参见 Q. 110, a. 2.
4. 参见 *De Somno*, II (459b 26).

above,[1] is the act of a corporeal organ. Therefore at the apprehension of the human soul, the sensitive appetite must needs be moved with an accompanying corporeal operation. But the apprehension of the human soul does not suffice to work a change in exterior bodies, except by means of a change in the body united to it, as was stated above.

Fourth Article
WHETHER THE SEPARATED HUMAN SOUL CAN MOVE BODIES AT LEAST LOCALLY?

We proceed thus to the Fourth Article:—

Objection 1. It seems that the separated human soul can move bodies at least locally. For a body naturally obeys a spiritual substance as to local motion, as was stated above.[2] But the separated soul is a spiritual substance. Therefore it can move exterior bodies by its command.

Obj. 2. Further, in the *Itinerary* of Clement it is said in the narrative of Nicetas to Peter that by sorcery Simon Magus retained power over the soul of a child that he had slain, and that through this soul he worked magical wonders.[3] But this could not have been without some corporeal change at least as to place. Therefore the separated soul has the power to move bodies locally.

On the contrary, the Philosopher says that the soul cannot move any other body whatsoever but its own.[4]

I answer that, The separated soul cannot by its natural power move a body. For it is manifest that, even while the soul is united to the body, it does not move the body except it be endowed with life; so that if one

1. 参见 Q. 81, a. 3.
2. 参见 Q. 110, a. 3.
3. 参见 *De Gestis S. Petri*, XXVII (PG 2, 492).
4. 参见 *De An.*, I, 3 (407b 19).

of the members should become lifeless, it does not obey the soul as to local motion. Now it is also manifest that no body is quickened by the separated soul. Therefore, within the limits of its natural power, the separated soul cannot command the obedience of a body; though, by the power of God, it can exceed these limits.

Reply Obj. 1. There are some spiritual substances whose powers are not determined to certain bodies, namely, the angels, who are naturally unfettered by a body. Consequently various bodies may obey them as to movement. But if the motive power of a separate substance is naturally determined to move a certain body, that substance will not be able to move a body of higher degree, but only one of lower degree; and thus, according to philosophers, the mover of the lower heavens could not move the higher heavens.[1] Therefore, since the soul is by its nature determined to move the body of which it is the form, it cannot by its natural power move any other body.

Reply Obj. 2. As Augustine[2] and Chrysostom[3] say, the demons often pretend to be the souls of the dead, in order to confirm the error of the Gentiles who believed this. It is therefore credible that Simon Magus was deceived by some demon who pretended to be the soul of the child whom Simon Magus had slain.

---

1. 参见 Cf. above, q. 57, a. 2; q. 52, a. 2.
2. 参见 *De Civit. Dei*, X, 11 (PL 41, 290).
3. 参见 *In Matt.*, hom. XXVIII (PG 57, 353).

Question CXVIII
THE PRODUCTION OF MAN FROM MAN AS TO THE SOUL
(*In Three Articles*)

WE now consider the production of man from man: first, as to the soul; secondly, as to the body.[1]

Under the first head there are three points of inquiry: (1) Whether the sensitive soul is transmitted with the semen? (2) Whether the intellectual soul is thus transmitted? (3) Whether all souls were created at the same time?

First Article
WHETHER THE SENSITIVE SOUL IS TRANSMITTED WITH THE SEMEN?

We proceed thus to the First Article:—

Objection 1. It would seem that the sensitive soul is not transmitted with the semen, but created by God. For every perfect substance, not composed of matter and form, that begins to exist, acquires existence not by generation, but by creation, for nothing is generated save from matter. But the sensitive soul is a perfect substance, or otherwise it could not move the body; and since it is the form of a body, it is not composed of matter and form. Therefore it begins to exist not by generation but by creation.

---

1. 参见 Q. 119.

Obj. 2. Further, in living things the principle of generation is the generating power, which, since it is one of the powers of the vegetative soul, is of a lower order than the sensitive soul. Now nothing acts beyond its species. Therefore the sensitive soul cannot be caused by the animal's generating power.

Obj. 3. Further, the generator begets its like. Hence the form of the generator must be actually in the cause of generation. But neither the sensitive soul itself nor any part of it is actually in the semen, for no part of the sensitive soul is elsewhere than in some part of the body; while in the semen there is not even a particle of the body, because there is not a particle of the body which is not made from the semen and by its power. Therefore the sensitive soul is not produced through the semen.

Obj. 4. Further, if there be in the semen any principle productive of the sensitive soul, this principle either remains after the animal is begotten, or it does not remain. Now it cannot remain. For either it would be identified with the sensitive soul of the begotten animal (which is impossible, for thus there would be identity between begetter and begotten, maker and made), or it would be distinct from it (and this again is impossible, for it has been proved above that in one animal there is but one formal principle, which is the one soul[1]). If on the other hand, the aforesaid principle does not remain, this again seems to be impossible; for thus an agent would act to its own destruction, which cannot be. Therefore the sensitive soul cannot be generated from the semen.

On the contrary, The power in the semen is to the animal seminally generated as the power in the elements of the world is to animals produced from these elements,—for instance, by putrefaction[2]. But in the latter animals the soul is produced by the elemental power,

---

1. 参见 Q. 76, a. 4.
2. putrefaction: 腐败物；腐败

according to *Genesis* i. 20: *Let the waters bring forth the creeping creatures having life.* Therefore also the souls of animals seminally generated are produced by the seminal power.

I answer that, Some have held that the sensitive souls of animals are created by God.[1] This opinion would hold if the sensitive soul were subsistent, having being and operation through itself. For thus, as having being and operation through itself, to be made would needs be proper to it. And since a simple and subsistent being cannot be made except by creation, it would follow that the sensitive soul would come to be by creation.

But this principle is false,—namely, that being and operation are proper to the sensitive soul, as has been made clear above;[2] for in that case it would not cease to exist when the body perishes. Since, therefore, it is not a subsistent form, its relation to being is that of the other corporeal forms, to which being does not belong as proper to them, but which are said to be inasmuch as the subsistent composites exist through them. Therefore to be made is proper to composites. And since the generator is like the generated, it follows of necessity that both the sensitive soul and all other like forms are naturally brought into being by certain corporeal agents that reduce the matter from potentiality to act, through some corporeal power of which they are possessed.

Now the more powerful an agent, the greater scope its action has. For instance, the hotter a body, the greater the distance to which its heat carries. Therefore bodies not endowed with life, which are the lowest in the order of nature, generate their like, not through some medium, but by themselves; and thus fire by itself generates fire. But living bodies, as being more powerful, act so as to generate their like, both without and with a medium. Without a medium—in the work of

1. 参见 A like opinion is attributed to Plato by Averroes, *In Metaph.*, VII, comm. 31 (VIII, 85r). Cf. St. Thomas, *De Pot.*, q. 3, a. 11; *In De An.*, I, lect. 10.
2. 参见 Q. 75, a. 3.

nutrition, in which flesh generates flesh; with a medium—in the act of generation, because the semen of the animal or plant derives a certain active force from the soul of the generator, just as the instrument derives a certain motive power from the principal agent. And as it matters not whether we say that something is moved by the instrument or by the principal agent, so neither does it matter whether we say that the soul of the generated is caused by the soul of the generator, or by some seminal power derived therefrom.

Reply Obj. 1. The sensitive soul is not a perfect self-subsistent substance. We have said enough on this point,[1] nor need we repeat it here.

Reply Obj. 2. The generating power begets not only by its own virtue, but by that of the whole soul, of which it is a power. Therefore the generating power of a plant generates a plant, and that of an animal begets an animal. For the more perfect the soul is, to so much a more perfect effect is its generating power ordained.

Reply Obj. 3. This active force which is in the semen, and which is derived from the soul of the generator, is, as it were, a certain movement of this soul itself; nor is it the soul or a part of the soul, save virtually, just as the form of a bed is not in the saw or the axe, but what is there is a certain movement towards that form. Consequently there is no need for this active force to have an actual organ; but it is based on the [vital] spirit in the semen which is frothy, as is attested by its whiteness. In this spirit, moreover, there is a certain heat derived from the power of the heavenly bodies, in whose power the inferior bodies also act towards the production of the species, as was stated above.[2] And since in this spirit the power of the soul is concurrent with the power of a heavenly body, it has been said that *man and the sun generate man.*[3] Moreover, elemental heat is employed instrumentally by

1. 参见 Q. 75, a. 3.
2. 参见 Q. 115, a. 3, ad 2.
3. 参见 Aristotle, *Phys.*, II, 2 (194b 13).

the soul's power, as also by the nutritive power, as Aristotle states.[1]

Reply Obj. 4. In perfect animals, generated by coition, the active force is in the semen of the male, as the Philosopher says;[2] but the foetal matter is provided by the female. In this matter the vegetative soul exists from the very beginning, not as to the second act, but as to the first act, as the sensitive soul is in one who sleeps. But as soon as it begins to attract nourishment, then it already operates in act. This matter therefore is transmuted by the power which is in the semen of the male, until it is actually informed by the sensitive soul. This does not mean that the force itself which was in the semen becomes the sensitive soul, for thus the generator and generated would be identical, and, moreover, this would be more like nourishment and growth than generation, as the Philosopher says.[3] And after the sensitive soul, by the power of the active principle in the semen, has been produced in one of the principal parts of the thing generated, then it is that the sensitive soul of the offspring begins to work towards the perfection of its own body, by nourishment and growth. As to the active power which was in the semen, it ceases to exist, when the semen is dissolved and its [vital] spirit vanishes. Nor is there anything unreasonable in this, because this force is not the principal but the instrumental agent; and the movement of an instrument ceases when once the effect has been produced.

Second Article
WHETHER THE INTELLECTUAL SOUL IS PRODUCED FROM THE SEMEN?

We proceed thus to the Second Article:—

Objection 1. It would seem that the intellectual soul is produced from

---

1. 参见 Aristotle, *De An.*, II, 4 (416a 9; a 28).
2. 参见 *De Gener. Anim.*, II, 4 (740b 24).
3. 参见 *De Gener.*, I, 5 (321a 22).

the semen. For it is written (*Gen.* xlvi. 26): *All the souls that came out of* Jacob's *thigh, sixty-six.* But nothing is produced from the thigh of a man, except from the semen. Therefore the intellectual soul is produced from the semen.

Obj. 2. Further, as was shown above, the intellectual, sensitive and nutritive souls are, in substance, one soul in man.[1] But the sensitive soul in man is generated from the semen, as in other animals; and therefore the Philosopher says that *the animal and the man are not made at the same time*, but first of all the animal is made having a sensitive soul.[2] Therefore the intellectual soul is also produced from the semen.

Obj. 3. Further, it is one and the same agent whose action is terminated in the matter and in the form; or else from matter and form there would not result something absolutely one. But the intellectual soul is the form of the human body, which is produced by the power of the semen. Therefore the intellectual soul also is produced by the power of the semen.

Obj. 4. Further, man begets his like in species. But the human species is constituted by the rational soul. Therefore the rational soul is from the begetter.

Obj. 5. Further, it cannot be said that God concurs in sin. But if the rational soul be created by God, sometimes God concurs in the sin of adultery, since sometimes offspring is begotten of illicit intercourse. Therefore the rational soul is not created by God.

On the contrary, It is written in *De Eccles. Dogm.* xiv., that *the rational soul is not engendered by coition.*[3]

I answer that, It is impossible for an active power existing in matter to extend its action to the production of an immaterial effect. Now it is manifest that the intellectual principle in man transcends matter,

---

1. 参见 Q. 76, a. 3.
2. 参见 *De Gener. Anim.*, II, 3 (736b 2).
3. 参见 Gennadius, *De Eccles. Dogm.*, XIV (PL 58, 984).

for it has an operation in which the body takes no part whatever. It is therefore impossible for the seminal power to produce the intellectual principle.

Again, the seminal power acts by virtue of the soul of the begetter, according as the soul of the begetter is the act of the body, making use of the body in its operation. Now the body has nothing whatever to do in the operation of the intellect. Therefore the power of the intellectual principle, as intellectual, cannot reach to the semen. Hence the Philosopher says: *It follows that the intellect alone comes from without.*[1]

Again, since the intellectual soul has an operation independent of the body, it is subsistent, as was proved above;[2] and so, to be and to be made are proper to it. Moreover, since it is an immaterial substance it cannot be caused through generation, but only through creation by God. Therefore to hold that the intellectual soul is caused by the begetter is nothing else than to hold the soul to be non-subsistent, and consequently to perish with the body. It is therefore heretical to say that the intellectual soul is transmitted with the semen.

Reply Obj. 1. In the passage quoted, the part is put instead of the whole, the soul for the whole man, by the figure of synecdoche[3].

Reply Obj. 2. Some say that the vital functions observed in the embryo are not from its soul, but from the soul of the mother,[4] or from the formative power of the semen.[5] Both of these explanations are false, for vital functions, such as feeling, nourishment and growth cannot be from an extrinsic principle. Consequently, it must be said that the soul is in the embryo: the nutritive soul from the beginning, then the sensitive, lastly the intellectual soul.

---

1. 参见 *De Gener. Anim.*, II, 3 (736b 27).
2. 参见 Q. 75, a. 2.
3. synecdoche: 提喻法；借代
4. 参见 Cf. Aristotle, *De Gener. Anim.*, II, 1 (733b 32). —Cf. also Alex, of Hales, *Summa Theol.*, II, I, no. 489 (II, 683).
5. 参见 Cf. Avicenna, *De Anim.*, XV, 2 (60rb).

Therefore some[1] say that in addition to the vegetative soul which existed first, another, namely the sensitive, soul supervenes; and in addition to this, again another, namely the intellectual soul. Thus there would be in man three souls of which one would be in potentiality to another. This has been disproved above.[2]

Therefore others[3] say that the same soul, which was at first merely vegetative, afterwards through the action of the seminal power becomes a sensitive soul; and finally this same soul becomes intellectual, not indeed through the active seminal power, but by the power of a higher agent, namely God, illumining it from without. For this reason the Philosopher says that the intellect comes from without.[4]—But this will not hold. First, because no substantial form is susceptive of more or less; but the addition of greater perfection constitutes another species, just as the addition of unity constitutes another species of number. Now it is not possible for the same identical form to belong to different species. Secondly, because it would follow that the generation of an animal would be a continuous movement, proceeding gradually from the imperfect to the perfect, as happens in alteration. Thirdly, because it would follow that the generation of a man or an animal is not generation absolutely, because the subject thereof would be a being in act. For if the vegetative soul is from the beginning in the matter of the offspring, and is subsequently gradually brought to perfection, this will imply addition of further perfection without corruption of the preceding perfection. And this is contrary to the nature of generation properly so called. Fourthly, because either that which is caused by the action of God is something subsistent (and

---

1. 参见 Cf. above, q. 76, a. 3.—Cf. also Avicebron, *Fons Vitae*, III, 46 (p. 181).
2. 参见 Q. 76, a. 3.
3. 参见 St. Albert, *In De Anim.*, XVI, tr. 1, ch. 11 (XII, 157); *Summa De Creatur.*, II, q. 17, a. 3 (XXXV, 155); *De Nat. et Orig. An.*, I, 4 (IX, 385).
4. 参见 *De Gener. Anim.*, II, 3 (736b 27).

thus it must needs be essentially distinct from the pre-existing form, which was non-subsistent; and we shall then come back to the opinion of those who held the existence of several souls in the body), or else it is not subsistent, but a perfection of the pre-existing soul (and from this it follows of necessity that the intellectual soul perishes with the body, which cannot be admitted).

There is again another explanation, according to those who held that all men have but one intellect in common. But this has been disproved above.[1]

We must therefore say that since the generation of one thing is the corruption of another, it follows of necessity both in men and in other animals that when a more perfect form supervenes the previous form is corrupted; yet so that the supervening form contains the perfection of the previous form, and something in addition. It is in this way that through many generations and corruptions we arrive at the ultimate substantial form, both in man and other animals. This indeed is apparent to the senses in animals generated from putrefaction. We conclude therefore that the intellectual soul is created by God at the end of human generation, and this soul is at the same time sensitive and nutritive, for the pre-existing forms have been corrupted.

Reply Obj. 3. This argument holds in the case of diverse agents not ordered to one another. But where there are many agents ordered to one another, nothing hinders the power of the higher agent from reaching to the ultimate form; while the powers of the inferior agents extend only to some disposition of matter. Just as in the generation of an animal, the seminal power disposes the matter, but the power of the soul gives the form. Now it is manifest from what has been said above that the whole of corporeal nature acts as the instrument of a spiritual power, especially that of God.[2] Therefore nothing hinders the

1. 参见 Q. 76, a. 2.
2. 参见 Q. 105, a. 5; q. 110, a. 1.

formation of the body from being due to a corporeal power, while the intellectual soul is from God alone.

Reply Obj. 4. Man begets his like, inasmuch as by his seminal power the matter is disposed for the reception of a particular kind of form.

Reply Obj. 5. In the action of the adulterer, what is of nature is good, and in this God concurs. But what there is of inordinate lust is evil, and in this God does not concur.

Third Article
WHETHER HUMAN SOULS WERE CREATED TOGETHER AT THE BEGINNING OF THE WORLD?

We proceed thus to the Third Article:—

Objection 1. It would seem that human souls were created together at the beginning of the world. For it is written (*Gen.* ii. 2): *God rested Him from all His work which He had done.* This would not be true if He created new souls every day. Therefore all souls were created at the same time.

Obj. 2. Further, spiritual substances before all others belong to the perfection of the universe. If therefore souls were created with the bodies, every day innumerable[1] spiritual substances would be added to the perfection of the universe. Consequently, at the beginning the universe would have been imperfect. This is contrary to *Genesis* ii. 2, where it is said that *God ended* all *His work.*

Obj. 3. Further, the end of a thing corresponds to its beginning. But the intellectual soul remains when the body perishes. Therefore it began to exist before the body.

On the contrary, it is said that *the soul is created together with the body.*[2]

I answer that, Some have maintained that it is accidental to the

1. innumerable：无数的
2. 参见 Gennadius, *De Eccles. Dogm.*, XIV; XVIII (PL 58, 984; 985).

intellectual soul to be united to the body, asserting that the soul is of the same nature as those spiritual substances which are not united to a body.[1] These, therefore, stated that the souls of men were created together with the angels at the beginning. But this opinion is false. First, in the very principle on which it is based. For if it were accidental to the soul to be united to the body, it would follow that man who results from this union is a being by accident; or that the soul is a man, which is false, as was proved above.[2] Moreover, that the human soul is not of the same nature as the angels is proved from the different mode of understanding, as was shown above.[3] For man understands by being informed through the senses, and turning to phantasms, as was stated above.[4] For this reason the soul needs to be united to the body, which is necessary to it for the operation of the sensitive part; whereas this cannot be said of an angel.

Secondly, this opinion can be proved to be false in itself. For if it is natural to the soul to be united to the body, it is unnatural to it to be without a body, and as long as it is without a body it is deprived of its natural perfection. Now it was not fitting that God should begin His work with things imperfect and unnatural, for He did not make man without a hand or a foot, which are natural parts of a man. Much less, therefore, did He make the soul without the body.

But if someone were to say that it is not natural to the soul to be united to the body, then we must seek the reason why it is united to a body. And the reason must be either because the soul so willed, or for some other reason. If because the soul willed it,—this seems incongruous. First, because it would be unreasonable of the soul to wish to be united to the body, if it did not need the body; for if it did need

1. 参见 Origen, *Peri Archon*, I, 6; 8; II, 9 (PG 11, 166; 178; 229).
2. 参见 Q. 75, a. 4.
3. 参见 Q. 55, a. 2; q. 85, a. 1.
4. 参见 Q. 85, a. 1.

it, it would be natural for it to be united to it, since nature does not fail in what is necessary. Secondly, because there would be no reason why, having been created from the beginning of the world, the soul should, after such a long time, come to wish to be united to the body. For a spiritual substance is above time, and superior to the heavenly revolutions. Thirdly, because it would seem that this body was united to this soul by chance; since for this union to take place two wills would have to concur, namely, that of the incoming soul, and that of the begetter. —If, however, this union be neither voluntary nor natural on the part of the soul, then it must be the result of some violent cause, and would be for the soul something penal and afflicting. This is in keeping with the opinion of Origen, who held that souls were embodied in punishment of sin. Since, therefore, all these opinions are unreasonable, we must absolutely acknowledge that souls were not created before bodies, but are created at the same time as they are infused into them.

Reply Obj. 1. God is said to have rested on the seventh day, not from all work, since we read (*Jo.* v. 17) : *My Father worketh until now*, but from the creation of any new genera and species, which did not in some way exist in the first works. For in this sense, the souls which are created now existed already, as to the likeness of the species, in the first works, which included the creation of Adam's soul.

Reply Obj. 2. Something can be added every day to the perfection of the universe, as to the number of individuals, but not as to the number of species.

Reply Obj. 3. That the soul remains without the body is due to the corruption of the body, which was a result of sin. Consequently it was not fitting that God should make the soul without the body from the beginning; for as it is written (*Wis.* i. 13, 16): *God made not death ... but the wicked with works and words have called it to them.*

Question CXIX
THE PROPAGATION OF MAN AS TO THE BODY
(*In Two Articles*)

WE now consider the propagation of man, as to the body. Concerning this there are two points of inquiry: (1) Whether any part of food is changed into true human nature? (2) Whether the semen, which is the principle of human generation, is produced from the surplus food?

First Article
WHETHER SOME PART OF FOOD IS CHANGED INTO TRUE HUMAN NATURE?

We proceed thus to the First Article:—

Objection 1. It would seem that none of the food is changed into true human nature. For it is written (*Matt.* xv. 17): *Whatsoever entereth into the mouth, goeth into the belly, and is cast out into the privy.* But what is cast out is not changed into the reality of human nature. Therefore none of the food is changed into true human nature.

Obj. 2. Further, the Philosopher distinguishes flesh according to *species* from flesh according to *matter*, and says that the latter *comes and goes.*[1] Now what is formed from food comes and goes. Therefore what is produced from food is flesh according to matter, not to the species. But

1. 参见 *De Gener.*, I, 5 (321b 21).

what belongs to true human nature belongs to the species. Therefore food is not changed into true human nature.

Obj. 3. Further, the *radical humor* seems to belong to the reality of human nature; and if it be lost, it cannot be recovered, according to physicians.[1] But it could be recovered if food were changed into the humor. Therefore food is not changed into true human nature.

Obj. 4. Further, if food were changed into true human nature, whatever is lost in man could be restored. But man's death is due only to the loss of something. Therefore man would be able by taking food to insure himself against death in perpetuity.

Obj. 5. Further, if food is changed into true human nature, there is nothing in man which may not be lost or be repaired: for what in a man is generated from food can both be lost and repaired. If therefore a man lived long enough, it would follow that in the end nothing would be left in him of what belonged to him at the beginning. Consequently he would not be numerically the same man throughout his life, since for a being to be numerically the same, identity of matter is necessary. But this is incongruous. Therefore food is not changed into true human nature.

On the contrary, Augustine says: *The bodily food when corrupted, that is, having lost its form, is changed into the texture of the members.*[2] But the texture of the members belongs to true human nature. Therefore food is changed into the reality of human nature.

I answer that, According to the Philosopher, *The relation of a thing to truth is according to its relation to being.*[3] Therefore that belongs to the true nature of any thing which enters into the constitution of that nature. But nature can be considered in two ways: first, in general according

---

1. 参见 References to Avicenna will be found in the notes of the editors of the works of St. Bonaventure (II, p. 736, notes 2, 3).
2. 参见 *De Vera Relig.*, XL (PL 34, 155).
3. 参见 *Metaph.*, Ia, 1 (993b 30).

to the essence of the species; secondly, as in the individual. Now form and common matter belong to a thing's true nature considered in general, while designated individual matter and the form individuated by that matter belong to the true nature as found in this particular individual. Thus *soul* and *body* belong to true human nature in general, but to the true human nature of Peter and Martin belong *this soul* and *this body*.

Now there are some things whose form can exist only in one individual matter; and thus, the form of the sun cannot exist save in the matter in which it actually is. And in this sense some have said that the human form can exist only in a certain designated matter, which, they said, was given that form in the beginning in the first man.[1] This meant that whatever may have been added to that which was derived by posterity from the first parent, does not belong to the true reality of human nature, as not receiving in truth the form of human nature.

But (said they) that matter, which in the first man was the subject of the human form, was multiplied in itself; and in this way is derived the multitude of human bodies from the body of the first man. According to these thinkers, food is not changed into true human nature. What they say is that we take food in order to help nature to resist the action of natural heat, and prevent the consumption of the *radical humor*; just as lead or tin is mixed with silver to prevent its being consumed by fire.

But this is unreasonable in many ways. First, because it comes to one and the same thing that a form can be produced in another matter and that it can cease to be in its proper matter; and therefore all things that can be generated are corruptible, and conversely. Now it is manifest that the human form can cease to exist in this particular matter which is its subject, or else the human body would not be corruptible. Consequently it can begin to exist in another matter,

1. 参见 Peter Lombard, *Sent.*, II, xxx, 14 (I, 467).

when something else is changed into true human nature.—Secondly, because in all beings whose entire matter is contained in one individual there is only one individual in the species, as is clearly the case with the sun, moon and the like. Thus there would be only one individual of the human species.—Thirdly, because the multiplication of matter cannot be understood otherwise than either in respect of quantity only as in rarefied things, whose matter increases in dimensions, or in respect of the substance itself of the matter. But as long as the substance alone of matter remains, it cannot be said to be multiplied, for multitude cannot consist in the addition of a thing to itself, since of necessity it can result only from division. Therefore some other substance must be added to matter, either by creation, or by the change of something else into it. Consequently no matter can be multiplied save either by rarefaction (as when air is made from water), or by the change of some other thing (as fire is multiplied by the addition of wood), or lastly by creation. Now it is manifest that the multiplication of matter in the human body does not occur by rarefaction, for thus the body of a mature man would be more imperfect than the body of a child. Nor does it occur by the creation of fresh matter, for, according to Gregory, *all things were created together as to the substance of matter, but not as to the specific form.*[1] Consequently the increase of the human body can come about only because food is changed into the reality of human nature.—Fourthly, because, since man does not differ from animals and plants in regard to the vegetative soul, it would follow that the bodies of animals and plants also do not increase through a change of the nourishment into the nourished body, but through some kind of multiplication. And this multiplication cannot be natural, since the matter cannot naturally extend beyond a certain fixed quantity, nor again does

1. 参见 *Moral.*, XXXII, 12 (PL 76, 644).

anything increase naturally, save either by rarefaction or the change of something else into it. Consequently the whole work of what we call the generative and nutritive powers would be miraculous. Which is altogether inadmissible.

And so others have said that the human form can indeed begin to exist in some other matter, if we consider human nature in general, but not if we consider it according as it is in this individual.[1] For in the individual, the form remains confined to a certain determinate matter, on which it is first imprinted at the generation of that individual, so that it never leaves that matter until the ultimate dissolution of the individual. And it is this matter, say they, that principally belongs to true human nature. But since this matter does not suffice for the requisite quantity of the body, some other matter must be added, through the change of food into the substance of the individual partaking of it, in such a quantity as suffices for the increase required. This matter, they state, belongs secondarily to true human nature, because it is not required for the first being of the individual, but for the quantity due him. And if anything further is produced from the food, this does not, properly speaking, belong to true human nature.

However, this too is inadmissible.—First, because this opinion judges of living bodies after the manner of inanimate bodies, in which, though there be a power of generating their like in species, there is not the power of generating their like in the individual; which power in living bodies is the nutritive power. Nothing, therefore, would be added to living bodies by their nutritive power, if their food were not changed into their true nature.—Secondly, because the active seminal power is a certain impression derived from the soul of the begetter, as was stated above.[2] Hence it cannot have a greater power in acting than does the soul from which it is derived. If, therefore, by the power of the

1. 参见 Cf. St. Bonaventure, *In II Sent.*, d. xxx, a. 3, q. 1 (II, 730); q. 2 (II, 735).
2. 参见 Q. 118, a. 1.

semen a certain matter truly assumes the form of human nature, much more can the soul, by the nutritive power, imprint the true form of human nature on the food which is assimilated. Thirdly, because food is needed not only for growth (or otherwise at the term of growth food would no longer be needful), but also to renew that which is lost by the action of natural heat. But there would be no renewal, unless what is formed from the food took the place of what was lost. Therefore, just as that which was there previously belonged to true human nature, so also does that which is formed from the food.

Therefore, according to others,[1] it must be said that food is really changed into the true reality of human nature by reason of its assuming the specific form of flesh, bones and other like parts. This is, in fact, what the Philosopher says, namely, that food *nourishes inasmuch as it is potentially flesh.*[2]

Reply Obj. 1. Our Lord does not say that the *whole* of what enters into the mouth, but *all,*—because something from every kind of food is cast out into the privy. It may also be said that whatever is generated from food can be dissolved by natural heat, and be cast aside through the pores, as Jerome expounds the passage.[3]

Reply Obj. 2. By flesh according to the species some have understood that which first receives the human species, which is derived from the begetter; and this, they say, lasts as long as the individual does.[4] By flesh according to the matter they understand what is generated from food; and this, they say, does not always remain, but as it comes so it goes. But this is contrary to the mind of Aristotle. For he says in that passage that *just as in things which have their species in matter* —for instance, wood or stone—*so in flesh, there is something according to*

1. 参见 Averroes, *In De Gener.*, I, comm. 38 (V, 161r).
2. 参见 *De An.*, II, 4 (416b 10); cf. *De Gener.*, I, 5 (322a 27).
3. 参见 *In Matt.*, II, super XV, 17 (PL 26, 112).
4. 参见 St. Bonaventure, *In II Sent.*, d. xxx, a. 3, q. 2 (II, 735).

the species, and something according to matter.[1] Now it is clear that this distinction has no place in inanimate things, which are not generated seminally, or nourished. Again, since what is generated from food is united to the nourished body by mixing with it (just as water is mixed with wine, as the Philosopher there says by way of example),[2] that which is added, and that to which it is added, cannot be of different natures, since they are already made one by being truly mixed together. Therefore there is no reason for saying that one is destroyed by natural heat, while the other remains.

It must therefore be said that this distinction of the Philosopher is not a distinction of diverse bodies of flesh, but of the same flesh considered from different points of view. For if we consider the flesh according to the species, that is, according to that which is formal in it, in this sense the flesh always remains, because the nature of flesh always remains together with its natural disposition. But if we consider flesh according to matter, then it does not remain, but is gradually destroyed and renewed; just as in the fire of a furnace, the form of fire remains, but the matter is gradually consumed, and other matter is substituted in its place.

Reply Obj. 3. The *radical humor* is said to comprise whatever the virtue of the species is founded on. If this be taken away, it cannot be renewed, as when a man's hand or foot is amputated[3]. But the *nutritive humor* is that which has not yet received perfectly the specific nature, but is on the way to it: *e.g.*, the blood, and the like. Therefore if such be taken away, the virtue of the species remains in its root, which is not destroyed.

Reply Obj. 4. Every virtue of a passible body is weakened by continuous action, because such agents are themselves subject to

---

1. 参见 *De Gener.*, I, 5 (321b 20).
2. 同上 (322a 9).
3. amputate: 切断；删除

action. Therefore the transforming virtue is at first strong enough to be able to transform not only enough for the renewal of what is lost, but also for growth. Later on it can transform only enough for the renewal of what is lost, and then growth ceases. At length it cannot do even this, and then begins decline. And finally, when this virtue fails altogether, the animal dies. In the same way, the virtue of wine that transforms the water added to it is weakened by further additions of water, until it becomes at length watery, as the Philosopher says by way of example.[1]

Reply Obj. 5. As the Philosopher says, when a certain matter is itself transformed into fire, then fire is said to be generated anew; but when matter is transformed into a fire already existing, then fire is said to be fed.[2] Hence, if the entire matter together loses the form of fire, and another matter is transformed into fire, there will be another distinct fire. But if, while one piece of wood is burning, other wood is laid on, and so on until the first piece is entirely consumed, the same identical fire will remain all the time, for that which is added passes into what pre-existed. It is the same with living bodies, in which by means of nourishment that is replenished which was consumed by natural heat.

Second Article
WHETHER THE SEMEN IS PRODUCED FROM SURPLUS FOOD?

We proceed thus to the Second Article:—

Objection 1. It would seem that the semen is not produced from the surplus food, but from the substance of the begetter. For Damascene says that *generation is a work of nature, producing, from the substance of the*

1. 参见 *De Gener.*, I, 5 (322a 31).
2. 同上 (322a 14).

begetter, that which is begotten.[1] But that which is generated is produced from the semen. Therefore the semen is produced from the substance of the begetter.

Obj. 2. Further, the son is like his father, according to that which he receives from him. But if the semen, from which something is generated, is produced from the surplus food, a man would receive nothing from his grandfather and his ancestors in whom the food never existed. Therefore a man would not bear more resemblance to his grandfather or ancestors than to any other men.

Obj. 3. Further, the food of the generator is sometimes the flesh of cows, pigs and the like. If, therefore, the semen were produced from surplus food, the man begotten of such semen would be more akin to a cow and a pig than to his father or other relations.

Obj. 4. Further, Augustine says that we were in Adam *not only by a seminal principle but also in the very substance of the body.*[2] But this would not be, if the semen were produced from surplus food. Therefore the semen is not produced therefrom.

On the contrary, The Philosopher proves in many ways that *the semen is surplus food.*[3]

I answer that, This question depends to some extent on what has been stated above.[4] For if human nature has the power to communicate its form to alien matter not only in another, but also in its own subject, it is clear that the food which at first is dissimilar becomes at length similar through the form communicated to it. Now it belongs to natural order that a thing should be reduced from potentiality to act gradually; and hence in generated things we observe that at first each is imperfect and is afterwards perfected. But it is clear

1. 参见 *De Fide Orth.*, I, 8 (PG 94, 813).
2. 参见 *De Genesi ad Litt.*, X, 20 (PL 34, 424).
3. 参见 *De Gener. Anim.*, I, 18 (726a 26).
4. 参见 A. 1; q. 118, a. 1.

that the common is to the proper and determinate as the imperfect is to the perfect; and we see that in the generation of an animal the animal is generated before the man or the horse. In the same way, food first of all receives a certain common virtue in regard to all the parts of the body, and is subsequently determined to this or that part of the body.

Now it is not possible that the semen be a kind of solution from what is already transformed into the substance of the members. For if this solution does not retain the nature of the member it is taken from, it would no longer be of the nature of the begetter, and would be on the way to corruption; and consequently it would not have the power of transforming something else into the likeness of that nature. But if it retained the nature of the member it is taken from, then, since it is limited to a certain part of the body, it would not have the power of acting towards [the production of] the whole nature, but only the nature of that part.—Unless one were to say that the solution is taken from all the parts of the body, and that it retains the nature of each part. Thus the semen would be a small animal in act, and then the generation of animal from animal would be a mere division, as mud is generated from mud, and as happens antong animals which continue to live after being cut in two: all of which is inadmissible[1].

It remains to be said, therefore, that the semen is not something separated from what before was the actual whole; rather is it the whole, though potentially, having the power, derived from the soul of the begetter, to produce the whole body, as was stated above.[2] Now that which is in potentiality to the whole is that which is generated from food, before being transformed into the substance of the members. Therefore the semen is taken from this. In this sense, the

1. inadmissible：不能允许的；不可接受的
2. 参见 A. 1; q. 118, a. 1.

nutritive power[1] is said to serve the generative power[2], because what is transformed by the nutritive power is employed as semen by the generative power. A sign of this, according to the Philosopher,[3] is that animals of great size, which require much food, have little semen in proportion to the size of their bodies, and generate seldom; and in like manner fat men, and for the same reason.

Reply Obj. 1. Generation is from the substance of the begetter in animals and plants, inasmuch as the semen owes its power to the form of the begetter, and inasmuch as it is in potentiality to the substance of the begetter.

Reply Obj. 2. The likeness of the begetter to the begotten is not because of the matter, but because of the form of the agent that generates its like. Therefore, in order that a man be like his grandfather, there is no need that the corporeal seminal matter should have been in the grandfather, but that there be in the semen a power derived from the soul of the grandfather through the father. In like manner, the third objection is answered. For kinship is not in relation to matter, but rather according to the derivation of the form.

Reply Obj. 4. These words of Augustine are not to be understood as though the immediate seminal principle, or the corporeal substance from which this individual was formed, was actually in Adam. Rather, both were in Adam as in their principle. For even the corporeal matter which is supplied by the mother, and which he calls corporeal substance, is originally derived from Adam; and so is the active power in the semen of the father, which is the immediate seminal principle of this man.

But Christ is said to have been in Adam according to *corporeal substance* not according to a seminal principle. For the matter from

1. nutritive power：营养力
2. generative power：生殖力
3. 参见 *De Gener. Anim.*, I, 18 (725a 28).

which His Body was formed, and which was supplied by the Virgin Mother[1], was derived from Adam; whereas the active virtue was not derived from Adam, because His Body was not formed by the seminal virtue[2] of a man, but by the operation of the Holy Ghost. For such a birth was becoming to Him, WHO IS ABOVE ALL GOD FOREVER BLESSED.[3] Amen.

---

1. the Virgin Mother：童贞的母亲，指圣母玛利亚
2. the seminal virtue：精子的力量。耶稣借着圣神的德能以童贞女玛利亚的净血成胎，所以没有精卵结合的生命孕育过程
3. WHO IS ABOVE ALL GOD FOREVER BLESSED.：祂是在一切之上永受赞美者。

术语汇编与简释

accident：偶然性

指本身不独立存在或自足存在，只存在于实体（substance）中的那些属性。实体的存在方式多少是固定的，而它的偶然性则可以消失或改变。

apostle：宗徒；使徒

该词源于希腊文 apostellein，apostolos，有派遣、被派遣者、使者的意思。特指耶稣的十二位主要门徒。有时候也指各地方传教的前驱，如保禄被称为外邦人的宗徒；方济各·沙勿略被称为东方宗徒；帕特里克被称为爱尔兰的宗徒。

atheism：无神论

对信仰神的否认。其理由或是认为说神存在虽有意义但属虚构，或者是如逻辑实证主义者认为的那样，说神存在是毫无意义的，因而无所谓是否是虚构的。可以说，无神论只有与某种神的观念相关时才能存在，公开的无神论者总会被合理地追问：你否认的是什么神？此外，还有为无神论辩解的种种权威性论证。例如：有神论者认为神本身必然存在，但必然存在这一概念在逻辑上是不一致的，神之存在与世上罪恶的存在是矛盾的，诉诸第一因或宇宙设计者只能造成解释上的错觉。

beatitude：真福；全福；至福

指圆满的幸福。《圣经》将真福视为与天主的共融，是人追求的最高和最圆满的价值。旧约特别强调现世的幸福，但也不忽略来世的真福。耶稣指出，属于天国的人“真是有福的”（玛 5：1–12）。祂预许要将永远的真福赐予那些与祂结合的人（默 19：9–10）。

being：存有

在早期希腊哲学中，存有与改变相对：存有是不变的，完满的存有物只能变坏，不能变得更好。然而世界却是在变，因此，世界只有某种程度的存有（或不完满的存有）。柏拉图认为不变的观念是最真实的实体，是事物的完美模式。但亚里士多德认为存有是已经实现的潜能，绝对存有就是那完全实现其所有的潜能者，也是不动的主动者，即天主。托马斯继承和发展了亚里士多德有关存有的思想，他认为天主是潜能完全的实现，没有丝毫未实现的潜能，因此，祂是不变的，也是不可能变的。祂是必然的存有者，祂是存有本身（the Being），祂是唯一能完全适当地说“我是”的存有者。其他存有物只是由于天主的意志或创造而产生的偶然的存有。存有是所有概念中最抽象的一个概念；而《圣经》中的天主则是生活的、位格化的实体。这两种概念怎么能结合在一起呢？可能的答案是：尽管天主存有的奥秘超越人的想象，然而，天主却已经从奥秘中走出来了，并且向那些听从祂的人启示了自己。再者，天主也在祂所创造的万物中留下了足迹，尤其那按照祂的肖像而造成的人。因此，天主之为存有（the Being）与人之为存有（human beings）之间便有了类比性。

belief：信念

信念是一种认识的态度，即当对命题 P 的真理性有某种证据但不是结论性证据的时候，坚持 P 为真。信念显然与知识有关，其特点是：比纯粹无根据的意见强，但比完全的知识弱。一般认为，认知 P 尤其意味着 P 为真；而相信 P 则与 P 其实为假不相矛盾。

Catholic：天主教；公教；天主教教友

希腊文原义为大公的、普遍的，107 年安提约基亚的圣依纳爵（St. Ignatius of Antioch）开始用该词称呼由耶稣亲自建立的至一、至圣、至公、传自宗徒的教会。

Christ：基督

该词源自希腊文的 Christos，本义是希伯来文的“默西亚”

（Messiah），意思是“受傅油者”，引申为救主及品位尊高者，通用为耶稣之名号。

Christian：基督徒；基督宗教的；表现基督精神的

公元43年，在安提约基亚首次使用该词称呼耶稣基督的追随者，即“基督徒”（见《圣经·宗徒大事录》第11章26节）。

council：会议，教会会议，宗教会议

天主教普世教会或地方教会的代表聚在一起，共同商讨教会事务的聚会。天主教最高级别的会议也叫大公会议（ecumenical council），是指由教宗召开，全球主教与教宗共同参与的会议。此类会议在天主教会拥有最高的司法权、裁判权和牧职权。从325年召开的第一届大公会议至今，已经召开了21届，最近的一次是1962—1965年举行的梵蒂冈第二届大公会议。

faith：信仰；信德；信心

人在生活中持有的信任、信赖的基本态度，若缺乏此态度，则无法成为成熟、完全的人。在宗教层面上，这种态度表现在相信超越的奥迹或神的启示。在《圣经》中，信仰是整个宗教生活的根源，是天人交往，即天主启示与人的信仰，一体两面中的一面。另外，该词也指所相信的对象、事理及教义等。

First Mover：原始推动者

宇宙中一切运动的源泉，其本身则是不动的。这一思想由亚里士多德提出，并由犹太教、基督宗教和伊斯兰教这三个一神教的哲学和神学加以发展。它给托马斯的五项论证提供了第一项论证，而且托马斯本人认为这是最显著的一项。托马斯主张：“每一物的运动均是被另一物致动的，但并不能这样无穷地推论下去，否则，便不再存在原始推动者了，也就根本不存在其他推动者，因为除非被原始推动者致动，否则第二推动者便不会运动。

这正像若不是用手挥动手杖，手杖便不会运动一样。所以，我们必须追至不受任何致动的原始推动者。人们都认为这个原始推动者就是天主。”

form：型式；形式；模式；格式

拉丁文字根为forma，指某事物的外在形状、轮廓。亚里士多德型质论的基本概念，指一物之所以为该物的式样；包括其内在、外在、有形、无形等。他认为形式是使某物成为可理解的、而且是被理智所把握的东西。亚里士多德反对柏拉图关于“形式都是可分离的”，即具有独立存在的观点，他认为，独立存在的东西是实体，而实体（除了极少数重大例外，如天主）是由质料和形式构成的。质料是具有形式的那种东西，例如，人的灵魂是人的肉体的形式，人的肉体是人的灵魂的质料。

genus：属

是托马斯哲学中一个极为广泛而综合的类别，其子类是种(species)。一般来说，在哲学上，无论是属还是种的概念都不具有特殊的生物学含义。

grace：恩宠；圣宠；恩典

该词源自拉丁文gratia和希腊文的charism，是神学的核心词汇之一。依据新旧约圣经的启示，指天主圣三以多种方式临在于人间，将自己通传给受造物。是天主的赠予，人白白获得；是天主的自由给予，人自由地接受。基督信仰认为，耶稣是恩宠的化身。

immortality：永生

托马斯认为人是灵魂和肉身的结合体，人的今生与来世的连续性及由此而来的人格统一性，将由离开肉体的不死的灵魂而得以维持。托马斯认为，灵魂是一个实体，是一个精神性的实体。

impossibility：不可能性

不可能的事是指一件事实上永远不会出现或者事实上不能做到的事（也许只是在某些情况下不会出现或某些人不能做到）。按照这种说法，在自然界中不可能的，或者对于人不可能的，或者在某些情况下对于某些人不可能的事，在任何时候对于天主都会不仅是可能的，而且是轻而易举的，因为天主是全能的。于是有人或许会说，就连天主也不能做到逻辑上不可能的事，例如，祂不能造一个自己搬不起来的石头。不过这种假设是似是而非的，因为它暗示着已经规定了一项甚至超乎全知全能者的能力的任务。但是，通过说自相矛盾的话或别的不可理喻的胡言乱语根本就规定不了任何任务。

individual：个体

指能被分割的和个体化的任何事物，或能作为一个句子或思想的主语（主体）的指称物的东西。个体虽然有时被狭指具体事物，如一个人或一本书，但也能是共相事物，如白色或善。

infinity：无限

自古希腊以来就被使用的概念，但该概念是含混的，不严格地被看成是“没有开端或终结的东西”或“没有内外界限的东西”。但是关于是潜在的无限还是现实的无限，亚里士多德承认前者而不承认后者。托马斯也认为自然界现实的无限是不可能，但天主在本质上是无限的，因为祂是纯粹的现实（pure actuality），只有祂既是现实的又是无限的。

matter：物质；质料；材料、质素

物理学、哲学及神学的基本词汇，是与形式或与精神相对之物，这两种相对物并非完全不相关。在这个意义上，物质只是基本材料或原料（质料），由此组成了世界上各种元素。

mystery：奥迹；奥理；奥秘

该词源自希腊文 myeein 及 mystes，一般而言，它指的是将人带入到秘密的、一般人无法接触的宗教与灵性的仪式或情况之中。从神学角度来看，富有神圣特性的隐秘或神秘之事迹是非经天主启示，理性无从得知的，或者仅知其然而不知其所以然的真理。比如圣三奥迹、降生奥迹、恩宠奥迹等。天主本身和祂的救恩计划以及耶稣基督的事迹，构成奥秘的核心意义。

person：位格；位；人格；人物

此词源自希腊文 prosopon 和拉丁文 persona，即假面具、舞台、角色、人格、身份、个性等。在一般的对话、戏剧中，用来描写一个演员的特殊角色、身份、地位与性格。为保护及说明圣经有关耶稣基督身上有天人合一以及天主圣三的奥迹，古代教会思想家，依据希腊、罗马文化思想特别发挥了该词的内涵。托马斯认为位格是“在理性内有区别的个别自立体”。近代较动态的神哲学思想特别发挥了位格的整体性、行动的主体性及关系性，认为整个存在及其活动与关系的最后主体，为整个人的尊严的基础。Divine Persons，是指天主的位格，指三位一体的天主父、子、圣神三位实在各有不同而又是同一个天主内的三个位格。

sacrament：圣事

该词来自拉丁文 sacer，sacramentum，而 sacramentum 演变自希腊文的 mysterion 及拉丁文的 mysterium，指天主教的初期教会依据耶稣的生活与福音而发展起来的有形可见的宗教仪式中的象征及标记，教会籍着这些象征和标记将天主无形可见的恩宠赐予领受的人。圣事是耶稣基督的行为，是祂的救恩行动；它是基督在世使命在时空中现实化的延续；是教会协同基督对天父的朝拜行为；是赋予人无形恩宠的祝圣行为；它不仅是赐予人恩宠的象征行为，而且是所象征的事实本身。天主教共有圣洗、坚振、圣体、忏悔、圣秩、傅油和婚姻七件圣事。

speculative：观看的，鉴赏的

该词的拉丁文 speculativa 来自动词 speculari，其主要意义是观看和鉴赏。人通过理智观看，需要经过一连串的组合、分解等推理的步骤才能达到认知的终点或目的，因此，一般都把这一形容词译为“理解的”或“思辨的”。但这种译法并不适用于天主，因为按照托马斯的看法，对天主的认知并不需要组合、分解或推理，而是从整体的角度观看一切。所以，针对天主的知识，这一形容词宜译为“观看的”或“鉴赏的”。

soul：魂，灵魂

托马斯像亚里士多德那样，在使用 soul（拉丁文：amina）这个名词时，是指“魂”，即我们四周生物的生命的第一根源。今天一般人把“魂”理解为灵魂，但托马斯所说的“anima”是等于亚里士多德所说的“psyche”，是生物的本源或组成因素，它使一样东西成为活的，就好像它躲在这东西的一切行动的背后似得。托马斯把“魂”分为三个种类：植物的“生魂”(vegetative soul)、动物的觉魂（sensitive soul）和人的“灵魂”(rational soul/anima intellectiva)。他认为只有人的“灵魂”是不朽的、不灭的，当它与肉身分离后会继续存在。

substance：实体

托马斯对实体的定义利用了逻辑的主词和谓语理论。如果 S 是谓语的主词，而它又不能成为任何其他主词的谓语，那么 S 就是一个实体。可以说实体就是能独立存在的事物。

theology：神学

此词源自希腊文 theos 及 logos。就广义而言，神学是论述神、研究神及神与宇宙关系的学问。就狭义而言，神学是指主流宗教，如佛教、印度教、伊斯兰教、犹太教及基督宗教对其宗教教义、生活体验及灵性修养的科学性研究。最狭义而言，指基督宗教神学，即依据天主在旧约、新约中的启示而发展出来的神学。分为实证神学、理论神学、实践神学三个领域，每一个领域都有其特殊的研究方法，但三者在理论与实践的整体性基础上，彼此构成神学的动态整体。传统神学比较强调“真”和“善”的幅度，“美”的面向不很明显。今日神学在整体学术领域中，一方面维持其独特性，另一面亦强调向其他学科开放交流的态度。

Trinity：天主圣三

天主三位一体的奥迹包含两个要素：圣父、圣子和圣神这三位是一个天主（trinity in unity）和一个天主是三位（unity in trinity）。首先，基督宗教肯定，神只有一个，没有别的神。从静态的体验来看，天主就是“一”；若由动态的一面来看，祂是一个正在实现中的事件；若由哲学概念来表达，就是绝对自主的存有。天主的本性是爱，天主就是爱（若一4：8）。天父是这爱的“自我给予”，天主子是这爱的“自我接受与答复”；圣神是这爱的“自我合一”。而在爱的内在生命中，基本上有两个动力：一是展开，一是集合。展开被称为“生”（generate），是爱的给予，即父毫无保留的给予；子是展开的接受与答复，即受生。这就是所谓的子由父而生。而集合是天主在爱的行动中所表现的第二动力，意谓父子的合一，即爱的合一，这就是圣神的来源，基督宗教称之为“发”（proceed）。既然展开导致集合，那么“生”也同样导致“发”，所以，子由父生，导致父与子共发圣神，因为父与子在爱中是合一的。所以，天主是父、天主是子、天主是圣神；父是天主、子是天主、圣神也是天主；但父不是子、不是圣神，子不是父、不是圣神，圣神不是父、不是子。因此，父对子的关系是主动的产生，这是父的特殊面，也就是“爱的给予”；子对父的关系是被动的产生，这是子的特殊面，就是“爱的接受与答复”；而圣神由于父子的关系是被动的发生，就是恩惠，就是爱的合一。

Word，the：圣言，道

圣言一词从广义上来说，指天主的一切言语；从狭义来说，指耶稣基督本身。在圣经旧约中，天主藉着言语启示祂的能力和智慧；在圣咏中，天主的话是创造性的也是救赎性的；先知蒙召最主要的任务是传达天主的话。整个旧约的启示都可以被称为是天主的话，但是新约却把天主的话和耶稣基督联系在一起，比如在若望的著作里，耶稣基督被视为成了血肉的天主圣言，因此，祂代表救赎的最终力量。圣言进入人类历史的顶峰就是耶稣基督。为新约而言，在耶稣基督内降生的圣言仍然留驻在教会内。而对圣言的宣讲必须是教会恒久的制度，不管是口头的宣讲还是笔录下来的圣言都有同样的权威。

World Academic Classics
世界学术经典·英文版

Marxism
马克思主义

The Communist Manifesto (Marx & Engels)
共产党宣言（马克思、恩格斯）

Chinese Classics
中国经典

论语（汉英对照）
Confucius' Analects

道德经（汉英对照）
Dao De Jing

孟子（汉英对照）
Mencius

庄子（汉英对照）
Zhuangzi

孙子兵法（汉英对照）
Sun Tzu on the Art of War

大学、中庸（汉英对照）
The Way of Learning and The Way to Harmony

Philosophy
哲 学

Republic (Plato)
理想国（柏拉图）

Metaphysics (Aristotle)
形而上学（亚里士多德）

Meditations on First Philosophy (René Descartes)
第一哲学沉思录（笛卡尔）

A Discourse on Method (René Descartes)
方法论（笛卡尔）

Pascal's Pensées (Blaise Pascal)
思想录（帕斯卡尔）

A Treatise of Human Nature (David Hume)
人性论（休谟）

Critique of Pure Reason (Kant)
纯粹理性批判（康德）

Critique of Judgement (Kant)
判断力批判（康德）

The Phenomenology of Mind (Hegel)
精神现象学（黑格尔）

The Logic of Hegel (Hegel)
小逻辑（黑格尔）

The World as Will and Representation (Schopenhauer)
作为意志与表象的世界（叔本华）

Thus Spake Zarathustra (Nietzsche)
查拉图斯特拉如是说（尼采）

Either / Or (Kierkegaard)
非此即彼（克尔凯郭尔）

Ideas: General Introduction to Pure Phenomenology (Husserl)
纯粹现象学导论（胡塞尔）

On First Philosophy (Husserl)
论第一哲学（胡塞尔）

Tractatus Logico-Philosophicus (Wittgenstein)
逻辑哲学论（维特根斯坦）

Philosophical Investigations (Wittgenstein)
哲学研究（维特根斯坦）

Pragmatism (William James)
实用主义（威廉·詹姆斯）

Reconstruction in Philosophy (John Dewey)
哲学的改造（杜威）

Time and Free Will (Henri Bergson)
时间与自由意志（伯格森）

A Discourse on the Positive Spirit (Auguste Comte)
论实证精神（孔德）

Novum Organum (Francis Bacon)
新工具（培根）

Ethics
伦理学

The Nicomachean Ethics of Aristotle (Aristotle)
尼各马可伦理学（亚里士多德）

The Theory of Moral Sentiments (Adam Smith)
道德情操论（亚当・斯密）

A Discourse on Inequality (Rousseau)
论人类不平等的起源与基础（卢梭）

Critique of Practical Reason (Kant)
实践理性批判（康德）

Utilitarianism (Mill)
功利主义（密尔）

Principia Ethica (Moore)
伦理学原理（摩尔）

Religion
宗教学

Confessions (St. Augustine)
忏悔录（圣・奥古斯丁）

Basic Writings of Saint Thomas Aquinas (Thomas Aquinas)
圣托马斯基本著作（阿奎那）

Basic Theological Writings (Martin Luther)
路德基本著作选（马丁・路德）

The Courage to Be (Paul Tillich)
存在的勇气（蒂利希）

The Essence of Christianity (Ludwig Feuerbach)
基督教的本质（费尔巴哈）

Politics
政治学

The Politics of Aristotle (Aristotle)
政治学（亚里士多德）

The Prince (Machiavelli)
君主论（马基雅维利）

The Social Contract (Rousseau)
社会契约论（卢梭）

Leviathan (Thomas Hobbes)
利维坦（霍布斯）

Two Treatises of Government (John Locke)
政府论（洛克）

The Spirit of the Laws (Montesquieu)
论法的精神（孟德斯鸠）

Democracy in America (Tocqueville)
论美国民主（托克维尔）

Considerations on Representative Government (Mill)
代议制政府（密尔）

The Federalist Papers (Hamilton)
联邦党人文集（汉密尔顿）

The Ancien Régime and the Revolution (Tocqueville)
旧制度与大革命（托克维尔）

Utopia (Thomas More)
乌托邦（莫尔）

On Liberty (Mill)
论自由（密尔）

Reflections on the Revolution in France (Edmund Burke)
法国革命论（伯克）

The Will to Power (Nietzsche)
权力意志（尼采）

On War (Carl von Clausewitz)
战争论（克劳塞维茨）

Mutual Aid: A Factor of Evolution (Pyotr Alexeyevich Kropotkin)
互助论（克鲁泡特金）

Economics
经济学

The Economics of Welfare (Pigou)
福利经济学（庇古）

Principles of Economics (Alfred Marshall)
经济学原理（马歇尔）

The General Theory of Employment, Interest and Money (Keynes)
就业、利息与货币通论（凯恩斯）

Capitalism, Socialism and Democracy (Schumpeter)
资本主义、社会主义与民主（熊彼特）

The Theory of Economic Development (Schumpeter)
经济发展理论（熊彼特）

An Essay on Population (Thomas Robert Malthus)
人口原理（马尔萨斯）

An Inquiry into the Nature and Causes of the Wealth of Nations (Adam Smith)
国民财富的性质和原因的研究（亚当・斯密）

The Principles of Scientific Management (Frederick Winslow Taylor)
科学管理原理（泰勒）

Sociology
社会学

Suicide: A Study in Sociology (Durkheim)
自杀：社会学研究（迪尔凯姆）

Ideology and Utopia (Mannheim)
意识形态与乌托邦（曼海姆）

The Protestant Ethic and the Spirit of Capitalism (Max Weber)
新教伦理与资本主义精神（韦伯）

First Principles (Herbert Spencer)
基本原理（斯宾塞）

The Philosophy of Money (Georg Simmel)
货币哲学（西美尔）

The Theory of Leisure Class (Thorstein B. Veblen)
论闲逸阶级（凡勃伦）

A Treatise on General Sociology (Vilfredo Pareto)
社会学总论（帕累托）

Anthropology
人类学

The Golden Bough (Frazer)
金枝（弗雷泽）

Race, Language and Culture (Franz Boas)
种族・语言・文化（鲍斯）

Argonauts of the Western Pacific (Malinowski)
西太平洋的航海者（马林诺夫斯基）

The Savage Mind (Claude Lévi-Strauss)
野性思维（列维-斯特劳斯）

Structure and Function in Primitive Society (Redcliffe-Brown)
原始社会的结构和功能（拉迪克利夫-布朗）

Psychology
心理学

The Principles of Psychology (William James)
心理学原理（威廉・詹姆斯）

The Interpretation of Dreams (Sigmund Freud)
梦的解析（弗洛伊德）

Principles of Physiological Psychology (Wundt)
生理心理学原理（冯特）

The Archetypes and the Collective Unconscious (Jung)
原型与集体无意识（荣格）

Law
法　学

Ancient Law (Maine)
古代法（梅因）

Lectures on Jurisprudence (Austin)
法理学演讲录（奥斯丁）

English Law and the Renaissance (Maitland)
英国法律与文艺复兴（梅特兰）

Fundamental Principles of the Sociology of Law (Ehrlich)
法律社会学基本原理（埃利希）

History
历史学

The Histories (Herodotus)
历史（希罗多德）

The Peloponnesian War (Thucydides)
伯罗奔尼撒战争史（修昔底德）

The Annals of Imperial Rome (Tacitus)
编年史（塔西佗）

The City of God (St. Augustine)
上帝之城（圣・奥古斯丁）

On Heroes, Hero Worship, and the Heroic in History (Thomas Carlyle)
论历史上的英雄、英雄崇拜和英雄业绩（卡莱尔）

The Idea of History (Collingwood)
历史的观念（科林伍德）

History of Civilization in Europe (Francois Guizot)
欧洲文明史（基佐）

The Influence of Sea Power (Alfred T. Mahan)
海权对历史的影响（马汉）

Theory & History of Historiography (Benedetto Croce)
史学理论与史学史（克罗齐）

A Short Account of the Destruction of the Indies (Bartolomé de las Cases)
西印度毁灭述略（卡萨斯）

Literary Theory and Aesthetics
文学理论与美学

On the Art of Poetry (Aristotle)
诗学（亚里士多德）

On the Art of Poetry (Horace)
诗艺（贺拉斯）

On the Sublime (Longinus)
论崇高（朗吉努斯）

Theory of Aesthetic / History of Aesthetic (Benedetto Croce)
美学理论 / 美学史（克罗齐）

Hegel's Aesthetics Lectures on Fine Art (Hegel)
黑格尔美学讲演录（黑格尔）

The Birth of Tragedy (Nietzsche)
悲剧的诞生（尼采）

Linguistics
语言学

Course in General Linguistics (Saussure)
普通语言学教程（索绪尔）

On Language (Wilhelm Humboldt)
论语言（威廉・洪堡特）

Scientific Philosophy
自然科学哲学

On the Origin of Species (Charles Darwin)
物种起源（达尔文）

Mathematical Principles of Natural Philosophy and Its System of the World (Issac Newton)
自然哲学及其宇宙体系的数学原理（牛顿）

Natural History (Pliny the Elder)
自然史（老普林尼）